W9-BSL-775

The Contemporary Management Online Learning Center

www.mhhe.com/jones3e

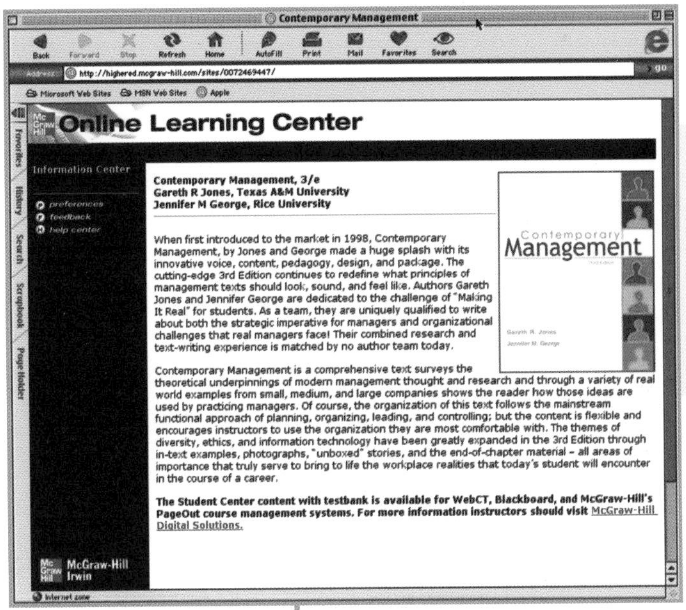

Access online study materials, regular text updates, and other Internet resources at the Contemporary Management website.

- Chapter Reviews--Review and apply text concepts with interactive practice quizzes, Flashcards, PowerPoint slides, World Wide Web exercises, and other materials.
- Business Week Cases--Read about the latest trends and problems facing managers in cases based on articles from the popular magazine.
- News Updates--Check out news briefs that relate the latest management news stories to chapter concepts.

A password-protected portion of the site is also available to instructors, offering downloadable supplements and other teaching resources.

Contemporary Management

Third Edition

Gareth R. Jones
Texas A&M University

Jennifer M. George
Rice University

McGraw-Hill Irwin

Boston Burr Ridge, IL Dubuque, IA Madison, WI New York San Francisco St. Louis
Bangkok Bogotá Caracas Kuala Lumpur Lisbon London Madrid Mexico City
Milan Montreal New Delhi Santiago Seoul Singapore Sydney Taipei Toronto

For Nicholas and Julia

McGraw-Hill Higher Education

*A Division of The **McGraw-Hill** Companies*

CONTEMPORARY MANAGEMENT

Published by McGraw-Hill, a business unit of The McGraw-Hill Companies, Inc. 1221 Avenue of the Americas, New York, NY, 10020. Copyright © 2003, 2000, 1998 by The McGraw-Hill Companies, Inc. All rights reserved. No part of this publication may be reproduced or distributed in any form or by any means, or stored in a database or retrieval system, without the prior written consent of The McGraw-Hill Companies, Inc., including, but not limited to, in any network or other electronic storage or transmission, or broadcast for distance learning.

Some ancillaries, including electronic and print components, may not be available to customers outside the United States.

This book is printed on acid-free paper.

domestic 1 2 3 4 5 6 7 8 9 0 WCK/WCK 0 9 8 7 6 5 4 3 2
international 1 2 3 4 5 6 7 8 9 0 WCK/WCK 0 9 8 7 6 5 4 3 2

ISBN 0-07-246944-7

Publisher: *John E. Biernat*
Senior Sponsoring editor: *Andy Winston*
Managing developmental editor: *Laura Hurst Spell*
Senior marketing manager: *Ellen Cleary*
Lead project manager: *Mary Conzachi*
Production supervisor: *Debra R. Sylvester*
Coordinator freelance designer: *Artemio Ortiz Jr.*
Supplement producer: *Betty Hadala*
Producer, Media Technology: *Jennifer Becka*
Photo research coordinator: *Judy Kausal*
Photo researcher: *Charlotte Goldman*
Cover and interior design: *Artemio Ortiz Jr.*
Typeface: *10.5/12 Baskerville*
Compositor: *Precision Graphics*
Printer: *Quebecor World Versailles Inc.*

Library of Congress Cataloging-in-Publication Data

Jones, Gareth R.
Contemporary management / Gareth R. Jones, Jennifer M. George.–3rd ed.
p. cm.
Includes index.
ISBN 0-07-246944-7 – ISBN 0-07-115121-4 (International ed.)
1. Management. I. George, Jennifer M. II. Title.
HD31.J597 2003
658–dc21

2002025530

INTERNATIONAL EDITION ISBN 0-07-115121-4

Copyright © 2003. Exclusive rights by The McGraw-Hill Companies, Inc. for manufacture and export. This book cannot be re-exported from the country to which it is sold by McGraw-Hill. The International Edition is not available in North America.

http://www.mhhe.com

Brief Contents

Contents

Chapter One

Chapter Two

Examples

Management in Action

Examples

Management in Action

Contents

Chapter Three

Chapter Four

Examples

Management in Action

Examples

Management in Action

Contents

Chapter Five

A Manager's Challenge
Ups and Downs in the Dot-Coms 151

Managing the Organizational Environment 150

Topics

Chapter Six

A Manager's Challenge
Expanding Globally in a Wired World 183

Managing the Global Environment 182

Topics

Examples

Management in Action

Examples

Management in Action

Contents

Chapter Seven

Chapter Eight

Examples

Management in Action

Examples

Management in Action

Contents

Chapter Nine

Chapter Ten

Examples

Management in Action

Examples

Management in Action

Contents

Chapter Eleven

Chapter Twelve

Examples

Management in Action

Examples

Management in Action

Contents

Chapter Thirteen

Chapter Fourteen

Examples

Management in Action

Examples

Management in Action

Contents

Chapter Fifteen

Communication 510

Chapter Sixteen

Organizational Conflict, Negotiation, Politics, and Change 546

Examples

Management in Action

Examples

Management in Action

Contents

Examples

Management in Action

Examples

Management in Action

Contents

Examples

Management in Action

Preface

The business world has changed dramatically in the three years since we last revised our book. There are increasing pressures on managers at all levels to integrate new information technology into all aspects of an organization's operations to improve efficiency and customer responsiveness. The increasing diversity of the workforce has made it imperative for managers to understand how and why people differ so that they can effectively manage diversity. The continuing need to innovate and improve the quality of goods and services to allow an organization to compete effectively, especially on a global level, has continued to confront managers. The tasks that managers must perform effectively have become more complex and challenging than ever before.

Encouraged by the favorable reception and high level of support that greeted the first two editions of *Contemporary Management* we set out to revise and develop the third edition of our book in significant ways based on the reactions and suggestions of both users and reviewers. Both users and reviewers were very supportive of our attempts to integrate contemporary management theories and approaches into the analysis of management and organizations. Our goal has been to distill new and classic theorizing and research into a contemporary framework that is compatible with the traditional focus on management as planning, leading, organizing, and controlling, but which transcends this traditional approach.

Users and reviewers report that students appreciate and enjoy our presentation of management, a presentation that makes its relevance obvious even to those who lack exposure to "a real-life" management context. Students like both the book's content and the way we relate management theory to real life examples to drive home the message that management matters both because it determines how well organizations perform, and because managers and organizations affect the lives of people who work inside them and people outside the organization, such as customers and shareholders.

The contemporary nature of our approach can be seen most clearly by examining our table of contents, and by perusing our treatment of management issues, especially with reference to the kinds of issues and organizations we discuss in our opening cases and many insights throughout the book. In keeping with this tradition, we've added many new and updated topics and issues throughout all of the chapters in the book. Some highlights include: fall of the dot-coms and problems and challenges encountered by dot-coms; moods and emotions; emotional intelligence; how managers create culture; attraction-selection-attrition framework; ethical organizational cultures; different kinds of diversity–age, gender, race and ethnicity, religion, capabilities/disabilities, socioeconomic background, sexual orientation; business case for diversity; schemas and gender schemas; gender discrimination; global supply chain management and its importance in light of increasing globalization; how IT is making the world smaller; designing global IT systems; B2Bnetworks and IT; knowledge management and IT; control systems and IT; Six Sigma quality improvement programs; 360-degree appraisals; cafeteria-style benefits; need for work-life balance; overpayment and underpayment inequity; equity and the dot-com bust; employee stock options; intellectual stimulation; development consideration; transformation leadership; gender and leadership; emotional intelligence and leadership; how virtual storefronts compare to traditional brick-and-mortar storefronts.

Unique Coverage

As you will see, we have some chapters that are not contained in any other management book. Our new Chapter 3, for example, takes the former chapter on "The Manager as a Person," (which discussed managers as real people with their own personalities, strengths, weaknesses, opportunities, and problems) and now combines it with an in-depth discussion of ethics and culture. This unique chapter now shows students how managers shape all aspects of the way an organization works, and students will grasp that managers are people like themselves and subject to the same kinds of forces that govern their choices and actions. Another unique chapter for a management book, Chapter 16, "Organizational Conflict, Negotiation, Politics, and Change," discusses how managers can successfully manage organizational politics, conflict, negotiation, and change. Students will also appreciate the challenges managers face and how, as future managers, they can successfully meet them. The chapter gives students a hands-on look at managing crucial organizational processes. Similarly, our book has always had the greatest coverage of communication and information technology (IT) of any book in the market, and the practical, hands on significance of understanding IT is obvious today like never before. We show in every chapter in rich detail how IT is impacting the jobs or managers and employees alike.

Emphasis on Applied Management

Our contemporary approach also is illustrated by the way we have chosen to organize and discuss contemporary management issues. We have gone to great lengths to bring the manager back into the subject matter of management. That is, we have written our chapters from the perspective of current or future managers to illustrate, in a hands-on way, the problems and opportunities they face and how they can effectively meet them. For example, in Chapter 3 we provide an integrated treatment of personality, ethics, and culture; in Chapter 4 a hands-on account of diversity, and sexual harassment that clearly explains their significance to practicing managers. In Chapter 7, on planning and strategy we provide an integrated treatment of highlighting the choices managers face as they go about performing the planning role. We emphasize important issues managers face and how management theory, research, and practice can help them and their organizations be effective. This chapter is one of our book's most popular chapters with both instructors and students.

This applied approach can also be clearly seen in the last three chapters of the book in which we cover the topics of managing information systems, technology, and operations management, topics that have tended to be difficult to teach to new management students in an interesting and novel way. Our chapters provide a student-friendly, behavioral approach to understanding the management processes entailed in information systems, operations management, and innovation and entrepreneurship. As our reviewers noted, while most books' treatment of these issues is dry and quantitative, ours comes alive with its focus on how managers can manage the people and processes necessary to give an organization a competitive advantage. In fact, the management of information technology to create and sustain a competitive advantage has always been a major theme of our book, as discussed earlier. In the new edition, our communications chapter, information systems chapter, abundant IT examples, and Internet exercises continue to provide a state-of-the-art account of new developments in computer information systems that students will understand and enjoy.

Flexible Organization

Another factor of interest to instructors concerns the way we have designed the grouping of chapters to allow instructors to teach the chapter material in the order that best suits their needs. For example, the more micro-oriented instructor can follow Chapters 1 through 4 with 12 through 16 and then do the more macro chapters. The more macro-oriented professor can follow Chapters 1 and 2 with 5 through 10, jump to 17, 18, 19, and then do the micro Chapters 2 and 3 and 11 through 16. Our sequencing of parts and chapters gives the instructor considerable freedom to design the course that best suits him or her. Instructors are not tied to the planning, organizing, leading, controlling framework, even though our presentation remains consistent with this approach.

Acknowledgments

Finding a way to integrate and present the rapidly growing literature on contemporary management and make it interesting and meaningful for students is not an easy task. In writing and revising the several drafts of *Contemporary Management,* we have been fortunate to have had the assistance of several people who have contributed greatly to the book's final form. First, we are grateful to Andy Winston, our sponsoring editor, for his ongoing support and commitment to our project, and for always finding ways to provide the resources that we needed to continually improve and refine our book. Second, we are grateful to Laura Spell, our developmental editor, for so ably coordinating the book's progress and to her and Ellen Cleary, our marketing manager, for providing us with concise and timely feedback and information from professors and reviewers that have allowed us to shape the book to the needs of its intended market. We also thank Artemio Ortiz for executing an awe-inspiring design, Mary Conzachi for coordinating the production process, and Alexander Ruiz (Rice University) for his research assistance, and Elaine Morris (Rice University) and Patsy Hartmangruber (Texas A&M) for providing excellent word-processing and graphic support. We are also grateful to the many colleagues and reviewers who provided us with useful and detailed feedback, perceptive comments and valuable suggestions for improving the manuscript.

Producing any competitive work is a challenge. Producing a truly market-driven textbook requires tremendous effort beyond simply obtaining reviews on a draft manuscript. Our goal was simple with the development of *Contemporary Management:* to be the most customer-driven principles of management text and supplement package ever published! With the goal to exceed the expectations of both faculty and students, we executed one of the most aggressive product development plans ever undertaken in textbook publishing. Hundreds of faculty have taken part in developmental activities ranging from regional focus groups to manuscript and supplement reviews and surveys. Consequently, we're confident in assuring you and your students, our customers, that every aspect of our text and support package reflects your advice and needs. As you review it we're confident that over and over your reaction will be "they listened!"

Our thanks to the faculty who contributed greatly to previous editions of *Contemporary Management:*

Fred Anderson, *Indiana University of Pennsylvania*
Jacquelyn Appeldorn, *Dutchess Community College*
Barry Armandi, *SUNY–Old Westbury*
Douglas E. Ashby, *Lewis & Clark Community College*
Barry S. Axe, *Florida Atlantic University*
Jeff Bailey, *University of Idaho*
Robert M. Ballinger, *Siena College*
Donita Whitney-Bammerlin, *Kansas State University*
Sandy Jeanquart Barone, *Murray State University*
Lorraine P. Bassette, *Prince George's Community College*
Gene Baten, *Central Connecticut State University*
Josephine Bazan, *Holyoke Community College*
Hrach Bedrosian, *New York University*
Jack C. Blanton, *University of Kentucky*
David E. Blevins, *University of Arkansas at Little Rock*
Karen Boroff, *Seton Hall University*
Barbara Boyington, *Brookdale Community College*
Charles Braun, *Marshall University*
Gil Brookins, *Siena College*
Patricia M. Buhler, *Goldey-Beacom College*
David Cadden, *Quinnipiac College*
Thomas Campbell, *University of Texas–Austin*
Thomas Carey, *Western Michigan University*
Daniel P. Chamberlin, *Regents University–CRB*
Nicolette DeVille Christensen, *Guilford College*
Anthony A. Cioffi, *Lorain County Community College*
Sharon F. Clark, *Lebanon Valley College*
Sharon Clinebell, *University of Northern Colorado*
Dianne Coleman, *Wichita State University*
Elizabeth Cooper, *University of Rhode Island*
Thomas D. Craven, *York College of Pennsylvania*
Kent Curran, *University of North Carolina*
Arthur L. Darrow, *Bowling Green State University*
Ron DiBattista, *Bryant College*
Thomas Duening, *University of Houston*
Charles P. Duffy, *Iona College*
Subhash Durlabhji, *Northwestern State University*
Robert A. Eberle, *Iona College*
Robert R. Edwards, *Arkansas Tech University*
William Eldridge, *Kean College*
Pat Ellsberg, *Lower Columbia College*
Stan Elsea, *Kansas State University*
Dale Finn, *University of New Haven*
Charles Flaherty, *University of Minnesota*
Robert Flemming, *Delta State University*
Jeanie M. Forray, *Eastern Connecticut State University*
Ellen Frank, *Southern Connecticut State University*

Joseph A. Gemma, *Providence College*
Neal Gersony, *University of New Haven*
Donna H. Giertz, *Parkland College*
Leo Giglio, *Dowling College*
David Glew, *Texas A&M University*
Carol R. Graham, *Western Kentucky University*
Matthew Gross, *Moraine Valley Community College*
John Hall, *University of Florida*
Eric L. Hansen, *California State University–Long Beach*
Justin U. Harris, *Strayer College*
Allison Harrison, *Mississippi State University*
Eileen Bartels Hewitt, *University of Scranton*
Stephen R. Hiatt, *Catawba College*
Tammy Bunn Hiller, *Bucknell University*
Jerry Horgesheiner, *Southern Utah State*
Gordon K. Huddleston, *South Carolina State University*
John Hughes, *Texas Tech University*
Charleen Jaeb, *Cuyahoga Community College*
Richard E. Johe, *Salem College*
Jehan G. Kavoosi, *Clarion University of Pennsylvania*
Ken Lehmenn, *Forsyth Technical Community College*
Lianlian Lin, *California State Polytechnic University*
Grand Lindstrom, *University of Wyoming*
Mary Lou Lockerby, *College of DuPage*
Esther Long, *University of Florida*
Bryan Malcolm, *University of Wisconsin*
Z. A. Malik, *Governors State University*
Mary J. Mallott, *George Washington University*
Reuben McDaniel, *University of Texas*
John A. Miller, *Bucknell University*
Thomas C. Neil, *Clark Atlanta University*
Brian Niehoff, *Kansas State University*
Judy Nixon, *University of Tennessee*
Cliff Olson, *Southern Adventists University*
Dane Partridge, *University of Southern Indiana*
Sheila J. Pechinski, *University of Maine*
Fred Pierce, *Northwood University*
Laynie Pizzolatto, *Nicholls State University*
Eleanor Polster, *Florida International University*
Paul Preston, *University of Texas-San Antonio*
Samuel Rabinowitz, *Rutgers University-Camden*
Gerald Ramsey, *Indiana University Southeast*
Charles Rarick, *Transylvania University*
Robert A. Reber, *Western Kentucky University*
Bob Redick, *Lincoln Land Community College*
Deborah Britt Roebuck, *Kennesaw State University*
Harvey Rothenberg, *Regis University*
George Ruggiero, *Community College of Rhode Island*
Cyndy Ruszkowski, *Illinois State University*
Michael Santoro, *Rutgers University*
Amit Shah, *Frostburg State University*
Richard Ray Shreve, *Indiana University Northwest*
Sidney Siegel, *Drexel University*
Raymond D. Smith, *Towson State University*
William Soukup, *University of San Diego*
H. T. Stanton, Jr., *Barton College*
Nestor St. Charles, *Dutchess Community College*
Lynda St. Clair, *Bryant College*
Gerald Schoenfeld, Jr., *James Madison University*
Michael Shapiro, *Dowling College*
Sharon Sloan, *Northwood University*
William A. Sodeman, *University of Southern Indiana*
Carl J. Sonntag, *Pikes Peak Community College*
Charles I. Stubbart, *Southern Illinois University at Carbondale*
James K. Swenson, *Moorhead State University*
Karen Ann Tarnoff, *East Tennessee State University*
Jerry L. Thomas, *Arapahoe Community College*
Kenneth Thompson, *DePaul University*
John Todd, *University of Arkansas*
Thomas Turk, *Chapman University*
Linn Van Dyne, *Michigan State University*
Jaen Vanhoegaerden, *Ashridge Management College*
Stuart H. Warnock, *University of Southern Colorado*
Toomy Lee Waterson, *Northwood University*
Philip A. Weatherford, *Embry-Riddle Aeronautical University*
Ben Weeks, *St. Xavier University*
W. J. Williams, *Chicago State University*
Robert Williams, *University of North Alabama*
Shirley A. Wilson, *Bryant College*
Michael A. Yahr, *Robert Morris College*
D. Kent Zimmerman, *James Madison University*

And special thanks to the faculty who gave us their feedback during the development of the third edition:

Dave Arnott, *Dallas Baptist University*
Kenneth E. Aupperle, *The University of Akron*
Frank Barber, *Cuyahoga Community College*
Ellen A. Benowitz, *Mercer County Community College*
Mary Jo Boehms, *Jackson State Community College*
Anne Cowden, *California State University–Sacramento*
Raul Chavez, *Eastern Mennonite University*
Steve Dunphy, *The University of Akron*

Karen Eboch, *Bowling Green State University*
Marilyn L. Fox, *Minnesota State University, Mankato*
Alisa Fleming, *University of Phoenix*
Brad D. Hays, *North Central State College*
Robert A. Herring, III, *Winston-Salem State University*
Eileen Hogan, *Kutztown University*
Velma Jesser, *Lane Community College*
Gwendolyn Jones, *The University of Akron*
Peggi Koenecke, *California State University–Sacramento*
George S. Lowry, *Randolph-Macon College*
Jennifer Martin, *York College of Pennsylvania*
Robert L. McKeage, *The University of Scranton*
Richard R. J. Morin, *James Madison University*
Behnam Nakhai, *Millersville University of Pennsylvania*
Ralph W. Parrish, *University of Central Oklahoma*
Mary Pisnar, *Baldwin Wallace College*
Tina L. Robbins, *Clemson University*
Kathleen Rust, *Elmhurst College*
Don Schreiber, *Baylor University*
John L. Schmidt, Jr., *George Mason University*
Robert Schwartz, *University of Toledo*
Roy L. Simerly, *East Carolina University*
Randi L. Sims, *Nova Southeastern University*
Robert W. Sosna, *Menlo College*
Raymond Shea, *Monroe Community College*
William A. Stoever, *Seton Hall University*
Joe Thomas, *Middle Tennessee State University*
Gloria Walker, *Florida Community College*
Emilia S. Westney, *Texas Tech University*
Robert H. Woodhouse, *University of St. Thomas*

GUIDED TOUR

RICH AND RELEVANT EXAMPLES

An important feature of our book is the way we use real-world examples and stories about managers and companies to drive home the applied lessons to students. Our reviewers were unanimous in their praise of the sheer range and depth of the rich, interesting examples we use to illustrate the chapter material and make it come alive. Moreover, unlike other books, our boxes are seamlessly integrated in the text: they are an integral part of the learning experience, and not tacked on and unrelated to the text itself. This is central to our pedagogical approach.

Each chapter now opens with "A Manager's Challenge" which poses a chapter-related challenge and then discusses how managers in one or more organizations responded to that challenge. "A Manager's Challenge" helps demonstrate the uncertainty surrounding the management process.

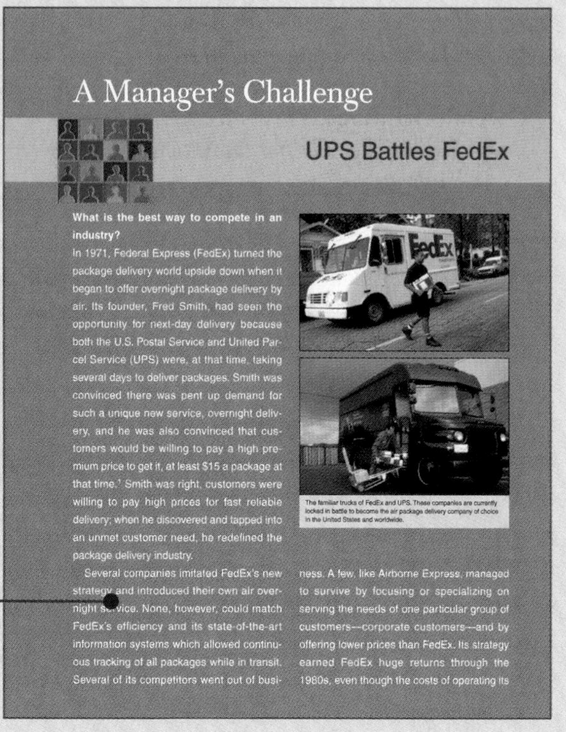

A Manager's Challenge

UPS Battles FedEx

What is the best way to compete in an industry?

In 1971, Federal Express (FedEx) turned the package delivery world upside down when it began to offer overnight package delivery by air. Its founder, Fred Smith, had seen the opportunity for next-day delivery because both the U.S. Postal Service and United Parcel Service (UPS) were, at that time, taking several days to deliver packages. Smith was convinced there was pent up demand for such a unique new service, overnight delivery, and he was also convinced that customers would be willing to pay a high premium price to get it, at least $15 a package at that time.[1] Smith was right, customers were willing to pay high prices for fast reliable delivery; when he discovered and tapped into an unmet customer need, he redefined the package delivery industry.

Several companies imitated FedEx's new strategy and introduced their own air overnight service. None, however, could match FedEx's efficiency and its state-of-the-art information systems which allowed continuous tracking of all packages while in transit. Several of its competitors went out of business. A few, like Airborne Express, managed to survive by focusing or specializing on serving the needs of one particular group of customers—corporate customers—and by offering lower prices than FedEx. Its strategy earned FedEx huge returns through the 1980s, even though the costs of operating its

The familiar trucks of FedEx and UPS. These companies are currently locked in battle to become the air package delivery company of choice in the United States and worldwide.

Managing Diverse Employees in a Diverse Environment

On the one hand, some people with real disabilities warranting workplace accommodations are hesitant to reveal their disabilities to their employers so that they can receive the accommodations they deserve.[40] On the other hand, there are anecdotes of employees abusing the ADA and seeking unnecessary accommodations for disabilities that may or may not exist.[41] Thus, perhaps, it is not surprising that the passage of the ADA does not appear to have increased employment rates significantly for those with disabilities.[42] A key challenge for managers is to promote an environment in which those needing accommodations feel comfortable disclosing their need to managers while making sure that the accommodations both enable disabled employees to effectively perform their jobs and are perceived to be fair by those not disabled.[43]

In addressing this challenge, often managers must educate both themselves and their employees about the disabilities, as well as the very real capabilities, of those who are disabled. For example, during Disability Awareness Week 2001, administrators at the University of Houston (UH) sought to increase the public's knowledge of disabilities while also h
disabled. Their program was called
Amoruso, director of the UH Center
are unaware of the prevalence of dis
consequences. For example, she sug
able to see, they can still excel in thei
such students to perform up to their c

The ADA also protects employe
drome (AIDS) from being discrimi
caused by the human immunodeficie
sexual contact, infected needles, and
spread through casual, nonsexual co
dice, some people wish to avoid all
Infected individuals may not necess
with HIV are able to remain effective
others at risk.[46]

AIDS awareness training can help
vide managers with a tool to prevent
employees. Such training focuses c
AIDS, dispelling myths, communica
emphasizing the rights of HIV-posit
ment that allows them to be product
ing is underscored by some of the p
ence once others in their workplace
following "Focus on Diversity").

Focus on Diversity

The ADA and HI
in the Workplace

The Equal Employment Opportu
plaints from 1992 to 1999 from in
nated against because of HIV. Su
of a recent Supreme Court ruling
crimination based on testing posit
required to make reasonable acco
to effectively perform their jobs.

Managing the Organizational Environment

ronment. Managing the match between the organization and its environment so that the organization's structure responds well to the forces in the task and general environments is a vital management task. In the long run, the ability of managers to perform this task is one key factor that separates high-performing from low-performing organizations and we discuss this issue in depth in Chapters 9, 10, and 11.

Utilizing IT and the Internet

Information technology (IT) and the Internet are being increasingly used by managers to help them deal with many of the forces in their task environment. On the supply side, many companies are taking advantage of business to business (B2B) networks to acquire their inputs more reliably and at less cost. Although there is currently great uncertainty over exactly how these B2B networks will evolve over time, the way they work is clear. At the industry level, all the companies in an industry agree to use the same IT software to link to each other and to the industry's suppliers, who also use the same software. As a result, purchasing managers can compare the features and prices of the different suppliers' products on-line and negotiate for the best price. At the same time, the buying companies might jointly decide that in the future they require inputs to have certain new specifications. They can use the network to inform suppliers about these changes and then allow suppliers to bid for the contract to supply the input. For example, car makers may jointly decide that in the future all the tires for SUVs should be built to higher quality specifications. Then through the B2B network they can inform all tire makers what those specifications are so they can respond quickly to these changes and bid for a particular car maker's business.

On the distribution side, the Internet can be used as an important new avenue for informing potential customers about new and existing products and providing a vehicle for selling those products to customers. The value of products sold on the Internet is expected to rise to $300 billion by 2010, something that Wal-Mart is keen to take advantage of as discussed in the "Information Technology Byte."

Information Technology Byte

Wal-Mart's New On-line Store

As Kmart found out, Wal-Mart's sophisticated inventory control IT gives it an important competitive advantage over other retailers because it allows Wal-Mart to charge lower prices to customers. Wal-Mart has always been a leader in IT. From the beginning all its stores have been connected to its head office in Bentonville, Arkansas, by satellite dish so that managers there have immediate access to information about store sales. Wal-Mart was a pioneer in using satellite TV to deliver training programs to its store managers and employees, and it now uses the Internet to handle the increased volume of programming that is necessary as it has grown globally over time.[30]

Given Wal-Mart's IT expertise, it was only natural that the company's top managers decided to establish an on-line store, walmart.com, to find yet another avenue to increase its annual $300 billion in sales. Imagine the surprise then when Wal-Mart announced a few months after opening its on-line store that it would be closing it for several weeks of "remodeling."

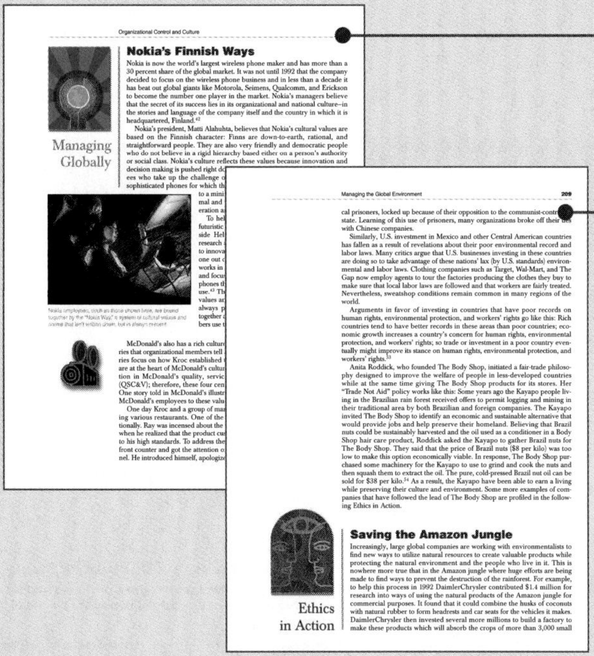
Organizational Control and Culture

Managing Globally

Nokia's Finnish Ways

Nokia is now the world's largest wireless phone maker and has more than a 30 percent share of the global market. It was not until 1992 that the company decided to focus on the wireless phone business and in less than a decade it has beat out global giants like Motorola, Seimens, Qualcomm, and Erickson to become the number one player in the market. Nokia's managers believe that the secret of its success lies in its organizational and national culture–in the stories and language of the company itself and the country in which it is headquartered, Finland.[42]

Nokia's president, Matti Alahuhta, believes that Nokia's cultural values are based on the Finnish character: Finns are down-to-earth, rational, and straightforward people. They are also very friendly and democratic people who do not believe in a rigid hierarchy based either on a person's authority or social class. Nokia's culture reflects these values because innovation and decision making is pushed right do

Nokia employees, such as those shown here, are bound together by the "Nokia Way," a system of cultural values and norms that isn't written down, but is always present.

Managing the Global Environment 209

cal prisoners, locked up because of their opposition to the communist-contr state. Learning of this use of prisoners, many organizations broke off their ties with Chinese companies.

Similarly, U.S. investment in Mexico and other Central American countries has fallen as a result of revelations about their poor environmental record and labor laws. Many critics argue that U.S. businesses investing in these countries are doing so to take advantage of these nations' lax (by U.S. standards) environmental and labor laws. Clothing companies such as Target, Wal-Mart, and The Gap now employ agents to tour the factories producing the clothes they buy to make sure that local labor laws are followed and that workers are fairly treated. Nevertheless, sweatshop conditions remain common in many regions of the world.

Arguments in favor of investing in countries that have poor records on human rights, environmental protection, and workers' rights go like this: Rich countries tend to have better records in these areas than poor countries; economic growth increases a country's concern for human rights, environmental protection, and workers' rights; so trade or investment in a poor country eventually might improve its stance on human rights, environmental protection, and workers' rights.[53]

Anita Roddick, who founded The Body Shop, initiated a fair-trade philosophy designed to improve the welfare of people in less-developed countries while at the same time giving The Body Shop products for its stores. Her "Trade Not Aid" policy works like this: Some years ago the Kayapo people living in the Brazilian rain forest received offers to permit logging and mining in their traditional area by both Brazilian and foreign companies. The Kayapo invited The Body Shop to identify an economic and sustainable alternative that would provide jobs and help preserve their homeland. Believing that Brazil nuts could be sustainably harvested and the oil used as a conditioner in a Body Shop hair care product, Roddick asked the Kayapo to gather Brazil nuts for The Body Shop. They said that the price of Brazil nuts ($8 per kilo) was too low to make this option economically viable. In response, The Body Shop purchased some machinery for the Kayapo to use to grind and cook the nuts and then squash them to extract the oil. The pure, cold-pressed Brazil nut oil can be sold for $38 per kilo.[54] As a result, the Kayapo have been able to earn a living while preserving their culture and environment. Some more examples of companies that have followed the lead of The Body Shop are profiled in the following Ethics in Action.

Ethics in Action

Saving the Amazon Jungle

Increasingly, large global companies are working with environmentalists to find new ways to utilize natural resources to create valuable products while protecting the natural environment and the people who live in it. This is nowhere more true that in the Amazon jungle where huge efforts are being made to find ways to prevent the destruction of the rainforest. For example, to help this process in 1992 DaimlerChrysler contributed $1.4 million for research into ways of using the natural products of the Amazon jungle for commercial purposes. It found that it could combine the husks of coconuts with natural rubber to form headrests and car seats for the vehicles it makes. DaimlerChrysler then invested several more millions to build a factory to make these products which will absorb the crops of more than 3,000 small

Additional in-depth examples appear in boxes throughout each chapter. "Management Insight" boxes illustrate the topics of the chapter, while the "Ethics in Action," "Managing Globally," "Focus on Diversity," and "Information Technology Byte" boxes examine the chapter topics from each of these perspectives. These are not "boxes" in the traditional sense, meaning they're not disembodied from the chapter narrative. These thematic applications are fully integrated into the reading. Students will no longer be forced to decide whether to read "boxed" material. It is also important to make these features interesting to students so that they engage students while illustrating the chapter material.

392 Chapter Eleven

In following these guidelines, managers need to remember why they are giving performance feedback: to encourage high levels of motivation and performance. Moreover, the information that managers gather through performance appraisal and feedback helps them determine how to distribute pay raises and bonuses.

Tips for New Managers

Performance Appraisal

1. Be sure to provide frequent informal appraisals and give performance feedback often.
2. Focus on results for performance appraisal and feedback when high performance can be reached by different kinds of behaviors and how employees perform their jobs is not important.
3. Focus on specific behaviors or outcomes, when providing performance feedback, adopt a problem-solving mode, express confidence in employees, praise instances of high performance, and agree to a timetable for improvements.
4. Avoid personal criticisms and treat employees with respect.
5. Seek honest appraisals of, and feedback on, your own behavior and take steps to improve your performance.

Pay and Benefits Pay includes employees' base salaries, pay raises, and bonuses and is determined by a number of factors including characteristics of the organization and the job and levels of performance. Employee benefits are based on membership in an organization (and not necessarily on the particular job held); they include sick days, vacation days, and medical and life insurance. In Chapter 12, we discuss the ways in which pay can motivate organizational members to perform at a high level, as well as the different kinds of pay plans managers can use to help an organization achieve its goals and gain a competitive advantage. Next we focus on establishing an organization's pay level and pay structure.

Pay Level

pay level The relative position of an organization's pay incentives in comparison with those of other organizations in the same industry employing similar kinds of workers.

Pay level is a broad comparative concept that refers to how an organization's pay incentives compare, in general, to those of other organizations in the same industry employing similar kinds of workers. Managers must decide if they want to offer relatively high wages, average wages, or relatively low wages. High wages help ensure that an organization is going to be able to recruit, select, and retain high performers, but high wages also raise costs. Low wages give an organization a cost advantage but may undermine the organization's ability to select and recruit high performers and to motivate current employees to perform at a high level. Either of these situations may lead to inferior quality or inadequate customer service.

This edition also continues the feature "Tips for New Managers" which distills the lessons that students can take from the chapter and use to develop their management skills.

EXPERIENTIAL LEARNING FEATURES

We have given considerable time and attention to developing state-of-the-art experiential end-of-chapter learning exercises that we hope will also drive home the meaning of management to students. Grouped together at the end of each chapter in the section called Management in Action, they include:

TOPICS FOR DISCUSSION AND ACTION A set of chapter-related questions and points for reflection some of which ask students to research actual management issues and learn first-hand from practicing managers.

BUILDING MANAGEMENT SKILLS A self-development exercise that asks students to apply what they have learned to their own experience of organizations and managers or to the experiences of others.

SMALL GROUP BREAKOUT EXERCISE This unique exercise is designed to allow instructors in large section classes to utilize interactive experiential exercises in groups of 3–4 students. The instructor calls on students to break up into small groups–simply by turning to people around them–and all students participate in the exercise in class, and a mechanism is provided for the different groups to share what they have learned with each other.

EXPLORING THE WORLD WIDE WEB Two Internet exercises are designed to draw students into the Web and give them experience of the new information systems, while applying what they have learned.

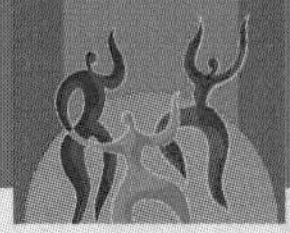

Management in Action

Topics for Discussion and Action

1. Describe the three steps of planning. Explain how they are related.
2. How can scenario planning help managers predict the future?
3. Ask a manager about the kinds of planning exercises he or she regularly uses. What are the purposes of these exercises, and what are their advantages or disadvantages?
4. What is the role of divisional and functional managers in the formulation of strategy?
5. Why is it important for functional managers to have a clear grasp of the organization's mission when developing strategies within their departments?
6. What is the relationship among corporate-, business-, and functional-level strategies and how do they create value for an organization?
7. Ask a manager to identify the corporate-, business-, and functional-level strategies used by his or her organization.

Building Management Skills

How to Analyze a Company's Strategy

Pick a well-known business organization that has received recent press coverage and for which you can get the annual reports or 10K filings from your school library for a number of years. For this organization do the following:

1. From the annual reports or 10K filings identify the main strategies pursued by the company over a ten-year period.
2. Try to identify why the company pursued these strategies. What reason was given in the annual reports, press reports, and so on?
3. Document whether and when any major changes in the strategy of the organization occurred. If changes did occur, try to identify the reason for them.
4. If changes in strategy occurred, try to determine the extent to which they were the result of long-term plans and the extent to which they were responses to unforeseen changes in the company's task environment.
5. What is the main industry that the company competes in?
6. What business-level strategy does the company seem to be pursuing in this industry?
7. What is the company's reputation with regard to productivity, quality, innovation, and responsiveness to customers in this industry? If the company has attained an advantage in any of these areas, how has it done so?
8. What is the current corporate-level strategy of the company? What is the company's stated reason for pursuing this strategy?
9. Has the company expanded internationally? If it has, identify its largest international market. How did the company enter this market? Did its mode of entry change over time?

280

Small Group Breakout Exercise

Low Cost or Differentiation?

Form groups of three or four people, and appoint one member as spokesperson who will communicate your findings to the class when called on by the instructor. Then discuss the following scenario.

You are a team of managers of a major national clothing chain, and you have been assigned with finding a way to restore your organization's competitive advantage. Recently, your organization has been experiencing increasing competition from two sources. First, discount stores such as Wal-Mart and Target have been undercutting your prices because they buy their clothes from low-cost foreign manufacturers while you buy most of yours from high-quality domestic suppliers. Discount stores have been attracting your customers who buy at the low end of the price range. Second, small boutiques opening in malls provide high-price designer clothing and are attracting away your customers at the high end of the market. Your company has become stuck in the middle, and you have to decide what to do: Should you start to buy abroad so that you can lower your prices and start to pursue a low-cost strategy? Should you focus on the high end of the market and become more of a differentiator? Or should you try to do both and pursue both a low-cost strategy and a differentiation strategy?

1. Using scenario planning, analyze the pros and cons of each alternative.
2. Think about the various clothing retailers in your local malls and city, and analyze the choices they have made about how to compete with one another along the low-cost and differentiation dimensions.

Exploring the World Wide Web

Search for a website that contains a good description of a company's strategy. What is the company's mission? Use the concepts and terminology of this chapter to describe the company's strategy to achieve its mission.

You're the Management Consultant

A group of investors in your city is considering opening a new upscale supermarket to compete with the major supermarket chains that are currently dominating the city's marketplace. They have called you in to help them determine what kind of upscale supermarket they should open. In other words, how can they best develop a competitive advantage against existing supermarket chains?

Questions

1. List the supermarket chains in your city and identify their strengths and weaknesses.
2. What business-level strategies are these supermarkets currently pursuing?
3. What kind of supermarket would do best against the competition? What kind of business-level strategy should it pursue?

BusinessWeek Cases in the News

Ford's Gamble on Luxury: Can It Make Its Portfolio of Acquired Brands Work Together?

Over the past decade, Ford Motor Co. has grown fat on profits from its pickup trucks and sport-utility vehicles. Last year, those trucks accounted for 80 percent of its pretax auto earnings in North America. But now that foreign auto makers have finally found their groove with light-truck vehicles that are truly competitive, those earnings are in jeopardy. Faced with such hot-selling models as the Toyota Sequoia and the BMW X5, Ford could see its share of the light-truck market fall by as

281

NEW! YOU'RE THE MANAGEMENT CONSULTANT This exercise presents a realistic scenario in which a manager/organization faces some kind of challenge, problem, or opportunity and the student plays the role of a management consultant offering advice and recommending a course of action based on the chapter content. Because managers and organizations frequently need this kind of help either internally (from other members of the organization) or externally (from consultants), these exercises provide students a real, hands-on way to take an action-oriented approach to solving "real" problems by applying what they've just learned in the chapter.

BUSINESS WEEK CASES IN THE NEWS Each chapter has two cases for analysis (or sometimes one longer case), which are shortened versions of actual *Business Week* articles. The accompanying discussion questions encourage students to read about and to analyze how real managers deal with real problems in the business world. Some of these cases, especially the longer ones, are to be found on the *Contemporary Management* website at www.mhhe.com/jones3e. These cases give instructors the opportunity to explore issues in more depth if they choose.

Our idea is that instructors can select from these exercises and vary them over the semester so that students can learn the meaning of management through many different avenues. These exercises complement the chapter material and have been class tested to add to the overall learning experience, and students report that they both learn from them and enjoy them.

INTEGRATED LEARNING SYSTEM

Great care was used in the creation of the supplemental materials to accompany *Contemporary Management*. Whether you are a seasoned faculty or a newly minted instructor, you'll find our support materials to be the most thorough and thoughtful ever created!

Instructor's Manual

Prepared by Anne Cowden of California State University-Sacramento, each chapter contains an overview, learning objectives, key terms, list of resources, notes for opening case, lecture outline, three lecture enhancers (at least one per chapter is new to this edition), notes for small group breakout exercises and World Wide Web exercises, notes for management cases, and video teaching notes.

Test Bank and Computerized Test Bank

The test bank has been thoroughly reviewed, revised and improved in response to customer feedback by a new author, Eileen Hogan, of Kutztown University. There are approximately 100 questions per chapter, including true-false, multiple-choice, and essay, each tagged with level of difficulty (corresponding to Bloom's taxonomy of educational objectives), correct answer, and page references to the text.

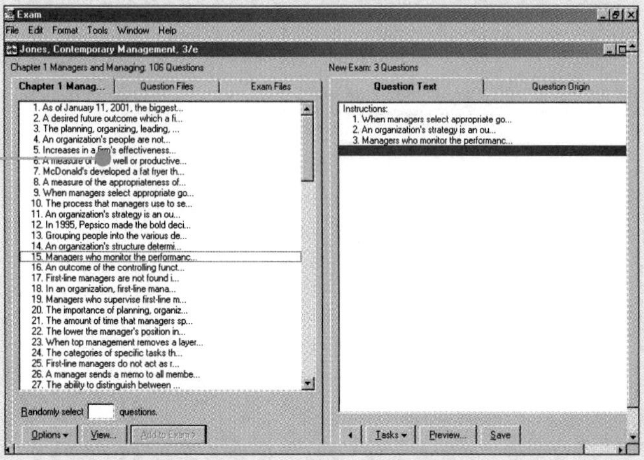

64 Chapter Two

Sony's Organic Structure

Managing Globally

Product engineers at Sony turn out an average of four ideas for new products every day. Despite the fact that Sony is now a huge, diversified organization employing more than 115,000 employees worldwide, the company continues to lead the way in innovation in the consumer electronics industry.[44] Why? A large part of the answer lies in the way the company uses its structure to organize and control its employees. First, a policy of self-promotion allows Sony engineers, without notifying their supervisors, to seek out projects anywhere in the company where they feel they can make a contribution. If they find new projects to which they can make contributions, their current bosses are expected to let them join the new teams. Sony has twenty-three business groups composed of hundreds of development teams, and this movement of people cross-pollinates ideas throughout the organization.[45]

Second, Sony deliberately emphasizes the lateral movement of people and ideas between design and engineering groups. The "Sony Way" emphasizes communication between groups to foster innovation and change.[46] Sony has a corporate research department full of people in integrating roles who coordinate the efforts of the business groups and product development teams. They make sure that each team knows what the others are doing, not only to share knowledge but also to avoid overlap or duplication of effort. Once a year, the corporate research department organizes an in-house three-day special event open only to Sony employees, where each product development team can display its work to its peers.

That Sony's organic structure works is evident from the company's success in the marketplace and from the number of innovative products Sony turns out. Like many other large Japanese companies, Sony has a policy of lifetime employment, which makes it easy for its engineers to take risks with ideas and encourages the development of norms and values that support innovative efforts. Moreover, Sony rewards its engineers with promotion and more control of resources when they are successful.

Sony is hard-headed, however, when it comes to making the best use of its resources. Top management takes pains to distance itself from decision making inside a team or even a business group, so that the magic of decentralized decision making can work. But it does intervene when different groups are duplicating one another's efforts. For example, when Sony made a big push into computers it reorganized the relationship between its audio, video, and computer groups so that they improved the way they coordinate new product developments. Once again, however, Sony takes a lateral view of the way the organization works, and its vertical chain of command is oriented toward finding ways to decentralize authority and still make the best use of resources. This lateral approach to organizing and controlling is working well as Sony is making record profits and has become the dominant global electronics competitor.

One of a stream of Sony's new Internet products that its engineers are turning out to secure the company's place in the growing market for digital electronic products.

Part 3 of this book is devoted to strategic management, the study of the relationship between organizations and their external environment and of the strategies organizations adopt to manage that environment.[47]

Videos

Two valuable sets of videos are now available with this text: a fresh line-up of case videos featuring programs from NBC and PBS news reports and a new series of management skills videos called the "Manager's Hot Seat." The case videos provide further coverage of topics, examples, and cases in each chapter that are identified with a distinctive video icon appearing in the book margins. New video titles include "Donna Dubinsky, Creator of Palm Pilot," "Dot Gone: Dot-Com Companies Failing," "MTV/Viacom China Manager Discusses the Changing Culture and Attitude in China," and "Daniel Goleman Discusses His Book, Emotional Intelligence." The Manager's Hot Seat videos show how real managers respond to simulated real-world scenarios that require the use of key management skills, including "Managing Personality Clashes/Conflict Resolution," "Self-Management: Disclosing Personal Information," "Using Active Listening to Resolve Issues," and "Managing Diversity: The Interview Process."

Chapter 1
Managers and Managing
Contemporary Management
Third Edition
Gareth R. Jones
Jennifer M. George
McGraw-Hill Irwin
PowerPoint Presentation by Charlie Cook
© Copyright McGraw-Hill. All rights reserved.

Instructor's Presentation Manager CD-ROM

This presentation CD-ROM allows instructors to easily create their own custom presentations using resources on the CD, like the instructor's manual, video clips, and PowerPoint®, or from their own PowerPoint® slides or Web screenshots.

PowerPoint® Presentation

Approximately 400 slides feature reproductions of key tables & figures from the text as well as original content, created by Charlie Cook of the University of West Alabama.

FOR STUDENTS

Student Study Guide
Prepared by Tom Quirk of Webster University, the study guide has been completely revised and updated with the goal of helping students master course content. Each chapter now includes learning objectives; chapter outline; and matching, true-false, multiple-choice, and essay questions, with answer keys including page references to the text.

Student CD-ROM
Every new copy of the Third Edition is packaged with a free Student CD-ROM, featuring an integrative case study on Yahoo!, with accompanying video, plus self-scoring chapter quizzes, chapter reviews, Web links, and interactive self-assessments such as "Active Listening Skills," "Team Roles Preference Scales," "What Is Your Primary Conflict Handling Style?" "Sources of Power," "Maslow's Hierarchy of Needs."

The Contemporary Management Online Learning Center
www.mhhe.com/jones3e
This website provides a convenient collection of online learning resources designed to reinforce and build on the text content, including chapter reviews, self-quizzes, exercises, cases, and news updates. (A password-protected section is also available to instructors, containing downloadable supplements, sample syllabi, and a message board.)

PowerWeb http://www.dushkin.com/powerweb.
Harness the assets of the Web to keep your course current with PowerWeb! This online resource provides high quality, peer-reviewed content including up-articles from leading periodicals and journals, current news, weekly updates with assessment, interactive exercises, Web research guide, study tips, and much more!

Business Week Edition
Students can subscribe to *Business Week* for a specially priced rate of $8.25 in addition to the price of this text.

Authors

Gareth R. Jones is a Professor of Management in the Lowry Mays College and Graduate School of Business at Texas A&M University. He received his B.A. in Economics/Psychology and his Ph.D. in Management from the University of Lancaster, U.K. He previously held teaching and research appointments at the University Warwick, Michigan State University, and the University of Illinois at Urbana–Champaign. He is a frequent visitor and speaker at universities in both the United Kingdom and the United States.

He specializes in strategic management and organizational theory and is well-known for his research that applies transaction cost analysis to explain many forms of strategic and organizational behavior. He is currently interested in strategy process, competitive advantage, and information technology issues. He is also investigating the relationships between ethics, trust, and organizational culture and studying the role of affect in the strategic decision-making process.

He has published many articles in leading journals of the field and his recent work has appeared in the *Academy of Management Review, Journal of International Business Studies, Human Relations.* An article on the role of information technology on many aspects of organizational functioning was recently published in the *Journal of Management.* One of his articles won the *Academy of Management Journal* Best Paper Award and he is one of the most prolific authors in the *Academy of Management Review.* He is or has served on the editorial boards of the *Academy of Management Review,* the *Journal of Management,* and *Management Inquiry.*

Gareth Jones has taken his academic knowledge and used it to craft leading textbooks in management, and three other major areas in the management discipline: organizational behavior, organizational theory, and strategic management. His books are widely recognized for their innovative, contemporary content, and for the clarity with which they communicate complex, real-world issues to students. He comes from a long line of educators and is happy that his two children, Nicholas who is 10, and Julia who is 9, seem to show similar interests, as they are always trying to teach him new things.

Jennifer M. George is the Mary Gibbs Jones Professor of Management and Professor of Psychology in the Jesse H. Jones Graduate School of Management at Rice University. She received her B.A. in Psychology/Sociology from Wesleyan University, her M.B.A. in Finance from New York University, and her Ph.D. in Management and Organizational Behavior from New York University. Prior to joining the faculty at Rice University, she was a Professor in the Department of Management at Texas A&M University.

She specializes in Organizational Behavior and is well known for her research on mood and emotion in the workplace, their determinants, and their effects on various individual and group level work outcomes. She is the author of many articles in leading peer-reviewed journals such as the *Academy of Management Journal,* the *Academy of Management Review,* the *Journal of Applied Psychology, Organizational Behavior and Human Decision Processes, Journal of Personality and Social Psychology,* and *Psychological Bulletin.* One of her papers won the Academy of Management's Organizational Behavior Division Outstanding Competitive Paper Award and another paper won the *Human Relations* Best Paper Award. She is, or has been, on the editorial review boards of the *Journal of Applied Psychology, Academy of Management Journal, Journal of Management, Organizational Behavior and Human Decision Processes,* and *Journal of Managerial Issues,* was a consulting editor for the *Journal of Organizational Behavior,* and is a member of the SIOP *Organizational Frontiers Series* editorial board. She is a Fellow in the American Psychological Association, the American Psychological Society, and the Society for Industrial and Organizational Psychology and a member of the Society for Organizational Behavior. Professor George is currently an Associate Editor for the *Journal of Applied Psychology.*

Chapter 1

Managers and Managing

Learning Objectives

After studying this chapter, you should be able to:

- Describe **what management is,** why management is important, what managers do, and how managers utilize organizational resources efficiently and effectively to achieve organizational goals.
- Distinguish among **planning, organizing, leading, and controlling** (the four principal managerial functions), and explain how managers' ability to handle each one can affect organizational performance.
- Differentiate among **three levels of management,** and understand the responsibilities of managers at different levels in the organizational hierarchy.
- Identify the **roles managers perform,** the skills they need to execute those roles effectively and the way new information technology is affecting these roles and skills.
- Discuss the principal **challenges managers face** in today's increasingly competitive global environment.

A Manager's Challenge

Bob Pittman's Big Job at AOL-Time Warner

What is high-performance management? On January 11, 2001, the biggest ever U.S. merger was finalized when two very different companies, America Online and Time Warner, joined together to form a $97 billion global entertainment media and information technology giant, AOL-Time Warner.[1] The combined AOL-Time Warner has interests in global Internet services and cable with more than 126 million subscribers. Its filmed entertainment interests include Warner Brothers and New Line Cinema; its television networks include CNN, TBS, and HBO; and its music and publishing interests include Warner Music, *Time* magazine, *Sports Illustrated,* and *People* magazine. The chairman of the new company, AOL founder Steve Case, and then chief executive officer (CEO), Time Warner's Gerald Levin chose Robert (Bob) Pittman, the company's chief operating officer, to perform the critical managerial job for the new company.[2]

Pittman's big job? To find the best way to efficiently and effectively combine the people and resources of both companies to use them to create more products and services, such as Internet TV and video on demand, for its customers and hence increase its profits. Pittman's challenge was to find a way to get all the company's managers to not just focus on their own particular task and role but to think about ways to make better use of the company's extensive resources organizationwide. For example, Pittman needed to get the managers of *Time* magazine to think about how they could use AOL's internet presence to increase the circulation or advertising revenues of their magazine. And, he needed to get AOL managers to think about how best to expand their service into Time Warner's cable networks, as well as to get cable customers to sign up for AOL Internet service.

Bob Pittman, pictured with his Harley-Davidson, loves to take long motorcycle trips when he has the time to get away from his difficult job of managing the AOL-Time Warner merger. A former radio show host, MTV executive, and TV show producer, he has spent all of his career in the entertainment industry.

To help AOL-Time Warner make the best use of its resources, Pittman immediately began to involve all managers in planning how the new company would operate in the future. He brought thousands of managers from different parts of the company together in weekly meetings to discuss, decide, and envision how they could create valuable new products or services that customers would want.[3] Countless meetings began to take place between managers from different parts and from all levels in the organization to decide what course of action or goals to set for the new company.[4]

One immediate obstacle he faced in developing a high-quality planning process was that the previously separated companies were organized very differently. The old Time Warner had been very hierarchical in nature, it was bureaucratic and decision making was slow. At AOL, on the other hand, managers were used to the fast-changing environment of the Internet and information technology industry. They were used to making decisions in teams and to making decisions quickly. Pittman, who was from AOL, decided that the AOL organizing model was the one that would be most successful in the new company. He created teams of AOL and Time Warner managers but made AOL managers responsible for taking the lead, and developing an organizational culture that would bring new products to market quickly.

Getting different kinds of managers to work together effectively is no easy task but Pittman was aided by the fact that he has good leadership qualities. He is renowned for his diplomacy and his ability to get what he wants done by persuasion rather than command. He used these leadership skills to forge a team among managers and make collaboration rather than competition the basis of the values in the company's new culture.

At the same time, however, one of the reasons for Pittman's success as a manager has been his concern for the bottom line—managing costs. His rise through the AOL hierarchy was achieved partly because he has great operational skills and recognizes ways to cut costs and speed new products to market quickly. Pittman accomplished this by his way of controlling the behavior of managers and their businesses. Pittman established challenging targets for each manager and for each part of the company to achieve. For example, one target was to justify the merger the company announced in 2001 by increasing annual revenues by 12 to 15 percent and realizing more than $1 billion in cost savings in the first year. To achieve these ambitious targets, Pittman set revenue and cost saving targets for his top managers to achieve, and they in turn set targets for their subordinates to achieve and so on down the organization. In August 2001, the company laid off several thousand employees to help it achieve its cost-saving goals.

Whether Pittman succeeds depends on whether AOL-Time Warner does in fact meet the targets it has set for itself. Pittman himself has a major personal stake in his success as a manager because it seems likely that if he makes his big job a success, he may become a future CEO of the company.

Overview

Bob Pittman's big job at AOL-Time Warner illustrates many of the challenges facing people who become managers: Managing a company or organization is a complex activity, and managers must learn the skills and acquire the knowledge necessary to become effective. Management is an unpredictable, risky process. Making the right decision is difficult; even effective managers often make mistakes, but the most effective managers are the ones, like Pittman, who rise to the top of the managerial hierarchy and bear the principal responsibility for an organization's success.

In this chapter, we look at what managers do and what skills and abilities they must develop if they are to manage their organizations successfully over time. We also identify the different kinds of managers that organizations need and the skills and abilities they must develop if they are to be successful. Finally, we identify some of the challenges that managers must address if their organizations are to grow and prosper.

What Is Management?

When you think of a manager, what kind of person comes to mind? Do you see someone who, like Bob Pittman, can determine the future prosperity of a large for-profit company? Or do you see the administrator of a not-for-profit organization such as a school, library, or charity, or the person in charge of your local McDonald's restaurant or Wal-Mart store, or the person you answer to if you have a part-time job? What do all these managers have in common? First, they all work in organizations. Organizations are collections of people who work together and coordinate their actions to achieve a wide variety of *goals,* or desired future outcomes.[5] Second, as managers, they are the people responsible for supervising the use of an organization's human and other resources to achieve its goals. **Management,** then, is the planning, organizing, leading, and controlling of human and other resources to achieve organizational goals effectively and efficiently. An organization's resources include assets such as people and their skills and knowledge; machinery, raw materials, computers and information technology, and financial capital.

management The planning, organizing, leading, and controlling of human and other resources to achieve organizational goals effectively and efficiently.

Achieving High Performance: A Manager's Goal

One of the most important goals that organizations and their members try to achieve is to provide some kind of good or service that customers desire. The principal goal of COO Bob Pittman is to manage the merger of AOL and Time Warner so that a new stream of goods and services, such as improved Internet service and TV, interactive games, movies on demand, and electronic books, are created that customers are willing to buy. The principal goal of doctors, nurses, and hospital administrators is to increase their hospital's ability to make sick people well. Likewise, the principal goal of each McDonald's restaurant manager is to produce burgers, fries, and shakes that people want to pay for and eat.

Organizational performance is a measure of how efficiently and effectively managers use resources to satisfy customers and achieve organizational goals. Organizational performance increases in direct proportion to increases in efficiency and effectiveness (see Figure 1.1).

organizational performance A measure of how efficiently and effectively a manager uses resources to satisfy customers and achieve organizational goals.

efficiency A measure of how well or productively resources are used to achieve a goal.

Efficiency is a measure of how well or how productively resources are used to achieve a goal.[6] Organizations are efficient when managers minimize the amount of input resources (such as labor, raw materials, and component parts) or the amount of time needed to produce a given output of goods or services. For example, McDonald's developed a more efficient fat frier that not only reduces the amount of oil used in cooking (by 30 percent) but also speeds up the cooking of french fries. Bob Pittman instructed his managers to search for ways to achieve $1 billion cost savings by streamlining the company's operations and eliminating duplication of services such as information and financial management and sales. A manager's responsibility is to ensure that an organization and its members perform as efficiently as possible all the activities needed to provide goods and services to customers.

Figure 1.1
Efficiency, Effectiveness, and Performance in an Organization

EFFICIENCY

EFFECTIVENESS	**LOW**	**HIGH**
HIGH	Low efficiency/ High effectiveness Manager chooses the right goals to pursue, but does a poor job of using resources to achieve these goals. Result: A product that customers want, but that is too expensive for them to buy.	High efficiency/ High effectiveness Manager chooses the right goals to pursue and makes good use of resources to achieve these goals. Result: A product that customers want at a quality and price that they can afford.
LOW	Low efficiency/ Low effectiveness Manager chooses wrong goals to pursue and makes poor use of resources. Result: A low-quality product that customers do not want.	High efficiency/ Low effectiveness Manager chooses inapppropriate goals, but makes good use of resources to pursue these goals. Result: A high-quality product that customers do not want.

High-performing organizations are efficient *and* effective.

effectiveness
A measure of the appropriateness of the goals an organization is pursuing and of the degree to which the organization achieves those goals.

Effectiveness is a measure of the appropriateness of the goals that managers have selected for the organization to pursue, and of the degree to which the organization achieves those goals. Organizations are effective when managers choose appropriate goals and then achieve them. Some years ago, for example, managers at McDonald's decided on the goal of providing breakfast service to attract more customers. The choice of this goal has proved very smart, for sales of breakfast food now account for more than 30 percent of McDonald's revenues. Pittman's goal is to create a constant flow of new kinds of innovative media and entertainment products. High-performing organizations such as AOL-Time Warner, McDonald's, Wal-Mart, Intel, Home Depot, Arthur Andersen, and the March of Dimes, are simultaneously efficient and effective, as shown in Figure 1.1. Managers who are effective are those who choose the right organizational goals to pursue and have the skills to utilize resources efficiently.

Why Study Management?

Today, more students are competing for places in business courses than ever before; the number of people wishing to pursue Master of Business Administration (MBA) degrees–today's passport to an advanced management position–is at an all time high. Why is the study of management currently so popular?

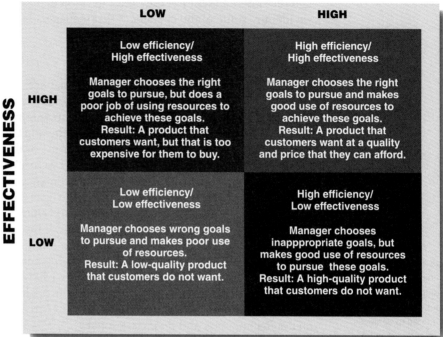

First, in any society or culture resources are valuable and scarce and the more efficient and effective use that organizations can make of those resources the greater the relative well-being and prosperity of people in that society. Because managers are the people who decide how to use many of a society's most valuable resources–its skilled employees, raw materials like oil and land, computers and information systems, and financial assets–they directly impact the well-being of a society and the people in it. Understanding what managers do and how they do it is of central importance to understanding how a society works and how it creates wealth.

Second, although most people are not managers, and many may never intend to become managers, almost all of us come into contact with managers because most people have jobs and bosses. Moreover, many people today are working in groups and teams and have to deal with co-workers. Studying management helps people to deal with their bosses and their co-workers. It reveals how to make decisions, plan, and organize tasks and resources that win the attention and support of the boss. Management also teaches people not yet in positions of authority how to lead co-workers, solve conflicts between them, and increase team performance.

Third, in any society people are in competition for a very important resource–a well-paying job and an interesting and satisfying career–and understanding management is one important path toward obtaining such a position. In general, jobs become more interesting the more complex or responsible they are. Any person who desires a motivating job that changes over time therefore might do well to develop management skills and become promotable. A person who has been working for several years and then returns to school for an MBA can usually find a more interesting, satisfying job and one that pays significantly more than the previous one. Moreover, salaries increase rapidly as people move up the organizational hierarchy whether it be a school system, a large for-profit business organization, or a not-for-profit charitable or medical institution.

Indeed, the salaries paid to top managers are enormous. For example, at AOL-Time Warner, CEO Gerald Levin received over $11 million in actual salary in 2000 and Bob Pittman was paid almost $1 million. However, even more staggering is the fact that most top executives also receive stock or shares in the company they manage and stock options that give them the right to sell these shares at a certain time in the future. If the value of the stock goes up then the managers keep the difference between the price they obtained the stock option for and what it is worth later. Since both AOL and Time Warner's stock prices have increased significantly over time, in January 2001 Levin's stock options were worth almost $300 million and Pittman's $182 million![7] These incredible amounts of money provide some indication of both the responsibilities and rewards that accompany the achievement of high management positions in major organizations. What is it that managers actually do to receive such rewards?

Managerial Functions

The job of management is to help an organization make the best use of its resources to achieve its goals. How do managers accomplish this objective? They do so by performing four essential managerial functions: *planning, organizing, leading,* and *controlling* (see Figure 1.2). The arrows linking these functions in Figure 1.2 suggest the sequence in which managers typically perform these functions. French manager Henri Fayol first outlined the nature of these managerial activities around the turn of the twentieth century in *General and Industrial Management,* a book that remains the classic statement of what managers must do to create a high-performing organization.[8]

Managers at all levels and in all departments–whether in small or large organizations, for-profit or not-for-profit organizations, or organizations that operate

Figure 1.2
Four Functions of Management

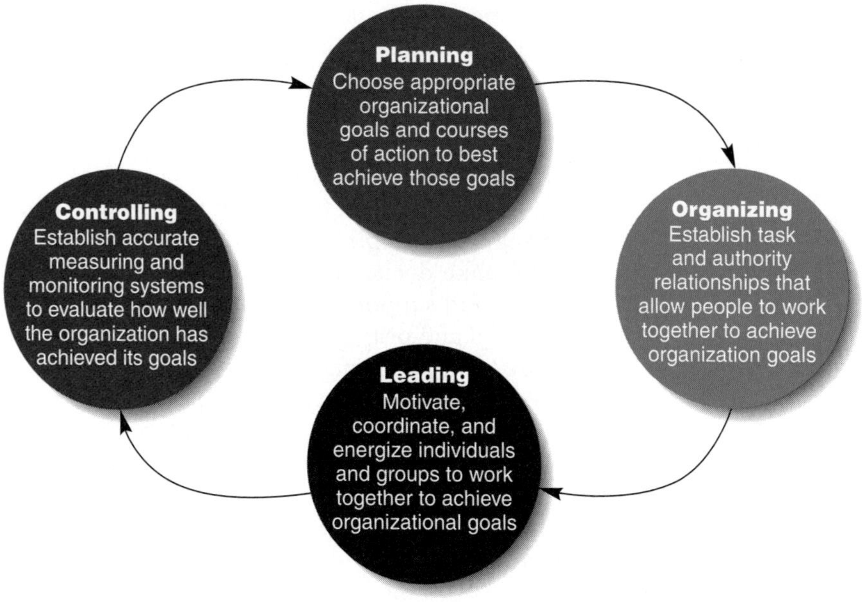

in one country or throughout the world–are responsible for performing these four functions that we look at next. How well managers perform these functions determines how efficient and effective their organizations are.

Planning

planning Identifying and selecting appropriate goals; one of the four principal functions of management.

Planning is a process that managers use to identify and select appropriate goals and courses of action. The three steps in the planning process are: (1) deciding which goals the organization will pursue, (2) deciding what courses of action to adopt to attain those goals, and (3) deciding how to allocate organizational resources to attain those goals. How well managers plan determines how effective and efficient their organization is–its performance level.[9]

As an example of planning in action consider the situation confronting Michael Dell, CEO of Dell Computer.[10] In 1984, the 19-year-old Dell saw an opportunity to enter the personal computer market by making personal computers and then selling them directly to customers. Dell began to plan how to put this idea into practice. First, he decided that his goal was to sell an inexpensive personal computer, to undercut the prices of companies like IBM and Apple Computer. Second, he had to decide on a course of action to achieve this goal. He decided to sell directly to customers by telephone and to bypass expensive computer stores. He also had to decide how to obtain low-cost components and how to tell potential customers about his products. Third, he had to decide how to allocate his limited funds (he only had $5,000) to buy labor and other resources. He chose to hire three people and work with them around a table to assemble his machines. Thus, to put his vision of making and selling personal computers into practice, Dell had to plan, and as his organization grew, his plans changed and became progressively more complex. In 2002, Dell and his managers are planning how to help the company maintain its position as the biggest and highest performing PC maker.[11] Bob Pittman has a similar goal of planning how to use AOL-Time Warner's resources to make it the most profitable global entertainment and media company.

Michael Dell sits in the dorm room at the University of Texas, Austin, where he launched his personal computer company as a college freshman. The room is now occupied by freshmen Russell Smith (left) and Jacob Frith, both from Plano, Texas.

strategy A cluster of decisions about what goals to pursue, what actions to take, and how to use resources to achieve goals.

The outcome of planning is a strategy, a cluster of decisions concerning what organizational goals to pursue, what actions to take, and how to use resources to achieve goals. The decisions that were the outcome of Michael Dell's planning formed a *low-cost strategy.* A low-cost strategy is a way of obtaining customers by making decisions that allow the organization to produce its goods or services cheaply so that prices can be kept low. Dell has been constantly refining this strategy and exploring new strategies to reduce costs; in 2001 Dell became the market leader as a result of this strategy. By contrast, AOL-Time Warner's strategy is to deliver new, exciting, and different entertainment products to its customers, a strategy known as differentiation.

Planning is a difficult activity because normally what goals an organization should pursue and how best to pursue them–which strategies to adopt–is not immediately clear. Managers take risks when they commit organizational resources to pursue a particular strategy. Either success or failure is a possible outcome of the planning process. Dell succeeded spectacularly, but many other PC makers either went out of business (such as Packard Bell and Digital) or lost huge sums of money (like IBM and AT&T) trying to compete in this industry. In Chapter 8 we focus on the planning process and on the strategies organizations can select to respond to opportunities or threats in an industry. The story of Indra Nooyi's rise to power at PepsiCo illustrates well how important planning and strategy making are to a manager's career success.

Managing Globally

Choosing the Right Strategy Pays off at PepsiCo

In 1995 Indra K. Nooyi found herself in a very enviable position. Both General Electric and PepsiCo were offering her a high-level position as one of the chief global strategists for their companies. In the end Nooyi chose to join Wayne Calloway, then CEO of PepsiCo, because he convinced her she would have the opportunity to use her conceptual and analytical skills to make a great global contribution to that company. From the beginning she worked closely with Calloway to chart PepsiCo's future global strategy. The company was not performing up to Wall Street's expectations, its share price was depressed, and management had to find out why and solve the problem.[12]

In 1995 beyond its huge global soda empire, PepsiCo owned the food chains Taco Bell, Kentucky Fried Chicken, and Pizza Hut which had operations throughout the world. The strategy behind owning these food chains was that PepsiCo could sell its soft drinks and snack products (it also owns Frito-Lay) in its restaurants. Nooyi and Calloway wondered if this strategy was working, however, so they spent months touring the restaurants and eating the food and trying to decide if ownership of these chains was central to PepsiCo's long-term goals. They also went abroad to get a close view of how PepsiCo's global operations were performing. In a bold move, they decided that these chains were really in a totally different business and they spun-off the food chains in 1997 to focus on PepsiCo's global soft drink business.[13]

Indra Nooyi, president and CFO of PepsiCo, stands next to Robert Morrison, Chairman and CEO of Quaker Oats, which PepsiCo acquired in 2000, former PepsiCo CEO Roger A. Enrico, and new CEO Steve Reinemund. This top management team has to manage the newly merged company and Nooyi is actively searching for new product opportunities to help increase its revenues.

Nooyi was convinced that what PepsiCo needed to do was to strengthen its global position in its core businesses of soft drinks and snacks. So she led the efforts to acquire Tropicana, the fruit juice maker that PepsiCo bought in 1998. Next, watching Coca-Cola sell off its bottling operations, she also carefully analyzed whether PepsiCo should bottle its own soft drinks or sell this business off, too. The result of this planning analysis was that she and Calloway came to the conclusion that it would be good to sell this business, too.

Wall Street also thought these changes in strategy were good; as Pepsi began to capture a bigger share of the global market from Coke, the company's stock price shot up.[14] In May 2001, Steven Reinemund took over as CEO of PepsiCo and immediately convinced Nooyi to stay on board as his second in command.[15] Nooyi's standing in PepsiCo shot up in 2001 when as a result of her incredibly hard work and long efforts she was promoted to president of PepsiCo.[16]

Organizing

organizing Structuring working relationships in a way that allows organizational members to work together to achieve organizational goals; one of the four principal functions of management.

organizational structure A formal system of task and reporting relationships that coordinates and motivates organizational members so that they work together to achieve organizational goals.

Organizing is a process that managers use to establish a structure of working relationships that allow organizational members to interact and cooperate to achieve organizational goals. Organizing involves grouping people into departments according to the kinds of job-specific tasks they perform. In organizing, managers also lay out the lines of authority and responsibility between different individuals and groups, and they decide how best to coordinate organizational resources, particularly human resources.

The outcome of organizing is the creation of an **organizational structure,** a formal system of task and reporting relationships that coordinates and motivates members so that they work together to achieve organizational goals. Organizational structure determines how an organization's resources can be best used to create goods and services. As Dell Computer grew, for example, Michael Dell faced the issue of how to structure the organization. Early on he was hiring 100 new employees a week and deciding how to design his managerial hierarchy to best motivate and coordinate their activities. As his organization grew he and his managers created progressively more complex kinds of organizational structures to help it achieve its goals. We examine the organizing process in detail in Chapters 9 through 11.

Leading

leading Articulating a clear vision and energizing and enabling organizational members so that they understand the part they play in achieving organizational goals; one of the four principal functions of management.

In **leading** managers not only articulate a clear vision for organizational members to follow but also energize and enable organizational members so that they understand the part they play in achieving organizational goals. Leadership depends on the use of power, influence, vision, persuasion, and communication skills to coordinate the behaviors of individuals and groups so that their activities and efforts are in harmony. Leaders also encourage employees to perform at a high level. The outcome of leadership is highly motivated and committed organizational members. Employees at Dell Computer, for example, have responded well to Michael Dell's hands-on leadership style; it has resulted in a hardworking, committed workforce. Managers at AOL-Time Warner appreciate Pittman's diplomatic leadership style, and his ability to help them resolve differences that could easily lead to bitter disputes and power struggles. We discuss the issues involved in managing and leading individuals and groups in Chapters 11 through 16.

Controlling

controlling Evaluating how well an organization is achieving its goals and taking action to maintain or improve performance; one of the four principal functions of management.

In **controlling,** managers evaluate how well an organization is achieving its goals and take action to maintain or improve performance. For example, managers monitor the performance of individuals, departments, and the organization as a whole to see whether they are meeting desired performance standards. AOL-Time Warner's Pittman learned early on in his career how important this is (see "A Manager's Challenge" at the beginning of the chapter). If standards are not being met, managers take action to improve performance.

The outcome of the control process is the ability to measure performance accurately and regulate organizational efficiency and effectiveness. To exercise control, managers must decide which goals to measure–perhaps goals pertaining to productivity, quality, or responsiveness to customers–and then they must design information and control systems that provide the data they need to assess performance. The controlling function also allows managers to evaluate how well they themselves are performing the other three functions of management–planning, organizing, and leading–and to take corrective action.

Michael Dell had difficulty establishing effective control systems because his company was growing so rapidly and he lacked experienced managers. In 1988 Dell's costs soared because no controls were in place to monitor inventory, which had built up rapidly. In 1993 financial problems arose because of ill-advised foreign currency transactions. In 1994 Dell's new line of laptop computers crashed because poor quality control resulted in defective products, some of which caught fire. To solve these and other control problems, Dell hired experienced managers to put the right control systems in place. As a result, by 1998 Dell was able to make computers for about 10 percent less than its competitors, a major source of competitive advantage. By 2001 Dell had become so efficient it was driving its competitors out of the market because it had realized a 15 to 20 percent cost advantage over them.[17] Controlling, like the other managerial functions, is an ongoing, fluid, always changing process that demands constant attention and action. We cover the most important aspects of the control function in Chapter 10 and in Chapters 17 through 19.

The four managerial functions–planning, organizing, leading, and controlling–are essential to a manager's job. At all levels in a managerial hierarchy, and across all departments in an organization, effective management means making decisions and managing these four activities successfully.

Types of Managers

To perform efficiently and effectively, organizations employ three types of managers–first-line managers, middle managers, and top managers–arranged in a hierarchy (see Figure 1.3). Typically, first-line managers report to middle managers, and middle managers report to top managers. Managers at each level have different but related responsibilities for utilizing organizational resources to increase efficiency and effectiveness. These three types of managers are grouped into departments according to their specific job responsibilities. A **department** such as manufacturing, accounting, or engineering is a group of people who work together and possess similar skills or use the same kind of knowledge, tools, or techniques to perform their jobs. Within each department are all three levels of management. Next we examine the reasons why organizations use a hierarchy of managers and group them into departments. We then examine some recent changes taking place in managerial hierarchies.

department A group of people who work together and possess similar skills or use the same knowledge, tools, or techniques to perform their jobs.

Levels of Management

As just discussed, organizations normally have three levels of management: first-line managers, middle managers, and top managers.

FIRST-LINE MANAGERS At the base of the managerial hierarchy are **first-line managers**, often called supervisors. They are responsible for the daily supervision of the nonmanagerial employees who perform many of the specific activities necessary to produce goods and services. First-line managers work in all departments of an organization.

first-line manager A manager who is responsible for the daily supervision of nonmanagerial employees.

Examples of first-line managers include the supervisor of a work team in the manufacturing department of a car plant, the head nurse in the obstetrics department of a hospital, and the chief mechanic overseeing a crew of mechanics in the service department of a new car dealership. At Dell Computer, first-line man-

Figure 1.3
Types of Managers

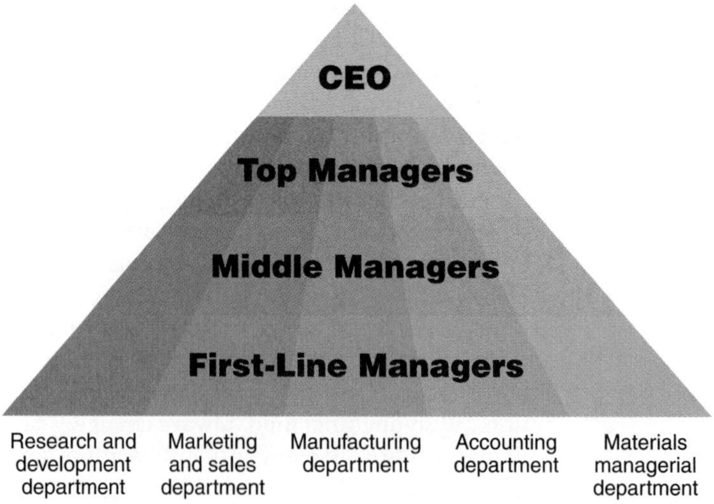

agers include the supervisors responsible for controlling the quality of Dell computers, or the level of customer service provided by Dell's telephone salespeople. When Michael Dell started his company, he personally controlled the computer assembly process and thus performed as a first-line manager or supervisor.

middle manager A manager who supervises first-line managers and is responsible for finding the best way to use resources to achieve organizational goals.

MIDDLE MANAGERS Supervising the first-line managers are **middle managers** responsible for finding the best way to organize human and other resources to achieve organizational goals. To increase efficiency, middle managers find ways to help first-line managers and nonmanagerial employees better utilize resources to reduce manufacturing costs or improve customer service. To increase effectiveness, middle managers evaluate whether the goals that the organization is pursuing are appropriate and suggest to top managers ways in which goals should be changed. Very often, the suggestions that middle managers make to top managers can dramatically increase organizational performance, as we explain in Chapter 8. A major part of the middle manager's job is to develop and fine-tune skills and know-how, such as manufacturing or marketing expertise, that allow the organization to be efficient and effective. Middle managers make the thousands of specific decisions about the production of goods and services: Which first-line supervisors should be chosen for this particular project? Where can we find the highest-quality resources? How should employees be organized to allow them to make the best use of resources?

Behind a first-class sales force look for the middle managers responsible for training, motivating, and rewarding salespeople. Behind a committed staff of high-school teachers look for the principal who energizes them to find ways to obtain the resources they need to do outstanding and innovative jobs in the classroom.

top manager A manager who establishes organizational goals, decides how departments should interact, and monitors the performance of middle managers.

TOP MANAGERS In contrast to middle managers, **top managers** are responsible for the performance of all departments.[18] They have cross-departmental responsibility. Top managers establish organizational goals, such as which goods and services the company should produce; they decide how the different departments should interact; and they monitor how well middle managers in each department utilize resources to achieve goals.[19] Top managers are ultimately responsible for the success or failure of an organization, and their performance (like that of Bill Pittman) is continually scrutinized by people inside and outside the organization, such as other employees and investors.[20]

The chief executive officer (CEO) is a company's most important manager to whom all other top managers report. Bill Pittman, for example, reported to Gerald Levin, the CEO of AOL-Time Warner. As the chief operating officer, Bill Pittman was second-in-command. Together the CEO and COO are responsible for developing good working relationships among the top managers of various departments (manufacturing and marketing, for example), usually top managers have the title vice president. A central concern of the CEO is the creation of a smoothly functioning **top-management team,** a group composed of the CEO, COO, and the department heads most responsible for helping achieve organizational goals.[21]

top-management team A group composed of the CEO, COO, and the heads of the most important departments.

The relative importance of planning, organizing, leading, and controlling–the four managerial functions–to any particular manager depends on the manager's position in the managerial hierarchy.[22] The amount of time that managers spend planning and organizing resources to maintain and improve organizational performance increases as they ascend the hierarchy (see Figure 1.4). Top managers devote most of their time to planning and organizing, the functions so

Figure 1.4
Relative Amount of Time That Managers Spend on the Four Managerial Functions

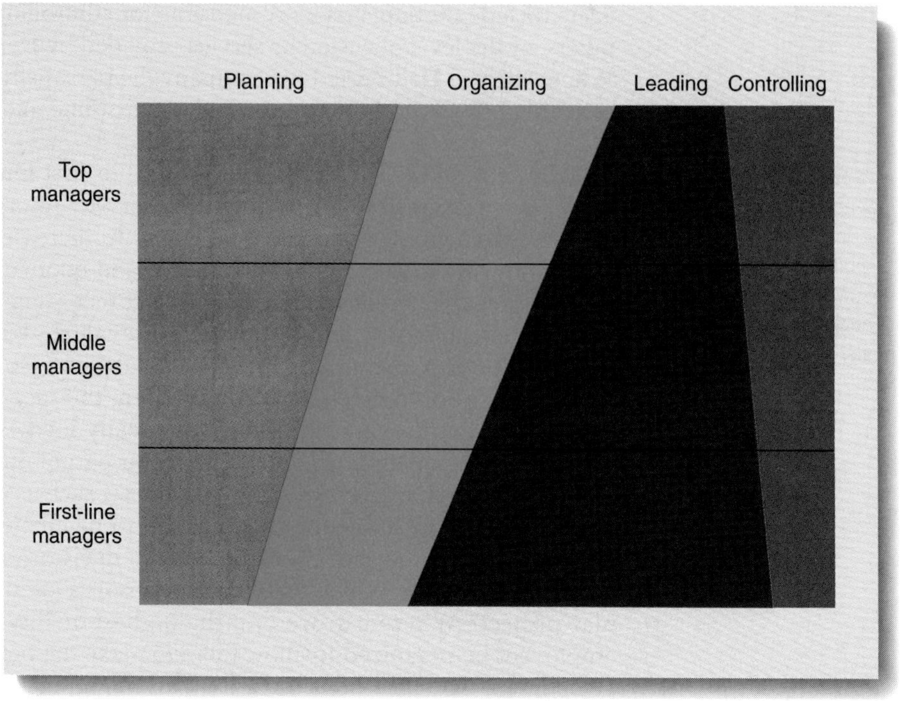

crucial to determining an organization's long-term performance. The lower managers positions are in the hierarchy, the more time they spend leading and controlling first-line managers or nonmanagerial employees.

Areas of Managers

Because so much of a manager's responsibility is to acquire and develop critical resources, managers are typically members of a specific department.[23] Managers inside a department possess job-specific skills and are known as, for example, marketing managers or manufacturing managers. As Figure 1.3 indicates, first-line, middle, and top managers, who differ from one another by virtue of their job-specific responsibilities, are found in each of an organization's major departments. Inside each department, the managerial hierarchy also emerges.

At Dell Computer, for example, Michael Dell hired experts to take charge of the marketing, sales, and manufacturing departments and to develop work procedures to help first-line managers control the company's explosive sales growth. The head of manufacturing quickly found that he had no time to supervise computer assembly, so he recruited manufacturing middle managers from other companies to assume this responsibility.

Recent Changes in Managerial Hierarchies

The tasks and responsibilities of managers at different levels have been changing dramatically in recent years. Two major factors that have led to these changes are global competition and advances in new information technologies (IT) and the development of e-commerce. Stiff competition for resources from organizations both at home and abroad has put increased pressure on all managers to improve efficiency, effectiveness, and organizational performance. Increasingly, top managers are encouraging lower-level managers to look beyond the goals of their own departments and take a cross-departmental view to find new opportunities to improve organizational performance, as AOL-Time Warner has done. New information technologies give managers at all levels access to more and better information and improve their ability to plan, organize, lead, and control; this has also revolutionized the way the managerial hierarchy works.[24]

RESTRUCTURING To take advantage of IT and e-commerce and their ability to reduce operating costs, CEOs and top-management teams have been restructuring organizations to reduce the employees on the payroll. **Restructuring** involves downsizing an organization or shrinking its operations by eliminating the jobs of large numbers of top, middle, or first-line managers and nonmanagerial employees. Restructuring promotes efficiency by reducing costs and allowing the organization to make better use of its remaining resources. For example, IT allows fewer employees to perform a given task because it increases each person's ability to process information and make decisions more quickly and accurately. The need to respond to low-cost global competition has also speeded restructuring efforts. In 2001 Gillette and Procter & Gamble Company both announced major plans to restructure and streamline their global operations to reduce costs; they also announced major job losses and will close plants and lay off more than 10 percent of their workforces worldwide.

restructuring Downsizing an organization by eliminating the jobs of large numbers of top, middle, and first-line managers and nonmanagerial employees.

Restructuring can produce some powerful negative outcomes. It can reduce the morale of the remaining employees worried about their own job security. And top managers of many downsized organizations are realizing that they downsized too far, because employees complain they are overworked and because more customers complain about poor-quality service.[25]

Large for-profit organizations today typically employ 10 to 15 percent fewer managers than they did 10 years ago. General Motors, IBM, AT&T, Du Pont, and many other organizations have eliminated several layers of middle management. The middle managers who still have jobs at these companies have had to assume additional responsibilities and are under increasing pressure to perform. Often, for example, middle managers who used to be responsible for coordinating and overseeing the work of first-line managers–but not for doing the work themselves–now have to perform specific job-related tasks while monitoring and coordinating the work of their subordinates.[26]

EMPOWERMENT AND SELF-MANAGED TEAMS Another major change in management has taken place at the level of first-line managers, who typically supervise the employees engaged in producing goods and services. By taking advantage of new information technologies, many organizations have taken two steps to reduce costs and improve quality. One is the **empowerment** of their workforces by using powerful new software programs to expand employees' knowledge, tasks, and responsibilities. The other is the creation of **self-managed teams**–groups of employees given responsibility for supervising their own activities and for monitoring the quality of the goods and services they provide.

empowerment Expanding employees' tasks and responsibilities.

self-managed team A group of employees who supervise their own activities and monitor the quality of the goods and services they provide.

Such teams input the results of their activities into computers, and through IT middle managers have immediate access to what is happening. As a result of IT, members of self-managed teams assume many of the responsibilities and duties

A self-managed team at Infocus Systems, a Portland, Oregon, software company use their laptop computers to show and exchange slides at a planning meeting where they are developing a presentation to promote the team's newest software product.

previously performed by first-line managers.[27] What is the role of the first-line manager in this new IT work context? First-line managers act as coaches or mentors whose job is not to tell employees what to do but to provide advice and guidance and help teams find new ways to perform their tasks more efficiently.[28]

The way in which Accenture, formerly Arthur Andersen Consulting, used IT to change the tasks and responsibilities of its managers and consultants illustrates the many important ways in which IT can affect management.

Information Technology Byte

Accenture's Bold New Management Style

Accenture, the biggest global management consulting company, has been one of the pioneers in using IT to revolutionize its management style. As it grew to employ over 70,000 employees in more than 46 countries by 2001, its CEO, Joe Forehand, and other top managers realized they needed a new way to organize and lead an army of global consultants. Specifically, top managers realized that because only Accenture's consultants in the field could diagnose and solve client problems, the firm needed a managerial hierarchy that facilitated creative, on-the-spot, decentralized decision making.

To accomplish this they decided to substitute direct control by managers with control through sophisticated IT systems.[29] First, they restructured the managerial hierarchy eliminating many levels of managers. Then, they went about setting up an organizationwide information management system to allow consultants to make their own decisions while providing them with expert backup advice when they needed help solving client problems.[30]

The change process began by equipping every consultant with a laptop computer. Using sophisticated in-house IT, each consultant is linked to all of the company's other consultants and becomes a member of a specific group that specializes in the needs of a particular kind of client such as consumer product firms or brokerage companies. To find a solution to a problem, the members of a specific group can email others in the group working at different client sites to see if they have faced similar client problems. If group members can't solve the problem, the consultant can then communicate with members of other groups by tapping into Accenture's large databases that contain volumes of potentially relevant information. They can also communicate directly with other firm members through a combination of phone, voice mail, email, and videoconferencing to gain access to the most current information being gathered and applied at existing client sites.[31] By utilizing these resources consultants stay abreast of the innovative practices within their own firm and within client firms.[32]

Accenture has found that IT's effects on flattening structure, decentralizing authority, and enlarging and enriching roles has increased its consultants' creativity and performance. By providing employees with more information to make a decision and enabling them to coordinate easily with other people, IT has given consultants much more freedom to make decisions. On the other hand, senior managers can easily manage what their consultants do by monitoring their progress electronically and taking corrective action as necessary. The end result is that Accenture has grown to be one of the most profitable of all global consulting companies.[33]

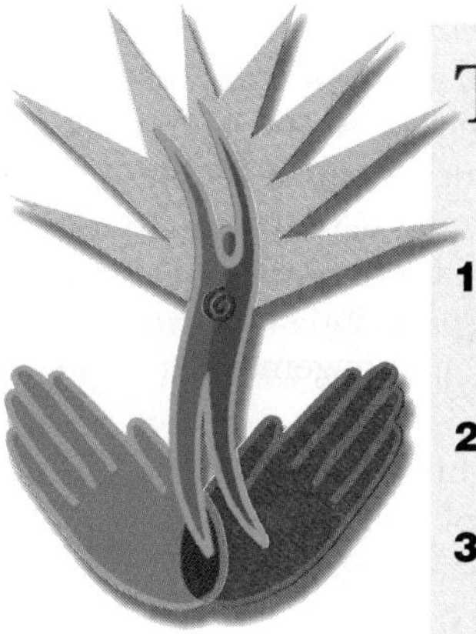

Tips for New Managers

Managing Resources

1. Talk to customers to assess whether the goods or services that an organization provides adequately meets their needs and how they might be improved.
2. Analyze how an organization can better obtain or use resources to increase efficiency and effectiveness.
3. Critically assess how the skills and know-how of departments is helping an organization achieve a competitive advantage. Take steps to improve skills whenever possible.
4. Count the number of managers at each level in the organization and analyze how to increase efficiency and effectiveness of the workforce.

IT and Managerial Roles and Skills

As the example of Accenture suggests, IT is having many important effects on the way managers perform their four functions. IT is also having major effects on the way managers perform their roles and on the skills they develop to perform those roles effectively. A **managerial role** is a set of specific tasks that a manager is expected to perform because of the position he or she holds in an organization. One well-known model of managerial roles was developed by Henry Mintzberg who detailed 10 specific roles that effective managers undertake. Although Mintzberg's roles overlap with Fayol's model, they are useful because they focus on what managers do in a typical hour, day, or week in an organization as they go about the actual job of managing.[34] Below, we discuss these roles and the skills managers need to develop to perform effectively in a time when information software systems and e-commerce are changing the way managers behave.

managerial role The specific tasks that a person is expected to perform because of the position he or she holds in an organization.

Managerial Roles Identified by Mintzberg

Henry Mintzberg reduced to 10 roles the thousands of specific tasks that managers need to perform as they plan, organize, lead, and control organizational resources.[35] Managers assume each of these roles to influence the behavior of individuals and groups inside and outside the organization. People inside the organization include other managers and employees. People outside the organization include shareholders, customers, suppliers, the local community in which an organization is located, and any local or government agency that has an interest in the organization and what it does.[36] Mintzberg grouped the 10 roles into three broad categories: *decisional, informational,* and *interpersonal* that are described in Table 1.1. Managers often perform many of these roles from minute to minute while engaged in the more general functions of planning, organizing, leading, or controlling. IT is changing how they do so.

DECISIONAL ROLES Decisional roles are closely associated with the methods managers use to plan strategy and utilize resources. IT helps a manager in the role of *entrepreneur* by providing more and better information to use in deciding which projects or programs to initiate and in investing resources to increase organizational performance. As a *disturbance handler,* IT gives a manager realtime information to manage the unexpected event or crisis that threatens the organization and to implement solutions quickly. As a resource allocator, human resource software systems from companies, such as Peoplesoft and SAP, give managers easy access to the detailed information they need to decide how best to use people and other resources to increase organizational performance. While engaged in that role, the manager must also be a *negotiator,* reaching agreements with other managers or groups claiming the first right to resources, or with the organization and outside groups such as suppliers or customers. The emergence of electronic markets and business-to-business (B2B) networks that link organizations to thousands of suppliers is but one example of the many ways IT helps managers perform the negotiator role.

INFORMATIONAL ROLES Informational roles are closely associated with the tasks necessary to obtain and transmit information and so have obviously been dramatically impacted by IT. The way in which managers at Accenture used IT systems to *monitor* the activities of consultants and organize and control them on a global level was discussed earlier. Acting as a *disseminator,* IT allows the manager to quickly and effectively transmit information to employees to influence their work attitudes and behavior. Wal-Mart, for example, has nationwide videoconferencing linking top managers to each individual store and uses the Internet to provide up-to-date training programs to its employees. In a similar way IT provides managers with much greater ability to act as a *spokesperson* and promote the organization so that people inside and outside the organization respond positively to it.

INTERPERSONAL ROLES Managers assume interpersonal roles to provide direction and supervision for both employees and the organization as a whole. IT can make managers much more visible throughout the organization. As a *figurehead,* the person who symbolizes an organization or a department, a CEO can use the Internet to inform employees and other interested parties, such as shareholders about what the organization's mission is and what it is seeking to achieve. At all levels managers can use email and the Internet to act as figureheads and role models who establish appropriate ways to behave in the organization. For example anybody in Microsoft is allowed to directly

Table 1.1
Managerial Roles Identified by Mintzberg

Type of Role	Specific Role	Examples of Role Activities
DECISIONAL	**Entrepreneur**	Commit organizational resources to develop innovative goods and services; decide to expand internationally to obtain new customers for the organization's products.
	Disturbance Handler	Move quickly to take corrective action to deal with unexpected problems facing the organization from the external environment, such as a crisis like an oil spill, or from the internal environment, such as producing faulty goods or services.
	Resource Allocator	Allocate organizational resources among different functions and departments of the organization; set budgets and salaries of middle and first-level managers.
	Negotiator	Work with suppliers, distributors, and labor unions to reach agreements about the quality and price of input, technical, and human resources; work with other organizations to establish agreements to pool resources to work on joint projects.
INTERPERSONAL	**Figurehead**	Outline future organizational goals to employees at company meetings; open a new corporate headquarters building; state the organization's ethical guidelines and the principles of behavior employees are to follow in their dealings with customers and suppliers.
	Leader	Provide an example for employees to follow; give direct commands and orders to subordinates; make decisions concerning the use of human and technical resources; mobilize employee support for specific organizational goals.
	Liaison	Coordinate the work of managers in different departments; establish alliances between different organizations to share resources to produce new goods and services.
INFORMATIONAL	**Monitor**	Evaluate the performance of managers in different functions and take corrective action to improve their performance; watch for changes occurring in the external and internal environment that may affect the organization in the future.
	Disseminator	Inform employees about changes taking place in the external and internal environment that will affect them and the organization; communicate to employees the organization's vision and purpose.
	Spokesperson	Launch a national advertising campaign to promote new goods and services; give a speech to inform the local community about the organization's future intentions.

email CEO Bill Gates if they think it necessary. For similar reasons IT allows managers to perform better as *leaders* because they have more and better quality information available to train, counsel, and mentor subordinates to help them reach their full potential. Finally, as a *liaison,* IT improves a manager's ability to link and coordinate the activities of people and groups both inside and outside the organization.

Ken Chenault, pictured here, is the President and CEO of the $19 billion American Express Company. Promoted in 1997, he climbed the ranks from their Travel Related Services Company, thanks to his "even temper and unrelenting drive." Respected by colleagues for his personality, most will say they can't remember him losing his temper or raising his voice. His open door policy for subordinates allows him to mentor AmEx managers and encourages all to enter and "speak their minds."

Terri Patsos Stanley, the manager of a small short-term rental business, has used IT to help her better perform many of these roles. At the same time the story of her company illustrates the importance of a hands-on personal touch as illustrated in the following "Management Insight."

Management Insight

Using IT to Improve Small Business Performance

Terri Patsos Stanley is the president of Boston Short-Term Rentals, a small company that pioneered the concept of providing business travelers with high-quality apartments as an alternative to staying in more expensive and often less convenient hotels. Since its start in 1995, her company has grown rapidly and she managed over 200 apartments in 2001. To keep costs down and customers happy, Patsos Stanley has had to learn all the different managerial roles.

As the president of a rapidly growing company, Patsos Stanley is continually required to make decisions. In the role of *entrepreneur,* she searches for opportunities to increase revenues by increasing the number of apartments that she manages. One solution she adopted was to use the Internet and develop a strong presence on the World Wide Web to attract customers. As a *disturbance handler,* she deals with unexpected problems such as plumbing breakdowns in the middle of the night; therefore, all staff members are connected by electronic paging and personal messaging devices to speed response to customer problems. As a *resource allocator,* she decides how much money to spend to refurbish and upgrade the apartments to maintain their luxury appeal. She maintains close contact with the apartment owners through the Internet–she sends digital images of the apartments over the Web, for example. As a *negotiator,* she contracts with other organizations such as cleaning or painting services to obtain the most economical services her business requires–once again the information available through the Internet makes this more efficient.

With more than 200 apartments to oversee, Boston Short-Term Rentals' information management is a vital activity, and Patsos Stanley's role as *monitor* is important. The sophisticated computer system she developed allows her to evaluate the performance of her business by occupancy rates, customer complaints, and other indicators of the quality of her service. The system facilitates her ability to respond quickly to problems as they arise. In her ongoing role as *disseminator,* she uses IT to update her staff with information about changes in visitor arrivals and departures, but as a *spokesperson* she is always on the phone to persuade visitors who may be somewhat hesitant about staying in an apartment that they know nothing about as opposed to staying with a hotel chain that has a well-recognized name.

In fact, Patsos Stanley has learned the importance of a very hands-on approach to managing her company. She and her employees personally greet the new arrivals and perform the activities that porters, the concierge, and front desk staff do in the typical hotel. In interpersonal terms, Patsos Stanley is the *figurehead* who provides the personal touch her guests expect; she is the person they can contact if problems arise. With her small staff of carpenters, electricians, interior decorators, and maintenance workers, she acts like a *leader,* energizing them to provide the quick service that guests expect. She is also a *liaison,* able to link her guests to organizations that provide services they may need such as dry cleaning, catering, or hairdressing. She enjoys the variety of her work and relishes the pleasure of meeting the senior managers, actors, and overseas visitors who stay in the apartments.[37]

The owner/manager of a small business like Boston Short-Term Rentals continually performs all these managerial roles. Apparently, Patsos Stanley uses the right mix of IT and personal service to perform her roles effectively; her company's size and revenues are constantly increasing.

Being a Manager

Our discussion of managerial roles may seem to suggest that a manager's job is highly orchestrated and that management is a logical, orderly process in which managers rationally calculate the best way to use resources to achieve organizational goals. In reality, being a manager often involves acting emotionally and relying on gut feelings. Quick, immediate reactions to situations rather than deliberate thought and reflection are an important aspect of managerial action.[38] Often, managers are overloaded with responsibilities, do not have time to spend in analyzing every nuance of a situation, and therefore make decisions in uncertain conditions without being sure which outcomes will be best.[39] Moreover, for top managers in particular, the current situation is constantly changing, and a decision that seems right today may prove to be wrong tomorrow.

The range of problems that managers face is enormous (*high variety*). Managers frequently must deal with many problems simultaneously (*fragmentation*), often must make snap decisions (*brevity*), and many times must rely on experience gained throughout their careers to do their jobs to the best of their abilities.[40] It is no small wonder that many managers claim that they are performing their jobs well if they are right just half of the time, and it is understandable why many experienced managers accept failure by their subordinates as a normal part of the learning experience. Managers and their subordinates learn both from their successes and from their failures.

Managerial Skills

Both education and experience enable managers to recognize and develop the skills they need to put organizational resources to their best use. Michael Dell realized from the start that he lacked enough experience and technical expertise in marketing, finance, and planning to guide his company alone. Thus, he recruited experienced managers from other information technology companies, such as IBM and Hewlett-Packard, to help him build his company. Research has shown that education and experience help managers acquire three principal types of skills: *conceptual, human,* and *technical.*[41] As you might expect, the level of these skills that managers need depend on their level in the managerial hierarchy. Typically planning and organizing require higher levels of conceptual skills, while leading and controlling require more human and technical skills (see Figure 1.5).

conceptual skills The ability to analyze and diagnose a situation and to distinguish between cause and effect.

CONCEPTUAL SKILLS Conceptual skills are demonstrated in the ability to analyze and diagnose a situation and to distinguish between cause and effect. Top managers require the best conceptual skills because their primary responsibilities are planning and organizing.[42] By all accounts, Bob Pittman was chosen for his demanding job because of his ability to identify new opportunities and mobilize his managers and other resources to take advantage of those opportunities.

Formal education and training are very important in helping managers develop conceptual skills. Business training at the undergraduate and graduate (MBA) levels provides many of the conceptual tools (theories and techniques in marketing, finance, and other areas) that managers need to perform their roles effectively. The study of management helps develop the skills that allow managers to understand the big picture confronting an organization. The ability to focus on the big picture lets managers see beyond the situation immediately at hand and consider choices while keeping in mind the organization's long-term goals.

Figure 1.5 Conceptual, Human, and Technical Skills Needed by Three Levels of Management

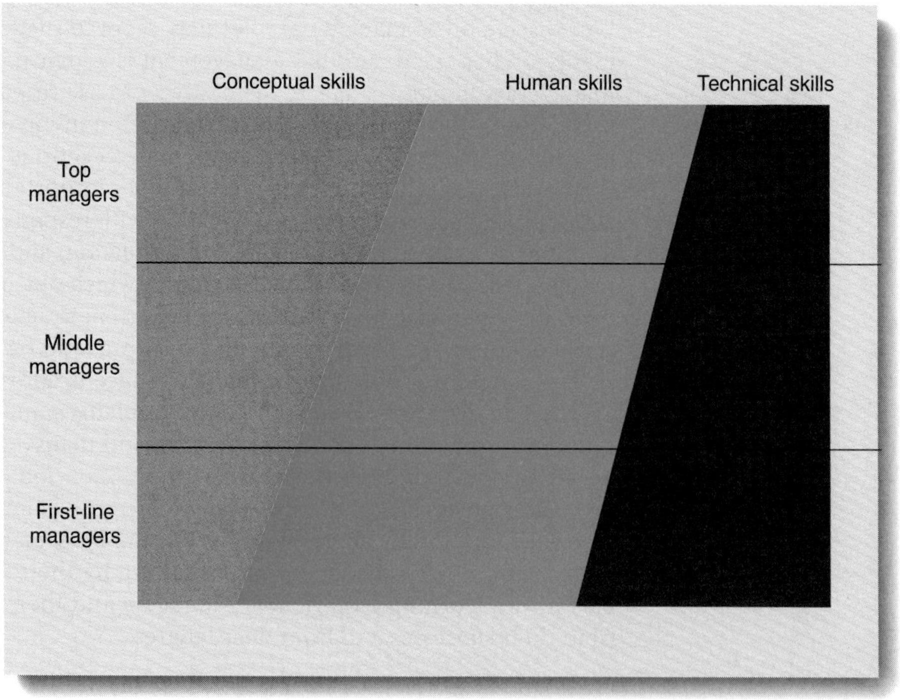

Today, continuing management education and training, including training in advanced IT, are an integral step in building managerial skills because new theories and techniques are constantly being developed to improve organizational effectiveness, such as B2B networks. A quick scan through a magazine such as *Business Week* or *Fortune* reveals a host of seminars in topics such as advanced marketing, finance, leadership, and managing human resources that are offered to managers at many levels in the organization, from the most senior corporate executives to middle managers. Microsoft, IBM, Motorola, and many other organizations designate a portion of each manager's personal budget to be used at the manager's discretion to attend management development programs.

In addition, organizations may wish to develop a particular manager's abilities in a specific skill area–perhaps to learn an advanced component of departmental skills, such as international bond trading, or to learn the skills necessary to implement a new IT system. The organization thus pays for managers to attend specialized programs to develop these skills. Indeed, one signal that a manager is performing well is an organization's willingness to invest in that manager's skill development. Similarly, many nonmanagerial employees who are performing at a high level (because they have studied management) are often sent to intensive management training programs to develop their management skills and to prepare them for promotion to first-level management positions.

human skills The ability to understand, alter, lead, and control the behavior of other individuals and groups.

HUMAN SKILLS **Human skills** include the ability to understand, alter, lead, and control the behavior of other individuals and groups. The ability to communicate, to coordinate, and to motivate people, and to mold individuals into a cohesive team distinguishes effective from ineffective managers. By all accounts, Bob Pittman, Michael Dell, and Terri Patsos Stanley all possess human skills.

Like conceptual skills, human skills can be learned through education and training, as well as developed through experience. Organizations increasingly utilize advanced programs in leadership skills and team leadership as they seek to capitalize on the advantages of self-managed teams. To manage interpersonal interactions effectively, each person in an organization needs to learn how to empathize with other people–to understand their viewpoints and the problems they face. One way to help managers understand their personal strengths and weaknesses is to have their superiors, peers, and subordinates provide feedback about their performance in the roles identified by Mintzberg. Thorough and direct feedback allows managers to develop their human skills.

technical skills Job-specific knowledge and techniques that are required to perform an organizational role.

TECHNICAL SKILLS **Technical skills** are the job-specific knowledge and techniques required to perform an organizational role. Examples include a manager's specific manufacturing, accounting, marketing, and increasingly IT skills. Managers need a range of technical skills to be effective. The array of technical skills managers need depends on their positions in organizations. The manager of a restaurant, for example, may need cooking skills to fill in for an absent cook, accounting and bookkeeping skills to keep track of receipts and costs and to administer the payroll, and aesthetic skills to keep the restaurant looking attractive for customers.

Effective managers need all three kinds of skills–conceptual, human, and technical. The absence of even one managerial skill can lead to failure. One of the biggest problems that people who start small businesses confront is their lack of appropriate conceptual and human skills. Someone who has the technical skills to start a new business does not necessarily know how to manage the venture successfully. Similarly, one of the biggest problems that scientists or engineers who switch careers from research to management confront is their lack of effective human skills. Management skills, roles, and functions are closely related, and wise managers or prospective managers are constantly in search of the latest educational contributions to help them develop the conceptual, human, and technical skills they need to function in today's changing and increasingly competitive global environment.

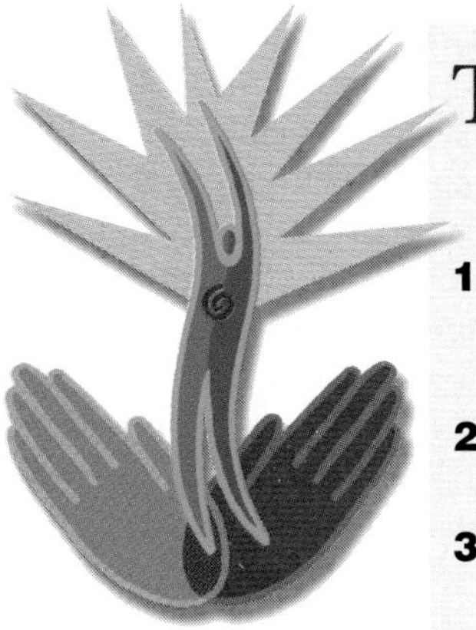

Tips for New Managers

Tasks and Roles

1. Estimate how much time managers spend performing each of the four tasks of planning, organizing, leading, and controling. Decide if managers are spending the right amount of time on each task.
2. Decide which of Mintzberg's 10 managerial roles managers are performing well or poorly.
3. Based on this analysis, take steps to ensure managers possess the right levels of conceptual, technical, and human skills to perform their jobs effectively.

Challenges for Management in a Global Environment

Because the world has been changing more rapidly than ever before, managers and other employees throughout an organization must perform at higher and higher levels. In the last 20 years, competition between organizations competing domestically (in the same country) and globally (in countries abroad) has increased dramatically. The rise of **global organizations,** organizations that operate and compete in more than one country, has put severe pressure on many organizations to improve their performance and to identify better ways to use their resources. The successes of German chemical companies Schering and Hoescht, Italian furniture manufacturer Natuzzi, Korean electronics companies Samsung and Lucky Goldstar, Brazilian plane maker Embraer, and Europe's Airbus Industries are putting pressure on organizations in other countries to raise their level of performance to compete successfully with these global companies.

global organizations Organizations that operate and compete in more than one country.

Even in the not-for-profit sector, global competition is spurring change. Schools, universities, police forces, and government agencies are reexamining their operations as a result of looking at the way things are done in other countries. For example, many curriculum and teaching changes in the United States have resulted from the study of methods that Japanese and European school systems use. Similarly, European and Asian hospital systems have learned much from the U.S. system–which may be the most effective, though not the most efficient, in the world.

Today, managers who make no attempt to learn and adapt to changes in the global environment find themselves reacting rather than innovating, and their organizations often become uncompetitive and fail.[43] Four major challenges stand out for managers in today's world: building a competitive advantage, maintaining ethical standards, managing a diverse workforce, and utilizing new information systems and technologies.

Building a Competitive Advantage

What are the most important lessons for managers and organizations to learn if they are to reach and remain at the top of the competitive environment of business? The answer relates to the use of organizational resources to build a competitive advantage. **Competitive advantage** is the ability of one organization to outperform other organizations because it produces desired goods or services more efficiently and effectively than its competitors. The four building blocks of competitive advantage are superior *efficiency; quality; speed, flexibility,* and *innovation;* and *responsiveness to customers* (see Figure 1.6).

competitive advantage The ability of one organization to outperform other organizations because it produces desired goods or services more efficiently and effectively than they do.

INCREASING EFFICIENCY Organizations increase their efficiency when they reduce the quantity of resources (such as people and raw materials) they use to produce goods or services. In today's competitive environment, organizations constantly are seeking new ways to use their resources to improve efficiency. Many organizations are training their workforces in the new skills and techniques needed to operate heavily computerized assembly plants. Similarly, cross-training gives employees the range of skills they need to perform many different tasks, and organizing employees in new ways, such as in self-managed teams, allows them to make good use of their skills. These are important steps in the effort to improve productivity. Japanese and German companies invest far more in training employees than do American or Italian companies.

Managers must improve efficiency if their organizations are to compete successfully with companies operating in Mexico, Malaysia, and other countries where employees are paid comparatively low wages. New methods must be devised either to increase efficiency or to gain some other competitive advantage–higher-quality goods, for example–if the loss of jobs to low-cost countries is to be prevented.

Figure 1.6
Building Blocks of Competitive Advantage

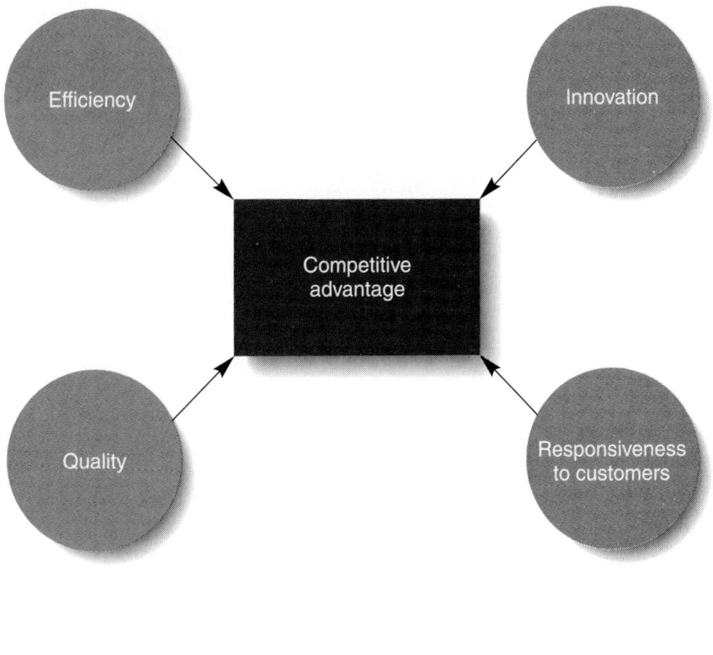

INCREASING QUALITY The challenge from global organizations such as Korean electronics manufacturers, Mexican agricultural producers, and European marketing and financial firms also has increased pressure on companies to improve the skills and abilities of their workforces to improve the quality of their goods and services. One major thrust to improve quality has been to introduce the quality-enhancing techniques known as *total quality management (TQM)*. Employees involved in TQM are often organized into quality control teams and are responsible for continually finding new and better ways to perform their jobs; they also must monitor and evaluate the quality of the goods they produce. TQM is based on a significant new philosophy of managing behavior in organizations; we thoroughly discuss this approach and ways of managing TQM successfully in Chapter 18.

INCREASING SPEED, FLEXIBILITY, AND INNOVATION Today, companies can win or lose the competitive race depending on their speed–how fast they can bring new products to market–or their flexibility–how easily they can change or alter the way they perform their activities to respond to the actions of their competitors. Companies that have speed and flexibility are agile competitors, their managers have superior planning and organizing abilities; they can think ahead, decide what to do, and then speedily mobilize their resources to respond to a changing environment. We examine how managers can build speed and flexibility in their organizations in later chapters. Bob Pittman's goal is to make AOL-Time Warner an agile company so that he will achieve the ambitious revenue and profit targets that the company has set for itself.

Innovation, the process of creating new or improved goods and services that customers want, or developing better ways to produce or provide goods and services, poses a special challenge. Managers must create an organizational setting in which people are encouraged to be innovative. Typically, innovation takes place in small groups or teams; management decentralizes control of work

A quality control team from Japanese television manufacturer, Sony, meet to discuss some ways to improve the design and manufacture of its new high-definition television sets for the U.S. market. Sony television sets are known for their high quality pictures and reliability.

activities to team members and creates an organizational culture that rewards risk taking. Understanding and managing innovation and creating a work setting that encourages risk taking are among the most difficult managerial tasks. Innovation is discussed in depth in Chapter 19.

INCREASING RESPONSIVENESS TO CUSTOMERS Organizations compete for customers with their products and services, so training employees to be responsive to customers' needs is vital for all organizations, but particularly for service organizations. Retail stores, banks, and hospitals, for example, depend entirely on their employees to perform behaviors that result in high-quality service at a reasonable cost.[44] As many countries (the United States, Canada, and Great Britain are just a few) move toward a more service-based economy (in part because of the loss of manufacturing jobs to China, Malaysia, and other countries with low labor costs), managing behavior in service organizations is becoming increasingly important. Many organizations are empowering their customer service employees and giving them the authority to take the lead in providing high-quality customer service. As noted previously, the empowering of nonmanagerial employees changes the role of first-line managers and often leads to the more efficient use of organizational resources.

Achieving a competitive advantage requires managers to use all their skills and expertise to develop resources and improve efficiency, quality, innovation, and responsiveness to customers. We revisit this theme often as we examine the ways managers plan strategies, organize resources and activities, and lead and control people and groups to effectively use human and other resources to achieve organizational goals.

Maintaining Ethical Standards

While mobilizing organizational resources, managers at all levels are under considerable pressure to increase the level at which their organizations perform. For example, top managers receive pressure from shareholders to increase the performance of the entire organization to boost the stock price, improve profits, or raise dividends. In turn, top managers may then pressure middle managers to find new ways to use organizational resources to increase efficiency or quality to attract new customers and earn more revenues.

Pressure to increase performance can be healthy for an organization because it causes managers to question the way the organization is working and it encourages them to find new and better ways to plan, organize, lead, and control. However, too much pressure to perform can be harmful.[45] It may induce managers to behave unethically in dealings with individuals and groups both inside and outside the organization.[46] For example, a purchasing manager for a large retail chain might buy inferior clothing as a cost-cutting measure; or to secure a large foreign contract, a sales manager in a large defense company might offer bribes to foreign officials. Two former Honda officials were convicted of accepting bribes from several large U.S. auto dealers to increase the supply of cars to the dealers and thus increase the dealers' profits.[47] Another example illustrating unethical managerial behavior is described in the following "Ethics in Action" feature.

Ethics in Action

Why the Price of Vitamins Was Too High

Recently, six global pharmaceutical companies admitted that they conspired to artificially raise the price of vitamins such as Vitamin A, B2, C, E and Beta Carotene and eliminate competition on a global basis. Swiss giant Hoffman-La Roche agreed to pay $500 million in criminal fines, the German company BASF paid $225 million in fines, and the others were fined large amounts.[48] How could this happen? How can it be prevented in the future?

Senior managers from each company's vitamin division jointly made the decision to inflate the division's profits and to act unethically at the expense of consumers. In several meetings around the world they worked out the details of the plot which went undiscovered for several years. One manager Kuno Summer, former director of worldwide marketing for Roche was fined $100,000 and put in a U.S. prison for several months. Many of the other top managers involved have been prosecuted in their home countries, and all have been fired by their companies. BASF, for example, has totally replaced its worldwide management team.[49]

What has been the end result of this fiasco for these companies? All have agreed to create a special position of ethics officer whose responsibility will be to develop new ethical standards to be used in these companies' planning processes. The ethics officer will also be responsible for listening to employees' complaints about unethical behavior, for training employees to make ethical decisions, and to counsel top managers so that nothing like this will happen again.

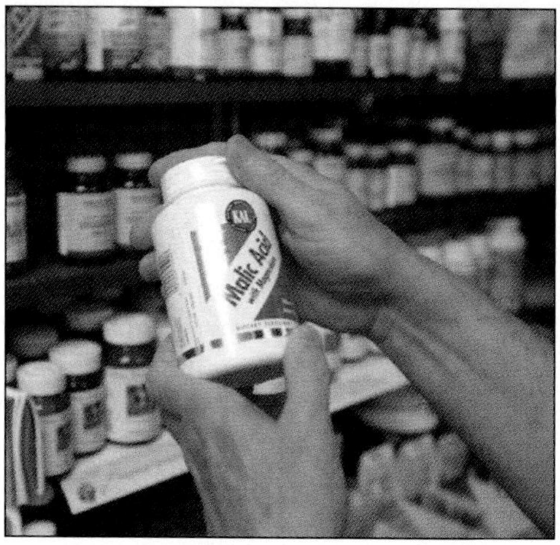

Taking advantage of the growing popularity of vitamins, managers at several global pharmaceutical companies conspired to raise the prices of key ingredients to inflate their profits at the expense of customers. Companies constantly need to reinforce their ethical standards to prevent such events from happening.

When managers act unethically, some individuals or groups may obtain short-term gains, but in the long run the organization and people inside and outside the organization will pay. Chapter 3 discusses the nature of ethics, the factors that influence ethical behavior, and the need for managers and all members of an organization to behave ethically as they pursue organizational goals.

Managing a Diverse Workforce

Another challenge for managers is to recognize the need to treat human resources in a fair and equitable manner. Today, the age, gender, race, ethnicity, religion, sexual preference, and socioeconomic makeup of the workforce present new challenges for managers. Managers must establish employment procedures and practices that are legal, fair, and do not discriminate against any organizational members.[50] In the past, white male employees dominated the ranks of management, but today increasing numbers of organizations are realizing that to motivate effectively and take advantage of the talents of a diverse workforce they must make promotion opportunities available to all employees, including women and minorities.[51] Managers must also recognize the performance-enhancing possibilities of a diverse workforce, such as the ability to take advantage of the skills and experiences of different kinds of people.[52] The following "Focus on Diversity" feature looks at how one company took advantage of diversity to enhance its competitive advantage.

Focus on Diversity

How Diversity Can Promote Customer Responsiveness

With assets of $36.5 billion in June 2001 Union Bank of California, based in San Francisco, is among the 30 largest banks in the United States.[53] It has enjoyed great success and growth throughout the last 10 years, in large part, because of the approach it has developed to diversity that reflects the needs of its employees, customers, and its environment.

Union Bank is based in one of the most diverse states in the nation, California, where more than half the population is Asian, African-American, Latino, or gay. Recognizing this fact, the bank always had a policy of hiring and recruiting diverse employees. However, not until 1996 did the bank realize that the diversity of its employees created a competitive advantage. In 1996, George Ramirez, a vice president at Union Bank suggested that the bank create a marketing group to develop a plan to attract customers who were Hispanic like himself. So successful was this venture that a group of African-American employees decided that they should create a marketing group to develop a marketing campaign to attract new African-American customers. After they enjoyed considerable success in recruiting new customers, it was clear to Union Bank's managers that they should use employee diversity as a way of improving customer service. For example, when customers walked into a bank branch in a predominately Latino neighborhood they would be greeted by substantial numbers of Latino employees.[54] Similarly, marketing campaigns could be tailored to the needs of each ethnic group.

Union Bank's customer service representatives, such as the employee pictured here, are well known for building relationships with their diverse customer groups to improve the level of customer service. The diverse nature of Union Bank's employees reflects the diverse customer groups the bank serves.

The bank, like many other organizations, also discovered that diversity can lead to competitive advantage because diverse employees view the same issue–for example, how to attract customers–with very different approaches. The bank found that creating diverse teams of employees helped improve the quality of decision making inside the organization. Furthermore, the bank's reputation of being a good place for minorities to work attracted highly skilled and motivated minority job candidates. As its former CEO Takahiro Moriguchi said in accepting a diversity award for the company, "By searching for talent from among the disabled, both genders, veterans, all ethnic groups and all nationalities, we gain access to a pool of ideas, energy, and creativity as wide and varied as the human race itself.[55] I expect diversity will become even more important as the world gradually becomes a truly global marketplace."

Managers who value their diverse employees not only invest in developing these employees' skills and capabilities but also link rewards to their performance. They are the managers who best succeed in promoting performance over the long run.[56] Today, more and more organizations are realizing that people are their most important resource and that developing and protecting human resources is an important challenge for management in a competitive global environment. We discuss the many issues surrounding the management of a diverse workforce in Chapter 4.

Utilizing Information Technology and E-commerce

As has already been discussed, another important challenge for managers is the efficient utilization of information technologies (IT) and e-commerce.[57] New technologies in the areas of computer-controlled manufacturing and information systems that link and enable employees in new ways are continually being developed. In a setting that uses self-managed teams, for example, sophisticated computer information systems link the activities of team members so that each team member knows what the others are doing. This coordination helps to improve quality and increase the pace of innovation. Microsoft, Hitachi, IBM, and other companies make extensive use of information systems, such as email, the Internet, and videoconferencing, accessible by means of personal computers, to build a competitive advantage. The importance of IT is discussed in great detail in Chapters 15 and 17, and throughout the text you will find icons that alert you to stories about how it is changing the way companies operate.

Summary and Review

WHAT IS MANAGEMENT? A manager is a person responsible for supervising the use of an organization's resources to meet its goals. An organization is a collection of people who work together and coordinate their actions to achieve a wide variety of goals. Management is the process of using organizational resources to achieve organizational goals effectively and efficiently through planning, organizing, leading, and controlling. An efficient organization makes the most productive use of its resources. An effective organization pursues appropriate goals and achieves these goals by using its resources to create the goods or services that customers want.

MANAGERIAL FUNCTIONS The four principal managerial functions are planning, organizing, leading, and controlling. Managers at all levels of the organization and in all departments perform these functions. Effective management means managing these activities successfully.

TYPES OF MANAGERS Organizations typically have three levels of management. First-line managers are responsible for the day-to-day supervision of nonmanagerial employees. Middle managers are responsible for developing and utilizing organizational resources efficiently and effectively. Top managers have cross-departmental responsibility. The top managers' job is to establish appropriate goals for the entire organization and to verify that department managers are utilizing resources to achieve those goals. To increase efficiency and effectiveness, some organizations have altered their managerial hierarchies by restructuring, by empowering their workforces, utilizing self-managed teams, and utilizing new information technology.

IT AND MANAGERIAL ROLES AND SKILLS According to Mintzberg, managers play 10 different roles: figurehead, leader, liaison, monitor, disseminator, spokesperson, entrepreneur, disturbance handler, resource allocator, and negotiator. Three types of skills help managers perform these roles effectively: conceptual, human, and technical skills. IT is changing both the way managers perform their roles and the skills they need to perform these roles because it provides richer and more meaningful information.

CHALLENGES FOR MANAGEMENT IN A GLOBAL ENVIRONMENT Today's competitive global environment presents many interesting challenges to managers: to build a competitive advantage by increasing efficiency; quality; speed, flexibility, and innovation; and customer responsiveness. To behave ethically toward people inside and outside the organization; to manage a diverse workforce; and to utilize new information systems and technologies.

Management in Action

Topics for Discussion and Action

1. Describe the difference between efficiency and effectiveness, and identify real organizations that you think are, or are not, efficient and effective.
2. In what ways can managers at each of the three levels of management contribute to organizational efficiency and effectiveness?
3. Identify an organization that you believe is high performing and one that you believe is low performing. Give 10 reasons why you think the performance levels of the two organizations differ so much.
4. Choose an organization such as a school or a bank; visit it; then list the different organizational resources it uses.
5. Visit an organization, and talk to first-line, middle, and top managers about their respective management roles in the organization and what they do to help the organization be efficient and effective.
6. Ask a middle or top manager, perhaps someone you already know, to give examples of how he or she performs the managerial functions of planning, organizing, leading, and controlling. How much time does he or she spend in performing each function?
7. Like Mintzberg, try to find a cooperative manager who will allow you to follow him or her around for a day. List the roles the manager plays, and indicate how much time he or she spends performing them.
8. What are the building blocks of competitive advantage? Why is obtaining a competitive advantage important to managers?
9. In what ways do you think managers' jobs have changed the most over the last 15 years? Why have these changes occurred?

Building Management Skills

Thinking About Managers and Management

Think of an organization that has provided you with work experience and the manager to whom you reported (or talk to someone who has had extensive work experience); then answer these questions.

1. Think of your direct supervisor. Of what department is he or she a member, and at what level of management is this person?
2. How do you characterize your supervisor's approach to management? For example, which particular management functions and roles does this person perform most often? What kinds of management skills does this manager have?
3. Do you think the functions, roles, and skills of your supervisor are appropriate for the particular job he or she performs? How could this manager improve his or her task performance? How can IT affect this?
4. How did your supervisor's approach to management affect your attitudes and behavior? For example, how well did you perform as a subordinate, and how motivated were you?
5. Think of the organization and its resources. Do its managers utilize organizational resources effectively? Which resources contribute most to the organization's performance?
6. Describe the way the organization treats its human resources. How does this treatment affect the attitudes and behaviors of the workforce?
7. If you could give your manager one piece of advice or change one management practice in the organization, what would it be?
8. How attuned are the managers in the organization to the need to increase efficiency, quality, innovation, or responsiveness to customers? How well do you think the organization performs its prime goals of providing the goods or services that customers want or need the most?

Small Group Breakout Exercise

Opening a New Restaurant

Form groups of three or four people, and appoint one group member as the spokesperson who will communicate your findings to the entire class when called on by the instructor. Then discuss the following scenario.

You and your partners have decided to open a large, full-service restaurant in your local community; it will be open from 7 A.M. to 10 P.M. to serve breakfast, lunch, and dinner. Each of you is investing $50,000 in the venture, and together you have secured a bank loan for $300,000 more to begin operations. You and your partners have little experience in managing a restaurant beyond serving meals or eating in restaurants, and you now face the task of deciding how you will manage the restaurant and what your respective roles will be.

1. Decide what your respective managerial roles in the restaurant will be. For example, who will be responsible for the necessary departments and specific activities? Describe your managerial hierarchy.
2. Which building blocks of competitive advantage do you need to establish to help your restaurant succeed? What criteria will you use to evaluate how successfully you are managing the restaurant?
3. Discuss the most important decisions that must be made about (a) planning, (b) organizing, (c) leading, and (d) controlling, to allow you and your partners to utilize organizational resources effectively and build a competitive advantage.
4. For each managerial function, list the issue that will contribute the most to your restaurant's success.

Exploring the World Wide Web

Search for the website of a company in which a manager discusses his or her approach to planning, organizing, leading, or controlling. What is that manager's approach to managing? What effects has this approach had on the company's performance?

You're the Management Consultant

Problems at Achieva

You have just been called in to help managers at Achieva, a fast-growing Internet software company that specializes in B2B network software. Your job is to help Achieva solve some management problems that have arisen because of its rapid growth.

Customer demand to license Achieva's software has boomed so much in just two years that more than 50 new software programmers have been added to help develop a new range of software products. Achieva's growth has been so swift that it still operates informally, its organizational structure is loose and flexible, and programmers are encouraged to find solutions to problems as they go along. Although this structure worked well in the past, you have been told that problems are arising.

There have been increasing complaints from employees that good performance is not being recognized in the organization and that they do not feel equitably treated. Moreover, there have been complaints about getting managers to listen to their new ideas and to act on them. A bad atmosphere is developing in the company, and recently several talented employees have left. Your job is to help Achieva's managers solve these problems quickly and keep the company on the fast track.

Questions

1. What kinds of organizing and controlling problems is Achieva suffering from?
2. What kinds of management changes need to be made to solve them?

BusinessWeek Cases in the News

The Lucky Charm of Steve Sanger

Most executives keep a wish list of competitors they would like to acquire. At cereal giant General Mills Inc., one name—Pillsbury Co.—had been near the top of the list "for about a hundred years," jokes CEO and Chairman Stephen W. Sanger.

Pillsbury, with its range of convenience foods, broad national distribution, and worldwide presence, not to mention a headquarters on the other side of Minneapolis, seemed a natural match. So when Paul S. Walsh, then chief operating officer of Pillsbury parent Diageo PLC, called last March to see if General Mills was interested in a merger, Sanger didn't hesitate. Did he want to meet for dinner? Are Cheerios round? Of course he did. "What motivated us was the belief that the companies would grow faster together than either would alone," says Sanger. "We didn't see a dozen combinations that would do that."

Tubular Yogurt

The $10.5 billion deal that Sanger agreed to in July will nearly double the size of General Mills, to roughly $13 billion in sales. And by pulling off one of the biggest mergers in the quickly consolidating food industry, Sanger has defined the task by which his nearly three-decade career at General Mills will be judged. Simply put: to integrate Pillsbury in a way that generates growth in a slow-growth business.

Sanger has little time to spare. Cereal sales have been declining since 1994; last year they were down 1.6 percent. By acquiring Pillsbury, he has with one stroke decreased General Mills' dependence on cereal from more than half of earnings to less than a third. Still, he'll have to find a way to sell more Wheaties, Cheerios, and Lucky Charms. And he'll probably have to strike some other deals, too. General Mills expects Federal Trade Commission approval of the Pillsbury merger any week now.

At first it might have seemed surprising that the 54-year-old Sanger, who made his name at General Mills as a savvy marketer, would turn out to be a bold dealmaker. Few would deny that he has a good feel for tastes and trends: Yoplait yogurt is now more popular than rival Dannon Co., in part because he correctly figured that kids would eat more if he put the yogurt in a tube. But some worried that the easygoing Sanger might not be tough enough to lead General Mills at a time when the whole food industry is slowing—cereal most of all.

So far, though, Sanger has acted more decisively and with greater effect than many expected. Since he took over in May 1995, sales have increased 6 percent a year, compared with 2 percent to 3 percent for total retail food sales, according to U.S. Bancorp Piper Jaffray. General Mills has done as well as it has because of Sanger's inventive cost-cutting and his risky decision to raise prices and boost advertising during a damaging cereal price war in 1997. As a result, profit margins were fattened and General Mills was able to eat into its competitor's market share. In 1999, it even took over the top spot from long-time rival Kellogg Co. and now has 32.2 percent of the U.S. market. "He's proven to be a more well-rounded CEO than I anticipated," says Prudential Securities Inc. food analyst John M. McMillin. "Initially, I saw a great marketing man who had less interest in numbers and more interest in innovation."

Purple Horseshoes

Sanger's rise through the ranks was propelled by his creativity and a knack for finessing seemingly trivial details into grand marketing plans and big gains for the company. When he was in charge of Lucky Charms in 1975, he followed a simple maxim: If consumers like something, give them more of it. In this case, Sanger added blue diamond-shaped marshmallows. When sales jumped 15 percent, he put in purple horseshoes. As head of the cereal division in 1988, he tweaked Cheerios. It's still General Mills' best-selling brand, mostly because he added new flavors such as apple cinnamon and honey nut.

Sanger got his first taste for marketing at DePauw University. As president of the student union board in the late 1960s, he started promoting Motown concerts on campus. "The main lesson I learned is that it's a lot easier to be a good marketer if you've got a good product," he says. "It was a lot easier to sell tickets to the Temptations than the Electric Prunes."

After graduating he considered a career as a concert promoter or lawyer but decided against both. Instead, he got an MBA at the University of Michigan and then joined Procter & Gamble Co. as a brand manager. A few years later, in 1974, he beat out his boss for a job at General Mills managing Wheaties. Sanger's competitive spirit and marketing acumen were apparent early on, says H. Brewster Atwater

Jr., the CEO and chairman from 1981 until 1995. "Steve was identified as someone with great potential," says Atwater. "He had interesting ideas about how to develop new products and get new business."

He also had some interesting ideas about how to manage the company. When he took over from the very reserved Atwater, Sanger quickly retired the General Mills uniform—a dark suit and white shirt—and closed the executive dining room. Then he changed the music on the company jet from classical to rock 'n' roll and told employees not to work past noon on Fridays in the summer. The night before his first board meeting as chairman, he attended a Rolling Stones concert rather than stay home worrying. "I got a little inspiration from Mick Jagger, and the board meeting went great," he recalls. William T. Esrey, chairman and CEO of Sprint Corp. and a board member, says Sanger seems "relatively low-key," but soon "you realize that you're dealing with an extremely capable, extremely mature, confident guy in his own right."

Add quirky to that description, too. Early in his tenure as CEO, Sanger was looking to cut costs and figured production-line changes could be made more efficiently. So he sent technicians to the NASCAR races in North Carolina to watch the pit crews. The technicians applied those techniques and managed to cut the changeover time from five hours to 20 minutes.

Colleagues say Sanger's demeanor encourages people to chance it. "If you're not failing, you're not doing enough," says Ian R. Friendly, president of the yogurt division. Sanger has set a good example: Eight years ago, he enthusiastically backed a new cereal that was sold as a snack, Fingos. It bombed. But he still thinks cereal can be more portable; he recently launched a cereal bar called Milk 'n Cereal.

Indeed, these days Sanger is even more convinced of the need for such hyperconvenient products—food that "you can eat with one hand while driving," as he says. That's why buying Pillsbury made so much sense to him. The company has all kinds of food—from Totino's Pizza Rolls to Old El Paso dinners—that Sanger believes have real potential in that regard. "Our goal is to keep innovating the way we have with our own products," he says.

Source: Julie Forster, "The Lucky Charm of Steve Sanger," *Business Week,* March 26, 2001, pp. 75–76.

Questions

1. What qualities make Steve Sanger a good manager?
2. How would you describe his approach to planning, leading, organizing, and controlling?

BusinessWeek Cases in the News

The New Calling

It's 8:30 on a Sunday evening in summer. Outside the Thomas & Mack Center in Las Vegas, where temperatures have hovered around 110°F all weekend, the desert heat is still oppressive. Inside is another matter. The air conditioning has made for a chilly stage as Andrea Jung waits in the wings to address the biggest crowd she has ever faced. And Jung herself couldn't be more cool and composed. In her red floor-length ball gown with spaghetti straps and white shoes with sharp-pointed toes, Jung, at 41, looks more like a movie star than the CEO of a $5.3 billion company. As she strides onto the stage, she is met by an explosion of applause from some 13,000 mostly forty- and fifty-something Avon women reps who have traveled to Las Vegas from all across the U.S. to see Avon's new product lines, listen to Englebert Humperdink, applaud Suzanne Somer's keynote speech, and do aerobics with Richard Simmons to songs like *Breaking Up is Hard to Do.* The contrast is striking: the svelte, fashionable, Ivy League-educated, New York fast-tracker preaching to the mostly middle American moms and grandmas whose fashion tastes lean toward slacks for dressy occasions and sweat suits and sneakers for the rest of the convention.

Still, with a mike in her hand and giant TV screens in the background projecting her image, Jung has no problem firing up the crowd. "Avon is first and foremost about you," she proclaims. "I stand here before you and promise you that that will never change." She vows that Avon Products Inc. can be as big in the women's beauty business as Walt Disney Co. is in entertainment. She confides her proudest moment: Jung, the daughter of Chinese immigrants, traveled to China last year for the first time in her life to meet and speak to women in a Chinese factory. "We will change the future of women around the world!" she exclaims. And as the audience rises to a standing ovation, Jung wraps up with the most amazing declaration of all: "I love you all!"

To the uninitiated, it all sounds like a lot of hooey. But for Jung the stakes are huge: She desperately needs the support of the company's 3 million sales reps worldwide to answer Avon's new calling: getting today's women to buy a brand that hit its peak when their mothers were first trying on lipstick. The pioneer of door-to-door selling, founded in 1886, Avon is at a critical turning point in its history. At the dawn of the Internet Age, when three-quarters of American women work, Avon's direct-sales model, dated for a generation, now seems positively antiquated. As direct selling gets redefined by such Web players as Dell Computer Corp. and Amazon.com Inc., Avon ladies seem in danger of going the way of the horse and buggy. If it weren't for Avon's success in such markets as Latin America and Asia, the company would surely have faded long ago. Indeed, according to industry trackers Kline & Co., direct selling represented only 6.8 percent of the $27 billion of cosmetics and toiletries sold in the U.S. in 1999, down from 8 percent in 1995. Avon itself has seen sales growth—up only 5 percent a year over the past decade—slow even further, to a 1.5 percent increase in 1999. And though the company reversed a two-year decline in operating profits last year to post a 16 percent increase to $549 million, over the past 10 years profits are up only an anemic 4 percent a year. "We're in one of the greatest economies of all times, and Avon's still finding it hard to increase sales," says Allan Mottus, a consultant to beauty and retail companies.

The huge task of fixing Avon falls squarely on Jung's shoulders. Jung landed the top job last November in the wake of a fourth-quarter sales and earnings shock that sent Avon shares down 50 percent. Soon afterward, Jung's predecessor, Charles R. Perrin, resigned. Jung, with very little operating experience under her belt, was suddenly running a company with millions of independent sales reps and operations in 137 countries. Now, with the need to reconcile the intersection of the Internet's explosive growth with the company's Old Economy direct-sales business model, Jung is faced with what is shaping up to be one of Corporate America's toughest consumer-products turnarounds.

Source: N. Byrnes, "Avon The New Calling: CEO Andrea Jung Wants to Sell More Than Makeup," *Business Week,* September 18, 2000, pp. 136–45.

Questions

1. What are the roles that are most important for Andrea Jung to perform successfully to help Avon transform itself?
2. How would you describe her approach to planning, leading, organizing, and controlling?

Chapter 2

The Evolution of Management Theory

Learning Objectives

After studying this chapter, you should be able to:

- Describe how **the need to increase organizational efficiency and effectiveness** has guided the evolution of management theory.
- Explain the principle of **job specialization and division of labor,** and tell why the study of person-task relationships is central to the pursuit of increased efficiency.
- Identify the **principles of administration and organization** that underlie effective organizations.
- Trace the changes in **theories about how managers should behave** to motivate and control employees.
- Explain the **contributions of management science** to the efficient use of organizational resources.
- Explain why the study of **the external environment and its impact on an organization** has become a central issue in management thought.

A Manager's Challenge

Finding Better Ways to Make Cars

What is the best way to utilize workers?
Car production has changed dramatically over the years as managers have applied different principles of management to organize and control work activities. Prior to 1900, small groups of skilled workers cooperated to hand-build cars with parts that often had to be altered and modified to fit together. This system, a type of small-batch production, was very expensive; assembling just one car took considerable time and effort; and skilled workers could produce only a few cars in a day. Although these cars were of high quality, they were too expensive. Managers of early car companies needed better techniques to increase efficiency, reduce costs, and sell more cars.

Henry Ford revolutionized the car industry. In 1913, Ford opened the Highland Park car plant in Detroit to produce the Model T. Ford and his team of manufacturing managers pioneered the development of mass-production manufacturing, a system that made the small-batch system almost obsolete overnight. In mass production, moving conveyor belts bring the cars to the workers. Each worker performs

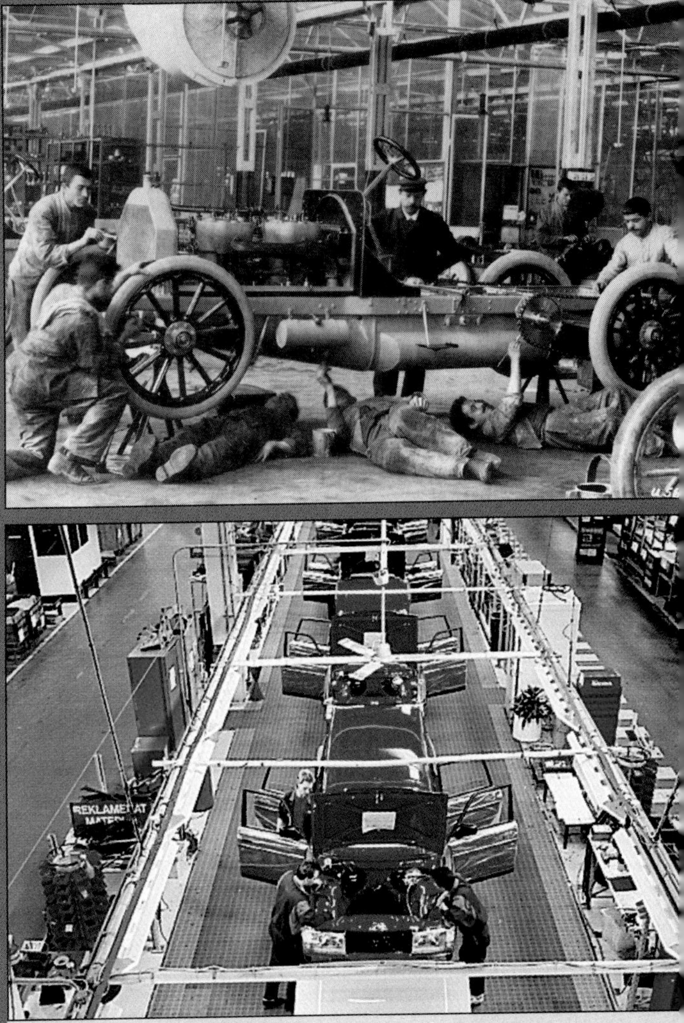

(a) The photo on top, taken in 1904 inside a Daimler Motor Company factory, is an example of the use of small-batch production, a production system in which small groups of people work together and perform all the tasks needed to assemble a product. (b) In 1913, Henry Ford revolutionized the production process of a car by pioneering mass production manufacturing, a production system in which a conveyor belt brings each car to the workers, and each individual worker performs a single task along the production line. Even today cars are still built using this system, as evidenced in the photo of workers along a modern-day computerized automobile assembly line.

a single assigned task along a production line, and the speed of the conveyor belt is the primary means of controlling workers' activities. Ford experimented to discover the most efficient way for each worker to perform an assigned task. The result was that each worker performed one narrow, specialized task, such as bolting on the door or attaching the door handle, and jobs in the Ford car plant became very repetitive. They required little use of a worker's skills.[1] Ford's management approach increased efficiency and reduced costs by so much that by 1920 he was able to reduce the price of a car by two-thirds and to sell more than 2 million cars a year.[2] Ford became the leading car company in the world, and competitors rushed to adopt the new mass-production techniques.

The next change in management thinking about car assembly occurred in Japan when Ohno Taiichi, a Toyota production engineer, pioneered the development of *lean manufacturing* in the 1960s after touring the U.S. plants of the Big Three car companies. The management philosophy behind lean manufacturing is to continuously find methods to improve the efficiency of the production process in order to reduce costs, increase quality, and reduce car assembly time. Lean production is based on the idea that if workers have input and can participate continually in the decision-making process, their skills and knowledge can be used to increase efficiency.

In lean manufacturing, workers work on a moving production line, but they are organized into small teams, each of which is responsible for a particular phase of car assembly, such as installing the car's transmission or electrical wiring system. Each team member is expected to learn the tasks of all members of that team, and each work group is responsible not only for assembling cars but also for continuously finding ways to increase quality and reduce costs. By 1970, Japanese managers had applied the new lean production system so efficiently that they were producing higher-quality cars at lower prices than their U.S. counterparts. By 1980 Japanese companies dominated the global car market.

To compete with the Japanese, managers of U.S. car makers visited Japan to learn the new management principles of lean production. As a result, companies such as General Motors (GM) established the Saturn plant to experiment with this new way of involving workers; GM also established a joint venture with Toyota called New United Motor Manufacturing Inc. (NUMMI) to learn how to achieve the benefits of lean production. Meanwhile Ford and Chrysler began to change their work processes to take advantage of workers' skills and knowledge.

In the 1990s global car companies increased the number of robots used on the production line and began to install sophisticated information technology (IT) to build and track the quality of cars being produced. Indeed, for a time it seemed that robots rather than workers would be building cars in the future. However, Toyota discovered something interesting at its fully roboticized car plant. When only robots build cars, efficiency does not continually increase because unlike people, robots cannot provide input to improve the work process. The crucial thing is to find the right balance between using people, computers, and IT so that global car companies are still in a race to improve and perfect better ways of making cars. •

Overview

As this sketch of the evolution of management thinking in global car manufacturing suggests, changes in management practices occur as managers, theorists, researchers, and consultants seek new ways to increase organizational efficiency and effectiveness. The driving force behind the evolution of management theory is the search for better ways to utilize organizational resources. Advances in management theory typically occur as managers and researchers find better ways to perform the principal management tasks: planning, organizing, leading, and controlling human and other organizational resources.

In this chapter, we examine how management theory concerning appropriate management practices has evolved in modern times and the central concerns that have guided its development. First, we examine the so-called classical management theories that emerged around the turn of the twentieth century. These include scientific management, which focuses on matching people and tasks to maximize efficiency; and administrative management, which focuses on identifying the principles that will lead to the creation of the most efficient system of organization and management. Next, we consider behavioral management theories developed both before and after the Second World War; these focus on how managers should lead and control their workforces to increase performance. Then we discuss management science theory, which developed during the Second World War and has become increasingly important as researchers have developed rigorous analytical and quantitative techniques to help managers measure and control organizational performance. Finally, we discuss business in the 1960s and 1970s and focus on the theories developed to help explain how the external environment affects the way organizations and managers operate.

By the end of this chapter you will understand the ways in which management theory has evolved over time. You will also understand how economic, political, and cultural forces have affected the development of these theories and the ways in which managers and their organizations behave. In Figure 2.1 we summarize the chronology of the management theories discussed in this chapter.

Scientific Management Theory

The evolution of modern management began in the closing decades of the nineteenth century, after the industrial revolution had swept through Europe and America. In the new economic climate, managers of all types of organizations–political, educational, and economic–were increasingly trying to find better ways to satisfy customers' needs. Many major economic, technical, and cultural changes were taking place at this time. The introduction of steam power and the development of sophisticated machinery and equipment changed the way goods

Figure 2.1
The Evolution of Management Theory

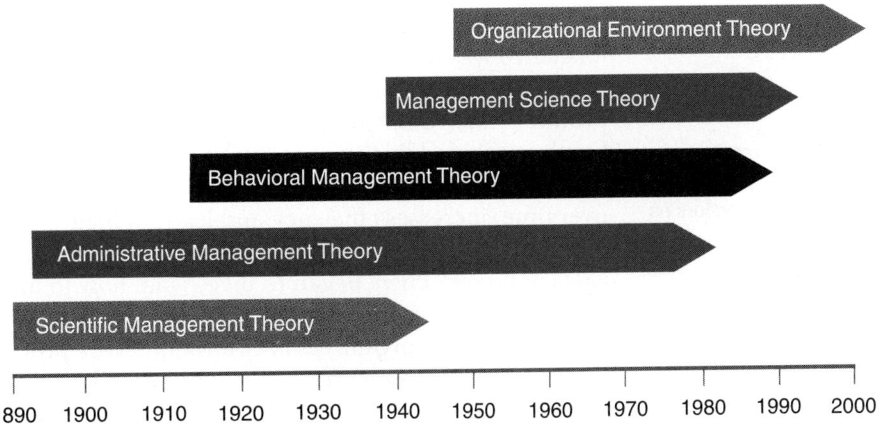

were produced, particularly in the weaving and clothing industries. Small workshops run by skilled workers who produced hand-manufactured products (a system called crafts production) were being replaced by large factories in which sophisticated machines controlled by hundreds or even thousands of unskilled or semiskilled workers made products. For example, raw cotton and wool, which in the past had been spun into yarn by families or whole villages working together were now shipped to factories where workers operated machines that spun and wove large quantities of yarn into cloth.

Owners and managers of the new factories found themselves unprepared for the challenges accompanying the change from small-scale crafts production to large-scale mechanized manufacturing. Moreover, many of the managers and supervisors in these workshops and factories were engineers who had only a technical orientation. They were unprepared for the social problems that occur when people work together in large groups in a factory or shop system. Managers began to search for new techniques to manage their organizations' resources, and soon they began to focus on ways to increase the efficiency of the worker-task mix.

Job Specialization and the Division of Labor

Initially, management theorists were interested in the subject of why the new machine shops and factory system were more efficient and produced greater quantities of goods and services than older, crafts-style production operations. Nearly 200 years before, Adam Smith had been one of the first writers to investigate the advantages associated with producing goods and services in factories. A famous economist, Smith journeyed around England in the 1700s studying the effects of the industrial revolution.[3] In a study of factories that produced various pins or nails, Smith identified two different manufacturing methods. The first was similar to crafts-style production, in which each worker was responsible for all of the 18 tasks involved in producing a pin. The other had each worker performing only 1 or a few of the 18 tasks that go into making a complete pin.

In a comparison of the relative performance of these different ways of organizing production, Smith found that the performance of the factories in which workers specialized in only 1 or a few tasks was much greater than the performance of the factory in which each worker performed all 18 pin-making tasks. In fact, Smith found that 10 workers specializing in a particular task could make 48,000 pins a day, whereas those workers who performed all the tasks could make only a few thousand at most.[4] Smith reasoned that this difference in performance was due to the fact that the workers who specialized became much more skilled at their specific tasks and as a group were thus able to produce a product faster than the group of workers who each performed many tasks. Smith concluded that increasing the level of **job specialization**–the process by which a division of labor occurs as different workers specialize in specific tasks over time–increases efficiency and leads to higher organizational performance.[5]

job specialization The process by which a division of labor occurs as different workers specialize in different tasks over time.

Armed with the insights gained from Adam Smith's observations, other managers and researchers began to investigate how to improve job specialization to increase performance. Management practitioners and theorists focused on how managers should organize and control the work process to maximize the advantages of job specialization and the division of labor.

Frederick W. Taylor, founder of Scientific Management, and one of the first people to study the behavior and performance of people at work.

F. W. Taylor and Scientific Management

Frederick W. Taylor (1856–1915) is best known for defining the techniques of **scientific management**, the systematic study of relationships between people and tasks for the purpose of redesigning the work process to increase efficiency. Taylor was a manufacturing manager who eventually became a consultant and taught other managers how to apply his scientific management techniques. Taylor believed that if the amount of time and effort that each worker expends to produce a unit of output (a finished good or service) can be reduced by increasing specialization and the division of labor, the production process will become more efficient. According to Taylor the way to create the most efficient division of labor could best be determined by scientific management techniques, rather than intuitive or informal rule-of-thumb knowledge. Based on his experiments and observations as a manufacturing manager in a variety of settings, he developed four principles to increase efficiency in the workplace:

scientific management The systematic study of relationships between people and tasks for the purpose of redesigning the work process to increase efficiency.

- Principle 1: *Study the way workers perform their tasks, gather all the informal job knowledge that workers possess, and experiment with ways of improving how tasks are performed.*

  To discover the most efficient method of performing specific tasks, Taylor studied in great detail and measured the ways different workers went about performing their tasks. One of the main tools he used was a time-and-motion study, which involves the careful timing and recording of the actions taken to perform a particular task. Once Taylor understood the existing method of performing a task, he then experimented to increase specialization. He tried different methods of dividing and coordinating the various tasks necessary to produce a finished product. Usually this meant simplifying jobs and having each worker perform fewer, more routine tasks, as at the pin factory or on Ford's car assembly line. Taylor also sought to find ways to improve each worker's ability to perform a particular task–for example, by reducing the number of motions workers made to complete the task, by changing the layout of the work area or the type of tools workers used, or by experimenting with tools of different sizes.

- Principle 2: *Codify the new methods of performing tasks into written rules and standard operating procedures.*

  Once the best method of performing a particular task was determined, Taylor specified that it should be recorded so that this procedure could be taught to all workers performing the same task. These new methods further standardized and simplified jobs–essentially making jobs even more routine. In this way efficiency could be increased throughout an organization.

- Principle 3: *Carefully select workers who possess skills and abilities that match the needs of the task, and train them to perform the task according to the established rules and procedures.*

  To increase specialization, Taylor believed workers had to understand the tasks that were required and be thoroughly trained to perform the task at the required level. Workers who could not be trained to this level were to be transferred to a job where they were able to reach the minimum required level of proficiency.[6]

- Principle 4: *Establish a fair or acceptable level of performance for a task, and then develop a pay system that provides a reward for performance above the acceptable level.*
  To encourage workers to perform at a high level of efficiency, and to provide them with an incentive to reveal the most efficient techniques for performing a task, Taylor advocated that workers benefit from any gains in performance. They should be paid a bonus and receive some percentage of the performance gains achieved through the more efficient work process.[7]

By 1910 Taylor's system of scientific management had become nationally known and in many instances was faithfully and fully practiced.[8] However, managers in many organizations chose to implement the new principles of scientific management selectively. This decision ultimately resulted in problems. For example, some managers using scientific management obtained increases in performance, but rather than sharing performance gains with workers through bonuses as Taylor had advocated, they simply increased the amount of work that each worker was expected to do. Many workers experiencing the reorganized work system found that as their performance increased, managers required them to do more work for the same pay. Workers also learned that increases in performance often meant fewer jobs and a greater threat of layoffs because fewer workers were needed. In addition, the specialized, simplified jobs were often monotonous and repetitive, and many workers became dissatisfied with their jobs.

Scientific management brought many workers more hardship than gain and a distrust of managers who did not seem to care about their well-being.[9] These dissatisfied workers resisted attempts to use the new scientific management techniques and at times even withheld their job knowledge from managers to protect their jobs and pay. It is not difficult for workers to conceal the true potential efficiency of a work system to protect their interests. Experienced machine operators, for example, can slow their machines in undetectable ways by adjusting the tension in the belts or by misaligning the gears. Workers sometimes even develop informal work rules that discourage high performance and encourage shirking as work groups attempt to identify an acceptable or fair performance level (a tactic discussed in the next section).

Unable to inspire workers to accept the new scientific management techniques for performing tasks, some organizations increased the mechanization of the work process. For example, one reason why Henry Ford introduced moving conveyor belts in his factory was the realization that when a conveyor belt controls the pace of work (instead of workers setting their own pace), workers can be pushed to perform at higher levels–levels that they may have thought were beyond their reach. Charlie Chaplin captured this aspect of mass production in one of the opening scenes of his famous movie *Modern Times* (1936). In the film, Chaplin caricatured a new factory employee fighting to work at the machine-imposed pace but losing the battle to the machine. Henry Ford also used the principles of scientific management to identify the tasks that each worker should perform on the production line and thus to determine the most effective way to create a division of labor to suit the needs of a mechanized production system.

From a performance perspective, the combination of the two management practices–(1) achieving the right mix of worker-task specialization and (2) linking people and tasks by the speed of the production line–makes sense. It pro-

Charlie Chaplin tries to extricate a fellow employee from the machinery of mass production in this scene from "Modern Times." The complex machinery is meant to represent the power that machinery has over the worker in the new work system.

duces the huge savings in cost and huge increases in output that occur in large, organized work settings. For example, in 1908 managers at the Franklin Motor Company using scientific management principles redesigned the work process, and the output of cars increased from 100 cars a month to 45 cars a day; workers' wages, however, increased by only 90 percent.[10] From other perspectives, however, scientific management practices raise many concerns. The definition of the workers' rights not by the workers themselves but by the owners or managers as a result of the introduction of the new management practices raised an ethical issue, which we examine in this "Ethics in Action."

Ethics in Action

Fordism in Practice

From 1908 to 1914, through trial and error, Henry Ford's talented team of production managers pioneered the development of the moving conveyor belt and thus changed manufacturing practices forever. Although the technical aspects of the move to mass production were a dramatic financial success for Ford and for the millions of Americans who could now afford cars, for the workers who actually produced the cars, many human and social problems resulted.

With simplification of the work process, workers grew to hate the monotony of the moving conveyor belt. By 1914 Ford's car plants were experiencing huge employee turnover–often reaching levels as high as 300 or 400 percent per year as workers left because they could not handle the work-induced stress.[11] Henry Ford recognized these problems and made an announcement: From that point on, to motivate his workforce, he would reduce the length of the workday from nine hours to eight hours, and the company would *double* the basic wage from $2.50 to $5.00 per day. This was a dramatic increase, similar to an announcement today of an overnight doubling of the minimum wage. Ford became an internationally famous figure, and the word Fordism was coined for his new approach.[12]

Ford's apparent generosity, however, was matched by an intense effort to control the resources–both human and material–with which his empire was built. He employed hundreds of inspectors to check up on employees, both inside and outside his factories. In the factory supervision was close and confining. Employees were not allowed to leave their places at the production line, and they were not permitted to talk to one another. Their job was to concentrate fully on the task at hand. Few employees could adapt to this system, and they developed ways of talking out of the sides of their mouths, like ventriloquists, and invented a form of speech that became known as the "Ford Lisp."[13] Ford's obsession with control brought him into greater and greater conflict with managers, who often were fired when they disagreed with him. As a result, many talented people left Ford to join a growing number of rivals.

Outside the workplace, Ford went so far as to establish what he called the Sociological Department to check up on how his employees lived and the ways they spent their time. Inspectors from this department visited the homes of employees and investigated their habits and problems. Employees who exhibited behaviors contrary to Ford's standards (for instance, if they drank too much or were always in debt) were likely to be fired. Clearly, Ford's effort to control his employees led him and his managers to behave in ways that today would be considered unacceptable and unethical and in the long run would impair an organization's ability to prosper.

Despite the problems of worker turnover, absenteeism, and discontent at Ford Motor Company, managers of the other car companies watched Ford reap huge gains in efficiency from the application of the new management principles. They believed that their companies would have to imitate Ford if they were to survive. They followed Taylor and used many of his followers as consultants to teach them how to adopt the techniques of scientific management. In addition, Taylor elaborated his principles in several books, including *Shop Management* (1903) and *The Principles of Scientific Management* (1911), which explain in detail how to apply the principles of scientific management to reorganize the work system.[14]

Taylor's work has had an enduring effect on the management of production systems. Managers in every organization, whether it produces goods or services, now carefully analyze the basic tasks that must be performed and try to devise the work systems that will allow their organizations to operate most efficiently.

The Gilbreths

Two prominent followers of Taylor were Frank Gilbreth (1868–1924) and Lillian Gilbreth (1878–1972), who refined Taylor's analysis of work movements and made many contributions to time-and-motion study.[15] Their aims were to (1) break up and analyze every individual action necessary to perform a particular task into each of its component actions, (2) find better ways to perform each component action, and (3) reorganize each of the component actions so that the action as a whole could be performed more efficiently–at less cost of time and effort.

The Gilbreths often filmed a worker performing a particular task and then separated the task actions, frame by frame, into their component movements. Their goal was to maximize the efficiency with which each individual task was performed so that gains across tasks would add up to enormous savings of time and effort. Their attempts to develop improved management principles were captured–at times quite humorously–in the movie *Cheaper by the Dozen,* which depicts how the Gilbreths (with their 12 children) tried to live their own lives according to these efficiency principles and apply them to daily actions such as shaving, cooking, and even raising a family.[16]

Eventually, the Gilbreths became increasingly interested in the study of fatigue. They studied how the physical characteristics of the workplace contribute to job stress that often leads to fatigue and thus poor performance. They isolated factors that result in worker fatigue, such as lighting, heating, the color of walls, and the design of tools and machines. Their pioneering studies paved the way for new advances in management theory.

This scene from "Cheaper by the Dozen" illustrates how "efficient families," such as the Gilbreths, use formal family courts to solve problems of assigning chores to different family members and to solve disputes when they arise.

In workshops and factories, the work of the Gilbreths, Taylor, and many others had a major effect on the practice of management. In comparison with the old crafts system, jobs in the new system were more repetitive, boring, and monotonous as a result of the application of scientific management principles, and workers became increasingly dissatisfied. Frequently, the management of work settings became a game between workers and managers: Managers tried to initiate work practices to increase performance, and workers tried to hide the true potential efficiency of the work setting to protect their own well-being.[17]

Administrative Management Theory

Side by side with scientific managers studying the person-task mix to increase efficiency, other researchers were focusing on **administrative management,** the study of how to create an organizational structure that leads to high efficiency and effectiveness. Organizational structure is the system of task and authority relationships that control how employees use resources to achieve the organization's goals. Two of the most influential views regarding the creation of efficient systems of organizational administration were developed in Europe: Max Weber, a German professor of sociology, developed one theory. Henri Fayol, the French manager who developed the model of management introduced in Chapter 1, developed the other.

administrative management The study of how to create an organizational structure that leads to high efficiency and effectiveness.

bureaucracy A formal system of organization and administration designed to ensure efficiency and effectiveness.

The Theory of Bureaucracy

Max Weber (1864–1920), wrote at the turn of the twentieth century, when Germany was undergoing its industrial revolution.[18] To help Germany manage its growing industrial enterprises at a time when it was striving to become a world power, Weber developed the principles of **bureaucracy**–a formal system of

Figure 2.2
Weber's Principles of Bureaucracy

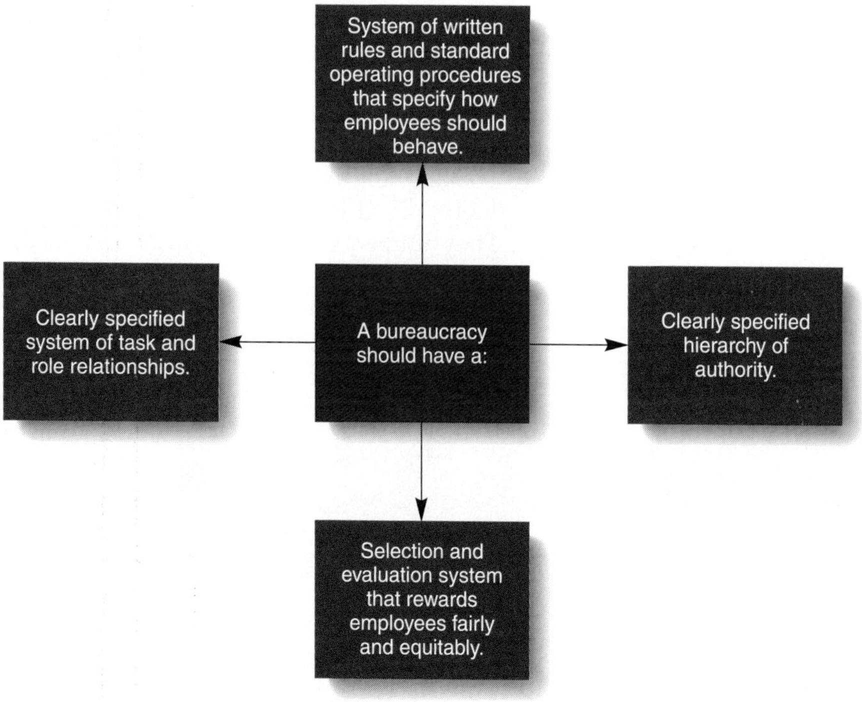

organization and administration designed to ensure efficiency and effectiveness. A bureaucratic system of administration is based on the five principles summarized in Figure 2.2.

authority The power to hold people accountable for their actions and to make decisions concerning the use of organizational resources.

- Principle 1: *In a bureaucracy, a manager's formal authority derives from the position he or she holds in the organization.*

  Authority is the power to hold people accountable for their actions and to make decisions concerning the use of organizational resources. Authority gives managers the right to direct and control their subordinates' behavior to achieve organizational goals. In a bureaucratic system of administration, obedience is owed to a manager, not because of any personal qualities–such as personality, wealth, or social status–but because the manager occupies a position that is associated with a certain level of authority and responsibility.[19]

- Principle 2: *In a bureaucracy, people should occupy positions because of their performance, not because of their social standing or personal contacts.*

  This principle was not always followed in Weber's time and is often ignored today. Some organizations and industries are still affected by social networks in which personal contacts and relations, not job-related skills, influence hiring and promotional decisions.

- Principle 3: *The extent of each position's formal authority and task responsibilities, and its relationship to other positions in an organization, should be clearly specified.*

  When the tasks and authority associated with various positions in the organization are clearly specified, managers and workers know what is expected of them and what to expect from each other. Moreover, an organization can hold all its employees strictly accountable for their actions when they know their exact responsibilities.

- Principle 4: *Authority can be exercised effectively in an organization when positions are arranged hierarchically, so employees know whom to report to and who reports to them.*[20]

  Managers must create an organizational hierarchy of authority that makes it clear who reports to whom and to whom managers and workers should go if conflicts or problems arise. This principle is especially important in the armed forces, FBI, CIA, and other organizations that deal with sensitive issues involving possible major repercussions. It is vital that managers at high levels of the hierarchy be able to hold subordinates accountable for their actions.

- Principle 5: *Managers must create a well-defined system of rules, standard operating procedures, and norms so that they can effectively control behavior within an organization.*

  rules Formal written instructions that specify actions to be taken under different circumstances to achieve specific goals.

  standard operating procedures Specific sets of written instructions about how to perform a certain aspect of a task.

  norms Unwritten, informal codes of conduct that prescribe how people should act in particular situations.

  Rules are formal written instructions that specify actions to be taken under different circumstances to achieve specific goals (for example, if A happens, do B). **Standard operating procedures (SOPs)** are specific sets of written instructions about how to perform a certain aspect of a task. A rule might state that at the end of the workday employees are to leave their machines in good order, and a set of SOPs specifies exactly how they should do so, itemizing which machine parts must be oiled or replaced. **Norms** are unwritten, informal codes of conduct that prescribe how people should act in particular situations. For example, an organizational norm in a restaurant might be that waiters should help each other if time permits.

  Rules, SOPs, and norms provide behavioral guidelines that increase the performance of a bureaucratic system because they specify the best ways to accomplish organizational tasks. Companies such as McDonald's and Wal-Mart have developed extensive rules and procedures to specify the behaviors required of their employees, such as "Always greet the customer with a smile."

Weber believed that organizations that implement all five principles establish a bureaucratic system that improves organizational performance. The specification of positions and the use of rules and SOPs to regulate how tasks are performed make it easier for managers to organize and control the work of subordinates. Similarly, fair and equitable selection and promotion systems improve managers' feelings of security, reduce stress, and encourage organizational members to act ethically and further promote the interests of the organization.[21]

If bureaucracies are not managed well, however, many problems can result. Sometimes, managers allow rules and SOPs, or "bureaucratic red tape," to become so cumbersome that decision making becomes slow and inefficient and organizations are unable to change. When managers rely too much on rules to solve problems and not enough on their own skills and judgment, their behavior becomes inflexible. A key challenge for managers is to use bureaucratic principles to benefit, rather than harm, an organization.

Fayol's Principles of Management

Henri Fayol (1841–1925) was the CEO of Comambault Mining. Working at the same time as, but independently from Weber, Fayol identified 14 principles (summarized in Table 2.1) that he believed essential to increase the efficiency of the management process.[22] We discuss these principles in detail here because, although they were developed at the turn of the twentieth century, they remain

Table 2.1
Fayol's 14 Principles of Management

Division of Labor Job specialization and the division of labor should increase efficiency, especially if managers take steps to lessen workers' boredom.
Authority and Responsibility Managers have the right to give orders and the power to exhort subordinates for obedience.
Unity of Command An employee should receive orders from only one superior.
Line of Authority The length of the chain of command that extends from the top to the bottom of an organization should be limited.
Centralization Authority should not be concentrated at the top of the chain of command.
Unity of Direction The organization should have a single plan of action to guide managers and workers.
Equity All organizational members are entitled to be treated with justice and respect.
Order The arrangement of organizational positions should maximize organizational efficiency and provide employees with satisfying career opportunities.
Initiative Managers should allow employees to be innovative and creative.
Discipline Managers need to create a workforce that strives to achieve organizational goals.
Remuneration of Personnel The system that managers use to reward employees should be equitable for both employees and the organization.
Stability of Tenure of Personnel Long-term employees develop skills that can improve organizational efficiency.
Subordination of Individual Interests to the Common Interest Employees should understand how their performance affects the performance of the whole organization.
Esprit de Corps Managers should encourage the development of shared feelings of comradeship, enthusiasm, or devotion to a common cause.

the bedrock on which much of the recent management theory and research are based. In fact, as the "Management Insight" following this discussion suggests, modern writers such as well-known management guru Tom Peters continue to extol these principles.

DIVISION OF LABOR A champion of job specialization and the division of labor for reasons already mentioned, Fayol was nevertheless among the first to point out the downside of too much specialization: boredom–a state of mind likely to cause a fall in product quality, worker initiative, and flexibility. As a result, Fayol advocated that workers be given more job duties to perform or be encouraged to assume more responsibility for work outcomes, a principle increasingly applied today in organizations that empower their workers.

AUTHORITY AND RESPONSIBILITY Like Weber, Fayol emphasized the importance of authority and responsibility. Fayol, however, went beyond Weber's formal authority, which derives from a manager's position in the hierarchy, to recognize the informal authority that derives from personal expertise, technical knowledge, moral worth, and ability to lead and to generate commitment from subordinates. (The study of authority is the subject of recent research into leadership, discussed in Chapter 13.)

unity of command A reporting relationship in which an employee receives orders from, and reports to, only one superior.

UNITY OF COMMAND The principle of **unity of command** specifies that an employee should receive orders from, and report to, only one superior. Fayol believed that *dual command*, the reporting relationship that exists when two supervisors give orders to the same subordinate, should be avoided except in exceptional circumstances. Dual command confuses the subordinate, undermines order and discipline, and creates havoc within the formal hierarchy of authority. Assessing any manager's authority and responsibility in a system of dual command is difficult, and the manager who is bypassed feels slighted and angry and may be uncooperative in the future.

line of authority The chain of command extending from the top to the bottom of an organization.

LINE OF AUTHORITY The **line of authority** is the chain of command extending from the top to the bottom of an organization. Fayol was one of the first management theorists to point out the importance of limiting the length of the chain of command by controlling the number of levels in the managerial hierarchy. The greater the number of levels in the hierarchy, the longer communication between managers at the top and bottom takes and the slower the pace of planning and organizing. Restricting the number of hierarchical levels to lessen these communication problems enables an organization to act quickly and flexibly; this is one reason for the recent trend toward restructuring (discussed in Chapter 1).

Fayol also pointed out that when organizations are split into different departments, each with its own hierarchy, it is important to allow middle and first-line managers in each department to interact with managers at similar levels in other departments. This interaction helps to speed decision making, because managers know each other and know whom to go to when problems arise. For cross-departmental integration to work, Fayol noted the importance of keeping one's superiors informed about what is taking place so that lower-level decisions do not harm activities taking place in other parts of the organization. One alternative to cross-departmental integration is to create cross-departmental teams controlled by a team leader (see Chapter 1).

centralization The concentration of authority at the top of the managerial hierarchy.

CENTRALIZATION Fayol also was one of the first management writers to focus on **centralization**, the concentration of authority at the top of the managerial hierarchy. Fayol believed that authority should not be concentrated at the top of the chain of command. One of the most significant issues that top managers face is how much authority to centralize at the top of the organization and what authority to decentralize to managers and workers at lower hierarchical levels. This is an important issue because it affects the behavior of people at all levels in the organization.

If authority is very centralized, only managers at the top make important decisions, and subordinates simply follow orders. This arrangement gives top managers great control over organizational activities and helps ensure that the organization is pursuing its strategy, but it makes it difficult for the people who are closest to problems and issues to respond to them in a timely manner. It also can lower the motivation of middle and first-line managers and make them less flexible and adaptable because they become reluctant to make decisions on their own, even when doing so is necessary. They get used to passing the buck. As we saw in Chapter 1, the pendulum is now swinging toward decentralization, as organizations seek to empower middle managers and create self-managed teams that monitor and control their own activities both to increase organizational flexibility and to reduce operating costs and increase efficiency.

unity of direction The singleness of purpose that makes possible the creation of one plan of action to guide managers and workers as they use organizational resources.

UNITY OF DIRECTION Just as there is a need for unity of command, there is also a need for **unity of direction,** the singleness of purpose that makes possible the creation of one plan of action to guide managers and workers as they use organizational resources. An organization without a single guiding plan becomes inefficient and ineffective; its activities become unfocused, and individuals and groups work at cross-purposes. Successful planning starts with top managers working as a team to craft the organization's strategy, which they communicate to middle managers, who decide how to use organizational resources to implement the strategy.

equity The justice, impartiality, and fairness to which all organizational members are entitled.

EQUITY As Fayol wrote: "For personnel to be encouraged to carry out their duties with all the devotion and loyalty of which they are capable, they must be treated with respect for their own sense of integrity, and equity results from the combination of respect and justice."[23] **Equity**–the justice, impartiality, and fairness to which all organizational members are entitled–is receiving much attention today; the desire to treat employees fairly is a primary concern for many managers. (Equity theory is discussed in Chapter 12.)

order The methodical arrangement of positions to provide the organization with the greatest benefit and to provide employees with career opportunities.

ORDER Like Taylor and the Gilbreths, Fayol was interested in analyzing jobs, positions, and individuals to ensure that the organization was using resources as efficiently as possible. To Fayol, **order** meant the methodical arrangement of positions to provide the organization with the greatest benefit and to provide employees with career opportunities to satisfy their needs. Thus, Fayol recommended the use of organizational charts to show the position and duties of each employee and to indicate which positions an employee might move to or be promoted into in the future. He also advocated that managers engage in extensive career planning to help ensure orderly career paths. Career planning is of primary interest today as organizations increase the resources they are willing to devote to training and developing their workforces.

initiative The ability to act on one's own, without direction from a superior.

INITIATIVE Although order and equity are important means to fostering commitment and loyalty among employees, Fayol believed that managers must also encourage employees to exercise **initiative,** the ability to act on their own, without direction from a superior. Used properly, initiative can be a major source of strength for an organization because it leads to creativity and innovation. Managers need skill and tact to achieve the difficult balance between the organization's need for order and employees' desire for initiative. Fayol believed that the ability to strike this balance was a key indicator of a superior manager.

discipline Obedience, energy, application, and other outward marks of respect for a superior's authority.

DISCIPLINE In focusing on the importance of **discipline**–obedience, energy, application, and other outward marks of respect for a superior's authority–Fayol was addressing the concern of many early managers: How to create a workforce that was reliable and hardworking and would strive to achieve organizational goals. According to Fayol, discipline results in respectful relations between organizational members and reflects the quality of an organization's leadership and a manager's ability to act fairly and equitably.

REMUNERATION OF PERSONNEL Fayol proposed reward systems including bonuses and profit-sharing plans, which are increasingly utilized today as organizations seek improved ways to motivate employees. Convinced from his own experience that an organization's payment system has important implications for organizational success, Fayol believed that effective reward systems should be equitable for both employees and the organization, encourage productivity by rewarding well-directed effort, not be subject to abuse, and be uniformly applied to employees.

STABILITY OF TENURE OF PERSONNEL Fayol also recognized the importance of long-term employment, and the idea has been echoed by contemporary management gurus such as Tom Peters, Jeff Pfeffer, and William Ouchi. When employees stay with an organization for extended periods of time, they develop skills that improve the organization's ability to utilize its resources.

SUBORDINATION OF INDIVIDUAL INTERESTS TO THE COMMON INTEREST The interests of the organization as a whole must take precedence over the interests of any one individual or group if the organization is to survive. Equitable agreements must be established between the organization and its members to ensure that employees are treated fairly and rewarded for their performance and to maintain the disciplined organizational relationships so vital to an efficient system of administration.

ESPRIT DE CORPS As this discussion of Fayol's ideas suggests, the appropriate design of an organization's hierarchy of authority and the right mix of order and discipline foster cooperation and commitment. Likewise, a key element in a successful organization is the development of **esprit de corps**, a French expression that refers to shared feelings of comradeship, enthusiasm, or devotion to a common cause among members of a group. Esprit de corps can result when managers encourage personal, verbal contact between managers and workers and by encouraging communication to solve problems and implement solutions.

esprit de corps Shared feelings of comradeship, enthusiasm, or devotion to a common cause among members of a group.

Some of the principles that Fayol outlined have faded from contemporary management practices, but most have endured. The characteristics of organizations that Tom Peters and Robert Waterman identified as being "excellently managed" in their best-selling book *In Search of Excellence* (1982) are discussed in this "Management Insight."[24]

Management Insight

Peters and Waterman's Excellent Companies

In the early 1980s, Tom Peters and Robert Waterman identified 62 organizations that they considered to be the best performing organizations in the United States. They asked the question, Why do these companies perform better than their rivals?, and discovered that successful organizations have managers who manage according to three sets of related principles. Those principles have a great deal in common with Fayol's principles.

First, Peters and Waterman argued, top managers of successful companies create principles and guidelines that emphasize managerial autonomy and entrepreneurship and encourage risk taking and initiative. For example, they allow middle managers to develop new products, even though there is no assurance that these products will be winners. In high-performing organizations, top managers are closely involved in the day-to-day operations of the company, provide unity of command and unity of direction, and do not simply make decisions in an isolated ivory tower. Top managers decentralize authority to lower-level managers and nonmanagerial employees and give them the freedom to get involved and the motivation to get things done.

The second approach that managers of excellent organizations use to increase performance is to create one central plan that puts organizational goals at center stage. In high-performing organizations, managers focus attention toward what the organization does best, and the emphasis is on continuously improving the goods and services the organization provides to its customers. Managers of top-performing companies resist the temptation to get sidetracked into pursuing ventures outside their area of expertise just because they seem to promise a quick return. These managers also focus on customers and establish close relationships with them to learn their needs, for responsiveness to customers increases competitive advantage.

The third set of management principles pertains to organizing and controlling the organization. Excellent companies establish a division of work and a division of authority and responsibility that will motivate employees to subordinate their individual interests to the common interest. Inherent in this approach is the belief that high performance derives from individual skills and abilities and that equity, order, initiative, and other indications of respect for the individual create the esprit de corps that fosters productive behavior. An emphasis on entrepreneurship and respect for every employee leads the best managers to create a structure that gives employees room to exercise initiative and motivates them to succeed. Because a simple, streamlined managerial hierarchy is best suited to achieve this outcome, top managers keep the line of authority as short as possible. They also decentralize authority to permit employee participation, but they keep enough control to maintain unity of direction.

As this insight into contemporary management suggests, the basic concerns that motivated Fayol continue to motivate management theorists.[25] The principles that Fayol and Weber set forth still provide a clear and appropriate set of guidelines that managers can use to create a work setting that makes efficient and effective use of organizational resources. These principles remain the bedrock of modern management theory; recent researchers have refined or developed them to suit modern conditions. For example, Weber's and Fayol's concerns for equity and for establishing appropriate links between performance and reward are central themes in contemporary theories of motivation and leadership.

Behavioral Management Theory

Because the writings of Weber and Fayol were not translated into English and published in the United States until the late 1940s, American management theorists in the first half of the twentieth century were unaware of the contributions of these European pioneers. American management theorists began where Taylor and his followers left off. Although their writings were all very different, the theorists all espoused a theme that focused on **behavioral management,** the study of how managers should personally behave to motivate employees and encourage them to perform at high levels and be committed to achieving organizational goals.

behavioral management The study of how managers should behave to motivate employees and encourage them to perform at high levels and be committed to the achievement of organizational goals.

The Work of Mary Parker Follett

If F. W. Taylor is considered the father of management thought, Mary Parker Follett (1868–1933) serves as its mother.[26] Much of her writing about management and about the way managers should behave toward workers was a response to her concern that Taylor was ignoring the human side of the organization. She pointed out that management often overlooks the multitude of ways in which employees can contribute to the organization when managers allow them to participate and exercise initiative in their everyday work lives.[27] Taylor, for example, never proposed that managers should involve workers in analyzing their jobs to identify better ways to perform tasks, or even ask workers how they felt about their jobs. Instead, he used time-and-motion experts to analyze workers' jobs for them. Follett, in contrast, argued that because workers know the most about their jobs, they should be involved in job analysis and managers should allow them to participate in the work development process.

Follett proposed that "Authority should go with knowledge . . . whether it is up the line or down." In other words, if workers have the relevant knowledge, then workers, rather than managers, should be in control of the work process itself, and managers should behave as coaches and facilitators–not as monitors and supervisors. In making this statement, Follett anticipated the current interest in self-managed teams and empowerment. She also recognized the importance of having managers in different departments communicate directly with each other to speed decision making. She advocated what she called cross-functioning: members of different departments working together in cross-departmental teams to accomplish projects–an approach that is increasingly utilized today.[28]

Mary Parker Follett, an early management thinker who advocated that "Authority should go with knowledge . . . whether it is up the line or down."

Fayol also mentioned expertise and knowledge as important sources of managers' authority, but Follett went further. She proposed that knowledge and expertise, and not managers' formal authority deriving from their position in the hierarchy, should decide who would lead at any particular moment. She believed, as do many management theorists today, that power is fluid and should flow to the person who can best help the organization achieve its goals. Follett took a horizontal view of power and authority, in contrast to Fayol, who saw the formal line of authority and vertical chain of command as being most essential to effective management. Follett's behavioral approach to management was very radical for its time.

The Hawthorne Studies and Human Relations

Probably because of its radical nature, Follett's work was unappreciated by managers and researchers until quite recently. Most continued to follow in the footsteps of Taylor and the Gilbreths. To increase efficiency, they studied ways to improve various characteristics of the work setting, such as job specialization or the kinds of tools workers used. One series of studies was conducted from

1924 to 1932 at the Hawthorne Works of the Western Electric Company.[29] This research, now known as the Hawthorne studies, began as an attempt to investigate how characteristics of the work setting–specifically the level of lighting or illumination–affect worker fatigue and performance. The researchers conducted an experiment in which they systematically measured worker productivity at various levels of illumination.

The experiment produced some unexpected results. The researchers found that regardless of whether they raised or lowered the level of illumination, productivity increased. In fact, productivity began to fall only when the level of illumination dropped to the level of moonlight, a level at which presumably workers could no longer see well enough to do their work efficiently.

The researchers found these results puzzling and invited a noted Harvard psychologist, Elton Mayo, to help them. Mayo proposed another series of experiments to solve the mystery. These experiments, known as the relay assembly test experiments, were designed to investigate the effects of other aspects of the work context on job performance, such as the effect of the number and length of rest periods and hours of work on fatigue and monotony.[30] The goal was to raise productivity.

During a two-year study of a small group of female workers, the researchers again observed that productivity increased over time, but the increases could not be solely attributed to the effects of changes in the work setting. Gradually, the researchers discovered that, to some degree, the results they were obtaining were influenced by the fact that the researchers themselves had become part of the experiment. In other words, the presence of the researchers was affecting the results because the workers enjoyed receiving attention and being the subject of study and were willing to cooperate with the researchers to produce the results they believed the researchers desired.

Subsequently, it was found that many other factors also influence worker behavior, and it was not clear what was actually influencing the Hawthorne workers' behavior. However, this particular effect–which became known as the **Hawthorne effect**–seemed to suggest that workers' attitudes toward their managers affect the level of workers' performance. In particular, the significant finding was that a manager's behavior or leadership approach can affect performance. This finding led many researchers to turn their attention to managerial behavior and leadership. If supervisors could be trained to behave in ways that would elicit cooperative behavior from their subordinates, then productivity could be increased. From this view emerged the **human relations movement**, which advocates that supervisors be behaviorally trained to manage subordinates in ways that elicit their cooperation and increase their productivity.

Hawthorne effect The finding that a manager's behavior or leadership approach can affect workers' level of performance.

human relations movement Advocates of the idea that supervisors receive behavioral training to manage subordinates in ways that elicit their cooperation and increase their productivity.

The importance of behavioral or human relations training became even clearer to its supporters after another series of experiments–the bank wiring room experiments. In a study of workers making telephone switching equipment, researchers Elton Mayo and F. J. Roethlisberger discovered that the workers, as a group, had deliberately adopted a norm of output restriction to protect their jobs. Workers who violated this informal production norm were subjected to sanctions by other group members. Those who violated group performance norms and performed above the norm were called ratebusters; those who performed below the norm were called chiselers.

The experimenters concluded that both types of workers threatened the group as a whole. Ratebusters threatened group members because they revealed to managers how fast the work could be done. Chiselers were looked down on because they were not doing their share of the work. Work-group members disciplined both ratebusters and chiselers to create a pace of work that the workers (not the managers) thought was fair. Thus, a work group's influence over output can be as great as the supervisors' influence. Since the work group can influence the behavior of its members, some management theorists argue that supervisors should be trained to behave in ways that gain the goodwill and cooperation of workers so that supervisors, not workers, control the level of work-group performance.

One of the main implications of the Hawthorne studies was that the behavior of managers and workers in the work setting is as important in explaining the level of performance as the technical aspects of the task. Managers must understand the workings of the **informal organization,** the system of behavioral rules and norms that emerge in a group, when they try to manage or change behavior in organizations. Many studies have found that, as time passes, groups often develop elaborate procedures and norms that bond members together, allowing unified action either to cooperate with management to raise performance or to restrict output and thwart the attainment of organizational goals.[31] The Hawthorne studies demonstrated the importance of understanding how the feelings, thoughts, and behavior of work-group members and managers affect performance. It was becoming increasingly clear to researchers that understanding behavior in organizations is a complex process that is critical to increasing performance.[32] Indeed, the increasing interest in the area of management known as **organizational behavior,** the study of the factors that have an impact on how individuals and groups respond to and act in organizations, dates from these early studies.

informal organization The system of behavioral rules and norms that emerge in a group.

organizational behavior The study of the factors that have an impact on how individuals and groups respond to and act in organizations.

Theory X and Theory Y

Several studies after the Second World War revealed how assumptions about workers' attitudes and behavior affect managers' behavior. Perhaps the most influential approach was developed by Douglas McGregor. He proposed that two sets of assumptions about how work attitudes and behaviors not only dominate the way managers think but also affect how they behave in organizations. McGregor named these two contrasting sets of assumptions Theory X and Theory Y (see Figure 2.3).[33]

THEORY X According to the assumptions of **Theory X,** the average worker is lazy, dislikes work, and will try to do as little as possible. Moreover, workers have little ambition and wish to avoid responsibility. Thus, the manager's task is to counteract workers' natural tendencies to avoid work. To keep workers' performance at a high level, the manager must supervise them closely and control their behavior by means of "the carrot and stick"–rewards and punishments.

Theory X Negative assumptions about workers that lead to the conclusion that a manager's task is to supervise them closely and control their behavior.

Managers who accept the assumptions of Theory X design and shape the work setting to maximize their control over workers' behaviors and minimize workers' control over the pace of work. These managers believe that workers must be made to do what is necessary for the success of the organization, and they focus on developing rules, SOPs, and a well-defined system of rewards and punishments to control behavior. They see little point in giving workers autonomy to solve their own problems because they think that the workforce neither expects nor desires cooperation. Theory X managers see their role as closely monitoring workers to ensure that they contribute to the production process and do not threaten product quality. Henry Ford, who closely supervised and managed his workforce, fits McGregor's description of a manager who holds Theory X assumptions.

Figure 2.3 Theory X versus Theory Y

THEORY X	THEORY Y
The average employee is lazy, dislikes work, and will try to do as little as possible.	Employees are not inherently lazy. Given the chance, employees will do what is good for the organization.
To ensure that employees work hard, managers should closely supervise employees.	To allow employees to work in the organization's interest, managers must create a work setting that provides opportunities for workers to exercise initiative and self-direction.
Managers should create strict work rules and implement a well-defined system of rewards and punishments to control employees.	Managers should decentralize authority to employees and make sure employees have the resources necessary to achieve organizational goals.

Theory Y Positive assumptions about workers that lead to the conclusion that a manager's task is to create a work setting that encourages commitment to organizational goals and provides opportunities for workers to be imaginative and to exercise initiative and self-direction.

THEORY Y In contrast, Theory Y assumes that workers are not inherently lazy, do not naturally dislike work, and, if given the opportunity, will do what is good for the organization. According to Theory Y, the characteristics of the work setting determine whether workers consider work to be a source of satisfaction or punishment; and managers do not need to closely control workers' behavior to make them perform at a high level because workers exercise self-control when they are committed to organizational goals. The implication of Theory Y, according to McGregor, is that "the limits of collaboration in the organizational setting are not limits of human nature but of management's ingenuity in discovering how to realize the potential represented by its human resources."[34] It is the manager's task to create a work setting that encourages commitment to organizational goals and provides opportunities for workers to be imaginative and to exercise initiative and self-direction.

When managers design the organizational setting to reflect the assumptions about attitudes and behavior suggested by Theory Y, the characteristics of the organization are quite different from those of an organizational setting based on Theory X. Managers who believe that workers are motivated to help the organization reach its goals can decentralize authority and give more control over the job to workers, both as individuals and in groups. In this setting, individuals and groups are still accountable for their activities, but the manager's role is not to control employees but to provide support and advice, to make sure employees have the resources they need to perform their jobs, and to evaluate them on their ability to help the organization meet its goals. Henri Fayol's approach to administration more closely reflects the assumptions of Theory Y, rather than Theory X. One company that has always operated with the type of management philosophy inherent in Theory Y is Hewlett-Packard, the subject of the next "Management Insight."

Management Insight

The Hewlett-Packard Way

Managers at the electronics company Hewlett-Packard consistently put into practice principles derived from Theory Y. (Go to the company's website at http://www.hp.com for additional information.) Founders William Hewlett and David Packard–Bill and Dave, as they are still known throughout the organization–established a philosophy of management known as the "HP

Way" that is people oriented, stresses the importance of treating every person with consideration and respect, and offers recognition for achievements.[35]

HP's philosophy rests on a few guiding principles. One is a policy of long-term employment. HP goes to great lengths not to lay off workers. At times when fewer people were needed, rather than lay off workers management cut pay and shortened the workday until demand for HP products picked up. This policy strengthened employees' loyalty to the organization.

The HP Way is based on several golden rules about how to treat members of the organization so that they feel free to be innovative and creative. HP managers believe that every employee of the company is a member of the HP team. They emphasize the need to increase the level of communication among employees, believing that horizontal communication between peers, not just vertical communication up and down the hierarchy, is essential for creating a positive climate for innovation.

To promote communication and cooperation between employees at different levels of the hierarchy, HP encourages informality. Managers and workers are on a first-name basis with each other and with the founders Bill and Dave. In addition, Bill and Dave pioneered the technique known as "managing by wandering around." People are expected to wander around learning what others are doing so that they can tap into opportunities to develop new products or find new avenues for cooperation. Bill and Dave also pioneered the principle that employees should spend 15 percent of their time working on projects of their own choosing, and they encouraged employees to take equipment and supplies home to experiment with them on their own time. HP's product design engineers leave their current work out in the open on their desks so that anybody can see what they are doing, can learn from it, or can suggest ways to improve it. Managers are selected and promoted because of their ability to engender excitement and enthusiasm for innovation in their subordinates. HP's offices have low walls and shared laboratories to facilitate communication and cooperation between managers and workers. In all these ways, HP managers seek to promote each employee's desire to be innovative and also to create a team and family atmosphere based on cooperation.[36]

The results of HP's practices have helped it become one of the leading electronics companies in the world and it has been very profitable. In 2001, however, HP, like most other high-tech companies was experiencing problems because of a downturn in the global economy, and it announced that it was searching for ways to reduce costs. However, in keeping with the management philosophy and values of its founders which continue to shape the company, CEO Carly Fiorino, announced that HP would not lay off employees but asked them to accept lower salaries and unpaid leave to help the company through this rough spot.[37]

Management Science Theory

Management science theory is a contemporary approach to management that focuses on the use of rigorous quantitative techniques to help managers make maximum use of organizational resources to produce goods and services. In essence, management science theory is a contemporary extension of scientific management, which, as developed by Taylor, also took a quantitative approach to measuring the worker-task mix to raise efficiency. There are many branches of management science and once again, IT, which is having significant impact on all

management science theory An approach to management that uses rigorous quantitative techniques to help managers make maximum use of organizational resources.

kinds of management practices, is affecting the tools managers use to make decisions.[38] Each branch of management science deals with a specific set of concerns:

- *Quantitative management* utilizes mathematical techniques, such as linear and nonlinear programming, modeling, simulation, queuing theory, and chaos theory, to help managers decide, for example, how much inventory to hold at different times of the year, where to locate a new factory, and how best to invest an organization's financial capital. IT offers managers new and improved ways of handling information to enable managers to make more accurate assessments of the situation and better decisions.
- *Operations management* provides managers with a set of techniques that they can use to analyze any aspect of an organization's production system to increase efficiency. IT, through the internet and through growing B2B networks is transforming the way managers handle the acquisition of inputs and the disposal of finished products.
- *Total quality management (TQM)* focuses on analyzing an organization's input, conversion, and output activities to increase product quality.[39] Once again, through sophisticated software packages and computer-controlled production, IT is changing the way managers and employees think about the work process and ways of improving it.
- *Management information systems (MIS)* help managers design information systems that provide information about events occurring inside the organization as well as in its external environment–information that is vital for effective decision making. Once again IT gives managers access to more and better information, and allows more managers at all levels to participate in the decision-making process.

All these subfields of management science, enhanced by sophisticated IT, provide tools and techniques that managers can use to help improve the quality of their decision making and increase efficiency and effectiveness. We discuss many of the important developments in management science theory thoroughly in Part 6 of this book. In particular, Chapter 17, "Managing Information Systems and Technologies," describes the management of information systems and technologies, and Chapter 18, "Operations Management: Managing Quality, Efficiency, and Responsiveness to Customers," focuses on IT, operations management, and TQM.

Organizational Environment Theory

An important milestone in the history of management thought occurred when researchers went beyond the study of how managers can influence behavior within organizations to consider how managers control the organization's relationship with its external environment, or **organizational environment**–the set of forces and conditions that operate beyond an organization's boundaries but affect a manager's ability to acquire and utilize resources. Resources in the organizational environment include the raw materials and skilled people that an organization requires to produce goods and services, as well as the support of groups including customers who buy these goods and services and provide the organization with financial resources. One way of determining the relative success of an organization is to consider how effective its managers are at obtaining scarce and valu-

organizational environment The set of forces and conditions that operate beyond an organization's boundaries but affect a manager's ability to acquire and utilize resources.

able resources.[40] The importance of studying the environment became clear after the development of open-systems theory and contingency theory during the 1960s.

The Open-Systems View

open system A system that takes in resources from its external environment and converts them into goods and services that are then sent back to that environment for purchase by customers.

One of the most influential views of how an organization is affected by its external environment was developed by Daniel Katz, Robert Kahn, and James Thompson in the 1960s.[41] These theorists viewed the organization as an **open system**—a system that takes in resources from its external environment and converts or transforms them into goods and services that are sent back to that environment, where they are bought by customers (see Figure 2.4).

At the input stage an organization acquires resources such as raw materials, money, and skilled workers to produce goods and services. Once the organization has gathered the necessary resources, conversion begins. At the conversion stage the organization's workforce, using appropriate tools, techniques, and machinery, transforms the inputs into outputs of finished goods and services such as cars, hamburgers, or flights to Hawaii. At the output stage the organization releases finished goods and services to its external environment, where customers purchase and use them to satisfy their needs. The money the organization obtains from the sales of its outputs allows the organization to acquire more resources so that the cycle can begin again.

closed system A system that is self-contained and thus not affected by changes occurring in its external environment.

entropy The tendency of a system to lose its ability to control itself and thus to dissolve and disintegrate.

The system just described is said to be open because the organization draws from and interacts with the external environment in order to survive; in other words, the organization is open to its environment. A **closed system,** in contrast, is a self-contained system that is not affected by changes in its external environment. Organizations that operate as closed systems, that ignore the external environment, and that fail to acquire inputs are likely to experience **entropy,** the tendency of a system to lose its ability to control itself and thus to dissolve and disintegrate.

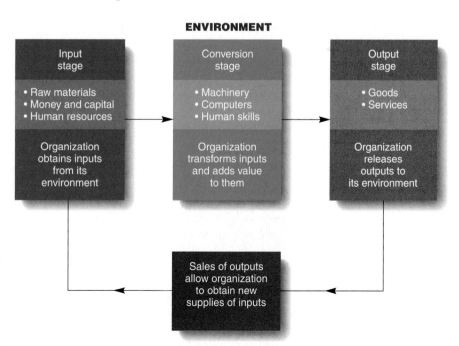

Figure 2.4
The Organization as an Open System

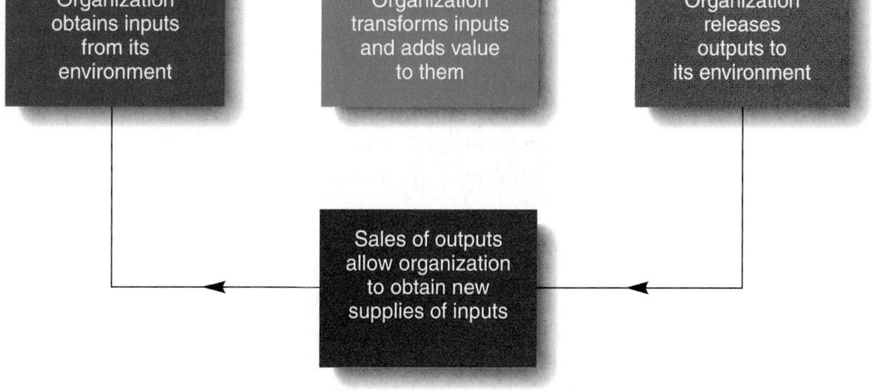

Management theorists can model the activities of most organizations by using the open-systems view. Manufacturing companies like Ford and General Electric, for example, buy inputs such as component parts, skilled and semi-skilled labor, and robots and computer-controlled manufacturing equipment; then at the conversion stage they use their manufacturing skills to assemble inputs into outputs of cars and appliances. As we discuss in later chapters, competition between organizations for resources is one of several major challenges to managing the organizational environment.

Researchers using the open-systems view are also interested in how the various parts of a system work together to promote efficiency and effectiveness. Systems theorists like to argue that the whole is greater than the sum of its parts; they mean that an organization performs at a higher level when its departments work together rather than separately. **Synergy,** the performance gains that result when individuals and departments coordinate their actions, is possible only in an organized system. The recent interest in using teams composed of people from different departments reflects systems theorists' interest in designing organizational systems to create synergy and thus increase efficiency and effectiveness.

synergy Performance gains that result when individuals and departments coordinate their actions.

Contingency Theory

contingency theory The idea that the organizational structures and control systems managers choose depend on—are contingent on—characteristics of the external environment in which the organization operates.

Another milestone in management theory was the development of **contingency theory** in the 1960s by Tom Burns and G. M. Stalker in Britain and Paul Lawrence and Jay Lorsch in the United States.[42] The crucial message of contingency theory is that there is no one best way to organize: The organizational structures and the control systems that managers choose depend on–are contingent on–characteristics of the external environment in which the organization operates. According to contingency theory, the characteristics of the environment affect an organization's ability to obtain resources; and to maximize the likelihood of gaining access to resources, managers must allow an organization's departments to organize and control their activities in ways most likely to allow them to obtain resources, given the constraints of the particular environment they face. In other words, how managers design the organizational hierarchy, choose a control system, and lead and motivate their employees is contingent on the characteristics of the organizational environment (see Figure 2.5).

An important characteristic of the external environment that affects an organization's ability to obtain resources is the degree to which the environment is changing. Changes in the organizational environment include changes in technology, which can lead to the creation of new products (such as compact discs) and result in the obsolescence of existing products (eight-track tapes); the entry of new competitors (such as global organizations that compete for available resources); and unstable economic conditions. In general, the more quickly the organizational environment is changing, the greater are the problems associated with gaining access to resources and the greater is managers' need to find ways to coordinate the activities of people in different departments to respond to the environment quickly and effectively.

MECHANISTIC AND ORGANIC STRUCTURES Drawing on Weber's and Fayol's principles of organization and management, Burns and Stalker proposed two basic ways in which managers can organize and control an organization's activities to respond to characteristics of its external environment: They can use a mechanistic structure or an organic structure.[43] As you will see, a

Figure 2.5 Contingency Theory of Organizational Design

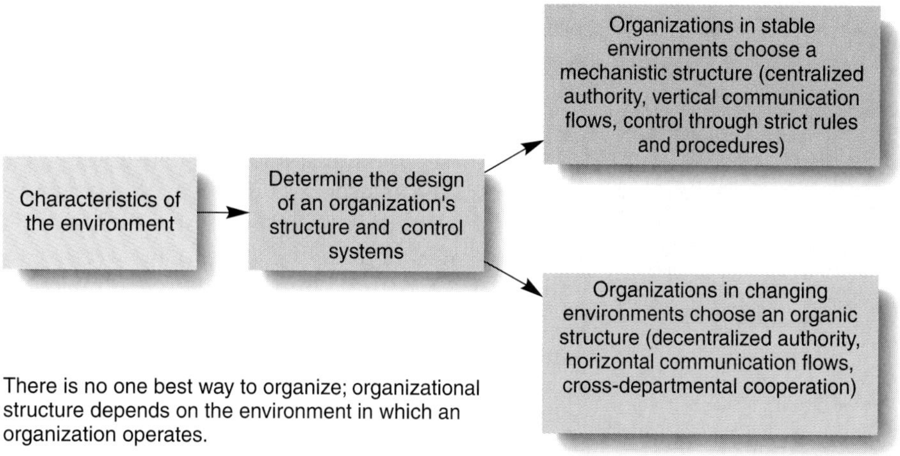

There is no one best way to organize; organizational structure depends on the environment in which an organization operates.

mechanistic structure typically rests on Theory X assumptions, and an organic structure typically rests on Theory Y assumptions.

When the environment surrounding an organization is stable, managers tend to choose a mechanistic structure to organize and control activities and make employee behavior predictable. In a **mechanistic structure,** authority is centralized at the top of the managerial hierarchy, and the vertical hierarchy of authority is the main means used to control subordinates' behavior. Tasks and roles are clearly specified, subordinates are closely supervised, and the emphasis is on strict discipline and order. Everyone knows his or her place, and there is a place for everyone. A mechanistic structure provides the most efficient way to operate in a stable environment because it allows managers to obtain inputs at the lowest cost, giving an organization the most control over its conversion processes and enabling the most efficient production of goods and services with the smallest expenditure of resources. McDonald's restaurants operate with a mechanistic structure. Supervisors make all important decisions; employees are closely supervised and follow well-defined rules and standard operating procedures.

mechanistic structure An organizational structure in which authority is centralized, tasks and rules are clearly specified, and employees are closely supervised.

In contrast, when the environment is changing rapidly, it is difficult to obtain access to resources, and managers need to organize their activities in a way that allows them to cooperate, to act quickly to acquire resources (such as new types of inputs to produce new kinds of products), and to respond effectively to the unexpected. In an **organic structure,** authority is decentralized to middle and first-line managers to encourage them to take responsibility and act quickly to pursue scarce resources. Departments are encouraged to take a cross-departmental or functional perspective, and, as in Mary Parker Follett's model, authority rests with the individuals and departments best positioned to control the current problems the organization is facing. In an organic structure, control is much looser than it is in a mechanistic structure, and reliance on shared norms to guide organizational activities is greater. Managers in an organic structure can react more quickly to a changing environment than can managers in a mechanistic structure. However, an organic structure is generally more expensive to operate because it requires more managerial time, money, and effort spent on coordination. So, it is used only when needed–when the organizational environment is unstable and rapidly changing. The way in which Sony uses an organic structure in the rapidly evolving electronics market is instructive.

organic structure An organizational structure in which authority is decentralized to middle and first-line managers and tasks and roles are left ambiguous to encourage employees to cooperate and respond quickly to the unexpected.

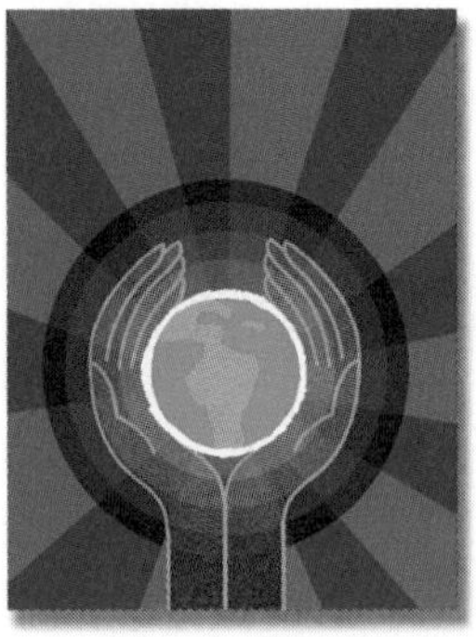

Managing Globally

Sony's Organic Structure

Product engineers at Sony turn out an average of four ideas for new products every day. Despite the fact that Sony is now a huge, diversified organization employing more than 115,000 employees worldwide, the company continues to lead the way in innovation in the consumer electronics industry.[44] Why? A large part of the answer lies in the way the company uses its structure to organize and control its employees. First, a policy of self-promotion allows Sony engineers, without notifying their supervisors, to seek out projects anywhere in the company where they feel they can make a contribution. If they find new projects to which they can make contributions, their current bosses are expected to let them join the new teams. Sony has twenty-three business groups composed of hundreds of development teams, and this movement of people cross-pollinates ideas throughout the organization.[45]

Second, Sony deliberately emphasizes the lateral movement of people and ideas between design and engineering groups. The "Sony Way" emphasizes communication between groups to foster innovation and change.[46] Sony has a corporate research department full of people in integrating roles who coordinate the efforts of the business groups and product development teams. They make sure that each team knows what the others are doing, not only to share knowledge but also to avoid overlap or duplication of effort. Once a year, the corporate research department organizes an in-house three-day special event open only to Sony employees, where each product development team can display its work to its peers.

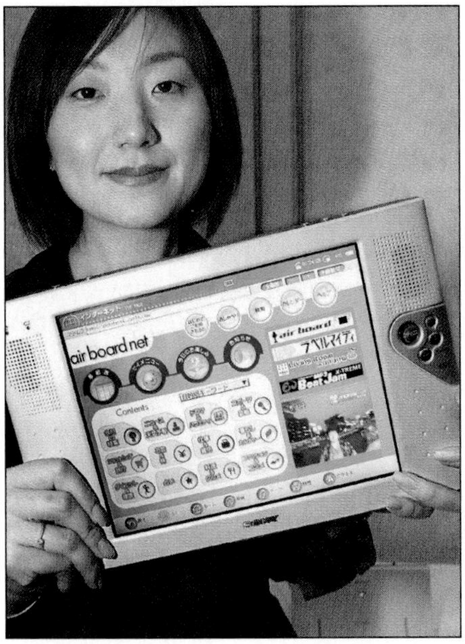

One of a stream of Sony's new Internet products that its engineers are turning out to secure the company's place in the growing market for digital electronic products.

That Sony's organic structure works is evident from the company's success in the marketplace and from the number of innovative products Sony turns out. Like many other large Japanese companies, Sony has a policy of lifetime employment, which makes it easy for its engineers to take risks with ideas and encourages the development of norms and values that support innovative efforts. Moreover, Sony rewards its engineers with promotion and more control of resources when they are successful.

Sony is hard-headed, however, when it comes to making the best use of its resources. Top management takes pains to distance itself from decision making inside a team or even a business group, so that the magic of decentralized decision making can work. But it does intervene when different groups are duplicating one another's efforts. For example, when Sony made a big push into computers it reorganized the relationship between its audio, video, and computer groups so that they improved the way they coordinate new product developments. Once again, however, Sony takes a lateral view of the way the organization works, and its vertical chain of command is oriented toward finding ways to decentralize authority and still make the best use of resources. This lateral approach to organizing and controlling is working well as Sony is making record profits and has become the dominant global electronics competitor.

Part 3 (Chapters 7–8) of this book is devoted to strategic management, the study of the relationship between organizations and their external environment and of the strategies organizations adopt to manage that environment.[47]

Tips for New Managers

Applying **Management Principles**

1. Analyze whether an organization's division of labor is meeting its current needs. Consider ways to change the level of job specialization to increase performance.
2. Examine the way an organization works in reference to Weber and Fayol's principles. Decide if the distribution of authority in the hierarchy best meets the organization's needs. Similarly, decide if the right system to discipline or remunerate employees is being used.
3. Examine organizational policies to see if managers are consistently behaving in an equitable manner and whether these policies lead to ethical employee behavior.

Summary and Review

In this chapter we examined the evolution of management theory and research over the last century. Much of the material in the rest of this book stems from developments and refinements of this work.

SCIENTIFIC MANAGEMENT THEORY The search for efficiency started with the study of how managers could improve person-task relationships to increase efficiency. The concept of job specialization and division of labor remains the basis for the design of work settings in modern organizations. New developments such as lean production and total quality management are often viewed as advances on the early scientific management principles developed by Taylor and the Gilbreths.

ADMINISTRATIVE MANAGEMENT THEORY Max Weber and Henri Fayol outlined principles of bureaucracy and administration that are as relevant to managers today as when they were written at the turn of the twentieth century. Much of modern management research refines these principles to suit contemporary conditions. For example, the increasing interest in the use of cross-departmental teams and the empowerment of workers are issues that managers also faced a century ago.

BEHAVIORAL MANAGEMENT THEORY Researchers have described many different approaches to managerial behavior, including Theories X and Y. Often, the managerial behavior researchers suggest reflects the context of their own historical era and culture. Mary Parker Follett advocated managerial behaviors that did not reflect accepted modes of managerial behavior at the time, but her work was largely ignored until conditions changed.

MANAGEMENT SCIENCE THEORY The various branches of management science theory provide rigorous quantitative techniques that give managers more control over each organization's use of resources to produce goods and services.

ORGANIZATIONAL ENVIRONMENT THEORY The importance of studying the organization's external environment became clear after the development of open-systems theory and contingency theory during the 1960s. A main focus of contemporary management research is to find methods to help managers improve the ways they utilize organizational resources and compete successfully in the global environment. Strategic management and total quality management are two important approaches intended to help managers make better use of organizational resources.

Management in Action

Topics for Discussion and Action

1. Choose a fast-food restaurant, a department store, or some other organization with which you are familiar, and describe the division of labor and job specialization it uses to produce goods and services. How might this division of labor be improved?
2. Apply Taylor's principles of scientific management to improve the performance of the organization you chose in item 1.
3. In what ways are Weber's and Fayol's ideas about bureaucracy and administration similar? In what ways do they differ?
4. Question a manager about his or her views of the relative importance of Fayol's 14 principles of management.
5. Which of Weber's and Fayol's principles seem most relevant to the creation of an ethical organization?
6. Why was the work of Mary Parker Follett ahead of its time? To what degree do you think it is appropriate today?
7. Visit various organizations in your community, and identify those that seem to operate with a Theory X or a Theory Y approach to management.
8. What is contingency theory? What kinds of organizations familiar to you have been successful or unsuccessful in dealing with contingencies from the external environment?
9. Why are mechanistic and organic structures suited to different organizational environments?

Building Management Skills

Managing Your Own Business

Now that you understand the concerns addressed by management thinkers over the last century, use this exercise to apply your knowledge to develop your management skills.

Imagine that you are the founding entrepreneur of a software company that specializes in developing games for home computers. Customer demand for your games has increased so much that over the last year your company has grown from a busy one-person operation to one with 16 employees. In addition to yourself, you employ six software developers to produce the software, three graphic artists, two computer technicians, two marketing and sales personnel, and two secretaries. In the next year you expect to hire 30 new employees, and you are wondering how best to manage your growing company.

1. Use the principles of Weber and Fayol to decide on the system of organization and management that you think will be most effective for your growing organization. How many levels will the managerial hierarchy of your organization have? How much authority will you decentralize to your subordinates? How will you establish the division of labor between subordinates? Will your subordinates work alone and report to you or work in teams?
2. Which management approach (for example, Theory X or Y) do you propose to use to run your organization? In 50 words or less write a statement describing the management approach you believe will motivate and coordinate your subordinates, and tell why you think this style will be best.

Small Group Breakout Exercise

Modeling an Open System

Form groups of three to five people, and appoint one group member as the spokesperson who will communicate your findings to the class when called on by the instructor. Then discuss the following scenario.

Think of an organization with which you are all familiar, such as a local restaurant, store, or bank. After choosing an organization, model it from an open-systems perspective. Identify its input, conversion, and output processes; and identify forces in the external environment that help or hurt the organization's ability to obtain resources and dispose of its goods or services.

Exploring the World Wide Web

Search for a website that contains a time line or a short history of a company, detailing the way the organization has developed over time. What are the significant stages in the company's development, and what problems and issues have confronted managers at these stages? (For example, you might investigate the history of Ford Motor Company by utilizing the extensive resources of Ford's historical library. Research Ford's website [www.ford.com], and locate and read the material on Ford's history and evolution over time.)

You're the Management Consultant

How to Manage a Hotel

You have been called in to advise the owners of an exclusive new luxury hotel. For the venture to succeed, hotel employees must focus on providing customers with the highest-quality customer service possible. The challenge is to devise a way of organizing and controlling employees that will promote high-quality service, that will encourage employees to be committed to the hotel, and that will reduce the level of employee turnover and absenteeism—which are typically high in the hotel business.

Questions

1. How do the various theories of management discussed in this chapter offer clues for organizing and controlling hotel employees?
2. Which parts would be the most important for an effective system to organize and control employees?

BusinessWeek Cases in the News

Downfall X: The Inside Story of the Management Fiasco at Xerox

For the text of this in-depth *Business Week* case, log on to the *Contemporary Management* website at www.mhhe.com/Jones3e.

Questions

1. How would you characterize Xerox's managers' approach to planning, organizing, leading, and controlling over time?
2. Why did management problems arise at Xerox?
3. What kind of CEO does Xerox need to help turn the company around?

Cases in the News

From the pages of *The Wall Street Journal*

Mr. Edens Profits from Watching His Worker's Every Move

Control is one of Ron Edens's favorite words. "This is a controlled environment," he says of the blank brick building that houses his company, Electronic Banking System Inc.

Inside, long lines of women sit at spartan desks, slitting envelopes, sorting contents and filling out "control cards" that record how many letters they have opened and how long it has taken them. Workers here, in "the cage," must process three envelopes a minute. Nearby, other women tap keyboards, keeping pace with a quota that demands 8,500 strokes an hour.

The room is silent. Talking is forbidden. The windows are covered. Coffee mugs, religious pictures and other adornments are barred from workers' desks.

In his office upstairs, Mr. Edens sits before a TV monitor that flashes images from eight cameras posted through the plant. "There's a little bit of Sneaky Pete to it," he says, using a remote control to zoom in on a document atop a worker's desk. "I can basically read that and figure out how someone's day is going."

This day, like most others, is going smoothly, and Mr. Edens's business has boomed as a result. "We maintain a lot of control," he says. "Order and control are everything in this business."

Mr. Edens's business belongs to a small but expanding financial service known as "lockbox processing." Many companies and charities that once did their paperwork in-house now "out-source" clerical tasks to firms like EBS, which processes donations to groups such as Mothers Against Drunk Driving, the Doris Day Animal League, Greenpeace and the National Organization for Women.

More broadly, EBS reflects the explosive growth of jobs in which workers perform low-wage and limited tasks in white-collar settings. This has transformed towns like Hagerstown—a blue-collar community hit hard by industrial layoffs in the 1970s—into sites for thousands of jobs in factory-sized offices.

Many of these jobs, though, are part time and most pay far less than the manufacturing occupations they replaced. Some workers at EBS start at the minimum wage of $4.25 an hour and most earn about $6 an hour. The growth of such jobs—which often cluster outside major cities—also completes a curious historic circle. During the Industrial Revolution, farmers' daughters went to work in textile towns like Lowell, Mass. In post-industrial America, many women of modest means and skills are entering clerical mills where they process paper instead of cloth (coincidentally, EBS occupies a former garment factory).

"The office of the future can look a lot like the factory of the past," says Barbara Garson, author of *The Electronic Sweatshop* and other books on the modern workplace. "Modern tools are being used to bring 19th-century working conditions into the white-collar world."

The time-motion philosophies of Frederick Taylor, for instance, have found a 1990s correlate in the phone, computer and camera, which can be used to monitor workers more closely than a foreman with a stopwatch ever could. Also, the nature of the work often justifies a vigilant eye. In EBS workers handle thousands of dollars in checks and cash, and Mr. Edens says cameras help deter would-be thieves. Tight security also reassures visiting clients. "If you're disorderly, they'll think we're out of control and that things could get lost," says Mr. Edens, who worked as a financial controller for the National Rifle Association before founding EBS in 1983.

But tight observation also helps EBS monitor productivity and weed out workers who don't keep up. "There's multiple uses," Mr. Edens says of surveillance. His desk is covered with computer printouts recording the precise toll of keystrokes tapped by each data-entry worker. He also keeps a day-to-day tally of errors. The work floor itself resembles an enormous classroom in the throes of exam period. Desks point toward the front, where a manager keeps watch from a raised platform that workers call "the pedestal" or "the birdhouse." Other supervisors are positioned toward the back of the room. "If you want to watch someone," Mr. Edens explains, "it's easier from behind because they don't know you're watching." There also is a black globe hanging from the ceiling, in which cameras are positioned.

Mr. Edens sees nothing Orwellian about this omniscience. "It's not a Big Brother attitude," he says. "It's more of a calming attitude."

But studies of workplace monitoring suggest otherwise. Experts say that surveillance can create a hostile environment in which workers feel pressured, paranoid and prone to stress-related illness. Surveillance also can be used punitively, to intimidate workers or to justify their firing.

Following a failed union drive at EBS, the National Labor Relations Board filed a series of complaints against the company, including charges that EBS threatened, interrogated, and spied on workers. As part of an out-of-court settlement, EBS reinstated a fired worker and posted a notice that it would refrain from illegal practices during a second union vote, which also failed.

"It's all noise," Mr. Edens says of the unfair labor charges. As to the pressure that surveillance creates, Mr. Edens sees that simply as "the nature of the beast." He adds: "It's got to add stress when everyone knows their production is being monitored. I don't apologize for that."

Mr. Edens also is unapologetic about the Draconian work rules he maintains, including one that forbids all talk unrelated to the completion of each task. "I'm not paying people to chat. I'm paying them to open envelopes," he says. Of the blocked windows. Mr. Edens adds: "I don't want them looking out—it's distracting. They'll make mistakes."

This total focus boosts productivity but it makes many workers feel lonely and trapped. Some try to circumvent the silence rule, like kids in a school library. "If you don't turn your head and sort of mumble out of the side of your mouth, supervisors won't hear you most of the time," Cindy Kesselring explains during her lunch break. Even so, she feels isolated and often longs for her former job as a waitress. "Work is your social life, particularly if you've got kids," says the 27-year-old mother. "Here it's hard to get to know people because you can't talk."

During lunch, workers crowd in the parking lot outside, chatting nonstop. "Some of us don't eat much because the more you chew the less you can talk," Ms. Kesselring says. There aren't other breaks and workers aren't allowed to sip coffee or eat at their desks during the long stretches before and after lunch. Hard candy is the only permitted desk snack.

New technology, and the breaking down of labor into discrete, repetitive tasks, also have effectively stripped jobs such as those at EBS of whatever variety and skills clerical work once possessed. Workers in the cage (an antiquated banking term for a money-handling area) only open envelopes and sort contents; those in the audit department compute figures; and data-entry clerks punch in the information that the others have collected. If they make a mistake, the computer buzzes and a message such as "check digit error" flashes on the screen.

"We don't ask these people to think—the machines think for them," Mr. Edens says. "They don't have to make any decisions." This makes the work simpler but also deepens its monotony. In the cage, Carol Smith says she looks forward to envelopes that contain anything out of the ordinary, such as letters reporting that the donor is deceased. Or she plays mental games. "I think to myself, A goes in this pile, B goes here and C goes there—sort of like Bingo." She says she sometimes feels "like a machine," particularly when she fills out the "control card" on which she lists "time in" and "time out" for each tray of envelopes. In a slot marked "cage operator" Ms. Smith writes her code number, 3173. "That's me," she says.

Barbara Ann Wiles, a keyboard operator, also plays mind games to break up the boredom. Tapping in the names and addresses of new donors, she tries to imagine the faces behind the names, particularly the odd ones. "Like this one, Mrs. Fittizzi," she chuckles. "I can picture her as a very stout lady with a strong accent, hollering on a street corner." She picks out another: "Doris Angelroth—she's very sophisticated, a monocle maybe, drinking tea on an overstuffed mohair couch."

It is a world remote from the one Ms. Wiles inhabits. Like most EBS employees, she must juggle her low-paying job with child care. On this Friday, for instance, Ms. Wiles will finish her eight-hour shift at about 4 P.M., go home for a few hours, then return for a second shift from midnight to 8 A.M. Otherwise, she would have to come in on Saturday to finish the week's work.

This way I can be home on the weekend to look after my kids," she says.

Others find the work harder to leave behind at the end of the day. In the cage, Ms. Smith says her husband used to complain because she often woke him in the middle of the night. "I'd be shuffling my hands in my sleep," she says, mimicking the motion of opening envelopes.

Her cage colleague, Ms. Kesselring, says her fiancé has a different gripe. "He dodges me for a couple of hours after work because I don't shut up—I need to talk, talk, talk," she says. And there is one household task she can no longer abide.

"I won't pay bills because I can't stand to open another envelope," she says. "I'll leave letters sitting in the mailbox for days."

Source: Tony Horwitz, "Mr. Edens Profits from Watching His Workers' Every Move," The *Wall Street Journal,* December 1, 1994.

Questions

1. Which of the management theories described in the chapter does Ron Edens make most use of?
2. What is your view of Edens's management approach?

Chapter 3

Attitudes, Values, Ethics, and Culture: The Manager as a Person

Learning Objectives

After studying this chapter, you should be able to:

- Describe the various personality traits that affect how managers think, feel, and behave.
- Explain what values, attitudes, and moods and emotions are and describe their impact on managerial action.
- Illustrate how ethics help managers determine the right or proper way to behave when dealing with different stakeholder groups.
- Define organizational culture and explain the role managers play in creating it.
- Explain why managers should strive to create ethical organizational cultures.

A Manager's Challenge

Promoting Positive Attitudes and Ethical Values at Medtronic

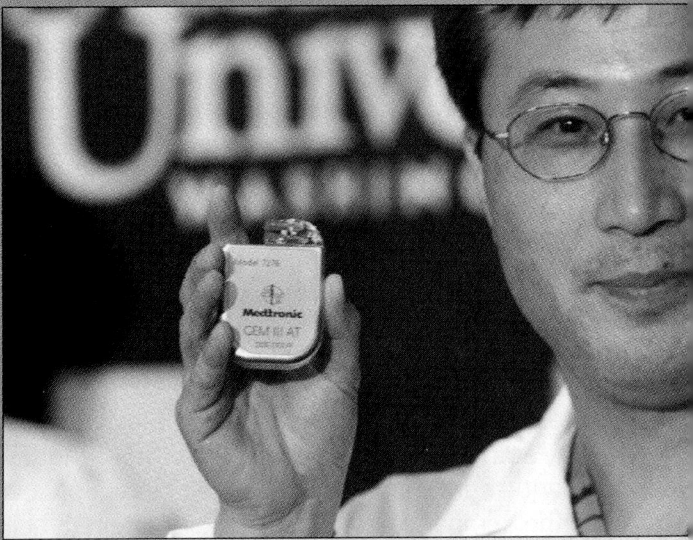

Vice President Dick Cheney's doctor, Sung Lee, holds up a Medtronic 3DR pacemaker plus during a news conference at George Washington University Hospital in Washington on June 30, 2001. Dr. Lee implanted a similar device in Cheney.

How can managers promote and sustain performance-enhancing attitudes and values throughout an organization?

Medtronic, based in Fridley, Minnesota, invents and manufactures medical devices, such as pacemakers, stents, and neurostimulators, to lessen pain, improve health, and extend life. Medtronic stands out as an organization whose employees—regardless of their position in the organizational hierarchy—perform at a high level, are satisfied with their jobs, and are committed to their organization. Why? Because Medtronic's culture, the set of shared values, norms, and expectations that guide its employees' behavior, reinforces and sustains positive employee attitudes and sound ethical values. Moreover, this culture is constantly maintained by managers from those in the very highest positions at Medtronic to lower-level managers. What kind of people are these managers and what kinds of attitudes and values do they uphold?

Executive managers at Medtronic, including former CEO Bill George, and current CEO Art Collins have had a major influence on the culture of this company. From the time he joined the company in 1989 until he retired in 2001, Bill George was instrumental in shaping the values, norms, and attitudes of its members. As you can imagine, ethical considerations are one of Medtronic's managers' major concerns because of the importance of ensuring high standards of patient safety. Also, many scientists and engineers join health-related companies because they wish to use their skills and talents to help others and they wish to join companies that have demonstrated their concern for people's well-being.

George and other top managers at Medtronic, therefore, go to great lengths to show their commitment to the highest ethical values and standards for patient care. Recruiting top scientists who possess the drive to excel is one important aspect of this. Creating the desire to perform highly and help people sets the scene for the development of positive work attitudes. For example, at Medtronic, Mark Rise, who has a Ph.D. in biomedical engineering, has the opportunity to work with great thinkers and use his creativity to invent new products to improve the quality of life for people with health problems ranging from heart and Parkinson's diseases to epilepsy and schizophrenia. These challenges raise his job performance and ensure both his job satisfaction and commitment to Medtronic.[1]

On a daily basis managers reinforce Medtronic's values and norms which further its mission to save and extend lives through the use of advanced medical devices. For example, managers invite people who use Medtronic devices to come to the company and share with employees their stories of how the company has prolonged or improved their lives. This annual celebration is a tangible sign to employees of the importance of their work.[2] One of the founders of Medtronic, Earl Bakken, periodically travels from his home in Hawaii to corporate headquarters to bestow on new employees engraved medallions with some of the company's core values: "Alleviate Pain, Restore Health, and Extend Life."[3]

While such events reinforce to employees the importance of their work, managers also seek to develop positive attitudes and moods by addressing employees' needs to reduce stress and balance work and family demands. George has always been concerned with work-life balance and ensuring that Medtronic provides a work environment that allows employees to flourish both on and off the job. For example, George himself stopped coming into work on Saturdays when he realized that his subordinates believed that if he came in on weekends then they needed to come in on weekends, too. Another example is middle manager Justine Fritz who embraces and reinforces Medtronic's values and ensures that her 12 team members are satisfied and find meaning in their work. However, as a mother, work-life balance is important to Fritz and she shares George's and current CEO Art Collins's appreciation of the need for balance.[4] Nonetheless, like Rise, Fritz and her fellow team members find great challenge, meaning, and a sense of accomplishment in their work especially when they launch a major new product that has just received approval from the U.S. Food and Drug Administration. Fritz manages more than 100 projects and as she puts it, "I've just never worked on anything that so visibly, so dramatically changes the quality of somebody's life."[5]

In a recent article in *Fortune* magazine, Bill George sums it up this way, "I always dreamt since I was 18 years old of being the head of a major corporation where the values of the company and my own values were congruent . . . where the product that you represent is doing good for people. We make mistakes . . . But at least the intent is there."[6] Medtronic's values and culture, espoused and reinforced by managers throughout the company ensure that employees are satisfied and committed and support Medtronic's ethical culture.

Overview

Like people everywhere, managers Bill George and Justine Fritz have their own distinctive personalities, ways of viewing things, personal challenges and disappointments, and shortcomings. In this chapter, we focus on the manager as a feeling, thinking human being. We start by describing enduring characteristics that influence how managers "manage," as well as how they view other people, their organizations, and the world around them. We discuss as well how managers' values, attitudes, and moods play out in organizations, shaping organizational ethics and culture. By the end of this chapter, you will have a good appreciation of how the personal characteristics of managers influence the process of management in general, and organizational ethics and culture in particular.

Enduring Characteristics: Personality Traits

All people, including managers, have certain enduring characteristics that influence how they think, feel, and behave both on and off the job. These characteristics are **personality traits**, particular tendencies to feel, think, and act in certain ways that can be used to describe the personalities of all individuals. It is important to understand the personalities of managers because their personalities influence their behavior and their approach to managing people and resources.

personality traits Enduring tendencies to feel, think, and act in certain ways.

Some managers, like Procter & Gamble's former chairman Edwin Artzt, are demanding, difficult to get along with, and highly critical of other people.[7] Other managers, like Southwest Airlines' former CEO Herb Kelleher, may be as concerned about effectiveness and efficiency as highly critical managers but are easier to get along with and likable and frequently praise the people around them. Both styles of management may produce excellent results, but their effects on employees are quite different. Do managers deliberately decide to adopt one or the other of these approaches to management? Although they may do so part of the time, in all likelihood their personalities also account for their different approaches. And, preliminary research suggests that the way people react to different conditions depends, in part, on their personalities.[8]

The Big Five Personality Traits

We can think of an individual's personality as being composed of five general traits or characteristics: extraversion, negative affectivity, agreeableness, conscientiousness, and openness to experience.[9] Researchers often consider these the Big Five personality traits.[10] Each of them can be viewed as a continuum along which every individual or, more specifically, every manager falls (see Figure 3.1).

Some managers may be at the high end of one trait continuum, others at the low end, and still others somewhere in between. An easy way to understand how these traits can affect a person's approach to management is to describe what people are like at the high and low ends of each trait continuum. As will become evident as you read about each trait, no single trait is right or wrong for being an effective manager. Rather, effectiveness is determined by a complex interaction between characteristics of managers (including personality traits) and the nature of the job and organization in which they are working. Moreover, personality traits that enhance managerial effectiveness in one situation may actually impair it in another situation.

extraversion The tendency to experience positive emotions and moods and to feel good about oneself and the rest of the world.

EXTRAVERSION **Extraversion** is the tendency to experience positive emotions and moods and feel good about oneself and the rest of the world. Managers who are high on extraversion (often called *extraverts*) tend to be sociable, affectionate, outgoing, and friendly. Managers who are low on extraversion (often called *introverts*) tend to be less inclined toward social interactions and to have a less positive outlook. Being high on extraversion may be an asset for managers whose jobs entail especially high levels of social interaction.

Figure 3.1
The Big Five Personality Traits

Manager's personalities can be described by determining which point on each of the following dimensions best characterizes the manager in question:

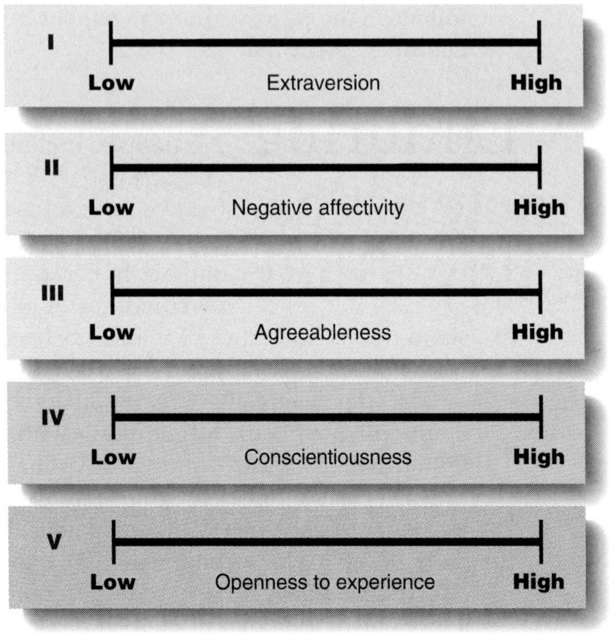

Managers who are low on extraversion may nevertheless be highly effective and efficient, especially when their jobs do not require excessive social interaction. Their more "quiet" approach may enable them to accomplish quite a bit of work in a limited time.

negative affectivity The tendency to experience negative emotions and moods, to feel distressed, and to be critical of oneself and others.

NEGATIVE AFFECTIVITY Negative affectivity is the tendency to experience negative emotions and moods, feel distressed, and be critical of oneself and others. Managers high on this trait may often feel angry and dissatisfied and complain about their own and others' lack of progress. Managers who are low on negative affectivity do not tend to experience many negative emotions and moods and are less pessimistic and critical of themselves and others. On the plus side, the critical approach of a manager high on negative affectivity may sometimes be effective if it spurs both the manager and others to improve their performance. Nevertheless, it is probably more pleasant to work with a manager who is low on negative affectivity; the better working relationships that such a manager is likely to cultivate also can be an important asset. Figure 3.2 is an example of a scale developed to measure a person's level of negative affectivity.

agreeableness The tendency to get along well with other people.

AGREEABLENESS Agreeableness is the tendency to get along well with others. Managers who are high on the agreeableness continuum are likeable, tend to be affectionate, and care about other people. Managers who are low on agreeableness may be somewhat distrustful of others, unsympathetic, uncooperative, and even at times antagonistic. Being high on agreeableness may be especially important for managers whose responsibilities require them to develop good, close relationships with others. Nevertheless, a low level of agreeableness may be an asset in managerial jobs that actually require managers to be antagonistic, such as drill sergeants, and some other kinds of military managers.

Figure 3.2
A Measure of Negative Affectivity

Instructions: Listed below are a series of statements a person might use to describe her/his attitudes, opinions, interests, and other characteristics. If a statement is true or largely true, put a "T" in the space next to the item. Or , if the statement is false or largely false, mark an "F" in the space.

Please answer every statement, even if you are not completely sure of the answer. Read each statement carefully, but don't spend too much time deciding on the answer.

____ **1.** I often find myself worrying about something.

____ **2.** My feelings are hurt rather easily.

____ **3.** Often I get irritated at little annoyances.

____ **4.** I suffer from nervousness.

____ **5.** My mood often goes up and down.

____ **6.** I sometimes feel "just miserable" for no good reason.

____ **7.** Often I experience strong emotions—anxiety, anger—without really knowing what causes them.

____ **8.** I am easily startled by things that happen unexpectedly.

____ **9.** I sometimes get myself into a state of tension and turmoil as I think of the day's events.

____ **10.** Minor setbacks sometimes irritate me too much.

____ **11.** I often lose sleep over my worries.

____ **12.** There are days when I'm "on edge" all of the time.

____ **13.** I am too sensitive for my own good.

____ **14.** I sometimes change from happy to sad, or vice versa, without good reason.

Scoring: Level of negative affectivity is equal to the number of items answered "True."

Source: Tellegen, *Brief Manual for the Differential Personality Questionnaire* (unpublished manuscript, University of Minnesota, 1982).

conscientiousness The tendency to be careful, scrupulous, and persevering.

CONSCIENTIOUSNESS Conscientiousness is the tendency to be careful, scrupulous, and persevering. Managers who are high on conscientiousness continuum are organized and self-disciplined; those who are low on this trait might sometimes appear to lack direction and self-discipline. Conscientiousness has been found to be a good predictor of performance in many kinds of jobs, including managerial jobs in a variety of organizations.[11] CEOs of major companies, such as Carly Fiorino of Hewlett-Packard, and Scott McNealy of Sun Microsystems often show signs of being high on conscientiousness–the long hours they work, their attention to detail, and their ability to handle their multiple responsibilities in an organized manner.

openness to experience The tendency to be original, have broad interests, be open to a wide range of stimuli, be daring, and take risks.

OPENNESS TO EXPERIENCE Openness to experience is the tendency to be original, have broad interests, be open to a wide range of stimuli, be daring, and take risks.[12] Managers who are high on this trait continuum may be especially likely to take risks and be innovative in their planning and decision making. Entrepreneurs who start their own businesses–like Bill Gates of

Microsoft, Jeff Bezos of Amazon.com, and Anita Roddick of The Body Shop–are, in all likelihood, high on openness to experience, which has contributed to their success as entrepreneurs and managers. The Medtronic managers featured in "A Manager's Challenge" are also likely to be high on openness to experience, as they are all involved in pushing forward the frontier for life saving and enhancing medical devices. Managers who are low on openness to experience may be less prone to take risks and more conservative in their planning and decision making. In certain organizations and positions, this tendency might be an asset. The manager of the fiscal office in a public university, for example, must ensure that all university departments and units follow the university's rules and regulations pertaining to budgets, spending accounts, and reimbursements of expenses.

By now it should be clear that successful managers occupy a variety of positions on the Big Five personality-trait continua. One highly effective manager may be high on extraversion and negative affectivity, another equally effective manager may be low on both these traits, and still another may be somewhere in between. Members of an organization must understand these differences across managers because they can shed light on how managers behave and on their approach to planning, leading, organizing, or controlling. If subordinates realize, for example, that their manager is low on extraversion, they will not feel slighted when their manager seems to be aloof because they will realize that by nature he or she is simply not outgoing.

Managers themselves also need to be aware of their own personality traits and the traits of others, including their subordinates and fellow managers. A manager who knows that he has a tendency to be highly critical of other people might try to tone down his negative approach. Similarly, a manager who realizes that her chronically complaining subordinate tends to be so negative because of his personality may take all his complaints with a grain of salt and realize that things probably are not as bad as this subordinate says they are.

In order for all members of an organization to work well together and with people outside the organization, such as customers and suppliers, they must understand each other. Such understanding comes, in part, from an appreciation of some of the fundamental ways in which people differ from one another–that is, an appreciation of personality traits.

Other Personality Traits That Affect Managerial Behavior

Many other specific traits in addition to the Big Five describe people's personalities. Here we look at traits that are particularly important for understanding managerial effectiveness: locus of control, self-esteem, and the needs for achievement, affiliation, and power.

internal locus of control The tendency to locate responsibility for one's fate within oneself.

LOCUS OF CONTROL People differ in their views about how much control they have over what happens to and around them. The locus of control trait captures these beliefs.[13] People with an **internal locus of control** believe that they themselves are responsible for their own fate; they see their own actions and behaviors as being important and decisive determinants of important outcomes such as levels of job performance, promotion, or being turned down for a choice job assignment. Some managers with an internal locus of control see the success of a whole organization resting on their shoulders. One example is Medtronic managers described in "A Manager's Challenge." An internal locus of control also helps to ensure ethical behavior and decision making in an organization because people feel accountable and responsible for their own actions. People with an **external locus of control** believe that outside forces are responsible for what happens to and around them; they do not think that their own actions make much of a difference. As such, they tend not to intervene to try to change a situation or solve a problem, leaving it to someone else.

external locus of control The tendency to locate responsibility for one's fate within outside forces and to believe that one's own behavior has little impact on outcomes.

Managers need to have an internal locus of control because they *are* responsible for what happens in organizations; they need to believe that they can and do make a difference as did Bill George at Medtronic. Moreover, managers are responsible for ensuring that organizations and their members behave in an ethical fashion and for this as well, they need to have an internal locus of control—they need to know and feel they can make a difference.

self-esteem The degree to which individuals feel good about themselves and their capabilities.

SELF-ESTEEM **Self-esteem** is the degree to which individuals feel good about themselves and their capabilities. People with high self-esteem believe that they are competent, deserving, and capable of handling most situations, as do George, Collins, Fritz, Rise, and Vang in "A Manager's Challenge." People with low self-esteem have poor opinions of themselves, are unsure about their capabilities, and question their ability to succeed at different endeavors.[14] Research suggests that people tend to choose activities and goals consistent with their levels of self-esteem. High self-esteem is desirable for managers because it facilitates their setting and keeping high standards for themselves, pushes them ahead on difficult projects, and gives them the confidence they need to make and carry out important decisions.

NEEDS FOR ACHIEVEMENT, AFFILIATION, AND POWER Psychologist David McClelland has extensively researched the needs for achievement, affiliation, and power.[15] The **need for achievement** is the extent to which an individual has a strong desire to perform challenging tasks well and to meet personal standards for excellence. People with a high need for achievement often set clear goals for themselves and like to receive performance feedback. The **need for affiliation** is the extent to which an individual is concerned about establishing and maintaining good interpersonal relations, being liked, and having other people around them get along with each other. The **need for power** is the extent to which an individual desires to control or influence others.[16]

need for achievement The extent to which an individual has a strong desire to perform challenging tasks well and to meet personal standards for excellence.

need for affiliation The extent to which an individual is concerned about establishing and maintaining good interpersonal relations, being liked, and having other people get along.

need for power The extent to which an individual desires to control or influence others.

Research suggests that high needs for achievement and for power are assets for first-line and middle managers; and that a high need for power is especially important for upper-level managers.[17] One study found that U.S. presidents with a relatively high need for power tended to be especially effective during their terms of office.[18] A high need for affiliation may not always be desirable in managers because it might lead them to try too hard to be liked by others (including subordinates) rather than doing all they can to ensure that performance is as high as it can and should be. Although most research on these needs has been done in the United States, some studies suggest that these findings may also be applicable to people in other countries, such as India and New Zealand.[19]

Taken together, these personality traits desirable in managers—an internal locus of control, high self-esteem, and high needs for achievement and power—suggest that managers need to be take-charge people who believe not only that their own actions are decisive in determining their own and their organization's fate but also in their own capabilities. They have a personal desire for accomplishment and influence over others.

Values, Attitudes, and Moods and Emotions

What are managers striving to achieve? How do they think they should behave? What do they think about their jobs and organizations? And, how do they actually feel at work? Some answers to these questions can be found by exploring managers' values, attitudes, and moods.

Values, attitudes, and moods capture how managers experience their jobs as individuals. *Values* describe what managers are trying to achieve through work and how they think they should behave. *Attitudes* capture their thoughts and feelings about their specific jobs and organizations. *Moods and emotions* encompass how managers actually feel when they are managing. Although these three aspects of managers' work experience are highly personal, they also have important implications for understanding how managers behave, how they treat and respond to others, and how, through their efforts, they help contribute to organizational effectiveness through planning, leading, organizing, and controlling.

Values: Terminal and Instrumental

terminal value A lifelong goal or objective that an individual seeks to achieve.

instrumental value A mode of conduct that an individual seeks to follow.

norms Informal rules of conduct for behaviors that are considered important by most members of a group or organization.

value system The terminal and instrumental values that are guiding principles in an individual's life.

The two kinds of personal values are *terminal* and *instrumental.* A **terminal value** is a personal conviction about lifelong goals or objectives; an **instrumental value** is a personal conviction about desired modes of conduct or ways of behaving.[20] Terminal values often lead to the formation of **norms** or informal rules of conduct for behaviors considered important by most members of a group or organization, such as behaving honestly or courteously.

Milton Rokeach, one of the leading researchers in the area of human values, identified 18 terminal values and 18 instrumental values that describe each person's value system (see Figure 3.3).[21] By rank ordering the terminal values from 1 (most important as a guiding principle in one's life) to 18 (least important as a guiding principle in one's life) and then rank ordering the instrumental values from 1 to 18, people can give good pictures of their **value systems**—what they are striving to achieve in life and how they want to behave.[22] (You can gain a good understanding of your own values by rank ordering first the terminal values and then the instrumental values listed in Figure 3.3).

Several of the terminal values listed in Figure 3.3 seem to be especially important for managers—such as *a sense of accomplishment (a lasting contribution), equality (brotherhood, equal opportunity for all), and self-respect (or self-esteem).* A manager who thinks a sense of accomplishment is of paramount importance might focus on making a lasting contribution to an organization by developing a new product that can save or prolong lives as is true of Rise and Fritz at Medtronic or by opening a new foreign subsidiary. A manager who places equality at the top of his or her list of terminal values may be at the forefront of an organization's efforts to support, provide equal opportunities to, and capitalize on the many talents of an increasingly diverse workforce.

Figure 3.3
Terminal and Instrumental Values

Terminal Values	Instrumental Values
A comfortable life (a prosperous life)	Ambitious (hard-working, aspiring)
An exciting life (a stimulating, active life)	Broad-minded (open-minded)
A sense of accomplishment (lasting contribution)	Capable (competent, effective)
A world at peace (free of war and conflict)	Cheerful (lighthearted, joyful)
A world of beauty (beauty of nature and the arts)	Clean (neat, tidy)
Equality (brotherhood, equal opportunity for all)	Courageous (standing up for your beliefs)
Family security (taking care of loved ones)	Forgiving (willlng to pardon others)
Freedom (independence, free choice)	Helpful (working for the welfare of others)
Happiness (contentedness)	Honest (sincere, truthful)
Inner harmony (freedom from inner conflict)	Imaginative (daring, creative)
Mature love (sexual and spiritual intimacy)	Independent (self-reliant, self-sufficient)
National security (protection from attack)	Intellectual (intelligent, reflective)
Pleasure (an enjoyable, leisurely life)	Logical (consistent, rational)
Salvation (saved, eternal life)	Loving (affectionate, tender)
Self-respect (self-esteem)	Obedient (dutiful, respectful)
Social recognition (respect, admiration)	Polite (courteous, well-mannered)
True friendship (close companionship)	Responsible (dependable, reliable)
Wisdom (a mature understanding of life)	Self-controlled (restrained, self-disciplined)

Source: Reprinted with permission of The Free Press, a Division of Simon & Schuster, Inc., from *The Nature of Human Values* by Milton Rokeach. Copyright © 1973 by The Free Press.

Other values are likely to be considered important by many managers, such *as a comfortable life (a prosperous life), an exciting life (a stimulating, active life), freedom (independence, free choice), and social recognition (respect, admiration).* The relative importance that managers place on each terminal value helps explain what they are striving to achieve in their organizations and what they will focus their efforts on.

Several of the instrumental values listed in Figure 3.3 seem to be important modes of conduct for managers, such as being ambitious (*hard-working, aspiring*), broad-minded (*open-minded*), capable (*competent, effective*), responsible (*dependable, reliable*), and *self-controlled (restrained, self-disciplined).* Moreover, the relative importance a manager places on these and other instrumental values may be a significant determinant of actual behaviors on the job. A manager who considers being *imaginative (daring, creative)* to be highly important, for example, is more likely to be innovative and take risks than is a manager who considers this to be less important (all else being equal). A manager who considers being *honest (sincere, truthful)* to be of paramount importance may be a driving force for taking steps to ensure that all members of a unit or organization behave ethically.

Although much of Rokeach's research was based in the United States, the terminal and instrumental values he identified can describe the values of people from other cultures as well, as indicated in this "Managing Globally."

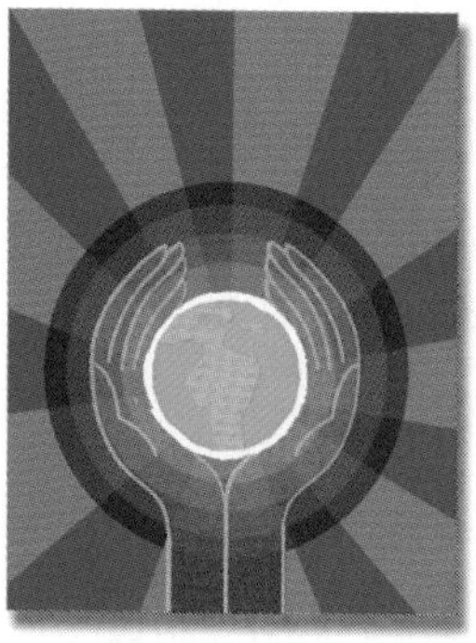

Managing Globally

Values of the Overseas Chinese

Over 55 million Chinese people work outside China, manage much of the trade and investment in all East Asia (except for Korea and Japan), and now are expanding beyond Asia to Europe and the United States. Often referred to as the "Overseas Chinese," they are prominent in businesses such as real estate and investment in countries such as Singapore and Malaysia.[23] They tend to be successful at what they do, so successful that some of them are now running multibillion-dollar companies.

Cheng Yu-tong, a Hong Kong-based real-estate manager, owns the Stouffer and Renaissance United States hotel chains and has taken control of some of Donald Trump's New York City real-estate ventures. President Enterprises, a Taiwanese food company, produces Girl Scout cookies in eight of its United States bakeries and also owns the bakery that makes Famous Amos chocolate chip cookies. Chinese managers are also forming agreements with companies in other countries to produce their products and sell them in local markets. For example, Chinese manufacturer TCL has entered into an agreement with the Indian firm, Baron India, to assemble its TVs and sell them in the Indian market.[24]

One distinguishing characteristic of some Overseas Chinese–whether managing a bank in Hong Kong or a truly global organization–is their values. Above all else, they value hard work, ambition, strong family ties, family security, responsibility, self-control, and competence. Billionaire Y. C. Wang has never taken a day off, and Kao Chin-yen, vice chairman of President Enterprises, says that he would feel sick if he had no work to do. Many of the businesses managed and owned by Overseas Chinese are family businesses, and parents work hard to ensure that their children have both the education and the experience they will need to assume responsible positions in their companies. That many Overseas Chinese are very disciplined and responsible managers who are highly competent is evident from their successes around the world.

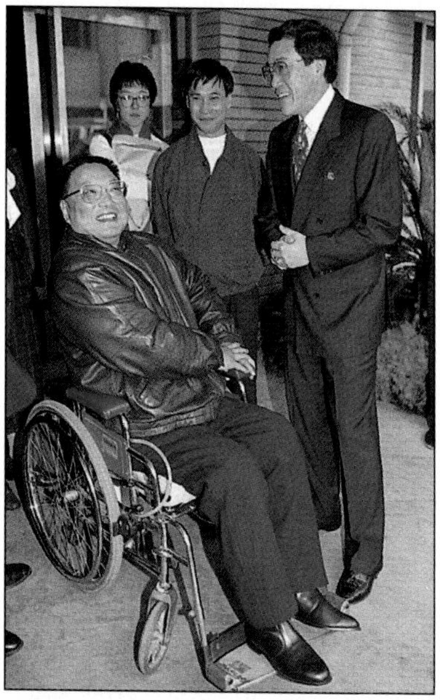

Chinese-American businessman Charles Wang, right, visits with Deng Pufang (son of Chinese leader Deng Ziaoping) during a visit to the Disabled Person's Federation headquarters in Beijing. Born in Shanghai, Wang is the founder of one of the world's largest software companies.

Given these values, you might think that the Overseas Chinese are somewhat risk-averse, but they are not. They also consider being daring and being creative to be important guiding principles, as evidenced by their multimillion-dollar investments around the world. Y. C. Wang is building one of the largest manufacturing facilities in the world in Taiwan at an estimated cost of $9 billion.

Respect, admiration, and social recognition also are important for these entrepreneurial managers. Many of the business deals between organizations owned and managed by Overseas Chinese are conducted through networks of managers who have developed close relationships of mutual trust and respect over decades. Personal relationships and connections built on respect and admiration are called *guanxi* and are the modus operandi for many Overseas Chinese. Similarly, *xinyong,* having a good reputation and a good credit rating, is a most valued asset for many Overseas Chinese managers.[25]

All in all, managers' value systems signify what they as individuals are trying to accomplish and be like in their personal lives and at work. Thus, managers' value systems are fundamental guides to their behavior and efforts at planning, leading, organizing, and controlling.

Attitudes

attitude A collection of feelings and beliefs.

An **attitude** is a collection of feelings and beliefs. Like everyone else, managers have attitudes about their jobs and organizations, and these attitudes affect how they approach their jobs. Two of the most important attitudes in this context are job satisfaction and organizational commitment.

job satisfaction The collection of feelings and beliefs that managers have about their current jobs.

JOB SATISFACTION **Job satisfaction** is the collection of feelings and beliefs that managers have about their current jobs.[26] Managers who are high in job satisfaction generally like their jobs, feel that they are being fairly treated, and believe that their jobs have many desirable features or characteristics (such as interesting work, good pay and job security, autonomy, or nice coworkers). Figure 3.4 shows sample items from two scales that managers can use to measure job satisfaction. Levels of job satisfaction tend to increase as one moves up the hierarchy in an organization. Upper managers, in general, tend to be more satisfied with their jobs than entry-level employees. Managers' levels of job satisfaction can range from very low to very high and anywhere in between.

organizational citizenship behaviors Behaviors that are not required of organizational members but that contribute to and are necessary for organizational efficiency, effectiveness, and gaining a competitive advantage.

In general, it is desirable for managers to be satisfied with their jobs, for at least two reasons. First, satisfied managers may be more likely to go the extra mile for their organization or perform **organizational citizenship behaviors (OCBs),** behaviors that are not required of organizational members but that contribute to and are necessary for organizational efficiency, effectiveness, and gaining a competitive advantage.[27] Managers who are satisfied with their jobs are more likely to perform these "above and beyond the call of duty" behaviors, which can range from putting in extra-long hours when needed to coming up with truly creative ideas and overcoming obstacles to implement them (even when doing so is not part of the manager's job), to going out of one's way to help a coworker, subordinate, or a superior (even when doing so entails considerable personal sacrifice).[28]

A second reason why it is desirable for managers to be satisfied with their jobs is that satisfied managers may be less likely to quit.[29] A manager who is highly satisfied may never even think about looking for another position; a dissatisfied manager may always be on the lookout for new opportunities. Turnover can hurt an organization because it results in the loss of the experience and knowledge that managers have gained about the company, industry, and the business environment.

A growing source of dissatisfaction for many lower- and middle-level managers, as well as for nonmanagerial employees, is the threat of unemployment and increased workloads from organizational downsizings. A recent study of 4,300 workers conducted by Wyatt Co. found that 76 percent of the employees of expanding companies are satisfied with their jobs but only 57 percent of the employees of companies that have downsized are satisfied.[30] Organizations that try to improve their efficiency through restructuring often eliminate a sizable number of first-line and middle management positions. This decision obviously hurts the managers who are laid off, and it also can reduce the job satisfaction levels of managers who remain. They might fear that they may be the next to be let go. In addition, the workloads of remaining managers often are dramatically increased as a result of restructuring, which also can contribute to dissatisfaction.

organizational commitment The collection of feelings and beliefs that managers have about their organization as a whole.

ORGANIZATIONAL COMMITMENT **Organizational commitment** is the collection of feelings and beliefs that managers have about their organization as a whole. Managers who are committed to their organizations believe in

Figure 3.4
Sample Items from Two Measures of Job Satisfaction

Sample items from the Minnesota Satisfaction Questionnaire:
People respond to each of the items in the scale by checking whether they are:

[ ] Very dissatisfied
[ ] Dissatisfied
[ ] Can't decide whether satisfied or not
[ ] Satisfied
[ ] Very satisfied

On my present job, this is how I feel about . . .

____ **1.** Being able to do things that don't go against my conscience.

____ **2.** The way my job provides for steady employment.

____ **3.** The chance to do things for other people.

____ **4.** The chance to do something that makes use of my abilities.

____ **5.** The way company policies are put into practice.

____ **6.** My pay and the amount of work I do.

____ **7.** The chances for advancement on this job.

____ **8.** The freedom to use my own judgment.

____ **9.** The working conditions.

____ **10.** The way my co-workers get along with each other.

____ **11.** The praise I get for doing a good job.

____ **12.** The feeling of accomplishment I get from the job.

The Faces Scale
Workers select the face which best expresses how they feel about their job in general.

11 10 9 8 7 6 5 4 3 2 1

Sources: D. J. Weiss, R. V. Dawis, G. W. England, and L. H. Lofquist, Manual for the Minnesota Satisfaction Questionnaire, 1967, Minnesota Studies in Vocational Rehabilitation: XXII University of Minnesota; R. B Dunham and J. B. Herman, "Development of a Female Faces Scale for Measuring Job Satisfaction," *Journal of Applied Psychology* 60 (1975): 629–31. Copyright © 1975 by the American Psychological Association. Reprinted with permission.

what their organizations are doing, are proud of what these organizations stand for, and feel a high degree of loyalty toward their organizations. Committed managers are more likely to go above and beyond the call of duty to help their company and are less likely to quit.[31] Organizational commitment can be especially strong when employees and managers truly believe in organizational values, it also leads to a strong organizational culture as found in Medtronic.

Organizational commitment is likely to help managers perform some of their figurehead and spokesperson roles (see Chapter 1). It is much easier for a manager to persuade others both inside and outside the organization of the merits of what the organization has done and is seeking to accomplish if the manager truly believes in and is committed to the organization. Figure 3.5 is an example of a scale that managers can use to measure a person's level of organizational commitment.

Figure 3.5
A Measure of Organizational Commitment

People respond to each of the items in the scale by checking whether they:

[ ] Strongly disagree
[ ] Moderately disagree
[ ] Slightly disagree
[ ] Neither disagree nor agree
[ ] Slightly agree
[ ] Moderately agree
[ ] Strongly agree

____ **1.** I am willing to put in a great deal of effort beyond that normally expected in order to help this organization be successful.

____ **2.** I talk up this organization to my friends as a great organization to work for.

____ **3.** I feel very little loyalty to this organization.*

____ **4.** I would accept almost any type of job assignment in order to keep working for this organization.

____ **5.** I find that my values and the organization's values are very similar.

____ **6.** I am proud to tell others that I am part of this organization.

____ **7.** I could just as well be working for a different organization as long as the type of work were similar.*

____ **8.** This organization really inspires the very best in me in the way of job performance.

____ **9.** It would take very little change in my present circumstances to cause me to leave this organization.*

____ **10.** I am extremely glad that I chose this organization to work for over others I was considering at the time I joined.

____ **11.** There's not too much to be gained by sticking with this organization indefinitely.*

____ **12.** Often, I find it difficult to agree with this organization's policies on important matters relating to its employees.*

____ **13.** I really care about the fate of this organization.

____ **14.** For me this is the best of all possible organizations for which to work.

____ **15.** Deciding to work for this organization was a definite mistake on my part.*

Scoring: Responses to items 1, 2, 4, 5, 6, 8, 10, 13, and 14 are scored such that 1 = strongly disagree; 2 = moderately disagree; 3 = slightly disagree; 4 = neither disagree nor agree; 5 = slightly agree; 6 = moderately agree; and 7 = strongly agree. Responses to "*" items 3, 7, 9, 11, 12, and 15 are scored 7 = strongly disagree; 6 = moderately disagree; 5 = slightly disagree; 4 = neither disagree nor agree; 3 = slightly agree; 2 = moderately agree; and 1 = strongly agree. Responses to the 15 items are averaged for an overall score from 1 to 7; the higher the score, the higher the level of organizational commitment.

Source: L. W. Porter and F. J. Smith, "Organizational Commitment Questionnaire," in J. D. Cook, S. J. Hepworth, T. D. Wall, and P. B. Warr, eds., *The Experience of Work: A Compendium and Review of 249 Measures and Their Use* (New York: Academic Press, 1981), 84–86.

Do managers in different countries have similar or different attitudes? Differences in the levels of job satisfaction and organizational commitment among managers in different countries are likely because these managers have different kinds of opportunities and rewards and because they face different economic, political, or sociocultural forces in their organizations' general environments. In countries with relatively high unemployment rates, such as France, levels of job satisfaction may be higher among employed managers because they may be happy simply to have a job.

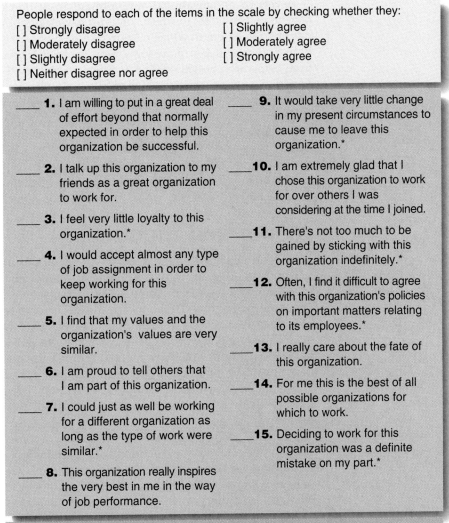

Levels of organizational commitment from one country to another may depend on the extent to which countries have legislation affecting firings and layoffs and the extent to which citizens of a country are geographically mobile. In both France and Germany legislation protects workers (including managers) from being fired or laid off. U.S. workers, in contrast, have very little protection. In addition, managers in the United States are more willing to relocate than managers in France and Germany. In France, citizens have relatively strong family and community ties, and in Germany housing is expensive and difficult to find. For those reasons citizens in both countries tend to be less geographically mobile than Americans.[32] Managers who know that their jobs are secure and are reluctant to relocate (such as those in Germany and France) may be more committed to their organizations than managers who know that their organizations could lay them off any day and who would not mind geographic relocations.

Moods and Emotions

mood A feeling or state of mind.

Just as you sometimes are in a bad mood and at other times in a good mood, so too are managers. A **mood** is a feeling or state of mind. When people are in a positive mood, they feel excited, enthusiastic, active, or elated.[33] When people are in a negative mood, they feel distressed, fearful, scornful, hostile, jittery, or nervous.[34] People who are high on extraversion are especially likely to experience positive moods; people who are high on negative affectivity are especially likely to experience negative moods. People's situations or circumstances also determine their moods, however, receiving a raise is likely to put most people in a good mood regardless of their personality traits. People who are high on negative affectivity are not always in a bad mood, and people who are low on extraversion still experience positive moods.[35]

emotions Intense, relatively short-lived feelings.

Another kind of feeling state, **emotions,** are more intense than moods, are often directly linked to whatever caused the emotion and are more short-lived. However, once whatever has triggered the emotion has been dealt with, the feelings may linger in the form of a less intense mood.[36] For example, a manager who gets very angry when one of his subordinates has engaged in an unethical behavior may find his anger decreasing in intensity once he has decided how to address the problem. Yet, he continues to be in a bad mood the rest of the day, even though he is not directly thinking about the unfortunate incident.[37]

Research on how moods affect the behavior of managers and other members of an organization has just begun. Preliminary studies suggest that the subordinates of managers who experience positive moods at work may perform at somewhat higher levels and be less likely to resign and leave the organization than the subordinates of managers who do not tend to be in a positive mood at work.[38] Other research suggests that under certain conditions, creativity might be enhanced by positive moods, whereas under other conditions, negative moods might push people to work harder to come up with truly creative ideas.[39]

Other research suggests that moods and emotions (which are more intense and short-lived feelings that are triggered by something specific) may play an important role in ethical decision making. For example, researchers at Princeton University found that when people are trying to solve difficult personal moral dilemmas, the parts of their brains that are responsible for emotions and moods are especially active.[40]

Recognizing the benefits of positive moods, the Northbrook, Illinois, accounting firm of Lipschultz, Levin, & Gray has gone to great lengths to promote positive feelings among its employees. Chief executive Steven Siegel claims that positive feelings promote relaxation and alleviate stress, increase revenues and attract clients, and reduce turnover. Positive moods are promoted in a variety of ways at Lipschultz, Levin, & Gray. Siegel has been known to put on a gorilla mask at especially busy times; clerks sometimes don chicken costumes; a foghorn announces the signing of a new client; employees can take a break and play miniature golf in the office, play darts, or exercise with a hula-hoop (even during tax time). A casual dress code also lightens things up at the firm. By all counts, positive moods seem to be paying off for this group of accountants, whose good feelings seem to be attracting new clients.

Patrick Corboy, president and chief executive of Austin Chemical, switched his account from a bigger firm to Lipschultz, Levin, & Gray because he found the people at the bigger firm to be "too stuffy and dour for us." Of the accountant William Finestone, who manages the Austin Chemical account, Corboy says the following: "[he] is a barrel of laughs . . . Bill not only solves our problems more quickly but he puts us at ease, too."[41]

Nevertheless, sometimes negative moods can have their advantages. Some studies suggest that critical thinking and devil's advocacy may be promoted by a negative mood, and sometimes especially accurate judgments may be made by managers in negative moods.[42]

Managers and other members of an organization need to realize that how they feel affects how they treat others and how others respond to them, including their subordinates. For example, a subordinate may be more likely to approach a manager with a somewhat far-out but potentially useful idea if the subordinate thinks the manager is in a good mood. Likewise, when managers are in very bad moods, their subordinates might try to avoid them at all costs. Figure 3.6 is an example of a scale that managers can use to measure the extent to which a person experiences positive and negative moods at work.

Figure 3.6
A Measure of Positive and Negative Mood at Work

People respond to each item by indicating the extent to which the item descibes how they felt at work during the past week on the following scale:

1 = Very slightly or not at all
2 = A little
3 = Moderately
4 = Quite a bit
5 = Very much

____ **1.** Active	____ **7.** Enthusiastic
____ **2.** Distressed	____ **8.** Fearful
____ **3.** Strong	____ **9.** Peppy
____ **4.** Excited	____**10.** Nervous
____ **5.** Scornful	____**11.** Elated
____ **6.** Hostile	____**12.** Jittery

Scoring: Responses to items 1, 3, 4, 7, 9, and 11 are summed for a positive mood score; the higher the score, the more positive mood is experienced at work. Responses to items 2, 5, 6, 8, 10, and 12 are summed for a negative mood score; the higher the score, the more negative mood is experienced at work.

Source: A. P. Brief, M. J. Burke, J. M. George, B. Robinson, and J. Webster, "Should Negative Affectivity Remain an Unmeasured Variable in the Study of Job Stress?" *Journal of Applied Psychology* 73 (1988): 193–98. M. J. Burke, A. P. Brief, J. M. George, L. Roberson, and J. Webster, "Measuring Affect at Work: Confirmatory Analyses of Competing Mood Structures with Conceptual Linkage to Cortical Regulatory Systems," *Journal of Personality and Social Psychology* 57 (1989): 1091–1102.

Emotional Intelligence

emotional intelligence The ability to understand and manage one's own moods and emotions and the moods and emotions of other people.

In understanding the effects of managers' and all workers' moods and emotions, it is important to take into account their levels of emotional intelligence. **Emotional intelligence** is the ability to understand and manage one's own moods and emotions and the moods and emotions of other people.[43] Managers with a high level of emotional intelligence are more likely to understand how they are feeling and why, and are more able to effectively manage their feelings. When managers are experiencing stressful feelings and emotions such as fear or anxiety, emotional intelligence enables them to understand why and manage these feelings so that they do not get in the way of effective decision making.[44]

Emotional intelligence also can help managers perform their important roles such as their interpersonal roles (figurehead, leader, and liaison). Understanding how your subordinates feel, why they feel that way, and how to manage these feelings is central to developing strong interpersonal bonds with them. Moreover, emotional intelligence has the potential to contribute to effective leadership in multiple ways.[45] Recognizing the benefits of emotional intelligence, some managers are taking active steps to promote emotional competencies, as indicated in the following "Ethics in Action."

Ethics in Action

Promoting Emotional Competencies at American Express

Managers at American Express were facing a vexing problem.[46] More than 60 percent of their clients, whose portfolios suggested a need for life insurance, were declining coverage when approached by their financial advisors. A special team was put together by Jim Mitchell, who was then the president of the insurance division of American Express located in Minneapolis, Minnesota, to figure out ways to make clients understand the merits of life insurance. The team's conclusions were startling–clients were not shying away from life insurance due to policy provisions or cost. Rather, the problem appeared to be emotional.[47]

It turned out that clients experienced a whole range of negative feelings when thinking about life insurance including distrust, fear, and a loss of control. These feelings were relayed to the financial advisors who, using a "hard sell" approach, tried harder to convince clients to purchase life insurance. This pattern set in motion a negative spiral by which both parties' negative emotions increased and financial advisors started questioning whether the use of "hard sell" tactics in such a situation was ethical. Not all advisors had this problem, however, and the successful advisors were able to understand both how and why clients were feeling the way they did. The successful advisors were able to empathize with their clients, see things from their perspective, as well as manage their own emotions throughout the process.[48]

Kate Cannon, who headed up the team, decided to experiment with training advisors to understand emotions and how to manage them. She trained employees to better understand how to interpret their own and their customers feelings. Results were so encouraging that she expanded the training sessions. She also sought the support of Doug Lennick, a vice president at American Express to develop a more in-depth program. Lennick was impressed with the results and mandated that all new financial advisors receive eight hours of emotional competency training. Cannon has since left

American Express and licenses the emotional competency training she developed to other companies such as Motorola.[49] American Express's experience suggests that emotional competence can not only reduce stress levels but also increase performance and encourage ethical behavior.

Ethics and Stakeholders

organizational stakeholders Shareholders, employees, customers, suppliers, and others who have an interest, claim, or stake in an organization and in what it does.

Who managers are as people, what they believe, and what they value are not just important determinants of their own behavior and the behaviors of their subordinates. Personality, attitudes, and values also affect the way managers view their responsibility for the well-being of the individuals and groups that have an interest, claim, or stake in their organizations.[50] Known as **organizational stakeholders,** these individuals and groups include shareholders, managers, nonmanagerial employees, customers, suppliers, the local community in which an organization operates, and citizens of countries in which an organization operates. In order to survive and prosper, an organization must effectively satisfy its stakeholders.[51] Stockholders want dividends, managers and workers want salaries and stable employment, and customers want high-quality products at reasonable prices. If stakeholders do not receive these benefits, they may withdraw their support for the organization: Stockholders will sell their stock, managers and workers will seek jobs in other organizations, and customers will take their business elsewhere.

Managers are the stakeholder group with the responsibility to decide which goals an organization should pursue to most benefit stakeholders and how to make the most efficient use of resources to achieve those goals. In making such decisions, managers are frequently in the position of having to juggle the interests of different stakeholders, including themselves.[52] These decisions are sometimes very difficult and challenge managers to uphold ethical values because sometimes decisions that benefit some stakeholder groups (managers and stockholders) harm other groups (individual workers and local communities). For example, in economic downturns or when a company experiences performance shortfalls, layoffs may help to cut costs (thus, benefiting shareholders) at the expense of the employees laid off. Many U.S. managers have recently been faced with this same very difficult decision–over 700,000 layoffs were announced in the first six months of 2001 according Challenger, Gray, and Christmas (a firm specializing in outplacement services).[53] Layoff decisions are always difficult as they not only take a heavy toll on workers, their families, and local communities but also mean the loss of the contributions of valued employees to an organization. Whenever decisions such as these are made that benefit some groups at the expense of others, ethics come into play.

ethics Moral principles or beliefs about what is right or wrong.

Ethics are moral principles or beliefs about what is right or wrong. These beliefs guide individuals in their dealings with other individuals and groups (stakeholders) and provide a basis for deciding whether behavior is right and proper.[54] Ethics help people determine moral responses to situations in which the best course of action is unclear. Ethics guide managers in their decisions about what to do in various situations. Ethics also help managers decide how best to respond to the interests of various organizational stakeholders.

Managers often experience an ethical dilemma when they confront a situation that requires them to choose between two courses of action, especially if each of them is likely to serve the interests of one particular stakeholder group to the detriment of the other.[55] To make an appropriate decision, managers must weigh the competing claims or rights of the various stakeholder groups. Sometimes, making a decision is easy because some obvious standard, value, or norm of behavior applies. For example, the terminal and instrumental values that make up managers' value systems may guide their behavior. In other cases, managers have trouble deciding what to do and sometimes even determining what the relevant facts are, as indicated in the following "Ethics in Action."

Ethics in Action

The Firestone versus Ford Case

Problems with Firestone tires led to a 6.5 million tire recall in August of 2000 and an additional 3.5 million recall in October of 2001. Over 250 traffic fatalities have been attributed to the faulty tires, and in particular, to problems with tread separations and rollovers.[56] Clearly, it is unfortunate that these problems weren't addressed earlier so needless deaths could have been avoided. However, even after the latest recall, controversy surrounds the faulty tires.

At issue is the fact that the majority of the deaths and injuries involved with the faulty tires occurred with Ford Explorers. Firestone claims that its tires have less problems on other vehicles (e.g., Ford Rangers and GM pickups) while Ford claims that Explorers have fewer problems with tread separations and rollovers when equipped with other brands of tires (e.g., Goodyear tires). Firestone tires and Ford Explorers might not be inherently unsafe; but when used together, they can result in disastrous outcomes. Ironically, the tire in question, the Wilderness AT, was designed especially for the Ford Explorer.[57]

However, as early as 1989, questions were raised about the stability of the Explorer and potential rollover problems. When the nonprofit consumers' organization, the Consumers Union, tested the Explorer prior to its mass production, test engineer, Roger Stornant noted that there were potential problems with the performance of the tire Ford had chosen to equip the Explorer with, and fewer problems were experienced with another Firestone tire. The Explorer continued to have problems and in 1996, a trainee test driver experienced a rollover while turning at less than 55 miles per hour.[58]

Prior to the massive recalls, rollovers involving Explorers (as well as Mercury Mountaineers) were increasing in the United States and other countries. In fact, Ford replaced the tires on these vehicles in nine countries without notifying U.S. authorities. While Firestone maintains that the Explorer is at least partially to blame for the problems, Ford and the National Highway Traffic Safety Administration have maintained otherwise.[59] Further investigation may help determine all of the contributing factors in this dangerous combination of tires and vehicles. From an ethical standpoint, however, one wonders why action wasn't taken sooner before so many lives were lost.

Tim Underhill rolls a tire into place to replace a Firestone Wilderness AT tire on a Ford Explorer at Super Tire Discount in Taylor, Michigan, a day after Ford recalled 13 million Firestone tires.

Philosophers have debated for centuries about the specific criteria that should be used to determine whether decisions are ethical or unethical. Three models of what determines whether a decision is ethical–the *utilitarian, moral rights,* and *justice* models–are summarized in Table 3.1.[60]

Table 3.1
Utilitarian, Moral Rights, and Justice Models of Ethics

	Managerial Implication	Problems for Managers
Utilitarian Model An ethical decision is a decision that produces the greatest good for the greatest number of people.	Managers should compare and contrast alternative courses of action based on the benefits and costs of those alternatives for different organizational stakeholder groups. They should choose the course of action that provides the most benefits to stakeholders. For example, managers should locate a new manufacturing plant at the place that will most benefit its stakeholders.	How do managers decide on the relative importance of each stakeholder group? How are managers to precisely measure the benefits and harms to each stakeholder group? For example, how do managers choose between the interests of stockholders, workers, and customers?
Moral Rights Model An ethical decision is a decision that best maintains and protects the fundamental rights and privileges of the people affected by it. For example, ethical decisions protect people's rights to freedom, life and safety, privacy, free speech, and freedom of conscience.	Managers should compare and contrast alternative courses of action based on the effect of those alternatives on stakeholders' rights. They should choose the course of action that best protects stakeholders' rights. For example, decisions that would involve significant harm to the safety or health of employees or customers are unethical.	If a decision will protect the rights of some stakeholders and hurt the rights of others, how do managers choose which stakeholder rights to protect? For example, in deciding whether it is ethical to snoop on an employee, does an employee's right to privacy outweigh an organization's right to protect its property or the safety of other employees?
Justice Model An ethical decision is a decision that distributes benefits and harms among stakeholders in a fair, equitable, or impartial way.	Managers should compare and contrast alternative courses of action based on the degree to which the action will promote a fair distribution of outcomes. For example, employees who are similar in their level of skill, performance, or responsibility should receive the same kind of pay. The allocation of outcomes should not be based on arbitrary differences such as gender, race, or religion.	Managers must learn not to discriminate between people because of observable differences in their appearance or behavior. Managers must also learn how to use fair procedures to determine how to distribute outcomes to organizational members. For example, managers must not give people they like bigger raises than they give to people they do not like or bend the rules to help their favorites.

In theory, each model offers a different and complementary way of determining whether a decision or behavior is ethical, and all three models should be used to sort out the ethics of a particular course of action. Ethical issues, however, are seldom clear-cut, and the interests of different stakeholders often conflict, so it is frequently extremely difficult for a decision maker to use these models to ascertain the most ethical course of action. For this reason many ethics experts propose this practical guide to determine whether a decision or behavior is ethical.[61] A decision is probably acceptable on ethical grounds if a manager can answer "yes" to each of these questions:

1. Does my decision fall within the accepted values, norms, or standards that typically apply in the organizational environment?
2. Am I willing to see the decision communicated to all stakeholders affected by it–for example, by having it reported in newspapers or on television?
3. Would the people with whom I have a significant personal relationship, such as family members, friends, or even managers in other organizations, approve of the decision? What would be their attitude?

ethical decision A decision that reasonable or typical stakeholders would find acceptable because it aids stakeholders, the organization, or society.

unethical decision A decision that a manager would prefer to disguise or hide from other people because it enables a company or a particular individual to gain at the expense of society or other stakeholders.

As you can see, values and attitudes are important determinants of what managers consider ethical behavior. From a management perspective, an **ethical decision** is a decision that reasonable or typical stakeholders, given their attitudes and values, would find acceptable because it aids stakeholders, the organization, or society. By contrast, an **unethical decision** is a decision a manager would prefer to disguise or hide from other people because it enables a company or a particular individual to gain at the expense of society or other stakeholders. Unethical people disguise their intentions because they know others would find their behavior unacceptable.

Which Behaviors Are Ethical?

A key ethical decision facing managers is how to apportion harms and benefits among stakeholder groups.[62] Suppose a company has a few very good years and makes high profits. Who should receive these profits–managers, workers, or stockholders? In the early 1990s, Chrysler made record profits. Stakeholders at Chrysler–stockholders, managers, and workers–started to fight about how to divide them up. Chrysler had amassed $9 billion in cash. Its managers wanted to use this money to protect the company against future economic downturns, a tactic that would give the managers themselves security. Stockholders, however, and in particular billionaire Kirk Kekorian (who owned more than 10 percent of Chrysler's stock), thought that this was the wrong choice. Kekorian saw that Chrysler's managers and workers were receiving record salaries and bonuses to reward them for their high performance, and he thought that stockholders (who had a strong claim on the organization's profits because they were the owners of the company) were being treated unethically because they were not receiving a larger share of the profits. Acting on his belief, Kekorian launched a takeover bid for the company to force out Chrysler's top managers so that stockholders could receive what he regarded as their proper share of the rewards. His takeover attempt failed, but he did succeed in forcing Chrysler's managers to substantially raise stockholder dividends.

The decision about how to divide profits among managers, workers, and stockholders might not seem to be an ethical issue, but it is, and in the same manner as how to apportion harms or costs among stakeholders when things go wrong.[63] Chrysler almost went bankrupt in the 1970s, and Lee Iacocca was appointed CEO to try to reverse the company's fortunes. Under Iacocca, Chrysler laid off over 65 percent of its workers and managers; many of them were unemployed for years in the hard-hit car industry of the 1970s. In 2001, DaimlerChrysler, the company formed when the German company Daimler Benz merged with Chrysler, again announced it would lay off thousands of U.S. workers because of large losses brought about by its high costs and falling demand for its cars.

Were these layoffs of managers and workers ethical? Managers at other companies did not take such drastic steps. AT&T, Kodak, and IBM, for example, laid off fewer workers or spread the layoffs over a much longer time period to reduce the harm done to their employees. Even when layoffs became inevitable, managers of these companies made the layoffs as painless as possible by introducing generous early retirement programs that gave workers full pension rights if they retired early. To reduce harm to employees, they also paid workers a month's or several months' salary for each year of service to the company.

In the United States, severance payments are not required by law, so the decision to pay layoff benefits is typically an ethical choice made by a company's top managers in light of their organization's code of ethics and cultural values. Many managers believe that employees who have worked for a long time for a company should receive layoff payments because they have made an investment in the company–providing their skills and loyalty–just as a stockholder invests in a company by providing capital. Workers, however, have a weaker claim on a company than do stockholders because they usually have no legally enforceable ownership rights in the company. Stockholders are the legal owners of a corporation. Moreover, when top managers decide to give layoff benefits to workers, the decision can harm stockholders, whose dividend payments may be reduced. Thus, deciding how to distribute organizational resources becomes an ethical issue. Top managers must choose the right or proper way to balance the interests of their different stakeholders, and their code of ethics helps them to do so.

Ethical issues loom large when a manager's decision is not governed by legal requirements and it is up to the manager to determine the appropriate actions to take. In western Europe, organizations are required by law to give employees layoff payments based on their years of service. Germany, France, and Britain specify how much managers and workers are entitled to receive if they are laid off. Managers in these organizations simply follow the rules in deciding how to behave. As noted above, there are no such laws in the United States. Although many organizations in the United States voluntarily provide layoff benefits, many do not. In general, the poorer a country is, the more likely are employees to be treated with little regard.

Managers also face ethical dilemmas when choosing how to deal with certain stakeholders. For example, suppliers provide an organization with its inputs and expect to be paid within a reasonable amount of time. Some managers, however, consistently delay payment to make the most use of their organization's money. This practice can hurt a supplier's cash flow and threaten its very survival.

An organization that is a powerful customer and buys large amounts of particular suppliers' products is in a position to demand that suppliers reduce their prices. If an organization does this, suppliers earn lower profits and the organization earns more. Is this behavior just "business as usual," or is it unethical?

In the early 1990s, Wal-Mart pressured suppliers to reduce prices, and for a short time suppliers were forced to do so in order to stay in business. However, the inequity of the arrangement upset the suppliers, and eventually they found new customers and reduced their dependence on Wal-Mart. The suppliers refused to spend their resources to develop the kinds of products that Wal-Mart wanted them to make. In addition, they slowed their deliveries to Wal-Mart's warehouses to keep their costs down. When Wal-Mart managers realized what was happening, they finally acknowledged they had to work with their suppliers to find ways to reduce costs for all parties involved.

Consider a different scenario. Suppose a supplier, to keep its costs down and profits high, secretly reduces the quality of the inputs it provides to an organization. This practice is obviously unethical because it is deceptive and dishonest. If suppliers do reduce the quality of their products, organizations are likely to stop buying from them when they discover the ruse, and the unethical suppliers ultimately will lose their customers. For this reason, many suppliers refrain from behaving unethically. Nevertheless, some companies do act unethically, especially if they expect to do little repeat business. One reason why McDonald's, for example, retains ownership of its restaurants along freeways is its fear that unscrupulous franchisees will provide poor-quality food because they think they are unlikely to see the same customers more than once. Were this to happen, McDonald's good name would be tarnished.

Customers are a critical stakeholder group because, as noted in Chapter 1, organizations depend on them for their very survival. Customers have the right to expect an organization to provide goods and services that will not harm them. A complex system of laws protects consumers in the United States, and they have legal rights for recourse if organizations provide unsafe products.

Local communities and the general public also have an interest or stake in whether the decisions that managers make are ethical. The quality of a city's school system or police department, the economic health of its downtown area, and its general level of prosperity all depend on choices made by managers of organizations. Kellogg, for example, is a major employer in Battle Creek, Michigan, and its decision to lay off 800 workers caused major economic problems for the city as tax revenues, business sales, and house prices fell because fewer workers were employed. When Wal-Mart decides to open a store outside a small city, it frequently destroys the businesses in the downtown area because they cannot compete with Wal-Mart's low prices. Are these decisions just ordinary business decisions, or are they unethical?

In sum, managers face many ethical choices as they deal with the different and sometimes conflicting interests of organizational stakeholders. Deciding what behavior is ethical is often a difficult task requiring managers to make tough choices that will benefit some stakeholders and harm others. Attitudes, values, and norms guide managers in making ethical choices.

Why Would Managers Behave Unethically Toward Other Stakeholders?

Typically, *unethical behavior*–behavior that falls outside the bounds of accepted standards or values–occurs because managers put their personal interests above the interests of other organizational stakeholders or choose to ignore the harm that they are inflicting on others.[64] Managers confront ethical dilemmas every time they have to balance the claims of one stakeholder group against the claims of another, and they might feel tempted to engage in unethical acts if the harm done to stakeholders is indirect or seems insignificant relative to the benefits that the managers themselves or their organization will receive from the unethical activity.[65]

In some countries, but not in the United States, bribing government officials to get business is an acceptable practice. Suppose that bribery will ensure that an American expatriate manager can secure for her company a large contract that in turn will net her a huge bonus and promotion. Bribery is not illegal in the country in which she is doing business; her competitors are actively engaging in it, and nobody really gets hurt. Is such bribery really unethical behavior, and does the U.S. government really have the right to say that for American citizens living abroad it is illegal? Similarly, if all members of a company's sales force routinely pad their expense accounts, is this behavior really unethical, since it is the common practice in the company? As discussed previously, family, upbringing, and religion help teach people how to distinguish between right and wrong behavior and how to be productive members of society. Managers who let self-interest take control of their decision making in such situations and ignore societal ethics as well are often those who have a poor or undeveloped code of individual ethics.[66]

Beyond the pursuit of ruthless self-interest, managers or workers may have other reasons to act unethically, such as feeling pressured by the situation they are in.[67] Sometimes the behavior of other managers (particularly superiors) may cause managers to behave unethically. Often, managers who find themselves under intense pressure to perform and to help their organization succeed encourage subordinates to act in dubious ways, such as bribing foreign officials, overcharging customers, or delivering substandard products. An example of this type of activity occurred in 1992 when the state of California accused Sears of consistently overcharging customers for car repairs.[68] Apparently, to improve a very weak financial position, Sears created a bonus system that encouraged its car repair employees to convince customers that they needed repairs that actually were unnecessary. Subsequently Sears changed its bonus system, but only after considerable harm had been done to the company's reputation.

Why Should Managers Behave Ethically?

Managers and other stakeholders must strongly resist pressures to behave unethically and to ignore widely accepted societal standards and values because of the harm that unethical behavior inflicts on others. Where is the source of this harm?

Perhaps the easiest way to illustrate how unethical behavior results in harm and ethical action brings universal benefits is to consider the "Tragedy of the Commons" scenario. Suppose that in an agricultural community there is common land that everybody has an equal right to use. Pursuing self-interest, each farmer acts to make the maximum use of the free resource to graze his or her own cattle and sheep. Collectively, the farmers overgraze the land, which quickly becomes worn-out. Then a strong wind blows away the exposed topsoil, so the common land is destroyed. The pursuit of individual self-interest with no consideration for societal interests leads to disaster for each individual and for the whole society because scarce resources are destroyed.[69]

As noted in Chapter 1, one of the major tasks of managers is to protect and nurture the resources under their control. Any organizational stakeholders–managers, workers, stockholders, suppliers–who advance their own interests by behaving unethically toward other stakeholders, either by taking resources or by denying resources to others, wastes collective resources. If other individuals or groups copy the behavior of the unethical stakeholder ("if he can do it, we can do it, too"), the rate at which collective resources are misused increases, and eventually there are few resources for producing goods and services. Unethical behavior that goes unpunished creates incentives for people to put their unbridled self-interest above the rights of others. When this happens, the benefits that people reap from joining together in organizations disappear very quickly.

reputation The esteem or high repute that individuals or organizations gain when they behave ethically.

An important safeguard against unethical behavior is the potential for loss of reputation.[70] **Reputation,** the esteem or high repute that individuals or organizations gain when they behave ethically, is a valuable asset. Stakeholders have valuable reputations that they must protect because their ability to earn a living and obtain resources in the long run depends on the way they behave on a day-to-day, week-to-week, and month-to-month basis.

If a manager misuses resources, and other parties regard that behavior as at odds with acceptable standards, the manager's reputation will suffer. Behaving unethically in the short run can have serious long-term consequences. A manager who has a poor reputation will have difficulty finding employment with other companies. Stockholders who see managers behaving unethically may refuse to invest in their companies, which will decrease the stock price, undermine the companies' reputations, and ultimately put the managers' jobs at risk.

All stakeholders have reputations to lose. Suppliers who provide shoddy inputs find that organizations learn over time not to deal with them, and eventually they go out of business. Powerful customers who demand ridiculously low prices find that their suppliers become less willing to deal with them, and resources ultimately become harder for them to obtain. Workers who shirk responsibilities on the job find it hard to get new jobs when they are fired.

In general, if a manager or company is known for being unethical, other stakeholders are likely to view that individual or organization with suspicion and hostility, and the reputation of each will be poor. But if a manager or company is known for ethical business practices, each will develop a good reputation. Beech-Nut, a maker of baby food, is a company that lost its reputation.[71] During the 1980s, Beech-Nut was in danger of going bankrupt; to cut costs, the company contracted with a low-cost supplier of apple juice concentrate. Shortly thereafter, one of Beech-Nut's quality control managers discovered that instead of being pure the apple juice contained large quantities of corn syrup. The manager quickly informed top managers. They, however, decided to ignore this information because of their need to keep costs down. Even when the quality control manager eventually went public, Beech-Nut's top managers conspired to mislead government investigators, distort information, and hide the truth. Eventually, the company was fined more than $2 million, and its top managers were convicted of fraud. In addition, Beech-Nut's managers destroyed not only their own reputations but also the reputation of their organization. Customers lost confidence in Beech-Nut products, and, once again on the brink of bankruptcy, the company was sold off cheaply to Ralston Purina, a move that resulted in substantial losses for stockholders.

Often, unethical behavior comes back to haunt those who engage in it. If all stakeholders are alert to the need to stop it–because it reduces their own benefits in the long run–then the level of unethical behavior falls. Ethical standards, attitudes, and rules help to increase the value and wealth of people individually and countries collectively. Countries tend to become more ethical as they become wealthier because people see how their behavior affects, and is affected by, the behavior of people around them.

Sources of an Organization's Code of Ethics

Codes of ethics are formal standards and rules, based on beliefs about right or wrong, that managers can use to help themselves make appropriate decisions with regard to the interests of their stakeholders.[72] Ethical standards embody views

Figure 3.7
Sources of an Organization's Code of Ethics

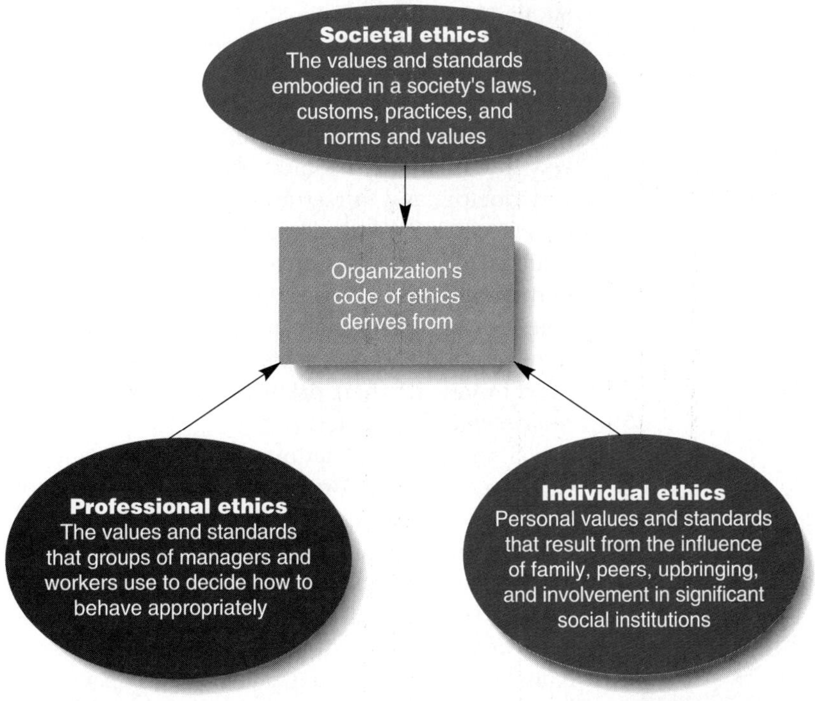

about abstractions such as justice, freedom, equity, and equality (see Table 3.1). An organization's code of ethics derives from three principal sources in the organizational environment: *societal* ethics, *professional* ethics, and the *individual* ethics of the organization's managers and employees (see Figure 3.7).

societal ethics
Standards that govern how members of a society are to deal with each other on issues such as fairness, justice, poverty, and the rights of the individual.

SOCIETAL ETHICS Societal ethics are standards that govern how members of a society deal with each other in matters involving issues such as fairness, justice, poverty, and the rights of the individual. Societal ethics emanate from a society's laws, customs, and practices, and the unwritten attitudes, values, and norms that influence how people interact with each other. People in a particular country may automatically behave ethically because they have internalized values and norms that specify how they should behave in certain situations. Not all values and norms are internalized, however. The typical ways of doing business in a society and laws governing the use of bribery and corruption are the result of decisions made and enforced by people with the power to determine what is appropriate.

Societal ethics vary among societies. For example, ethical standards accepted in the United States are not accepted in all other countries. In many economically poor countries bribery is standard practice to get things done, such as getting a telephone installed or a contract awarded. In the United States and many other Western countries, bribery is considered unethical and often illegal.

Societal ethics control self-interested behavior by individuals and organizations; that is, behavior threatening society's collective interests. Laws spelling out what is good or appropriate business practice provide benefits to everybody. Free and fair competition among organizations is possible only when laws and rules level the playing field and define what behavior is acceptable or unacceptable in certain situations. For example, it is ethical for a manager to compete with managers in other companies by producing a higher-quality or lower-priced product, but it is not ethical (or legal) to do so by spreading false claims about competitors' products, bribing stores to exclude competitors' products, or blowing up competitors' factories.

professional ethics Standards that govern how members of a profession are to make decisions when the way they should behave is not clear-cut.

PROFESSIONAL ETHICS Professional ethics are standards that govern how members of a profession, managers or workers, make decisions when the way in which they should behave is not clear-cut.[73] Medical ethics govern the way doctors and nurses are to treat patients. Doctors are expected to perform only necessary medical procedures and to act in the patient's interest and not in their own. The ethics of scientific research require scientists to conduct their experiments and present their findings in ways that ensure the validity of their conclusions. Like society at large, most professional groups can impose punishments for violations of ethical standards. Doctors and lawyers can be prevented from practicing their professions if they disregard professional ethics and put their own interests first.

Within an organization, professional rules and norms often govern how employees such as lawyers, researchers, and accountants make decisions and act in certain situations, and these rules and norms may become part of the organization's code of ethics. When they do, workers internalize the rules and norms of their profession (just as they do those of society) and often follow them automatically when deciding how to behave.[74] Because most people follow established rules of behavior, people often take ethics for granted. However, when professional ethics are violated, such as when scientists fabricate data to disguise the harmful effects of products, ethical issues rise to the forefront of attention.

individual ethics Personal standards that govern how individuals are to interact with other people.

INDIVIDUAL ETHICS Individual ethics are personal values (both terminal and instrumental) and attitudes that govern how individuals interact with other people.[75] Sources of individual ethics include the influence of one's family, peers, and upbringing in general, and an individual's personality and experience. The experiences gained over a lifetime–through membership in significant social institutions such as schools and religions, for example–also contribute to the development of the personal standards and values that a person applies to decide what is right or wrong, and whether to perform certain actions or make certain decisions. Many decisions or behaviors that one person finds unethical, such as using animals for cosmetics testing, may be acceptable to another person because of differences in their personality, values, and attitudes. Thus, before we look at how organizations and managers can promote ethical behavior, it is useful to take an in-depth look at the various factors that cause managers to think and act as they do.

Organizational Culture

organizational culture The set of values, norms, standards for behavior, and shared expectations that influence the ways in which individuals, groups, and teams interact with each other and cooperate to achieve organizational goals.

An organization's code of ethics is one manifestation of a wider set of influences on organizational members' behaviors, namely organizational culture. Organizational culture is the set of shared values, norms, standards for behavior, and expectations that influence the ways in which individuals, groups, and teams interact with each other and cooperate to achieve organizational goals (organizational culture is also discussed in Chapters 5 and 10). Just as managers differ from each other along a number of dimensions such as the Big Five personality traits, so too do their organizations' values and norms, and members' attitudes and behavior. In fact, one can think about organizational culture as being the "personality" of an organization.

How Managers Influence Organizational Culture

While all members of an organization can contribute to the development and maintenance of organizational culture, managers play a particularly important part in influencing organizational culture, given their multiple and important roles (see Chapter 1). How managers create culture is most vividly evident in start-ups of new companies. Entrepreneurs who start their own companies are typically also the start-up's top managers until the companies grow and/or become profitable. Often referred to as the firms' founders, these managers literally create their organizations' cultures.

Often, the founders' personal characteristics play an important role in the creation of organizational culture. Benjamin Schneider, a well-known management researcher at the University of Maryland, developed a model that helps to explain the role that founders' personal characteristics play in determining organizational culture.[76] His model, called the **attraction-selection-attrition (ASA) framework,** posits that when founders hire employees for their new ventures, they tend to be attracted to and choose employees whose personalities are similar to their own. These similar employees are more likely to stay, while employees dissimilar in personality might be hired, they are more likely to leave the organization. As a result of these attraction, selection, and attrition processes, people in the organization tend to have similar personalities and the typical or dominant personality profile of organizational members determines and shapes organizational culture.[77]

attraction-selection-attrition framework
A model that explains how personality may influence organizational culture.

For example, Mary Stevens started her own software company, Comp-Ease. Stevens is high on openness to experience and conscientiousness and low on extraversion; she likes to take risks, experiment with new things, and break down barriers to creativity and innovation. And she goes about these entrepreneurial activities with a quiet sense of determination. When Stevens interviewed prospective employees for her venture, she was especially attracted to those who shared her propensity toward taking risks and being creative, those, like herself who were determined to be successful and not overly outgoing in the interview. As Comp-Ease grew Stevens delegated responsibilities for interviewing and hiring to her subordinates who tended to attract and select employees similar to themselves. Whenever employees who don't like to experiment and take risks were inadvertently hired, they often left after a few months on the job.

While ASA processes are most evident in small firms such as Stevens' Comp-Ease, they also can operate in large companies. According to the ASA model, this is a naturally occurring phenomenon to the extent that managers and new hires are free to make the kinds of choices the model specifies. While people tend to get along well with others who are similar to themselves, too much similarity in an organization can actually impair organizational effectiveness. That is, similar people tend to view conditions and events in similar ways and thus, can be resistant to change. Moreover, organizations benefit from a diversity of perspectives rather than similarity in perspectives (see Chapter 4). Getting back to Comp-Ease, luckily Stevens realized this fact just in time. A series of decisions had gone wrong leading to the loss of one client and several potential clients. This forced Stevens to consider the strengths and weaknesses of her organization. After analyzing what went wrong in each case, she realized that Comp-Ease was not only taking far too many unnecessary risks but also was not as aggressive as it should be in pursuing new clients. Since Comp-Ease was continuing to grow, Stevens decided to hire some new employees who would be more cautious and less prone to take risks to complement the risk-takers in her company. She also decided to hire some very outgoing individuals with industrial sales experience to build relationships with new and existing clients.

In addition to personality, other personal characteristics of managers shape organizational culture; these include managers' values, attitudes, moods and emotions, and emotional intelligence.[78] For example, both terminal and instrumental values of managers play a role in determining organizational culture. Managers who highly value freedom and equality, for example, might be more likely to stress the importance of autonomy and empowerment in their organizations as well as fair treatment for all. As another example, managers who highly value being helpful and forgiving may be prone to emphasize the importance of organizational members being kind and helpful to each other as well as be tolerant of mistakes.

Managers who are satisfied with their jobs, committed to their organizations, and experience positive moods and emotions might also encourage these attitudes and feelings in others. The result would be an organizational culture emphasizing positive attitudes and feelings. Research suggests that attitudes like job satisfaction and organizational commitment can be affected by the influence of others. Managers are in a particularly strong position to engage in social influence given their multiple roles. Moreover, research suggests that moods and emotions can be "contagious" and spending time with people who are excited and enthusiastic can increase one's own levels of excitement and enthusiasm, as discussed in the following "Management Insight."[79]

Management Insight

How to Create a High-Performing Organizational Culture

Herb Kelleher, the flamboyant founder, former CEO, and current chairman of the board of Southwest Airlines, exemplifies many of the ways in which founders and managers shape organizational culture.[80] Southwest Airlines' culture values fun, high-quality customer service, commitment to employees, empowerment, an entrepreneurial spirit, high performance, and commitment to employees. Why? Because Kelleher embodies and expresses these values in his own behavior. He has always emphasized the importance of having fun while providing superior customer service throughout Southwest. The story of the way he grew Southwest is a story of entrepreneurship, risk taking, challenge, and "having fun."

Southwest is one of the most profitable companies in the airline industry and ranked fourth in *Fortune* magazine's, "100 Best Companies to Work For."[81] Southwest Airlines demonstrates its commitment to its employees (in addition to its customers) in numerous ways including a no layoff policy.[82] How do Herb Kelleher and managers maintain Southwest Airlines high-performing culture which has its own personality that distinguishes it from other airlines?

One way in which they do this to ensure that they hire (i.e., attract and select) new employees who will fit in the Southwest culture. For example, in 2000, Southwest received over 200,000 resumes from which it eventually ended up selecting 5,134 new employees.[83] Moreover, Southwest employees are the ones who select new members and decide if they would be happy working with the newcomers. Given the culture's emphasis on high-quality

Southwest Airlines' no-layoff policy was severely tested in the aftermath of the September 11 terrorist attacks. But company execs stood firm: Southwest was the only major airline that did not lay off employees after the tragedy.

customer service, feeling good, and having fun, it would be hard to imagine Southwest hiring employees who were overly critical or grouchy.

With a committed workforce in place, Southwest then builds employee motivation by providing all employees with stock options and linking rewards to performance. Employees become "owners" of the company and this also makes them more committed to it. Over time too, Kelleher and his managers build reinforcing norms and values by emphasizing the importance of all employees to the organization. Barriers between managers, pilots, flight attendants, and baggage handlers are minimized; they all share similar norms of providing high-quality customer service and work together to do so. Southwest holds frequent parties for its employees, gives many awards, and in many other ways recognizes the contributions of its members. Small wonder it has strong terminal and instrumental values and is one of the strongest airlines flying today.

Ethical Organizational Cultures

Managers can emphasize the importance of ethical behavior and social responsibility by ensuring that ethical values and norms are a central component of organizational culture. While an organization's code of ethics guides decision making when ethical questions arise, managers can go one step further by ensuring that important ethical values and norms are key features of an organization's culture. For example, Herb Kelleher and Southwest Airlines' culture value employee well-being; this translates into norms dictating that layoffs should be avoided.[84] Ethical values and norms such as these that are part of an organization's culture help organizational members resist self-interested action and recognize that they are part of something bigger than themselves.[85]

Managers' role in developing ethical values and standards in other employees is very important. Employees naturally look to those in authority to provide leadership, and managers become ethical role models whose behavior is scrutinized by their subordinates. If top managers are not ethical, their subordinates are not likely to behave in an ethical manner. Employees may think that if it's all right for a top manager to engage in dubious behavior, it's all right for them, too. The actions of top managers such as CEOs and the president of the United States are scrutinized so closely for ethical improprieties because their actions represent the values of their organizations and, in the case of the president, the values of the nation.

ethics ombudsman An ethics officer who monitors an organization's practices and procedures to be sure they are ethical.

Managers can also provide a visible means of support to develop an ethical culture. Increasingly, organizations are creating the role of ethics officer, or **ethics ombudsman,** to monitor their ethical practices and procedures. The ethics ombudsman is responsible for communicating ethical standards to all employees, for designing systems to monitor employees' conformity to those standards, and for teaching managers and nonmanagerial employees at all levels of the organization how to respond to ethical dilemmas appropriately.[86] Because the ethics ombudsman has organizationwide authority, organizational members in any department can communicate instances of unethical behavior by their managers or coworkers without fear of retribution. This arrangement makes it easier for everyone to behave ethically. In addition, ethics ombudsmen can provide guidance when organizational members are uncertain about whether an action is ethical. Some organizations have an organizationwide ethics committee to provide guidance on ethical issues and help write and update the company code of ethics.

Social Responsibility

There are many reasons why it is important for managers and organizations to act ethically and to do everything possible to avoid harming stakeholders. However, what about the other side of the coin? What responsibility do managers have to provide benefits to their stakeholders and to adopt courses of action that enhance the well-being of society at large? The term **social responsibility** refers to a manager's duty or obligation to make decisions that nurture, protect, enhance, and promote the welfare and well-being of stakeholders and society as a whole. Many kinds of decisions signal an organization's interest in being socially responsible (see Table 3.2).

social responsibility A manager's duty or obligation to make decisions that promote the welfare and well-being of stakeholders and society as a whole.

APPROACHES TO SOCIAL RESPONSIBILITY The strength of organizations' commitment to social responsibility ranges from low to high (see Figure 3.8).[87] At the low end of the range is an obstructionist approach. Obstructionist managers choose not to behave in a socially responsible way. Instead, they behave unethically and illegally and do all they can to prevent knowledge

Table 3.2
Forms of Socially Responsible Behavior

Managers are being socially responsible and showing their support for their stakeholders when they

- Provide severance payments to help laid-off workers make ends meet until they can find other jobs
- Provide workers with opportunities to enhance their skills and acquire additional education so they can remain productive and do not become obsolete because of changes in technology
- Allow employees to take time off when they need to and provide health care and pension benefits for employees
- Contribute to charities or support various civic-minded activities in the cities or towns in which they are located (Target and Levi Strauss both contribute 5 percent of their profits to support schools, charities, the arts, and other good works.)
- Decide to keep open a factory whose closure would devastate the local community
- Decide to keep a company's operations in the United States to protect the jobs of American workers rather than move abroad
- Decide to spend money to improve a new factory so that it will not pollute the environment
- Decline to invest in countries that have poor human rights records
- Choose to help poor countries develop an economic base to improve living standards

Figure 3.8 Approaches to Social Responsibility

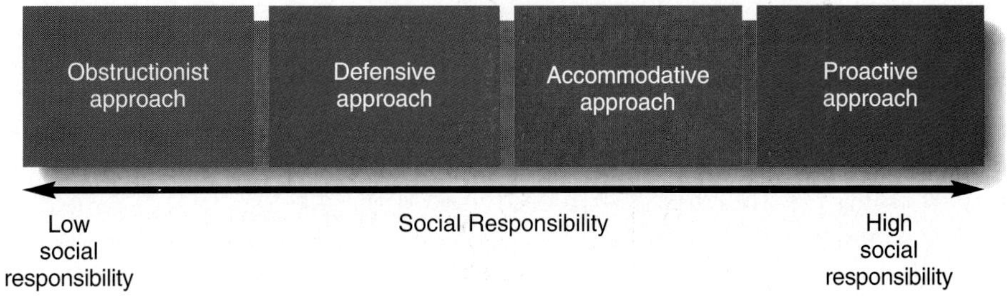

of their behavior from reaching other organizational stakeholders and society at large. Managers at the Mansville Corporation adopted this approach when they surpressed evidence that asbestos causes lung damage. Managers at Beech-Nut who sought to hide evidence about the use of corn syrup in their apple juice also adopted this approach. These managers chose an obstructionist approach. The result was not only a loss of reputation but devastation for their organizations and for all stakeholders involved.

A defensive approach indicates at least a commitment to ethical behavior. Defensive managers stay within the law and abide strictly with legal requirements but make no attempt to exercise social responsibility beyond what the law dictates. Managers adopting this approach do all they can to ensure that their employees behave legally and do not harm others. But when making ethical choices, these managers put the claims and interests of their shareholders first, at the expense of other stakeholders.

The very nature of a capitalist society in which managers' primary responsibility is to the owners of the corporation–its shareholders–probably encourages the defensive response. Some economists believe that managers in a capitalist society should always put stockholders' claims first, and that if these choices are not acceptable to other members of society and are considered unethical, then society must pass laws and create rules and regulations to govern the choices managers make.[88] From a defensive perspective, it is not managers' responsibility to make socially responsible choices; their job is to abide by the rules that have been legally established. Thus, defensive managers have little active interest in social responsibility.

An accommodative approach is an acknowledgment of the need to support social responsibility. Accommodative managers agree that organizational members ought to behave legally and ethically, and they try to balance the interests of different stakeholders against one another so that the claims of stockholders are seen in relation to the claims of other stakeholders. Managers adopting this approach want to make choices that are reasonable in the eyes of society and want to do the right thing when called on to do so.

Managers taking a proactive approach actively embrace the need to behave in socially responsible ways, go out of their way to learn about the needs of different stakeholder groups, and are willing to utilize organizational resources to promote the interests not only of stockholders but of the other stakeholders. Such companies–Hewlett-Packard, The Body Shop, McDonald's, Johnson & Johnson–are at the forefront of campaigns for causes such as a pollution-free environment, recycling and conservation of resources, minimizing or avoiding the use of animals in drug and cosmetic testing, and reducing crime, illiteracy, and poverty. Ethical organizational cultures also encourage organizational

Figure 3.9
Johnson & Johnson's Credo

Our Credo

We believe our first responsibility is to the doctors, nurses and patients,
to mothers and fathers and all others who use our products and services.
In meeting their needs everything we do must be of high quality.
We must constantly strive to reduce our costs
in order to maintain reasonable prices.
Customers' orders must be serviced promptly and accurately.
Our suppliers and distributors must have an opportunity
to make a fair profit.

We are responsible to our employees,
the men and women who work with us throughout the world.
Everyone must be considered as an individual.
We must respect their dignity and recognize their merit.
They must have a sense of security in their jobs.
Compensation must be fair and adequate,
and working conditions clean, orderly and safe.
We must be mindful of ways to help our employees fulfill
their family responsibilities.
Employees must feel free to make suggestions and complaints.
There must be equal opportunity for employment, development
and advancement for those qualified.
We must provide competent management,
and their actions must be just and ethical.

We are responsible to the communities in which we live and work
and to the world community as well.
We must be good citizens—support good works and charities
and bear our fair share of taxes.
We must encourage civic improvements and better health and education.
We must maintain in good order
the property we are privileged to use,
protecting the environment and natural resources.

Our final responsibility is to our stockholders.
Business must make a sound profit.
We must experiment wlth new ideas.
Research must be carried on, innovative programs developed
and mistakes paid for.
New equipment must be purchased, new facilities provided
and new products launched.
Reserves must be created to provide for adverse times.
When we operate according to these principles,
the stock holders should realize a fair return.

Johnson & Johnson

Source: Johnson & Johnson Annual Report.

members to behave in a socially responsible manner. In fact, managers at Johnson & Johnson take social responsibility so seriously that their organization is frequently mentioned as an example of a socially responsible firm. Their Credo (see Figure 3.9) is one of the many ways in which social responsibility is emphasized at Johnson & Johnson. As discussed in "Ethics in Action" on the next page, Johnson & Johnson's ethical organizational culture provides the company and its various stakeholder groups with numerous benefits.

Ethics in Action

Johnson & Johnson's Ethical Culture

Johnson & Johnson is so well known for its ethical culture that it has been judged to have the best corporate reputation for two years in a row based on a survey of over 26,000 consumers conducted by Harris Interactive and the Reputation Institute at New York University.[89] Johnson & Johnson grew from a family business lead by General Robert Wood Johnson in the 1930s to become a major maker of pharmaceutical and medical products. Attesting to the role of managers in creating ethical organizational cultures, Johnson emphasized the importance of ethics and responsibility to stakeholders and wrote the first Johnson & Johnson credo in 1943.[90]

The credo continues to guide employees at Johnson & Johnson today and outlines the company's commitments to its different stakeholder groups emphasizing that the organization's first responsibility is to doctors, nurses, patients, and consumers. Following this group are suppliers and distributors, employees, communities, and lastly, stockholders.[91] This credo has served managers and employees at Johnson & Johnson well and guided some difficult decision making such as the decision to recall all Tylenol capsules in the U.S. market after cyanide-laced capsules were responsible for seven deaths in Chicago.

True to its ethical culture and outstanding reputation, consumer well-being always comes before profit considerations at Johnson & Johnson. For example, around 20 years ago, Johnson & Johnson's baby oil was used as a tanning product at a time when the harmful effects of sun exposure were much less well known by the public.[92] The product manager for baby oil at the time, Carl Spalding, was making a presentation to top management about marketing plans when the President David Clare mentioned that tanning might not be healthy.[93] Before launching his planned marketing campaign, Spalding looked into the health-related concerns connected with tanning and discovered some evidence suggested health-related problems from too much exposure to the sun. Even though the evidence was not definitive, Spalding recommended that baby oil no longer be marketed as a tanning aid, which resulted in a 50 percent decrease in sales of baby oil to the tune of $5 million.[94]

An employee removes Tylenol from a Chicago store's shelves on Johnson & Johnson's instructions after the discovery of contaminated supplies in 1982.

The ethical values and norms in Johnson & Johnson's culture, along with its credo, guide managers such as Spalding to make the right decision in difficult situations such as this one. Hence, it is understandable why Johnson & Johnson is renowned for its corporate reputation. An ethical culture and outstanding reputation have other benefits in addition to helping employees make the right decisions in questionable situations. Jeanne Hamway, vice president for recruiting, finds that Johnson & Johnson's reputation helps them recruit and attract a diverse workforce.[95] Moreover, when organizations develop an outstanding reputation, their employees often are less tempted to act in a self-interested or unethical manner. For example, managers at Johnson & Johnson suggest that since employees in the company never accept bribes, the company is known as one in which bribes should not be offered in the first place.[96] All in all, ethical cultures such as Johnson & Johnson's benefit various stakeholder groups in multiple ways.

Summary and Review

PERSONALITY TRAITS Personality traits are enduring tendencies to feel, think, and act in certain ways. The Big Five general traits are extraversion, negative affectivity, agreeableness, conscientiousness, and openness to experience. Other personality traits that affect managerial behavior are locus of control, self-esteem, and the needs for achievement, affiliation, and power.

VALUES, ATTITUDES, AND MOODS AND EMOTIONS A terminal value is a personal conviction about lifelong goals or objectives; an instrumental value is a personal conviction about modes of conduct. Terminal and instrumental values have an impact on what managers try to achieve in their organization and the kinds of behaviors they engage in. An attitude is a collection of feelings and beliefs. Two attitudes important for understanding managerial behaviors include job satisfaction (the collection of feelings and beliefs that managers have about their jobs) and organizational commitment (the collection of feelings and beliefs that managers have about their organization). A mood is a feeling or state of mind; emotions are more intense feelings. Managers' moods, or how they feel at work on a day-to-day basis, have the potential to impact not only their own behavior and effectiveness but also their subordinates. Emotional intelligence is ability to understand and manage one's own and other people's moods and emotions.

ETHICS AND STAKEHOLDERS Ethics are moral principles or beliefs about what is right or wrong. These beliefs guide people in their dealings with other individuals and groups (stakeholders) and provide a basis for deciding whether behavior is right and proper. Many organizations have a formal code of ethics derived primarily from societal ethics, professional ethics, and the individual ethics of the organization's top managers. Managers can apply ethical standards to help themselves decide on the proper way to behave toward organizational stakeholders.

ORGANIZATIONAL CULTURE Organizational culture is the set of values, norms, standards for behavior, and shared expectations that influence the ways in which individuals, groups, and teams interact with each other and cooperate to achieve organizational goals. Founders of new organizations and managers play an important role in creating and maintaining organizational cultures. Ethical organizational cultures are those in which ethical values and norms are emphasized. Ethical organizational cultures can help organizations and their members behave in a socially responsible manner.

Management in Action

Topics for Discussion and Action

1. Discuss why managers who have different types of personalities can be equally effective and successful.
2. Interview a manager in a local organization. Ask the manager to describe situations in which he or she is especially likely to act in accordance with his or her values. Ask the manager to describe situations in which he or she is less likely to act in accordance with his or her values.
3. Can managers be too satisfied with their jobs? Can they be too committed to their organizations? Why or why not?
4. Assume that you are a manager of a restaurant. Describe what it is like to work for you when you are in a negative mood.
5. Why might managers be disadvantaged by low levels of emotional intelligence?
6. When are ethics and ethical standards especially important in organizations?
7. Why might managers do things that conflict with their own ethical values?
8. How can managers ensure that they create ethical organizational cultures?

Building Management Skills

Diagnosing Culture

Think about the culture of the last organization you worked for, your current university, or another organization or club to which you belong. Then, answer the following questions.

1. What values and norms are emphasized in this culture?
2. How are ethics addressed in this culture?
3. Who seems to have played an important role in creating the culture?
4. How does the culture address the needs of different stakeholder groups?

Small Group Breakout Exercise

Making Difficult Decisions in Hard Times

Form groups of three or four people, and appoint one member as the spokesperson who will communicate your findings to the whole class when called on by the instructor. Then discuss the following scenario.

You are on the top-management team of a medium-size company that manufactures cardboard boxes, containers, and other cardboard packaging materials. Your company is facing increasing levels of competition for major corporate customer accounts and profits have declined significantly. You have tried everything you can to cut costs and remain competitive, with the exception of laying off employees. Your company has had a no layoff policy for the past 20 years and you believe it is an important part of the organization's ethical culture. However, you are experiencing mounting pressure to increase your firm's performance and your no layoff policy has been questioned by shareholders. Even though you haven't decided whether to lay off employees and thus, break with a 20-year tradition for your company, rumors are rampant in your organization that something is afoot and employees are worried. You are meeting today to address this problem.

1. Develop a list of options and potential courses of action to address the heightened competition and decline in profitability that your company has been experiencing.
2. Choose your preferred course of action and justify why you will take this route.
3. Describe how you will communicate your decision to employees.
4. If your preferred option involves a layoff, justify why. If it doesn't involve a layoff, explain why.

Exploring the World Wide Web

Find the website of a company that is undertaking initiatives to enhance levels of job satisfaction or organizational commitment among employees. What are those initiatives? Do you think they will be successful in promoting job satisfaction or organizational commitment? Why or why not?

You're the Management Consultant

Sam Bernstein was recently hired as the vice president for human resources in an advertising agency. The agency has been plagued by accusations that certain employees engage in unethical conduct ranging from conflicts of interest with clients to using expense accounts for family vacations. While a task force composed of high-ranking managers in the agency has been formed to investigate these allegations and propose a course of action to deal with any lapses in ethical conduct on the part of the agency's employees, Bernstein has been asked to proactively address the issue of organizational ethics as part of his objectives for the year. He has found out that the agency actually does not have a Code of Ethics per se. Whenever legal questions arise, the agency employs freelance attorneys for advice, and if necessary, action. The organization does have policies forbidding conflicts of interest with clients and use of expense accounts for personal travel. However, top management is concerned that these policies are too vague and not taken seriously.

As an expert in ethics and ethical organizational cultures, Bernstein has come to you for help. He doesn't know where to start to address this seemingly monumental task as well as how to proceed and what he should even be striving to accomplish. Advise Bernstein.

BusinessWeek Cases in the News

What's A Fair Price For Drugs?

In the past few months, drugmakers like Merck & Co. and Abbott Laboratories Inc. have slashed prices for anti-HIV drugs in AIDS-ravaged Africa. Instead of charging $10,000 to $15,000 per year as in the U.S., they will sell their medicines for as little as $600 a year.

This dramatic move gets drugmakers off the hot seat. No longer can they be accused of raking in billions in profits while ignoring the suffering and deaths of millions. But the result will be a stark difference in prices, which will raise the perennial question of why drug prices are so high in the U.S. compared with the rest of the world. "The humanitarian effort could come back and hit them in the eye," says Nancy Myers, senior research analyst at Lehman Brothers Inc.

The deep discounts raise other issues as well. All along, drugmakers have said they need high prices to pay the steep cost of research and development. But do they really? If they can sell AIDS drugs or other medicines for pennies a pill in Africa—or at 60 percent of the U.S. price in Europe—doesn't that undercut the R&D argument?

The industry's critics think so. Public Citizen notes that the 11 biggest drugmakers raked in $28 billion in profits last year—and for eight of them, profits were higher than R&D spending. "They don't have to make that money in order to do R&D," says Abbey S. Meyers, president of the National Organization for Rare Disorders. "That's the excuse they've been using for years—and no one believes it anymore."

So who's right? There's no simple answer. But here's a step-by-step journey through the thicket of arguments surrounding drug prices:

Should drugmakers offer deep discounts to developing nations?

Unequivocally, yes—and not just for the humanitarian reasons. "The economic theory and evidence is clear: Differential pricing can benefit consumers in low-income countries without harming—and perhaps even benefiting—consumers in high-income countries," observes Dr. Jonathan D. Quick, director of essential drugs and medicines policy at the World Health Organization.

Here's why. Most drugs cost only pennies per pill to make. Selling them cheaply to poor nations therefore costs drugmakers nothing—and can even bring in profits that help support new R&D. "It's a win-win. Drugmakers would be doing good in the world, creating markets—and making marginal profits," explains Barry R. Bloom, dean of the Harvard School of Public Health.

O.K., but does this mean Americans are shouldering the burden for paying for R & D through high prices?

Yes. And Americans may actually be paying a bit too much—as we'll see below. But at the same time, the U.S. gets the benefits.

Even at today's prices, with the nation's total pharmaceutical bill soaring from $51 billion in 1993 to a projected $136 billion in 2001, there are plenty of economists who consider drugs a bargain. Cholesterol-lowering drugs such as Merck & Co.'s Zocor or Pfizer Inc.'s Lipitor, for instance, can prevent heart disease, saving big bucks on surgery and hospitalizations. "We should be happy that pharmaceuticals are the fastest-growing component of the health-care budget, because it means that other components aren't growing as fast as they otherwise would," says pharmaceutical economist Eugene Mick Kolassa at the University of Mississippi.

Is expensive R & D the determining factor in drug pricing?

Contrary to industry's claims, not really. The way a drug's price is set has little or nothing to do with how much that drug costs to develop. Instead, pharmaceuticals are just like any other product: Companies charge what the market will bear. An improved version of heparin, a blood thinner used to prevent clots during procedures such as hip surgery, saves an average of $200 in medical costs each time it's used. So companies charge 100 times more than they did for their original heparin—and still produce overall health-care savings.

Setting prices on considerations such as these is just Economics 101 for drugmakers. Contends Stanford health-care economist Dr. Alan M. Garber: "It would be unfair to portray them as greedy or irresponsible if they charge what they can get."

In this context, are prices really too high in the U.S.?

Yes, may economists say—and they blame our health-care system. In short, it's not a free market. Among purchasers, there's little competition that would exert downward pressures on prices. And under most insurance schemes, neither doctors nor consumers have incentives to seek out and buy the drugs that offer the best value. "Resources are best allocated when markets determine the price, based on value to consumers," says Joseph A. DiMasi, director of economic analysis at the Tufts University Center for the Study of Drug Development. "We're a good distance from that."

High prices do mean that companies can do more R&D. But how much does R&D really cost?

Industry likes to claim that drug development takes a dozen years and costs up the $500 million. The number originally comes from a 1991 study in which DiMasi and colleagues collected data from 12 pharmaceutical companies on 93 drugs. They concluded that the total average cost was $231 million in 1987 dollars. DiMasi now puts the price tag at $318 million in 1999 dollars, while others argue that since clinical trials have become more complex and expensive, the actual cost must be closer to the cited $500 million.

In fact, the amount spent on each drug is a fraction of that amount. About half of the $300 million to $500 million is what companies could have earned with the money by investing it elsewhere—the so-called opportunity cost. And since only about one in 10 drugs tested in human trials makes it to the market, more than half of the rest is the cost of all the failed projects. As a result, cutting either the time to market or the failure rate can dramatically reduce the total R&D cost. Ultimately, if drug prices did come down, companies would have no choice but to get smarter about their research. After all, their very future depends on being able to produce a steady stream of new drugs.

How can the U.S. get prices that are appropriate?

Not with price controls. Instead, the nation needs to let the market work better. How? By freeing up big purchasers to negotiate discounts irrespective of the prices the government gets. Consumers and doctors also need to be made aware of the relative costs and benefits of individual drugs. If consumers had to pay more out of pocket for expensive drugs, many would opt for cheaper but still effective alternatives. As for Americans who can't afford drugs, the solution is more insurance coverage.

And what's the right policy for the Third World?

Washington and drugmakers need to embrace the idea of different prices in different countries, as long as those prices are based on ability to pay. There's a sobering lesson from recent history. In the late 1980s, U.S. vaccine makers were bashed by Congress at the first sign that they might cost more in the U.S. than elsewhere. In the end, they stopped selling vaccines to developing countries. Europeans stepped into the breach and took over the markets. Indeed, the right approach is not to complain that Americans are paying too much but to figure out ways to get more drugs to more people around the world—at prices they can afford. Moving beyond the knee-jerk reaction that Americans are being gouged if others can buy drugs more cheaply would be a major step toward a healthier world for everyone.

Source: J. Carey, "What's a Fair Price for Drugs?" *Business Week,* April 30, 2001, pp. 105–06.

Questions

1. Is it ethical to charge high prices for drugs?
2. From an ethical standpoint, how should prices for different drugs be set?

Cases in the News

Savaged By the Slowdown: How Families are Coping—or not—With the Fallout

Until the downturn, 40-year-old Steve Jackson's blood pressure was an ultralow 105 over 60. After surviving a plane crash in 1984, in which his United Air Lines 727 hit a radio tower on takeoff and ripped the fuselage under his seat, he nonchalantly boarded the next available flight. Seemingly unflappable, his family and friends thought of him as a cool-hand Luke.

Until the night of February 15, when Jackson stared at the news on the computer screen in his cluttered Chapel Hill office and couldn't believe what he saw. Jackson, a university research coordinator for Nortel Networks Corp., had always thought of his Nortel options as a reward for the lean years when he and his wife lived in a two-window dump so dark it killed the plants. But news that Nortel would miss earnings was sending the stock into a tailspin, one that ultimately wiped out his one-time, million-dollar fortune and left him with a $400,000 tax bill on money he would never see. Turns out that by hanging on to the shares after he exercised the options instead of selling, Jackson had triggered the alternative minimum tax. That move, in turn ended up destroying his kids' college savings and the family's net worth.

At first, Jackson had trouble keeping food down. Then he could not sleep. Acne sprouted all over his face. His doctor prescribed Valium, which Jackson says he ate "like M&Ms." To cope with the debt, he took a second mortgage on his house which he says he'll be lucky to keep, and another job as an electrician's assistant on the night shift, paying $20 an hour. "It's like Kafka," says Jackson, who worries when his phone rings that it's a layoff call. "Work-family balance? I have no balance. From the moment I wake up until I fall asleep, this problem consumes me."

The downturn has done plenty of damage, ravaging market caps, decimating earnings, and extinguishing all sorts of entrepreneurial dreams. Less visible has been the slowdown's effect on families. As companies gear up for what is predicted to be a third round of job cuts this fall, economists say unemployment could rise to 5 percent by early next year.

Fantasy World

Not that those who are still employed are without their worries. Businesses across the country are saddling their reduced ranks with bigger workloads, causing stress levels to spike beyond their boomtime levels. They are also cutting bonuses, which will likely leave many families strapped, having financed their luxury lifestyles on the extra compensation. Already, some boomers are angry about being able to afford retirement, while many elderly are disappointed about derailed plans to move into posh, concierge-equipped retirement communities. These downbeat expectations for the near term appears to be catching up with consumers, who sent the Conference Board's confidence gauge down two points in August to a two-month low. "Almost any market indicator you look at points to significant and increasing amounts of stress on households," says Mark M. Zandi, chief economist at researcher Economy.com. "And I get no sense that it's going to come to an end any time soon."

Employee assistance and outplacement professionals say this dampened outlook, coupled with dwindling severance packages, are causing new and disturbing tensions among employees and their families, especially now that Corporate America's paternalism has largely vanished. "The downturn is now hitting them very hard," says Richard A. Chaifetz, chairman and CEO of Compsych, the world's largest privately held employee assistance firm, whose clients include American Express, J.P. Morgan, and Krispy Kreme.

Indeed, Chaifetz says Compsych is receiving record levels of calls for help from employees and their families. Since the downturn, counselors say they have seen a marked increase in "crisis calls" involving problems such as online affairs, addictions in adolescents, and spousal abuse (which counselors say is occurring more and more against men). "People feel like they had the rug pulled out from under them," says Chaifetz. "They were living in a fantasy world."

Now, they're finding out how harsh reality can be. Sure, plenty of families stashed it away during the boom, protecting themselves, from the economic whiplash. Others, who haven't suffered a layoff or a big economic reversal, are humming along just fine. In fact, these sorts of families have helped support what until recently has been a surprisingly upbeat mood among customers. But Economy.com's Zandi warns that the number of families feeling the strain may well grow over the coming months. That's largely because Americans are sitting on huge piles of debt. Delinquencies on car loans and credit cards are at or near record levels, as are those on mortgages for lower-income homeowners. Household debt service has also hit an all-time high, along with personal bankruptcies (charts). And for those who still have jobs, their incomes, hours, and bonuses, like those of executives at Ford Motor Co. and Sun Microsystems Inc., are being cut.

These financial troubles are not being lost on companies. Human resource professionals figure that when workers worry about family finances, they waste 13 percent of the workday on calling creditors and other distractions. Money woes also lead to medical problems, lower productivity, more absenteeism, and accidents. Indeed, research shows that family members who survive a layoff face workplaces that are more stressful, political, and cutthroat than before the downsizing, leaving them with even less time for family. Some employee assistance firms have added financial counseling, as well as survivor seminars, to their offerings to help workers cope.

Nowhere is that help needed more than in the Bay Area, where the jobless rate has jumped from 1.7 percent in January to a recent 4.7 percent. During the boom, the lines at Frankie Johnnie & Luigi's in Mountain View, CA, were two blocks long, filled with dot-commers celebrating stock prices over the sausage bread and salami strombolis. Today, only a small clump waits to get in. Instead, the long lines are forming across the railroad tracks at the nonprofit food bank, Community Services Agency.

Priorities

Each morning, about 75 or so laid-off high-tech workers line up for the 10 AM opening, when they can get bread, butter, and milk—when it's available. Last year, most of the agency's clients were low-income workers who showed up in their fast-food uniforms. Today, it's laid-off dot-commers in khakis, especially single parents and those fresh out of college. "The kind of people we're seeing has drastically changed," says Tom Myers.

Some who have suffered huge reversals are finding the crisis can help them set new priorities, like the ex-dot-com CEO who postponed having kids during the boom, only to realize now that she really does want a family, even though she and her husband lost their millions and can barely afford the rent. But mostly, the newly jobless and suddenly unwealthy are distressed, and they are flocking to newly formed support groups, like Transitions at Mountain View's St. Timothy's Episcopal Church. Members participate in role-playing exercises, where some of the downturn-induced family pressures are vented and worked through. Leading the sessions is James Thomas, a minister and Jungian analyst who likes the pain of the families he sees to those he counseled in the 1980s through the Oklahoma oil crisis, when the suicide rate got so high the state started a gun-giveback program. "People held on for a couple of months in Oklahoma before they crashed and burned," Thomas says. "It's déjà vu here."

Angry and Afraid

Group member Ivan Temes, who has had a 30-year career in Silicon Valley in consumer support at stalwarts such as Levi Strauss & Co. and Apple Computer Inc., has no trouble believing that. Temes has been laid off before, but the most recent downsizing, from Internet privacy company Privada Inc., was the worst, coming with no warning, no benefits, and no severance. His wife is angry and afraid, especially since the family has run through its savings and Temes recently called about food stamps. Their 6-year-old son, Joshua, also feels the financial fear. Recently, when Temes was on the way out the door, he recounts, he needed some change and asked Joshua for a quarter. Running out of the room, Joshua waved a bill in his hand, shouting excitedly, "Here, Daddy—here's a dollar." Says Temes: "He gets what is going on."

Temes is hoping his next job will last long enough for the family to regain its footing. But with hiring-and-firing frenzies a part of the new employment landscape, getting a new job doesn't mean the end of uncertainty. No one knows that better than George deWalder, a specialty-materials manager in Mocksville, N.C. The 55-year-old has been a casualty of serial layoffs, losing nine jobs in 10 years, a volatility he says nearly ruined his relationship with his 23-year-old son. He also blames the downsizings for playing a role in the end of his 28-year marriage to a woman he still loves but who couldn't take the roller coaster. "I wouldn't wish her on me, either," he says. It didn't make things any easier, he adds, that she worked for SAS Institute—a company that never lays off workers. "In all my times of job hunting, I've never seen it this bad," deWalder says. Lately, he says, he has begun to ask himself: What's the point?

Others who made and lost fortunes, who got and lost promotions, who were and then weren't CEOs, are asking themselves the same question. For many families in the downturn, all the euphoria on the way up is being followed by equal doses of pain on the way down.

Source: M. Conlin, "Savaged by the Slowdown: How Families Are Coping—or not—With the Fallout," *Business Week,* September 17, 2001, pp. 74–77.

Questions

1. What ethical obligations do organizations have to employees and their families when times are tough due to economic downturns?
2. Do these obligations apply to all members of an organization equally? Why or why not?

Chapter 4

Managing Diverse Employees in a Diverse Environment

Learning Objectives

After studying this chapter, you should be able to:

- Appreciate the increasing diversity of the workforce and of the organization environment.
- Grasp the central role that managers play in the effective management of diversity.
- Understand why the effective management of diversity is both an ethical and a business imperative.
- Appreciate how perception and the use of schemas can result in unfair treatment.
- Appreciate the steps managers can take to effectively manage diversity.
- Understand the two major forms of sexual harassment and how they can be eliminated.

A Manager's Challenge

Retaining Talented Minorities and Women at DeLoitte & Touche

How can managers retain talented minorities and women?

In the early 1990s, top management at Deloitte & Touche (D&T), now the second largest accounting and consulting firm in the United States, realized they had a problem. It seemed that minorities and women were quitting their jobs in disproportionate numbers when compared to white males. Thus, although the firm was committed to recruiting talented minorities and women, for some reason many of these high-performing employees were quitting their jobs. Women of all colors, in particular, were highly likely to leave the firm; this resulted in D&T's hierarchy of authority being increasingly dominated by men, especially at high levels. In 1991, out of 50 candidates for partner, only 4 were women.[1]

Kris Haworth, head of the computer forensics lab at Deloitte & Touche, sits at her desk in her San Francisco office.

Why were so many diverse women leaving D&T, and was this a significant problem? Some managers thought these women were leaving for personal reasons and/or to raise families, so they concluded it wasn't a management problem. Fortunately for D&T, then CEO Mike Cooke thought differently. When he established a taskforce to find out if and why there was a problem, the taskforce learned that women were not leaving D&T for personal reasons or to have families. Rather, they didn't think their future would be that bright in D&T's male-dominated culture.[2]

Cooke resolved to change this state of affairs through a multipronged approach. Key to this approach was getting all of D&T's managers to realize how men, women, and minorities were viewed in the firm. While men were often viewed in terms of their potential, women and minorities were typically evaluated on their current performance. Even though they considered the performance of many women and minority employees excellent, managers did expect them to rise through the corporate hierarchy. Thus, women and diverse employees were often passed over for top assignments and excluded from important networking opportunities, such as golf games with clients or networking over drinks after work. For example, when a partner had to assign a particularly difficult case—say, a manufacturing company that was difficult to deal with—managers would implicitly and sometimes explicitly assume that a female subordinate wouldn't be able to handle it. The implicit belief was that a male subordinate would be able to succeed in such a tough environment even though the only difference between the two subordinates was their gender.[3]

D&T's recognition that its increasingly diverse employees presented special management problems resulted in a commitment by top management to understand and resolve the many issues involved. D&T took many major steps to effectively manage diversity. An organizationwide mentorship program was initiated for minorities and women who were paired with senior managers of other ages, genders, and ethnicities to encourage the development of an organization culture that valued and appreciated diversity. Top managers discovered that in the high-pressure world of accountancy work-life balance and family issues were the concern of not just their female employees who did wish to have children at some point in their careers but also many of their male employees. So, D&T initiated a major flextime initiative that allows all employees to develop more flexible work schedules if they choose. Many other diversity initiatives followed that have paid off. D&T is currently more successful at retaining talented women and minorities than other accountancy firms and is consistently voted as one of the best companies to work for in the United States. The number of its female partners and directors has increased by 98 percent.[4]

D&T's top management realizes, however, that the effective management of diversity needs to be a continuing effort. This is why it has taken many steps to build a strong culture that values diversity and corrects faulty perceptions and stereotypes. These and other natural human tendencies had resulted in women and minorities being treated differently than white men even though there are no work-related reasons to expect them to behave or perform any differently. As D&T puts it, "A diverse workforce provides the talent, creativity, flexibility, world-vision, and strength that we need to successfully compete in global markets."[5] •

Overview

As managers at Deloitte & Touche realized, the effective management of diversity means much more than hiring diverse employees. It means learning to appreciate and respond appropriately to the needs, attitudes, beliefs, and values that diverse people bring to an organization. It also means correcting misconceptions about why and how different kinds of employee groups are different from one another and finding the most effective way to utilize the skills and talents of diverse employees.

In this chapter, we focus on the effective management of diversity in an environment that is becoming increasingly diverse in all respects. Not only is the diversity of the U.S. workforce increasing, suppliers and customers are also becoming increasingly diverse. Indeed, Deloitte & Touche has instituted a program to encourage minority suppliers to compete for its business, and sponsors schools and colleges which supply a stream of well-trained recruits. Moreover, many companies, including D&T, are global companies and operate in a diverse global environment.

Members of Nike's Diversity Council share their views during a meeting. Collectively, the council has over 100 years of experience at Nike and represents a diversity of ages, races, gender, living orientations, nationalities, cultures, and abilities. Its goal is to lead and validate Nike's efforts dedicated to diversity. To stay competitive, Nike believes that it must be able to recruit and retain individuals who have different backgrounds and views and who will contribute new ideas and help "raise the bar."

As was true at D&T, sometimes even well-intentioned managers inadvertently treat one group of employees differently from another group, even though there are no performance-based differences between the two groups. This chapter also explores why differential treatment occurs and the steps managers and organizations can take to ensure that diversity, in all respects, is effectively managed for the good of all organizational stakeholders.

The Increasing Diversity of the Workforce and the Environment

One of the most important management issues to emerge over the last 30 years has been the increasing diversity of the workforce. **Diversity** is dissimilarities–differences–among people due to age, gender, race, ethnicity, religion, sexual orientation, socioeconomic background, and capabilities/ disabilities (see Figure 4.1).

diversity Differences among people in age, gender, race, ethnicity, religion, sexual orientation, socioeconomic background, and capabilities/disabilities.

Diversity raises important ethical issues and social responsibility issues as well (see Chapter 3). It is also a critical issue for organizations, one that if not handled well can bring an organization to its knees, especially in our increasingly global environment. There are several reasons why diversity is such a pressing concern and issue both in the popular press and for managers and organizations:

- There is a strong ethical imperative in many societies that diverse people receive equal opportunities and be treated fairly and justly. Unfair treatment is also illegal.
- Effectively managing diversity can improve organizational effectiveness. When managers effectively manage diversity, they not only encourage other managers to treat diverse members of an organization fairly and justly but also realize that diversity is an important organizational resource that can help an organization gain a competitive advantage.
- There is substantial evidence that diverse individuals continue to experience unfair treatment in the workplace as a result of biases, stereotypes, and overt discrimination. In one study, résumés of equally qualified men and women

Figure 4.1
Sources of Diversity in the Workforce

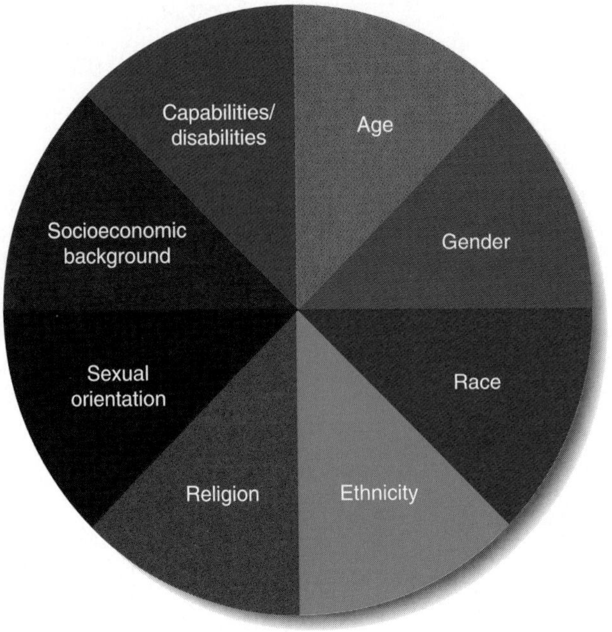

were sent to high-priced Philadelphia restaurants (where potential earnings are high). Though equally qualified, men were more than twice as likely as women to be called for a job interview and more than five times as likely to receive a job offer.[6] Findings from another study suggest that both women and men tend to believe that women will accept lower pay than men; this is a potential explanation for the continuing gap in pay between men and women.[7]

Figure 4.2
2008: Projected New Entrants in the U.S. Labor Force

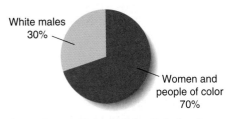

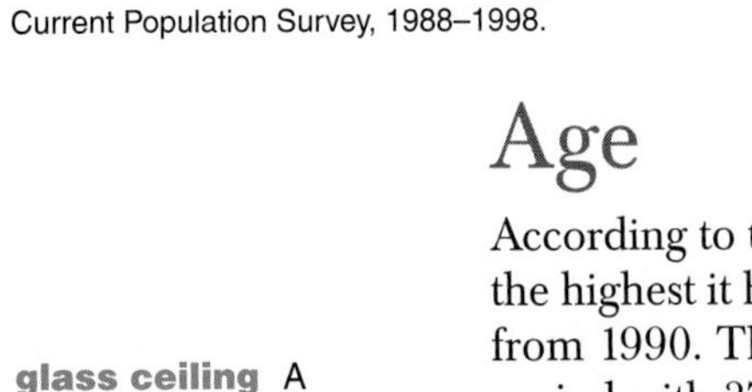

Source: Bureau of Labor Statistics, Projections from Current Population Survey, 1988–1998.

Other kinds of diverse employees may face even greater barriers. For example, the federal Glass Ceiling Commission Report indicated that African Americans have the hardest time being promoted and climbing the corporate ladder, that Asians are often stereotyped into technical jobs, and that Hispanics are assumed to be less well educated than other minority groups.[8] The term **glass ceiling** alludes to the invisible barriers that prevent minorities and women from being promoted to top corporate positions.

Before we can discuss the multitude of issues surrounding the effective management of diversity, we must document just how diverse the U.S. workforce is becoming (see Figure 4.2).

Age

glass ceiling A metaphor alluding to the invisible barriers that prevent minorities and women from being promoted to top corporate positions.

According to the 2000 Census, the median age of a person in the United States is the highest it has ever been, 35.3 years, which is a two-and-one-half-year increase from 1990. The 45–54 age cohort saw the greatest population growth over this period with 37.7 million U.S. residents in 2000.[9] Title VII of the Civil Rights Act of 1964 as well as the Age Discrimination in Employment Act of 1967 are the major federal laws prohibiting age discrimination.[10] While we discuss federal employment legislation in more depth in Chapter 11, major equal employment opportunity legislation that prohibits discrimination among diverse groups is summarized in Table 4.1.

Table 4.1
Major Equal Employment Opportunity Laws Affecting HRM

Year	Law	Description
1963	Equal Pay Act	Requires men and women to be paid equally if they are performing equal work
1964	Title VII of the Civil Rights Act	Prohibits discrimination in employment decisions on the basis of race, religion, sex, color, or national origin; covers a wide range of employment decisions, including hiring, firing, pay, promotion, and working conditions
1967	Age Discrimination in Employment Act	Prohibits discrimination against workers over the age of 40 and restricts mandatory retirement
1978	Pregnancy Discrimination Act	Prohibits discrimination against women in employment decisions on the basis of pregnancy, childbirth, and related medical decisions
1990	Americans with Disabilities Act	Prohibits discrimination against disabled individuals in employment decisions and requires employers to make accommodations for disabled workers to enable them to perform their jobs
1991	Civil Rights Act	Prohibits discrimination (as does Title VII) and allows for the awarding of punitive and compensatory damages, in addition to back pay, in cases of intentional discrimination
1993	Family and Medical Leave Act	Requires employers to provide 12 weeks of unpaid leave for medical and family reasons including paternity and illness of a family member

The aging of the population suggests managers need to be vigilant that employees are not discriminated against because of age. Moreover, managers need to ensure that the policies and procedures they have in place treat all workers fairly, regardless of their ages, as indicated in the following "Focus on Diversity."

Focus on Diversity

Age Discrimination at Ford?

One of Ford Motor Company's initiatives in 1999 was to increase diversity, put a younger management team in place, and reorient Ford's culture toward change, new technology, and new markets.[11] Ford created a new performance appraisal process (see Chapter 11) for its 18,000 salaried, white-collar workers that required supervisors to give each of their subordinates a yearly grade of A, B, or C. Subordinates who receive a C cannot receive a pay raise or a promotion and those who receive a C in two consecutive years can be demoted or fired. In 2000, Ford required that supervisors distribute "grades" so that 10 percent of their subordinates received As, 80 percent received Bs, and the remaining 10 percent received Cs. In 2001, Ford modified the process by requiring 10 percent As, 85 percent Bs, and 5 percent Cs.[12]

How was the new process received by the managers affected by it? Negatively, to put it mildly. In fact, 42 employees have filed two class-action lawsuits against Ford claiming that the new process was used to terminate older managers. Attorneys for these employees suggest that Ford is stereotypically assuming that older workers are slow to change or learn new things and thus, trying to diminish their numbers.[13] Take the case of John Wyrwas, a 60-year-old manager who recently participated in Ford's Six Sigma program to improve quality and attained "blackbelt" status. Blackbelts are top performers in the program with leadership, math, and statistical expertise. As a blackbelt, Wyrwas worked on upgrading the process used to prototype products. Thus, he was shocked to learn that he received a C; as he put it, the process was "devoid of any objective criteria."[14]

While the outcomes of these lawsuits have yet to be determined, managers' work attitudes have been undermined by the new process which forces supervisors to compare and evaluate managers in a relative sense rather than based on objective criteria. Ford had hoped that the new process would both help to remove poor performers and promote teamwork.[15] Some managers wonder how a process that pits them against each other could promote teamwork. As Pam Tucker, a 48-year-old manager who has participated in the lawsuit indicates, "If anything, this has caused extensive navel-gazing rather than staring out at the horizon at the consumer and competition . . . . People are constantly looking over their shoulders."[16]

Gender

Women and men are almost equally represented in the U.S. workforce (approximately 54 percent of the U.S. workforce is male and 46 percent female),[17] yet women's median earnings are estimated to be $18,996 per year compared to $30,132 for men.[18] Thus, the gender pay gap appears to be as alive and well as the glass ceiling. According to the nonprofit organization Catalyst that studies women in business, while women comprise about 49 percent of the employees in managerial and professional positions, only around 12 percent of corporate officers in the 500 largest U.S. companies (i.e., Fortune 500) are women, only 4 percent of the top earners are women, only 6.2 percent of those with the highest ranking titles in corporate America are women (e.g., CEO or executive vice president), and less than 5 women occupy CEO positions in the Fortune 500 companies.[19] These women, such as Andrea Jung, CEO of Avon Products, and Carly S. Fiorina, CEO of Hewlett-Packard, stand out among their male peers and often receive a disparate amount of attention in the media. (We address this issue later when we discuss the effects of being salient.) Women are also very underrepresented on boards of directors–they currently hold 12 percent of Standard & Poor's 500 board seats.[20] However, as Sheila Wellington, President of Catalyst, indicates, "Women either control or influence nearly all consumer purchases, so it's important to have their perspective represented on boards."[21]

Additionally, research conducted by consulting firms suggests that female executives outperform their male colleagues on skills such as being able to motivate others, promoting good communication, turning out high quality work, and being a good listener.[22] For example, the Hagberg Group performed in-depth evaluations of 425 top executives in a variety of industries and each executive was rated by approximately 25 people. Of the 52 skills assessed, women received higher ratings than men on 42 skills, though at times the differences were small.[23] All in all, studies such as these make one wonder why the glass ceiling continues to hamper the progress of women in business (a topic we address later in the chapter).

Race and Ethnicity

The U.S. Census Bureau typically distinguishes between the following races: American Indian or Alaska Native (native Americans or origins in North, Central, or South America), Asian (origins in the Far East, Southeast Asia, or India), African American (origins in Africa), Native Hawaiian or Pacific Islander (origins in the Pacific Islands such as Hawaii, Guam, or Somoa), and white (origins in Europe, the Middle East, or North Africa). Ethnicity refers to whether a person is Hispanic or not Hispanic. Hispanics, also referred to as Latinos, are people whose origins are in Spanish cultures such as Cuba, Mexico, Puerto Rico, and South and Central America. Hispanics can be of different races.[24]

The racial and ethnic diversity of the U.S. population is increasing as is the composition of the workforce. For example, the Bureau of Labor Statistics projects the following annual growth rates in the working population for the 10-year period from 1998 to 2008: .9 percent for whites, 1.8 percent for African Americans, and 3.2 percent for Hispanics.[25] According to the U.S. Census in 2000, 75.1 percent of the population was white, 12.9 percent was African American, 12.5 percent was Hispanic, and 3.6 percent was Asian.[26] Mexican Americans are estimated to comprise over 60 percent of the U.S. Hispanic population, with the remainder of Hispanics having diverse countries of origin. According to a recent poll, most Hispanics prefer to be identified by their country of origin (e.g., Mexican, Cuban, or Salvadoran) rather than by the overarching term, *Hispanic*.[27]

The increasing racial and ethnic diversity of the workforce and population as a whole underscores the importance of effectively managing diversity. In the remainder of the chapter, we focus on the fair treatment of diverse employees, why this is such an important challenge, and what managers can do. We begin by taking a broader perspective and considering how increasing racial and ethnic diversity in an organization's environment (e.g., customers and suppliers) affects decision making and organizational effectiveness.

At a general level, managers and organizations are increasingly being reminded that stakeholders in the environment are diverse and expect organizational decisions and actions to reflect this diversity. For example, the NAACP (National Association for Colored People) and Children Now (an advocacy group) have lobbied the entertainment industry to increase the diversity in television programming, writing, and producing.[28] The need for such increased diversity is more than apparent. For example, while Hispanics make up 12.5 percent of the U.S. population (or 35 million potential TV viewers), only about 2 percent of the characters in prime time TV shows are Hispanics (i.e., of the 2,251 characters in prime time shows, only 47 are Hispanic), according to a study conducted by Children Now.[29] Moreover, only about 1.3 percent of the evening network TV news stories are reported by Hispanic correspondents, according to the Center for Media and Public Affairs.[30]

Pressure is mounting on networks to increase diversity for a variety of reasons revolving around the diversity of the population as a whole, TV viewers, and consumers. For example, home and automobile buyers are increasingly diverse, reflecting the increasing diversity of the population as a whole.[31] Moreover, managers have to be especially sensitive to avoid stereotyping different groups when they communicate with potential customers. For example, Toyota Motor Sales USA made a public apology to the Reverend Jesse Jackson and his Rainbow Coalition for using a print advertisement depicting an African American man with a Toyota RAV4 sport utility image embossed on his gold front tooth.[32]

One of Toyota's competitors, Nissan Motor Co., has also come under pressure for its treatment of diverse customers. According to the *New York Times,* Nissan charges African American customers more for car loans than they do white buyers. In the two states with the highest amount of overcharging, Maryland and Wisconsin, African-American customers paid, on average, $800 more in financing fees than white customers.[33] Some of the customers who have been overcharged are suing Nissan. Their attorney, Gary Klein, indicated that other automakers engage in similar discriminatory practices. Nissan has stated that discrimination is prohibited in their company. The courts will ultimately decide the outcome of the case.[34] Actions such as these and those by the Rainbow Coalition are beneficial in that they signal to managers and their organizations that diverse stakeholders not only expect to be treated fairly and with respect but also if they are not treated in this manner, organizational effectiveness might suffer.[35] For example, in response to the Toyota ad that stereotyped African Americans as well as another offensive ad published a few years earlier, Jesse Jackson threatened to start a boycott of Toyota vehicles. As Jackson put it, "As Toyota's profits continue to climb, so does its obligation to market its products in a professional and respectful manner."[36]

Religion

Title VII of the Civil Rights Act prohibits discrimination based on religion (as well as based on race/ethnicity, country of origin, and sex, see Table 4.1 and Chapter 11). In addition to Title VII, in 1997 the federal government issued "The White House Guidelines on Religious Exercise and Expression in the Federal Workplace."[37] These guidelines, while technically only applicable in federal offices, also are frequently relied on by large corporations. The guidelines require employers to make reasonable accommodations for religious practices such as observances of holidays as long as it does not entail major costs or hardships.[38]

A key issue for managers when it comes to religious diversity is recognizing and being aware of different religions and their beliefs with particular attention being paid to when religious holidays fall. For example, critical meetings should not be scheduled during a holy day for members of a certain faith and managers should be willing to be flexible in allowing people time off for religious observances. According to Lobna Ismail, director of a diversity training company in Silver Spring, Maryland, when managers acknowledge, respect, and make even small accommodations for religious diversity, employee loyalty is often enhanced. For example, allowing employees to leave work early on certain days instead of taking a lunch break or posting holidays for different religions on the company calendar can go a long way toward making individuals of diverse religions feel respected and valued as well as enabling them to practice their faith.[39]

Capabilities/Disabilities

The Americans with Disabilities Act (ADA) of 1990 prohibits discrimination against those with disabilities and also requires employers to make reasonable accommodations to allow the disabled to effectively perform their jobs. In force for more than a decade, the ADA is not uncontroversial. On the surface, few would argue with the intent of this legislation. However, as managers attempt to implement policies and procedures to comply with the ADA, they face a number of interpretation and fairness challenges.

On the one hand, some people with real disabilities warranting workplace accommodations are hesitant to reveal their disabilities to their employers so that they can receive the accommodations they deserve.[40] On the other hand, there are anecdotes of employees abusing the ADA and seeking unnecessary accommodations for disabilities that may or may not exist.[41] Thus, perhaps, it is not surprising that the passage of the ADA does not appear to have increased employment rates significantly for those with disabilities.[42] A key challenge for managers is to promote an environment in which those needing accommodations feel comfortable disclosing their need to managers while making sure that the accommodations both enable disabled employees to effectively perform their jobs and are perceived to be fair by those not disabled.[43]

In addressing this challenge, often managers must educate both themselves and their employees about the disabilities, as well as the very real capabilities, of those who are disabled. For example, during Disability Awareness Week 2001, administrators at the University of Houston (UH) sought to increase the public's knowledge of disabilities while also heightening awareness of the abilities of the disabled. Their program was called "Think Ability."[44] According to Cheryl Amoruso, director of the UH Center for Students with Disabilities, many people are unaware of the prevalence of disabilities as well as misinformed about their consequences. For example, she suggests that just because students may not be able to see, they can still excel in their coursework.[45] Accommodations enabling such students to perform up to their capabilities are covered under the ADA.

The ADA also protects employees with acquired immune deficiency syndrome (AIDS) from being discriminated against in the workplace. AIDS is caused by the human immunodeficiency virus (HIV) and is transmitted through sexual contact, infected needles, and contaminated blood products. HIV is not spread through casual, nonsexual contact. Yet, out of ignorance, fear, or prejudice, some people wish to avoid all contact with anyone infected with HIV. Infected individuals may not necessarily develop AIDS and some individuals with HIV are able to remain effective performers of their jobs, while not putting others at risk.[46]

AIDS awareness training can help people overcome their fears and also provide managers with a tool to prevent illegal discrimination against HIV-infected employees. Such training focuses on educating employees about HIV and AIDS, dispelling myths, communicating relevant organizational policies, and emphasizing the rights of HIV-positive employees to privacy and an environment that allows them to be productive.[47] The need for AIDS awareness training is underscored by some of the problems HIV-positive employees experience once others in their workplace become aware of their condition (see the following "Focus on Diversity").

Focus on Diversity

The ADA and HIV/AIDS in the Workplace

The Equal Employment Opportunity Commission received over 2,100 complaints from 1992 to 1999 from individuals who claimed they were discriminated against because of HIV. Such complaints are likely to increase in light of a recent Supreme Court ruling indicating that federal laws prohibit discrimination based on testing positive for HIV.[48] Moreover, organizations are required to make reasonable accommodations to enable people with AIDS to effectively perform their jobs.

Thus, managers have an obligation to educate employees about HIV and AIDS, dispel myths and the stigma of AIDS, and ensure that HIV-related discrimination is not occurring in the workplace. For example, Home Depot has provided HIV training and education to more than 700 store managers; such training was sorely needed given over half of the managers indicated it was the first time they had the opportunity to talk about AIDS.[49] Currently, an estimated 900,000 people in the United States are infected with HIV and approximately 40,000 new HIV infections occur each year. Most of these new cases are in the working population (18–49 year olds) and advances in medication and treatment mean that more infected individuals are able to continue working or are able to return to work after their condition improves.[50] On a global level, AIDS is at epidemic levels in Africa and South and Southeast Asia; unfortunately many infected individuals in these countries are not receiving treatment nor are enough steps being taken to halt the spread of AIDS.[51] According to the World Health Organization, over 23.4 million adults in subSaharan Africa alone have AIDS.[52]

In the United States, managers and organizations that do not treat HIV-positive employees in a fair manner as well as provide reasonable accommodations (e.g., allowing time off for doctor visits or to take medicine) risk costly lawsuits. Take the case of Richard Kelly, a 43-year old investment banker who has filed a $75 million lawsuit against a unit of the Canadian Imperial Bank of Commerce.[53] According to Kelly, he was viewed as a star performer and received positive feedback from his superiors until they learned that he was HIV-positive. Once his HIV status was known in the company, Kelly was discriminated against, demoted, and eventually fired. While representatives for the bank deny these allegations, the courts will ultimately decide the merits of the suit.[54] In any case, lawsuits such as Kelly's underscore the importance of HIV/AIDS education and training in the workplace to ensure that discrimination on this basis does not occur and is not tolerated.

Socioeconomic Background

Socioeconomic background typically refers to a combination of social class and income-related factors. From a management perspective, socioeconomic diversity (and in particular, diversity in income levels) requires managers to be sensitive and responsive to the needs and concerns of those who might not be as well off as others. U.S. welfare reform in the mid- to late-1990s emphasized the need for single mothers and others receiving public assistance to join or return to the workforce. In conjunction with a strong economy, this led to record declines in the number of families, households, and children living below the poverty level, according to the 2000 U.S. census.[55] However, the economic downturn in the early 2000s, along with increased terrorism, and the tragic collapse of the World Trade Center in New York City, resulted in domestic and international repercussions. These suggest that some past gains which lifted families out of poverty, have been reversed. In a very strong economy, it is much easier for poor people with few skills to find jobs; in a weak economy when companies lay off employees in hard times, unfortunately people who need their income the most are often the first to lose their jobs.[56]

In any case, even with all the gains from the 1990s, the U.S. Census estimates that 6,825,399 families' income was below the poverty level in 2000, with 3,581,475 of these families being headed by single women.[57] The U.S. Census Bureau relies on predetermined threshold income figures, based on family size and composition, adjusted annually for inflation, to determine the poverty level. Families whose income falls below the threshold level are considered poor.[58] Thus, for example, in 2000 a family of four with two children under 18 was considered poor if their annual income fell below $17,463.[59] When workers earn less than $10 or $15 per hour, it is often difficult, if not impossible, for them to meet their families' needs.[60] Moreover, increasing numbers of families are facing the challenge of finding suitable child care arrangements that enable them to work long hours and/or through the night to maintain an adequate income level. New information technology has also lead to more and more businesses operating 24 hours a day, creating real challenges for workers on the night shift, especially those with children.[61]

Hundreds of thousands of parents across the country are scrambling to find someone to care for their children while working the night shift, commuting several hours a day, working weekends and holidays, or putting in long hours on one or more jobs. This has led to the opening of day care facilities that operate round the clock as well as managers seeking to provide such care for their employees with children. For example, the Children's Choice Learning Center in Las Vegas, Nevada, operates round the clock for employees working nights in neighboring casinos as cashiers and dealers as well as nurses, hospital workers, and call-center operators on the night shift. Randy Donahue, a security guard who works until midnight picks his children up from the center when he gets off work; his wife is a nurse on the night shift. There currently are five Children's Choice Learning Centers in the U.S. operating 24 hours a day and plans are underway to add seven more.[62]

Judy Harden, who focuses on families and child care issues for the United Auto Workers Union, indicates that the demands families are facing necessitate round-the-clock and odd-hours child care options. Many parents simply do not have the choice of working hours that allow them to take care of their children at night and/or on weekends, never mind when the children are sick.[63] In 1993, Ford Motor Company built a round the clock child care facility for 175 children of employees in Livonia, Michigan. However, a recent survey of child care needs indicated that many employees in other locations such as Detroit and Kansas City require such a facility. Some parents and psychologists feel uneasy having children separated from their families for so much time and particularly at night. Most agree that unfortunately for many families this is not a choice but a necessity.[64]

Socioeconomic diversity suggests that managers need to be sensitive and responsive to the needs and concerns of workers who may be less fortunate than themselves in terms of income and financial resources, child care and elder care options, housing opportunities, and sources of social and family support. Moreover–and equally important–managers should try to provide such individuals opportunities to learn, advance, and make meaningful contributions to their organizations while improving their economic well-being (see the following "Ethics in Action").

Ethics in Action

Martha Williams: Successful and Socially Responsible

Martha Williams grew up in poverty in one of Chicago's public housing projects.[65] Her first job after graduating from high school was an entry level position in Republic Molding, a plastics molding plant in Niles, Illinois.[66] Williams commuted two hours each way for her position that paid the minimum wage. And the rest has been history.[67]

From her first few days on the job, Williams was intrigued and motivated to learn as much as she could about plastics manufacturing. She worked her way up the hierarchy to the position of plant manager within eight years. After remaining in that position for 10 years, Williams realized that the glass ceiling was hampering her progress and she decided to start her own business. In 1991, Williams launched Stylemaster and her company has gone on to win awards for its plastic containers.[68] Stylemaster is growing and successful, a tribute to William's determination even in the face of adversity (e.g., a bankruptcy in the 1990s and a cancer diagnosis).[69]

Williams is also determined to give back to the community in which she grew up and provide its young people with opportunities she didn't have herself. For example, rather than move her company to a building in the suburbs to accommodate the need for more space, Williams decided to locate her company in economically depressed southwest Chicago to give back to this area and create several hundred new jobs. In fact, Williams was the first to commit to turning an illegal dumpsite into an industrial park by building the new Stylemaster plant on the site (of course, after an appropriate waste cleanup process). Other companies are now following her lead and the new Greater Southwest Industrial Park will enrich the area as well as provide jobs and income for nearby workers and their families.[70] As Williams puts it, "I truly wanted to be able to give back to the community, and to work with the city."[71]

Martha Williams, founder of Stylemaster, grew up in the housing projects on the south side of Chicago. After years of hard work, Williams returned to the area to celebrate the grand opening of her company's new factory, which is expected to bring 400 new jobs to the economically depressed area.

Sexual Orientation

A recent survey suggests that approximately 2.8 percent of men in the United States self-identify themselves as gay and 1.4 percent of women self-identify themselves as lesbian.[72] While no federal law prohibits discriminations based on sexual orientation, 11 states have such laws, and a 1998 executive order prohibits sexual orientation discrimination in civilian federal offices. However, an increasing number of organizations recognize the minority status of gay and lesbian employees, affirm their rights to fair and equal treatment, and provide benefits to same-sex partners of gay and lesbian employees. For example, over 20 percent of the Fortune 500 companies provide domestic-partner benefits, and DaimlerChrysler, Ford, General Motors, and the United Auto Workers Union have endorsed the provision of domestic-partner benefits to the more than 400,000 workers they employ.[73]

For many managers and organizations providing these benefits is simply an ethical decision. There are also some very sound business rationales behind provision of domestic-partner benefits to gay and lesbian employees, as well as unmarried people, namely the attraction and retention of valuable employees.[74] Because gay and lesbian employees most commonly do not have young children to care for, these employees are frequently able to be flexible and assume jobs with work schedules that would be very difficult for employees with small children, such as shift or night work. For the same reason gay and lesbian employees are able to travel much more easily and spend considerable time away from their homes, which makes them especially suitable for jobs in sales, consulting, and travel services, especially on a global level. Additionally, many gays and lesbians are particularly attracted to and suited for jobs in entertainment, arts, and advertising, as well as to those involving helping and providing service to other people such as nurses, doctors, and teachers.

Managers and the Effective Management of Diversity

The increasing diversity of the environment which, in turn, increases the diversity of an organization's workforce, increases the challenges managers face in effectively managing diversity. Each of the eight kinds of diversity discussed above presents managers with a particular set of issues and problems they need to appreciate before they can respond to them effectively. Understanding these issues is not always a simple matter as the managers at Deloitte & Touche discovered. Frequently research has to be done to help managers become aware of the many subtle and unobtrusive ways in which diverse employee groups can come to be treated unfairly over time. There are many more steps managers can take to become sensitive to the ongoing effects of diversity in their organizations and to avoid the pitfalls.

Critical Managerial Roles

In each of their managerial roles (see Chapter 1), managers can either promote the effective management of diversity or derail such efforts; thus, they are critical to this process. For example, in their interpersonal roles, managers can convey that the effective management of diversity is a valued goal and objective (figurehead role), can serve as a role model and institute policies and procedures to ensure that diverse organizational members are treated fairly (leader role), and enable diverse individuals and groups to coordinate their efforts and cooperate with each other both inside the organization and at the organization's boundaries (liaison role). In Table 4.2 we summarize some of the ways in which managers can ensure that diversity is effectively managed as they perform their different roles.

Given the formal authority that managers have in organizations, they typically have more influence than rank-and-file employees. When managers commit to supporting diversity, as was true at Deloitte & Touche, their authority and positions of power and status influence other members of an organization to make a similar commitment.[75] Research on social influence supports such a link as people are more likely to be influenced and persuaded by others who have high status.[76]

Moreover, when managers commit to diversity, their commitment legitimizes the diversity management efforts of others.[77] In addition, resources are devoted to such efforts and all members of an organization believe that their diversity-related efforts are supported and valued. Consistent with this reasoning, top management commitment and rewards for the support of diversity are often cited as critical ingredients for the success of diversity management initiatives.[78] Additionally, seeing managers express confidence in the abilities and talents of diverse employees causes other members to be similarly confident and help to reduce any misconceived misgivings they may have as a result of ignorance or stereotypes.[79]

Another important reason that managers are so central to the effective management of diversity hinges on two factors. The first factor is that women,

Table 4.2
Managerial Roles and the Effective Management of Diversity

Type of Role	Specific Role	Example
Interpersonal	Figurehead	Convey that the effective management of diversity is a valued goal and objective.
	Leader	Serve as a role model and institute policies and procedures to ensure that diverse members are treated fairly.
	Liaison	Enable diverse individuals to coordinate their efforts and cooperate with each other.
Informational	Monitor	Evaluate the extent to which diverse employees are being treated fairly.
	Disseminator	Inform employees about diversity policies and initiatives and the intolerance of discrimination.
	Spokesperson	Support diversity initiatives in the wider community and speak to diverse groups to interest them in career opportunities.
Decisional	Entrepreneur	Commit resources to develop new ways to effectively manage diversity and eliminate biases and discrimination.
	Disturbance Handler	Take quick action to correct inequalities and curtail discriminatory behavior.
	Resource Allocator	Allocate resources to support and encourage the effective management of diversity.
	Negotiator	Work with organizations (e.g., suppliers) and groups (e.g., labor unions) to support and encourage the effective management of diversity.

African Americans, Hispanics, and other minorities often start out at a slight disadvantage due to the ways in which they are perceived by others in organizations, particularly in work settings where they are a numerical minority. As Virginia Valian, a psychologist at Hunter College who studies gender indicates, "in most organizations women begin at a slight disadvantage. A woman does not walk into the room with the same status as an equivalent man, because she is less likely than a man to be viewed as a serious professional."[80]

The second factor is that research suggests slight differences in treatment can cumulate to result in major disparities over time. Even small differences–such as a very slight favorable bias for men receiving promotions–can lead to major differences in the number of male and female managers over time.[81] Thus, while women and other minorities are sometimes advised not to make "a mountain out of a molehill" when they perceive they have been unfairly treated, research conducted by Valian and others suggests that molehills (i.e., slight differences in treatment based on irrelevant distinctions such as race, gender, or ethnicity) can turn into mountains over time (i.e., major disparities in important outcomes such as promotions) if they are ignored.[82] Once again, managers play a crucial role in ensuring that neither large nor small disparities in treatment and outcomes due to irrelevant distinctions such as race or ethnicity occur in organizations. Moreover, managers have the obligation, both from an ethical and business perspective, to ensure that such disparities do not occur and are not tolerated in organizations.

The Ethical Imperative to Manage Diversity Effectively

Effectively managing diversity not only makes good business sense (which is discussed in the next section) but also is an ethical imperative in U.S. society. Two moral principles provide managers with guidance in their efforts to meet this imperative: distributive justice and procedural justice.

distributive justice
A moral principle calling for the distribution of pay raises, promotions, and other organizational resources to be based on meaningful contributions that individuals have made and not on personal characteristics over which they have no control.

DISTRIBUTIVE JUSTICE The principle of distributive justice dictates the fair distribution of pay raises, promotions, job titles, interesting job assignments, office space, and other organizational resources among members of an organization. The distribution of these outcomes should be based on the meaningful contributions that individuals have made to the organization (such as time, effort, education, skills, abilities, and performance levels) and not on irrelevant personal characteristics over which individuals have no control (such as gender, race, or age).[83] Managers have an obligation to ensure that distributive justice exists in their organizations. This does not mean that all members of an organization receive identical or similar outcomes; rather it means that members who receive more outcomes than others have made substantially higher or more significant contributions to the organization.

Is distributive justice common in organizations in corporate America? Probably the best way to answer this question is by saying that things are getting better. Fifty years ago, overt discrimination against women and minorities was not uncommon; today, organizations are inching closer toward the ideal of distributive justice. Statistics comparing the treatment of women and minorities with the treatment of white men suggest that most managers would need to take a proactive approach to achieve distributive justice in their organizations.

Women, for example, represent approximately 46 percent of the U.S. workforce yet only about 12 percent of corporate officers and boards of directors are women, less than 6 percent of employees with the highest status job titles are women, and only about 4 percent of women occupy positions with the highest earning levels.[84] And there are fewer than five female CEOs of Fortune 500 companies. These statistics should be considered in light of the fact that women hold 49 percent of professional and managerial positions in organizations.[85]

Women of color face an even harder glass ceiling to crack.[86] According to a recent study, women of color cite a lack of sponsors, mentors, networks, visible assignments, and role models as factors that can inhibit or slow their advancement in corporate America (see Figure 4.3).[87] According to the U.S. Bureau of Labor Statistics, for each dollar earned by white men, Hispanic, African American, and white women earn 56 cents, 67 cents, 78 cents respectively.[88]

In many countries, managers have not only an ethical obligation to strive to achieve distributive justice in their organizations but also a legal obligation to treat all employees fairly. They risk being sued by employees who believe that they are not being fairly treated. That is precisely what six African-American employees at Texaco did when they experienced racial bias and discrimination.[89]

procedural justice
A moral principle calling for the use of fair procedures to determine how to distribute outcomes to organizational members.

PROCEDURAL JUSTICE The principle of procedural justice requires managers to use fair procedures to determine how to distribute outcomes to organizational members.[90] This principle applies to typical procedures such as appraising subordinates' performance, deciding who should receive a raise or a promotion, and deciding whom to lay off when an organization is forced to

Figure 4.3
Women-of-color Managers Cite Barriers to Their Advancement

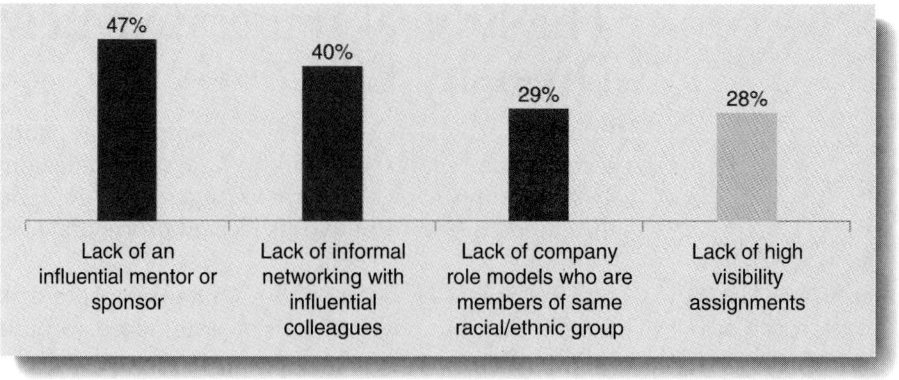

Source: 1999 Census of Women Corporate Officers and Top Earners and 1999 Census of Women Board Directors of Fortune 1000, and Catalyst Women of Color in Corporate Management: Opportunities and Barriers, 1999, www.catalystwomen.org, October 21, 2001.

downsize. Procedural justice exists, for example, when managers (1) carefully appraise a subordinate's performance, (2) take into account any environmental obstacles to high performance beyond the subordinate's control, such as lack of supplies, machine breakdowns, or dwindling customer demand for a product, and (3) ignore irrelevant personal characteristics such as the subordinate's age or ethnicity. Like distributive justice, procedural justice is necessary not only to ensure ethical conduct but also to avoid costly lawsuits, as illustrated in this "Focus on Diversity."

Focus on Diversity

Age Discrimination at Schering-Plough

A New Jersey court ordered Schering-Plough, a pharmaceutical maker based in Bordentown, New Jersey, to pay Fred Maiorino, a former salesman who was fired, $435,000 in punitive damages and $8 million in compensatory damages based on evidence that Maiorino's supervisors had engaged in age discrimination. Although Schering-Plough plans to appeal the decision, at the heart of the case is a series of actions and decisions that denied Maiorino procedural justice.

Maiorino worked for Schering-Plough for 35 years and had been commended for his sales performance. In his 60s, he repeatedly declined offers of early retirement. He reported that management's response to his decision was to institute a series of unfair procedures to make him look bad and to build a paper trail to justify his dismissal. Maiorino indicated that he was given very difficult sales goals to reach and was held to different and higher standards than other salespeople. He was accused of failing to meet work requirements without being informed of the requirements in advance. Schering-Plough's managers also spied on his house to see how early in the morning he left to start his sales rounds (while failing to take into account how late he worked in the evenings).

Even the procedures used to inform Maiorino, a 35-year company veteran, of his dismissal seem unjust. Maiorino's boss invited Maiorino to meet him one morning in a local diner for coffee. Maiorino assumed they were just going to chat prior to beginning their familiar routine of visiting doctors to discuss Schering-Plough's prescription drugs. Instead of having a pleasant conversation, however, the boss handed Maiorino a letter announcing his immediate termination. A few minutes later, Maiorino drove home and was followed by his boss and another Schering-Plough employee, who took all of Maiorino's sales materials and his company car. Maiorino was literally left standing in his driveway, unemployed–the last thing he had expected when he left home an hour earlier to start the workday.

Schering-Plough maintains that its treatment of Maiorino was appropriate and plans to appeal the court's decision. Several of Maiorino's former customers, however, agreed with the court and actually stopped prescribing Schering-Plough's drugs to protest the company's violation of procedural justice.[91]

Effectively Managing Diversity Makes Good Business Sense

The diversity of organizational members can be a source of competitive advantage, helping an organization provide customers with better goods and services.[92] The variety of points of view and approaches to problems and opportunities that diverse employees provide can improve managerial decision making. Suppose the Budget Gourmet frozen-food company is trying to come up with some creative ideas for new frozen dishes that will appeal to health-conscious time-conscious customers tired of the same old frozen-food fare. Which group do you think is likely to come up with the most creative ideas: a group of white women with master's degrees in marketing from Yale University who grew up in upper-middle-class families in the Northeast or a racially mixed group of men and women who grew up in families with varying income levels in different parts of the country and attended a mix of business schools (New York University, Oklahoma State, University of Michigan, UCLA, Cornell University, Texas A&M University, and Iowa State)? Most people would agree that the diverse group is likely to come up with a wider range of creative ideas. Although this example is simplistic, it underscores one way in which diversity can lead to a competitive advantage.

Just as the workforce is becoming increasingly diverse, so too are the customers who buy an organization's goods or services. In an attempt to suit local customers' needs and tastes, managers of Target's chain of 623 discount stores vary the selection of products available in stores in different cities and regions. For example, the Target store in Phoenix, Arizona, stocks religious candles and Spanish-language diskettes and Disney videos to appeal to local Hispanic Catholics; the Target store in Scottsdale, Arizona, stocks in-line skates and bicycle baby trailers that appeal to well-to-do yuppies.[93]

Diverse members of an organization are likely to be attuned to what goods and services diverse segments of the market want and do not want. Major car companies, for example, are increasingly assigning women to their design teams to ensure that the needs and desires of female customers (a growing segment of the market) are taken into account in new car design.

For Darden Restaurants, the business case for diversity rests on market share and growth. Darden seeks to satisfy the needs and tastes of diverse customers by providing menus in Spanish in communities with large Hispanic populations.[94] Similarly, market share and growth and the identification of niche markets lead Tracey Campbell to cater to disabled travelers.[95] She heads InnSeekers, a telephone and on-line listing resource for bed-and-breakfasts. Nikki Daruwala works for the Calvert Group in Bethesda, Maryland. This mutual fund emphasizes social responsibility and diversity. She indicates that profit alone is more than enough of an incentive to effectively manage diversity. As she puts it, "You can look at an automaker. There are more women making decisions about car buying or home buying . . . $3.72 trillion per year are spent by women."[96]

Another way in which the effective management of diversity can positively affect profitability is through increasing retention of valued employees by decreasing the costs of hiring replacements for those who quit as well as ensuring that all employees are highly motivated. In terms of retention, given the current legal environment, more and more organizations are attuned to the need to emphasize the importance of diversity in hiring. Once hired, if diverse employees think they are being unfairly treated, however, they will be likely to seek opportunities elsewhere. Thus, the recruiting of diverse employees has to be followed up by the ongoing effective management of diversity to retain these valued organizational members.

If diversity is not effectively managed so that turnover rates are higher for certain groups than others, profitability will suffer on several counts and most immediately and directly in the costs of hiring replacement workers. According to the Employment Management Association, on average it costs more than $10,000 to hire a new employee; other estimates are significantly higher. For example, Ernst & Young estimates it costs about $1,200,000 to replace 10 professionals and the diversity consulting firm Hubbard & Hubbard estimates replacement costs average one-and-a-half times an employee's annual salary.[97] Moreover, additional costs from failing to effectively manage diversity stem from time lost due to the barriers diverse members of an organization perceive as thwarting their progress and advancement.[98]

Effectively managing diversity makes good business sense for another reason. More and more, managers and organizations concerned about diversity are insisting that their suppliers also support diversity. Managers of American Airlines, for example, recently announced that all the law firms they hire must submit quarterly reports indicating the extent to which diverse employees worked on the airline's account. Similarly, managers at Chrysler, Aetna Life & Casualty, and General Motors all consider information about the extent to which law firms support diversity when they are deciding which law firms will represent them.[99] Managers in the Teachers Insurance and Annuity Association–College Retirement Equities Fund (TIAA-CREF) are putting pressure on Nucor Corporation to add women and minorities to its board of directors, which currently consists entirely of white men. TIAA-CREF owns 912,900 shares in Nucor, and its managers feel that their heavy investment in Nucor gives them enough clout to bring diversity to the board of directors.[100]

Finally, from both a business and an ethical perspective, the effective management of diversity is necessary to avoid costly lawsuits such as those settled by Advantica (owner of the Denny's chain) and the Coca-Cola Company. Recently Coca-Cola settled a class-action suit brought by African American employees to the tune of $192 million. The damage such lawsuits cause goes beyond the monetary awards to the injured parties and can tarnish a company's image. One positive outcome of Coca-Cola's recent settlement is their recognition of the need to commit additional resources to diversity management initiatives. In this regard, Coke is increasing its use of minority suppliers, instituting a formal mentoring program, and instituting days to celebrate diversity with its workforce.[101]

By now, it should be clear that effectively managing diversity is a necessity on both ethical and business grounds. This brings us to the question of why diversity presents managers and all of us with so many challenges; a question we address in the next section on perception.

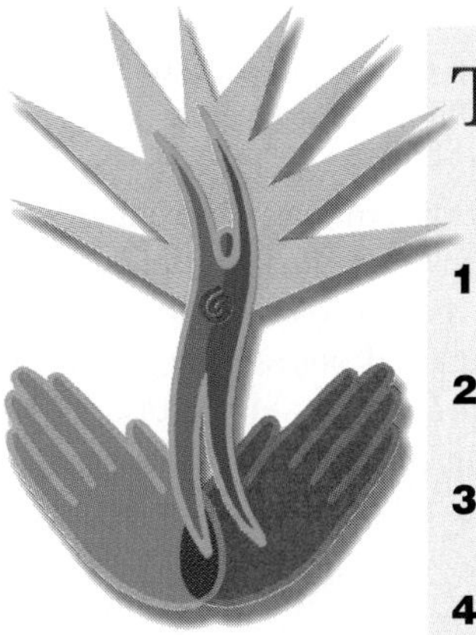

Tips for New Managers

Managing an **Increasingly Diverse** Workforce

1. Familiarize yourself with Economic Opportunity legislation and recent court rulings pertaining to diversity in the workforce.
2. Consider how you can more effectively manage diversity in the different roles you perform.
3. Periodically audit the units you oversee to ensure that diverse organizational members are being treated fairly and with respect.
4. Determine the business case for diversity in your units and share it with others.

Perception

Most people tend to think that the decisions managers make in organizations and the actions they take are the result of some objective determination of the issues involved and the surrounding situation. However, each manager's interpretation of a situation or even another person is precisely that–an interpretation. Nowhere are the effects of perception more likely to lead to different interpretations than in the area of diversity. This is because each person's interpretation of a situation, and subsequent response to it, is affected by his or her own age, race, gender, religion, socioeconomic status, capabilities, and sexual orientation. For example, different managers may see the same 21-year-old, black, male, gay, gifted and talented subordinate in different ways: One may see a creative maverick with a great future in the organization while another may see a potential troublemaker who needs to be watched closely. Different managers may even view what appears to be an objectively negative event–such as the increasing departure of talented women in "A Manager's Challenge"–in different ways. As happened in Deloitte & Touche some may see it as a future threat to the profitability of the company while others may view it as a result of women's desire to leave the workforce to have children. **Perception** is the process through which people select, organize, and interpret sensory input–what they see, hear, touch, smell, and taste–to give meaning and order to the world around them.[102] All decisions and actions that managers take are based on their subjective perceptions. When these perceptions are relatively accurate–close to the true nature of what is actually being perceived–good decisions are likely to be made and appropriate actions taken. Managers of fast-food restaurant chains such as McDonald's, Pizza Hut, and Wendy's accurately perceived that their customers were becoming more health conscious in the 1980s and 1990s and added salad bars and low-fat entrees to their menus. Managers at Kentucky Fried Chicken, Jack-in-the-Box, and Burger King took much longer to perceive this change in what customers wanted.

perception The process through which people select, organize, and interpret what they see, hear, touch, smell, and taste, to give meaning and order to the world around them.

One reason why McDonald's is so successful is that its managers go to great lengths to make sure that their perceptions of what customers want are accurate. McDonald's has 4,700 restaurants outside the United States (including 1,070 in Japan, 694 in Canada, 550 in Britain, 535 in Germany, 411 in Australia, 314 in France, 23 in China, and 3 in Russia) that generate approximately $3.4 billion in annual revenues. Key to McDonald's success in these diverse markets are managers' efforts to perceive accurately a country's culture and taste in food and then to act on these perceptions. For instance, McDonald's serves veggie burgers in Holland and black currant shakes in Poland.[103]

When managers' perceptions are relatively inaccurate, managers are likely to make bad decisions and take inappropriate actions, which hurt organizational effectiveness. Bad decisions concerning diversity for reasons of age, ethnicity, or sexual orientation may range from (1) not hiring qualified people, (2) failing to promote top-performing subordinates, who subsequently decide to take their skills to competing organizations, and (3) promoting poorly performing managers because they have the same "diversity profile" as the manager or managers making the decision.

Factors That Influence Managerial Perception

Several managers' perceptions of the same person, event, or situation are likely to differ because managers differ in personality, values, attitudes, and moods (see Chapter 3). Each of these factors can influence the way someone perceives a person or situation. An older middle manager who is high on openness to experience is likely to perceive the recruitment of able young managers as a positive learning opportunity; a similar middle manager who is low on openness to experience may perceive able younger subordinates as a threat. A manager who has high levels of job satisfaction and organizational commitment may perceive a job transfer to another department or geographic location which has very different employees (age, ethnicity, and so on) as an opportunity to learn and develop new skills. A dissatisfied, uncommitted manager may perceive the same transfer as a demotion.

schema An abstract knowledge structure that is stored in memory and makes possible the interpretation and organization of information about a person, event, or situation.

Managers' and all organizational members' perceptions about each other also are affected by their past experience and acquired knowledge about people, events, and situations organized into pre-existing schemas. **Schemas** are abstract knowledge structures stored in memory that allow people to organize and interpret information about a person, an event, or a situation.[104] Once a person develops a schema for a kind of person or event, any newly encountered person or situation that is related to the schema activates it and information is processed in ways consistent with the information stored in the schema. Thus, people tend to perceive others by using the expectations or preconceived notions contained in their schemas.[105] Once again, these expectations are derived from past experience and knowledge.

People tend to pay attention to information that is consistent with their schemas and ignore or discount inconsistent information. Thus, schemas tend to be reinforced and strengthened over time because people pay attention to information that is seen as confirming the schemas. This also results in schemas being resistant to change.[106] This does not mean that schemas never change; if that were the case, people could never adapt to changing conditions and learn from their mistakes. Rather, it suggests that schemas are slow to change and a considerable amount of contradictory information needs to be encountered for people to change their schemas.

Schemas, when they are relatively accurate depictions of the true nature of a person or situation, are functional because they help people make sense of the world around them. People are typically confronted with so much information that it is not possible to make sense of it without relying on schemas.

Schemas are dysfunctional when they are inaccurate because they cause managers and all members of an organization to perceive people and situations inaccurately and assume certain things that are not necessarily true. Recall from the opening case how some managers at Deloitte & Touche were guided by inaccurate schemas, leading to a male-dominated culture that caused women to leave the firm. For example, these schemas caused the managers to view a male subordinate as more capable of meeting a difficult challenge or interacting with high-level executives than a female simply based on the fact that he was a man rather than a woman.

gender schemas Preconceived beliefs or ideas about the nature of men and women, their traits, attitudes, behaviors, and preferences.

Psychologist Virginia Valian refers to these inaccurate preconceived notions of men and women as gender schemas. **Gender schemas** are a person's preconceived notions about the nature of men and women, their traits, attitudes, behaviors, and preferences.[107] Research suggests that among white, middle-class Americans, the following gender schemas are prevalent: men are action-oriented, assertive, independent, and task-focused; women are expressive, nurturing, and oriented toward and caring of other people.[108] Any schemas such as these that assume a single visible characteristic such as one's sex causes a person to possess specific traits and tendencies is bound to be inaccurate. For example, not all women are alike and not all men are alike and there are many women who are more independent and task-focused than men. Gender schemas can be learned in childhood and are reinforced in a number of ways in society. For example, while young girls may be encouraged by their parents to play with trucks and play tools (stereotypically masculine toys), boys generally are not encouraged, and sometimes actively discouraged from playing with dolls (stereotypically feminine toys).[109] As children grow up, they learn that occupations dominated by men have higher status than occupations dominated by women. Prior to the diversity initiatives at Deloitte & Touche in "A Manager's Challenge," women professionals learned that they would not advance as quickly or as far as their male counterparts despite their high performance. Why? Essentially because of managers' inaccurate gender schemas which led them to believe that women were less capable of handling difficult situations than men. Thus, managers shied away from giving women difficult assignments, assignments that typically lead to advancement in an organization.

Perception As a Determinant of Unfair Treatment

Even though most people would agree that distributive justice and procedural justice are desirable goals, diverse organizational members are sometimes treated unfairly, as previous examples illustrate. Why is this problem occurring? One important overarching reason is because of inaccurate perceptions. To the extent that managers and other members of an organization rely on inaccurate schemas such as gender schemas to guide their perceptions of each other, unfair treatment is likely to occur.

stereotype Simplistic and often inaccurate beliefs about the typical characteristics of particular groups of people.

Gender schemas are a kind of **stereotype,** simplistic and often inaccurate beliefs about the typical characteristics of particular groups of people. Stereo-

Harvard Pilgrim, a healthcare provider, uses role-playing training exercises to demonstrate to its employees the ways in which they may inadvertently stereotype their co-workers and customers. The workers all have cards on their caps that designate each of them with a certain attitude or personality. For example, the middle woman's card reads, "Agreeable."

types are usually based on a highly visible characteristic such as a person's age, gender, or race.[110] Managers who allow stereotypes to influence their perceptions assume erroneously that a person possesses a whole host of characteristics simply because she or he happens to be an Asian woman, a white man, or a lesbian, for example. African-American men are often stereotyped as good athletes, Hispanic women as subservient.[111] Obviously, there is no reason to assume that every African-American man is a good athlete or that every Hispanic woman is subservient. Stereotypes, however, lead people to make such erroneous assumptions. A manager who accepts stereotypes might, for example, decide not to promote a highly capable Hispanic woman into a management position because the manager is certain that she will not be assertive enough to supervise others.

bias The systematic tendency to use information about others in ways that result in inaccurate perceptions.

Inaccurate perceptions leading to unfair treatment of diverse members of an organization also can be due to biases. **Biases** are systematic tendencies to use information about others in ways that result in inaccurate perceptions. Because of the way biases operate, people often are unaware that their perceptions of others are inaccurate. There are several types of biases.

The similar-to-me effect is the tendency to perceive others who are similar to ourselves more positively than we perceive people who are different.[112] The similar-to-me effect is summed up by the saying, "Birds of a feather flock together." It can lead to unfair treatment of diverse employees simply because they are different from the managers who are perceiving them, evaluating them, and making decisions that affect their future in the organization.

Managers (particularly top managers) are likely to be white men. Although these managers may endorse the principles of distributive and procedural justice, they may unintentionally fall into the trap of perceiving other white men more positively than they perceive women and minorities. This is the similar-to-me effect. Being aware of this bias as well as using objective information about employees' capabilities and performance as much as possible in decision making about job assignments, pay raises, promotions, and other outcomes can help managers avoid the similar-to-me effect.

Social status, a person's real or perceived position in a society or an organization, can be the source of another bias. The social status effect is the tendency to perceive individuals with high social status more positively than we perceive those with low social status. A high-status person may be perceived as smarter and more believable, capable, knowledgeable, and responsible than a low-status person, even in the absence of objective information about either person.

Imagine being introduced to two people at a company Christmas party. Both are white men in their late 30s, and you learn that one is a member of the company's top-management team and the other is a supervisor in the mailroom. From this information alone, you are likely to assume that the top manager is smarter, more capable, more responsible, and even more interesting than the mailroom supervisor. Because women and minorities have traditionally had lower social status than white men, the social status effect may lead some people to perceive women and minorities less positively than they perceive white men.

Have you ever stood out in a crowd? Maybe you were the only man in a group of women, or maybe you were dressed formally for a social gathering when everyone else was in jeans. Salience–or conspicuousness–is another source of bias. The salience effect is the tendency to focus attention on individuals who are conspicuously different from us. When people are salient, they often feel as though all eyes are watching them, and this perception is not too far off the mark. Salient individuals are more often the object of attention than are other members of a work group, for example. A manager who has six white subordinates and one Hispanic subordinate reporting to her may inadvertently pay more attention to the Hispanic in group meetings because of the salience effect.

Individuals who are salient are often perceived to be primarily responsible for outcomes and operations and are evaluated more extremely, in either a positive or a negative direction.[113] Thus, when the Hispanic subordinate does a good job on a project, she receives excessive praise, and when she misses a deadline, she is excessively chastised.

Overt Discrimination

overt discrimination Knowingly and willingly denying diverse individuals access to opportunities and outcomes in an organization.

Inaccurate schemas and perceptual biases can lead well-meaning managers and organizational members to unintentionally discriminate against others due to their inaccurate perceptions. On the other hand, **overt discrimination,** or knowingly and willingly denying diverse individuals access to opportunities and outcomes in an organization, is intentional and deliberate. Overt discrimination is not only unethical but also illegal. Unfortunately, just as some managers steal from their organizations, others engage in overt discrimination.

Overt discrimination is a clear violation of the principles of distributive and procedural justice. Moreover, when managers are charged with overt discrimination, costly lawsuits can ensue as indicated in the following "Focus on Diversity".

Focus on Diversity

Charges of Gender Discrimination at Wal-Mart

In June of 2001, six Wal-Mart employees filed a class-action lawsuit against the retailer alleging widespread discrimination against women. Potentially the largest discrimination lawsuit targeting a private employer, the suit claims that women are assigned to the lowest-level positions in Wal-Mart and have little chance of advancement.[114]

While 72 percent of Wal-Mart employees are women, only about 33 percent of the managers at Wal-Mart are women. At Wal-Mart's main competitors, 56 percent of managers, on average, are women.[115] Kim Miller, a Wal-Mart sales associate and a party to the lawsuit, indicates that her performance was appraised positively, she received compliments from customers, and was honored with the Employee-of-the-Year Award. Yet she repeatedly was passed over for promotions over a nine year period and sometimes less qualified men received the promotions. Miller's complaints to managers fell on deaf ears and she believes she was even retaliated against for complaining in the first place.[116]

Stephanie Odle, another party to the lawsuit, commented that "I guess you could say I was Wal-Martized . . . I gave up my nights, my days, my weekends, my holidays. Time and again the jobs I should have had were given to men."[117] While six women are listed in the lawsuit, they are seeking class-action status on behalf of more than 700,000 former and current female Wal-Mart employees; this would allow them to collect damages on their behalf.[118] Joe Sellers, one of the lawyers for the women named in the suit puts it this way, "Wal-Mart has operated the largest glass ceiling for its women employees in the country and we want to shatter it . . . We want to dismantle the procedures and practices by which Wal-Mart has kept its female employees from getting promoted."[119] Wal-Mart denied the charges and it will be up to the courts to decide the ultimate outcome of this case.

How to Manage Diversity Effectively

Various kinds of barriers arise to managing diversity effectively in an organization. Some barriers have their origins in the person doing the perceiving; some in the information and schemas that have built up over time concerning the person being perceived. To overcome these barriers and effectively manage diversity, managers (and other organizational members) must possess or develop certain attitudes and values and the skills needed to change other people's attitudes and values.

Steps in Managing Diversity Effectively

Managers can take a number of steps to change attitudes and values and promote the effective management of diversity. Here, we describe these steps, some of which we have referred to previously (see Table 4.3).

SECURE TOP MANAGEMENT COMMITMENT As we mentioned earlier in the chapter, top management's commitment to diversity is crucial for the success of any diversity-related initiatives. Top managers need to develop the correct ethical values, and performance or business-oriented attitudes that allow them to make appropriate use of their human resources.

STRIVE TO INCREASE THE ACCURACY OF PERCEPTIONS One aspect of developing the appropriate values and attitudes is to take steps to increase the accuracy of their perceptions. Managers should consciously attempt to be open to other points of view and perspectives, seek them out, and encourage their subordinates to do the same.[120] Organizational members who are open to other perspectives put their own beliefs and knowledge to an important reality test and will be more inclined to modify or change them when nec-

Table 4.3
Promoting the Effective Management of Diversity

- Secure top management commitment.
- Increase the accuracy of perceptions.
- Increase diversity awareness.
- Increase diversity skills.
- Encourage flexibility.
- Pay close attention to how employees are evaluated.
- Consider the numbers.
- Empower employees to challenge discriminatory behaviors, actions, and remarks.
- Reward employees for effectively managing diversity.
- Provide training utilizing a multipronged, ongoing approach.
- Encourage mentoring of diverse employees.

essary. Managers should not be afraid to change their views about a person, issue, or event; moreover, they should encourage their subordinates to be open to changing their views in the light of disconfirming evidence.

INCREASE DIVERSITY AWARENESS It is natural for managers and other members of an organization to view other people from their own perspectives, because their own feelings, thoughts, attitudes, and experiences guide their perceptions and interactions. The ability to appreciate diversity, however, requires people to become aware of other perspectives and the various attitudes and experiences of others. Many diversity awareness programs in organizations strive to increase managers' and workers' awareness of (1) their own attitudes, biases, and stereotypes and (2) the differing perspectives of diverse managers, subordinates, coworkers, and customers. Diversity awareness programs often have these goals:[121]

- Providing organizational members with accurate information about diversity
- Uncovering personal biases and stereotypes
- Assessing personal beliefs, attitudes, and values and learning about other points of view
- Overturning inaccurate stereotypes and beliefs about different groups
- Developing an atmosphere in which people feel free to share their differing perspectives and points of view
- Improving understanding of others who are different from oneself

INCREASE DIVERSITY SKILLS Efforts to increase diversity skills focus on improving the way managers and their subordinates interact with each other and on improving their ability to work with different kinds of people.[122] An important issue here is being able to communicate with diverse employees. Diverse organizational members may have different styles of communication, may differ in their language fluency, may use words differently, may differ in the nonverbal signals they send through facial expression and body language, and may differ in the way they perceive and interpret information. Managers and their subordinates must learn to communicate effectively with one another if an organization is to take advantage of the skills and abilities of its diverse workforce. Educating organizational members about differences in ways of communicating is often a good starting point.

Organizational members should also feel comfortable enough to "clear the air" and solve communication difficulties and misunderstandings as they occur rather than letting problems grow and fester without acknowledgment.

Diversity education can help managers and subordinates gain a better understanding of how people may interpret certain kinds of comments. Diversity education also can help employees learn how to resolve misunderstandings.

ENCOURAGE FLEXIBILITY Managers and their subordinates must learn how to be open to different approaches and ways of doing things. This does not mean that organizational members have to suppress their personal styles. Rather, it means that they must be open to, and not feel threatened by, different approaches and perspectives, and they must have the patience and flexibility needed to understand and appreciate diverse perspectives.

To the extent it is feasible, managers should also be flexible enough to incorporate the differing needs of diverse employees. Earlier we mentioned how religious diversity suggests that people of certain religions might need time off for holidays that are traditionally workdays in the United States; managers need to anticipate and respond to such requests with flexibility (e.g., letting people skip the lunch hour so they can leave work early). Moreover, flexible work hours, having the option to work from home, and cafeteria style benefit plans (see Chapter 11) are just a few of the many ways in which managers can be responsive to the differing needs of diverse employees while enabling them to be effective contributors to an organization.

PAY CLOSE ATTENTION TO HOW ORGANIZATIONAL MEMBERS ARE EVALUATED Whenever feasible, it is desirable to rely on objective performance indicators (see Chapter 11) as these are less subject to bias. When objective indicators are not available or are inappropriate, managers should ensure that adequate time and attention are focused on the evaluation of employees' performance and evaluators are held accountable for their evaluations.[123] Moreover, vague performance standards should be avoided.[124]

CONSIDER THE NUMBERS Recall from "A Manager's Challenge" how Deloitte & Touche realized it had a diversity problem by the fact that very few women held high positions in the firm. Looking at the numbers of members of different minority groups and women in various positions, at various levels in the hierarchy, in locations that differ in their desirability, and in any other relevant categorizations in an organization can provide managers with important information about potential problems and ways to rectify them, as it did for Deloitte & Touche.[125]

EMPOWER EMPLOYEES TO CHALLENGE DISCRIMINATORY BEHAVIORS, ACTIONS, AND REMARKS Managers should strive to create an organizational culture (see Chapter 3) that has zero tolerance for discrimination. As part of such a culture, organizational members should feel empowered to challenge discriminatory behavior whether the behavior is directed at them or they witness discriminatory behavior being directed at another employee.[126]

REWARD EMPLOYEES FOR EFFECTIVELY MANAGING DIVERSITY If the effective management of diversity is a valued organizational objective, then employees should be rewarded for their contributions to this objective.[127] For example, after settling a major race discrimination lawsuit, Coca-Cola Company now ties managers' pay to their achievement of diversity goals.

PROVIDE TRAINING UTILIZING A MULTIPRONGED, ONGOING APPROACH Many managers such as Cooke in "A Manager's Challenge" use a multipronged approach to increase diversity awareness and skills in their organizations; they use films and printed materials supplemented by experiential exercises to uncover hidden biases and stereotypes. Sometimes simply providing a forum for people to learn about and discuss their differing attitudes, values, and experiences can be a powerful means for increasing awareness. Also useful are role-plays that enact problems resulting from lack of awareness and indicate the increased understanding that comes from appreciating others' viewpoints. Accurate information and training experiences can debunk stereotypes. Group exercises, role-plays, and diversity-related experiences can help organizational members develop the skills they need to work effectively with a variety of people.

Managers sometimes hire outside consultants to provide diversity training. Some organizations have their own diversity experts in-house. Digital Equipment Corporation, for example, has a diversity management department, called "Valuing Differences," similar to other departments such as marketing or finance.[128]

United Parcel Service (UPS), a package delivery company, developed an innovative community internship program to increase the diversity awareness and skills of its managers and at the same time benefit the wider community. Upper- and middle-managers participating in the program take one month off

UPS managers, as part of its "Community Internship Program," work in a soup kitchen for the homeless to learn about problems and opportunities in dealing with people who are different from themselves.

the job to be community interns. They work in community organizations helping people who in many instances are very different from themselves–such organizations include a detention center in McAllen, Texas, for Mexican immigrants; homeless shelters; AIDS centers; Head Start programs; migrant farmworker assistance groups; and groups aiming to halt the spread of drug abuse in inner cities. Approximately 40 managers a year are community interns at an annual cost to UPS of $400,000.

Since the program began in 1968, 800 managers have been community interns. Interacting with and helping diverse people enhances the interns' awareness of diversity because they experience it firsthand. Bill Cox, a UPS division manager who spent a month in the McAllen detention center, summed up his experience of diversity: "You've got these [thousands of] migrant workers down in McAllen . . . and they don't want what you have. All they want is an opportunity to earn what you have. That's a fundamental change in understanding that only comes from spending time with these people."[129]

Many managers who complete the UPS community internship program have superior diversity skills as a result of their experiences. During their internships, they learn about different cultures and approaches to work and life; they learn to interact effectively with people with whom they ordinarily do not come into contact; and they are forced to learn flexibility because of the dramatic difference between their role at the internship site and their role as manager at UPS.

ENCOURAGE MENTORING OF DIVERSE EMPLOYEES Unfortunately, African Americans and other minorities continue to be less likely to attain high level positions in their organizations, and for those who do, their climb up the corporate ladder typically takes longer than for white men. David Thomas, a professor at the Harvard Business School has studied the careers of minorities in corporate America. One of his major conclusions is that mentoring is very important for minorities, most of whom have reached high levels in their organizations by having a solid network of mentors and contacts.[130] **Mentoring** is a process by which an experienced member of an organization (the mentor) provides advice and guidance to a less experienced member (the protégé) and helps the less experienced member learn how to advance in the organization and in his or her career. This was the system adopted by DeLoitte & Touche.

mentoring A process by which an experienced member of an organization (the mentor) provides advice and guidance to a less experienced member (the protégé) and helps the less experienced member learn how to advance in the organization and in his or her career.

According to Thomas, effective mentoring is more than providing instruction, offering advice, helping build skills, and sharing technical expertise. Of course, these aspects of mentoring are important and necessary. However, equally important is developing a high quality, close, and supportive relationship with a mentor. Emotional bonds between a mentor and a protégé can enable a protégé, for example, to express fears and concerns, and sometimes even reluctance to follow a mentor's advice. The mentor can then help the protégé build his or her confidence and feel comfortable engaging in unfamiliar work behaviors.[131]

Pat Carmichael, a senior vice president at JP Morgan Chase who happens to be an African-American woman has mentored hundreds of protégés throughout her career and exemplifies effective mentoring.[132] She encourages her protégés to seek out difficult assignments and feedback from their supervisors. She also helps her protégés build networks of contacts and has a very extensive network herself. She serves as both a coach and a counselor to her protégés and encourages them to seek out opportunities to address their weaknesses and broaden their horizons.[133]

Tips for New Managers

Managing **Diversity**

1. Consider ways in which your perceptions of your subordinates might be unintentionally biased or inaccurate.
2. Make sure your subordinates receive training to increase their diversity awareness and skills.
3. Find creative ways to flexibly address the needs of diverse employees.
4. Communicate the importance of zero tolerance for discrimination and empower your subordinates to actively promote this policy.
5. Make sure your subordinates are being effectively mentored.

Sexual Harassment

Sexual harassment seriously damages both the people who are harassed and the reputation of the organization in which it occurs. It also can cost organizations large amounts of money. In 1995, for example, Chevron Corporation agreed to pay $2.2 million to settle a sexual harassment lawsuit filed by four women who worked at Chevron Information Technology Company in San Ramon, California. One woman involved in the suit said that she had received violent pornographic material through the company mail. Another, an electrical engineer, said that she had been asked to bring pornographic videos to Chevron workers at an Alaska drill site.[134] More recently, TWA settled a lawsuit to the tune of $2.6 million which alleged that female employees were sexually harassed at JFK International Airport in New York. According to the EEOC, sexual harassment was not only tolerated at TWA but also company officials did little to curtail it when it was brought to their attention.[135]

Unfortunately, what happened at Chevron and TWA are not isolated incidents. Sixty percent of the 607 women surveyed by the National Association for Female Executives indicated that they had experienced some form of sexual harassment.[136] Women are the most frequent victims of sexual harassment; particularly those in male-dominated occupations or those who occupy positions stereotypically associated with certain gender relationships such as a female secretary reporting to a male boss. Less frequently, men can be victims of sexual harassment. For instance, several male employees at Jenny Craig who filed a lawsuit said that they were subject to lewd and inappropriate comments from female coworkers and managers.[137] Sexual harassment is not only unethical; it is also illegal. Managers have an ethical obligation to ensure that they, their coworkers, and their subordinates never engage in sexual harassment, even unintentionally.

Forms of Sexual Harassment

quid pro quo sexual harassment Asking for or forcing an employee to perform sexual favors in exchange for some reward or to avoid negative consequences.

There are two basic forms of sexual harassment: quid pro quo sexual harassment and hostile work environment sexual harassment. **Quid pro quo sexual harassment** occurs when a harasser asks or forces an employee to perform sexual favors to keep a job, receive a promotion, receive a raise, obtain some other work-related opportunity, or avoid receiving negative consequences such as demotion or dismissal.[138] This "Sleep with me, honey, or you're fired" form of harassment is the more extreme form of harassment and leaves no doubt in anyone's mind that sexual harassment has taken place.[139]

hostile work environment sexual harassment Telling lewd jokes, displaying pornography, making sexually oriented remarks about someone's personal appearance, and other sex-related actions that make the work environment unpleasant.

Hostile work environment sexual harassment is more subtle. **Hostile work environment sexual harassment** occurs when organizational members are faced with an intimidating, hostile, or offensive work environment because of their sex.[140] Lewd jokes, sexually oriented comments, displays of pornography, displays or distribution of sexually oriented objects, and sexually oriented remarks about one's physical appearance are examples of hostile work environment sexual harassment. A hostile work environment interferes with organizational members' ability to perform their jobs effectively and has been deemed illegal by the courts. Managers who engage in hostile work environment harassment or allow others to do so risk costly lawsuits for their organizations, as evidenced by the experience of Chevron.

Steps Managers Can Take to Eradicate Sexual Harassment

Managers have an ethical obligation to eradicate sexual harassment in their organizations. There are many ways to accomplish this objective. Here are four initial steps that managers can take to deal with the problem.[141]

- Develop and clearly communicate a sexual harassment policy endorsed by top management. This policy should include prohibitions against both quid pro quo and hostile work environment sexual harassment. It should contain (1) examples of types of behavior that are unacceptable, (2) a procedure for employees to use to report instances of harassment, (3) a discussion of the disciplinary actions that will be taken when harassment has taken place, and (4) a commitment to educate and train organizational members about sexual harassment.
- Use a fair complaint procedure to investigate charges of sexual harassment. Such a procedure should (1) be managed by a neutral third party, (2) ensure that complaints are dealt with promptly and thoroughly, (3) protect and fairly treat victims, and (4) ensure that alleged harassers are fairly treated.
- When it has been determined that sexual harassment has taken place, take corrective actions as soon as possible. These actions can vary depending on the severity of the harassment. When harassment is extensive, prolonged over a period of time, of a quid pro quo nature, or severely objectionable in some other manner, corrective action may include firing the harasser.
- Provide sexual harassment education and training to organizational members, including managers. The majority of Fortune 500 firms currently provide this education and training for their employees. Managers at Du Pont, for example, developed Du Pont's "A Matter of Respect" program to help educate employees about sexual harassment and eliminate its occurrence. The program includes a four-hour workshop in which participants are given information that defines sexual harassment, sets forth the company's policy against it, and explains how to report complaints and access a 24-hour hotline. Participants watch video clips showing actual instances of harassment. One clip shows a saleswoman having dinner with a male client who, after much negotiating, seems about to give her company his business when he suddenly suggests that they continue their conversation in his hotel room.

The Navy is not alone in its fight against sexual harassment. Shown here is a U.S. Army anti-sexual harassment poster, introduced as a part of the Army's campaign to discourage and eliminate incidents of sexual harassment such as those that surfaced in 1996

The saleswoman is confused about what to do. Will she be reprimanded if she says no and the deal is lost? After watching a video, participants discuss what they have seen, why the behavior is inappropriate, and what organizations can do to alleviate the problem.[142] Throughout the program, managers stress to employees that they do not have to tolerate sexual harassment or get involved in situations in which harassment is likely to occur.

Other organizations that are proactively addressing the sexual harassment problem are Corning, Digital Equipment, and the U.S. Navy. Digital Equipment Corporation offers a full-day training program that educates employees about the different forms of sexual harassment and makes extensive use of role-playing.[143] In the wake of the much-publicized Tailhook scandal–Navy and Marine Corps pilots sexually harassed naval aviators at a convention in Las Vegas–the Navy is trying to eradicate sexual harassment and improve its managing of diversity (and its pubic image). All members of the Navy, regardless of rank, are educated about appropriate and inappropriate behavior. Men and women who have committed sexual harassment offenses have been discharged. Eighteen courses are offered on issues surrounding sexual harassment, and all members of the Navy are required to participate in continuous training. Evidence that these initiatives were sorely needed comes from the Navy's toll-free sexual harassment advice line. During its first four months of operation, 500 calls were received.[144]

In June 1998 the Supreme Court announced some important rulings concerning both an employee's and a company's responsibilities in trying to prevent sexual harassment. These guidelines are summarized in the following "Ethics in Action" reprinted from *Business Week*.[145]

Ethics in Action

Finally, a Corporate Tip Sheet on Sexual Harassment

A chill wind ran through corporate boardrooms on June 26 as the Supreme Court handed down two landmark rulings on sexual harassment. The justices ruled that companies can be held liable for a supervisor's sexually harassing behavior even if the offense was never reported to management. And the high court said an employer can be liable when a supervisor threatens to punish a worker for resisting sexual demands–even if such threats aren't carried out.

At first blush, the decisions sound like a prescription for a flood of new lawsuits. But take a deep breath, Corporate America. There's actually some good news for employers in the fine print of the justices' decisions. For the first time, the court is giving companies guidelines on how to protect themselves against sexual-harassment charges. There are no guarantees, of course. But, if companies get serious about stamping out harassment and sustain the efforts, they can be better protected in court–and their employees can feel safer at work.

The court's advice: Develop a zero-tolerance policy on harassment, communicate it to employees, and ensure that victims can report abuses without fear of retaliation. "Employers should feel safe as long as they are vigorous," says Susan R. Meisinger, senior vice president at the Society for Human Resource Management.

So even though the court has broadened the conditions under which suits can be brought, a company can deflect sexual-harassment charges with a two-pronged "affirmative defense," the justices said. First, it must take "reasonable care to prevent and correct promptly any sexually harassing behavior." Then, it must show that an employee failed to use internal procedures for reporting abusive behavior. This defense won't work when a supervisor retaliates against a worker for resisting sexual advances. But it will protect a company from charges that it tolerates a hostile work environment.

That means if a company has a strong antiharassment policy and a worker doesn't report an incident of sexual harassment and later sues, an employer can use that as part of a defense. Says Boston employment lawyer Marily D. Stempler: "The court places obligations on employers to set up policies, but it also places an obligation on the victim to come forward."

Not every nuance is spelled out. The court didn't describe, for example, what constitutes "reasonable care" for preventing or halting harassment. But employment consultants say companies should now publicize the policies as aggressively and regularly as possible–in handbooks, on posters, in training sessions, and in reminders in paychecks. Line supervisors and employees should be given real-life examples of what could constitute offensive conduct.

Companies also must ensure that workers won't face reprisals if they report offending behavior. Employment experts say companies should designate several managers to take these complaints, so that employees don't find themselves reporting to their immediate supervisor–very often the abuser. Managers should be trained in sexual-harassment issues. And, experts say, punishment against harassers should be swift and sure.

With legal costs for a jury trial running as high as $200,000, it's cheaper for most companies to put in place a basic sexual-harassment program. Still, none of this is simple. Small companies may not have the expertise to investigate complaints. And for all companies, once a complaint is filed, employers will face increased pressure to sort out who's telling the truth and to mete out serious punishments.

But by both expanding a company's potential liability and offering a valid defense, the Supreme Court noted that it was giving employers "an incentive to prevent and eliminate harassment." That means companies can protect themselves while doing right by their workers. That's an opportunity for Corporate America, not a threat.

Summary and Review

MANAGERS' CRITICAL ROLE IN MANAGING DIVERSITY Both the workforce and the organizational environment are increasingly diverse and effectively managing this diversity is an essential component of management. In each of their managerial roles, managers can encourage the effective management of diversity which is both an ethical and a business imperative.

PERCEPTION Perception is the process through which people select, organize, and interpret sensory input to give meaning and order to the world around them. It is inherently subjective. Schemas guide perception; when schemas are based on a single visible characteristic such as race or gender, they are stereotypes and highly inaccurate leading to unfair treatment. Unfair treatment also can result from biases and overt discrimination.

HOW TO MANAGE DIVERSITY EFFECTIVELY There are a number of steps that managers can take to effectively manage diversity. The effective management of diversity is an ongoing process that requires frequent monitoring.

SEXUAL HARASSMENT Two forms of sexual harassment are quid pro quo sexual harassment and hostile work environment sexual harassment. Steps that managers can take to eradicate sexual harassment include development and communication of a sexual harassment policy endorsed by top management, use of fair complaint procedures, prompt corrective action when harassment occurs, and sexual harassment training and education.

Management in Action

Topics for Discussion and Action

1. Discuss why violations of the principles of distributive and procedural justice continue to occur in modern organizations. What can managers do to uphold these principles in their organizations?
2. Why do gay and lesbian workers and workers who test positive for HIV sometimes get discriminated against?
3. Why would some employees resent accommodations made for the disabled that are dictated by the Americans with Disabilities Act?
4. Discuss the ways in which schemas can be functional and dysfunctional.
5. Discuss an occasion when you may have been treated unfairly because of stereotypical thinking. What stereotypes were applied to you? How did they result in you being treated unfairly?
6. How does the similar-to-me effect influence your own behavior and decisions?
7. Why is mentoring particularly important for minorities?
8. Why is it important to consider the numbers of different groups of employees at various levels in an organization's hierarchy?
9. Think about a situation in which you would have benefited from mentoring but a mentor was not available. What could you have done to try to get the help of a mentor in this situation?
10. Choose a Fortune 500 company not mentioned in the chapter. Conduct library research to determine what steps this organization has taken to effectively manage diversity and eliminate sexual harassment.

Building Management Skills

Solving Diversity-Related Problems

Think about the last time that you (1) were treated unfairly because you differed from a decision maker on a particular dimension of diversity or (2) observed someone else being treated unfairly because that person differed from a decision maker on a particular dimension of diversity. Then answer these questions.

1. Why do you think the decision maker acted unfairly in this situation?
2. In what ways, if any, were biases, stereotypes, or overt discrimination involved in this situation?
3. Was the decision maker aware that he or she was acting unfairly?
4. What could you or the person who was treated unfairly have done to improve matters and rectify the injustice on the spot?
5. Was any sexual harassment involved in this situation? If so, what kind was it?
6. If you had authority over the decision maker (for example, if you were his or her manager or supervisor), what steps would you take to ensure that the decision maker no longer treated diverse individuals unfairly?

Small Group Breakout Exercise

Determining if a Problem Exists

Form groups of three or four people, and appoint one member as the spokesperson who will communicate your findings to the whole class when called on by the instructor. Then discuss the following scenario.

You and your partners own and manage a local chain of restaurants with moderate to expensive prices that are open for lunch and dinner during the week and for dinner on weekends. Your staff is diverse and you believe that you are effectively managing diversity. Yet, on visits to the different restaurants you have noticed that your African-American employees tend to congregate together and communicate with each other. The same is true for your Hispanic employees and your white employees. You are meeting with your partners today to discuss this observation.

1. Discuss why the patterns of communication that you observed might be occurring in your restaurants.
2. Discuss whether your observation reflects an underlying problem. If so, why? If not, why not?
3. Discuss whether you should address this issue with your staff and in your restaurants. If so, how and why? If not, why not?

Exploring the World Wide Web

Find the website of a company that is taking active steps to effectively manage diversity. What are these steps and why are they being taken? Can you identify anything that is particularly innovative in this company's approach to managing diversity? Anything that might be inadvertently dysfunctional?

You're the Management Consultant

Maria Herrera was recently promoted to the position of director of financial analysis for a medium-size consumer goods firm. During her first few weeks on the job, she took the time to have lunch with each of her subordinates to try to get to know them better. Herrera has 12 direct reports who are junior and senior financial analysts that support different product lines. Susan Epstein, one of the female financial analysts she had lunch with made the following statement, "I'm so glad we finally have a woman in charge. Now, hopefully things will get better around here." Herrera pressed Epstein to elaborate but Epstein clammed up. She indicated that she didn't want to bias Herrera and that the problems were pretty self-evident. In fact, Epstein was surprised that Herrera didn't know what she was talking about and jokingly mentioned that perhaps she should spend some time undercover, observing her group and their interactions with others.

Herrera spoke with both her supervisor and the former director who had been promoted and volunteered to be on-call if Herrera had any questions. Neither man knew of any diversity-related issues in her group. In fact, her supervisor's response was, "We've got a lot of problems, but fortunately, that's not one of them."

As an expert in the effective management of diversity, Herrera has come to you for help. She doesn't know what she should do next to address this issue (or even if it is an issue at all) and but feels she should do something. Advise Herrera.

BusinessWeek Cases in the News

A Settlement That's Not Settled

In the struggle against sexual discrimination on Wall Street, Pamela K. Martens is a latter-day Rosa Parks—a woman who, metaphorically speaking, refused to sit in the back of the bus. The soft-spoken West Virginia native was a broker at the Garden City (N.Y.) branch of Smith Barney, whose locker-room atmosphere was epitomized by its notorious boys-only basement playpen, the "Boom-Boom Room."

After years of petty harassment and stymied promotion, Martens fought back. She was lead plaintiff in a landmark 1996 class action lawsuit that resulted, two years later, in a wide-ranging settlement with the firm, now merged with Salomon Brothers. To its defenders, the outcome was a masterpiece of justice that has resulted in dramatic change, not just at Salomon Smith Barney but also on Wall Street in general—where affirmative action is, in public at least, a rallying cry. Smith Barney agreed to set up an independent dispute-resolution process (DRP) for aggrieved women and to introduce various programs to encourage the hiring and promotion of women. "There was a lot of good done by that lawsuit, a lot of change," says Chicago attorney Linda D. Friedman, whose law firm, Stowell & Friedman, filed the suit. "The company has done some amazing things"—firing objectional managers and vastly increasing its hiring of women, she says.

Skewed?

But Martens—and some other former Smith Barney employees who initiated the suit—have a far less glowing view of the settlement. They have raised troubling questions about its fairness and execution—concerns rejected by U. S. District Court Judge Constance Baker Motley, who approved the settlement in July 1998. Critics among the plaintiffs assert that the DRP is skewed toward Smith Barney, and unnecessarily shrouded in secrecy that even Smith Barney agrees is not required by the settlement.

One claimant who may wind up not getting a penny in compensation is Martens—who opted out of the settlement and has since had her case tossed out by Motley on a technicality. The continued legal wrangling has cast a pall over the settlement that was widely hailed at the time as a model for dealing with thorny gender-discrimination issues.

For Martens, a former journalist who joined the branch in 1985, its suburban offices were a throwback to an earlier era—the Stone Age, perhaps. In the basement was the infamous Boom-Boom Room, a kind of frat-house bar with a garbage bin filled with Bloody Marys and a rusty bike hanging from the ceiling. The atmosphere was so Neanderthal, Martens says, that she rarely strayed from her office. She complained to management, to no avail. In October 1995, Martens was fired—because, she was told, she missed a meeting.

That was the first salvo in a war that has dragged on to the present day. On one side are Martens and other dissatisfied plaintiffs, backed by the New York chapter of the National Organization for Women. On the other are Stowell & Friedman, some of the plaintiffs, the national NOW, which supported the settlement—and Judge Motley, who has firmly sided with Stowell & Friedman since the settlement. Salomon defends the deal's fairness, but general counsel Joan Guggenheimer declined to comment on the legal wrangling.

"Stonewalled"

The issues are complex, but they boil down to this: Are women treated fairly in the settlement? There are 22,000 potential claimants—every woman who worked at Smith Barney from 1993 to 1998. Some 1,900 members of the class filed claims, and 1,300 of them were settled. Friedman insists that the DRP has worked splendidly. At the sessions, she says, women are treated fairly and with courtesy and are not required to undergo humiliating mental examinations that, she says, are common in other types of legal proceedings. At one typical mediation session, she says, attorneys for Smith Barney apologized for the treatment that was meted out to a claimant. One of those attorneys, she says, was even reduced to tears—something that, she insists, was heartening to the claimant. And, above all, she asserts, the women have received generous settlements. How much? Critics' estimates averaging under $16,000 are hotly disputed by Freidman, who says the figure is higher. How much higher? She won't say—and neither will Smith Barney. Friedman notes that claimants have individually agreed not to disclose their settlements, which is standard practice, she says.

Critics insist that, based on the limited information that has emerged, the DRP process has been a failure. "Women are being stonewalled in their attempts to proceed to mediation, obtain discovery material . . . and obtain awards that bear a relationship to the egregious civil rights violations committed by Smith Barney," argued the New York chapter of NOW in a friend-of-the-court brief in May. Nonsense, says Friedman, who attacks the settlement's opponents as misguided or self-interested.

One central criticism of the settlement, however, is not in dispute. Not only are individual settlements secret, but so is the total amount paid to claimants. That number is known only to Smith Barney and to Friedman & Stowell—and they're not telling. Salomon general counsel Guggenheimer says the settlement doesn't prohibit disclosure of individual amounts or the total but that the firm doesn't believe it's appropriate to release such data. Friedman declines to give a precise number and will say that "when it's all finished," the total cost to the firm will be in the "hundreds of millions." Guggenheimer won't comment on that, either.

Such secrecy is a main grievance of the dissenting plantiffs. But an effort to get a detailed status report on the settlement—as well as a court-appointed Special Master to oversee its implementation—has failed, big time. In May, Judge Motley summarily rejected an effort to get such relief by Kent Spriggs, a Florida attorney hired by some of the dissenting plaintiffs. In a stinging decision, Motley levied fines of $5,000 a piece on Spriggs and his law partner and revoked their permission to appear before the court. Motley acidly commented that Spriggs had made "serious allegations which were unsupported by affidavits" and that "by all credible reports, the [dispute resolution process] is running smoothly and serving class members well."

Doubletalk

In recent days, Spriggs has appealed Motley's rulings—as has Martens. In a separate decision, Motley threw out an effort by Martens and co-plaintiff Judith P. Mione to pursue their cases separately. In her ruling, which Martens is vigorously contesting, Motley makes the ironic allegation that Martens and Mione failed to pursue their claims vigorously enough. She accused the two women of "pettifoggery" that "focused on interloping in the affairs of the class."

If the judge's ruling stands, Pamela Martens won't get a dime for the years of petty harassment she suffered at Smith Barney. Usually, such a decisive legal defeat would be fatal—the last chapter in the saga of the Boom-Boom Room. But if you think that—well, you don't know Pamela Martens. While her attorney files briefs seeking to overturn the decision, Martens has filed an ethics complaint against the judge (who did not return calls seeking comment).

And despite all the frustrations, Martens looks back on the past few years without a tinge of regret. "I hear people say they would never go through it again, it has taken such a toll," she says. "For me, it's been so enriching. I opened my eyes and took action." But as long as the sums paid out to claimants are shrouded in mystery, the public will never know for sure whether the women received justice—or were sold down the river.

Source: G. Weiss, "A Settlement That's Not Settled," *Business Week,* October 30, 2000, pp. 164–65.

Questions

1. Why isn't the Smith Barney settlement settled?
2. Should secrecy surround some of the settlements and the dispute resolution process? Why or why not?

BusinessWeek Cases in the News

Women in the Boardroom

Over the past decade, more and more corporations have added women to their boards of directors. This trend reflects both public pressure and the growing perception by boards that women can be as effective corporate managers as men and may even bring different and valuable perspectives to a board's decision-making process.

Writing in the current issue of *Global Focus,* management consultants Nanette Fondas and Susan Sassalos offer evidence that having women directors does indeed have a positive impact on board performance. Using a survey of 115 large public companies in the early 1990s, Fondas and Sasalos examine how factors such as the share of inside directors on a board, the degree of institutional ownership, the role of top management in choosing directors, and the presence of women directors affected the reported ability of boards to influence key management decisions.

The results indicate that boards with one or more female directors have substantially more influence over management decisions than all-male boards. Among the other variables, only the degree of institutional ownership significantly enhanced board involvement.

Why this positive effect on corporate governance? While it may simply be that influential boards tend to seek out female directors, the authors think otherwise. Women have tended to be outside directors, they note, and often bring a broader perspective to the table. They may also have to pass higher hurdles in the direction-selection process—which could well reinforce their determination to fulfill their responsibilities.

Whatever the reason, the team's findings bolster the view that women directors can improve board functioning.

Source: G. Koretz, "Women in the Boardroom," *Business Week,* September 25, 2000, p. 30.

Questions

1. Is it important for corporate boards of directors to be diverse? Why or why not?
2. Why are there no women on some boards of directors? What might be the potential consequences of their absence?

Chapter 5

Managing the Organizational Environment

Learning Objectives

After studying this chapter you should be able to:

- Explain why the ability to **perceive, interpret, and respond** appropriately to the organizational environment is crucial for managerial success.
- Identify the main forces in an **organization's task and general environments,** and describe the challenges that each force presents to managers.
- Discuss the main **ways in which managers can manage** the organizational environment.
- Explain why **boundary-spanning activities** are important.

A Manager's Challenge

Ups and Downs in the Dot-Coms

Could managers have anticipated the future?

By 1995 the growing business opportunities possible because of the expanding use of the Internet and World Wide Web were becoming apparent to savvy people. Many managers began to leave other organizations to join or start their own dot-com companies that offered customers new kinds of products and services. For example, ebay.com, the auction house, was started by a former Microsoft manager, and Amazon.com by a former business consultant.[1] Other people founded organizations like Cisco Systems and Oracle to supply the hardware, like routers, and software platforms that form the backbone of the Internet. Still others such as Federal Express and UPS could see the prospective growth of their business because the dot-coms would need companies to distribute their products to customers worldwide. Existing "bricks and mortar (B&M)" companies also realized that they needed a Web presence to compete with the dot-coms and take advantage of an important new way to reach customers. Companies such as Barnes & Noble and Toys 'Я' Us raced to open their own on-line stores. At

The "bricks and mortar" store and "virtual" storefront of bookseller Barnes and Noble. As of 2001, Barnes and Noble had still not yet made a profit from its on-line activities and the company as a whole was experiencing losses.

the same time, entrepreneurs were racing to establish dot-coms that offered an on-line equivalent to products or services offered by B&M companies. For example, E*Trade, the on-line stockbroker, began to compete with Merrill Lynch; and Travelocity and Expedia began to compete with the thousands of small travel agencies that operate throughout the United States.

The Internet environment was rapidly changing and developing, opportunities were everywhere. The 'Net seemed to hold the promise of being the new industry of the new century in which every stakeholder—suppliers, distributors, customers, and investors—would reap big rewards. Venture capitalists pumped billions of dollars into the new dot-coms, investors flocked to buy shares in these companies and their share prices rose to astronomical heights. However, in 2000 the bottom fell out of the dot-com market and by June 2001, hundreds of dot-coms had gone belly-up. Why? Because most dot-coms had failed to earn any profits and had run out of money. Others like Walt Disney's on-line portal go.com were being shut down by their B&M parents because they were losing millions of dollars. Even hardware companies like Cisco and Lucent saw their stock prices plunge as customers either couldn't pay for their Internet hardware or cut back their purchases.

What kinds of threats had emerged in the dot-com and Internet environment that had caused this huge turnaround in the fortunes of all stakeholders? First, many dot-com companies had failed to anticipate the high costs associated with efficiently warehousing and distributing their products to customers. Although it seemed that using the Web was a relatively inexpensive way to reach new customers, it turned out that getting products to them was not. Distribution required sophisticated and well-designed information systems and experienced employees. Second, the economy took a downturn in 2000 and both companies and consumers began to spend less. B&M companies, for example, began to spend much less on advertising on dot-coms like Yahoo! which sent Yahoo!'s stock price down 85 percent from its peak. Third, both the hardware and software technology used to access the World Wide Web and link dot-coms to customers was changing rapidly. Cisco Systems, the high-flying Internet hardware supplier, stumbled badly in 2001 when it became clear that new optical routers would become the hardware of choice in the future. In addition, Cisco had many small agile competitors who, in the short run at least, had more expertise in this area. Investors began to realize that dot-coms might have difficulty making any money in this new environment, so they sold their shares. The stock prices of dot-coms plunged so far they wiped $1 trillion of value from the stock market.

The weakest dot-coms have already gone as a result of this shakeout but the inability of the survivors to make significant profits is also troubling. Many of the managers who joined the dot-coms have rejoined B&M companies to help strengthen their Internet skills. Many other dot-coms also have formed alliances with B&M companies so, for example, all the toys sold by Amazon.com are distributed by Toys 'Я' Us's Internet division. It is clear that big challenges lie ahead for managers of both dot-coms and B&M companies seeking to build a strong on-line presence and become "bricks and clicks" companies.

Overview

The rapidly changing fortunes of dot-com companies illustrates an important lesson that all managers need to learn. The organizational environment is uncertain and unpredictable because it is complex and constantly changing. Managers face in the environment a rich array of forces that they must recognize and respond to quickly and appropriately if their organizations are to survive and prosper. Managers must position their organizations to deal efficiently and effectively with new developments.

In this chapter, we examine the organizational environment in detail. We describe it and identify the principal forces–both task and general–that create pressure and influence managers and thus affect the way organizations operate. Next, we discuss several methods that managers can use to help organizations adjust and respond to forces in the organizational environment. By the end of the chapter, you will understand the steps managers must take to ensure that organizations adequately address and appropriately respond to their environments.

What is the Organizational Environment?

organizational environment The set of forces and conditions that operate beyond an organization's boundaries but affect a manager's ability to acquire and utilize resources.

The **organizational environment** is a set of forces and conditions outside the organization's boundaries that have the potential to affect the way the organization operates.[2] These forces change over time and thus present managers with opportunities and threats. Changes in the environment, such as the introduction of new technology or the opening of global markets, create opportunities for managers to obtain resources or enter new markets and thereby strengthen their organizations. In contrast, the rise of new competitors, an economic recession, or an oil shortage poses a threat that can devastate an organization if managers are unable to obtain resources or sell the organization's goods and services. The quality of managers' understanding of organizational environment forces, and their ability to respond appropriately to those forces, are critical factors affecting organizational performance.

In this chapter we explore the nature of these forces and consider how managers can respond to them. A detailed discussion of the way the external environment affects the planning and organizing processes is presented in Parts 3 and 4. Our focus now is on understanding the organizational environment and its impact on managers and organizations.

To identify opportunities and threats caused by forces in the organizational environment, it is helpful for managers to distinguish between the task environment and the more encompassing general environment (see Figure 5.1).

task environment The set of forces and conditions that originate with suppliers, distributors, customers, and competitors and affect an organization's ability to obtain inputs and dispose of its outputs because they influence managers on a daily basis.

general environment The wide-ranging economic, technological, sociocultural, demographic, political and legal, and global forces that affect an organization and its task environment.

The **task environment** is the set of forces and conditions that originate with suppliers, distributors, customers, and competitors; these forces and conditions affect an organization's ability to obtain inputs and dispose of its outputs. The task environment contains the forces that have the most immediate and direct effect on managers because they pressure and influence managers on a daily basis. When managers turn on the radio or television, arrive at their offices in the morning, open their mail, or look at their computer screens, they are likely to learn about problems facing them because of changing conditions in their organization's task environment.

The **general environment** includes the wide-ranging economic, technological, sociocultural, demographic, political and legal, and global forces that affect the organization and its task environment. For the individual manager, opportunities and threats resulting from changes in the general environment are often more difficult to identify and respond to than are events in the task environment. However, as in the dot-com story above, changes in these forces can have major impact on managers and their organizations.

The Task Environment

Forces in the task environment result from the actions of suppliers, distributors, customers, and competitors (see Figure 5.1). These four groups affect a manager's ability to obtain resources and dispose of outputs on a daily, weekly, and monthly basis and thus have a significant impact on short-term decision making.

Figure 5.1
Forces in the Organizational Environment

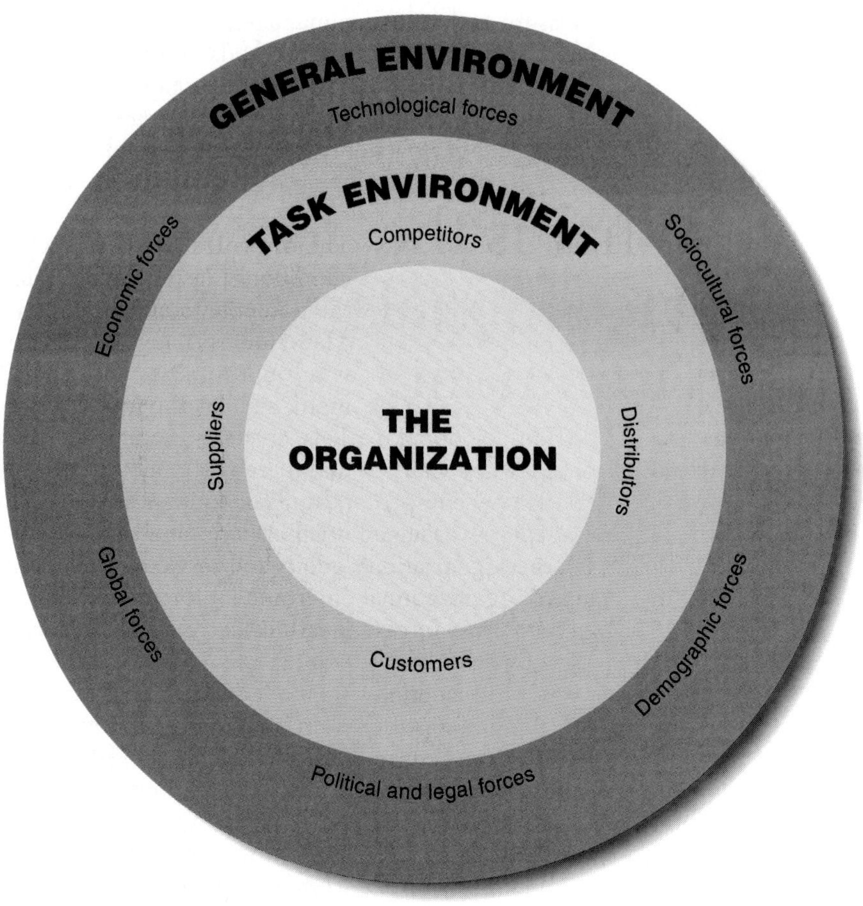

Suppliers

suppliers Individuals and organizations that provide an organization with the input resources that it needs to produce goods and services.

Suppliers are the individuals and companies that provide an organization with the input resources (such as raw materials, component parts, or employees) that it needs to produce goods and services. In return, the supplier receives compensation for those goods and services. An important aspect of a manager's job is to ensure a reliable supply of input resources.

Take Dell Computer, for example, the company we focused on in Chapter 1. Dell has many suppliers of component parts such as microprocessors (Intel and AMD) and disk drives (Quantum and Seagate Technologies). It also has suppliers of preinstalled software including the operating system (Microsoft), and specific applications software (IBM, Oracle, and America Online). Dell's providers of capital, such as banks and financial institutions, are also important suppliers. Cisco Systems and Oracle are important providers of Internet hardware and software for dot-coms.

There are several suppliers of labor to Dell. One is the educational institutions that train future Dell employees and therefore provide the company with skilled workers. Another is trade unions, organizations that represent employee interests and can control the supply of labor by exercising the right of unionized workers to strike. Unions also can influence the terms and conditions under which labor is employed. Dell's workers are not unionized; when layoffs became necessary due to an economic slowdown in 2001, Dell had few problems in laying off workers to reduce costs. In organizations and industries where unions are very strong, however, an important part of a manager's job is negotiating and administering agreements with unions and their representatives.

Changes in the nature, numbers, or types of any supplier result in forces that produce opportunities and threats to which managers must respond if their organizations are to prosper. Dell, for example, is constantly searching for global low-cost suppliers to keep its PC prices competitive. If managers do not respond to a threat, for example, failing to utilize low-cost foreign suppliers– they put their organization at a competitive disadvantage. Levi Strauss, for example, could not compete with the low-priced jeans sold by Wal-Mart and other retailers and was forced to close almost all of its U.S. jean factories and utilize low-cost foreign suppliers to keep the price of its jeans low.

Another major supplier-related threat that confronts managers arises when suppliers' bargaining position is so strong that they can raise the prices of the inputs they supply to the organization. A supplier's bargaining position is especially strong when (1) the supplier is the sole source of an input and (2) the input is vital to the organization.[3] For example, for 17 years G. D. Searle was the sole supplier of NutraSweet, the artificial sweetener used in most diet soft drinks. Not only was NutraSweet an important ingredient in diet soft drinks, it also was one for which there was no acceptable substitute (saccharin and other artificial sweeteners raised health concerns). Searle earned its privileged position because it invented and held the patent for NutraSweet. Patents prohibit other organizations from introducing competing products for 17 years. In 1992, Searle's patent expired, and many companies began to produce products similar to NutraSweet. Prior to 1992, Searle was able to demand a high price for NutraSweet, charging twice as much as the price of an equivalent amount of sugar. Paying that price raised the costs of soft-drink manufacturers, including Coca-Cola and PepsiCo, which had no alternative but to buy the product.[4] Today, NutraSweet is still the artificial sweetener of choice, but soft drink companies pay much less for it.

In contrast, when an organization has many suppliers for a particular input, it is in a relatively strong bargaining position with those suppliers and can demand low-cost, high-quality inputs from them. Oftentimes, an organization can use its power with suppliers to force them to reduce their prices, as Dell often does, or even force them to abide by more ethical or humane operating standards, as McDonald's did in this "Ethics in Action."

Ethics in Action

McDonald's Chicken and Egg Problem

In response to rising public concern about the treatment of animals reared for human consumption, McDonald's recently announced that it "will be a leader in animal welfare" and that henceforth it would only deal with egg suppliers who abide by two standards: First, suppliers must agree to no longer withdraw food and water from chickens to increase the rate at which they lay eggs. And second, suppliers must agree not to trim the birds' beaks to stop them from hurting one another, something which should lead suppliers to house chickens in bigger cages (at present the chickens have no room to spread their wings). McDonald's announced that it would work with its 26 suppliers to share the increased costs of following these new guidelines. Why will its suppliers bear the increased costs? As a McDonald's spokesperson said, "The bottom line is that when McDonald's speaks people listen because of our massive purchasing power. Our suppliers understand where we're going with this and the ones who want to come along can come along. We suspect they will."[5] After all, McDonald's buys 2 billion eggs annually for its Egg McMuffins and other food items.[6]

In 2001 McDonald's announced new standards that would require egg suppliers to improve the conditions under which chickens are housed and treated. Since McDonald's is an important customer, suppliers are likely to follow these new standards.

Distributors

distributors Organizations that help other organizations sell their goods or services to customers.

Distributors are organizations that help other organizations sell their goods or services to customers. The decisions that managers make about how to distribute products to customers can have important effects on organizational performance. As we saw in the dot-com story, package delivery companies such as Federal Express, UPS, and the United States Postal Service became the distributors for the millions of items bought on-line and shipped to customers.

The changing nature of distributors and distribution methods can also bring opportunities and threats for managers. If distributors are so large and powerful that they can control customers' access to a particular organization's goods and services, they can threaten the organization by demanding that it reduce the prices of its goods and services.[7] For example, the huge retail distributor Wal-Mart controls its suppliers' access to a great number of customers and thus often demands that its suppliers reduce their prices. If an organization such as Procter & Gamble refuses to reduce its prices, Wal-Mart might respond by buying products only from Procter & Gamble's competitors–companies such as Unilever and Dial.

In contrast, the power of a distributor may be weakened if there are many options. This has been the experience of the three broadcast television networks–ABC, NBC, and CBS. Their ability to demand lower prices from the producers of television programs has been weakened. The presence of hundreds of new cable television channels has reduced the three networks' clout by reducing their share of the viewing audience to less than 50 percent, down from more than 90 percent a decade ago. Similarly, because there are many package delivery companies, the dot-coms would not really be threatened if one firm tried to increase prices because they could switch delivery companies.

Customers

customers Individuals and groups that buy the goods and services that an organization produces.

Customers are the individuals and groups that buy the goods and services that an organization produces. For example, Dell's customers can be segmented into several distinct groups: (1) individuals who purchase PCs for home use, (2) small companies, (3) large companies, (4) government agencies, (5) educational institutions. Changes in the number and types of customers or changes in customers' tastes and needs also result in opportunities and threats. An organization's success depends on its response to customers. In the PC industry, customers are demanding lower prices and increased multimedia capability, and PC companies must respond to the changing types and needs of customers.[8] A school too must adapt to the changing needs of its customers. For example, if more Spanish-speaking students enroll, additional English as a second language classes may need to be scheduled. A manager's ability to identify an organization's main customers and produce the goods and services they want is a crucial factor affecting organizational and managerial success.

Competitors

competitors
Organizations that produce goods and services that are similar to a particular organization's goods and services.

One of the most important forces that an organization confronts in its task environment is competitors. **Competitors** are organizations that produce goods and services similar to a particular organization's goods and services. In other words, competitors are organizations vying for the same customers. Dell's competitors include other domestic manufacturers of PCs (such as Apple, Compaq, and Gateway) as well as foreign competitors (such as Sony and Toshiba in Japan and Group Bull in France). Dot-com stock broker, E*Trade, has other dot-com competitors like Ameritrade and TD Waterhouse, as well as bricks & clicks competitors such as Merrill Lynch and Charles Schwab.

Rivalry between competitors is potentially the most threatening force that managers must deal with. A high level of rivalry often results in price competition, and falling prices reduce access to resources and lower profits. In 2001, competition in the personal computer industry became intense because of an economic slowdown and because Dell was aggressively cutting costs and prices to try to increase its market share. In June 2001 Michael Dell announced that he wanted to increase Dell's market share from 13 to 40 percent–and Dell is already the global leader.[9] In 2001, IBM announced it was exiting the PC business because it was losing millions in its battle against low-cost rivals such as Dell and Gateway.

potential competitors
Organizations that presently are not in a task environment but could enter if they so chose.

Although the rivalry between existing competitors is a major threat, so is the potential for new competitors to enter the task environment. **Potential competitors** are organizations that are not presently in a task environment but could enter if they so chose. Amazon.com, for example, is not currently in the retail furniture or appliance business, but it could enter the businesses if its managers decided it could profitably sell these products. When new competitors enter an industry, competition increases and prices decrease.

barriers to entry
Factors that make it difficult and costly for an organization to enter a particular task environment or industry.

In general, the potential for new competitors to enter a task environment (and thus boost the level of competition) is a function of barriers to entry.[10] **Barriers to entry** are factors that make it difficult and costly for an organization to enter a particular task environment or industry.[11] In other words, the more difficult and costly it is to enter the task environment, the higher are the barriers to entry. The higher the barriers to entry, the fewer the competitors in an organization's task environment and thus the lower the threat of competition. With fewer competitors, it is easier to obtain customers and keep prices high.

economies of scale
Cost advantages associated with large operations.

Barriers to entry result from two main sources: economies of scale and brand loyalty (see Figure 5.2). **Economies of scale** are the cost advantages associated with large operations. Economies of scale result from factors such as being able to manufacture products in very large quantities, buy inputs in bulk, or make more effective use of organizational resources than competitors by fully utilizing employees' skills and knowledge. If organizations already in the task environment are large and enjoy significant economies of scale, then their costs are

Figure 5.2
Barriers to Entry and Competition

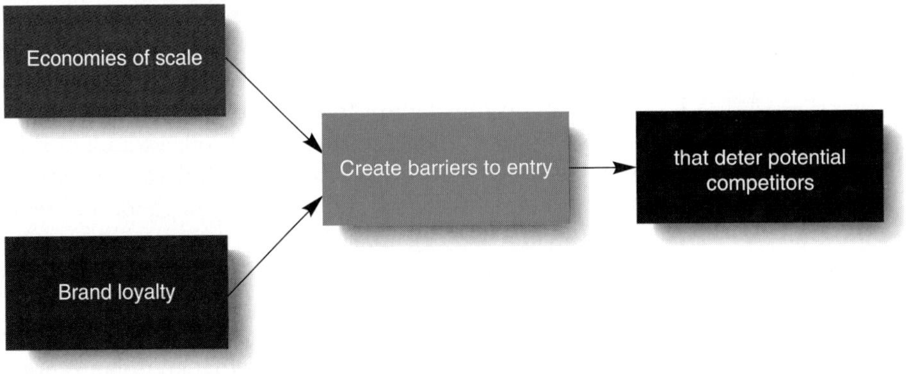

lower than the costs of potential entrants will be, and newcomers will find it very expensive to enter the industry. Amazon.com, for example, enjoys significant economies of scale relative to most other dot-com companies.[12]

brand loyalty Customers' preference for the products of organizations currently existing in the task environment.

Brand loyalty is customers' preference for the products of organizations currently existing in the task environment. If established organizations enjoy significant brand loyalty, then a new entrant will find it extremely difficult and costly to obtain a share of the market. Newcomers must bear huge advertising costs to build customer awareness of the good or service they intend to provide.[13] Both Amazon.com and Yahoo!, for example, two of the first dot-coms to go on-line, enjoy a high level of brand loyalty and have some of the highest website hit rates of all dot-coms (which also allows them to increase their advertising revenues).

In some cases, government regulations function as a barrier to entry. Many industries which were deregulated, such as air transport, trucking, utilities, and telecommunications saw a high level of new entry into their industries after deregulation, something which forced existing companies in those industries to operate more efficiently or risk being put out of business.

In summary, intense rivalry among competitors creates a task environment that is highly threatening and causes difficulty for managers trying to gain access to the resources an organization needs. Conversely, low rivalry results in a task environment where competitive pressures are more moderate and managers have greater opportunities to acquire the resources they need for their organizations to be effective. Kmart's battle with Wal-Mart illustrates many of the issues surrounding the force of competition and rivalry.

Management Insight

Kmart's Most Important Battle

In 1995, Kmart almost went bankrupt because declines in revenues led to major losses as its customers increasingly switched to its main competitors, Wal-Mart and Target. Why did its customers switch?

Wal-Mart's managers developed state-of-the-art information technology that gave it a major cost advantage in inventory distribution over Kmart. Moreover, Wal-Mart's ability to buy products in huge volumes led to economies of scale in purchasing, sales, and distribution. Its low costs also allowed it to charge low prices and its advertising slogan "everyday low prices" attracted price-conscious customers from Kmart. Target, on the other hand, had developed a hip-fashion image and had gained a reputation for providing customers with good quality products at reasonable prices. It

Charles Conaway, CEO of Kmart is joined by actress Jaclyn Smith, model Kathy Ireland, and Martha Stewart, all of whom have featured lines of products in Kmart stores, at festivities reintroducing the company's "blue light specials."

enjoyed increasing brand loyalty from customers who enjoyed shopping in its colorful, brightly lit, and well-designed stores.

Kmart was under attack from these two aggressive competitors who had taken the initiative and were providing customers with more perceived value. Kmart was being squeezed in the middle and to make matters worse it had internal organizing problems that made it difficult to fight back. Compared to Wal-Mart, Kmart's purchasing and inventory system was in abysmal condition, the shelves in its stores were often understocked so customers could not get what they wanted, and it simply could not match the efficiency of Wal-Mart's operations. On the other hand, compared to Target its stores were old and outdated, and it did not offer its customers a good shopping experience. Kmart was doing badly on many competitive fronts, hence its financial troubles.[14]

In 2000, new CEO Charles C. Conaway took control and began to focus on how Kmart could better manage the forces in its task environment. On the supply side he decided to invest more than $2 billion in new purchasing and inventory control IT that would substantially reduce costs and allow Kmart to charge lower prices like Wal-Mart.[15] He also announced plans to increase the Martha Stewart lines that Kmart had began to carry to increase its appeal to its main customer group–mothers with small children. He also decided to bring back Kmart's well-known "Blue Light Specials" to give Kmart a more exciting image to help it fight back against its competitors and to retain if not increase its customers. Conaway's attempt to fight back against Wal-Mart failed. In January 2002 Kmart declared Chapter 11 bankruptcy just as Wal-Mart announced record sales.

Not only for-profit organizations but also not-for-profit organizations have customers, suppliers, and competitors that influence and pressure managers because of the opportunities and threats they create. Consider a business school at a state-supported college or university. The customers of the business school are the organizations that hire its graduates, society at large (which benefits from an educated workforce), and the students themselves. Competitors of the business school include other business schools, both state and private, and in-house corporate education programs, such as Motorola's "Motorola U," which produces customized programs that satisfy many of Motorola's immediate business education needs. Suppliers include the university administration and the state government, both of which supply financial resources to the business school. The ultimate suppliers of these resources, of course, are taxpayers.

The Industry Life Cycle

industry life cycle The changes that take place in an industry as it goes through the stages of birth, growth, shakeout, maturity, and decline.

An important determinant of the nature and strength of the forces in an organization's task environment (and thus of the nature of opportunities and threats) is the **industry life cycle**–the changes that take place in an industry as it goes through the stages of birth, growth, shakeout, maturity, and decline (see Figure 5.3). Each stage in the life cycle is associated with particular kinds of forces in the task environment. Managers need to understand which life-cycle stage their organization is in to accurately perceive the opportunities and threats that it faces.

BIRTH The birth stage of an industry is characterized by competition among companies to develop the winning technology–the one that will allow them to provide the goods or services that customers want. Early in an industry's evolution, managers of new companies experiment with different ways of producing the product or delivering it to customers. In the Internet or dot-com industry, for example, different on-line auction houses, or search engine portals, or online bookstores competed to develop the storefront software that would be the easiest for customers to use or the most attractive or informative. Companies like Amazon.com, Yahoo!, and E*Trade were the most successful. In the birth stage, an organization's relationships with its suppliers, distributors, and customers are fluid and likely to change quickly, making the environment uncertain and difficult to predict and control.

GROWTH The growth stage begins at the point when a product gains customer acceptance and an influx of consumers enters the market. Rapid growth in customer demand attracts many new organizations into the industry, increasing the level of competition, as happened in the Internet industry. The newcomers, like the new dot-coms, pioneer new varieties of the industry's products and improved ways of producing and delivering those products to customers. This is also occurring in the cellular phone and wireless communication industry today where new generations of mobile phones and handheld communication devices from companies such as Nokia, Motorola, and Sony offer new services like email, instant messaging, and soon even video.[16] These changes lead to a complex set of forces in the task environment as the relationships among suppliers, distributors, and competitors all change rapidly.

SHAKEOUT Near the end of the growth stage there is a marked change in an industry's task environment because slowing customer demand for the industry's product raises the level of competition in the industry. In response, organizations often reduce their prices, and the result can be a price war, which causes prices to fall rapidly. In the shakeout stage, the least-efficient companies are driven out of the industry; consequently, there is significant uncertainty until the shakeout is complete. The Internet industry has just gone through one major shakeout: In the brokerage segment of the market the cost of buying and selling shares dropped from over $50 a transaction to under $10 in less than three years forcing many companies out of the market.

Figure 5.3
Stages in the Industry Life Cycle

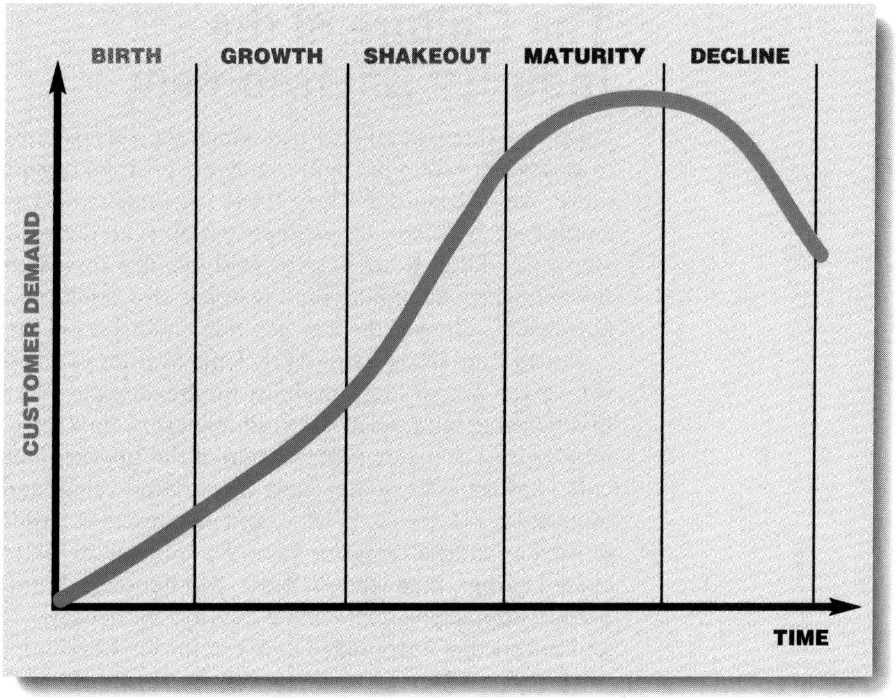

MATURITY By the time an industry reaches maturity, most customers have bought the product and demand is growing slowly or is constant. The task environment is more stable because relationships between suppliers, distributors, and competitors are more predictable. Customers have developed brand loyalty for the products of certain companies, and managers have developed good working relationships with suppliers and distributors. A few large companies usually dominate mature industries, so the level of competition is lower, or at least more predictable, because each company can predict how its competitors will behave. Finally, organizations that have survived into maturity are often protected from new competition by relatively high barriers to entry.

This stable situation may persist for a long time, allowing companies to enjoy high profits. But in a mature industry with low barriers to entry, competitors may enter the market, and if this happens, rapid change may occur. For example, prior to 1990 the U.S. retail clothing industry was a stable, mature industry dominated by Sears, Kmart, Montgomery Ward, and J.C. Penney. However, the emergence of low-cost foreign clothes manufacturers, and aggressive new competitors like Wal-Mart and Target which focused on selling attractive low-cost clothing totally changed the competitive environment in the retail clothing industry as discussed earlier. All four of the old, established companies lost billions of dollars fighting the challenge from the new competitors. Three companies were forced to close hundreds of their now unprofitable stores and Montgomery Ward finally exited the industry in 2001.

DECLINE In the final stage in the evolution of an industry, customer demand for the industry's product decreases. Falling demand typically leads to a situation in which organizations in the industry are making more of the product than customers want to buy. As in the shakeout period, companies often respond to this situation by cutting prices, and competition increases. Once again, the most inefficient companies are driven out of the industry.

The Culture of the Industry Environment

Chapter 2 discussed the way in which the values, norms, and beliefs held by an organization's founders and managers form an organizational culture. Furthermore, we discussed the way those organizational values and norms influence employees' behavior; for example, employees' desire to be conscientious or innovative or ethical. It has been argued too, that the nature of the industry environment in which an organization operates also results in certain kinds of values and norms that influence the way company managers in the industry behave.[17]

Recall from the story of AOL-Time Warner in Chapter 1 that AOL managers were given primary responsibility for creating the new combined company's way of organizing because, as dot-com managers, they were used to the dynamic, fast-moving and changing environment of the Internet industry. In other words, dot-com companies have managers who shared values and norms of being creative, innovative, risk taking, flexible, and responsive to customers because they operate in such an industry environment. By contrast, in the retail clothing industry discussed earlier, managers in Sears, Montgomery Ward, and Kmart had become used to dominating the retailing industry for decades. They had developed values and norms that encouraged concern for the bottom line, caution, and conservative behavior. Managers respected traditions and authority and were reluctant to rock the boat. When new companies used foreign suppliers to produce either low-cost or new chic clothing, these companies were in big trouble, and they were forced to bring in new managers, like Kmart's Conaway, to try to change their operating values and norms and turn their performance around.

When managers leave organizations for career reasons, they often move to another organization in the same industry where they can use their skills and experience. As a result, values and norms they take become widespread throughout an industry and result in the same approach to planning, organizing, and so on.[18] This is why companies that are in trouble because of agile new competitors often pick a new CEO from outside the business who will have a new perspective on how to improve a company's declining performance. Two examples: IBM picked Lou Gerstner who had no experience in computing to head its turnaround, and Kmart's new CEO Charles Conaway had no previous experience with retailing clothes.

The bottom line then is that effective managers must understand the way forces in the task environment may change over time and learn to respond appropriately. The quality of managers' planning, organizing, and decision making depends on their ability to correctly perceive and understand the forces operating in the task and general environments.

The General Environment

Economic, technological, sociocultural, demographic, political and legal, and global forces in an organization's general environment can have profound effects on the organization's task environment, effects that may not be evident to managers. For example, the sudden, dramatic upheavals in the Internet and dot-com industry environment were brought about by a combination of changing Internet technology, a softening U.S. stock market and economy, and increasing fears about the health of the global economy, too. These changes triggered intense competition between dot-com companies which further worsened the industry situation.

The implication is clear: Managers must constantly analyze forces in the general environment because these forces affect ongoing decision making and planning. Next, we discuss the major forces in the general environment, and examine their impacts on an organization's task environment.

Economic Forces

economic forces Interest rates, inflation, unemployment, economic growth, and other factors that affect the general health and well-being of a nation or the regional economy of an organization.

Economic forces affect the general health and well-being of a country or world region. They include interest rates, inflation, unemployment, and economic growth. Economic forces produce many opportunities and threats for managers. Low levels of unemployment and falling interest rates mean a change in the customer base: More people have more money to spend and as a result organizations have an opportunity to sell more goods and services. Good economic times affect supplies: Resources become easier to acquire, and organizations have an opportunity to flourish, as high-tech companies did throughout the 1990s when they made record profits as the economy boomed in large part because of advances in information technology and growing global trade.

In contrast, worsening macroeconomic conditions pose a threat because they limit managers' ability to gain access to the resources their organizations need. Profit-oriented organizations such as retail stores and hotels have fewer customers for their goods and services during economic downturns. Not-for-profit organizations such as charities and colleges receive fewer donations during economic downturns. Even a moderate deterioration in national or regional economic conditions can seriously affect performance. During 2000, a relatively mild recession was a major factor in the staggering collapse of dot-com companies; it also caused major losses to many high-tech companies such as Lucent, Palm, and Compaq. Managers at these enterprises faced momentous challenges.

Poor economic conditions make the environment more complex and managers' jobs more difficult and demanding. Managers may need to reduce the number of individuals in their departments and increase the motivation of remaining employees, and managers and workers alike may need to identify ways to acquire and utilize resources more efficiently. Successful managers realize the important effects that economic forces have on their organizations and they pay close attention to what is occurring in the national and regional economy in order to respond appropriately.

Technological Forces

technology The combination of skills and equipment that managers use in the design, production, and distribution of goods and services.

technological forces Outcomes of changes in the technology that managers use to design, produce, or distribute goods and services.

Technology is the combination of tools, machines, computers, and skills, information, and knowledge that managers use in the design, production, and distribution of goods and services. **Technological forces** are outcomes of changes in the technology that managers use to design, produce, or distribute goods and services. The overall pace of technological change has accelerated greatly in the last decade; because of advances in microprocessors and computer hardware and software, and technological forces have increased in magnitude.[19]

Technological forces can have profound implications for managers and organizations. Technological change can make established products obsolete–for example, typewriters, black and white televisions, bound sets of encyclopedias–forcing managers to find new ways to satisfy customer needs. Although technological change can threaten an organization, it also can create a host of new opportunities for designing, making, or distributing new and better kinds of goods and services. More powerful microprocessors, primarily developed by Intel, caused a revolution in information technology that spurred demand for PCs, contributed to the success of companies such as Dell and Compaq, and led to the decline of others such as IBM.[20] IBM and other producers of mainframe computers have seen demand for their products decrease as organizationwide networks of PCs have replaced mainframes in many computing applications.[21] However, IBM has responded in the last decade by changing its emphasis from providing computer hardware to computer services and consulting and is once again in a strong position. Managers must move quickly to respond to such changes if their organizations are to survive and prosper.

Changes in information technology also are altering the very nature of work itself within organizations and, in addition, the manager's job. Telecommuting along the information superhighway and videoconferencing are now everyday activities that provide opportunities for managers to supervise and coordinate geographically dispersed employees. Salespeople in many companies work from home offices and commute electronically to work. Salespeople communicate with other employees through companywide electronic mail networks and use video cameras attached to PCs for "face-to-face" meetings with fellow workers who may be across the country. New IT is pervading all kinds of organizations as the following "Information Technology Byte" suggests.

Information Technology Byte

A High-Tech Winery?

Cakebread Cellars, a specialty wine maker in California's Napa Valley, is known internationally for the quality of its wines; it was ranked seventh in overall quality in 2000. To keep its costs under control so that it can continue to improve product quality and protect the health of its vines, Cakebread Cellars's managers developed state-of-the-art information technology for their winery. This technology has several different components.

First, because the quality of wine depends upon how much water a vine receives and when, at the root of each of its thousands of vines Cakebread installed an electronic measuring device that monitors the water intake of each vine. The device also allows Cakebread to keep a lifetime record of the history of each vine to keep each in peak condition. Second, information on its vines is fed into a complex computer software program which allows Cakebread's wine experts to monitor the vines and determine the optimum watering and feeding schedule. They can also pinpoint the right time to pick the grapes–the time when the grapes' sugar content is at its highest. Third, Cakebread is electronically linked to a local weather-forecasting service that informs

The process of grape growing and wine production in many U.S. wineries, like Cakebread Cellars, is now infused with advanced information technologies that are designed to improve the quality of the wines. Cakebread, like many U.S. wineries now regularly wins international wine competitions.

vintners quickly of any adverse weather conditions that might emerge during the harvesting period.

Once the grapes are picked, the fourth step in the monitoring process begins. Monitoring devices are placed in all the large wine fermentation vessels so that wine makers can study the fermentation process and monitor the progress of the wine.[22] In this way they can seek to influence the taste of the final product by altering the length of the fermentation process or by making a decision to blend different varieties of wine to create the optimum product. Fifth, the bottling process is also electronically monitored to ensure the quality of the final product. According to Cakebread's wine makers, IT provides them with the information that allows them to make the final decisions that result in the production of a great wine as opposed to a good one.

Sociocultural Forces

sociocultural forces Pressures emanating from the social structure of a country or society or from the national culture.

social structure The arrangement of relationships between individuals and groups in a society.

Sociocultural forces are pressures emanating from the social structure of a country or society or from the national culture. Pressures from both sources can either constrain or facilitate the way organizations operate and managers behave. **Social structure** is the arrangement of relationships between individuals and groups in a society. Societies differ substantially in social structure. In societies that have a high degree of social stratification, there are many distinctions among individuals and groups. Caste systems in India and Tibet and the recognition of numerous social classes in Great Britain and France produce a multilayered social structure in each of those countries. In contrast, social stratification is lower in relatively egalitarian New Zealand and in the United States, where the social structure reveals few distinctions among people. Most top managers in France come from the upper classes of French society, but top managers in the United States come from all strata of American society.

Societies also differ in the extent to which they emphasize the individual over the group. For example, the United States emphasizes the primacy of the individual, and Japan emphasizes the primacy of the group. This difference may dictate the methods managers need to use to motivate and lead employees.

national culture The set of values that a society considers important and the norms of behavior that are approved or sanctioned in that society.

National culture is the set of values that a society considers important and the norms of behavior that are approved or sanctioned in that society. Societies differ substantially in the values and norms that they emphasize. For example, in the United States individualism is highly valued, and in Korea and Japan individuals are expected to conform to group expectations.[23] National culture also affects the way managers motivate and coordinate employees and the way organizations do business. Ethics, an important aspect of national culture, was discussed in detail in Chapter 3.

Social structure and national culture not only differ across societies but also change within societies over time. In the United States, attitudes toward the roles of women, love, sex, and marriage changed in each past decade. Many people in Asian countries such as Hong Kong, Singapore, Korea, and Japan think that the younger generation is far more individualistic and "American-like" than previous generations. Currently, throughout much of eastern Europe, new values that emphasize individualism and entrepreneurship are replacing communist values based on collectivism and obedience to the state. The pace of change is accelerating.

Individual managers and organizations must be responsive to changes in, and differences among, the social structures and national cultures of all the countries in which they operate. In today's increasingly integrated global economy, managers are likely to interact with people from several countries, and many managers live and work abroad. Effective managers are sensitive to differences between societies and adjust their behaviors accordingly.

Managers and organizations also must respond to social changes within a society. During the 1980s and 1990s, for example, Americans became more interested in their personal health and fitness. Managers who recognized this trend early and exploited the opportunities that resulted from it were able to reap significant gains for their organizations. PepsiCo used the opportunity presented by the fitness trend and took market share from arch rival Coca-Cola by being the first to introduce diet colas and fruit-based soft drinks. Quaker Oats made Gatorade the most popular sports drink and brought out a whole host of low-fat food products. The health trend, however, did not offer opportunities to all companies; to some it posed a threat. Tobacco companies came under intense pressure due to consumers' greater awareness of negative health impacts from smoking. Hershey Foods and other manufacturers of candy bars have been threatened by customers' desires for low-fat, healthy foods.

Demographic Forces

demographic forces Outcomes of changes in, or changing attitudes toward, the characteristics of a population, such as age, gender, ethnic origin, race, sexual orientation, and social class.

Demographic forces are outcomes of changes in, or changing attitudes toward, the characteristics of a population, such as age, gender, ethnic origin, race, sexual orientation, and social class. Like the other forces in the general environment, demographic forces present managers with opportunities and threats and can have major implications for organizations. We examined the nature of these challenges in depth in our discussion of diversity in Chapter 3 so we will not discuss these forces again here.

We will just note one important change occurring today, namely, most industrialized nations are experiencing the aging of their populations as a consequence of falling birth and death rates and the aging of the baby-boom generation. In Germany, for example, the percentage of the population over age 65 is expected to rise to 20.7 percent in 2010 from 15.4 percent in 1990. Comparable figures for Canada are 14.4 and 11.4 percent; for Japan, 19.5 and 11.7 percent; and for the United States, 13.5 and 12.6 percent.[24] In the United States the percentage increase is far smaller because of the huge wave of immigration during the 1990s and the large families that new immigrants typically have. However, the absolute number of older people has also increased substantially and is increasing opportunities for organizations that cater to older people; the home health care and recreation industries, for example, are seeing an upswing in demand for their services.

The aging of the population also has several implications for the workplace. Most significant are a relative decline in the young people joining the workforce and an increase in active employees willing to postpone retirement past the traditional retirement age of 65. These changes suggest that organizations need to find ways to motivate and utilize the skills and knowledge of older employees, an issue that many Western societies have yet to tackle.

Political and Legal Forces

political and legal forces Outcomes of changes in laws and regulations, such as the deregulation of industries, the privatization of organizations, and increased emphasis on environmental protection.

Political and legal forces are outcomes of changes in laws and regulations. They result from political and legal developments within society and significantly affect managers and organizations. Political processes shape a society's laws. Laws constrain the operations of organizations and managers, and thus create both opportunities and threats.[25] For example, throughout much of the industrialized world there has been a strong trend toward deregulation of industries previously controlled by the state and privatization of organizations once owned by the state.

In the United States, deregulation of the airline industry in 1978 ushered into the task environment of commercial airlines major changes that are still working themselves out. Deregulation allowed 29 new airlines to enter the industry between 1978 and 1993. The increase in airline-passenger carrying capacity after deregulation led to excess capacity on many routes, intense competition, and fare wars. To respond to this more competitive task environment, in the 1980s airlines looked for ways to reduce operating costs. The development of hub-and-spoke systems, the rise of nonunion airlines, and the introduction of no-frills discount service are all responses to increased competition in the airlines' task environment. By the 1990s, once again in control of their environments, airlines were making record profits. However, soaring oil prices in 2000 wiped out these profits and airlines found themselves once again under pressure.

Deregulation and privatization are just two examples of political and legal forces that can challenge organizations and managers. Others include increased emphasis on environmental protection and the preservation of endangered species, increased emphasis on safety in the workplace, and legal constraints against discrimination on the basis of race, gender, or age. Successful managers carefully monitor changes in laws and regulations to take advantage of the opportunities they create and counter the threats they pose in an organization's task environment.

Global Forces

global forces
Outcomes of changes in international relationships; changes in nations' economic, political, and legal systems; and changes in technology, such as falling trade barriers, the growth of representative democracies, and reliable and instantaneous communication.

Global forces are outcomes of changes in international relationships; changes in nations' economic, political, and legal systems; and changes in technology. The global environment is the subject of Chapter 6, so here we are limiting our discussion to a few introductory comments. Perhaps the most important global force affecting managers and organizations is the increasing economic integration of countries around the world.[26] Free trade agreements such as the General Agreement on Tariffs and Trade (GATT) and the North American Free Trade Agreement (NAFTA), and the growth of the European Union (EU), have led to a lowering of barriers to the free flow of goods and services between nations.[27]

Falling trade barriers have created enormous opportunities for organizations in one country to sell goods and services in other countries. By allowing companies from other countries to compete for an organization's domestic customers, however, falling trade barriers also pose a serious threat because they increase competition in the task environment. Between 1973 and 2000, for example, U.S. car makers saw Japanese competitors increase their share of the U.S. car market from 3 to nearly 27 percent. This growth would not have been possible without relatively low trade barriers, which allowed producers in Japan to export cars to the United States. Competition from Toyota, Honda, and other Japanese companies forced managers of the U.S. car companies to find ways to improve their operations. To remain competitive, they had to transform the way their organizations designed and manufactured cars. Managers at Chrysler and Ford, for example, now use decentralized structures and cross-functional teams to design, manufacture, and market cars. As a result of these changes, U.S. companies gained ground against their foreign competitors, otherwise the percentage of foreign cars sold in 2000 in the United States would be far higher. However, if global forces had not increased the intensity of competition in the task environment of U.S. car companies, U.S. managers might have been slow to make such changes. The U.S. car industry's culture used to be very conservative and slow moving, but no more because it has learned new global values and norms, such as product quality and reliability.

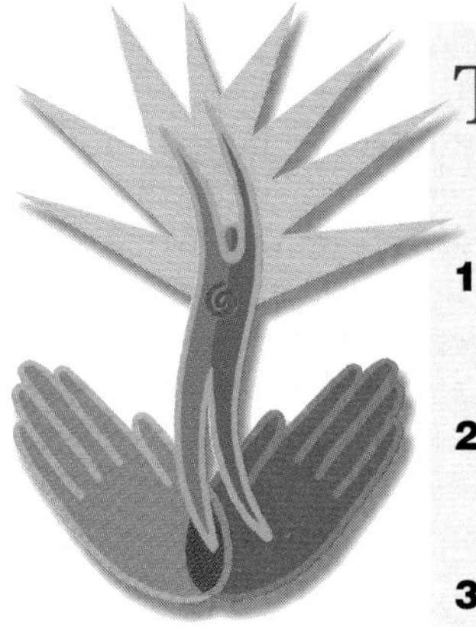

Tips for New Managers

Forces in the Environment

1. List the forces in an organization's task environment that affect it the most. Analyze changes taking place that may result in opportunities or threats for the organization.
2. List the forces in the general environment that affect an organization the most. Analyze changes taking place that may result in opportunities or threats for the organization.
3. Devise a plan indicating how your managers propose to take advantage of opportunities or counter threats that arise from environmental forces and what kinds of resources they will need to do so.

Managing the Organizational Environment

As previously discussed, an important task for managers is to understand how forces in the task and general environments generate opportunities for, and threats to, their organizations. To analyze the importance of opportunities and threats in the organizational environment, managers must measure (1) the level of complexity in the environment and (2) the rate at which the environment is changing. With this information, they can plan appropriately and choose the best goals and courses of action.

The complexity of the organizational environment is a function of the number and potential impact of the forces to which managers must respond in both the task and the general environments. A force that seems likely to have a significant negative impact is a potential threat to which managers must devote a high level of organizational resources. A force likely to have a marginal impact poses little threat to an organization and requires only a minor commitment of managerial time and attention. A force likely to make a significant positive impact warrants a considerable commitment of managerial time and effort to take advantage of the opportunity.

In general, the larger an organization is, the greater the number of environmental forces that managers must respond to. Compare, for example, the organizational environment facing the manager of a roadside diner with that facing top managers at Taco Bell's headquarters. At the local level, the main concern of a restaurant manager is to ensure an adequate supply of inputs, such as food supplies and restaurant employees, to provide customers with fast and efficient service. In contrast, top managers at Taco Bell must determine how to distribute food supplies to restaurants in the most efficient ways; how to ensure that the organization's practices do not discriminate against any ethnic groups or older workers; how to respond to customers' new preference for tacos made with low-fat cheese and sour cream; and how to deal with competition from McDonald's, which has reduced the cost of its hamburgers to compete with Taco Bell's low-cost tacos and burritos. Clearly, the more forces managers must deal with, the more complicated is the management process.

environmental change The degree to which forces in the task and general environments change and evolve over time.

Environmental change is the degree to which forces in the task and general environments change and evolve over time. Change is problematic for an organization and its managers because the consequences of change can be difficult to predict.[28] For example, managers in the computer and telecommunications industries know that technological advances such as the increasing power and falling cost of microprocessors and the development of broadband and wireless transmission will produce dramatic changes in their task environments, but they do not know what the magnitude or effects of those changes will be. Managers can attempt to forecast or simply guess about future conditions in the task environment, such as where and how strong the new competition may be. But, confronted with a complex and changing task environment, managers cannot be sure that decisions and actions taken today will be appropriate in the future. This uncertainty makes their jobs especially challenging. It also makes it vitally important for managers to understand the forces that shape the organizational environment.

As a first step in managing the organizational environment, managers need to list the number and relative strength of the forces that affect their organization's task and general environments the most. Second, they need to analyze the way changes in these forces may result in opportunities or threats for their organizations. Third, they need to draw up a plan indicating how they propose to take advantage of those opportunities or counter those threats and what kinds of resources they will need to do so. An understanding of the organizational environment is necessary so that managers can anticipate how the task environment might look in the future and decide on the actions to pursue if the organization is to prosper.

Reducing the Impact of Environmental Forces

Often managers can counter threats in the task environment by reducing the potential impact of forces in that environment. Finding ways to reduce the number and potential impact of forces in the organizational environment is the job of all managers in an organization. The principal task of the CEO and top-management team is to devise strategies that will allow an organization to take advantage of opportunities and counter threats in its general and task environments. (See Part 3 for a discussion of this vital topic.) Middle managers in an organization's departments collect relevant information about the task environment, such as (1) the future intentions of the organization's competitors, (2) the identity of new customers for the organization's products, and (3) the identity of new suppliers of crucial or low-cost inputs. First-line managers find ways to use resources more efficiently to hold down costs or to get close to customers and learn what they want.

Creating an Organizational Structure

Another way to respond to a complex and changing organizational environment is to increase the complexity of the organization's structure and its control systems. (We discuss organizational structure and control systems in detail in Part 4.) To do this, top managers assign various departments to deal with the

Figure 5.4
How Managers Use Functions to Manage Forces in the Task and General Environments

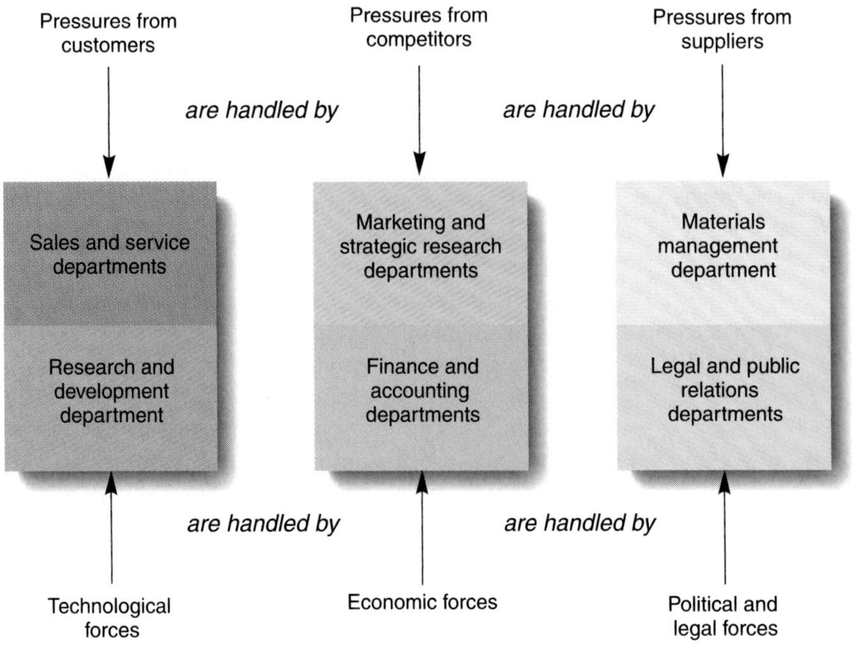

various forces affecting the task and general environments (see Figure 5.4). For example, the sales and service departments develop the skills and knowledge necessary to handle relationships with customers. The research and development department identifies changes in technology that will impact the organization and uses that technology to develop new goods and services to attract customers. The finance and accounting departments scan and monitor economic forces and assess their impact on the organization.

Middle managers within an organization's departments are responsible for identifying what is happening in the environment as it relates to their functional area and for forecasting how environmental forces are likely to affect their departments and the organization as a whole. The ability of department managers to (1) develop the skills they need to manage the segment of the environment they are responsible for and (2) cooperate with other departments to get products to customers in a timely fashion determines organizational performance–the organization's ability to acquire and utilize resources efficiently and effectively. Effective organizations have departments that respond quickly and appropriately to unforeseen situations and to take advantage of unexpected opportunities. Ineffective organizations lack not only the ability to respond to changes in the task and general environments but also the skills needed to secure scarce and valuable resources. Indeed, a recent book, *Competing on the Edge,* argues that the most important challenge facing managers is not just the need to respond quickly to changing conditions in the environment but to time their responses to the cycles or rhythms in their environments, such as the changing patterns of their customers' needs so that they know when to change to respond to those needs.[29] Dell, for example, has shown itself to be the computer company that can best sense what customers are looking for in a new PC.

In essence, to reduce the impact of environmental forces, managers perform their organizing function and design an organizational structure that allows them to respond appropriately to the specific forces and conditions in the environment. Managing the match between the organization and its environment so that the organization's structure responds well to the forces in the task and general environments is a vital management task. In the long run, the ability of managers to perform this task is one key factor that separates high-performing from low-performing organizations and we discuss this issue in depth in Chapters 9, 10, and 11.

Utilizing IT and the Internet

Information technology (IT) and the Internet are being increasingly used by managers to help them deal with many of the forces in their task environment. On the supply side, many companies are taking advantage of business to business (B2B) networks to acquire their inputs more reliably and at less cost. Although there is currently great uncertainty over exactly how these B2B networks will evolve over time, the way they work is clear. At the industry level, all the companies in an industry agree to use the same IT software to link to each other and to the industry's suppliers, who also use the same software. As a result, purchasing managers can compare the features and prices of the different suppliers' products on-line and negotiate for the best price. At the same time, the buying companies might jointly decide that in the future they require inputs to have certain new specifications. They can use the network to inform suppliers about these changes and then allow suppliers to bid for the contract to supply the input. For example, car makers may jointly decide that in the future all the tires for SUVs should be built to higher quality specifications. Then through the B2B network they can inform all tire makers what those specifications are so they can respond quickly to these changes and bid for a particular car maker's business.

On the distribution side, the Internet can be used as an important new avenue for informing potential customers about new and existing products and providing a vehicle for selling those products to customers. The value of products sold on the Internet is expected to rise to $300 billion by 2010, something that Wal-Mart is keen to take advantage of as discussed in the "Information Technology Byte."

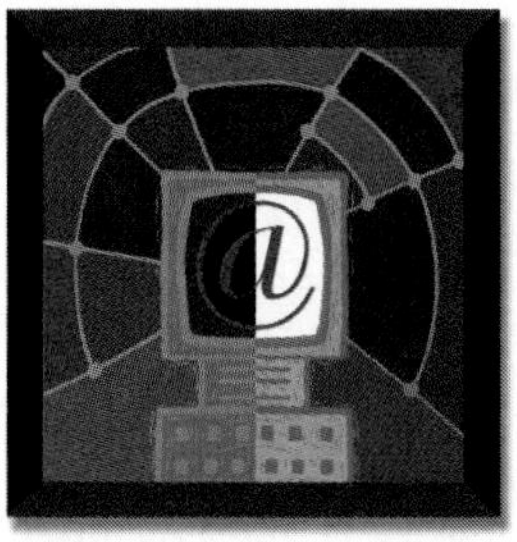

Information Technology Byte

Wal-Mart's New On-line Store

As Kmart found out, Wal-Mart's sophisticated inventory control IT gives it an important competitive advantage over other retailers because it allows Wal-Mart to charge lower prices to customers. Wal-Mart has always been a leader in IT. From the beginning all its stores have been connected to its head office in Bentonville, Arkansas, by satellite dish so that managers there have immediate access to information about store sales. Wal-Mart was a pioneer in using satellite TV to deliver training programs to its store managers and employees, and it now uses the Internet to handle the increased volume of programming that is necessary as it has grown globally over time.[30]

Given Wal-Mart's IT expertise, it was only natural that the company's top managers decided to establish an on-line store, walmart.com, to find yet another avenue to increase its annual $300 billion in sales. Imagine the surprise then when Wal-Mart announced a few months after opening its on-line store that it would be closing it for several weeks of "remodeling."

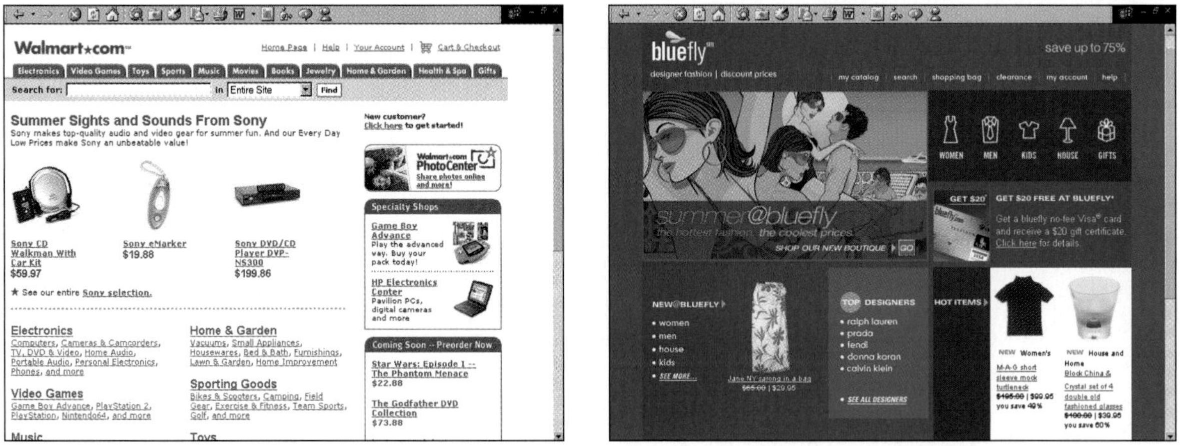

The virtual storefronts of Kmart's bluefly.com and Wal-Mart's walmart.com. These companies are competing to develop new information technology that gives customers a better shopping experience.

It turns out that managing an on-line store was a much more difficult proposition than Wal-Mart had imagined. The leader in distributing huge volumes of products to its stores, it found reliably distributing single packages to individual customers very difficult. Wal-Mart found out that it had not yet developed either the software or the physical capabilities to handle on-line selling and distribution, and it lagged far behind Amazon.com which is the market leader in this form of technology.

Jeanne Jackson, walmart.com's president, talks about Wal-Mart's Web strategy during Wal-Mart's annual company meeting. She is leading the fight to make walmart.com the number one consumer goods on-line store of choice with customers.

Determined to succeed in its on-line venture because of the enormous future potential of on-line selling, Wal-Mart decided to solve its problems. It hired a new CEO, Jeanne P. Jackson, the former CEO of Gap Inc.'s Banana Republic unit and the head of its on-line sales unit to head up walmart.com. One of her main tasks is to decide what kinds of products walmart.com should stock.[31] Wal-Mart then decided to pump $100 million into developing the IT and physical warehousing necessary for it to compete with Amazon.com and establish itself as a leading on-line vendor. At a time when many dot-coms are exiting the market because of lack of cash, Wal-Mart's deep pockets and expertise give it the opportunity to succeed where many other dot-coms have failed.

Finally, one of the main uses of information technology and the Internet is to provide information to other stakeholders interested in an organization and what it does. For example, as just discussed companies can easily inform customers about their new products; suppliers, distributors, and even competitors

Figure 5.6
Change in the Environment as a Two-Way Process

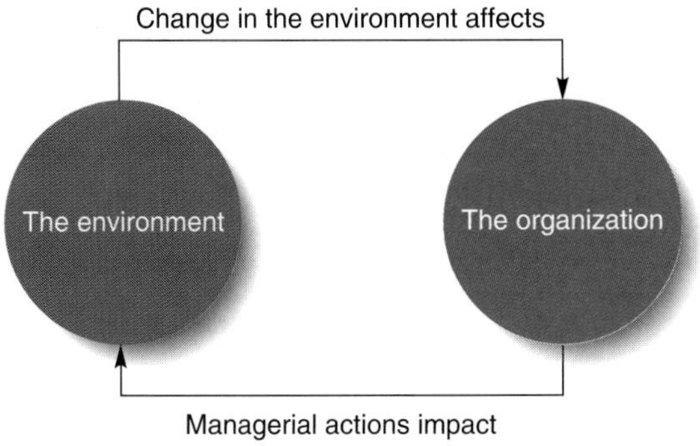

legal challenge to AT&T's monopoly of telephone services in the United States. MCI claimed that the AT&T monopoly was not in the best public interest and violated antitrust regulations. Ultimately, MCI won this David versus Goliath battle, and in 1984 the U.S. Supreme Court ordered AT&T to separate into a long-distance company and seven regional telephone companies (the "Baby Bells"). The Court also opened the door for MCI to compete head-to-head with AT&T in the long-distance market. The result of MCI managers' actions was to usher in a new era of competition in the now-deregulated U.S. telecommunications industry. MCI has been a major beneficiary of this change, capturing more than 20 percent of the U.S. long-distance market, it is now part of Worldcom. Occasionally the actions of just one manager can bring profound changes to an organization's external environment, as this "Management Insight" indicates.

Management Insight

IBM's Bill Lowe Changes the Rules of the Game

In 1980 Bill Lowe was a manager at IBM's entry systems division in Boca Raton, Florida. Lowe had watched the growth of the personal computer industry–dominated by Apple, Atari, and Radio Shack–with growing interest and apprehension. He believed that IBM, the dominant force in the mainframe computer industry, should also be a leading player in the fast-growing PC segment. Thus, in mid-1980, acting on his own initiative, he assembled a team of managers to draft a proposal describing how IBM could build a viable personal computer within a year.

Lowe's plan called for IBM to adopt an open-system architecture for the new personal computer. This meant that Lowe proposed a departure from the company's normal practice of producing key components and software in-house so other companies could not buy them. Instead, he recommended that IBM buy components "off-the-shelf" from other producers. The key components that Lowe proposed to buy included Intel's 8088 microprocessor and a software operating system known as MS-DOS from Microsoft, then a little-known Seattle company. The advantage of this approach was that it would enable IBM to get a personal computer to the market quickly. The disadvantage was that it would allow other companies to produce IBM-compatible PCs by simply buying the same Intel microprocessor and MS-DOS operating system. Such a strategy represented a radical departure for IBM, which in the past had tried to stop imitation of its products by producing all key components in-house.[35]

Lowe's team submitted the plan to IBM's powerful corporate management committee and in August 1980 received the authorization to go ahead. Just over a year later the first IBM PC was introduced into the marketplace. It was an overnight sensation and quickly grabbed the market lead from Apple. More important, however, Lowe's decision to go with an open system architecture enabled a flood of imitators to enter the market.

Within two years, the imitators were producing PCs that were compatible with the IBM standard. The first of these imitators was Compaq Computer. Compaq was soon followed by myriad other companies, including current industry stars such as Dell and Gateway. The result was the creation of today's highly competitive PC industry–an industry that IBM is no longer a part of–it exited in 2000 after experiencing huge losses. Thus, Lowe's fateful decision to adopt open-system architecture forever changed the task environment in the personal computer industry.

Tips for New Managers

Managing the Organizational Environment

1. To assess the level of uncertainty in the environment, analyze its level of complexity and rate of change.
2. Once the number and importance of the forces in the environment have been determined, decide how to build and develop departments to respond to them.
3. After analyzing your customers, competitors, and suppliers, decide which managers should be responsible for identifying and responding to their needs.
4. Once the rate of change in the task and general environment has been determined, decide whether a mechanistic or an organic structure is most appropriate for the organization.

Summary and Review

WHAT IS THE ORGANIZATIONAL ENVIRONMENT? The organizational environment is the set of forces and conditions that operate beyond an organization's boundaries but affect a manager's ability to acquire and utilize resources. The organizational environment has two components, the task environment and the general environment. The task environment is the set of forces and conditions that originate with suppliers, distributors, customers, and competitors that influence managers on a daily basis. The general environment is wider-ranging economic, technological, sociocultural, demographic, political and legal, and global forces that affect an organization and its task environment.

MANAGING THE ORGANIZATIONAL ENVIRONMENT Two factors affect the nature of the opportunities and threats that organizations face: (1) the level of complexity in the environment and (2) the rate of change in the environment. Managers must learn how to analyze the forces in the environment in order to respond effectively to opportunities and threats.

ORGANIZATIONAL-ENVIRONMENT RELATIONSHIPS The principal ways in which managers increase their organizations' ability to manage the environment is (1) by creating an organizational structure and control systems to allow managers throughout the organization to deal with the specific parts of the environment for which they are responsible; (2) by utilizing IT and the Internet to obtain more and better information and (3) by engaging in boundary-spanning activities that lead managers to have a better appreciation for their environments so that they can avoid management mistakes.

Management in Action

Topics for Discussion and Action

1. Why is it important for managers to understand the nature of the environmental forces that are acting on them and their organization?
2. Choose an organization, and ask a manager in that organization to list the number and strengths of forces in the organization's task environment. Ask the manager to pay particular attention to identifying opportunities and threats that result from pressures and changes in customers, competitors, and suppliers.
3. Which organization is likely to face the most complex task environment, a biotechnology company trying to develop a new cure for cancer or a large retailer like the Gap or Macy's? Why?
4. The population is aging because of declining birth rates, declining death rates, and the aging of the baby-boom generation. What might some of the implications of this demographic trend be for (a) a pharmaceutical company, (b) the home construction industry, and (c) the agendas of political parties?
5. As a result of deregulation, soon the average business and household will be able to choose from among several competing electricity suppliers. How might this development alter the task environment facing a manager in an electric utility?
6. Choose an organization, and ask its managers to describe the organizational structure and control systems that help that organization respond to its environment. Do you think managers in this organization are doing a good job of matching the organization to its task and general environments?
8. List five ways in which managers in a biotechnology company can help their company by engaging in boundary-spanning activities.

Building Management Skills

Analyzing an Organization's Task and General Environments

Pick an organization with which you are familiar. It can be an organization in which you have worked or currently work, or one that you interact with regularly as a customer (such as the college that you are currently attending). For this organization do the following.

1. Describe the main forces in the task environment that are affecting the organization.
2. Describe the main forces in the general environment that are affecting the organization.
3. Try to determine whether the organization's task and general environments are relatively stable or changing rapidly.
4. Explain how environmental forces affect the job of an individual manager within this organization. How do they determine the opportunities and threats that its managers must confront?

Small Group Breakout Exercise

How to Enter the Copying Business

Form groups of three to five people, and appoint one group member as the spokesperson who will communicate your findings to the whole class when called on by the instructor. Then discuss the following scenario.

You and your partners have decided to open a small printing and copying business in a college town of 100,000 people. Your business will compete with companies like Kinko's. You know that over 50 percent of small businesses fail in their first year, so to increase your chances of success, you have decided to do a detailed analysis of the task environment of the copying business to discover what opportunities and threats you would encounter. As a group:

1. Decide what you must know about (a) your future customers, (b) your future competitors, and (c) other critical forces in the task environment, if you are to be successful.
2. Evaluate the main barriers to entry into the copying business.
3. Based on this analysis, list some of the steps you will take to help your new copying business succeed.

Exploring the World Wide Web

Search for the website of a company that has a complex, rapidly changing environment. What forces in its organizational environment are creating the strongest opportunities and threats? How are managers attempting to respond to these opportunities and threats?

You're the Management Consultant

The Changing Environment of Retailing

You have been called in to advise the top managers of a major clothing store who are facing a crisis. This clothing store has been the leader in its market for the last 15 years. In the last three years, however, two other major clothing store chains have opened up and they have steadily been attracting your customers—your sales are down 30 percent. To find out why, the managers surveyed former customers and learned customers perceive the store is just not keeping up with changing fashion trends and new forms of customer service. In examining the way the store operates, managers realize that over time the 10 buyers who purchase the clothing and accessories for your store have been buying increasingly from the same clothing suppliers and have become reluctant to try new ones. Moreover, salespeople rarely, if ever, make suggestions for changing the way the store operates, and the culture of the store has become conservative and risk averse.

Questions

1. Analyze the major forces in the task environment of a retail clothing store.
2. Devise a program that will help managers and employees to better understand and respond to their store's task environment.

BusinessWeek Cases in the News

Who Will Hold the Cards? As the plastic wars heat up, look for more consolidation

Stand by for the next wave of consolidation in the credit-card business. As American consumers gorge themselves on $675 billion of credit-card debt, the stakes have never been higher for card issuers. Today, the industry's Big Five—Citigroup, MBNA, First USA, American Express, and Discover—control over half the market, up from about a third a decade ago, according to *The Nilson Report*. But the pressure to get even bigger is intense as the critical mass for a profitable operation soars.

The costs of staying in the game are enormous. Analysts estimate that Citigroup alone plows about $1 billion annually into marketing consumer credit-card services to stay at the top of the pile with its $96 billion of receivables. Such massive outlays are unthinkable for even the 10th-largest bank-card issuer, Wells Fargo, with $9.9 billion of receivables, let alone the throngs of small and midsize banks. Besides, says Mark C. Alpert, specialty finance analyst at Deutsche Banc Alex. Brown, credit-card outfits may now need portfolios of at least $50 billion to profitably grow, double what they needed five years ago. "The majority of bank-owned credit-card companies will be sold in the coming years," predicts Kenneth Posner, specialty finance analyst at Morgan Stanley Dean Witter.

Lethal Combination

Indeed, since late 1997, 17 of the top 35 bank holding companies including Key Corp., Sun-Trust Banks Inc., and First Union Corp., have sold credit-card units to rivals. Once, they invested heavily to compete with a rising legion of specialty issuers such as Delaware-based MBNA Corp. The lethal combination of thinning margins and a possible rise in bad debts because of the slowing U.S. economy is prompting even more survivors to rethink their strategies. "The amount of receivables for sale has exploded," says Oliver Sarkozy, a managing director at Credit Suisse First Boston, which advised on sales of $15 billion worth of credit-card portfolios over the past 12 months.

Now Wachovia Corp. is considering throwing in the towel. One of the most successful midsize card operators, the Winston-Salem (N.C.) bank hired CSFB on February 6, 2001, to advise it on what to do with its $8 billion credit-card portfolio. Just over a year ago it acquired a $2 billion portfolio from Partners First Holdings LLC, but now it's contemplating a sale—even though the business racked up 16 percent of Wachovia's earnings in 2000. If Wachovia does sell, it would be the largest deal sine Advanta Corp. sold $11.5 billion of receivables to Fleet Boston Financial Corp. in 1998.

Even trophy franchises like American Express and Morgan Stanley's Discover could become takeover targets. As recently as January 24, 2001, Wall Street was abuzz with scuttlebutt that Morgan Stanley Chairman and Chief Executive Philip Purcell was mulling selling the Discover unit to MBNA or Citigroup. Purcell denies that he plans to sell Discover, which analysts say could fetch as much as $14 billion. Later, rumors circulated within Morgan Stanley that Purcell wanted to buy American Express. Morgan Stanley neither confirmed nor denied the possible purchase.

Short List

American Express will not comment on the speculation, either. But analysts believe the company is more likely to be a predator. With a market cap close to $60 billion, it would be an expensive morsel to swallow. Moreover, since Kenneth I. Chenault took over as CEO in January 2001, the company has made it clear that it does not plan to sell its own $50 billion portfolio. Instead, Alfred F. Kelly Jr., president of American Express' U.S. consumer services, sees the economic downturn as an opportunity to gain market share through more portfolio acquisitions. Indeed, American Express recently snapped up a $226 million credit-card portfolio from Bank of Hawaii. And it's on a short list to buy Wachovia's portfolio, investment bankers say.

A wild card that could change American Express' and Discover's fortunes is a Justice Department antitrust suit against MasterCard International, Visa USA Inc., and Visa International, expected to be decided this month. If the U.S. District Court of Manhattan eliminates Visa and MasterCard rules that prevent thousands of banks from also offering Amex and Discover cards, then the Discover franchise will become much more valuable—and Amex would likely push hard to grab back market share from archrivals Visa and MasterCard.

As the gulf between large and small credit-card players widens, there's plenty for American Express and others to go for. Analysts say that all midsize banks risk being scarfed up, though most of the larger ones insist they do not plan to axe their credit-card businesses. For example, although Chairman and CEO James Dimon of Chicago's Bank One told financial analysts on February 12, 2001, that he expects revenues from the bank's credit-card business to be flat this year, he recently told *BusinessWeek:* "We love the business. We intend to be a winner in it."

To survive, Bank One and other middle-tier players such as Fleet Boston, Wells Fargo, and Bank of America will need to chase after valuable portfolios to develop a stronghold. Deutsche Banc's Alpert figures there are probably a dozen credit-card portfolios in the $500 million to $2 billion range that could be snapped up by larger players. "The first step is to try and buy," adds an investment banker who asks not to be named. "But if [the middle tier] fail in that, they may be sellers."

The smaller fry may not have much time to decide whether to get out or fight furiously to bulk up their businesses. Just as consolidation heats up, the industry is showing signs of slowing growth. Receivables of credit-card issuers may swell by only 6 percent in 2001, versus a solid 10.4 percent rise the previous year. And new charges—key grist for the future growth of receivables—rose just 5.7 percent in the fourth quarter of 2000, to $225 billion, versus 8.8 percent in the same period of 1999, according to Deutsche Banc Alex. Brown.

Indeed, the credit-card industry could experience its worst operating environment in a decade. For the last two years, bad debts declined as consumer confidence rose. But recently, charge-offs have swelled as consumer confidence has fallen. Even large players are worried. Although he did not give specifics, American Express' Chenault warned financial analysts in a meeting that credit-card spending slowed in the fourth quarter of 2000. "If spending slows further and credit weakens, we will be impacted—not to the same extent as some of our competitors—but impacted nonetheless," he said. The average delinquency rates for the top 15 credit-card issuers crept up to 4.32 percent in the fourth quarter of 2000, from 4.11 percent. Echoes Robert B. Willumstad, head of the global consumer business at Citigroup: "There are concerns that we'll have a hard landing that will ripple through the consumer lending business," though there are no signs of weakness at present.

If there is a slowdown, it will also be tougher to sell expensive credit-card portfolios. "These deals for the most part are in cash," says Michael Hughes, specialty finance analyst at Merrill Lynch & Co. "You have to go out and raise money to do them. And that's tough to do." Analysts estimate that American Express paid as much as a 32 percent premium for Bank of Hawaii's credit-card portfolio. But "a slowdown in consumer spending could dampen any potential buyer's enthusiasm," says E. Reilly Tierney, a Fox-Pitt, Kelton financial services analyst.

Nevertheless, the credit-card wars won't be over any time soon. After all, when the going gets tough, the tough go shopping.

Source: E. Thornton, H. Timmons, and J. Weber, "Who Will Hold the Cards? As the Plastic Wars Heat Up Look for More Consolidation," *Business Week,* March 19, 2001, pp. 90–91.

Questions

1. What environmental forces are changing in the credit card industry?
2. How are these changes going to affect managers and their companies?

BusinessWeek Cases in the News

Why E-Brokers are Broker and Broker

Barely a year ago, online brokers looked poised to take over Wall Street. Discounters E*Trade, Ameritrade, and Datek were sending shivers down the spines of hidebound mammoths like Merrill Lynch & Co. Their cheap trades drew in a growing legion of retail investors. These upstarts suddenly seemed on track to become as highly valued as Wall Street veterans. By last March, E*Trade Group's $9.4 billion market capitalization topped that of Bear Stearns Cos.

Not anymore. These days, it's the online brokers who are trembling. On January 8, 2001, Ameritrade Holding Corp. laid off 350 employees, 14 percent of its workforce, after announcing an expected first-quarter loss of 12¢ to 14¢ per share, versus analysts' estimates of 5¢. A week earlier, J. P. Morgan Chase & Co. halved its Morgan Online staff to 150. A similar fate may await most pure online brokers. "It wouldn't surprise me to see all of these guys announce layoffs," says Jaime Punishill, a senior analyst at consultants Forrester Research Inc.

Brainless Bulls?

What went wrong? Consider a familiar Wall Street motto: Don't confuse a bull market with brains. Online brokers and cheap trades were in vogue when markets were rising. But now, investors who thought they knew it all are finding that they needed advice all along. Many are too scared to make their own trades and are high-tailing it out of the markets. Or they are scrambling to find a good adviser. The trend is punishing discount brokers, who need transactions to survive and have little advice to give. "The current [online broker] model is inadequate for the pressures they are facing now," says Eric J. Rajendra, global head of e-financial services at consultant A. T. Kearney.

Of course, traditional brokers have also suffered severe blows from the turbulent stock market. But with deep pockets, they are poised to wreak revenge. They're set to bury or buy any online broker that insists on slogging it out as a transaction-oriented business. So the online crowd needs partners to build up competitive research and advisory services quickly. E*Trade, for example, tied up with Ernst & Young last year. The pure online discount broker is dead. "There will be a time when the term 'Internet brokerage' is no longer relevant," predicts Julio Gómez, chairman of online researcher Gómez Inc.

A devastating shakeout among the nation's 140 or so online brokers lies ahead. "We think you need 5 to 10," says Henry McVey, financial-services analyst at Morgan Stanley Dean Witter.

Analysts figure that online brokers are geared up to handle a total of 1.2 million trades a day. But since the stock market started its lengthy decline in spring 2000, online brokers' daily trades have dropped 30 percent, to 834,000, according to investment bank Robertson Stephens Inc.

The pain is particularly acute for discount online brokers, sine they are such young companies. The end of dot-com euphoria combined with the rapidly rising cost of acquiring new clients online is putting a serious dent in their revenue growth and in their ability to raise funding to expand. "It's a double whammy," says Richard H. Repetto, online brokerage analyst at Putnam Lovell Securities Inc.

Last Laugh

But Wall Street itself is also learning some harsh lessons from its forays into the online world. J. P. Morgan laid off marketing personnel partly because it discovered that while Morgan Online helps its private bankers, even its comprehensive online advice offerings aren't a surefire draw for droves of millionaire Net-savvy clients. A recent Forrester Research study shows that despite aggressive marketing, only 4 percent of 3,500 millionaires have visited J. P. Morgan's website, versus 28 percent who have seen E*Trade.

Nevertheless, traditional Wall Street firms may have the last laugh. Their broader Net offerings make it increasingly difficult for the online crowd to steal clients away. And, like it or not, the Net has become a mandatory component of financial advice. Hence, J. P. Morgan, Merrill Lynch, Morgan Stanley Dean Witter, Goldman Sachs, and Credit Suisse First Boston are all investing heavily in sophisticated online offerings.

Short of a huge boom in stock trading, the online brokers' woes are set to endure. That means if they can't beat Wall Street's Old Economy firms, they'll have to join them.

Source: E. Thornton, "Why E-Brokers Are Broker and Broker," *Business Week,* January 22, 2001, p. 94.

Questions

1. What factors in the environment are giving rise to opportunities and threats for brokerage companies?
2. How are managers of these companies trying to manage these opportunities and threats?

Chapter 6

Managing the Global Environment

Learning Objectives

After studying this chapter, you should be able to:

- Explain why the **global environment** is becoming more open and competitive and why barriers to the global transfer of goods and services are falling, increasing the opportunities, complexities, and challenges that managers face.
- Identify each of the **forces in the global task environment,** and explain why they create opportunities and threats for global managers.
- Describe the way in which **political and legal, economic, and sociocultural forces** in the general environment can affect managers and the way in which global organizations operate.
- List the **impediments to the development** of a more open global environment.

A Manager's Challenge

Expanding Globally in a Wired World

What is the best way to go global?
Although most of the best known dot-coms, such as Amazon.com, eBay.com, and Yahoo.com, were founded in the mid-1990s, some dot-coms immediately began a strong push to expand their activities globally. Why? Because many dot-com managers thought that once they had established a good operating or business model for the U.S. market they could then easily take this model and adapt it to the needs of countries worldwide. In this way dot-coms could quickly generate global revenues and become global powerhouses, a belief which boosted their stock price enormously.

Similarly, many bricks & mortar (B&M) companies like Land's End, the catalog clothing company, and Wal-Mart, saw opportunities to use the Internet to boost their global sales. Many managers felt that every company needed a global wired presence if they were going to be able to compete in the 21st century. Some dot-coms and B&M companies made no push to expand overseas; however, for example, Barnesandnoble.com, amazon.com's major bookstore competitor, made no attempt to establish a presence

Both Amazon.com and Land's End operate in many different countries around the world. They have found that when they establish global operations in a particular country they also have to establish a global distribution system to handle the sale of their products to customers in that country.

overseas. Its main goal was to compete with Amazon.com to obtain a share of the U.S. market. What are the opportunities and threats that confront dot-coms and B&M companies as they expand globally? What is the best way to go global?

Amazon.com has been the most aggressive of the dot-coms in its foreign expansion plans. In 1996, it acquired Bookpages, an independent online bookstore in the United Kingdom, and renamed it amazon.com.uk and installed its proprietary in-house information systems. In 1998, it started its German subsidiary from scratch and subsequently started online stores in France and Japan. By 2001, 29 million people in over 160 countries bought products from Amazon.[1] eBay has been similarly aggressive, taking over small online auction houses in different parts of the world and incorporating them into its auction store empire.[2]

Some dot-coms have run into trouble expanding abroad. While eBay has had few problems because it does not have to physically ship the products that it sells—the buyers and sellers at its auction sites handle shipping—this has not been true for companies such as Amazon.com which have to both obtain and ship their products to customers quickly. Amazon.com was forced to establish a very expensive distribution network to ship its products to customers in every country in which it operates. Moreover, it has run into problems that stem from language and cultural differences between countries in the way people buy and sell products, and has had to customize its information systems to suit local conditions. Like many other companies that have expanded beyond their borders, Amazon.com has found that everything has to be built from the ground up and this is very expensive—not a good thing for young companies that lack money. Amazon.com has never made a profit because the costs of its growth and expansion have been so great and there are few economies of scale in selling in multiple countries.[3] The potential reward, however, is huge global sales. Indeed, in November 2001 Amazon.com announced record international sales.

The company that has succeeded best at global expansion is Land's End. Land's End was and still is a clothing mail-order company; in 2001, for example, it shipped over 150 million catalogs to customers worldwide. Land's End established catalog operations in the United Kingdom in 1991, in Japan in 1993, and in Germany in 1996. In all these countries Land's End set up the distribution and call centers it needed to get its products to customers. So, given that it already had in place an efficient distribution network, the emergence of the Internet was an enormous opportunity for Land's End. It moved quickly to establish www.Landsend.com in 1995 to take advantage of the Internet and has continued to build websites in Ireland, France, Italy, and many other countries.

Land's End's experience has been the opposite of Amazon.com's because it has achieved economies of scale. First, it already had an efficient worldwide distribution/sales infrastructure in place. Second, its clothes, unlike books and videos which have to be translated or recorded into many different languages, require less customization to the needs of customers in different countries.[4]

Thus, it appears that there is no easy path to successful global expansion for dot-coms or other companies. Each new foreign venture has to be carefully planned and charted because having a competitive advantage in one country does not necessarily translate into an advantage for another company. •

Overview

As the global activities of the dot-coms suggest, managers of organizations large and small, for-profit and not-for-profit, cannot afford to ignore the forces in the global environment. Many organizations and managers have concluded that in order to survive in the 21st century, they need to adopt a global perspective. Most organizations must become **global organizations,** organizations that operate and compete in more than one country.

global organization An organization that operates and competes in more than one country.

If organizations are to adapt to the global environment, their managers must learn to understand the global forces that operate in it and how these forces give rise to opportunities and threats. In this chapter, we examine why the global environment has become more open, vibrant, and competitive. We examine how forces in the global task and general environments affect global organizations and their managers. We examine the different ways in which organizations can expand internationally. And we examine impediments to the creation of an even more open global environment. By the end of this chapter, you will appreciate the changes that have been taking place in the global environment and understand why it is important for managers to develop a global perspective as they strive to increase organizational efficiency and effectiveness.

The Changing Global Environment

In the 21st century, any idea that the world is composed of a set of distinct national countries and markets that are separated physically, economically, and culturally from one another has vanished. Managers now recognize that organizations exist and compete in a truly global market. Today, managers regard the global environment as a source of important opportunities and threats that they must respond to (see Figure 6.1). As suggested by the dot-coms's experience, managers constantly confront the challenges of global competition, establishing operations in a foreign country, obtaining inputs from foreign suppliers, or the challenges of managing in a foreign culture.

In essence, managers view the global environment as *open;* that is, as an environment in which they and their organizations are free to buy goods and services from, and sell goods and services to, whichever countries they choose. An open environment is also one in which global organizations are free not only to compete against each other to attract customers but also to establish foreign subsidiaries to become the strongest competitors throughout the world. Coca-Cola and PepsiCo, for example, have competed aggressively for 20 years to develop the strongest global soft drink empire, the dot-coms in the opening case are doing the same. Table 6.1 lists the 100 largest global organizations in 2000 by revenues.

In this section, we explain why the global environment has become more open and competitive and why this development is so significant for managers today. We examine how economic changes such as the lowering of barriers to trade and investment have led to greater interaction and exchanges between organizations and countries. We discuss how declines in barriers of distance and culture have increased the interdependencies between organizations and countries. And we consider the specific implications of these changes for managers and organizations.

Declining Barriers to Trade and Investment

During the 1920s and 1930s, many countries erected formidable barriers to international trade and investment in the belief that this was the best way to promote their economic well-being. Many of these barriers were high tariffs on imports of manufactured goods. A **tariff** is a tax that a government imposes on imported or, occasionally, on exported goods. The U.S. government, for example, currently levies a 25 percent tariff on the price of four-wheel-drive vehicles imported to the United States. The aim of import tariffs is to protect domestic industries and jobs, such as those in the auto or steel industry, from foreign competition by raising the price of goods from abroad.

tariff A tax that a government imposes on imported or, occasionally, exported goods.

Figure 6.1
The Global Environment

Very often, however, when one country imposes an import tariff, others follow suit and the result is a series of retaliatory moves as countries progressively raise tariff barriers against each other. In the 1920s this behavior depressed world demand and helped usher in the Great Depression of the 1930s and massive unemployment. In short, rather than protecting jobs and promoting economic well-being, governments of countries that resort to raising high tariff barriers ultimately reduce employment and undermine economic growth.[5]

GATT AND THE RISE OF FREE TRADE Having learned from the Great Depression, after the Second World War advanced Western industrial countries committed themselves to the goal of removing barriers to the free flow of resources between countries. This commitment was reinforced by acceptance of the principle that free trade, rather than tariff barriers, was the best way to foster a healthy domestic economy and low unemployment.[6]

free-trade doctrine The idea that if each country specializes in the production of the goods and services that it can produce most efficiently, this will make the best use of global resources.

The **free trade doctrine** predicts that if each country agrees to specialize in the production of the goods and services that it can produce most efficiently, this will make the best use of global resources and will result in lower prices. For example, if Indian companies are highly efficient in the production of textiles and U.S. companies are highly efficient in the production of computer software, then under a free-trade agreement production of textiles would shift to India and computer software to the United States. Under these conditions, prices of textiles and software should fall because both goods are being produced in the location where they can be made at the lowest cost, benefiting consumers and making the best use of scarce resources.

Table 6.1
Largest Global Corporations

Global 100 Rank	Company	Revenues ($ million)	Global 100 Rank	Company	Revenues ($ million)
1	Exxon Mobil	210,392.0	51	Texaco	51,130.0
2	Wal-Mart Stores	193,295.0	52	Fujitsu	49,603.5
3	General Motors	184,632.0	53	Duke Energy	49,318.0
4	Ford Motor	180,598.0	54	Kroger	49,000.4
5	DaimlerChrysler	150,069.7	55	NEC	48,928.0
6	Royal Dutch/Shell Group	149,146.0	56	Hewlett-Packard	48,782.0
7	BP	148,062.0	57	HSBC Holdings	48,632.8
8	General Electric	129,853.0	58	Koninklijke Ahold	48,491.7
9	Mitsubishi	126,579.4	59	Nestlé	48,225.0
10	Toyota Motor	121,416.2	60	Chevron	48,069.0
11	Mitsui	118,013.7	61	State Farm Insurance Cos.	47,863.1
12	Citigroup	111,826.0	62	Tokyo Electric Power	47,555.7
13	Itochu	109,756.5	63	UBS	47,315.8
14	Total Fina Elf	105,869.6	64	Dai-chi Mutual Life Insurance	46,435.6
15	Nippon Telegraph & Telephone	103,234.7	65	American International Group	45,972.0
16	Enron	100,789.0	66	Home Depot	45,738.0
17	AXA	92,781.6	67	Morgan Stanley Dean Witter	45,413.0
18	Sumitomo	91,168.4	68	Sinopec	45,346.0
19	Intl. Business Machines	88,396.0	69	ENI	45,139.0
20	Marubeni	85,351.0	70	Merrill Lynch	44,872.0
21	Volkswagen	78,851.9	71	Fannie Mae	44,088.9
22	Hitachi	76,126.8	72	Unilever	43,973.6
23	Siemens	74,858.3	73	Fortis	43,830.9
24	ING Group	71,195.9	74	ABN AMRO Holding	43,389.6
25	Allianz	71,022.3	75	Metro	43,371.1
26	Matsushita Electric Industrial	69,475.3	76	Prudential	43,125.5
27	E.ON	68,432.6	77	State Power Corporation	42,548.7
28	Nippon Life Insurance	68,054.8	78	Rwe Group	42,513.7
29	Deutsche Bank	67,133.2	79	Compaq Computer	42,383.0
30	Sony	66,158.4	80	Repsol YPF	42,273.2
31	AT&T	65,981.0	81	Pemex	42,166.8
32	Verizon Communications	64,707.0	82	McKesson HBOC	42,010.0
33	U.S. Postal Service	64,540.0	83	China Petroleum	41,683.7
34	Philip Morris	63,276.0	84	Lucent Technologies	41,420.0
35	CGNU	61,498.7	85	Sears Roebuck	40,937.0
36	J.P. Morgan Chase	60,065.0	86	Peugeot	40,830.6
37	Carrefour	59,887.8	87	Munich Re Group	40,671.6
38	Credit Suisse	59,315.5	88	Merck	40,363.2
39	Nissho Iwai	58,557.3	89	Procter & Gamble	39,951.0
40	Honda Motor	58,461.6	90	WorldCom	39,090.0
41	Bank of America Corp.	57,747.0	91	Vivendi Universal	38,628.3
42	BNP Paribas	57,611.6	92	Samsung Electronics	38,490.7
43	Nissan Motor	55,077.1	93	TIAA-CREF	38,063.5
44	Toshiba	53,826.6	94	Deutsche Telekom	37,834.4
45	PDVSA	53,680.0	95	Motorola	37,580.0
46	Assicurazioni Generali	53,333.1	96	Sumitomo Life Insurance	37,535.8
47	Fiat	53,190.4	97	Zurich Financial Services	37,431.0
48	Mizuho Holdings	52,068.5	98	Mitsubishi Electric	37,348.9
49	SBC Communications	51,476.0	99	Renault	37,128.4
50	Boeing	51,321.0	100	Kmart	37,028.0

Source: *Fortune.com,* July 7, 2001, www.fortune.com.

Countries that accepted this free-trade doctrine set as their goal the removal of barriers to the free flow of goods between countries. They attempted to achieve this through an international treaty known as the General Agreement on Tariffs and Trade (GATT). In the half-century since World War II, there have been eight rounds of GATT negotiations aimed at lowering tariff barriers. The last round, the Uruguay Round, involved 117 countries and was completed in December 1993. This round succeeded in lowering tariffs by over 30 percent from the previous level. On average, the tariff barriers among the governments of developed countries declined from over 40 percent in 1948 to about 3 percent in 2000, causing a dramatic increase in world trade.[7]

Declining Barriers of Distance and Culture

Barriers of distance and culture also closed the global environment and kept managers inward looking. The management problems Unilever, a large British soap and detergent maker, experienced at the turn of the 20th century illustrate the effect of these barriers.

Founded in London during the 1880s by William Lever, Unilever had a worldwide reach by the early 1900s and operated subsidiaries in most major countries of the British empire, including India, Canada, and Australia. Lever had a very hands-on, autocratic management style and found his far-flung business empire difficult to control. The reason for Lever's control problems was that communication over great distances was difficult. It took six weeks to reach India by ship from England, and international telephone and telegraph services were very unreliable.

Another problem that Unilever encountered was the difficulty of doing business in societies that were separated from Britain by barriers of language and culture. Different countries have different sets of national beliefs, values, and norms, and Lever found a management approach that worked in Britain did not necessarily work in India or Persia (now Iran). As a result, management practices had to be tailored to suit each unique national culture. After Lever's death in 1925, top management at Unilever decentralized decision-making authority to the managers of the various national subsidiaries so that they could develop a management approach that suited the country in which they were operating. One result of this strategy was that the subsidiaries grew distant and remote from one another.[8]

Since the end of World War II, major advances in communications and transportation technology have been reducing the barriers of distance and culture that affected Unilever and other global organizations. Over the last 30 years, global communications have been revolutionized by developments in satellites, digital switching, and optical fiber telephone lines–and most recently, by the exploding growth of the Internet. Satellites and optical fibers can carry hundreds of thousands of messages simultaneously, making possible global video teleconferencing and allowing companies to develop global intranets, company-specific information and decision making systems, and global email.[9] As a result of such developments, reliable, secure, and instantaneous communication is now possible with nearly any location in the world. Fax machines in Sri Lanka, cellular phones in the Brazilian rain forest, satellite dishes in Russia, video phones in Manhattan, and videoconferencing facilities in Japan are all part of the communications revolution that is changing the way the world works. This

In the middle of a maize field, villagers in Niger, Africa, gather to view worldwide news and events on their village's communal television.

revolution has made it possible for a global organization–a tiny garment factory or a huge company such as Unilever–to do business anywhere, anytime, and to search out customers and suppliers from around the world.

Several major innovations in transportation technology since World War II also have made the global environment more open. Most significant, the growth of commercial jet travel has reduced the time it takes to get from one location to another. Because of jet travel, New York is now closer to Tokyo than it was to Philadelphia in the days of the 13 colonies–a fact that makes control of far-flung international businesses much easier today than in William Lever's era.

In addition to making travel faster, modern communications and transportation technologies have also helped reduce the cultural distance between countries. The Internet and its millions of websites facilitate the development of global communications networks and media which are helping to create a worldwide culture above and beyond unique national cultures. Moreover, television networks such as CNN, MTV, BBC, and HBO can now be received in many countries around the world, and Hollywood films are shown around the globe.

Effects of Free Trade on Managers

The lowering of barriers to trade and investment and the decline of distance and culture barriers have created enormous opportunities for organizations to expand the market for their goods and services through exports and investments in foreign countries. Although managers at some organizations, like Barnes & Noble, have shied away from trying to sell their goods and services overseas, the situation of Amazon.com and Land's End is more typical. The shift toward a more open global economy has created not only more opportunities to sell goods and services in foreign markets, but also the opportunity to buy more from foreign countries. Indeed, the success in the United States of Land's End has been based in part on its managers' willingness to import low-cost clothes and bedding from foreign manufacturers. Land's End purchases clothing from manufacturers in Hong Kong, Malaysia, Taiwan, and China because

U.S. textile makers often do not offer the same quality, styling, flexibility, or price.[10] Indeed, most clothing companies such as Levi Strauss, Wal-Mart, and Target are major players in the global environment by virtue of their purchasing activities, even if like Target or Dillard's they sell only inside the United States.

The manager's job is also more challenging in a dynamic global environment because of the increased intensity of competition that goes hand in hand with the lowering of barriers to trade and investment. Thus, the job of the average manager in a U.S. car company became a lot harder from the mid-1970s on as a result of the penetration of the U.S. market by efficient Japanese and German competitors and the resulting increase in competition. Levi Strauss closed its last U.S. clothing factory in 2001 because it could not match the prices of low-cost foreign jeans manufacturers who compete with Levi's to sell to clothing chains such as Dillard's, Target, and Macy's.

NAFTA The growth of regional trade agreements such as the North American Free Trade Agreement (NAFTA) also presents opportunities and threats for managers and their organizations. NAFTA, which became effective on January 1, 1994, aims to abolish the tariffs on 99 percent of the goods traded between Mexico, Canada, and the United States by 2004. NAFTA also removes most barriers on the cross-border flow of resources, giving, for example, financial institutions and retail businesses in Canada and the United States unrestricted access to the Mexican marketplace. After NAFTA was signed, there was a flood of investment into Mexico from the United States, and many other countries such as Japan, into Mexico. Wal-Mart, Price Club, Radio Shack, and other major U.S. retail chains plan to expand their operations in Mexico.

The establishment of free-trade areas creates an opportunity for manufacturing organizations because it allows them to reduce their costs. They can do this either by shifting production to the lowest-cost location within the free-trade area (for example, U.S. auto and textile companies shifting production to Mexico) or by serving the whole region from one location, rather than establishing separate operations in each country.

Some managers, however, might see regional free-trade agreements as a threat because they expose a company based in one member country to increased competition from companies based in the other member countries. Managers in Mexico, the United States, and Canada are experiencing this now that NAFTA is here. For the first time, Mexican managers find themselves facing a threat: head-to-head competition in some industries against efficient U.S. and Canadian organizations. But the opposite is true as well: U.S. and Canadian managers are experiencing threats in labor-intensive industries, such as the flooring tile and textile industries, where Mexican businesses have a cost advantage.

The three current NAFTA members have announced that they hope to expand the treaty in the future to include other countries in Central and South America to increase economic prosperity throughout the Americas. Chile is a possible future member as are Brazil and Argentina. However the recent currency and economic problems that these countries have been experiencing have slowed down the attempt to expand NAFTA, as has political resistance within the United States.

In essence, the shift toward a more open, competitive global environment has increased both the opportunities that managers can take advantage of and the threats they must respond to in performing their jobs effectively. Next, we look in detail at the forces in the global task and general environments to see where these opportunities and threats are arising.

The Global Task Environment

As managers operate in the global environment, they confront forces that differ from country to country and from world region to world region.[11] In this section, we examine some of the forces in the global task environment that increase opportunities or threats for managers. The major forces in the global task environment are similar to those introduced in Chapter 3: suppliers, distributors, customers, and competitors (see Figure 6.2).

Suppliers

At a global level, managers have the opportunity to buy products from foreign suppliers or to become their own suppliers and manufacture their own products abroad. For example, as noted in the opening case, to lower costs and increase product quality, Amazon.com and Land's End import low-cost clothes, books, and electronics from foreign manufacturers as well as sell this merchandise in countries across the globe. Organizations such as Levi Strauss, AT&T, and GE also have prospered by manufacturing their own low-cost products abroad, which has enabled them to charge their U.S. customers lower prices.

A common problem facing managers of large global organizations such as Ford, Procter & Gamble, and IBM is the development of a global network of suppliers that will allow their companies to keep costs down and quality high. For example, the building of Boeing's newest jet airliner, the 777, required 132,500 engineered parts produced around the world by 545 suppliers.[12] While Boeing makes the majority of these parts, eight Japanese suppliers make parts for the 777's fuselage, doors, and wings; a Singapore supplier makes the doors for the plane's forward landing gear; and three Italian suppliers manufacture wing flaps. Boeing's rationale for buying so many inputs from foreign suppliers is that these suppliers are the best in the world at performing their particular activity, and doing business with them helps Boeing to produce a high-quality final product, a vital requirement given the need for aircraft safety and reliability.[13]

Figure 6.2
Forces in the Global Task Environment

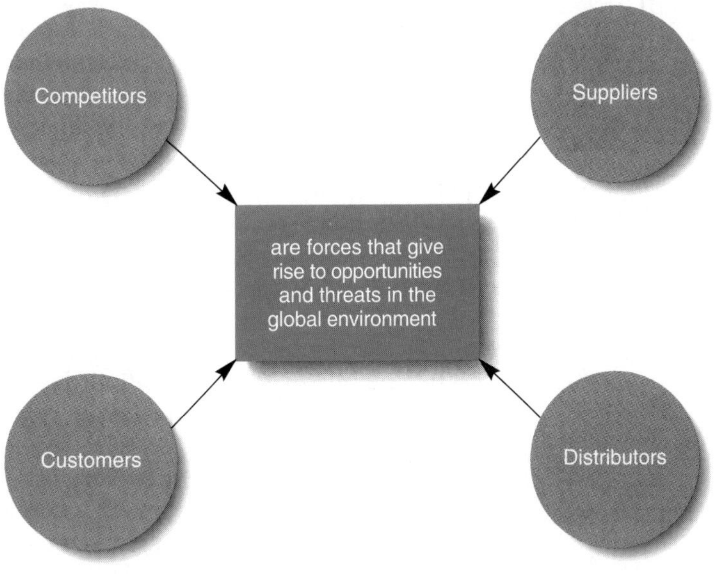

The purchasing activities of global companies have become increasingly complicated as a result of the development of a whole range of skills and competencies in different countries around the world. It is clearly in their interests to search out the lowest cost, best quality suppliers no matter where they may be. Also, the Internet makes it possible for companies to coordinate complicated, arm's-length exchanges involving the purchasing of inputs and the disposal of outputs.

global outsourcing The purchase of inputs from foreign suppliers, or the production of inputs abroad, to lower production costs and improve product quality or design.

Global outsourcing is the process by which organizations purchase inputs from other companies or produce inputs themselves throughout the world, to lower their production costs and improve the quality or design of their products. To take advantage of national differences in the cost and quality of resources such as labor or raw materials, General Motors might build its own engines in one country, transmissions in another, brakes in a third, and buy other components from hundreds of global suppliers. Trade expert Robert Reich once calculated that of the $20,000 that customers pay GM for a Pontiac Le Mans, about $6,000 goes to South Korea, where the Le Mans is assembled; $3,500 to Japan for advanced components such as engines, transaxles, and electronics; $1,500 to Germany, where the Le Mans was designed; $800 to Taiwan, Singapore, and Japan for small components; $500 to Britain for advertising and marketing services; and about $100 to Ireland for data-processing services. The remaining $7,000 goes to GM–and to the lawyers, bankers, and insurance agents that GM retains in the United States.[14]

Is the Le Mans a U.S. product? Yes, but it is also a Korean product, a Japanese product, and a German product. Today, such global exchanges are becoming so complex that specialized organizations are emerging to help manage global organizations supply chains, that is, the flow of inputs necessary to produce a product. One example is Li & Fung profiled in Managing Globally.

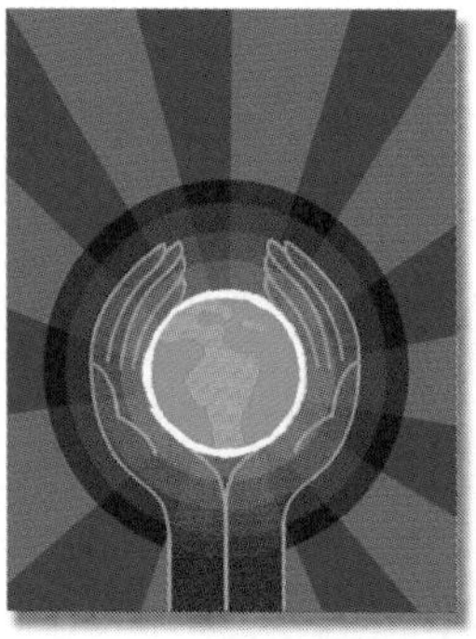

Managing Globally

Li & Fung's Global Supply Chain Management

Finding the foreign suppliers that offer the lowest-priced and highest-quality products is an important task facing the managers of global organizations. Since these suppliers are located in thousands of cities in many countries around the world finding them is a difficult business. Often, global companies use the services of foreign intermediaries or brokers, located near these suppliers, to find the one that best meets their input requirements. Li & Fung, now run by brothers Victor and William Fung, is one of these brokers that has helped hundreds of global companies to locate suitable foreign suppliers, especially suppliers in mainland China.[15]

In 2001, however, managing global companies' supply chains became a more complicated task. To reduce costs, foreign suppliers were increasingly specializing in just one part of the task of producing a product. For example, in the past, a company such as Target might have negotiated with a foreign supplier to manufacture 1 million units of some particular shirt at a certain cost per unit. But with specialization, Target might find it can reduce the costs of producing the shirt even further by splitting apart the operations involved in producing the shirt and having different foreign suppliers, often in different countries perform each operation. For example, to get the lowest cost per unit, rather than just negotiate with a foreign supplier over the price of making a particular shirt, Target might first negotiate with a yarn manufacturer in Vietnam to make the yarn; then ship the yarn to a Chinese supplier to weave it into cloth; and then to several different factories in Malaysia and the Philippines to cut the cloth and sew the shirts. Then, another foreign company might take responsibility for packaging and shipping the shirts to wherever in the world they are required. Because a company such as Target has thousands of different clothing products under production, and these change all the time, the problems of managing such a supply chain to get the full cost savings from global expansion are clear.

Li & Fung has capitalized on this opportunity. Realizing that many global companies do not have the time or expertise to find such specialized low-price suppliers, they moved quickly to provide such a service. Li & Fung employ 3,600 agents who travel across 37 countries to find new suppliers and inspect existing suppliers to find new ways to help their global clients get lower prices or higher-quality products. Global companies are happy to outsource their supply chain management to Li & Fung because they realize significant cost savings. Even though they pay a hefty fee to Li & Fung, they avoid the costs of employing their own agents. As the complexity of supply chain management continues to increase more and more companies like Li & Fung are appearing.

Distributors

Another force that creates opportunities and threats for global managers is the nature of a country's distribution system. For example, consider how Japan's systems of distributing Japanese-made products caused problems for Toys 'Я' Us managers when they were seeking to establish a chain of stores in Japan. Traditionally, Japanese manufacturers sold their products only by means of wholesalers with which they had developed long-term business relationships. Because the wholesalers added their own price markup, the price Toys 'Я' Us had to pay for Japanese toys increased and this thwarted the U.S. company's attempt to establish a competitive advantage in Japan based on price discounting. To keep its costs low, Toys 'Я' Us insisted on buying directly from Japanese manufacturers, but the manufacturers refused.

This standoff was finally broken by Japan's deep recession in the early 1990s. Faced with slumping orders, computer-game maker Nintendo reversed its earlier decision and agreed to sell merchandise directly to Toys 'Я' Us. Soon a host of other Japanese toy companies followed Nintendo's lead. With these major problems solved, average sales in Toys 'Я' Us's Japanese stores were between $15 million and $20 million a year, roughly double the sales per store in the United States. As Toys 'Я' Us discovered in Japan, the traditional means by which goods and services are distributed and sold to customers can present challenges to managers of organizations pursuing international expansion. Managers must identify the hidden problems surrounding the distribution and sale of goods and services–such as anti-competitive government regulations–in order to discover hidden threats early and find ways to overcome them before significant resources are invested.

Customers

The most obvious opportunity associated with expanding into the global environment is the prospect of selling goods and services to new customers, as Amazon.com's CEO Jeff Bezos discovered. Similarly, Arthur Andersen and PricewaterhouseCoopers, two large accounting companies, have established

Two newly affluent Chinese consumers enjoy Coca-Cola, a global brand, whose recipe has nevertheless been specially altered to satisfy the taste of Chinese consumers.

foreign operations throughout the world and recruit and train thousands of foreign accountants to serve the needs of customers in a wide variety of countries.

Today, once-distinct national markets are merging into one huge global marketplace where the same basic product can be sold to customers worldwide. This consolidation is occurring both for consumer goods and for business products and has created enormous opportunities for managers. The global acceptance of Coca-Cola, Sony Walkmans, McDonald's hamburgers, Doc Martin boots, and Nokia cell phones is a sign that the tastes and preferences of consumers in different countries are beginning to become more similar.[16] Similarly, large global markets currently exist for business products such as telecommunications equipment, electronic components, computer services, and financial services. Thus, Motorola sells its telecommunications equipment, Intel its microprocessors, and SAP its business systems management software, to customers throughout the world.

Nevertheless, despite evidence that the same goods and services are receiving acceptance from customers worldwide, it is important not to place too much emphasis on this development. Because national cultures differ in many ways, significant differences between countries in consumer tastes and preferences still remain. These differences often require managers to customize goods and services to suit the preferences of local consumers. For example, despite McDonald's position as a leading global organization, its management has recognized a need for local customization. In Brazil, McDonald's sells a soft drink made from the guarana, an exotic berry that grows along the Amazon River. In Malaysia, McDonald's sells milk shakes flavored with durian, a strong-smelling fruit that local people consider an aphrodisiac.[17] Similarly, when Mattel decided to begin selling Barbie dolls in Japan, it had to redesign the doll's appearance (color of hair, facial features, and so on) to suit the tastes of its prospective customers.

Competitors

Although finding less-expensive or higher-quality supplies and attracting new customers are global opportunities for managers, entry into the global environment also leads to major threats in the form of increases in competition both at home and abroad. U.S. managers in foreign markets, for example, face the problem of competing against local companies familiar with the local market that have generated considerable brand loyalty. As a result, U.S. managers might find it difficult to break into a foreign market and obtain new customers. Of course, foreign competitors trying to enter a U.S. company's domestic market face the same challenges. U.S. car companies faced strong global competition at home in the 1970s, when foreign competitors aggressively entered the U.S. market. In the global environment, the level of competition can increase rapidly, and managers must be alert to the changes taking place in order to respond appropriately.

The Global General Environment

Despite evidence that countries are becoming more similar to one another and that the world is on the verge of becoming a global village, countries still differ across a range of political, legal, economic, and cultural dimensions. When an organization operates in the global environment, it confronts in the global general environment a series of forces that differ from country to country and world region to world region. In this section we consider how forces in the global general environment, such as political and legal, economic, and sociocultural forces, create opportunities and threats for managers of global organizations (see Figure 6.3).

Political and Legal Forces

Global political and legal forces result from the diverse and changing nature of various countries' political and legal systems. Because the global range of political systems includes everything from representative democracies to totalitarian regimes, managers must understand how these different political systems work to manage global organizations effectively.

representative democracy A political system in which representatives elected by citizens and legally accountable to the electorate form a government whose function is to make decisions on behalf of the electorate.

In **representative democracies,** such as Britain, Canada, Germany, and the United States, citizens periodically elect individuals to represent their interests. These elected representatives form a government whose function is to make decisions on behalf of the electorate. To guarantee that voters can hold elected representatives legally accountable for their actions, an ideal representative democracy incorporates a number of safeguards into the law. These include (1) an individual's right to freedom of expression, opinion, and organization; (2) free media; (3) regular elections in which all eligible citizens are allowed to vote; (4) limited terms for elected representatives; (5) a fair court system that is independent from the political system; (6) a nonpolitical police force and armed service; and (7) relatively free access to state information.[18]

Figure 6.3 Forces in the Global General Environment

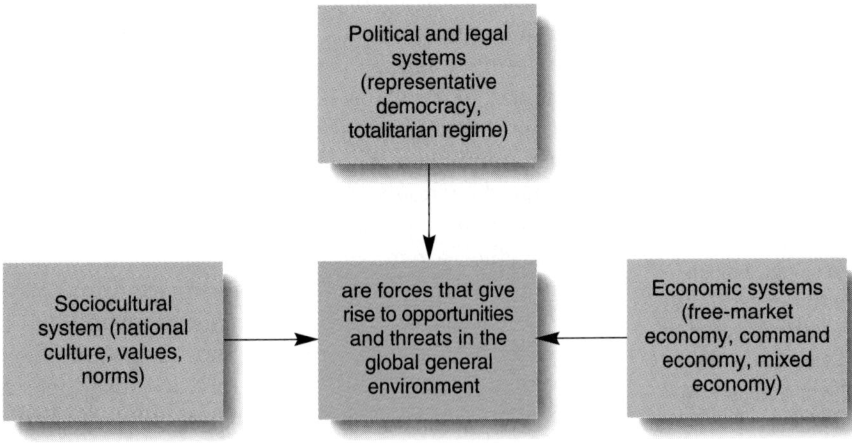

totalitarian regime A political system in which a single party, individual, or group holds all political power and neither recognizes nor permits opposition.

In contrast, in **totalitarian regimes** a single political party, individual, or group of individuals holds all political power. Typically, totalitarian regimes neither recognize nor permit opposition from individuals or groups. Most of the constitutional guarantees on which representative democracies are based are denied to the citizens of totalitarian states. In most totalitarian countries, political repression is widespread. Those who question the policies of the rulers and their right to rule find themselves imprisoned or worse. Totalitarian regimes are found in countries such as China, Iraq, and Iran.

Why must managers be concerned about the political makeup of a foreign country in which they are doing business? First, stable democratic countries with a high degree of political freedom tend to be characterized by economic freedom and a well-defined legal system. In turn, economic freedom and a well-defined legal system protect the rights of individuals and corporations and are conducive to business.[19] Second, totalitarian regimes' lack of respect for human rights raises the question of whether it is ethical to trade with, or invest in, those countries.

Economic Forces

Economic forces are caused by the changing nature of countries' economic systems. Around the globe, economic systems range from free-market economies to command economies, and managers must learn how different economic systems work in order to understand the opportunities and threats associated with them.

free-market economy An economic system in which private enterprise controls production and the interaction of supply and demand determines which and how many goods and services are produced and how much consumers pay for them.

In a **free-market economy,** the production of goods and services is left in the hands of private (as opposed to government) enterprise. The goods and services that are produced, and the quantities that are produced, are not specified by a central authority. Rather, production is determined by the interaction of the forces of supply and demand. If demand for a product exceeds supply, the price of the product will rise, prompting managers and organizations to produce more. If supply exceeds demand, prices will fall, causing managers and organizations to produce less. In a free-market economy the purchasing patterns of consumers, as signaled to managers by changes in demand, determine what and how much is produced.

command economy An economic system in which the government owns all businesses and specifies which and how many goods and services are produced and the prices at which they are sold.

In a **command economy,** the goods and services that a country produces, the quantity in which they are produced, and the prices at which they are sold are all planned by the government. In a pure command economy, all businesses are government owned and private enterprise is forbidden. As recently as 1990, the communist countries of eastern Europe and the Soviet Union had command economies; other communist countries such as China and Vietnam still do. The overall failure of these economies to perform as well as the free-market-oriented systems of western Europe, North America, and areas of the Pacific Rim helped precipitate the collapse of communism in many of these countries and the subsequent dismantlement of command economies. Even in China and Vietnam, which remain communist controlled, there has been a marked shift away from a command economy.

mixed economy An economic system in which some sectors of the economy are left to private ownership and free-market mechanisms and others are owned by the government and subject to government planning.

Between free market economies, on the one hand, and command economies, on the other, are mixed economies. In a **mixed economy,** certain sectors of the economy are left to private ownership and free-market mechanisms, and other sectors are characterized by significant government ownership and government planning. Mixed economies are most commonly found in the democratic countries of western Europe, but they are disappearing as these countries shift toward the free-market model. For example, in Britain in the 1980s the government owned a majority stake in many important industries, including airlines, rail, health care, steel, and telecommunications. Since then, following a trend toward privatization, the British government has sold its airline, steel, and telecommunications interests to private investors, and a significant private health care sector has emerged to compete with government-provided health care. Similar privatization efforts have been undertaken in other western European countries and are growing in eastern Europe.

The manager of a global organization generally prefers a free-market system, for two reasons. First, because much of the economy is in private hands, there tend to be few restrictions on organizations that decide to invest in countries with free-market economies. For example, U.S. companies face fewer impediments to investing in Britain, with its largely free-market system, than they do in China, where a free market is allowed in only certain sectors of the economy. Second, free-market economies tend to be more economically developed and have higher rates of economic growth than command or mixed economies, so their citizens tend to have higher per capita incomes and more spending power.[20] As a result, for companies attempting to export or to establish foreign subsidiaries, they are more attractive markets than are mixed economies or command economies, which are closely regulated by government.

Changes in Political and Legal and Economic Forces

In recent years, two large and related shifts in political and economic forces have occurred globally (see Figure 6.4).[21] One–the shift away from totalitarian dictatorships and toward more democratic regimes–has been most dramatic in eastern Europe and the former Soviet Union, where totalitarian communist regimes collapsed during the late 1980s and early 1990s. The other–the shift toward representative democracy–has occurred from Latin America to Africa. For the most part, the movement toward democracy has been precipitated by the failure of totalitarian regimes with command or mixed economies to improve the well-being of their citizens. This failure has been particularly noticeable in comparisons of these countries with democratic, free-market countries such as Germany, Japan, and the United States.

Accompanying this change in political forces has been a worldwide shift away from command and mixed economies and toward the free-market model, as noted previously.[22] This economic shift was triggered by the realization that government involvement in economic activity often impedes economic growth. Thus, a wave of privatization and deregulation has swept throughout the world, from the former communist countries to Latin America, Asia, and western Europe. Governments have sold off government-owned organizations to private investors and have dismantled regulations that inhibit the operation of the free market.

These trends are good news for managers of global organizations because they result in the expansion of opportunities for exporting and investment abroad. A decade ago, few Western companies exported to or invested in eastern Europe because the combination of totalitarian political regimes and command economies created a hostile environment for Western businesses. Since 1990, however, the environment in eastern Europe has become far more favorable for Western businesses; from 1990 to 2000, Western businesses have invested more than $150 billion in eastern Europe.[23] A similar story has unfolded in China, where despite the continued presence of a totalitarian communist regime, a move toward greater economic freedom has produced a surge

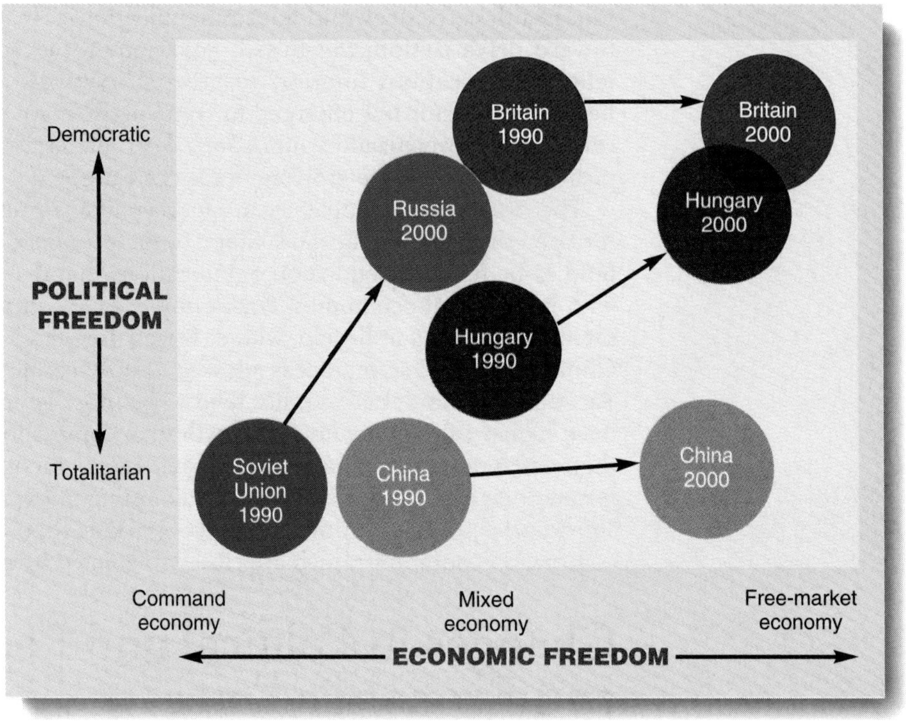

Figure 6.4
Changes in Political and Economic Forces

of Western and Japanese business activity in this region of the world. From 1990 to 2000, foreign companies invested over $500 billion in China and by 2001 China accounted for 60 percent of all foreign investment in South East Asia.[24]

After making these huge investments, the managers of many Western companies have experienced considerable difficulty in their attempts to establish business operations in eastern Europe and China. For example, when the Chiquita Brands International entered the Czech Republic, the company was hoping to take advantage of that nation's rapid move toward a free-market economy. However, Chiquita found that the premium bananas it sold in the West could not be marketed in the Czech Republic. After decades of communism, Czech citizens apparently had difficulty understanding why something of better quality should cost more. Chiquita was forced to switch to lower-quality bananas after discovering that consumers were unwilling to pay higher prices for superior bananas.[25] Managers who want to take advantage of the opportunities created by changing global political and legal and economic forces face a major challenge, and nowhere has this been seen more clearly than in the global car industry.

Managing Globally

The Changing Face of Global Car Manufacturing

In the last decade, a huge wave of mergers and alliances between global car manufacturers resulted from changing economic and political conditions. Ford, for example, bought Jaguar and Volvo, and owns the majority share in Mazda.[26] GM owns Germany's Opel, Sweden's Saab, and Japan's Isuzu; Chrysler and Mercedes-Benz merged, and bought Mitsubishi in 2000; and Renault bought Nissan in 2000.[27]

These global mergers have occurred because car makers realize that they need to have a strong presence in every region of the world if they are to obtain the full benefits from globalization. Car companies have been merging rapidly to achieve global economies of scale. The goal of these companies is to design and produce cars that can be sold throughout the world, making it easier to recoup the huge costs of developing a new vehicle. Also, global car companies can enjoy the low costs that can be obtained from having global supply chains, as discussed earlier. Moreover, they can obtain and share valuable design or car-making skills that may be present in one car company but not in another, such as Mercedes-Benz's safety features, or Mitsubishi's low-cost small car design skills.

Chrysler and Mitsubishi are expected to achieve considerable cost savings from their merger for this reason, and the merger between Renault and Nissan is also expected to pay off handsomely.[28] However, such expected savings from the merger between Mercedes-Benz and Chrysler were not forthcoming. Indeed, many of the mergers between car companies have not proved profitable and have resulted in many losses. GM, for example, has lost over a billion dollars from its investments in Saab and Isuzu, as has Mercedes-Benz from its takeover of Chrysler.[29]

Despite such short-term economic problems, however, these mergers are expected to pay off during the next decades as car companies jockey for position as world leaders. Indeed, politically, as the world divides into economic regions, only a global presence will allow a car company to play in the world league. Also, to enter new largely untapped markets such as eastern Europe and China, car companies have to be able to respond to the different political and cultural forces that characterize business in different countries; hence, the need for operations on a truly global level. Indeed, the takeover of Japanese car companies has been due to a combination of a severe recession in Japan combined with an increasing political willingness by the Japanese government to allow foreign firms to control Japanese companies.[30] The same situation is occurring in Korea where bankrupt Korean car companies are being targeted by U.S. car companies as well.

Sociocultural Forces

What is interesting about the experiences of companies such as Chiquita in the Czech Republic is that many of their problems are the result of critical differences in the values, norms, and attitudes of Western cultures and of eastern European cultures conditioned by communism and a command economy. National culture is an important sociocultural force that global managers must take into account when they do business in foreign countries. National culture includes the values, norms, knowledge, beliefs, moral principles, laws, customs, and other practices that unite the citizens of a country.[31] National culture shapes individual behavior by specifying appropriate and inappropriate behavior and interaction with others. People learn national culture in their everyday lives by interacting with those around them. This learning starts at an early age and continues throughout their lives.

national culture The set of values that a society considers important and the norms of behavior that are approved or sanctioned in that society.

VALUES AND NORMS The basic building blocks of national culture are values and norms. Values are ideas about what a society believes to be good, right, desirable, or beautiful. They provide the basic underpinnings for notions of individual freedom, democracy, truth, justice, honesty, loyalty, social obligation, collective responsibility, the appropriate roles for men and women, love,

values Ideas about what a society believes to be good, right, desirable, or beautiful.

sex, marriage, and so on. Values are more than merely abstract concepts; they are invested with considerable emotional significance. People argue, fight, and even die over values such as freedom.

Though deeply embedded in society, values are not static–however, change in a country's values is likely to be slow and painful. For example, the value systems of many formerly communist states, such as Russia, are undergoing significant changes as those countries move away from a value system that emphasizes the state and toward one that emphasizes individual freedom. Social turmoil often results when countries undergo major changes in their values.

norms Unwritten rules and codes of conduct that prescribe how people should act in particular situations.

folkways The routine social conventions of everyday life.

Norms are unwritten rules and codes of conduct that prescribe appropriate behavior in particular situations and shape the behavior of people toward one another. Two types of norms play a major role in national culture: folkways and mores. Folkways are the routine social conventions of everyday life. They concern customs and practices such as dressing appropriately for particular situations, good social manners, eating with the correct utensils, and neighborly behavior. Although folkways define the way people are expected to behave, violation of folkways is not a serious or moral matter. People who violate folkways are often thought to be eccentric or ill mannered, but they are not usually considered to be evil or bad. In many countries, initially foreigners may be excused for violating folkways because they are unaccustomed to local behavior, but repeated violations are not excused because foreigners are expected to learn appropriate behavior.

mores Norms that are considered to be central to the functioning of society and to social life.

Mores are norms that are considered to be central to the functioning of society and to social life. They have much greater significance than folkways. Accordingly, the violation of mores can be expected to bring serious retribution. Mores include proscriptions against theft, adultery, and incest. In many societies mores have been enacted into law. Thus, all advanced societies have laws against theft and incest. However, there are many differences in mores from one society to another.[32] In the United States, for example, drinking alcohol is widely accepted; but in Saudi Arabia, the consumption of alcohol is viewed as a violation of social norms and is punishable by imprisonment (as many U.S. citizens working in Saudi Arabia have discovered).

HOFSTEDE'S MODEL OF NATIONAL CULTURE Researchers have spent considerable time and effort identifying similarities and differences in the values and norms of different countries. One model of national culture was developed by Gert Hofstede.[33] As a psychologist for IBM, Hofstede collected data on employee values and norms from more than 100,000 IBM employees in 64 countries. Based on his research, Hofstede developed five dimensions along which national cultures can be placed (see Figure 6.5).

individualism A worldview that values individual freedom and self-expression and adherence to the principle that people should be judged by their individual achievements rather than by their social background.

collectivism A worldview that values subordination of the individual to the goals of the group and adherence to the principle that people should be judged by their contribution to the group.

INDIVIDUALISM VERSUS COLLECTIVISM The first dimension, which Hofstede labeled individualism versus collectivism, has a long history in human thought. Individualism is a worldview that values individual freedom and self-expression and adherence to the principle that people should be judged by their individual achievements rather than by their social background. In Western countries, individualism usually includes admiration for personal success, a strong belief in individual rights, and high regard for individual entrepreneurs.[34]

In contrast, collectivism is a worldview that values subordination of the individual to the goals of the group and adherence to the principle that people should be judged by their contribution to the group. Collectivism was widespread in communist countries but has become less prevalent since the collapse of communism in those countries. Japan is a noncommunist country where collectivism is highly valued.

Figure 6.5
Hofstede's Model of National Culture

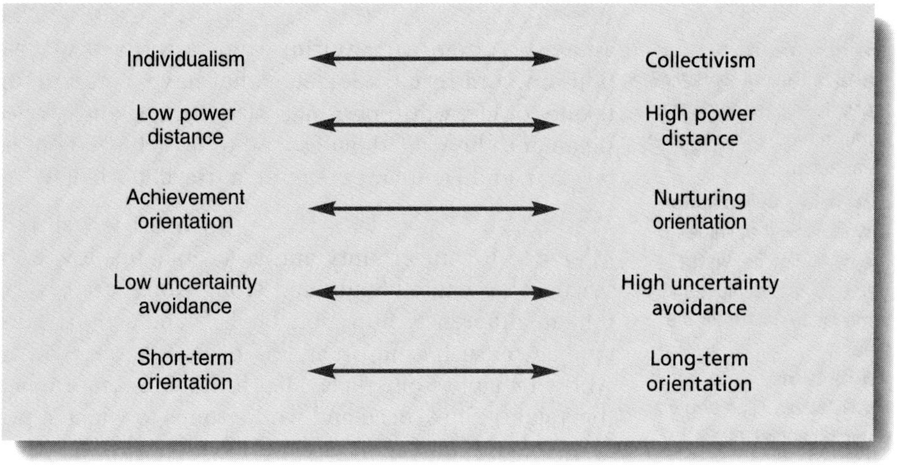

Collectivism in Japan traces its roots to the fusion of Confucian, Buddhist, and Shinto thought that occurred during the Tokugawa period in Japanese history (1600–1870s).[35] One of the central values that emerged during this period was strong attachment to the group–whether a village, a work group, or a company. Strong identification with the group is said to create pressures for collective action in Japan, as well as strong pressure for conformity to group norms and a relative lack of individualism.[36]

Managers must realize that organizations and organizational members reflect their national culture's emphasis on individualism or collectivism. Indeed, one of the major reasons why Japanese and American management practices differ is that Japanese culture values collectivism and U.S. culture values individualism.[37]

power distance The degree to which societies accept the idea that inequalities in the power and well-being of their citizens are due to differences in individuals' physical and intellectual capabilities and heritage.

POWER DISTANCE By power distance Hofstede meant the degree to which societies accept the idea that inequalities in the power and well-being of their citizens are due to differences in individuals' physical and intellectual capabilities and heritage. This concept also encompasses the degree to which societies accept the economic and social differences in wealth, status, and well-being that result from differences in individual capabilities.

Societies in which inequalities are allowed to persist or grow over time have *high power distance.* In high-power-distance societies, workers who are professionally successful amass wealth and pass it on to their children, and as a result, inequalities may grow over time. In such societies, the gap between rich and poor, with all the attendant political and social consequences, grows very large. In contrast, in societies with *low power distance,* large inequalities between citizens are not allowed to develop. In low-power-distance countries, the government uses taxation and social welfare programs to reduce inequality and improve the welfare of the least fortunate. These societies are more attuned to preventing a large gap between rich and poor and minimizing discord between different classes of citizens.

Advanced Western countries such as the United States, Germany, the Netherlands, and the United Kingdom have relatively low power distance and high individualism. Economically poor Latin American counties such as Guatemala and Panama, and Asian countries such as Malaysia and the Philippines, have high power distance and low individualism.[38] These findings suggest that the cultural values of richer countries emphasize protecting the rights of individuals and, at the same time, provide a fair chance of success to every member of society.

achievement orientation A worldview that values assertiveness, performance, success, and competition.

nurturing orientation A worldview that values the quality of life, warm personal friendships, and services and care for the weak.

uncertainty avoidance The degree to which societies are willing to tolerate uncertainty and risk.

long-term orientation A worldview that values thrift and persistence in achieving goals.

short-term orientation A worldview that values personal stability or happiness and living for the present.

ACHIEVEMENT VERSUS NURTURING ORIENTATION Societies that have an **achievement orientation** value assertiveness, performance, success, competition, and results. Societies that have a **nurturing orientation** value the quality of life, warm personal relationships, and services and care for the weak. Japan and the United States tend to be achievement oriented; the Netherlands, Sweden, and Denmark are more nurturing oriented.

UNCERTAINTY AVOIDANCE Societies as well as individuals differ in their tolerance for uncertainty and risk. Societies low on **uncertainty avoidance** (such as the United States and Hong Kong) are easygoing, value diversity, and tolerate differences in personal beliefs and actions. Societies high on uncertainty avoidance (such as Japan and France) are more rigid and skeptical about people whose behaviors or beliefs differ from the norm. In these societies, conformity to the values of the social and work groups to which a person belongs is the norm, and structured situations are preferred because they provide a sense of security.

LONG-TERM VERSUS SHORT-TERM ORIENTATION The last dimension that Hofstede described is orientation toward life and work.[39] A national culture with a **long-term orientation** rests on values such as thrift (saving) and persistence in achieving goals. A national culture with a **short-term orientation** is concerned with maintaining personal stability or happiness and living for the present. Societies with a long-term orientation include Taiwan and Hong Kong, well known for their high rate of per capita savings. The United States and France have a short-term orientation, and their citizens tend to spend more and save less.

NATIONAL CULTURE AND GLOBAL MANAGEMENT Differences among national cultures have important implications for managers. First, because of cultural differences, management practices that are effective in one country might be troublesome in another. General Electric's (GE) managers learned this while trying to manage Tungsram, a Hungarian lighting products company it acquired for $150 million. GE was attracted to Tungsram, widely regarded as one of Hungary's best companies, because of Hungary's low wage rates and the possibility of using the company as a base from which to export lighting products to western Europe. GE transferred some of its best managers to Tungsram and hoped it would soon become a leader in Europe. Unfortunately, many problems arose.

One of the problems resulted from major misunderstandings between the American managers and the Hungarian workers. The Americans complained that the Hungarians were lazy; the Hungarians thought the Americans were pushy. The Americans wanted strong sales and marketing functions that would pamper customers. In the prior command economy, sales and marketing activities were unnecessary. In addition, Hungarians expected GE to deliver Western-style wages, but GE came to Hungary to take advantage of the country's low-wage structure.[40] As Tungsram's losses mounted, GE managers had to admit that, because of differences in basic attitudes between countries, they underestimated the difficulties they would face in turning Tungsram around. Nevertheless, by 2001, these problems were solved; GE's Hungarian operations made it a major player in the European lighting market, causing it to invest another $1 billion.[41]

Often, management practices must be tailored to suit the cultural contexts within which an organization operates. An approach effective in the United States might not work in Japan, Hungary, or Mexico, because of differences in national culture. For example, American-style pay-for-performance systems that emphasize the performance of individuals alone might not work well in Japan, where individual performance in pursuit of group goals is the value that receives emphasis.

Managers doing business with individuals from another country must be sensitive to the value systems and norms of that country and behave accordingly. For example, Friday is the Islamic Sabbath. Thus, it would be impolite and inappropriate for a U.S. manager to schedule a busy day of activities for Saudi Arabian managers visiting on a Friday.

A culturally diverse management team can be a source of strength for an organization participating in the global marketplace. Organizations that employ managers from a variety of cultures appreciate better than do organizations with culturally homogeneous management teams how national cultures differ, and they tailor their management systems and behaviors to the differences. Indeed, one of the advantages that many Western companies have over their Japanese competitors is greater willingness to build an international team of senior managers.[42] For example, Ford, is headed by Lebanese-born CEO, Jacques Nasser, and Coca-Cola's CEO is Douglas Daft who was born in Australia. Japanese companies, in contrast, tend to have almost all Japanese-born senior managers and consequently have a more culturally narrow view of doing business across borders.

culture shock The feelings of surprise and disorientation that people experience when they do not understand the values, folkways, and mores that guide behavior in a culture.

expatriate managers Managers who go abroad to work for a global organization.

Culture shock is a phrase that sums up the feelings of surprise and disorientation that people experience when they enter a foreign culture and do not understand the values, folkways, and mores that guide behavior in that culture. Many managers and their families experience culture shock when they move abroad. If they have received no training, they may not understand how to do business in a foreign country or how local stores and school systems operate. Learning a different culture takes time and effort, and global organizations must devote considerable resources to helping **expatriate managers** (managers who go abroad to work for a global organization) adapt to local conditions and learn the local culture.

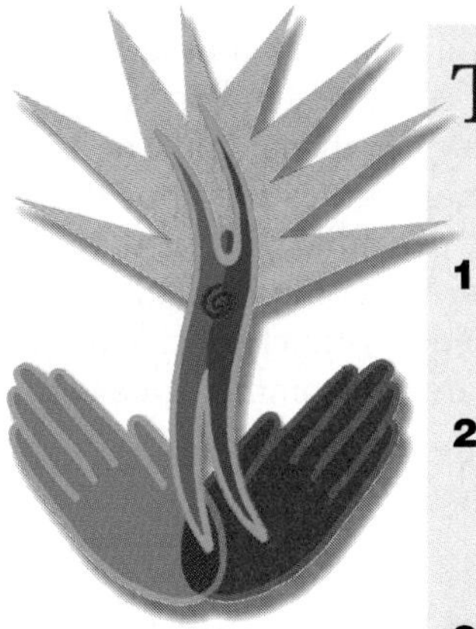

Tips for New Managers

Understanding the Global Environment

1. Carefully analyze forces in the global task environment to identify opportunities and threats, and then select the most appropriate way to operate in that task environment.
2. Find opportunities to take advantage of the global environment by, for example, finding new kinds of customers to export goods and services to, or new avenues to invest in foreign countries, or new ways to buy and make products overseas.
3. Identify the threats in the global environment, such as strong foreign companies poised to invade the home market or powerful suppliers who might withhold inputs.
4. Be sensitive to the differences between countries, and carefully analyze their political, economic, and sociocultural systems to find the best way to operate in those countries.
5. Recognize the need to become internationally and cross-culturally aware.

Choosing a Way to Expand Internationally

As we have discussed, the trend toward a more open, competitive global environment has proved to be both an opportunity and a threat for organizations and managers. The opportunity is that organizations that expand globally are able to open new markets and reach more customers and gain access to new sources of raw materials and to low-cost suppliers of inputs. The threat is that organizations that expand globally are likely to encounter new competitors in the foreign countries they enter and must respond to new political, economic, and cultural conditions.

Before setting up foreign operations, managers of companies such as Amazon.com, Land's End, GE, Toys 'Я' Us, and Boeing, needed to analyze the forces in the environment of a particular country (such as Korea or Brazil) in order to choose the right method to expand and respond to those forces in the most appropriate way. In general, four basic ways to operate in the global environment are importing and exporting, licensing and franchising, strategic alliances, and wholly owned foreign subsidiaries. We briefly discuss each one, moving from the lowest level of foreign involvement and investment required of a global organization and its managers, and the least amount of risk, to the high end of the spectrum (see Figure 6.6).[43]

Importing and Exporting

exporting Making products at home and selling them abroad.

importing Selling at home products that are made abroad.

The least complex global operations are exporting and importing. A company engaged in **exporting** makes products at home and sells them abroad. An organization might sell its own products abroad or allow a local organization in the foreign country to distribute its products. Few risks are associated with exporting because a company does not have to invest in developing manufacturing facilities abroad. It can further reduce its investment abroad if it allows a local company to distribute its products.

A company engaged in **importing** sells at home products that are made abroad (products it makes itself or buys from other companies). For example, most of the products that Pier 1 Imports, The Bombay Company, and The Limited sell to their customers are made abroad. In many cases the appeal of a product–Irish glass, French wine, Italian furniture, or Indian silk–is that it is made abroad. The Internet has made it much easier for companies to inform potential foreign buyers about their products; detailed product specifications, and features are available online, and informed buyers can communicate easily with prospective sellers.

Licensing and Franchising

licensing Allowing a foreign organization to take charge of manufacturing and distributing a product in its country or world region in return for a negotiated fee.

In **licensing,** a company (the licenser) allows a foreign organization (the licensee) to take charge of both manufacturing and distributing one or more of its products in the licensee's country or world region in return for a negotiated fee. Chemical maker Du Pont might license a local factory in India to produce nylon or Teflon. The advantage of licensing is that the licenser does not have to bear the development costs associated with opening up in a foreign country; the licensee bears the costs. The risks associated with this strategy are that the company granting the license has to give its foreign partner access to its technological know-how and so risks losing control over its secrets.

Figure 6.6 Four Ways of Expanding Internationally

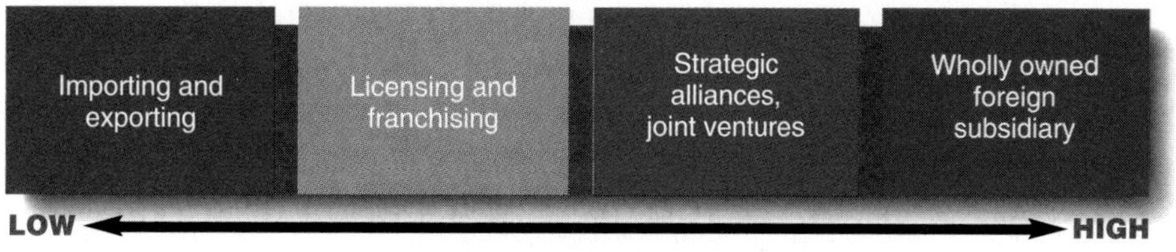

franchising Selling to a foreign organization the rights to use a brand name and operating know-how in return for a lump-sum payment and a share of the profits.

Whereas licensing is pursued primarily by manufacturing companies, franchising is pursued primarily by service organizations. In **franchising,** a company (the franchiser) sells to a foreign organization (the franchisee) the rights to use its brand name and operating know-how in return for a lump-sum payment and share of the franchiser's profits. Hilton Hotels might sell a franchise to a local company in Chile to operate hotels under the Hilton name in return for a franchise payment. The advantage of franchising is that the franchiser does not have to bear the development costs of overseas expansion and avoids the many problems associated with setting up foreign operations. The downside is that the organization that grants the franchise may lose control over the way in which the franchisee operates and product quality may fall. In this way, franchisers, such as Hilton, Avis, and McDonald's, risk losing their good names. American customers who buy McDonald's hamburgers in Korea may reasonably expect those burgers to be as good as the ones they get at home. If they are not, McDonald's reputation will suffer over time. Once again, the Internet facilitates communication between partners and allows them to better meet each other's expectations.

Strategic Alliances

strategic alliance An agreement in which managers pool or share their organization's resources and know-how with a foreign company, and the two organizations share the rewards and risks of starting a new venture.

One way to overcome the loss-of-control problems associated with exporting, licensing, and franchising is to expand globally by means of a strategic alliance. In a **strategic alliance,** managers pool or share their organization's resources and know-how with those of a foreign company, and the two organizations share the rewards or risks of starting a new venture in a foreign country. Sharing resources allows a U.S. company, for example, to take advantage of the high-quality skills of foreign manufacturers and the specialized knowledge of foreign managers about the needs of local customers, and to reduce the risks involved in a venture. At the same time, the terms of the alliance give the U.S. company more control over how the good or service is produced or sold in the foreign country than it would have as a franchiser or licenser.

joint venture A strategic alliance among two or more companies that agree to jointly establish and share the ownership of a new business.

A strategic alliance can take the form of a written contract between two or more companies to exchange resources, or it can result in the creation of a new organization. A **joint venture** is a strategic alliance among two or more companies that agree to jointly establish and share the ownership of a new business.[44] An organization's level of involvement abroad increases in a joint venture because it normally involves a capital investment in production facilities abroad in order to produce goods or services outside its home country. Risk, however, is reduced. The Internet and global teleconferencing provide the increased communication and coordination necessary for partners to work together on a global basis. In 2001, for example, Coca-Cola and Nestlé announced that they would form a joint venture and cooperate in marketing their teas, coffees, and health-oriented beverages to more than 50 countries in the world.[45] Similarly, BP Amoco and Italy's ENI announced that they would form a joint venture to build a $2.5 billion gas-liquefaction plant in Egypt.[46]

Wholly Owned Foreign Subsidiaries

wholly owned foreign subsidiary Production operations established in a foreign country independent of any local direct involvement.

When managers decide to establish a **wholly owned foreign subsidiary,** they invest in establishing production operations in a foreign country independent of any local direct involvement. Many Japanese car component companies, for example, have established their own operations in the United States to supply U.S.-based Japanese car makers such as Toyota and Honda with high-quality components.

Operating alone, without any direct involvement from foreign companies, an organization receives all of the rewards and bears all of the risks associated with operating abroad.[47] This method of international expansion is much more expensive than the others because it requires a higher level of foreign investment and presents managers with many more threats. However, investment in a foreign subsidiary or division offers significant advantages: It gives an organization high potential returns because the organization does not have to share its profits with a foreign organization, and it reduces the level of risk because the organization's managers have full control over all aspects of their foreign subsidiary's operations. Moreover, this type of investment allows managers to protect their technology and know-how from foreign organizations. Large, well-known companies like Du Pont, General Motors, and Arthur Andersen, which have plenty of resources, make extensive use of wholly owned subsidiaries. No matter what means they choose to expand globally, however, companies have to be careful to design and select the right kind of information systems and websites to allow customers to buy their products.

Information Technology Byte

Designing Global Information Systems

As more and more customers buy products on-line the importance of a company's website is increasing. Good design is essential for attracting not only domestic customers but also those overseas. Domestically, the problems involved in designing a good website caused even information technology expert Wal-Mart to close down its website for two weeks in 2000 while it reworked its search and ordering system.[48] Dell Computer, however, has one of the easiest-to-use websites of a U.S. company so imagine its surprise when, after creating a Japanese website, it found that Japanese customers were not attracted to it at all.

The reason? Dell's designers decided to give the website a thick black border around the outside of the screen and in Japan black is the sign of negative feelings and emotions.[49] Dell's designers moved quickly to solve this problem and now, whenever they create a website in a foreign company they are careful to work with local managers to make sure that their screen color or icons do not offend local tastes or customs. Another common problem involves making sure that designers are making correct use of the country's language to avoid embarrassing mistakes, something that is particularly important in Asia where local scripts are easy to misinterpret. Also, companies must take into consideration how customers like to pay for their on-line products. Unlike the

United States where consumers make constant use of credit cards, consumers in Germany and Japan like to avoid debt and pay by cash or debit card.

To respond to these problems, companies such as Yahoo, Dell, and Lycos are increasingly developing local management teams based in each country in which they operate to oversee their businesses. Often, this can involve giving domestic managers foreign assignments to help develop their global expertise. For example, managers can learn about each country's different regulatory environment; they can also help develop a strategy to customize products to suit local tastes; in this way a company's global knowledge increases.

Beyond websites directed at customers, companies also have to be sure they are developing information systems and intranets that are understandable and usable not only by domestic and foreign managers but also by their suppliers worldwide. For example, Wal-Mart's push to become a global company has led it to develop a global knowledge management system that tells foreign suppliers what kinds of products it requires and what it is willing to pay for them.[50] Foreign suppliers can then bid for Wal-Mart's business; in this way Wal-Mart makes sure it is securing the lowest prices. This global knowledge system is also used to enable the sharing of merchandising information from country to country so Wal-Mart can quickly take advantage of changing trends and ideas.

Impediments to an Open Global Environment

To this point, we have emphasized the trend toward the creation of a more open, competitive global environment and the advantages that result from this, such as access to more customers or to higher-quality or cheaper inputs. However, as every manager of a global organization knows, we live in an imperfect world, and significant barriers to cross-border exchanges between countries continue to make global expansion risky and expensive.

Government Imposed Impediments

One reason why barriers exist is that governments have ways of getting around free-trade agreements such as the GATT. GATT aims primarily to lower tariff barriers, but there are various nontariff barriers to trade that governments can erect. In other words, there are many loopholes in the GATT that countries can exploit. One class of nontariff impediments to international trade and investment is known as administrative barriers. Administrative barriers are government policies that in theory have nothing to do with international trade and investment but in practice have the intended effect of limiting imports of goods and inward investment by foreign corporations.

Japan is well-known for the many ways in which it attempts to restrict the entry of foreign competitors or lessen their impact on Japanese firms. For example, Japan's Large Scale Retail Store Law allows small retailers to block large retailers from entering a particular market for up to 10 years; it slowed the entry of U.S. firms like Toys 'Я' Us into the Japanese market. Another kind of administrative trade barrier prevents Dutch companies from exporting tulip bulbs to Japan. Why do Dutch companies export tulip bulbs to almost every country in the world except Japan? Japanese customs inspectors insist on checking every tulip bulb by cutting the stems vertically down the middle, and even Japanese ingenuity cannot put them back together.[51] Japan has come under intense pressure to relax and abolish these regulations, as the following "Managing Globally" suggests.

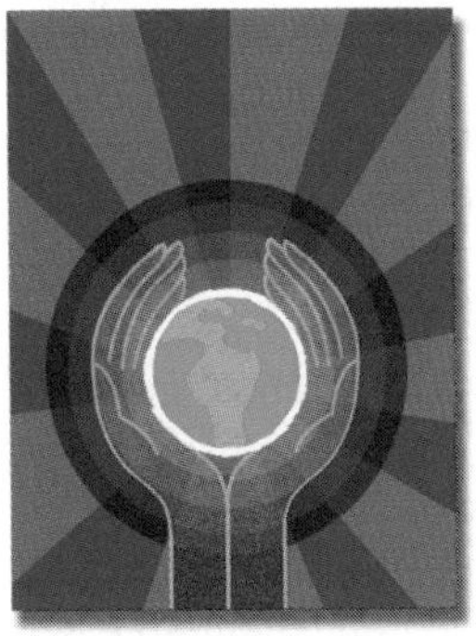

Managing Globally

American Rice Invades Japan

The Japanese rice market, similar to many other of its markets, was closed to foreign competitors until 1993 to protect Japan's thousands of high–cost small rice farmers. Rice cultivation is expensive in Japan because of its mountainous terrain, and Japanese consumers have always paid high prices for rice. Under foreign pressure, the Japanese government opened the market, and foreign competitors are now allowed to export to Japan 8 percent of its annual rice consumption. Despite the still-present hefty foreign tariff on rice of $2.33 per 2.2 pounds, U.S. rice sells for $14 dollars a pound bag while Japanese rice sells for about $19. With the recession affecting Japan, price conscious consumers are turning to foreign rice which has hurt domestic farmers.

In 2001, however, an alliance between organic rice grower Lundberg Family Farms of California and the Nippon Restaurant Enterprise Co. found a new way to break into the Japanese rice market. Because there is no tariff on rice used in processed foods, Nippon takes the U.S. organic rice and converts it into "O-bento" an organic hot boxed lunch packed with rice, vegetables, chicken, beef, and salmon all imported from the United States. These new lunches, which cost about $4 compared to a Japanese rice bento which costs about $9 are sold at railway stations and other outlets around Japan.[52] They are proving to be very popular and are creating a storm of protest from Japanese rice farmers who already have been forced to leave 37 percent of their rice fields idle and grow less-profitable crops because of the entry of U.S. rice growers. Japanese and foreign companies are increasingly forming alliances to find new ways to break into the high-price Japanese market and, little by little, Japan's restrictive trade practices are being whittled away.

A Japanese businessman receives a lunch box at a Nippon restaurant shop at the Tokyo Railway Station. Nippon began selling lunch boxes prepared from US rice, frozen, and imported from the United States in 2001, drawing harsh protests from Japanese rice farmers.

Self-Imposed Ethical Impediments

Organizations impose on themselves other impediments to cross-border trade and investment. Why would managers choose to limit their own options for engaging in international trade and investment? In many countries, human rights, workers' rights, and environmental protection are of such low priority that managers decline to have their organizations trade with, or invest in, these countries on ethical grounds.

The human rights issue has recently been raised in the United States in connection with the importing of goods from China. China is not a democracy, and its human rights record is poor. Some of the goods imported into the United States from China are made by prison labor. Many prisoners in China are political prisoners, locked up because of their opposition to the communist-controlled state. Learning of this use of prisoners, many organizations broke off their ties with Chinese companies.

Similarly, U.S. investment in Mexico and other Central American countries has fallen as a result of revelations about their poor environmental record and labor laws. Many critics argue that U.S. businesses investing in these countries are doing so to take advantage of these nations' lax (by U.S. standards) environmental and labor laws. Clothing companies such as Target, Wal-Mart, and The Gap now employ agents to tour the factories producing the clothes they buy to make sure that local labor laws are followed and that workers are fairly treated. Nevertheless, sweatshop conditions remain common in many regions of the world.

Arguments in favor of investing in countries that have poor records on human rights, environmental protection, and workers' rights go like this: Rich countries tend to have better records in these areas than poor countries; economic growth increases a country's concern for human rights, environmental protection, and workers' rights; so trade or investment in a poor country eventually might improve its stance on human rights, environmental protection, and workers' rights.[53]

Anita Roddick, who founded The Body Shop, initiated a fair-trade philosophy designed to improve the welfare of people in less-developed countries while at the same time giving The Body Shop products for its stores. Her "Trade Not Aid" policy works like this: Some years ago the Kayapo people living in the Brazilian rain forest received offers to permit logging and mining in their traditional area by both Brazilian and foreign companies. The Kayapo invited The Body Shop to identify an economic and sustainable alternative that would provide jobs and help preserve their homeland. Believing that Brazil nuts could be sustainably harvested and the oil used as a conditioner in a Body Shop hair care product, Roddick asked the Kayapo to gather Brazil nuts for The Body Shop. They said that the price of Brazil nuts ($8 per kilo) was too low to make this option economically viable. In response, The Body Shop purchased some machinery for the Kayapo to use to grind and cook the nuts and then squash them to extract the oil. The pure, cold-pressed Brazil nut oil can be sold for $38 per kilo.[54] As a result, the Kayapo have been able to earn a living while preserving their culture and environment. Some more examples of companies that have followed the lead of The Body Shop are profiled in the following Ethics in Action.

Ethics in Action

Saving the Amazon Jungle

Increasingly, large global companies are working with environmentalists to find new ways to utilize natural resources to create valuable products while protecting the natural environment and the people who live in it. This is nowhere more true that in the Amazon jungle where huge efforts are being made to find ways to prevent the destruction of the rainforest. For example, to help this process in 1992 DaimlerChrysler contributed $1.4 million for research into ways of using the natural products of the Amazon jungle for commercial purposes. It found that it could combine the husks of coconuts with natural rubber to form headrests and car seats for the vehicles it makes. DaimlerChrysler then invested several more millions to build a factory to make these products which will absorb the crops of more than 3,000 small

A worker harvests plants in the Amazon rainforest. More and more companies are investing in the environmentally friendly ways to use natural products of the Amazon jungle.

coconut farmers and bring prosperity to the Brazilian state of Marajo.[55] Honda and Toyota have also agreed to utilize these natural, environmentally friendly products, so that more growth in the region seems likely.

Following the lead of The Body Shop, Estee Lauder Companies also has been discovering ways to use natural dyes from plants to color its lipsticks and other products. For example, one of its lipsticks marketed by Arveda contains a reddish pigment from shrubs grown by Yawanawa Indians. Finally, Hermes, the French fashion house, developed a chic handbag made from natural rubber, and its Amazonia collection of bags now sell for $1,000 each. Even though efforts by these and other companies have created many thousands of jobs for farmers and workers in the rainforest, the fight continues to find ways to slow down the disappearance of the Amazon jungle and the displacement of the many Indian tribes who live within it.

Tips for New Managers

Managing the Global Environment

1. Identify the ways that the shift to a more open global environment has resulted in a more complex, competitive, and changing environment and how this affects a manager's job.
2. Analyze the changes taking place in relations between countries and world regions to forecast where new opportunities and threats may come from.
3. Try to foresee the way that impediments to trade and investment will make doing business in other countries difficult. Develop a plan to overcome these impediments.

Summary and Review

THE GLOBAL ENVIRONMENT In recent years there has been a marked shift away from a closed global environment, in which countries are cut off from each other by barriers to international trade and investment and by barriers of distance and culture, and toward a more open global environment. The emergence of an open global environment and the reduction of barriers to the free flow of goods, services, and investment owe much to the rise of global trade agreements such as GATT; to the growing global acceptance of a free-market philosophy; and to the poor performance of countries that protected their markets from international trade and investment.

THE GLOBAL TASK ENVIRONMENT Forces in the global task environment are more complex than those inside only one country and present managers with greater opportunities and threats. Managers must analyze forces in their global task environment to determine how best to operate abroad.

THE GLOBAL GENERAL ENVIRONMENT In the general environment, managers must recognize the substantial differences among countries' political, legal, economic, and sociocultural systems. Political, legal, and economic differences range from democratic states with free-market systems to totalitarian states with mixed or command economies. These differences impact on the attractiveness of a nation as a trading partner or as a target for foreign investment. Substantial differences in national culture can also be observed, such as those described in Hofstede's model of national culture. Management practices must be tailored to the particular culture in which they are to be applied. What works in the United States, for example, might not be appropriate in France, Peru, or Vietnam.

IMPEDIMENTS TO AN OPEN GLOBAL ENVIRONMENT Despite the shift toward a more open, competitive global environment, many impediments to international trade and investment still remain. Some are imposed by governments. Others are self-imposed by organizations.

Management in Action

Topics for Discussion and Action

1. In what ways does a more open global environment increase opportunities and threats in the global task environment?
2. How do political, legal, and economic forces shape national culture? What characteristics of national culture do you think have the most important effect on how successful a country is in doing business abroad?
3. Ask an expatriate manager about the most important problems and challenges that he or she confronted during an assignment abroad.
4. The textile industry has a labor-intensive manufacturing process that utilizes unskilled and semiskilled workers. What are the implications of the shift to a more open global environment for textile companies whose manufacturing operations are based in high-wage countries such as Australia, Britain, and the United States?
5. "Over the next decade we will see the emergence of enormous global markets for standardized products such as cars, blue jeans, food products, and recorded music." In your view is this an accurate statement or an exaggeration?
6. After the passage of the North American Free Trade Agreement, many U.S. companies shifted production operations to Mexico to take advantage of lower labor costs and lower standards for environmental and worker protection. As a result, they cut their costs and were better able to survive in an increasingly competitive global environment. Was their behavior ethical—that is, did the ends justify the means?
7. Go to the library and gather information that allows you to compare and contrast the political, economic, and cultural systems of the United States, Mexico, and Canada. In what ways are the countries similar? How do they differ? How might the similarities and differences influence the activities of managers at an enterprise such as Ford or Wal-Mart that do business in all three countries?

Building Management Skills

Studying a Global Organization

Pick one of the following companies—Ford Motor Company, Compaq Computer, Procter & Gamble, or Kellogg. Collect information about the company from its annual reports or from articles in business magazines such as *Fortune* or *Business Week;* then do the following.

1. Identify the three largest foreign markets in which the company operates.
2. List the forces in the global task environment that you think have most affected the company's organization, and try to determine how its managers have responded to those forces.
3. Identify the political, economic, and sociocultural forces that have the most effect on the company, paying particular attention to differences in national culture. What implications, if any, do such differences have for the way in which this company sells its product in different national markets?
4. Determine how the shift toward a more open global environment has affected the opportunities and threats facing managers in the company.

Small Group Breakout Exercise

How to Become Globally Aware

Form groups of three to five people, and appoint one group member as the spokesperson who will communicate your findings to the whole class when called on by the instructor. Then discuss the following scenario.

You are store managers who work for a large U.S. retailer that is planning to open a chain of new stores in France. Each of you has been given the responsibility to manage one of these stores, and you are meeting to develop a plan of action to help you and your families adjust to the conditions that you will encounter in France. As a group, do the following.

1. Decide which forces in the environment will most affect your ability and your family's ability to adjust to the French culture.
2. Identify the best ways to gather information about the French business and social environment to enable you to understand these forces.
3. Decide what steps you and your family can take before you leave for France to smooth your transition into the French culture and help you avoid culture shock.

Exploring the World Wide Web

Search for the website of a company with a strong global presence. What are the main forces in the task and general global environments that most affect the way this company operates? How are managers responding to these forces?

You're the Management Consultant

You have been approached by the senior managers of Lartor, a high-tech company, to advise them on whether to outsource the production of a range of new electronic video products that are currently under development to foreign manufacturers or whether to establish a foreign subsidiary to manufacture its own. While keeping manufacturing costs low is important, product quality is very important as well and specifications will need to be tailored to suit the needs of many different countries.

Questions

1. What forces in the environment will be the most important to analyze to decide which is the best manufacturing option?
2. What kind of management and information system will you need to design to make sure Lartor has sufficient control over cost and quality?

BusinessWeek Cases in the News

Car Power: With Trade Barriers Falling, Latin America's Auto Industry Enters an Era of Innovation

For the text of this in-depth *Business Week* case, log on to the *Contemporary Management* website at www.mhhe.com/jones3e.

Questions

1. How are changes in the global (a) task environment and (b) general environment affecting foreign car makers' decisions to operate in Latin American countries?
2. What are the main ways in which foreign car makers are entering Latin America?

Source: G. Smith, J. Wheatly, and J. Green, "Car Power: With Trade Barriers Falling, Latin America's Auto Industry Is Entering a New Era of Innovation," *Business Week,* October 23, 2000, pp.73–82.

BusinessWeek

Cases in the News

Surprise! Nokia Doesn't Walk on Water; Its About-face on Growth Will Harm Its Credibility

A year ago, the vision looked so alluring. As Europeans surfed the Web via their mobile phones, a new generation of speedy, data-friendly handsets would fly off store shelves. No one embraced this idea more enthusiastically than Jorma Ollila, chief of Finland's Nokia, the world's largest and most profitable mobile-phone maker.

Then, on June 12, 2001, the company stunned the investors with a profits warning, slashing second-quarter sales growth estimates in half, to 10 percent. The sell orders that followed wiped more than $31 billion off Nokia's market cap in one day. The suddenly gloomy Ollila blamed a deterioration "driven by economic uncertainty, the ongoing technology transition, and less aggressive marketing by the operators."

Translation: Europe's economy is in worse shape than expected, and mobile data transmission, the big hope of companies like Nokia and its next-door rival, Sweden's Ericsson, has so far proved a dud. The networks to provide all the promised gee-whiz services won't be up and running until this summer at the earliest. The phones aren't coming soon. And in Europe, just about everybody who wants an ordinary cell phone has one.

Ouch!

Until Ollila's announcement, stock-pickers assumed Nokia would somehow defy gravity, despite the woes of rivals such as Ericsson and Motorola Inc. Until recently, Nokia predicted a global market of 550 million cell phones by year-end, with the Finnish company selling 40 percent of the haul. Now Nokia pegs demand at 405 million phones. Analysts at Merrill Lynch & Co. reckon it will be more like 390 million.

Nokia says its earlier optimism reflected only what it was seeing in the first quarter and that it didn't expect America's problems to spread so quickly to Europe. Still, the volte-face is "a blow to Nokia's credibility" says Mark Davies Jones, managing director for telecom equipment research at Schroder Salomon Smith Barney in London. Delays from Nokia are contributing to the mobile-Net malaise. The company's phones for the next stage, so-called 2.5G, are late. Analysts see a decline in Nokia profits of 12 percent this year, to around $4.3 billion on sales of $26 billion.

Adding to the pressure, many European cell-phone operators struggling under massive debts are slashing the subsidies that supercharged handset sales. Meanwhile, the drop in European demand makes Nokia more dependent on bargain-basement markets like China. Nokia had also counted on an increase in its telecom equipment business to offset any volatility in consumer handsets. How, Nokia admits its infrastructure sales will grow only as fast as the market, a big shock to investors.

To shore up margins, Nokia is moving some production to lower-cost countries such as Mexico and China. But what it really needs to do is deliver the promised wonders of the mobile Net. Only then will this Finnish wonder regain its star status.

Source: K. Capell and W. Echikson, "Surprise! Nokia Doesn't Walk on Water," *Business Week,* June 25, 2001, p. 49.

Questions

1. What forces in the global environment shocked Nokia's managers?
2. How have they started to respond to these forces?

Chapter 7

The Manager as a Decision Maker

Learning Objectives:

After studying this chapter, you should be able to:

- Differentiate between **programmed and nonprogrammed decisions,** and explain why nonprogrammed decision making is a complex, uncertain process.
- Describe the **six steps** that managers should take to make the best decisions.
- Explain how **cognitive biases** can affect decision making and lead managers to make poor decisions.
- Identify the advantages and disadvantages of **group decision making,** and describe techniques that can improve it.
- Explain the role that **organizational learning and creativity play** in helping managers to improve their decisions.

A Manager's Challenge

Decision Making Troubles at Nike

How can managers make good decisions in a changing environment?

Phil Knight started Nike by selling athletic shoes from the trunk of his car. His company has grown to be the major player in the athletic shoe industry and was one of the most profitable companies in the world in the 1980s and 1990s.[1] Nike's image as a hip company with cool products was epitomized by famed basketball player Michael Jordan who helped popularize the brand with teenagers across the country.[2] Because Nike seemingly could do no wrong and almost all of Knight's past decisions led to increased growth and profits, the current turn of events at Nike is puzzling.

In the 2000s, CEO Knight has not only missed a number of important business opportunities that Nike could have benefited from but also failed to adequately respond to emerging challenges and threats. Nike has experienced declining profits because of lackluster sales due to inventory shortages of popular products and surpluses of unpopular ones. In addition to a lack of responsiveness to changing customer needs, Nike has been charged with operating sweatshops and other labor abuses in overseas manufacturing facilities. Knight was slow to respond to these charges. It appears that Knight has made some questionable decisions and Nike's performance has suffered.[3] How could the tide have turned for a much admired company?

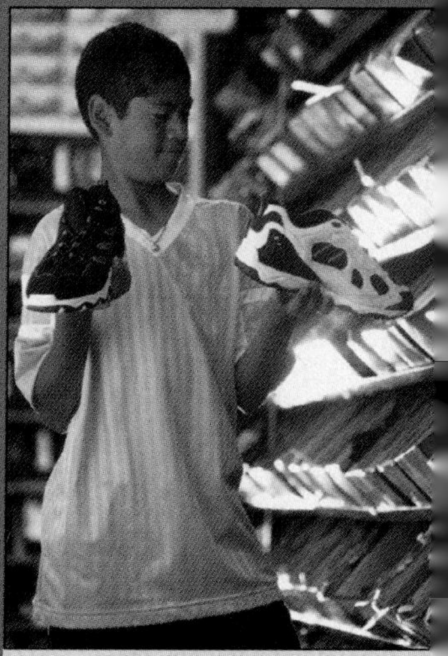

A shoe customer makes a tough decision. One reason for Nike's declining profits may be a cultural mindset that has led designers to emphasize shoe performance over fashion.

Many of Nike's current problems stem from faulty decision making at the top and the failure of its managers to change the basis on which they make decisions as conditions in the environment changed. Nike's managers' mindset emphasizes the importance of the internal development of products believing that Nike's designers know best how to develop popular products. Their almost fanatical emphasis on doing things the "Nike Way" led to an inward looking approach to decision making.[4] Nike's strong corporate culture prevented both its designers and managers from noticing how customer demands and the environment were changing.

Interestingly enough, Knight had hired outsiders who brought new ideas and tried to help the company change with the times. Frequently Knight and other managers vetoed the initiatives these outsiders championed because they did not seem to fit with Nike's culture. One example is Gordon O. McFadden, who was hired as president of outdoor products at Nike. He tried to persuade Knight to acquire North Face Inc., an outdoor products company, to take advantage of the booming hiking market. McFadden thought the North Face acquisition would put Nike at the top of the outdoor gear market. Knight eventually shot the idea down because Nike has not been in the habit of growth via acquisition—Nike's company culture dictated that designers knew best how to develop the "right" products.[5]

Nike's cultural mind-set also led its designers to emphasize the performance of athletic shoes, over the trendy or fashionable styles in vogue. This caused Nike to miss out on shifts in certain segments of the market; for example, a shift away from white athletic shoes to more versatile darker shoes for city living. In its emphasis on performance, Nike also devoted too many resources to developing very expensive high-performance shoes like the Shox line of shoes which sells for over $140 a pair at the expense of midpriced athletic shoes in the $60 to $90 range, which are responsible for around half of Nike's annual revenues.[6]

Although managers were brought in to change Nike's rigid mind-set and help it to make decisions in tune with the times, their efforts were thwarted. Often they left the company. McFadden, for example, left after Knight would not take his advice. Similarly, a former top manager at Kinko's Inc., Ellen Turner, was hired as chief marketing officer; she was bent on overhauling Nike's marketing and sales departments. She soon understood that she had little support within Nike to back her initiation of needed changes and left the company within six months.[7] Decision makers at Nike need to realize that conditions in the market and the environment changed. Because times have changed, what may have worked in the Michael Jordan era might not work today.

Overview

"A Manager's Challenge" describes how difficult and challenging effective decision making can be in an organization. Nike, a very successful company that seemingly could do no wrong for so long has recently been troubled by a failure to seize opportunities and respond appropriately to challenges. Decision making is so difficult and challenging precisely because of the changes occurring in the environment that bring uncertainty. Decision makers in organizations such as Nike have a natural tendency to view decisions from a we've-always-done-it-this-way perspective. For example, recent decisions at Nike that have been questioned in the business press concern its focus on performance rather than fashion and the internal development of new products over the acquisition of innovative small companies.[8]

The purpose of this chapter is to examine how managers make decisions and to explore how individual, group, and organizational factors affect the quality of the decisions they make and thus determine organizational performance. We discuss the nature of managerial decision making and examine some models of the decision-making process that help reveal the complexities of successful decision making. Then we outline the main steps of the decision-making process; in addition, we explore the biases that may cause capable managers to make poor decisions both as individuals and as members of a group. Finally, we examine how managers can promote organizational learning and creativity and improve the quality of their decision making. By the end of this chapter you will understand the crucial role decision making plays in creating a high-performing organization.

The Nature of Managerial Decision Making

Every time managers act to plan, organize, direct, or control organizational activities, they make a stream of decisions. In opening a new restaurant, for example, managers have to decide where to locate it, what kinds of food to provide to customers, which people to employ, and so on. Decision making is a basic part of every task managers perform. In this chapter we study how these decisions are made.

As we discussed in the last three chapters, one of the main tasks facing a manager is to manage the organizational environment. Forces in the external environment give rise to many opportunities and threats for managers and their organizations. In addition, inside an organization managers must address many opportunities and threats that may arise during the course of utilizing organizational resources. To deal with these opportunities and threats, managers must make decisions–that is, they must select one solution from a set of alternatives. **Decision making** is the process by which managers respond to the opportunities and threats that confront them by analyzing the options and making determinations, or *decisions*, about specific organizational goals and courses of action. A good decision results in the selection of appropriate goals and courses of action that increase organizational performance; bad decisions result in lower performance.

decision making The process by which managers respond to opportunities and threats by analyzing options and making determinations about specific organizational goals and courses of action.

Decision making in response to opportunities occurs when managers search for ways to improve organizational performance to benefit customers, employees, and other stakeholder groups. In "A Manager's Challenge," Gordon McFadden saw a growth opportunity in the hiking market and thus was pushing Nike top management to acquire North Face Inc. to ultimately improve Nike's standing and performance in this market.[9] *Decision making in response to threats* occurs

Opening a new business such as this restaurant involves a long list of managerial decisions—from where to locate the restaurant to what to put on the menu. Decisions like these are critical to the success of a business enterprise.

when events inside or outside the organization are adversely affecting organizational performance and managers are searching for ways to increase performance.[10] For example, Nike's managers had to decide quickly how to react to aggressive competitors such as Reebok and Adidas which had developed new kinds of sports shoes or to charges that its shoe manufacturers were operating sweatshops. Decision making is central to being a manager, and whenever managers engage in planning, organizing, leading, and controlling–their four principal functions–they are constantly making decisions.

Managers are always searching for ways to improve their decision making to improve organizational performance. At the same time, they do their best to avoid costly mistakes that will hurt organizational performance. Examples of spectacularly good decisions include Liz Claiborne's decision in the 1980s to focus on producing clothes for the growing number of women entering the workforce–a decision that contributed to making her company one of the largest clothing manufacturers. Also, Bill Gates's decision to buy a computer operating system for $50,000 from a small company in Seattle and sell it to IBM for the new IBM personal computer resulted in Gates and Microsoft, respectively, becoming the richest man and richest software company in the United States. Examples of spectacularly bad decisions include the decision by managers at NASA and Morton Thiokol to launch the *Challenger* space shuttle–a decision that resulted in the deaths of six astronauts in 1986. Also the decision of Ken Olsen, founder of Digital Equipment Corporation, to stay with mainframe computers in the 1980s and not allow his engineers to spend the company's resources to create new kinds of personal computers because of his belief that "personal computers are just toys" was a decision that cost Olsen his job as CEO and almost ruined his company.

Programmed and Nonprogrammed Decision Making

Regardless of the specific decision that a manager is responsible for, the decision-making process is either programmed or nonprogrammed.[11]

programmed decision making Routine, virtually automatic decision making that follows established rules or guidelines.

PROGRAMMED DECISION MAKING Programmed decision making is a *routine,* virtually automatic process. Programmed decisions are decisions that have been made so many times in the past that managers have developed rules or guidelines to be applied when certain situations inevitably occur. Programmed decision making takes place when a school principal asks the school board to hire a new teacher whenever student enrollment increases by 40 students; when a manufacturing supervisor hires new workers whenever existing workers' overtime increases by more than 10 percent; and when an office manager orders basic office supplies, such as paper and pens, whenever the inventory of supplies on hand drops below a certain level. Furthermore, in the last example, the office manager probably orders the same amount of supplies each time.

This decision making is called *programmed* because office managers, for example, do not need to continually make judgments about what should be done. They can rely on long-established decision rules such as these:

- Rule 1: When the storage shelves are three-quarters empty, order more copy paper.
- Rule 2: When ordering paper, order enough to fill the shelves.

Managers can develop rules and guidelines to regulate all routine organizational activities. For example, rules can specify how a worker should perform a certain task, and rules can specify the quality standards that raw materials must meet to be acceptable. Most decision making that relates to the day-to-day running of an organization is programmed decision making. Examples include decision making about how much inventory to hold, when to pay bills, when to bill customers, and when to take nonpaying customers to court is likely to fall into the programmed category. Programmed decision making is possible when managers have the information they need to create rules that will guide decision making. There is little ambiguity involved in assessing when the stockroom is empty or counting the number of new students in class.

NONPROGRAMMED DECISION MAKING Suppose, however, managers are not at all certain that a course of action will lead to a desired outcome. Or, in even more ambiguous terms, suppose managers are not even clear about what they are really trying to achieve. Obviously, rules cannot be developed to predict uncertain events. **Nonprogrammed decision making** is required for these *nonroutine* decisions. Nonprogrammed decisions are made in response to unusual or novel opportunities and threats. Nonprogrammed decision making occurs when there are no ready-made decision rules that managers can apply to a situation. Rules do not exist because the situation is unexpected and managers lack the information they would need to develop rules to cover it. Examples of nonprogrammed decision making include decisions to invest in a new kind of technology, develop a new kind of product, launch a new promotional campaign, enter a new market, or expand internationally.

Nonprogrammed decision making Nonroutine decision making that occurs in response to unusual, unpredictable opportunities and threats.

How do managers make decisions in the absence of decision rules? First they must search for information about alternative courses of action; second, they must rely on intuition and judgment to choose wisely among alternatives. **Intuition** is a person's ability to make sound decisions based on one's past experience and immediate feelings about the information at hand. **Judgment** is a person's ability to develop a sound opinion because of the way he or she evaluates the importance of the information available in a particular context. "Exercising" one's judgment is a more rational process than "going with" one's intuition. For reasons that we examine later in this chapter, both intuition and judgment often are flawed and can result in poor decision making. Thus, the likelihood of error is much greater in nonprogrammed decision making than in programmed decision making.[12] In the remainder of this chapter, when we talk about decision making, we are referring to *nonprogrammed* decision making because it causes the most problems for managers.

intuition Ability to make sound decisions based on one's past experience and immediate feelings about the information at hand.

judgment Ability to develop a sound opinion based on one's evaluation of the importance of the information at hand.

The classical and the administrative decision-making models reveal many of the assumptions, complexities, and pitfalls that affect decision making. These models help reveal the factors that managers and other decision makers must be aware of to improve the quality of their decision making. Remember that the classical and administrative models are just that–guides that can help managers understand the decision-making process. In real life, the process is typically not cut-and-dried; these models, however, can help guide a manager through it.

Classical decision-making model A prescriptive approach to decision making based on the assumption that the decision maker can identify and evaluate all possible alternatives and their consequences and rationally choose the most appropriate course of action.

The Classical Model

One of the earliest models of decision making, the **classical model,** is *prescriptive,* which means that it specifies how decisions *should* be made. Managers using the classical model make a series of simplifying assumptions about the nature of

Figure 7.1
The Classical Model of Decision Making

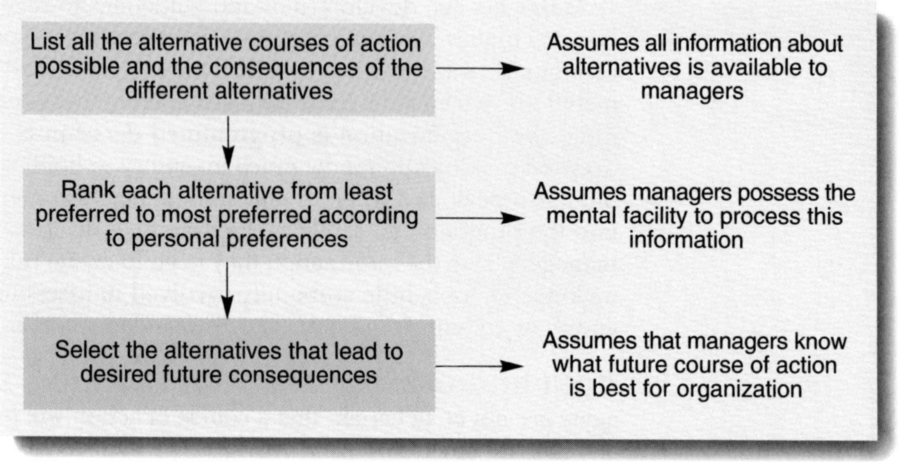

the decision-making process (see Figure 7.1). The premise of the classical model is that once managers recognize the need to make a decision, they should be able to generate a complete list of *all* alternatives and consequences and make the best choice. In other words, the classical model assumes that managers have access to *all* the information they need to make the **optimum decision,** which is the most appropriate decision possible in light of what they believe to be the most desirable future consequences for their organization. Furthermore, the classical model assumes that managers can easily list their own preferences for each alternative and rank them from least to most preferred to make the optimum decision.

optimum decision The most appropriate decision in light of what managers believe to be the most desirable future consequences for their organization.

The Administrative Model

James March and Herbert Simon disagreed with the underlying assumptions of the classical model of decision making. In contrast, they proposed that managers in the real world do *not* have access to all the information they need to make a decision. Moreover, they pointed out that even if all information were readily available, many managers would lack the mental or psychological ability to absorb and evaluate it correctly. As a result, March and Simon developed the **administrative model** of decision making to explain why decision making is always an inherently uncertain and risky process–and why managers can rarely make decisions in the manner prescribed by the classical model. The administrative model is based on three important concepts: *bounded rationality, incomplete information,* and *satisficing.*

administrative model An approach to decision making that explains why decision making is inherently uncertain and risky and why managers usually make satisfactory rather than optimum decisions.

BOUNDED RATIONALITY March and Simon pointed out that human decision-making capabilities are bounded by people's cognitive limitations–that is, limitations in their ability to interpret, process, and act on information.[13] They argued that the limitations of human intelligence constrain the ability of decision makers to determine the optimum decision. March and Simon coined the term **bounded rationality** to describe the situation in which the number of alternatives a manager must identify is so great and the amount of information so vast that it is difficult for the manager to even come close to evaluating it all before making a decision.[14]

bounded rationality Cognitive limitations that constrain one's ability to interpret, process, and act on information.

Figure 7.2
Why Information Is Incomplete

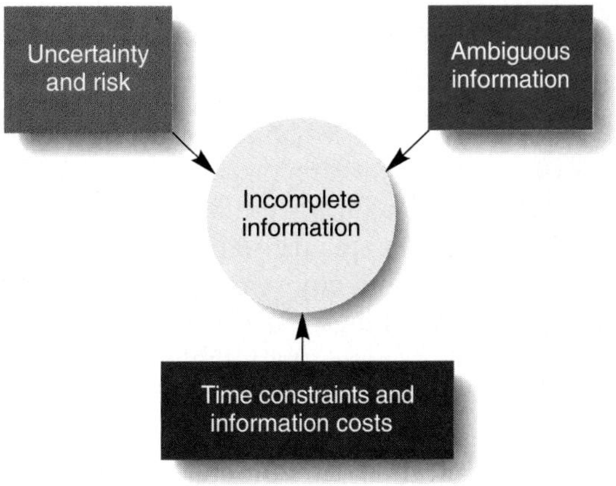

INCOMPLETE INFORMATION Even if managers did have an unlimited ability to evaluate information, they still would not be able to arrive at the optimum decision because they would have incomplete information. Information is incomplete because the full range of decision-making alternatives is unknowable in most situations and the consequences associated with known alternatives are uncertain as is true at Nike in "A Manager's Challenge."[15] In other words, information is incomplete because of risk and uncertainty, ambiguity, and time constraints (see Figure 7.2).

risk The degree of probability that the possible outcomes of a particular course of action will occur.

RISK AND UNCERTAINTY As we saw in Chapter 3, forces in the organizational environment are constantly changing. **Risk** is present when managers know the possible outcomes of a particular course of action and can assign probabilities to them. For example, managers in the biotechnology industry know that new drugs have a 10 percent probability of successfully passing advanced clinical trials and a 90 percent probability of failing. These probabilities reflect the experiences of thousands of drugs that have gone through advanced clinical trials. Thus, when managers in the biotechnology industry decide to submit a drug for testing, they know that there is only a 10 percent chance that the drug will succeed, but at least they have some information on which to base their decision.

uncertainty Unpredictability.

When **uncertainty** exists, the probabilities of alternative outcomes *cannot* be determined, and future outcomes are *unknown.* Managers are working blind. The probability of a given outcome occurring is *not* known, and managers have little information to use in making a decision. For example, in 1993, when Apple Computer introduced the Newton, its personal digital assistant (PDA), managers had no idea what the probability of a successful product launch for a PDA might be. Because Apple was the first to market this totally new product, there was no body of well-known data that Apple's managers could draw on to calculate the probability of a successful launch. Uncertainty plagues most managerial decision making.[16] Although Apple's initial launch of its PDA was a disaster due to technical problems, an improved version was more successful. In fact, Apple created the PDA market that has boomed during the 2000s as new and different wireless products have been introduced. As indicated in the following "Information Technology Byte," a major source of uncertainty for top managers revolves around being unable to accurately predict or forecast future demand for products and services.

Information Technology Byte

Lucent's Optimistic Projections Come Back to Haunt Them

Richard McGinn, former CEO of Lucent Technologies, was fired by its board of directors after revenues fell because customers were dissatisfied with its products, employees had lost faith in the company, and returns to shareholders plummeted. Henry Schacht, who had preceded McGinn as CEO and subsequently retired, was called back to take over the top spot at Lucent and turn things around. What went wrong at Lucent? At least part of their troubles were attributable to an inability to accurately predict future demand amid over-optimist projections of growth.[17]

Lucent Technologies was spun off of AT&T and specializes in telecommunications equipment. Just when Lucent became a publicly traded company, the telecommunications industry entered a period of rapid growth as did use of the Internet and wireless communication. Lucent experienced phenomenal sales and revenue growth and was riding high. However, rather than realistically trying to forecast the extent to which current growth of the industry would continue into the future, top managers such as McGinn simply assumed (optimistically) that growth would continue.[18]

Moreover, they became so convinced of the merits of their optimistic projections that they engaged in practices to help push growth along. For example, Lucent lent money to customers to purchase Lucent equipment (referred to as vendor financing), confident that these customers would be successful and able to pay the money back to Lucent. When many of these customers struggled in a declining economy, Lucent's prospects of collecting on its loans diminished. Lucent also gave large discounts to encourage some of its biggest customers to increase their current equipment purchases. This caused problems for Lucent when demand slackened because it was producing too much equipment. Lucent faced both increasing balances of accounts receivable from customers as well as rising inventories that outstripped demand.

Former CEO of Lucent Technologies, Richard McGinn.

While it is difficult for any manager to predict future demand in uncertain times, these overly optimistic projections were a recipe for disaster, especially because there was no indication that such optimism was not warranted. For example, Stephanie Mehta, a reporter for *Fortune* magazine wrote that, "Just days before warnings of a fourth-quarter shortfall . . . McGinn told *Fortune* that strong demand for wireless and Internet gear would buoy sales."[19] As a result of its bad decisions Lucent was forced to layoff more than half its workforce in the early 2000s, hopefully, its new managers now realize how uncertain the future really is.

AMBIGUOUS INFORMATION A second reason why information is incomplete is that much of the information managers have at their disposal is **ambiguous information.** Its meaning is not clear–it can be interpreted in multiple and often conflicting ways.[20] Take a look at Figure 7.3. Do you see a young woman or an old woman? In a similar fashion, managers often interpret the same piece of information differently and make decisions based on their own interpretations. Recall from "A Manager's Challenge" how McFadden viewed

ambiguous information Information that can be interpreted in multiple and often conflicting ways.

Figure 7.3
Ambiguous Information: Young Woman or Old Woman?

the acquisition of North Face Inc. as an opportunity in the hiking gear market while Knight and other top managers at Nike vetoed the acquisition because they interpreted it as being too troublesome and favored internal development of new products instead.[21]

TIME CONSTRAINTS AND INFORMATION COSTS The third reason why information is incomplete is that managers have neither the time nor the money to search for all possible alternative solutions and evaluate all the potential consequences of those alternatives. Consider the situation confronting a Ford Motor Company purchasing manager who has one month to choose a supplier for a small engine part. There are thousands of potential suppliers for this part (there are 20,000 auto suppliers in the United States alone). Given the time available, the purchasing manager cannot contact all potential suppliers and ask each for its terms (price, delivery schedules, and so on). Moreover, even if the time were available, the costs of obtaining the information, including the manager's own time, would be prohibitive.

SATISFICING March and Simon argue that managers do not attempt to discover every alternative when faced with bounded rationality, an uncertain future, unquantifiable risks, considerable ambiguity, time constraints, and high information costs. Rather, they use a strategy known as **satisficing**, exploring a limited sample of all potential alternatives.[22] When managers satisfice, they search for and choose acceptable, or satisfactory ways to respond to problems and opportunities rather than trying to make the optimum decision.[23] In the case of the Ford purchasing manager's search, for example, it may involve asking a limited number of suppliers for their terms, trusting that they are representative of suppliers in general, and making a choice from that set. Although this course of action is reasonable from the perspective of the purchasing manager, it may mean that a potentially superior supplier is overlooked.

satisficing Searching for and choosing an acceptable, or satisfactory, response to problems and opportunities, rather than trying to make the best decision.

March and Simon pointed out that managerial decision making is often more art than science. In the real world, managers must rely on their intuition and judgment to make what seems to them to be the best decision in the face of uncertainty and ambiguity.[24] Moreover, managerial decision making is often fast paced, as managers use their experience and judgment to make crucial decisions under conditions of incomplete information. Although there is nothing wrong with this approach, decision makers should be aware that human judgment is often flawed. As a result, even the best managers sometimes end up making very poor decisions.[25] Another major problem is decision makers who have a difficult time making timely decisions and delay seizing opportunities and responding to challenges and problems, as indicated in the following "Information Technology Byte."

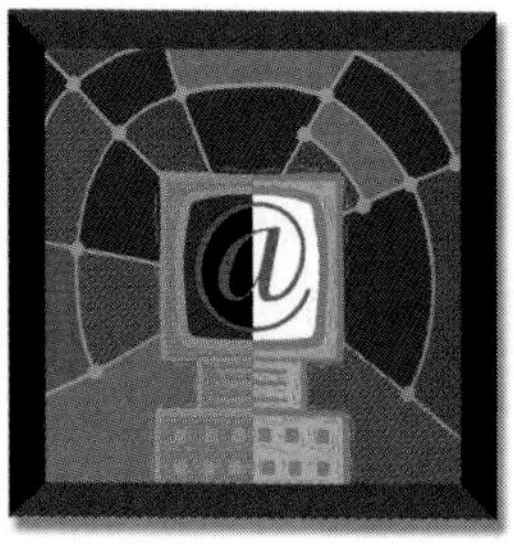

Information Technology Byte

Decision-Making Delays Hinder Motorola

Christopher Galvin became CEO of Motorola in 1997 and since then, the company has experienced lackluster performance which some observers attribute to the difficulty Galvin seems to have in making timely decisions to respond to ongoing competitive challenges. For example, delays in bringing out new kinds of wireless phones resulted in Motorola's share of the wireless phone market plummeting while Nokia, which continues to introduce new phones, has increased its share.[26]

Examples of Galvin's reluctance to make quick decisions at Motorola are not hard to find. For instance, when Geoffrey Frost a top marketing manager at Motorola recommended that the company switch advertising agencies for its line of wireless telephones, a year transpired before the switch was actually implemented.[27] Galvin was reluctant to make a switch and wanted to give the current agency another chance; one wonders what the sales picture would have looked like had the switch taken place when Frost recommended it.

Why does Galvin appear to be a slow decision maker? Although he claims he is not slow, others suggest that Galvin wants every question explored and answered in detail before he can make a decision. However, when the competitive environment is changing rapidly often this is not possible, and the resulting delay in introducing new products can be costly.

As another example, several top Motorola managers recognized the need to retreat from Iridium, Motorola's global portable phone satellite system in late 1999. Two important reasons for this were that these portable phones would not work inside buildings and these phones would cost hundreds of dollars each! However, Galvin stuck with Iridium another year which was a disaster as Motorola wrote off a $2.6 billion loss on Iridium in late 2000. In another case, managers say that 18 months transpired before Galvin agreed to sell Motorola's semiconductor components business, a move recommended by the president of the unit in which the business was housed to improve profitability and focus.[28]

Interestingly, insiders indicate that Galvin is intelligent, smart, and visionary as well as being a nice guy, private, and down to earth. In fact, some suggest that Galvin might better help Motorola as a visionary chairman, whose commitment to the wireless Internet and biotechnology are noteworthy. In any case, Galvin indicates that he has no intention of abandoning ship and is taking a more hands-on, demanding approach to leading Motorola through troubled times.[29]

Steps in the Decision-Making Process

Using the work of March and Simon as a basis, researchers have developed a step-by-step model of the decision-making process and the issues and problems that managers confront at each step. Perhaps the best way to introduce this model is to examine the real-world nonprogrammed decision making that Scott McNealy had to engage in at a crucial point in Sun Microsystems' history.

In early August 1985, Scott McNealy, CEO of Sun Microsystems (a computer workstation manufacturer based in Mountain View, California) had to decide whether to go ahead with the launch of the new Carrera workstation computer, scheduled for September 10. Sun's managers had chosen the September 10 date nine months earlier when the development plan for the Carrera was first proposed. McNealy knew that it would take at least a month to prepare for the September 10 launch and that the decision could not be put off.

Customers were waiting for the new machine, and McNealy wanted to be the first to provide a workstation that took advantage of Motorola's powerful 16 megahertz 68020 microprocessor. Capitalizing on this opportunity would give Sun a significant edge over Apollo, its main competitor in the workstation market. McNealy knew, however, that committing to the September 10 launch date was risky. Motorola was having production problems with the 16 megahertz 68020 microprocessor and could not guarantee Sun a steady supply of these chips. Moreover, the operating system software was not completely free of bugs.

If Sun launched the Carrera on September 10, the company might have to ship some machines with software that was not fully operational and prone to crash the system and that utilized Motorola's less-powerful 12 megahertz 68020 microprocessor instead of the 16 megahertz version.[30] Of course, Sun could later upgrade the microprocessor and operating system software in any machines purchased by early customers, but the company's reputation would suffer as a result. If Sun did not go ahead with the September launch, the company would miss an important opportunity.[31] Rumors were circulating in the industry that Apollo would be launching a new machine of its own in December. McNealy wondered what he should do. The microprocessor and operating system problems might be resolved by September 10, but then again they might not be.

Scott McNealy clearly had a difficult decision to make. He had to decide quickly whether to launch the Carrera, but he was not in possession of all the facts. He did not know, for example, whether the microprocessor or operating system problems could be resolved by September 10; nor did he know whether Apollo was going to launch a competing machine in December. But he could not wait to find these things out–he had to make a decision. We'll see what he decided later in the chapter.

Many managers who must make important decisions with incomplete information face a dilemma similar to McNealy's. There are six steps that managers should consciously follow to make a good decision (see Figure 7.4).[32] We review them in the remainder of this section.

Figure 7.4
Six Steps in Decision Making

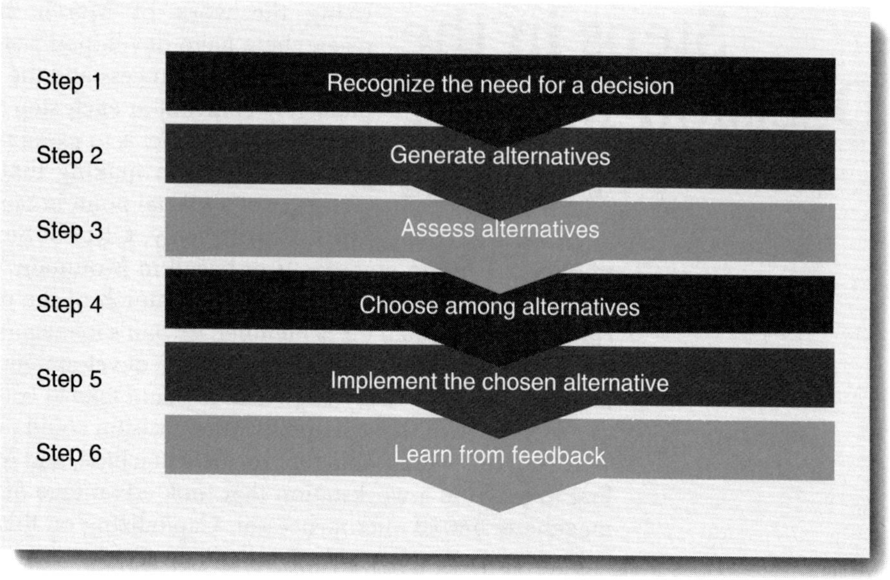
Step 1
Recognize the need for a decision
Step 2
Generate alternatives
Step 3
Assess alternatives
Step 4
Choose among alternatives
Step 5
Implement the chosen alternative
Step 6
Learn from feedback

Recognize the Need for a Decision

The first step in the decision-making process is to recognize the need for a decision. Scott McNealy recognized this need, and he realized that a decision had to be made quickly because it would take a month to get ready for the September 10 launch. McNealy also knew that the September 10 launch was a critical goal because Sun needed to beat Apollo to the market with a new machine to gain a competitive advantage over this strong challenger.

Some stimuli usually spark the realization that there is a need to make a decision. These stimuli often become apparent because changes in the organizational environment result in new kinds of opportunities and threats. This happened at Sun Microsystems. The September 10 launch date had been set when it seemed that Motorola chips would be readily available. Later, with the supply of chips in doubt and bugs remaining in the system software, Sun was in danger of failing to meet its launch date.

The stimuli that spark decision making are as likely to result from the actions of managers inside an organization as they are from changes in the external environment.[33] An organization possesses a set of skills, competencies, and resources in its employees and in departments such as marketing, manufacturing, and research and development. Managers who actively pursue opportunities to use these competencies create the need to make decisions. Managers thus can be proactive or reactive in recognizing the need to make a decision, but the important issue is that they must recognize this need and respond in a timely and appropriate way.[34]

Generate Alternatives

Having recognized the need to make a decision, a manager must generate a set of feasible alternative courses of action to take in response to the opportunity or threat. Management experts cite failure to properly generate and consider different alternatives as one reason why managers sometimes make bad decisions.[35] In the Sun Microsystems decision, the alternatives seem clear: to go ahead with the September 10 launch or to delay the launch until the Carrera was 100 percent ready for market introduction. Often, however, the alternatives are not so obvious or so clearly specified.

One major problem is that managers may find it difficult to come up with creative alternative solutions to specific problems. Perhaps some of them are used to seeing the world from a single perspective–they have a certain "managerial mind-set." In a manner similar to Digital's Olsen, many managers find it difficult to view problems from a fresh perspective. According to best-selling management author Peter Senge, we all are trapped within our personal mental models of the world–our ideas about what is important and how the world works.[36] Generating creative alternatives to solve problems and take advantage of opportunities may require that we abandon our existing mind-sets and develop new ones–something that usually is difficult to do.

The importance of getting managers to set aside their mental models of the world and generate creative alternatives is reflected in the growth of interest in the work of authors such as Peter Senge and Edward de Bono, who have popularized techniques for stimulating problem solving and creative thinking among managers.[37] Later in this chapter, we discuss the important issues of organizational learning and creativity in detail.

Evaluate Alternatives

Once managers have generated a set of alternatives, they must evaluate the advantages and disadvantages of each one.[38] The key to a good assessment of the alternatives is to define the opportunity or threat exactly and then specify the criteria that *should* influence the selection of alternatives for responding to the problem or opportunity. One reason for bad decisions is that managers often fail to specify the criteria that are important in reaching a decision.[39] In general, successful managers use four criteria to evaluate the pros and cons of alternative courses of action (see Figure 7.5):

1. *Legality*: Managers must ensure that a possible course of action is legal and will not violate any domestic and international laws or government regulations.
2. *Ethicalness*: Managers must ensure that a possible course of action is ethical and will not unnecessarily harm any stakeholder group. Many of the decisions that managers make may help some organizational stakeholders and harm others (see Chapter 3). When examining alternative courses of action, managers need to be very clear about the potential effects of their decisions.
3. *Economic feasibility*: Managers must decide whether the alternatives are economically feasible–that is, whether they can be accomplished given the organization's performance goals. Typically, managers perform a cost-benefit analysis of the various alternatives to determine which one will have the best net financial payoff.
4. *Practicality*: Managers must decide whether they have the capabilities and resources required to implement the alternative, and they must be sure that the alternative will not threaten the attainment of other organizational goals. At first glance, an alternative might seem to be economically superior to other alternatives, but if managers realize that it is likely to threaten other important projects, they might decide that it is not practical after all.

Figure 7.5
General Criteria for Evaluating Possible Courses of Action

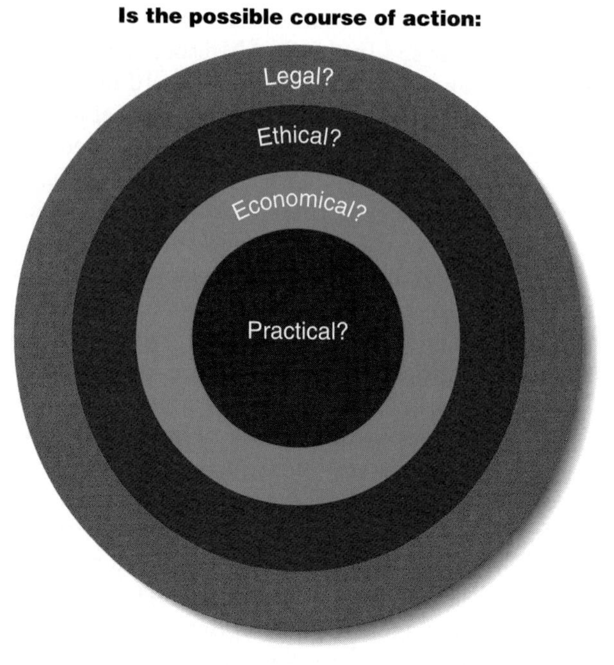
Is the possible course of action:
Legal?
Ethical?
Economical?
Practical?

Very often, a manager must consider these four criteria simultaneously. Scott McNealy framed the problem at hand at Sun Microsystems quite well. The key question was whether to go ahead with the September 10 launch date. Two main criteria were influencing McNealy's choice: the need to ship a machine that was as "complete" as possible (the *practicality* criterion) and the need to beat Apollo to market with a new workstation (the *economic feasibility* criterion). These two criteria conflicted. The first suggested that the launch should be delayed, the second that the launch should go ahead. McNealy's actual choice was based on the relative importance that he assigned to these two criteria. In fact, Sun Microsystems went ahead with the September 10 launch, which suggests that McNealy thought the need to beat Apollo to market was the more important criterion.

The disastrous launch of the *Challenger* space shuttle illustrates the importance of bringing all available information to bear on the decision-making processes and making sure the alternative courses of action are evaluated using all relevant criteria.

Some of the worst managerial decisions can be traced to poor assessment of the alternatives, such as the decision to launch the *Challenger* space shuttle mentioned earlier. In that case, the desire of NASA and Morton Thiokol managers to demonstrate to the U.S. public the success of the U.S. space program in order to ensure future funding (*economic feasibility*) conflicted with the need to ensure the safety of the astronauts (*ethicalness*). Managers deemed the economic criterion more important and decided to launch the space shuttle. At Digital Equipment, Olsen's remark that "personal computers are just toys" showed his lack of understanding of the economic considerations affecting competition in the computer industry. Selecting the right set of criteria by which to assess alternatives is never easy. Often it becomes necessary to collect additional information to make a satisfactory evaluation. Unfortunately, some managers get so caught up in practicality and economic feasibility issues that they lose sight of the legal and ethical implications of alternatives, as indicated in the following "Ethics in Action."

Ethics in Action

The Dark Side of High Tech

Some of the last century's high-tech success stories have turned sour as revelations of unethical and illegal behavior come to light. Take the case of Rambus, a successful technology design firm, which was humbled by the decisions some managers took to increase revenues by patenting others' ideas and requesting royalties once those ideas were actually implemented by their originators. For example, in the 1990s, Rambus employees sat in on collaborative meetings held by IBM, Hewlett-Packard, Samsung, and Toshiba to develop standards for computer chips. Discussions turned to "programmable CAS latency"–a new feature.[40] Richard Crisp, one of the Rambus employees present at the meeting subsequently had Rambus attorneys seek a patent for programmable latency. Similar patents had been taken out under equally suspicious circumstances for other products by Rambus such as dynamic random access memory chips.[41]

Rambus didn't act on the patents right away but waited until a patented technology or product was widely used; managers then sought to collect hefty royalty fees because of their existing patents–patents based on ideas Rambus stole from others. Some of the companies Rambus sought royalty fees from figured out what was going on and now Rambus faces 11 lawsuits in the United States and Europe related to the patents; these lawsuits have been brought by companies larger and more powerful than Rambus. In the first case that went to trial, Rambus was indicted for defrauding Infineon, a Siemens spinoff.[42]

Managers at Avant! were also charged with theft, in this case, theft of software code developed by Cadence. Avant! was founded by former Cadence employees; however, when they left Cadence, they took a copy of the company's database code which they then used in their own software products.[43] In May of 2001, Chairman Gerry Hsu was fined $2.7 million for the software heist and four of Avant!'s top managers received jail sentences. Moreover, the company faces $230 million in criminal penalties.[44] Clearly economic gain should never overshadow legal and ethical criteria in choosing among alternative courses of action and making decisions.

Choose Among Alternatives

Once the set of alternative solutions has been carefully evaluated, the next task is to rank the various alternatives (using the criteria discussed in the previous section) and make a decision. When ranking alternatives, managers must be sure *all* the information available be brought to bear on the problem or issue at hand. As the Sun Microsystems case indicates, however, identifying all *relevant* information for a decision does not mean that the manager has *complete* information; in most instances, information is incomplete.

Perhaps more serious than the existence of incomplete information is the often-documented tendency of managers to ignore critical information, even when it is available We discuss this tendency in detail below when we examine the operation of cognitive biases and groupthink.

Implement the Chosen Alternative

Once a decision has been made and an alternative has been selected, it must be implemented, and many subsequent and related decisions must be made. Once a course of action has been decided (for example, to develop a new line of women's clothing), thousands of subsequent decisions are necessary to implement it. These decisions would involve recruiting dress designers, obtaining fabrics, finding high-quality manufacturers, and signing contracts with clothing stores to sell the new line.

Although the need to make subsequent decisions to implement the chosen course of action may seem obvious, many managers make a decision and then fail to act on it. This is the same as not making a decision at all. To ensure that a decision is implemented, top managers must assign to middle managers the responsibility for making the follow-up decisions necessary to achieve the goal. They must give middle managers sufficient resources to achieve the goal and they must hold the middle managers accountable for their performance. If the middle managers are successful at implementing the decision, they should be rewarded; if they fail, they should be subject to sanctions.

Learning from Feedback

The final step in the decision-making process is learning from feedback. Effective managers always conduct a retrospective analysis to see what they can learn from past successes or failures. Managers who do not evaluate the results of their decisions do not learn from experience; instead, they stagnate and are likely to make the same mistakes again and again.[45] To avoid this problem, managers must establish a formal procedure with which they can learn from the results of past decisions. The procedure should include these steps:

1. Compare what actually happened to what was expected to happen as a result of the decision.
2. Explore why any expectations for the decision were not met.
3. Derive guidelines that will help in future decision making.

Managers who always strive to learn from past mistakes and successes are likely to continuously improve the decisions they make. A significant amount of learning can take place when the outcomes of decisions are evaluated, and this assessment can produce enormous benefits.

Tips for New Managers

Managing the Decision Making Process

1. Recognize that it is impossible for you to make optimum decisions and orient your actions to making the best decision possible.
2. To make the best decision possible, learn to use intuition and judgment to uncover acceptable alternatives and to choose between them.
3. Constantly monitor changes in organizational performance and in the environmental forces to discover if there are any opportunities or threats that need to be addressed.

4. Create a set of clearly defined criteria to frame opportunities and threats and apply these criteria consistently.
5. Encourage your subordinates to make problem solving a major part of their jobs and to generate as many feasible alternatives as possible.
6. Be aware of the role people's preferences and interests play in generating alternative courses of action and learn how to manage coalitions to promote effective decision making.
7. Learn from your successes and mistakes.

Cognitive Biases and Decision Making

heuristics Rules of thumb that simplify decision making.

systematic errors Errors that people make over and over and that result in poor decision making.

In the 1970s psychologists Daniel Kahneman and Amos Tversky suggested that because all decision makers are subject to bounded rationality, they tend to use heuristics, rules of thumb that simplify the process of making decisions.[46] Kahneman and Tversky argued that rules of thumb are often useful because they help decision makers make sense of complex, uncertain, and ambiguous information. Sometimes, however, the use of heuristics can lead to systematic errors in the way decision makers process information about alternatives and make decisions. Systematic errors are errors that people make over and over and that result in poor decision making. Because of cognitive biases, which are caused by systematic errors, otherwise capable managers may end up making bad decisions.[47] Four sources of bias that can adversely affect the way managers make decisions are prior hypotheses, representativeness, the illusion of control, and escalating commitment (see Figure 7.6).

Prior Hypothesis Bias

prior hypothesis bias A cognitive bias resulting from the tendency to base decisions on strong prior beliefs even if evidence shows that those beliefs are wrong.

Decision makers who have strong prior beliefs about the relationship between two variables tend to make decisions based on those beliefs *even when presented with evidence that their beliefs are wrong.* In doing so they are falling victim to prior hypothesis bias. Moreover, decision makers tend to seek and use information that is consistent with their prior beliefs and to ignore information that contradicts those beliefs. At Nike, profiled in "A Manager's Challenge," we saw how Knight and other top managers rejected McFadden's initiative to acquire North Face Inc. because it was not consistent with their belief that the internal development of new products was better than the acquisition of new products.[48]

Representativeness Bias

representativeness bias A cognitive bias resulting from the tendency to generalize inappropriately from a small sample or from a single vivid event or episode.

Many decision makers inappropriately generalize from a small sample or even from a single vivid case or episode. An interesting example of the representativeness bias occurred after World War II, when Seawell Avery, the CEO of

Figure 7.6
Sources of Cognitive Bias at the Individual and Group Levels

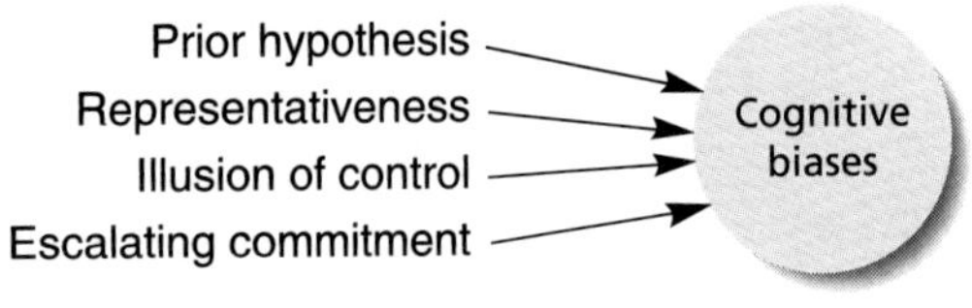

Montgomery Ward, shelved plans for national expansion to meet competition from Sears because he believed there would be a depression after the war. The basis for Avery's belief was the occurrence of the Great Depression after World War I. However, there was no second Great Depression, and Avery's poor decision allowed Sears to establish itself as the number one nationwide retailer. Avery's mistake was to generalize from the post-World War I experience and assume that "depressions always follow wars."

Illusion of Control

illusion of control A source of cognitive bias resulting from the tendency to overestimate one's own ability to control activities and events.

Other errors in decision making result from the **illusion of control,** the tendency of decision makers to overestimate their ability to control activities and events. Top-level managers seem to be particularly prone to this bias. Having worked their way to the top of an organization, they tend to have an exaggerated sense of their own worth and are overconfident about their ability to succeed and to control events.[49] The illusion of control causes managers to overestimate the odds of a favorable outcome and, consequently, to make inappropriate decisions. For example, Nissan used to be controlled by Katsuji Kawamata, an autocratic CEO who thought he had the ability to run the car company single-handedly. He made all the decisions some of which resulted in a series of spectacular mistakes, including changing the company's name from Datsun to Nissan. It is possible that Phil Knight and his top managers at Nike suffered from the same kind of thinking because of their many past successes.

Escalating Commitment

escalating commitment A source of cognitive bias resulting from the tendency to commit additional resources to a project even if evidence shows that the project is failing.

Having already committed significant resources to a course of action, some managers commit more resources to the project *even if they receive feedback that the project is failing.*[50] Feelings of personal responsibility for a project apparently bias the analysis of decision makers and lead to this **escalating commitment.** They decide to increase their investment of time and money in a course of action and ignore evidence that it is illegal, unethical, uneconomical, or impractical (see Figure 7.5). Often, the more appropriate decision would be to cut their losses and run.

A tragic example of where escalating commitment can lead is the *Challenger* disaster. Apparently, managers at both NASA and Morton Thiokol were so anxious to keep the shuttle program on schedule that they ignored or discounted any evidence that would slow the program down. Thus, the information offered by two Thiokol engineers who warned about O-ring failure in cold weather was discounted, and the shuttle was launched on a chilly day in January 1986.

Another example of escalating commitment occurred during the 1960s and 1970s when large U.S. steelmakers responded to low-cost competition from minimills and foreign steelmakers by increasing their investments in the technologically obsolete steelmaking facilities they already possessed, rather than investing in new, cutting-edge technology.[51] This decision was irrational because investment in obsolete technology would never enable them to lower their costs and compete successfully. Similarly, overly optimistic top managers at Lucent Technologies escalated their commitment to growth, engaging in practices like discounting and vendor loans that ultimately may have hurt organizational performance.[52]

Be Aware of Your Biases

How can managers avoid the negative effects of cognitive biases and improve their decision-making and problem-solving abilities? Managers must become aware of biases and their effects, and they must identify their own personal style of making decisions.[53] One useful way for managers to analyze their decision-making style is to review two decisions that they made recently–one decision that turned out well and one that turned out poorly. Problem-solving experts recommend that managers start by determining how much time to spend on each of the decision-making steps, such as gathering information to identify the pros and cons of alternatives or ranking the alternatives, to make sure that they spend sufficient time on each step.[54]

Another recommended technique for examining decision-making style is for managers to list the criteria they typically use to assess and evaluate alternatives–the heuristics (rules of thumb) they typically employ, their personal biases, and so on–and then critically evaluate the appropriateness of these different factors.

Many individual managers are likely to have difficulty identifying their own biases, so it is often advisable for managers to scrutinize their own assumptions by working with other managers to help expose weaknesses in their decision-making style. In this context, the issue of group decision making becomes important.

Group Decision Making

Many, perhaps most, important organizational decisions are made by groups of managers rather than by individuals. Group decision making is superior to individual decision making in several respects. When managers work as a team to make decisions and solve problems, their choices of alternatives are less likely to fall victim to the biases and errors discussed previously. They are able to draw on the combined skills, competencies, and accumulated knowledge of group members and thereby improve their ability to generate feasible alternatives and make good decisions. Group decision making also allows managers to process more information and to correct each other's errors. And in the implementation phase, all managers affected by the decisions agree to cooperate. When a group of managers makes a decision (as opposed to one top manager making a decision and imposing it on subordinate managers), the probability that the decision will be implemented successfully increases. (We discuss how to encourage employee participation in decision making in Chapter 13.)

Nevertheless, some disadvantages are associated with group decision making. Groups often take much longer than individuals to make decisions. Getting two or more managers to agree to the same solution can be difficult because managers' interests and preferences are often different. In addition, just like decision making by individual managers, group decision making can be undermined by biases. A major source of group bias is *groupthink*.

groupthink A pattern of faulty and biased decision making that occurs in groups whose members strive for agreement among themselves at the expense of accurately assessing information relevant to a decision.

The Perils of Groupthink

Groupthink is a pattern of faulty and biased decision making that occurs in groups whose members strive for agreement among themselves at the expense of accurately assessing information relevant to a decision.[55] When managers are subject to groupthink, they collectively embark on a course of action without developing appropriate criteria to evaluate alternatives. Typically, a group rallies around one central manager, such as the CEO, and the course of action that manager supports. Group members become blindly committed to that course of action without evaluating its merits. Commitment is often based on an emotional, rather than an objective, assessment of the optimal course of action.

The decision President Kennedy and his advisors made to launch the unfortunate Bay of Pigs invasion in Cuba in 1962, the decisions made by President Johnson and his advisors from 1964 to 1967 to escalate the War in Vietnam, the decision made by President Nixon and his advisors in 1972 to cover up the Watergate break-in, and the decision made by NASA and Morton Thiokol to launch the ill-fated *Challenger* shuttle that exploded after take-off all were likely influenced by groupthink. After the fact, decision makers such as these who may fall victim to groupthink are often surprised that their decision-making process and outcomes were so flawed.

When groupthink occurs, pressures for agreement and harmony within a group have the unintended effect of discouraging individuals from raising issues that run counter to majority opinion. For example, when managers at NASA and Morton Thiokol fell victim to groupthink, they convinced each other that all was well and that there was no need to delay the launch of the *Challenger* space shuttle.

Devil's Advocacy and Dialectical Inquiry

The existence of cognitive biases and groupthink raises the question of how to improve the quality of group and individual decision making so that managers make decisions that are realistic and based on a thorough evaluation of alternatives. Two techniques known to counteract groupthink and cognitive biases are devil's advocacy and dialectic inquiry (see Figure 7.7).[56]

devil's advocacy Critical analysis of a preferred alternative, made in response to challenges raised by a group member who, playing the role of devil's advocate, defends unpopular or opposing alternatives for the sake of argument.

Devil's advocacy is a critical analysis of a preferred alternative to ascertain its strengths and weaknesses before it is implemented.[57] Typically, one member of the decision-making group plays the role of devil's advocate. The devil's advocate critiques and challenges the way the group evaluated alternatives and chose one over the others. The purpose of devil's advocacy is to identify all the reasons that might make the preferred alternative unacceptable after all. In this way, decision makers can be made aware of the possible perils of recommended courses of action.

Figure 7.7 Devil's Advocacy and Dialectical Inquiry

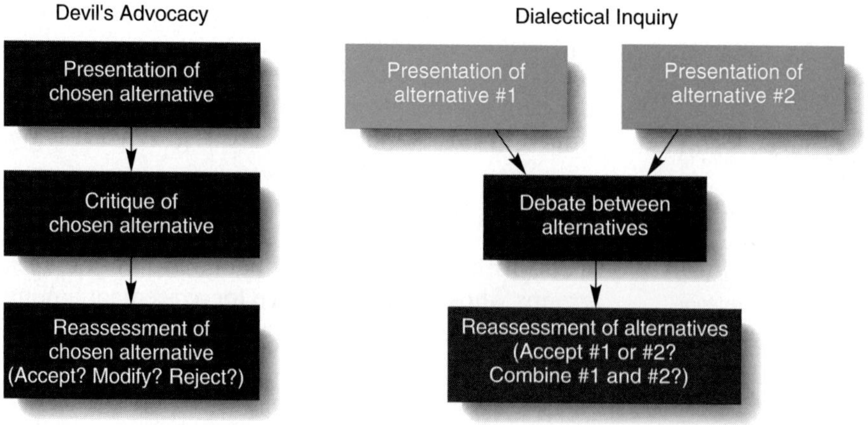

dialectical inquiry Critical analysis of two preferred alternatives in order to find an even better alternative for the organization to adopt.

Dialectical inquiry goes one step further. Two groups of managers are assigned to a problem, and each group is responsible for evaluating alternatives and selecting one of them.[58] Top managers hear each group present its preferred alternative, and then each group critiques the other's position. During this debate, top managers challenge both groups' positions to uncover potential problems and perils associated with their solutions. The goal is to find an even better alternative course of action for the organization to adopt.

Both devil's advocacy and dialectical inquiry can help counter the effects of cognitive biases and groupthink.[59] In practice, devil's advocacy is probably the easier method to implement because it involves less commitment in managerial time and effort than does dialectical inquiry.

Diversity among Decision Makers

Another way to improve group decision making is to promote diversity in decision-making groups (see Chapter 4).[60] Bringing together managers of both genders from various ethnic, national, and functional backgrounds broadens the range of life experiences and opinions that group members can draw from as they generate, assess, and choose among alternatives. Moreover, diverse groups are sometimes less prone to groupthink because group members already differ from each other and thus are less subject to pressures for uniformity.

Organizational Learning and Creativity

The quality of managerial decision making ultimately depends on innovative responses to opportunities and threats. How can managers increase their ability to make nonprogrammed decisions, decisions that will allow them to adapt to, modify, and even drastically alter their task environments so that they can continually increase organizational performance? The answer is by encouraging organizational learning.[61]

organizational learning The process through which managers seek to improve employees' desire and ability to understand and manage the organization and its task environment.

learning organization An organization in which managers try to maximize the ability of individuals and groups to think and behave creatively and thus maximize the potential for organizational learning to take place.

creativity A decision maker's ability to discover original and novel ideas that lead to feasible alternative courses of action.

Organizational learning is the process through which managers seek to improve employees' desire and ability to understand and manage the organization and its task environment so that employees can make decisions that continuously raise organizational effectiveness.[62] A **learning organization** is one in which managers do everything possible to maximize the ability of individuals and groups to think and behave creatively and thus maximize the potential for organizational learning to take place. At the heart of organizational learning is **creativity**, the ability of a decision maker to discover original and novel ideas that lead to feasible alternative courses of action. Encouraging creativity among managers is such a pressing organizational concern that many organizations hire outside experts to help them develop programs to train their managers in the art of creative thinking and problem solving.

Creating a Learning Organization

How do managers go about creating a learning organization? Learning theorist Peter Senge identified five principles for creating a learning organization (see Figure 7.8).[63]

1. For organizational learning to occur, top managers must allow every person in the organization to develop a sense of *personal mastery*. Managers must empower employees and allow them to experiment and create and explore what they want.

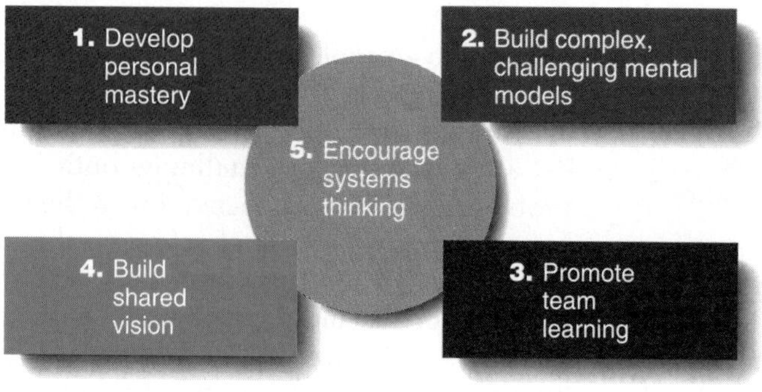
1. Develop personal mastery
2. Build complex, challenging mental models
5. Encourage systems thinking
4. Build shared vision
3. Promote team learning

Figure 7.8
Senge's Principles for Creating a Learning Organization

2. As part of attaining personal mastery, organizations need to encourage employees to develop and use *complex mental models*–sophisticated ways of thinking that challenge them to find new or better ways of performing a task–to deepen their understanding of what is involved in a particular activity. Here Senge is arguing that managers must encourage employees to develop a taste for experimenting and risk taking.[64]

3. Managers must do everything they can to promote group creativity. Senge thinks that *team learning* (learning that takes place in a group or team) is more important than individual learning in increasing organizational learning. He points out that most important decisions are made in subunits such as groups, functions, and divisions.

4. Managers must emphasize the importance of *building a shared vision*–a common mental model that all organizational members use to frame problems or opportunities.

5. Managers must encourage *systems thinking* (a concept drawn from systems theory, discussed in Chapter 2). Senge emphasizes that to create a learning organization, managers must recognize the effects of one level of learning on another. Thus, for example, there is little point in creating teams to facilitate team learning if managers do not also take steps to give employees the freedom to develop a sense of personal mastery.

Building a learning organization requires managers to change their management assumptions radically. Developing a learning organization is neither a quick nor an easy process. Senge has been working with Ford Motor Company for the last eight years to help managers make Ford a learning organization. Why does Ford want this? Top management believes that to compete successfully into the next century Ford must improve its members' ability to be creative and make the right decisions. Increasingly, managers are being called on to promote global organizational learning, as indicated in the following "Managing Globally" box.

Managing Globally

Global Organizational Learning at Wal-Mart

In recent years, Wal-Mart has been making major strides to become a global retail company. For example, Wal-Mart is currently the largest retail company in Mexico and Canada and international operations account for approximately 17 percent of Wal-Mart's revenues and around 12 percent of its profits.[65]

While it has had many global successes, its globalization efforts have resulted in several failures because of decision-making errors. Managers at Wal-Mart use the lessons derived from its failures and successes in one country to promote global organizational learning across the many countries in which it now operates. For example, when Wal-Mart entered Malaysia it was convinced customers there would respond to its one-stop shopping format. It found however, that Malaysians enjoy the social experience of shopping in a lively market or bazaar and they did not like the impersonal efficiency of the typical Wal-Mart store. As a result, Wal-Mart has learned the importance of designing store layouts to appeal to the customers of each country in which it operates.

When purchasing and operating a chain of stores in another country such as the British ASDA chain, Wal-Mart now strives to retain what customers value in the local market while taking advantage of all of Wal-Mart's accumulated organizational learning. For example, Wal-Mart improved ASDA's information technology used for inventory and sales tracking in stores and enrolled ASDA in Wal-Mart's global purchasing operations which has enabled them to pay less for certain products, sell them for less, and overall, significantly increase sales. At the same time, Wal-Mart empowered local ASDA managers to run the stores; as the president of ASDA indicates, "This is still essentially a British business in the way it's run day to day."[66]

A Wal-Mart store in Germany. Wal-Mart managers have learned to take into account the local market preferences when opening stores in another country.

John B. Menzer, head of the international division, is the champion behind promoting organizational learning. Menzer has learned that it is advantageous to empower local employees to manage operations and encourage the sharing of proven practices around the world. Consistent with global learning, Menzer is also encouraging the spreading of best practices from overseas to the United States such as ASDA's system for stocking fresh food.[67] Consistent with empowering local employees, Menzer has reduced the staff in the international division at Wal-Mart in Bentonville, Arkansas, from 450 to 137 which has resulted in further cost savings.[68] Clearly, global organizational learning is essential for companies such as Wal-Mart with significant operations in multiple countries.

Promoting Individual Creativity

Research suggests that when certain conditions are met, managers are more likely to be creative. First, as just discussed, people must be given the opportunity and freedom to generate new ideas. Creativity declines when managers look over the shoulders of talented employees and try to "hurry up" a creative solution. How would you feel if your boss said you had one week to come up with a new product idea to beat the competition? Creativity results when managers have an opportunity to experiment, to take risks, and to make mistakes and learn from them. Highly innovative companies like 3M, Hewlett-Packard, and Newell Rubbermaid are well known for the wide degree of freedom they give their managers. An informal norm at each of these companies is the expectation that managers will spend at least 10 percent of their time on projects of their own choosing, a policy that fosters creativity.

Once managers have generated alternatives, creativity can be fostered by providing them with constructive feedback so that they know how well they are doing. Ideas that seem to be going nowhere can be eliminated and creative energies refocused in other directions. Ideas that seem promising can be promoted, and help from other managers can be obtained as well.[69]

Top managers must also stress the importance of looking for alternative solutions and visibly reward employees who come up with creative ideas. Being creative can be demanding and stressful. Employees who believe that they are working on important, vital issues are motivated to put forth the high levels of effort that creativity demands. Creative people like to receive the acclaim of others, and innovative organizations have many kinds of ceremonies and rewards to recognize creative employees. For example, 3M established the Carlton Hall of Fame to recognize successful innovators. They not only become members of the hall of fame but also receive financial rewards through the Golden Step program.

Promoting Group Creativity

To encourage creativity at the group level, organizations can make use of group problem-solving techniques that promote creative ideas and innovative solutions. These techniques can also be used to prevent groupthink and to help managers uncover biases. Here, we look at three group decision-making techniques: *brainstorming*, the *nominal group technique*, and the *Delphi technique*.

BRAINSTORMING Brainstorming is a group problem-solving technique in which managers meet face-to-face to generate and debate a wide variety of alternatives from which to make a decision.[70] Generally, from 5 to 15 managers meet in a closed-door session and proceed like this:

- One manager describes in broad outline the problem the group is to address.
- Group members then share their ideas and generate alternative courses of action.
- As each alternative is described, group members are not allowed to criticize it, and everyone withholds judgment until all alternatives have been heard. One member of the group records the alternatives on a flip chart.
- Group members are encouraged to be as innovative and radical as possible. Anything goes; and the greater the number of ideas put forth, the better. Moreover, group members are encouraged to piggyback or build on each other's suggestions.
- When all alternatives have been generated, group members debate the pros and cons of each and develop a short list of the best alternatives.

production blocking A loss of productivity in brainstorming sessions due to the unstructured nature of brainstorming.

nominal group technique A decision-making technique in which group members write down ideas and solutions, read their suggestions to the whole group, and discuss and then rank the alternatives.

Brainstorming is very useful in some problem-solving situations–for example, when managers are trying to find a new name for a perfume or for a model of car. But sometimes individuals working alone can generate more alternatives. The main reason for this loss of productivity appears to be **production blocking** that occurs because group members cannot always simultaneously make sense of all the alternatives being generated, think up additional alternatives, and remember what they were thinking.[71]

NOMINAL GROUP TECHNIQUE To avoid production blocking, the **nominal group technique** is often used. It provides a more structured way of generating alternatives in writing and gives each manager more time and opportunity to generate alternative solutions. The nominal group technique is especially useful when an issue is controversial and when different managers might be expected to champion different courses of action. Generally, a small group of managers meet in a closed-door session and adopt the following procedures:

- One manager outlines the problem to be addressed, and 30 or 40 minutes are allocated for each group member to write down ideas and solutions. Group members are encouraged to be innovative.
- Managers take turns reading their suggestions to the group. One manager writes the alternatives on a flip chart. No criticism or evaluation of alternatives is allowed until all alternatives have been read.
- The alternatives are then discussed, one by one, in the sequence in which they were first proposed. Group members can ask for clarifying information and critique each alternative to identify its pros and cons.
- When all alternatives have been discussed, each group member ranks all the alternatives from most preferred to least preferred, and the alternative that receives the highest ranking is chosen.[72]

DELPHI TECHNIQUE Both nominal group technique and brainstorming require managers to meet together to generate creative ideas and engage in joint problem solving. What happens if managers are in different cities or in different parts of the world and cannot meet face-to-face? Videoconferencing is one way to bring distant managers together to brainstorm. Another way is to use the **Delphi technique**, a written approach to creative problem solving.[73] The Delphi technique works like this:

delphi technique A decision-making technique in which group members do not meet face to face but respond in writing to questions posed by the group leader.

- The group leader writes a statement of the problem and a series of questions to which participating managers are to respond.
- The questionnaire is sent to the managers and departmental experts who are most knowledgeable about the problem; they are asked to generate solutions and mail the questionnaire back to the group leader.
- A team of top managers records and summarizes the responses. The results are then sent back to the participants, with additional questions to be answered before a decision can be made.
- The process is repeated until a consensus is reached and the most suitable course of action is apparent.

Promoting Creativity at the Global Level

The Delphi technique is particularly useful when managers are separated by barriers of time and distance, a situation that is common in the global environment. Today, organizations are under increasing pressure to reduce costs and develop global products. To do so, they typically centralize their research and development (R&D) expertise by bringing R&D managers together at one location. Encouraging creativity among teams of R&D experts from different countries poses special problems, however. First, R&D experts often have difficulty communicating their ideas to one another because of language problems and because of cultural differences in their approaches to problem solving. Second, the decision-making process differs from country to country. In Japan, for example, decisions tend to be made in a very participative manner, and the group as a whole must agree on a course of action before a decision gets made. In contrast, decision making is very centralized in Mexico; top managers decide what to do with little input from subordinates.

Managers must take special steps to encourage creativity among people from different countries who are supposed to be working together. They must develop training programs that promote awareness and understanding so that diverse individuals can cooperate and brainstorm new ideas and approaches to problems, opportunities, and threats.

Tips for New Managers

Improving Decision Making

1. Be aware of cognitive biases and test assumptions you use to frame problems, select alternatives, and make decisions.
2. Recognize the advantages of using diverse decision making groups.
3. Use devil's advocacy and dialectic inquiry to guard against groupthink.
4. Take all possible steps to promote creativity at the individual and group level and make a technique like brainstorming a routine part of the problem-solving process.

Summary and Review

THE NATURE OF MANAGERIAL DECISION MAKING Programmed decisions are routine decisions made so often that managers have developed decision rules to be followed automatically. Nonprogrammed decisions are made in response to situations that are unusual or novel; they are nonroutine decisions. The classical model of decision making assumes that decision makers have complete information; are able to process that information in an objective, rational manner; and make optimum decisions. March and Simon argue that managers are boundedly rational, rarely have access to all the information they need to make optimum decisions, and consequently satisfice and rely on their intuition and judgment when making decisions.

STEPS IN THE DECISION-MAKING PROCESS When making decisions, managers should take these six steps: recognizing the need for a decision, generating alternatives, assessing alternatives, choosing among alternatives, implementing the chosen alternative, and learning from feedback.

COGNITIVE BIASES AND DECISION MAKING Most of the time, managers are fairly good decision makers. On occasion, however, problems can result because human judgment can be adversely affected by the operation of cognitive biases that result in poor decisions. Cognitive biases are caused by systematic errors in the way decision makers process information and make decisions. Sources of these errors include prior hypotheses, representativeness, the illusion of control, and escalating commitment. Managers should undertake a personal decision audit to become aware of their biases to improve their decision making.

GROUP DECISION MAKING Many advantages are associated with group decision making, but there are also several disadvantages. One major source of poor decision making is groupthink. Afflicted decision makers collectively embark on a dubious course of action without questioning the assumptions that underlie their decision. Managers can improve the quality of group decision making by using techniques such as devil's advocacy and dialectic inquiry and by increasing diversity in the decision-making group.

ORGANIZATIONAL LEARNING AND CREATIVITY Organizational learning is the process through which managers seek to improve employees' desire and ability to understand and manage the organization and its task environment so that employees can make decisions that continuously raise organizational effectiveness. Managers must take steps to promote organizational learning and creativity at the individual and group levels to improve the quality of decision making.

Management in Action

Topics for Discussion and Action

1. What are the main differences between programmed decision making and nonprogrammed decision making?
2. In what ways do the classical and administrative models of decision making help managers appreciate the complexities of real-world decision making?
3. Ask a manager to recall the best and the worst decisions he or she ever made. Try to determine why these decisions were so good or so bad.
4. Why do capable managers sometimes make bad decisions? What can individual managers do to improve their decision-making skills?
6. In what kinds of groups is groupthink most likely to be a problem? When is it least likely to be a problem? What steps can group members take to ward off groupthink?
7. What is organizational learning, and how can managers promote it?

Building Management Skills

How Do You Make Decisions?

Pick a decision that you made recently and that has had important consequences for you. This decision may be your decision about which college to attend, which major to select, whether to take a part-time job, or which part-time job to take. Using the material in this chapter, analyze the way in which you made the decision—in particular:

1. Identify the criteria you used, either consciously or unconsciously, to guide your decision making.
2. List the alternatives you considered. Were these all possible alternatives? Did you unconsciously (or consciously) ignore some important alternatives?
3. How much information did you have about each alternative? Were you making the decision on the basis of complete or incomplete information?
4. Try to remember how you reached the decision. Did you sit down and consciously think through the implications of each alternative, or did you make the decision on the basis of intuition? Did you use any rules of thumb to help you make the decision?
5. In retrospect, do you think that your choice of alternative was shaped by any of the cognitive biases discussed in this chapter?
6. Having answered those five questions, do you think in retrospect that you made a reasonable decision? What, if anything, might you do to improve your ability to make good decisions in the future?

Small Group Breakout Exercise

Brainstorming

Form groups of three or four people, and appoint one member as the spokesperson who will communicate your findings to the whole class when called on by the instructor. Then discuss the following scenario.

You and your partners are trying to decide which kind of restaurant to open in a centrally located shopping center that has just been built in your city. The problem confronting you is that the city already has many restaurants that provide different kinds of food in all price ranges. You have the resources to open any type of restaurant. Your challenge is to decide which type is most likely to succeed.

Use the brainstorming technique to decide which type of restaurant to open. Follow these steps.

1. As a group, spend 5 or 10 minutes generating ideas about the alternative restaurants that you think will be most likely to succeed. Each group member should be as innovative and creative as possible, and no suggestions should be criticized.
2. Appoint one group member to write down the alternatives as they are identified.
3. Spend the next 10 or 15 minutes debating the pros and cons of the alternatives. As a group try to reach a consensus on which alternative is most likely to succeed.

After making your decision, discuss the pros and cons of the brainstorming method, and decide whether any production blocking occurred.

When called on by the instructor, the spokesperson should be prepared to share your group's decision with the class, as well as the reasons you made your decision.

Exploring The World Wide Web

Search for a website that describes a company whose managers have just made a major decision. What was the decision? Why did they make it? How successful has it been?

You're The Management Consultant

Michael Silverstein is a top manager who was recently hired by an oil field services company in Oklahoma to help them respond more quickly and proactively to potential opportunities in their market. He reports to the chief operating officer (COO) who reports to the CEO and has been on the job eight months. Thus far, he has come up with three initiatives he carefully studied, thought were noteworthy, and proposed and justified to the COO. The COO seemed cautiously interested when Silverstein presented the proposals and each time indicated he would think about them and discuss them with the CEO as considerable resources were involved. Each time, Silverstein never heard back from the COO and when a few weeks elapsed, he casually asked the COO if there was any news on the proposal in question. For the first proposal, the COO said, "We think it's a good idea but the timing is off. Let's shelve it for the time being and reconsider it next year." For the second proposal, the COO said, "Mike [the CEO] reminded me that we tried that two years ago and it wasn't well received in the market. I am surprised I didn't remember it myself when you first described the proposal but it came right back to me once Mike mentioned it." For the third proposal, the COO simply said, "We're not convinced it will work."

Silverstein has come to you for advice. He believes that his three proposed initiatives are viable ways to seize opportunities in the marketplace yet cannot proceed with any of them. Moreover, with each proposal, he has invested considerable amounts of time and has even worked to bring others on board to support the proposal just to have it shot down by the CEO. When he interviewed for the position, both the COO and the CEO claimed they wanted "an outsider to help them step out of the box and innovate" yet, his experience to date has just been the opposite. As an expert in decision making, he has come to you for advice. What should Silverstein do?

BusinessWeek Cases in the News

Repairing the Coke Machine: Doug Daft Finds Restructuring Tougher Than Anticipated

For the text of this in-depth *Business Week* case, log on to the *Contemporary Management* website at www.mhhe.com/jones3e.

Questions

1. How would you characterize Doug Daft's approach to decision making at Coke? What are the pros and cons of his approach?
2. Do you think he will be effective at transforming Coca-Cola? Why or why not?

Source: D. Foust and G. Khermouch, "Repairing the Coke Machine," *Business Week,* March 19, 2001, BusinessWeek.com.

BusinessWeek

Cases in the News

Under the Knife

When Koji Nishigaki became CEO of NEC Corp. 2 1/2 years ago, Japan's top chip- and computer maker was in trouble. Nishigaki knew he'd have to impose drastic measures. And by Japanese standards, he did. Nishigaki cut NEC's workforce by 15,000, or 10 percent. He streamlined management, unloaded some unprofitable businesses, and introduced the kind of transparent decision making that is as rare in Japan as shareholder value.

Nishigaki now has to find dramatic new ways to cut costs—fast. "This IT recession is so tough," he says, "it's forcing us into another round of restructuring."

Since he announced another series of deep cost cuts in July, Toshiba Corp. and Fujitsu Ltd. have unveiled their own restructuring plans. Like NEC, they are seeing a scary drop in demand for a wide range of info-tech devices.

Analysts say Japan's electronics makers are focusing on cutting costs when they should be reinventing themselves. Right now, they make everything from hard-disk drives to submarine cables. "CEOs should be asking themselves: 'Which businesses should I focus on to win? Which business should I exit altogether?'"

If the giants do manage to fix themselves by cutting divisions as well as jobs, investors and lenders will favor them at the expense of other Japanese industries, which will feel pressure to pare down, too. "This is the start of a restructuring wave that could spread to other sectors."

Nishigaki was the first to forge joint ventures with Japanese rivals—a memory-chip alliance with Hitachi Ltd., and one with Matsushita Electric Industrial Co. (Panasonic) to develop next-generation cell phone software.

Sounds good, but analysts are clamoring for more. "I think there has to be a drastic restructuring of chip operations, for starters." Nishigaki will sell off some plants to contract manufacturers and convert others to system-chip production. But he's not about to pull out of chip production altogether.

If the prospects for NEC are less than bright, they're downright gloomy for Fujitsu and Toshiba. "They're mistaken if they think they'll return to profit just by cutting costs." What's required for Japan's fabled electronics titans is nothing less than a wholesale makeover.

Source: I. M. Kunii, "Under the Knife: The Global Tech Crunch Forces Chip Giants to Pare Down," *Business Week*, September 10, 2001, p. 62.

Questions

1. What mindset do top managers at NEC, Toshiba, and Fujitsu appear to have adopted in response to the economic downturn? Do you think their orientation will facilitate or hamper effective decision making? Why or why not?
2. How might these major players in the IT field turn their current problems into opportunities?

Chapter 8

The Manager as a Planner and Strategist

Learning Objectives

After studying this chapter, you should be able to:

- Describe the **three steps of the planning process.**
- Explain the relationship between **planning and strategy.**
- Explain the role of planning in **predicting the future** and in mobilizing organizational resources to meet future contingencies.
- Outline the main steps in **SWOT analysis.**
- Differentiate among **corporate-, business-, and functional-level strategies.**
- Describe the vital role played by **strategy implementation** in determining managers' ability to achieve an organization's mission and goals.

A Manager's Challenge

UPS Battles FedEx

What is the best way to compete in an industry?

In 1971, Federal Express (FedEx) turned the package delivery world upside down when it began to offer overnight package delivery by air. Its founder, Fred Smith, had seen the opportunity for next-day delivery because both the U.S. Postal Service and United Parcel Service (UPS) were, at that time, taking several days to deliver packages. Smith was convinced there was pent up demand for such a unique new service, overnight delivery, and he was also convinced that customers would be willing to pay a high premium price to get it, at least $15 a package at that time.[1] Smith was right, customers were willing to pay high prices for fast reliable delivery; when he discovered and tapped into an unmet customer need, he redefined the package delivery industry.

The familiar trucks of FedEx and UPS. These companies are currently locked in battle to become the air package delivery company of choice in the United States and worldwide.

Several companies imitated FedEx's new strategy and introduced their own air overnight service. None, however, could match FedEx's efficiency and its state-of-the-art information systems which allowed continuous tracking of all packages while in transit. Several of its competitors went out of business. A few, like Airborne Express, managed to survive by focusing or specializing on serving the needs of one particular group of customers—corporate customers—and by offering lower prices than FedEx. Its strategy earned FedEx huge returns through the 1980s, even though the costs of operating its vast air delivery system were, and still are, very high.

Previously only a road delivery package service, in 1988 UPS initiated an overnight air delivery service of its own.[2] UPS managers realized that the future of package delivery lay both on the road and in the air because different customer groups, with different needs were emerging. It began to aggressively imitate FedEx's operating and information systems, especially its tracking systems. Slowly and surely UPS increased the number of overnight packages that it was delivering but it was still way behind FedEx. Even its well-developed, highly efficient road delivery system that could reach every customer in the United States—its major strength—was not really helping it to catch up.

Then, in 1999, UPS announced two major innovations: First, it introduced a new tracking and shipping information system which matched, and even exceeded, the sophistication of that used by FedEx because it could work with any IT system used by corporate customers. By contrast, customers had to install and use FedEx's proprietary IT, causing more work and cost for them. Second, UPS integrated its overnight air service into this nationwide delivery service and now has a seamless interface between these two different aspects of its business. This has given it a competitive advantage over FedEx because UPS can more efficiently deliver short-range and mid-distance packages, those around 500 miles, than FedEx, as well as match FedEx's long-range operations. Moreover, UPS can also offer customers lower prices because it has lower costs than FedEx.

In 2000 FedEx delivered 3 million overnight packages and had a 39 percent market share compared to UPS's 2.2 million packages; but while UPS's overnight business was growing at 8 percent FedEx's was growing at 3.6 percent.[3] Some analysts believe that the efficiency and flexibility of UPS's delivery systems will make it the market leader in even overnight delivery (it already is in surface package delivery) and that it is the company poised to become the global leader this century. Not only has FedEx been shaken by these new developments, small delivery companies like Airborne Express have come under increased pressure and it appears that major changes in the industry are ahead.

Overview

As the battle between FedEx and UPS suggests, there is more than one way to compete in an industry. To find a viable way to enter and compete in an industry, managers must study the way other organizations behave and identify their strategies. By studying the strategies of FedEx, UPS was able to devise a strategy that allowed it to enter the overnight package industry and take on FedEx. So far, it has had considerable success and appears to have achieved a competitive advantage over FedEx.

In an uncertain competitive environment, managers must engage in thorough planning to find a strategy that will allow them to compete effectively. This chapter explores the manager's role both as planner and as strategist. We discuss the different elements involved in the planning process, including its three major steps: (1) determining an organization's mission and major goals, (2) choosing strategies to realize the mission and goals, and (3) selecting the appropriate way of organizing resources to implement the strategies. We also discuss scenario planning and SWOT analysis, important techniques that managers use to analyze their current situation. By the end of this chapter, you will understand the role managers play in the planning and strategy-making process to create high-performance organizations.

An Overview of the Planning Process

planning Identifying and selecting appropriate goals and courses of action; one of the four principal functions of management.

strategy A cluster of decisions about what goals to pursue, what actions to take, and how to use resources to achieve goals.

mission statement A broad declaration of an organization's purpose that identifies the organization's products and customers and distinguishes the organization from its competitors.

Planning, as we noted in Chapter 1, is a process that managers use to identify and select appropriate goals and courses of action for an organization.[4] The organizational plan that results from the planning process details the goals of the organization and specifies how managers intend to attain those goals. The cluster of decisions and actions that managers take to help an organization attain its goals is its strategy. Thus, planning is both a goal-making and a strategy-making process.

In most organizations, planning is a three-step activity (see Figure 8.1). The first step is determining the organization's mission and goals. A mission statement is a broad declaration of an organization's overriding purpose; this statement is intended to identify an organization's products and customers as well as to distinguish the organization in some way from its competitors. The second step is formulating strategy. Managers analyze the organization's current situation and then conceive and develop the strategies necessary to attain the organization's mission and goals. The third step is implementing strategy. Managers decide how to allocate the resources and responsibilities required to implement those strategies between people and groups within the organization.[5] In subsequent sections of this chapter we look in detail at the specifics of each of these steps. But first, we examine the general nature and purpose of planning, one of the four managerial functions identified by Henri Fayol.

Levels of Planning

In large organizations planning usually takes place at three levels of management: corporate, business or division, and department or functional. Figure 8.2 shows the link between the three steps in the planning process and these three levels. To understand this model, consider how General Electric (GE), a large organization that competes in many different businesses, operates.[6] GE has three main levels of management: corporate level, business level, and functional level (see Figure 8.3). At the corporate level are CEO and Chairman Jeffrey Immelt, three other top managers, and their corporate support staff. Below the corporate level is the business level. At the business level are the different divisions of the

Figure 8.1
Three Steps in Planning

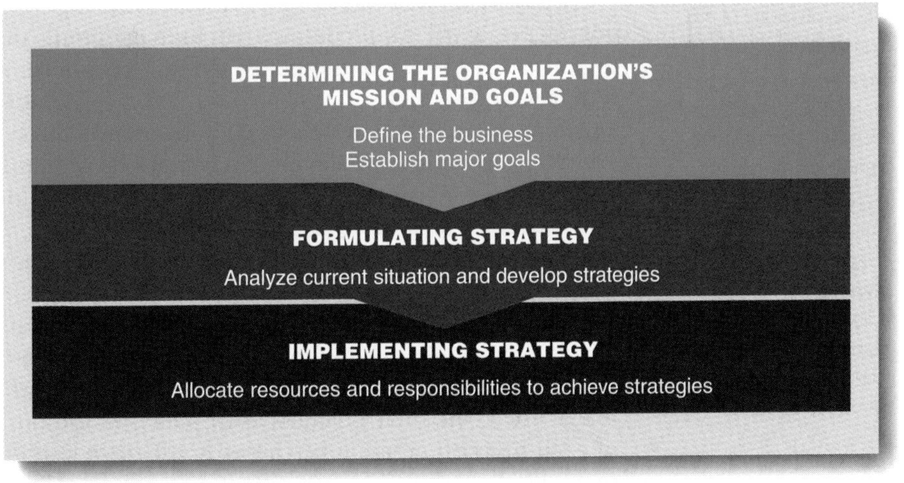
DETERMINING THE ORGANIZATION'S MISSION AND GOALS
Define the business
Establish major goals
FORMULATING STRATEGY
Analyze current situation and develop strategies
IMPLEMENTING STRATEGY
Allocate resources and responsibilities to achieve strategies

Figure 8.2
Levels and Types of Planning

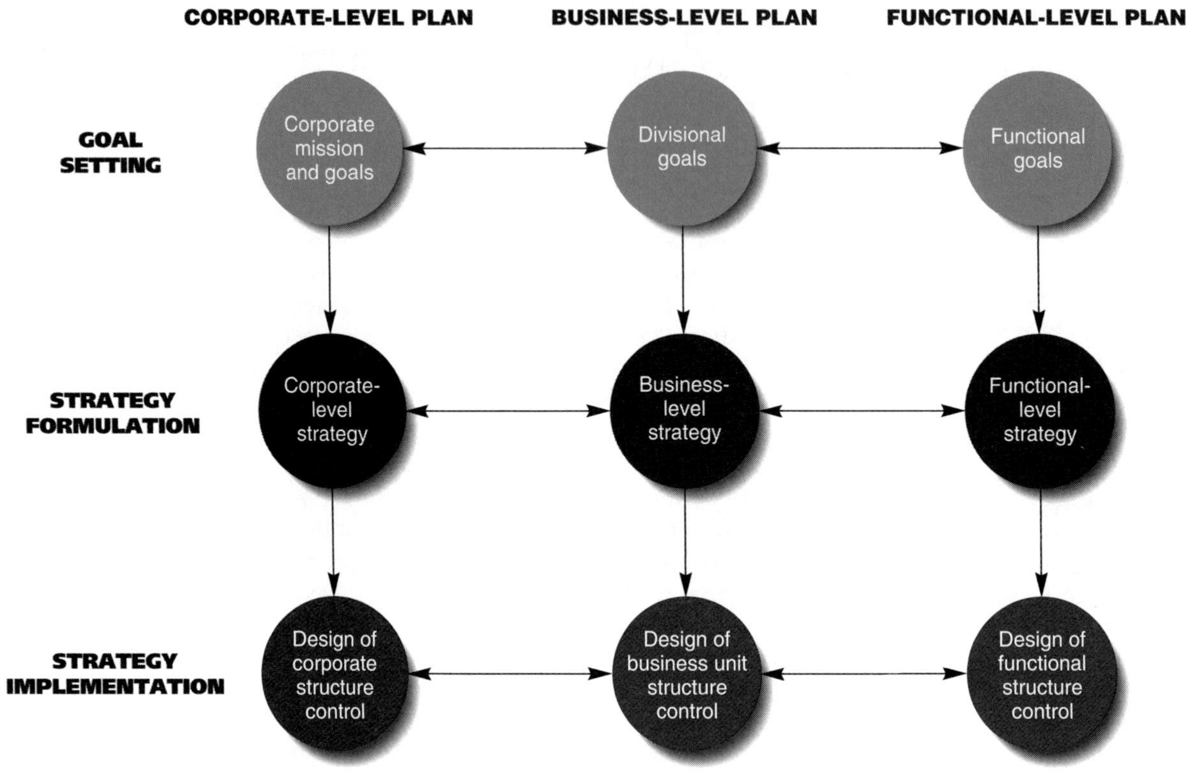

division A business unit that has its own set of managers and functions or departments and competes in a distinct industry.

divisional managers Managers who control the various divisions of an organization.

corporate-level plan Top management's decisions pertaining to the organization's mission, overall strategy, and structure.

corporate-level strategy A plan that indicates in which industries and national markets an organization intends to compete.

company. A **division** is a business unit that competes in a distinct industry; GE has over 150 divisions, including GE Aircraft Engines, GE Financial Services, GE Lighting, GE Motors, GE Plastics, and NBC. Each division has its own set of **divisional managers.** In turn, each division has its own set of functions or departments–manufacturing, marketing, human resource management, R&D, and so on. Thus, GE Aircraft has its own marketing function, as do GE Lighting, GE Motors, and NBC.

At GE, as at other large organizations, planning takes place at each level. The **corporate-level plan** contains top management's decisions pertaining to the organization's mission and goals, overall (corporate-level) strategy, and structure (see Figure 8.2). **Corporate-level strategy** indicates in which industries and national markets an organization intends to compete. One of the goals stated in GE's corporate-level plan is that GE should be first or second in market share in every industry in which it competes. A division that cannot attain this goal may be sold to another company. GE Medical Systems was sold to Thompson of France for this reason. Another GE goal is the acquisition of other companies to help build market share. Over the last decade, GE has acquired several financial services companies and has transformed the GE Financial Services Division into one of the largest financial service operations in the world.

The corporate-level plan provides the framework within which divisional managers create their business-level plans. At the business level, the managers of each division create a **business-level plan** that details (1) long-term goals that will allow the division to meet corporate goals and (2) the division's busi-

Figure 8.3
Levels of Planning at General Electric

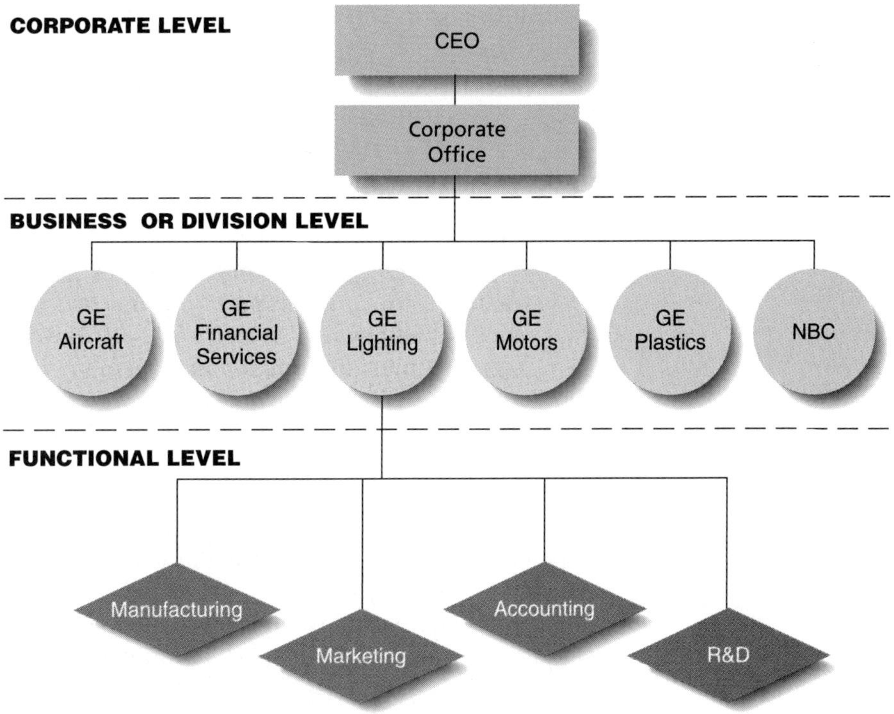

business-level plan Divisional managers' decisions pertaining to divisions' long-term goals, overall strategy, and structure.

business-level strategy A plan that indicates how a division intends to compete against its rivals in an industry.

function A unit or department in which people have the same skills or use the same resources to perform their jobs.

functional managers Managers who supervise the various functions, such as manufacturing, accounting, and sales, within a division.

functional-level plan Functional managers' decisions pertaining to the goals that they propose to pursue to help the division attain its business-level goals.

functional-level strategy A plan that indicates how a function intends to achieve its goals.

ness-level strategy and structure. **Business-level strategy** states the methods a division or business intends to use to compete against its rivals in an industry. Managers at GE Lighting (currently number two in the global lighting industry behind the Dutch company Philips NV) develop strategies designed to help the division take over the number-one spot and better contribute to GE's corporate goals. The lighting division's competitive strategy might emphasize, for example, trying to reduce costs in all departments in order to lower prices and gain market share from Philips. GE is currently planning to expand its European lighting operations, which as we discussed in Chapter 6, is based in Hungary.[7]

A **function** is a unit or department in which people have the same skills or use the same resources to perform their jobs. Examples include manufacturing, accounting, and sales. The business-level plan provides the framework within which **functional managers** devise their plans. A **functional-level plan** states the goals that functional managers propose to pursue to help the division attain its business-level goals, which, in turn, allow the organization to achieve its corporate goals. **Functional-level strategy** sets forth the actions that managers intend to take at the level of departments such as manufacturing, marketing, and R&D to allow the organization to attain its goals. Thus, for example, consistent with GE Lighting's strategy of driving down costs, the manufacturing function might adopt the goal "To reduce production costs by 20 percent over three years," and its functional strategy to achieve this goal might include (1) investing in state-of-the-art European production facilities, and (2) developing an electronic global business-to-business network to reduce the cost of inputs and inventory-holding costs.

An important issue in planning is ensuring consistency in planning across the three different levels. Functional goals and strategies should be consistent with divisional goals and strategies, which in turn should be consistent with corporate goals and strategies, and vice versa. Once complete, each function's plan is normally linked to its division's business-level plan, which, in turn, is linked to the corporate plan. Although few organizations are as large and complex as GE, most plan as GE does and have written plans to guide managerial decision making.

Who Plans?

In general, corporate-level planning is the primary responsibility of top managers.[8] At General Electric, the corporate-level goal that GE be first or second in every industry in which it competes was first articulated by former CEO, Jack Welch who stepped down in September 2001. Now, Welch's hand-selected successor, Jeffrey Immelt, and his top-management team decide which industries GE should compete in. Corporate-level managers are responsible for approving business- and functional-level plans to ensure that they are consistent with the corporate plan.

Corporate planning decisions are not made in a vacuum. Other managers do have input to corporate-level planning. At General Electric and many other companies, divisional and functional managers are encouraged to submit proposals for new business ventures to the CEO and top managers, who evaluate the proposals and decide whether to fund them.[9] Thus, even though corporate-level planning is the responsibility of top managers, lower-level managers can and usually are given the opportunity to become involved in the process.

This approach is common not only at the corporate level but also at the business and functional levels. At the business level, planning is the responsibility of divisional managers, who also review functional plans. Functional managers also typically participate in business-level planning. Similarly, although the functional managers bear primary responsibility for functional-level planning, they can and do involve their subordinates in this process. Thus, although ultimate responsibility for planning may lie with certain select managers within an organization, all managers and many nonmanagerial employees typically participate in the planning process.

Time Horizons of Plans

time horizon The intended duration of a plan.

Plans differ in their **time horizon,** or intended duration. Managers usually distinguish among *long-term plans* with a horizon of five years or more, intermediate-term plans with a horizon between one and five years, and *short-term plans* with a horizon of one year or less.[10] Typically, corporate- and business-level goals and strategies require long- and intermediate-term plans, and functional-level goals and strategies require intermediate- and short-term plans.

Although most organizations operate with planning horizons of five years or more, it would be inaccurate to infer from this that they undertake major planning exercises only once every five years and then "lock in" a specific set of goals and strategies for that time period. Most organizations have an annual planning cycle, which is usually linked to their annual financial budget (although a major planning effort may be undertaken only every few years).

Although a corporate- or business-level plan may extend over five years or more, it is typically treated as a *rolling plan,* a plan that is updated and amended every year to take account of changing conditions in the external environment. Thus, the time horizon for an organization's 2002 corporate-level plan might be 2007; for the 2003 plan it might be 2008; and so on. The use of rolling plans is essential because of the high rate of change in the environment and the difficulty of predicting competitive conditions five years in the future. Rolling plans allow managers to make midcourse corrections if environmental changes warrant, or to change the thrust of the plan altogether if it no longer seems appropriate. The use of rolling plans allows managers to plan flexibly, without losing sight of the need to plan for the long term. As discussed earlier, UPS is a master at using rolling plans to improve its long-run efficiency. It constantly updates its plans as its systems experts develop improved IT systems that provide it with new opportunities to improve its operating effectiveness as discussed in the "Information Technology Byte."

Information Technology Byte

Rolling Plans and Global Supply Chain Management

As discussed in the opening case, UPS is gaining on FedEx because its managers are committed to constantly upgrading and developing the potential of its IT systems as new technology becomes ever more powerful and useful. Using this new technology, UPS has also gained ground on FedEx in providing another important service that is becoming increasingly important given the growth of B2B networks–global supply chain management.

Both UPS and FedEx offer companies such as Compaq, Ford, and Dell a complete global pickup, warehousing, transportation, tracking, and delivery service of their products to customers. Also, they can manage the delivery of inputs these companies require to make their products so that they do not have to carry large stocks of inventory which is expensive. Thus, UPS and FedEx are now in the business of using IT to manage the flow of a company's inputs and the distribution of its outputs–global supply chain management.

FedEx had the early lead in this business, it had opened such a service in Japan and in the United States, building warehouses near major customers to facilitate the flow of Japanese products to the United States. However in the 1990s, UPS managers realized the huge growth potential of the supply chain management business because of soaring international trade and the growth of foreign specialist suppliers that could supply low-cost inputs. They initiated a series of rolling plans and set targets to develop an IT system that would continuously improve customer service and increase UPS's efficiency.

By contrast, FedEx managers did not capitalize on their early lead in the business. Although they used to have the best tracking and IT systems, they apparently did not set in place a program to update and improve them, believing their competitive advantage was too strong. This was a mistake. By 2000, the constant improvements in its IT systems had given UPS the lead; large corporate customers were increasingly choosing UPS to manage their supply chains. In 2000, Ford, for example, saved $250 million by allowing UPS to manage the shipping, tracking, and distribution of its new cars to dealers throughout the United States. Some analysts believe that UPS currently has the best supply-chain services in place.

Currently, both companies are competing to redefine and control the global shipping business, something largely made possible by the growth of new IT systems and the Internet. Indeed, the emergence of the dot-coms, and companies like Amazon.com, which ship hundreds of millions of packages a year was a major factor in shaping the competitive strategies of these two companies. Interestingly, because of its lower prices in 2001, UPS was the shipper of choice for Amazon.com.

Standing Plans and Single-Use Plans

Another distinction often made between plans is whether they are standing plans or single-use plans. Managers create standing and single-use plans to help achieve an organization's specific goals. *Standing plans* are used in situations in which programmed decision making is appropriate. When the same situations occur repeatedly, managers develop policies, rules, and standard operating procedures (SOP) to control the way employees perform their tasks. A *policy* is a general guide to action; a *rule* is a formal, written guide to action; and a *standing operating procedure* is a written instruction describing the exact series of actions that should be followed in a specific situation. For example, an organization may have a standing plan about ethical behavior by employees. This plan includes a *policy* that all employees are expected to behave ethically in their dealings with suppliers and customers; a rule that requires any employee who receives from a supplier or customer a gift larger than $10 to report the gift; and an SOP that obliges the recipient of the gift to make the disclosure in writing within 30 days.

In contrast, *single-use plans* are developed to handle nonprogrammed decision making in unusual or one-of-a-kind situations. Examples of single-use plans include *programs,* which are integrated sets of plans for achieving certain goals, and *projects,* which are specific action plans created to complete various aspects of a program. One of NASA's major programs was to reach the moon, and one project in this program was to develop a lunar module capable of landing on the moon and returning to the earth.

Why Planning Is Important

Essentially, planning is ascertaining where an organization is at the present time and deciding where it should be in the future and how to move it forward. When managers plan, they must consider the future and forecast what may happen in order to take actions in the present and mobilize organizational resources to deal with future opportunities and threats. As we have discussed in previous chapters, however, the external environment is uncertain and complex, and managers typically must deal with incomplete information and bounded rationality. This is one reason why planning is so complex and difficult.

Almost all managers engage in planning, and all should participate because they must try to predict future opportunities and threats. The absence of a plan often results in hesitations, false steps, and mistaken changes of direction that can hurt an organization or even lead to disaster. Planning is important for four main reasons:

1. Planning is a useful way of getting managers to participate in decision making about the appropriate goals and strategies for an organization. Effective planning gives all managers the opportunity to participate in decision making. At Intel, for example, top managers, as part of their annual planning process, regularly request input from lower-level managers to determine what the organization's goals and strategies should be.
2. Planning is necessary to give the organization a sense of direction and purpose.[11] A plan states what goals an organization is trying to achieve and what strategies it intends to use to achieve them. Without the sense of direction and purpose that a formal plan provides, managers may interpret their own tasks and roles in ways that best suit themselves. The result will be an organization

that is pursuing multiple and often conflicting goals and a set of managers who do not cooperate and work well together. By stating which organizational goals and strategies are important, a plan keeps managers on track so that they use the resources under their control effectively.

3. A plan helps coordinate managers of the different functions and divisions of an organization to ensure that they all pull in the same direction. Without a good plan, it is possible that the members of the manufacturing function will produce more products than the members of the sales function can sell, resulting in a mass of unsold inventory. Implausible as this might seem, it happened to the high-flying Internet router supplier, Cisco Systems in 2000 when manufacturing, which had been able to sell all the routers that it produced, had over $2 billion of unsold inventory because of the combination of an economic recession and customers' demands for new kinds of optical routers that Cisco did not have in stock.

4. A plan can be used as a device for controlling managers within an organization. A good plan specifies not only which goals and strategies the organization is committed to but also who is responsible for putting the strategies into action to attain the goals. When managers know that they will be held accountable for attaining a goal, they are motivated to do their best to make sure the goal is achieved.

Henri Fayol, the originator of the model of management we discussed in Chapter 1, said that effective plans should have four qualities: unity, continuity, accuracy, and flexibility.[12] *Unity* means that at any one time only one central, guiding plan is put into operation to achieve an organizational goal; more than one plan to achieve a goal would cause confusion and disorder. *Continuity* means that planning is an ongoing process in which managers build and refine previous plans and continually modify plans at all levels–corporate, business, and functional–so that they fit together into one broad framework. *Accuracy* means that managers need to make every attempt to collect and utilize all available information at their disposal in the planning process. Of course, managers must recognize the fact that uncertainty exists and that information is almost always incomplete (for reasons we discussed in Chapter 7). Despite the need for continuity and accuracy, however, Fayol emphasized that the planning process should be *flexible* enough so that plans can be altered and changed if the situation changes; managers must not be bound to a static plan.

Scenario Planning

scenario planning
The generation of multiple forecasts of future conditions followed by an analysis of how to respond effectively to each of those conditions; also called contingency planning.

One way in which managers can try to create plans that have the four qualities that Fayol described is by utilizing scenario planning, one of the most widely used planning techniques. **Scenario planning** (also known as *contingency planning*) is the generation of multiple forecasts of future conditions followed by an analysis of how to respond effectively to each of those conditions.

As noted previously, planning is about trying to forecast and predict the future in order to be able to anticipate future opportunities and threats. The future, however, is inherently unpredictable. How can managers best deal with this unpredictability? This question preoccupied managers at Royal Dutch Shell, the third largest global oil company in the 1980s. In 1984, oil was $30 a barrel, and most analysts and managers, including Shell's, believed that it would hit $50 per barrel by 1990. Nevertheless, Shell conducted a scenario-planning exercise for its managers. Shell's managers were asked to use scenario planning to generate different future scenarios of conditions in the oil market, and then to develop a set of plans that detailed how they would respond to these opportunities and threats if any such scenario occurred.

One scenario used the assumption that oil prices would fall to $15 per barrel and managers had to decide what they should do in such a case. Managers went to work with the goal of creating a plan consisting of a series of recommendations. The final plan included proposals to cut oil exploration costs by investing in new technologies, to accelerate investments in cost-efficient oil-refining facilities, and to weed out unprofitable gas stations.[13] In reviewing these proposals, top management came to the conclusion that even if oil prices continued to rise, all of these actions would benefit Shell by widening the company's profit margin. They decided to put the plan into action. As it happened, in the mid-1980s oil prices did collapse to $15 a barrel, but Shell, unlike its competitors, had already taken steps to be profitable in a low-oil-price world. Consequently, by 1990, the company was twice as profitable as its major competitors, and of course when oil prices once again rose beyond $30 in 2000 Shell enjoyed record profits.

Because the future is unpredictable the only reasonable approach to planning is first to generate "multiple futures"–or scenarios of the future–based on different assumptions about conditions that *might prevail* in the future, and then to develop different plans that detail what a company *should do* in the event that any of these scenarios actually occurs. Managers at Shell believe that the advantages of scenario planning were not only the plans that were generated but also the education of managers at all levels about the dynamic and complex nature of Shell's environment and the breadth of strategies available to Shell. Scenario planning is a learning tool that raises the quality of the planning process and can bring real benefits to an organization.[14]

Shell's success with scenario planning influenced many other companies to adopt similar systems. By 1990, more than 50 percent of Fortune 500 companies were using some version of scenario planning (it is also called *contingency planning*), and the number has increased since then.[15] The great strength of scenario planning is its ability not only to anticipate the challenges of an uncertain future but also to educate managers to think about the future–to think strategically.[16]

Tips For New Managers

Planning

1. Think ahead by using exercises like scenario planning on a regular basis.
2. See plans as a guide to action. Don't become straitjacketed by plans that may no longer be appropriate in a changing environment.
3. Make sure that the plans created at each of the three organizational levels are compatible with one another and that managers at all levels recognize how their actions fit into the overall corporate plan.
4. Give managers at all levels the opportunity to participate in the planning process to best analyze an organization's present situation and the future scenarios that may affect it.

Determining the Organization's Mission and Goals

Determining the organization's mission and goals is the first step of the planning process. Once the mission and goals are agreed upon and formally stated in the corporate plan, they guide the next steps by defining which strategies are appropriate and which are inappropriate.[17]

Defining the Business

To determine an organization's mission, managers must first define its business so that they can identify what kind of value they will provide to customers. To define the business, managers must ask three questions: (1) Who are our customers? (2) What customer needs are being satisfied? (3) How are we satisfying customer needs?[18] They ask these questions to identify the customer needs that the organization satisfies and the way the organization satisfies those needs. Answering these questions helps managers to identify not only what customer needs they are satisfying now but what needs they should try to satisfy in the future and who their true competitors are. All of this information helps managers plan and establish appropriate goals. The case of Mattel shows the important role that defining the business has in the planning process.

Management Insight

Mattel Rediscovers Itself

In the 1990s, Mattel Inc., the well-known maker of such classic toys as Barbie dolls and Hot Wheels believed that the toy market and customer preferences for toys were changing rapidly. This was because of the growing popularity of electronic toys and computer games. Sales of computer games had increased dramatically as more and more parents saw the educational opportunities offered by games that children would also enjoy playing. Moreover, many kinds of computer games could be played with other people over the Internet so it seemed that in the future the magic of electronics and information technology would turn the toy world upside down.

Mattel's managers feared that core products, such as its range of Barbie dolls, might lose their appeal and become old given the future possibilities opened up by chips, computers, and the Internet. Mattel's managers believed that its customers' needs were changing, and that it needed to find new ways to satisfy those needs if it was to remain the biggest toy seller in the United States. Fearing they would lose their customers to the new computer game companies, Mattel's managers decided that the quickest and easiest way to redefine its business and become a major player in the computer game market would be to acquire one of these companies. So, in 1998 Mattel paid \$3.5 billion for The Learning Company, the maker of such popular games as "Thinking Things." Its goal was to use this company's expertise and knowledge both to build an array of new computer games, and to take Mattel's toys such as Barbie and create new games around them. In this way it hoped to better meet the needs of its existing customers and cater to the needs of the new computer game customers.[19]

In addition, while some classic toys like Barbie have the potential to satisfy customers' needs for generations, the popularity of many toys is temporary and is often linked to the introduction of a new movie from Disney, Pixar, or Dreamworks. To ensure that it could meet the changing needs of customers for these kinds of toys, Mattel signed contracts with these companies to become the supplier of the toys linked to these movies. For example in 2001 it agreed to pay Warner Brothers, 15 percent of the gross revenues, and a guaranteed $20 million, for the rights to produce toys linked to the Harry Potter movie, based upon the books of the same name. It plans to fill many of these toys with electronics to allow them to move and make sounds and also to create Harry Potter computer games that will give it even greater ability to satisfy its customers' needs.[20]

One of the new Harry Potter products: a life sized replica of "Fluffy" the three-headed dog that guards the Sorcerer's Stone in the popular book series. Mattel has a license to manufacture and sell a whole range of Harry Potter products.

While Mattel's managers correctly sensed that customers' needs were changing, the way in which it decided to satisfy these customer needs–namely by buying The Learning Company–was not the right decision. It turned out that the skills to rapidly develop new games linked to Mattel's products were not present in The Learning Company and few popular games were forthcoming. Moreover, it had underestimated the need to promote and update its core toys and that the $3.5 billion could have been much better spent boosting and developing these toys. In 2001, CEO Bob Eckert sold off The Learning Company and decided that henceforth it would hire independent specialist companies to develop new electronic toys and computer games, including many related to its well-known products.

In the fast-changing toy market where customers'needs change and evolve, and where new groups of customers do emerge as new technologies result in new kinds of toys, toy companies like Mattel must learn to define and redefine their businesses to satisfy those needs. By 2001, Mattel had begun to turn out whole new ranges of electronic products linked to Barbie, a new Diva Starz doll line, and new electronic games, and its profits started to recover. Companies have to listen closely to their customers and decide how best to meet their changing needs and preferences.

Establishing Major Goals

Once the business is defined, managers must establish a set of primary goals to which the organization is committed. Developing these goals gives the organization a sense of direction or purpose. In most organizations, articulating major goals is the job of the CEO, although other managers have input into the process. Thus, as noted previously, under the leadership of Jack Welch, General Electric operated with the primary goal that it be first or second in every business in which it competes.

The best statements of organizational goals are ambitious–that is, they stretch the organization and require managers to improve its performance capabilities.[21] For example, in 2001 Cisco Systems CEO John Chambers outlined a very challenging goal. This high-flying Internet hardware company has been the success story of the 1990s. It has enjoyed yearly growth of 30 to 50 percent in sales revenue, but was hit in 2000 with over $2.2 billion in excess inventory it could not sell as many of the dot-com companies went belly up and its sales plummeted.[22] Nevertheless Chambers announced that the company intended to return to its 30 to 50 percent growth rate within three years and was taking the

Figure 8.4
Four Mission Statements

COMPANY	MISSION STATEMENT
Cisco	Cisco solutions provide competitive advantage to our customers through more efficient and timely exchange of information, which in turn leads to cost savings, process efficiencies, and closer relationships with their customers, prospects, business partners, suppliers, and employees.
Compaq	Compaq, along with our partners, will deliver compelling products and services of the highest quality that will transform computing into an intuitive experience that extends human capability on all planes—communication, education, work, and play.
Wal-Mart	We work for you. We think of ourselves as buyers for our customers, and we apply our considerable strengths to get the best value for you. We've built Wal-Mart by acting on behalf of our customers, and that concept continues to propel us. We're working hard to make our customers' shopping easy.
AT&T	We are dedicated to being the world's best at bringing people together–giving them easy access to each other and to the information and services they want and need–anytime, anywhere.

appropriate steps to get there. Steps that included the firing of thousands of employees, a big push to increase global sales, and the investment of billions in research to produce new generations of optical networking equipment. This goal represents a significant challenge for Cisco because by the top-management team's own admission, many of its largest customers are cutting back on Internet expenditures, the dot-com boom has ended, and evolving technology may well require a change in strategic direction. Cisco's managers' vision of the mission and goals of their company, and those of Compaq, AT&T, and Wal-Mart, are presented in Figure 8.4.

Although goals should be challenging, they should be realistic. Challenging goals give managers an incentive to look for ways to improve an organization's operation, but a goal that is unrealistic and impossible to attain may prompt managers to give up.[23] For example, Cisco set a challenging goal to reduce its costs by $1 billion a year and managers moved to make many significant improvements in the efficiency of Cisco's operations to achieve this goal.[24] Experience at other companies, like Compaq, Dell, and IBM, however, has shown that it is possible to achieve these cost reductions provided that managers at all levels are involved in these efforts to increase efficiency.[25]

The time period in which a goal is expected to be achieved should be stated. Cisco's managers have committed themselves to achieving the sales increases by 2004. Time constraints are important because they emphasize that a goal must be attained within a reasonable period; they inject a sense of urgency into goal attainment and act as a motivator.

Formulating Strategy

Strategy formulation involves managers analyzing an organization's current situation and then developing strategies to accomplish its mission and achieve its goals.[26] Strategy formulation begins with managers analyzing the factors within an organization and outside, in the task and general environments,

strategy formulation Analysis of an organization's current situation followed by the development of strategies to accomplish its mission and achieve its goals.

SWOT analysis A planning exercise in which managers identify organizational strengths (S), weaknesses (W), environmental opportunities (O), and threats (T).

that affect or may affect the organization's ability to meet its goals now and in the future. SWOT analysis and the Five Forces Model are two useful techniques managers use to analyze these factors.

SWOT Analysis

SWOT analysis is a planning exercise in which managers identify organizational strengths (S), and weaknesses (W), and environmental opportunities (O), and threats (T). Based on a SWOT analysis, managers at the different levels of the organization select the corporate-, business-, and functional-level strategies to best position the organization to achieve its mission and goals (see Figure 8.5). Because SWOT analysis is the first step in strategy formulation at any level, we consider it first, before turning specifically to corporate-, business-, and functional-level strategies.

In Chapters 5 and 6 we discussed forces in the task and general environments that have the potential to affect an organization. We noted that changes in these forces can produce opportunities that an organization might take advantage of and threats that may harm its current situation. The first step in SWOT analysis is to identify an organization's strengths and weaknesses. Table 8.1 lists many important strengths (such as high-quality skills in marketing and in research and development) and weaknesses (such as rising manufacturing costs and outdated technology). The task facing managers is to identify the strengths and weaknesses that characterize the present state of their organization.

The second step in SWOT analysis begins when managers embark on a full-scale SWOT planning exercise to identify potential opportunities and threats in the environment that affect the organization at the present or may affect it in the future. Examples of possible opportunities and threats that must be anticipated (many of which were discussed in Chapter 5) are listed in Table 8.1.

With the SWOT analysis completed, and strengths, weaknesses, opportunities, and threats identified, managers can begin the planning process and determine strategies for achieving the organization's mission and goals. The resulting strategies should enable the organization to attain its goals by taking advantage of opportunities, countering threats, building strengths, and correcting organizational weaknesses. To appreciate how managers use SWOT analysis to formulate strategy, consider how Douglas Conant, CEO of Campbell Soup, used it to select strategies to try to turn around this troubled food products maker in 2001.

Figure 8.5 Planning and Strategy Formulation

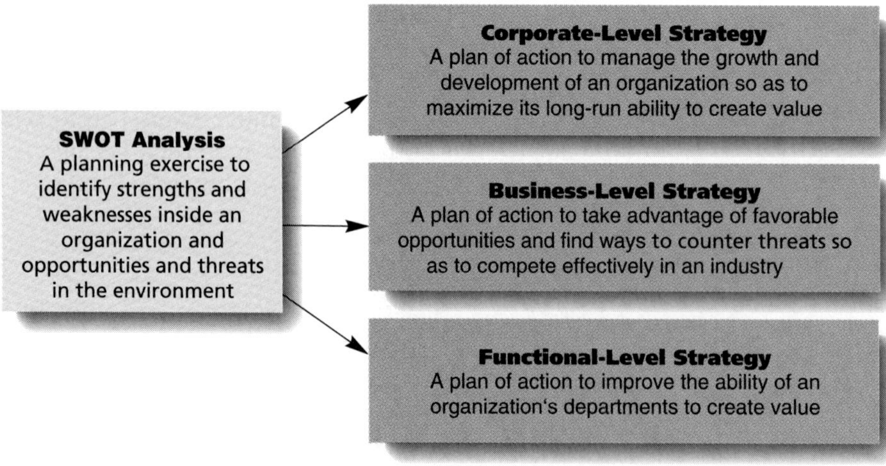

Table 8.1
Questions for SWOT Analysis

Potential Strengths	Potential Opportunities	Potential Weaknesses	Potential Threats
Well-developed strategy? Strong product lines? Broad market coverage? Manufacturing competence? Good marketing skills? Good materials management systems? R&D skills and leadership? Human resource competencies? Brand-name reputation? Cost of differentiation advantage? Appropriate management style? Appropriate organizational structure? Appropriate control systems? Ability to manage strategic change? Others?	Expand core business(es)? Exploit new market segments? Widen product range? Extend cost or differentiation advantage? Diversify into new growth businesses? Expand into foreign markets? Apply R&D skills in new areas? Enter new related businesses? Vertically integrate forward? Vertically integrate backward? Overcome barriers to entry? Reduce rivalry among competitors? Apply brand-name capital in new areas? Seek fast market growth? Others?	Poorly developed strategy? Obsolete, narrow product lines? Rising manufacturing costs? Decline in R&D innovations? Poor marketing plan? Poor materials management systems? Loss of customer goodwill? Inadequate human resources? Loss of brand name? Growth without direction? Loss of corporate direction? Infighting among divisions? Loss of corporate control? Inappropriate organizational structure and control systems? High conflict and politics? Others?	Attacks on core business(es)? Increase in domestic competition? Increase in foreign competition? Change in consumer tastes? Fall in barriers to entry? Rise in new or substitute products? Increase in industry rivalry? New forms of industry competition? Potential for takeover? Changes in demographic factors? Changes in economic factors? Downturn in economy? Rising labor costs? Slower market growth? Others?

Management Insight

A Transformation at Campbell's Soup

Campbell's Soup Co. is one of the oldest and best known companies in the world. However, in recent years Campbell's has seen demand for its major products like condensed soup plummet as customers have switched from high-salt, processed soups to healthier low-fat, low-salt varieties. Indeed, its condensed soup business fell by 20 percent between 1998 and 2000. By 2001, Campbell's market share and profits were falling, and its new CEO Douglas Conant had to decide what to do to turn around the company and maintain its market position.

One of Conant's first actions was to initiate a thorough SWOT planning exercise. An analysis of the environment identified the growth of the organic and health food segment of the food market and the increasing number of other kinds of convenience foods as a threat to Campbell's core soup business. The analysis of the environment also revealed three growth opportunities. One opportunity was in a growing market for health and sports drinks in which Campbell's already was a competitor with its V8 juice, the second was the growing market for salsas in which Campbell's competed with its Pace salsa, and the third was in chocolate products where Campbell's Godiva brand had enjoyed increasing sales throughout the 1990s.

As part of an attempt to turnaround its ailing condensed soup business, Campbell's used some innovative marketing ploys. Here, Steve Solomon puts the finishing touches on a 10-foot tall Campbell's Tomato Soup can displaying the company's newly designed soup label. It was unveiled at the Andy Warhol Museum in Pittsburgh, the home of many of Warhol's pop art Campbell's Soup pictures.

With the analysis of the environment complete, Conant turned his attention to his organization's resources and capabilities. His internal analysis of Campbell's identified a number of major weaknesses. These included staffing levels that were too high relative to its competitors, and high costs associated with manufacturing its soups because of the use of old, outdated machinery. Also, Conant noted that Campbell's had a very conservative culture, people seemed to be afraid to take risks, something that was a real problem in the fast-changing food industry where customer tastes are always changing and new products must be developed constantly. At the same time, the SWOT analysis identified an enormous *strength.* Campbell's enjoyed huge economies of scale because of the enormous quantity of food products that it makes, and it also had a first-rate research and development division which had the capability to develop exciting new food products.

Using the information gained from this SWOT analysis, Conant and his managers decided that Campbell's needed to use its product development skills to revitalize its core products and modify or reinvent them in ways that would appeal to increasingly health conscious and busy consumers who did not want to take the time to prepare old-fashioned condensed soup. Campbell's needed to reinvent them to suit the changing needs of its customers. Moreover, it needed to expand its franchise in the health and sports, snack, and luxury food segments of the market.

Another major need that managers saw was to find new ways to deliver its products to customers. To increase sales Campbell's needed to tap into new food outlets, such as corporate cafeterias, college dining halls, and other mass eateries to expand consumers' access to its foods. Finally, Campbell's had to decentralize authority to managers at lower levels in the organization and give them the responsibility to bring new kinds of soups, salsas, and chocolate products to the market. In this way he hoped to revitalize Campbell's slow-moving culture and speed the flow of improved and new products to the market.

Analysts are waiting to see if Conant can make the changes necessary to turn around and revitalize the company. Its competitors like Pillsbury, which acquired Progresso soup, and Heinz are driving ahead with their own product innovations and their goal is also to increase their share of the food market.

The Five Forces Model

A well-known model that helps managers isolate particular forces in the external environment that are potential threats is Michael Porter's five forces model. We discussed the first four in Chapter 5. Porter identified these five factors that are major threats because they affect how much profit organizations competing within the same industry can expect to make:

- *The level of rivalry among organizations in an industry.* The more that companies compete against one another for customers–for example, by lowering the prices of their products or by increasing advertising–the lower is the level of industry profits (low prices mean less profit).
- *The potential for entry into an industry.* The easier it is for companies to enter an industry–because, for example, barriers to entry, such as brand loyalty, are low–the more likely it is for industry prices and therefore industry profits to be low.
- *The power of suppliers.* If there are only a few suppliers of an important input, then suppliers can drive up the price of that input, and expensive inputs result in lower profits for the producer.
- *The power of customers.* If only a few large customers are available to buy an industry's output, they can bargain to drive down the price of that output. As a result, producers make lower profits.
- *The threat of substitute products.* Often, the output of one industry is a substitute for the output of another industry (plastic may be a substitute for steel in some applications, for example). Companies that produce a product with a known substitute cannot demand high prices for their products, and this constraint keeps their profits low.

Porter argued that when managers analyze opportunities and threats they should pay particular attention to these five forces because they are the major threats that an organization will encounter. It is the job of managers at the corporate, business, and functional levels to formulate strategies to counter these threats so that an organization can respond to its task and general environments, perform at a high level, and generate high profits.

Formulating Corporate-Level Strategies

Corporate-level strategy is a plan of action concerning which industries and countries an organization should invest its resources in to achieve its mission and goals. In developing a corporate-level strategy, managers ask: How should the growth and development of the company be managed in order to increase its ability to create value for its customers (and thus increase performance) over the long run? Managers of most organizations have the goal to grow their companies and actively seek out new opportunities to use the organization's resources to create more goods and services for customers. Examples of organizations growing rapidly are AOL Time Warner and Microsoft, whose CEOs Gerald Levin and Bill Gates pursue any feasible opportunity to use their companies' skills to provide customers with new products.

In addition, some managers must help their organizations respond to threats due to changing forces in the task or general environment. For example, customers may no longer be buying the kinds of goods and services a company is producing (typewriters or black and white televisions), or other organizations may have entered the market and attracted away customers (this happened to FedEx when UPS entered the overnight delivery market). Top managers aim to find the best strategies to help the organization respond to these changes and improve performance.

The principal corporate-level strategies that managers use to help a company grow, to keep it on top of its industry, and to help it retrench and reorganize to stop its decline are (1) concentration on a single business, (2) diversification, (3) international expansion and (4) vertical integration. These four strategies are all based on one idea: An organization benefits from pursuing any one of them only when the strategy helps *further increase the value of the organization's goods and services for customers.* To increase the value of goods and services, a corporate-level strategy must help an organization, or one of its divisions, differentiate and add value to its products either by making them unique or special or by lowering the costs of value creation.

Concentration on a Single Business

Most organizations begin their growth and development with a corporate-level strategy aimed at concentrating resources in one business or industry in order to develop a strong competitive position within that industry. For example, McDonald's began as one restaurant in California, but its managers' long-term goal was to focus its resources in the fast-food business and use those resources to quickly expand across the United States.

Sometimes, concentration on a single business becomes an appropriate corporate-level strategy when managers see the need to reduce the size of their organizations to increase performance. Managers may decide to get out of certain industries, for example, when particular divisions lose their competitive advantage. Managers may sell off those divisions, lay off workers, and concentrate remaining organizational resources in another market or business to try to improve performance. This happened to electronics maker Hitachi in 2001 when it was forced to get out of the CTR computer monitor business. Intense low-price competition existed in the computer monitor market because customers were increasingly switching from bulky CTR monitors to the newer flat, LCD monitors. In July 2001, Hitachi announced it was closing three factories in Japan, Singapore, and Malaysia that produced CTR monitors and would use its resources to invest in the new LCD technology.[27] In contrast, when organizations are performing effectively, they often decide to enter new industries in which they can use their resources to create more value.

Diversification

diversification
Expanding operations into a new business or industry and producing new goods or services.

Diversification is the strategy of expanding operations into a new business or industry and producing new goods or services.[28] Examples of diversification include PepsiCo's diversification into the snack-food business with the purchase of Frito Lay, tobacco giant Philip Morris's diversification into the brewing industry with the acquisition of Miller Beer, and General Electric's move into broadcasting with its acquisition of NBC. There are two main kinds of diversification: related and unrelated.

related diversification Entering a new business or industry to create a competitive advantage in one or more of an organization's existing divisions or businesses.

synergy Performance gains that result when individuals and departments coordinate their actions.

RELATED DIVERSIFICATION Related diversification is the strategy of entering a new business or industry to create a competitive advantage in one or more of an organization's existing divisions or businesses. Related diversification can add value to an organization's products if managers can find ways for its various divisions or business units to share their valuable skills or resources so that synergy is created.[29] Synergy is obtained when the value created by two divisions cooperating is greater than the value that would be created if the two divisions operated separately. For example, suppose two or more divisions within a diversified company can utilize the same manufacturing facilities, distribution channels, advertising campaigns, and so on. Each division that shares resources has to invest less in the shared functions than it would have to invest if it had full responsibility for the activity. In this way, related diversification can be a major source of cost savings.[30] Similarly, if one division's R&D skills can be used to improve another division's products, the second division's products may receive a competitive advantage.

Procter & Gamble's disposable diaper and paper towel businesses offer one of the best examples of the successful production of synergies. These businesses share the costs of procuring inputs such as paper and developing new technology to reduce manufacturing costs. In addition, a joint sales force sells both products to supermarkets, and both products are shipped by means of the same distribution system. This resource sharing has enabled both divisions to reduce their costs, and as a result, they can charge lower prices than their competitors and thus attract more customers.[31]

In pursuing related diversification, managers often seek to find new businesses where they can use the existing skills and resources in their departments to create synergies, add value to the new business, and hence improve the competitive position of the company. Alternatively, managers may acquire a company in a new industry because they believe that some of the skills and resources of the acquired company might improve the efficiency of one or more of their existing divisions. If successful, such skill transfers can help an organization to lower its costs or better differentiate its products because they create synergies between divisions.

unrelated diversification Entering a new industry or buying a company in a new industry that is not related in any way to an organization's current businesses or industries.

UNRELATED DIVERSIFICATION Managers pursue unrelated diversification when they enter new industries or buy companies in new industries that are not related in any way to their current businesses or industries. One main reason for pursuing unrelated diversification is that, sometimes, managers can buy a poorly performing company, transfer their management skills to that company, turn around its business, and increase its performance, all of which creates value.

Another reason for pursuing unrelated diversification is that purchasing businesses in different industries lets managers engage in *portfolio strategy,* which is apportioning financial resources among divisions to increase financial returns or spread risks among different businesses, much as individual investors do with their own portfolios. For example, managers may transfer funds from a rich division (a "cash cow") to a new and promising division (a "star") and, by appropriately allocating money between divisions, create value. Though used as a popular explanation in the 1980s for unrelated diversification, portfolio strategy has run into increasing criticism in the 1990s.[32]

Today, many companies and their managers are abandoning the strategy of unrelated diversification because there is evidence that too much diversification can cause managers to lose control of their organization's core business.

Management experts suggest that although unrelated diversification might initially create value for a company, managers sometimes use portfolio strategy to expand the scope of their organization's businesses too much. When this happens, it becomes difficult for top managers to be knowledgeable about all of the organization's diverse businesses. Managers do not have the time to process all of the information required to adequately assess the strategy and performance of each division objectively, and organizational performance often suffers.

This problem began to occur at General Electric in the 1970s. As former CEO Reg Jones commented: "I tried to review each business unit plan in great detail. This effort took untold hours and placed a tremendous burden on the corporate executive office. After awhile I began to realize that no matter how hard we would work, we could not achieve the necessary in-depth understanding of the 40-odd business unit plans."[33] Unable to handle so much information, top managers are overwhelmed and eventually make important resource allocation decisions on the basis of only a superficial analysis of the competitive position of each division. This usually results in value being lost rather than created.[34]

Thus, although unrelated diversification can create value for a company, research evidence suggests that many diversification efforts have reduced value rather than created it.[35] As a consequence, during the 1990s there has been a trend among many diversified companies to divest many of their unrelated divisions. Managers have sold off divisions and concentrated organizational resources on their core business and focused more on related diversification.[36] In the 1990s, for example, Sears divested all of the stock brokerage, insurance, and real-estate businesses it acquired during the 1980s, to concentrate on strengthening its core retailing activities and survive in its fight with Wal-Mart and Target.

International Expansion

As if planning the appropriate level of diversification was not a difficult enough decision, corporate-level managers also must decide on the appropriate way to compete internationally. A basic question confronts the managers of any organization that competes in more than one national market: To what extent should the organization customize features of its products and marketing campaign to different national conditions?[37]

global strategy Selling the same standardized product and using the same basic marketing approach in each national market.

multidomestic strategy Customizing products and marketing strategies to specific national conditions.

If managers decide that their organization should sell the same standardized product in each national market in which it competes, and use the same basic marketing approach, they adopt a **global strategy**.[38] Such companies undertake very little, if any, customization to suit the specific needs of customers in different countries. But if managers decide to customize products and marketing strategies to specific national conditions, they adopt a **multidomestic strategy**. Matsushita has traditionally pursued a global strategy, selling the same basic TVs and VCRs in every market in which it does business and often using the same basic marketing approach. Unilever, the European food and household products company, has pursued a multidomestic strategy. Thus, to appeal to German customers, Unilever's German division sells a different range of food products and uses a different marketing approach than its North American division.

Global and multidomestic strategies both have advantages and disadvantages. The major advantage of a global strategy is the significant cost savings associated with not having to customize products and marketing approaches to different national conditions. For example, products like Rolex watches, Ralph Lauren or Tommy Hilfiger clothing, Channel or Armani accessories or perfume, Dell computers, Chinese-made plastic toys and buckets, and U.S. grown rice and wheat are all products that are sold using the same marketing across many countries by simply changing the language. Thus, companies can save a significant amount of money.

The major disadvantage of pursuing a global strategy is that, by ignoring national differences, managers may leave themselves vulnerable to local competitors that do differentiate their products to suit local tastes. This occurred in the British consumer electronics industry. Amstrad, a British computer and electronics company, got its start by recognizing and responding to local consumer needs. Amstrad captured a major share of the British audio market by ignoring the standardized inexpensive music centers marketed by companies pursuing a global strategy, such as Sony and Matsushita. Instead, Amstrad's product was encased in teak rather than metal and featured a control panel tailor-made to appeal to British consumers' preferences. To remain competitive in this market, Matsushita had to place more emphasis on local customization of its Panasonic and JVC brands.

The advantages and disadvantages of a multidomestic strategy are the opposite of those of a global strategy. The major advantage of a multidomestic strategy is that by customizing product offerings and marketing approaches to local conditions, managers may be able to gain market share or charge higher prices for their products. The major disadvantage is that customization raises production costs and puts the multidomestic company at a price disadvantage because it often has to charge prices higher than the prices charged by competitors pursuing a global strategy. Obviously, the choice between these two strategies calls for trade-offs. Managers at Gillette have created a strategy that combines the best features of both international strategies, as profiled in this "Managing Globally" feature.

Managing Globally

Gillette's New International Strategy

Gillette, the well-known razor blade maker, has been a global company from the beginning as its managers quickly saw the advantages of selling its products abroad. By 2000, 60 percent of Gillette's revenues came from global sales and this percentage is expected to increase.[39] Gillette's strategy over the years has been pretty constant: Find a new foreign country with a growing market for razor blades, form a strategic alliance with a local razor blade company and take a majority stake in it; invest in a large marketing campaign and then build a modern factory to make razor blades and other products for the local market. For example, when Gillette entered Russia after the break up of the Soviet Union it saw a huge opportunity to increase sales. It formed a joint venture with a local company called Leninets Concern which made a razor known as the Sputnik, and then with this base began to import its own brands into Russia. When sales growth rose sharply it decided to offer more products in the market and built a new plant in St. Petersburg.[40]

Today, Gillette operates 54 manufacturing facilities in more than 20 countries.[41] It establishes its factories in countries where labor and other costs are low, and then distributes and markets its products to countries in that region of the world. So, in this sense it pursues a global strategy. However, all of Gillette's research and development and design takes place in the United States. As it develops new kinds of razors it equips its foreign factories to manufacture them when it decides that local customers are ready to trade up to the new product. So, for example, Gillette's latest razor may be introduced in a foreign country years later than in the United States. Thus, Gillette is customizing its product

A large part of Gillette's profitability depends on the global sales of its razors and shaving products. Here, a potential customer in India is informed about the advantages of Gillette's latest razor.

offering to the needs of different countries and also pursues a multidomestic strategy. By pursuing this international strategy Gillette achieve low costs and still differentiates and customizes its product range to suit the needs of each country or world region. This strategy has proved very effective for Gillette. In 2001 Gillette Chairman and CEO James F. Kilts reported that, "There are few consumer products companies with more powerful global brands than Gillette. I believe that there is a huge opportunity to maximize the potential of Gillette's global brands by tailoring its products to the needs of different countries."

Vertical Integration

When an organization is doing well in its business, managers often see new opportunities to create value by either producing their own inputs or distributing their own outputs. Managers at E. & J. Gallo Winery, for example, realized that they could lower Gallo's costs if they produced their own wine bottles rather than buying them from a glass company. As a result, Gallo established a new division to produce glass bottles.

vertical integration A strategy that allows an organization to create value by producing its own inputs or distributing and selling its own outputs.

Vertical integration is the corporate-level strategy through which an organization becomes involved in producing its own inputs (*backward* vertical integration) or distributing and selling its own outputs (*forward* vertical integration).[42] A steel company that supplies its iron ore needs from company-owned iron ore mines is engaging in backward vertical integration. A personal computer company that sells its computers through company-owned distribution outlets, as Tandy did through its Radio Shack stores, is engaging in forward vertical integration.

Figure 8.6 illustrates the four main stages in a typical raw-materials-to-consumer value chain; value is added at each stage. Typically, the primary operations of an organization take place in one of these stages. For a company based in the assembly stage, backward integration would involve establishing a new division in intermediate manufacturing or raw-material production, and forward integration would involve establishing a new division to distribute its

Figure 8.6
Stages in a Vertical Value Chain

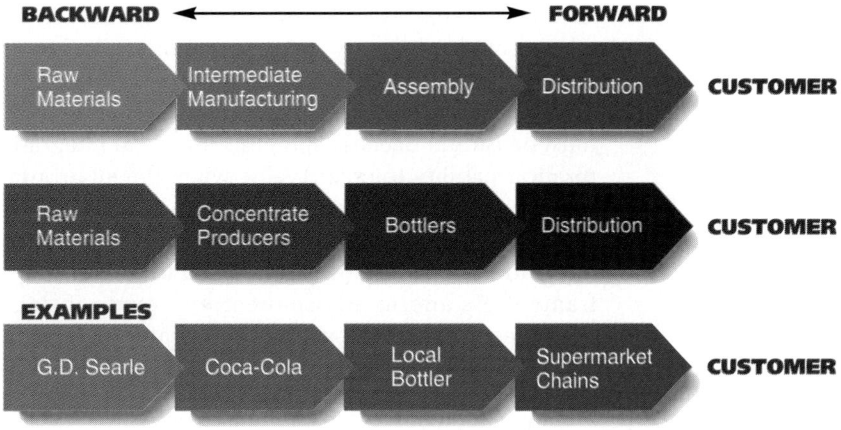

products to wholesalers or to sell directly to customers. A division at one stage receives the product produced by the division in the previous stage, transforms it in some way–adding value–and then transfers the output at a higher price to the division at the next stage in the chain.

As an example of how the value chain works, consider the cola segment of the soft-drink industry. Raw-materials suppliers include sugar companies and G. D. Searle, manufacturer of the artificial sweetener NutraSweet, which is used in diet colas. These companies sell their products to companies that make concentrate–such as Coca-Cola and PepsiCo that mix these inputs with others to produce the cola concentrate that they market. In the process, they add value to these inputs. The concentrate producers then sell the concentrate to bottlers, who add carbonated water to the concentrate and package the resulting drink–again adding value to the concentrate. Next, the bottlers sell the packaged product to various distributors, including retail stores such as Price Costco and Wal-Mart, and fast-food chains such as McDonald's. These distributors add value by making the product accessible to customers. Thus, value is added by companies at each stage in the raw-materials-to-consumer chain.

A major reason why managers pursue vertical integration is that it allows them either to add value to their products by making them special or unique or to lower the costs of value creation. For example, Coca-Cola and PepsiCo, in a case of forward vertical integration to build brand loyalty and enhance the differentiated appeal of their colas, decided to buy up their major bottlers to increase control over marketing and promotion efforts that had been handled by the bottlers.[43] An example of using forward vertical integration to lower costs is Matsushita's decision to open company-owned stores to sell its Panasonic and JVC products and thus keep the profit that otherwise would be earned by independent retailers.[44]

Although vertical integration can help an organization to grow rapidly, it can be a problem when forces in the environment counter the strategies of the organization and make it necessary for managers to reorganize or retrench. Vertical integration can reduce an organization's flexibility to respond to changing environmental conditions. For example, IBM used to produce most of its own components for mainframe computers. While this made sense in the 1970s, it became a major handicap for the company in the fast-changing computer industry of the 1990s. The rise of organizationwide networks of personal computers meant slumping demand for mainframes. As demand fell, IBM found itself with an excess-capacity problem, not only in its mainframe assembly operations but also in component operations. Closing down this capacity cost IBM over $5 billion.[45]

When considering vertical integration as a strategy to add value, managers must be careful because sometimes vertical integration actually reduces an organization's ability to create value when the environment changes. This is why so many companies now outsource the production of component parts to other companies. IBM, however, has found a new opportunity for forward vertical integration in the 1990s.[46] It decided to provide IT consulting services to mainframe users and to advise them on how to install and manage any software packages they chose on their mainframes. Providing such IT services was so profitable for IBM that by 2000 it had recovered its market position.

Formulating Business-Level Strategies

Michael Porter, the researcher who developed the five forces model discussed earlier, also formulated a theory of how managers can select a business-level strategy, a plan to gain a competitive advantage in a particular market or industry.[47] According to Porter, managers must choose between the two basic ways of increasing the value of an organization's products: differentiating the product to add value or lowering the costs of value creation. Porter also argues that managers must choose between serving the whole market or serving just one segment or part of a market. Based on those choices, managers choose to pursue one of four business-level strategies: low-cost, differentiation, focused low-cost, or focused differentiation (see Table 8.2).

Low-Cost Strategy

low-cost strategy Driving the organization's costs down below the costs of its rivals.

With a **low-cost strategy,** managers try to gain a competitive advantage by focusing the energy of all the organization's departments or functions on driving the organization's costs down below the costs of its rivals. This strategy, for example, would require manufacturing managers to search for new ways to reduce production costs, R&D managers to focus on developing new products that can be manufactured more cheaply, and marketing managers to find ways to lower the costs of attracting customers. According to Porter, organizations pursuing a low-cost strategy can sell a product for less than their rivals sell it and yet still make a profit because of their lower costs. Thus, organizations that pursue a low-cost strategy hope to enjoy a competitive advantage based on their low prices. For example, BIC pursues a low-cost strategy; it offers customers razor blades priced lower than Gillette's and ballpoint pens less expensive than those offered by Cross or Waterford.

Differentiation Strategy

differentiation strategy Distinguishing an organization's products from the products of competitors in dimensions such as product design, quality, or after-sales service.

With a **differentiation strategy,** managers try to gain a competitive advantage by focusing all the energies of the organization's departments or functions on distinguishing the organization's products from those of competitors in one or more important dimensions, such as product design, quality, or after-sales service and support. Often, the process of making products unique and different is expensive. This strategy, for example, often requires managers to increase

Table 8.2
Porter's Business-Level Strategies

	Number of Market Segments Served	
Strategy	**Many**	**Few**
Low-cost	✓	
Focused low-cost		✓
Differentiation	✓	
Focused differentiation		✓

spending on product design or R&D to differentiate the product, and costs rise as a result. Organizations that successfully pursue a differentiation strategy may be able to charge a premium price for their products, a price usually much higher than the price charged by a low-cost organization. The premium price allows organizations pursuing a differentiation strategy to recoup their higher costs. Coca-Cola, PepsiCo and Procter & Gamble, are some of the many well-known companies that pursue a strategy of differentiation. They spend enormous amounts of money on advertising to differentiate, and create a unique image for, their products.

"Stuck in the Middle"

According to Porter's theory, managers cannot simultaneously pursue both a low-cost strategy and a differentiation strategy. Porter identified a simple correlation: Differentiation raises costs and thus necessitates premium pricing to recoup those high costs. For example, if BIC suddenly began to advertise heavily to try to build a strong global brand image for its products, BIC's costs would rise. BIC then could no longer make a profit simply by pricing its blades or pens lower than Gillette or Cross. According to Porter, managers must choose between a low-cost strategy and a differentiation strategy. He refers to managers and organizations that have not made this choice as being "stuck in the middle." According to Porter, organizations stuck in the middle tend to have lower levels of performance than do those that pursue a low-cost or differentiation strategy. To avoid being stuck in the middle, top managers must instruct departmental managers to take actions that will result in either low cost or differentiation.

However, exceptions to this rule can be found. In many organizations managers have been able to drive costs below those of rivals and simultaneously differentiate their products from those offered by rivals.[48] For example, Toyota's production system is reportedly the most efficient in the world. This efficiency gives Toyota a low-cost strategy vis-à-vis its rivals in the global car industry. At the same time, Toyota has differentiated its cars from those of rivals on the basis of superior design and quality. This superiority allows the company to charge a premium price for many of its popular models.[49] Thus, Toyota seems to be simultaneously pursuing both a low-cost and a differentiated business-level strategy. This example suggests that although Porter's ideas may be valid in most cases, very well managed companies such as Toyota, McDonald's, and Dell Computer may have both low costs and differentiated products.

Focused Low-Cost and Focused Differentiation Strategies

Both the differentiation strategy and the low-cost strategy are aimed at serving many or most segments of a particular market such as for cars or computers. Porter identified two other business-level strategies that aim to serve the needs of customers in only one or a few market segments.[50] Managers pursuing a **focused low-cost strategy** serve one or a few segments of the overall market and aim to be the lowest-cost company serving that segment.

focused low-cost strategy Serving only one segment of the overall market and being the lowest-cost organization serving that segment.

For example, Cott Corporation is the world's leading supplier of *retailer* brandname carbonated soft drinks. With production facilities in Canada, the United States and the United Kingdom, it produces, packages, and distributes a wide selection of retailer brand beverages for grocery, mass-merchandise, drugstore, and convenience store chains. For example, all Wal-Mart soda sold under the Sam's brand-name is made by Cott. However, note that while it is the world's leading supplier of *retailer-brand name* sodas, it is focusing on a low cost strategy. It makes no attempt to compete with Coke and Pepsi, which, as noted earlier, pursue a differentiation strategy, and whose brand-name sodas dominate the global soda market.

By contrast, managers pursuing a **focused differentiation** *strategy* serve just one or a few segments of the market and aim to be the most differentiated company serving that segment. BMW, for example, pursues a focused strategy, producing cars exclusively for higher-income customers. By contrast, Toyota pursues a differentiation strategy and produces cars that appeal to consumers in almost all segments of the car market, from basic transportation (Toyota Tercel), through the middle of the market (Toyota Camry), to the high-income end of the market (Lexus).

focused differentiation strategy Serving only one segment of the overall market and trying to be the most differentiated organization serving that segment.

As these examples suggest, companies pursuing either of these focused strategies have chosen to *specialize* in some way by directing their efforts at a particular kind of customer (such as serving the needs of babies or affluent customers) or even the needs of customers in a specific geographical region (customers on the east or west coast). An excellent example of how a company can pursue both a low-cost and a differentiated focused strategy at the same time by using new information technologies is provided by Zara, a manufacturer of fashionable Spanish clothing.

Managing Globally

IT and Just-in-Time Low-Cost Fashion

Well-known fashion houses like Channel, Dior, and Armani can charge thousands of dollars for the fashionable collections of suits and dresses that they introduce twice yearly in the fall and in the spring. Only the very rich can afford such differentiated and expensive clothing and this has opened up a gap in the fashion market for companies that can supply fashionable clothes at lower prices. Essentially, these companies have the capabilities to pursue a focused differentiation and cost-leadership strategy.

While many clothing companies, such as the United States's The Gap, Sweden's Hennes & Mauritz, and England's Jaeger and Laura Ashley, have attempted to supply fashionable clothes at lower prices, none has succeeded as well as Spanish clothes maker, Zara, whose sales have soared in recent years.[51] Zara has managed to position itself as the low price/cost leader in the fashion segment of the clothing market because of the way it uses information technology. It has created an information system that allows it to manage its design and manufacturing process in a way that minimizes the inventory it has to carry–the major cost borne by a clothing retailer. However, its IT also gives instantaneous feedback on which clothes are selling well, and in which countries, which gives it a competitive advantage from differentiation. Specifically, Zara can manufacture more of a particular kind of dress or suit to meet high customer demand, decide which clothing should be sold in its rapidly expanding network of global stores, and constantly change the mix of clothes it offers customers to keep up with fashion. Moreover, it can do this at relatively small output levels, something which is also a part of a specialized, focused strategy.

One of Spanish clothes-maker Zara's new high fashion stores. While this store is in Madrid, former delivery boy Amancio Ortega who founded Zara intends to establish a store in all the major cities of the world in the next decade.

Zara's IT also allows it to manage the interface between its design and manufacturing operations more efficiently. Zara only takes five weeks to design a new collection and then a week to make it. Other fashion houses, by contrast, can take six or more months to design the collection and then three more before it is available in stores.[52] This short time-to-market gives Zara great flexibility and allows the company to respond quickly to the rapidly changing fashion market which fashions can change several times a year. Because of the quick manufacturing to sales cycle and just-in-time fashion, Zara offers its clothes collections at relatively low prices and still makes profits that are the envy of the fashion clothing industry.

When Zara offered its shares to the public for the first time in 2001, its shares soared in price.[53] Investors believe that there will soon be a Zara store in most major cities across the world and that its name will become as common to customers as the more well-known clothes designers.

Formulating Functional-Level Strategies

Functional-level strategy is a plan of action to improve the ability of an organization's departments to create value. It is concerned with the actions that managers of individual departments (such as manufacturing or marketing) can take to add value to an organization's goods and services and thereby increase the value customers receive. The price that customers are prepared to pay for a product indicates how much they value an organization's products. The more customers value a product, the more they are willing to pay for it.

functional-level strategy A plan that indicates how a function intends to achieve its goals.

There are two ways in which departments can add value to an organization's products:

1. Departmental managers can lower the costs of creating value so that an organization can attract customers by keeping its prices lower than its competitors' prices.

2. Departmental managers can add value to a product by finding ways to differentiate it from the products of other companies.

If customers see more value in one organization's products than in the products of its competitors, they may be willing to pay premium prices. Thus, there must be a fit between functional- and business-level strategies if an organization is to achieve its mission and goal of maximizing the amount of value it gives customers. The better the fit between functional- and business-level strategies, the greater will be the organization's competitive advantage–its ability to attract customers and the revenue they provide.

Each organizational function has an important role to play in the process of lowering costs or adding value to a product (see Table 8.3). Manufacturing can find new ways to lower production costs or to build superior quality into the product to add value. Marketing, sales, and after-sales service and support can add value by, for example, building brand loyalty (as Coca-Cola and PepsiCo have done in the soft-drink industry) and finding more effective ways to attract customers. Human resource management can lower the costs of creating value by recruiting and training a highly productive workforce. The R&D function can lower the costs of creating value by developing more efficient production processes. Similarly, R&D can add value by developing new and improved products that customers value over established product offerings. Managers can lower the costs of creating value and can add value through their effective leadership and coordination of the whole organization (see Chapter 13).

In trying to add value or lower the costs of creating value, all functional managers should attend to these four goals:[54]

1. *To attain superior efficiency.* Efficiency is a measure of the amount of inputs required to produce a given amount of outputs. The fewer the inputs required to produce a given output, the higher is the efficiency and the lower the cost of outputs. For example, in 1990 it took the average Japanese auto company 16.8 employee-hours to build a car, while the average American auto company took 25.1 employee-hours. Japanese companies at that time were more efficient and had lower costs than their American rivals.[55] By 2000, U.S. companies adopted more efficient manufacturing methods and narrowed that gap significantly; matching Japanese quality levels, however, has been more difficult.

2. *To attain superior quality.* Quality here means producing goods and services that are reliable–they do the job they were designed for and do it well.[56] Providing high-quality products creates a brand-name reputation for an organization's products. In turn, this enhanced reputation allows the organization to charge a higher price. In the automobile industry, for example, not only does Toyota have an efficiency-based cost advantage over many American and European competitors, but the higher quality of Toyota's products has also enabled the company to earn more money because customers are willing to pay a premium price for its cars.

3. *To attain superior innovation.* Anything new or novel about the way an organization operates or the goods and services it produces is the result of innovation. Innovation leads to advances in the kinds of products, production processes, management systems, organizational structures, and strategies that an organization develops. Successful innovation gives an organization something unique that its rivals lack. This uniqueness may enhance value added and thereby allow the organization to differentiate itself from its rivals and attract customers who will pay a premium price for its product. For example, Toyota is widely credited with pioneering a number of critical innovations in the way cars

Table 8.3
How Functions Can Lower the Costs and Create Value or Add Value to Create a Competitive Advantage

Value-Creating Function	Ways to Lower the Cost of Creating Value (Low-Cost Advantage)	Ways to Add Value (Differentiation Advantage)
Sales and marketing Materials management Research and development Manufacturing Human resource management	• Find new customers • Find low-cost advertising methods • Use just-in-time inventory system/computerized warehousing • Develop long-term relationships with suppliers and customers • Improve efficiency of machinery and equipment • Design products that can be made more cheaply • Develop skills in low-cost manufacturing • Reduce turnover and absenteeism • Raise employee skills	• Promote brand-name awareness and loyalty • Tailor products to suit customers' needs • Develop long-term relationships with suppliers to provide high-quality inputs • Reduce shipping time to customers • Create new products • Improve existing products • Increase product quality and reliability • Hire highly skilled employees • Develop innovative training programs

are built, and these innovations have helped Toyota achieve superior productivity and quality–the basis of Toyota's competitive advantage.

4. *To attain superior responsiveness to customers.* An organization that is responsive to customers tries to satisfy their needs and give them exactly what they want. An organization that treats customers better than its rivals treats them provides a valuable service for which customers may be willing to pay a higher price.

Attaining superior efficiency, quality, innovation, and responsiveness to customers requires the adoption of many state-of-the-art management techniques and practices, such as total quality management, flexible manufacturing systems, just-in-time inventory, self-managing teams, cross-functional teams, process reengineering, and employee empowerment. It is the responsibility of managers at the functional level to identify these techniques and develop a functional-level plan that contains the strategies necessary to develop them. We discuss these techniques at length in Part 6 where we focus on the management of operations and processes. The important issue to remember here is that all of these techniques can help an organization achieve a competitive advantage by lowering the costs of creating value, or by adding value above and beyond that offered by rivals.

Planning and Implementing Strategy

After identifying appropriate strategies to attain an organization's mission and goals, managers confront the challenge of putting those strategies into action. Strategy implementation is a five-step process:

1. Allocating responsibility for implementation to the appropriate individuals or groups

2. Drafting detailed action plans that specify how a strategy is to be implemented
3. Establishing a timetable for implementation that includes precise, measurable goals linked to the attainment of the action plan
4. Allocating appropriate resources to the responsible individuals or groups
5. Holding specific individuals or groups responsible for the attainment of corporate, divisional, and functional goals

As an example of how the strategy implementation process works in practice, consider the situation of Citibank, one of the largest financial institutions in the United States. While analyzing the strengths and weaknesses of Citibank (during a SWOT analysis), managers identified poor responsiveness to customers, and a lack of innovation within the organization as major weaknesses. Customers who are forced to wait in line, or wait several days for an answer to their personal banking inquiries, are not satisfied customers.

To correct this weakness, Citibank's managers decided to reengineer or redesign the bank's customer service processes to reduce waste and inefficiencies and to speed responsiveness to customers.[57] Managers at all levels from the top down were charged with the implementation of this initiative. At each level, managers were requested to draft a plan that specified how this initiative would be implemented.

The plan called for the bank to train a small group of its own employees in reengineering techniques designed to build new customer service skills and to use this group as a reengineering team. The action plan also established a formal process for identifying reengineering opportunities within the organization and for deciding which customer service problems the reengineering team should tackle first. A detailed timetable was established; it laid out deadlines for identifying and training the reengineering team, for identifying reengineering opportunities, for prioritizing opportunities, and for beginning the actual reengineering process. The individuals responsible were given a budget to provide them with the financial resources necessary to complete the project. Finally, top management informed the individuals responsible that they would be held accountable for meeting the timetable associated with the plan and for the overall success of the strategic initiative.

As the case of Citibank illustrates, the planning process goes beyond the mere identification of strategies; it also includes actions taken to ensure that the organization actually puts its strategies into action. It should be noted that the plan for implementing a strategy may require radical redesign of the structure of the organization, the development of new control systems, and the adoption of a program for changing the culture of the organization. These are all issues that we address in the next three chapters.

Tips for New Managers

Strategy

1. Periodically define an organization's business to determine how well it is achieving its mission. Use this planning exercise to determine its future goals.

2. Make SWOT analysis an integral part of the planning process.
3. Always be alert for opportunities to increase the value of an organization's goods and services so it can better serve its customers' needs.
4. Ensure that functional managers focus on finding new ways in which to lower the costs of value creation or to add value to products so that an organization can pursue both a low-cost strategy and a differentiation strategy.
5. Carefully assess the costs and benefits associated with using a corporate-level strategy and only enter a new business when it can clearly demonstrate that it will increase the value of your products.

Summary and Review

PLANNING Planning is a three-step process: (1) determining an organization's mission and goals; (2) formulating strategy; (3) implementing strategy. Managers use planning to identify and select appropriate goals and courses of action for an organization and to decide how to allocate the resources they need to attain those goals and carry out those actions. A good plan builds commitment for the organization's goals, gives the organization a sense of direction and purpose, coordinates the different functions and divisions of the organization, and controls managers by making them accountable for specific goals. In large organizations planning takes place at three levels: corporate, business or divisional, and functional or department. Although planning is typically the responsibility of a well-defined group of managers, the subordinates of those managers should be given every opportunity to have input into the process and to shape the outcome. Long-term plans have a time horizon of five years or more; intermediate-term plans, between one and five years; and short-term plans, one year or less.

DETERMINING MISSION AND GOALS AND FORMULATING STRATEGY Determining the organization's mission requires managers to define the business of the organization and establish major goals. Strategy formulation requires managers to perform a SWOT analysis and then choose appropriate strategies at the corporate, business, and functional levels. At the corporate level, organizations use strategies such as concentration on a single business, diversification, international expansion, and vertical integration to help increase the value of the goods and services provided to customers. At the business level, managers are responsible for developing a successful low-cost or differentiation strategy, either for the whole market or for a particular segment of it. At the functional level, departmental managers strive to develop and use their skills to help the organization either to add value to its products by differentiating them or to lower the costs of value creation.

IMPLEMENTING STRATEGY Strategy implementation requires managers to allocate responsibilities to appropriate individuals or groups, draft detailed action plans that specify how a strategy is to be implemented, establish a timetable for implementation that includes precise, measurable goals linked to the attainment of the action plan, allocate appropriate resources to the responsible individuals or groups, and hold individuals or groups accountable for the attainment of goals.

Management in Action

Topics for Discussion and Action

1. Describe the three steps of planning. Explain how they are related.
2. How can scenario planning help managers predict the future?
3. Ask a manager about the kinds of planning exercises he or she regularly uses. What are the purposes of these exercises, and what are their advantages or disadvantages?
4. What is the role of divisional and functional managers in the formulation of strategy?
5. Why is it important for functional managers to have a clear grasp of the organization's mission when developing strategies within their departments?
6. What is the relationship among corporate-, business-, and functional-level strategies and how do they create value for an organization?
7. Ask a manager to identify the corporate-, business-, and functional-level strategies used by his or her organization.

Building Management Skills

How to Analyze a Company's Strategy

Pick a well-known business organization that has received recent press coverage and for which you can get the annual reports or 10K filings from your school library for a number of years. For this organization do the following:

1. From the annual reports or 10K filings identify the main strategies pursued by the company over a ten-year period.
2. Try to identify why the company pursued these strategies. What reason was given in the annual reports, press reports, and so on?
3. Document whether and when any major changes in the strategy of the organization occurred. If changes did occur, try to identify the reason for them.
4. If changes in strategy occurred, try to determine the extent to which they were the result of long-term plans and the extent to which they were responses to unforeseen changes in the company's task environment.
5. What is the main industry that the company competes in?
6. What business-level strategy does the company seem to be pursuing in this industry?
7. What is the company's reputation with regard to productivity, quality, innovation, and responsiveness to customers in this industry? If the company has attained an advantage in any of these areas, how has it done so?
8. What is the current corporate-level strategy of the company? What is the company's stated reason for pursuing this strategy?
9. Has the company expanded internationally? If it has, identify its largest international market. How did the company enter this market? Did its mode of entry change over time?

Small Group Breakout Exercise

Low Cost or Differentiation?

Form groups of three or four people, and appoint one member as spokesperson who will communicate your findings to the class when called on by the instructor. Then discuss the following scenario.

You are a team of managers of a major national clothing chain, and you have been assigned with finding a way to restore your organization's competitive advantage. Recently, your organization has been experiencing increasing competition from two sources. First, discount stores such as Wal-Mart and Target have been undercutting your prices because they buy their clothes from low-cost foreign manufacturers while you buy most of yours from high-quality domestic suppliers. Discount stores have been attracting your customers who buy at the low end of the price range. Second, small boutiques opening in malls provide high-price designer clothing and are attracting away your customers at the high end of the market. Your company has become stuck in the middle, and you have to decide what to do: Should you start to buy abroad so that you can lower your prices and start to pursue a low-cost strategy? Should you focus on the high end of the market and become more of a differentiator? Or should you try to do both and pursue both a low-cost strategy and a differentiation strategy?

1. Using scenario planning, analyze the pros and cons of each alternative.
2. Think about the various clothing retailers in your local malls and city, and analyze the choices they have made about how to compete with one another along the low-cost and differentiation dimensions.

Exploring the World Wide Web

Search for a website that contains a good description of a company's strategy. What is the company's mission? Use the concepts and terminology of this chapter to describe the company's strategy to achieve its mission.

You're the Management Consultant

A group of investors in your city is considering opening a new upscale supermarket to compete with the major supermarket chains that are currently dominating the city's marketplace. They have called you in to help them determine what kind of upscale supermarket they should open. In other words, how can they best develop a competitive advantage against existing supermarket chains?

Questions

1. List the supermarket chains in your city and identify their strengths and weaknesses.
2. What business-level strategies are these supermarkets currently pursuing?
3. What kind of supermarket would do best against the competition? What kind of business-level strategy should it pursue?

BusinessWeek Cases in the News

Ford's Gamble on Luxury: Can It Make Its Portfolio of Acquired Brands Work Together?

Over the past decade, Ford Motor Co. has grown fat on profits from its pickup trucks and sport-utility vehicles. Last year, those trucks accounted for 80 percent of its pretax auto earnings in North America. But now that foreign auto makers have finally found their groove with light-truck vehicles that are truly competitive, those earnings are in jeopardy. Faced with such hot-selling models as the Toyota Sequoia and the BMW X5, Ford could see its share of the light-truck market fall by as much as 10 percent in the next two years, by some estimates.

Now, the question is: Can Ford turn the tables on BMW, Mercedes-Benz, and Toyota Motor's Lexus division through its $12 billion investment in luxury brands? Former Ford CEO Jaques A. Nasser thinks his luxury-growth strategy is a winner. "No one else in the business can duplicate what we've done," he says. Through a series of acquisitions, Ford has built an impressive portfolio of luxury brands—Jaguar, Volvo, Land Rover, Aston Martin, and Lincoln—and hired an army of former BMW executives to run the combined operation. The man at the top of Ford's Premier Automotive Group is Wolfgang Reitzle, the charismatic former president of BMW, whose job as group vice-president is to build Ford's luxury brands into a profit machine as powerful as its trucks.

If Reitzle can whip Ford's luxury brands into shape, the auto maker may be sitting on a gold mine. Fueled by the stock market gains of aging baby boomers, sales of those autos have been growing faster than the rest of the market. And traditionally, wealthy car buyers are somewhat insulated in a downturn. Last year, Ford's luxury brands sold 915,000 vehicles worldwide, putting it 140,000 vehicles ahead of BMW and about 400,000 vehicles behind industry leader Mercedes-Benz. By 2005, Ford wants to sell 1.3 million luxury vehicles. The company doesn't break out financial results for its premium group, but analysts estimate that the unit had revenues of $26.5 billion last year and operating income of $1.3 billion, about 19 percent of Ford's total. Merrill, Lynch & Co. analyst John Casesa predicts that profit margins for the group could more than double, from 3 percent to 8.3 percent, in five years, spurring a 27 percent jump in Ford's overall earnings.

But Reitzle faces difficult challenges. While Ford's premium brand names are strong, all are underperforming, analysts say. Reitzle has to find a way to boost efficiency by sharing parts and factories and to broaden each marque's vehicle lineup without damaging the brands' venerable images, even as rivals step up their own offerings. And he has to act fast. "They're in a race to grow their luxury portfolio to offset the deterioration that will ultimately come in trucks," says Deutsche Banc Alex. Brown analyst Rod Lache. "I don't know if they'll win."

Eclectic

Reitzle certainly has an ambitious game plan. Unlike Mercedes or BMW, which are expanding their lineups under a single brand, Ford will cover the luxury segment with a portfolio of brands, each catering to a different lifestyle or type of buyer. Volvo, for instance, is positioned as a maker of safe family cars, while Jaguar connotes British elegance, and Land Rover caters to the off-road safari set. Ford argues that it doesn't have to spend money developing a Jaguar SUV, for instance, because customers can opt for a Range Rover or a Lincoln Navigator instead. Says Victor H. Doolan, executive director for the premium auto group: "We don't have to stretch our brands beyond their core values."

The key to Ford's multi-brand strategy is Reitzle's goal to eventually sell all five luxury nameplates in one dealership. The dealer-owner would operate five separate showrooms under one roof, with separate sales staffs but combined service operations and back-office functions. Doolan says the idea will work because most luxury car buyers own three or four vehicles. Ford, he says, can "fill all the needs of their garage" at a single dealership. Contruction recently began near Phoenix on the first of about 10 such dealerships that are scheduled to open in the next 18 months. Those dealerships will include a quarter-mile test track so that while an owner's car is being serviced, the customer can test-drive another luxury marque.

Most dealers would jump at the chance to own a megastore selling all of Ford's luxury brands. But many are worried that investing in such a dealership, which could cost up to $25 million, would be too expensive. "Most of us are waiting to see how it will work," says Harold Kuhn, owner of Park Lincoln Mercury in Detroit. One big issue: Ford has to persuade dealers of different brands to sell their stores to other car dealers to form the consolidated luxury operations. Already, Ford has encouraged Lincoln Mercury dealers to sell their businesses to reduce the number of dealers in certain regions.

Some critics say the idea won't fly because Ford's premium lineup just can't encompass everything luxury owners want. Susan Jacobs, president of Jacobs & Associates, a Rutherford (N.J.) firm specializing in luxury-market analysis, gives this example: A Jaguar enthusiast who likes sporty cars is more likely to want the European high-performance experience of a BMW or Mercedes for his new SUV than a Lincoln Navigator or Land Rover. With rivals adding SUVs and entry-level models to their lineups, Ford can forget about stealing customers from European brands, says Jacobs. "The mistake they're making, in a very crowded market," Jacobs says, "is that you just can't manage all these boutique brands."

Reitzle believes that by carefully deciding which new models to add under each brand name, collisions between brands can be avoided. "You can only do what we're doing when you have a brand portfolio that is complementary. Our setup is unique," he says.

So are the problems. And Reitzle can't ignore each brand's particular issues as he pursues his integrated luxury strategy. Jaguar, having overcome longstanding quality problems, has perhaps the most aggressive growth plans. Its sales grew about 25 percent last year, to 87,000 units, with the addition of the $45,000 S-type, a sedan built on the same platform as Ford's Lincoln LS and the upcoming Ford Thunderbird. Jaguar is moving further downscale with the $30,000 X-type, a competitor to BMW's 3-series, which goes on sale this summer. And to expand its market, Jaguar is also going after younger drivers and African-American purchasers by using marketing that is geared toward them. But the low end of the luxury category is perhaps the most competitive segment, and as the economy softens, it's the one that could be subject to a price war.

Fixer-Upper

Ford also has to find a way to make Land Rover profitable, something its previous owner, BMW, couldn't do. Land Rover isn't as bad off as Jaguar was when Ford purchased it in 1989, but company execs estimate that it will take as long as two years just to shore up the British auto maker. Long term, the plan is to share platforms with Ford's trucks to lower costs and improve quality. For now, growth will come from the addition of lower-priced models, such as the Freelander, which debuts in the United States later this year.

Perhaps the toughest challenge is turning around Ford's own Lincoln brand. Even though sales climbed in the late 90s with the success of the big Lincoln Navigator SUV, the brand was eclipsed by faster-growing import rivals Mercedes and Lexus. Ford execs are trying to reshape Lincoln around the theme "American luxury." This spring, the $52,000 Lincoln Blackwood, an SUV-pickup hybrid, goes on sale. And within a few years, Lincoln will add an entry-level sedan and a compact SUV. More Lincolns are also on the drawing board.

Even Volvo, the Swedish carmaker known for its boxy sedans and wagons, is beginning to introduce more stylish models, such as the new S60 sedan now on sale. Volvo is Ford's biggest luxury brand, selling 477,000 units worldwide, but the goal is to boost that figure to 600,000 within five years. More important, Volvo's growth is key to Ford's turnaround efforts in Europe, where Ford can stem losses by building Volvos in underutilized Ford factories.

Building the Premier Automotive Group into the profit machine Ford envisions will take time. "We are now on a 10-year journey," says Reitzle. With so many brands under its belt, Ford is hoping for a comfortable ride.

Source: J. Muller and D. Welch, "Ford's Gamble on Luxury," *Business Week,* March 5, 2001, pp. 69–70.

Questions

1. What is Ford's business-level strategy? What are its main features? Why does it have so many different brandname cars?
2. What are the main problems, opportunities, and threats Ford's managers encounter in managing this strategy?

BusinessWeek Cases in the News

Sorry, Steve: Here's Why It Won't Work

For years, Apple Computer CEO Steven P. Jobs has tried working with retailers to make shopping for Apple's stylish products as appealing as using them—everything from setting up kiosks to special sections adorned with Apple's Think Different posters. Still, the computer maker's share has fallen, and Jobs figures he knows why. "Buying a car is no longer the worst purchasing experience. Buying a computer is now No. 1," he griped at the MacWorld trade show in January.

Now, he's taking matters into his own hands. On May 19, Apple will open a swanky new retail store—the first of as many 110 nationwide—at Tyson's Corner Galleria mall outside Washington. While Apple execs won't comment on their plans, the idea seems clear: Well-trained Apple salespeople in posh Apple stores can convince would-be buyers of the Mac's unique advantages, including its well-regarded iMovie software for making home videos and its iTunes program for burning custom CDs.

"Caviar"

With its top-notch brand and proven marketing panache, Apple should have a shot at improving on the Gateway Country Store model. And it will give Apple fresh outlets to sell its own products such as the titanium PowerBook and other companies' consumer gadgets such as Handspring Inc.'s Visor handheld line. The company would gain new revenue as a reseller of other electronic goodies and have more control over marketing and servicing of its products. What's more, Apple could boost margins by cutting out middlemen and wooing buyers to higher-priced models.

The way Jobs sees it, the stores look to be a sure thing. But even if they attain a measure of success, few outsiders think new stores, no matter how well-conceived, will get Apple back on the hot-growth path. Jobs's focus on selling just a few consumer Macs has helped boost profits, but it is keeping Apple from exploring potential new markets. And his perfectionist attention to aesthetics has resulted in beautiful but pricey products with limited appeal outside the faithful: Apple's market share is a measly 2.8 percent. "Apple's problem is it still believes the way to grow is serving caviar in a world that seems pretty content with cheese and crackers," gripes former Chief Financial Officer Joseph Graziano.

Rather than unveil a Velveeta Mac, Jobs thinks he can do a better job than experienced retailers at moving the beluga. Problem is, the numbers don't add up. Given the decision to set up shop in high-rent districts in Manhattan, Boston, Chicago, and Jobs's hometown of Palo Alto, Calif., the leases for Apple's stores could cost $1.2 million a year each, says David A. Goldstein, president of researcher Channel Marketing Corp. Since PC retailing gross margins are normally 10 percent or less, Apple would have to sell $12 million a year per store to pay for the space. Gateway does about $8 million annually at each of its Country Stores. Then there's the cost of construction, hiring experienced staff. "I give them two years before they're turning out the lights on a very painful and expensive mistake," says Goldstein.

Harsh words. Still, Jobs' instinct that Apple has to take some dramatic steps is on target. In recent years, Apple has succeeded mainly by getting its 25 million-strong customer base to upgrade to pricier machines with higher margins. But only 12 million of them are due for upgrades in the next couple of years, analysts estimate. Meantime, Dell Computer Corp. and Compaq Computer Corp. have been stealing share from Apple in the key education market.

Source: C. Edwards, "Sorry, Steve: Here's Why it Won't Work," *Business Week,* May 21, 2001, p. 44.

Questions

1. Why is Steve Jobs' opening Apple retail stores? How will this help it build competitive advantage? What is Apple's business-level strategy?
2. Why does *Business Week* think these stores will have a problem? Now, search the Internet and find out how well these stores are doing today. Was *Business Week* correct?

Chapter 9
Managing Organizational Structure

Learning Objectives

After studying this chapter, you should be able to:

- Identify the **factors that influence** managers' choice of an **organizational structure.**
- Explain **how managers group tasks into jobs** that are motivating and satisfying for employees.
- Describe the **types of organizational structures** managers can design, and explain why they choose one structure over another.
- Explain why there is a need to both **centralize and decentralize authority.**
- Explain **why managers must coordinate and integrate** between jobs, functions, and divisions as an organization grows.
- Explain why managers who seek new ways to increase efficiency and effectiveness are using **strategic alliances** and **network structures.**

A Manager's Challenge

Lucent Reorganizes for Survival

How should managers organize to improve performance?

In the early 2000s, an economic recession and falling sales led managers at many companies to examine whether they should change their way of organizing to increase their efficiency and effectiveness. For some companies the issue was that increasing competition made it imperative that they restructure and find a simpler and more streamlined and efficient way of organizing their activities. For other companies, the need was to restructure to differentiate their products to sustain or increase their competitive advantage and better meet the needs of their customers. For still others, the problem was that their rapid global expansion in the 1990s was now causing many problems of communication and coordination and managers needed to rethink the way they were organized at the global level.

Take Lucent Technologies which makes Internet routers and other communications equipment. As one of the high-flying high-tech companies of the 1990s, Lucent was severely affected by all three of these problems. In 2001, Lucent's stock plunged to less than \$7 a share from a high of more than \$70 because of falling sales and mounting losses.[1] The reason? Its managers had backed the development of the wrong kind of router, one based on capacity rather than speed, and speed turned out to be what customers wanted. By contrast, Nortel Networks, one of its major competitors had developed fast optical or light-based routers and it now had 45 percent of the market compared to Lucent's 15 percent.

A total of over one-third of Lucent employees received "pink slips" from the company during a recent series of layoffs. Moving to a simpler, easier to manage, organizational structure may help Lucent to compete more effectively and avoid such layoffs in the future.

Among the many reasons for its poor decision making, was the incredibly complex way it had been organized by former CEO, Richard McGinn. To promote the speedy development of new products McGinn had decided that Lucent should be set up as 11 different business divisions, each of which would focus on a particular product and market.[2] However, enormous communications and coordination problems arose since managers in one division did not know what managers in the others were doing. Incompatible kinds of products were being developed, new technology was not being shared across divisions, and it was a nightmare trying to sell Lucent's range of products globally since the 11 business units were each handling their own global sales.

McGinn was forced to leave the company in October 2000. His successor, Henry Schacht, decided efficiency and effectiveness would increase if Lucent reorganized the 11 different units into just 5 business units. This would make managers more accountable for their actions and they would be better able to communicate and avoid the problems noted above. Schacht and his managers spent hundreds of millions of dollars to restructure the company and laid off over 15,000 employees.

In 2001, however, it was clear that Lucent could no longer even afford the luxury of having five divisions because of mounting losses and the need to reduce costs. In July and October, Schacht announced that Lucent would reorganize again both to reduce costs and allow it to better focus its resources to speed up the new product development process. Another 20,000 employees were to be laid off (a total of almost one half of Lucent's employees were laid off as a result of the restructuring). And, Lucent announced that it was combining the five units into only two business divisions.[3] First, an Integrated Network Solutions Division would handle all its "land-line" products such as routers, switching, and data software. Second, a Mobility Solutions Division would handle the company's wireless products.

Managers hoped this new structure would perform more flexibly and organically and allow it to respond faster and more effectively to the rapidly changing information technology environment. They also knew it would save billions of dollars and would be a much more efficient method of organizing. Finally, they hoped that with just two major divisions it would be far easier to coordinate and manage global sales, something vital if Lucent was to achieve a turnaround. In 2001, it began to reorganize activities and move toward its new product division structure. The jury was out though, on whether these changes would be enough to turnaround its fortunes and if it would survive in its battle with Nortel and Cisco. •

Overview

As "A Manager's Challenge" suggests, the challenge facing Lucent was to identify the best way to operate in the new, more competitive industry environment. Lucent's managers were forced to radically change the way it organized its employees and other resources to meet that challenge, many thousands of its employees were laid off and suffered the results of poor managerial decision making.

In Part 4 of this book, we examine how managers can organize and control human and other resources to create high-performing organizations. To organize and control (two of the four functions of management identified in Chapter 1), managers must design an organizational architecture that makes the best use of resources to produce the goods and services customers want. **Organizational architecture** is the combination of organizational structure, control systems, culture, and human resource management systems that together determine how efficiently and effectively organizational resources are used.

organizational architecture The organizational structure, control systems, culture, and human resource management systems that together determine how efficiently and effectively organizational resources are used.

By the end of this chapter, you will be familiar not only with various organizational structures but also with various factors that determine the organizational design choices that managers make. Then, in Chapters 10 and 11 we examine issues surrounding the design of an organization's control systems, culture, and human resource management systems.

Designing Organizational Structure

Organizing is the process by which managers establish the structure of working relationships among employees to allow them to achieve organizational goals efficiently and effectively. **Organizational structure** is the formal system of task and job reporting relationships that determines how employees use resources to achieve organizational goals.[4] **Organizational design** is the process by which managers make specific organizing choices about tasks and job relationships that result in the construction of a particular organizational structure.[5]

organizational structure A formal system of task and reporting relationships that coordinates and motivates organizational members so that they work together to achieve organizational goals.

organizational design The process by which managers make specific organizing choices that result in a particular kind of organizational structure.

As noted in Chapter 2, according to *contingency theory,* managers design organizational structures to fit the factors or circumstances that are affecting the company the most and causing them the most uncertainty.[6] Thus, there is no one best way to design an organization: Design reflects each organization's specific situation and researchers have argued that in some situations stable, mechanistic structures may be most appropriate while in others flexible, organic structures might be the most effective. Four factors are important determinants of the type of organizational structure or organizing method managers select: the nature of the organizational environment, the type of strategy the organization pursues, the technology (and particularly *information technology*) the organization uses, and the characteristics of the organization's human resources (see Figure 9.1).[7]

The Organizational Environment

In general, the more quickly the external environment is changing and the greater the uncertainty within it, the greater are the problems facing managers in trying to gain access to scarce resources. In this situation, to speed decision making and communication and make it easier to obtain resources, managers typically make organizing choices that bring flexibility to the organizational structure.[8] They are likely to decentralize authority and empower lower-level employees to make important operating decisions–a more organic structure. In contrast, if the external environment is stable, resources are readily available, and uncertainty is low, then less coordination and communication among people and functions is needed to obtain resources, and managers can make organizing choices that bring more stability or formality to the organizational structure.

Figure 9.1
Factors Affecting Organizational Structure

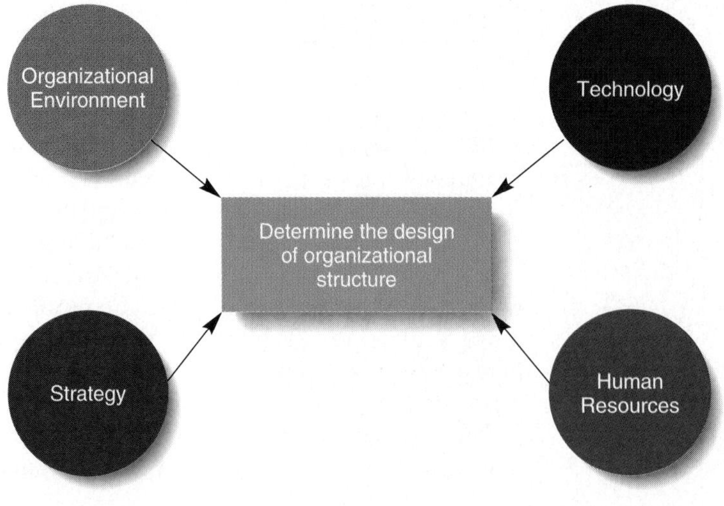

Managers in this situation prefer to make decisions within a clearly defined hierarchy of authority and use extensive rules and standard operating procedures to govern activities–a more mechanistic structure.

As we have seen in Chapters 3 and 4, change is rapid in today's marketplace, and increasing competition both at home and abroad is putting greater pressure on managers to attract customers and increase efficiency and effectiveness. Consequently, interest in finding ways to structure organizations–such as through empowerment and self-managed teams–to allow people and departments to behave flexibly has been increasing.

Strategy

As discussed in Chapter 7, once managers decide on a strategy, they must choose the right means to implement it. Different strategies often call for the use of different organizational structures. For example, a differentiation strategy aimed at increasing the value customers perceive in an organization's goods and services usually succeeds best in a flexible structure; flexibility facilitates a differentiation strategy because managers can develop new or innovative products quickly–an activity that requires extensive cooperation among functions or departments. In contrast, a low-cost strategy that is aimed at driving down costs in all functions usually fares best in a more formal structure, which gives managers greater control over the expenditures and actions of the organization's various departments.[9]

In addition, at the corporate level, when managers decide to expand the scope of organizational activities by vertical integration or diversification, for example, they need to design a flexible structure to provide sufficient coordination among the different business divisions.[10] As discussed in Chapter 8, many companies have been divesting businesses because managers have been unable to create a competitive advantage to keep them up to speed in fast-changing industries. By moving to a more flexible structure, such as a product division structure, divisional managers gain more control over their different businesses. Finally, expanding internationally and operating in many different countries challenges managers to create organizational structures that allow organizations to be flexible on a global level.[11] As we discuss later, managers can group their departments or functions and divisions in several ways to allow them to effectively pursue an international strategy.

Technology

Technology is the combination of skills, knowledge, tools, machines, computers, and equipment that are used in the design, production, and distribution of goods and services. As a rule, the more complicated the technology that an organization uses, the more difficult it is for managers and workers to impose strict control on technology or to regulate it efficiently. Thus, the more complicated the technology, the greater is the need for a flexible structure to enhance managers' ability to respond to unexpected situations and give them the freedom to work out new solutions to the problems they encounter. In contrast, the more routine the technology, the more appropriate is a formal structure, because tasks are simple and the steps needed to produce goods and services have been worked out in advance.

What makes a technology routine or complicated? One researcher who investigated this issue, Charles Perrow, argued that two factors determine how

complicated or nonroutine technology is: task variety and task analyzability.[12] *Task variety* is the number of new or unexpected problems or situations that a person or function encounters in performing tasks or jobs. *Task analyzability* is the degree to which programmed solutions are available to people or functions to solve the problems they encounter. Nonroutine or complicated technologies are characterized by high task variety and low task analyzability; this means that many varied problems occur and that solving these problems requires significant nonprogrammed decision making. In contrast, routine technologies are characterized by low task variety and high task analyzability; this means that the problems encountered do not vary much and are easily resolved through programmed decision making.

Examples of nonroutine technology are found in the work of scientists in a research and development laboratory who develop new products or discover new drugs, or in the planning exercises an organization's top-management team uses to chart the organization's future strategy. Examples of routine technology include typical mass-production or assembly operations, where workers perform the same task repeatedly and where managers have already identified the programmed solutions necessary to perform a task efficiently. Similarly, in service organizations such as fast-food restaurants, the tasks that crew members perform in making and serving fast food are very routine.

The extent to which the process of actually producing or creating goods and services depends on people or machines is another factor that determines how nonroutine a technology is. The more the technology used to produce goods and services is based on the skills, knowledge, and abilities of people working together on an ongoing basis and not on automated machines that can be programmed in advance, the more complex the technology is. Joan Woodward, a professor who investigated the relationship between technology and organizational structure, differentiated among three kinds of technology on the basis of the relative contribution made by people or machines.[13]

small-batch technology Technology that is used to produce small quantities of customized, one-of-a-kind products and is based on the skills of people who work together in small groups.

mass-production technology Technology that is based on the use of automated machines that are programmed to perform the same operations over and over.

continuous-process technology Technology that is almost totally mechanized and is based on the use of automated machines working in sequence and controlled through computers from a central monitoring station.

Small-batch technology is used to produce small quantities of customized, one-of-a-kind products and is based on the skills of people who work together in small groups. Examples of goods and services produced by small-batch technology include custom-built cars, such as Ferraris and Rolls-Royces, highly specialized metals and chemicals that are produced by the pound rather than by the ton, and the process of auditing in which a small team of auditors is sent to a company to evaluate and report on its accounts. Because small-batch goods or services are customized and unique, workers need to respond to each situation as required; thus, a structure that decentralizes authority to employees and allows them to respond flexibly is most appropriate with small-batch technology.

Woodward's second kind of technology, **mass-production technology,** is based primarily on the use of automated machines that are programmed to perform the same operations time and time again. Mass production works most efficiently when each person performs a repetitive task. There is less need for flexibility, and a formal organizational structure is the preferred choice because it gives managers the most control over the production process. Mass production results in an output of large quantities of standardized products such as tin cans, Ford Tauruses, washing machines, and light bulbs, or even services such as a car wash or dry cleaning.

The third kind of technology that Woodward identified, **continuous-process technology,** is almost totally mechanized. Products are produced by automated machines working in sequence and controlled through computers from a central monitoring station. Examples of continuous-process technology include

Small teams of highly skilled workers assemble Ferraris, which cost in excess of $250,000. The hand-built nature of exclusive motorcars is a part of their appeal to wealthy customers.

large steel mills, oil refineries, nuclear power stations, and large-scale brewing operations. The role of workers in continuous-process technology is to watch for problems that may occur unexpectedly and cause dangerous or even deadly situations. The possibility of a machinery or computer breakdown, for example, is a major source of uncertainty associated with this technology. If an unexpected situation does occur, employees must be able to respond quickly and appropriately to prevent a disaster from resulting (such as an explosion in a chemical complex), and the need for a flexible response makes a flexible organizational structure the preferred choice with this kind of technology.

INFORMATION TECHNOLOGY As we have seen in previous chapters, new information technologies are having profound effects on the way an organization operates. At the level of organizational structure, IT is changing methods of organizing. IT-enabled organizational structure allows for new kinds of tasks and job reporting relationships among electronically connected people that promotes superior communication and coordination. For example, one type of IT-enabled organizational relationship is **knowledge management,** the sharing and integrating of expertise within and between functions and divisions through real-time, interconnected IT.[14] Some benefits from these arrangements include the development of synergies that may result in competitive advantage in the form of product or service differentiation–something Lucent was seeking to achieve. Unlike more rigid bureaucratic organizing methods, new IT-enabled organizations can respond more quickly to changing environmental conditions such as increased global competition. In summary, the nature of an organization's technology is an important determinant of its structure. Today, many companies are trying to use IT in innovative ways to make their structures more flexible and to take advantage of the value-creating benefits of complex technology. Many of the ways in which IT can affect organizing are discussed in this and later chapters.

knowledge management The sharing and integrating of expertise within and between functions and divisions through real-time, interconnected IT.

Human Resources

A final important factor affecting an organization's choice of structure is the characteristics of the human resources it employs. In general, the more highly skilled an organization's workforce is and the more people are required to work together in groups or teams to perform their tasks, the more likely is an organization to use a flexible, decentralized structure. Highly skilled employees or employees who have internalized strong professional values and norms of behavior as part of their training usually desire freedom and autonomy and dislike close supervision. Accountants, for example, have learned the need to report company accounts honestly and impartially, and doctors and nurses have absorbed the obligation to give patients the best care possible.

Flexible structures, characterized by decentralized authority and empowered employees, are well suited to the needs of highly skilled people. Similarly, when people work in teams, they must be allowed to interact freely, which also is possible in a flexible organizational structure. Thus, when designing an organizational structure, managers must pay close attention to the workforce and to the work itself.

In summary, an organization's external environment, strategy, technology, and human resources are the factors to be considered by managers in seeking to design the best structure for an organization. The greater the level of uncertainty in the organization's environment, the more complex its strategy and technologies, and the more highly qualified and skilled its workforce, the more likely are managers to design a structure that is flexible and that can change quickly. The more stable the organization's environment, the less complex and more well understood its strategy or technology, and the less skilled its workforce, the more likely are managers to design an organizational structure that is formal and controlling.

How do managers design a structure to be either flexible or formal? The way an organization's structure works depends on the organizing choices managers make about four issues:

- How to group tasks into individual jobs
- How to group jobs into functions and divisions
- How to allocate authority in the organization among jobs, functions, and divisions
- How to coordinate or integrate among jobs, functions, and divisions

Grouping Tasks into Jobs: Job Design

The first step in organizational design is **job design**, the process by which managers decide how to divide into specific jobs the tasks that have to be performed to provide customers with goods and services. Managers at McDonald's, for example, have decided how best to divide the tasks required to provide customers with fast, cheap food in each McDonald's restaurant. After experimenting with different job arrangements, McDonald's managers decided on a basic division of labor among chefs and food servers. Managers allocated all the tasks involved in actually cooking the food (putting oil in the fat fryers, opening packages of frozen french fries, putting beef patties on the grill, making salads, and so on) to the job

job design The process by which managers decide how to divide tasks into specific jobs.

Workers at a Subway sandwich shop follow the carefully designed work procedures that allow the company to provide a large variety of sandwiches to customers quickly at peak times.

of chef. They allocated all the tasks involved in giving the food to customers (such as greeting customers, taking orders, putting fries and burgers into bags, adding salt, pepper, and napkins, and taking money) to food servers. In addition, they created other jobs–the job of dealing with drive-in customers, the job of keeping the restaurant clean, and the job of shift manager responsible for overseeing employees and responding to unexpected events. The result of the job design process is a *division of labor* among employees, one that McDonald's managers have discovered through experience is most efficient.

Establishing an appropriate division of labor among employees is a critical part of the organizing process, one that is vital to increasing efficiency and effectiveness. At McDonald's, the tasks associated with chef and food server were split into different jobs because managers found that, for the kind of food McDonald's serves, this approach was most efficient. It is efficient because when each employee is given fewer tasks to perform (so that each job becomes more specialized), employees become more productive at performing the tasks that constitute each job.

At Subway sandwich shops, however, managers chose a different kind of job design. At Subway, there is no division of labor among the people who make the sandwiches, wrap the sandwiches, give them to customers, and take the money. The role of chef and food server is combined into one. This different division of tasks and jobs is efficient for Subway and not for McDonald's because Subway serves a limited menu of mostly submarine-style sandwiches that are prepared to order. Subway's production system is far simpler than McDonald's, because McDonald's menu is much more varied and its chefs must cook many different kinds of foods.

job simplification The process of reducing the number of tasks that each worker performs.

Managers of every organization must analyze the range of tasks to be performed and then create jobs that best allow the organization to give customers the goods and services they want. In deciding how to assign tasks to individual jobs, however, managers must be careful not to take **job simplification,** the process of reducing the number of tasks that each worker performs, too far.[15]

Too much job simplification may reduce efficiency rather than increase it if workers find their simplified jobs boring and monotonous, become demotivated and unhappy, and as a result perform at a low level.

Job Enlargement and Job Enrichment

In an attempt to create a division of labor and design individual jobs to encourage workers to perform at a higher level and be more satisfied with their work, several researchers have proposed ways other than job simplification to group tasks into jobs: job enlargement and job enrichment.

job enlargement Increasing the number of different tasks in a given job by changing the division of labor.

job enrichment Increasing the degree of responsibility a worker has over his or her job.

Job enlargement is increasing the number of different tasks in a given job by changing the division of labor.[16] For example, because Subway food servers make the food as well as serve it, their jobs are "larger" than the jobs of McDonald's food servers. The idea behind job enlargement is that increasing the range of tasks performed by a worker will reduce boredom and fatigue and may increase motivation to perform at a high level–increasing both the quantity and quality of goods and services provided.

Job enrichment is increasing the degree of responsibility a worker has over a job by, for example, (1) empowering workers to experiment to find new or better ways of doing the job, (2) encouraging workers to develop new skills, (3) allowing workers to decide how to do the work and giving them the responsibility for deciding how to respond to unexpected situations, and (4) allowing workers to monitor and measure their own performance.[17] The idea behind job enrichment is that increasing workers' responsibility increases their involvement in their jobs and thus increases their interest in the quality of the goods they make or the services they provide.

In general, managers who make design choices that increase the job enrichment and job involvement are likely to increase the degree to which people behave flexibly rather than rigidly or mechanically. Narrow, specialized jobs are likely to lead people to behave in predictable ways; workers who perform a variety of tasks and who are allowed and encouraged to discover new and better ways to perform their jobs are likely to act flexibly and creatively. Thus, managers who enlarge and enrich jobs create a flexible organizational structure, and those who simplify jobs create a more formal structure. If workers are also grouped into self-managed work teams, the organization is likely to be flexible because team members provide support for each other and can learn from one another.

The Job Characteristics Model

J. R. Hackman and G. R. Oldham's job characteristics model is an influential model of job design that explains in detail how managers can make jobs more interesting and motivating.[18] Hackman and Oldham's model (see Figure 9.2) also describes the likely personal and organizational outcomes that will result from enriched and enlarged jobs.

According to Hackman and Oldham, every job has five characteristics that determine how motivating the job is. These characteristics determine how employees react to their work and lead to outcomes such as high performance and satisfaction and low absenteeism and turnover:

- *Skill variety:* The extent to which a job requires an employee to use a wide range of different skills, abilities, or knowledge. Example: The skill variety required by the job of a research scientist is higher than that called for by the job of a McDonald's food server.

- *Task identity:* The extent to which a job requires a worker to perform all the tasks required to complete the job from the beginning to the end of the production process. Example: A craftsworker who takes a piece of wood and transforms it into a custom-made piece of furniture such as a desk has higher task identity than does a worker who performs only one of the numerous operations required to assemble a television.
- *Task significance:* The degree to which a worker feels his or her job is meaningful because of its affect on people inside the organization such as coworkers or to people outside the organization such as customers. Example: A teacher who sees the effect of his or her efforts in a well-educated and well-adjusted student enjoys high task significance compared to a dishwasher who monotonously washes dishes as they come to the kitchen.
- *Autonomy:* The degree to which a job gives an employee the freedom and discretion needed to schedule different tasks and decide how to carry them out. Example: Salespeople who have to plan their schedules and decide how to allocate their time among different customers have relatively high autonomy compared to assembly-line workers whose actions are determined by the speed of the production line.
- *Feedback:* The extent to which actually doing a job provides a worker with clear and direct information about how well he or she has performed the job. Example: An air traffic controller whose mistakes may result in a midair collision receives immediate feedback on job performance; a person who compiles statistics for a business magazine often has little idea of when he or she makes a mistake or does a particularly good job.

Hackman and Oldham argue that those five job characteristics affect an employee's motivation because they affect three critical psychological states (see Figure 9.2). The more employees feel that their work is *meaningful* and that they are *responsible for work outcomes* and *responsible for knowing how those outcomes affect others,* the more motivating work becomes and the more likely employees are to be satisfied and to perform at a high level. Moreover, employees who have jobs that are highly motivating are called on to use their skills more and to perform more tasks, and they are given more responsibility for doing the job. All of the foregoing are characteristic of jobs and employees in flexible structures where

Figure 9.2
The Job Characteristics Model

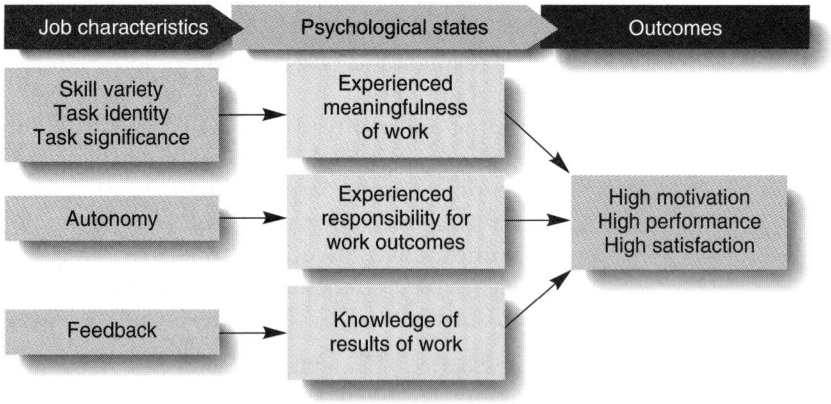

Source: Adapted from J. R. Hackman and G. R. Oldham, *Work Redesign* (Reading, MA: Addison-Wesley, 1980).

authority is decentralized and where employees commonly work with others and must learn new skills to complete the range of tasks for which their group is responsible.

Tips for New Managers

Designing Structure and Jobs

1. Carefully analyze an organization's environment, strategy, technology, and human resources to decide which type of organizational structure to use.
2. To create a more formal structure, carefully define the limits of each employee's job, create clear job descriptions, and evaluate each worker on his or her job performance.
3. To create a more flexible structure, enlarge and enrich jobs and allow workers to expand their jobs over time. Also, encourage workers to work together and evaluate both individual and group performance.
4. Use the job characteristics model to guide job design and recognize that most jobs can be enriched to make them more motivating and satisfying

Grouping Jobs into Functions and Divisions

Once managers have decided which tasks to allocate to which jobs, they face the next organizing decision: how to group jobs together to best match the needs of the organization's environment, strategy, technology, and human resources. Most top-management teams decide to group jobs into departments and develop a functional structure to use organizational resources. As the organization grows, managers design a divisional structure or a more complex matrix or product team structure.

Choosing a structure and then designing it so that it works as intended is a significant challenge. As noted in Chapter 7, managers reap the rewards of a well-thought-out strategy only if they choose the right type of structure to implement and execute the strategy. The ability to make the right kinds of organizing choices is often what differentiates effective from ineffective managers.

Functional Structure

A *function* is a group of people, working together, who possess similar skills or use the same kind of knowledge, tools, or techniques to perform their jobs. Manufacturing, sales, and research and development are often organized into functional departments. A **functional structure** is an organizational structure composed of all the departments that an organization requires to produce its goods or services. Figure 9.3 shows the functional structure that Pier 1 Imports, the home furnishings company, uses to supply its customers with a range of goods from around the world to satisfy their desires for new and innovative products.

functional structure An organizational structure composed of all the departments that an organization requires to produce its goods or services.

Pier 1's main functions are finance and administration, merchandising (purchasing the goods), stores (managing the retail outlets), logistics (managing

Figure 9.3
The Functional Structure of Pier 1 Imports

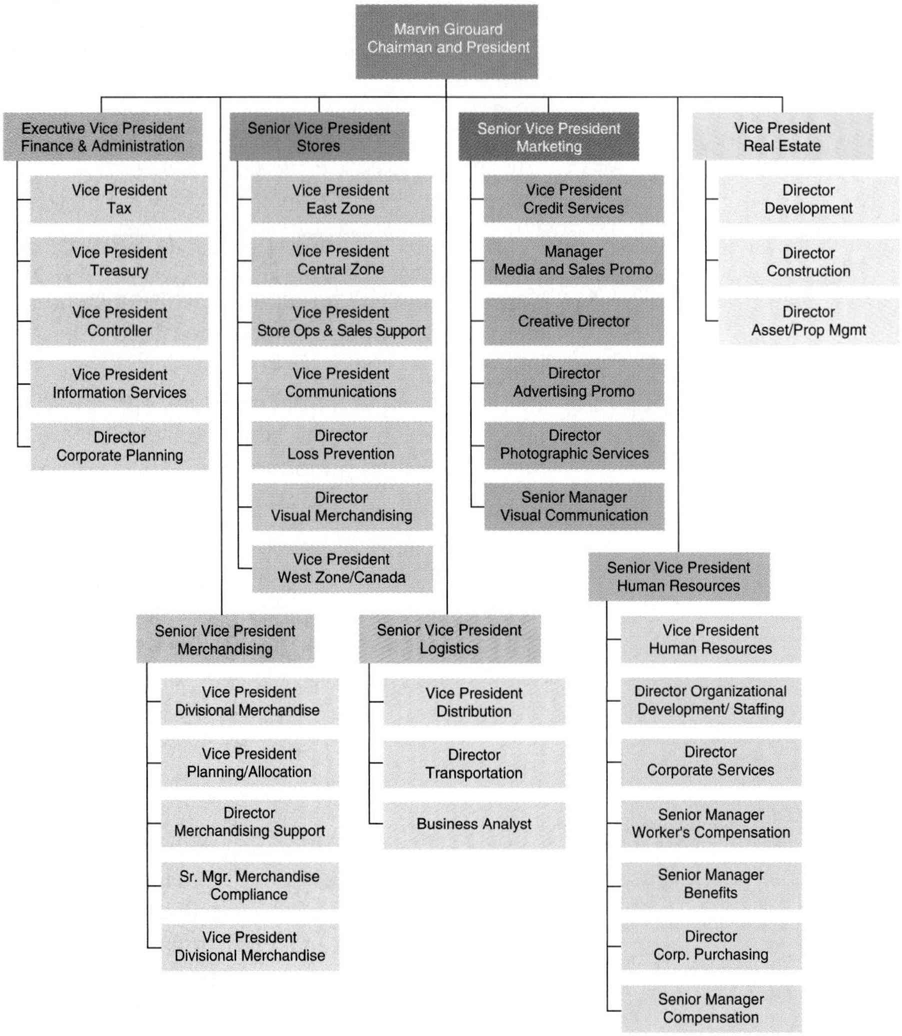

product distribution), marketing, human resources, and real estate. Each job inside a function exists because it helps the function perform the activities necessary for high organizational performance. Thus, within the logistics department are all the jobs necessary to efficiently distribute and transport products to stores, and inside the marketing department are all the jobs (such as promotion, photography, and visual communication) that are necessary to increase the appeal of Pier 1's products to customers.

There are several advantages to grouping jobs according to function. First, when people who perform similar jobs are grouped together, they can learn from observing one another and thus become more specialized and can perform at a higher level. The tasks associated with one job often are related to the tasks associated to another job, which encourages cooperation within a function. In Pier 1's marketing department, for example, the person designing the photography program for an ad campaign works closely with the person responsible for designing store layouts and with visual communication experts. As a result, Pier 1 is able to develop a strong, focused marketing campaign to differentiate its products.

Second, when people who perform similar jobs are grouped together, it is easier for managers to monitor and evaluate their performance.[19] Imagine if marketing experts, logistics experts, and real-estate experts were grouped together in one function and supervised by a manager from merchandising. Obviously, the merchandising manager would not have the expertise to evaluate all these different people appropriately. However a functional structure allows coworkers to evaluate how well other coworkers are performing their jobs, and if some coworkers are performing poorly, more experienced coworkers can help them develop new skills.

Finally, as we saw in Chapter 3, managers appreciate functional structure because it allows them to create the set of functions they need in order to scan and monitor the task and general environments.[20] With the right set of functions in place, managers are in a good position to develop a strategy that allows the organization to respond to its particular situation. Employees in marketing can specialize in monitoring new marketing developments that will allow Pier 1 to better target its customers. For example, in 2001, Pier 1 installed new call center information technology that allows it to personalize its relationship with its customers.[21] Employees in merchandising can monitor all potential suppliers of home furnishings both at home and abroad to find the goods most likely to appeal to Pier 1's customers and manage Pier 1's global supply chain.

As an organization grows, and particularly as its task environment and strategy change because it is beginning to produce a wider range of goods and services for different kinds of customers, several problems can make a functional structure less efficient and effective.[22] First, managers in different functions may find it more difficult to communicate and coordinate with one another when they are responsible for several different kinds of products, especially as the organization grows both domestically and internationally. Second, functional managers may become so preoccupied with supervising their own specific departments and achieving their departmental goals that they lose sight of organizational goals. If that happens, organizational effectiveness will suffer because managers will be viewing issues and problems facing the organization only from their own, relatively narrow, departmental perspectives.[23] Both of these problems can reduce efficiency and effectiveness.

Divisional Structures: Product, Market, and Geographic

As the problems associated with growth and diversification increase over time, managers must search for new ways to organize their activities to overcome the problems associated with a functional structure. Most managers of large organizations choose a **divisional structure** and create a series of business units to produce a specific kind of product for a specific kind of customer. Each *division* is a collection of functions or departments that work together to produce the product. The goal behind the change to a divisional structure is to create smaller, more manageable units within the organization. There are three forms of divisional structure (see Figure 9.4).[24] When managers organize divisions according to the *type of good or service* they provide, they adopt a product structure. When managers organize divisions according to the *area of the country or world* they operate in, they adopt a geographic structure. When managers organize divisions according to the *types of customer* they focus on, they adopt a market structure.

divisional structure
An organizational structure composed of separate business units within which are the functions that work together to produce a specific product for a specific customer.

Figure 9.4
Product, Market, and Geographic Structures

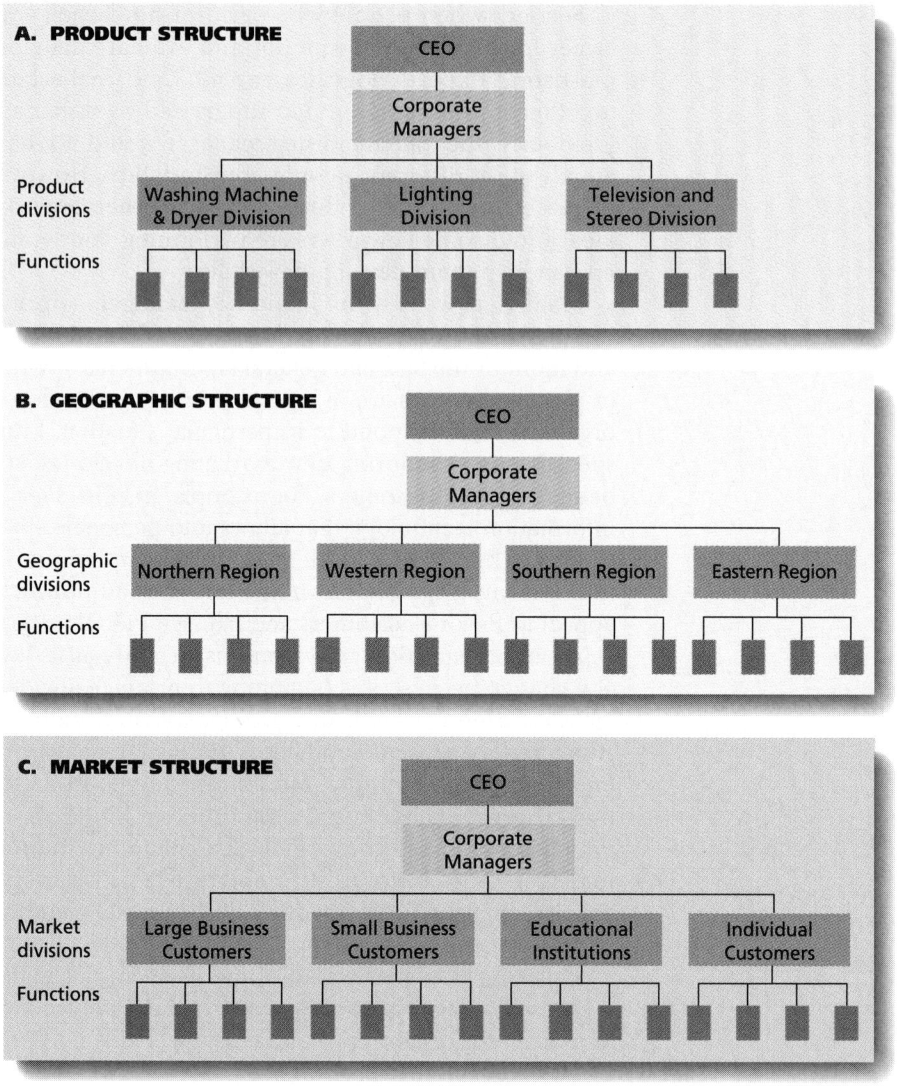

PRODUCT STRUCTURE Imagine the problems that managers at Pier 1 would encounter if they decided to diversify into producing and selling cars, fast food, and health insurance–in addition to home furnishings–and tried to use their existing set of functional managers to oversee the production of all four kinds of product. No manager would have the necessary skills or abilities to oversee those four products. No individual marketing manager, for example, could effectively market cars, fast food, health insurance, and home furnishings at the same time. To perform a functional activity successfully, managers must have experience in specific markets or industries. Consequently, if managers decide to diversify into new industries or to expand their range of products, they commonly design a product structure to organize their operations (see Figure 9.4A).

product structure An organizational structure in which each product line or business is handled by a self-contained division.

Using a **product structure,** managers place each distinct product line or business in its own self-contained division and give divisional managers the responsibility for devising an appropriate business-level strategy to allow the division to compete effectively in its industry or market.[25] Each division is self-contained because it has a complete set of all the functions–marketing, R&D,

finance, and so on–that it needs to produce or provide goods or services efficiently and effectively. Functional managers report to divisional managers, and divisional managers report to top or corporate managers.

Grouping functions into divisions focused on particular products has several advantages for managers at all levels in the organization. First, a product structure allows functional managers to specialize in only one product area, so they are able to build expertise and fine-tune their skills in this particular area. Second, each division's managers can become experts in their industry; this expertise helps them choose and develop a business-level strategy to differentiate their products or lower their costs while meeting the needs of customers. Third, a product structure frees corporate managers from the need to supervise directly each division's day-to-day operations; this latitude allows corporate managers to create the best corporate-level strategy to maximize the organization's future growth and ability to create value. Corporate managers are likely to make fewer mistakes about which businesses to diversify into or how to best expand internationally, for example, because they are able to take an organizationwide view.[26] Corporate managers also are likely to evaluate better how well divisional managers are doing, and they can intervene and take corrective action as needed.

The extra layer of management, the divisional management layer, can improve the use of organizational resources. Moreover, a product structure puts divisional managers close to their customers and lets them respond quickly and appropriately to the changing task environment. The way in which Viacom's managers created a product structure is profiled in the following "Management Insight."

Management Insight

Viacom's 2001 Product Structure

Sumner Redstone, the billionaire chairman of Viacom, is continually making acquisitions that add to the range of products the huge media entertainment company provides to its customers. Under Redstone, Viacom started in the cable and television business and expanded into several fields: entertainment, networks and broadcasting, video, music, and theme parks, publishing, and television. In 2000, for example, Viacom acquired CBS television and BET.[27]

To manage Viacom's many different businesses effectively, Redstone decided to design a product structure (see Figure 9.5). He put each business in a separate division and gave managers in each division responsibility for making their business the number-one performer in its industry. Redstone recognized, however, that the different divisions could help each other and create synergies for Viacom by sharing their skills and resources. Blockbuster, for example, could launch a major advertising campaign to publicize the movies that Paramount makes and thus boost the visibility of both divisions' products, and Simon & Schuster could produce and publish specific books to tie in with the opening of a movie and thus boost ticket and book sales. To achieve these synergies, Redstone created a team of corporate managers who are responsible for working with the different divisional managers to identify new opportunities to create value. So far, this method of organizing has served Viacom well, and it has become one of the top four media and entertainment companies.[28]

GEOGRAPHIC STRUCTURE When organizations expand rapidly both at home and abroad, functional structures can create special problems, because managers in one central location may find it increasingly difficult to deal with

Figure 9.5
Viacom's 2001 Product Structure

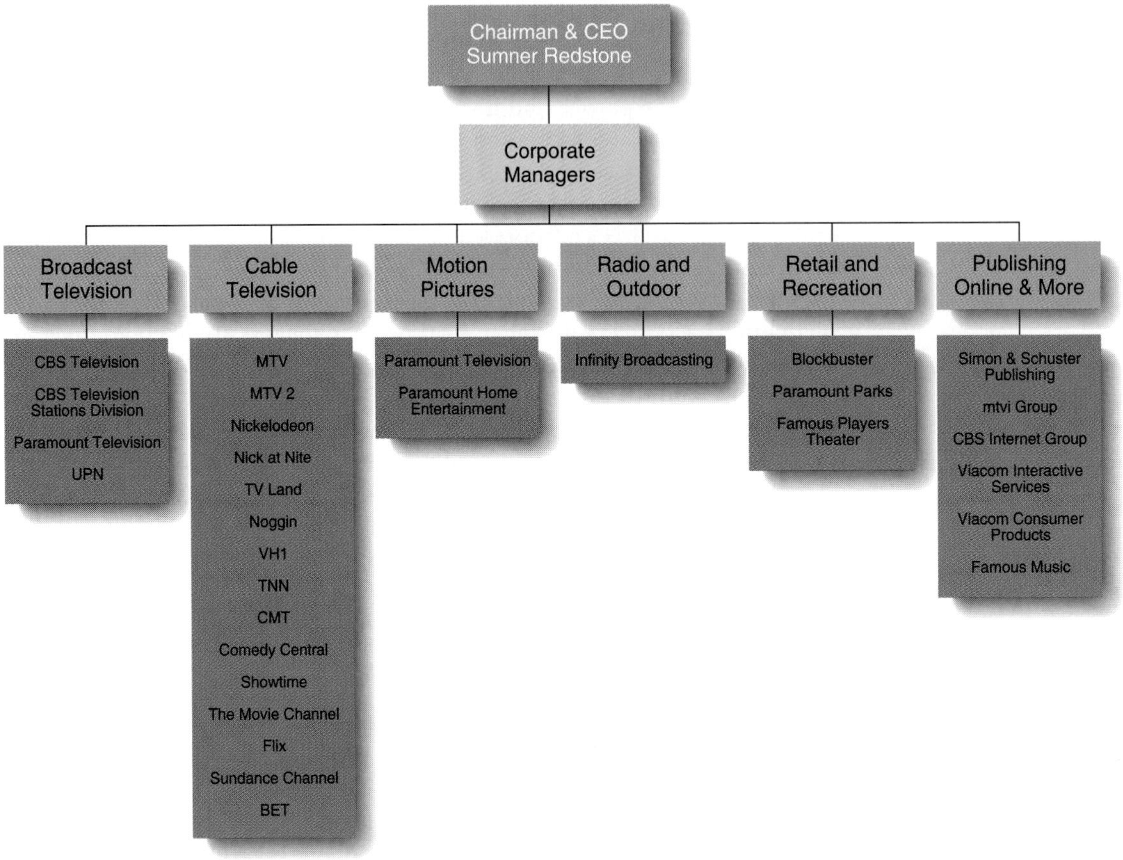

geographic structure An organizational structure in which each region of a country or area of the world is served by a self-contained division.

the different problems and issues that may arise in each region of a country or area of the world. In these cases, a **geographic structure,** in which divisions are broken down by geographical location, is often chosen (see Figure 9.4B). To achieve the corporate mission of providing next-day mail service, Fred Smith, CEO of Federal Express, chose a geographic structure and divided up operations by creating a division in each region. Large retailers like Macy's, Neiman Marcus, and Brooks Brothers also use a geographic structure. Since the needs of retail customers differ by region–for example, surfboards in California and down parkas in the Midwest–a geographic structure gives retail regional managers the flexibility they need to choose the range of products that best meets the needs of regional customers.

In adopting a *global geographic structure,* such as shown in Figure 9.6A, managers locate different divisions in each of the world regions where the organization operates. Managers are most likely to do this when they pursue a multidomestic strategy because customer needs vary widely by country or world region. For example, if products that appeal to U.S. customers do not sell in Europe, the Pacific Rim, or South America, then managers must customize the products to meet the needs of customers in those different world regions; a global geographic structure with global divisions will allow them to do this.

Figure 9.6
Global Geographic and Global Product Structures

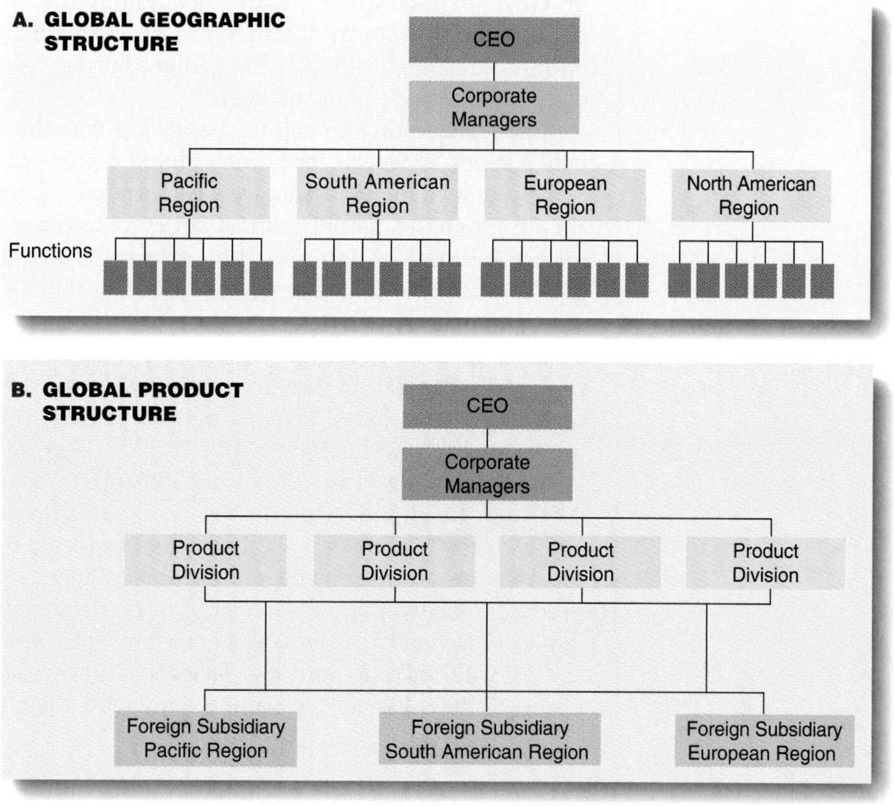

In contrast, to the degree that customers abroad are willing to buy the same kind of product, or slight variations thereof, managers are more likely to pursue a global strategy. In this case they are more likely to use a *global product structure.* In a global product structure, the product divisions, not the country and regional managers take responsibility for deciding where to manufacture its products and how to market its products in foreign countries worldwide (see Figure 9.6B). Product division managers manage their own global value chains and decide where to establish foreign subsidiaries to distribute and sell their products to customers in these foreign countries. As we noted at the beginning of this chapter, an organization's strategy is a major determinant of its structure both at home and abroad, and the way in which Exide, the battery manufacturer, moved from a global geographic to a global product structure is instructive as discussed next.

Managing Globally

Exide's New Global Structure

Exide is the world's biggest producer of automotive and industrial batteries but it continued to lose money through the 1990s. Former Chrysler COO, Robert A. Lutz, was hired to turn around Exide's performance and in 2000 he decided that the source of the problem lay in the way Exide organized its global activities. Exide was organized by geographical areas, 10 regional or country organizations managed the production and sale of all Exide's batteries within their geographical area. These 10 organizations operated separately and often competed for the same customers. Many of Exide's customers–Ford or GM, for example–operate throughout the world. Several of Exide's regional organizations competed to be Ford's major global supplier, often undercutting each other's prices to get Ford's business and maximize their own organization's performance!

Lutz realized that he had to change the way these managers operated. He held a series of retreats for Exide's global senior managers and he got them to agree that a change in structure was necessary. Lutz's answer was that Exide should move to a global product structure and organize its activities according to the kind of batteries the company made and sold worldwide. Six global product divisions were formed around the major product lines such as automotive, network-power, industrial, and motive power batteries. Thousands of Exide managers who had previously worked for a country or regional organization now found themselves working for a global product unit, their focus shifted from manufacturing and selling in their local market to serving the world market.

By 2001, Exide's losses had vanished and it was once again making a modest profit. Its global structure was working more efficiently and effectively although many problems such as where to locate research and development activities, and how to manage the global value chain across product divisions still had to be worked out. In fact, Exide's managers realized after the change that the process of organizing never ends. "Come back in a year from now and we will look different" was Exide's managers new understanding of organizing, as they–like all companies–cope with today's complex global world.[29]

MARKET STRUCTURE Sometimes the pressing issue facing managers is how to group functions according to the type of customer buying the product, in order to tailor the products the organization offers to each customer's unique demands. A computer company like Dell, for example, has several kinds of customers, including large businesses (which might demand networks of computers linked to a mainframe computer), small companies (which may need just a few

The way in which Gerber adapted its baby foods to the Japanese market is an example of a global product structure. Here, Salesclerk Miki Yoshida of the Meidi-Ya Co. displays a package of flounder and spinach stew, left, and jars of whitebait porridge, center, and wild duck cream stew, produced by Gerber, at her Tokyo store. Such dishes may not appeal to many American toddlers, but dishes like these are big business in Japan.

PCs linked together), educational users in schools and universities (which might want thousands of independent PCs for their students); and individual users (who may want a high-quality multimedia PC so that they can play the latest video games).

market structure
An organizational structure in which each kind of customer is served by a self-contained division; also called customer structure.

To satisfy the needs of diverse customers, a company might adopt a market structure (also called a *customer structure*), which groups divisions according to the particular kinds of customers they serve (see Figure 9.4C). A market structure allows managers to be responsive to the needs of their customers and allows them to act flexibly to make decisions in response to customers' changing needs.

Matrix and Product Team Designs

Moving to a product, market, or geographic divisional structure allows managers to respond more quickly and flexibly to the particular set of circumstances they confront. However, when the environment is dynamic and is changing rapidly, and uncertainty is high, even a divisional structure may not provide managers with enough flexibility to respond to the environment quickly. When customer needs or information technology are changing rapidly and the environment is very uncertain, managers must design the most flexible kind of organizational structure available: a matrix structure or a product team structure (see Figure 9.7).

matrix structure An organizational structure that simultaneously groups people and resources by function and by product.

MATRIX STRUCTURE In a matrix structure, managers group people and resources in two ways simultaneously: by function and by product.[30] Employees are grouped by functions to allow them to learn from one another and become more skilled and productive. In addition, employees are grouped into *product teams* in which members of different functions work together to develop a specific product. The result is a complex network of reporting relationships among product teams and functions that makes the matrix structure very flexible (see Figure 9.7A). Each person in a product team reports to two bosses: (1) a functional boss, who assigns individuals to a team and evaluates their performance from a functional perspective, and (2) the boss of the product team, who evaluates their performance on the team. Thus, team members are known as *two-boss employees* because they report to two managers. The functional employees assigned to product teams change over time as the specific skills that the team needs change. At the beginning of the product development process, for example, engineers and R&D specialists are assigned to a product team because their skills are needed to develop new products. When a provisional design has been established, marketing experts are assigned to the team to gauge how customers will respond to the new product. Manufacturing personnel join when it is time to find the most efficient way to produce the product. As their specific jobs are completed, team members leave and are reassigned to new teams. In this way the matrix structure makes the most use of human resources.

To keep the matrix structure flexible, product teams are empowered and team members are responsible for making most of the important decisions involved in product development.[31] The product team manager acts as a facilitator, controlling the financial resources and trying to keep the project on time and within budget. The functional managers try to ensure that the product is the best that it can be in order to maximize its differentiated appeal.

Matrix structures have been used successfully for many years by high-tech companies that operate in environments where new product development takes

Figure 9.7
Matrix and Product Team Structures

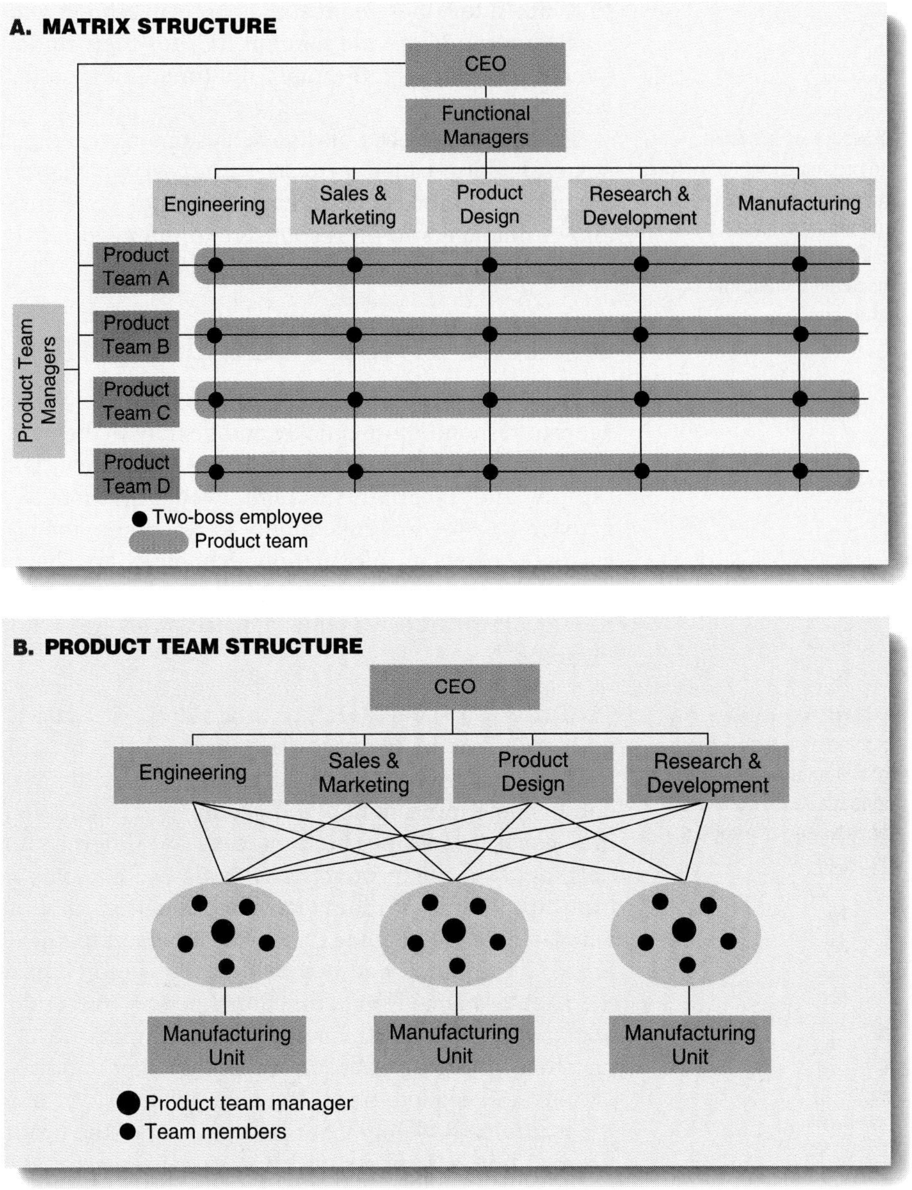

place monthly or yearly, and the need to innovate quickly is vital to the organization's survival. The flexibility afforded by a matrix structure allows managers to keep pace with a changing and increasingly complex environment.[32]

PRODUCT TEAM STRUCTURE The dual reporting relationships that are at the heart of a matrix structure have always been difficult for managers and employees to deal with. Often, the functional boss and the product boss make conflicting demands on team members, who do not know which boss to satisfy first. Also, functional and product team bosses may come into conflict over precisely who is in charge of which team members and for how long. To avoid these problems, managers have devised a way of organizing people and resources that still allows an organization to be flexible but makes its structure easier to operate: a product team structure.

Hallmark uses product teams that work intensively together to develop new kinds of greeting cards. The use of these teams also speed up the development of its cards so that it can react to changes in customers tastes and preferences.

The **product team structure** differs from a matrix structure in two ways: (1) It does away with dual reporting relationships and two-boss managers, and (2) functional employees are permanently assigned to a cross-functional team that is empowered to bring a new or redesigned product to market. A **cross-functional team** is a group of managers brought together from different departments to perform organizational tasks. When managers are grouped into cross-departmental teams, the artificial boundaries between departments disappear, and a narrow focus on departmental goals is replaced with a general interest in working together to achieve organizational goals. The results of such changes have been dramatic: DaimlerChrysler can introduce a new model of car in two years, down from five; Black & Decker can innovate new products in months, not years; and Hallmark Cards can respond to changing customer demands for types of cards in weeks, not months.

product team structure An organizational structure in which employees are permanently assigned to a cross-functional team and report only to the product team manager or to one of his or her direct subordinates.

cross-functional team A group of managers from different departments brought together to perform organizational tasks.

Members of a cross-functional team report only to the product team manager or to one of his or her direct subordinates. The heads of the functions have only an informal, advisory relationship with members of the product teams–the role of functional managers is only to counsel and help team members, share knowledge among teams, and provide new technological developments that can help improve each team's performance (see Figure 9.7B).[33]

Increasingly, organizations are making empowered cross-functional teams an essential part of their organizational architecture to help them gain a competitive advantage in fast-changing organizational environments. For example, Newell Rubbermaid the well-known maker of more than 5,000 household products moved to a product team structure because its managers wanted to speed up the rate of product innovation. Managers created 20 cross-functional teams composed of five to seven people from marketing, manufacturing, R&D, finance, and other functions.[34] Each team focuses its energies on a particular product line such as garden products, bathroom products, or kitchen products. These teams developed more than 365 new products a year. Owens-Corning, the insulation maker, offers an extreme example of how to use teams in a factory setting. One hundred employees work in its Tennessee plant, and all of them report directly to the plant manager![35] Owens-Corning has eliminated every level in the hierarchy between the plant manager and employees by putting all its employees in teams and making them jointly responsible for all operational decision making. The plant manager intervenes only when requested to do so by a team member, and even then only to act as a facilitator to help the empowered work teams solve their problems.

hybrid structure The structure of a large organization that has many divisions and simultaneously uses many different organizational structures.

Hybrid Structure

A large organization that has many divisions and simultaneously uses many different structures has a **hybrid structure.** Most large organizations use product division structures and create self-contained divisions; then each division's managers select the structure that best meets the needs of the particular environment, strategy, and so on. Thus, one product division may choose to operate with a functional structure, a second may choose a geographic structure, and a third may choose a product team structure because of the nature of the division's products or the desire to be more responsive to customers' needs. Target offers an example of one kind of hybrid structure based on grouping by customer and by geography as shown in the "Management Insight."

Management Insight

Target's Hybrid Structure

Target Stores used to be a division of the Dayton Hudson Company, the famous retailer and owner of the Marshall Field's store chain. In 2000, however, in recognition of the fact that Target Stores was contributing most of its profits, Dayton Hudson changed its name to the Target Corporation.[36] Dayton Hudson acquired Target in 1962 in order to enter the discount merchandising, low-price segment of the retail market. Before, its Marshall Field's and Mervyns stores had catered to the needs of affluent customers; now it wanted to compete for customers who had modest incomes. Target's managers focused on providing shoppers with a pleasant shopping experience, brightly lit stores with wide aisles, and attractive chic merchandise. They found the right formula; today Target has more than 1,000 stores and is extremely profitable.

Dayton Hudson had always operated its different store chains as independent divisions in a market division structure, as shown in Figure 9.8. Its top managers recognized that each store chain needed to be given a free hand to develop the strategy that best suited its market and its customers' needs. This method of organizing had paid off, Target Stores was the success story. However, Marshall Field's had not fared so well in its struggle at the top end of the market against Neiman Marcus, Nordstrom, and Saks Fifth Avenue.

Beneath this market structure, which in 2001 had four parts, Target, Mervyns, Marshall Field's, and target.direct, Target's Internet division, was another layer of organization. Both Target Stores and Marshall Field's operate with a geographic structure that groups stores by region. Individual stores

Figure 9.8
Target's Hybrid Structure

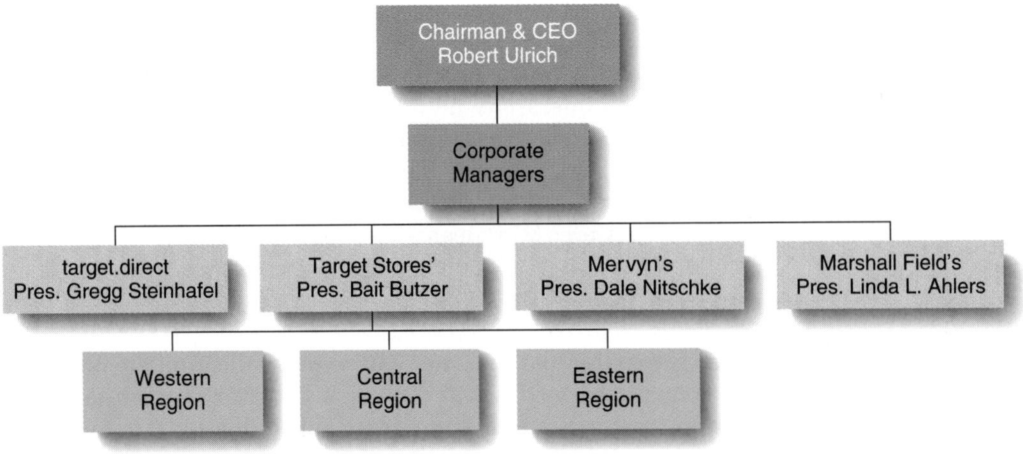

are under the direction of a regional office, which is responsible for coordinating the market needs of the stores in its region and for responding to regional customer needs. The regional office feeds information back to divisional headquarters where centralized merchandising functions make decisions for all Target or Marshall Field's stores.

Organizational structure may thus be likened to the layers of an onion. The outer layer provides the overarching organizational framework–most commonly a product or market division structure–and each inner layer is the structure that each division selects for itself in response to the contingencies it faces–such as a geographic or product team structure. The ability to break a large organization into smaller units or divisions makes it much easier for managers to change structure when the need arises–for example, when a change in technology or an increase in competition in the environment necessitates a change from a functional to a product team structure. For example, Lucent shed several layers of structure and moved from a complex 11 product-team hybrid structure to a far more simple two-division product structure when its performance declined.

Coordinating Functions and Divisions

In organizing, managers have several tasks; to group functions and divisions and create the organizational structures best suited to the contingencies they face. Their next task is to ensure that there is sufficient coordination or integration among functions and divisions so that organizational resources are used efficiently and effectively. Having discussed how managers divide organizational activities into jobs, functions, and divisions to increase efficiency and effectiveness, we now look at how they put the parts back together.

We look first at the way in which managers design the hierarchy of authority to coordinate functions and divisions so that they work together effectively. Then we focus on integration and examine the many different integrating mechanisms that managers can use to coordinate functions and divisions.

Allocating Authority

authority The power to hold people accountable for their actions and to make decisions concerning the use of organizational resources.

hierarchy of authority An organization's chain of command, specifying the relative authority of each manager.

span of control The number of subordinates who report directly to a manager.

As organizations grow and produce a wider range of goods and services, the size and number of their functions and divisions increase. To coordinate the activities of people, functions, and divisions and to allow them to work together effectively, managers must develop a clear hierarchy of authority.[37] **Authority** is the power vested in a manager to make decisions and use resources to achieve organizational goals by virtue of his or her position in an organization. The **hierarchy of authority** is an organization's chain of command–the relative authority that each manager has–extending from the CEO at the top down through the middle managers and first-line managers, to the nonmanagerial employees who actually make goods or provide services. Every manager, at every level of the hierarchy, supervises one or more subordinates. The term **span of control** refers to the number of subordinates who report directly to a manager.

Figure 9.9 shows a simplified picture of the hierarchy of authority and the span of control of managers at McDonald's in 2001. At the top of the hierarchy is Jack Greenberg, CEO and chairman of McDonald's board of directors. Greenberg is the manager who has ultimate responsibility for McDonald's performance, and he

Figure 9.9
The Hierarchy of Authority and Span of Control at McDonald's Corporation

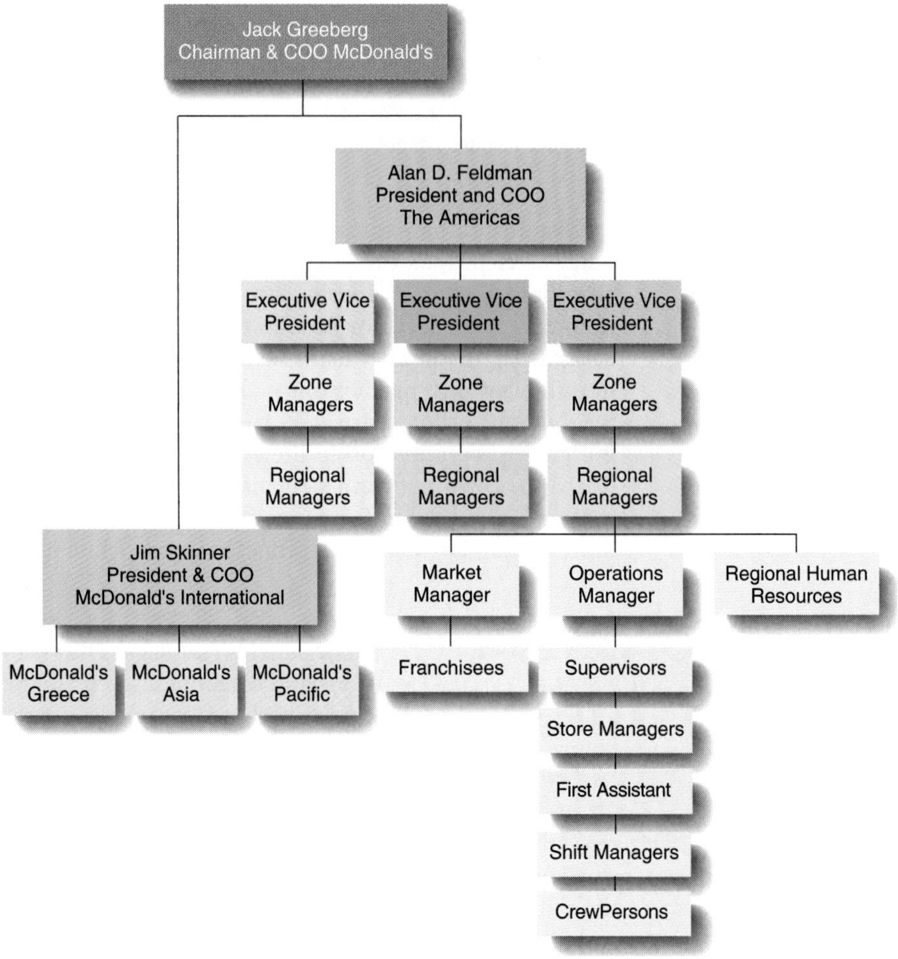

has the authority to decide how to use organizational resources to benefit McDonald's stakeholders.[38] Both Alan Feldman and Jim Skinner report directly to Greenberg. Feldman is the president and COO of McDonald's The Americas and Skinner is the head of McDonald's International, all of its global operations: they are next in the chain of command under Greenberg. Of special mention here is Mats Lederhausen who in July 2001 was appointed executive vice president for strategy and business development. He also reports to Greenberg, but unlike Greenberg, Feldman, and Skinner, he is not a **line manager,** someone in the direct line or chain of command who has formal authority over people and resources. Rather, Lederhausen is the **staff manager** responsible for one of McDonald's specialist functions, planning. He is responsible for "growing our existing businesses and identifying new opportunities" at the corporate level.[39]

line manager Someone in the direct line or chain of command who has formal authority over people and resources lower down.

staff manager A manager responsible for managing one of McDonald's specialist functions, like finance or marketing.

Managers at each level of the hierarchy confer on managers at the next level down the authority to make decisions about how to use organizational resources. Accepting this authority, those lower-level managers then become responsible for their decisions and are accountable for how well they make those decisions. Managers who make the right decisions are typically promoted, and organizations motivate managers with the prospects of promotion and increased responsibility within the chain of command.

Below Feldman are the other main levels or layers in the McDonald's USA chain of command- executive vice president, zone managers, regional managers, and supervisors. A hierarchy is also evident in each company-owned McDonald's restaurant. At the top is the store manager; at lower levels are the first assistant, shift managers, and crew personnel. McDonald's managers have decided that this hierarchy of authority best allows the company to pursue its business-level strategy of providing fast food at reasonable prices.

TALL AND FLAT ORGANIZATIONS As an organization grows in size (normally measured by the number of its managers and employees), its hierarchy of authority normally lengthens, making the organizational structure taller. A tall organization has many levels of authority relative to company size; a flat organization has fewer levels relative to company size (see Figure 9.10).[40] As a hierarchy becomes taller, problems that make the organization's structure less flexible and slow managers' response to changes in the organizational environment may result.

Figure 9.10
Tall and Flat Organizations

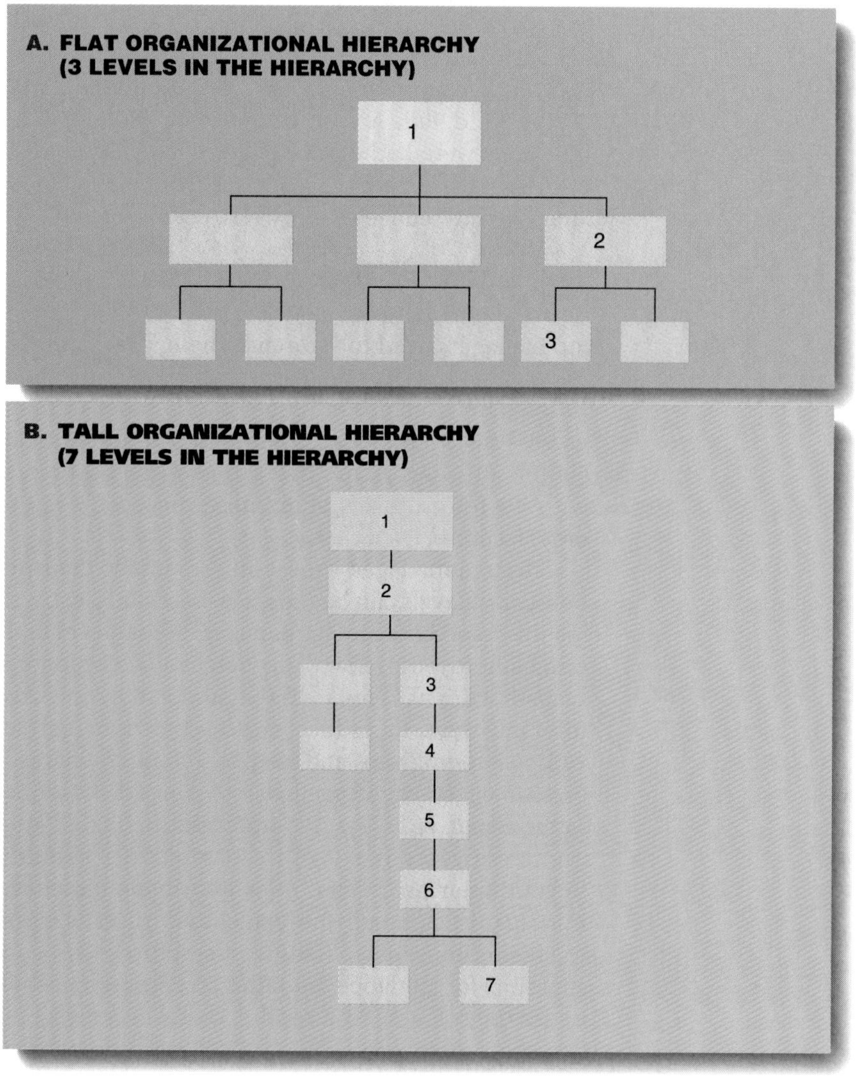

Communication problems may arise when an organization has many levels in the hierarchy. It can take a long time for the decisions and orders of upper-level managers to reach managers farther down in the hierarchy, and it can take a long time for top managers to learn how well their decisions worked out. Feeling out of touch, top managers may want to verify that lower-level managers are following orders and may require written confirmation from them. Middle managers, who know they will be held strictly accountable for their actions, start devoting more time to the process of making decisions to improve their chances of being right. They might even try to avoid responsibility by making top managers decide what actions to take.

Another communication problem that can result is the distortion of commands and orders being transmitted up and down the hierarchy, which causes managers at different levels to interpret what is happening differently. Distortion of orders and messages can be accidental, occurring because different managers interpret messages from their own narrow functional perspectives. Or it can be intentional, occurring because managers low in the hierarchy decide to interpret information to increase their own personal advantage.

Another problem with tall hierarchies is that they usually indicate that an organization is employing many managers, and managers are expensive. Managerial salaries, benefits, offices, and secretaries are a huge expense for organizations. Large companies such as IBM and General Motors pay their managers billions of dollars a year. In the early 2000s, hundreds of thousands of middle managers were laid off as dot-coms collapsed and high-tech companies such as Hewlett-Packard and Lucent, discussed at the beginning of the chapter, attempted to reduce costs by restructuring and downsizing their workforces.

THE MINIMUM CHAIN OF COMMAND To ward off the problems that result when an organization becomes too tall and employs too many managers, top managers need to ascertain whether they are employing the right number of middle and first-line managers and see whether they can redesign their organizational architecture to reduce the number of managers. Top managers might well follow a basic organizing principle–the principle of the minimum chain of command–which states that top managers should always construct a hierarchy with the fewest levels of authority necessary to efficiently and effectively use organizational resources.

Effective managers constantly scrutinize their hierarchies to see whether the number of levels can be reduced–for example, by eliminating one level and giving the responsibilities of managers at that level to managers above and empowering employees below. This practice has become increasingly common in the United States as companies that are battling low-cost foreign competitors search for new ways to reduce costs. One manager who is constantly trying to empower employees and keep the hierarchy flat is Colleen C. Barrett, the number-two executive of Southwest Airlines.[41] Barrett is the highest-ranking woman in the airline industry. At Southwest, she is well known for continually reaffirming Southwest's message that employees should feel free to go above and beyond their prescribed roles to provide better customer service. Her central message is that Southwest values and trusts its employees, who are empowered to take responsibility. Southwest employees are encouraged not to look to their superiors for guidance but rather to take responsibility to find ways to do the job better themselves. As a result, Southwest keeps the number of its middle managers to a minimum.

CENTRALIZATION AND DECENTRALIZATION OF AUTHORITY

Another way in which managers can keep the organizational hierarchy flat is to decentralize authority to lower-level managers and nonmanagerial employees.[42] If managers at higher levels give lower-level employees the responsibility to make important decisions and only manage by exception, then the problems of slow and distorted communication noted previously are kept to a minimum. Moreover, fewer managers are needed because their role is not to make decisions but to act as coach and facilitator and to help other employees make the best decisions. In addition, when decision making is low in the organization and near the customer, employees are better able to recognize and respond to customer needs.

Decentralizing authority allows an organization and its employees to behave in a flexible way even as the organization grows and becomes taller. This is why managers are so interested in empowering employees, creating self-managed work teams, establishing cross-functional teams, and even moving to a product team structure. These design innovations help keep the organizational architecture flexible and responsive to complex task and general environments, complex technologies, and complex strategies.

Although more and more organizations are taking steps to decentralize authority, too much decentralization has certain disadvantages. If divisions, functions, or teams are given too much decision-making authority, they may begin to pursue their own goals at the expense of organizational goals. Managers in engineering design or R&D, for example, may become so focused on making the best possible product that they fail to realize that the best product may be so expensive that few people will be willing or able to buy it. Also with too much decentralization, lack of communication among functions or among divisions may prevent possible synergies among them from ever materializing, and organizational performance suffers.

Top managers must seek the balance between centralization and decentralization of authority that best meets the four major contingencies an organization faces (see Figure 9.1). If managers are in a stable environment, using well-understood technology, and producing staple kinds of products (such as cereal, canned soup, books, or televisions), then there is no pressing need to decentralize authority, and managers at the top can maintain control of much of organizational decision making.[43] However, in uncertain, changing environments where high-tech companies are producing state-of-the-art products, top managers must empower employees and allow teams to make important strategic decisions so that the organization can keep up with the changes taking place. Two companies that saw different reasons to centralize or decentralize authority are DaimlerChrysler and Volkswagen, discussed next.

Managing Globally

DaimlerChrysler, Volkswagen, and Decentralization

In 2001, two German car companies, DaimlerChrysler and Volkswagen, came to different conclusions about whether they should centralize or decentralize authority. Jurgen Schrempp, CEO of DaimlerChrysler, was furious about the billions of dollars of losses its U.S. Chrysler division experienced in the early 2000s. He attributed the problem to too much decentralization of authority. After their merger in 1999, Schrempp had allowed Chrysler's U.S.

managers to retain too much control of decision making and they had not made the tough choices required to reduce costs and improve quality.[44] Indeed, Chrysler seemed to have lost its early lead to Ford, and GM was catching up fast. He decided to install a German management team to oversee Chrysler's operations, managers who would not only report directly to him but also give him the ability to make the key decisions that would affect Chrysler's future.

Volkswagen, on the other hand, had a different problem. It was enjoying great success with its Volkswagen division, but poor success with its luxury lines of cars which include Audi, Bugatti, and Bentley.[45] The reason? Some of its managers blamed the fact that Volkswagen's purchasing, research and development, and engineering decisions were centralized at the top of the organization. Decisions about how different cars should look and which components they should share were made at very high levels and often for cost reasons. Managers believed this had led to a public perception that Audi cars were not really any higher quality than ordinary Volkswagens, and so Audi's sales had languished, while those of BMW and Mercedes had taken off because Audi has lost its luxury differentiated appeal. The solution Volkswagen managers proposed was to create separate luxury-car and mass-car divisions and to decentralize decision making responsibility to managers in those divisions.

Types of Integrating Mechanisms

integrating mechanisms Organizing tools that managers can use to increase communication and coordination among functions and divisions.

Much coordination takes place through the hierarchy of authority. In addition, managers can use various **integrating mechanisms** to increase communication and coordination among functions and divisions. The greater the complexity of an organization's structure, the greater is the need for coordination among people, functions, and divisions to make the organizational structure work efficiently and effectively.[46] Thus, when managers choose to adopt a divisional, matrix, or product team structure, they must use complex kinds of integrating mechanisms to achieve organizational goals. UPS and FedEx, for example, have complex geographic structures that need an enormous amount of coordination among regions to achieve the goal of next-day package delivery. They achieve this through the innovative use of integrating mechanisms such as computer-controlled tracking equipment and customer-liaison personnel to manage transactions quickly and efficiently.

Six integrating mechanisms are available to managers to increase communication and coordination.[47] These mechanisms–arranged on a continuum from simplest to most complex–are listed in Figure 9.11 with examples of the individuals or groups that might use them. In the remainder of this section we examine each one, moving from the simplest to most complex.

DIRECT CONTACT Direct contact among managers creates a context within which managers from different functions or divisions can work together to solve mutual problems. However, several problems are associated with establishing contact among managers in different functions or divisions. Managers from different functions may have different views about what must be done to achieve organizational goals. But if the managers have equal authority (as functional managers typically do), the only manager who can tell them what to do is the CEO. If functional and divisional managers cannot reach agreement, no mechanism exists to resolve the conflict apart from the authority of the boss.

Figure 9.11 Types and Examples of Integrating Mechanisms

SIMPLE

Direct contact Marketing manager and research and development manager meet to brainstorm new product ideas.

Liason roles Assistant manager and project team leader indentify best product suggestions to put into development.

Task forces Representatives from marketing, research and development, and manufacturing meet to discuss launch of new product.

Cross-functional team A cross-functional team composed of all functions is formed to manage product to its launch in the market.

Integrating roles and departments Senior managers provide members of cross-functional team with relevant information from other teams and from other divisions.

Matrix structures Top managers decide to move to a matrix structure to develop many new products simultaneously.

COMPLEX

The need to solve everyday conflicts, however, wastes top-management time and effort and slows decision making. In fact, one sign of a poorly performing organizational structure is the number of problems sent up the hierarchy for top managers to solve. To increase coordination among functions and divisions and to prevent these problems from emerging, top managers can incorporate more complex integrating mechanisms into their organizational architecture.

LIAISON ROLES Managers can increase coordination among functions and divisions by establishing liaison roles. When the volume of contacts between two functions increases, one way to improve coordination is to give one manager in each function or division the responsibility for coordinating with the other. These managers may meet daily, weekly, monthly, or as needed. Figure 9.12A depicts a liaison role; the small dot represents the person within a function who has responsibility for coordinating with the other function. The responsibility for coordination is part of the liaison's full-time job, and usually an informal relationship forms between the people involved, greatly easing strains between functions. Furthermore, liaison roles provide a way of transmitting information across an organization, which is important in large organizations whose employees may know no one outside their immediate function or division.

task force A committee of managers from various functions or divisions who meet to solve a specific, mutual problem; also called an ad hoc committee.

TASK FORCES When more than two functions or divisions share many common problems, direct contact and liaison roles may not provide sufficient coordination. In these cases, a more complex integrating mechanism, a task force, may be appropriate (see Figure 9.12B). One manager from each relevant function or division is assigned to a task force that meets to solve a specific, mutual problem; members are responsible for reporting back to their departments on the issues addressed and the solutions recommended. Task forces are often called *ad hoc committees* because they are temporary; they may meet on a regular basis or only a few times. When the problem or issue is solved, the task force is no longer needed, and members return to their normal roles in their departments or are assigned to other task forces. Typically, task force members also perform many of their normal duties while serving on the task force.

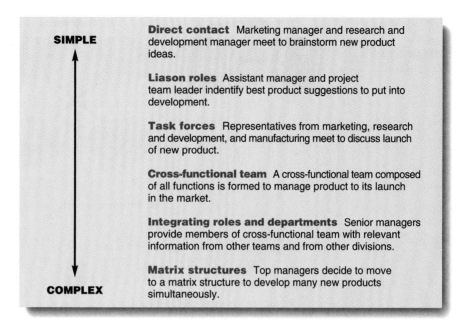

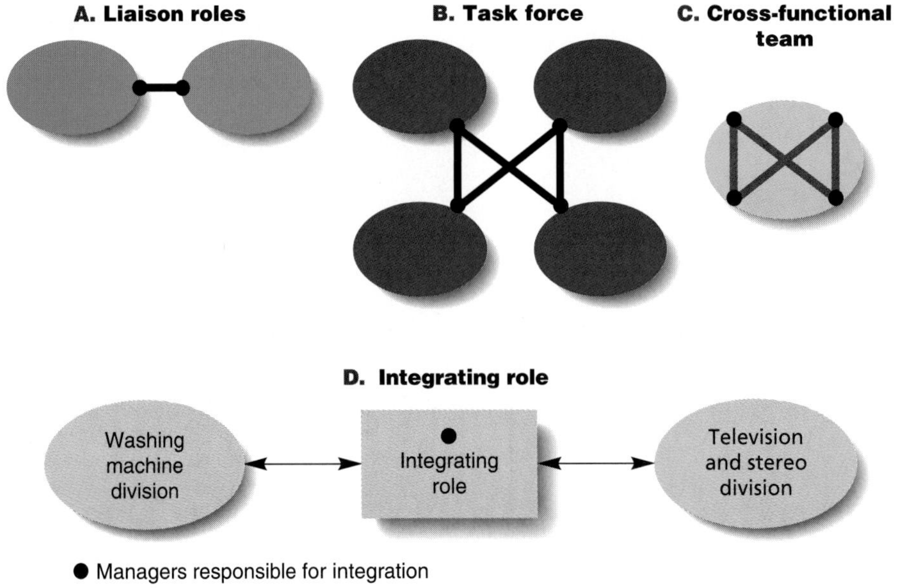

Figure 9.12 Forms of Integrating Mechanisms

CROSS-FUNCTIONAL TEAMS In many cases, the issues addressed by a task force are recurring problems such as the need to develop new products or find new kinds of customers. To address recurring problems effectively, managers are increasingly using permanent integrating mechanisms such as cross-functional teams (see Figure 9.12C). An example of such a cross-functional team is a new product development committee that is responsible for the choice, design, manufacturing, and marketing of a new product. Such an activity obviously requires a great deal of integration among functions if new products are to be successfully introduced, and using a complex integrating mechanism such as a cross-functional team accomplishes this. Intel, for instance, emphasizes cross-functional teamwork. Its structure consists of over 90 cross-functional groups that meet regularly to set functional strategy in areas such as engineering and marketing and to develop business-level strategy.

The more complex an organization, the more important cross-functional teams become. Westinghouse, for example, has established a cross-functional team system to promote integration among divisions and improve organizational performance. As discussed previously, the product team structure is based on cross-functional teams to speed products to market. These teams assume responsibility for all aspects of product development.

INTEGRATING ROLES An integrating role is a role whose only function is to increase coordination and integration among functions or divisions to achieve performance gains from synergies (see Figure 9.12D). Usually, managers who perform integrating roles are experienced senior managers who can envisage how to use the resources of the functions or divisions to obtain new synergies. One study found that Du Pont, the giant chemical company, had created 160 integrating roles to provide coordination among the different divisions of the company and improve corporate performance.[48] Once again, the more complex an organization and the greater the number of its divisions, the more important integrating roles are.

MATRIX STRUCTURE When managers must be able to respond quickly to the task and general environments, they often use a matrix structure. The reason for choosing a matrix structure is clear. It contains many of the integrating mechanisms already discussed: The two-boss managers integrate between functions and product teams; the matrix is built on the basis of temporary teams or task forces; and each member of a team performs a liaison role. The matrix structure is flexible precisely because it is formed from complex integrating mechanisms.

In summary, to keep an organization responsive to changes in its task and general environments, as the organization grows and becomes more complex, managers must increase coordination among functions and divisions by using complex integrating mechanisms. Managers must decide on the best way to organize their structures to create an organizational architecture that allows them to make the best use of organizational resources.

Strategic Alliances, B2B Network Structures, and IT

Recently, increasing globalization and the use of new IT have brought about two innovations in organizational architecture that have been sweeping through U.S. and European companies: strategic alliances, and business-to-business (B2B) network structures. A **strategic alliance** is a formal agreement that commits two or more companies to exchange or share their resources in order to produce and market a product.[49] Most commonly strategic alliances are formed because the companies share similar interests and believe they can benefit from cooperating. For example, Japanese car companies such as Toyota and Honda form many strategic alliances with particular suppliers of inputs such as car axles, gearboxes, and air-conditioning systems. Over time, these companies work closely with their suppliers to improve the efficiency and effectiveness of these inputs so that the final product–the car produced–is of higher quality and very often can be produced at lower cost. Today, Japanese companies have also established these alliances with suppliers throughout the United States and Mexico because both companies now build several models of cars in these countries.

strategic alliance An agreement in which managers pool or share their organization's resources and know-how with a foreign company, and the two organizations share the rewards and risks of starting a new venture.

network structure A series of strategic alliances that an organization creates with suppliers, manufacturers, and distributors to produce and market a product.

Throughout the 1990s, the growing sophistication of IT with global intranets and teleconferencing has made it much easier to manage strategic alliances and allow managers to share information and cooperate. One outcome of this has been the growth of strategic alliances into a network structure. A **network structure** is a series of global strategic alliances that one or several organizations create with suppliers, manufacturers, and/or distributors to produce and market a product. Network structures allow an organization to manage its global value chain in order to find new ways to reduce costs and increase the quality of products–without incurring the high costs of operating a complex organizational structure (such as the costs of employing many managers). More and more U.S. and European companies are relying on global network structures to gain access to low-cost foreign sources of inputs, as discussed in Chapter 6. Shoemakers such as Nike and Adidas are two companies that have used this approach extensively.

Nike is the largest and most profitable sports shoe manufacturer in the world. The key to Nike's success is the network structure that Nike founder and CEO

Philip Knight created to allow his company to produce and market shoes. As noted in Chapter 8, the most successful companies today are trying to pursue simultaneously a low-cost and a differentiation strategy. Knight decided early that to do this at Nike he needed organizational architecture that would allow his company to focus on some functions, such as design, and leave others, such as manufacturing, to other organizations.

By far the largest function at Nike's Oregon headquarters is the design function, composed of talented designers who pioneered innovations in sports shoe design such as the air pump and Air Jordans that Nike introduced so successfully. Designers use computer-aided design (CAD) to design Nike shoes, and they electronically store all new product information, including manufacturing instructions. When the designers have finished their work, they electronically transmit all the blueprints for the new products to a network of Southeast Asian suppliers and manufacturers with which Nike has formed strategic alliances.[50] Instructions for the design of a new sole may be sent to a supplier in Taiwan; instructions for the leather uppers, to a supplier in Malaysia. The suppliers produce the shoe parts and send them for final assembly to a manufacturer in China with whom Nike has established another strategic alliance. From China these shoes are shipped to distributors throughout the world. Ninety-nine percent of the 99 million pairs of shoes that Nike makes each year are made in Southeast Asia.

This network structure gives Nike two important advantages: First, Nike is able to respond to changes in sports shoe fashion very quickly. Using its global IT system, Nike literally can change the instructions it gives each of its suppliers overnight, so that within a few weeks its foreign manufacturers are producing new kinds of shoes.[51] Any alliance partners that fail to perform up to Nike's standards are replaced with new partners.

outsource To use outside suppliers and manufacturers to produce goods and services.

Second, Nike's costs are very low because wages in Southeast Asia are a fraction of what they are in the United States and this difference gives Nike a low-cost advantage. Also, Nike's ability to outsource and use foreign manufacturers to produce all its shoes abroad allows Knight to keep the organization's U.S. structure flat and flexible. Nike is able to use a relatively inexpensive functional structure to organize its activities. Sports shoe manufacturers' attempts to keep their costs low have led to many charges that Nike and others are supporting sweat shops that harm foreign workers as the following "Ethics in Action" suggests.

Ethics in Action

Of Shoes and Sweatshops

As the production of all kinds of goods and services are being increasingly outsourced to poor regions and countries of the world, the behavior of companies that outsource production to subcontractors in these countries has come under increasing scrutiny. Nike, the giant sports shoe maker with sales of more than $9 billion a year was one of the first to experience a backlash when critics revealed how workers in these countries were being treated. Indonesian workers were stitching together shoes in hot noisy factories for only 80 cents a day or about $18 a month.[52] Workers in Vietnam and China fared better; they could earn $1.60 a day. In all cases however, critics charged that at least $3 a day was needed to maintain an adequate living standard.

These facts generated an outcry in the United States where Nike was roundly attacked for its labor practices; a backlash against sales of Nike products forced Phil Knight, Nike's billionaire owner, to reevaluate Nike's labor practices. Nike announced that henceforth all the factories producing its

Members of United Students against Nike unfurl a banner at the Niketown store in New York accusing Nike of using sweatshop labor to produce its athletic apparel. Nike and other athletic apparel companies have since taken steps to ensure better working conditions for foreign workers.

shoes and clothes would be independently monitored and inspected. After its competitor Reebok, which also had been criticized for similar labor practices, announced that it was raising wages in Indonesia by 20 percent, Nike raised them by 25 percent to $23 a month.[53] Small though this may seem, it was a huge increase to workers in these countries.

In Europe, another sportswear company–Adidas–had largely escaped such criticism. But in 1999 it was reported that in El Salvador, a Taiwan-based Adidas subcontractor was employing girls as young as 14 in its factories and making them work for more than 70 hours a week. They were allowed to go to the restroom only twice a day and if they stayed longer than three minutes they lost a day's wages.[54] Adidas moved swiftly to avoid the public relations nightmare that Nike had experienced. Adidas announced that henceforth its subcontractors would also be required to abide by more strict labor standards.

What has happened in the sports shoe industry has happened throughout the clothing industry and other industries like electronics and toys as well. Companies such as Wal-Mart, Target, The Gap, Sony, and Mattel have all been forced to reevaluate the ethics of their labor practices and to promise to keep a constant watch on subcontractors in the future. A statement to this effect can be found on many of these companies' webpages, for example, Nike's (www.nikebiz.com) and The Gap's (www.thegap.com).

boundaryless organization An organization whose members are linked by computers, faxes, computer-aided design systems, and videoteleconferencing and who rarely, if ever, see one another face-to-face.

knowledge management system A company-specific virtual information system that allows workers to share their knowledge and expertise and find others to help solve ongoing problems.

business to business (B2B) network A group of organizations that join together and use IT to link themselves to potential global suppliers to increase efficiency and effectiveness.

The ability of managers to develop a network structure to produce or provide the goods and services customers want, rather than create a complex organizational structure to do so, has led many researchers and consultants to popularize the idea of a **boundaryless organization.** Such an organization is composed of people linked by IT–computers, faxes, computer-aided design systems, and videoteleconferencing–who may rarely, if ever, see one another face-to-face. People are utilized when their services are needed, much as in a matrix structure, but they are not formal members of an organization; they are functional experts who form an alliance with an organization, fulfill their contractual obligations, and then move on to the next project.

Large consulting companies, such as Arthur Andersen and McKinsey & Co., utilize their global consultants in this way. Consultants are connected by laptops to an organization's **knowledge management system,** its company-specific information system that systematizes the knowledge of its employees and provides them with access to other employees who have the expertise to solve the problems that they encounter as they perform their jobs.

The use of outsourcing and the development of network structures is increasing rapidly as organizations recognize the many opportunities they offer to reduce costs and increase organizational flexibility. U.S. companies spent $300 billion on global supply chain management in 2000. This push to lower costs has led to the development of electronic **business-to-business (B2B) networks** in which most or all of the companies in an industry (for example, car makers) use the same software platform to link to each other and establish industry specifications and standards. Then, these companies jointly list the quantity and specifications of the inputs they require and invite bids from the thousands of potential suppliers around the world. Suppliers also use the same software platform so electronic bidding, auctions, and transactions are possible between buyers and sellers around the world. The idea is that high-volume standardized transactions can help drive down costs at the industry level.

Today, with advances in IT, designing organizational architecture is becoming an increasingly complex management function. To maximize efficiency and effectiveness, managers must assess carefully the relative benefits of having their own organization perform a functional activity versus forming an alliance with another organization to perform the activity. It is still not clear how B2B networks and other forms of electronic alliances between companies will develop in the future.

Tips for New Managers

Choosing a Structure

1. If an organization begins to produce a wider range of products, and especially if it enters new businesses or industries, evaluate whether a move to a product structure will keep the organization organic.
2. If an organization grows and expands regionally or nationally, evaluate whether a move to a geographic structure will keep the organization organic.
3. If an organization begins to serve different kinds of customers, evaluate whether a move to a market structure will keep the organization organic.
4. To increase efficiency, quality, innovation, or responsiveness to customers, consider moving to a matrix or product team structure and find ways of decentralizing authority and empowering employees.
5. No matter what kind of structure an organization uses, periodically analyze its hierarchy of authority and keep the number of levels in the hierarchy to a minimum.
6. Analyze if strategic alliances, network structure, and IT are organizing choices that will help keep an organization flatter and more organic.

Summary and Review

DESIGNING ORGANIZATIONAL STRUCTURE The four main determinants of organizational structure are the external environment, strategy, technology, and human resources. In general, the higher the level of uncertainty associated with these factors, the more appropriate is a flexible, adaptable structure as opposed to a formal, rigid one.

GROUPING TASKS INTO JOBS Job design is the process by which managers group tasks into jobs. To create more interesting jobs, and to get workers to act flexibly, managers can enlarge and enrich jobs. The job characteristics model provides a tool managers can use to measure how motivating or satisfying a particular job is.

GROUPING JOBS INTO FUNCTIONS AND DIVISIONS

Managers can choose from many kinds of organizational structures to make the best use of organizational resources. Depending on the specific organizing problems they face, managers can choose from functional, product, geographic, market, matrix, product team, and hybrid structures.

COORDINATING FUNCTIONS AND DIVISIONS No matter which structure managers choose, they must decide how to distribute authority in the organization, how many levels to have in the hierarchy of authority, and what balance to strike between centralization and decentralization to keep the number of levels in the hierarchy to a minimum. As organizations grow, managers must increase integration and coordination among functions and divisions. Six integrating mechanisms are available to facilitate this: direct contact, liaison roles, task forces, cross-functional teams, integrating roles, and the matrix structure.

STRATEGIC ALLIANCES AND NETWORK STRUCTURE

To avoid many of the communications and coordination problems that emerge as organizations grow, managers are attempting to use IT to develop new ways of organizing. In a strategic alliance, managers enter into an agreement with another organization to provide inputs or to perform a functional activity. If managers enter into a series of these agreements they create a network structure. A network structure, most commonly based on some shared form of IT, can be formed around one company, or a number of companies can join together to create an industry B2B network.

Management in Action

Topics for Discussion and Action

1. Would a flexible or a more formal structure be appropriate for these organizations: (a) a large department store, (b) a Big Five accountancy firm, (c) a biotechnology company? Explain your reasoning.
2. Using the job characteristic model as a guide, discuss how a manager can enrich or enlarge subordinates' jobs.
3. How might a salesperson's job or a secretary's job be enlarged or enriched to make it more motivating?
4. When and under what conditions might managers change from a functional to (a) a product, (b) a geographic, or (c) a market structure?
5. How do matrix structure and product team structure differ? Why is product team structure more widely used?
6. Find a manager and identify the kind of organizational structure that his or her organization uses to coordinate its people and resources. Why is the organization using that structure? Do you think a different structure would be more appropriate? Which one?
7. With the same or another manager, discuss the distribution of authority in the organization. Does the manager think that decentralizing authority and empowering employees is appropriate?
8. Compare the pros and cons of using a network structure to perform organizational activities and performing all activities in-house or within one organizational hierarchy.
9. What are the advantages and disadvantages of business-to-business networks?

Building Management Skills

Understanding Organizing

Think of an organization with which you are familiar, perhaps one you have worked in—such as a store, restaurant, office, church, or school. Then answer the following questions.

1. Which contingencies are most important in explaining how the organization is organized? Do you think it is organized in the best way?
2. Using the job characteristics model, how motivating do you think the job of a typical employee in this organization is? Can you think of any ways in which a typical job could be enlarged or enriched?
3. What kind of organizational structure does the organization use? If it is part of a chain, what kind of structure does the entire organization use? What other structures discussed in the chapter might allow the organization to operate more effectively? For example, would the move to a product team structure lead to greater efficiency or effectiveness? Why or why not?
4. How many levels are there in the organization's hierarchy? Is authority centralized or decentralized? Describe the span of control of the top manager and of middle or first-line managers.
5. Is the distribution of authority appropriate for the organization and its activities? Would it be possible to flatten the hierarchy by decentralizing authority and empowering employees?
6. What are the principal integrating mechanisms used in the organization? Do they provide sufficient coordination among individuals and functions? How might they be improved?
7. Now that you have analyzed the way this organization is organized, what advice would you give its managers to help them improve the way it operates?

Small Group Breakout Exercise

Bob's Appliances

Form groups of three or four people, and appoint one member as the spokesperson who will communicate your findings to the whole class when called on by the instructor. Then discuss the following scenario.

Bob's Appliances sells and services household appliances such as washing machines, dishwashers, ranges, and refrigerators. Over the years, the company has developed a good reputation for the quality of its customer service, and many local builders patronize the store. Recently, some new appliance retailers, including Circuit City and REX, have opened stores that also provide numerous appliances. In addition to appliances, however, to attract more customers these stores carry a complete range of consumer electronics products—televisions, stereos, and computers. Bob Lange, the owner of Bob's Appliances, has decided that if he is to stay in business he must widen his product range and compete directly with the chains.

In 2002, he decided to build a 20,000-square-foot store and service center, and he is now hiring new employees to sell and service the new line of consumer electronics. Because of his company's increased size, Lange is not sure of the best way to organize the employees. Currently, he uses a functional structure; employees are divided into sales, purchasing and accounting, and repair. Bob is wondering whether selling and servicing consumer electronics is so different from selling and servicing appliances that he should move to a product structure (see figure) and create separate sets of functions for each of his two lines of business.[55]

You are a team of local consultants that Bob has called in to advise him as he makes this crucial choice. Which structure do you recommend? Why?

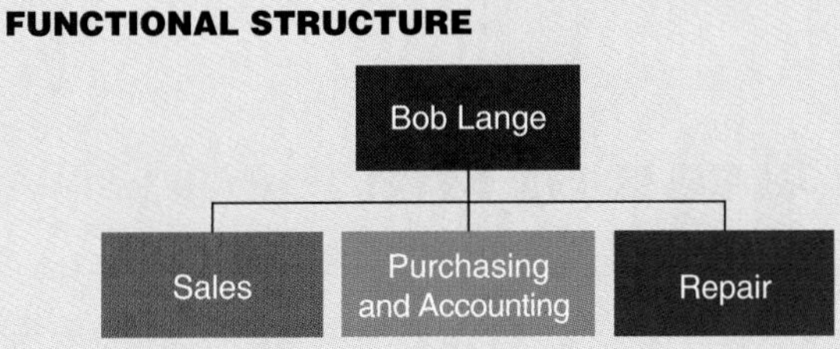

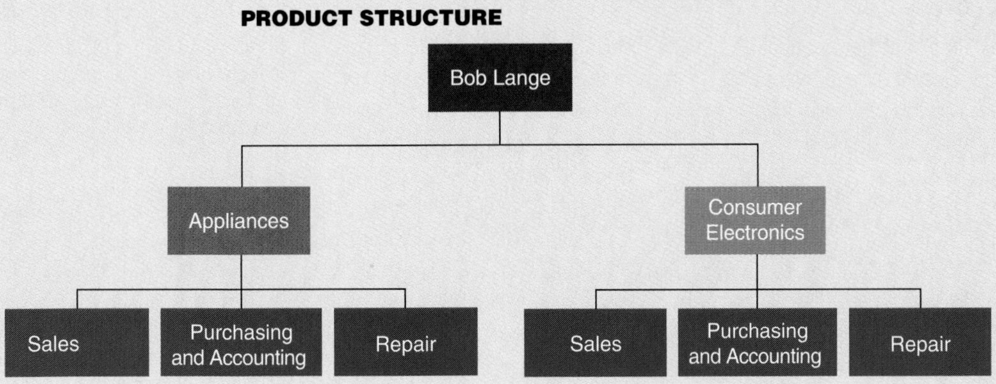

Exploring the World Wide Web

Search for a website that tells the story of how an organization changed its structure in some way to increase its efficiency and effectiveness.

You're the Management Consultant

Speeding Up Website Design

You have been called in as a consultant by the top functional managers of a website design, production, and hosting company whose new animated website designs are attracting a lot of attention and a lot of customers. Currently, your employees are organized into different functions such as hardware, software design, graphic art, website hosting as well as functions such as marketing and human resources. Each function takes its turn to work on a new project from initial customer request to final online website hosting.

The problem this company is experiencing is that it typically takes one year from the initial idea stage to the time that the website is up and running and the company wants to shorten this time by half to protect and expand its market niche. The managers believe their current functional structure is the source of the problem, it is not allowing employees to develop websites fast enough to satisfy customers' demands. They want you to suggest a better one.

Questions

1. Discuss ways in which you can improve the way the current functional structure operates to speed website development.
2. Discuss the pros and cons of moving to a (a) multidivisional, (b) matrix, and (c) product-team structure to reduce website development time.
3. Which of these structures do you think is most appropriate and why?

BusinessWeek Cases in the News

Radical Bold Management Experiment at HP

For the text of this in-depth *Business Week* case, log on to the *Contemporary Management* website at www.mhhe.com/jones3e.

Questions

1. What kind of structure did HP use to organize its activities before Fiorino changed it? What problems did the structure cause?
2. What changes did Fiorino make? Why? How does Fiorino hope its new structure will affect the behavior of HP employees?

Source: P. Burrows, "Radical: Bold Management Experiment at Hewlett-Packard," *Business Week,* February 19, 2001, pp. 71–80.

BusinessWeek

Cases in the News

Meet the "Completely Different EDS"

When Electronic Data Systems Corp. landed the U.S. government's biggest-ever technology outsourcing deal—a $7 billion contract to build and maintain computer networks for the U.S. Navy and Marine Corps—Champagne corks popped and Sousa marches played over loudspeakers at the sprawling EDS headquarters in Plano, Tex. For CEO Richard H. Brown and his team, the surprise win over three rivals was proof positive that the once foundering technology-services giant was back. Wall Street was impressed, too. The company's stock jumped nearly 10 percent after the October 6 announcement.

But for many investors, it's too soon to celebrate. Despite nearly two years of painful cost-cutting and reorganizing and six consecutive quarters of rising profit margins, EDS still must prove that it can reignite its sluggish top-line growth. Brown has done "an exceptional job" of restructuring EDS and boosting profitability, says analyst David M. Togut of Morgan Stanley Dean Witter. "But [revenue] growth is much more difficult than restructuring."

Brown, a New Jersey native, who joined EDS in January 1999, isn't the only IT-services chief struggling with sluggish growth. Computer Sciences Corp., Perot Systems, and other industry players have had similar disappointments. Heavy spending on Y2K fixes and frenzied Net initiatives in 1999 dampened sales earlier this year. And the strong dollar is pinching international players such as EDS, which gets 42 percent of its revenues from overseas.

Still, EDS faces some self-made hurdles. As part of Brown's $1 billion cost-cutting effort, the company terminated about 125 contracts and sold units with subpar profits. That left a $600 million hold in revenues to fill this year. Brown let a third of his salesforce go to make room for better performers but only recently staffed up to prior levels. And a massive shuffling of executives followed some 13,500 layoffs and early retirements, hurting critical sales relationships with existing customers.

Brown's drastic medicine was sorely needed. The scrappy business founded by Ross Perot and sold to GM in 1984 had grown fat and complacent. Some 48 "strategic business units" operated as separate fiefdoms, bloating costs and confusing customers. By the mid-90s, EDS was an also-ran in the budding world of the Internet—and had ceded leadership in services to a revitalized IBM. In 1996, EDS was spun off by GM and forced to cut prices for its former parent to lock in a new, long-term services deal. EDS quickly found itself struggling to meet sales and earnings targets.

Brown hit EDS like a neutron bomb. Only 10 of the 37 top officers who were there when he arrived remain. The 48 fiefdoms have been streamlined into four business divisions: A weekly report ranks the top 40 managers against their sales targets and is shared with all of them. A computerized "service excellence dashboard" shows how more than 1,000 contracts are performing—with red highlights on the trouble spots, as ranked by customers and EDS executives. Brown regularly visits customers and employees and responds to the hundreds of e-mails he gets monthly from workers. "There's a sense of urgency that hasn't been there before," says EDS Vice President Robb R. Rasmussen.

Pleased customers have taken notice. William C. Van Fraasen, CEO of Blue Cross & Blue Shield of Massachusetts Inc., says Brown stopped by for a visit to hear his concerns within two months of taking the top job at EDS. In seven years as CEO, it was the first one-on-one meeting Van Fraasen had had with an EDS chief. "They listen better" now, he says. Jack Sandner, CEO of FreeDrive Inc.—which offers data storage services via the Net—was astonished at EDS's newfound focus. In more than a decade as chairman of the Chicago Mercantile Exchange, Sandner had worked with EDS and found the experience to be "like rowing a boat in mud." But less than two weeks after Sandner and Brown chatted at a White House dinner in August, EDS teams were combing through FreeDrive. Ten days later, EDS had agreed to invest in FreeDrive and to provide Web-hosting and data-storage services to the startup. "This is a completely different EDS," marvels Sandner.

EDS has no choice but to be faster and nimbler. Even its bread-and-butter outsourcing business—handling data centers, networks, and other tech chores for customers—is rapidly changing. Outsourcing chief Douglas L. Frederick says such deals, still 75 percent of EDS's revenues, are getting smaller and shorter than the 10-year mega-contracts typical a few years ago.

And profit margins are getting slimmer as competition heats up. Customers are looking for outsourcing deals built around specific technologies or business processes, like taking over the management of the human resources or accounting department, says IDC analyst Traci Gere. That kind of flexibility "has not been a hallmark of EDS in the past," she says.

Need for Speed

EDS will need to be even speedier if it wants to be a big player in e-business services, the fastest-growing tech-services market: Research house GartnerGroup expects it to increase more than sixfold by 2004, to $158 billion. EDS's e-business customers often cite the company's good work, but give it mixed reviews when it comes to providing "really innovative, cutting-edge types of solutions," says Gartner analyst Frances Karamouzis.

To improve on that score, EDS in November launched bluesphere, a new unit to offer customers Web design integrated with back-end applications, such as billing and procurement. Analyst Karl E. Keirstead of Lehman Brothers Inc. figures giants like EDS and IBM are well positioned to take market share from e-business niche players such as Sapient and Razorfish. "The projects that are left are larger, more complex deals" requiring global companies with experience integrating heavyweight computer systems, Keirstead says.

With most of the jolting changes behind it, will EDS finally take off? Merrill Lynch & Co. analyst Stephen T. McClellan thinks so. He figures non-GM revenues—the number most analysts follow—will grow 11 percent next year, after a paltry 4 percent increase in 2000. Earnings should jump 15 percent, to $1.3 billion. Still, he admits, profitably implementing these complex deals is where the real risk lies.

Even EDS executives concede they've done the easy part in pruning costs. Now they've got to deliver on their growth promises to reap their rewards on Wall Street. Until then, they'd do best to turn down the Sousa and keep those Champaign flutes in storage.

Source: W. Zelner, "Meet the Completely Different EDS," *Business Week,* December 18, 2000, pp. 204–06.

Questions

1. What kind of organizational structure did the old EDS have? How did this affect its performance?
2. What changes did Brown make to EDS's structure and how did they affect its performance?

Chapter 10

Organizational Control and Culture

Learning Objectives

After studying this chapter, you should be able to:

- Define **organizational control,** and describe the four steps of the control process.
- Identify the **main output controls,** and discuss their advantages and disadvantages as means of coordinating and motivating employees.
- Identify the **main behavior controls,** and discuss their advantages and disadvantages as means of coordinating and motivating employees.
- Explain the **role of organizational culture** in creating an effective organizational architecture.

A Manager's Challenge

Gateway's New Rules Result in Low Customer Satisfaction

How should managers control to improve performance?

In 2001, Gateway, the personal computer maker, saw its customer satisfaction rating plummet from third to fifth in consumer satisfaction with personal computer makers. This drop caused Gateway's managers considerable anxiety because they use this measure of customer satisfaction as an important indicator of their company's ongoing performance. Such a drop is very serious to a computer maker because the volume of its on-line sales depends on how easy it is for customers to put their mail-order computer together when it reaches their homes, and how easy it is for them to get advice and good service when they encounter a software or hardware problem. Customer satisfaction ratings also directly affect a company's profits, and as Gateway's computer shipments slipped by more than 11 percent in 2001 compared to 2000, it began to lose money.

Gateway Computer's familiar cow-patterned computer boxes speed down the production line as the company attempts to rebuild its market share in the fiercely competitive personal computer industry.

Why did customer satisfaction fall? Gateway randomly surveys its customers 30 days after they receive their computers to inquire about the nature of their buying experience. Mike Ritter, director of Gateway consumer marketing, discovered that the source of customer dissatisfaction was a series of new rules and policies the company had instituted for its customer-service reps to follow because of its desire to reduce the increasing costs of after-sales service. As Gateway's product line had broadened and many different software and hardware options were made available to customers, so had the complexity of its customer-service procedures. Employees had to have a great deal more information at their disposal to solve customer problems. These problems were often made more serious when customers installed additional software on their computers which then caused problems with the software already installed on the Gateway machine. As everybody who has installed new software knows, it can take considerable time to iron out the problems and get the new installation to work. Gateway was spending millions of dollars in employee time to solve these problems and desired to reduce these costs.

Ritter reported to Gateway CEO Ted Wiatt that of the 15 rules and procedures the company had instituted for its customer-service reps to follow, two rules in particular were the source of customer dissatisfaction. The first rule concerned the issue of customer-installed software. Gateway had told its service reps to inform customers that if they installed any other software on their machines this would invalidate Gateway's warranty. This infuriated customers who asked why shouldn't they install other necessary software? The second rule was one that rewarded customer-support reps on the basis of how quickly they handled customer calls, meaning that the more calls they handled in an hour or day the higher their bonuses.

The joint effect of these two rules was customer reps were now motivated to minimize the length of a service call, and in particular, were unwilling to help solve customer problems that resulted from installation of "outlawed software" since this took a lot of time. Obviously customers resented this treatment and the result was the big decline in customer satisfaction. Moreover, customer reps were not happy because they felt they were violating Gateway's cultural values and norms about providing excellent customer service. When they were hired, Gateway had prided itself on having a strong corporate culture.

Once Gateway's managers realized the source of the problem they abolished the 15 rules immediately. Within one month in 2001 the 30 day survey saw customer satisfaction jump by over 10 percent. In retrospect, Gateway's managers described these new rules and policies as "misguided and stupid," they hope that the company's sales will now start to increase and it will regain some market share it lost to Dell and Compaq. However, in July 2001 Gateway announced that it was closing down its global computer making operations and it is in a tough race against Dell Computer, which now has over 25 percent market share compared with less that 10 percent for Gateway. As Gateway's managers discovered, it is necessary to carefully choose and evaluate the rules and policies used to control employees' behavior to prevent unexpected problems.

Overview

As the experience of Gateway suggests, the ways in which managers decide to control the behavior of their employees can have very different effects on the way employees behave. When managers make choices about how to influence and regulate their employees's behavior and performance, they establish the second foundation of organizational architecture, organizational control.

As discussed in Chapter 9, the first task facing managers is to establish the structure of task and job reporting relationships that allow organizational members to use resources most efficiently and effectively. Structure alone, however, does not provide the incentive or motivation for people to behave in ways that help achieve organizational goals. The purpose of organizational control is to provide managers with a means to direct and motivate subordinates to work toward achieving organizational goals and to provide managers with specific feedback on how well an organization and its members are performing. Gateway's 15 rules were intended to direct and motivate employee behavior: its market share, profits, and customer satisfaction rating are measures that give it feedback on how well it is performing.

Organizational structure provides an organization with a skeleton, and control and culture give it the muscles, sinews, nerves, and sensations that allow managers to regulate and govern its activities. The managerial functions of organizing and controlling are inseparable, and effective managers must learn to make them work together in a harmonious way.

In this chapter, we look in detail at the nature of organizational control and describe the steps in the control process. We discuss three types of control available to managers to control and influence organizational members–output control, behavior control, and clan control (which operates through the values and norms of an organization's culture).[1] By the end of this chapter, you will appreciate the rich variety of control systems available to managers and understand why developing an appropriate control system is vital to increasing the performance of an organization and its members.

What is Organizational Control?

As noted in Chapter 1, *controlling* is the process whereby managers monitor and regulate how efficiently and effectively an organization and its members are performing the activities necessary to achieve organizational goals. As discussed in previous chapters, when *planning* and *organizing,* managers develop the organizational strategy and structure that they hope will allow the organization to use resources most effectively to create value for customers. In *controlling,* managers monitor and evaluate whether the organization's strategy and structure are working as intended, how they could be improved, and how they might be changed if they are not working.

Control, however, does not mean just reacting to events after they have occurred. It also means keeping an organization on track and anticipating events that might occur. Control is concerned with keeping employees motivated, focused on the important problems confronting the organization, and working together to take advantage of opportunities that will help an organization perform more highly over time.

The Importance of Organizational Control

To understand the importance of organizational control, consider how it helps managers obtain superior efficiency, quality, responsiveness to customers, and innovation–the four building blocks of competitive advantage.

To determine how *efficiently* they are using their resources, managers must be able to accurately measure how many units of inputs (raw materials, human resources, and so on) are being used to produce a unit of output. Managers also must be able to measure how many units of outputs (goods and services) are being produced. A control system contains the measures or yardsticks that allow managers to assess how efficiently the organization is producing goods and services. Moreover, if managers experiment with changing the way the organization produces goods and services to find a more efficient way of producing them, these measures tell managers how successful they have been. For example, when managers at Ford decided to adopt a product-team structure to design, engineer, and manufacture new car models, they used measures such as time taken to design a new car and cost savings per car produced to evaluate how well the new structure worked in comparison with the old structure. They found that the new one performed better. Without a control system in place, managers have no idea how well their organization is performing and how its performance can be improved–information that is becoming increasingly important in today's highly competitive environment.

Today, much of the competition among organizations revolves around increasing the *quality* of goods and services. In the car industry, for example, cars within each price range compete against one another in features, design, and reliability. Thus, whether a customer will buy a Ford Taurus, Chevy Cavalier, Dodge Intrepid, Toyota Camry, or Honda Accord depends significantly on the quality of each product. Organizational control is important in determining the quality of goods and services because it gives managers feedback on product quality. If the managers of car makers consistently measure the number of customer complaints and the number of new cars returned for repairs, or if school principals measure how many students drop out of school or how achievement scores on nationally based tests vary over time, they have a good indication of how much quality they have built into their product–be it an educated student or a car that does not break down. Effective managers create a control system that consistently monitors the quality of goods and services so that they can make continuous improvements to quality–an approach that can give them a competitive advantage.

Managers can also help make their organizations more *responsive to customers* if they develop a control system that allows them to evaluate how well customer-contact employees are performing their jobs, as Gateway does. Monitoring employee behavior can help managers find ways to increase employees' performance levels, perhaps by revealing areas in which skill training can help employees or by finding new procedures that allow employees to perform their jobs better. When employees know that their behaviors are being monitored, they may also have more incentive to be helpful and consistent in how they act toward customers. To improve customer service, for example, Ford regularly surveys customers about their experiences with particular Ford dealers. If a dealership receives too many customer complaints, Ford's managers investigate the dealership to uncover the sources of the problems and suggest solutions; if necessary, they might even threaten to reduce the numbers of cars a dealership receives to force the dealer to improve the quality of its customer service.

Finally, controlling can raise the level of *innovation* in an organization. Successful innovation takes place when managers create an organizational setting in which employees feel empowered to be creative and in which authority is decentralized to employees so that they feel free to experiment and take risks. Deciding on the appropriate control systems to encourage risk taking is an important management challenge; organizational culture (discussed later in this chapter) becomes important in this regard. To encourage product teams at Ford to perform highly, top managers monitored the performance of each team separately–by examining how each team reduced costs or increased quality, for example–and used a bonus system related to performance to pay each team. The product team manager then evaluated each team member's individual performance, and the most innovative employees received promotions and rewards based on their superior performance.

Control Systems and IT

control systems Formal target-setting, monitoring, evaluation, and feedback systems that provide managers with information about how well the organization's strategy and structure are working.

Control systems are formal target-setting, monitoring, evaluation, and feedback systems that provide managers with information about whether the organization's strategy and structure are working efficiently and effectively.[2] Effective control systems alert managers when something is going wrong and give them time to respond to opportunities and threats. An effective control system has three characteristics: It is flexible enough to allow managers to respond as necessary to unexpected events; it provides accurate information and gives managers a true picture of organizational performance; and it provides managers with the information in a timely manner because making decisions on the basis of outdated information is a recipe for failure.

New forms of IT have revolutionized control systems because they facilitate the flow of accurate and timely information up and down the organizational hierarchy and between functions and divisions. Today, employees at all levels of the organization routinely feed information into a company's information system or network and start the chain of events that affect decision making at some other part of the organization. This could be the department store clerk whose scanning of purchased clothing tells merchandise managers what kinds of clothing need to be reordered; or the salesperson in the field who feeds into a wireless laptop information about customers' changing needs or problems.

feedforward control Control that allows managers to anticipate problems before they arise.

Control and information systems are developed to measure performance at each stage in the process of transforming inputs into finished goods and services (see Figure 10.1). At the *input* stage, managers use **feedforward control** to anticipate problems before they arise so that problems do not occur later, during the conversion process.[3] For example, by giving stringent product specifications to suppliers in advance (a form of performance target), an organization can control the quality of the inputs it receives from its suppliers and thus avoid potential problems during the conversion process. Also, IT can be used to keep in contact with suppliers and to monitor their progress. Similarly, by screening job applicants, often by viewing their resumes electronically, and using several interviews to select the most highly skilled people, managers can lessen the chance that they will hire people who lack the necessary skills or experience to perform effectively. In general, the development of management information systems promote feedforward control that provides managers with timely information about changes in the task and general environments that may impact their organization later on. Effective managers always monitor trends and changes in the external environment to try to anticipate problems. (We discuss management information systems in detail in Chapter 17.)

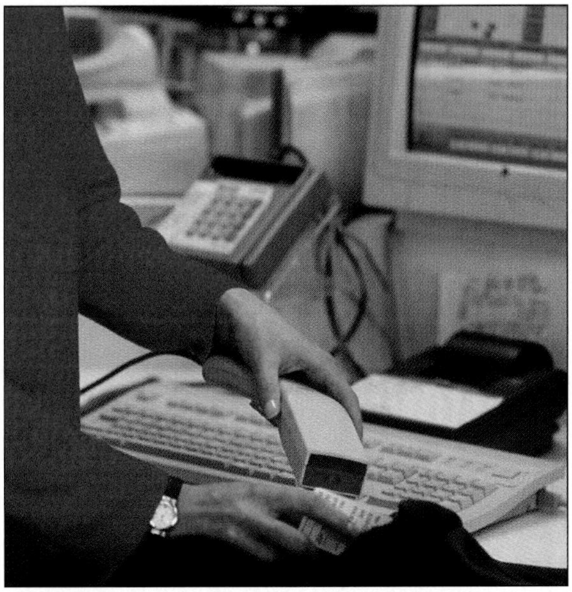

Scanning devices, such as the one shown here, are becoming common in all types of work processes, as more companies require real-time information about their products and customers.

At the *conversion* stage, **concurrent control** gives managers immediate feedback on how efficiently inputs are being transformed into outputs so that managers can correct problems as they arise. Concurrent control through IT alerts managers to the

Figure 10.1
Three Types of Control

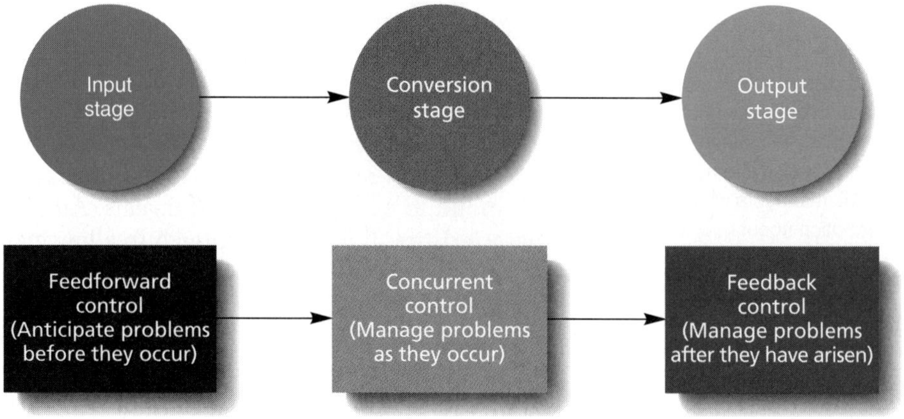

concurrent control Control that gives managers immediate feedback on how efficiently inputs are being transformed into outputs so that managers can correct problems as they arise.

feedback control Control that gives managers information about customers' reactions to goods and services so that corrective action can be taken if necessary.

need to react quickly to whatever is the source of the problem, be it a defective batch of inputs, a machine that is out of alignment, or a worker who lacks the skills necessary to perform a task efficiently. Concurrent control is at the heart of total quality management programs (discussed at length in Chapter 18), in which workers are expected to constantly monitor the quality of the goods or services they provide at every step of the production process and inform managers as soon as they discover problems. One of the strengths of Toyota's production system, for example, is that individual workers are given the authority to push a button to stop the assembly line whenever they discover a quality problem. When all problems have been corrected, the result is a finished product that is much more reliable.

At the *output* stage, managers use **feedback control** to provide information about customers' reactions to goods and services so that corrective action can be taken if necessary. For example, a feedback control system that monitors the number of customer returns alerts managers when defective products are being produced, and a management information system that measures increases or decreases in relative sales of different products alerts managers to changes in customer tastes so they can increase or reduce the production of specific products.

The Control Process

The control process, whether at the input, conversion, or output stage, can be broken down into four steps: establishing standards of performance, then measuring, comparing, and evaluating actual performance (see Figure 10.2).[4]

- Step 1: *Establish the standards of performance, goals, or targets against which performance is to be evaluated.*

At Step 1 in the control process managers decide on the standards of performance, goals, or targets that they will use in the future to evaluate the performance of the entire organization or part of it (such as a division, a function, or an individual). The standards of performance that managers select measure efficiency, quality, responsiveness to customers, and innovation.[5] If managers decide to pursue a low-cost strategy, for example, then they need to measure efficiency at all levels in the organization.

At the corporate level, a standard of performance that measures efficiency is *operating costs,* the actual costs associated with producing goods and services, including all employee-related costs. Top managers might set a corporate goal

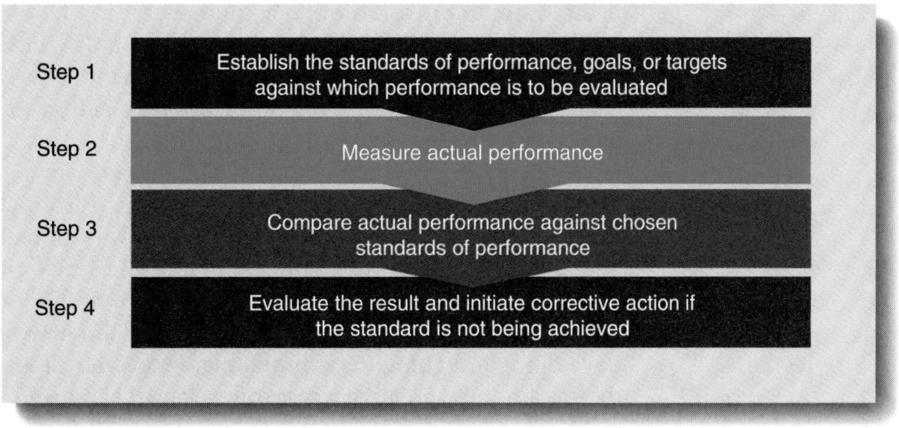
Step 1
Establish the standards of performance, goals, or targets against which performance is to be evaluated
Step 2
Measure actual performance
Step 3
Compare actual performance against chosen standards of performance
Step 4
Evaluate the result and initiate corrective action if the standard is not being achieved

Figure 10.2 Four Steps in Organizational Control

of "reducing operating costs by 10 percent for the next three years" to increase efficiency. Corporate managers might then evaluate divisional managers for their ability to reduce operating costs within their respective divisions, and divisional managers might set cost-savings targets for functional managers. Thus, performance standards selected at one level affect those at the other levels, and ultimately the performance of individual managers is evaluated in terms of their ability to reduce costs. For example, in 2001 struggling Xerox Corp., named Anne Mulcahy as CEO and gave her the challenging task of turning around the company's fortunes. She was selected because of her 25-year reputation as a person who had been most successful in reducing costs and increasing efficiency in Xerox's general markets division.[6]

The number of standards of performance that an organization's managers use to evaluate efficiency, quality, and so on, can run into the thousands or hundreds of thousands. Managers at each level are responsible for selecting those standards that will best allow them to evaluate how well the part of the organization they are responsible for is performing.[7] Managers must be careful to choose the standards of performance that allow them to assess how well they are doing with *all four* of the building blocks of competitive advantage. If managers focus on just one (such as efficiency in the example above) and ignore others (such as determining what customers really want and innovating a new line of products to satisfy them), managers may end up hurting their organization's performance. This is what happened to Gateway Computer, its managers tried to increase efficiency and reduce costs by using policies that led customer-service representatives to cut short customer calls. Although this might have saved costs, it resulted in a large decrease in customer satisfaction which hurt Gateway's effectiveness.

- Step 2: *Measure actual performance.*

Once managers have decided which standards or targets they will use to evaluate performance, the next step in the control process is to measure actual performance. In practice, managers can measure or evaluate two things: (1) the actual *outputs* that result from the behavior of their members and (2) the *behaviors* themselves (hence the terms *output control* and *behavior control* used below).[8]

Sometimes both outputs and behaviors can be easily measured. Measuring outputs and evaluating behavior is relatively easy in a fast-food restaurant, for example, because employees are performing routine tasks. Managers at Gateway, in measuring the number of customer calls each employee handled, were using output control. Similarly, managers of a fast-food restaurant can quite easily measure outputs by counting how many customers their employees serve and how much money customers spend. Managers can easily observe each employee's behavior and quickly take action to solve any problems that may arise.

When an organization and its members perform complex, nonroutine activities that are intrinsically difficult to measure, it is much more difficult for managers to measure outputs or behavior.[9] It is very difficult, for example, for managers in charge of R&D departments at Merck or Microsoft to measure performance or to evaluate the performance of individual members because it can take 5 or 10 years to determine whether the new products that scientists are developing are going to be profitable. Moreover, it is impossible for a manager to measure how creative a research scientist is by watching his or her actions.

In general, the more nonroutine or complex organizational activities are, the harder it is for managers to measure outputs or behaviors.[10] Outputs, however, are usually easier to measure than behaviors because they are more tangible and objective. Therefore, the first kind of performance measures that managers tend to use are those that measure outputs. Then managers develop performance measures or standards that allow them to evaluate behaviors to determine whether employees at all levels are working toward organizational goals. Some simple behavior measures are, Do employees come to work on time? Do employees consistently follow the established rules for greeting and serving customers? Each type of output and behavior control and the way it is used at the different organizational levels–corporate, divisional, functional, and individual–is discussed in detail subsequently.

- Step 3: *Compare actual performance against chosen standards of performance.*

During Step 3, managers evaluate whether–and to what extent–performance deviates from the standards of performance chosen in Step 1. If performance is higher than expected, managers might decide that they set performance standards too low and may raise them for the next time period to challenge their subordinates.[11] Managers at Japanese companies are well known for the way they try to raise performance in manufacturing settings by constantly raising performance standards to motivate managers and workers to find new ways to reduce costs or increase quality.

However, if performance is too low and standards were not reached, or if standards were set too high so that employees could not achieve them, managers must decide whether to take corrective action.[12] It is easy to take corrective action when the reasons for poor performance can be identified–for instance, high labor costs. To reduce costs, managers can search for low-cost foreign sources of supply or invest more in technology or implement cross-functional teams. More often, however, the reasons for poor performance are hard to identify. Changes in the environment such as the emergence of a new global competitor, a recession, or an increase in interest rates might be the source of the problem. Within an organization, perhaps the R&D function underestimated the problems it would encounter in developing the new product or the extra costs of doing unforeseen research. If managers are to take any form of corrective action, Step 4 is necessary.

- Step 4: *Evaluate the result and initiate corrective action if the standard is not being achieved.*

The final step in the control process is to evaluate the results. Whether performance standards have been met or not, managers can learn a great deal during this step. If managers decide that the level of performance is unacceptable, they must try to solve the problem. Sometimes, performance problems occur because the standard was too high; for example, a sales target was too optimistic and impossible to achieve. In this case, adopting more realistic standards can reduce the gap between actual performance and desired performance. However, if managers determine that something in the situation is causing the problem, then to raise performance they will need to change the way resources are being utilized.[13] Perhaps the latest technology is not being used; perhaps workers lack the advanced training needed to perform at a higher level; perhaps the organization needs to buy its inputs or assemble its products abroad to compete against low-cost rivals; perhaps it needs to restructure itself or reengineer its work processes to increase efficiency.

The simplest example of a control system is the thermostat in a home. By setting the thermostat, you establish the standard of performance with which actual temperature is to be compared. The thermostat contains a sensing or monitoring device, which measures the actual temperature against the desired temperature. Whenever there is a difference between them, the furnace or air-conditioning unit is activated to bring the temperature back to the standard: In other words, corrective action is initiated. This is a simple control system, for it is entirely self-contained and the target (temperature) is easy to measure.

Establishing targets and designing measurement systems is much more difficult for managers because the high level of uncertainty in the organizational environment causes managers to rarely know what might happen. Thus, it is vital for managers to design control systems to alert them to problems so that they can be dealt with before they become threatening. Another issue is that managers are not just concerned about bringing the organization's performance up to some predetermined standard; they want to push that standard forward, to encourage employees at all levels to find new ways to raise performance.

In the following sections, we consider the three most important types of control that managers use to coordinate and motivate employees to ensure they pursue superior efficiency, quality, innovation, and responsiveness to customers: output control, behavior control, and organizational culture or clan control (see Figure 10.3). Managers use all three to govern and regulate organizational activities, no matter what specific organizational structure is in place.

Figure 10.3 Three Organizational Control Systems

Type of control	Mechanisms of control
Output control	Financial measures of performance Organizational goals Operating budgets
Behavior control	Direct supervision Management by objectives Rules and standard operating procedures
Organizational culture/clan control	Values Norms Socialization

Output Control

All managers develop a system of output control for their organizations. First, they choose the goals or output performance standards or targets that they think will best measure efficiency, quality, innovation, and responsiveness to customers. Then they measure to see whether the performance goals and standards are being achieved at the corporate, divisional or functional, and individual levels of the organization. The three main mechanisms that managers use to assess output or performance are financial measures, organizational goals, and operating budgets.

Financial Measures of Performance

Top managers are most concerned with overall organizational performance and use various financial measures to evaluate performance. The most common are profit ratios, liquidity ratios, leverage ratios, and activity ratios. They are discussed below and summarized in Table 10.1.[14]

- *Profit ratios* measure how efficiently managers are using the organization's resources to generate profits. *Return on investment (ROI),* an organization's net income before taxes divided by its total assets, is the most commonly used financial performance measure because it allows managers of one organization to compare performance with that of other organizations. ROI allows managers to assess an organization's competitive advantage. *Gross profit margin* is the difference between the amount of revenue generated by a product and the resources used to produce the product. This measure provides managers with information about how efficiently an organization is utilizing its resources and about how attractive customers find the product. It also provides managers with a way to assess how well an organization is building a competitive advantage.
- *Liquidity ratios* measure how well managers have protected organizational resources to be able to meet short-term obligations. The *current ratio* (current assets divided by current liabilities) tells managers whether they have the resources available to meet the claims of short-term creditors. The *quick ratio* tells whether they can pay these claims without selling inventory.
- *Leverage ratios* such as the *debt-to-assets ratio* and the *times- covered ratio* measure the degree to which managers use debt (borrow money) or equity (issue new shares) to finance ongoing operations. An organization is highly leveraged if it uses more debt than equity, and debt can be very risky when profits fail to cover the interest on the debt.
- *Activity ratios* provide measures of how well managers are creating value from organizational assets. *Inventory turnover* measures how efficiently managers are turning inventory over so that excess inventory is not carried. *Days sales outstanding* provides information on how efficiently managers are collecting revenue from customers to pay expenses.

The objectivity of financial measures of performance is the reason why so many managers use them to assess the efficiency and effectiveness of their organizations. When an organization fails to meet performance standards such as ROI, revenue, or stock price targets, managers know that they must take corrective action. Thus, financial controls tell managers when a corporate reorganization might be necessary, when they should sell off divisions and exit from businesses, or when they should rethink their corporate-level strategies.[15]

Table 10.1
Four Measures of Financial Performance

Profit Ratios			
Return on investment	=	$\frac{\text{Net profit before taxes}}{\text{Total assets}}$	Measures how well managers are using the organization's resources to generate profits.
Gross profit margin	=	$\frac{\text{Sales revenues} - \text{cost of goods sold}}{\text{Sales revenues}}$	The differences between the amount of revenue generated from the product and the resources used to produce the product.
Liquidity Ratios			
Current ratio	=	$\frac{\text{Current assets}}{\text{Current liabilities}}$	Do managers have resources available to meet claims of short-term creditors?
Quick ratio	=	$\frac{\text{Current assets} - \text{inventory}}{\text{Current liabilities}}$	Can managers pay off claims of short-term creditors without selling inventory?
Leverage Ratios			
Debt-to-assets ratio	=	$\frac{\text{Total debt}}{\text{Total assets}}$	To what extent have managers used borrowed funds to finance investments?
Times-covered ratio	=	$\frac{\text{Profit before interest and taxes}}{\text{Total interest charges}}$	Measures how far profits can decline before managers cannot meet interest changes. If ratio declines to less than 1, the organization is technically insolvent.
Activity Ratios			
Inventory turnover	=	$\frac{\text{Cost of goods sold}}{\text{Inventory}}$	Measures how efficiently managers are turning inventory over so excess inventory is not carried.
Days sales outstanding	=	$\frac{\text{Accounts receivable}}{\frac{\text{Total Sales}}{300}}$	Measures how efficiently managers are collecting revenues from customers to pay expenses.

Although financial information is an important output control, financial information by itself does not provide managers with all the information they need about the four building blocks of competitive advantage. Financial results inform managers about the results of decisions they have already made; they do not tell managers how to find new opportunities to build competitive advantage in the future. To encourage a future-oriented approach, top managers must establish organizational goals that encourage middle and first-line managers to achieve superior efficiency, quality, innovation, and responsiveness to customers.

Organizational Goals

Once top managers consult with lower-level managers, and set the organization's overall goals, they establish performance standards for the divisions and functions. These standards specify for divisional and functional managers the level at which their units must perform if the organization is to achieve its overall goals.[16] Each division is given a set of specific goals to achieve (see Figure 10.4). We saw

Figure 10.4 Organizationwide Goal Setting

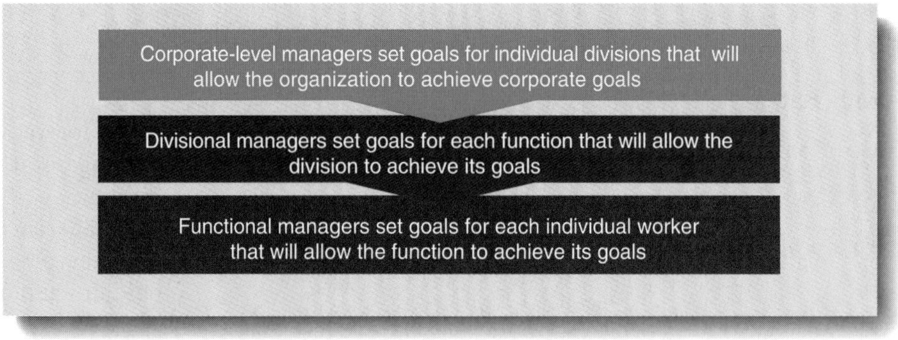

in Chapter 8, for example, that former General Electric CEO Jack Welch and his successor Jeffery Immelt declare that the goal of each division is to be first or second in its industry in profit. Divisional managers then develop a business-level strategy (based on achieving superior efficiency or innovation) that they hope will allow them to achieve that goal.[17] In consultation with functional managers, they specify the functional goals that the managers of different functions need to achieve to allow the division to achieve its goals. For example, sales managers might be evaluated for their ability to increase sales; materials management managers, for their ability to increase the quality of inputs or lower their costs; R&D managers, for the number of products they innovate or the number of patents they receive. In turn, functional managers establish goals that first-line managers and nonmanagerial employees need to achieve to allow the function to achieve its goals.

Output control is used at every level of the organization, and it is vital that the goals set at each level harmonize with the goals set at other levels so that managers and other employees throughout the organization work together to attain the corporate goals that top managers have set.[18] It is also important that goals be set appropriately so that managers are motivated to accomplish them. If goals are set at an impossibly high level, managers might work only half-heartedly to achieve them because they are certain they will fail. In contrast, if goals are set so low that they are too easy to achieve, managers will not be motivated to use all their resources as efficiently and effectively as possible. Research suggests that the best goals are *specific difficult goals*–goals that will challenge and stretch managers' ability but are not out of reach and will not require an impossibly high expenditure of managerial time and energy. Such goals are often called *stretch goals*.

Deciding what is a specific, difficult goal and what is a goal that is too difficult or too easy is a skill that managers must develop. Based on their own judgment and work experience, managers at all levels must assess how difficult a certain task is, and they must assess the ability of a particular subordinate manager to achieve the goal. If they do so successfully, challenging, interrelated goals–goals that reinforce one another and focus on achieving overall corporate objectives–will energize the organization.

operating budget A budget that states how managers intend to use organizational resources to achieve organizational goals.

Operating Budgets

Once managers at each level have been given a goal or target to achieve, the next step in developing an output control system is to establish operating budgets that regulate how managers and workers attain those goals. An **operating budget** is a blueprint that states how managers intend to use organizational resources to achieve organizational goals efficiently. Typically, managers at one level allocate to subordinate managers a specific amount of resources to use to produce goods and services. Once they have been given a budget, these lower-level managers must decide how to allocate money for different organizational activities. They are then evaluated for their ability to stay within the budget and to make the best use of available resources. For example, managers at GE's washing machine division might have a budget of $50 million to spend to develop and sell a new line of washing machines. They must decide how much money to allocate to the various functions such as R&D, engineering, and sales so that the division generates the most customer revenue and makes the biggest profit.

Large organizations often treat each division as a singular or stand-alone responsibility center. Corporate managers then evaluate each division's contribution to corporate performance. Managers of a division may be given a fixed budget for resources and evaluated for the amount of goods or services they can produce using those resources (this is a *cost* or *expense* budget approach). Or managers may be asked to maximize the revenues from the sales of goods and services produced (a *revenue* budget approach). Or managers may be evaluated on the difference between the revenues generated by the sales of goods and services and the budgeted cost of making those goods and services (a *profit* budget approach). Japanese companies' use of operating budgets and challenging goals to increase efficiency is instructive in this context.

In summary, three components–objective financial measures, challenging goals and performance standards, and appropriate operating budgets–are the essence of effective output control. Most organizations develop sophisticated output control systems to allow managers at all levels to keep accurate account of the organization so that they can move quickly to take corrective action as needed.[19] Output control is an essential part of management.

Problems with Output Control

When designing an output control system, managers must be careful to avoid some pitfalls. For example, they must be sure that the output standards they create motivate managers at all levels and do not cause managers to behave in inappropriate ways to achieve organizational goals.

Suppose top managers give divisional managers the goal of doubling profits over a three-year period. This goal seems challenging and reachable when it is jointly agreed upon, and in the first two years profits go up by 70 percent. In the third year, however, an economic recession hits and sales plummet. Divisional managers think it is increasingly unlikely that they will meet their profit goal. Failure will mean losing the substantial monetary bonus tied to achieving the goal. How might managers behave to try to preserve their bonus?

One course of action they might take is to find ways to reduce costs, since profit can be increased either by raising revenues or reducing costs. Thus, divisional managers might cut back on expensive research and development activities, delay maintenance on machinery, reduce marketing expenditures, and lay off middle managers and workers to reduce costs so that at the end of the year they will make their target of doubling profits and receive their bonuses. This tactic might help them achieve a short-run goal–doubling profits–but such actions could hurt long-term profitability or ROI (because a cutback in R&D can reduce the rate of product innovation, a cutback in marketing will lead to the loss of customers, and so on). Problems of this sort occurred at Gillette as described in the next "Management Insight."

Management Insight

Gillette Changes Its Goals and Objectives

In 2001 Gillette Company's new chairman, James M. Kilts, announced that the poorly performing company would not be experiencing a turnaround anytime in the near future. He attributed a large part of Gillette's problems to the overly ambitious sales and profit goals that his predecessor had set for managers of its divisions (razors and toiletries, Braun appliances, and Duracell batteries). To achieve these ambitious sales targets divisional managers had slashed advertising budgets and loaded up on inventory hoping to sell it quickly and generate large revenues. However, this had backfired when customer demand dropped and a recession occurred.

Kilts saw that Gillette's managers had not been focusing on the right way to reduce costs. Because managers' salaries and bonuses were based on their ability to meet the ambitious goals that had been set for them, they had acted with a short-term mindset. Managers had not been thinking about the long-term goal of trying to find the best balance between keeping costs under control, keeping customers happy, and keeping the pipeline of new products full.

Kilts announced that henceforth Gillette would no longer provide specific and unrealistic sales and earning targets that created a "circle of doom" and led managers to behave in just the ways that would prevent them from achieving the goals–by reducing advertising to reduce costs, for example. Henceforth, Kilts decided that Gillette would set long-term goals based on carefully drawn marketing plans that targeted products customers wanted and would lead to long-term sales growth. Also, Gillette would carefully examine its product line to focus its resources on products that offered the most payoff and weed out poorly performing products that did not contribute much to the bottom line. Finally, he announced that Gillette would layoff more than 4,000 employees as a short-term solution to its falling sales and profits. Thus, an unhappy outcome often results when organizations use the wrong set of goals to control and motivate their employees–goals that are too stretching and specific.

As Gillette's experience suggests, long-run effectiveness is what managers should be most concerned about. Thus, managers must consider carefully how flexible they should be when using output control. If conditions change (as they will because of uncertainty in the task and general environments), it is probably better for top managers to communicate to managers lower in the hierarchy that they are aware of the changes taking place and are willing to revise and lower goals and standards. Indeed, many organizations schedule yearly revisions of their five-year plan and goals, and use scenario planning to avoid the problems Gillette experienced.

The message is clear: Although output control is a useful tool for keeping managers and employees at all levels motivated and the organization on track, it is only a guide to appropriate action. Managers must be sensitive to how they use output control and constantly monitor its effects at all levels in the organization.

Behavior Control

Organizational structure by itself does not provide any mechanism that motivates managers and nonmanagerial employees to behave in ways that make the structure work or even improve the way it works–hence the need for control. Put another way, managers can develop an elegant organizational structure with highly appropriate task and reporting relationships, but it will work as designed only if managers also establish control systems that allow them to motivate and shape employee behavior.[20] Output control is one method of motivating employees; behavior control is another method. This section examines three mechanisms of behavior control that managers can use to keep subordinates on track, and make organizational structures work as they are designed to work: direct supervision, management by objectives, and rules and standard operating procedures (see Figure 10.3).

Direct Supervision

The most immediate and potent form of behavior control is direct supervision by managers who actively monitor and observe the behavior of their subordinates, teach subordinates the behaviors that are appropriate and inappropriate, and intervene to take corrective action as needed. Moreover, when managers personally supervise subordinates, they lead by example and in this way can help subordinates develop and increase their own skill levels (leadership is the subject of Chapter 13). Thus, control through personal supervision can be a very effective way of motivating employees and promoting behaviors that increase efficiency and effectiveness.[21]

Nevertheless, certain problems are associated with direct supervision. First, it is very expensive because a manager can personally manage only a small number of subordinates effectively. Therefore, if direct supervision is the main kind of control being used in an organization, a lot of managers will be needed and costs will increase. For this reason, output control is usually preferred to behavior control; indeed, output control tends to be the first type of control that managers at all levels use to evaluate performance.

Second, direct supervision can demotivate subordinates if they feel that they are under such close scrutiny that they are not free to make their own decisions. Moreover, subordinates may start to pass the buck and avoid responsibility if they feel that their manager is waiting in the wings ready to reprimand anyone who makes the slightest error.

Third, as noted previously, for many jobs direct supervision is simply not feasible. The more complex a job is, the more difficult it is for a manager to evaluate how well a subordinate is performing. The performance of divisional and functional managers, for example, can be evaluated only over relatively long time periods (this is why an output control system is developed), so it makes little sense for top managers to continually monitor their performance.

Management by Objectives

To provide a framework within which to evaluate subordinates' behavior and, in particular, to allow managers to monitor progress toward achieving goals, many organizations implement some version of management by objectives (MBO). **Management by objectives** is a system of evaluating subordinates for their ability to achieve specific organizational goals or performance standards and to meet operating budgets.[22] Most organizations make some use of management by objectives because it is pointless to establish goals and then fail to evaluate whether or not they are being achieved. Management by objectives involves three specific steps:

management by objectives A goal-setting process in which a manager and his or her subordinates negotiate specific goals and objectives for the subordinate to achieve and then periodically evaluate the extent to which the subordinate is achieving those goals.

- Step 1: *Specific goals and objectives are established at each level of the organization.*

Management by objective starts when top managers establish overall organizational objectives, such as specific financial performance targets. Then objective setting cascades down throughout the organization as managers at the divisional and functional levels set their objectives to achieve corporate objectives.[23] Finally, first-level managers and workers jointly set objectives that will contribute to achieving functional goals.

- Step 2: *Managers and their subordinates together determine the subordinates' goals.*

An important characteristic of management by objectives is its participatory nature. Managers at every level sit down with the subordinate managers who report directly to them and together they determine appropriate and feasible goals for the subordinate and bargain over the budget that the subordinate will need to achieve his or her goals. The participation of subordinates in the objective-setting process is a way of strengthening their commitment to achieve their goals and meet their budgets.[24] Another reason why it is so important for subordinates (both individuals and teams) to participate in goal setting is so they can tell managers what they think they can realistically achieve.[25]

- Step 3: *Managers and their subordinates periodically review the subordinates' progress toward meeting goals.*

Once specific objectives have been agreed upon for managers at each level, managers are accountable for meeting those objectives. Periodically, they sit down with their subordinates to evaluate their progress. Normally, salary raises and promotions are linked to the goal-setting process, and managers who achieve their goals receive greater rewards than those who fall short. (The issue of how to design reward systems to motivate managers and other organizational employees is discussed in Chapter 10.)

In the companies that have decentralized responsibility for the production of goods and services to empowered teams and cross-functional teams, management by objectives works somewhat differently. Managers ask each team to develop a set of goals and performance targets that the team hopes to achieve–goals that are consistent with organizational objectives. Managers then negotiate with each team to establish its final goals and the budget the team will need to achieve them. The reward system is linked to team performance, not to the performance of any one team member. An interesting example of how IT can be used to manage the MBO process quickly and effectively is discussed in the "Information Technology Byte."

Information Technology Byte

Cypress Semiconductor's On-Line MBO System

In the fast-moving semiconductor business a premium is placed on organizational adaptability. At Cypress Semiconductor CEO T. J. Rodgers was facing a problem. How could he control his growing, 1,500-employee organization without developing a bureaucratic management hierarchy? Rodgers believed that a tall hierarchy hinders the ability of an organization to adapt to changing conditions. He was committed to maintaining a flat and decentralized organizational structure with a minimum of management layers. At the same time, he needed to control his employees to ensure that they perform in a manner consistent with the goals of the company.[26] How could he achieve this without resorting to direct supervision and the management hierarchy that it implies?

Technicians check electronic equipment at Cypress Semiconductor in California. Any delays or problems can be quickly identified and corrected because of the MBO system Cypress CEO, T. J. Rodgers uses to track employee performance.

The solution that Rodgers adopted was to implement a computer-based on-line information system through which he can manage what every employee and team is doing in his fast-moving and decentralized organization. Each employee maintains a list of 10 to 15 goals, such as "Meet with marketing for new product launch" or "Make sure to check with customer X." Noted next to each goal is when it was agreed upon, when it is due to be finished, and whether it has been finished. All of this information is stored on a central computer. Rodgers claims that he can review the goals of all employees in about four hours, and that he does so each week.[27] How is this possible? He manages by exception and looks only for employees who are falling behind. He then calls them, not to scold, but to ask whether there is anything he can do to help them get the job done. It takes only about half an hour each week for employees to review and update their lists. This system allows Rodgers to exercise control over his organization without resorting to the expensive layers of a management hierarchy and direct supervision.

Bureaucratic Control

bureaucratic control Control of behavior by means of a comprehensive system of rules and standard operating procedures.

When direct supervision is too expensive and management by objectives is inappropriate, managers might turn to another mechanism to shape and motivate employee behavior: bureaucratic control. **Bureaucratic control** is control by means of a comprehensive system of rules and standard operating procedures (SOPs) that shape and regulate the behavior of divisions, functions, and individuals. In Chapter 2, we discussed Weber's theory of bureaucracy and noted that all organizations use bureaucratic rules and procedures but some use them more than others.[28]

Rules and SOPs guide behavior and specify what employees are to do when they confront a problem that needs a solution. It is the responsibility of a manager to develop rules that allow employees to perform their activities efficiently and effectively. When employees follow the rules that managers have developed, their behavior is *standardized*–actions are performed the same way time and time again–and the outcomes of their work are predictable. And, to the degree that managers can make employees' behavior predictable, there is no need to monitor the outputs of behavior because standardized behavior leads to standardized outputs.

Suppose a worker at Toyota comes up with a way to attach exhaust pipes that reduces the number of steps in the assembly process and increases efficiency. Always on the lookout for ways to standardize procedures, managers make this idea the basis of a new rule that says: "From now on, the procedure for attaching the exhaust pipe to the car is as follows." If all workers followed the rule to the letter, every car would come off the assembly line with its exhaust pipe attached in the new way, and there would be no need to check exhaust pipes at the end of the line. In practice, mistakes and lapses of attention do happen, so output control is used at the end of the line, and each car's exhaust system is given a routine inspection. However, the number of quality problems with the exhaust system is minimized because the rule (bureaucratic control) is being followed.

Service organizations such as retail stores and fast-food restaurants attempt to standardize the behavior of employees by instructing them on the correct way to greet customers or the appropriate way to serve and bag food. Employees are trained to follow the rules that have proved to be most effective in a particular situation, and the better trained the employees are, the more standardized is their behavior, and the more trust managers can have that outputs (such as food quality) will be consistent. The following "Information Technology Byte" describes the way in which rules and SOPS can help companies perform better and build a competitive advantage even in the supposedly "informal" dot-com industry.

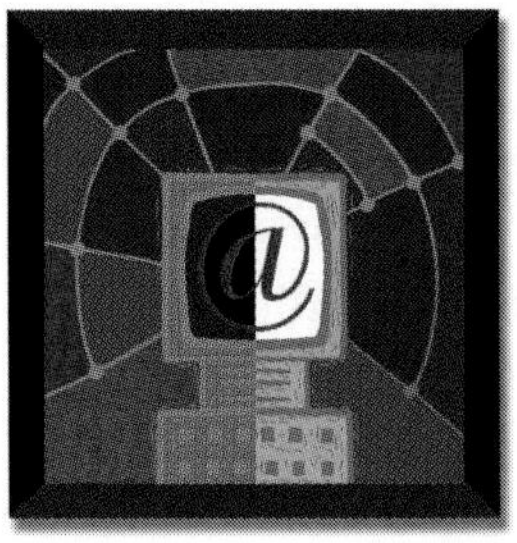

Information Technology Byte

siteROCK's Military Management Runs on Rules

The high tech, dot-com image is not usually associated with the military image. However, managers of the thousands of dot-coms which went belly-up in the early 2000s might have benefited from some military-style discipline. Indeed, a few dot-coms which survived the shakeout did so because their managers used military style procedures to control their employees and ensure high performance. One of these companies is siteROCK based in Emeryville, California, whose COO, Dave Lilly, is an ex-nuclear submarine commander.

siteROCK is in the business of hosting and managing other companies' websites and keeping them up and running and error free. A customer's site that goes down or runs haywire is the major enemy. To maximize the performance of his employees and to increase their ability to respond to unexpected on-line events, Lilly decided that they needed a comprehensive set of rules and standard operating procedures to cover all the major known problems.[29] Lilly insisted that every problem solving procedure should be written down. siteROCK now has over 30 thick binders listing all the processes and checklists that employees need to follow when an unexpected event happens. Their job is to try to solve the problem using these procedures.

Moreover, again drawing from his military experience, Lilly instituted a "two-man rule" that whenever the unexpected happens each employee must immediately tell a co-worker and the two together should attempt to solve the problem. The goal is simple: Use the rules to achieve a quick resolution of a complex issue. If the existing rules don't work, then employees must experiment, and when they find a solution, the solution is turned into a new rule to be included in the procedures book to aid the future decision making of all employees in the organization.

At siteROCK, these written rules and SOPs are used to control employee behavior to achieve high levels of customer service. Because the goal is 100 percent reliability, detailed blueprints guide planning and decision making, not seat-of-the-pants problem solving which might be brilliant 80 percent of the time but result in disaster the rest. Before siteROCK employees are allowed in the control room each day they must read over the most important rules and SOPs. And, at the end of a shift they spend 90 minutes doing paperwork that logs what they have done and states any new or improved rules that they have come up with.

Problems with Bureaucratic Control

siteROCK, like all organizations, makes extensive use of bureaucratic control because rules and SOPs effectively control routine organizational activities. With a bureaucratic control system in place, managers can manage by exception and intervene and take corrective action only when necessary. However, managers need to be aware of a number of problems associated with bureaucratic control, because they can reduce organizational effectiveness.[30]

First, establishing rules is always easier than discarding them. Organizations tend to become overly bureaucratic over time as managers do everything according to the rule book. If the amount of "red tape" becomes too great, decision making slows and managers react slowly to changing conditions. This sluggishness can imperil an organization's survival if agile new competitors emerge. Once a siteROCK employee has found a better rule the old one is discarded.

Second, because rules constrain and standardize behavior and lead people to behave in predictable ways, there is a danger that people become so used to automatically following rules that they stop thinking for themselves. Thus, too much standardization can actually reduce the level of learning taking place in an organization and get the organization off track if managers and workers focus on the wrong issues. An organization thrives when its members are constantly thinking of new ways to increase efficiency, quality, and customer responsiveness. By definition, new ideas do not come from blindly following standardized procedures. Similarly, the pursuit of innovation implies a commitment by managers to discover new ways of doing things; innovation, however, is incompatible with the use of extensive bureaucratic control.

Managers must therefore be sensitive about the way they use bureaucratic control. It is most useful when organizational activities are routine and well understood and when employees are making programmed decisions such as in mass-production settings or in a routine service setting of stores such as Ford, Target, or Midas Muffler. Bureaucratic control is much less useful in situations where nonprogrammed decisions have to be made and managers have to react quickly to changes in the organizational environment.

To use output control and behavior control, managers must be able to identify the outcomes they want to achieve and the behaviors they want employees to perform to achieve these outcomes. For many of the most important and significant organizational activities, however, output control and behavior control are inappropriate for several reasons:

- A manager cannot evaluate the performance of workers such as doctors, research scientists, or engineers by observing their behavior on a day-to-day basis.
- Rules and SOPs are of little use in telling a doctor how to respond to an emergency situation or a scientist how to discover something new.
- Output controls such as the amount of time a surgeon takes for each operation or the costs of making a discovery are very crude measures of the quality of performance.

How can managers attempt to control and regulate the behavior of their subordinates when personal supervision is of little use, when rules cannot be developed to tell employees what to do, and when outputs and goals cannot be measured at all or can be measured usefully only over long periods? One source of control increasingly being used by organizations is a strong organizational culture.

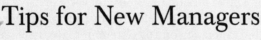

Tips for New Managers

Control

1. Identify the source(s) of an organization's competitive advantage (efficiency, quality, innovation, and customer responsiveness). Then design control systems that allow managers to evaluate how well they are building competitive advantage.
2. Involve employees in the goal-setting process and make MBO an organizationwide activity.
4. Choose the right balance of direct supervision and bureaucratic controls to allow managers to monitor progress toward goals and to take corrective action as needed.
5. Periodically evaluate the output and behavior control system to keep it aligned with your current strategy and structure.

Organizational Culture and Clan Control

Organizational culture is another important control system that regulates and governs employee attitudes and behavior. As we discussed in Chapters 3 and 5, **organizational culture** is the set of values, norms, standards of behavior, and common expectations that control the ways in which individuals and groups in an organization interact with each other and work to achieve organizational goals. **Clan control** is the control exerted on individuals and groups in an organization by shared values, norms, standards of behavior, and expectations. Organizational culture is not an externally imposed system of constraints, such as direct supervision or rules and pro-

organizational culture The set of values, norms, standards of behavior, and common expectations that control the ways in which individuals and groups in an organization interact with each other and work to achieve organizational goals.

clan control The control exerted on individuals and groups in an organization by shared values, norms, standards of behavior, and expectations.

cedures. Rather, employees internalize organizational values and norms, and then let these values and norms guide their decisions and actions. Just as people in society at large generally behave in accordance with socially acceptable values and norms–such as the norm that people should line up at the checkout counters in supermarkets–so are individuals in an organizational setting mindful of force of organizational values and norms.

Organizational culture is an important source of control for two reasons. First, it makes control possible in situations where managers cannot use output or behavior control. Second and more important, when a strong and cohesive set of organizational values and norms is in place, employees focus on thinking about what is best for the organization in the long run–all their decisions and actions become oriented toward helping the organization perform well. For example, a teacher spends personal time after school coaching and counseling students; an R&D scientist works 80 hours a week, evenings, and weekends, to help speed up a late project; a sales clerk at a department store runs after a customer who left a credit card at the cash register. Many researchers and managers believe that employees of some organizations go out of their way to help their organization because the organization has a strong and cohesive organizational culture–a culture that controls employee attitudes and behaviors.

Values and Norms: Creating a Strong Organizational Culture

In Chapter 6, we discussed values and norms in the context of national culture. *Values* are beliefs and ideas about the kinds of goals members of a society should pursue and about the kinds or modes of behavior people should use to achieve these goals.[31] *Norms* are unwritten, informal rules or guidelines that prescribe appropriate behavior in particular situations. Norms emerge from values.[32] In an organization, values and norms inform organizational members about what goals they should pursue and how they should behave to reach those goals. Thus, values and norms perform the same function as formal goals, written rules, or direct supervision.

Managers can influence the kinds of values and norms that develop in an organization. Some managers might cultivate values and norms that let subordinates know that they are welcome to perform their roles in innovative, creative ways and to be innovative and entrepreneurial, willing to experiment and go out on a limb even if there is a significant chance of failure. Top managers at organizations such as Intel, Microsoft, and Sun Microsystems encourage employees to adopt such values to support their commitment to innovation as a source of competitive advantage.

Other managers, however, might cultivate values and norms that let employees know that they should always be conservative and cautious in their dealings with others and should always consult with their superiors before making important decisions and should always put their actions in writing so they can be held accountable for whatever happens. In any setting where caution is needed–nuclear power stations, large oil refineries, chemical plants, financial institutions, insurance companies–a conservative, cautious approach to making decisions might be highly appropriate.[33] In a nuclear power plant, for example, the catastrophic consequences of a mistake make a high level of supervision vital. Similarly, in a bank or mutual fund company the risk of losing investors' money also makes a cautious approach to investing highly appropriate.

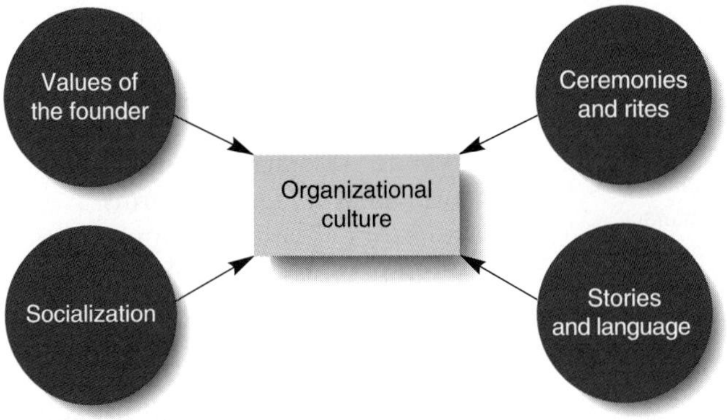

Figure 10.5 Factors Creating a Strong Organizational Culture

The managers of different kinds of organizations may deliberately cultivate and develop the organizational values and norms that are best suited to their task and general environments, strategy, or technology. Organizational culture is transmitted to organizational members through the values of the founder, the process of socialization, ceremonies and rites, and stories and language (see Figure 10.5).

VALUES OF THE FOUNDER One manager who has a very important impact on the kind of organizational culture that emerges in an organization is the founder. An organization's founder and his or her personal values and beliefs have a substantial influence on the values, norms, and standards of behavior that develop over time within the organization.[34] Founders set the scene for the way cultural values and norms develop because they hire other managers to help them run their organizations. It is reasonable to assume that founders select managers who share their vision of the organization's goals and what it should be doing; in any case, new managers quickly learn from the founder what values and norms are appropriate in the organization and thus what is desired of them. Subordinates imitate the style of the founder and, in turn, transmit his or her values and norms to their subordinates. Gradually over time, the founder's values and norms permeate the organization.[35]

A founder who requires a great display of respect from subordinates and insists on proprieties such as formal job titles and formal modes of dress encourages subordinates to act in this way toward their subordinates. Often, a founder's personal values affect an organization's competitive advantage. For example, McDonald's founder Ray Kroc insisted from the beginning on high standards of customer service and cleanliness at McDonald's restaurants; these became core sources of McDonald's competitive advantage. Similarly, Bill Gates, the founder of Microsoft, pioneered certain cultural values in Microsoft. Employees are expected to be creative and to work hard, but they are encouraged to dress informally and to personalize their offices. Gates also established a host of company events such as cookouts, picnics, and sports events to emphasize to employees the importance of being both an individual and a team player.

organizational socialization The process by which newcomers learn an organization's values and norms and acquire the work behaviors necessary to perform jobs effectively.

SOCIALIZATION Over time, organizational members learn from each other which values are important in an organization and the norms that specify appropriate and inappropriate behaviors. Eventually, organizational members behave in accordance with the organization's values and norms–often without realizing they are doing so. **Organizational socialization** is the process by which newcomers learn an organization's values and norms and acquire the work behaviors necessary to perform jobs effectively.[36] As a result of their socialization experiences, organizational members internalize an organization's

Texas A&M's Fish Camp is an annual orientation program designed to help freshmen (or Fish) make the transition from high school to college life. Texas A&M's Fish Camp runs for four days and is attended by over 4,500 freshmen each year.

values and norms and behave in accordance with them not only because they think they have to but because they think that these values and norms describe the right and proper way to behave.[37]

At Texas A&M University, for example, all new students are encouraged to go to "Fish Camp" to learn how to be an "Aggie" (the traditional nickname of students at the university). They learn about the ceremonies that have developed over time to commemorate significant events or people in A&M's history. In addition, they learn the way to behave at football games and in class and what it means to be an Aggie. As a result of this highly organized socialization program, by the time new students arrive on campus and start their first semester they have been socialized into what a Texas A&M student is supposed to do, and they have relatively few problems adjusting to the college environment.

Most organizations have some kind of socialization program to help new employees learn the ropes–the values, norms, and culture of that organization. The military, for example, is well known for the rigorous socialization process it uses to turn raw recruits into trained soldiers. Organizations such as Arthur Andersen also put new recruits through a rigorous training program to provide them with the knowledge they need not only to perform well in their jobs but also to represent the company to its clients. New recruits attend a six-week training program at Arthur Andersen's Chicago training center, where they learn from experienced organizational members how to behave and what they should be doing. Thus, through the organizational socialization program, the founder and top managers of an organization can transmit to employees the cultural values and norms that shape the behavior of organizational members.

CEREMONIES AND RITES Another way in which managers can attempt to create or influence an organizational culture is by developing organizational ceremonies and rites–formal events that recognize incidents of importance to the organization as a whole and to specific employees.[38] The most common rites that organizations use to transmit cultural norms and values to their members are rites of passage, of integration, and of enhancement (see Table 10.2).[39]

Table 10.2
Organizational Rites

Type of Rite	Example of Rite	Purpose of Rite
Rite of passage	Induction and basic training	Learn and internalize norms and values
Rite of integration	Office Christmas party	Build common norms and values
Rite of enhancement	Presentation of annual award	Motivate commitment to norms and values

Rites of passage determine how individuals enter, advance within, or leave the organization. The socialization programs developed by military organizations (such as the U.S. Army) or by large accountancy firms (such as Arthur Andersen) described above are rites of passage. Likewise, the ways in which an organization prepares people for promotion or retirement are rites of passage.

Rites of integration, such as shared announcements of organizational successes, office parties, and company cookouts, build and reinforce common bonds among organizational members. Southwest Airlines is well known for its efforts to develop ceremonies and rituals to bond employees to the organization by showing them that they are valued members. Southwest holds cookouts in the parking lot of its Dallas headquarters, and Herb Kelleher, its founder personally attends each employee Christmas party throughout the country. Because there are so many Christmas parties to attend, Kelleher often finds himself attending parties in July!

A company's annual meeting also may be used as a ritual of integration, offering an opportunity to communicate organizational values to managers, other employees, and shareholders. Wal-Mart, for example, makes its annual stockholders' meeting an extravagant ceremony that celebrates the company's success. The company often flies thousands of its highest-performing employees to its annual meeting at its Bentonville, Arkansas, headquarters for a huge weekend entertainment festival complete with performances by country and western stars. Wal-Mart believes that entertainment that rewards its supporters reinforces the company's high-performance values and culture. The proceedings are shown live over closed-circuit television in all Wal-Mart stores so that all employees can join in the rites celebrating the company's achievements.[40]

Rites of enhancement, such as awards dinners, newspaper releases, and employee promotions, let organizations publicly recognize and reward employees' contributions and thus strengthen their commitment to organizational values. By bonding members within the organization, rites of enhancement help promote clan control.

STORIES AND LANGUAGE Stories and language also communicate organizational culture. Stories (whether fact or fiction) about organizational heroes and villains and their actions provide important clues about values and norms. Such stories can reveal the kinds of behaviors that are valued by the organization and the kinds of practices that are frowned on.[41] Nokia provides a particularly good example of a company whose stories and language form an integral part of its culture.

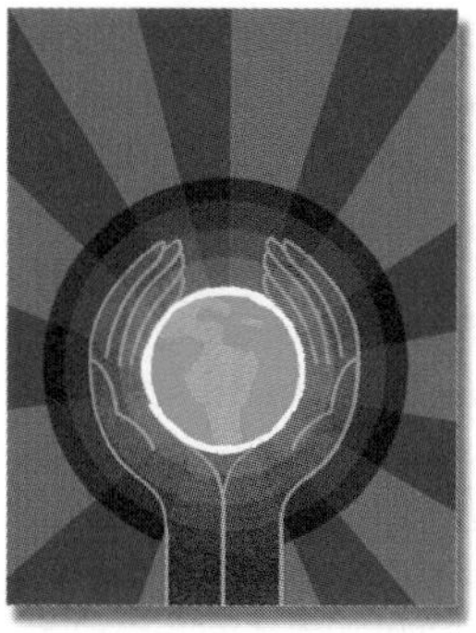

Managing Globally

Nokia's Finnish Ways

Nokia is now the world's largest wireless phone maker and has more than a 30 percent share of the global market. It was not until 1992 that the company decided to focus on the wireless phone business and in less than a decade it has beat out global giants like Motorola, Seimens, Qualcomm, and Erickson to become the number one player in the market. Nokia's managers believe that the secret of its success lies in its organizational and national culture–in the stories and language of the company itself and the country in which it is headquartered, Finland.[42]

Nokia's president, Matti Alahuhta, believes that Nokia's cultural values are based on the Finnish character: Finns are down-to-earth, rational, and straightforward people. They are also very friendly and democratic people who do not believe in a rigid hierarchy based either on a person's authority or social class. Nokia's culture reflects these values because innovation and decision making is pushed right down to the bottom line, to teams of employees who take up the challenge of developing the ever smaller and more sophisticated phones for which the company is known. Bureaucracy is kept to a minimum at Nokia, its culture is based on informal and personal relationships and norms of cooperation and teamwork.

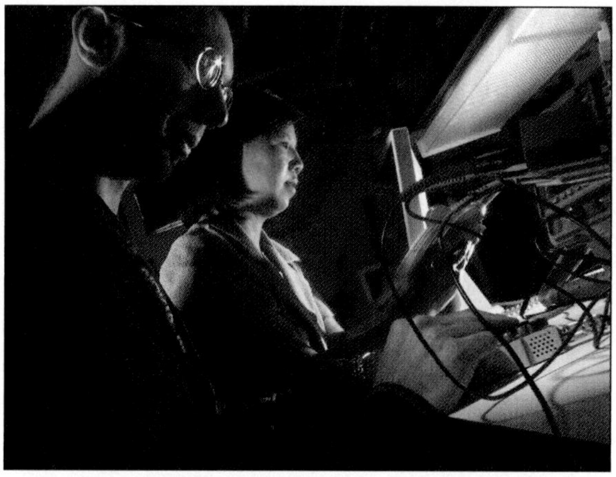

Nokia employees, such as those shown here, are bound together by the "Nokia Way," a system of cultural values and norms that isn't written down, but is always present.

To help strengthen its culture Nokia has built a futuristic open plan steel and glass building just outside Helsinki. Here in an open environment its research and development people can work together to innovate new kinds of wireless phones. More than one out of every three of Nokia's 60,000 employees works in research; what keeps these people together and focused is Nokia's company mission to produce phones that are better, cheaper, smaller, and easier to use.[43] This is the "Nokia Way" a system of cultural values and norms that can't be written down but is always present in the values that cement people together and in the language and stories that its members use to orient themselves to the company.

McDonald's also has a rich culture at the heart of which are hundreds of stories that organizational members tell about founder Ray Kroc. Most of these stories focus on how Kroc established the strict operating values and norms that are at the heart of McDonald's culture. Kroc was dedicated to achieving perfection in McDonald's quality, service, cleanliness, and value for the money (QSC&V); therefore, these four central values permeate McDonald's culture. One story told in McDonald's illustrates well how Kroc went about socializing McDonald's employees to these values.

One day Kroc and a group of managers from the Houston region were touring various restaurants. One of the restaurants was having a bad day operationally. Ray was incensed about the long lines of customers, and he was furious when he realized that the product customers were receiving that day was not up to his high standards. To address the problem, he jumped up and stood on the front counter and got the attention of all customers and operating crew personnel. He introduced himself, apologized for the long wait and cold food, and told the customers that they could have freshly cooked food or their money back–whichever they wanted. As a result, the customers left happy, and when Kroc checked on the restaurant later, he found that his message had gotten through to its managers and crew–performance had improved. Other stories describe Kroc scrubbing dirty toilets and picking up litter inside or outside a restaurant. These and similar stories are spread around the organization by McDonald's employees. They are the stories that have helped establish Kroc as McDonald's "hero."

Because spoken language is a principal medium of communication in organizations, the characteristic slang or jargon–that is, organization-specific words or phrases–that people use to frame and describe events provides important clues about norms and values. "McLanguage," for example, is prevalent at all levels of McDonald's. A McDonald's employee described as having "ketchup in their blood" is someone who is truly dedicated to the McDonald's way–someone who has been completely socialized to its culture. McDonald's has an extensive training program teaching new employees "McDonald's speak," and new employees are welcomed into the family with a formal orientation that illustrates Kroc's dedication to QSC&V.

The concept of organizational language encompasses not only spoken language but how people dress, the offices they occupy, the cars they drive, and the degree of formality they use when they address one another. Casual dress reflects and reinforces Microsoft's entrepreneurial culture and values. Formal business attire supports Arthur Andersen's conservative culture, which emphasizes the importance of conforming to organizational norms such as respect for authority and staying within one's prescribed role. Traders in the Chicago Futures and Options trading pits frequently wear garish and flamboyant ties and jackets to make their presence known in a sea of faces. The demand for magenta, lime green, and silver lamé jackets featuring bold images such as the Power Rangers–anything that helps the traders stand out and attract customers–is enormous.[44] When employees speak and understand the language of their organization's culture, they know how to behave in the organization and what attitudes are expected of them.

Culture and Managerial Action

The way in which organizational culture shapes and controls employee behavior is evident in the way managers perform their four main functions: planning, organizing, leading, and controlling. As we consider these functions, we continue to distinguish between top managers who create organizational values and norms that encourage creative, innovative behavior and top managers who encourage a conservative, cautious approach by their subordinates. We noted earlier that both kinds of values and norms may be appropriate in different situations.

PLANNING Top managers in an organization with an innovative culture are likely to encourage lower-level managers to participate in the planning process and develop a flexible approach to planning. They are likely to be willing to listen to new ideas and to take risks involving the development of new products. In contrast, top managers in an organization with conservative values are likely to emphasize formal top-down planning. Suggestions from lower-level managers are likely to be subjected to a formal review process, which can significantly slow decision making. Although this deliberate approach may improve the quality of decision making in a nuclear power plant, it can have unintended consequences. In the past, at conservative IBM, the planning process became so formalized that managers spent most of their time assembling complex slide shows and overheads to defend their current positions rather than thinking about what they should be doing to keep IBM abreast of the changes taking place in the computer industry. When CEO Lou Gerstner took over, he used every means at his disposal to abolish this culture, even building a brand new campus-style headquarters to change managers' mindsets.

ORGANIZING What kinds of organizing will managers in innovative and in conservative cultures encourage? Valuing creativity, managers in innovative cultures are likely to try to create an organic structure, one that is flat with few levels in the hierarchy, and in which authority is decentralized so that employees are encouraged to work together to find solutions to ongoing problems. A product team structure may be very suitable for an organization with an innovative culture. In contrast, managers in a conservative culture are likely to create a well-defined hierarchy of authority and establish clear reporting relationships so that employees know exactly whom to report to and how to react to any problems that arise.

LEADING In an innovative culture, managers are likely to lead by example, encouraging employees to take risks and experiment. They are supportive regardless of whether employees succeed or fail. In contrast managers in a conservative culture are likely to use management by objectives and to constantly monitor subordinates' progress toward goals, overseeing their every move. We examine leadership in detail in Chapter 13 when we examine the leadership styles that managers can adopt to influence and shape employee behavior.

CONTROLLING As this chapter makes clear, there are many control systems that managers can adopt to shape and influence employee behavior. The control systems they choose represent a choice about how they want to motivate organizational members and keep them focused on organizational goals. Managers who want to encourage the development of innovative values and norms that encourage risk taking choose output and behavior controls that match this objective. They are likely to choose output controls that measure performance over the long run and develop a flexible MBO system suited to the long and uncertain process of innovation. In contrast, managers who want to encourage the development of conservative values choose the opposite combination of output and behavior controls. They develop specific, difficult goals for subordinates, frequently monitor progress toward these goals, and develop a clear set of rules that subordinates are expected to adhere to.

The values and norms of an organization's culture strongly affect the way managers perform their management functions. The extent to which managers buy into the values and norms of their organization shapes their view of the world and their actions and decisions in particular circumstances.[45] In turn, the actions that managers take can have an impact on the performance of the organization. Thus, organizational culture, managerial action, and organizational performance are linked together.

This linkage is apparent at Hewlett-Packard (HP), a leader in the electronic instrumentation and computer industries. Established in the 1940s, HP developed a culture that is an outgrowth of the strong personal beliefs of the company's founders, William Hewlett and David Packard. Bill and Dave, as they are known within the company, formalized HP's culture in 1957 in a statement of corporate objectives known as the "HP Way," discussed in Chapter 2. The basic values informing the HP Way stress serving everyone who has a stake in the company with integrity and fairness, including customers, suppliers, employees, stockholders, and society in general. Bill and Dave helped build this culture within HP by hiring like-minded people and by letting the HP Way guide their own actions as managers. One outgrowth of their commitment to employees was a policy that HP would not be a "hire and fire company." This principle was severely tested on several occasions most recently in 2001 when declines in its business forced the company to ask employees to take early retirement, unpaid leave, and cuts in salaries. Tens of thousands of HP employees signed up for pay cuts and the company was able to avoid layoffs unlike other companies which have laid off many employees.[46] The linkage among organizational culture, managerial actions, and organizational performance is also evident at Merck, as discussed next.

Ethics in Action

Merck & Co. Develops a Free Treatment for River Blindness

Merck & Co. is one of the largest producers of prescription drugs in the world. Much of Merck's success can be attributed to its ability to attract the very best research scientists who come because its corporate culture nurtures scientists and emphasizes value and norms of innovation. Scientists are given great freedom to pursue intriguing ideas even if the commercial payoff is questionable. Moreover, researchers are inspired to think of their work as a quest to alleviate human disease and suffering worldwide and Merck has a reputation as an ethical company that has values that put people above profits. As George Merck, son of the company's founder and its former chairman, said: "We try never to forget that medicine is for the people . . . It is not for the profits. The profits follow . . . they have never failed to appear."

In 1978, Dr. Roy Vagelos, director of Merck's research labs, received a memo from a senior research scientist, Dr. William Campbell. Campbell thought that a compound that Merck was developing to treat parasites in cattle–Ivermectin–could be effective against river blindness, a parasitic disease that by 1978 was plaguing around 18 million people and had blinded more than 340,000, principally in Africa. Both Vagelos and Campbell knew that developing a treatment would be costly. Moreover, even if Merck succeeded, it seemed unlikely that the afflicted Third World populations would be able to afford the drug. Vagelos, however, felt that failure to investigate such a promising drug candidate was counter to Merck's ethical values and could demoralize Merck's scientists. So he authorized funds to support the development of a drug from Ivermectin.

Nearly 10 years and $50 million later, Merck received regulatory approval for the treatment, called Mectizan. Merck hoped that an agency such as the U.S. government or the World Health Organization would provide aid to help the company recoup its costs by paying the $3 per year dose fee for the drug treatment. However, no aid materialized, and in 1987 Merck announced that it would donate Mectizan free of charge to anyone who needed the drug. In 1997 alone, approximately 18 million people were treated with Mectizan in the areas of the world most affected by river blindness.[47]

Although the Hewlett-Packard and Merck examples indicate that organizational culture can give rise to managerial actions that ultimately benefit the organization, this is not always the case. The cultures of some organizations become dysfunctional and encourage managerial actions that harm the organization and discourage actions that might lead to an improvement in performance.[48] For example, Sunflower Electric Power Corporation, a generation and transmission cooperative, almost went bankrupt in 2000. A state committee of inquiry set up to find out the source of the problem put the blame on its CEO. They decided that he had created an abusive culture based on fear and blame that encouraged managers to fight over and protect their turf. Managers were afraid to rock the boat or make suggestions, they could not predict what would happen to them. The CEO was fired and a new CEO, Chris Hauck, was appointed to change the cooperative's culture. He found it very hard too, his senior managers were so used to the old value and norms. One top manager, for example, frequently engaged in the practice of berating one supervisor until the man became physically sick.[49] Hauck fired this and other managers as a signal that such behavior would no longer be tolerated. With the help of consultants he went about the slow process of changing values and norms to emphasize cooperation, teamwork, and respect for others. Clearly, managers can influence the way their organizational culture develops over time.[50]

Summary and Review

WHAT IS ORGANIZATIONAL CONTROL? Controlling is the process whereby managers monitor and regulate how efficiently and effectively an organization and its members are performing the activities necessary to achieve organizational goals. Controlling is a four-step process: (1) establishing performance standards, (2) measuring actual performance, (3) comparing actual performance against performance standards, and (4) evaluating the results and initiating corrective action if needed.

OUTPUT CONTROL To monitor output or performance, managers choose goals or performance standards that they think will best measure efficiency, quality, innovation, and responsiveness to customers at the corporate, divisional, departmental or functional, and individual levels. The main mechanisms that managers use to monitor output are financial measures of performance, organizational goals, and operating budgets.

BEHAVIOR CONTROL In an attempt to shape behavior and induce employees to work toward achieving organizational goals, managers utilize direct supervision, management by objectives, and bureaucratic control by means of rules and standard operating procedures.

ORGANIZATIONAL CULTURE Organizational culture is the set of values, norms, standards of behavior, and common expectations that control the ways individuals and groups in an organization interact with each other and work to achieve organizational goals. Clan control is the control exerted on individuals and groups by shared values, norms, standards of behavior, and expectations. Organizational culture is transmitted to employees through the values of the founder, the process of socialization, organizational ceremonies and rites, and stories and language. The way managers perform their management functions influences the kind of culture that develops in an organization.

Management in Action

Topics for Discussion and Action

1. What is the relationship between organizing and controlling?
2. How do output control and behavior control differ?
3. Ask a manager to list the main performance measures that he or she uses to evaluate how well the organization is achieving its goals.
4. Ask the same or a different manager to list the main forms of output control and behavior control that he or she uses to monitor and evaluate employee behavior.
5. Why is it important for managers to involve subordinates in the control process?
6. What is organizational culture, and how does it affect the way employees behave?
7. Interview some employees of an organization, and ask them about the organization's values, norms, socialization practices, ceremonies and rites, and special language and stories. Referring to this information, describe the organization's culture.
8. What kind of controls would you expect to find most used in (a) a hospital, (b) the Navy, (c) a city police force. Why?

Building Management Skills

Understanding Controlling

For this exercise you will analyze the control systems used by a real organization such as a department store, restaurant, hospital, police department, or small business. It can be the organization that you investigated in Chapter 8 or a different one. Your objective is to uncover all the different ways in which managers monitor and evaluate the performance of the organization and employees.

1. At what levels does control take place in this organization?
2. Which output performance standards (such as financial measures and organizational goals) do managers use most often to evaluate performance at each level?
3. Does the organization have a management by objectives system in place? If it does, describe it. If it does not, speculate about why not.
4. How important is behavior control in this organization? For example, how much of managers' time is spent directly supervising employees? How formalized is the organization? Do employees receive a book of rules to instruct them about how to perform their jobs?
5. What kind of culture does the organization have? What are the values and norms? Do employees tell any particular stories that reveal the organization's norms and values? What effect does the organizational culture have on the way employees behave or treat customers?
6. Based on this analysis, do you think there is a fit between the organization's control systems and its culture? What is the nature of this fit? How could it be improved?

Small Group Breakout Exercise

How Best to Control the Sales Force?

Form groups of three or four people, and appoint one member as the spokesperson who will communicate your findings to the whole class when called on by the instructor. Then discuss the following scenario.

You are the regional sales managers of an organization that supplies high-quality windows and doors to building supply centers nationwide. Over the last three years, the rate of sales growth has slackened. There is increasing evidence that, to make their jobs easier, salespeople are primarily servicing large customer accounts and ignoring small accounts. In addition, the salespeople are not dealing promptly with customer questions and complaints, and this inattention has resulted in a drop in after-sales service. You have talked about these problems, and you are meeting to design a control system to increase both the amount of sales and the quality of customer service.

1. Design a control system that you think will best motivate salespeople to achieve these goals.
2. What relative importance do you put on (a) output control, (b) behavior control, and (c) organizational culture in this design?

Exploring the World Wide Web

Search for the website of a company that actively uses organizational culture (or one of the other types of control) to build competitive advantage. What kind of values and norms is the culture based on? How does it affect employee behavior?

You're the Management Consultant

You have been called in to advise the managers in charge of teams of web-design and web-hosting specialists and programmers. Each team is working on a different aspect of website production and while each is responsible for the quality of their own performance, their performance also depends on how well the other teams perform. You are meeting to design a control system that will be used to motivate and reward all the teams. Your objective is to create a control system that will help to increase the performance of each team separately and facilitate cooperation between the teams, something that is necessary because the various projects are interlinked and affect one another—just as the different parts of the car must fit together. Since competition in the website production market is intense, it is imperative that the website be up and running as quickly as possible and incorporate all the latest advances in website software technology.

Questions

1. What kind of outputs controls will best facilitate positive interactions both within the teams and between the teams?
2. What kind of behavior controls will best facilitate positive interactions both within the teams and between the teams?
3. How would you go about helping managers develop a culture to promote high team performance?

BusinessWeek

Cases in the News

Warm and Fuzzy Won't Save Procter & Gamble

Procter and Gamble Co. employees, particularly those in management, are breathing a sigh of relief. "Crazy Man Durk"—known to the outside world as Durk I. Jager, CEO and chairman—is out, having resigned under pressure from the board. "Gentleman John" E. Pepper, P&G's CEO until 1998, and Alan "A.G." Lafley, a man known for his people skills, are in charge. Who says nice guys finish last?

Unfortunately, the elation at one of the nation's biggest packaged-goods producers is destined to be short-lived. For all his abrasive ways—and his failure, in 17 months at the helm, to bring about a real turnaround—Jager may have been the company's best hope for recovery. Without him, P&G is likely to remain an entrenched bureaucracy with the same bottom-line problems it has struggled with for a decade.

At first blush, P&G does not look like a company on the road to recovery. Jager recently conceded that he would not fulfill his promise of a 15 percent growth in profits for the quarter, and P&G will fall below target the next two quarters as well. And since January, shares have collapsed from $118 to $56.

Not Enough

Egged on by a short-term-minded Wall Street, however, P&G pulled the plug too soon on what could have been the company's turnaround. Jager had less than two years to implement massive changes in a rigidly structured company. That was clearly not enough.

While major brands such as Tide, Ivory, and Pampers may have shown only meager growth, Jager had some successes. The purchase of Iams premium dog food, for example, is looking like a hit. P&G took this $800 million private brand and began shipping it to its vast array of supermarket customers. Market share has grown; sales should hit $1 billion for the year ending in June. Says Jim Holbrook, a P&G alum and now president of the Zipatoni Group consulting firm: "This is a high-margin, high-turn business, and Jager saw a way to take it to the mass market."

Dog food is not the only bright spot. Jager also wins praise from otherwise critical analysts for creating global identities for his brands while still allowing local execs to determine marketing tactics. The practice is showing some promise in North America. In recent months, P&G has won back market share in hair care, detergent, and toilet paper lines. "He changed the company from one that was inwardly focused on cost efficiencies to one outwardly focused on gaining global market share," says William Steele, an analyst at Bane America Securities.

To achieve this, Jager, confronting a roster of old-line, slow-growing products, became almost obsessed with new-product development. He ramped up R&D, cut in half the time it took P&G to introduce new products, and doubled the rate of launches. It took Jager's P&G 18 months instead of the typical three years to launch Swiffer, its electrostatic dust mop. The first year out, P&G sold a stunning $400 million worth.

All this required Jager to attack what is probably P&G's most serious problem: its entrenched, risk-averse culture. He torpedoed the old-fashioned international network of 144 regional managers and reorganized the company into seven global business units built around product lines. That process broke up decades-old fiefdoms and gave P&G the ability to respond more quickly and efficiently to global trends. The move was praised by customers such as Wal-Mart Stores. He also encouraged managers to leave behind the company's traditional consensus management, to be more innovative, and to take more risks.

Unfortunately for Jager, the benefits of this restructuring have not worked their way to the bottom line yet. The investments in acquisitions, research and development, and marketing of new products all hit earnings hard. To counterbalance all the spending, plans to cut 15,000 jobs and close 10 plants were in progress. But they were not expected to produce savings until 2001. In the face of his extensive cash outlays, however, Jager made a major error by promising Wall Street double-digit earnings gains by this spring. It was the second time in his short reign that he failed to meet expectations—unforgivable by today's market standards.

Some of this might have been overlooked if Jager had been a different man, certainly if he had been a different leader. He didn't play up to Wall Street analysts or investors, and his abrasive style cost him support from managers and rank-and-file employees. Many of them have the added power of being company stockholders.

"By Your Sword"

In the consensus-building atmosphere of P&G, lack of popular support is the kiss of death, says John Bissell, a former P&G brand manager now at Gundersen Partners, a management consulting firm. "If you are a well-liked member of the management community, you're given some leeway if you make a mistake or two," he says. "But if you are disliked and people are rebelling under your leadership, you live and die by your sword."

By the end, the combination added up to a corporate rejection of Jager and everything he stood for—even to the most petty detail: While other ex-chiefs such as Edward Arnst and John Pepper maintained offices at Cincinnati headquarters, Jager will get no such perk. The P&G Establishment wants him gone. With him will go much of the change that could eventually have made a difference.

Now, P&G is in what can only be described as retreat. Lafley has already said the company changed too much, too fast, and he plans to reverse the trend. A dozen new product launches already on the calendar are being reconsidered, he says. Pepper—who stepped aside two years ago when management decided new, tough changes were called for—is also back. But revisiting the good old days of the 1990s at P&G isn't much of a formula for growth either.

Source: Ellen Neuborne and Robert Berner, "Warm and Fuzzy Won't Save Procter & Gamble," *Business Week,* June 26, 2000, pp. 48–49.

Questions

1. What were the values and norms in Procter & Gamble's culture before Jager? How did they affect its performance?
2. How did Jager change Procter & Gamble's culture? Why was he forced out of the company?
3. How has Procter & Gamble been performing recently?

Chapter 11

Human Resource Management

Learning Objectives

After studying this chapter, you should be able to:

- Explain why strategic human resource management can help an organization gain a **competitive advantage.**
- Describe the **steps managers take to recruit and select** organizational members.
- Discuss the **training and development** options that ensure organizational members can effectively perform their jobs.
- Explain why **performance appraisal and feedback** is such a crucial activity, and list the choices managers must make in designing effective performance appraisal and feedback procedures.
- Explain the issues managers face in **determining levels of pay and benefits.**

A Manager's Challenge

Managing Human Resources at Trilogy Software

How can managers effectively recruit, train, and integrate new hires in rapidly growing organizations?

A key managerial challenge in rapidly growing organizations is finding new hires to fill the ever increasing need for human resources, and then assuring that they get up to speed quickly and make real contributions within their first several months on the job. This is easier said than done, unless, of course, you are Joe Liemandt, CEO of Trilogy Software headquartered in Austin, Texas. Liemandt and four other Stanford University students founded Trilogy in 1989 and the rest has been, literally, history.[1] Trilogy currently has more than 1,400 employees in Austin, Boston, and Paris who provide e-business solutions to clients as well as technical training and consulting worldwide. For large companies such as IBM, Hewlett-Packard, Motorola, and Boeing, Trilogy also designs software that enables salespeople to not only configure products to meet their customers' unique needs but also price the products on their laptops. In 2000, Trilogy managers increased the size of the workforce by 45 percent by hiring 450 employees to join the existing 1,000 employees; annual revenues are in the $200 million range.[2]

Trilogy chief recruiter Jeff Daniel (right) and star interviewer Graham Hesselroth show their Trilogy spirit.

Successfully integrating a high percentage of new hires into an organization on an annual basis is a challenge in any industry, and perhaps more so in one that is both rapidly changing and technology-intensive. How do managers at Trilogy do it? Essentially, by painstaking efforts to effectively manage people, Trilogy's most important resource.

Early on, managers at Trilogy realized that they would need to hire the best and the brightest to maintain their competitive advantage. To this end, they spare no expense in finding and hiring top talent from universities around the country. Once they find prospective employees, they engage in a full court press to attract them to Trilogy. Trilogy recruits at around 20 universities including Stanford, MIT, the University of Pennsylvania, and the University of Michigan. While some new hires have masters and even doctoral degrees, the majority of recruits have recently received their bachelors degrees (many majoring in computer science but also some in the social sciences and liberal arts).[3]

Early on, Liemandt tackled a major challenge: How to integrate new hires into the company and instill in them a willingness to take risks, achieve the impossible, and cooperate with, and trust, each other. Enter Trilogy University, the three-month boot camp which not only trains new hires but also indoctrinates them into Trilogy's culture that emphasizes such values as humility, creativity and innovation, teamwork, and change.[4]

Training at Trilogy University is action-based. For example, during the first month, classes are held from 8:00 A.M. until midnight. Trainees work on real projects in teams whether it be modifying and improving an existing product, developing a new product, or designing a new human resource management process (for example, a new way to recruit employees). While functional training is important, so too is the valuable experience trainees gain working in teams, learning to trust each other, and communicating their ideas in presentations to top management. Moreover, trainees learn the power of humility, as well as how to take risks, learn from failure, and come up with truly creative ideas.[5] Every effort is made to ensure that each and every new hire successfully completes Trilogy University. As manager Danielle Rios puts it, "We want everyone here to be a star."[6]

Liemandt believes that the millions of dollars his company spends on training each year is well worth it not only because of the learning that goes on but also as a means of retaining top talent.[7] Being challenged, working with talented people, and making creative contributions in an atmosphere of cooperation and trust are important aspects of the Trilogy experience that are emphasized at Trilogy University and serve to motivate and retain top talent.

Overview

Managers are responsible for acquiring, developing, protecting, and utilizing the resources that an organization needs to be efficient and effective. One of the most important resources in all organizations is human resources–the people involved in the production and distribution of goods and services. Human resources include all members of an organization, ranging from top managers to entry-level employees. Effective managers like Joe Liemandt in "A Manager's Challenge" realize how valuable human resources are and take active steps to make sure that their organizations build and fully utilize their human resources to gain a competitive advantage.

This chapter examines how managers can tailor their human resource management system to their organization's strategy and structure. We discuss in particular the major components of human resource management: recruitment and selection, training and development, performance appraisal, pay and benefits, and labor relations. By the end of this chapter, you will understand the central role human resource management plays in creating a high performing organization.

Strategic Human Resource Management

Organizational architecture (see Part 4) is the combination of organizational structure, control systems, culture, and a human resource management system that managers develop to use resources efficiently and effectively. **Human resource management (HRM)** includes all the activities managers engage in to attract and retain employees and to ensure that they perform at a high level and contribute to the accomplishment of organizational goals. These activities make up an organization's human resource management system, which has five major components: recruitment and selection, training and development, performance appraisal and feedback, pay and benefits, and labor relations (see Figure 11.1).

human resource management Activities that managers engage in to attract and retain employees and to ensure that they perform at a high level and contribute to the accomplishment of organizational goals.

strategic human resource management The process by which managers design the components of a human resource management system to be consistent with each other, with other elements of organizational architecture, and with the organization's strategy and goals.

Strategic human resource management is the process by which managers design the components of an HRM system to be consistent with each other, with other elements of organizational architecture, and with the organization's strategy and goals.[8] The objective of strategic HRM is the development of an HRM system that enhances an organization's efficiency, quality, innovation, and responsiveness to customers–the four building blocks of competitive advantage.

As part of strategic human resource management, some managers have adopted "Six Sigma" quality improvement plans. These plans ensure that an organization's products and services are as free of error or defects as possible through a variety of human resource-related initiatives. Jack Welch, former CEO of General Electric Company, has indicated that these initiatives have saved his company millions of dollars and other companies such as Whirlpool and Motorola also have implemented Six Sigma initiatives. In order for such initiatives to be effective, however, top managers have to be committed to Six Sigma, employees must be motivated, and there must be demand for the products or services of the organization in the first place. David Fitzpatrick, head of

Figure 11.1 Components of a Human Resource Management System

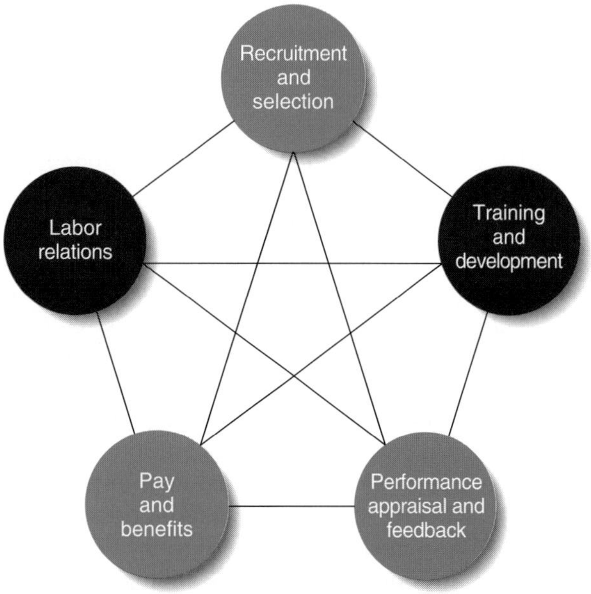

Each component of an HRM system influences the others, and all five must fit together

Deloitte Consulting's Lean Enterprise Practice estimates that most Six Sigma plans are not effective because these conditions for effective Six Sigma are not in place. For example, if top managers are not committed to the quality initiative, they may not devote the necessary time and resources to make it work and may lose interest in it prematurely.[9]

Overview of the Components of HRM

Managers use recruitment and *selection,* the first component of an HRM system, to attract and hire new employees who have the abilities, skills, and experiences that will help an organization achieve its goals. Microsoft Corporation, for example, has the goal of remaining the premier computer software company in the world. To achieve this goal, Bill Gates realized the importance of hiring only the best software designers. When Microsoft hires new software designers, hundreds of highly qualified candidates with excellent recommendations are interviewed and rigorously tested; only the very best are hired. This careful attention to selection has contributed to Microsoft's competitive advantage. Microsoft has little trouble recruiting top programmers because candidates know they will be at the forefront of the industry if they work for Microsoft, utilizing the latest technology and working with the best people.[10]

After recruiting and selecting employees, managers use the second component, training and development, to ensure that organizational members develop the skills and abilities that will enable them to perform their jobs effectively in the present and the future as is true at Trilogy Software in "A Manager's Challenge." Training and development is an ongoing process; changes in technology and the environment, as well as in an organization's goals and strategies, often require organizational members to learn new techniques and ways of working. At Microsoft Corporation, newly hired program designers receive on-the-job training by joining small teams that include experienced employees who serve as mentors or advisors. New recruits learn firsthand from team members how to go about developing computer systems that are responsive to customers' programming needs.[11]

The third component, *performance appraisal and feedback,* serves two different purposes in HRM. First, performance appraisal can provide managers with the information they need to make good human resources decisions–decisions about how to train, motivate, and reward organizational members.[12] Thus, the performance appraisal and feedback component is a kind of *control system* that can be used with management by objectives (discussed in Chapter 10). Second, performance feedback from performance appraisal serves a developmental purpose for members of an organization. When managers regularly evaluate their subordinates' performance, they can provide them with valuable information about their strengths and weaknesses and the areas in which they need to concentrate.

On the basis of performance appraisals, managers distribute *pay* to employees, part of the fourth component of an HRM system. By rewarding high-performing organizational members with pay raises, bonuses, and the like, managers increase the likelihood that an organization's most valued human resources are motivated to continue their high levels of contribution to the organization. Moreover, by linking pay to performance, high-performing employees are more likely to stay with the organization, and managers are more likely to fill positions that become open with highly talented individuals. Benefits such as health insurance, are important outcomes that employees receive by virtue of their membership in an organization.

Jesus Corona instructs future union organizers at the United Farm Workers offices in Salinas, California, on how to conduct "home meetings," as the union prepares for a winter-long blitz with pickers. In the heart of the nation's most productive strawberry fields, growers, workers, and lawyers are preparing for another season of harvest and labor disputes.

Last, but not least, labor relations encompass the steps that managers take to develop and maintain good working relationships with the labor unions that may represent their employees' interests. For example, an organization's labor relations component can help managers establish safe working conditions and fair labor practices in their offices and plants.

Managers must ensure that all five of these components fit together and complement their company's structure and control systems.[13] For example, if managers decide to decentralize authority and empower employees, they need to invest in training and development to ensure that lower level employees have the knowledge and expertise they need to make the decisions that top managers would make in a more centralized structure.

Each of the five components of HRM influences the others (see Figure 11.1).[14] The kinds of people that the organization attracts and hires through recruitment and selection, for example, determine (1) the kind of training and development that are necessary, (2) the way performance is appraised, and (3) the appropriate levels of pay and benefits. Managers at Microsoft ensure that their organization has highly qualified program designers by (1) recruiting and selecting the best candidates, (2) providing new hires with the guidance of experienced team members so that they learn how to be responsive to customers' needs when designing programs and systems, (3) appraising program designers' performance in terms of their individual contributions and their team's performance, and (4) basing programmers' pay on individual and team performance.

The Legal Environment of HRM

In the rest of this chapter we focus in detail on the choices managers must make in strategically managing human resources to attain organizational goals and gain a competitive advantage. Effectively managing human resources is a complex undertaking for managers and we provide an overview of some of the major issues they face. Before we do, however, we need to look at how the legal environment affects human resource management.

The local, state, and national laws and regulations that managers and organizations must abide by add to the complexity of HRM. For example, the U.S. government's commitment to **equal employment opportunity (EEO)** has resulted in the creation and enforcement of a number of laws that managers must abide by. The goal of EEO is to ensure that all citizens have an equal opportunity to obtain employment regardless of their gender, race, country of origin, religion, age, or disabilities. Table 11.1 summarizes some of the major EEO laws affecting HRM. Other laws, such as the Occupational Safety and Health Act of 1970, require managers to ensure that employees' health is protected from workplace hazards and safety standards are met.

equal employment opportunity The equal right of all citizens to the opportunity to obtain employment regardless of their gender, age, race, country of origin, religion, or disabilities.

In Chapter 4, we discussed how effectively managing diversity is an ethical and business imperative. EEO laws and their enforcement make the effective management of diversity a legal imperative as well. The Equal Employment Opportunity Commission (EEOC) is the division of the Department of Justice

Table 11.1
Major Equal Employment Opportunity Laws Affecting HRM

Year	Law	Description
1963	Equal Pay Act	Requires men and women to be paid equally if they are performing equal work
1964	Title VII of the Civil Rights Act	Prohibits discrimination in employment decisions on the basis of race, religion, sex, color, or national origin; covers a wide range of employment decisions, including hiring, firing, pay, promotion, and working conditions
1967	Age Discrimination in Employment Act	Prohibits discrimination against workers over the age of 40 and restricts mandatory retirement
1978	Pregnancy Discrimination Act	Prohibits discrimination against women in employment decisions on the basis of pregnancy, childbirth, and related medical decisions
1990	Americans with Disabilities Act	Prohibits discrimination against disabled individuals in employment decisions and requires employers to make accommodations for disabled workers to enable them to perform their jobs
1991	Civil Rights Act	Prohibits discrimination (as does Title VII) and allows for the awarding of punitive and compensatory damages, in addition to back pay, in cases of intentional discrimination
1993	Family and Medical Leave Act	Requires employers to provide 12 weeks of unpaid leave for medical and family reasons including paternity and illness of a family member

that enforces most of the EEO laws and handles discrimination complaints. In addition, the EEOC issues guidelines for managers to follow to ensure that they are abiding by EEO laws. For example, the Uniform Guidelines on Employee Selection Procedures issued by the EEOC (in conjunction with the Departments of Labor and Justice and the Civil Service Commission) provide managers with guidance about how to ensure that the recruitment and selection component of human resource management complies with Title VII of the Civil Rights Act (which prohibits discrimination based on gender, race, color, religion, and national origin).[15]

Contemporary challenges that managers face related to the legal environment include how to eliminate sexual harassment (see Chapter 4), how to make accommodations for disabled employees, how to deal with employees with substance abuse problems, and how to manage HIV-positive employees and employees with AIDS.[16] HIV-positive employees are infected with the virus that causes AIDS, but may show no AIDS symptoms and may not develop AIDS in the near future. Often, such employees are able to perform their jobs effectively, and managers must take steps to ensure that they are able to do so and are not discriminated against in the workplace.[17] Employees with AIDS may or may not be able to perform their jobs effectively, and, once again, managers need to ensure that they are not unfairly discriminated against.[18] Many organizations have instituted AIDS awareness training programs to educate organizational members about HIV and AIDS, dispel unfounded myths about how HIV is spread, and ensure that individuals infected with the HIV virus are treated fairly and are able to be productive as long as they can while not putting others at risk.[19]

The multitude of recent failures, bankruptcies, and layoffs in high-technology start-ups and dot-coms have resulted in some managers being confronted with a new set of ethical (and in some cases legal) challenges, as seen in the following "Ethics in Action."

Ethics in Action

Don't Make Promises You May Not Be Able to Keep

In the first quarter of 2001, over 50,000 dot-com jobs were eliminated, with the majority of them being around San Francisco Bay.[20] Some laid-off dot-commers actually enjoyed the relief from 14-hour workdays and used their sudden dramatic increase in free time to renew their interests in hobbies and sports, travel, or spend more time with their children.[21] Others, not as financially secure, were furiously networking to find new positions and doing part-time consulting work. While all their stories are different, they do share one thing in common: broken promises.

Workers flocked to dot-coms with promises of getting rich quick, working in a vibrant and stimulating environment, and being able to cash in on lucrative stock options. Not only have many of these promises been broken, but instead of riches and glory, dot-commers received pink slips and some were even escorted from their workplaces by security guards.[22] Was it ethical for dot-com owners and managers to make lofty promises to prospective employees (some of whom left well-paying secure jobs in Fortune 500 companies for the excitement and riches of working in a dot-com), promises which we now know they were not able to keep?

High-tech workers network with recruiters in Austin Texas at a dot-com "pink slip" party in a local nightclub.

Some laid-off employees think not and are seeking legal remedies. Employment law firms are seeing a dramatic increase in their case work; many new clients are disgruntled former dot-commers who are seeking legal redress for what they consider unethical behavior on the part of failing dot-com owners and managers. For example, former employees of wwrrr.inc, a dot-com focused on on-line learning in Minneapolis, do not like the treatment they received when wwrrr.inc went out of business. Some of these employees were not paid for the last two weeks they worked for the defunct dot-com, they were not reimbursed for work-related expenses they paid for out of their own pockets, their health insurance was cancelled, and their promised valuable stock options were worthless. These employees have brought their case before the U.S. Labor Department for an investigation.[23]

Other laid-off dot-commers are seeking redress through WARN (worker adjustment and retraining notification), a federal law stipulating that organizations with more than 100 employees are required to provide 60 days' notice when undertaking a large layoff.[24] Such notice was not given at Walker Digital when founder Jay Walker let go 100 of his 115 employees without any warning. Walker Digital's action got the attention of Connecticut Attorney General Richard Blumenthal, who questioned its legality.[25] While the legal issues surrounding the rise and fall of dot-coms may take years for the courts to settle, clearly, on ethical grounds, managers can learn a valuable lesson from this piece of business history: Be careful not to make promises that you may not be able to keep.

Recruitment and Selection

Recruitment includes all the activities managers engage in to develop a pool of qualified candidates for open positions.[26] **Selection** is the process by which managers determine the relative qualifications of job applicants and their potential for performing well in a particular job. Prior to actually recruiting and selecting employees, managers need to engage in two important activities: human resource planning and job analysis (Figure 11.2).

recruitment Activities that managers engage in to develop a pool of qualified candidates for open positions.

selection The process that managers use to determine the relative qualifications of job applicants and their potential for performing well in a particular job.

human resource planning Activities that managers engage in to forecast their current and future needs for human resources.

Human Resource Planning

Human resource planning includes all the activities managers engage in to forecast their current and future human resource needs. Current human resources are the employees an organization needs today to provide high-quality goods and services to customers. Future human resource needs are the employees the organization will need at some later date to achieve its longer-term goals.

As part of human resource planning, managers must make both demand forecasts and supply forecasts. *Demand forecasts* estimate the qualifications and numbers of employees an organization will need given its goals and strategies. *Supply forecasts* estimate the availability and qualifications of current employees now and in the future, and the supply of qualified workers in the external labor market.

As a result of their human resource planning, managers sometimes decide to **outsource** to fill some of their human resources needs. Instead of recruiting and selecting employees to produce goods and services, managers contract with people who are not members of their organization to produce goods and services. Managers in publishing companies, for example, frequently contract with freelance editors to copyedit new books that they intend to publish. Kelly Services is an organization that provides temporary typing, clerical, and secretarial workers to managers who want to use outsourcing to fill some of their human resource requirements in these areas. Outsourcing is increasingly being used on a global level as well.

Figure 11.2
The Recruitment and Selection System

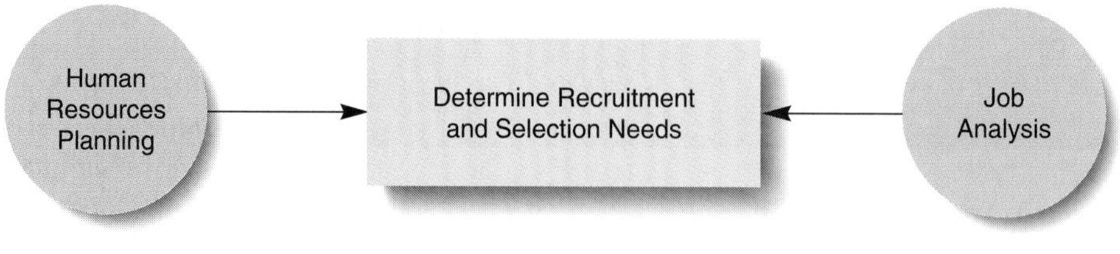

outsource To use outside suppliers and manufacturers to produce goods and services.

Two reasons why human resources planning sometimes leads managers to outsource are flexibility and cost. First, outsourcing can give managers increased flexibility, especially when accurately forecasting human resource needs is difficult, human resource needs fluctuate over time, or finding skilled workers in a particular area is difficult. Second, outsourcing can sometimes allow managers to make use of human resources at a lower cost. When work is outsourced, costs can be lower for a number of reasons: The organization does not have to provide benefits to workers; managers are able to contract for work only when the work is needed; and managers do not have to invest in training. Outsourcing can be used for functional activities such as after-sales service on appliances and equipment, legal work, and the management of information systems. Roy Richie, general counsel for the Chrysler Corporation, uses temporary attorneys to write contracts and fill some of his department's human resource needs. As he says, "The math works...Savings can be tremendous."[27]

Outsourcing does have its disadvantages, however. When work is outsourced, managers may lose some control over the quality of goods and services. Also, individuals performing outsourced work may have less knowledge of organizational practices, procedures, and goals and less commitment to an organization than regular employees. In addition, unions resist outsourcing because it has the potential to eliminate some of their members. To gain some of the flexibility and cost saving of outsourcing and avoid some of outsourcing's disadvantages, some organizations, such as Microsoft and IBM, rely on a pool of temporary employees to, for example, debug programs. However, as indicated in the following "Information Technology Byte," managers need to be careful to ensure that temporary employees are, in fact, temporary and are treated fairly.

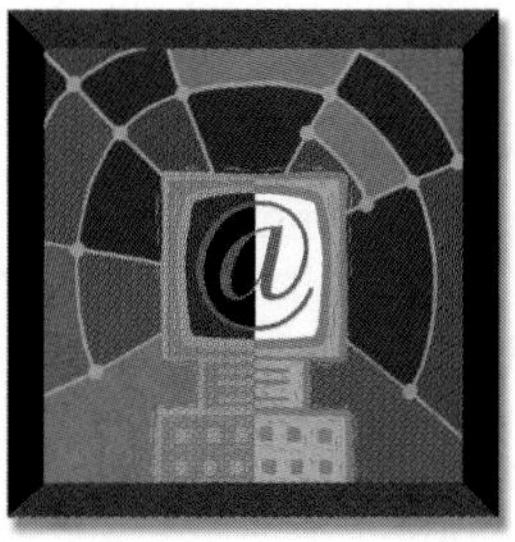

Information Technology Byte

Permatemps at Microsoft

Large corporations often rely on a large staff of temporary employees. For example, IBM employs more than 40,000 temporary workers per year and Microsoft has a staff of 5,000 temporary employees.[28] However, managers who regularly rely on temporary employees to fill some of their human resource needs are advised to make sure that "temporary" workers are, in fact, temporary and that they are treated fairly. This advice comes in the wake of Microsoft settling a class action lawsuit filed by 8,000 former temporary workers to the tune of $97 million. The workers complained that they were regular employees in every way except for their financial compensation, benefits, and inability to purchase Microsoft stock at a discount as participants in its employee stock purchase plan.[29]

In response to the settlement, Microsoft has taken steps to ensure that its "permatemps" are considered temporary in the eyes of the law. For example, temporary workers must now stop working at Microsoft for 100 days after they have worked for one full year.[30] While this policy may help Microsoft avoid future costly settlements, one wonders how socially responsible it is.

Moreover, by some accounts, temporary workers at Microsoft are treated like second-class citizens. These permatemps work in a variety of positions in customer service, software testing, and programming and some of them are employed by Microsoft for years (with gaps in between). Yet, they aren't entitled to stock options nor do the benefits their employment agencies pay usually compare with the attractive benefit package Microsoft provides to permanent workers.[31] Moreover, their ID badges distinguish them as temporary employees and sometimes they are made to feel like second class citizens. Consider the experience of software tester David Larsen, who has worked at Microsoft on and off for several years, "I made the mistake of telling my boss' boss that I was going to take advantage of things like brown-bag lunches. . . . My boss later told me, 'They don't want you to go to those things; they want you at your computer finding bugs."[32]

Clearly, there are sound business reasons for hiring temporary workers and companies like Microsoft and IBM will likely continue to do so. But, from both a legal and a social responsibility perspective, managers need to take steps to ensure that temporary workers are, in fact, temporary and treated fairly.

Job Analysis

job analysis Identifying the tasks, duties, and responsibilities that make up a job and the knowledge, skills, and abilities needed to perform the job.

Job analysis is a second important activity that managers need to undertake prior to recruitment and selection.[33] **Job analysis** is the process of identifying (1) the tasks, duties, and responsibilities that make up a job (the job description), and (2) the knowledge, skills, and abilities needed to perform the job (the job specifications).[34] For each job in an organization, a job analysis needs to be done.

A job analysis can be done in a number of ways including observing current employees as they perform the job or interviewing them. Often, managers rely on questionnaires compiled by jobholders and their managers. The questionnaires ask about the skills and abilities needed to perform the job, job tasks and the amount of time spent on them, responsibilities, supervisory activities, equipment used, reports prepared, and decisions made.[35] The Position Analysis Questionnaire (PAQ) is a comprehensive standardized questionnaire that many managers rely on to conduct job analyses.[36] It focuses on behaviors jobholders perform, working conditions, and job characteristics and can be used for a variety of jobs.[37] The PAQ contains 194 items organized into six divisions: (1) information input (where and how the job holder acquires information to perform the job), (2) mental processes (reasoning, decision making, planning, and information-processing activities that are part of the job), (3) work output (physical activities performed on the job and machines and devices used), (4) relationships with others (interactions with other people that are necessary to perform the job), (5) job context (the physical and social environment of the job), and (6) other job characteristics (such as work pace).[38] A trend, in some organizations, is toward more flexible jobs in which tasks and responsibilities change and cannot be clearly specified in advance. For these kinds of jobs, job analysis focuses more on determining the skills and knowledge workers need to be effective and less on specific duties.

After managers have completed human resource planning and job analyses for all jobs in an organization, they will know their human resources needs and the jobs they need to fill. They will also know the knowledge, skills, and abilities potential employees need to perform those jobs. At this point, recruitment and selection can begin.

External and Internal Recruitment

As noted earlier, recruitment is what managers do to develop a pool of qualified candidates for open positions.[39] They traditionally have used two main types of recruiting: external and internal which is now supplemented by recruiting over the Internet.

EXTERNAL RECRUITING When managers recruit externally to fill open positions, they look outside the organization for people who have not worked for the organization previously. There are multiple means through which managers can recruit externally–advertisements in newspapers and magazines, open houses for students and career counselors at high schools and colleges or on-site at the organization, career fairs at colleges, and recruitment meetings with groups in the local community.

Many large organizations send teams of interviewers to college campuses to recruit new employees. External recruitment can also take place through informal networks such as when current employees inform friends about open positions in their companies or recommend people they know to fill vacant spots. Some organizations use employment agencies for external recruitment, and some external recruitment takes place simply through walk ins–jobhunters coming to an organization and inquiring about employment possibilities.

With all the downsizings and corporate layoffs that have taken place in recent years, you might think that external recruiting would be a relatively easy task for managers. However, it often is not, because even though many people may be looking for jobs, many of the jobs that are opening up require skills and abilities that these jobhunters do not have. As profiled in the following "Managing Globally," managers looking to fill vacant positions and jobhunters seeking employment opportunities are increasingly relying on the Internet to make connections with each other.

Managing Globally

Electronic Recruiting at Monster.com and Jobline International

Jeff Taylor founded what has become the world's largest electronic recruiting website, Monster.com, in 1994. In 1995, while maintaining his position as CEO, Taylor sold his company to TMP Worldwide, Inc., a New York-based search and employment ad agency, to have the financial resources of a large and more established organization to fund an ad campaign promoting his recruiting website on national TV.[40]

Taylor is as unconventional as the name of his company and website; after dropping out of college, he did promotional work for entertainers, worked as a dejay in nightclubs in Boston, and founded other companies including a recruitment agency. In fact, this last endeavor led Taylor to think about the idea of Monster.com. His agency specialized in the high tech field and he was lamenting the difficult time his corporate clients were having finding the right people to fill their open positions using traditional newspaper advertisements. He came up with a solution to this problem–an on-line job board or Monster Board and the rest was history.[41]

Monster.com is the leading on-line recruiting company with over 30 percent of this market and approximately 10 million resumes of job seekers. It continued to earn a profit in the period from 1999 to 2001 when many other dot-coms went out of business and competitors were losing money. Job seekers can post their resumes for free on Monster.com while employers pay a fee to post their positions available and search for suitable applicants.[42]

Through Monster.com, job seekers also can search for jobs on a global basis. On the Monster.com website, those seeking jobs in other countries can

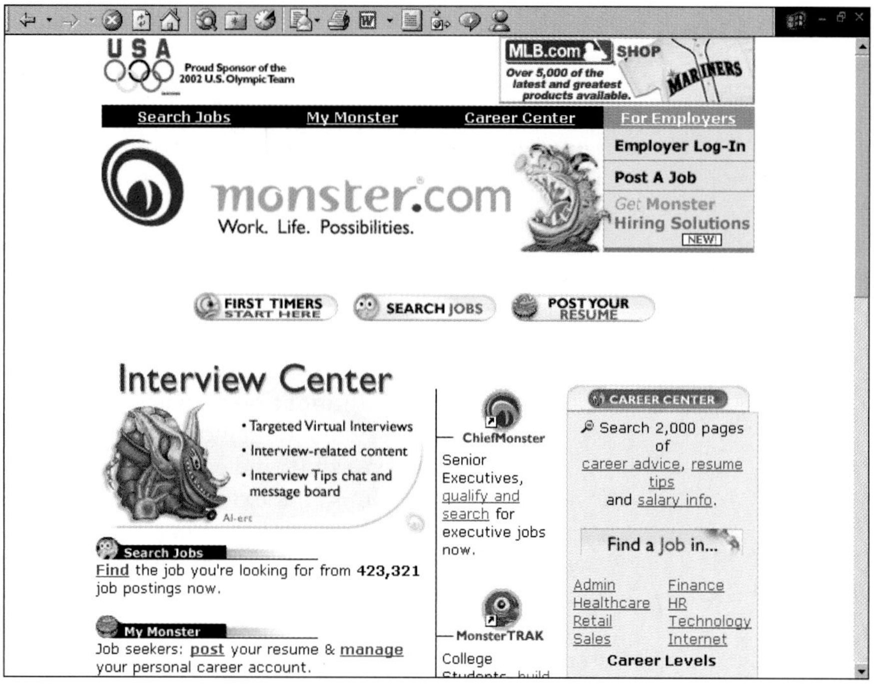

Jeff Taylor came up with the idea for monster.com, the leading on-line recruiting company, when his recruitment agency was having trouble finding the right people to fill open high-tech positions using traditional newpaper ads.

click on monster global gateway, whereby they are directed to Jobline International, Europe's largest electronic recruiting site with operations in 12 countries, over 800,000 users, and more than 600,000 resumes.[43] Major corporations such as Coca-Cola, Cisco, Ernst & Young, Canon, and Telia have relied on Jobline International to fill global positions.[44] Clearly, web-based recruiting companies like Monster.com and Jobline International have vastly increased the external recruiting options for managers seeking to fill vacant positions as well as put managers in contact with many more potential applicants than ever before. Time will tell if managers of these successful dot-coms can continue their current trajectory of growth in revenues and profits.

External recruiting has both advantages and disadvantages for managers. Advantages include having access to a potentially large applicant pool, being able to attract people who have the skills, knowledge, and abilities that an organization needs to achieve its goals, and being able to bring in newcomers who may have a fresh approach to problems and be up-to-date on the latest technology. These advantages have to be weighed against the disadvantages, including the relatively high costs of external recruitment. Employees recruited externally also lack knowledge about the inner workings of the organization and may need to receive more training than those recruited internally. Finally, when employees are recruited externally, there is always uncertainty concerning whether they will actually be good performers.

lateral move A job change that entails no major changes in responsibility or authority levels.

INTERNAL RECRUITING When recruiting is internal, managers turn to existing employees to fill open positions. Employees recruited internally are either seeking **lateral moves** (job changes that entail no major changes in responsibility or authority levels) or promotions. Internal recruiting has several advantages. First, internal applicants are already familiar with the organization (including its goals, structure, culture, rules, and norms). Second, managers already know candidates; they have considerable information about their skills and abilities and actual behavior on the job. Third, internal recruiting can help boost levels of employee motivation and morale, both for the employee who gets the job and for other workers. Those who are not seeking a promotion or who may not be ready for a promotion can see that it is a possibility for the future; or a lateral move can alleviate boredom once a job has been fully mastered and also provide a useful way to learn new skills. Finally, internal recruiting is normally less time-consuming and expensive.

Given the advantages of internal recruiting, why do managers rely on external recruiting as much as they do? The answer is because of the disadvantages of internal recruiting–among them, a limited pool of candidates and a tendency among those candidates to be set in the organization's ways. Often, the organization simply does not have suitable internal candidates. Sometimes, even when suitable internal applicants are available, managers may rely on external recruiting to find the very best candidate or to help bring new ideas and approaches into their organization. When organizations are in trouble and performing poorly, external recruiting is often relied on to bring in managerial talent with a fresh approach. For example, when IBM's performance was suffering in the 1990s and the board of directors was looking to recruit a new CEO, rather than consider any of IBM's existing top managers for this position, the board recruited Lou Gerstner, an outsider who had no previous experience in the computer industry.

HONESTY IN RECRUITING At times, when trying to recruit the most qualified applicants, managers may be tempted to paint overly rosy pictures of both the open positions and the organization as a whole. They may worry that if they are totally honest about advantages and disadvantages, they either will not be able to fill positions or will have fewer or less qualified applicants. A manager trying to fill a secretarial position, for example, may emphasize the high level of pay and benefits the job offers and fail to mention the fact that the position is usually a dead-end job offering few opportunities for promotion.

Research suggests that painting an overly rosy picture of a job and organization is not a wise recruiting strategy. Recruitment is more likely to be effective when managers provide potential applicants with an honest assessment of both the advantages and disadvantages of a job and the organization. Such an assessment is called a **realistic job preview (RJP)**.[45] RJPs can be effective because they can reduce the number of new hires who quit when their jobs and organizations fail to meet their unrealistic expectations and they help applicants decide for themselves if the job is right for them.

realistic job preview An honest assessment of the advantages and disadvantages of a job and organization.

Take the earlier example of the manager trying to recruit a secretary. The manager who paints a rosy picture of the job might have an easier time filling it but might end up hiring a secretary who expects to be promoted quickly to an administrative assistant position. After a few weeks on the job, the secretary may realize that a promotion is highly unlikely no matter how good his or her performance, become dissatisfied, and look for and accept another job. The manager then has to recruit, select, and train another new secretary. The manager could have avoided this waste of valuable organizational resources by using a realistic job preview. An RJP would have increased the likelihood that a secretary comfortable with few promotional opportunities was hired and subsequently would have been satisfied to remain on the job.

The Selection Process

Once managers develop a pool of applicants for open positions through the recruitment process, they need to find out whether each applicant is qualified for the position and likely to be a good performer. If more than one applicant meets these two conditions, managers must further determine which applicants are likely to be better performers than others. They have several selection tools to help them sort out the relative qualifications of job applicants and appraise their potential for being good performers in a particular job. Those tools include background information, interviews, paper-and-pencil tests, physical ability tests, performance tests, and references (see Figure 11.3).[46]

BACKGROUND INFORMATION To aid in the selection process, managers obtain background information from job applications and from résumés. Such information might include the highest levels of education obtained, college majors and minors, type of college or university attended, years and type of work experience, and mastery of foreign languages. Background information can be helpful both to screen out applicants who are lacking key qualifications (such as a college degree) and to determine which qualified applicants are more promising than others. For example, applicants with a BS may be acceptable, but those who also have an MBA are preferable.

INTERVIEWS Virtually all organizations use interviews during the selection process. Interviews may be structured or unstructured. In a *structured interview,* managers ask each applicant the same standard questions (such as What are your unique qualifications for this position? and What characteristics of a job are most important for you?). Particularly informative questions may be those that prompt an interviewee to demonstrate skills and abilities needed for the job by answering the question. Sometimes called *situational interview questions,* these often present interviewees with a scenario that they would likely encounter on the job and ask them to indicate how they would handle it.[47] For example, applicants for a sales job may be asked to indicate how they would

Figure 11.3
Selection Tools

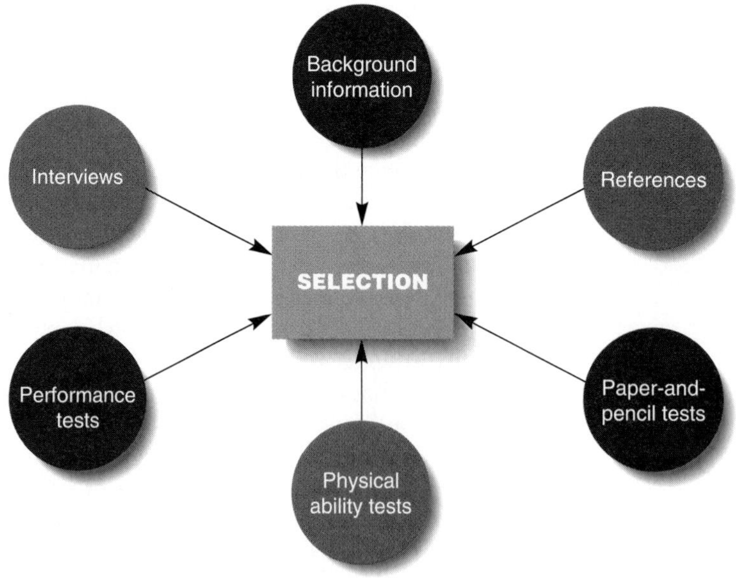

respond to a customer who complains about waiting too long for service, a customer who is indecisive, and a customer whose order is lost.

An *unstructured interview* proceeds more like an ordinary conversation. The interviewer feels free to ask probing questions to discover what the applicant is like and does not ask a fixed set of questions determined in advance. In general, structured interviews are superior to unstructured interviews because they are more likely to yield information that will help identify qualified candidates and are less subjective. Also, evaluations based on structured interviews may be less influenced by the interviewer's biases than evaluations based on unstructured interviews.

Even when structured interviews are used, however, the potential exists for the interviewer's biases to influence his or her judgment. Recall from Chapter 4 how the similar-to-me effect can cause people to perceive others who are similar to themselves more positively than those who are different and how stereotypes can result in inaccurate perceptions. Interviewers must be trained to avoid these biases and sources of inaccurate perceptions as much as possible. Many of the approaches to increasing diversity awareness and diversity skills described in Chapter 5 are used to train interviewers to avoid the effects of biases and stereotypes. In addition, using multiple interviewers can be advantageous as their individual biases and idiosyncrasies may cancel one another out.[48]

When conducting interviews, managers cannot ask questions that are irrelevant to the job in question; otherwise their organizations run the risk of costly lawsuits. It is inappropriate and illegal, for example, to inquire about an interviewee's spouse or to ask questions about whether an interviewee plans to have children. Because questions such as these are irrelevant to job performance, they are discriminatory and violate EEO laws (see Table 11.1). Thus, interviewers also need to be instructed in EEO laws and informed about questions that may violate those laws.

Managers can use interviews at various stages in the selection process. Some use interviews as initial screening devices; others use them as a final hurdle that applicants must jump. Regardless of when they are used, managers typically use other selection tools in conjunction with interviews because of the potential for bias and for interviewers forming inaccurate assessments of interviewees. Even though training and using structured rather than unstructured interviews can eliminate the effects of some of these biases, interviewers can still come to erroneous conclusions about interviewees' qualifications. Interviewees, for example, who make a bad initial impression or are overly nervous in the first minute or two of an interview tend to be judged more harshly than other less nervous candidates, even if the rest of the interview goes well.

PAPER-AND-PENCIL TESTS The two main kinds of paper-and-pencil tests used for selection purposes are ability tests and personality tests. *Ability tests* assess the extent to which applicants possess the skills necessary for job performance, such as verbal comprehension or numerical skills. Autoworkers hired by General Motors, Chrysler, and Ford, for example, are typically tested for their ability to read and to do mathematics.[49]

Personality tests measure personality traits and characteristics relevant to job performance. Some retail organizations, for example, give job applicants honesty tests to determine how trustworthy they are. The use of personality tests (including honesty tests) for hiring purposes is controversial. Some critics maintain that honesty tests do not really measure honesty (that is, they are not valid) and can

Lisa Cedars grimaces as she hauls a 165-lb. dummy to the finish line during a physical fitness test for firefighting applicants at the fire department in Alexandria, Louisiana. The physical test is just one of many used to determine the top candidates.

be faked by job applicants. Before using any paper-and-pencil tests for selection purposes, managers must have sound evidence that the tests are actually good predictors of performance on the job in question. Managers who use tests without such evidence may be subject to costly discrimination lawsuits.

PHYSICAL ABILITY TESTS For jobs requiring physical abilities, such as fire fighting, garbage collecting, and package delivery, managers use physical ability tests that measure physical strength and stamina as selection tools. Autoworkers are typically tested for mechanical dexterity because this physical ability is an important skill for high job performance in many auto plants.[50]

PERFORMANCE TESTS *Performance tests* measure job applicants' performance on actual job tasks. Applicants for secretarial positions, for example, typically are required to complete a typing test that measures how quickly and accurately they type. Applicants for middle- and top-management positions are sometimes given short-term projects to complete–projects that mirror the kinds of situations that arise in the job being filled–to assess their knowledge and problem-solving capabilities.[51]

Assessment centers, first used by AT&T, take performance tests one step further. In a typical assessment center, about 10 to 15 candidates for managerial positions participate in a variety of activities over a few days. During this time they are assessed for the skills an effective manager needs–problem-solving skills, organization skills, communication skills, and conflict resolution skills. Some of the activities are performed individually; others are performed in groups. Throughout the process, current managers observe the candidates' behavior and measure performance. Summary evaluations are then used as a selection tool.

REFERENCES Applicants for many jobs are required to provide references from former employers or other knowledgeable sources (such as a college instructor or advisor) who know the applicants' skills, abilities, and other personal characteristics. These individuals are asked to provide candid information about the applicant. References are often used at the end of the selection process to confirm a decision to hire. Yet the fact that many former employers are reluctant to provide negative information in references sometimes makes it difficult to interpret what a reference is really saying about an applicant.

In fact, several recent lawsuits filed by applicants who felt that they were unfairly denigrated or had their privacy invaded by unfavorable references from former employers have caused managers to be increasingly wary of providing any negative information in a reference, even if it is accurate. For jobs in which the jobholder is responsible for the safety and lives of other people, however, failing to provide accurate, negative information in a reference does not just mean that the wrong person might get hired; it may also mean that other people's lives will be at stake, as indicated in the following "Ethics in Action."

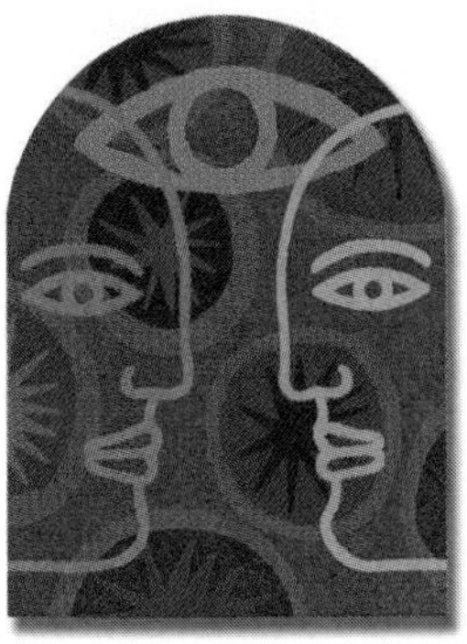

Ethics in Action

Withholding Negative Information and the Importance of Background Checks

When an American Airlines pilot mistakenly thought there was engine failure, the commuter plane he was piloting crashed near Raleigh, North Carolina. Subsequent inquiries indicated that the same pilot had been found unfit to fly on his previous job. However, American Airlines did not have access to this information when they hired him. Why? Airlines that have provided negative references and documented poor performance have been sued by former employees for invasion of privacy. The former employer of this particular pilot was unwilling to risk getting sued and thus failed to provide an accurate negative reference.[52] Is it ethical to withhold negative information when lives are at stake? This question haunts many managers, including Stephen Sayler of Kansas City, who did not mention in a reference that a former employee and truck driver for his company had been fired for drinking. Donna Salinas of Salt Lake City did not report that a health care worker she supervised had been fired for stealing from an elderly patient. Salinas indicated that "It absolutely made me sick that I couldn't tell."[53] Managers like Sayler and Salinas who withhold negative information from references often do so because they fear that their companies may be subject to costly lawsuits if they give a negative reference for a former employee, even if it is accurate.

Realizing the ethical dilemma faced by these managers and the potential risks to human life and well-being, legislators have taken steps to protect former employers who give accurate, negative information in references for former employees. In Utah, for example, former employees can win defamation suits only if they can prove that information in the reference was false or disregarded the truth. Georgia, too, provides protection to former employers against lawsuits arising from references for health care workers and bank employees.[54] Similar initiatives at the national level are taking place, particularly to provide airlines with liability protection so that accurate information can be provided in references for former pilots seeking new positions.[55] Clearly, rights to privacy and protection against defamation are important societal values, when human lives and well-being are at stake, former employers need to be able to provide accurate information in references, even if it is negative and prevents an applicant from obtaining a job.

Additionally, the potential for withholding negative information on the part of former employers suggests that managers should carefully check the backgrounds of prospective employees. Fortunately, managers can turn to a number of on-line resources for help as well as organizations specializing in background checks. For example, www.frauddefense.com has a variety of free resources on its website, KnowX.com provides services for a fee to check whether prospective employees were party to any lawsuits or bankruptcies, Employeescreen.com does a thorough background investigation for under $100 per applicant, and the Association of Certified Fraud Examiners (cfenet.com) helps put managers in touch with security professionals.[56] Managers at Clik Communications, Inc., a New York firm that creates reports for consulting companies to give to their customers, were glad they relied on a security professional to check the background of a promising applicant for the position of director of finance. As it turned out, this individual was not so promising after all–he lacked both the MBA and the work experience he claimed on his resume.[57]

THE IMPORTANCE OF RELIABILITY AND VALIDITY Whatever the selection tools a manager uses, these tools need to be both reliable and valid. Reliability is the degree to which a tool or test measures the same thing each time it is administered. Scores on a selection test should be very similar if the same person is assessed with the same tool on two different days; if there is quite a bit of variability, the tool is unreliable. For interviews, determining reliability is more complex because the dynamic is personal interpretation. That's why the reliability of interviews can be increased if two or more different qualified interviewers interview the same candidate. If the interviews are reliable, the interviewers should come to similar conclusions about the interviewees' qualifications.

reliability The degree to which a tool or test measures the same thing each time it is used.

Validity is the degree to which a tool measures what it purports to measure–for selection tools, that is the degree to which the test predicts performance on the tasks or job in question. Does a physical ability test used to select firefighters, for example, actually predict on-the-job performance? Do assessment center ratings actually predict managerial performance? Do typing tests predict secretarial performance? These are all questions of validity. Honesty tests, for example, are controversial because it is not clear that they validly predict honesty in such jobs as retailing and banking.

validity The degree to which a tool or test measures what it purports to measure.

Managers have an ethical and legal obligation to use reliable and valid selection tools. Yet reliability and validity are a matter of degree rather than all-or-nothing characteristics. Thus, managers should strive to use selection tools in such a way that they can achieve the greatest degree of reliability and validity. For ability tests of a particular skill, managers should keep up-to-date on the latest advances in the development of valid paper-and-pencil tests and use the test with the highest reliability and validity ratings possible for their purposes. Regarding interviews, managers can improve reliability by having more than one person interview job candidates.

Training and Development

Training and development helps to ensure that organizational members have the knowledge and skills needed to perform jobs effectively, take on new responsibilities, and adapt to changing conditions. Training primarily focuses on teaching organizational members how to perform their current jobs and helping them acquire the knowledge and skills they need to be effective performers. Development focuses on building the knowledge and skills of organizational members so that they are prepared to take on new responsibilities and challenges. Training tends to be used more frequently at lower levels of an organization; development tends to be used more frequently with professionals and managers. Trilogy University, described in "A Manager's Challenge," focuses, in large part, on ensuring that new college graduates have the skills and capabilities needed to perform their jobs effectively.

training Teaching organizational members how to perform their current jobs and helping them acquire the knowledge and skills they need to be effective performers.

development Building the knowledge and skills of organizational members so that they will be prepared to take on new responsibilities and challenges.

Before creating training and development programs, managers should perform a needs assessment to determine which employees need training or development and what type of skills or knowledge they need to acquire (see Figure 11.4).[58] In "A Manager's Challenge," Joe Liemandt's needs assessment suggested that new hires at Trilogy Software needed training not only in functional areas but also in taking risks, being creative, working in a team, and communicating effectively.

Figure 11.4
Training and Development

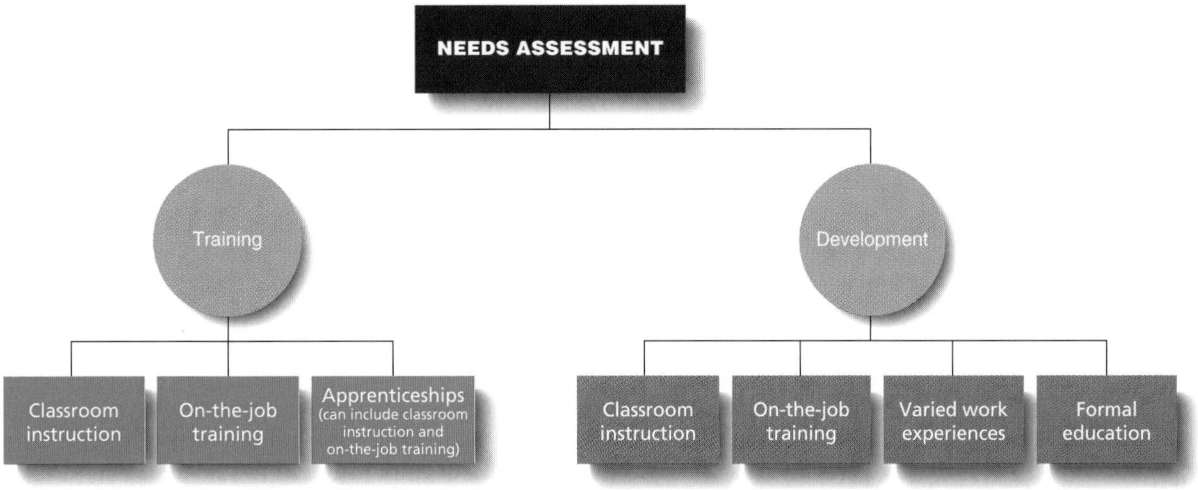

needs assessment
An assessment of which employees need training or development and what type of skills or knowledge they need to acquire.

Types of Training

The training new hires receive at Trilogy University represents a mix of two types of training: classroom instruction and on-the-job training.

CLASSROOM INSTRUCTION Through classroom instruction, employees acquire knowledge and skills in a classroom setting. This instruction may take place within the organization or outside of it, such as when employees are encouraged to take courses at local colleges and universities. Many organizations actually establish their own formal instructional divisions–some are even called colleges–to provide needed classroom instruction.

At Ethan Allen Interiors Inc., for example, employees from stores around the country attend Ethan Allen College at company headquarters in Danbury, Connecticut. During classes, employees acquire in-depth knowledge about the company's products and learn how to listen to customers and accurately assess their needs. In addition, the college provides instruction on such diverse topics as floor plans and window treatments. Training at Ethan Allen is an ongoing process. Veteran employees attending two- or three-day sessions at the college to brush up on their skills and keep abreast of the latest developments. M. Farooq Kathwari, chairman and CEO of Ethan Allen, believes that the classroom instruction that employees receive at Ethan Allen College has contributed significantly to his company's competitive advantage.[59]

Classroom instruction frequently includes the use of videos and role-playing in addition to traditional written materials, lectures, and group discussions. Videos can be used to demonstrate appropriate and inappropriate job behaviors. For example, by watching an experienced salesperson effectively deal with a loud and angry customer in a video clip, inexperienced salespeople can develop skills in handling similar situations. During role-playing, trainees either directly participate in or watch others perform actual job activities in a simulated setting. At McDonald's Hamburger University, for example, role playing helps franchisees acquire the knowledge and skills they need to manage their restaurants.

Simulations also can be part of classroom instruction, particularly on complicated jobs that require an extensive amount of learning and in which errors carry a high cost. In a simulation, key aspects of the work situation and job tasks are duplicated as closely as possible in an artificial setting. For example, air traffic controllers are trained by simulations because of the complicated nature of the work, the extensive amount of learning involved, and the very high costs of air traffic control errors.

on-the-job training Training that takes place in the work setting as employees perform their job tasks.

ON-THE-JOB TRAINING In on-the-job training, learning occurs in the work setting as employees perform their job tasks. On-the-job training can be provided by co-workers or supervisors or occur simply as jobholders gain experience and knowledge from doing the work. Newly hired waiters and waitresses in chains such as Red Lobster or The Olive Garden often receive on-the-job training from experienced employees. The supervisor of a new bus driver for a campus bus system may ride the bus for a week to ensure that the driver has learned the routes and follows safety procedures. Chefs learn to create new and innovative dishes by experimenting with different combinations of ingredients and cooking techniques. For all on-the-job training employees learn by doing. At Trilogy University on-the-job training means that new hires work in teams on real projects that are important for the success of the company.

Managers often use on-the-job training on a continuing basis to ensure that their subordinates keep up-to-date with changes in goals, technology, products, or customer needs and desires. For example, sales representatives in Mary Kay Cosmetics Inc. receive ongoing training so that they are not only knowledgeable about new cosmetic products and currently popular colors but also reminded of Mary Kay's guiding principles. Mary Kay's expansion into Russia has been very successful, in part because of ongoing training that Mary Kay's Russian salespeople receive.[60]

In Chapter 4, you learned about why diversity training is so important in organizations and the different options managers have to choose from. As indicated in the following "Focus on Diversity," training can solve real business problems while bringing diverse individuals together and promoting bonds between them.

Focus on Diversity

Action-Oriented Training Solves Business Problems and Fosters Diversity

Action-oriented training is growing in popularity and has several advantages, as is true at Trilogy Software in "A Manager's Challenge." When employees are trained by working on real business problems or projects in teams, they develop not only their technical skills but also their teamwork skills and communication networks. An additional benefit is that diverse individuals can be brought together to work on problems; these team members might never have come in contact with each other before. Once the training is completed, these diverse individuals have the opportunity to keep in contact with each other and serve as important resources for information and guidance.[61]

This is certainly the case at Siemens, the huge German conglomerate that competes with General Electric. Siemens University, responsible for the training of analysts and engineers, puts trainees and managers on teams to solve real problems Siemens is facing. Moreover, team makeup is often diverse;

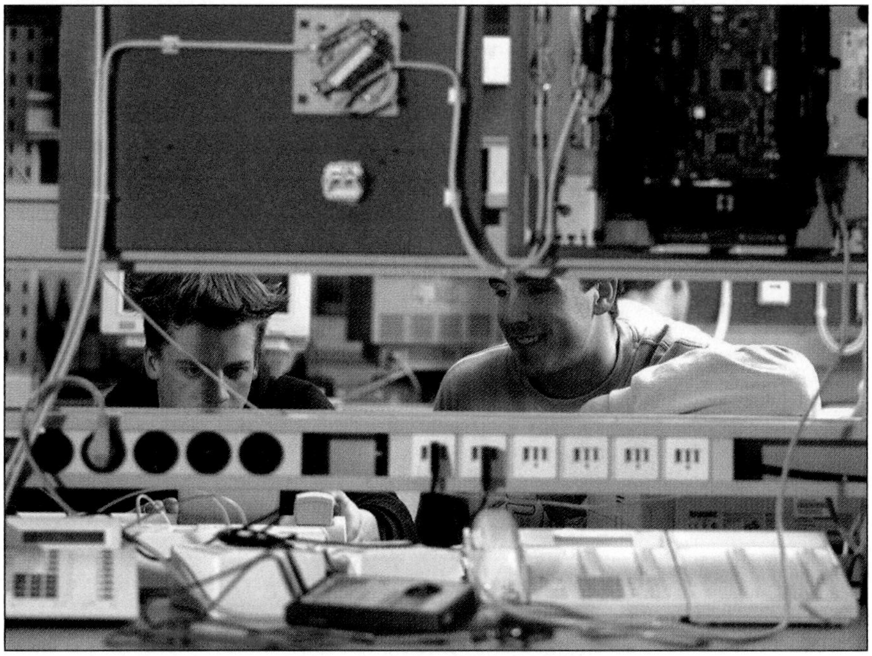

Two trainees set up a HICOM system in Siemens' Professional Education Center in Munich. The company is currently training over 300 people as electronic communications engineers.

Siemens operates in over 150 countries and teams are often composed of members who may work not only in different divisions but also in different countries. Team members (including the managers) have the opportunity to work with people they would not have come in contact with otherwise; this facilitates problem solving due to the diversity of ideas and approaches, as well as promotes diversity. Moreover, such training expands trainees' communication network of contacts within Siemens. The training has financial benefits for Siemens as well–the solutions teams come up with as part of their training typically save Siemens more than $10 million per year.[62]

Siemens' managers also create unique training programs to promote important values and objectives. For example, Joachim Doring, a Siemens' vice president, wanted 60 managers in the Telecommunications Division to understand the need for, and value of, sharing knowledge. He brought them to a lake near Munich, gave them logs, drums, rope, and pontoons, and instructed them to build rafts without talking to each other. While the managers accomplished their task, they also learned the value of knowledge sharing. Back on the job, Doring and the managers are promoting knowledge sharing at Siemens through ShareNet, a website on which employees can post information, communicate with each other, and search for information. ShareNet also enables interactions between diverse individuals who may be working in different units and in different countries.[63] All in all, well thought out and designed training programs can have multiple benefits.

Types of Development

Although both classroom instruction and on-the-job training can be used for development purposes as well as training, development often includes additional activities such as varied work experiences and formal education.

VARIED WORK EXPERIENCES Top managers need to develop an understanding of, and expertise in, a variety of functions, products and services, and markets. To develop executives who will have this expertise, managers frequently make sure that employees with high potential have a wide variety of different job experiences, some in line positions and some in staff positions. Varied work experiences broaden employees' horizons and help them think more about the big picture. For example, one- to three-year stints overseas are being used increasingly to provide managers with international work experiences. With organizations becoming more global, managers need to develop an understanding of the different values, beliefs, cultures, regions, and ways of doing business in different countries.

FORMAL EDUCATION Many large corporations reimburse employees for tuition expenses they incur while taking college courses and obtaining advanced degrees. This is not just benevolence on the part of the employer or even a simple reward given to the employee; it is an effective way to develop employees who are able to take on new responsibilities and more challenging positions. For similar reasons, corporations spend thousands of dollars sending managers to executive development programs such as executive MBA programs. In these programs, experts teach managers the latest in business and management techniques and practices.

To save time and travel costs, managers are increasingly relying on long-distance learning to formally educate and develop employees. Using videoconferencing technologies, business schools such as the Harvard Business School, the University of Michigan, and Babson College are teaching courses on video screens in corporate conference rooms. Business schools are also customizing courses and degrees to fit the development needs of employees in a particular company. The University of Michigan uses long-distance learning, for example, to provide instruction for customized MBA degrees for employees of the Daewoo Corporation in Korea and Cathay Pacific Airways Ltd. in Hong Kong. In conjunction with Westcott Communications Inc., eight business schools have actually formed a new venture, Executive Education Network, to create and operate satellite classrooms in major corporations; almost 100 companies have already signed on, including Eastman Kodak Company, Walt Disney Company, and Texas Instruments.[64]

Transfer of Training and Development

Whenever training and development takes place off the job or in a classroom setting, it is vital for managers to promote the transfer of the knowledge and skills acquired to the actual work situation. Trainees should be encouraged and expected to use their new-found expertise on the job.

Performance Appraisal and Feedback

The recruitment and selection and training and development, components of a human resource management system ensure that employees have the knowledge and skills needed to be effective now and in the future. **Performance appraisal** and feedback complement recruitment, selection, training, and development. Performance appraisal is the evaluation of employees' job performance and contributions to their organizations. **Performance feedback** is the process through which managers share

performance appraisal The evaluation of employees' job performance and contributions to their organization.

performance feedback The process through which managers share performance appraisal information with subordinates, give subordinates an opportunity to reflect on their own performance, and develop, with subordinates, plans for the future.

performance appraisal information with their subordinates, give subordinates an opportunity to reflect on their own performance, and develop, with subordinates, plans for the future. Before performance feedback, performance appraisal must take place. Performance appraisal could take place without providing performance feedback, but wise managers are careful to provide feedback because it can contribute to employee motivation and performance.

Performance appraisal and feedback contribute to the effective management of human resources in two ways. Performance appraisal gives managers important information on which to base human resource decisions.[65] Decisions about pay raises, bonuses, promotions, and job moves all hinge on the accurate appraisal of performance. Performance appraisal can also help managers determine which workers are candidates for training and development, and in what areas. Performance feedback encourages high levels of employee motivation and performance. It lets good performers know that their efforts are valued and appreciated. It also lets poor performers know that their lackluster performance needs improvement. Performance feedback can provide both good and poor performers with insight into their strengths and weaknesses and ways in which they can improve their performance in the future.

Types of Performance Appraisal

Performance appraisal focuses on the evaluation of traits, behaviors, and results.[66]

TRAIT APPRAISALS When trait appraisals are used, managers assess subordinates on personal characteristics that are relevant to job performance, such as skills, abilities, or personality. A factory worker, for example, may be evaluated based on her ability to use computerized equipment and perform numerical calculations. A social worker may be appraised based on his empathy and communication skills.

Three disadvantages of trait appraisals often lead managers to rely on other appraisal methods. First, possessing a certain personal characteristic does not ensure that the personal characteristic will actually be used on the job and result in high performance. For example, a factory worker may possess superior computer and numerical skills but be a poor performer due to low motivation. The second disadvantage of trait appraisals is linked to the first. Because traits do not always show a direct association with performance, workers and courts of law may view them as unfair and potentially discriminatory. The third disadvantage of trait appraisals is that they often do not enable managers to provide employees with feedback that they can use to improve performance. Because trait appraisals focus on relatively enduring human characteristics that only change over the long term, employees can do little to change their behavior in response to performance feedback from a trait appraisal. Telling a social worker that he lacks empathy provides him with little guidance about how to improve his interactions with clients, for example. These disadvantages suggest that managers should use trait appraisals only when they can demonstrate that the assessed traits are accurate and important indicators of job performance.

BEHAVIOR APPRAISALS Through behavior appraisals, managers assess how workers perform their jobs–the actual actions and behaviors that workers exhibit on the job. Whereas trait appraisals assess what workers are *like*, behavior appraisals assess what workers *do*. For example, with a behavior appraisal, a manager might evaluate a social worker on the extent to which he looks clients in the eye when talking with them, expresses sympathy when they are upset, and refers them to community counseling and support groups geared toward the specific problem they are encountering. Behavior appraisals are especially useful when *how* workers perform their jobs is important. In educational organizations such as high schools, for example, the numbers of classes and students are important, but how students are taught or the methods teachers use to ensure that learning takes place are also important.

Behavior appraisals have the advantage of providing employees with clear information about what they are doing right and wrong and how they can improve their performance. And, because behaviors are much easier for employees to change than traits, performance feedback from behavior appraisals is more likely to lead to performance improvements.

RESULT APPRAISALS For some jobs, *how* people perform the job is not as important as *what* they accomplish or the results they obtain. With results appraisals, managers appraise performance by the results or the actual outcomes of work behaviors. Take the case of two new car salesmen. One salesman strives to develop personal relationships with his customers. He spends hours talking to them and frequently calls them up to see how their decision-making process is going. The other salesman has a much more hands-off approach. He is very knowledgeable, answers customers' questions, and then waits for them to come to him. Both salesmen sell, on average, the same number of cars, and the customers of both are satisfied with the customer service they receive according to postcards that the dealership mails to customers asking for an assessment of their satisfaction. The manager of the dealership appropriately uses results appraisals (sales and customer satisfaction) to evaluate the salespeople's performance because it does not matter which behavior salespeople use to sell cars as long as they sell the desired number and satisfy customers. If one salesperson sells too few cars, however, the manager can give the salesperson performance feedback that he is not selling enough.

OBJECTIVE AND SUBJECTIVE APPRAISALS Whether managers appraise performance in terms of traits, behaviors, or results, the information they assess is either *objective* or *subjective*. **Objective appraisals** are based on facts and are likely to be numerical–the number of cars sold, the number of meals prepared, the number of times late, the number of audits completed. Managers often use objective appraisals when results are being appraised, because results tend to be easier to quantify than traits or behaviors. When how workers perform their jobs is important, however, subjective behavior appraisals are more appropriate than results appraisals.

objective appraisal An appraisal that is based on facts and is likely to be numerical.

Subjective appraisals are based on managers' perceptions of traits, behaviors, or results. Because subjective appraisals rest on managers' perceptions, there is always the chance that they are inaccurate (we discuss managerial perception in more detail in the next chapter). This is why both researchers and managers have spent considerable time and effort to determine the best way to develop reliable and valid subjective measures of performance.

subjective appraisal An appraisal that is based on perceptions of traits, behaviors, or results.

Some of the more popular subjective measures such as the graphic rating scale, the behaviorally anchored rating scale (BARS), and the behavior observation scale (BOS) are illustrated in Figure 11.5.[67] When graphic rating scales are used, performance is assessed along a continuum with specified intervals. With a BARS, performance is assessed along a scale with clearly defined scale points containing examples of specific behaviors. BOS assess performance by how often specific

Figure 11.5 Subjective Measures of Performance

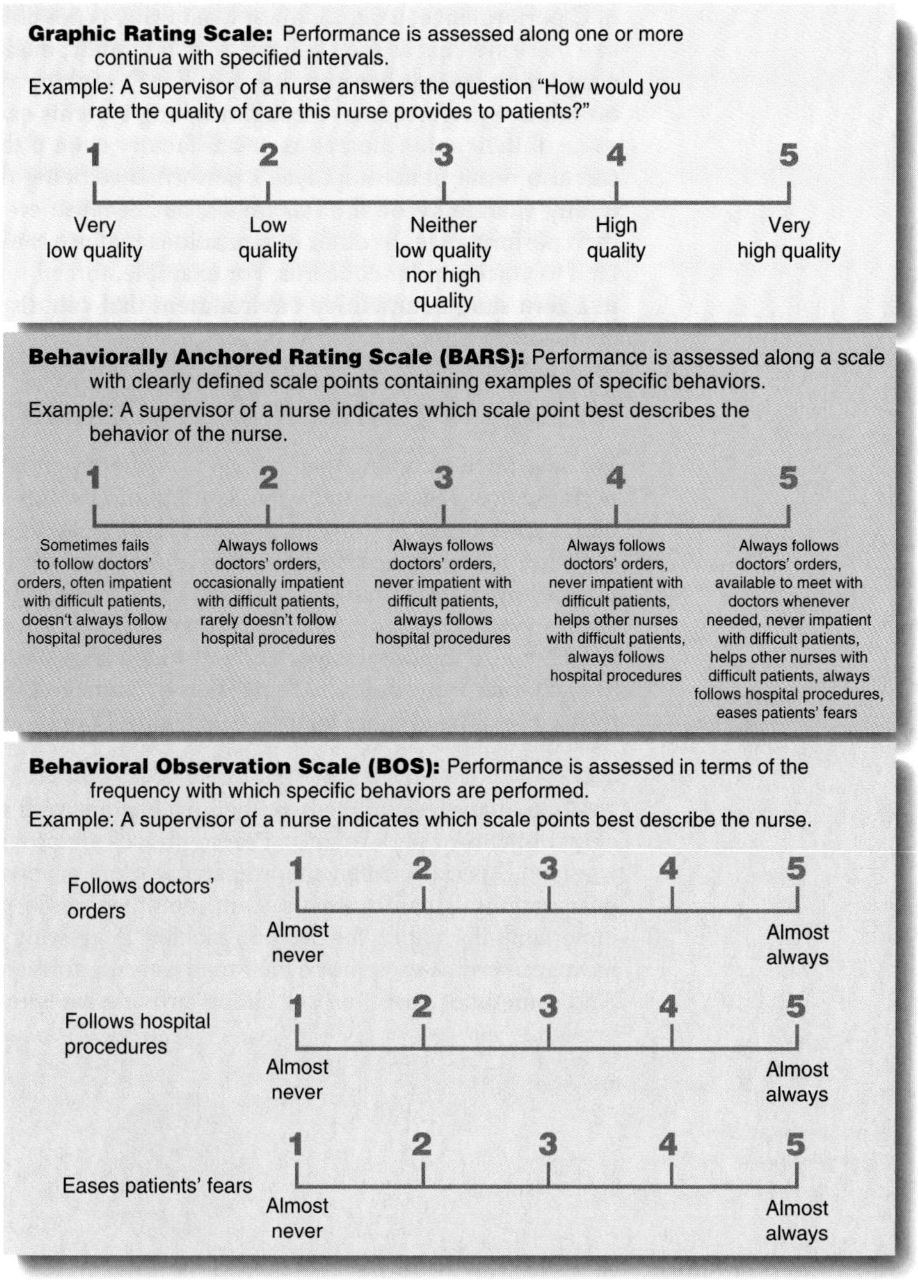
Graphic Rating Scale: Performance is assessed along one or more continua with specified intervals.
Example: A supervisor of a nurse answers the question "How would you rate the quality of care this nurse provides to patients?"
1
2
3
4
5
Very low quality
Low quality
Neither low quality nor high quality
High quality
Very high quality
Behaviorally Anchored Rating Scale (BARS): Performance is assessed along a scale with clearly defined scale points containing examples of specific behaviors.
Example: A supervisor of a nurse indicates which scale point best describes the behavior of the nurse.
1
2
3
4
5
Sometimes fails to follow doctors' orders, often impatient with difficult patients, doesn't always follow hospital procedures
Always follows doctors' orders, occasionally impatient with difficult patients, rarely doesn't follow hospital procedures
Always follows doctors' orders, never impatient with difficult patients, always follows hospital procedures
Always follows doctors' orders, never impatient with difficult patients, helps other nurses with difficult patients, always follows hospital procedures
Always follows doctors' orders, available to meet with doctors whenever needed, never impatient with difficult patients, helps other nurses with difficult patients, always follows hospital procedures, eases patients' fears
Behavioral Observation Scale (BOS): Performance is assessed in terms of the frequency with which specific behaviors are performed.
Example: A supervisor of a nurse indicates which scale points best describe the nurse.
Follows doctors' orders
1
2
3
4
5
Almost never
Almost always
Follows hospital procedures
1
2
3
4
5
Almost never
Almost always
Eases patients' fears
1
2
3
4
5
Almost never
Almost always

behaviors are performed. Many managers may use both objective and subjective appraisals. For example, a salesperson may be appraised both on the dollar value of sales (objective) and the quality of customer service (subjective).

In addition to subjective appraisals, some organizations employ *forced rankings* whereby supervisors must rank their subordinates and assign them to different categories according to their performance (which is subjectively appraised). For example, middle managers at Ford Motor Company are ranked by their supervisors in a forced distribution from A to C with 10 percent of them receiving As, 80 percent receiving Bs, and 10 percent receiving Cs.[68] The first year an employee receives a C, he or she does not receive a bonus and after two years of C performance, a demotion or even firing is possible. Employees tend not to like these systems as they believe they are unfair; managers at Ford have filed a class-action lawsuit because they feel Ford's ranking system is unfair.[69] Relying on relative performance through ranking systems can force managers to rate some of their subordinates as unsatisfactory even if this might not be true and can also result in an employee's performance being downgraded, not because of any change he or she has made, but because co-workers have improved their performance. In other organizations that use rankings systems, employees tend to voice similar concerns. For example, forced rankings systems can result in a zero-sum, competitive environment that can discourage cooperation and teamwork.[70]

Who Appraises Performance?

We have been assuming that managers or the supervisors of employees evaluate performance. This is a pretty fair assumption, for supervisors are the most common appraisers of performance; indeed each year, 70 million U.S. citizens have their job performance appraised by their managers or supervisors.[71] Performance appraisal is an important part of most managers' job duties. Managers are responsible for not only motivating their subordinates to perform at a high level but also making many decisions hinging on performance appraisals, such as pay raises or promotions. Appraisals by managers can be usefully augmented by appraisals from other sources (see Figure 11.6).

SELF, PEERS, SUBORDINATES, AND CLIENTS When self-appraisals are used, managers supplement their evaluations with an employee's assessment of his or her own performance. Peer appraisals are provided by an employee's co-workers. Especially when subordinates work in groups or teams, feedback from peer appraisals can motivate team members while providing managers with important information for decision making. A growing number of companies are having subordinates appraise their managers' performance and leadership as well. And sometimes customers or clients provide assessments of employee perfor-

Figure 11.6
Who Appraises Performance?

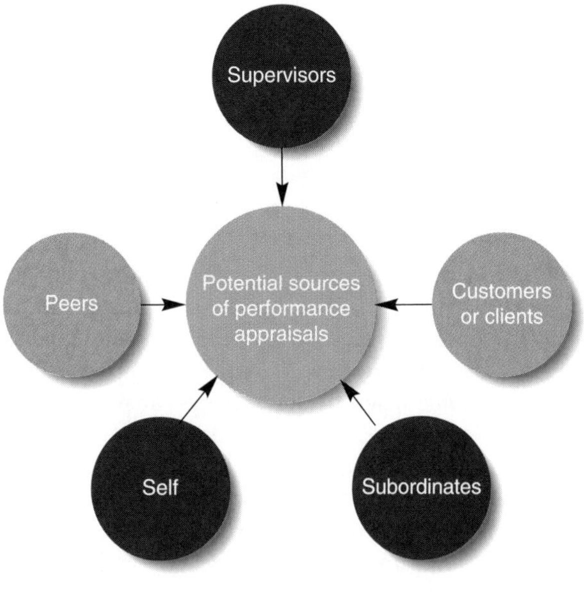

mance in terms of responsiveness to customers and quality of service. Although appraisals from each of these sources can be useful, managers need to be aware of potential issues that may arise when they are used. Subordinates sometimes may be inclined to inflate self-appraisals, especially if organizations are downsizing and they are worried about their job security. Managers who are appraised by their subordinates may fail to take needed but unpopular actions out of fear that their subordinates will appraise them negatively.

360-DEGREE PERFORMANCE APPRAISALS To improve motivation and performance, some organizations include 360-degree appraisals and feedback in their performance appraisal systems, especially for managers. In a **360-degree appraisal,** a manager's performance is appraised by a variety of people, beginning with the manager's self-appraisal and including peers or co-workers, subordinates, superiors, and sometimes even customers or clients. The manager receives feedback based on evaluations from these multiple sources.

360-degree appraisal A performance appraisal by peers, subordinates, superiors, and sometimes clients who are in a position to evaluate a manager's performance.

The growing number of companies using 360-degree appraisals and feedback include AT&T Corp., Allied Signal Inc., Eastman Chemical Co., and Baxter International Inc.[72] A 360-degree appraisal and feedback is not always as clear-cut as it might seem. On the one hand, some subordinates try to get back at their bosses by giving managers negative evaluations, especially when evaluations are anonymous (to encourage honesty and openness). A top manager at Citicorp indicated that he received a highly negative appraisal from a subordinate who tried to smear him personally. The manager was pretty sure that the evaluation came from a very poor performer.[73] On the other hand, some managers coach subordinates to give, or even threaten sanctions if they fail to give, positive evaluations.

Peers often are very knowledgeable about performance, but may be reluctant to provide an accurate and negative appraisal of someone they like or a positive appraisal of someone they dislike. At Baxter International, when peer appraisals were used in the information technology unit, workers tended to provide each other with uniformly positive evaluations because they knew the evaluations were going to be used for pay raise decisions and they were not able to provide negative feedback anonymously. Managers at Baxter continued conducting the peer appraisals but decided to use them primarily for self-development activities and not for pay decisions.[74]

In addition, whenever peers, subordinates, or anyone else evaluates a worker's performance, managers must be sure that the evaluators are actually knowledgeable about the performance dimensions being assessed. For example, subordinates should not evaluate their supervisor's decision making if they have little opportunity to observe this dimension of performance.

These potential problems with 360-degree appraisals and feedback do not mean that they are not useful. Rather they suggest that for 360-degree appraisals and feedback to be effective, there has to be trust throughout an organization. More generally, trust is a critical ingredient in any performance appraisal and feedback procedure. In addition, research suggests that 360-degree appraisals should focus on behaviors rather than traits or results, and that managers need to carefully select appropriate raters. Moreover, appraisals tend to be more honest when made anonymously and when raters have been trained in how to use 360-degree appraisal forms.[75] Additionally, managers need to think carefully about the extent to which 360-degree appraisals are appropriate for certain jobs and be willing to modify any system they implement when they become aware of unintended problems the appraisal system is responsible for.[76]

Even when 360-degree appraisals are used, it is sometimes difficult to design an effective process by which subordinates' feedback can be communicated to their managers. Advances in information technology provide organizations with a potential solution to this problem. For example, ImproveNow.com has on-line questionnaires that subordinates can fill out to evaluate the performance of their managers and provide the managers with feedback. Each subordinate of a particular manager completes the questionnaire on-line independently, all responses are tabulated, and the manager is given specific feedback on behaviors in a variety of areas such as rewarding good performance, looking out for the subordinates' best interest and being supportive, and having a vision for the future.[77]

For example, Sonia Russomanno, a manager at Alliance Funding, a New Jersey mortgage lending organization, received feedback from her nine subordinates on-line from Improve.Now. She received an overall grade of B and specific feedback on a variety of dimensions. This experience drove home to Russomanno the importance of getting honest feedback from her subordinates and listening to it to improve her performance as a manager. She has changed how she rewards her subordinates as a result and plans on using this service in the future to see how she is doing.[78]

Effective Performance Feedback

formal appraisal An appraisal conducted at a set time during the year and based on performance dimensions and measures that were specified in advance.

For the performance appraisal and feedback component of a human resource management system to encourage and motivate high performance, managers must provide their subordinates with performance feedback. To generate useful information to feed back to their subordinates, managers can use both formal and informal appraisals. **Formal appraisals** are conducted at set times during the year and are based on performance dimensions and measures that have been specified in advance. A salesperson, for example, may be evaluated by his or her manager twice a year on the performance dimensions of sales and customer service, sales being objectively measured from sales reports and customer service being measured with a BARS (see Figure 11.5).

Managers in most large organizations use formal performance appraisals on a fixed schedule dictated by company policy such as every six months or every year. An integral part of a formal appraisal is a meeting between the manager and the subordinate in which the subordinate is given feedback on performance. Performance feedback lets subordinates know in which areas they are excelling and which areas need improvement; it also should provide them with guidance for improving performance.

Realizing the value of formal appraisals, managers in many large corporations have committed substantial resources to updating their performance appraisal procedures and training low-level managers in how to use them and provide accurate feedback to employees. Top managers at the pharmaceutical company Hoffmann-La Roche Inc., for example, recently spent $1.5 million updating and improving their performance appraisal procedures. Alan Rubino, vice president of human resources for Hoffmann-La Roche, believes that this was money well spent because "people need to know exactly where they stand and what's required of them." Before Hoffmann-La Roche's new system was implemented, managers attended a three-day training and development session to improve their performance appraisal skills. The new procedures call for every manager and subordinate to develop a performance plan for subordinates for the coming year–a plan that is linked to the company's strategy and goals and approved by the manager's own superiors. Formal performance appraisals are conducted every six months during which actual performance is compared to planned performance.[79]

Formal performance appraisals supply both managers and subordinates with valuable information, but subordinates often want feedback on a more frequent basis, and managers often want to motivate subordinates as the need arises. For these reasons many companies, including Hoffman-La Roche, supplement formal performance appraisal with frequent **informal appraisals,** for which managers and their subordinates meet as the need arises to discuss ongoing progress and areas for improvement. Moreover, when job duties, assignments, or goals change, informal appraisals can provide workers with timely feedback concerning how they are handling their new responsibilities.

informal appraisal An unscheduled appraisal of ongoing progress and areas for improvement.

Managers often dislike providing performance feedback, especially when the feedback is negative, but doing so is an important managerial activity. Here are some guidelines for giving effective performance feedback that contributes to employee motivation and performance:

- Be specific and focus on behaviors or outcomes that are correctable and within a worker's ability to improve. *Example:* Telling a salesperson that he is too shy when interacting with customers is likely to do nothing more than lower his self-confidence and prompt the salesperson to become defensive. A more effective approach would be to give the salesperson feedback about specific behaviors to engage in–greeting customers as soon as they enter the department; asking customers whether they need help; volunteering to help customers find items if they seem to be having trouble.
- Approach performance appraisal as an exercise in problem solving and solution finding, not criticizing. *Example:* Rather than criticize a financial analyst for turning in reports late, the manager helps the analyst determine why the reports are late and identify ways to better manage his time.
- Express confidence in a subordinate's ability to improve. *Example:* Instead of being skeptical, a first-level manager tells a subordinate that she is confident that the subordinate can increase quality levels.
- Provide performance feedback both formally and informally. *Example:* The staff of a preschool receives feedback from formal performance appraisals twice a year. The director of the school also provides frequent informal feedback such as complimenting staff members on creative ideas for special projects, noticing when they do a particularly good job handling a difficult child, and pointing out when they provide inadequate supervision.
- Praise instances of high performance and areas of a job in which a worker excels. *Example:* Rather than focusing on just the negative, a manager discusses the areas her subordinate excels in as well as the areas in need of improvement.
- Avoid personal criticisms and treat subordinates with respect. *Example:* An engineering manager acknowledges her subordinates' expertise and treats them as professionals. Even when the manager points out performance problems to subordinates, she refrains from criticizing them personally.
- Agree to a timetable for performance improvements. *Example:* A first-level manager and his subordinate decide to meet again in one month to determine if quality levels have improved.

In following these guidelines, managers need to remember why they are giving performance feedback: to encourage high levels of motivation and performance. Moreover, the information that managers gather through performance appraisal and feedback helps them determine how to distribute pay raises and bonuses.

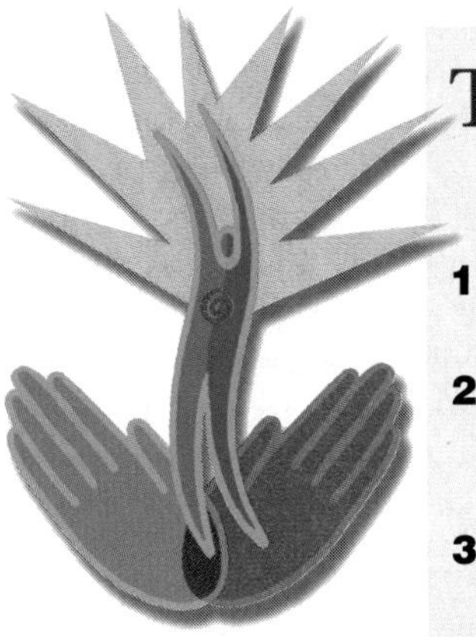

Tips for New Managers

Performance Appraisal

1. Be sure to provide frequent informal appraisals and give performance feedback often.
2. Focus on results for performance appraisal and feedback when high performance can be reached by different kinds of behaviors and how employees perform their jobs is not important.
3. Focus on specific behaviors or outcomes, when providing performance feedback, adopt a problem-solving mode, express confidence in employees, praise instances of high performance, and agree to a timetable for improvements.
4. Avoid personal criticisms and treat employees with respect.
5. Seek honest appraisals of, and feedback on, your own behavior and take steps to improve your performance.

Pay and Benefits

Pay includes employees' base salaries, pay raises, and bonuses and is determined by a number of factors including characteristics of the organization and the job and levels of performance. Employee benefits are based on membership in an organization (and not necessarily on the particular job held); they include sick days, vacation days, and medical and life insurance. In Chapter 12, we discuss the ways in which pay can motivate organizational members to perform at a high level, as well as the different kinds of pay plans managers can use to help an organization achieve its goals and gain a competitive advantage. Next we focus on establishing an organization's pay level and pay structure.

Pay Level

pay level The relative position of an organization's pay incentives in comparison with those of other organizations in the same industry employing similar kinds or workers.

Pay level is a broad comparative concept that refers to how an organization's pay incentives compare, in general, to those of other organizations in the same industry employing similar kinds of workers. Managers must decide if they want to offer relatively high wages, average wages, or relatively low wages. High wages help ensure that an organization is going to be able to recruit, select, and retain high performers, but high wages also raise costs. Low wages give an organization a cost advantage but may undermine the organization's ability to select and recruit high performers and to motivate current employees to perform at a high level. Either of these situations may lead to inferior quality or inadequate customer service.

In determining pay levels, managers should take into account their organization's strategy. A high pay level may prohibit managers from effectively pursuing a low-cost strategy. But a high pay level may be well worth the added costs in an organization whose competitive advantage lies in superior quality and excellent customer service. As one might expect, hotel and motel chains with a low-cost strategy such as Days Inn and Hampton Inns have lower pay levels than chains striving to provide high-quality rooms and services such as Four Seasons and Hyatt Regency.

Pay Structure

pay structure The arrangement of jobs into categories reflecting their relative importance to the organization and its goals, level of skill required, and other characteristics.

After deciding on a pay level, managers have to establish a pay structure for the different jobs in the organization. A **pay structure** clusters jobs into categories reflecting their relative importance to the organization and its goals, levels of skill required, and other characteristics managers consider to be important. Pay ranges are established for each job category. Individual job-holders' pay within job categories is then determined by factors such as performance, seniority, and skill levels.

There are some interesting global differences in pay structures. Large corporations based in the United States tend to pay their CEOs and top managers higher salaries than their European or Japanese counterparts. There also is a much greater pay differential between employees at the bottom of the corporate hierarchy and those higher up the hierarchy in U.S. companies than in European or Japanese companies. In 1994, for example, European CEOs' average annual salary was $389,711 while U.S. CEOs's average annual salary was $819,428.[80]

Concerns have been raised over whether it is equitable or fair for CEOs of large companies in the United States to be making hundreds of thousands or even millions of dollars in years when their companies are restructuring and laying off a good portion of their workforces. In 1995, CEO pay levels in the United States rose an average of 30 percent while massive layoffs were also taking place.[81] Robert Allen, for example, the CEO of AT&T, came under intense scrutiny in 1996 because he was earning $5 million a year when AT&T announced plans to layoff thousands of employees.

Stride-Rite, the children's shoe maker, has established an intergenerational day care center for its employees in which the families of employees are encouraged to take an active interest in the care of its employees' children.

Benefits

Organizations are legally required to provide certain benefits to their employees, including workers' compensation, Social Security, and unemployment insurance. Workers' compensation provides employees with financial assistance if they become unable to work due to a work-related injury or illness. Social Security provides financial assistance to retirees and disabled former employees. Unemployment insurance provides financial assistance to workers who lose their jobs due to no fault of their own. The legal system in the United States views these three benefits as ethical requirements for organizations and thus mandates that they be provided.

Other benefits such as health insurance, dental insurance, vacation time, pension plans, life insurance, flexible working hours, company-provided day care, and employee assistance and wellness programs are provided at the option of employers. Benefits enabling workers to simultaneously balance the demands of their jobs and their life away from the office or factory are of growing importance for many workers who have competing demands on their all too scarce time and energy.

cafeteria benefit plan A plan from which employees can choose the benefits that they want.

In some organizations, top managers determine which benefits might best suit the employees and organization and offer the same benefit package to employees. Other organizations, realizing that employees' needs and desires might differ, offer **cafeteria-style benefit plans** that let employees themselves choose the benefits they want. Cafeteria-style benefit plans sometimes assist managers in dealing with employees that feel unfairly treated because they are unable to take advantage of certain benefits available to other employees who, for example, have children. Some organizations have success with cafeteria-style benefit plans; others find them difficult to manage.

Labor Relations

labor relations The activities that managers engage in to ensure that they have effective working relationships with the labor unions that represent their employees' interests.

Labor relations are the activities that managers engage in to ensure that they have effective working relationships with the labor unions that represent their employees' interests. Although the U.S. government has responded to the potential for unethical organizations and managers treating workers unfairly–by creating and enforcing laws regulating employment (including the EEO laws listed in Table 11.1)–some workers believe that a union will ensure that their interests are fairly represented in their organizations.

Before we describe unions in more detail, let's take a look at some examples of important employment legislation. In 1938 the government passed the Fair Labor Standards Act, which prohibited child labor and made provisions for minimum wages, overtime pay, and maximum working hours to protect workers' rights. In 1963 the Equal Pay Act mandated that men and women performing equal work (work requiring the same levels of skill, responsibility, and effort performed in the same kind of working conditions) receive equal pay (see Table 11.1). In 1970 the Occupational Safety and Health Act mandated procedures for managers to follow to ensure workplace safety. These are just a few of the U.S. government's efforts to protect workers' rights. State legislatures also have been active in promoting safe, ethical, and fair workplaces.

Unions

Unions exist to represent workers' interests in organizations. Given that managers have more power than rank-and-file workers and that organizations have multiple stakeholders, there is always the potential that managers might take steps that benefit one set of stakeholders such as shareholders while hurting another such as employees. For example, managers may decide to speed up a production line to lower costs and increase production in the hopes of increasing returns to shareholders. Speeding up the line, however, could hurt employees forced to work at a rapid pace, and may increase the risk of injuries. Also, employees receive no additional pay for the extra work they are performing. Unions represent workers' interests in a scenario such as this.

The U.S. Congress acknowledged the role that unions could play in ensuring safe and fair workplaces when it passed the National Labor Relations Act of

1935. This act made it legal for workers to organize into unions to protect their rights and interests and declared certain unfair or unethical organizational practices to be illegal. The National Labor Relations Act also established the National Labor Relations Board (NLRB) to oversee union activity. Currently, the NLRB conducts certification elections, which are held among the employees of an organization to determine whether they want a union to represent their interests. The NLRB also makes judgments concerning unfair labor practices and specifies practices that managers must refrain from.

Employees might vote to have a union represent them for any number of specific reasons.[82] They may think that their wages and working conditions are in need of improvement. They may believe that managers are not treating them with respect. They may think that their working hours are unfair or that they need more job security or a safer work environment. Or they may be dissatisfied with management and find it difficult to communicate their concerns to their bosses. Regardless of the specific reason, one overriding reason is power: A united group inevitably wields more power than an individual, and this type of power may be especially helpful to employees in some organizations.

Although these would seem to be potent forces for unionization, some workers are reluctant to join unions. Sometimes this reluctance is due to the perception that union leaders are corrupt. Some workers may simply believe that belonging to a union might not do them much good or may actually cause more harm than good while costing them money in membership dues. Employees also might not want to be forced into doing something they do not want to–such as striking–because the union thinks it is in their best interest. Moreover, although unions can be a positive force in organizations, sometimes they also can be a negative force, impairing organizational effectiveness. For example, when union leaders resist needed changes in an organization or are corrupt, organizational performance can suffer.

The percentage of U.S. workers represented by unions today is smaller than in the 1950s, an era when unions were especially strong.[83] The American Federation of Labor–Congress of Industrial Organizations (AFL–CIO) includes 64 voluntary member unions representing 13 million workers.[84] Union influence in manufacturing and heavy industries has been on the decline, presumably because these workers no longer see the need to be represented by unions. Recently unions have made inroads in other segments of the workforce, however, particularly the low-wage end. Garbage collectors in New Jersey, poultry plant workers in North Carolina, and janitors in Baltimore are among the growing numbers of low-paid workers who are currently finding union membership attractive. North Carolina poultry workers voted in a union in part because they thought it was unfair that they had to buy their own gloves and hairnets used on the job and had to ask their supervisors' permission to go to the restroom.[85] Union membership and leadership, traditionally dominated by white men, is also becoming increasingly diverse. For example, Linda Chavez-Thompson is the executive vice president of the AFL-CIO and the first woman and Hispanic to hold a top management position in the federation.[86]

Labor officials in Washington, D.C., also are becoming increasingly diverse. Elaine L. Chao, the 24th U.S. Secretary of Labor, is the first Asian-American woman to hold an appointment in a U.S. president's cabinet. Chao, who has extensive management experience as a former CEO of the United Way of America and also as a former director of the Peace Corps, is committed to equal opportunity in the workplace, the well-being of workers and their families, and increased flexibility in the workplace.[87]

Collective Bargaining

collective bargaining Negotiation between labor unions and managers to resolve conflicts and disputes about issues such as working hours, wages, benefits, working conditions, and job security.

Collective bargaining is negotiation between labor unions and managers to resolve conflicts and disputes and important issues such as working hours, wages, working conditions, and job security. Before sitting down with management to negotiate, union members sometimes go on strike to drive home their concerns to managers. Once an agreement that union members support has been reached (sometimes with the help of a neutral third party called a *mediator*), union leaders and managers sign a contract spelling out the terms of the collective bargaining agreement. We discuss conflict and negotiation in depth in Chapter 16, but some brief observations are in order here because collective bargaining is an ongoing consideration in labor relations.

The signing of a contract, for example, does not bring the collective bargaining process to a halt. Disagreement and conflicts can arise over the interpretation of the contract. In these cases, a neutral third party called an *arbitrator,* is usually called in to resolve the conflict. An important component of a collective bargaining agreement is a *grievance procedure* through which workers who believe they are not being fairly treated are allowed to voice their concerns and have their interests represented by the union. Workers who think that they were unjustly fired in violation of a union contract, for example, may file a grievance, have the union represent them, and get their jobs back if an arbitrator agrees with them.

Union members sometimes go on strike when managers make decisions that they think will hurt them and are not in their best interests. This is precisely what happened in 1996 when General Motors' North American assembly plants employing 177,000 workers were idled for 18 days. The strike originated in GM's Dayton, Ohio, brake assembly plants due to management's decision to buy some parts from other companies rather than make them in GM's own plants.[88] The United Auto Workers Union called a strike because outsourcing threatens union members' jobs. The agreement that the union and management, bargaining collectively, reached allowed the outsourcing to continue but contained provisions for the creation of hundreds of new jobs as well as for improvements in working conditions.[89]

Summary and Review

STRATEGIC HUMAN RESOURCE MANAGEMENT Human resource management (HRM) includes all the activities that managers engage in to ensure that their organizations are able to attract, retain, and effectively utilize human resources. Strategic HRM is the process by which managers design the components of a human resource management system to be consistent with each other, with other elements of organizational architecture, and with the organization's strategies and goals.

RECRUITMENT AND SELECTION Before recruiting and selecting employees, managers must engage in human resource planning and job analysis. Human resource planning includes all the activities managers engage in to forecast their current and future needs for human resources. Job analysis is the process of identifying (1) the tasks, duties, and responsibilities that make up a job and (2) the knowledge, skills, and abilities needed to perform the job. Recruitment includes all the activities that managers engage in to develop a pool of qualified applicants for open positions. Selection is the process by which managers determine the relative qualifications of job applicants and their potential for performing well in a particular job.

TRAINING AND DEVELOPMENT Training focuses on teaching organizational members how to perform effectively in their current jobs. Development focuses on broadening organizational members' knowledge and skills so that they will be prepared to take on new responsibilities and challenges.

PERFORMANCE APPRAISAL AND FEEDBACK Performance appraisal is the evaluation of employees' job performance and contributions to their organization. Performance feedback is the process through which managers share performance appraisal information with their subordinates, give them an opportunity to reflect on their own performance, and develop with them plans for the future. Performance appraisal provides managers with useful information for decision making purposes. Performance feedback can encourage high levels of motivation and performance.

PAY AND BENEFITS Pay level is the relative position of an organization's pay incentives in comparison with those of other organizations in the same industry employing similar workers. A pay structure clusters jobs into categories according to their relative importance to the organization and its goals, the levels of skills required, and other characteristics. Pay ranges are then established for each job category. Organizations are legally required to provide certain benefits to their employees; other benefits are provided at the discretion of employers.

LABOR RELATIONS Labor relations includes all the activities managers engage in to ensure that they have effective working relationships with the labor unions that may represent their employees' interests. The National Labor Relations Board oversees union activity. Collective bargaining is the process through which labor unions and managers resolve conflicts and disputes and negotiate agreements.

Management in Action

Topics for Discussion and Action

1. Discuss why it is important for human resource management systems to be in sync with an organization's strategy and goals and with each other.
2. Interview a manager in a local organization to determine how that organization recruits and selects employees.
3. Discuss why training and development is an ongoing activity for all organizations.
4. Describe the type of development activities you think middle managers are most in need of.
5. Evaluate the pros and cons of 360-degree performance appraisals and feedback. Would you like your performance to be appraised in this manner? Why or why not?
6. Discuss why two restaurants in the same community might have different pay levels.
7. Explain why union membership is becoming more diverse.

Building Management Skills

Analyzing Human Resources Systems

Think about your current job or a job that you have had in the past. If you have never had a job, then interview a friend or family member who is currently working. Answer the following questions about the job you have chosen.

1. How are people recruited and selected for this job? Are the recruitment and selection procedures that the organization uses effective or ineffective? Why?
2. What training and development do people who hold this job receive? Is it appropriate? Why or why not?
3. How is performance of this job appraised? Does performance feedback contribute to motivation and high performance on this job?
4. What levels of pay and benefits are provided on this job? Are these levels of pay and benefits appropriate? Why or why not?

Small Group Breakout Exercise

Building a Human Resource Management System

Form groups of three or four people, and appoint one group member as the spokesperson who will communicate your findings to the whole class when called upon by the instructor. Then, discuss the following scenario.

You and your two or three partners are engineers with a business minor who have decided to start a consulting business. Your goal is to provide manufacturing-process engineering and other engineering services to large and small organizations. You forecast that there will be an increased use of outsourcing for these activities. You discussed with managers in several large organizations the services you plan to offer, and they expressed considerable interest. You have secured funding to start your business and now are building the HRM system. Your human resource planning suggests that you need to hire between five and eight experienced engineers with good communication skills, two clerical/secretarial workers, and two MBAs who between them will have financial, accounting, and human resources skills. You are striving to develop your human resources in a way that will enable your new business to prosper.

1. Describe the steps you will take to recruit and select (a) the engineers, (b) the clerical/secretarial workers, and (c) the MBAs.

2. Describe the training and development the engineers, the clerical/secretarial workers, and the MBAs will receive.

3. Describe how you will appraise the performance of each group of employees and how you will provide feedback.

4. Describe the pay level and pay structure of your consulting firm.

Exploring the World Wide Web

Find websites of two companies that try to recruit new employees by means of the World Wide Web. Are their approaches to recruitment on the World Wide Web similar or different? What are the potential advantages of the approaches of each? What are the potential disadvantages?

You're the Management Consultant

Walter Michaels has just received some disturbing feedback. Michaels is the director of human resources for Maxi Vision Inc., a medium-size window and glass door manufacturer. Michaels recently initiated a 360-degree performance appraisal system for all middle and upper managers at Maxi Vision, including himself but excluding the most senior executives and the top management team.

Michaels was eagerly awaiting the feedback he would receive from the managers who report to him; he had recently implemented several important initiatives that affected them and their subordinates including a complete overhaul of the organization's performance appraisal system. While the managers who reported to Michaels were evaluated based on 360-degree appraisals, their own subordinates were evaluated using a 20 question BARS scale Michaels recently created that focuses on behaviors. Conducted annually, appraisals were an important input into pay raise and bonus decisions.

Michaels was so convinced that the new performance appraisal procedures were highly effective that he hoped his own subordinates would mention them in their feedback to him. And boy did they! Michaels was amazed to learn that the managers and their subordinates thought the new BARS scales were unfair, inappropriate, and a waste of time. In fact, the managers' feedback to Michaels was that their own performance was suffering, based on the 360-degree appraisals they received, because their subordinates hated the new appraisal system and partially blamed their bosses who were part of management. Some managers even admitted giving all their subordinates around the same scores on the scales so their pay raises and bonuses would not be affected by their performance appraisals.

Michaels couldn't believe his eyes when he read these comments. He had spent so much time developing what he thought was the ideal rating scale for this group of workers. Evidently for some unknown reason, they were being very closed-minded and wouldn't give it a chance. Michaels' own supervisor was aware of these complaints and said that it was a top priority for Michaels to fix "this mess" (with the implication that Michaels was responsible for creating it). Michaels has come to you, an expert in human resource management, for advice. What should he do?

BusinessWeek Cases in the News

Job Security, No. Tall Latte, Yes.

When dot-coms started building gourmet coffee bars modeled on Central Perk from the TV show *Friends*—complete with mood lighting, overstuffed sofas, and 14 varieties of premium brews—some wondered if the New Economy frills were getting out of hand. It was one thing to hand out signing bonuses to janitors, and maids to summer interns. If a slowdown occurred, these perks could easily be whacked. But caffeine-addicted employees swarmed the espresso machines like druggies angling for a fix. Yanking this freebie could send them into convulsions of revolt.

Not to worry. The dot-com era may be dead, but, for the most part, connoisseur office coffee is here to stay. In fact, instead of worrying about being cut off from their caffeine supplies, employees can also look forward to mainlining free bottled water and subsidized snacks, both of which are in the offing at many companies—despite the slowdown-induced emphasis on cost-cutting.

Souped Up

What began as a dot-com dividend has "spilled over into a legacy," says Richard Wyckoff, president of corporate America's top coffee supplier, Aramark Refreshment Services, which reports that sales of souped-up coffee machines tripled in the past year. Many companies such as Philadelphia-based Omicrom say that no matter how bad things get, they wouldn't dare pull the perk. Even managers at MCI Worldcom Inc., who post-merger were told to can the coffee, have resumed re-ordering.

The any-kind-of-coffee-you-want largesse is not the only New Economy legacy. Far from being fads that will evaporate like so many market caps, many of the workplace revolutions developed to coddle employees and warehouse them in offices for as long as possible might very well strengthen during the next 15 years. Part of the reason is economic. Even with the slow-down, companies must still compete for valued knowledge workers. And as employees are forced to clock workaholic hours in the global, 24/7 economy, companies will have to make offices seem more and more like home.

Out Gen Yers

Attitudinal shifts about the workplace are also a key factor. Earlier in their lives, many of the boomers now running the show spat on bourgeois values, disdained all things corporate, and fancied themselves as bohemians. In fact, today's corporate chieftains make up the first generation that didn't serve in the armed forces and wasn't weaned on military models of organization. Thus, some have refashioned offices in the image of their freewheeling, anti-establishment values. They want to succeed, but they also want to be cool.

In Return of the Suit

Of course, not everything about the loosey-goosey New Economy workplace will stick. Skin-tight spandex and scruffy facial hair at the office are fading as fast as knee-length skirts on the runway. Underscored by a President who requires crisp, company-man dress, the suit is making a big comeback. Some firms such as recruiter Korn/Ferry have even reinstituted the button-down codes of yore—except in Silicon Valley. Already, retailer Men's Warehouses Inc. and fashion design Joseph Abboud are forming a marketing alliance aimed at the resurgence of professional dress.

Waning, too, is the reign of the unwrinkled. Seasoned, over-40 types bring a level of comfort to employers that post-pubescent wireheads never could. Another casualty: résumé puffery. Gone are the days when employers skipped the background and reference checks, allowing fakers to sail through. And the corporate carpetbaggers who bounced from job to job, collecting fatter paychecks and more options along the way, are no longer laughing at those "loyalist losers." They're asking them for jobs.

Bur for the most part, dot-com style perks will become permanent fixtures of the work landscape. Cultural changes wrought by the New Economy stem from when all those startups were siphoning off Old Economy workers amid the worst labor shortage in modern history. Rather than sit back and take it, Big Five accounting firms, Rust Belt stalwarts, investment banks, and law firms were forced to remake themselves in the image of their worker-snatching rivals. The strategy shifted the balance of power in employees' favor, and companies still haven't been able to completely regain their upper hand. That's why the recent pileup in layoffs isn't going to magically turn everyone back into a gold-watch seeker. Those days have been replaced by the free-agent mentality, in which the most talented workers can still afford to seek better deals within their companies and on the open market.

The smartest companies know this. Instead of ensnaring employees financially with more signing bonuses and huge salaries, they are trying to hook them emotionally with management retreats, specials awards, and assistance with elder and dependent care. And rather than resorting to their old strategy of assembling secret SWAT teams to psychologically pressure would-be defectors into staying, they are rechristening these leave-takers "alumni" and bidding them to boomerang back to the firm—if and when it's still hiring.

That's why Ernst & Young renamed its Office for Retention to the Center for the New Workforce. "People will have nine jobs by the time they are 30," says E&Y job czar Deborah K. Holmes. "We'd be delighted to be two or three of those jobs." And when skilled workers take those jobs, they'll do so with dot-com-style employment contracts in hand that protect them from mergers and downturns. After all, the Nasdaq may be in shreds, but if talented workers learned anything from the boom, it's that their careers—and offices—don't have to be.

Source: M. Conlin, "Job Security, No. Tall Latte, Yes," *Business Week,* April 2, 2001, pp. 62, 64.

Questions

1. Why does it appear that managers are preserving some traditions from the dot-com heyday and eliminating others?
2. How important are job benefits, perks, and work environment factors for organizational effectiveness?

BusinessWeek

Cases in the News

How to Enable the Disabled

It's a puzzle that is perplexing the economics fraternity. While the expansion of the 1990s boosted jobs and incomes for most Americans, it seems to have bypassed a key group: the nearly 10 percent of the working age population with disabilities.

A study by Richard V. Burkhauser and Andrew J. Houtenville of Cornell University and Mary C. Daly of the Federal Reserve Bank of San Francisco tells the story. Despite rising demand for workers, the employment rates of disabled men and women fell steadily from 1989 to 1999 (chart). Further, their household incomes lagged behind the income gains of other households, as earnings declines were only partly offset by higher payments from such programs as Social Security Disability Insurance and Supplemental Security Income (SSI).

Why hasn't employment of the disabled grown during this expansion, as it did in other cyclical upturns such as that of the 1980s? The question is touching off a hot debate among economists.

Some, such as Massachusetts Institute of Technology economists Daron Acemoglu and Joshua Angrist, believe the Americans With Disabilities Act (ADA) which took effect in 1992 and was supposed to enhance hiring of the disabled, actually backfired. Their analysis of survey data suggests the costs of accommodating disabled employees—and lawsuits if they are fired—have dissuaded employers from adding disabled workers to their payrolls.

The law's defenders argue that the survey data are flawed. People who are successfully integrated into the workforce, for example, may no longer describe themselves as "disabled" in government surveys—thus lowering the employment estimate for the disabled population. Researchers Douglas Kruse and Lisa Schur or Rutgers University find that employment of people with functional disabilities who did not describe themselves as "work-disabled" rose after the ADA was passed.

Still others stress a sharp rise in people receiving disability payments via Social Security or SSI. In this view, the decline in employer-sponsored health insurance along with relaxed government eligibility standards in the 1990s induced many of the disabled to opt for transfer programs rather than work. Indeed, a study by John Bound and Timothy Waidmann of the University of Michigan attributes much of the drop in disabled employment rates to the growth in government disability insurance rolls.

Of course, it's likely that all of these theories have some validity—that the ADA hurt hiring prospects for some people and helped others, for example, and that many were attracted by the greater availability of government transfer programs. What everyone agrees is that more has to be done to bring the disabled into the world of work and off the government dole.

Thus, hopes are now focused on the new "Ticket to Work" federal law about to go into effect. Under this program, private agencies that successfully train and place the disabled in continuing employment will receive as payment some of the funds they save the government.

Source: G. Koretz, "How to Enable the Disabled" *Business Week,* November 6, 2000, Department: Economic Trends, *Business Week* Archives.

Scant Progress for People with Disabilities

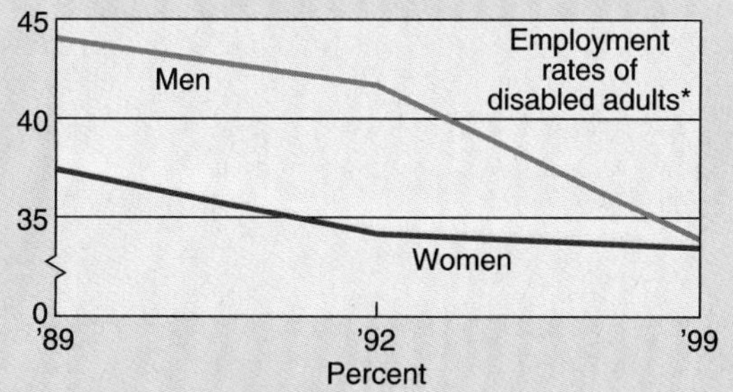

*Data, Richard V. Burkhauser, Mary C. Daly, and Andrew J. Houtenville ©6W

Questions

1. Why might the disabled have difficulty in obtaining jobs for which they are qualified and in earning appropriate levels of income given their education and skills?
2. How can managers take steps to ensure that the ADA has positive rather than negative effects on the fate of the disabled?

Chapter 12

Motivation

Learning Objectives:

After studying this chapter, you should be able to:

- Explain what **motivation** is and why managers need to be concerned about it.
- Describe from the perspectives of **expectancy theory** and **equity theory** what managers should do to have a highly motivated workforce.
- Explain how **goals and needs** motivate people and what kinds of goals are especially likely to result in high performance.
- Identify the motivation lessons that managers can learn from **operant conditioning theory** and **social learning theory.**
- Explain why and how managers can use **pay** as a major motivation tool.

A Manager's Challenge

Consistently Ranking as a Best Company to Work for: Tindell and Boone Inspire and Motivate at The Container Store

How can managers motivate employees in an industry known for high levels of turnover and low levels of motivation?

An employee at The Container Store provides customer assistance with a smile.

Kip Tindell and Garrett Boone founded The Container Store in Dallas, Texas, in 1978 and currently serve as CEO and chairman, respectively. When they opened their first store, they were out on the floor trying to sell customers their storage and organization products that would economize on space and time and make their lives a little less complicated. The Container Store has grown to include 25 stores in 10 states; although the original store in Dallas had only 1,600 square feet, their stores today average around 25,000 square feet. The phenomenal growth in the size of the stores has been matched by a 20 to 25 percent overall company growth.[1] Surprising enough, Tindell and Boone can still be found on the shop floor tidying shelves and helping customers carry out their purchases.[2] And that, perhaps, is an important clue to the secret of their success and their record as the first company to be ranked number one in *Fortune*'s annual survey of the best companies to work for two years running.[3]

Early on, Tindell and Boone recognized that people are The Container Store's most valuable asset and that after hiring great people, one of the most important managerial tasks is motivating them. One would think that motivating employees might be especially challenging in the retail industry which has an average annual turnover rate for full-time salespeople of more than 70 percent and an annual turnover rate for store managers over 30 percent. The Container Stores' comparable figures are fractions of these industry statistics, a testament to Tindell and Boone's ability to motivate.[4] As part of the *Fortune* survey, 97 percent of employees at The Container Store indicate that "people care about each other here."[5]

How do Tindell and Boone do it? Essentially, by being clear about what is important at The Container Store, enabling employees to be high performers, rewarding employees in multiple ways, creating a fair and stimulating work environment, and treating employees like the highly capable individuals that they are.[6] Maintaining excellent customer service and a motivated, enthusiastic workforce that is treated well are top priorities at The Container Store as are honesty, openness, and trust.

While the majority of full-time salespeople have college degrees, they nonetheless receive more than 235 hours of training during their first year on the job (compared to an industry average of under 10 hours).[7] This focus on training continues throughout employees' careers with The Container Store, consistent with Tindell and Boone's emphasis on customer service and employee motivation. Training focuses on the characteristics and advantages of each product, how to sell and provide superior customer service, and how to creatively meet customers' container and storage needs. Thus, employees feel confident that they can help customers—even those with very unusual container needs—and provide truly excellent service.

Tindell and Boone also recognize the importance of rewarding employees for a job well done. For example, employees receive 50 to 100 percent higher wages than industry average and merit pay increases for superior sales performance can reach 8 percent per year. To encourage high individual performance as well as teamwork and cooperation, both individual and team-based rewards are utilized at The Container Store. Some high-performing salespeople earn more than their store managers which suits the store managers fine as long as equitable procedures are used and rewards are distributed fairly.[8]

Professional development is a valued outcome employees obtain from working at The Container Store. Employees are respected and are given the autonomy to best meet customers' needs however they see fit. Given all the training they receive, employees are confident that they can do this. As Garrett Boone puts it, "Everybody we hire, we hire as a leader. Anybody in our store can take an action that you might think of typically being a manager's action."[9] Thus, employees really have the opportunity to learn and develop on the job, somewhat of a rarity in retail sales.

Additionally, employees are treated with respect and have access to what is often privileged information in other companies such as the amount of annual store sales. Employees also have flexible work options and flexible benefits; medical, dental, and 401K (retirement) plans; job security; and a casual dress code. Equally important are the opportunity to work with other highly motivated individuals in an environment that exudes enthusiasm and excitement. Not only are The Container Store's employees motivated but they also look forward to coming to work and feel like their co-workers and managers are part of their family. Employees feel pride in what they do—helping customers organize their lives, save space and time, and have a better sense of well-being. Hence, they not only personally benefit from high performance but they also feel good about the products they sell and helping customers satisfy their needs.[10] Tindell and Boone evidently have never lost sight of the importance of motivation for both organizations and their members. •

Overview

Even with the best strategy in place and an appropriate organizational architecture, an organization will be effective only if its members are motivated to perform at a high level. Tindell and Boone clearly realize this. One reason why leading is such an important managerial activity is that it entails ensuring that each member of an organization is motivated to perform highly and help the organization achieve its goals. When managers are effective, the outcome of the leading process is a highly motivated workforce. A key challenge for managers of organizations both large and small is to encourage employees to perform at a high level.

In this chapter we describe what motivation is, where it comes from, and why managers need to promote high levels of it for an organization to be effective and achieve its goals. We examine important theories of motivation: expectancy theory, need theories, equity theory, goal-setting theory, and learning theories. Each provides managers with important insights about how to motivate organizational members. The theories are complementary in that each focuses on a somewhat different aspect of motivation. Considering all of the theories together helps managers gain a rich understanding of the many issues and problems involved in encouraging high levels of motivation throughout an organization. Last, we consider the use of pay as a motivation tool. By the end of this chapter, you will understand what it takes to have a highly motivated workforce.

The Nature of Motivation

motivation Psychological forces that determine the direction of a person's behavior in an organization, a person's level of effort, and a person's level of persistence.

Motivation may be defined as psychological forces that determine the direction of a person's behavior in an organization, a person's level of effort, and a person's level of persistence in the face of obstacles.[11] The *direction of a person's behavior* refers to the many possible behaviors that a person could engage in. For example, employees at The Container Store know that they should do whatever is required to meet a customer's container needs and don't have to ask permission to do something out of the ordinary.[12] *Effort* refers to how hard people work. Employees at The Container Store exert high levels of effort to provide superior customer service. *Persistence* refers to whether, when faced with roadblocks and obstacles, people keep trying or give up. For example, when Hayden Tidwell, a salesperson at The Container Store in Dallas couldn't find a box in the store that would hold a customer's painting, rather than giving up and telling the customer he was sorry, he persisted and made a custom-size box with cardboard and tape.[13]

Motivation is so central to management because it explains *why* people behave the way they do in organizations–why employees at The Container Store provide such excellent customer service and enjoy doing so. Motivation also explains why a waiter is polite or rude, and why a kindergarten teacher really tries to get children to enjoy learning or just goes through the motions. It explains why some managers themselves truly put their organizations' best interests first whereas others are more concerned with maximizing their salaries, and why–more generally–some workers put forth twice as much effort as others.

intrinsically motivated behavior Behavior that is performed for its own sake.

Motivation can come from *intrinsic* or *extrinsic* sources. **Intrinsically motivated behavior** is behavior that is performed for its own sake; the source of motivation is actually performing the behavior, and motivation comes from doing the work itself. Many managers are intrinsically motivated; they derive a sense of accomplishment and achievement from helping their organizations to achieve their goals and gain competitive advantages. Jobs that are interesting and challenging or high on the five characteristics described by the job characteristics model (see Chapter 9) are more likely to lead to intrinsic motivation than are jobs that are boring or do not make use of a person's skills and abilities. An elementary school teacher who really enjoys teaching children, a computer programmer who loves solving programming problems, and a commercial photographer who relishes taking creative photographs are all intrinsically motivated. For these individuals, motivation comes from performing their jobs whether it be teaching children, finding bugs in computer programs, or taking pictures.

extrinsically motivated behavior Behavior that is performed to acquire material or social rewards or to avoid punishment.

Extrinsically motivated behavior is behavior that is performed to acquire material or social rewards or to avoid punishment; the source of motivation is the consequences of the behavior, not the behavior itself. A car salesperson who is motivated by receiving a commission on all cars sold, a lawyer who is motivated by the high salary and status that go along with the job, and a factory worker who is motivated by the opportunity to earn a secure income are all extrinsically motivated. Their motivation comes from the consequences they receive as a result of their work behaviors.

People can be intrinsically motivated, extrinsically motivated, or both intrinsically and extrinsically motivated. A top manager who derives a sense of accomplishment and achievement from managing a large corporation and strives to reach year-end targets to obtain a hefty bonus is both intrinsically and extrinsically motivated. Similarly, a nurse who enjoys helping and taking care of patients and is motivated by having a secure job with good benefits is both intrinsically and extrinsically motivated. At The Container Store, employees are both extrinsically motivated by their relatively high salary and generous benefits and intrinsically motivated because they genuinely enjoy and get a sense of satisfaction out of their work and serving customers and look forward to coming to work each day. Whether workers are intrinsically motivated, extrinsically motivated, or both depends on a wide variety of factors: (1) workers' own personal characteristics (such as their personalities, abilities, values, attitudes, and needs); (2) the nature of their jobs (such as whether they have been enriched or where they are on the five core characteristics of the job characteristics model); and (3) the nature of the organization (such as its structure, its culture, its control systems, its human resource management system, and the ways in which rewards such as pay are distributed to employees).

Regardless of whether people are intrinsically or extrinsically motivated, they join and are motivated to work in organizations to obtain certain outcomes. An **outcome** is anything a person gets from a job or organization. Some outcomes, such as autonomy, responsibility, a feeling of accomplishment, and the pleasure of doing interesting or enjoyable work, result in intrinsically motivated behavior. Other outcomes, such as pay, job security, benefits, and vacation time, result in extrinsically motivated behavior.

outcome Anything a person gets from a job or organization.

input Anything a person contributes to his or her job or organization.

Organizations hire people to obtain important inputs. An **input** is anything a person contributes to the job or organization, such as time, effort, education, experience, skills, knowledge, and actual work behaviors. Inputs such as these are necessary for an organization to achieve its goals. Managers strive to motivate members of an organization to contribute inputs–through their behavior, effort, and persistence–that help the organization achieve its goals. How do managers do this? They ensure that members of an organization obtain the outcomes they desire when they make valuable contributions to the organization. Managers use outcomes to motivate people to contribute their inputs to the

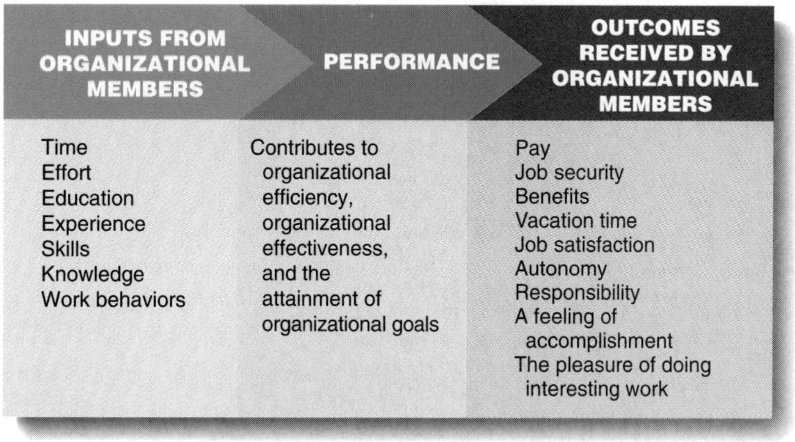

Figure 12.1 The Motivation Equation

organization. Giving people outcomes when they contribute inputs and perform well aligns the interests of employees with the goals of the organization as a whole because when employees do what is good for the organization, they personally benefit.

This alignment between employees and organizational goals as a whole can be described by the motivation equation depicted in Figure 12.1. Managers seek to ensure that people are motivated to contribute important inputs to the organization, that these inputs are put to good use or focused in the direction of high performance, and that high performance results in workers obtaining the outcomes they desire.

Each of the theories of motivation discussed in this chapter focuses on one or more aspects of this equation. Each theory focuses on a different set of issues that managers need to address to have a highly motivated workforce. Together, the theories provide a comprehensive set of guidelines for managers to follow to promote high levels of employee motivation. Effective managers, such as Tindell and Boone in "A Manager's Challenge" tend to follow many of these guidelines, whereas ineffective managers often fail to follow them and seem to have trouble motivating organizational members.

Expectancy Theory

expectancy theory The theory that motivation will be high when workers believe that high levels of effort lead to high performance and high performance leads to the attainment of desired outcomes.

Expectancy theory, formulated by Victor H. Vroom in the 1960s, posits that motivation is high when workers believe that high levels of effort lead to high performance and high performance leads to the attainment of desired outcomes. Expectancy theory is one of the most popular theories of work motivation because it focuses on all three parts of the motivation equation: inputs, performance, and outcomes. Expectancy theory identifies three major factors that determine a person's motivation: *expectancy*, *instrumentality*, and *valence* (see Figure 12.2).[14]

Expectancy

expectancy In expectancy theory, a perception about the extent to which effort results in a certain level of performance.

Expectancy is a person's perception about the extent to which effort (an input) results in a certain level of performance. A person's level of expectancy determines whether he or she believes that a high level of effort results in a high level of performance. People are motivated to put forth a lot of effort on their jobs

Figure 12.2
Expectancy, Instrumentality, and Valence

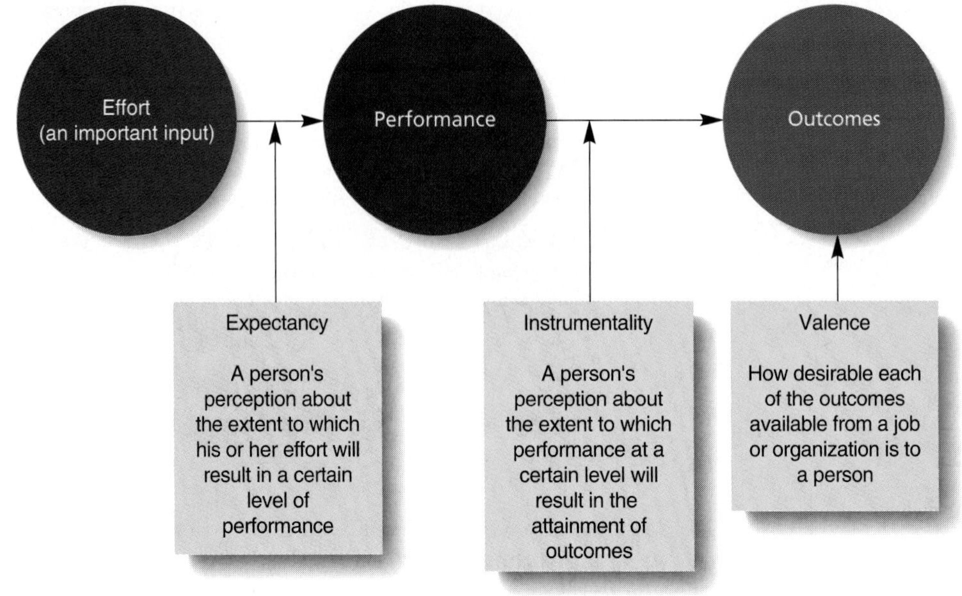

only if they think that their effort will pay off in high performance–that is, if they have a high expectancy. Think about how motivated you would be to study for a test if you thought that no matter how hard you tried you would get a D. Think about how motivated a marketing manager would be who thought that no matter how hard he or she worked there was no way to increase sales of an unpopular product. In these cases, expectancy is low, so overall motivation is also low.

Members of an organization are motivated to put forth a high level of effort only if they think that doing so leads to high performance. In other words, in order for people's motivation to be high, expectancy must be high. Thus, in attempting to influence motivation, managers need to make sure that their subordinates believe that if they do try hard they can actually succeed. One way managers can boost expectancies is through expressing confidence in their subordinates capabilities. Garrett Boone in "A Manager's Challenge" expressed confidence in his subordinates when he indicated that, "Everybody we hire, we hire as a leader. Anybody in our store can take an action that you might think of typically being a manager's action."[15]

In addition to expressing confidence in subordinates, another way for managers to boost subordinates' expectancy levels and motivation is by providing training so that people have all the expertise needed for high performance. Managers at Julius Blum GmbH, a manufacturing company that produces hinges in Hoechst, Austria, boost their employees' expectancy and motivation through a four-year apprenticeship program combining classroom and on-the-job instruction that costs practically $5 million a year. The program is well worth its cost, however. Blum has some of the best-trained employees in Austria, and the combination of their training, high expectancy, and motivation has resulted in the company being very successful.[16] Similarly, the hundreds of hours that managers at The Container Store devote to training helps ensure that their employees have high expectancy for providing excellent customer service.

Instrumentality

instrumentality In expectancy theory, a perception about the extent to which performance results in the attainment of outcomes.

Expectancy captures a person's perceptions about the relationship between effort and performance. **Instrumentality,** the second major concept in expectancy theory, is a person's perception about the extent to which performance at a certain level results in the attainment of outcomes (see Figure 12.2). According to expectancy theory, employees are motivated to perform at a high level only if they think that high performance will lead to (or is *instrumental* for attaining) outcomes such as pay, job security, interesting job assignments, bonuses, or a feeling of accomplishment. In other words, instrumentalities must be high for motivation to be high–people must perceive that because of their high performance they will receive outcomes.

Managers promote high levels of instrumentality when they clearly link performance to desired outcomes. In addition, managers must clearly communicate this linkage to subordinates. By making sure that outcomes available in an organization are distributed to organizational members on the basis of their performance, managers promote high instrumentality and motivation. When outcomes are linked to performance in this way, high performers receive more outcomes than low performers. In "A Manager's Challenge," Boone and Tindell raise levels of instrumentality and motivation for The Container Store employees by linking pay raises to performance.

Another example of high instrumentality contributing to high motivation can be found in the Cambodian immigrants who own, manage, and work in more than 80 percent of the doughnut shops in California.[17] These immigrants see high performance as leading to many important outcomes such as income, a comfortable existence, family security, and the autonomy provided by working in a small business. Their high instrumentality contributes to their high motivation to succeed.

Valence

valence In expectancy theory, how desirable each of the outcomes available from a job or organization is to a person.

Although all members of an organization must have high expectancies and instrumentalities, expectancy theory acknowledges that people differ in their preferences for outcomes. For many people, pay is the most important outcome of working. For others, a feeling of accomplishment or enjoying one's work is more important than pay. The term **valence** refers to how desirable each of the outcomes available from a job or organization is to a person. To motivate organizational members, managers need to determine which outcomes have high valence for them–are highly desired–and make sure that those outcomes are provided when members perform at a high level. From "A Manager's Challenge," it appears that in addition to pay, autonomy, a stimulating work environment, enthusiastic co-workers, and generous benefits are highly valent outcomes for many employees at The Container Store.

Bringing It All Together

According to expectancy theory, high motivation results from high levels of expectancy, instrumentality, and valence (see Figure 12.3). If any one of these factors is low, motivation is likely to be low. No matter how tightly desired outcomes are linked to performance, if a person thinks it is practically impossible

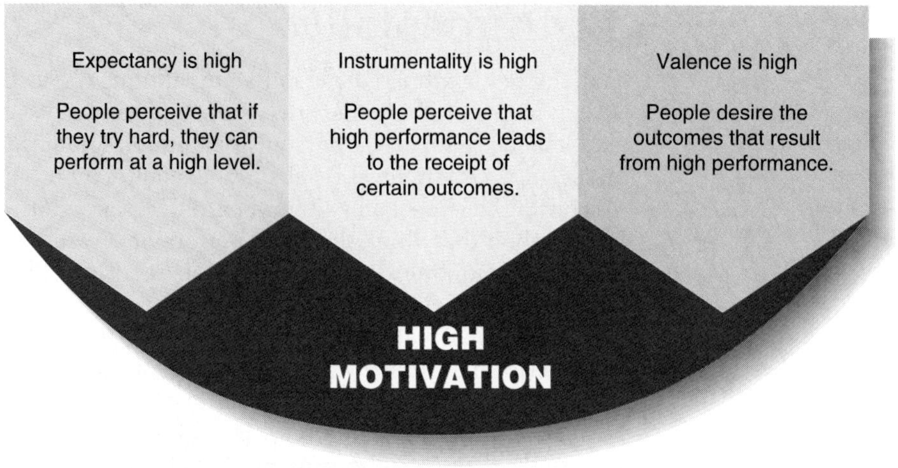

Figure 12.3
Expectancy Theory

to perform at a high level, then motivation to perform at a high level is exceedingly low. Similarly, if a person does not think that outcomes are linked to high performance, or if a person does not desire the outcomes that are linked to high performance, then motivation to perform at a high level is low.

Need Theories

A **need** is a requirement or necessity for survival and well-being. The basic premise of **need theories** is that people are motivated to obtain outcomes at work that will satisfy their needs. Need theory complements expectancy theory by exploring in depth which outcomes motivate people to perform at a high level. Need theories suggest that to motivate a person to contribute valuable inputs to a job and perform at a high level, a manager must determine what needs the person is trying to satisfy at work and ensure that the person receives outcomes that help to satisfy those needs when the person performs at a high level and helps the organization achieve its goals.

need A requirement or necessity for survival and well-being.

need theories Theories of motivation that focus on what needs people are trying to satisfy at work and what outcomes will satisfy those needs.

There are several need theories. Here we discuss Abraham Maslow's hierarchy of needs, Clayton Alderfer's ERG theory, Frederick Herzberg's motivator-hygiene theory, and David McClelland's needs for achievement, affiliation, and power. These theories describe needs that people try to satisfy at work. In doing so, they provide managers with insights about what outcomes motivate members of an organization to perform at a high level and contribute inputs to help the organization achieve its goals.

Maslow's Hierarchy of Needs

Psychologist Abraham Maslow proposed that all people seek to satisfy five basic kinds of needs: physiological needs, safety needs, belongingness needs, esteem needs, and self-actualization needs (see Table 12.1).[18] He suggested that these needs constitute a **hierarchy of needs,** with the most basic or compelling needs–physiological and safety needs–at the bottom. Maslow argued that these lowest-level needs must be met before a person strives to satisfy needs higher up in the hierarchy, such as self-esteem needs. Once a need is satisfied, Maslow proposed, it ceases to operate as a source of motivation. The lowest level of *unmet* needs in the hierarchy is the prime motivator of behavior; if and when this level is satisfied, needs at the next highest level in the hierarchy motivate behavior.

Maslow's hierarchy of needs An arrangement of five basic needs that, according to Maslow, motivate behavior. Maslow proposed that the lowest level of unmet needs is the prime motivator and that only one level of needs is motivational at a time.

Table 12.1
Maslow's Hierarchy of Needs

	Needs	Description	Examples of How Managers Can Help People Satisfy These Needs at Work
Highest-level needs ↑	**Self-actualization needs**	The needs to realize one's full potential as a human being	By giving people the opportunity to use their skills and abilities to the fullest extent possible
	Esteem needs	The needs to feel good about oneself and one's capabilities, to be respected by others, and to receive recognition and appreciation	By granting promotions and recognizing accomplishments
	Belongingness needs	Needs for social interaction, friendship, affection, and love	By promoting good interpersonal relations and organizing social functions such as company picnics and holiday parties
	Safety needs	Needs for security, stability, and a safe environment	By providing job security, adequate medical benefits, and safe working conditions
↓ **Lowest-level needs (most basic or compelling)**	**Physiological needs**	Basic needs for things such as food, water, and shelter that must be met in order for a person to survive	By providing a level of pay that enables a person to buy food and clothing and have adequate housing

The lowest level of unsatisfied needs motivates behavior; once this level of needs is satisfied, a person tries to satisfy the needs at the next level.

Although this theory identifies needs that are likely to be important sources of motivation for many people, research does not support Maslow's contention that there is a need hierarchy or his notion that only one level of needs is motivational at a time.[19] Nevertheless, a key conclusion can be drawn from Maslow's theory: People try to satisfy different needs at work. To have a motivated workforce, managers must determine which needs employees are trying to satisfy in organizations and then make sure that individuals receive outcomes that satisfy their needs when they perform at a high level and contribute to organizational effectiveness. By doing this, managers align the interests of individual members with the interests of the organization as a whole. By doing what is good for the organization (that is, performing at a high level), employees receive outcomes that satisfy their needs.

In our increasingly global economy, managers must realize that citizens of different countries might differ in the needs they seek to satisfy through work.[20] Some research suggests, for example, that people in Greece and Japan are especially motivated by safety needs and that people in Sweden, Norway, and Denmark are motivated by belongingness needs.[21] In less-developed countries with low standards of living, physiological and safety needs are likely to be the prime motivators of behavior. As countries become wealthier and have higher standards of living, needs related to personal growth and accomplishment (such as esteem and self-actualization) become important as motivators of behavior.

Alderfer's ERG Theory

Alderfer's ERG theory The theory that three universal needs—for existence, relatedness, and growth—constitute a hierarchy of needs and motivate behavior. Alderfer proposed that needs at more than one level can be motivational at the same time.

Clayton Alderfer's ERG theory collapses the five categories of needs in Maslow's hierarchy into three universal categories–existence, relatedness, and growth–also arranged in a hierarchy (see Table 12.2). Alderfer agrees with Maslow that as lower-level needs become satisfied, a person seeks to satisfy higher-level needs. Unlike Maslow, however, Alderfer believes that a person can be motivated by needs at more than one level at the same time. A cashier in a supermarket, for example, may be motivated both by existence needs and by relatedness needs. The existence needs motivate the cashier to come to work regularly and not make mistakes so that his job will be secure and he will be able to pay his rent and buy food. The relatedness needs motivate the cashier to become friends with some of the other cashiers and have a good relationship with the store manager. Alderfer also suggests that when people experience *need frustration* or are unable to satisfy needs at a certain level, they will focus all the more on satisfying the needs at the next lowest level in the hierarchy.[22]

As with Maslow's theory, research does not support some of the specific ideas outlined in ERG theory, such as the existence of the three-level need hierarchy that Alderfer proposed.[23] However, for managers, the important message from ERG theory is the same as that from Maslow's theory: Determine what needs your subordinates are trying to satisfy at work, and make sure that they receive outcomes that satisfy these needs when they perform at a high level to help the organization achieve its goals.

Herzberg's Motivator-Hygiene Theory

Herzberg's motivator-hygiene theory A need theory that distinguishes between motivator needs (related to the nature of the work itself) and hygiene needs (related to the physical and psychological context in which the work is performed) and proposes that motivator needs must be met for motivation and job satisfaction to be high.

Adopting an approach different from Maslow's and Alderfer's, Frederick Herzberg focuses on two factors: (1) outcomes that can lead to high levels of motivation and job satisfaction and (2) outcomes that can prevent people from being dissatisfied. According to Herzberg's motivator-hygiene theory, people have two sets of needs or requirements: motivator needs and hygiene needs.[24] *Motivator needs* are related to the nature of the work itself and how challenging it is. Outcomes such as interesting work, autonomy, responsibility, being able to grow and develop on the job, and a sense of accomplishment and achievement help to satisfy motivator needs. To have a highly motivated and satisfied workforce, Herzberg suggested, managers should take steps to ensure that employees' motivator needs are being met.

Hygiene needs are related to the physical and psychological context in which the work is performed. Hygiene needs are satisfied by outcomes such as pleasant and comfortable working conditions, pay, job security, good relationships with co-workers, and effective supervision. According to Herzberg, when hygiene needs are not met, workers are dissatisfied, and when hygiene needs are met, workers are not dissatisfied. Satisfying hygiene needs, however, does not result in high levels of motivation or even high levels of job satisfaction. For motivation and job satisfaction to be high, motivator needs must be met.

Many research studies have tested Herzberg's propositions, and, by and large, the theory fails to receive support.[25] Nevertheless, Herzberg's formulations have contributed to our understanding of motivation in at least two ways. First, Herzberg helped to focus researchers' and managers' attention on the important distinction between intrinsic motivation (related to motivator needs)

Table 12.2
Alderfer's ERG Theory

	Needs	Description	Examples of How Managers Can Help People Satisfy These Needs at Work
Highest-level needs ↑	**Growth needs**	The needs for self-development and creative and productive work	By allowing people to continually improve their skills and abilities and engage in meaningful work
	Relatedness needs	The needs to have good interpersonal relations, to share thoughts and feelings, and to have open two-way communication	By promoting good interpersonal relations and by providing accurate feedback
Lowest-level needs ↓	**Existence needs**	Basic needs for food, water, clothing, shelter, and a secure and safe environment	By promoting enough pay to provide for the basic necessities of life and safe working conditions

As lower-level needs are satisfied, a person is motivated to satisfy higher-level needs. When a person is unable to satisfy higher-level needs (or is frustrated), motivation to satisfy lower-level needs increases

and extrinsic motivation (related to hygiene needs), covered earlier in the chapter. Second, his theory prompted researchers and managers to study how jobs could be designed or redesigned so that they are intrinsically motivating.

McClelland's Needs for Achievement, Affiliation, and Power

need for achievement The extent to which an individual has a strong desire to perform challenging tasks well and to meet personal standards for excellence.

need for affiliation The extent to which an individual is concerned about establishing and maintaining good interpersonal relations, being liked, and having other people around them get along with each other.

need for power The extent to which an individual desires to control or influence others.

Psychologist David McClelland has extensively researched the needs for achievement, affiliation, and power.[26] The **need for achievement** is the extent to which an individual has a strong desire to perform challenging tasks well and to meet personal standards for excellence. People with a high need for achievement often set clear goals for themselves and like to receive performance feedback. The **need for affiliation** is the extent to which an individual is concerned about establishing and maintaining good interpersonal relations, being liked, and having other people around them get along with each other. The **need for power** is the extent to which an individual desires to control or influence others.[27]

While each of these needs is present in each of us to some degree, their importance in the workplace depends upon the position one occupies. For example, research suggests that high needs for achievement and for power are assets for first-line and middle managers and that a high need for power is especially important for upper managers.[28] One study found that U.S. presidents with a relatively high need for power tended to be especially effective during their terms of office.[29] A high need for affiliation may not always be desirable in managers and other leaders because it might lead them to try too hard to be liked by others (including subordinates) rather than doing all they can to ensure that performance is as high as it can and should be. Although most research on these needs has been done in the United States, some studies suggest that the findings may be applicable to people in other countries as well, such as India and New Zealand.[30]

Other Needs

Clearly more needs motivate workers than the needs described by these four theories. For example, more and more workers are feeling the need for work-life balance and time to take care of their loved ones while simultaneously being highly motivated at work. Interestingly enough recent research suggests that being exposed to nature (even just be being able to see some trees from your office window) has many salutary effects and a lack of such exposure can actually impair well-being and performance.[31] Thus, having some time during the day when one can at least see nature may be another important need.

Managers of successful companies often strive to ensure that as many of their valued employees' needs as possible are satisfied in the workplace. This is illustrated by the following "Information Technology Byte" on the SAS Institute.

Information Technology Byte

High Motivation Rules at the SAS Institute

Right behind The Container Store in *Fortune* magazine's list of the 100 best companies to work for is the SAS Institute, which ranked second in 2001.[32] The SAS Institute is the world's largest privately owned software company with 8,000 employees worldwide and approximately $1.1 billion in sales.[33] Every indicator suggests that SAS employees are highly motivated and perform well while also working 35-hour weeks. How do managers at SAS do it? In large part, by ensuring that employees are highly motivated and the variety of needs they bring to the workplace are satisfied by doing a good job at SAS.[34]

Satisfying the need for intrinsically motivating work has also been a key priority at SAS. Managers strive to make sure that each employee is motivated by the work he or she performs, and employees are encouraged to change jobs to prevent becoming bored with their work (even if these job changes require SAS to provide additional training). Moreover, in contrast to some of their competitors, all new product development work at SAS is performed in-house so employees have the opportunity to experience the excitement of developing a new product and seeing it succeed.[35]

The SAS Institute also satisfies employees' needs for economic security by paying them fairly and providing them with secure jobs. Employees have their own offices and the work environment is rich in pleasant vistas whether it be artwork on the walls or views of the rolling hills of Cary, North Carolina, at the company headquarters. Managers at SAS realize that needs for work-life balance are a top priority for many of their employees and seek to satisfy these needs in a variety of ways including 35-hour workweeks, on-site day care and medical care, unlimited sick days, and high chairs in the company cafeteria for those wishing to dine with their kids. Moreover,

An SAS Institute employee makes her way to the dining hall on the 200-acre SAS campus located in Cary, N.C. SAS Institute is known as one of the best companies in the country, offering jogging paths, a gymnasium, and a Montessori pre-school on the campus.

employees and their families are encouraged to use the 200 acres that surrounds company headquarters for family walks and picnics.[36] While chief executive, James Goodnight, and John Sall, cofounders and co-owners of SAS are considering an Initial Public Offering (IPO) of SAS stock, Goodnight (who owns two-thirds of SAS) has indicated that he will maintain control of SAS.[37] Thus, employees will most likely continue to be treated the way Goodnight would like to be treated himself, an enduring value at SAS since its founding in 1977.[38]

Equity Theory

equity theory A theory of motivation that focuses on people's perceptions of the fairness of their work outcomes relative to their work inputs.

Equity theory is a theory of motivation that concentrates on people's perceptions of the fairness of their work *outcomes* relative to, or in proportion to, their work *inputs.* Equity theory complements expectancy and need theories by focusing on how people perceive the relationship between the outcomes they receive from their jobs and organizations and the inputs they contribute. Equity theory was formulated in the 1960s by J. Stacy Adams, who stressed that what is important in determining motivation is the *relative* rather than the *absolute* level of outcomes a person receives and inputs a person contributes. Specifically, motivation is influenced by the comparison of one's own outcome/input ratio with the outcome/input ratio of a referent.[39] The *referent* could be another person or a group of people who are perceived to be similar to oneself; the referent also could be oneself in a previous job or one's expectations about what outcome/input ratios should be. In a comparison of one's own outcome/input ratio to a referent's outcome/input ratio, one's *perceptions* of outcomes and inputs (not any objective indicator of them) are key.

Equity

equity The justice, impartiality, and fairness to which all organizational members are entitled.

Equity exists when a person perceives his or her own outcome/input ratio to be equal to a referent's outcome/input ratio. Under conditions of equity (see Table 12.3), if a referent receives more outcomes than you receive, the referent contributes proportionally more inputs to the organization, so his or her outcome/input ratio still equals your outcome/input ratio. Maria Sanchez and Claudia King, for example, both work in a shoe store in a large mall. Sanchez is paid more per hour than King but also contributes more inputs, including being responsible for some of the store's bookkeeping, closing the store, and periodically depositing cash in the bank. When King compares her outcome/input ratio to Sanchez's (her referent's), she perceives the ratios to be equitable because Sanchez's higher level of pay (an outcome) is proportional to her higher level of inputs (bookkeeping, closing the store, and going to the bank).

Similarly, under conditions of equity, if you receive more outcomes than a referent, then your inputs are perceived to be proportionally higher. Continuing with our example, when Sanchez compares her outcome/input ratio to King's (her referent's) outcome/input ratio, she perceives them to be equitable because her higher level of pay is proportional to her higher level of inputs.

When equity exists, people are motivated to continue contributing their current levels of inputs to their organizations to receive their current levels of outcomes. If people wish to increase their outcomes under conditions of equity, they are motivated to increase their inputs.

Inequity

inequity Lack of fairness.

Inequity, lack of fairness, exists when a person's outcome/input ratio is not perceived to be equal to a referent's. Inequity creates pressure or tension inside people and motivates them to restore equity by bringing the two ratios back into balance.

underpayment inequity The inequity that exists when a person perceives that his or her own outcome/input ratio is less than the ratio of a referent.

overpayment inequity The inequity that exists when a person perceives that his or her own outcome/input ratio is greater than the ratio of a referent.

There are two types of inequity: underpayment inequity and overpayment inequity (see Table 12.3). **Underpayment inequity** exists when a person's own outcome/input ratio is perceived to be *less* than that of a referent. In comparing yourself to a referent, you think that you are *not* receiving the outcomes you should be, given your inputs. **Overpayment inequity** exists when a person perceives that his or her own outcome/input ratio is *greater* than that of a referent. In comparing yourself to a referent, you think that the referent is receiving *more* outcomes than he or she should be, given his or her inputs.

Ways to Restore Equity

According to equity theory, both underpayment inequity and overpayment inequity create tension that motivates most people to restore equity by bringing the ratios back into balance.[40] When people experience *underpayment* inequity, they may be motivated to lower their inputs by reducing their working hours, putting forth less effort on the job, or being absent, or they may be motivated to increase their outcomes by asking for a raise or a promotion. Susan Richie, a financial analyst at a large corporation, noticed that she was working longer hours and getting more work accomplished than a co-worker who had the same position, yet they both received the exact same pay and other outcomes. To

Table 12.3
Equity Theory

Condition	Person		Referent	Example
Equity	$\frac{\text{Outcomes}}{\text{Inputs}}$	=	$\frac{\text{Outcomes}}{\text{Inputs}}$	An engineer perceives that he contributes more inputs (time and effort), and receives proportionally more outcomes (a higher salary and choice job assignments), than his referent.
Underpayment inequity	$\frac{\text{Outcomes}}{\text{Inputs}}$	< (less than)	$\frac{\text{Outcomes}}{\text{Inputs}}$	An engineer perceives that he contributes more inputs but receives the same outcomes as his referent.
Overpayment inequity	$\frac{\text{Outcomes}}{\text{Inputs}}$	> (greater than)	$\frac{\text{Outcomes}}{\text{Inputs}}$	An engineer perceives that he contributes the same inputs but receives more outcomes than his referent.

restore equity, Richie decided to stop coming in early and staying late. Alternatively, she could have tried to restore equity by trying to increase her outcomes by, for example, asking her boss for a raise.

When people experience *overpayment* inequity, they may try to restore equity by changing their perceptions of their own or their referents' inputs or outcomes. Equity can be restored when people realize that they are contributing more inputs than they originally thought. Equity also can be restored by perceiving the referent's inputs to be lower or the referent's outcomes to be higher than one originally thought. When equity is restored in this way, actual inputs and outcomes are unchanged and no real action is taken by the person being overpaid. What is changed is how people think about or view their or the referent's inputs and outcomes. For instance, Mary McMann experienced overpayment inequity when she realized that she was being paid $2 an hour more than a co-worker who had the same job as she did in a record store and who contributed the same amount of inputs. McMann restored equity by changing her perceptions of her inputs. She realized that she worked harder than her co-worker and solved more problems that came up in the store.

Experiencing either overpayment or underpayment inequity, you might decide that your referent is not appropriate because, for example, the referent is too different from yourself. Choosing a more appropriate referent may bring the ratios back into balance. Angela Martinez, a middle manager in the engineering department of a chemical company, experienced overpayment inequity when she realized that she was being paid quite a bit more than her friend who was a middle manager in the marketing department of the same company. After thinking about the discrepancy for a while, Martinez decided that engineering and marketing were so different that she should not be comparing her job to her friend's job even though they were both middle managers. Martinez restored equity by changing her referent; she picked a fellow middle manager in the engineering department as a new referent.

When people experience *underpayment* inequity and other means of equity restoration fail, they can change their perceptions of their own or the referents' inputs or outcomes. For example, they may realize that their referent is really working on more difficult projects than they are or that they really take more time off from work than their referent does. Alternatively, if people who feel that they are underpaid have other employment options, they may leave the organization. As an example, John Steinberg, an assistant principal in a high school, experienced underpayment inequity when he realized that all of the other assistant principals of high schools in his school district had received promotions to the position of principal even though they had been in their jobs for a shorter time than he had been. Steinberg's performance had always been appraised as being high, so after his repeated requests for a promotion went unheeded, he found a job as a principal in a different school district.

Motivation is highest when as many people as possible in an organization perceive that they are being equitably treated–their outcomes and inputs are in balance. Top contributors and performers are motivated to continue contributing a high level of inputs because they are receiving the outcomes they deserve. Mediocre contributors and performers realize that if they want to increase their outcomes, they have to increase their inputs. Managers of effective organizations, like Tindell and Boone at The Container Store, realize the importance of equity for motivation and performance and continually strive to ensure that employees believe they are being equitably treated.

The dot-com boom and subsequent bust, along with increased global competition, has resulted in some workers putting in longer and longer working hours (i.e., increasing their inputs) without any kind of increase in their outcomes. For those whose referents are not experiencing a similar change, perceptions of inequity are likely. Moreover, some of these individuals have turned to the legal system to try to redress these perceived inequities as indicated in the following "Ethics in Action."

Ethics in Action

Are Long and Uncompensated Hours Equitable?

Jill Andresky Fraser spent five years researching the work lives of managers, accountants, consultants, and other white-collar employees for her recently published book, *White Collar Sweatshop*. Her findings are discouraging, to say the least. It seems that many office workers are working longer and longer hours without corresponding increases in their compensation. According to Andresky Fraser, over 25 million U.S. workers work more than 49 hours per week in the office, almost 11 million work more than 60 hours per week in the office, and many also put in additional work hours at home. In addition, advances in information technology, such as email and cell phones, have resulted in work intruding on home time, vacation time, and even special occasions. For example, Andresky Fraser tells the story of a middle manager at American Express who worked on her computer at home until 5:00 A.M. on the day of her own wedding.[41]

Resentment is building over these uncompensated, long hours and some of the overworked are seeking legal remedies. The U.S. Fair Labor Standards Act mandates that nonmanagerial workers receive overtime pay at a rate of one and one-half times their regular hourly rate for any hours worked beyond the standard 40-hour week.[42] According to the act, managers are

Whether or not this employee receives pay for overtime depends on her status as an exempt or nonexempt employee.

defined as employees who make important decisions affecting their organizations, supervise two or more subordinates, or can hire and fire employees. More and more workers are claiming that their employers are classifying them as managers so that they don't have to pay them overtime. For example, General Dynamics, U-Haul, Taco Bell, Borders Books, Pepsi-Cola, and other companies have had lawsuits filed against them pertaining to overtime pay.[43]

James Horner, a manager at the U-Haul moving center in Barstow, California, believed he was unfairly treated when he was regularly expected to work at least 60 hours per week at his regular pay rate. U-Haul hadn't paid Horner overtime pay because he was a manager; Horner thought, and the California Superior Court found, that Horner spent most of his time doing the same kinds of tasks as hourly workers at the center who do receive overtime pay.[44] In the past, it was more prestigious to be an "exempt" employee (i.e., exempt from overtime) as this signified that one was not an hourly or blue collar worker. Given the excessive hours now expected of some employees, fair and equitable compensation seems to be outweighing any concerns with maintaining one's status as an exempt employee.[45]

Goal-Setting Theory

goal-setting theory A theory that focuses on identifying the types of goals that are most effective in producing high levels of motivation and performance and explaining why goals have these effects.

Goal-setting theory focuses on motivating workers to contribute their inputs to their jobs and organizations; in this way it is similar to expectancy theory and equity theory. But goal-setting theory takes this focus a step further by considering as well how managers can ensure that organizational members focus their inputs in the direction of high performance and the achievement of organizational goals.

Ed Locke and Gary Latham, the leading researchers on goal-setting theory, suggest that the goals that organizational members strive to attain are prime determinants of their motivation and subsequent performance. A *goal* is what a person is trying to accomplish through his or her efforts and behaviors.[46] Just as you may have a goal to get a good grade in this course, so do members of an organization have goals that they strive to meet. For example, salespeople at Neiman Marcus strive to meet sales goals while top managers pursue market share and profitability goals.

Goal-setting theory suggests that to stimulate high motivation and performance, goals must be *specific* and *difficult*.[47] Specific goals are often quantitative–a salesperson's goal to sell $200 worth of merchandise per day, a scientist's goal to finish a project in one year, a CEO's goal to reduce debt by 40 percent and increase revenues by 20 percent, a restaurant manager's goal to serve 150 customers per evening. In contrast to specific goals, vague goals such as "doing your best" or "selling as much as you can" do not have much motivational impact.

Difficult goals are hard but not impossible to attain. In contrast to difficult goals, easy goals are those that practically everyone can attain, and moderate goals are goals that about one-half of the people can attain. Both easy and moderate goals have less motivational power than difficult goals.

Regardless of whether specific, difficult goals are set by managers, workers, or teams of managers and workers, they lead to high levels of motivation and performance. When managers set goals for their subordinates, their subordinates must accept the goals or agree to work toward them; also they should be committed to them or really want to attain them. Some managers find having subordinates participate in the actual setting of goals boosts their acceptance of and commitment to the goals. In addition, organizational members need to receive *feedback* about how they are doing; feedback can often be provided by the performance appraisal and feedback component of an organization's human resource management system (see Chapter 11). More generally, goals and feedback are integral components of performance management systems in organizations such as management by objectives (see Chapter 10).

Specific, difficult goals affect motivation in two ways: First, they motivate people to contribute more inputs to their jobs. Specific, difficult goals cause people to put forth high levels of effort, for example. Just as you would study harder if you were trying to get an A in a course instead of a C, so too will a salesperson work harder to reach a $200 sales goal instead of a $100 goal. Specific, difficult goals also cause people to be more persistent than easy, moderate, or vague goals when they run into difficulties. Salespeople who are told to sell as much as possible might stop trying on a slow day, whereas having a specific, difficult goal to reach causes them to keep trying.

A second way in which specific, difficult goals affect motivation is by helping people focus their inputs in the right direction. These goals let people know what they should be focusing their attention on, be it increasing the quality of customer service or sales or lowering new product development times. The fact that the goals are specific and difficult also frequently causes people to develop *action plans* for reaching them.[48] Action plans can include the strategies to attain the goals and timetables or schedules for the completion of different activities crucial to goal attainment. Like the goals themselves, action plans also help ensure that efforts are focused in the right direction and that people do not get sidetracked along the way.

Although specific, difficult goals have been found to increase motivation and performance in a wide variety of jobs and organizations both in the United States and abroad, recent research suggests that they may detract from performance under certain conditions. When people are performing complicated and very challenging tasks that require a considerable amount of learning, specific, difficult goals may actually impair performance.[49] All of a person's attention needs to be focused on learning complicated and difficult tasks. Striving to reach a specific, difficult goal may detract from performance on complex tasks because some of a person's attention is directed away from learning about the task and toward trying to figure out how to achieve the goal. Once a person has learned the task and it no longer seems complicated or difficult, then the assignment of specific, difficult goals is likely to have its usual effects.

Tips for New Managers

Expectancy and Equity Theories

1. Let your subordinates know that you think they are terrific and expect them to succeed (if this is true).
2. Distribute outcomes based on important inputs and performance levels and let your subordinates know that you do this.
3. Determine which outcomes your subordinates desire and try to gain control over as many of these as possible (i.e., have the authority to distribute or withhold outcomes).
4. Let your subordinates know which inputs are most valuable for them to contribute to their jobs and the organization to receive desired outcomes.

Learning Theories

The basic premise of **learning theories** as applied to organizations is that managers can increase employee motivation and performance by the ways they link the outcomes that employees receive to the performance of desired behaviors in an organization and the attainment of goals. Thus, learning theory focuses on the linkage between performance and outcomes in the motivation equation (see Figure 12.1).

learning theories Theories that focus on increasing employee motivation and performance by linking the outcomes that employees receive to the performance of desired behaviors and the attainment of goals.

learning A relatively permanent change in knowledge or behavior that results from practice or experience.

Learning can be defined as a relatively permanent change in a person's knowledge or behavior that results from practice or experience.[50] Learning takes place in organizations when people learn to perform certain behaviors to receive certain outcomes. For example, a person learns to perform at a higher level than in the past or to come to work earlier because he or she is motivated to obtain the outcomes that result from these behaviors, such as a pay raise or praise from a supervisor. In "A Manager's Challenge," The Container Store's emphasis on training ensures that new hires learn how to provide excellent customer service and all employees continue their learning throughout their careers with The Container Store.

Of the different learning theories, operant conditioning theory and social learning theory provide the most guidance to managers in their efforts to have a highly motivated workforce.

Operant Conditioning Theory

operant conditioning theory The theory that people learn to perform behaviors that lead to desired consequences and learn not to perform behaviors that lead to undesired consequences.

According to **operant conditioning theory,** developed by psychologist B. F. Skinner, people learn to perform behaviors that lead to desired consequences and learn not to perform behaviors that lead to undesired consequences.[51] Translated into motivation terms, Skinner's theory means that people will be motivated to perform at a high level and attain their work goals to the extent that high performance and goal attainment allow them to obtain outcomes they desire. Similarly, people avoid performing behaviors that lead to outcomes they

Workers at a Lincoln Electric plant assemble electric generators. Lincoln Electric is well known for its policy of positively reinforcing work behaviors that promote safety and productivity.

do not desire. By linking the performance of *specific behaviors* to the attainment of *specific outcomes*, managers can motivate organizational members to perform in ways that help an organization achieve its goals.

Operant conditioning theory provides four tools that managers can use to motivate high performance and prevent workers from engaging in absenteeism and other behaviors that detract from organizational effectiveness. These tools are positive reinforcement, negative reinforcement, punishment, and extinction.[52]

positive reinforcement Giving people outcomes they desire when they perform organizationally functional behaviors.

negative reinforcement Eliminating or removing undesired outcomes when people perform organizationally functional behaviors.

POSITIVE REINFORCEMENT Positive reinforcement gives people outcomes they desire when they perform organizationally functional behaviors. These desired outcomes, called *positive reinforcers*, include any outcomes that a person desires, such as pay, praise, or a promotion. Organizationally functional behaviors are behaviors that contribute to organizational effectiveness; they can include producing high-quality goods and services, providing high-quality customer service, and meeting deadlines. By linking positive reinforcers to the performance of functional behaviors, managers motivate people to perform the desired behaviors.

NEGATIVE REINFORCEMENT Negative reinforcement also can encourage members of an organization to perform desired or organizationally functional behaviors. Managers using negative reinforcement actually eliminate or remove undesired outcomes once the functional behavior is performed. These undesired outcomes, called *negative reinforcers*, can range from a manager's constant nagging or criticism, to unpleasant assignments, to the ever-present threat of losing one's job. When negative reinforcement is used, people are motivated to perform behaviors because they want to stop receiving or avoid undesired outcomes. Managers who try to encourage salespeople to sell more by threatening them with being fired are using negative reinforcement. In this case, the negative reinforcer is the threat of job loss, which is removed once the functional behaviors are performed.

Whenever possible, managers should try to use positive reinforcement. Negative reinforcement can make for a very unpleasant work environment and even a negative culture in an organization. No one likes to be nagged, threatened, or exposed to other kinds of negative outcomes. The use of negative reinforcement sometimes causes subordinates to resent managers and try to get back at them.

IDENTIFYING THE RIGHT BEHAVIORS FOR REINFORCEMENT Even managers who use positive reinforcement (and refrain from using negative reinforcement) can get into trouble if they are not careful to identify the right behaviors to reinforce–behaviors that are truly functional for the organization. Doing this is not always as straightforward as it might seem. First, it is crucial for managers to choose behaviors over which subordinates have control; in other words, subordinates must have the freedom and opportunity to perform the behaviors that are being reinforced. Second, it is crucial that these behaviors contribute to organizational effectiveness.

extinction Curtailing the performance of dysfunctional behaviors by eliminating whatever is reinforcing them.

EXTINCTION Sometimes members of an organization are motivated to perform behaviors that actually detract from organizational effectiveness. According to operant conditioning theory, all behavior is controlled or determined by its consequences; one way for managers to curtail the performance of dysfunctional behaviors is to eliminate whatever is reinforcing the behaviors. This process is called **extinction.**

Suppose a manager has a subordinate who frequently stops by his office to chat–sometimes about work-related matters but at other times about various topics ranging from politics to last night's football game. The manager and the subordinate share certain interests and views, so these conversations can get quite involved, and both seem to enjoy them. The manager, however, realizes that these frequent and sometimes lengthy conversations are actually causing him to stay at work later in the evenings to make up for the time he loses during the day. The manager realizes that he is actually reinforcing his subordinate's behavior by acting interested in the topics the subordinate brings up and responding at length to them. To extinguish this behavior, the manager stops acting interested in these non-work-related conversations and keeps his responses polite and friendly but brief. No longer being reinforced with a pleasurable conversation, the subordinate eventually ceases to be motivated to interrupt the manager during working hours to discuss non-work-related issues.

punishment Administering an undesired or negative consequence when dysfunctional behavior occurs.

PUNISHMENT Sometimes managers cannot rely on extinction to eliminate dysfunctional behaviors because they do not have control over whatever is reinforcing the behavior or because they cannot afford the time needed for extinction to work. When employees are performing dangerous behaviors or behaviors that are illegal or unethical, the behavior needs to be eliminated immediately. Sexual harassment, for example, is an organizationally dysfunctional behavior that cannot be tolerated. In such cases, managers often rely on **punishment,** administering an undesired or negative consequence to subordinates when they perform the dysfunctional behavior. Punishments used by organizations range from verbal reprimands to pay cuts, temporary suspensions, demotions, and firings. Punishment, however, can have some unintended side effects–resentment, loss of self-respect, a desire for retaliation–and should be used only when necessary.

To avoid the unintended side effects of punishment, managers should keep in mind these guidelines:

- Downplay the emotional element involved in punishment. Make it clear that you are punishing a person's performance of a dysfunctional behavior, not the person himself or herself.
- Try to punish dysfunctional behaviors as soon after they occur as possible, and make sure the negative consequence is a source of punishment for the individuals involved. Be certain that organizational members know exactly why they are being punished.
- Try to avoid punishing someone in front of others, for this can hurt a person's self-respect and lower esteem in the eyes of co-workers as well as make co-workers feel uncomfortable.[53] Even so, making organizational members aware of the fact that an individual who has committed a serious infraction has been punished can sometimes be effective in preventing future infractions and teaching all members of the organization that certain behaviors are unacceptable. For example, when organizational members are informed

that a manager who has sexually harassed subordinates has been punished, they learn or are reminded of the fact that sexual harassment is not tolerated in the organization.

Managers and students alike often confuse negative reinforcement and punishment. To avoid such confusion, keep in mind the two major differences between them. First, negative reinforcement is used to promote the performance of functional behaviors in organizations; punishment is used to stop the performance of dysfunctional behaviors. Second, negative reinforcement entails the *removal* of a negative consequence when functional behaviors are performed; punishment entails the *administration* of negative consequences when dysfunctional behaviors are performed.

Effectively administering rewards and careful, judicious use of punishment are key strategies for managers to motivate their workforce, as indicated in the following "Information Technology Byte."

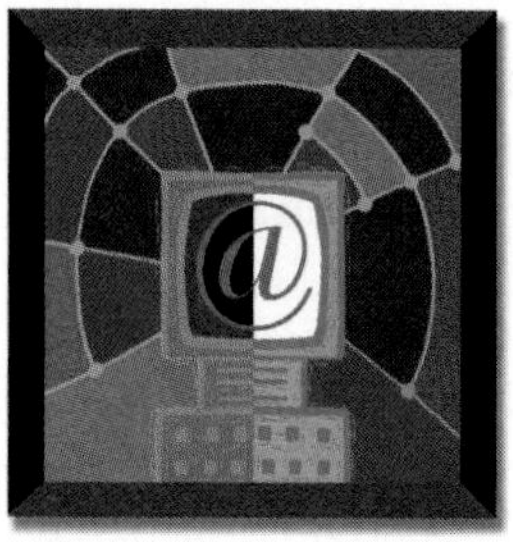

Information Technology Byte

J. Crew Outfits by Bricks and Clicks

J. Crew, headquartered in New York City, is one of the most successful clothing companies in the United States. J. Crew was founded by Arthur Cinader in the early 1980s.[54] His idea was to sell a line of clothes with the then very popular and trendy Ralph Lauren look at about one-half the price. A key part of Cinader's approach and J. Crew's ongoing strategy is an outstanding clothing catalog that looks more like a fashion magazine with full-page photographs of models in seemingly natural poses. The models look like real people (very attractive ones, of course) and the catalog makes J. Crew clothing very appealing and accessible to potential customers. Cinader's daughter, Emily, joined J. Crew in 1982 after she graduated from college and made significant contributions to J. Crew's unique style and approach.[55]

The company grew and prospered through the 1980s and 1990s but hit upon hard times in 1997. The Cinaders decided to sell 60 percent of J. Crew to the Texas Pacific Group, Arthur retired, Emily kept 19 percent of the company and became the chairman, and Mark Sarvary was appointed CEO. Sarvary worked wonders at J. Crew through expanding its presence on the Web, and even more important, by adding more than 100 new stores. Currently, J. Crew sells around 22 percent of its merchandise through its mainstay catalog, 14 percent through its Website, and 64 percent through its stores.[56] J. Crew boasts over 150 stores in more than 35 states.[57]

In addition to the rapid expansion, Sarvary also ensured that J. Crew employees are rewarded for a job well done and punishment is kept to a minimum and only used when necessary. This wasn't always the case. Clearly the Cinaders' contributions to the success of J. Crew are profound–both Arthur and Emily contributed to J. Crew's unique style, the catalog was a real innovation, and their intelligence and ingenuity continues to make its mark on the company. However, they were less adept at managing people. For example, a story is told about how Arthur angrily ended a meeting with a subordinate because that person had used an incomplete abbreviation. A certain degree of confidence was needed to stand up to Arthur and Emily who had their own ideas about how things should be done.[58]

Sarvary changed all that. Punishment is rarely, if ever used, and employees are positively reinforced for desired behaviors. For example, sales associates receive monthly financial incentives based on their sales performance,

J. Crew's new CEO Mark Savary has worked wonders at the company by expanding its presence on the Web, adding over 100 new stores, and ensuring employees are rewarded for their efforts.

various contests are staged to promote desired behaviors with winners receiving valued rewards, and employees receive bonuses for referring potential job applicants.[59] Moreover, working at J. Crew is exciting and fun.[60] If J. Crew continues on its current trajectory, more and more customers will be outfitted by its catalog, website, or one of its many stores.

organizational behavior modification The systematic application of operant conditioning techniques to promote the performance of organizationally functional behaviors and discourage the performance of dysfunctional behaviors.

ORGANIZATIONAL BEHAVIOR MODIFICATION When managers systematically apply operant conditioning techniques to promote the performance of organizationally functional behaviors and discourage the performance of dysfunctional behaviors, they are engaging in **organizational behavior modification (OB MOD)**.[61] OB MOD has been successfully used to improve productivity, efficiency, attendance, punctuality, compliance with safety procedures, and other important behaviors in a wide variety of organizations such as Michigan Bell, Connecticut General Life Insurance, Emery Air Freight, General Electric, Standard Oil of Ohio, B. F. Goodrich, and Weyerhaeuser. The five basic steps in OB MOD are described in Figure 12.4.

OB MOD works best for behaviors that are specific, objective, and countable, such as attendance and punctuality, making sales, or putting telephones together, all of which lend themselves to careful scrutiny and control. OB MOD may be questioned because of its lack of relevance to certain work behaviors (for example, the many work behaviors that are not specific, objective, and countable). Some people also have questioned it on ethical grounds. Critics of OB MOD suggest that it is overly controlling and robs workers of their dignity, individuality, freedom of choice, and even their creativity. Supporters counter that OB MOD is a highly effective means of promoting organizational efficiency. There is some merit to both sides of this argument. What is clear, however, is that when used appropriately, OB MOD provides managers with a technique to motivate the performance of at least some organizationally functional behaviors.

Figure 12.4
Five Steps in OB MOD

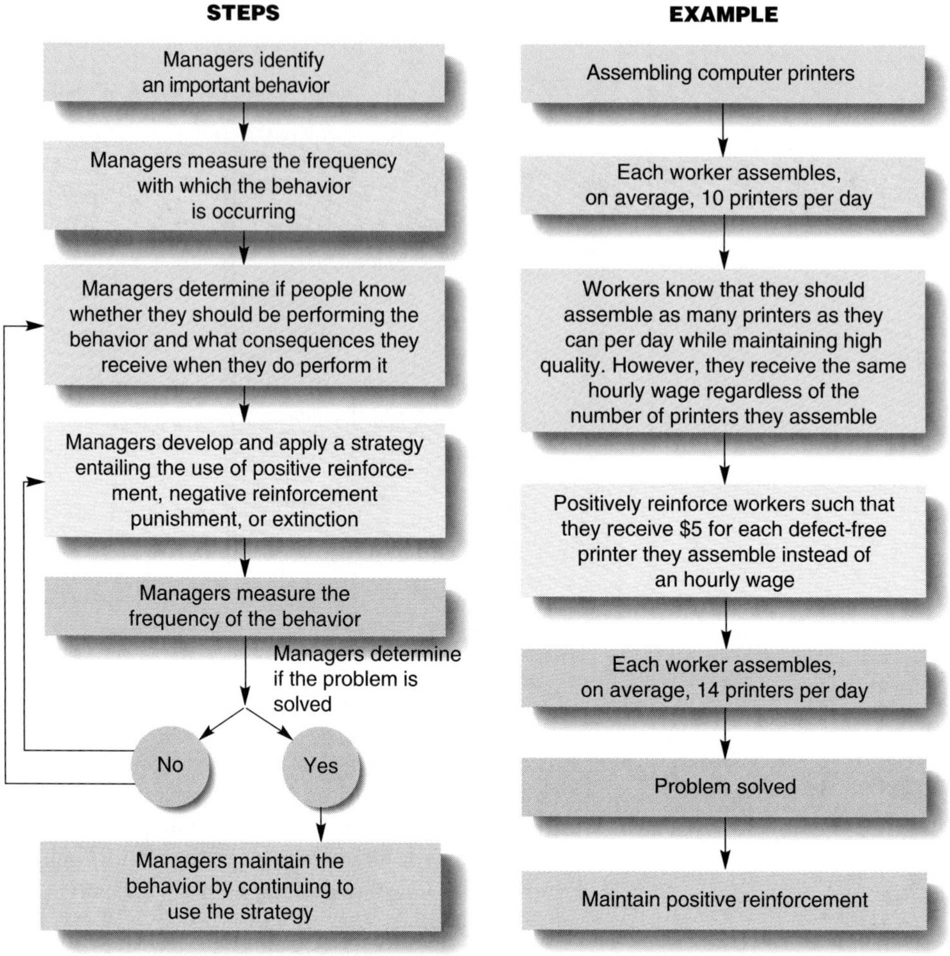

Source: Adapted from *Organizational Behavior Modification and Beyond* by F. Luthans and R. Kreitner (Scott, Foresman, 1985). With permission of the authors.

Social Learning Theory

social learning theory A theory that takes into account how learning and motivation are influenced by people's thoughts and beliefs and their observations of other people's behavior.

vicarious learning Learning that occurs when the learner becomes motivated to perform a behavior by watching another person perform it; also called observational learning.

Social learning theory proposes that motivation results not only from direct experience of rewards and punishments but also from a person's thoughts and beliefs. Social learning theory extends operant conditioning's contribution to managers' understanding of motivation by explaining (1) how people can be motivated by observing other people perform a behavior and be reinforced for doing so (*vicarious learning*), (2) how people can be motivated to control their behavior themselves (*self-reinforcement*), and (3) how people's beliefs about their ability to successfully perform a behavior affect motivation (*self-efficacy*).[62] We look briefly at each of these motivators.

VICARIOUS LEARNING **Vicarious learning,** often called *observational learning,* occurs when a person (the learner) becomes motivated to perform a behavior by watching another person (the model) perform the behavior and be positively reinforced for doing so. Vicarious learning is a powerful source of motivation on many jobs in which people learn to perform functional behaviors by watching others. Salespeople learn how to be helpful to customers, medical school students learn how to treat patients, law clerks learn how to practice law, and nonmanagers learn how to be managers, in part, by observing experienced members of an organization perform these behaviors properly and being reinforced for them. In general, people are more likely to be motivated to imitate the behavior of models who are highly competent, are (to some extent) experts in the behavior, have high status, receive attractive reinforcers, and are friendly or approachable.[63]

To promote vicarious learning, managers should strive to have the learner meet the following conditions:

- The learner observes the model performing the behavior.
- The learner accurately perceives the model's behavior.
- The learner remembers the behavior.
- The learner has the skills and abilities needed to perform the behavior.
- The learner sees or knows that the model is positively reinforced for the behavior.[64]

self-reinforcer Any desired or attractive outcome or reward that a person gives to himself or herself for good performance.

SELF-REINFORCEMENT Although managers are often the providers of reinforcement in organizations, sometimes people motivate themselves through self-reinforcement. People can control their own behavior by setting goals for themselves and then reinforcing themselves when they achieve the goals.[65] **Self-reinforcers** are any desired or attractive outcomes or rewards that people can give to themselves for good performance, such as a feeling of accomplishment, going to a movie, having dinner out, buying a new CD, or taking time out for a golf game. When members of an organization control their own behavior through self-reinforcement, managers do not need to spend as much time as they ordinarily would trying to motivate and control behavior through the administration of consequences because subordinates are controlling and motivating themselves. In fact, this self-control is often referred to as the self-management of behavior.

Chinese students at the prestigious Jiaotong University in Shanghai exemplify how strong motivation through self-control can be. These students, many of whom are aspiring engineers, live in Spartan conditions (a barely lit small room is home for seven students) and take exceptionally heavy course loads. They spend their spare time reading up on subjects not covered in their classes, and many ultimately hope to obtain engineering jobs overseas with high-tech companies. Illustrating high self-control, 22-year-old Yan Kangrong spends his spare time reading computer textbooks and designing software for local companies. As Kangrong puts it, "We learn the basics from teachers. . . . But we need to expand on this knowledge by ourselves."[66]

self-efficacy A person's belief about his or her ability to perform a behavior successfully.

SELF-EFFICACY **Self-efficacy** is a person's belief about his or her ability to perform a behavior successfully. Even with all the most attractive consequences or reinforcers hinging on high performance, people are not going to be motivated if they do not think that they can actually perform at a high level. Similarly, when people control their own behavior, they are likely to set for themselves difficult goals that will lead to outstanding accomplishments only if they think that they have the capability to reach those goals. Thus, self-efficacy influences motivation both when managers provide reinforcement and when workers themselves provide it.[67] The greater the self-efficacy, the greater is the motivation and performance. In "A Manager's Challenge," Tindell and Boone boost self-efficacy when they express confidence in their employees and view them all as leaders. Verbal persuasion provided by Tindell and Boone as well as a person's own past performance and accomplishments and the accomplishments of other people play a role in determining a person's self-efficacy.

Pay and Motivation

In Chapter 11, we discussed how managers establish a pay level and structure for an organization as a whole. Here we focus on how, once a pay level and structure is in place, managers can use pay to motivate employees to perform at a high level and attain their work goals. Pay is used to motivate entry-level workers, first-line and middle managers, and even top managers such as CEOs. Pay can be used to motivate people to perform behaviors that help an organization achieve its goals, and it can be used to motivate people to join and remain with an organization.

Each of the theories described in this chapter alludes to the importance of pay and suggests that pay should be based on performance:

- *Expectancy theory*: Instrumentality, the association between performance and outcomes such as pay, must be high for motivation to be high. In addition, pay is an outcome that has high valence for many people.
- *Need theories*: People should be able to satisfy their needs by performing at a high level; pay can be used to satisfy several different kinds of needs.
- *Equity theory*: Outcomes such as pay should be distributed in proportion to inputs (including performance levels).
- *Goal-setting theory*: Outcomes such as pay should be linked to the attainment of goals.
- *Learning theories*: The distribution of outcomes such as pay should be contingent on the performance of organizationally functional behaviors.

merit pay plan A compensation plan that bases pay on performance.

As these theories suggest, to promote high motivation, managers should base the distribution of pay to organizational members on performance levels so that high performers receive more pay than low performers (other things being equal).[68] At General Mills, for example, the pay of all employees ranging from mailroom clerks to senior managers is based, at least in part, on performance.[69] A compensation plan basing pay on performance is often called a **merit pay plan.** Once managers have decided to use a merit pay plan, they face two important choices: whether to base pay on individual, group, or organizational performance or to use salary increases or bonuses.

Basing Merit Pay on Individual, Group, or Organizational Performance

Managers can base merit pay on individual, group, or organizational performance. When individual performance (such as the dollar value of merchandise a salesperson sells, the number of loudspeakers a factory worker assembles, and a lawyer's billable hours) can be accurately determined, individual motivation is likely to be highest when pay is based on individual performance.[70] When members of an organization work closely together and individual performance cannot be accurately determined (as in a team of computer programmers developing a single software package), pay cannot be based on individual performance, and a group- or organization-based plan must be used. When the attainment of organizational goals hinges on members working closely together and cooperating with each other (as in a small construction company that builds custom homes), group- or organization-based plans may be more appropriate than individual-based plans.[71]

It is possible to combine elements of an individual-based plan with a group- or organization-based plan to motivate each individual to perform highly while at the same time motivating all individuals to work well together, cooperate with each other, and help each other as needed. Lincoln Electric, a very successful company and a leading manufacturer of welding machines, uses a combination individual- and organization-based plan.[72] Pay is based on individual performance. In addition, each year the size of a bonus fund depends on organizational performance. Money from the bonus fund is distributed to people on the basis of their contributions to the organization, attendance, levels of cooperation, and other indications of performance. Employees of Lincoln Electric are motivated to cooperate and help each other because when the firm as a whole performs well, everybody benefits by having a larger bonus fund. Employees also are motivated to contribute their inputs to the organization because their contributions determine their share of the bonus fund.

Salary Increase or Bonus?

Managers can distribute merit pay to people in the form of a salary increase or a bonus on top of regular salaries. Although the dollar amount of a salary increase or bonus might be identical, bonuses tend to have more motivational impact for at least three reasons. First, salary levels are typically based on performance levels, cost-of-living increases, and so forth from the day people start working in an organization, which means that the absolute level of the salary is based largely on factors unrelated to *current* performance. A 5 percent merit increase in salary, for example, may seem relatively small in comparison to one's total salary. Second, a current salary increase may be affected by other factors in addition to performance, such as cost-of-living increases or across-the-board market adjustments. Third, because organizations rarely reduce salaries, salary levels tend to vary less than performance levels do. Related to this point is the fact that bonuses give managers more flexibility in distributing outcomes. If an organization is doing well, bonuses can be relatively high to reward employees for their contributions. However, unlike salary increases, bonus levels can be reduced when an organization's performance lags. All in all, bonus plans have more motivational impact than salary increases because the amount of the bonus can be directly and exclusively based on performance.[73]

Consistent with the lessons from motivation theories, bonuses can be linked directly to performance and vary from year to year and employee to employee, as at Gradient Corporation, a Cambridge, Massachusetts, environmental consulting firm.[74] Another example of an organization that successfully uses bonuses is Nucor Corporation. Steelworkers at Nucor tend to be much more productive than steelworkers in other companies–probably because they can receive bonuses tied to performance and quality that are from 130 to 150 percent of their regular or base pay.[75]

employee stock option A financial instrument that entitles the bearer to buy shares of an organization's stock at a certain price during a certain period of time or under certain conditions.

In addition to pay raises and bonuses, high-level managers and executives are sometimes granted employee stock options. **Employee stock options** are financial instruments that entitle the bearer to buy shares of an organization's stock at a certain price during a certain period of time or under certain conditions.[76] For example, in addition to their salaries stock options are sometimes used to attract high-level managers. The exercise price is the stock price that the bearer can buy the stock at and the vesting conditions specify when the bearer can actually buy the stock at the exercise price. The option's exercise price is generally set equal to the market price of the stock on the date it is granted, and the vesting conditions might specify that the manager has to have worked at the organization for 12 months or perhaps met some performance target (increase in profits) before being able to exercise the option. In high-technology firms and start-ups, options are sometimes used in a similar fashion for employees at various levels in the organization.[77]

From a motivation standpoint, stock options are not so much used as rewards for past individual performance but rather to motivate employees to work in the future for the good of the company as a whole. This is true because stock options issued at current stock prices only have value in the future if an organization does well and its stock price appreciates; thus, giving employees stock options should encourage them to help the organization improve its performance over time.[78] In high-technology start-ups and dot-coms, stock options have often motivated potential employees to leave promising jobs in larger companies and work for the start-ups. In the late 1990s and early 2000s, many dot-commers were devastated to learn that not only were their stock options worthless because their companies went out of business or were doing poorly but also they were unemployed.

Examples of Merit Pay Plans

Managers can choose among several merit pay plans, depending on the work that employees perform and other considerations. Using *piece-rate pay*, an individual-based merit plan, managers base employees' pay on the number of units each employee produces, whether televisions, computer components, or welded auto parts. Managers at Lincoln Electric use piece-rate pay to determine individual pay levels. Advances in information technology are currently simplifying the administration of piece-rate pay in a variety of industries. For example, farmers have typically allocated piece-rate pay to farm workers through a laborious, time-consuming process. Now, they can rely on metal buttons the size of a dime that farmworkers clip to their shirts or put in their pockets. Made by Dallas Semiconductor Corporation, these buttons are customized for use in farming by Agricultural Data Systems based in Laguna Niguel, California.[79] Each button contains a semiconductor linked to payroll computers by a wandlike probe in the field.[80] The wand relays the number of boxes of fruit or vegetables that each worker picks as well as the type and quality of the produce picked, the location it was picked in, and the time and the date. The buttons are activated by touching them with the probe; hence, they are called Touch Memory Buttons. Managers generally find that the buttons save time, improve accuracy, and provide valuable information about their crops and yields.[81]

Using *commission pay*, another individual-based merit pay plan, managers base pay on a percentage of sales. Managers at the successful real-estate company Re/Max International Inc. use commission pay for their agents, who are paid a percentage of their sales. Some department stores, such as Neiman Marcus, use commission pay for their salespeople.

Examples of organizational-based merit pay plans include the Scanlon plan and profit sharing. The *Scanlon plan* (developed by Joseph Scanlon, a union leader in a steel and tin plant in the 1920s) focuses on reducing expenses or cutting costs; members of an organization are motivated to come up with and implement cost-cutting strategies because a percentage of the cost savings achieved during a specified time is distributed back to employees.[82] Under *profit sharing*, employees receive a share of an organization's profits. Approximately 16 percent of the employees in medium or large firms receive profit sharing, and about 25 percent of small firms give their employees a share of the profits.[83] Regardless of the specific kind of plan that is used, managers should always strive to link pay to the performance of behaviors that help an organization achieve its goals.

Japanese managers in large corporations have long shunned merit pay plans in favor of plans that reward seniority. However, as indicated in the following "Managing Globally," this is starting to change.

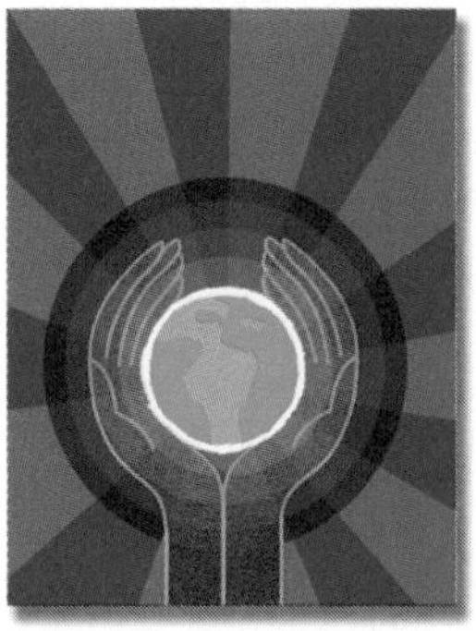

Managing Globally

Merit Pay Catches on in Japan

Top managers in Japan's large organizations have traditionally allocated outcomes like pay and promotion based on seniority. Workers expected to spend years with the same company before they would be promoted to very responsible positions and receive top salaries. Signs indicate that this is changing for a number of reasons. First, more and more young Japanese professionals are leaving their relatively secure jobs in large companies for more interesting work in Internet start-ups, often taking pay cuts. For example, Kiyonori Takechi left his position with NEC Corp. to join eBay; Takechi decided to leave NEC Corp. because he realized it would take years for him to have enough seniority in the company to receive a promotion. As another example, Seiichiro Nakagawa left positions at the Bank of Tokyo, the World Bank, and Ito-Yakado Co. (a Japanese retail organization) to join software company SiteDesign. Takechi and Nakagawa have been joined by many other young Japanese professionals who switch jobs to learn new skills and have greater responsibility on the job.[84]

Ebank President Taiichi Matsuo, center, joins hands with Vice President Takehiko Wakayama, left, and Makoto Arima, managing director of Yahoo Japan, as they brief reporters about their new online bank in Tokyo in July, 2001.

Interestingly enough, on their new jobs, these same young professionals are implementing management practices traditionally uncommon in Japanese companies, such as merit pay. For example, Nakagawa, the chief financial officer at SiteDesign, instituted a merit pay plan and merit-based promotions at SiteDesign.[85]

Managers of large Japanese companies have taken note of these new developments and are making changes to try to retain valuable employees. For instance, Tokio Marine and Fire Insurance, Hitachi, and Hissho Iwai no longer use seniority for pay and promotion decisions; now their plans take into account performance and are more merit-based. In an effort to attract new employees, Hissho Iwai, a trading organization, even offers new hires employee stock options.[86] From a motivational standpoint, managers instituting these changes are taking a major step in the right direction.

Tips for New Managers

Learning **Theory**

1. Distribute outcomes to workers based on their performance of desired behaviors.
2. Use positive reinforcement instead of negative reinforcement whenever possible.
3. When feasible, use extinction rather than punishment to curtail dysfunctional behaviors. When punishment is necessary, focus on the behavior, not the person, and downplay the emotional element.
4. Make sure that good performer models are available for others to imitate, especially when someone is new to a job or organization.
5. Make sure that members of an organization see top performers being positively reinforced for their contributions.
6. Have high expectations for your subordinates and express confidence in their ability to succeed.
7. For subordinates who have low self-efficacy, encourage small successes by assigning them tasks they are likely to succeed at. Progressively increase the difficulty level of the tasks so success builds on itself.

Summary and Review

THE NATURE OF MOTIVATION Motivation encompasses the psychological forces within a person that determine the direction of a person's behavior in an organization, a person's level of effort, and a person's level of persistence in the face of obstacles. Managers strive to motivate people to contribute their inputs to an organization, to focus these inputs in the direction of high performance, and to ensure that people receive the outcomes they desire when they perform at a high level.

EXPECTANCY THEORY According to expectancy theory, managers can promote high levels of motivation in their organizations by taking steps to ensure that expectancy is high (people think that if they try, they can perform at a high level), instrumentality is high (people think that if they perform at a high level, they will receive certain outcomes), and valence is high (people desire these outcomes).

NEED THEORIES Need theories suggest that to motivate their workforces, managers should determine what needs people are trying to satisfy in organizations and then ensure that people receive outcomes that satisfy these needs when they perform at a high level and contribute to organizational effectiveness.

EQUITY THEORY According to equity theory, managers can promote high levels of motivation by ensuring that people perceive that there is equity in the organization or that outcomes are distributed in proportion to inputs. Equity exists when a person perceives that his or her own outcome/input ratio equals the outcome/input ratio of a referent. Inequity motivates people to try to restore equity.

GOAL-SETTING THEORY Goal-setting theory suggests that managers can promote high motivation and performance by ensuring that people are striving to achieve specific, difficult goals. It also is important for people to accept the goals, be committed to them, and receive feedback about how they are doing.

LEARNING THEORIES Operant conditioning theory suggests that managers can motivate people to perform highly by using positive reinforcement or negative reinforcement (positive reinforcement being the preferred strategy). Managers can motivate people to avoid performing dysfunctional behaviors by using extinction or punishment. Social learning theory suggests that people can also be motivated by observing how others perform behaviors and receive rewards, by engaging in self-reinforcement, and by having high levels of self-efficacy.

PAY AND MOTIVATION Each of the motivation theories discussed in this chapter alludes to the importance of pay and suggests that pay should be based on performance. Merit pay plans can be individual-, group-, or organization-based and can entail the use of salary increases or bonuses.

Management in Action

Topics for Discussion and Action

1. Discuss why two people with similar abilities may have very different expectancies for performing at a high level.
2. Describe why some people have low instrumentalities even when their managers distribute outcomes based on performance.
3. Interview four people who have the same kind of job (such as salesperson, waiter/waitress, or teacher), and determine what kinds of needs they are trying to satisfy at work.
4. Analyze how professors try to promote equity to motivate students.
5. Describe three techniques or procedures that managers can use to determine whether a goal is difficult.
6. Discuss why managers should always try to use positive reinforcement instead of negative reinforcement.
7. Interview a manager in an organization in your community to determine the extent to which the manager takes advantage of vicarious learning to promote high motivation among subordinates.

Building Management Skills

Diagnosing Motivation

Think about the ideal job that you would like to obtain upon graduation. Describe this job, the kind of manager you would like to report to, and the kind of organization you would be working in. Then answer the following questions.

1. What would be your levels of expectancy and instrumentality on this job? Which outcomes would have high valence for you on this job? What steps would your manager take to influence your levels of expectancy, instrumentality, and valence?
2. Whom would you choose as a referent on this job? What steps would your manager take to make you feel that you were being equitably treated? What would you do if, after a year on the job, you experienced underpayment inequity?
3. What goals would you strive to achieve on this job? Why? What role would your manager play in determining your goals?
4. What needs would you strive to satisfy on this job? Why? What role would your manager play in helping you satisfy these needs?
5. What behaviors would your manager positively reinforce you for on this job? Why? What positive reinforcers would your manager use?
6. Would there be any vicarious learning on this job? Why or why not?
7. To what extent would you be motivated by self-control on this job? Why?
8. What would be your level of self-efficacy on this job? Why would your self-efficacy be at this level? Should your manager take steps to boost your self-efficacy? If not, why not? If so, what would these steps be?

Small Group Breakout Exercise

Increasing Motivation

Form groups of three or four people, and appoint one member as the spokesperson who will communicate your findings to the whole class when called on by the instructor. Then discuss the following scenario.

You are a group of partners who own a chain of 15 dry-cleaning stores in a medium-size town. You are meeting today to discuss a problem in customer service that has surfaced recently. When any one of you spends the day, or even part of the day in a particular store, clerks seem to provide excellent customer service, spotters are making sure all stains are removed from garments, and pressers are doing a good job of pressing difficult items such as silk blouses. Yet during those same visits customers complain to you about such things as stains not being removed and items being poorly pressed in some of their previous orders; indeed, several customers have brought garments in to be redone. Customers also sometimes comment on having waited too long for service on previous visits. You are meeting today to address this problem.

1. Discuss the extent to which you believe that you have a motivation problem in your stores.
2. Given what you have learned in this chapter, design a plan to increase the motivation of clerks to provide prompt service to customers even when they are not being watched by a partner.
3. Design a plan to increase the motivation of spotters to remove as many stains as possible even when they are not being watched by a partner.
4. Design a plan to increase the motivation of pressers to do a top-notch job on all clothes they press, no matter how difficult.

Exploring the World Wide Web

Find the website of a company that bases pay on performance for some or all of its employees. Describe the merit pay plan in use at this company. Which employees are covered by the plan? Do you think this pay plan will foster high levels of motivation? Why or why not?

You're the Management Consultant

Eva Hernandez supervises a team of marketing analysts who work on different snack products in a large food products company. The marketing analysts have recently received undergraduate degrees in business or liberal arts and have been on the job between one and three years. Their responsibilities include analyzing the market for their respective products including competitors, tracking current marketing initiatives, and planning future marketing campaigns. They also need to prepare quarterly sales and expense reports for their products and estimated budgets for the next three quarters; to prepare these reports, they need to obtain data from financial and accounting analysts assigned to their products.

When they first started on the job, Hernandez took each marketing analyst through the reporting cycle, explaining what needs to be done, how to accomplish it, and emphasizing the need for timely reports. While preparing the reports can be tedious, she thinks it is pretty straightforward and easily accomplished if the analysts plan ahead and allocate sufficient time for these tasks. When reporting time approaches, she reminds the analysts through emails and emphasizes the need for accurate and timely reports in team meetings.

According to Hernandez, this element of the analysts' jobs couldn't be more straightforward. However, at the end of each quarter, the majority of the analysts turn their reports in a day or two late, and worse yet, Hernandez's own supervisor (who the reports are eventually turned in to) has indicated that information is missing often in the reports and sometimes even has errors. Once Hernandez starting getting flak from her own supervisor about this problem, she realized she better fix things, and quick. She met with the marketing analysts, explained the problem, told them to turn the reports in to her a day or two early so she could look them over, and more generally emphasized that they really needed to get their act together. Unfortunately, things have not improved much and Hernandez is spending more and more of her own time doing the reports. Hernandez has come to you for advice because you are an expert in motivation. What should she do?

BusinessWeek

Cases in the News

What Exactly Is a 'Living Wage'?

Another spring, another student protest. But this time, undergrads at Harvard University won significant national attention for their cause. For three weeks starting in April, they staged a sit-in to demand that Harvard pay a "living wage" to its 1,000 or so janitors and other service workers, including those working for subcontractors. Students folded their tent city on May 8, after Harvard agreed to form a committee with student and worker representatives to look at raising pay rates that start at $6.50 an hour. The students argued that Harvard should pay at least $10.25, enough to lift a family of four above the federal poverty line.

Their effort cast a spotlight on a national movement to force universities, cities, and other public employers to pay a living wage. Religious, student, and labor groups all have become involved in the cause. Here's an overview of what they're doing and why.

What is the living-wage movement?

It's a grassroots effort to help low-wage workers earn enough to support their families above the poverty line, defined in 1999 as $17,029 a year for a family of four. This equates to $8.19 an hour for a full-time job and is 60 percent higher than the $10,700 or so a worker would earn in a year at the federal minimum wage of $5.15 an hour.

How did the movement begin?

Religious groups and labor unions started talking about living wages in the early 1900s, which led to the passage of the federal minimum in 1938. The contemporary version dates back to 1994, when Baltimore clergy members running food pantries noticed that many regular visitors were working full time but still couldn't feed their families. The clergy turned to the city for help. Eventually, they got an ordinance passed that requires city subcontractors to pay their employees a living wage, now $8.03 an hour.

How many of these laws are there, and who do they cover?

To date, 63 living-wage ordinances have been enacted since 1994. Religious and labor groups have campaigns going in another 75 communities, while students are pushing the idea at about 22 universities. So far, most of the 63 laws passed have been in cities, though some counties, a few school boards, and two universities—the University of Wisconsin and Wesleyan University—have enacted them.

Most of the laws cover companies that provide services to cities but not workers on city payrolls. Some laws apply only to a few kinds of subcontractors, such as janitorial services. Others, such as those in Detroit and Hartford, require businesses to comply if they receive tax abatements or other financial assistance. Only a handful of cities, including Durham, N.C., and Omaha, require living wages for all municipal workers.

How many workers are covered?

Only about 100,000 so far—a fraction of the working poor. Though the number of workers earning a below-poverty wage has declined sharply in recent years, 25 percent of the workforce, or 30 million people, fell into this category in 1999. Many have working spouses, so only 12 percent of all families were in poverty.

If advocates somehow passed laws covering every city in the country, that would lift the pay of roughly 1 million subcontractor employees who now earn less than the poverty rate. If the laws also covered all those workers employed directly by municipalities, it would add another 1.3 million people, for a total of 2.3 million.

Do all the laws require a minimum wage of $8.19 an hour?

No, the amounts vary. The highest wage currently is in Santa Cruz, Calif., where it is $12 without health benefits or $11 with them. More than 35 ordinances require or encourage some form of health benefits.

How much does all this cost, and who's footing the bill?

The business impact has been minimal, researchers say, because the laws affect so few people and because higher wages are offset by higher productivity and lower turnover. So far, there's little evidence that living-wage laws raise taxes, although they likely would if they covered more workers.

Opponents have long argued that minimum wage laws destroy jobs. Is that true of living-wage laws? Many economists have backed away from the argument that minimum wages lead to fewer jobs. But even those who still think so say the logic doesn't apply to living-wage laws, because they mostly target municipal workers, so taxpayers absorb any extra costs. David Neumark, a visiting Fellow at the Public Policy Institute of California and a leading minimum-wage opponent, found that when living-wage laws raise pay by 50 percent, say from $5.15 an hour to $7.73 an hour, poverty declines by 1 percent.

What's the argument against such laws?

Business groups insist that higher wages could force them to cut jobs. Opponents also fear that the laws erode their profits and could spur broader increases in the minimum wage. They are working in state legislatures to make local ordinances illegal. So far, five states have passed laws banning local minimum wage hikes, and seven others have had similar debates. After Missouri passed a ban, St. Louis approved its own living-wage ordinance, the legality of which will soon be decided in court.

Why don't living-wage advocates push for a higher federal minimum wage, which covers most of the workforce?

Because they run into less political resistance at the local level. Business groups are more powerful in Congress, where last year they blocked attempts to lift the federal minimum to $6.15 an hour. Washington lawmakers plan to debate similar legislation again soon, but living-wage advocates know they have no chance of getting the minimum pegged to the poverty line. So they chip away at the problem locally.

Source: R. Sharpe, "What Exactly Is A 'Living Wage'?" *Business Week*, May 28, 2001, pp. 78–79.

Questions

1. What are the pros and cons of living wages?
2. Why don't more living wage ordinances exist?
3. Why don't activists in favor of living wages lobby for an increase in the federal minimum wage?

BusinessWeek Cases in the News

The Artificial Sweetener in CEO Pay

For Chief Executive Officer George M.C. Fisher, 1999 was not exactly a Kodak moment. As a withering price war with Fuji cost his company market share in film, and with little to show for his much-vaunted digital strategy, Eastman Kodak Co.'s chief found himself in a financial quagmire. Profit growth was flat and shareholder returns fell by 5.4 percent, a fact board members found distressing. But that didn't stop them from richly rewarding him with a $2.5 million bonus, up 47 percent from 1998, and options valued at more than $2.9 million.

In this age of pay for performance, giving an underperforming CEO a raise seems to defy logic. But things become clearer when you read the fine print in the proxy. Fisher, who has since left Kodak, got his bonus increase in part because of the company's 5 percent revenue growth—and his option grant in part because of a practice that compares CEOs' pay with their peers'. Kodak spokesman Gerard Meuchner notes that Fisher's base salary hadn't changed since he joined the company in 1993, and in 2000 both his bonus and option grant declined significantly, despite profit growth of 1.4 percent. Still, why did Kodak use industry pay data to set Fisher's option grant? Says Meuchner: Because Kodak competes with those companies for executive talent.

The technique is called competitive benchmarking, and in the 1990s, it became widespread. By one estimate, 96 percent of companies in the Standard & Poor's 500-stock index use it to set pay. Company boards figure that if a CEO doesn't earn as much as his peers, he'll take a hike.

It's logical that companies would want to use some comparison in deciding on pay rates. But it may be time to reconsider the extent to which companies lean on benchmarking in pay decisions. A new study suggests that the practice was a main culprit in the skyrocketing CEO pay of the 1990s, when average compensation of chief execs at top U.S. companies grew more than 500 percent, from $1.9 million to $12.4 million. And that's not all. The authors of the study—John Bizjak of Oregon's Portland State University, Michael L. Lemmon of the University of Utah, and Lalitha Naveen of Arizona State University, all finance professors—found that the "underpaid" CEOs, who are benchmarking's main beneficiaries, are the worst performers of the bunch. While no one was looking, Bizjak says, corporations institutionalized a practice that rewards the least deserving. "It weakens the link between pay and performance," he says.

Pinpointing the inflationary effect of benchmarking is tricky. Companies don't say how much of an exec's raise is designed to bring him into line with industry peers. Still, Bizjak and his colleagues found that CEOs who earn less than the median for their peer group get salary and bonus raises twice as big as those granted to CEOs paid above the median. As an example, he cites wholesale trade. In five of the six years covered by the study, "underpaid" CEOs got raises in base salaries and bonuses that far exceeded those of their higher-paid brethren.

Vicious Circle

In most industries, CEOs paid above and below the median get annual raises, with those allotted to "underpaid" execs being much bigger. When that happens, the median grows by leaps and bounds, prompting new raises for the underpaid, and the cycle continues. From 1993 to 1998, in the wholesale trade example, salaries and bonuses grew 65 percent, from $737,900 to $1.2 million. Bizjak won't venture a guess as to how much of the increase came from benchmarking, but others will. Fred Cook, managing director of Frederick W. Cook & Co., a New York compensation consultant, estimates that up to half the 1990s increase was from benchmarking.

What makes this research rise above the ordinary are the data on performance. Bizjak and company found that the CEOs who got the biggest raises didn't generate commensurate performance. Companies giving big raises to their below-median CEOs trailed their less generous counterparts in sales growth, return on assets, and total return.

To be sure, there are valid reasons for boards to make pay comparisons. More often than not, the reason cited by board members is retention. Without assurances of comparable pay, many feel their CEOs would head for the door. Apparel maker Russell Corp. (RML) gave John F. Ward an increase in 1999 after its stock plunged 15 percent, in part because he met earnings goals, and in part because of benchmarking. "We want to make our CEO happy, and the best way to make him happy is to pay him commensurate with our competitors," says Russell compensation committee member Herschel M. Bloom. "What our competitors are paying plays a role."

Many company directors, not surprisingly, deny they're paying big dollars just to keep the boss from walking. Says Jess T. Hay, compensation committee chairman for SBC Communications Inc. (SBC), which used benchmarking to boost the '99 pay of CEO Edward E. Whitacre Jr.: "We're playing for the very long haul. Ed Whitacre has been as able a chief executive as there is in the country today."

When that isn't the case—when a CEO is not performing up to par—companies do shareholders no favors by increasing their pay. The more logical course: Pay him exactly what he's worth, sending a powerful message that poor performance will not be tolerated. Some CEOs will buckle down and start earning their keep. Others will threaten to leave. Let them. Sure, a CEO search will be disruptive, but in a weakening economy, finding a replacement becomes easier every day. In either case, the company wins.

Source: L. Lavelle, "The Artificial Sweetener in CEO Pay" *Business Week*, March 26, 2001, pp. 102, 104.

Questions

1. What are the motivational implications of benchmarking CEO pay?
2. What are the ethical implications of this practice?

Chapter 13

Leadership

Learning Objectives

After studying this chapter, you should be able to:

- Describe what leadership is, when leaders are effective and ineffective, and the sources of power that enable managers to be effective leaders.
- Identify the traits that show the strongest relationship to leadership, the behaviors leaders engage in, and the limitations of the trait and behavior models of leadership.
- Explain how contingency models of leadership enhance our understanding of effective leadership and management in organizations.
- Describe what transformational leadership is, and explain how managers can engage in it.
- Characterize the relationship between gender and leadership.

A Manager's Challenge

Maintaining Growth and Profitability in an Internet Company: Meg Whitman Continues to Transform eBay

How can a manager provide the leadership to succeed in an industry in which so many others are struggling?

eBay CEO Meg Whitman holds up an eBay promotional toy truck in her office in San Jose, California.

Meg Whitman has continued to transform eBay since she first joined the small start-up in 1998. While time will tell if eBay is able to sustain its enviable record of growth and profitability, Whitman has truly transformed this company during her tenure as CEO. Interestingly enough, Whitman originally turned down the request for an interview with eBay when she was first contacted by an executive search firm. When the firm called back a few weeks later, she agreed to an interview only to maintain good terms with the search firm in case she needed their help herself in the future.[1] The rest has literally been history.

Pierre Omidyar, eBay's chairman, founded the company in 1995. When Whitman interviewed for the position of CEO in 1998, the company was called Auction Web, its website was in black and white, and it included a section devoted to the Ebola virus (an interest and concern of Omidyar) and a section with Omidyar's fiancée's webpage. The company had 20 employees in a small Silicon Valley office and approximately $4.5 million in annual sales. Currently, eBay has around 2,000 employees, over $425 million in annual sales, and literally encompasses a global community of buyers and sellers. In 2000, eBay's profits increased by over 350 percent to $48.3 million when $5.5 billion in sales were transacted over eBay.[2] The company has always earned a profit since its stock has been publicly traded, unlike many other Internet companies.[3]

What are the keys to Whitman's success as a leader of this growing company? Vision, values, balance, confidence and trust in her employees, and excitement and enthusiasm. She had the vision to identify the unique features of communication and doing business over the World Wide Web and made sure that eBay capitalizes on these features. EBay provides an electronic community in which millions of collectors, buyers, sellers, and increasingly, businesses, can efficiently communicate and transact with each other. EBay provides auction and fixed price sales for products ranging from small businesses and equipment to automobiles and real estate to toys, baseball cards, and jewelry.[4] Whitman is always looking to the future for ways to actualize her vision and increase eBay's revenues and profits. For example, in June 2001 eBay started eBay Stores that enable individual sellers, small business, and large companies like IBM and the Hard Rock Café to set up electronic stores on eBay that help them better serve their customers or the on-line buyers of their products.[5]

Whitman trusts and empowers her employees, believes in their capabilities, thinks that each employee can make an important contribution to the eBay community, and treats every employee with respect.[6] She is very task-oriented, works hard, and expects the same from her employees. For example, when eBay was having trouble with its website in 1999, Whitman would work well into the night with her subordinates trying to alleviate the difficulties.[7] She also has the experience and discipline needed to lead a large company. Prior to joining eBay, she held top management positions at Hasbro toys, Florists Transworld Delivery, and Stride Rite. This experience reinforced the need to be responsive to customers, keep costs down and profits up, and have motivated managers and employees. As Whitman puts it, "how is managing in the New Economy different from managing in the Old Economy? Actually, it's a lot the same."[8]

Yet, her business sense and drive are balanced by the recognition that work should also be fun, people have other needs and desires in addition to work, and managers need to look out for the well-being of their subordinates.[9] EBay hosts a variety of social events for its employees such as picnics and parties, gives out free T-shirts and sodas, and has periodic special days like "slipper day" and "bagel Wednesday" as well as fun contests. Recognizing the importance of motivation, Whitman ensures that her employees are rewarded for a job well done both as individuals and as members of teams. For example, given the importance of cooperation and teamwork at eBay, bonuses are distributed to employees based on the performance of their teams. Other rewards and benefits include stock options, a tuition reimbursement plan, complete medical and dental insurance, and generous vacation time.[10] All in all, Meg Whitman embodies many of the keys to effective leadership.

Overview

Meg Whitman exemplifies how effective leadership results in a high-performing organization. In Chapter 1 we explained that one of the four primary tasks of managers is leading. Thus, it should come as no surprise that leadership is a key ingredient in effective management. When leaders are effective, their subordinates or followers are highly motivated, committed, and high performing. When leaders are ineffective, chances are good that their subordinates do not perform up to their capabilities, are demotivated, and may be dissatisfied as well. CEO Whitman is a leader at the very top of an organization, but leadership is an important ingredient for managerial success at all levels of an organization: top management, middle management, and first-line management. Moreover, leadership is a key ingredient for managerial success for organizations large and small.

In this chapter we describe what leadership is and examine the major leadership models that shed light on the factors that contribute to a manager being an effective leader. We look at trait and behavior models, which focus on what leaders are like and what they do, and contingency models–Fiedler's contingency model, path-goal theory, and the leader substitutes model–each of which takes into account the complexity surrounding leadership and the role of the situation in leader effectiveness. We also describe how managers can use transformational leadership to dramatically affect their organizations. By the end of this chapter, you will have a good appreciation of the many factors and issues that managers face in their quest to be effective leaders.

The Nature of Leadership

leadership The process by which an individual exerts influence over other people and inspires, motivates, and directs their activities to help achieve group or organizational goals.

leader An individual who is able to exert influence over other people to help achieve group or organizational goals.

Leadership is the process by which a person exerts influence over other people and inspires, motivates, and directs their activities to help achieve group or organizational goals.[11] The person who exerts such influence is a **leader.**

When leaders are effective, the influence they exert over others helps a group or organization achieve its performance goals. When leaders are ineffective, their influence does not contribute to, and often detracts from, goal attainment. As the "Manager's Challenge" makes clear, Meg Whitman is an effective leader: she exerts strong influence over her followers, and the way she motivates and rewards them has helped eBay achieve its goals.

Beyond performance goals, effective leadership increases an organization's ability to meet all the contemporary challenges discussed throughout this book, including the need to obtain a competitive advantage, the need to foster ethical behavior, and the need to manage a diverse workforce fairly and equitably. Leaders who exert influence over organizational members to help meet these goals increase their organizations' chances of success.

In considering the nature of leadership, we first look at leadership styles and how they affect managerial tasks and at the influence of culture on leadership styles. We then focus on the key to leadership, power, which can come from a variety of sources. Finally, we consider the contemporary dynamic of empowerment and how it relates to effective leadership.

Personal Leadership Style and Managerial Tasks

A manager's *personal leadership style*–that is, the specific ways in which a manager chooses to influence other people–shapes the way that manager approaches planning, organizing, and controlling (the other principal tasks of managing). Consider Meg Whitman's personal leadership style in the "Manager's Challenge," she trusts and respects her employees, treats them well, yet strives to ensure that they are motivated and work hard. She works hard herself and recognizes the importance of each of the principal tasks of managing, even in a New Economy company. And she is very forward looking and visionary.

Managers at all levels and in all kinds of organizations have their own personal leadership styles that determine not only how they lead their subordinates but also how they perform the other management tasks. Michael Kraus, owner and manager of a dry-cleaning store in the northeastern United States, for example, takes a very hands-on approach to leadership. He has the sole authority for determining work schedules and job assignments for the 15 employees in his store (an organizing task), makes all important decisions by himself (a planning task), and closely monitors his employees' performance and rewards top performers with pay increases (a control task). Kraus's personal leadership style is effective in his organization. His employees are generally motivated, perform highly, and are satisfied, and his store is highly profitable.

Developing an effective personal leadership style often is a challenge for managers at all levels in an organization. This challenge is often exacerbated when times are tough, due, for example, to an economic downturn or decline in customer demand. The dot-com boom and bust and the slowing economy in the very early 2000s provided many leaders with just such a challenge. Top managers who weathered this period can provide insights into effectively leading when times are tough, as indicated in the following "Information Technology Byte."

Information Technology Byte

Effective Leadership Styles for Tough Times: Lessons from Howard Schulz, Richard Schulze, David Farr, and Lou Gerstner

If you didn't recognize some of the names in the title of this Byte, think top managers. Each of these leaders is a current or former chairman or CEO. While their companies are in dramatically different businesses, one characteristic they have in common is that they adopted effective leadership styles in the tough times of the early 2000s.[12]

Howard Schulz, chairman of coffee giant Starbucks, declared in the late 1990s that Starbucks was going to be doing more and more of its business on the Internet. Then came the dot-com bust and Schulz quickly recognized the need to hone in on Starbucks' key sources of competitive advantage. The plans for the Internet were put on hold, more new stores were opened, and rather than selling on the Web, stores are being wired for Web access so customers can communicate electronically while sipping their cappuccinos. In addition to concentrating on key strengths, another part of Schulz's leadership style is paying attention to important details such as the location of Starbuck's stores to maximize customer traffic and ease of access.[13]

Compaq CEO Michael Capellas (left) joins Howard Schulz at a Houston Starbucks store to announce their partnership to create a high-speed connected environment in Starbucks across North America.

Richard Schulze, CEO and founder of consumer electronics chain Best Buy, adopted a similar style during this period. He focused on Best Buy's key goals for expansion and continued with the planned acquisition of Musicland while at the same time trying to cut costs and improve efficiency at Best Buy.[14] David Farr, CEO of Emerson Electric, also emphasized efficiency, cutting costs, and careful planning to weather the economic downturn. Emerson manufactures a variety of products ranging from measuring equipment for large industrial manufacturing and processing companies to power tools sold in hardware stores.

Likewise, CEO Lou Gerstner kept his eye on IBM's major objectives–finding the right customers and providing them with products they need and excellent customer service.[15] At IBM, attention to detail focuses on having highly satisfied customers; employees–including high-level managers–are held responsible for keeping customers happy and maintaining regular and frequent contact with them. All in all, these four top managers have adopted personal styles for tough times that have helped their organizations weather tough times with less fallout than some of their competitors.[16]

Leadership Styles across Cultures

Some evidence suggests that leadership styles vary not only among individuals but also among countries or cultures. Some research suggests that European managers tend to be more humanistic or people oriented than both Japanese and American managers. The collectivistic culture in Japan places prime emphasis on the group rather than the individual, so the importance of individuals' own personalities, needs, and desires is minimized. Organizations in the United States tend to be very profit oriented and thus tend to downplay the importance of individual employees' needs and desires. Many countries in Europe have a more individualistic perspective than Japan and a more humanistic perspective than the United States, which may result in some European managers being more people oriented than their Japanese or American counterparts. European managers, for example, tend to be reluctant to lay off employees, and when a layoff is absolutely necessary, they take careful steps to make it as painless as possible.[17]

Another cross-cultural difference is in time horizons. Managers in any one country often differ in their time horizons, but there are also cultural differences. For example, U.S. organizations tend to have a short-run profit orientation, which results in U.S. managers' personal leadership styles emphasizing short-run performance. Japanese organizations tend to have a long-run growth orientation, which results in Japanese managers' personal leadership styles emphasizing long-run performance. Justus Mische, a personnel manager at the European organization Hoechst suggests that "Europe, at least the big international firms in Europe, have a philosophy between the Japanese, long term, and the United States, short term."[18] Research on these and other global aspects of leadership is in its infancy; as it continues, more cultural differences in managers' personal leadership styles may be discovered.

Power: The Key to Leadership

No matter what one's leadership style, a key component of effective leadership is found in the power the leader has to affect other people's behavior and get them to act in certain ways.[19] There are several types of power: legitimate, reward, coercive, expert, and referent power (see Figure 13.1).[20] Effective leaders take steps to ensure that they have sufficient levels of each type and that they use the power they have in beneficial ways.

legitimate power The authority that a manager has by virtue of his or her position in an organization's hierarchy.

LEGITIMATE POWER **Legitimate power** is the authority a manager has by virtue of his or her position in an organization's hierarchy. Personal leadership style often influences how a manager exercises legitimate power. Take the case

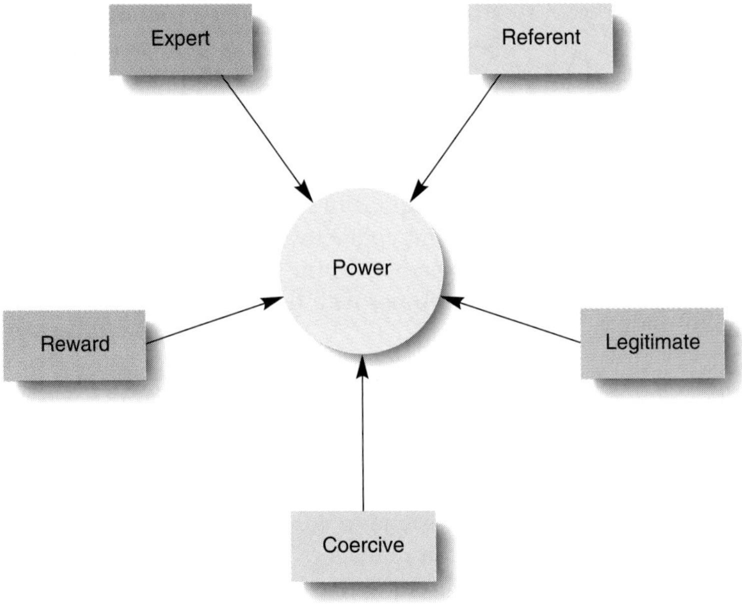

Figure 13.1
Sources of Managerial Power

of Carol Loray, who is a first-line manager in a greeting card company and leads a group of 15 artists and designers. Loray has the legitimate power to hire new employees, assign projects to the artists and designers, monitor their work, and appraise their performance. She uses this power effectively. She always makes sure that her project assignments match the interests of her subordinates as much as possible so they will enjoy their work. She monitors their work to make sure they are on track but does not engage in close supervision, which can hamper creativity. She makes sure her performance appraisals are developmental, providing concrete advice for areas where improvements could be made. Recently, Loray negotiated with her manager to increase her legitimate power so that now she can initiate and develop proposals for new card lines.

reward power The ability of a manager to give or withhold tangible and intangible rewards.

REWARD POWER **Reward power** is the ability of a manager to give or withhold tangible rewards (pay raises, bonuses, choice job assignments) and intangible rewards (verbal praise, a pat on the back, respect). As you learned in Chapter 12, members of an organization are motivated to perform at a high level by a variety of rewards. Being able to give or withhold rewards based on performance is a major source of power that allows managers to have a highly motivated workforce. Managers of salespeople in retail organizations like Neiman Marcus and Dillard's Department Stores, in car dealerships like DaimlerChrysler and Ford, and in travel agencies like Liberty Travel and the Travel Company often use their reward power to motivate their subordinates. Subordinates in organizations such as these often receive a commission on whatever they sell and rewards for the quality of their customer service, which motivate them to do the best they can.

Effective managers use their reward power in such a way that subordinates feel that their rewards signal that they are doing a good job and their efforts are appreciated. Ineffective managers use rewards in a more controlling manner (offering the "carrot" instead of wielding the "stick") that signals to subordinates that the manager has the upper hand. Managers also can take steps to increase their reward power.

Carol Loray had the legitimate power to appraise her subordinates' performance, but she lacked the reward power to distribute raises and end-of-year bonuses until she discussed with her own manager why this would be a valuable motivational tool for her to use. Loray now receives a pool of money each year for salary increases and bonuses and has the reward power to distribute them as she sees fit.

coercive power The ability of a manager to punish others.

COERCIVE POWER Coercive power is the ability of a manager to punish others. Punishment can range from verbal reprimands, to reductions in pay or working hours, to actual dismissal. In the last chapter, we discussed how punishment can have negative side effects such as resentment and retaliation and should be used only when necessary (for example, to curtail a dangerous behavior). Managers who rely heavily on coercive power tend to be ineffective as leaders and sometimes even get fired themselves. William J. Fife is one example; he was fired from his position as CEO of Giddings and Lewis Inc., a manufacturer of factory equipment, because of his overreliance on coercive power. In meetings, Fife often verbally criticized, attacked, and embarrassed top managers. Realizing how destructive Fife's use of punishment was for them and the company, these managers complained to the board of directors, who, after a careful consideration of the issues, asked Fife to resign.[21]

Excessive use of coercive power seldom produces high performance and is questionable ethically. Sometimes it amounts to a form of mental abuse, robbing workers of their dignity and causing excessive levels of stress. Overuse of coercive power can even result in dangerous working conditions. Better results can be obtained by using reward power, as Ricardo Semler realized when he took control of his family business, Semco, a Brazilian manufacturer of industrial products such as pumps, mixers, and propellers, at the age of 21.[22] Use of coercive power had been the norm rather than the exception at Semco. Fear was rampant, guards policed the factory, workers were frisked when they left for the day, their visits to the restroom were timed, and anyone who broke a piece of equipment had to pay for it. Though some other traditional Brazilian companies were and still are managed in a similar fashion, Semler found managing Semco in this manner to be so stressful that after collapsing one day on a business trip, he vowed to make Semco "a true democracy, a place run on trust and freedom, not fear."[23] His goal was to create an ethical workplace in which all employees were treated with respect and dignity. By all reports, he has achieved his goal.

How did Semler achieve this feat? After careful planning and analysis, he decided to use reward power instead of coercive power to get things done. Workers are no longer closely monitored and actually can come and go when they want. Workers are allowed to choose their own bosses.[24] Aside from creating more ethical working conditions that have lowered levels of fear, distrust, and stress for Semco employees, Semler's radical changes have also dramatically improved Semco's performance. In fact, managers from global organizations such as Mobil and IBM have traveled to Brazil to see firsthand what has happened at Semco.[25] Semler has written a best seller entitled, *Maverick,* and two articles in the *Harvard Business Review,* describing his approach to management.[26]

expert power Power that is based in the special knowledge, skills, and expertise that a leader possesses.

EXPERT POWER Expert power is based on the special knowledge, skills, and expertise that a leader possesses. The nature of expert power varies, depending on the leader's level in the hierarchy. First-level and middle managers often have technical expertise relevant to the tasks that their subordinates perform. Their expert power gives them considerable influence over subordinates. Carol

Loray has expert power: She is an artist herself and has drawn and designed some of her company's top-selling greeting cards.

Some top managers derive expert power from their technical expertise. Andrew Grove, CEO of Intel, has a PhD in chemical engineering and is very knowledgeable about the ins and outs of Intel's business–producing semiconductors and microprocessors.[27] Similarly, Bill Gates, chairman of Microsoft, has expertise in software design; and Roy Vagelos, former CEO of Merck, a major pharmaceutical company, was an outstanding research scientist in his own right. Many top-level managers, however, lack technical expertise and derive their expert power from their abilities as decision makers, planners, and strategists. Jack Welch, the former well-known leader and CEO of General Electric summed it up this way: "The basic thing that we at the top of the company know is that we don't know the business. What we have, I hope, is the ability to allocate resources, people, and dollars."[28]

Effective leaders take steps to ensure that they do have an adequate amount of expert power to perform their leadership roles. They may obtain additional training or education in their fields, make sure they keep up-to-date with the latest developments and changes in technology, stay abreast of changes in their fields through involvement in professional associations, and read widely to be aware of momentous changes in the organization's task and general environments. Expert power tends to be best used in a guiding or coaching manner rather than in an arrogant, high-handed manner.

referent power Power that comes from subordinates' and coworkers' respect, admiration, and loyalty.

REFERENT POWER Referent power is more informal than the other kinds of power. Referent power is a function of the personal characteristics of a leader; it is the power that comes from subordinates' and coworkers' respect, admiration, and loyalty. Leaders who are likeable and whom subordinates wish to use as a role model are especially likely to possess referent power. Rochelle Lazarus, a top manager at the advertising agency Ogilvy & Mather, won IBM's worldwide advertising account in part because of her referent power.[29]

In addition to being a valuable asset for top managers like Lazarus, referent power can help first- line and middle managers be effective leaders as well. Sally Carruthers, for example, is the first-level manager of a group of secretaries in the finance department of a large state university. Carruthers's secretaries are known to be among the best in the university. Much of their willingness to go above and beyond the call of duty has been attributed to Carruthers's warm and caring nature, which makes each of them feel important and valued. Managers can take steps to increase their referent power, such as taking time to get to know their subordinates and showing interest in and concern for them.

Empowerment: An Ingredient in Modern Management

empowerment Expanding employees' tasks and responsibilities.

More and more managers today are incorporating in their personal leadership styles an aspect that at first glance seems to be the opposite of being a leader. In Chapter 1, we described how empowerment the process of giving employees at all levels in the organization the authority to make decisions, be responsible for their outcomes, improve quality, and cut costs–is becoming increasingly popular in organizations. When leaders empower their subordinates, the subordinates typically take over some of the responsibilities and authority that used to reside with the leader or manager, such as the right to reject parts that do not meet quality standards, the right to check one's own work, and the right to schedule work activities. Empowered subordinates are given the power to make some of the decisions that their leaders or supervisors used to make.

At first glance, empowerment might seem to be the opposite of effective leadership because managers are allowing subordinates to take a more active role in leading themselves. In actuality, however, empowerment can contribute to effective leadership for several reasons:

- Empowerment increases a manager's ability to get things done because the manager has the support and help of subordinates who may have special knowledge of work tasks.
- Empowerment often increases workers' involvement, motivation, and commitment, which helps ensure that they are working toward organizational goals.
- Empowerment gives managers more time to concentrate on their pressing concerns because they spend less time on day-to-day supervisory activities.

Effective managers like Meg Whitman realize the benefits of empowerment. The personal leadership style of managers who empower subordinates often entails developing their ability to make good decisions as well as being subordinates' guide, coach, and source of inspiration. Empowerment is a popular trend in the United States at companies as diverse as United Parcel Service (a package delivery company) and Coram Healthcare Corporation (a provider of medical equipment and services). Empowerment is also taking off around the world.[30] For instance, even companies in South Korea (such as Samsung, Hyundai, and Daewoo), in which decision making typically was centralized with the founding families, are empowering managers at lower levels to make decisions.[31]

Trait and Behavior Models of Leadership

Leading is such an important process in all organizations—nonprofit organizations, government agencies, and schools as well as for-profit corporations—that it has been researched for decades. Early approaches to leadership, called the *trait model* and the *behavior model,* sought to determine what effective leaders are like as people and what they do that makes them so effective.

The Trait Model

The trait model of leadership focused on identifying those personal characteristics that cause effective leadership. Researchers thought effective leaders must have certain personal qualities that set them apart from ineffective leaders and from people who never become leaders. Decades of research (beginning in the 1930s) and hundreds of studies indicate that certain personal characteristics do appear to be associated with effective leadership. (See Table 13.1 for a list of these.)[32] Notice that although this model is called the "trait" model, some of the personal characteristics that it identifies are not personality traits per se but rather are concerned with a leader's skills, abilities, knowledge, and expertise. As the "Manager's Challenge" shows, Meg Whitman certainly appears to possess many of these characteristics (such as intelligence, self-confidence, and integrity and honesty). Leaders who do not possess these traits may be ineffective.

Traits alone are not the key to understanding leader effectiveness, however. Some effective leaders do not possess all of these traits, and some leaders who

Table 13.1
Traits and Personal Characteristics Related to Effective Leadership

TRAIT	DESCRIPTION
Intelligence	Helps managers understand complex issues and solve problems
Knowledge and expertise	Helps managers make good decisions and discover ways to increase efficiency and effectiveness
Dominance	Helps managers influence their subordinates to achieve organizational goals
Self-confidence	Contributes to managers' effectively influencing subordinates and persisting when faced with obstacles or difficulties
High energy	Helps managers deal with the many demands they face
Tolerance for stress	Helps managers deal with uncertainty and make difficult decisions
Integrity and honesty	Helps managers behave ethically and earn their subordinates' trust and confidence
Maturity	Helps managers avoid acting selfishly, control their feelings, and admit when they have made a mistake

do possess them are not effective in their leadership roles. This lack of a consistent relationship between leader traits and leader effectiveness led researchers to shift their attention away from traits and to search for new explanations for effective leadership. Rather than focusing on what leaders are like (the traits they possess), researchers began to turn their attention to what effective leaders actually do–in other words, to the behaviors that allow effective leaders to influence their subordinates to achieve group and organizational goals.

The Behavior Model

After extensive study in the 1940s and 1950s, researchers at the Ohio State University identified two basic kinds of leader behaviors that many leaders in the United States, Germany, and other countries engaged in to influence their subordinates: *consideration* and *initiating structure*.[33]

consideration Behavior indicating that a manager trusts, respects, and cares about subordinates.

CONSIDERATION Leaders engage in consideration when they show their subordinates that they trust, respect, and care about them. Managers who truly look out for the well-being of their subordinates and do what they can to help subordinates feel good and enjoy their work perform consideration behaviors. In the "Manager's Challenge," Meg Whitman engages in consideration when she treats her subordinates with respect, trusts them, and strives to make eBay a fun work community.[34]

initiating structure Behavior that managers engage in to ensure that work gets done, subordinates perform their jobs acceptably, and the organization is efficient and effective.

INITIATING STRUCTURE Leaders engage in initiating structure when they take steps to make sure that work gets done, subordinates perform their jobs acceptably, and the organization is efficient and effective. Assigning tasks to individuals or work groups, letting subordinates know what is expected of them, deciding how work should be done, making schedules, encouraging adherence to rules and regulations, and motivating subordinates to do a good job are all examples of initiating structure.[35] Michael Teckel, the manager of an upscale store selling imported men's and women's shoes in a midwestern city, engages in initiating structure when he establishes weekly work, lunch, and break schedules to ensure that the store has enough salespeople on the floor. Teckel also initiates structure when he discusses the latest shoe designs with his subordinates so that they are knowledgeable with customers, when he encourages adherence to the store's refund and exchange policies, and when he encourages his staff to provide high-quality customer service and to avoid a hard-sell approach.

Initiating structure and consideration are independent leader behaviors. Leaders can be high on both, low on both, or high on one and low on the other. As indicated in the following "Ethics in Action," Bob Nardelli, CEO of Home Depot, appears to engage in both of these behaviors.

Ethics in Action

Consideration and Initiating Structure at Home Depot

Bernie Marcus and Arthur Blank, founders and co-chairmen of Home Depot, hired Bob Nardelli to fill the position of CEO (formerly held by Blank) because they realized that Home Depot was in need of some initiating structure.[36] Home Depot has grown rapidly from a single store in Atlanta to more than 1,150 stores in South and North America with sales close to $50 billion.[37] In fact, Marcus and Blank's focus on growth, coupled with a slowing economy, motivated them to bring in a new leader to initiate some structure and keep Home Depot on the right track.

Nardelli, a former top manager at General Electric, emphasized initiating structure his first few weeks on the job. He has flattened Home Depot's hierarchy by scaling back the number of managerial levels, has reassigned key employees to better take advantage of their expertise, and is reorienting Home Depot to be focused on profits rather than primarily growth. He is also emphasizing quality and is not afraid to make needed changes, which are more apparent to him as a newcomer than to Blank and Marcus who have been with Home Depot from the start.[38]

Home Depot Chairman Bernie Marcus, left center, Home Depot CEO and President Arthur Blank, center, and Co-Founder Ken Langone, right center, applaud after ringing the opening bell at the NYSE on July 10, 2000, celebrating their 1,000th store.

Nonetheless, Nardelli also recognizes the need for consideration. Maintaining high levels of motivation and job satisfaction among Home Depot's employees are key priorities for him as well as looking out for their well-being and understanding what is important to them. Moreover, Nardelli has promoted environmental and socially responsible initiatives at Home Depot such as environmentally friendly lumber supply programs supported by the Rainforest Action Network.[39] Large and complex organizations like Home Depot require leaders who engage in initiating structure and consideration, as Marcus and Blank recognized when they hired Nardelli.

Leadership researchers have identified leader behaviors similar to consideration and initiating structure. Researchers at the University of Michigan, for example, identified two categories of leadership behaviors, *employee-centered behaviors* and *job-oriented behaviors,* that correspond roughly to consideration and initiating structure, respectively.[40] Models of leadership popular with consultants also tend to zero in on these two kinds of behaviors. For example, Robert Blake and Jane Mouton's Managerial Grid® focuses on *concern for people* (similar to consideration) and *concern for production* (similar to initiating structure). Blake and Mouton advise that effective leadership often requires both a high level of concern for people and a high level of concern for production.[41] As another example, Paul Hersey and Kenneth Blanchard's model focuses on supportive behaviors (similar to consideration) and task-oriented behaviors (similar to initiating structure). According to Hersey and Blanchard, leaders need to consider the nature of their subordinates when trying to determine the extent to which they should perform these two behaviors.[42]

You might expect that effective leaders and managers would perform both kinds of behaviors, but research has found that this is not necessarily the case. The relationship between performance of consideration and initiating structure behaviors and leader effectiveness is not clear-cut. Some leaders are effective even when they do not perform consideration behaviors or initiate structure behaviors, and some leaders are ineffective even when they do perform both kinds of behaviors. Like the trait model of leadership, the behavior model alone cannot explain leader effectiveness. Realizing this, researchers began building more complicated models of leadership, models focused not only on the leader and what he or she does but also on the situation or context in which leadership occurs.

Contingency Models of Leadership

Simply possessing certain traits or performing certain behaviors does not ensure that a manager will be an effective leader in all situations calling for leadership. Some managers who seem to possess the "right" traits and perform the "right" behaviors turn out to be ineffective leaders. Managers lead in a wide variety of situations and organizations and have various kinds of subordinates performing diverse tasks in a multiplicity of environmental contexts. Given the wide variety of situations in which leadership occurs, what makes a manager an effective leader in one situation (such as certain traits or certain behaviors) is not necessarily what that manager needs to be equally effective in a different situation. An effective army general might not be an effective university president, an effective manager of a restaurant might not be an effective manager of a clothing store, an effective coach of a football team might not be an effective manager of a fitness center, and an effective first-line manager in a manufacturing company might not be an effective middle manager. The traits or behaviors that may contribute to a manager being an effective leader in one situation might actually result in the same manager being an ineffective leader in another situation.

Contingency models of leadership take into account the situation or context within which leadership occurs. According to contingency models, whether or not a manager is an effective leader is the result of the interplay between what the manager is like, what he or she does, and the situation in which leadership takes place. Contingency models propose that whether a leader who possesses certain traits or performs certain behaviors is effective depends on, or is contingent on, the situation or context. In this section, we discuss three prominent contingency models developed to shed light on what makes managers effective leaders: Fred Fiedler's contingency model, Robert House's path-goal theory, and the leader substitutes model. As you will see, these leadership models are complementary; each focuses on a somewhat different aspect of effective leadership in organizations.

Fiedler's Contingency Model

Fred E. Fiedler was among the first leadership researchers to acknowledge that effective leadership is contingent on, or depends on, the characteristics of the leader *and* of the situation. Fiedler's contingency model helps explain why a manager may be an effective leader in one situation and ineffective in another; it also suggests which kinds of managers are likely to be most effective in which situations.[43]

LEADER STYLE Like the trait approach, Fiedler hypothesized that personal characteristics can influence leader effectiveness. He used the term *leader style* to refer to a manager's characteristic approach to leadership and identified two basic leader styles: *relationship-oriented* and *task-oriented.* All managers can be described as having one style or the other.

relationship-oriented leaders Leaders whose primary concern is to develop good relationships with their subordinates and to be liked by them.

Relationship-oriented leaders are primarily concerned with developing good relationships with their subordinates and being liked by them. Relationship-oriented managers focus on having high-quality interpersonal relationships with subordinates. This does not mean, however, that the job does not get done when relationship-oriented leaders are at the helm. But it does mean that the quality of interpersonal relationships with subordinates is a prime concern for relationship-oriented leaders. Lawrence Fish, for example, is the chairman of Citizens Financial Group Inc. of Providence, Rhode Island, which has tripled its assets in the last three years. As the top manager who helped to engineer this rapid growth, Fish has never lost sight of the importance of good relationships and personally writes a thank you note to at least one of his subordinates each day.[44]

task-oriented leaders Leaders whose primary concern is to ensure that subordinates perform at a high level.

Task-oriented leaders are primarily concerned with ensuring that subordinates perform at a high level. Task-oriented managers focus on task accomplishment and making sure the job gets done. Some task-oriented leaders like the top managers of the family-owned C. R. England Refrigerated Trucking Company based in Salt Lake City, Utah, go so far as to closely measure and evaluate performance on a weekly basis to ensure subordinates are performing as well as they can.[45]

In his research, Fiedler measured leader style by asking leaders to rate the coworker with whom they have had the most difficulty working (called the *least-preferred coworker* or LPC) on a number of dimensions such as whether the person is boring or interesting, gloomy or cheerful, enthusiastic or unenthusiastic, cooperative or uncooperative. Relationship-oriented leaders tend to describe the LPC in relatively positive terms; their concern for good relationships leads them to think about others in positive terms. Task-oriented leaders tend to describe the LPC in negative terms; their concern for task accomplishment causes them to think badly about others who make getting the job done difficult. Thus, relationship-oriented and task-oriented leaders are sometimes referred to as *high* LPC and *low* LPC leaders, respectively.

SITUATIONAL CHARACTERISTICS According to Fiedler, leadership style is an enduring characteristic; managers cannot change their style, nor can they adopt different styles in different kinds of situations. With this is mind, Fiedler identified three situational characteristics that are important determinants of how favorable a situation is for leading: leader-member relations, task structure, and position power. When a situation is favorable for leading, it is relatively easy for a manager to influence subordinates so that they perform at a high level and contribute to organizational efficiency and effectiveness. In a situation unfavorable for leading, it is much more difficult for a manager to exert influence.

leader-member relations The extent to which followers like, trust, and are loyal to their leader; a determinant of how favorable a situation is for leading.

LEADER-MEMBER RELATIONS The first situational characteristic that Fiedler described, **leader-member relations,** is the extent to which followers like, trust, and are loyal to their leader. Situations are more favorable for leading when leader-member relations are good.

task structure The extent to which the work to be performed is clear-cut so that a leader's subordinates know what needs to be accomplished and how to go about doing it; a determinant of how favorable a situation is for leading.

TASK STRUCTURE The second situational characteristic that Fiedler described, task structure, is the extent to which the work to be performed is clear-cut so that a leader's subordinates know what needs to be accomplished and how to go about doing it. When task structure is high, situations are favorable for leading. When task structure is low, goals may be vague, subordinates may be unsure of what they should be doing or how they should do it, and the situation is unfavorable for leading.

Task structure was low for Geraldine Laybourne when she was a top manager at Nickelodeon, the children's television network. It was never precisely clear what would appeal to her young viewers, whose tastes can change dramatically, or how to motivate her subordinates to come up with creative and novel ideas.[46] In contrast, Herman Mashaba, founder and owner of Black Like Me, a hair care products company based in South Africa, seems to have relatively high task structure in his leadership situation. His company's goals are to produce and sell inexpensive hair care products to native Africans, and managers accomplish these goals by using simple yet appealing packaging and distributing the products through neighborhood beauty salons.[47]

position power The amount of legitimate, reward, and coercive power that a leader has by virtue of his or her position in an organization; a determinant of how favorable a situation is for leading.

POSITION POWER The third situational characteristic that Fiedler described, position power, is the amount of legitimate, reward, and coercive power a leader has by virtue of his or her position in an organization. Leadership situations are more favorable for leading when position power is strong.

COMBINING LEADER STYLE AND THE SITUATION By taking all possible combinations of good and poor leader-member relations, high and low task structure, and strong and weak position power, Fiedler identified eight leadership situations, which vary in their favorability for leading (see Figure 13.2). After extensive research, he determined that relationship-oriented leaders are most effective in moderately favorable situations (situations IV, V, VI, and VII in Figure 13.2) and task-oriented leaders are most effective in very favorable (situations I, II, and III) or very unfavorable situations (situation VIII).

PUTTING THE CONTINGENCY MODEL INTO PRACTICE Recall that, according to Fiedler, leader style is an enduring characteristic that managers cannot change. This suggests that to be effective, either managers need to be placed in

Figure 13.2
Fiedler's Contingency Theory of Leadership

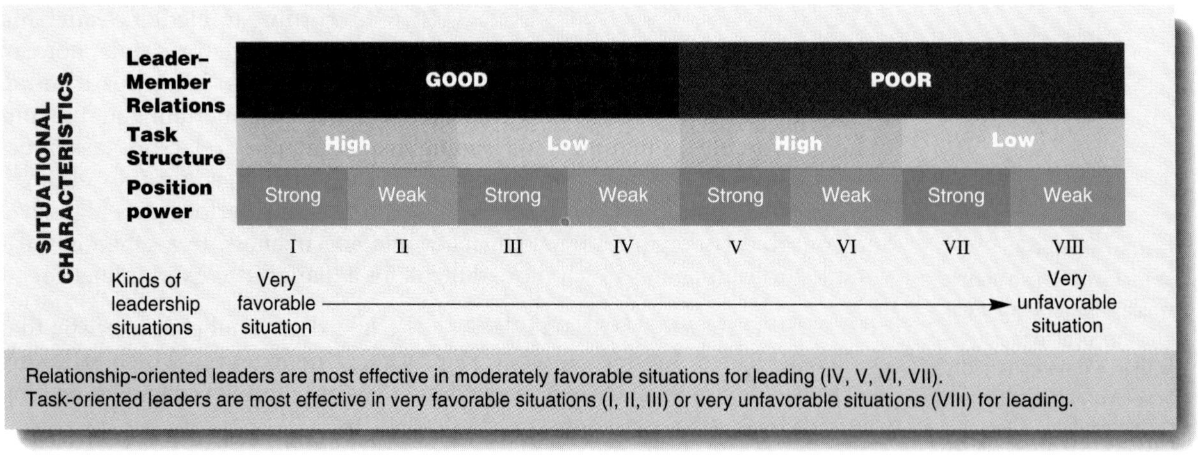

leadership situations that fit their style, or situations need to be changed to suit the manager. Situations can be changed, for example, by giving a manager more position power or taking steps to increase task structure such as by clarifying goals.

Take the case of Mark Compton, a relationship-oriented leader employed by a small construction company who was in a very unfavorable situation and having a rough time leading his construction crew. His subordinates did not trust him to look out for their well-being (poor leader-member relations), the construction jobs he supervised tended to be novel and complex (low task structure), and he had no control over the rewards and disciplinary actions his subordinates received (weak position power). Recognizing the need to improve matters, Compton's supervisor gave him the power to reward crew members with bonuses and overtime work as he saw fit and to discipline crew members for poor-quality work and unsafe on-the-job behavior. As his leadership situation improved to be moderately favorable, so too did Compton's effectiveness as a leader and the performance of his crew.

Research studies tend to support some aspects of Fiedler's model but also suggest that, like most theories, it needs some modifications.[48] Some researchers have questioned what the LPC scale really measures. Others find fault with the model's premise that leaders cannot alter their styles. That is, it is likely that at least some leaders can diagnose the situation they are in and when their style is inappropriate for the situation, modify their style so it is more in line with what the leadership situation calls for.

House's Path-Goal Theory

path-goal theory A contingency model of leadership proposing that leaders can motivate subordinates by identifying their desired outcomes, rewarding them for high performance and the attainment of work goals with these desired outcomes, and clarifying for them the paths leading to the attainment of work goals.

In what he called **path-goal theory,** leadership researcher Robert House focused on what leaders can do to motivate their subordinates to achieve group and organizational goals.[49] The premise of path-goal theory is that effective leaders motivate subordinates to achieve goals by (1) clearly identifying the outcomes that subordinates are trying to obtain from the workplace, (2) rewarding subordinates with these outcomes for high performance and the attainment of work goals, and (3) clarifying for subordinates the *paths* leading to the attainment of work *goals*. Path-goal theory is a contingency model because it proposes that the steps managers should take to motivate subordinates depend on both the nature of the subordinates and the type of work they do.

Based on the expectancy theory of motivation (see Chapter 12), path-goal theory provides managers with three guidelines to follow to be effective leaders:

1. *Find out what outcomes your subordinates are trying to obtain from their jobs and the organization.* These outcomes can range from satisfactory pay and job security to reasonable working hours and interesting and challenging job assignments. After identifying these outcomes, the manager should have the *reward power* needed to distribute or withhold these outcomes. Mark Crane, for example, is the vice principal of a large elementary school. Crane determined that the teachers he leads are trying to obtain the following outcomes from their jobs: pay raises, autonomy in the classroom, and the choice of which grades they teach. Crane had reward power for the latter two outcomes, but the school's principal determined how the pool of money for raises was to be distributed each year. Because Crane was the first-line manager who led the teachers and was most familiar with their performance, he asked the principal (his boss) to give him some say in determining pay raises. Realizing that this made a lot of sense, his principal gave Crane full power to distribute raises and requested only that Crane review his decisions with him prior to informing the teachers about them.

2. *Reward subordinates for high performance and goal attainment with the outcomes they desire.* The teachers and administrators at Crane's school considered several dimensions of teacher performance critical to achieving their goal of providing high-quality education–high-quality in-class instruction, special programs to enhance student interest and learning (such as science and computer projects), and availability for meetings with parents to discuss their children's progress and special needs. Crane distributed pay raises to the teachers based on the extent to which they performed highly on each of these dimensions. The top-performing teachers were given first choice of grade assignments and also had practically complete autonomy in their classrooms.

3. *Clarify the paths to goal attainment for subordinates, remove any obstacles to high performance, and express confidence in subordinates' capabilities.* This does not mean that a manager needs to tell subordinates what to do. Rather, it means that a manager needs to make sure that subordinates are clear about what they should be trying to accomplish and have the capabilities, resources, and confidence levels needed to be successful. Crane made sure that all the teachers understood the importance of these three targeted goals and asked them whether, to reach them, they needed any special resources or supplies for their classes. Crane also gave additional coaching and guidance to teachers who seemed to be struggling. For example, Patrick Conolly, in his first year of teaching after graduate school, was unsure about how to use special projects in a third-grade class and how to react to parents who were critical. Conolly's actual teaching was excellent, but he even felt insecure about how he was doing on this dimension. To help build Conolly's confidence, Crane told Conolly that he truly thought he could be one of the school's top teachers (which was true). He gave Conolly some ideas about special projects that worked particularly well with the third grade, such as a writing project. Crane also role-played teacher-parent interactions with Conolly. Conolly played the role of a particularly dissatisfied or troubled parent while Crane played the role of a teacher trying both to solve the underlying problem while making the parent feel that his or her child's needs were being met. Crane's efforts to clarify the paths to goal attainment for Conolly paid off: Within two years the local PTS voted Conolly teacher of the year.

Path-goal theory identifies four kinds of leadership behaviors that motivate subordinates:

- *Directive behaviors* are similar to initiating structure and include setting goals, assigning tasks, showing subordinates how to complete tasks, and taking concrete steps to improve performance.
- *Supportive behaviors* are similar to consideration and include expressing concern for subordinates and looking out for their best interests.
- *Participative behaviors* give subordinates a say in matters and decisions that affect them.
- *Achievement-oriented behaviors* motivate subordinates to perform at the highest level possible by, for example, setting very challenging goals, expecting that they be met, and believing in subordinates' capabilities.

Which of these behaviors should managers use to lead effectively? The answer to this question depends, or is contingent, on the nature of the subordinates and the kind of work they do.

Directive behaviors may be beneficial when subordinates are having difficulty completing assigned tasks, but they might be detrimental when subordinates are independent thinkers who work best when left alone. *Supportive* behaviors are often advisable when subordinates are experiencing high levels of stress. *Participative* behaviors can be particularly effective when subordinates' support of a decision is required. *Achievement-oriented* behaviors may increase motivation levels of highly capable subordinates who are bored from having too few challenges, but they might backfire if used with subordinates who are already pushed to their limit.

Effective managers seem to have a knack for determining what kinds of leader behaviors are likely to work in different situations and result in increased effectiveness, as indicated in this "Management Insight."

Management Insight

Supporting Creativity

What do playing in an orchestra and designing high-status automobiles have in common? Both activities require creativity from artistic individuals. Effectively leading workers who are engaged in creative activities can be a challenge. For example, too much initiating structure can inhibit their creativity. Roger Nierenberg, conductor of the Stamford, Connecticut, Symphony Orchestra has long recognized this and rather than being overly controlling with musicians, he emphasizes supportive behaviors. Nierenberg utilizes positive feedback to support his musicians, never blames them when things go wrong, and provides direction in an encouraging manner.[50]

Nierenberg's positive, encouraging style of leading and conducting also can be applied in more traditional work environments. For example, in his leadership classes for managers at major corporations, such as Lucent Technologies and Georgia-Pacific, he coaches the managers on how to commit to a course of action and direct their subordinates to attain it in a supportive, uncritical manner.[51]

A positive, encouraging style of leadership often gets the best results from employees—whether they're performing on stage or working in the back office.

This approach to leading creative workers is applied in other countries as well. For example, Chris Bangle, who heads BMW's global design efforts in Munich, Germany, takes great pains to shield creative designers of BMW interiors and exteriors from critical comments or negative feedback from others in the organization such as market analysts and engineers. Rather than critiques, above all else, designers need support from leadership and the freedom to explore different designs, as well as encouraging direction to reach closure in a reasonably timely fashion.[52] Bangle sees this kind of encouraging and supportive leadership as key to BMW's competitive advantage in designing cars like "moving works of art that express the driver's love of quality."[53]

The Leader Substitutes Model

leadership substitute Characteristics of subordinates or characteristics of a situation or context that act in place of the influence of a leader and make leadership unnecessary.

The leader substitutes model suggests that leadership is sometimes unnecessary because substitutes for leadership are present. A **leadership substitute** is something that acts in place of the influence of a leader and makes leadership unnecessary. This model suggests that under certain conditions managers do not have to play a leadership role–that members of an organization sometimes can perform highly without a manager exerting influence over them.[54] The leader substitutes model is a contingency model because it suggests that in some situations leadership is unnecessary.

Take the case of David Cotsonas, who teaches English at a foreign language school in Cypress, an island in the Mediterranean Sea. Cotsonas is fluent in Greek, English, and French, an excellent teacher, and highly motivated. Many of his students are businesspeople who have some rudimentary English skills and wish to increase their fluency to be able to conduct more of their business in English. He enjoys not only teaching them English but also learning about the work they do, and he often keeps in touch with his students after they finish his classes. Cotsonas meets with the director of the school twice a year to discuss semiannual class schedules and enrollments.

With practically no influence from a leader, Cotsonas is a highly motivated top performer at the school. In his situation, leadership is unnecessary because substitutes for leadership are present. Cotsonas's teaching expertise, his motivation, and his enjoyment of his work all are substitutes for the influence of a leader–in this case, the school's director. If the school's director were to try to exert influence over the way Cotsonas goes about performing his job, Cotsonas would probably resent this infringement on his autonomy, and it is unlikely that his performance would improve because he is already one of the school's best teachers.

As in Cotsonas's case, *characteristics of subordinates*–such as their skills, abilities, experience, knowledge, and motivation–can be substitutes for leadership.[55] *Characteristics of the situation or context*–such as the extent to which the work is interesting and enjoyable–also can be substitutes. When work is interesting and enjoyable, as it is for Cotsonas, jobholders do not need to be coaxed into performing because performing is rewarding in its own right. Similarly, when managers *empower* their subordinates or use *self-managed work* teams (discussed in detail in Chapter 14), the need for leadership influence from a manager is decreased because team members manage themselves.

Substitutes for leadership can increase organizational efficiency and effectiveness because they free up some of managers' valuable time and allow managers to focus their efforts on discovering new ways to improve organizational effectiveness. The director of the language school, for example, was able to spend much of his time making arrangements to open a second school in Rhodes, an island in the Aegean Sea, because of the presence of leadership substitutes not only in the case of Cotsonas but for most of the other teachers at the school as well.

Bringing It All Together

Effective leadership in organizations occurs when managers take steps to lead in a way that is appropriate for the situation or context in which leadership occurs and for the subordinates who are being led. The three contingency models of leadership discussed above help managers hone in on the necessary ingredients for effective leadership. They are complementary in that each one looks at the leadership question from a different angle. Fiedler's contingency model explores how a manager's leadership style needs to be matched to that person's leadership situation for maximum effectiveness. House's path-goal theory focuses on how managers should motivate subordinates and describes the specific kinds of behaviors that managers can engage in to have a highly motivated workforce. The leadership substitutes model alerts managers to the fact that sometimes they do not need to exert influence over subordinates and thus can free up their time for other important activities. Table 13.2 recaps these three contingency models of leadership.

Table 13.2
Contingency Models of Leadership

MODEL	FOCUS	KEY CONTINGENCIES
Fiedler's contingency model	Describes two leader styles, relationship-oriented and task-oriented, and the kinds of situations in which each kind of leader will be most effective	Whether or not a relationship-oriented or a task-oriented leader is effective is contingent on the situation
House's path-goal theory	Describes how effective leaders motivate their followers	The behaviors that managers should engage in to be effective leaders are contingent on the nature of the subordinates and the work they do
Leader substitutes model	Describes when leadership is unnecessary	Whether or not leadership is necessary for subordinates to perform highly is contingent on characteristics of the subordinates and the situation

Tips for New Managers

Contingency Models of Leadership

1. Take steps to ensure that your leadership approach is appropriate for the situation.
2. Determine what outcomes your subordinates are trying to obtain from their jobs, make sure you have reward power for these outcomes, and distribute the outcomes based on performance levels.
3. Express confidence in your subordinates' capabilities and do whatever you can to help them believe in their ability to succeed. Remove any obstacles to success.
4. Explore how you can take advantage of leadership substitutes to free up some of the time you spend supervising your subordinates.

Transformational Leadership

Time and time again, throughout business history, certain leaders seem to literally transform their organizations, making sweeping changes to revitalize and renew operations. For example, in the 1990s, the chief executive of the German electronics company Siemens, Heinrich von Pierer, dramatically transformed his company. When von Pierer took over in 1992, Siemens had a rigid hierarchy in place, was suffering from increased global competition, and was saddled with a conservative, perfectionist culture that stifled creativity and innovation and slowed decision making. Von Pierer's changes at Siemens have been nothing short of revolutionary.[56] At the new Siemens, subordinates critique their managers, who receive training in how to be more democratic and participative and spur creativity. Employees are no longer afraid to speak their minds, and the quest for innovation is a driving force throughout the company.

Von Pierer is literally transforming Siemens and its thousands of employees to be more innovative and take the steps needed to gain a competitive advantage. When managers have such dramatic effects on their subordinates and on an organization as a whole, they are engaging in transformational leadership. **Transformational leadership** occurs when managers change (or transform) their subordinates in three important ways:[57]

transformational leadership Leadership that makes subordinates aware of the importance of their jobs and performance to the organization and aware of their own needs for personal growth and that motivates subordinates to work for the good of the organization.

1. *Transformational managers make subordinates aware of how important their jobs are for the organization and how necessary it is for them to perform those jobs as best they can so that the organization can attain its goals.* Von Pierer sent the message throughout Siemens not only that innovating, cost cutting, and increasing customer service and satisfaction were everyone's responsibilities but also that improvements could be and needed to be made in these areas. For example, when von Pierer realized that managers in charge of microprocessor sales were not realizing the importance of their jobs and of performing them in a top-notch fashion, he had managers from Siemens's top microprocessor customers give the Siemens's microprocessor managers feedback about their poor service and unreliable delivery schedules. The microprocessor managers quickly realized how important it was for them to take steps to improve customer service.
2. *Transformational managers make their subordinates aware of the subordinates' own needs for personal growth, development, and accomplishment.* Von Pierer has made Siemens's employees aware of their own needs in this regard through numerous workshops and training sessions, through empowering employees throughout the company, through the development of fast-track career programs, and through increased reliance on self-managed work teams.[58]
3. *Transformational managers motivate their subordinates to work for the good of the organization as a whole, not just for their own personal gain or benefit.* Von Pierer's message to Siemens's employees has been clear: Dramatic changes in the way they perform their jobs are crucial for the future viability and success of Siemens. As von Pierer puts it, "We have to keep asking ourselves: Are we flexible enough? Are we changing enough?"[59] One way von Pierer has tried to get all employees thinking in these terms is by inserting in the company magazine distributed to all employees self-addressed postcards urging them to send in their ideas for making improvements directly to him.

When managers transform their subordinates in these three ways, subordinates trust the manager, are highly motivated, and help the organization achieve its goals. As a result of von Pierer's transformational leadership, for example, a team of Siemens's engineers working in blue jeans in a rented house developed a tool control system in one-third the time and at one-third the cost of other similar systems developed at Siemens.[60] How do managers like von Pierer transform subordinates and produce dramatic effects in their organizations? There are at least three ways in which managers and other transformational leaders can influence their followers: by being a charismatic leader, by intellectually stimulating subordinates, and by engaging in developmental consideration (see Table 13.3).

charismatic leader An enthusiastic, self-confident leader able to clearly communicate his or her vision of how good things could be.

Being a Charismatic Leader

Transformational managers are **charismatic leaders.** They have a vision of how good things could be in their work groups and organizations that is in contrast

Table 13.3
Transformational Leadership

Transformational Managers

- Are charismatic
- Intellectually stimulate subordinates
- Engage in developmental consideration

Subordinates of Transformational Managers

- Have increased awareness of the importance of their jobs and high performance
- Are aware of their own needs for growth, development, and accomplishment
- Work for the good of the organization and not just their own personal benefit

with the status quo. Their vision usually entails dramatic improvements in group and organizational performance as a result of changes in the organization's structure, culture, strategy, decision making, and other critical processes and factors. This vision paves the way for gaining a competitive advantage. From the "Manager's Challenge" it is clear that part of Meg Whitman's vision for eBay is that the company continue to grow and find new ways to take as much advantage as possible of the unique communication features of doing business on the Internet.

Charismatic leaders are excited and enthusiastic about their vision and clearly communicate it to their subordinates, as does Meg Whitman. The excitement, enthusiasm, and self-confidence of a charismatic leader contribute to the leader's being able to inspire followers to enthusiastically support his or her vision.[61] As Mal Ransom, vice president of marketing at Packard Bell Computers, puts it, "we all buy into the dream; we all buy into the vision."[62] People often think of charismatic leaders or managers as being "larger than life." The essence of charisma, however, is having a vision and enthusiastically communicating it to others. Thus, managers who appear to be quiet and earnest can also be charismatic.

Stimulating Subordinates Intellectually

Transformational managers openly share information with their subordinates so that they are aware of problems and the need for change. The manager causes subordinates to view problems in their groups and throughout the organization from a different perspective, consistent with the manager's vision. Whereas in the past subordinates might not have been aware of some problems, may have viewed problems as a "management issue" beyond their concern, or may have viewed problems as insurmountable, the transformational manager's **intellectual stimulation** leads subordinates to view problems as challenges that they can and will meet and conquer. The manager engages and empowers subordinates to take personal responsibility for helping solve problems.[63]

intellectual stimulation Behavior a leader engages in to make followers aware of problems and view these problems in new ways, consistent with the leader's vision.

Engaging in Developmental Consideration

When managers engage in **developmental consideration,** they not only perform the consideration behaviors described earlier, such as demonstrating true concern for the well-being of subordinates, but go one step further. The manager

developmental consideration Behavior a leader engages in to support and encourage followers and help them develop and grow on the job.

goes out of his or her way to support and encourage subordinates, giving them opportunities to enhance their skills and capabilities and to grow and excel on the job.[64] Heinrich von Pierer engages in developmental consideration in numerous ways, such as providing counseling sessions with a psychologist for managers who are having a hard time adapting to the changes at Siemens and sponsoring hiking trips to stimulate employees to think and work in new ways.[65]

All organizations, no matter how large or small, successful or unsuccessful, can benefit when their managers engage in transformational leadership. Moreover, while the benefits of transformational leadership are often most apparent when an organization is in trouble, as indicated in the following "Managing Globally," transformational leadership can be an enduring approach to leadership, leading to long-run organizational effectiveness.

Managing Globally

Enduring Transformational Leadership at Colgate-Palmolive

Since Reuben Mark became the CEO of Colgate-Palmolive over 15 years ago, the company has consistently been a high performer, often outperforming such admired companies as GE, IBM, and Coca-Cola in terms of earnings per share.[66] These outstanding results as well as other evidence suggest that Mark is a transformational leader who continues to steer Colgate-Palmolive in the right direction.

Mark's vision for Colgate-Palmolive emphasizes efficiency, cost-cutting, and a very focused approach emphasizing oral and personal care products such as toothpaste, deodorant, and soap.[67] Moreover, globalization is another key element of Mark's vision. For example, less than half of the company's revenues are derived from sales in the United States and Canada; sales to Latin America, Asia, Africa, and Europe are the key revenue generators.[68]

Mark intellectually stimulates his followers by emphasizing the importance of their own efforts in finding ways to cut costs and boost efficiency. He also cares about them personally and prefers having the spotlight focused on their contributions to the company instead of his own. To top it off, Mark, who has a good sense of humor, is very accessible and acts like other employees rather than the CEO (e.g., he flies on low-cost Southwest Airlines rather than booking first-class flights like other CEOs).[69] All in all, Mark's ongoing transformational leadership at Colgate-Palmolive demonstrates that this kind of leadership can be enduring over the long term.

A concert stage sponsored by Colgate-Palmolive at the Calle Ocho carnival in Little Havana, Miami, Florida, an event celebrating the cultural diversity of the area. What does it take to lead a global corporation like Colgate-Palmolive? For Reuben Marks it's been a matter of maintaining a clear business focus, a low-key profile, and a sense of humor.

The Distinction between Transformational and Transactional Leadership

transactional leadership Leadership that motivates subordinates by rewarding high performance and reprimanding them for low performance.

Transformational leadership is often contrasted with transactional leadership. Transactional leadership involves managers using their reward and coercive power to encourage high performance. When managers reward high performers, reprimand or otherwise punish low performers, and motivate subordinates by reinforcing desired behaviors and extinguishing or punishing undesired ones, they are engaging in transactional leadership.[70] Managers who effectively influence their subordinates to achieve goals yet do not seem to be making the kind of dramatic changes that are part of transformational leadership are engaging in transactional leadership.

Many transformational leaders engage in transactional leadership. They reward subordinates for a job well done and notice and respond to substandard performance. But they also have their eyes on the bigger picture of how much better things could be in their organizations, how much more their subordinates are capable of achieving, and how important it is to treat their subordinates with respect and to help them reach their full potential.

Research has found that when leaders engage in transformational leadership, their subordinates tend to have higher levels of job satisfaction and performance.[71] Additionally, subordinates of transformational leaders may be more likely to trust their leaders and their organizations and feel that they are being fairly treated, which in turn, may positively influence their work motivation (see Chapter 12).[72]

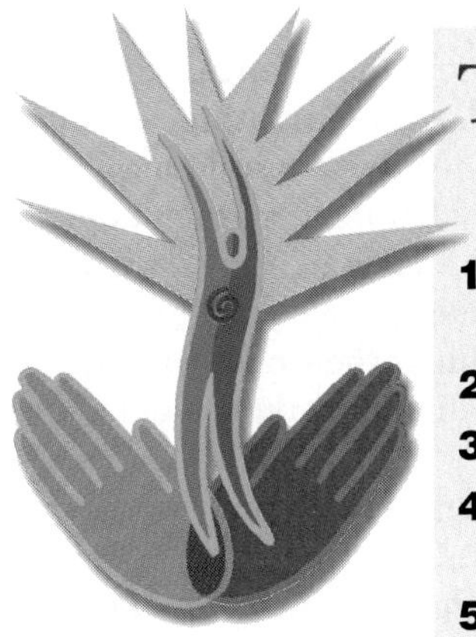

Tips for New Managers

Transformational Leadership

1. Let subordinates know how their own jobs and performance contribute to organizational effectiveness.
2. Help subordinates learn and use new skills.
3. Enthusiastically communicate your vision for changes and improvements.
4. Share organizational problems and challenges with subordinates and engage them in problem-solving efforts.
5. Take a personal interest in your subordinates.

Gender and Leadership

The increasing number of women entering the ranks of management as well as the problems some women face in their efforts to be hired as managers or promoted into management positions has prompted researchers to explore the relationship between gender and leadership. Although there are relatively more women in management positions today than there were ten years ago, there are still relatively few women in top management and, in some organizations, even in middle management.

When women do advance to top-management positions, special attention often is focused on the fact that they are women. In 1992, Ellen M. Knapp was appointed to a top-management position, vice chair of technology, at Coopers & Lybrand, a Big Six accounting firm. She was the only woman to reach this level in the hierarchy of any of the Big Six firms at that time. Coopers & Lybrand was thought to have a "men's club atmosphere," and the vast majority of the partners in the firm were men.[73] When Knapp first assumed her position, some observers likened her appointment to anarchy. However, her superior capabilities and determination have earned her the respect of her predominantly male coworkers. Her transformational leadership over the past several years has dramatically upgraded Cooper & Lybrand's technology base–an upgrade that was sorely needed and late in coming prior to Knapp's assuming her top-management position.[74] Nevertheless, when she was appointed to this position, much attention was focused on the simple fact that she was a woman. If she had been a man, gender would never have entered the picture. Unfortunately, professional women and women in managerial positions are continuing to be confronted with some of the same kinds of challenges that Knapp experienced at Coopers.[75]

A widespread stereotype of women is that they are nurturing, supportive, and concerned with interpersonal relations. Men are stereotypically viewed as being directive and focused on task accomplishment. Such stereotypes suggest that women tend to be more relationship oriented as managers and engage in more consideration behaviors, whereas men are more task oriented and engage in more initiating structure behaviors. Does the behavior of actual male and female managers bear out these stereotypes? Do women managers lead in different ways than men? Are male or female managers more effective as leaders?

Research suggests that male and female managers who have leadership positions in organizations behave in similar ways.[76] Women do not engage in more consideration than men, and men do not engage in more initiating structure than women. Research does suggest, however, that leadership style may vary between women and men. Women tend to be somewhat more participative as leaders than men, involving subordinates in decision making and seeking their input.[77] Male managers tend to be less participative than female managers, making more decisions on their own and wanting to do things their own way. Moreover, research suggests that men tend to be harsher when they punish their subordinates than women.[78]

There are at least two reasons why female managers may be more participative as leaders than male managers.[79] First, subordinates may try to resist the influence of female managers more so than they do the influence of male managers. Some subordinates may never have reported to a woman before, some may inappropriately see a management role as being more appropriate for a man than for a woman, and some may just resist being led by a woman. To overcome this resistance and encourage subordinates' trust and respect, women managers may adopt a participative approach.

A second reason why female managers may be more participative is that they sometimes have better interpersonal skills than male managers.[80] A participative approach to leadership requires high levels of interaction and involvement between a manager and his or her subordinates, sensitivity to subordinates' feelings, and the ability to make decisions that may be unpopular with subordinates but necessary for goal attainment. Good interpersonal skills may help female managers have the effective interactions with their subordinates that are crucial to a participative approach.[81] To the extent that male managers have more difficulty managing interpersonal relationships, they may shy away from the high levels of interaction with subordinates necessary for true participation.

The key finding from research on leader behaviors, however, is that male and female managers do *not* differ significantly in their propensities to perform different leader behaviors. Even though they may be more participative, female managers do not engage in more consideration or less initiating structure than male managers.

Perhaps a question even more important than whether male and female managers differ in the leadership behaviors they perform is whether they differ in effectiveness. Consistent with the findings for leader behaviors, research suggests that across different kinds of organizational settings, male and female managers tend to be *equally effective* as leaders.[82] Thus, there is no logical basis for stereotypes favoring male managers and leaders or for the existence of the glass ceiling (an invisible barrier that seems to prevent women from advancing as far as they should in some organizations). Because women and men are equally effective as leaders, the increasing number of women in the workforce should result in a larger pool of highly qualified candidates for management positions in organizations, ultimately enhancing organizational effectiveness.[83]

Emotional Intelligence and Leadership

Do the moods and emotions leaders experience on the job influence their behavior and effectiveness as leaders? Preliminary research suggests that this is likely to be the case. For example, one study found that when store managers experienced positive moods at work, salespeople in the stores they led provided high-quality customer service and were less likely to quit.[84]

Moreover, a leader's level of emotional intelligence (see Chapter 3) may play a particularly important role in leadership effectiveness.[85] For example, emotional intelligence may help leaders develop a vision for their organizations, motivate their subordinates to commit to this vision, and energize them to enthusiastically work to achieve this vision. Moreover, emotional intelligence may enable leaders to develop a significant identity for their organization and instill high levels of trust and cooperation throughout the organization while maintaining the flexibility needed to respond to changing conditions.[86]

Summary and Review

THE NATURE OF LEADERSHIP Leadership is the process by which a person exerts influence over other people and inspires, motivates, and directs their activities to help achieve group or organizational goals. Leaders are able to influence others because they possess power. The five types of power available to managers are legitimate power, reward power, coercive power, expert power, and referent power. Many managers are using empowerment as a tool to increase their effectiveness as leaders.

TRAIT AND BEHAVIOR MODELS OF LEADERSHIP The trait model of leadership describes personal characteristics or traits that contribute to effective leadership. However, some managers who possess these traits are not effective leaders, and some managers who do not possess all the traits are nevertheless effective leaders. The behavior model of leadership describes two kinds of behavior that most leaders engage in: consideration and initiating structure.

CONTINGENCY MODELS OF LEADERSHIP Contingency models take into account the complexity surrounding leadership and the role of the situation in determining whether a manager is an effective or ineffective leader. Fiedler's contingency model explains why managers may be effective leaders in one situation and ineffective in another. According to Fiedler's model, relationship-oriented leaders are most effective in situations that are moderately favorable for leading, and task-oriented leaders are most effective in situations that are very favorable or very unfavorable for leading. House's path-goal theory describes how effective managers motivate their subordinates by determining what outcomes their subordinates want, rewarding subordinates with these outcomes when they achieve their goals and perform at a high level, and clarifying the paths to goal attainment. Managers can engage in four different kinds of behaviors to motivate subordinates: directive behaviors, supportive behaviors, participative behaviors, or achievement-oriented behaviors. The leader substitutes model suggests that sometimes managers do not have to play a leadership role because their subordinates perform highly without the manager having to exert influence over them.

TRANSFORMATIONAL LEADERSHIP Transformational leadership occurs when managers have dramatic effects on their subordinates and on the organization as a whole and inspire and energize subordinates to solve problems and improve performance. These effects include making subordinates aware of the importance of their own jobs and high performance, making subordinates aware of their own needs for personal growth, development, and accomplishment, and motivating subordinates to work for the good of the organization and not just their own personal gain. Managers can engage in transformational leadership by being charismatic leaders, by intellectually stimulating subordinates, and by engaging in developmental consideration. Transformational managers also often engage in transactional leadership by using their reward and coercive powers to encourage high performance.

GENDER AND LEADERSHIP Female and male managers do not differ in the leadership behaviors that they perform, contrary to stereotypes suggesting that women are more relationship oriented and men more task oriented. Female managers sometimes are more participative than male managers, however. Research has found that women and men are equally effective as managers and leaders.

EMOTIONAL INTELLIGENCE AND LEADERSHIP The moods and emotions leaders experience on the job may affect their leadership effectiveness. Moreover, emotional intelligence has the potential to contribute to leadership effectiveness in multiple ways.

Management in Action

Topics for Discussion and Action

1. Describe the steps managers can take to increase their power and ability to be effective leaders.
2. Think of specific situations in which it might be especially important for a manager to engage in consideration and in initiating structure.
3. Interview an actual manager to find out how the three situational characteristics that Fiedler identified are affecting the manager's ability to provide leadership.
4. For your current job or for a future job you expect to hold, describe what your supervisor could do to strongly motivate you to be a top performer.
5. Discuss why managers might want to change the behaviors they engage in, given their situation, their subordinates, and the nature of the work being done. Do you think managers are able to readily change their leadership behaviors? Why or why not?
6. Discuss why substitutes for leadership can contribute to organizational effectiveness.
7. Describe what transformational leadership is, and explain how managers can engage in it.
8. Find an example of a company that has dramatically turned around its fortunes and improved its performance. Determine whether a transformational manager was behind the turnaround and, if one was, what this manager did.
9. Discuss why some people still think that men make better managers than women even though research indicates that men and women are equally effective as managers and leaders.

Building Management Skills

Analyzing Failures of Leadership

Think about a situation you are familiar with in which a leader was very ineffective. Then answer the following questions.

1. What sources of power did this leader have? Did the leader have enough power to influence his or her followers?
2. What kinds of behaviors did this leader engage in? Were they appropriate for the situation? Why or why not?
3. From what you know, do you think this leader was a task-oriented leader or a relationship-oriented leader? How favorable was this leader's situation for leading?
4. What steps did this leader take to motivate his or her followers? Were these steps appropriate or inappropriate? Why?
5. What signs, if any, did this leader show of being a transformational leader?

Small Group Breakout Exercise

Improving Leadership Effectiveness

Form groups of three to five people, and appoint one member as the spokesperson who will communicate your findings and conclusions to the whole class when called on by the instructor. Then discuss the following scenario.

You are a team of human resource consultants who have been hired by Carla Caruso, an entrepreneur who has started her own interior decorating business. A highly competent and creative interior decorator, Caruso established a working relationship with most of the major home builders in her community. At first, she worked on her own as an independent contractor. Then because of a dramatic increase in the number of new homes being built, she became swamped with requests for her services and decided to start her own company.

She hired a secretary/bookkeeper and four interior decorators, all of whom are highly competent. Caruso still does decorating jobs herself and has adopted a hands-off approach to leading the four decorators who report to her because she feels that interior design is a very personal, creative endeavor. Rather than pay the decorators on some kind of commission basis (such as a percentage of their customers' total billings), she pays them a premium salary higher than average so that they are motivated to do what's best for a customer's needs and not what will result in higher billings and commissions.

Caruso thought everything was going smoothly until customer complaints started coming in. These complaints ranged from the decorators' being hard to get a hold of, promising unrealistic delivery times, and being late for or failing to keep appointments, and being impatient and rude when customers had a trouble making up their minds. Caruso knows that her decorators are very competent and is concerned that she must not be effectively leading and managing them. She wonders, in particular, if her hands-off approach is to blame and if she should change the manner in which she rewards or pays her decorators. She has asked for your advice.

1. Analyze the sources of power that Caruso has available to her to influence the decorators. What advice can you give her to either increase her power base or use her existing power more effectively?
2. Given what you have learned in this chapter (for example, from the behavior model and path-goal theory), does Caruso seem to be performing appropriate leader behaviors in this situation? What advice can you give her about the kinds of behaviors she should perform?
3. What steps would you advise Caruso to take to increase the decorators' motivation to deliver high-quality customer service?
4. Would you advise Caruso to try to engage in transformational leadership in this situation? If not, why not? If so, what steps would you advise her to take?

Exploring the World Wide Web

Find the website of a company that provides information on the company's missions, goals, and values. Also, scan the website for information about this company's top managers and their personal leadership styles. How do you think the company's missions, goals, and values may impact the process of leadership in this company?

You're the Management Consultant

Jim Zhou is the CEO of a medium-size company that makes window coverings such as Hunter Douglas blinds and Douttes. His company has a real cost advantage in terms of being able to make custom window coverings at costs that are relatively low in the industry. However, the performance of his company has been lackluster. In order to make needed changes and improve performance, he met with the eight other top managers in his company and charged them with identifying problems and missed opportunities in each of their areas and coming up with an action plan to address these problems and take advantage of opportunities.

Once their action plans received the "go ahead" from Zhou, the managers were charged with implementing their action plans in a timely fashion and monitoring the effects of their initiatives on a monthly basis for the next 8 to 12 months.

Each of the manager's action plans were approved by Zhou and a year later, most of them were reporting that their initiatives had been successful in addressing the problems and opportunities they had identified a year ago. However, overall company performance continued to be lackluster and showed no signs of improvement. Zhou is confused, troubled, and starting to question both his leadership capabilities as well as his approach to change. He has come to you for help because you are an expert in leadership. He wants you to tell him why his company continues to have lackluster performance and to advise him about what he should do next.

BusinessWeek Cases in the News

Who's Afraid of a Little Mud?

Joe Luter likes to tell a story about an old man who was walking with his grandson around a cemetery. They see a tombstone that reads: "Here lies Charles W. Johnson, a man who had no enemies." The little boy says: "Gee, granddad, this man must have been a great man. He had no enemies." "Son," the grandfather replies, "if a man didn't have any enemies, he didn't do a damn thing witha his life."

By that measure, Joseph W. Luter III, 61, has certainly lived a rich, full life. Environmentalists, animal-rights activists, and independent farmers all rail against Luter, the chairman, CEO, and president of Smithfield Foods Inc., the largest hog butcher in the world. North Carolina, worried about hog-waste spilling from huge lagoons into its water-ways, imposed a moratorium on Smithfield's expansion. Animal-welfare folks say the company cruelly confines pigs to narrow pens. And small farmers blame big corporations for depressing hog prices. "These guys are not businessmen making a buck. They're bullies," says Robert F. Kennedy, Jr., the environmental attorney who is leading a court battle against Smithfield. Luter shrugs off the attacks: "I think in America today if you become too successful, you draw criticism, whether it's Smithfield in the pork business or Microsoft in the computer business or Exxon in the oil business."

But one group still adores Luter and his Smithfield (Va.)-based company: shareholders. After muscling its way into hog farming and riding a wave of processing consolidation, Smithfield has more than doubled sales since 1996. It now controls 12 percent of hog farming—triple the size of its nearest competition—and 20 percent of processing. The company expects sales to rise another 14 percent, to $5.9 billion, in the fiscal year ended April 29. It says net income should more than double, to $169 million. Investors have reaped the rewards of Luter's feeding frenzy, with a nearly hundred-fold increase in Smithfield's share price since 1981, to a split-adjusted $34. "He does it by following Warren Buffett's creed: Be greedy when others are fearful and fearful when others are greedy," says analyst David C. Nelson of Credit Suisse First Boston.

Still, with mounting political opposition to corporate pig farming and a need to diversify his offering to supermarkets, he has to find new avenues of growth. That is what drove Smithfield's attempt last November to buy IBP Inc., the largest U.S. beef packer. Smithfield lost to Tyson Foods Inc., which later backed out of its deal amid a welter of lawsuits. Smithfield then agreed to buy Moyer Packing Co., a smaller beef processor. That broadens its line of prepackaged, branded meat, which commands twice the profit margins of commodity meats, and boosts distribution in the Northeast.

No boots needed

These days, though, the closest Luter gets to pigs are the emblems on his distinctive ties. He may still sound like a man of the earth, eschewing corporate babble, but Luter conducts much of his business from an apartment on Park Avenue in Manhattan, leaving day-to-day operations to the presidents of each of Smithfield's subsidiary companies. He can go weeks and weeks without talking to them. "I'm a risk-taker. I'm an opportunist," he says. "I'm not a professional manager."

It's a far cry from how Luter got his start as a teenager working on the kill floor of his father's business, Luter Packing Co., back in Smithfield. He went on to major in business administration at Wake Forest University and was mulling law school when his father died in 1962. That drew him back into the business. Luter started in sales but had much bigger plans. Borrowing every cent he could, he bought out nonfamily investors and made himself president at 26. "I was surviving on Alka-Seltzer for three years," he recalls. "I had bitten off more than I could chew." Overwhelmed, he sold out in 1969 to conglomerate Liberty Equities Corp. for $20 million. But Liberty ran Smithfield into the ground, and its banks called upon Luter to manage a turnaround. He cut a whole layer of management, and divested anything that wasn't related to slaughtering or processing.

By 1981, Luter was in a position to expand. He bought Gwaltney's, his major local competitor, making Smithfield the dominant East Coast pork processor. He built the largest processing operation in the world in Bladen County, N.C.—today, it kills 32,000 hogs a day, twice that of a typical plant. Realizing there was more money in raising pigs than slaughtering them, Luter bought out his hog-farm partners in 1999 and 2000, as the price of hogs sank to a historic low of 8¢ a pound. Today, massive economies of scale enable him to raise pigs substantially cheaper than other producers. On average, the industry uses three pounds of feed to produce a pound of pork; Smithfield's rate is 2.6 to 1.

"Visionary"

Owning both the raw material and the processing protects Luter's operations from the cyclical nature of commodity price swings and lets him sell a consistent-quality product. But rivals still aren't sure whether Luter is ahead of them or just further out on a limb. "The gamble to invest enormously in hog production and to control the source of supply and quality of hogs is visionary," says Timothy T. Day, chairman and CEO of competing processor Bar-S Foods Co. "The question is, over 10 years, will it prove to be the right strategy?" Smithfield racked up $1.1 billion in debt and has a 1-to-1 debt-to-equity ratio. But with $500 million in earnings before interest, taxes, depreciation, and amortization, "this is not an overwhelming burden," says analyst Jeffrey G. Kanter of Prudential Securities Inc.

For now, Luter says he's content to watch the court battle between Tyson and IBP from the sidelines while studying how his own purchase of the smaller Moyer beef-processing operation unfolds. But that could quickly change as environmental and other concerns prohibit Smithfield from expanding in some of the richest hog-producing areas of the country. Laws aimed at limiting corporate farms are piling up in states like Iowa and North Dakota. And complaints about environmental hazards of huge hog farms are mounting. Luter claims his company's methods are safe and that by spraying the accumulated waste onto surrounding croplands, "it's really organic farming." But environmentalists assert that it will cost $10 billion just to clean up North Carolina's Neuse River. South Carolina Governor Jim Hodges said in April the company was not welcome in that state either. Luter may be out in front of his industry, but he's got a barnyard full of detractors close behind who would love to tan his hide.

Source: J. Forster, "Who's Afraid of a Little Mud," *Business Week,* May 21, 2001, pp. 112–13.

Questions

1. How would you characterize Joe Luter's personal leadership style?
2. Do you think his leadership behavior is questionable on ethical grounds? Why or why not?

BusinessWeek

Cases in the News

Boeing Attempts a U-Turn at High Speed

For much of last year, a dozen of Boeing Co.'s best engineers locked themselves in an unmarked office in a secured area of the jet maker's suburban Renton (Wash.) operations. Unknown to most of the company's nearly 200,000 workers, the group was busily redesigning Boeing's future. To the outside world, Boeing was heavily promoting a remade 747 jumbo jet to compete with rival Airbus Industrie. But inside the skunk works operation, known by its code name 20xx, Boeing was hedging its bets. What the engineers came up with is the Sonic Cruiser, a much smaller jet that looks like a stealth bomber and can travel nearly at the speed of sound.

Radical? Absolutely. But no more so than the broader shakeup that's sweeping Boeing these days. Frustrated with the slow pace of change at the stodgy $51.3 billion aerospace company, CEO Philip M. Condit has embarked on a bold plan to restructure it along the lines of General Electric Co. That means targeting more high-margin service, space, and defense business. Division chiefs are getting more autonomy but will have to compete more than ever for corporate funding.

Something to Prove

Condit is beefing up Boeing Capital Corp. as a separate unit and pushing it to finance more than just aircraft purchases. And he even opened a Jack Welch-like corporate learning center in St. Louis. The most dramatic statement: Boeing's announcement last month that it is packing up its headquarters and moving out of Seattle.

It's easy to see why Condit wants to get past airliners and defense contracts. Commercial jet sales are growing only by 5% a year. And Airbus Industrie, Boeing's European competitor, has been eating its lunch. In the past five years, Airbus has captured roughly half the airliner market. Besides, Condit is eager to raise Boeing's meager price-earnings ratio of 15 by convincing a skeptical Wall Street that the company has been freed from aviation's cycles of boom and bust. But first he has to prove that this is more than just another dubious diversification move, like the company's past forays into pleasure boats and furniture. "They are putting a lot of money and effort into projects that could become dry wells," says Richard L. Aboulafia, analyst for the Teal Group, a Virginia-based consulting group.

Condit bristles at calling his strategy "diversification," and swears it is all about making smart bets in markets the company already serves. Example: Boeing's plan to deliver fully capable Internet links to airliners. "We want to push boundaries, but by bringing technology to the customers we already know," Condit says. "In the past, we didn't understand the market. We are trying very hard not to do that here."

A couple of years ago, it wasn't clear that Condit would be around to pull off such a bold bet. He and President Harry C. Stonecipher were struggling with a massive restructuring of airliner production that coincided with a huge bulge of orders. They laid off tens of thousands of workers, slashed costs, streamlined production, and outsourced more jet fabrication work. The moves paid off. Earnings have beaten Wall Street estimates for eight successive quarters, and operating income climbed 14 percent in 2000, to $3.5 billion. That helped boost annual cash flow to more than $4 billion last year. The stock hit $70 a share last December, up from $35 in May, though it has since fallen back to about $55 along with the overall market. "Today the company is a much improved business," says Richard J. Glasebrook II, managing director for Oppenheimer Capital, which owns 9 million shares.

Delegation

Now Condit wants to change Boeing's culture, too. Taking a page from Welch's playbook, Condit is making the three key operating units—commercial airplanes, military aircraft, and space and communication—accountable to tough new performance standards. He is giving the heads of those units new CEO titles and the freedom to run their businesses as independent companies. Condit says he will concentrate on longer-term strategy and allocating resources to new business ideas and acquisitions. "We will be focused on where we go next, what's the next opportunity, and how do we grow this business," he says.

It won't be easy to find the answers within Boeing's other two core businesses. With the C-17 cargo program and the F/A-18 fighter jet in full production, the $12 billion military aircraft division has been generating double-digit profit margins, and Boeing figures to be a key player in any national missile defense system. But overall defense spending on projects like its proposed Joint Strike Fighter is likely to remain constrained. The $9 billion space and communication division holds the most promise. Last year, Boeing spent $3.9 billion to buy Hughes Satellite division, and Condit expects the unit to double its sales to $8 billion over the next five years. However, Hughes reported a loss of $323 million last year, and the space unit is struggling with rocket failures and soaring costs of new launch systems.

One of Boeing's first efforts to apply its existing technology, developed by Boeing's defense engineers, uses satellites and ground-based servers to provide high-speed Internet access to air travelers so they can watch video streaming over the Web or download big data files from work. However, Connexion has yet to land an order, while a more limited system, marketed by Seattle-based Tenzing Communications Inc., has deals with several foreign airlines.

To have the cash it needs to invest in those budding markets, Boeing can't keep ceding ground to Airbus in its biggest business, commercial jets, which still accounts for 60 percent of total sales. Condit hopes the shakeup will make Boeing more nimble in negotiating airplane sales. While Airbus chief salesman John Leahy and his staff can make decisions on the spot, airline executives say, Boeing handles pricing and other concessions by committee, tying up deals with layers of bureaucracy. "I'm hoping they give more authority and support to individuals to work the deals so they don't have to call Seattle for every little thing," says John L. Plueger, chief operating officer for Los Angeles-based International Lease Finance Corp., one of the biggest airplane leasing companies.

The Sonic Cruiser could also alter the dynamics of the Boeing-Airbus dogfight. It would be a huge commitment to Boeing's conviction that airlines will demand smaller, more efficient jets flying directly to smaller cities, rather than lots of 500-seat superjumbos that serve central "hub" airports. Boeing says that more than 85 percent of the people flying into Tokyo's Narita airport, for example, aren't going to Tokyo, but are heading to Singapore, Hong Kong, or elsewhere in Asia.

There are many unanswered questions about the Sonic Cruiser. It may cut 25 percent from transpacific flight times, as Boeing claims, but how much fuel will it guzzle? Alan R. Mulally, CEO for Boeing's Commercial Airplane division, says he can design and build it for about the cost of a conventional jet liner. But some analysts estimate total development could cost $10 billion. Airbus officials see Boeing's decision to scrap the 747X as vindication of their large-plane strategy. Some of the biggest airlines have been enthusiastic about the project, though. Rono J. Dutta, president of United Airlines Inc. parent UAL Corp., confirms his company worked with Boeing to develop the Sonic Cruiser. "This industry is always hungry for new technology," he says.

Still, the Sonic Cruiser is just a side bet for Condit. Ultimately, he's hoping to pilot his company from a low p/e ratio airplane maker stuck in a cyclical industry to a high-value, diversified aerospace company. With such an ambitious flight plan, it's time to strap on the seatbelts.

Source: S. Holmes, C. Matlack, M. Arndt, and W. Zellner, "Boeing Attempts a U-Turn at High Speed," *Business Week,* April 16, 2001, pp. 126, 128

Questions

1. In what ways is Philip Condit engaging in transformational leadership at Boeing?
2. To what extent might Boeing's existing practices and culture hamper his efforts to make major changes?

Chapter 14

Groups and Teams

Learning Objectives

After studying this chapter, you should be able to:

- Explain why groups and teams are key contributors to **organizational effectiveness.**
- Identify the **different types of groups and teams** that help managers and organizations achieve their goals.
- Explain how different elements of **group dynamics** influence the functioning and effectiveness of groups and teams.
- Explain why it is important for groups and teams to have a balance of **conformity** and **deviance** and a moderate level of **cohesiveness.**
- Describe **how managers can motivate group members** to achieve organizational goals and reduce social loafing in groups and teams.

A Manager's Challenge

Motivating Teams in Manufacturing

How can managers motivate employees working in teams in traditional manufacturing environments?

Groups and teams are relied on in all kinds of organizations from those specializing in heavy industrial manufacturing to those in high-tech fields ranging from computer software development to biotechnology. And, motivating members of groups and teams on an ongoing basis is a significant challenge for managers. This managerial challenge is particularly salient in heavy manufacturing organizations in which the work itself might not be intrinsically interesting, working conditions not great, and economic conditions uncertain. Managers at Nucor have mastered this challenge and effectively motivate groups and teams throughout the company in the good times and the bad.

Nucor is the biggest steel producer and largest recycler in the United States with more than \$4.5 billion in annual revenues and over 8,000 employees. Headquartered in Charlotte, North Carolina, Nucor has operations in nine states manufacturing all kinds of steel products ranging from steel joists, bars, and beams to steel decks and metal building systems.[1]

Production workers at Nucor are organized into teams with from 8 to 40 members based on the kind of work the team is responsible for such as rolling steel or operating a furnace. Team members have considerable autonomy to make decisions and creatively respond to problems and opportunities as there are relatively few layers in the corporate hierarchy supporting the empowerment of teams.[2] Teams develop their own informal rules for behavior and make their own decisions. As long as team members follow organizational rules and policies (e.g., for safety) and meet quality standards, they are free to govern themselves. Managers act as coaches or advisors rather

Nucor steel employees join in a dedication ceremony at the company's new recycling facility in Cofield, N.C., in October 2000.

than supervisors, helping teams out when they need some additional assistance.[3]

To ensure that production teams are motivated to help Nucor achieve its goals, team members are eligible for weekly bonuses based on the team's performance. Essentially, these production workers receive weekly base pay that does not vary and are eligible to receive weekly bonus pay that can average from 80 to150 percent of their regular pay.[4] The bonus rate is predetermined by the kinds of work a team performs and the capabilities of the machinery they use. Given the immediacy of the bonus and its potential magnitude, team members are highly motivated to perform at a high level, develop informal rules that support high performance, and strive to help Nucor reach its goals. Moreover, because all members of a team receive the same amount of weekly bonus money, they are motivated to do their best for the team, cooperate, and help each other out. They are reluctant to take time off unless they really need it (e.g., due to illness).[5]

Fairness is an important value at Nucor and managers strive to ensure that team members are treated fairly and rewarded for their efforts. Consistent with an emphasis on fairness, top managers at Nucor earn relatively less than their counterparts in other large organizations and do not receive any extra benefits or perks not available to production workers.[6]

Nucor also believes in job security for its production workers both for their own peace of mind and to help ensure their loyalty and commitment to Nucor's success. When times are tough, managers and all employees strive to find creative ways to cut costs while minimizing layoffs. For example, during the economic downturn in the fall of 2001, some Nucor manufacturing facilities switched to four-day work weeks enabling them to cut costs by paying workers for four days rather than five. At an average annual pay rate of $50,000 per worker, the switch to four-day work weeks could result in a savings of $10,000 per employee per year. Moreover, senior executives' bonuses were eliminated (these bonuses can account for up to 66 percent of the executives' salaries).[7] Managers and employees alike agree that these creative ways to cut costs and preserve jobs are in everyone's best interest and contribute to high levels of motivation at Nucor. All in all, managers at Nucor seem to be doing all they can to ensure high levels of motivation in production teams.

Overview

Nucor is not alone in using groups and teams to produce goods and services that best meet customers' needs. Managers in large companies such as Du Pont, Microsoft, and Ford Motor Company and in small companies such as Web Industries, Perdue Farms, and Risk International Services are all relying on teams to help them gain a competitive advantage.[8] In this chapter we look in detail at how groups and teams can contribute to organizational effectiveness and the types of groups and teams used in organizations. We discuss how different elements of group dynamics influence the functioning and effectiveness of groups, and we describe how managers can motivate group members to achieve organizational goals and reduce social loafing in groups and teams. By the end of this chapter, you will appreciate why the effective management of groups and teams is a key ingredient for organizational performance and a source of competitive advantage.

Groups, Teams, and Organizational Effectiveness

A **group** may be defined as two or more people who interact with each other to accomplish certain goals or meet certain needs.[9] A **team** is a group whose members work *intensely* with each other to achieve a specific common goal or objective. As these definitions imply, all teams are groups but not all groups are teams. The two characteristics that distinguish teams from groups are the *intensity* with which team members work together and the presence of a *specific, overriding team goal or objective.*

group Two or more people who interact with each other to accomplish certain goals or meet certain needs.

team A group whose members work intensely with each other to achieve a specific, common goal or objective.

As described in "A Manager's Challenge," members of production teams in Nucor work intensely together to achieve the specific objective of high levels of weekly performance. In contrast, the accountants who work in a small CPA firm are a group: They may interact with each other to achieve goals such as keeping up-to-date on the latest changes in accounting rules and regulations, maintaining a smoothly functioning office, satisfying clients, and attracting new clients. But they are not a team because they do not work intensely with each other. Each accountant concentrates on serving the needs of his or her own clients.

Because all teams are also groups, whenever we use the term *group* in this chapter, we are referring to both groups *and* teams. As you might imagine, because members of teams do work intensely together, teams can sometimes be difficult to form, and it may take time for members to learn how to effectively work together. Groups and teams can help an organization gain a competitive advantage because they can (1) enhance its performance, (2) increase its responsiveness to customers, (3) increase innovation, and (4) increase employees' motivation and satisfaction (see Figure 14.1). In this section, we look at each of these contributions in turn.

Groups and Teams as Performance Enhancers

synergy Performance gains that result when individuals and departments coordinate their actions.

One of the main advantages of using groups is the opportunity to obtain a type of **synergy**: People working in a group are able to produce more or higher-quality outputs than would have been produced if each person had worked separately

Figure 14.1
Groups' and Teams' Contributions to Organizational Effectiveness

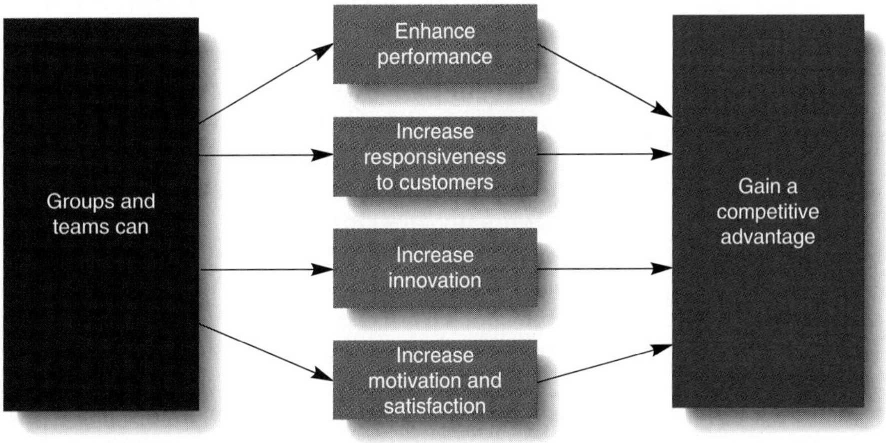

and all their individual efforts were combined. The essence of synergy is captured in the saying "The whole is more than the sum of its parts." Factors that can contribute to synergy in groups include the ability of group members to bounce ideas off one another, to correct each other's mistakes, to solve problems immediately as they arise, to bring a diverse knowledge base to bear on a problem or goal, and to accomplish work that is too vast or all-encompassing for individuals to achieve on their own. At Nucor in "A Manager's Challenge," the kinds of work the production teams are responsible for could not be performed by an individual acting alone; it is only through the combined efforts of eight or more team members that teams can manufacture products and recycle steel.

To take advantage of the potential for synergy in groups, managers need to make sure that groups are composed of members who have complementary skills and knowledge relevant to the group's work. For example, at Hallmark Cards synergies are created by placing all the members of departments and functions needed to create and produce a greeting card into a cross-functional team (see Chapter 9). For instance, artists, writers, designers, and marketing experts work together as team members to develop new cards.[10]

At Hallmark, the skills and expertise of the artists complement the contributions of the writers and vice versa. Managers also need to give groups enough autonomy so that the groups, rather than the manager, are solving problems and determining how to achieve goals and objectives. This is true in the cross-functional teams at Hallmark and the production teams at Nucor. To promote synergy, managers need to empower their subordinates by being coaches, guides, and resources for groups, while refraining from playing a more directive or supervisory role as is true at Nucor. The potential for synergy in groups may be the reason why more and more managers are incorporating empowerment in their personal leadership styles (see Chapter 13).

Groups, Teams, and Responsiveness to Customers

Being responsive to customers is not always easy. In manufacturing organizations, for example, customers' needs and desires for new and improved products have to be balanced against engineering constraints, production costs and feasibilities, government safety regulations, and marketing challenges. In service organizations such as health maintenance organizations (HMOs), being responsive to patients' needs and desires for prompt, high-quality medical care and treatment has to be balanced against meeting physicians' needs and desires and keeping health care costs under control. Being responsive to customers often requires the wide variety of skills and expertise found in different departments and at different levels in an organization's hierarchy. Sometimes, for example, employees at lower hierarchy levels, such as sales representatives for a computer company, are closest to its customers and most attuned to their needs. However, lower-level employees like salespeople often lack the technical expertise needed to come up with new product ideas; such expertise is found in the research and development department. Bringing salespeople, research and development experts, and members of other departments together in a group or cross-functional team can enhance responsiveness to customers. Consequently, when managers form a team, they need to make sure that the diversity of expertise and knowledge needed to be responsive to customers exists within the team; this is why cross-functional teams are so popular.

In a cross-functional team, the expertise and knowledge in different organizational departments are brought together in the skills and knowledge of the team members. Managers of high-performing organizations are careful to determine which types of expertise and knowledge are required for teams to be responsive to customers, and they use this information in forming teams.

As indicated in the following "Information Technology Byte," advances in information technology are allowing teams to work together to improve their responsiveness to customers.

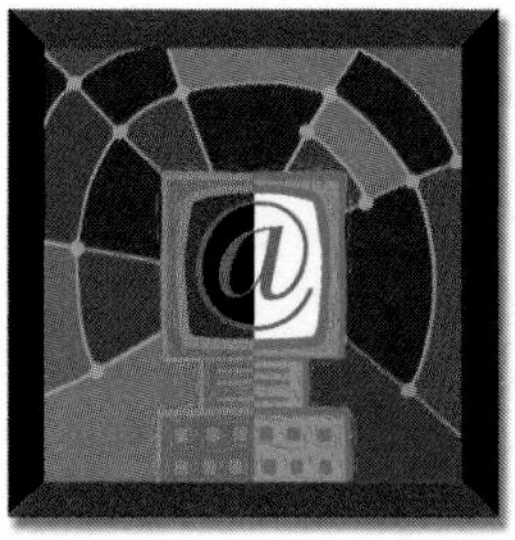

Information Technology Byte

3M Teams Excel at Responsiveness to Customers

Teams at 3M have been renowned for their innovativeness and responsiveness to customers in developing new products. 3M currently has more than $15 billion in revenues derived from sales of over 50,000 products sold in 200 countries.[11] Part of 3M's success can be attributed to its decentralization and use of empowered teams to develop and sell new products. Different divisions in 3M operate as if they were different companies. New product development teams have both the autonomy and resources to develop products from their own ideas. And, teams of sales representatives have the freedom to call on their own customers and approach them in the manner they see fit.

Ironically, while this approach to product development and sales has lead both to the creation and selling of a host of innovative products year in and year out, and responsiveness to customers at the product-level, managers realized that the relationship the company as a whole had with its customers was in need of an overhaul. Essentially, information was not being shared across teams and divisions so multiple reps from different teams and divisions called on the same customers, unbeknownst to each and causing confusion for the customer.

When 3M started selling over the Internet, the problem got worse rather than better as teams in different units developed their own websites requiring customers to log in to multiple Internet sites that operated differently to find out what products 3M had to offer.[12] Managers at 3M realized they needed to retain their decentralized, team approach to maintain 3M's innovative edge and that the solution to this problem did not lie in any kind of restructuring of operations per se. Rather, what was needed was a means of sharing information across teams and divisions and developing an integrated electronic interface across divisions of 3M with customers.

Managers at 3M committed $20 million to the development of a global, interactive, and integrative IT database that tracks sales and financial performance by products and by customers. New product development teams, sales reps, and managers can log into a single website and learn how different products are selling around the world as well as all the 3M products a major customer might currently be purchasing. Similarly, customers can log into the site to learn about all the 3M products that might satisfy their needs along with detailed information on product specifications and availabilities around the globe.[13] Fortunately for 3M and its customers, advances in information technology have enabled the company to carry on with its tradition of the continuous development of innovative new products while at the same time being responsive to customers' needs for a unified interface with the company.

Teams and Innovation

Innovation, the creative development of new products, new technologies, new services, or even new organizational structures, is a topic we discuss in detail in Chapter 18. Often, an individual working alone does not possess the extensive set of skills, knowledge, and expertise required for successful innovation. Managers can better encourage innovation by creating teams of diverse individuals who together have the knowledge relevant to a particular type of innovation rather than by relying on individuals working alone.

Using teams to innovate has other advantages as well. First, team members can often uncover each other's errors or false assumptions; an individual acting alone would not be able to do this. Second, team members can critique each other's approaches when need be and build off each other's strengths while compensating for weaknesses, one of the advantages of devil's advocacy and dialectical inquiry discussed in Chapter 6.

To further promote innovation, managers are well advised to empower teams and make their members fully responsible and accountable for the innovation process. The manager's role is to provide guidance, assistance, coaching, and the resources team members need, and not to closely direct or supervise their activities. To speed innovation, managers also need to form teams in which each member brings some unique resource to the team, such as engineering prowess, knowledge of production, marketing expertise, or financial savvy. Successful innovation sometimes requires that managers form teams with members from different countries and cultures.

Groups and Teams as Motivators

Managers often decide to form groups and teams to accomplish organizational goals, then find that using groups and teams brings additional benefits. Members of groups–and especially members of teams because of the higher intensity of interaction in teams–are likely to be more highly motivated and satisfied than they would be if they were working on their own. The experience of working alongside other highly charged and motivated people can be very stimulating. In addition, working on a team can be very motivating: Team members more readily see how their efforts and expertise directly contribute to the achievement of team and organizational goals, and they feel personally responsible for the outcomes or results of their work. This has been the case at Nucor and Hallmark Cards.

The increased motivation and satisfaction that can accompany the use of teams can also lead to other outcomes, such as lower turnover. This has been Frank B. Day's experience as founder and CEO of Rock Bottom Restaurants Inc. To provide high-quality customer service, Day has organized the restaurants' employees into wait staff teams, whose members work together to refill beers, take orders, bring hot chicken enchiladas to tables, or clear off the tables. Team members share the burden of undesirable activities and unpopular shift times; and customers no longer have to wait until a particular waitress or waiter is available. Motivation and satisfaction levels in the Rock Bottom Restaurants seem to be higher than in other restaurants, and turnover is about one-half of that experienced in other U.S. restaurant chains.[14]

Working in a group or team can also satisfy organizational members' needs for social interaction and feeling connected to other people. For workers who perform highly stressful jobs, such as hospital emergency and operating room staff, group membership can be an important source of social support and motivation.

Family members or friends may not be able to fully understand or appreciate some sources of work stress that these group members experience firsthand. Moreover, group members may cope better with work stressors when they are able to share them with other members of their group. In addition, groups often devise techniques to relieve stress, such as the telling of jokes among hospital operating room staff.

Why do managers in all kinds of organizations rely so heavily on groups and teams? Effectively managed groups and teams can help managers in their quest for high performance, responsiveness to customers, and employee motivation. Before explaining how managers can effectively manage groups, however, we describe the types of groups formed in organizations.

Types of Groups and Teams

To achieve their goals of high performance, responsiveness to customers, innovation, and employee motivation, managers can form various types of groups and teams (see Figure 14.2). **Formal groups** are those managers establish to achieve organizational goals. The formal work groups are cross-functional teams composed of members from different departments such as those at Hallmark Cards, and *cross-cultural* teams composed of members from different cultures or countries such as the teams at global car makers. As you will see, some of the groups discussed in this section also can be considered cross-functional (if they are composed of members from different departments) or cross-cultural (if they are composed of members from different countries or cultures).

formal group A group that managers establish to achieve organizational goals.

Sometimes organizational members, managers or nonmanagers, form groups because they believe that groups will help them achieve their own goals or meet their own needs (for example, the need for social interaction). Groups formed in this way are **informal groups.** Four nurses who work in a hospital and have lunch together twice a week constitute an informal group.

informal group A group that managers or nonmanagerial employees form to help achieve their own goals or meet their own needs

The Top-Management Team

A central concern of the CEO and president of a company is to form a **top-management team** to help the organization achieve its mission and goals. Top-management teams are responsible for developing the strategies that result in an

top-management team A group composed of the CEO, the president, and the heads of the most important departments.

Figure 14.2
Types of Groups and Teams in Organizations

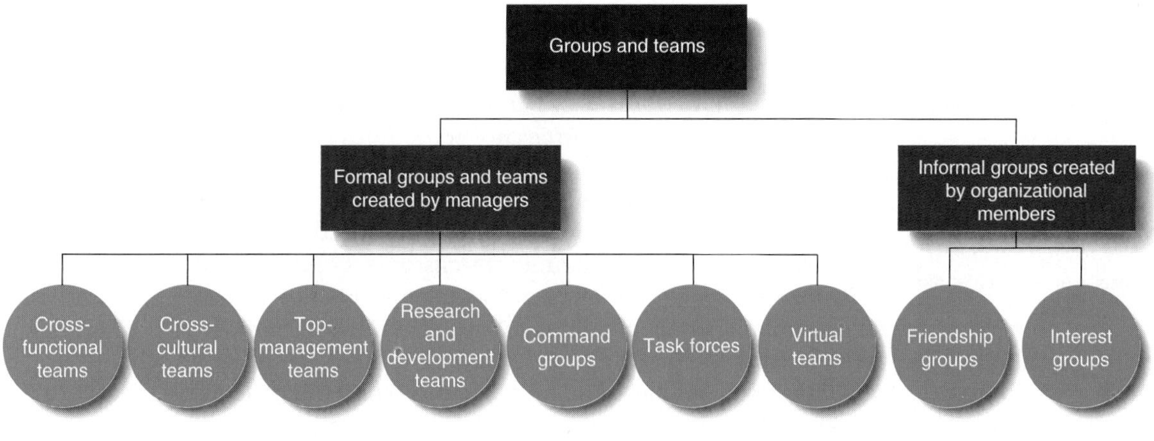

organization's competitive advantage; most have between five and seven members. In forming their top-management teams, CEOs are well advised to stress diversity–diversity in expertise, skills, knowledge, and experience. Thus, many top-management teams are also cross-functional teams: They are composed of members from different departments such as finance, marketing, production, and engineering. Diversity helps ensure that the top-management team will have all the background and resources it needs to make good decisions. Diversity also helps guard against *groupthink,* faulty group decision making that results when group members strive for agreement at the expense of an accurate assessment of the situation (see Chapter 6).

Research and Development Teams

research and development team A team whose members have the expertise and experience needed to develop new products.

Managers in pharmaceuticals, computers, electronics, electronic imaging and other high-tech industries often create **research and development teams** to develop new products. Eric Fossum, a researcher and manager with NASA's Jet Propulsion Laboratory at the California Institute of Technology, for example, formed and heads up a three-member R&D team that is developing a camera so small that its basic operational parts can fit on a single computer chip.[15] Managers select R&D team members on the basis of their expertise and experience in a certain area. Sometimes R&D teams are cross-functional teams with members from departments such as engineering, marketing, and production in addition to members from the research and development department.

Command Groups

command group A group composed of subordinates who report to the same supervisor; also called a department or unit.

Subordinates who report to the same supervisor compose a **command group.** When top managers design an organization's structure and establish reporting relationships and a chain of command, they are essentially creating command groups. Command groups, often called *departments* or *units,* perform a significant amount of the work in many organizations. In order to have command groups that help an organization gain a competitive advantage, managers need to motivate group members to perform at a high level, and managers need to be effective leaders. Examples of command groups include the salespeople in a large department store in New York who report to the same supervisor, the employees of a small swimming pool sales and maintenance company in Florida who report to a general manager, the telephone operators at the MetLife insurance company who report to the same supervisor, and workers on an automobile assembly line in the Ford Motor Company who report to the same first-line manager.

Task Forces

task force A committee of managers or nonmanagerial employees from various departments or divisions who meet to solve a specific, mutual problem; also called an ad hoc committee.

Managers form **task forces** to accomplish specific goals or solve problems in a certain time period; task forces are sometimes called ad hoc committees. For example, Michael Rider, owner and top manager of a chain of six gyms and fitness centers in the Midwest, created a task force composed of the general managers of each of the six gyms to determine whether the fitness centers should institute a separate fee schedule for customers who wanted to use the centers only for aerobics classes (and not use other facilities such as weights, steps, tracks, and swimming pools). The task force was given three months to prepare a report summarizing the pros and cons of the proposed change in fee schedules. Once the task force completed its report and reached the conclusion that the change in fee structure probably would reduce revenues rather than increase them and thus should not be implemented, it was disbanded. As in Rider's case, task forces can be a valuable tool for busy managers who do not have the time to personally explore an important issue in depth.

Sometimes managers need to form task forces whose work, so to speak, is never done. The task force may be addressing a long-term or enduring problem or issue facing an organization, such as how to most usefully contribute to the local community or how to make sure that the organization provides opportunities for potential employees with disabilities. Task forces that are relatively permanent are often referred to as *standing committees*. Membership in standing committees changes over time. Members may have, for example, a two- or three-year term on the committee, and memberships expire at varying times so that there are always some members with experience on the committee. Managers often form and maintain standing committees to make sure that important issues continue to be addressed.

Self-Managed Work Teams

self-managed work team A group of employees who supervise their own activities and monitor the quality of the goods and services they provide.

Self-managed work teams are teams in which team members are empowered and have the responsibility and autonomy to complete identifiable pieces of work. On a day-to-day basis, team members decide what the team will do, how it will do it, and which team members will perform which specific tasks.[16] Managers provide self-managed work teams with their overall goals (such as assembling defect-free computer keyboards) but let team members decide how to meet those goals. Managers usually form self-managed work teams to improve quality, increase motivation and satisfaction, and lower costs. Often, by creating self-managed work teams, they combine tasks that individuals working separately used to perform, so the team is responsible for the whole set of tasks that yields an identifiable output or end product.

In response to increasing competition, Johnson Wax, maker of well-known household products including Pledge furniture polish, Glade air freshener, and Windex window cleaner, formed self-managed work teams to find ways to cut costs. Traditionally, Johnson Wax used assembly-line production, in which workers were not encouraged or required to do much real thinking on the job, let alone determine how to cut costs. Things could not be more different at Johnson Wax now. Consider, for example, the nine-member self-managed work team that is responsible for molding plastic containers. Team members choose their own leader, train new members, have their own budget to manage, and are responsible for figuring out how to cut the costs of molding plastic containers. Kim Litrenta, a 17-year veteran of Johnson's Waxdale, Wisconsin, plant, sums up the effects of the change from assembly-line production to self-managed work teams this way: "In the past you'd have no idea how much things cost because you weren't involved in decisions. Now it's amazing how many different ways people try to save money."[17]

Managers can take a number of steps to ensure that self-managed work teams are effective and help an organization gain a competitive advantage:[18]

- Give teams enough responsibility and autonomy to be truly self-managing. Refrain from telling team members what to do or solving problems for them even if you (as a manager) know what should be done.
- Make sure that a team's work is sufficiently complex so that it entails a number of different steps or procedures that must be performed and results in some kind of finished end product.

- Carefully select members of self-managed work teams. Team members should have the diversity of skills needed to complete the team's work, have the ability to work with others, and want to be part of a team.
- As a manager, realize that your role vis-à-vis self-managed work teams calls for guidance, coaching, and supporting, not supervising. You are a resource for teams to turn to when needed.
- Analyze what type of training team members need and provide it. Working in a self-managed work team often requires that employees have more extensive technical and interpersonal skills.

Managers in a wide variety of organizations have found that self-managed work teams help the organization achieve its goals, as is true at Nucor in "A Manager's Challenge."[19] However, self-managed work teams can run into trouble. Members are often reluctant to discipline one another by withholding bonuses from members who are not performing up to par or by firing members.[20] Buster Jarrell, a manager who oversees self-managed work teams in AES Corporation's Houston plant, has found that although self-managed work teams are highly effective, they have a very difficult time firing team members who are performing poorly.[21]

The Dallas office of the New York Life Insurance Co. recently experimented with having members of self-managed teams evaluate each other's performance and determine pay levels. Team members did not feel comfortable assuming this role however, and managers ended up evaluating performance and determining pay levels.[22] One reason for team members' discomfort may be the close personal relationships they sometimes develop with each other. In addition, members of self-managed work teams actually do take longer to accomplish tasks, such as when team members have difficulties coordinating their efforts.

Virtual Teams

virtual team A team whose members rarely or never meet face to face and interact by using various forms of information technology such as email, computer networks, telephone, fax, and video conferences.

Virtual teams are teams whose members rarely or never meet face to face and interact by using various forms of information technology such as email, computer networks, telephone, fax, and video conferences. As organizations become increasingly global with operations in far-flung regions of the world, and as the need for specialized knowledge increases due to advances in technology, virtual teams allow managers to create teams to solve problems or explore opportunities without being limited by the fact that team members need to be working in the same geographic location.[23]

Take the case of an organization that has manufacturing facilities in Australia, Canada, the United States, and Mexico and is encountering a quality problem in a complex manufacturing process. Each of its manufacturing facilities has a quality control team headed up by a quality control manager. The vice president for production does not try to solve the problem by forming and leading a team at one of the four manufacturing facilities; instead she forms and leads a virtual team composed of the quality control managers of the four plants and the plants' general managers. When these team members communicate via email and videoconferencing, a wide array of knowledge and experience is brought to bear to solve the problem.

The principal advantage of virtual teams is that they enable managers to disregard geographic distances and form teams whose members have the knowledge, expertise, and experience to tackle a particular problem or take advantage of a specific opportunity.[24] Virtual teams also can include members who are not actually employees of an organization itself; a virtual team might include members of an organization that is used for outsourcing. More and more companies, including Compaq, Hewlett-Packard, PricewaterhouseCoopers, Lotus Development, Kodak, Whirlpool, and VeriFone, are either using or exploring the use of virtual teams.[25]

There are two forms of information technologies that members of virtual teams rely on, synchronous technologies and asynchronous technologies.[26] Synchronous technologies enable virtual team members to communicate and interact with each other in real time simultaneously through videoconferencing, teleconferencing, and electronic meetings. Asynchronous technologies delay communication as is true with email, electronic bulletin boards, and Internet websites. Many virtual teams use both kinds of technology depending on what projects they are working on.

Increasing globalization is likely to result in more organizations relying on virtual teams to a greater extent.[27] One of the major challenges members of virtual teams face is building a sense of camaraderie and trust among team members who rarely, if ever, meet face-to-face. To address this challenge, some organizations schedule recreational activities, such as ski trips, so virtual team members can get together. Other organizations make sure that virtual team members have a chance to meet in person soon after the team is formed and then schedule periodic face-to-face meetings to promote trust, understanding, and cooperation in the teams.[28] The need for such meetings is underscored by research which suggests that while some virtual teams can be as effective as teams that meet face-to-face, virtual team members might be less satisfied with teamwork efforts and have fewer feelings of camaraderie or cohesion. (Group cohesiveness is discussed in more detail later in the chapter.)[29]

At Thomson Financial, advances in information technology are enabling customers to interact with the organization in a virtual environment more responsive to their needs, as indicated in the following "Information Technology Byte."

Information Technology Byte

Thomson Becomes More Responsive to Customers

Thomson Financial specializes in providing electronic information to the global financial services industry. Thomson Financial is part of Thomson Corporation and has $2 billion in revenues. Different groups, units, and divisions of Thomson sell products to different customers; this means that a single customer such as Merrill Lynch might receive related product offerings from multiple groups at Thomson. As competition increased in this market and other firms such as Multex, Reuters, and Bloomberg were offering similar products and services, Thomson realized that its piecemeal approach to customer service needed an overhaul.[30]

Dick Harrington, CEO of Thomson Corporation, and Pat Tierney, CEO of Thomson Financial, teamed up to make major changes to the operations of Thomson Financial. Essentially, their goal was to become more responsive to customers as a unified company offering bundles of products. Early on, they identified three major customer groupings, traders, portfolio managers, and equity analysts who had different needs for electronic financial information.

For each customer grouping, the team utilized information technology to determine work flows and electronic information demands and requirements. They used this data to develop an integrative information technology

Friendship groups like the one pictured here can be beneficial to an organization. They help satisfy employees' needs for interpersonal interaction, provide social support in times of stress, and increase job satisfaction. Since group members often discuss work-related problems, they even end up generating solutions that can be used on the job.

network through which Thomson employees and customers could navigate to determine the right set and mix of Thomson products to best meet customers' needs. Having a single, integrated IT system benefits individual units and groups at Thomson as they no longer have to devote as many resources to their own individual IT systems. It also helps Thomson respond to increased competition in this market by offering customers sets of products that will meet their needs, making it easier to identify these products, and reducing the motivation of customers to shop around for different products. Moreover, customers can directly access this system at their convenience.[31] All in all, information technology has enabled Thomson to continue to use groups and teams to develop a wide variety of products suited for different customer groups while at the same time presenting customers with integrated sets of solutions to meet their needs.

Friendship Groups

friendship group An informal group composed of employees who enjoy each other's company and socialize with each other.

The groups described so far are formal groups created by managers. **Friendship groups** are informal groups composed of employees who enjoy each other's company and socialize with each other. Members of friendship groups may have lunch together, take breaks together, or meet after work for meals, sports, or other activities. Friendship groups help satisfy employees' needs for interpersonal interaction, can provide needed social support in times of stress, and can contribute to people feeling good at work and satisfied with their jobs. Managers themselves often form friendship groups. The informal relationships that managers build in friendship groups can help them solve work-related problems because members of these groups typically discuss work-related matters and offer advice.

interest group An informal group composed of employees seeking to achieve a common goal related to their membership in an organization.

Interest Groups

Employees form informal **interest groups** when they seek to achieve a common goal related to their membership in an organization. Employees may form interest groups, for example, to encourage managers to consider instituting flexible working hours, providing on-site child care, improving working conditions, or more proactively supporting environmental protection. Interest groups can provide managers with valuable insights into the issues and concerns that are foremost in employees' minds. They also can signal the need for change.

Group Dynamics

The ways in which groups function and, ultimately, their effectiveness hinge on group characteristics and processes known collectively as *group dynamics*. In this section, we discuss five key elements of group dynamics: group size, tasks, and roles; group leadership; group development; group norms; and group cohesiveness.

Group Size, Tasks, and Roles

Managers need to take group size, group tasks, and group roles into account as they create and maintain high-performing groups and teams.

GROUP SIZE The number of members in a group can be an important determinant of members' motivation and commitment and group performance. There are several advantages to keeping a group relatively small–between two and nine members. Compared with members of large groups, members of small groups tend to (1) interact more with each other and find it easier to coordinate their efforts; (2) be more motivated, satisfied, and committed; (3) find it easier to share information; and (4) be better able to see the importance of their personal contributions for group success. A disadvantage of small rather than large groups is that members of small groups have fewer resources available to accomplish their goals.

Large groups–with 10 or more members–also offer some advantages. They have at their disposal more resources to achieve group goals than do small groups. These resources include the knowledge, experience, skills, and abilities of group members as well as their actual time and effort. Large groups also enable managers to obtain the advantages stemming from the **division of labor**–splitting the work to be performed into particular tasks and assigning tasks to individual workers. Workers who specialize in particular tasks are likely to become skilled at performing those tasks and contribute significantly to high group performance.

division of labor Splitting the work to be performed into particular tasks and assigning tasks to individual workers.

The disadvantages of large groups include the problems of communication and coordination and the lower levels of motivation, satisfaction, and commitment that members of large groups sometimes experience. It is clearly more difficult to share information with, and coordinate the activities of, 16 people rather than 8 people. Moreover, members of large groups might not think that their efforts are really needed and sometimes might not even feel a part of the group.

In deciding on the appropriate size for any group, managers attempt to gain the advantages of small group size while at the same time forming groups with sufficient resources to accomplish their goals and have a well-developed division of labor, as is true at Nucor in "A Manager's Challenge." As a general rule of thumb, groups should have no more members than necessary to achieve a division of labor and provide the resources needed to achieve group goals. In R&D teams, for example, group size is too large when (1) members spend more time communicating what they know to others than applying what they know to solve problems and create new products, (2) individual productivity decreases, and (3) group performance suffers.[32]

task interdependence The degree to which the work performed by one member of a group influences the work performed by other members.

pooled task interdependence The task interdependence that exists when group members make separate and independent contributions to group performance.

GROUP TASKS The appropriate size of a high-performing group is affected by the kind of tasks the group is to perform. An important characteristic of group tasks that affects performance is **task interdependence,** the degree to which the work performed by one member of a group influences the work performed by other members.[33] As task interdependence increases, group members need to interact more frequently and intensely with each other, and their efforts have to be more closely coordinated if they are to perform at a high level. Management expert James D. Thompson identified three types of task interdependence: pooled, sequential, and reciprocal (see Figure 14.3).[34]

POOLED TASK INTERDEPENDENCE **Pooled task interdependence** exists when group members make separate and independent contributions to group performance; overall group performance is the sum of the performance of the individual members (see Figure 14.3A). Examples of groups that have pooled task interdependence include a group of teachers in an elementary school, a group of salespeople in a department store, a group of secretaries in an

Figure 14.3
Types of Task Interdependence

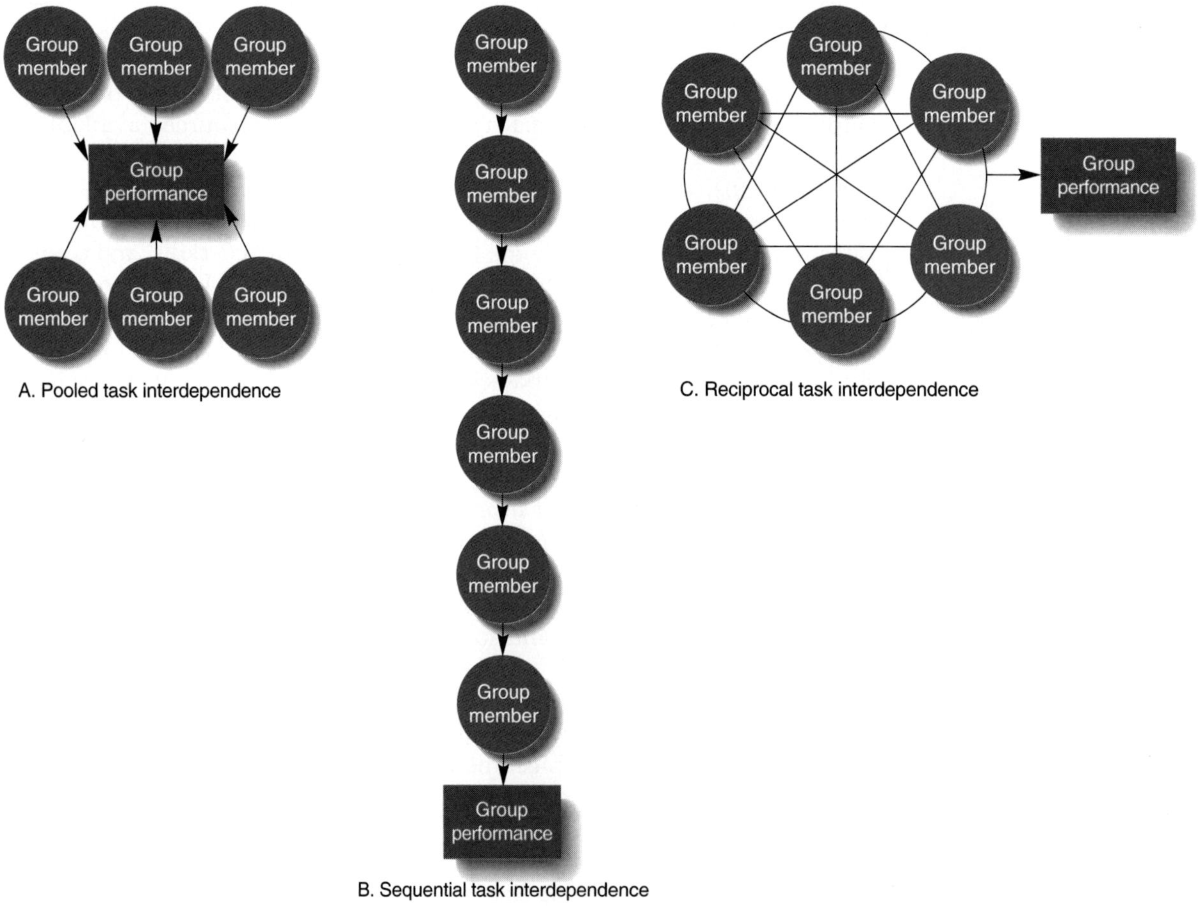

office, and a group of custodians in an office building. In these examples, group performance, whether it be the number of children who are taught and the quality of their education, the dollar value of sales, the amount of secretarial work completed, or the number of offices that are cleaned, is determined by summing the individual contributions of group members.

For groups with pooled interdependence, managers should determine the appropriate group size primarily from the amount of work to be accomplished. Large groups can be effective because group members work independently and do not have to interact frequently with each other. Motivation in groups with pooled interdependence will be highest when managers reward group members based on individual performance.

sequential task interdependence The task interdependence that exists when group members must perform specific tasks in a predetermined order.

SEQUENTIAL TASK INTERDEPENDENCE Sequential task interdependence exists when group members must perform specific tasks in a predetermined order; certain tasks have to be performed before others, and what one worker does affects the work of others (see Figure 14.3B). Assembly lines and mass-production processes are characterized by sequential task interdependence.

When group members are sequentially interdependent, group size is usually dictated by the needs of the production process–for example, the number of steps needed in an assembly line to efficiently produce a CD player. With sequential interdependence, it is difficult to identify individual performance because one group member's performance depends on how well others perform their tasks. A slow worker at the start of an assembly line, for example, causes all workers farther down to work slowly. Thus, managers are often advised to reward group members for group performance. Group members will be motivated to perform highly because if the group performs well, each member will benefit. In addition, group members may put pressure on poor performers to improve so that group performance and rewards do not suffer.

reciprocal task interdependence The task interdependence that exists when the work performed by each group member is fully dependent on the work performed by other group members.

RECIPROCAL TASK INTERDEPENDENCE Reciprocal task interdependence exists when the work performed by each group member is fully dependent on the work performed by other group members; group members have to share information, intensely interact with each other, and coordinate their efforts in order for the group to achieve its goals (see Figure 14.3C). In general, reciprocal task interdependence characterizes the operation of teams, rather than other kinds of groups. The task interdependence of R&D teams, top-management teams, and many self-managed work teams is reciprocal.

When group members are reciprocally interdependent, managers are advised to keep group size relatively small because of the necessity to coordinate team members' activities. Communication difficulties can arise in teams with reciprocally interdependent tasks because team members need to interact frequently with one another and be available when needed. As group size increases, communication difficulties increase and can impair team performance.

When a group's members are reciprocally interdependent, managers also are advised to reward group members on the basis of group performance. Individual levels of performance are often difficult for managers to identify, and group-based rewards help ensure that group members will be motivated to perform at a high level and make valuable contributions to the group. Of course, if a manager can identify instances of individual performance in such groups, they too can be rewarded to maintain high levels of motivation. Microsoft and many other companies reward group members for their individual performance and for the performance of their group.

group role A set of behaviors and tasks that a member of a group is expected to perform because of his or her position in the group.

GROUP ROLES A **group role** is a set of behaviors and tasks that a member of a group is expected to perform because of his or her position in the group. Members of cross-functional teams, for example, are expected to perform roles relevant to their special areas of expertise. In our earlier example of cross-functional teams at Hallmark Cards, it is the role of writers on the teams to create verses for new cards, the role of artists to draw illustrations, and the role of designers to put verse and artwork together in an attractive and appealing card design. The roles of members of top-management teams are shaped primarily by their areas of expertise–production, marketing, finance, research and development–but members of top-management teams also typically draw on their broad-based expertise as planners and strategists.

In forming groups and teams, managers need to clearly communicate their expectations for group members' roles in the group, what is required of them, and how the different roles in the group fit together to accomplish group goals. Managers also need to realize that group roles often change and evolve as a group's tasks and goals change and as group members gain experience and knowledge. Thus, to get the performance gains that come from experience or "learning by doing," managers should encourage group members to take the initiative to assume additional responsibilities as they see fit and modify their assigned roles. This process, called **role making,** can enhance individual and group performance.

role making Taking the initiative to modify an assigned role by assuming additional responsibilities.

In self-managed work teams and some other groups, group members themselves are responsible for creating and assigning roles. Many self-managed work teams also pick their own team leaders. When group members create their own roles, managers should be available to group members in an advisory capacity, helping them effectively settle conflicts and disagreements. At Johnsonville Foods, for example, the position titles of first-line managers have been changed to "advisory coach" to reflect the managers' new role vis-à-vis the self-managed work teams they oversee.[35]

Group Leadership

All groups and teams need leadership. Indeed, as we discussed in detail in Chapter 13, effective leadership is a key ingredient for high-performing groups, teams, and organizations. Sometimes managers assume the leadership role in groups and teams, as is the case in many command groups and top-management teams. Or a manager may appoint a member of a group who is not a manager to be group leader or chairperson, as is the case in a task force or standing committee. In other cases, group or team members may choose their own leaders, or a leader may emerge naturally as group members work together to achieve group goals. When managers empower members of self-managed work teams, they often let group members choose their own leaders. Some self-managed work teams find it effective to rotate the leadership role among their members. Whether leaders of groups and teams are managers or not, and whether they are appointed by managers or emerge naturally in a group, they play an important role in ensuring that groups and teams perform up to their potential.

Group Development over Time

President Richard (Skip) LeFauve of Saturn Corporation–which uses self-managed work teams–has learned that it sometimes takes a self-managed work team two or three years to perform up to its true capabilities.[36] As LeFauve's experience suggests, what a group is capable of achieving depends

Figure 14.4 Five Stages of Group Development

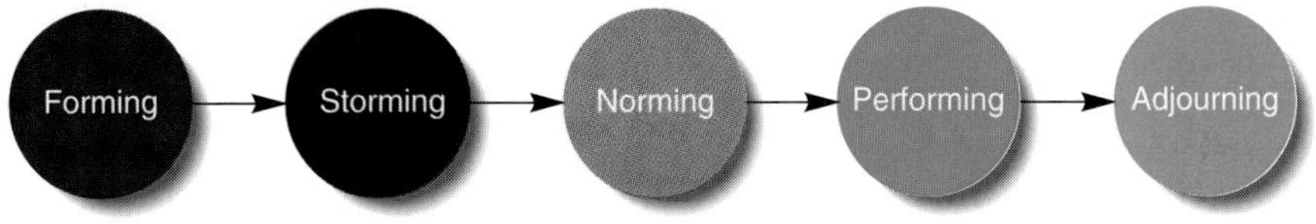

in part on its stage of development. Knowing that it takes considerable time for self-managed work teams to get up and running has helped LeFauve have realistic expectations for new teams at Saturn. He also knows that he has to provide new team members with considerable training and guidance.

Although every group's development over time is somewhat unique, researchers have identified five stages of group development that many groups seem to pass through (see Figure 14.4).[37] In the first stage, *forming,* members try to get to know each other and reach a common understanding of what the group is trying to accomplish and how group members should behave. During this stage, managers should strive to make each member feel a valued part of the group.

In the second stage, *storming,* group members experience conflict and disagreements because some members do not wish to submit to the demands of other group members. Disputes may arise over who should lead the group. Self-managed work teams can be particularly vulnerable during the storming stage. Managers need to keep an eye on groups at this stage to make sure that conflict does not get out of hand.

During the third stage, *norming,* close ties between group members develop, and feelings of friendship and camaraderie emerge. Group members arrive at a consensus about what goals they should be seeking to achieve and how group members should behave toward one another. In the fourth stage, *performing,* the real work of the group gets accomplished. Depending on the type of group in question, managers need to take different steps at this stage to help ensure that groups are effective. Managers of command groups need to make sure that group members are motivated and that they are effectively leading group members. Managers overseeing self- managed work teams have to empower team members and make sure that teams are given enough responsibility and autonomy at the performing stage.

The last stage, *adjourning,* applies only to groups that eventually are disbanded, such as task forces. During adjourning a group is dispersed. Sometimes, adjourning takes place when a group completes a finished product, such as when a task force evaluating the pros and cons of providing on-site child care produces a report supporting its recommendation.

Managers need a flexible approach to group development and need to keep attuned to the different needs and requirements of groups at the various stages.[38] Above all else, and regardless of the stage of development, managers need to think of themselves as resources for groups. Thus, managers always should be striving to find ways to help groups and teams function more effectively.

Group Norms

All groups, whether top-management teams, self-managed work teams, or command groups, need to control their members' behaviors to ensure that the group performs highly and meets its goals. Assigning roles to each group member is one way to control behavior in groups. Another important way in which groups influence members' behavior is through the development and enforcement of

group norms Shared guidelines or rules for behavior that most group members follow.

group norms.[39] **Group norms** are shared guidelines or rules for behavior that most group members follow. Groups develop norms concerning a wide variety of behaviors, including working hours, the sharing of information among group members, how certain group tasks should be performed, and even how members of a group should dress. At Nucor in "A Manager's Challenge," recall how production teams develop their own norms to ensure high performance and the attainment of the weekly bonus.

Managers should encourage members of a group to develop norms that contribute to group performance and the attainment of group goals. For example, group norms that dictate that each member of a cross-functional team should always be available for the rest of the team when his or her input is needed, return phone calls as soon as possible, inform other team members of travel plans, and give team members a phone number at which he or she can be reached when traveling on business, help to ensure that the team is efficient, performs highly, and achieves its goals. A norm in a command group of secretaries that dictates that secretaries who happen to have a light workload in any given week should help out secretaries with heavier workloads helps to ensure that the group completes all assignments in a timely and efficient manner. And a norm in a top-management team that dictates that team members should always consult with each other before making major decisions helps to ensure that good decisions are made with a minimum of errors.

CONFORMITY AND DEVIANCE Group members conform to norms for three reasons: (1) They want to obtain rewards and avoid punishments. (2) They want to imitate group members whom they like and admire. (3) They have internalized the norm and believe it is the right and proper way to behave.[40] Consider the case of Robert King, who conformed to his department's norm of attending a fund-raiser for a community food bank. King's conformity could be due to (1) his desire to be a member of the group in good standing and to have friendly relationships with other group members (rewards), (2) his copying the behavior of other members of the department whom he respects and who always attend the fund-raiser (imitating other group members), or (3) his belief in the merits of supporting the activities of the food bank (believing that is the right and proper way to behave).

Failure to conform, or deviance, occurs when a member of a group violates a group norm. Deviance signals that a group is not controlling one of its member's behaviors. Groups generally respond to members who behave defiantly in one of three ways:[41]

1. The group might try to get the member to change his or her deviant ways and conform to the norm. Group members might try to convince the member of the need to conform, or they might ignore or even punish the deviant. For example, in a Johnsonville Foods plant Liz Senkbiel, a member of a self-managed work team responsible for weighing sausages, failed to conform to a group norm dictating that group members should periodically clean up an untidy room used to interview prospective employees. Senkbiel refused to take part in the team's cleanup efforts, and team members reduced her monthly bonus by about $225 for a two-month period.[42] Senkbiel clearly learned the costs of deviant behavior in her team.
2. The group might expel the member.
3. The group might change the norm to be consistent with the member's behavior.

That last alternative suggests that some deviant behavior can be functional for groups. Deviance is functional for a group when it causes group members to stop and evaluate norms that may be dysfunctional but are taken for granted by the group. Often, group members do not think about why they behave in a certain way or why they follow certain norms. Deviance can cause group members to reflect on their norms and change them when appropriate.

Take the case of a group of receptionists in a beauty salon who followed the norm that all appointments would be hand-written in an appointment book and at the end of each day the receptionist on duty would enter the appointments into the salon's computer system, which printed out the hairdressers' daily schedules. One day, a receptionist decided to enter appointments directly into the computer system at the time they were being made, bypassing the appointment book. This deviant behavior caused the other receptionists to think about why they were using the appointment book in the first place since all appointments could be entered into the computer directly. After consulting with the owner of the salon, the group changed its norm. Now appointments are entered directly into the computer, which saves time and cuts down on scheduling errors.

ENCOURAGING A BALANCE OF CONFORMITY AND DEVIANCE

To effectively help an organization gain a competitive advantage, groups and teams need to have the right balance of conformity and deviance (see Figure 14.5). A group needs a certain level of conformity to ensure that it can control members' behavior and channel it in the direction of high performance and

Figure 14.5 Balancing Conformity and Deviance in Groups

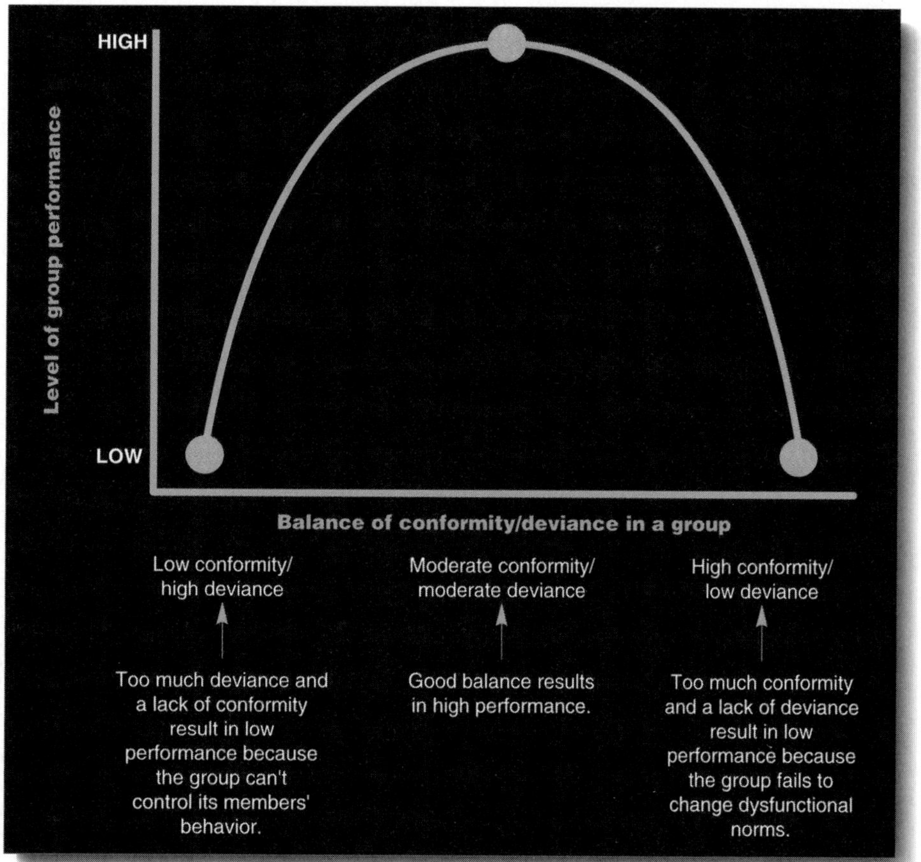

group goal accomplishment. A group also needs a certain level of deviance to ensure that dysfunctional norms are discarded and replaced with functional ones. Balancing conformity and deviance is a pressing concern for all groups, whether they are top-management teams, R&D teams, command groups, or self-managed work teams.

The extent of conformity and reactions to deviance within groups are determined by group members themselves. The three bases for conformity described above are powerful forces that more often than not result in group members' conforming to norms. Sometimes these forces are so strong that deviance rarely occurs in groups, and when it does, it is stamped out.

Managers can take several steps to ensure that there is enough tolerance of deviance in groups so that group members are willing to deviate from dysfunctional norms and, when deviance occurs in their group, reflect on the appropriateness of the violated norm and change the norm if necessary. First, managers can be role models for the groups and teams they oversee. When managers encourage and accept employees' suggestions for changes in procedures, do not rigidly insist that tasks be accomplished in a certain way, and admit when a norm that they once supported is no longer functional, they signal to group members that conformity should not come at the expense of needed changes and improvements. Second, managers should let employees know that there are always ways to improve group processes and performance levels and thus opportunities to replace existing norms with norms that will better enable a group to achieve its goals and perform at a high level. Third, managers should encourage members of groups and teams to periodically assess the appropriateness of their existing norms.

Managers in the innovative design firm Ideo, based in Palo Alto, California, have excelled at ensuring that design teams have the right mix of conformity and deviance, resulting in Ideo designing products in fields ranging from medicine to space travel to computing and personal hygiene, as indicated in the following "Focus on Diversity."

Focus on Diversity

Diversity of Thought and Respect for Ideas Reign at Ideo

Many products we now take for granted were designed by Ideo. Ideo designed the first Apple mouse, the Palm handheld organizer, stand-up toothpaste containers, flexible shelving for offices, self-sealing drink bottles for sports, blood analyzers, and even equipment used in space travel.[43] Managers and designers at Ideo pride themselves on being experts at the process of innovation, rather than in any particular domain. Of course, they have technical design experts such as mechanical and electrical engineers work on products requiring such specialized knowledge. But on the same teams with the engineers might be an anthropologist, a biologist, and a social scientist.

Essentially, a guiding principle at Ideo is that innovation comes in many shapes and sizes and it is only through diversity in thought that people can recognize opportunities for innovation. To promote such diversity in thought, new product development at Ideo is a team effort. Moreover, both conformity and deviance are encouraged on Ideo teams.

Deviance, thinking differently, and not conforming to expected ways of doing things and mind- sets are encouraged at Ideo. In fact, innovative ideas often flow when designers try to see things as they really are and are not blinded by thoughts of what is appropriate, possible, or the ways things should be. Often times, constraints on new product design are created by designers themselves conforming to a certain mind-set about the nature of a product or what a product can or should do and look like. Ideo designers are encouraged to actively breakdown these constraints in their design teams.

Managers at Ideo also realize the need for a certain amount of conformity so that members of design teams can work effectively together and achieve their goals. Thus, conformity to a few very central norms is emphasized in Ideo teams. These norms include understanding what the team is working on (e.g., the product, market, or client need), observing real people in their natural environments, visualizing how new products might work and be used, evaluating and refining product prototypes, encouraging wild ideas, and never rejecting an idea simply because it sounds too crazy.[44] As long as these norms are followed, diversity of thought and even deviance serve to promote innovation at Ideo. In fact, another norm at Ideo is to study "rule breakers"–people who don't follow instructions for products, for example, or try to put products to different uses–as these individuals might help designers identify problems with existing products and unmet consumer needs.[45] All in all, Ideo's focus on encouraging both deviance and conformity in design teams has benefitted all of us as we use Ideo-designed products that seem so familiar we take them for granted. We forget these products weren't in existence until a design team at Ideo was called on by a client to develop a new product or improve on an existing one.

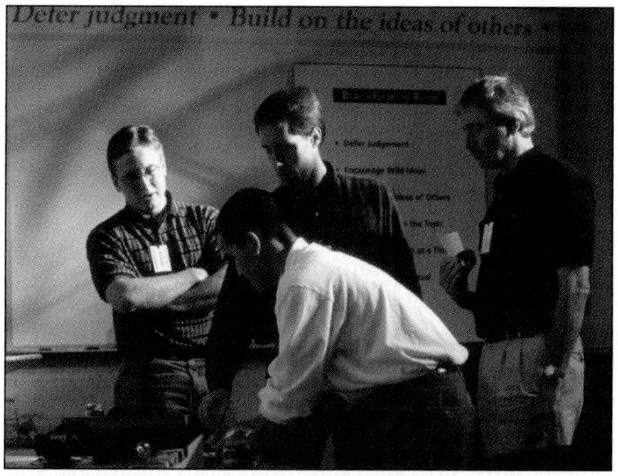

An Ideo team works on a project. Ideo design teams strive to break down constraints on innovation, while conforming to a few central norms that allow them to work effectively.

Group Cohesiveness

group cohesiveness The degree to which members are attracted or loyal to a group.

Another important element of group dynamics that affects group performance and effectiveness is **group cohesiveness,** the degree to which members are attracted or loyal to their group or team.[46] When group cohesiveness is high, individuals strongly value their group membership, find the group very appealing, and have strong desires to remain a part of the group. When group cohesiveness is low, group members do not find their group particularly appealing and have little desire to retain their group membership. Research suggests that managers should strive to have a moderate level of cohesiveness in the groups and teams they manage because that is most likely to contribute to an organization's competitive advantage.

CONSEQUENCES OF GROUP COHESIVENESS There are three major consequences of group cohesiveness: levels of participation within a group, levels of conformity to group norms, and emphasis on group goal accomplishment (see Figure 14.6).[47]

LEVEL OF PARTICIPATION WITHIN A GROUP As group cohesiveness increases, the extent of group members' participation within the group increases. Participation contributes to group effectiveness because group members are actively involved in the group, ensure that group tasks get accomplished, readily

Figure 14.6
Sources and Consequences of Group Cohesiveness

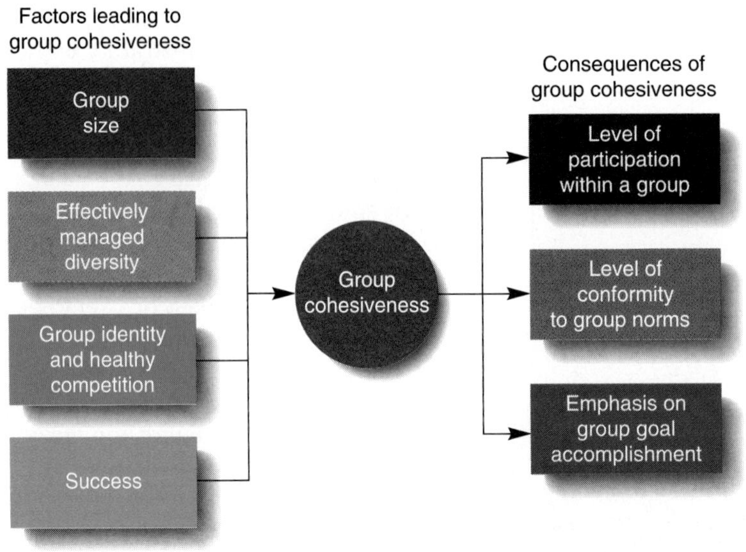

share information with each other, and have frequent and open communication (the important topic of communication is covered in depth in Chapter 15).

A moderate level of group cohesiveness helps to ensure that group members actively participate in the group and communicate effectively with each other. The reason why managers may not want to encourage high levels of cohesiveness is illustrated by the example of two cross-functional teams responsible for developing new toys. Members of the highly cohesive Team Alpha often have lengthy meetings that usually start with non-work-related conversations and jokes, meet more often than most of the other cross-functional teams in the company, and spend a good portion of their time communicating the ins and outs of their department's contribution to toy development to other team members. Members of the moderately cohesive Team Beta generally have efficient meetings in which ideas are communicated and discussed as needed; they do not meet more often than necessary, and share the ins and outs of their expertise with each other to the extent that it is needed for the development process. Teams Alpha and Beta have both developed some top-selling toys. However, it generally takes Team Alpha 30 percent longer than Team Beta to do so. This is why too much cohesiveness can be too much of a good thing.

LEVEL OF CONFORMITY TO GROUP NORMS Increasing levels of group cohesiveness result in increasing levels of conformity to group norms, and, when cohesiveness becomes high, there may be so little deviance in groups that group members conform to norms even when they are dysfunctional. In contrast, low cohesiveness can result in too much deviance and undermine the ability of a group to control its members' behaviors to get things done.

Teams Alpha and Beta in the toy company both had the same norm for toy development. It dictated that members of each team would discuss potential ideas for new toys, decide on a line of toys to pursue, and then have the team member from R&D design a prototype. Recently, a new animated movie featuring a family of rabbits produced by a small film company was an unexpected hit, and major toy companies were scrambling to reach licensing agreements to produce toy lines featuring the rabbits. The top-management team in the toy company assigned Teams Alpha and Beta to develop the new toy lines and to do so quickly to beat out the competition.

Members of Team Alpha followed their usual toy development norm even though the marketing expert on the team believed that the process could have been streamlined to save time. The marketing expert on Team Beta urged the team to deviate from its toy development norm. She suggested that the team not have R&D develop prototypes but instead modify top-selling toys the company already made to feature rabbits, and then reach a licensing agreement with the film company based on the high sales potential (given the company's prior success). Once the licensing agreement was signed, the company could take the time needed to develop innovative and unique rabbit toys with more input from R&D.

As a result of the willingness of the marketing expert on Team Beta to deviate from the norm for toy development, the toy company obtained an exclusive licensing agreement with the film company and had its first rabbit toys on the shelves of stores in a record three months. Groups need a balance of conformity and deviance, so a moderate level of cohesiveness often yields the best outcome, as it did in the case of Team Beta.

EMPHASIS ON GROUP GOAL ACCOMPLISHMENT As group cohesiveness increases, the emphasis placed on group goal accomplishment also increases within a group. A very strong emphasis on group goal accomplishment, however, does not always lead to organizational effectiveness. For an organization to be effective and gain a competitive advantage, the different groups and teams in the organization must cooperate with each other and be motivated to achieve *organizational goals,* even if doing so sometimes comes at the expense of the achievement of group goals. A moderate level of cohesiveness motivates group members to accomplish both group and organizational goals. High levels of cohesiveness can cause group members to be so focused on group goal accomplishment that they may strive to achieve group goals no matter what–even when doing so jeopardizes organizational performance.

At the toy company, the major goal of the cross-functional teams was to develop new toy lines that were truly innovative, utilized the latest in technology, and were in some way fundamentally distinct from other toys on the market. When it came to the rabbit project, Team Alpha's high level of cohesiveness contributed to its continued emphasis on its group goal of developing an innovative line of toys; thus, the team stuck with its usual design process. Team Beta, in contrast, realized that developing the new line of toys quickly was an important organizational goal that should take precedent over the group's goal of developing pathbreaking new toys, at least in the short run. Team Beta's moderate level of cohesiveness contributed to team members doing what was best for the toy company in this case.

FACTORS LEADING TO GROUP COHESIVENESS Four factors contribute to the level of group cohesiveness (see Figure 14.6).[48] By influencing these *determinants of group cohesiveness,* managers can raise or lower the level of cohesiveness to promote moderate levels of cohesiveness in groups and teams.

GROUP SIZE As we mentioned earlier, members of small groups tend to be more motivated and committed than members of large groups. Thus, to promote cohesiveness in groups, when feasible, managers should form groups that are small to medium in size (between around 2 and 15 members). If a group is low in cohesiveness and large in size, managers might want to consider the feasibility of dividing the group in two and assigning different tasks and goals to the two newly formed groups.

EFFECTIVELY MANAGED DIVERSITY In general, people tend to like and get along with others who are similar to themselves. It is easier to communicate with someone, for example, who shares your values, has a similar background, and has had similar experiences. However, as discussed in Chapter 4, diversity in groups, teams, and organizations can help an organization gain a competitive advantage. Diverse groups often come up with more innovative and creative ideas. One reason why cross-functional teams are so popular in organizations like Hallmark Cards is that the diversity in expertise represented in the teams results in higher levels of team performance.

In forming groups and teams, managers need to make sure that the diversity in knowledge, experience, expertise, and other characteristics necessary for group goal accomplishment is represented in the new groups. Managers then have to make sure that this diversity in group membership is effectively managed so that groups will be cohesive. We discuss the effective management of diversity in detail in Chapter 4, and the following "Focus on Diversity" provides additional insight into the steps managers can take to ensure that diverse groups and teams are cohesive.

Focus on Diversity

Integrating Theory and Practicality

Getting researchers in different scientific disciplines to work together is no easy task. Not only do they rely on different knowledge bases but they also speak different languages and approach the research process differently. Difficulties are compounded when some of those who concentrate on theory and theoretical development are teamed with those who focus on experimentation and practicality. Acknowledging the challenge of building cohesive groups under these conditions and the potential benefits in terms of innovation is the Science and Technology Center for Environmentally Responsible Solvents and Processes in Chapel Hill, North Carolina. It has assembled teams of scientists from different disciplines and orientations to develop new products, with the help of a team social scientist who helps other members understand and communicate with each other.[49]

The center was formed to discover ways to substitute liquid carbon dioxide (which is harmless) for environmentally hazardous chemical solvents in a variety of applications. For example, two widely used solvents in dry cleaning stores are perchloroethylene (contaminates ground water and may cause cancer) and petrol (extremely flammable). Alternatively, harmless liquid carbon dioxide can also be used to dry clean clothes as proven by the franchise, Hangers Cleaners, that uses it instead of traditional dry cleaning solvents.[50]

A library employee diligently returns books to their shelves. When employees at a New York public library seemed to have more time for reading the library books than for re-shelving them, the head librarian solved the problem of "social-loafing" by holding each employee responsible for re-shelving books in a particular location. Once employees knew that the head librarian could identify their efforts, there were rarely any backlogs of books to be re-shelved.

The center has scientists and engineers from a variety of universities working together in teams on different applications. Early on, the director of the center, Joe DeSimone, realized that teams with individuals from diverse disciplines and backgrounds might need help communicating with each other and building a cohesive effectively functioning team. Enter social scientist Diane Sonnenwald. Sonnenwald helps team members appreciate what each has to offer to the team's project, recognize the complementary nature of their talents, share information, and feel enough trust to admit when they don't understand something. Researchers on the teams such as Ruben Carbonell who heads a team exploring potential microelectronics applications of liquid carbon dioxide recognize the benefits of Sonnenwald's contributions to building team cohesiveness. A group of large chemical companies have found this approach has promise and are providing a portion of the funding for the center.[51] All in all, the center may enrich our understanding of environmentally friendly solvents as well as the effective management of diverse teams.

GROUP IDENTITY AND HEALTHY COMPETITION When group cohesiveness is low, managers can often increase it by encouraging groups to develop their own identities or personalities and to engage in healthy competition. This is precisely what managers at Eaton Corporation based in Lincoln, Illinois, did. Eaton's employees manufacture products such as engine valves, gears, truck axles, and circuit breakers. Managers at Eaton created self-managed work teams to cut costs and improve performance. They realized, however, that the teams would have to be cohesive to ensure that they would strive to achieve their goals. Managers promoted group identity by having the teams give themselves names such as "The Hoods," "The Worms," and "Scrap Attack" (a team striving to reduce costly scrap metal waste by 50 percent). Healthy competition among groups is promoted by displaying measures of each team's performance and the extent to which teams have met their goals on a large TV screen in the cafeteria and by rewarding team members for team performance.[52]

If groups are too cohesive, managers can try to decrease cohesiveness by promoting organizational (rather than group) identity and making the organization as a whole the focus of the group's efforts. Organizational identity can be promoted by making group members feel that they are valued members of the organization as a whole and by stressing cooperation across groups to promote the achievement of organizational goals. Excessive levels of cohesiveness also can be decreased by reducing or eliminating competition between groups and rewarding cooperation.

SUCCESS When it comes to promoting group cohesiveness, there is more than a grain of truth to the saying that "Nothing succeeds like success." As groups become more successful, they become increasingly attractive to their members, and their cohesiveness tends to increase. When cohesiveness is low, managers can increase cohesiveness by making sure that a group can achieve some noticeable and visible successes.

Take the case of a group of salespeople in the housewares department of a medium-size department store. The housewares department was recently moved to a corner of the store's basement. Its remote location resulted in low sales because of infrequent customer traffic in that part of the store. The salespeople, who were generally evaluated favorably by their supervisors and were valued members of the store, tried various initiatives to boost sales, but to no avail. As a result of this lack of success and the poor performance of their department, their cohesiveness started to plummet. To increase and preserve the cohesiveness of the group, the store manager implemented a group-based incentive across the store. In any month, members of the group with the best attendance and punctuality records would have their names and pictures posted on a bulletin board in the cafeteria and would each receive a $50 gift certificate. The housewares group frequently had the best records, and their success on this dimension helped to build and maintain their cohesiveness. Moreover, this initiative boosted attendance and discouraged lateness throughout the store. As another example, teams at Nucor in "A Manager's Challenge" are likely to become cohesive when they consistently perform at a high level and team members are rewarded for team performance with a weekly bonus.

Managing Groups and Teams for High Performance

Now that you have a good understanding of why groups and teams are so important for organizations, the types of groups that managers create, and group dynamics, we consider some additional steps that managers can take to make sure groups and teams perform highly and contribute to organizational effectiveness. Managers striving to have top-performing groups and teams need to (1) motivate group members to work toward the achievement of organizational goals, (2) reduce social loafing, and (3) help groups to manage conflict effectively.

Motivating Group Members to Achieve Organizational Goals

When work is difficult, tedious, or requires a high level of commitment and energy, managers cannot assume that group members will always be motivated to work toward the achievement of organizational goals. Consider the case of a group of house painters who paint the interiors and exteriors of new homes for a construction company and are paid on an hourly basis. Why should they strive to complete painting jobs quickly and efficiently if doing so will just make them feel more tired at the end of the day and they will not receive any tangible benefits? It makes more sense for the painters to adopt a more relaxed approach, to take frequent breaks, and to work at a leisurely pace. This relaxed approach, however, impairs the construction company's ability to gain a competitive advantage because it raises costs and increases the time needed to complete a new home.

Managers can motivate members of groups and teams to achieve organizational goals and create a competitive advantage by making sure that the members themselves benefit when the group or team performs highly as is true at Nucor in "A Manager's Challenge." If members of a self-managed work team know that they will receive a weekly bonus based on team performance, they will be highly motivated to perform at a high level.

Managers often rely on some combination of individual and group-based incentives to motivate members of groups and teams to work toward the achievement of organizational goals and a competitive advantage, as is true at Nucor in "A Manager's Challenge." When individual performance within a group can be assessed, pay is often determined by individual performance or by both individual and group performance. When individual performance within a group cannot be accurately assessed, then group performance should be the key determinant of pay levels. Approximately 75 percent of companies that use self-managed work teams base members' pay in part on team performance.[53] A major challenge for managers is to develop a fair pay system that will lead to both high individual motivation and high group or team performance.

Other benefits that managers can make available to high-performance group members–in addition to monetary rewards–include extra resources such as equipment and computer software, awards and other forms of recognition, and choice future work assignments. For example, members of self-managed work teams that develop new software at companies like Microsoft often value working on interesting and important projects; members of teams that have performed highly are rewarded by being assigned to interesting and important new projects.

At Ideo (profiled in an earlier "Focus on Diversity"), managers motivate team members by making them feel important. As Tom Kelley, Ideo's general manager puts it, "When people feel special, they'll perform beyond your wildest dreams."[54] To make Ideo team members feel special, Ideo managers plan unique and fun year-end parties, give teams the opportunity to take time off if they feel they need or want to, encourage teams to take field trips, and see harmless pranks as a way to incorporate fun into the workplace.[55]

Reducing Social Loafing in Groups

social loafing The tendency of individuals to put forth less effort when they work in groups than when they work alone.

We have been focusing on the steps that managers can take to encourage high levels of performance in groups. Managers, however, need to be aware of an important downside to group and team work: the potential for social loafing, which reduces group performance. **Social loafing** is the tendency of individuals to put forth less effort when they work in groups than when they work alone.[56] Have you ever worked on a group project in which one or two group members never seemed to be pulling their weight? Have you ever worked in a student club or committee in which some members always seemed to be missing meetings and never volunteered for activities? Have you ever had a job in which one or two of your coworkers seemed to be slacking off because they knew that you or other members of your work group would make up for their low levels of effort? If you have, you have witnessed social loafing in action.

Social loafing can occur in all kinds of groups and teams and in all kinds of organizations. It can result in lower group performance and may even prevent a group from attaining its goals. Fortunately, there are steps managers can take to reduce social loafing and sometimes completely eliminate it; we will look at three (see Figure 14.7).

1. *Make individual contributions to a group identifiable.*

Some people may engage in social loafing when they work in groups because they think that they can hide in the crowd–that no one will notice if they put forth less effort than they should. Other people may think that if they put forth high levels of effort and make substantial contributions to the group, their contribution will not be noticed and they will receive no rewards for their work–so why bother.[57]

One way in which managers can effectively eliminate social loafing is by making individual contributions to a group identifiable so that group members perceive that low and high levels of effort will be noticed and individual contributions

Figure 14.7
Three Ways to Reduce Social Loafing

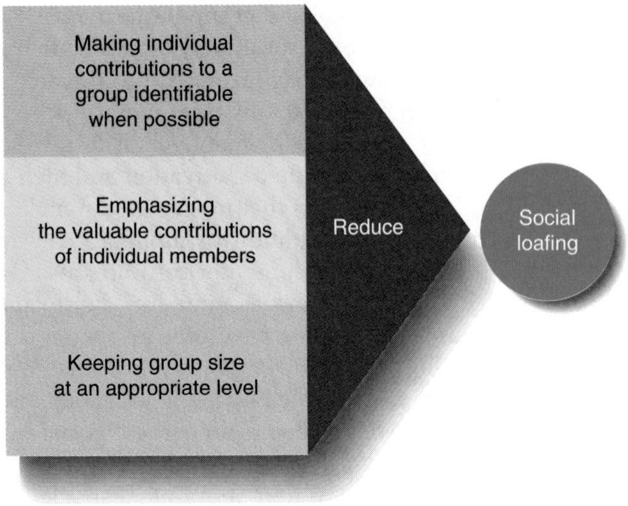

evaluated.[58] Managers can accomplish this by assigning specific tasks to group members and holding them accountable for their completion. Take the case of a group of eight employees responsible for reshelving returned books in a large public library in New York. The head librarian was concerned that there was always a backlog of seven or eight carts of books to be reshelved, even though the employees never seemed to be particularly busy and some even found time to sit down in the current periodicals section to read newspapers and magazines. The librarian decided to try to eliminate the apparent social loafing by assigning a particular section of the library that each employee was always responsible for reshelving. Because the library's front-desk employees sorted the books by section on the carts as they were returned, holding the shelvers responsible for particular sections was easily accomplished. Once the shelvers knew that the librarian could identify their effort or lack of effort, there were rarely any backlogs of books to be reshelved.

Sometimes the members of a group can cooperate to eliminate social loafing by making individual contributions identifiable. For example, in a small security company members of a self-managed work team assemble control boxes for home alarm systems. They start each day by deciding who will perform what tasks that day and how much work each member and the group as a whole should strive to accomplish. Each team member knows that, at the end of the day, the other team members will know exactly how much he or she has accomplished. With this system in place, social loafing never occurs in the team. Remember, however, that in some teams, individual contributions cannot be made identifiable as is true in teams whose members are reciprocally interdependent.

2. *Emphasize the valuable contributions of individual members.*

Another reason why social loafing may occur is that people sometimes think that their efforts are unnecessary or unimportant when they work in a group. They feel the group will accomplish its goals and perform at an acceptable level whether they personally perform at a high level. To counteract this belief, when managers form groups, they should assign individuals to groups on the basis of the valuable contributions that *each* person can make to the group as a whole. Clearly communicating to group members why each person's contribution is valuable to the group is an effective means by which managers and group members themselves can reduce or eliminate social loafing.[59] This is most clearly illustrated in cross-functional teams where each member's valuable contribution to the team derives from a personal area of expertise. By emphasizing why each member's skills are important, managers can reduce social loafing in such teams.

3. *Keep group size at an appropriate level.*

Group size is related to the causes of social loafing we just described. As size increases, identifying individual contributions becomes increasingly difficult, and members are increasingly likely to think that their individual contributions are not very important. To overcome this, managers should form groups with no more members than are needed to accomplish group goals and perform highly.[60]

Helping Groups to Manage Conflict Effectively

At some point or other, practically all groups experience conflict either within the group (intragroup conflict) or with other groups (intergroup conflict). In Chapter 16 we discuss conflict in depth and explore ways to manage it effectively. As you will learn there, managers can take several steps to help groups manage conflict and disagreements.

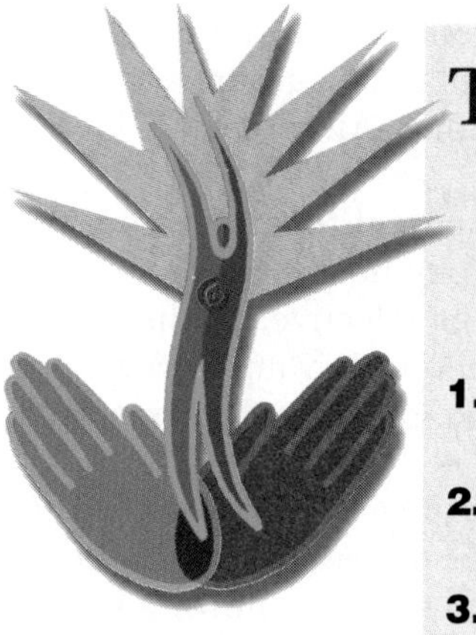

Tips for New Managers

Group Dynamics and Managing Groups and Teams for High Performance

1. Make sure that members of groups and teams personally benefit when the group or team performs highly.
2. Form groups and teams with no more members than are necessary to achieve group and team goals.
3. Reward members of groups whose tasks are characterized by pooled task interdependence based upon individual performance.
4. Reward members of groups or teams whose tasks are characterized by sequential task interdependence based upon group performance.
5. Reward team members whose tasks are characterized by reciprocal task interdependence based upon team performance or a combination of individual and team performance (if individual performance can be identified).
6. Clearly communicate to members of groups and teams the expectations for their roles and how the different roles in the group fit together.
7. Encourage group and team members to periodically assess the appropriateness of existing norms.

Summary and Review

GROUPS, TEAMS, AND ORGANIZATIONAL EFFECTIVENESS A group is two or more people who interact with each other to accomplish certain goals or meet certain needs. A team is a group whose members work intensely with each other to achieve a specific common goal or objective. Groups and teams can contribute to organizational effectiveness by enhancing performance, increasing responsiveness to customers, increasing innovation, and being a source of motivation for their members.

TYPES OF GROUPS AND TEAMS Formal groups are groups that managers establish to achieve organizational goals; they include cross-functional teams, cross-cultural teams, top-management teams, research and development teams, command groups, task forces, self-managed work teams, and virtual teams. Informal groups are groups that employees form because they believe that the groups will help them achieve their own goals or meet their needs; they include friendship groups and interest groups.

GROUP DYNAMICS Key elements of group dynamics are group size, tasks, and roles; group leadership; group development; group norms; and group cohesiveness. The advantages and disadvantages of large and small groups suggest that managers should form groups with no more members than are needed to provide the group with the human resources it needs to achieve its goals and use a division of labor. The type of task interdependence that characterizes a group's work gives managers a clue about the appropriate size of the group. A group role is a set of behaviors and tasks that a member of a group is expected to perform because of his or her position in the group. All groups and teams need leadership.

Five stages of development that many groups pass through are forming, storming, norming, performing, and adjourning. Group norms are shared rules for behavior that most group members follow. To be effective, groups need a balance of conformity and deviance. Conformity allows a group to control its members' behavior to achieve group goals; deviance provides the impetus for needed change.

Group cohesiveness is the attractiveness of a group or team to its members. As group cohesiveness increases, so, too, do the level of participation and communication within a group, the level of conformity to group norms, and the emphasis on group goal accomplishment. Managers should strive to achieve a moderate level of group cohesiveness in the groups and teams they manage.

MANAGING GROUPS AND TEAMS FOR HIGH PERFORMANCE To make sure that groups and teams perform highly, managers need to motivate group members to work toward the achievement of organizational goals, reduce social loafing, and help groups to effectively manage conflict. Managers can motivate members of groups and teams to work toward the achievement of organizational goals by making sure that members personally benefit when the group or team performs highly.

Management in Action

Topics for Discussion and Action

1. Why do all organizations need to rely on groups and teams to achieve their goals and gain a competitive advantage?
2. Interview one or more managers in an organization in your local community to identify the types of groups and teams that the organization uses to achieve its goals.
3. What kinds of employees would prefer to work in a virtual team? What kinds of employees would prefer to work in a team that meets face-to-face?
4. Think about a group that you are a member of, and describe your group's current stage of development. Does the development of this group seem to be following the forming-storming-norming-performing-adjourning stages described in the chapter?
5. Think about a group of employees who work in a McDonald's restaurant. What type of task interdependence characterizes this group? What potential problems in the group should the restaurant manager be aware of and take steps to avoid?
6. Discuss the reasons why too much conformity can hurt groups and their organizations.
7. Why do some groups have very low levels of cohesiveness?
8. Imagine that you are the manager of a hotel. What steps will you take to reduce social loafing by members of the cleaning staff who are responsible for keeping all common areas and guest rooms spotless?

Building Management Skills

Diagnosing Group Failures

Think about the last dissatisfying or discouraging experience you had as a member of a group or team. Perhaps the group did not accomplish its goals, perhaps group members could agree about nothing, or perhaps there was too much social loafing. Now answer the following questions.

1. What type of group was this?
2. Were group members motivated to achieve group goals? Why or why not?
3. How large was the group, what type of task interdependence existed in the group, and what group roles did members play?
4. What were the group's norms? How much conformity and deviance existed in the group?
5. How cohesive was the group? Why do you think the group's cohesiveness was at this level? What consequences did this level of group cohesiveness have for the group and its members?
6. Was social loafing a problem in this group? Why or why not?
7. What could the group's leader or manager have done differently to increase group effectiveness?
8. What could group members have done differently to increase group effectiveness?

Small Group Breakout Exercise

Creating a Cross-Functional Team

Form groups of three or four people, and appoint one member as the spokesperson who will communicate your findings to the whole class when called on by the instructor. Then discuss the following scenario.

You are a group of managers in charge of food services for a large state university in the Midwest. Recently a survey of students, faculty, and staff was conducted to evaluate customer satisfaction with the food services provided by the university's eight cafeterias. The results were disappointing, to put it mildly. Complaints ranged from dissatisfaction with the type and range of meals and snacks provided, operating hours, and food temperature, to unresponsiveness, to current concerns about the importance of low-fat/high-fiber diets and the needs of vegetarians. You have decided to form a cross-functional team to further evaluate reactions to the food services and to develop a proposal for changes to be made to increase customer satisfaction.

1. Indicate who should be on this important cross-functional team and why.
2. Describe the goals the team should be striving to achieve.
3. Describe the different roles that will need to be performed in this team.
4. Describe the steps you will take to help ensure that the team has a good balance between conformity and deviance and a moderate level of cohesiveness.

Exploring the World Wide Web

Find the website of a company that relies heavily on teams to accomplish its goals. What kinds of teams does this company use? What steps do managers take to ensure that team members are motivated to perform at a high level?

You're the Management Consultant

Jill Ruiz was recently hired in a boundary spanning role for the global unit of an educational and professional publishing company. The company is headquartered in New York (where Ruiz works) and has divisions in multiple countries. Each division is responsible for translating, manufacturing, marketing, and selling a set of books in its country. Part of Ruiz's responsibilities is interfacing with managers in each of the divisions in her region (Central and South America), overseeing their budgeting and financial reporting to headquarters, and heading up a virtual team consisting of herself and the top managers in charge of each of the divisions in her region. The virtual team is to promote global learning, explore new potential opportunities and markets, and address ongoing problems. She communicates directly with division managers via telephone and email, as well as written reports, memos, and faxes. When virtual team meetings are convened, videoconferencing is often used.

After her first few virtual team meetings, Ruiz noticed that the managers seemed to be reticent about speaking up. Interestingly enough, when each manager communicates with her individually, primarily in telephone conversations, they tend to be very forthcoming and frank and she feels she has a good rapport with each of them. However, getting them to communicate with each other as a virtual team has been a real challenge. At the last meeting, she tried to prompt some of the managers to raise issues relevant to the agenda that she knew were on their minds from her individual conversations with them. Surprisingly, the managers skillfully avoided informing their fellow teammates about the heart of the issues in question. Ruiz is confused and troubled. While she feels her other responsibilities are going well, she knows that her virtual team is not operating like a team at all and no matter what she tries, discussions in virtual team meetings are forced and generally unproductive. As an expert on team functioning, she has come to you for advice. What do you think is the cause of the problem and how should Ruiz address it?

BusinessWeek

Cases in the News

GE Capital's E-Biz Farm Team

On a June morning in the boardroom at General Electric Capital Corp. in Stamford, Conn., Anand Modak is telling a group of executives what he dislikes about the GE Financial Assurance website. "The information should be available within three clicks" of a mouse, he says, instead of seven in some cases. Sitting nearby, soaking it all in, are top GE Capital executives such as CEO Denis J. Nayden and Chief Technology & Information Officer Michael W. Stout. But Modak, 33, isn't a GE Capital employee or a top-dollar consultant. He's a second-year MBA student at the University of Connecticut's School of Business Administration, brought in to show GE Capital executives how he and his fellow students could lend a hand with the $56 billion company's e-business problems.

The GE execs came away impressed. "They've got smart people," says Nayden. Five months later, GE Capital has formed a partnership with UConn's B-school—and may establish a model for corporate and academic collaboration on new technologies. The company agreed to invest about $2.5 million and has promised an additional $1 million every year until 2005 to create and operate a new e-commerce lab on Uconn's two-year-old Stamford campus, just minutes from GE Capital's main offices. Forty students will work full time during a semester to study various e-commerce technologies and issues. Other students at Uconn's main campus in Storrs, Conn., will participate through projects, GE executives will be assigned to the lab, working closely with faculty to guide research.

For GE, the main benefit is a pipeline of potential recruits and an inexpensive team to noodle over e-biz solutions. "We're not interested in theoretical research—I need to transform my businesses radically, and quickly," says Nayden, who is an alumnus of UConn's B-school. "If I did this myself, I'd have to hire new people, engage consultants, or take [existing employees] off of another project."

The venture is the largest between a GE unit and a B-school. GE Industrial Systems has given $1.5 million to UConn's school of engineering, and Richard N. Dino, the UConn B-school's associate dean, says this school may soon become more involved in the e-lab, too. In this new venture, however, GE Capital execs have continuing commitment and closer supervision. And more such arrangements may be on the way: GE is considering similar deals with two or three other universities.

The relationship pushes to new levels the alliance between corporations and B-schools, which are seeking out financing that allows them to conduct more relevant research. Take, for instance, the year-old Center for eBusiness @ MIT, a venture between 16 corporate sponsors and Massachusetts Institute of Technology's Sloan School of Management, which *Business Week* ranks No. 5 in the U.S. Sponsors kick in $300,000 a year, half of which goes to have a faculty member, one or two master's students, and a PhD candidate work on an issue important to the company. The contracts involve fewer students than the GE e-lab, however, and don't focus on short-term business solutions.

Real World

Such collaborations are partly being driven by cost considerations. Faculty research alone costs the University of Maryland's Robert H. Smith School of Business $10 million a year, for instance. Organizations and foundations donate an additional $2 million to $3 million for research. Only $200,000 to $300,000 of that comes from corporations. Smith School Dean Howard Frank wants to boost that share to $3 million, but it's not as simple as saying: "We're smart. Give us money," he says. "You build a value-added relationship."

For students inside UConn's 10,000-square-foot e-lab offices, that relationship includes real-world case studies and access to top GE executives. If e-lab projects are later spun off into products or services, the school has a chance to share in profits. GE Capital may buy innovations that originate with faculty or that grow out of the e-lab. But the project also represents a bid for prestige for the 52-year-old Uconn B-school, which has a $16 million annual operating budget and a $17 million endowment. That's tiny compared with the $267.7 million endowment at the University of Michigan's business school, for example. Uconn's Dino says he's trying to drive the unranked school into the top 50 schools nationwide: "That's what this whole thing is about."

Feedback

Outside academics worry that too much hands-on involvement by executives in settings like the e-lab can skew results. "If executives are conducting research, then it is likely to be less rigorous," warns S. P. Kothari, professor of accounting and director of the New Economy Value Research Lab at MIT's Sloan School. But UConn faculty say any drawbacks are more than offset by the ability to test their ideas in real-world settings. They have the right to use research conducted in the e-lab as the basis for papers. "We're often approached to do research for money," says UConn's James Marsden. "But we can't write about it . . . because we have to sign nondisclosure agreements."

Lab results also will be fed back into curriculum. This spring, for example, students can take New Technology Evaluation, a course co-taught by a UConn professor and a GE Capital manager. Students will handle dozens of GE Capital projects in areas such as biometrics, e-auctions, digital piracy, and website design. And as projects demand, students will have access to early versions of new technology, such as souped-up Palm hand-held computers and iris-scanning personal identification systems. Says GE Capital Chief Technology Officer Chris Perretta: "We get good toys."

In return, GE Capital should gain a recruiting edge. Other close company-school relationships bear this out: Of the 200 MBAs that Maryland graduated last spring, 20 percent went to companies that the school had a close relationship with, says Frank. GE Capital's Nayden adds: "Students get a view of working with GE Capital, and we get a telescopic view into a talented pipeline. That's much different than a cold interview."

Just look at Modak, the second-year MBA. This month, he's wrapping up a feasibility study of a new idea from a GE Capital business. After he presents his findings on December 8, Modak will focus on getting a job. Will he apply at GE Capital? You bet. And once dozens of students have channeled through the e-lab, other companies may want a peek, too.

Source: M. Schneider, "GE Capital's E-Biz Farm Team," *Business Week,* November 27, 2000, pp. 110–11.

Questions

1. What are the benefits for the students participating in the E-Biz teams? What are the potential disadvantages?
2. How would you characterize the pros and cons of this initiative for the University of Connecticut? For GE Capital Corp.?
3. Do you think other companies and universities can strike up similar kinds of partnerships? Why or why not?

BusinessWeek Cases in the News

Kim's Fall From Grace

What an ignominious fall. As recently as two years ago, Kim Woo Choong, founder of South Korea's Daewoo Group, was revered as the man who built a small textile-trading house into Korea's second-largest industrial conglomerate. Since then, revelations of deep losses, corruption, and mismanagement at Daewoo have shredded his legend. Now the last vestiges of respect are gone.

In the first week of February, the Supreme Public Prosecution Office, Korea's top law-enforcement agency, announced it had arrested seven of Kim's top lieutenants on four criminal charges, including fraud and embezzlement. They were jailed to await formal indictment and trial. Those in custody include top current and former executives of the group's many divisions, among them Kang Byung Ho and Chang Byung Ju, ex-presidents of Daewoo Corp., and Kim Tae Gou, former chairman of Daewoo Motor. Kim Woo Choong, whose empire once produced 10 percent of South Korea's gross domestic product, is a fugitive, flitting between Europe and Africa to avoid prosecution on charges including fraud and embezzlement.

The prosecutors allege that Kim and his associates organized what they believe is Asia's biggest single financial fraud—false accounting between 1997 and 1998 that inflated the value of Daewoo's equity by $32 billion. More disclosures could come. "It's not over, with dozens of other people still being probed," says Kang Kap Jin, a spokesman for the prosecutor's office. One arrested executive, Yoo Ki Bum, admits the company, like many, manipulated the books, though not on his orders: He will "face the music," his lawyer, Surh Jeong Woo, says. However, says an official, "the most important part of the jigsaw puzzle that's missing is Kim Woo Choong, who masterminded the whole operation." Korean missions worldwide are on alert, and prosecutors plan to ask Interpol for help finding Kim.

Kim's lawyer couldn't be reached for comment, but local press reports have quoted the lawyer as saying Kim hasn't decided whether to return home. Prosecutors sound determined to get their man—though some cynical observers speculate that Kim hasn't yet been found because

Daewoo money ended up in politicians' pockets.

It's no secret that over the years, Korea's *chaebol* relied on accounting maneuvers to plump up profits, diminish liabilities, and generally make the business look good. But the scale at Daewoo was breathtaking. The government prosecutor's office has released only scant details. It appears, though, that its investigation centers on a few areas: asset-swapping between Daewoo entities to create fictitious profits; cover-ups of failed ventures; and a London-based slush fund that diverted money from Daewoo's trading arm, Daewoo Corp.

Unfortunately, says Lee Dong Gull, a former economic adviser to President Kim Dae Jung, much of what prosecutors are uncovering could have been detected long ago. "To send a strong message, the government must also hold responsible the accounting firms and regulatory officials who overlooked the fraud," he says. "Anyone carefully studying Daewoo's books could detect misconduct of that magnitude."

Fictitious Profits

Take Daewoo Corp., Daewoo Heavy Industries, and Daewoo Electronics. In 1998, they posted a combined net profit of $272 million, though South Korea was in the depths of its worst recession since the Korean War. Their publicly available income statements, however, list $2.7 billion in gains from asset sales carried out between Daewoo companies: One Daewoo business would sell an asset far above stated book value to an affiliate, and book the capital gain as profit. Government lawyers say the assets were actually worth far less. "By swapping their shares and other assets at inflated prices, they generated all the gains without exchanging even a single cent," Lee says. Once these fictitious profits were deleted, the three companies collectively lost $2.4 billion.

Some of the prosecutors' allegations border on the farcical, such as Daewoo Motor Co.'s attempt to cover up its failed $200 million investment in a car plant in Ukraine. When Daewoo Motor was unable to get parts to keep the plant running, the Ukrainian government complained. To placate it, Daewoo surreptitiously shipped cars built in Korea to the Ukrainian border, where they were taken apart and sent to the plant for reassembly. Prosecutors say the company claimed sales and profits from the bogus production and fraudulently obtained loans based on them.

The slush-fund accusation has a familiar ring. In November 1995, Kim and a group of top Korean executives were charged with paying bribes to Roh Tae Woo, who was President from 1988 to 1993, from a $650 million slush fund: Kim got a suspended jail sentence for that. In the current case, prosecutors say Kim set up a shell company called British Finance Center (BFC). In preliminary filings, prosecutors could not put a precise figure on how much cash was shifted to the fund. But they said that $2.6 billion made its way into the account after Daewoo forged documents to create an import-export transaction that never occurred. The group diverted an additional $1.5 billion from car-export revenues. Prosecutors did not say how the money was spent, but industry executives and analysts think at least part of it was earmarked for the chairman's personal use and for bribing government officials around the world and executives at client companies and banks. One former Daewoo executive told *Business Week:* "Chairman Kim carried with him bundles of money to lobby for projects in emerging markets."

Punishing the Innocent

The disclosures may explain why Ford Motor Co. last September dropped its bid for Daewoo Motor, which went bankrupt in November 2000. (The entire *chaebol* was declared insolvent in 1999, with more than $70 billion in debt.) The allegations of Kim's wrongdoing have complicated an already arduous restructuring and negotiations with General Motors corp. to buy the company. Management has pledged to lay off some 2,000 assembly-line workers this month. Understandably, the company's unionized workers resent the sacrifice. "Kim Woo Choong has been stealing money from the company, and we should not be punished for the mess he created," says Daewoo Motor Labor Union representative Choi Jong Hak.

The Daewoo arrests may give the government the political cover it needs for a fresh attack on the cronyism infecting *chaebol,* banks, and politicians. Ensuring transparency in business transactions would help the entire financial system. For decades, Kim Woo Choong has been a role model for ambitious Korean youths. The government could now hold him up as a model of a different kind.

Source: M. Ihlwan, "Kim's Fall From Grace," *Business Week,* February 19, 2001, pp. 50–51.

Questions

1. Why did Kim Woo Choong and his top management team engage in unethical behaviors?
2. How come it took so long for these problems to surface? How can similar fiascos be avoided in the future?

Chapter 15
Communication

Learning Objectives

After studying this chapter, you should be able to:

- Explain why effective communication helps an organization gain a **competitive advantage.**
- Describe the **communication process,** and explain the **role of perception** in communication.
- Define **information richness,** and describe the information richness of communication media available to managers.
- Describe the **communication networks** that exist in groups and teams.
- Explain how **advances in technology** have given managers new options for managing communication.
- Describe important **communication skills that managers need** as senders and as receivers of messages.

A Manager's Challenge

Bringing People Back into IT

How can managers humanize their use of IT so that customers, clients, and employees can use it as a tool to promote effective communication?

How often have you called a company or service organization and wasted valuable time choosing among seemingly limitless menu options just to have to repeat them again because all you need to do is speak to a human being and not an automated system? Or have you ever spent too much time navigating an Internet site to make a purchase only to have it not go through? Experiences such as these are all too common and point to an interesting paradox. Advances in information technology (IT) are presumably designed to facilitate effective communication among people whether they are friends, customers, employees, strangers, or salespeople. However, in their zeal to employ IT, some managers and organizations have lost sight of the human element in communication. When the human element is neglected, IT might not contribute to effective communication or even hinder it.

Intel CEO Craig Barrett (right) speaks at a recent Intel Developer's Forum. All the information that employees can access through its IT systems is available to suppliers and resellers.

Increasing numbers of managers and organizations are realizing this and trying to bring the human touch back into IT uses and applications.[1] Essentially, a people-oriented approach to the use of IT can improve internal communication within organizations, result in increased responsiveness to customers, and even help an organization develop new products.

Managers at Intel excel at using IT to not only improve communication within the company but also to improve organizational performance. Intel has always emphasized efficiency and does so with its use of IT. Intel's IT systems enable employees to not only access data and information but also get in touch with people who may hold the key to solving a problem or taking advantage of an opportunity. Moreover, all the information that employees can access through Intel's IT systems also is available to its suppliers and resellers. As Sandra Morris, vice president of the E-Business Group at Intel puts it, "We've taken the walls off of Intel and wrapped it in cellophane, and everybody can look inside."[2]

Alternatively, managers at eBay have mastered the humanization of IT from the customer's perspective. One of the reasons eBay is so popular with its customers, whether they are buying or selling, is its personal touch. Buyers are treated like people and sellers go out of their way to help them.[3] Users of eBay are interacting with real people via their computers and eBay goes out of its way to ensure that this human touch is ever present. One example is its feedback mechanisms for sellers where buyers can rate and comment on their purchasing experience with a particular seller so that future potential buyers know how reliable the seller is. The human touch is even more important in business to business Internet transactions. Forward looking companies like SciQuest.com Inc (a supplier of laboratory pharmaceutical products) not only hire salespeople but also ensure that personal relationships are maintained and supported electronically.[4]

Managers at other companies are using IT to learn more about their customers and be more responsive to their needs. For example, Hallmark Cards has an on-line bulletin board which brings people together to discuss a variety of issues. Hallmark recruited 200 people to interact using the bulletin board, referred to as an Idea Exchange.[5] These volunteers receive Hallmark gifts in return for their participation, some have made friends, and many look forward to their daily chats. With participants' permission, Hallmark listens in to these electronic conversations and gleans ideas for new products from them. Other companies undertaking similar kinds of initiatives include Coca-Cola, Stonyfield Farm, and Kraft Foods.[6] While the applications differ, what these initiatives have in common is the use of IT to gain a better sense of customers' preferences with the ultimate objective of being more responsive to their needs. Clearly, there are multiple benefits to humanizing the use of IT.

Overview

Even with all the advances in information technology available to managers, ineffective communication continues to take place in organizations. As illustrated in "A Manager's Challenge," some managers realize this and also the fact that IT is a tool to improve human communication, not a substitute for human communication. Hence, managers are emphasizing the humanization of IT and striving to bring people back into the center stage of effective communication. Ineffective communication is detrimental for managers, workers, and organizations; it can lead to poor performance, strained interpersonal relations, poor quality service, and dissatisfied customers. For an organization to be effective and gain a competitive advantage, managers at all levels need to be good communicators.

In this chapter, we describe the nature of communication and the communication process and explain why all managers and their subordinates must be effective communicators. We describe the communication media available to managers and the factors they need to consider in selecting a communication medium for each message they send. We consider the communication networks that organizational members rely on, and we explore how advances in information technology have expanded managers' range of communication options. We describe the communication skills that help managers be effective senders and receivers of messages. By the end of this chapter, you will have a good appreciation of the nature of communication and the steps that managers can take to ensure that they are effective communicators.

Communication and Management

communication The sharing of information between two or more individuals or groups to reach a common understanding.

Communication is the sharing of information between two or more individuals or groups to reach a common understanding.[7] "A Manager's Challenge" highlights some important aspects of this definition. First and foremost, no matter how electronically based, communication is a human endeavor and involves individuals and groups. Second, communication does not take place unless a common understanding is reached. Thus, when you call a business to speak to a person in customer service or billing and are bounced back and forth between endless automated messages and menu options and eventually hang up in frustration, communication has not taken place.

The Importance of Good Communication

In Chapter 1, we described how an organization can gain a competitive advantage when managers strive to increase efficiency, quality, responsiveness to customers, and innovation. Good communication is essential for obtaining each of these four goals and thus is a necessity for gaining a competitive advantage.

Managers can *increase efficiency* by updating the production process to take advantage of new and more efficient technologies and by training workers to operate the new technologies and expand their skills. Good communication is necessary for managers to learn about new technologies, implement them in their organizations, and train workers in how to use them. Similarly, *improving quality* hinges on effective communication. Managers need to communicate to all members of an organization the meaning and importance of high quality and the routes to attaining it. Subordinates need to communicate quality problems and suggestions for increasing quality to their superiors, and members of self-managed work teams need to share their ideas for improving quality with each other.

Good communication can also help to increase *responsiveness to customers.* When the organizational members who are closest to customers, such as department store salespeople and bank tellers, are empowered to communicate customers' needs and desires to managers, managers are better able to respond to these needs. Managers, in turn, must communicate with other organizational members to determine how best to respond to changing customer preferences.

Innovation, which often takes place in cross-functional teams, also requires effective communication. Members of a cross-functional team developing a new compact disc player, for example, must effectively communicate with each other to develop a disc player that customers will want, that will be of high quality, and that can be produced efficiently. Members of the team also must communicate with managers to secure the resources they need to develop the disc player and keep them informed of progress on the project.

Effective communication is necessary for managers and all members of an organization to increase efficiency, quality, responsiveness to customers, and innovation and thus gain a competitive advantage for the organization. Managers therefore must have a good understanding of the communication process if they are to perform effectively.

Lorenzo Zambrano is the CEO of Cemex, a cement company headquartered in Monterrey, Mexico, who has focused on helping developing countries. Zambrano uses IT to facilitate effective communication with resultant gains in efficiency, responsiveness to customers, and innovation, as indicated in the following "Managing Globally."

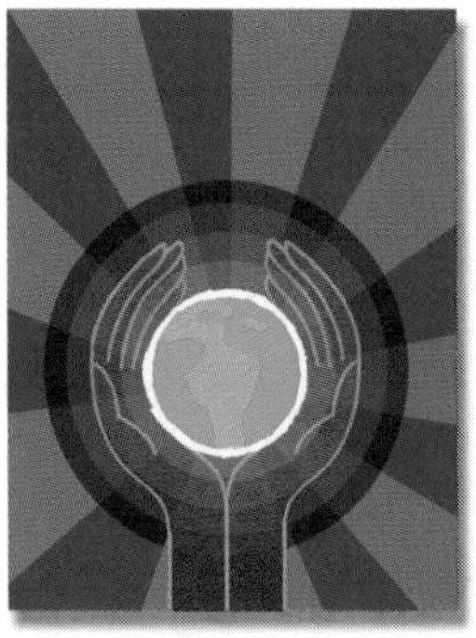

Managing Globally

Cemex Uses IT to Pave the Way in Cement

Cemex is more profitable than its competitors in the cement industry such as the French company, Lafarge, and the Swiss company, Holcim. And at least part of Cemex's secret for success lies in the way its CEO Lorenzo Zambrano embraces and takes advantage of information technology. Although Zambrano is the grandson of the founder of Cemex, he earned his current position as CEO by working hard and climbing the corporate hierarchy for 18 years until he was named CEO in 1985.[8] Ever since that, Zambrano has focused on how to use IT to improve efficiency, responsiveness to customers, and innovation at Cemex.

Early on, Zambrano focused on efficiency and lamented the lack of timely data on plant performance. To solve this problem, he hired computer programmers to develop a system to produce automated reports on factory performance, created an IT department in the 1980s in Mexico, and created a satellite system whereby data could be transmitted seamlessly to headquarters from the plants.[9] Zambrano has continued to embrace IT; one of his underlying philosophies has been to develop systems accessible to employees in the plants and the fields so they too can benefit from access to information.

Recently, Zambrano has pushed the IT envelope one step further. Cemex now provides employees with free computers and Internet connections for their homes for personal use. Moreover, Cemex trucks are equipped with computers and global positioning systems. Now dispatchers at Cemex know production output, customer orders, and truck locations so they can most efficiently deliver cement products to customers in a timely manner. With the new system in place, delivery times have been drastically shortened and each truck driver makes many more deliveries per day.[10] All in all, Zambrano has continued to put the latest in IT to good use at Cemex, and thus, maintained its competitive advantage in the cement industry.

Cemex executives join New York Stock Exchange President William Johnson (third from left) in ringing the opening bell at the NYSE as part of ceremonies held to mark the initial listing of Cemex shares on the NYSE in September, 1999.

The Communication Process

The communication process consists of two phases. In the *transmission phase,* information is shared between two or more individuals or groups. In the *feedback phase,* a common understanding is assured. In both phases, a number of distinct stages must occur for communication to take place (see Figure 15.1).[11]

Figure 15.1
The Communication Process

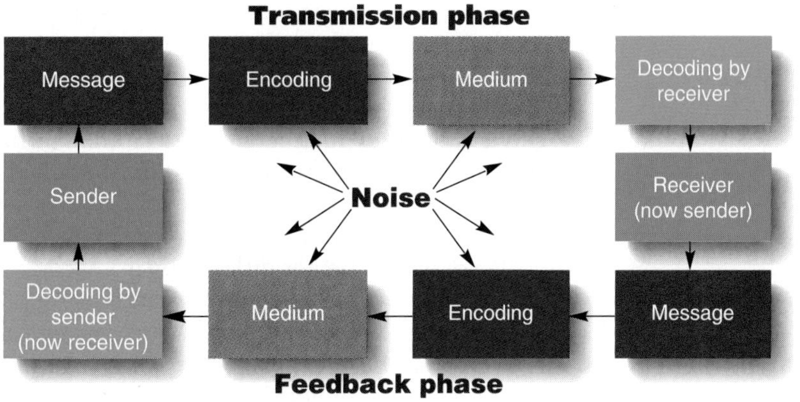

sender The person or group wishing to share information.

message The information that a sender wants to share.

encoding Translating a message into understandable symbols or language.

noise Anything that hampers any stage of the communication process.

receiver The person or group for which a message is intended.

medium The pathway through which an encoded message is transmitted to a receiver.

decoding Interpreting and trying to make sense of a message.

verbal communication The encoding of messages into words, either written or spoken.

nonverbal communication The encoding of messages by means of facial expressions, body language, and styles of dress.

Starting the transmission phase, the **sender,** the person or group wishing to share information with some other person or group, decides on the **message,** what information to communicate. Then the sender translates the message into symbols or language, a process called **encoding;** often messages are encoded into words. **Noise** is a general term that refers to anything that hampers any stage of the communication process.

Once encoded, a message is transmitted through a medium to the **receiver,** the person or group for which the message is intended. A **medium** is simply the pathway, such as a phone call, a letter, a memo, or face-to-face communication in a meeting, through which an encoded message is transmitted to a receiver. At the next stage, the receiver interprets and tries to make sense of the message, a process called **decoding.** This is a critical point in communication.

The feedback phase is initiated by the receiver (who becomes a sender). The receiver decides what message to send to the original sender (who becomes a receiver), encodes it, and transmits it through a chosen medium (see Figure 15.1). The message might contain a confirmation that the original message was received and understood or a restatement of the original message to make sure that it has been correctly interpreted; or it might include a request for more information. The original sender decodes the message and makes sure that a common understanding has been reached. If the original sender determines that a common understanding has not been reached, sender and receiver cycle through the whole process as many times as needed to reach a common understanding. Feedback eliminates misunderstandings, ensures that messages are correctly interpreted, and enables senders and receivers to reach a common understanding.

The encoding of messages into words, written or spoken, is **verbal communication.** We also encode messages without using written or spoken language. **Nonverbal communication** shares information by means of facial expressions (smiling, raising an eyebrow, frowning, dropping one's jaw), body language (posture, gestures, nods and shrugs), and even style of dress (casual, formal, conservative, trendy). Top managers in General Motors (GM), for example, wear slacks and sport jackets rather than suits when they walk around GM plants to communicate or signal that GM's old bureaucracy has been dismantled and that the company is decentralized and more informal than it used to be.[12] The trend toward increasing empowerment of the workforce has led some managers to dress informally to communicate that all employees of an organization are team members, working together to create value for customers.

Nonverbal communication can be used to back up or reinforce verbal communication. Just as a warm and genuine smile can back up words of appreciation for a job well done, a concerned facial expression can back up words of sympathy for a personal problem. In such cases, the congruence between verbal and the nonverbal communication helps to ensure that a common understanding is reached.

Sometimes when members of an organization decide not to express a message verbally, they inadvertently do so nonverbally. People tend to have less control over nonverbal communication, and often a verbal message that is withheld gets expressed through body language or facial expressions. A manager who agrees to a proposal that she or he actually is not in favor of may unintentionally communicate her disfavor by grimacing.

Sometimes nonverbal communication is used to send messages that cannot be sent through verbal channels. Many lawyers are well aware of this communication tactic. Lawyers are often schooled in techniques of nonverbal communication such as choosing where to stand in the courtroom for maximum effect and using eye contact during different stages of a trial. Lawyers sometimes get into trouble for using inappropriate nonverbal communication in an attempt to influence juries. In a Louisiana court, prosecuting attorney Thomas Pirtle was admonished and fined $2,500 by Judge Yada Magee for shaking his head in an expression of doubt, waving his arms indicating disfavor, and chuckling when the attorneys for the defense were stating their case.[13]

The Role of Perception in Communication

Perception plays a central role in communication and affects both transmission and feedback. In Chapter 4, we defined *perception* as the process through which people select, organize, and interpret sensory input to give meaning and order to the world around them. We mentioned that perception is inherently subjective and influenced by people's personalities, values, attitudes, and moods as well as by their experience and knowledge. When senders and receivers communicate with each other, they are doing so based on their own subjective perceptions. The encoding and decoding of messages and even the choice of a medium hinge on the perceptions of senders and receivers.

In addition, perceptual biases can hamper effective communication. Recall from Chapter 4 that *biases* are systematic tendencies to use information about others in ways that result in inaccurate perceptions. In Chapter 4, we described a number of biases that can result in diverse members of an organization being treated unfairly. These same biases also can lead to ineffective communication. For example, *stereotypes,* simplified and often inaccurate beliefs about the characteristics of particular groups of people, can interfere with the encoding and decoding of messages.

Suppose a manager stereotypes older workers as being fearful of change. When this manager encodes a message to an older worker about an upcoming change in the organization, she may downplay the extent of the change so as not to make the older worker feel stressed. The older worker, however, fears change no more than his younger colleagues fear it and decodes the message to mean that hardly any changes are going to be made. The older worker fails to adequately prepare for the change, and his performance subsequently suffers because of his lack of preparation for the change. Clearly, the ineffective communication was due to the manager's inaccurate assumptions about older workers. Instead of relying on stereotypes, effective managers strive to perceive other people accurately by focusing on their actual behaviors, knowledge, skills, and abilities. Accurate perceptions, in turn, contribute to effective communication.

The Dangers of Ineffective Communication

Because managers must communicate with others to perform their various roles and tasks, managers spend most of their time communicating, whether in meetings, in telephone conversations, through email, or in face-to-face interactions. Indeed, some experts estimate that managers spend approximately 85 percent of their time engaged in some form of communication.[14]

Effective communication is so important that managers cannot just concentrate on their own effective communication; they also have to help their subordinates be effective communicators. When all members of an organization are able to communicate effectively with each other and with people outside the organization, the organization is much more likely to perform highly and gain a competitive advantage.

When managers and other members of an organization are ineffective communicators, organizational performance suffers, and any competitive advantage the organization might have is likely to be lost. Moreover, poor communication sometimes can be downright dangerous and even lead to tragic and unnecessary loss of human life. For example, researchers from Harvard University recently studied the causes of mistakes, such as a patient receiving the wrong medication, in two large hospitals in the Boston area. They discovered that some mistakes in hospitals occur because of communication problems–physicians not having the information they need to correctly order medications for their patients or nurses not having the information they need to correctly administer medications. The researchers concluded that some of the responsibility for these mistakes lies with hospital management, which has not taken active steps to improve communication.[15]

Communication problems in the cockpit of airplanes and between flying crews and air traffic controllers are unfortunately all too common, sometimes with deadly consequences. In the late 1970s, two jets collided over Tenerife (one of the Canary Islands); because of miscommunication between a pilot and the control tower, 600 people were killed. The tower radioed to the pilot, "Clipper 1736 report clear of runway." The pilot mistakenly interpreted this message to mean that he was cleared for takeoff.[16] Unfortunately, errors like this one are not a thing of the past. A safety group at NASA tracked more than 6,000 unsafe flying incidents and found that communication difficulties caused approximately 529 of them.[17]

Information Richness and Communication Media

To be effective communicators, managers (and other members of an organization) need to select an appropriate communication medium for *each* message they send. Should a change in procedures be communicated to subordinates in a memo sent through email? Should a congratulatory message about a major accomplishment be communicated in a letter, in a phone call, or over lunch? Should a layoff announcement be made in a memo or at a plant meeting? Should the members of a purchasing team travel to Europe to cement a major agreement with a new supplier, or should they do so through faxes? Managers deal with these questions day in and day out.

There is no one best communication medium for managers to rely on. In choosing a communication medium for any message, managers need to consider three factors. The first and most important is the level of information richness that is needed. **Information richness** is the amount of information a communication medium can carry and the extent to which the medium enables the sender and receiver to reach a common understanding.[18] The communication media that managers use vary in their information richness (see Figure 15.2).[19] Media high in information richness are able to carry an extensive amount of information and generally enable receivers and senders to come to a common understanding.

information richness The amount of information that a communication medium can carry and the extent to which the medium enables the sender and receiver to reach a common understanding.

The second factor that managers need to take into account in selecting a communication medium is the *time* needed for communication, because managers' and other organizational members' time is valuable. Managers at United Parcel Service, for example, dramatically reduced the amount of time they spent by using video conferences instead of face-to-face communication, which required managers to travel overseas.[20]

The third factor that affects the choice of a communication medium is the *need for a paper or electronic trail* or some kind of written documentation that a message was sent and received. A manager may wish to document in writing, for example, that a subordinate was given a formal warning about excessive lateness.

In the remainder of this section we examine four types of communication media that vary along these three dimensions (information richness, time, and paper or electronic trail).[21]

Face-to-Face Communication

Face-to-face communication is the medium that is highest in information richness. When managers communicate face-to-face, they not only can take advantage of verbal communication but also can interpret each other's nonverbal signals such as facial expressions and body language. A look of concern or puzzlement can sometimes say more than a thousand words, and managers can respond to these nonverbal signals on the spot. Face-to-face communication also enables managers to receive instant feedback. Points of confusion, ambiguity, or misunderstanding can be resolved, and managers can cycle through the communication process as many times as they need to, to reach a common understanding.

management by wandering around A face-to-face communication technique in which a manager walks around a work area and talks informally with employees about issues and concerns.

Management by wandering around is a face-to-face communication technique that is effective for many managers at all levels in an organization.[22]

Figure 15.2
The Information Richness of Communication Media

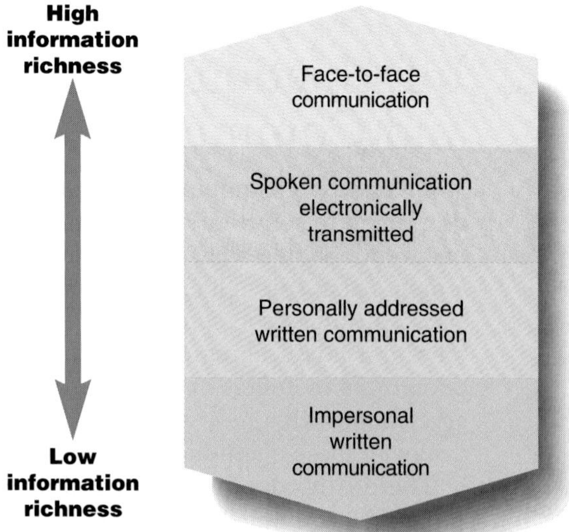

Rather than scheduling formal meetings with subordinates, managers walk around work areas and talk informally with employees about issues and concerns that both employees and managers may have. These informal conversations provide managers and subordinates with important information and at the same time foster the development of positive relationships. William Hewlett and David Packard, founders and former top managers of Hewlett-Packard, found management by wandering around a highly effective way to communicate with their employees.

Because face-to-face communication is highest in information richness, you might think that it should always be the medium of choice for managers. This is not the case, however, because of the amount of time it takes and the lack of a paper or electronic trail resulting from it. For messages that are important, personal, or likely to be misunderstood, it is often well worth managers' time to use face-to-face communication and, if need be, supplement it with some form of written communication documenting the message.

Advances in information technology are providing managers with new and close alternative communication media for face-to-face communication. Many organizations such as American Greetings Corp. and Hewlett-Packard are using *video conferences* to capture some of the advantages of face-to-face communication (such as access to facial expressions) while saving time and money because managers in different locations do not have to travel to meet with one another. During a video conference, managers in two or more locations communicate with each other over large TV or video screens; they not only hear each other but also see each other throughout the meeting.

In addition to saving travel costs, video conferences sometimes have other advantages. Managers at American Greetings have found that decisions get made more quickly when video conferences are used because more managers can be involved in the decision-making process and therefore fewer managers have to be consulted outside the meeting itself. Managers at Hewlett-Packard have found that video conferences have shortened new product development time by 30 percent for similar reasons. Video conferences also seem to lead to more efficient meetings. Some managers have found that their meetings are 20 to 30 percent shorter when video conferences are used instead of face-to-face meetings.[23]

Taking video conferences one step further, IBM and TelePort Corporation have joined forces to build virtual dining rooms in which top managers can actually have power meals with other managers in another location. Managers in one location are seated around a large, round table bisected by a huge video screen on which they are able to see their life-size dining partners in another location sitting around the same kind of table having the same kind of meal. Even though managers may be hundreds or thousands of miles apart, they can eat together as they discuss pressing concerns. The cameras enabling the transmission of the video images are hidden in flower arrangements so they do not unnerve the diners. The cost of these tables starts at $150,000, and major hotel chains such as Hilton, Hyatt, and Doubletree are interested in purchasing them for use by their business customers.[24]

Video conferencing allows for face-to-face communication between two or more people. It also saves on travel costs and the time involved to fly to other locations.

Spoken Communication Electronically Transmitted

After face-to-face communication, spoken communication electronically transmitted over phone lines is second highest in information richness (see Figure 15.2). Although managers communicating over the telephone do not have access to body language and facial expressions, they do have access to the tone of voice in which a message is delivered, the parts of the message the sender emphasizes, and the general manner in which the message is spoken, in addition to the actual words themselves. Thus, telephone conversations have the capacity to convey extensive amounts of information. Managers also can ensure that mutual understanding is reached because they can get quick feedback over the phone and answer questions.

Voice mail systems and answering machines also allow managers to send and receive verbal electronic messages over telephone lines. Voice mail systems are companywide systems that enable senders to record messages for members of an organization who are away from their desks and allow receivers to access their messages when hundreds of miles away from the office. Such systems are obviously a necessity when managers are frequently out of the office, and managers on the road are well advised to periodically check their voice mail.

Personally Addressed Written Communication

Lower than electronically transmitted verbal communication in information richness is personally addressed written communication (see Figure 15.2). One of the advantages of face-to-face communication and verbal communication electronically transmitted is that they both tend to demand attention, which helps ensure that receivers pay attention. Personally addressed written communication such as memos and letters also have this advantage. Because they are addressed to a particular person, the chances are good that the person will actually pay attention to (and read) them. Moreover, the sender can write the message in a way that the receiver is most likely to understand. Like voice mail, written communication does not enable a receiver to have his or her questions answered immediately, but when messages are clearly written and feedback is provided, common understandings can still be reached.

Even if managers use face-to-face communication, a follow-up in writing is often needed for messages that are important or complicated and need to be referred to later on. This is precisely what Karen Stracker, a hospital administrator, did when she needed to tell one of her subordinates about an important change in the way the hospital would be handling denials of insurance benefits. Stracker met with the subordinate and described the changes face-to-face. Once she was sure that the subordinate understood them, she handed her a sheet of instructions to follow, which essentially summarized the information they had discussed.

Email also fits into this category of communication media because senders and receivers are communicating through personally addressed written words. The words, however, are appearing on their personal computer screens rather than on pieces of paper. Email is becoming so widespread in the business world that managers are even developing their own email etiquette. To save time, Andrew Giangola, a manager at book publisher Simon & Schuster, used to type all his email messages in capital letters. He was surprised when a receiver of one of his messages responded, "Why are you screaming at me?" Messages in capital letters are often perceived as being shouted or screamed, and thus Giangola's routine use of capital letters was bad email etiquette. Here are some other guidelines from polite emailers: Always punctuate messages; do not ramble on or say more than you need to; do not act as though you do not understand something when in fact you do understand it; and pay attention to spelling and format (put a memo in memo form). To avoid embarrassments like Giangola's, managers at Simon & Schuster created a task force to develop guidelines for email etiquette.[25]

The growing popularity of email has also enabled many workers and managers to become *telecommuters,* people who are employed by organizations and work out of offices in their own homes. There are approximately 8.4 million telecommuters in the United States. Many telecommuters indicate that the flexibility of working at home enables them to be more productive while giving them a chance to be closer to their families and not waste time traveling to and from the office.[26] A recent study conducted by Georgetown University found that 75 percent of the telecommuters surveyed said their productivity increased and 83 percent said their home life improved once they started telecommuting.[27]

Unfortunately, the growing use of email has been accompanied by growing abuse of email. Some employees sexually harass coworkers through email, and divorcing spouses who work together sometimes sign their spouse's name to email and send insulting or derogatory messages to the spouse's boss. Robert Mirguet, information systems manager at Eastman Kodak, has indicated that some Kodak employees have used Kodak's email system to try to start their own businesses during working hours. Kodak managers monitor employees' email messages when they suspect some form of abuse. Top managers also complain that sometimes their email is clogged with junk mail. In a recent survey over half of the organizations surveyed acknowledged some problems with their email systems.[28]

To avoid these and other costly forms of email abuse, managers need to develop a clear policy specifying what company email can and should be used for and what is out of bounds. Managers also should clearly communicate this policy to all members of an organization, as well as the procedures that will be used when email abuse is suspected and the consequences that will result when email abuse is confirmed.

Email abuse often occurs in conjunction with surfing the Internet on company time. Troubling statistics suggest that approximately 70 percent of the total amount of time spent surfing the Internet is time when surfers are at work.[29] As indicated in the following "Ethics in Action," more and more organizations are cracking down on this extracurricular activity.

Ethics in Action

Web Surfers Beware

According to a study conducted by the American Management Association, close to 75 percent of the medium and large companies surveyed reported that they engaged in some kind of monitoring of employees' email and Internet activities.[30] Critics of such monitoring suggest that monitoring is an invasion of privacy. Proponents suggest that Web surfing costs millions in lost productivity and also exposes a company to potential lawsuits, given that the majority of visits to pornographic websites occur during the workday. Recently, Xerox fired 40 workers for visiting porn sites at work in violation of Xerox's Internet policy.[31]

In a sluggish economy with more job seekers than positions open, corporate crackdowns on Web surfing are on the rise whether it be for trading stocks on company time, conversing in chat rooms, or visiting porn sites. Websense, a company that provides monitoring systems for Internet usage, recently conducted a survey that indicated one in three companies have fired employees for abusing the Internet. E*Trade, JDS Uniphase, Allen Matkins (a law firm in Los Angeles), and Xerox join the growing number of companies relying on monitoring to curtail Internet abuse.[32]

Monitoring systems can scan for key words and then keep track of questionable words or phrases.[33] Alternatively, to reduce certain forms of temptation, some organizations install filters that prevent certain Internet sites, such as porn sites, from being accessed at work. According to Dr. David Greenfield, who manages the Center of Internet Addiction in West Hartford, Connecticut, porn sites are the most common nonwork-related sites people visit while they are supposed to be working.[34] Clearly, workers who want to keep their jobs are advised to send nonwork-related emails and surf the Web on their own time.

Impersonal Written Communication

Impersonal written communication is lowest in information richness and is well suited for messages that need to reach a large number of receivers. Because such messages are not addressed to particular receivers, feedback is unlikely, so managers must make sure that messages sent by this medium are written clearly in language that all receivers will understand.

Managers often find company newsletters useful vehicles for reaching large numbers of employees. Many managers give their newsletters catchy names to spark employee interest and also to inject a bit of humor into the workplace. Managers at the pork-sausage maker Bob Evans Farms Inc. called their newsletter "The Squealer" for many years but recently changed the title to "The Homesteader" to reflect the company's broadened line of products. Managers at American Greetings Corp., at Yokohama Tire Corp., and at Eastman Kodak call their newsletters "Expressions," "TreadLines," and "Kodakery," respectively. Managers at Quaker State Corp. held a contest to rename their newsletter. Among the 1,000 names submitted were "The Big Q Review," "The Pipeline," and "Q. S. Oil Press"; the winner was "On Q."[35]

Managers can use impersonal written communication for various messages, including rules, regulations, policies, newsworthy information, and announcements of changes in procedures or the arrival of new organizational members. Impersonal written communication also can communicate instructions about how to use machinery or how to process work orders or customer requests. For these kinds of messages, the paper or electronic trail left by this communication medium can be invaluable for employees.

information overload The potential for important information to be ignored or overlooked while tangential information receives attention.

Just as with personal written communication, impersonal written communication can be delivered and retrieved electronically, and this is increasingly the case in companies large and small. Unfortunately, the ease with which electronic messages can be spread has lead to their proliferation. Many managers' and workers' electronic in-boxes are so backlogged that often they do not have time to read all the electronic work-related information available to them. The problem with such **information overload** is the potential for important information to be ignored or overlooked while tangential information receives attention. Moreover, information overload can result in thousands of hours and millions in dollars in lost productivity. Realizing the hazards of overload, Nathan Zeldes, computing productivity manager for Intel's division in Israel, decided to tackle this problem head on.[36] In Zeldes' division, some 3 million emails are sent or received each day, and some employees receive more than 300 messages per day. On average, employees spend around two and a half hours per day dealing with this barrage of information. To combat this problem, Zeldes developed a training program to meet the overload problem head-on as well as educate employees about how email can improve productivity and be used in ways that limit overload. Reactions to the training program have been positive and it is now used around the globe in Intel divisions.[37] Some of Intel's organizational learning about email and overload are captured in their 10 commandments of email, reproduced in the following "Information Technology Byte."

Information Technology Byte

Intel's "10 Commandments of Email"

1. Don't use your inbox as a catchall folder for everything you need to work on. Read items once, and answer them immediately if necessary, delete them if possible, or move them to project-specific folders.
2. Set up a "Five Weeks Folder" that deletes its content automatically after five weeks. Use it as a repository for messages you're unsure about, such as that email you want to delete, but you're not sure if the guy's going to call you tomorrow and ask you about it.
3. Assist colleagues' inbox-filtering efforts by agreeing on acronyms to use in subject lines that quickly identify action items and other important messages. Sample acronyms: <AR>, Action Required; <MSR>, Monthly Status Report.
4. Send group mail only when it is useful to *all* recipients. Use "reply-to-all" and "CC:" buttons sparingly.
5. Ask to be removed from distribution lists that you don't need to be on.
6. To cut down on pileup, use the "out-of-office" feature of your email, in addition to your voice mail, to notify people when you are traveling.
7. When possible, send a message that is only a subject line, so recipients don't have to open the email to read a single line. End the subject line with <EOM>, the acronym for End of Message.
8. Graphics and attachments are fun, but they slow down your ability to download messages when you're on the road. Use them sparingly.
9. If you're sending an attachment larger than 5 MB to a large group of recipients, consider putting it on the company's website or intranet instead.
10. Be specific. If you send a 20-page attachment, tell the recipient that the important information is on pages 2 and 17.[38]

Communication Networks

Although various communication media are utilized, communication in organizations tends to flow in certain patterns. The pathways along which information flows in groups and teams and throughout an organization are called **communication networks**. Which communication network a group uses depends on the nature of the group's tasks and the extent to which group members need to communicate with each other to achieve group goals.

communication networks The pathways along which information flows in groups and teams and throughout the organization.

Communication Networks in Groups and Teams

As you learned in Chapter 14, groups and teams, whether they are cross-functional teams, top-management teams, command groups, self-managed work teams, or task forces, are the building blocks of organizations. Four communication networks can develop in groups and teams: the wheel, the chain, the circle, and the all-channel network (see Figure 15.3).

WHEEL NETWORK In a wheel network, information flows to and from one central member of the group. Other group members do not need to communicate with each other to perform well, and the group can accomplish its goals by directing all communication to and from the central member. Wheel networks are often found in command groups with pooled task interdependence. Picture a group of taxi cab drivers who report to the same dispatcher, who is also their supervisor. Each driver needs to communicate with the dispatcher, but the drivers do not need to communicate with each other. In groups such as this, the wheel network results in efficient communication, saving time without compromising performance. Though found in groups, wheel networks are not found in teams because they do not allow for the intense interactions characteristic of teamwork.

Figure 15.3 Communication Networks in Groups and Teams

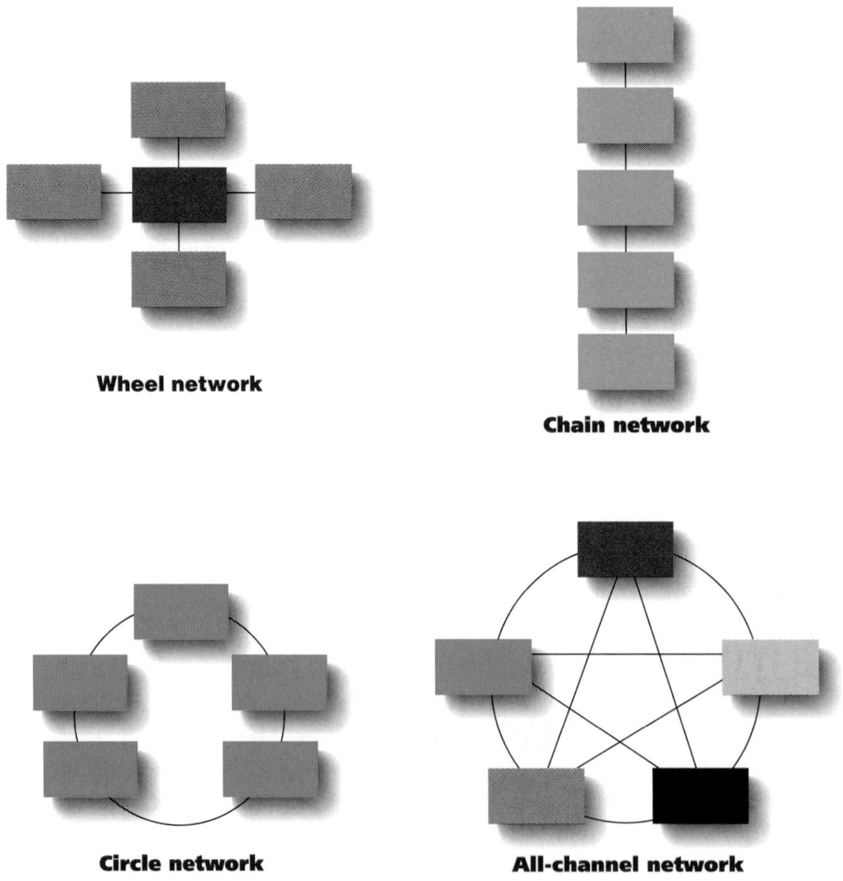

CHAIN NETWORK In a chain network, members communicate with each other in a predetermined sequence. Chain networks are found in groups with sequential task interdependence, such as an assembly line. When group work has to be performed in a predetermined order, the chain network is often found because group members need to communicate with those whose work directly precedes and follows their own. Like wheel networks, chain networks tend not to exist in teams because of the limited amount of interaction among group members.

CIRCLE NETWORK In a circle network, group members communicate with others who are similar to them in experiences, beliefs, areas of expertise, background, office location, or even where they sit when the group meets. Members of task forces and standing committees, for example, tend to communicate with others who have similar experiences or backgrounds. People also tend to communicate with people whose offices are next to their own. Like wheel and chain networks, circle networks are most often found in groups that are not teams.

ALL-CHANNEL NETWORK An all-channel network is found in teams. It is characterized by high levels of communication: Every team member communicates with every other team member. Top-management teams, cross-functional teams, and self-managed work teams frequently have all-channel networks. The reciprocal task interdependence often found in such teams requires information flows in all directions. Computer software specially designed for use by work groups can help maintain effective communication in teams with all-channel networks because it provides team members with an efficient way to share information with each other.

Organizational Communication Networks

An organization chart may seem to be a good summary of an organization's communication network, but often it is not. An organization chart summarizes *formal* reporting relationships in an organization and the formal pathways along which communication takes place. Often, however, communication is *informal* and flows around issues, goals, projects, and ideas instead of moving up and down the organizational hierarchy in an orderly fashion. Thus, an organization's communication network includes not only the formal communication pathways summarized in an organizational chart but also informal communication pathways along which a great deal of communication takes place (see Figure 15.4)

Communication can and should occur across departments and groups as well as within them and up and down and sideways in the corporate hierarchy. Communication up and down the corporate hierarchy is often called *vertical* communication. Communication among employees at the same level in the hierarchy or sideways is called *horizontal* communication. Managers obviously cannot determine in advance what an organization's communication network will be, nor should they try to. Instead, to accomplish goals and perform at a high level, organizational members should be free to communicate with whomever they need to contact. Because organizational goals change over time, so too do organizational communication networks. Informal communication networks can

Figure 15.4
Formal and Informal Communication Networks in an Organization

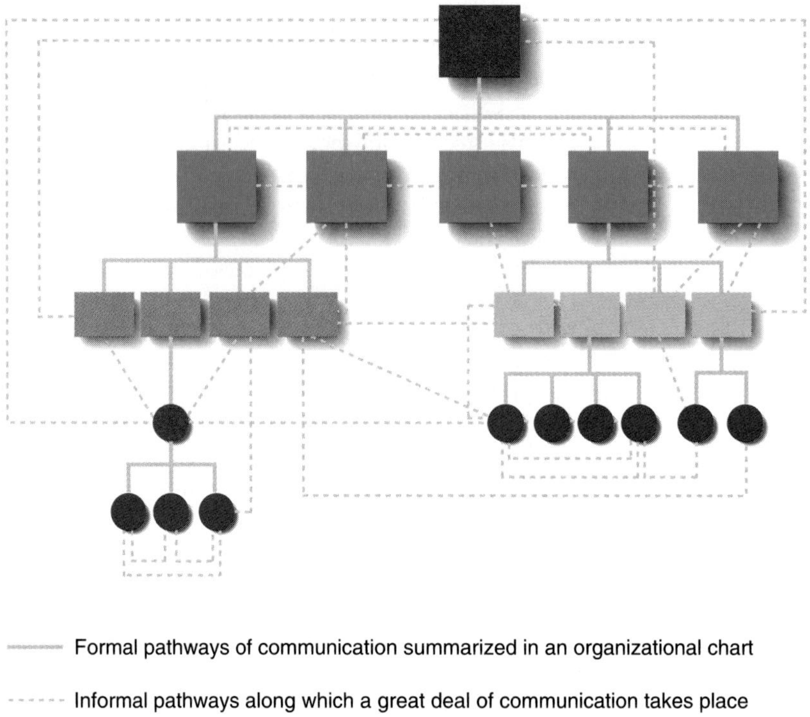

contribute to an organization's competitive advantage because they help ensure that organizational members have the information they need when they need it to accomplish their goals.

grapevine An informal communication network along which unofficial information flows.

One informal organizational communication network along which information flows quickly if not always accurately is the grapevine. The **grapevine** is an informal network along which unofficial information flows.[39] People in an organization who seem to know everything about everyone are prominent in the grapevine. Information spread over the grapevine can be on issues of either a business (an impending takeover) or a personal (the CEO's separation from his wife) nature.

External Networks

In addition to networks within an organization, managers, professional employees, and those with work-related ties outside of their employing organization often are part of external networks whose members span a variety of companies. For example, scientists working in universities and in corporations often communicate in networks formed around common underlying interests in a particular topic or subfield. As another example, physicians working around the country belong to specialty professional associations that help them keep up-to-date on the latest advances in their fields. For some managers and professionals, participation in these interest-oriented networks is just as important, or even more important, than internal company networks. Networks of contacts working in the same discipline or field or with similar expertise and knowledge can be very helpful, for example, when an individual is looking to change jobs or even find a job after a layoff. Unfortunately, discrimination and stereotypes have led to some of these networks being off-limits to certain individuals due to

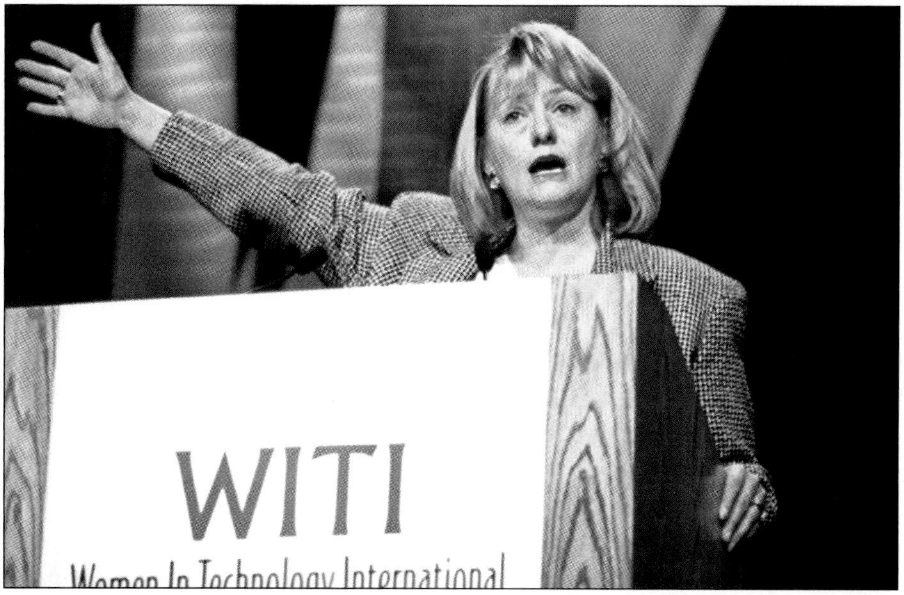

Autodesk, Inc., CEO Carol Bartz gives the opening keynote address to 3,000 professional women at the annual Women in Technology conference. Often excluded from external networks dominated by men, growing numbers of women are participating in networks of their own creation.

gender or race. For example, the term *old boys' network* alludes to the fact that networks of contacts for job leads, government contracts, or venture capital funding have often been dominated by men and off-limits to women, a state of affairs that some women are seeking to change, as indicated in the following "Focus on Diversity."[40]

Focus on Diversity

Women Benefit from External Networks of Contacts

Often excluded or unwelcome in external networks dominated by men, growing numbers of professional women are participating in networks of their own creation, and benefiting from them. For example, the Bohemian Grove is a 130-year-old network of men in high positions in the corporate world and government. They get together every summer for two weeks in the redwood forests in Northern California to network and participate in a variety of activities ranging from group discussions to recreational pastimes. Women are not allowed.[41]

Enter Belizean Grove, founded by Susan Stautberg, president of New York-based PartnerCom which creates advisory boards for companies around the globe. Belizean Grove is a by-invitation get-together of high-level women in the corporate world, academia, and government which convenes in Belize, Central America. A diverse group of women participate in Belizean Grove including venture capitalists, entrepreneurs, government appointees, and professors. Panel discussions cover a variety of topics and women attendees bond with each other emotionally, often creating lasting networks of contacts.[42]

Other networks of women professionals are also proliferating. For example, former and current female employees of certain companies such as Goldman Sachs and McKinsey have company-specific networks they can join similar to college alumni networks.[43] Women benefit from such networks in the same ways as men (e.g., access to job leads, funding sources for new ventures, advice, etc.). Additionally, such external networks may be even more important for women than men because professional women often have fewer role models and mentors available to them than their male counterparts.[44] This may be particularly true in male-dominated occupations such as construction. In this industry, one network women can turn to is the National Association of Women in Construction (NAWIC). It not only provides women in this industry with information and advice on a variety of issues that concern them but also provides them an opportunity to network with others. Clearly, external networks are important for all kinds of employees.

Technological Advances in Communication

Exciting advances in information technology have dramatically increased managers' abilities to communicate with others as well as to quickly access information to make decisions. Three advances that are having major impacts on managerial communication are the Internet, intranets, and groupware. However, as profiled in "A Manager's Challenge," managers must not lose sight of the fact that communication is essentially a human endeavor, no matter how it may be facilitated by IT.

The Internet

Internet A global system of computer networks.

The **Internet** is a global system of computer networks that is easy to join and used by employees of organizations around the world to communicate inside and outside their companies. Over 110 million people in the United States alone use the Internet on a regular basis and half of these users are women.[45] Managers in more than 21,000 companies use the Internet to communicate, and over 75 percent of new users are hooked up by means of their companies' Internet links.[46] Table 15.1 lists the 10 countries with the most Internet users.

Managers and companies use the Internet for a variety of communication purposes: to communicate with suppliers and contractors to maintain appropriate inventory levels and keep them informed of progress on projects and changes in schedules; to communicate within a company, primarily to and from

Table 15.1
The Global Top Ten Countries in Internet Use

Country	Internet Users
United States	110,825,000
Japan	18,156,000
Great Britain	13,975,000
Canada	13,277,000
Germany	12,285,000
Australia	6,837,000
Brazil	6,790,000
China	6,308,000
France	5,696,000
South Korea	5,688,000

Source: *ComputerIndustry Almanac*; obtained from an article in *Newsweek,* "We've All Got Mail," May 15, 2000.

distant offices to corporate headquarters by email; to advertise to potential customers; to sell goods and services to customers; to obtain information about other companies including competitors; to provide the general public with information about the company; to recruit new employees.[47]

The World Wide Web is the business district on the Internet with multimedia capabilities. Companies' home pages on the World Wide Web are like offices that potential customers can visit. In attractive graphic displays on home pages, managers communicate information about the goods and services they offer, why customers should want to purchase them, how to purchase them, and where to purchase them. By surfing the Web and visiting competitors' home pages, managers can see what their competitors are doing.[48] Each day, hundreds of new companies add themselves to the growing numbers of organizations on the World Wide Web.[49] Approximately 18 million people in the United States have used the World Wide Web within the last 24 hours.[50]

By all counts, use of the Internet for communication is burgeoning. Nevertheless, some managers and organizations do not conduct certain business transactions over the Internet because of security concerns. Ironically, the very reason why the Internet was created and why it is so popular–it allows millions of senders and receivers of messages to share vast amounts of information with each other–hampered its use for certain business transactions because of a lack of security. Just as managers do not want to freely distribute information about their accounts to the public, customers want to hide rather than share their credit card numbers. Experts suggest, however, that the Internet can be made reasonably secure so that accounts, credit cards, business documents, and even cash are relatively safe.

Gene Spafford, a professor who is working on Purdue University's computer-security research project called COAST, suggests that although perfect security can never be obtained with any form of communication, good security on the Internet is certainly possible.[51] In addition, when considering security on the Internet, managers need to consider the security of alternative communication media. Scott McNealy, chairman and CEO of Sun Microsystems, says that his email is much more secure and harder for unwanted intruders to access than is his regular mail, which is just dropped into an unlocked box.[52]

Intranets

Growing numbers of managers are finding that the technology on which the World Wide Web and the Internet are based has enabled them to improve communication within their own companies by creating a new type of communication medium. These managers are using the technology that allows information sharing over the Internet to share information within their own companies through company networks called **intranets.** Intranets are being used not just in high-tech companies such as Sun Microsystems and Digital Equipment but also in companies such as Chevron, Goodyear, Levi Strauss, Pfizer, Chrysler, Motorola, and Ford.[53]

intranet A companywide system of computer networks.

Intranets allow employees to have many kinds of information at their fingertips (or keyboards). Directories, phone books, manuals, inventory figures, product specifications, information about customers, biographies of top managers and the board of directors, global sales figures, minutes from meetings, annual reports, delivery schedules, and up-to-the-minute revenue, cost, and profit figures are just a few examples of the information that can be shared through intranets. Intranets can be accessed with different kinds of computers so that all members of an organization can be linked together. Intranets are protected from unwanted intrusions by hackers or by competitors with firewall security systems that request users to provide passwords and other pieces of identification before being able to access the intranet.[54]

The advantage of intranets lies in their versatility as a communication medium. They can be used for a number of purposes by people who may have little expertise in computer software and programming. While some managers complain that the Internet is too crowded and the World Wide Web too glitzy, informed managers are realizing that using the Internet's technology to create their own computer network may be one of the Internet's biggest contributions to organizational effectiveness.

Groupware

groupware Computer software that enables members of groups and teams to share information with each other.

Groupware is computer software that enables members of groups and teams to share information with each other to improve their communication and performance. Managers in the Bank of Montreal and other organizations have had success in introducing groupware into their organizations; managers in the advertising agency Young & Rubicam and other organizations have encountered considerable resistance to groupware.[55] Even in companies where the introduction of groupware has been successful, some employees resist using it. Some clerical and secretarial workers at the Bank of Montreal, for example, were dismayed to find that their neat and accurate files were being consolidated into computer files that would be accessible to many of their coworkers.

Managers are most likely to be able to successfully use groupware in their organizations as a communication medium when certain conditions are met:[56]

1. The work is group or team based, and members are rewarded, at least in part, for group performance.
2. Groupware has the full support of top management.
3. The culture of the organization stresses flexibility and knowledge sharing, and the organization does not have a rigid hierarchy of authority.
4. Groupware is being used for a specific purpose and is viewed as a tool for group or team members to use to work more effectively together, not as a personal source of power or advantage.
5. Employees receive adequate training in the use of computers and groupware.[57]

Employees are likely to resist using groupware and managers are likely to have a difficult time implementing it when people are working primarily on their own and are rewarded for their own individual performances.[58] Under these circumstances, information is often viewed as a source of power and people are reluctant to share information with others by means of groupware.

Take the case of three salespeople who sell insurance policies in the same geographic area; they are paid individually based on the number of policies each of them sells and the retention of their customers. The supervisor of the salespeople invested in some groupware and encouraged the salespeople to use the groupware to share information about their sales, sales tactics, customers, insurance providers, and claim histories. The supervisor told the salespeople that having all this information at their fingertips would allow them to be more efficient as well as sell more policies and provide better service to customers.

Even though they received extensive training in how to use the groupware, the salespeople never got around to using it. Why? They all were afraid that giving away their secrets to their coworkers might reduce their own commissions. In this situation, the salespeople were essentially competing with each other and thus had no incentive to share information. Under such circumstances, a groupware system may not be a wise choice of communication medium. Conversely, had the salespeople been working as a team and had they received bonuses based on team performance, groupware might have been an effective communication medium.

In order for an organization to gain a competitive advantage, managers need to keep up-to-date on advances in information technology such as groupware, intranets, and the Internet. But managers should not adopt these or other advances without first considering carefully how the advance in question might improve communication and performance in their particular groups, teams, or whole organization. Moreover, as highlighted in "A Manager's Challenge," managers need to keep in mind that all of these advances in IT are tools for people to use to facilitate effective communication and not ends in and of themselves.

Tips for New Managers

Information Richness and Communication Media

1. For messages that are important, personal, or likely to be misunderstood, consider using face-to-face communication or video conferences.
2. Consider using video conferences instead of face-to-face meetings to save time and travel costs.
3. Frequently check voice mail when out of the office.
4. For messages that are complex and need to be referred to later on, use written communication either alone or in conjunction with face-to-face communication, verbal communication electronically transmitted, or video conferences.
5. Develop a clear policy specifying what company email can and cannot be used for and communicate this policy to all organizational members.

Communication Skills for Managers

Some of the various barriers to effective communication in organizations have their origins in senders. When messages are unclear, incomplete, or difficult to understand, when they are sent over an inappropriate medium, or when no provision for feedback is made, communication suffers. Other communication barriers have their origins in receivers. When receivers pay no attention to or do not listen to messages or when they make no effort to understand the meaning of a message, communication is likely to be ineffective. Sometimes advanced information technology such as automated phone systems can hamper effective communication to the extent that the human element is missing, as profiled in "A Manager's Challenge."

To overcome these barriers and effectively communicate with others, managers (as well as other organizational members) must possess or develop certain communication skills. Some of these skills are particularly important when managers send messages; others are critical when managers *receive* messages. These skills help ensure that managers will be able to share information, will have the information they need to make good decisions and take action, and will be able to reach a common understanding with others.

Communication Skills for Managers as Senders

Organizational effectiveness depends on managers (as well as other organizational members) being able to effectively send messages to people inside and outside an organization. Table 15.2 summarizes seven communication skills that help ensure that when managers send messages, they are properly understood and the transmission phase of the communication process is effective. Let's see what each skill entails.

SEND CLEAR AND COMPLETE MESSAGES Managers need to learn how to send a message that is clear and complete. A message is clear when it is easy for the receiver to understand and interpret, and it is complete when it contains all the information that the sender and receiver need to reach a common understanding. In striving to send messages that are both clear and complete, managers must learn to anticipate how receivers will interpret messages and adjust messages to eliminate sources of misunderstanding or confusion.

ENCODE MESSAGES IN SYMBOLS THE RECEIVER UNDERSTANDS Managers need to appreciate that when they encode messages, they should use symbols or language that the receiver understands. When sending messages in English to receivers whose native language is not English, for example, it is important to use commonplace vocabulary and to avoid using clichés that, when translated, may make little sense and sometimes are either comical or insulting.

jargon Specialized language that members of an occupation, group, or organization develop to facilitate communication among themselves.

Jargon, specialized language that members of an occupation, group, or organization develop to facilitate communication among themselves, should never be used when communicating with people outside the occupation, group, or organization. For example, truck drivers refer to senior-citizen drivers as "doubleknits," compact cars as "rollerskates," highway dividing lines as "paints," double or triple freight trailers as "pups," and orange barrels around road construction areas as "Schneider eggs." Using this jargon among themselves results in effective

Table 15.2
Seven Communication Skills for Managers as Senders of Messages

- Send messages that are clear and complete.
- Encode messages in symbols that the receiver understands.
- Select a medium that is appropriate for the message.
- Select a medium that the receiver monitors.
- Avoid filtering and information distortion.
- Ensure that a feedback mechanism is built into messages.
- Provide accurate information to ensure that misleading rumors are not spread.

communication because they know precisely what is being referred to. But if a truck driver used this language to send a message to a receiver who did not drive trucks (such as "That rollerskate can't stay off the paint"), the receiver would have no clue to what the message meant.[59]

SELECT A MEDIUM APPROPRIATE FOR THE MESSAGE As you have learned, when relying on verbal communication, managers can choose from a variety of communication media, including face-to-face communication in person, written letters, memos, newsletters, phone conversations, email, voice mail, faxes, and video conferences. When choosing among these media, managers need to take into account the level of information richness required, time constraints, and the need for a paper/electronic trail. A primary concern in choosing an appropriate medium is the nature of the message. Is it personal, important, nonroutine and likely to be misunderstood and in need of further clarification? If it is, face-to-face communication is likely to be in order.

SELECT A MEDIUM THAT THE RECEIVER MONITORS Another factor that managers need to take into account when selecting a communication medium is whether the medium is one that the receiver monitors. Managers differ in the communication media they pay attention to. Many managers simply select the communication medium that they themselves use the most and are most comfortable with, but doing this can often lead to ineffective communication. Managers who dislike telephone conversations and too many face-to-face interactions may prefer to use email, send many email messages per day, and check their own email every few hours. Managers who prefer to communicate with people in person or over the phone may have email addresses but rarely use email and forget to check for email messages. No matter how much a manager likes email, sending email to someone who does not check his or her email is futile. Learning which managers like things in writing and which prefer face-to-face interactions and then using the appropriate medium enhances the chance that receivers will actually receive and pay attention to messages.

A related consideration is whether receivers have disabilities that hamper their ability to decode certain messages. A blind receiver, for example, cannot read a written message. Managers should ensure that their employees with disabilities have resources available to communicate effectively with others. For example, deaf employees can effectively communicate over the telephone by using text-typewriters that have a screen and a keyboard on which senders can type messages. The message travels along the phone lines to special operators called communication assistants, who translate the typed message into a text that receivers can listen to. Receivers' spoken replies are translated into typewritten text by the communication assistants and appear on the senders' screens. The communication assistants relay messages back and forth to each sender and receiver.[60] Additionally, use of fax and email instead of phone conversations can aid deaf employees.

filtering Withholding part of a message out of the mistaken belief that the receiver does not need or will not want the information.

AVOID FILTERING AND INFORMATION DISTORTION Filtering occurs when senders withhold part of a message because they (mistakenly) think that the receiver does not need the information or will not want to receive it. Filtering can occur at all levels in an organization and in both vertical and horizontal communication. As described in Chapter 8, rank-and-file workers may filter messages they send to first-line managers, first-line managers may filter messages to middle managers, and middle managers may filter messages to top managers. Such filtering is most likely to take place when messages contain bad news or problems that subordinates are afraid they will be blamed for.

information distortion Changes in the meaning of a message as the message passes through a series of senders and receivers.

Information distortion occurs when the meaning of a message changes as the message passes through a series of senders and receivers. Some information distortion is accidental–due to faulty encoding and decoding or to a lack of feedback. Other information distortion is deliberate. Senders may alter a message to make themselves or their groups look good and to receive special treatment.

Managers themselves should avoid filtering and distorting information. But how can they eliminate these barriers to effective communication throughout their organization? They need to establish trust throughout the organization. Subordinates who trust their managers believe that they will not be blamed for things beyond their control and will be treated fairly. Managers who trust their subordinates provide them with clear and complete information and do not hold things back.

INCLUDE A FEEDBACK MECHANISM IN MESSAGES Because feedback is essential for effective communication, managers should build a feedback mechanism into the messages they send. They either should include a request for feedback or indicate when and how they will follow up on the message to make sure that it was received and understood. When managers write letters and memos or send faxes, they can request that the receiver respond with comments and suggestions in a letter, memo, or fax; schedule a meeting to discuss the issue; or follow up with a phone call. By building feedback mechanisms such as these into their messages, managers ensure that they get heard and are understood.

rumors Unofficial pieces of information of interest to organizational members but with no identifiable source.

PROVIDE ACCURATE INFORMATION **Rumors** are unofficial pieces of information of interest to organizational members but with no identifiable source. Rumors spread quickly once they are started and usually they concern topics that organizational members think are important, interesting, or amusing. Rumors, however, can be misleading and can cause harm to individual employees and their organizations when they are false, malicious, or unfounded. Managers can halt the spread of misleading rumors by providing organizational members with accurate information on matters that concern them.

Communication Skills for Managers as Receivers

Managers receive as many messages as they send. Thus, managers must possess or develop communication skills that allow them to be effective receivers of messages. Table 15.3 summarizes three of these important skills, which we examine in greater detail.

Table 15.3
Three Communication Skills for Managers as Receivers of Messages

- Pay attention.
- Be a good listener.
- Be empathetic.

PAY ATTENTION Because of their multiple roles and tasks, managers often are overloaded and forced to think about several things at once. Pulled in many different directions, they sometimes do not pay sufficient attention to the messages they receive. To be effective, however, managers should always pay attention to messages they receive, no matter how busy they are. When discussing a project with a subordinate, an effective manager focuses on the project and not on an upcoming meeting with his or her own boss. Similarly, when managers are reading written forms of communication, they should focus their attention on understanding what they are reading; they should not be sidetracked into thinking about other issues.

BE A GOOD LISTENER Managers (and all other members of an organization) can do several things to be good listeners. First, managers should refrain from interrupting senders in the middle of a message so that senders do not lose their train of thought and managers do not jump to erroneous conclusions based on incomplete information. Second, managers should maintain good eye contact with senders so that senders feel their listeners are paying attention; doing this also helps managers focus on what they are hearing. Third, after receiving a message, managers should ask questions to clarify points of ambiguity or confusion. Fourth, managers should paraphrase, or restate in their own words, points senders make that are important, complex, or open to alternative interpretations; this is the feedback component so critical to successful communication.

Managers, like most people, often like to hear themselves talk rather than listen to others. Part of being a good communicator, however, is being a good listener, an essential communication skill for managers as receivers of messages transmitted face-to-face and over the telephone.

BE EMPATHETIC Receivers are empathetic when they try to understand how the sender feels and try to interpret a message from the sender's perspective, rather than viewing a message from only their own point of view. Marcia Mazulo, the chief psychologist in a public school system in the Northwest, recently learned this lesson after interacting with Karen Sanchez, a new psychologist on her staff. Sanchez was distraught after meeting with the parent of a child she had been working with extensively. The parent was difficult to talk to and argumentative and was not supportive of her own child. Sanchez told Mazulo how upset she was, and Mazulo responded by reminding Sanchez that she was a professional and that dealing with such a situation was part of her job. This feedback upset Sanchez further and caused her to storm out of the room.

In hindsight, Mazulo realized that her response had been inappropriate. She had failed to empathize with Sanchez, who had spent so much time with the child and was deeply concerned about the child's well-being. Rather than dismissing Sanchez's concerns, Mazulo realized, she should have tried to understand how Sanchez felt and given her some support and advice for dealing positively with the situation.

Understanding Linguistic Styles

Consider the following scenarios:

- A manager from New York is having a conversation with a manager from Iowa City. The Iowa City manager never seems to get a chance to talk. He keeps waiting for a pause to signal his turn to talk, but the New York manager never pauses long enough. The New York manager wonders why the Iowa City manager does not say much. He feels uncomfortable when he pauses and the Iowa City manager says nothing, so he starts talking again.
- Elizabeth compliments Bob on his presentation to upper management and asks Bob what he thought of her presentation. Bob launches into a lengthy critique of Elizabeth's presentation and describes how he would have handled it differently. This is hardly the response Elizabeth expected.
- Catherine shares with fellow members of a self-managed work team a new way to cut costs. Michael, another team member, thinks her idea is a good one and encourages the rest of the team to support it. Catherine is quietly

pleased by Michael's support. The group implements "Michael's" suggestion, and it is written up as such in the company newsletter.

- Robert was recently promoted and transferred from his company's Oklahoma office to its headquarters in New Jersey. Robert is perplexed because he never seems to get a chance to talk in management meetings; someone else always seems to get the floor. Robert's new boss wonders whether Robert's new responsibilities are too much for him, although Robert's supervisor in Oklahoma rated him highly and said he is a real "go-getter." Robert is timid in management meetings and rarely says a word.

linguistic style
A person's characteristic way of speaking.

What do these scenarios have in common? Essentially, they all describe situations in which a misunderstanding of linguistic styles leads to a breakdown in communication. The scenarios are based on the research of linguist Deborah Tannen, who describes **linguistic style** as a person's characteristic way of speaking. Elements of linguistic style include tone of voice, speed, volume, use of pauses, directness or indirectness, choice of words, credit-taking, and use of questions, jokes, and other manners of speech.[61] When people's linguistic styles differ and these differences are not understood, ineffective communication is likely.

The first and last scenarios illustrate regional differences in linguistic style.[62] The Iowa City manager and Robert from Oklahoma expect the pauses that signal turn-taking in conversations to be longer than the pauses made by their colleagues in New York and New Jersey. This difference causes communication problems. The Iowan and transplanted Oklahoman think that their eastern colleagues never let them get a word in edgewise, and the easterners cannot figure out why their colleagues from the Midwest and Southwest do not get more actively involved in conversations.

Differences in linguistic style can be a particularly insidious source of communication problems because linguistic style is often taken for granted. People rarely think about their own linguistic styles and often are unaware of how linguistic styles can differ. In the example above, Robert never realized that when dealing with his New Jersey colleagues, he could and should jump into conversations more quickly than he used to do in Oklahoma, and his boss never realized that Robert felt that he was not being given a chance to speak in meetings.

The aspect of linguistic style just described, length of pauses, differs by region in the United States. Much more dramatic differences in linguistic style occur cross-culturally.

CROSS-CULTURAL DIFFERENCES Managers from Japan tend to be more formal in their conversations and more deferential toward upper-level managers and people with high status than are managers from the United States. Japanese managers do not mind extensive pauses in conversations when they are thinking things through or when they think that further conversation might be detrimental. U.S. managers, in contrast (even managers from regions of the United States where pauses tend to be long), find very lengthy pauses very disconcerting and feel obligated to talk to fill the silence.[63]

Another cross-cultural difference in linguistic style concerns the appropriate physical distance separating speakers and listeners in business-oriented conversations.[64] The distance between speakers and listeners is greater in the United States, for example, than it is in Brazil or Saudia Arabia. Citizens of different countries also vary in how direct or indirect they are in conversations and the extent to which they take individual credit for accomplishments. Japanese culture, with its collectivist or group orientation, tends to encourage linguistic styles in which group rather than individual accomplishments are emphasized. The opposite tends to be true in the United States.

These and other cross-cultural differences in linguistic style can and often do lead to misunderstandings. For example, when a team of American managers presented a proposal for a joint venture to Japanese managers, the Japanese managers were silent as they thought about the implications of what they had just heard. The American managers took this silence as a sign that the Japanese managers wanted more information, so they went into more detail about the proposal. When they finished, the Japanese were silent again, not only frustrating the Americans but also making them wonder whether the Japanese were at all interested in the project. The American managers suggested that if the Japanese already had decided that they did not want to pursue the project, there was no reason for the meeting to continue. The Japanese were truly bewildered. They were trying to carefully think out the proposal, yet the Americans thought they were not interested!

Communication misunderstandings and problems like this can be overcome if managers make themselves familiar with cross-cultural differences in linguistic styles. If the American managers and the Japanese managers had realized that periods of silence are viewed differently in Japan and in the United States, their different linguistic styles might have been less troublesome barriers to communication. Before managers communicate with people from abroad, they should try to find out as much as they can about the aspects of linguistic style that are specific to the country or culture in question. Expatriate managers who have lived in the country in question for an extended period of time can be good sources of information about linguistic styles because they are likely to have experienced firsthand some of the differences that citizens of a country are not aware of. Finding out as much as possible about cultural differences also can help managers learn about differences in linguistic styles because the two are often closely linked.

GENDER DIFFERENCES Referring back to the four scenarios that open this section, you may be wondering why Bob launched into a lengthy critique of Elizabeth's presentation after she paid him a routine compliment on his presentation, or you may be wondering why Michael got the credit for Catherine's idea in the self-managed work team. Research conducted by Tannen and other linguists has found that the linguistic styles of men and women differ in practically every culture or language.[65] Men and women take their own linguistic styles for granted and thus do not realize when they are talking with someone of a different gender that differences in their styles may lead to ineffective communication.

In the United States, women tend to downplay differences between people, are not overly concerned about receiving credit for their own accomplishments, and want to make everyone feel more or less on an equal footing so that even poor performers or low-status individuals feel valued. Men, in contrast, tend to emphasize their own superiority and are not reluctant to acknowledge differences in status. These differences in linguistic style led Elizabeth to routinely compliment Bob on his presentation even though she thought that he had not done a particularly good job. She asked him how her presentation was so that he could reciprocate and give her a routine compliment, putting them on an equal footing. Bob took Elizabeth's compliment and question about her own presentation as an opportunity to confirm his superiority, never realizing that all she was expecting was a routine compliment. Similarly, Michael's enthusiastic support for Catherine's cost-cutting idea and her apparent surrender of ownership of the idea after she described it led team members to assume incorrectly that the idea was Michael's.[66]

Differences in linguistic style may come from early childhood, when girls and boys are inclined to play with their own gender. Research shows that girls tend to play in small groups trying to be and noting how they are all similar. Boys, on the other hand, tend to emphasize status differences, challenging each other and relying on a leader to emerge.

Do some women try to prove that they are better than everyone else, and are some men unconcerned about taking credit for ideas and accomplishments? Of course. The gender differences in linguistic style that Tannen and other linguists have uncovered are general tendencies evident in *many* women and men, not in *all* women and men.

Where do gender differences in linguistic style come from? Tannen suggests that they develop from early childhood on. Girls and boys tend to play with children of their own gender, and the ways in which girls and boys play are quite different. Girls play in small groups, engage in a lot of close conversation, emphasize how similar they are to each other, and view boastfulness negatively. Boys play in large groups, emphasize status differences, expect leaders to emerge who boss others around, and give each other challenges to try to meet. These differences in styles of play and interaction result in differences in linguistic styles when boys and girls grow up and communicate as adults. The ways in which men communicate emphasize status differences and play up relative strengths; the ways in which women communicate emphasize similarities and downplay individual strengths.[67]

Interestingly, gender difference are also turning up in the ways that women and men use email and electronic forms of communication. For example, Susan Herring, a researcher at Indiana University has found that in public electronic forums such as message boards and chat rooms, men tend to make stronger assertions, be more sarcastic, and more likely to use insults and profanity than women while women are more likely to be supportive, agreeable, and polite.[68] David Silver, a researcher at the University of Washington, has found that women are more expressive electronic communicators and encourage others to express their thoughts and feelings while men are briefer and to the point.[69] Interestingly enough, some men are finding email to be a welcome way to express their feelings to people they care about. For example, real estate broker Mike Murname finds it easier to communicate with, and express his love for, his grown children via email.[70]

MANAGING DIFFERENCES IN LINGUISTIC STYLES Managers should not expect to change people's linguistic styles or try to. Instead, to be effective, managers need to understand differences in linguistic styles. Knowing, for example, that some women are reluctant to speak up in meetings not because they have nothing to contribute but because of their linguistic style should lead managers to ensure that these women have a chance to talk. And a manager who knows that certain people are reluctant to take credit for ideas can be extra careful to give credit where it is deserved. As Tannen points out, "Talk is the lifeblood of managerial work, and understanding that different people have different ways of saying what they mean will make it possible to take advantage of the talents of people with a broad range of linguistic styles."[71]

Tips for New Managers

Sending and Receiving Messages

1. Make sure that the messages you send are clear, complete, encoded in symbols the receiver will understand, and sent over a medium the receiver monitors.
2. Establish a sense of trust in your organization to discourage filtering and information distortion.
3. Send your messages in a way that will ensure that you receive feedback.
4. Pay attention to the messages you receive, be a good listener, and try to understand the sender's perspective.
5. Be attuned to differences in linguistic style and try to understand the ways they affect communication in your organization.

Summary and Review

COMMUNICATION AND MANAGEMENT Communication is the sharing of information between two or more individuals or groups to reach a common understanding. Good communication is necessary for an organization to gain a competitive advantage. Communication occurs in a cyclical process that entails two phases, transmission and feedback.

INFORMATION RICHNESS AND COMMUNICATION MEDIA Information richness is the amount of information a communication medium can carry and the extent to which the medium enables the sender and receiver to reach a common understanding. Four categories of communication media in descending order of information richness are face-to-face communication (includes video conferences), spoken communication electronically transmitted (includes voice mail), personally addressed written communication (includes email), and impersonal written communication.

COMMUNICATION NETWORKS Communication networks are the pathways along which information flows in an organization. Four communication networks found in groups and teams are the wheel, the chain, the circle, and the all-channel network. An organizational chart summarizes formal pathways of communication, but communication in organizations is often informal, as is true of communication through the grapevine.

TECHNOLOGICAL ADVANCES IN COMMUNICATION The Internet is a global system of computer networks that managers around the world use to communicate within and outside their companies. The World Wide Web is the multimedia business district on the Internet. Intranets are internal communication networks that managers can create to improve communication, performance, and customer service. Intranets use the same technology that the Internet and World Wide Web are based on. Groupware is computer software that enables members of groups and teams to share information with each other to improve their communication and performance.

COMMUNICATION SKILLS FOR MANAGERS There are various barriers to effective communication in organizations. To overcome these barriers and effectively communicate with others, managers must possess or develop certain communication skills. As senders of messages, managers should send messages that are clear and complete, encode messages in symbols the receiver understands, choose a medium appropriate for the message and monitored by the receiver, avoid filtering and information distortion, include a feedback mechanism in the message, and provide accurate information to ensure that misleading rumors are not spread.

Communication skills for managers as receivers of messages include paying attention, being a good listener, and being empathetic. Understanding linguistic styles is also an essential communication skill for managers. Linguistic styles can vary by geographic region, gender, and country or culture. When these differences are not understood, ineffective communication can occur.

Management in Action

Topics for Discussion and Action

1. Interview a manager in an organization in your community to determine with whom he or she communicates on a typical day and what communication media he or she uses.
2. Which medium (or media) do you think would be appropriate for each of the following kinds of messages that a subordinate could receive from his or her boss: (a) a raise, (b) not receiving a promotion, (c) an error in a report prepared by the subordinate, (d) additional job responsibilities, and (e) the schedule for company holidays for the upcoming year? Explain your choices.
3. Discuss the pros and cons of using the Internet and World Wide Web to conduct business transactions such as purchasing goods and services.
4. Why do some organizational members resist using groupware?
5. Why do some managers find it difficult to be good listeners?
6. Explain why subordinates might filter and distort information about problems and performance shortfalls when communicating with their bosses.
7. Explain why differences in linguistic style, when not understood by senders and receivers of messages, can lead to ineffective communication.

Building Management Skills

Diagnosing Ineffective Communication

Think about the last time you experienced very ineffective communication with another person—someone you work with, a classmate, a friend, a member of your family. Describe the incident. Then answer the following questions.

1. Why was your communication ineffective in this incident?
2. What stages of the communication process were particularly problematic and why?
3. Describe any filtering or information distortion that occurred.
4. Do you think differences in linguistic styles adversely affected the communication that took place? Why or why not?
5. How could you have handled this situation differently so that communication would have been effective?

Small Group Breakout Exercise

Reducing Resistance to Advances in Information Technology

Form groups of three or four people, and appoint one member as the spokesperson who will communicate your findings to the whole class when called on by the instructor. Then discuss the following scenario.

You are a team of managers in charge of information and communications in a large consumer products corporation. Your company has already implemented many advances in information technology. Managers and workers have access to voice mail, email, the Internet, your company's own intranet, and groupware.

Many employees use the new technology, but the resistance of some is causing communication problems. For example, all managers have email addresses and computers in their offices, but some refuse to turn on their computers, let alone send and receive email. These managers think that they should be able to communicate as they always have done—in person, over the phone, or in writing. Consequently, when managers who are unaware of their preferences send them email messages, those messages are never retrieved. Moreover, the resistant managers never read company news sent over email. Another example of the resistance that your company is encountering concerns the use of groupware. Members of some work groups do not want to share information with each other electronically.

Although you do not want to force people to use the technology, you want them to at least try it and give it a chance. You are meeting today to develop strategies for reducing resistance to the new technologies.

1. One resistant group of employees is made up of top managers. Some of them seem computer-phobic. They never have used, and do not want to start using, personal computers for any purpose, including communication. What steps will you take to get these managers to give their PCs a chance?
2. A second group of resistant employees consists of middle managers. Some middle managers resist using your company's intranet. Although these middle managers do not resist the technology per se and use their PCs for multiple purposes, including communication, they seem to distrust the intranet as a viable way to communicate and get things done. What steps will you take to get these middle managers to take advantage of the intranet?
3. A third group of resistant employees is made up of members of groups and teams who do not want to use the groupware that has been provided to them. You think that the groupware could improve their communication and performance, but they seem to think otherwise. What steps will you take to get these members of groups and teams to start using groupware?

Exploring the World Wide Web

Find the website of a company that you know very little about. Scan the website of this company. Do you think this website effectively communicates important information about this company? Why or why not? Is there anything that you think customers or prospective employees would especially like to see on the website that is not currently there? Is there anything on the website that you think should not be there?

You're the Management Consultant

Mark Chen supervisors support staff for an Internet merchandising organization which sells furniture over the Internet. Chen has always thought that he needed to expand his staff and right when he was about to approach his boss with such a request, the economy slowed down and other areas of the company have experienced layoffs. Thus, Chen's plans for trying to add to his staff are on indefinite hold.

However, he has noticed a troubling pattern of communication with his staff. Ordinarily, when he wants one of his staff members to work on a task, he emails them with the pertinent information. For the last few months, his email requests have gone unheeded and his subordinates only complied with his request after he visited with them in person about it and gave them a specific deadline. Each time, they apologized for not getting to it sooner but said that they were so overloaded with requests that they sometimes even stop answering their phones. Unless someone asks for something more than once, they feel it is not that urgent and can put it on hold. Chen thinks this state of affairs is deplorable. Also, he realized that his subordinates have no way of prioritizing tasks—hence, some very important projects he asked them to complete were put on hold until he followed up about them. Knowing he cannot add to his staff in the short term, Chen has come to you for advice. In particular he wants to develop a system whereby his staff will provide some kind of response to requests within 24 hours, will be able to prioritize tasks, identifying their relative importance, and will not feel so overloaded that they ignore their boss's requests and don't answer their phones. As an expert in communication, advise Chen.

Cases in the News

Across the Geek Divide

The old joke goes: How can you tell an extroverted geek from an introverted one?

The extroverted geek looks at your shoes, rather than his, when he talks to you.

There is some truth to the stereotype that many technologically oriented employees would rather commune with computer code or hardware than the world at large, say those who head software companies—the same people who are now finding that potential customers want to hear from their techno wizards, *aka* geeks. Increasingly, software sales teams must include a programmer, one who is comfortable talking with a roomful of marketing and financial executives.

Talking the Talk

"You're kicking them out of their comfort zone," says Dov Goldman, founder and CEO of Cognet Corp. in Valhalla, N.Y. Like most companies that sell enterprise software, Cognet has a tech person on every sales team. It has to be someone who not only understands the nuts and bolts of the software, "but has gained some business experience and had some of his optimism about what works and doesn't work technologically tempered by experience with the real world." Lack of real-world business experience, Goldman says, is the reason the industry has so much great software in search of a problem to fix.

Technical degrees, traditionally, do not cover the communication and management skills that are part of, say, an MBA or marketing degree, so software companies find themselves doing in-house training. Vivek Wadhwa, founder and CEO of Relativity Technologies, which modernizes legacy software systems, uses trial-and-error coaching to get a programmer to be part of the sales team.

One of Relativity's best salespeople is also its Russian-born chief technology officer, Len Erlikh. Because Erlikh was a brilliant technician, "I would push him in front of customers, then critique him when it was over." After many such sessions, Erlikh has become "awesome" on sales calls, said Wadhwa, adding that experience tells him that about one-third of all techies have great potential as business people. One of the reasons he's willing to spend a lot of time coaching that one-third is because it is how he was transformed from a "clueless" programmer into a capable CEO.

Party with a Geek

Before founding Relativity Technologies, in the Research Triangle Park of North Carolina, Wadhwa was chief technology officer at Seer Technologies, founded by Gene Bedell in the early 1990s. "He got ahead because of his technical prowess and general aggressiveness," says Bedell. The trouble is, Wadhwa would say what was on his mind rather than listening to the customer. Bedell still winces, for example, at the memory of losing a big corporate client when Wadhwa told its team that they were, in effect, "a bunch of dopes." Adds Bedell: "Those guys would never talk to me again."

Fortunately, "constant coaching" transformed Wadhwa, says Bedell, unlike some technical people he has worked with who proved to be "constitutionally incapable of listening." Wadhwa says that what he learned from Bedell, author of *Three Steps to Yes: The Gentle Art of Getting Your Way,* is that "all the world's a sales call."

Why does the CEO bother to work so hard on the technology employees' communications skills? The way the salespeople get credibility with the customer is to bring the tech person with them. "We call it genius-on-a-string," Wadhwa says, alluding to a pull toy.

Why would the technology-minded work so hard to be a salesperson? Because the ones who help make the sales get the promotions and the biggest salaries.

The Techie Divide

"Those who can communicate literally raise themselves above the pack," says Harry E. Chambers, whose book, *Effective Communication Skills for Scientific and Technical Professionals,* was published in June 2001. His book quotes Elizabeth Haggerty, program manager for business and manufacturing process improvements at the Carrier Corp. in Hartford. She has both engineering and MBA degrees. "The path of being an engineer/scientist and spending the rest of your life as an individual contributor does not really exist anymore. If you really want to get promoted, get salary increases, and be recognized for your contributions, you need to have [communication] skills."

Things are changing, but they still have a way to go. In his work as a consultant, Chambers has noticed how, "Techies will roll their eyes and talk about all those other people, and all those other people will roll their eyes and talk about the techies. It impacts productivity in companies today." That's why, he says, at more companies, bridging that communication gap is increasingly part of the job. "If Susan is having trouble with her computer, it's no longer acceptable for the computer technician to say, 'Susan just doesn't get it.' Unless she is certified as below-average intelligence, it's part of the technician's job to get the information she needs across to her," Chambers said. He is optimistic that this "disconnect" between the technical and non-technical side will change "because it has to—but it ain't gonna be tomorrow."

Party with a Geek?

Goldman, too, thinks the problem eventually will disappear. Many of those who, traditionally, have been attracted to computer technology "are there because they want to avoid the problems of communicating with people," he says. But as technology becomes an ever more pervasive part of the knowledge economy, those techies with a broader array of skills and a more outgoing personality will begin to see technology as a career option.

"Society will adapt," Goldman says. "What happened in the dot-com explosion was that we saw those people could make a lot of money and have a lot of impact. People are now willing to date computer programmers. The problem will solve itself as it becomes cool to be a geek."

Whatever their communications difficulties today, it sounds as if those geniuses on a string are likely to have the last word.

Source: T. Forsman and R. J. Phillips, "Across the Geek Divide," *Business Week,* June 26, 2001, Business Week Online.

Questions

1. Why might it be important for software sales teams to include a programmer?
2. What can managers do to ensure that programmers and technical experts are able to effectively communicate with clients and customers?

BusinessWeek Cases in the News

Revenge of the Downsized Nerds

The agents on the computer intrusion squad at the San Francisco FBI bureau thought they had seen everything when it came to hackers. But since the tech meltdown began late last year, the Silicon Valley G-men have discovered a new breed: laid-off dot-commers and other techies who are out for revenge. In one case under investigation, an axed systems administrator hacked back into his former company's computers, then published user I.D.s, passwords, and secret company information in public chat rooms. Another pink-slipped worker sent bawdy emails—complete with a pornographic picture attached—to everyone at the high-tech company where he had worked. And at an import-export outfit, the CEO can't access any of his old email: A former employee wiped it all out.

These computer criminals are part of a new sort of cyber saboteur: the disgruntled ex-employee. In recent months, axed workers have posted a company's payroll on its intranet, planted data-destroying bugs, and handed over valuable intellectual property to competitors. Although exact numbers are hard to come by, computer security experts say it is fast becoming the top technical concern at many companies. "This is a major threat," says Internet Trading Technologies CEO Craig Goldberg.

Costly Damage

Take the FBI's San Francisco office, which saw just three cases of disgruntled ex-employees breaking into corporate networks last year. So far this year, it has 15. In Boston, no cases were reported in 2000; now, there are four. That may not sound like much, but most companies want to avoid negative publicity and don't report such crimes. "This is just the tip of the iceberg," says James Hegarty, supervisor of the FBI's computer crime squad in Boston. "We think it's phenomenally underreported."

Of course, fired workers have always exacted revenge on their former employers. But this time, they're capable of much greater damage. More than ever, companies depend on computer networks that are vulnerable to electronic sabotage. With more than 30,000 websites filled with hacking tools that any grade-schooler could use, today's brand of getting even is far easier for alienated workers to pull off. It's also far more costly for companies. The FBI estimates the cost of the average insider attack at $2.7 million.

Many of the attacks amount to low-level extortion. One systems administrator at a hospital encrypted patient files once she learned she would be laid off. She then offered to fix the problem immediately in exchange for severance, a cash payout, and a no-prosecution agreement. The hospital signed the "golden parachute," as computer-security experts call such deals, and subsequently was unable to press charges.

So who is the typical perpetrator of cyber sabotage? An introvert prone to nursing grudges, says Bethesda (Md.)–based Political Psychology Associates Ltd. Researchers have identified six common traits in attackers: a history of personal or social frustrations, heavy computer usage, loose ethics, reduced loyalty, a sense of entitlement, and lack of empathy.

Companies rarely know how many computers they have or who is authorized to use them. And they often don't immediately terminate their ex-workers' access. Worse, one computer-security consultant cites a case in which a laid-off worker even managed to use the password of a dead co-worker to log back into a company's network, because the dead man's profile hadn't yet been deleted. International Data Corp. estimates that as many as 30 percent of a company's approved users are no longer around. Many executives also make the mistake of assuming firewalls will protect them. But a third of companies using firewalls say they're still hacked into, according to the Computer Security Institute.

That's why taking some simple preventative steps to centralize computer access can save a lot of money. Companies such as E*Trade Group Inc. and Oppenheimer Funds Inc. are racing to install the latest in security software, which offers the ability to instantly block laid-off workers from their entire networks. How times have changed. A year ago, companies begged to get employees to stay. Now, they're doing everything they can to keep former workers away.

Source: M. Conlin and A. Salkever, "Revenge of the Downsized Nerds," *Business Week,* July 30, 2001, Business Week Online.

Questions

1. Why would laid off employees want to sabotage their former employers?
2. What can managers do to avoid potential sabotage when faced with an unavoidable layoff?

Chapter 16

Organizational Conflict, Negotiation, Politics, and Change

LEARNING OBJECTIVES

After studying this chapter, you should be able to:

- Explain why conflict arises, and identify the **types and sources of conflict** in organizations.
- Describe **conflict management strategies** that managers can use to resolve conflict effectively.
- Describe negotiation strategies that managers can use to resolve conflict through **integrative bargaining.**
- Explain why managers need to be attuned to **organizational politics,** and describe the political strategies that managers can use to become politically skilled.
- Identify the main steps in the **organizational change process.**

A Manager's Challenge

Shakeup at Ford

How can managers initiate major changes in organizations, stay focused on key concerns and objectives, and gain the support of important stakeholders?

When Jacques A. Nasser became CEO of Ford Motor Co. in 1999, spirits were high. Nasser was confident that he had good material to work with and he would recreate Ford into one of the best global companies. At the time he took over, Ford had $23 million in cash on hand and few threatening problems.[1] Yet, the company needed to remake itself according to Nasser to become more in tune with the Internet economy, operate more efficiently, improve quality, and expand to become a major global company (not just a global automaker). Nasser set about making significant changes to reinvent Ford.[2]

Less than three years later on October 30, 2001, Nasser was out of a job, and Ford was reeling from a series of problems, mishaps, and debacles ranging from the Firestone tire recall, recalls not associated with Firestone tires, and declining quality to higher costs, lower productivity, plummeting stock prices, and a class-action lawsuit filed on behalf of middle managers who claim that Nasser's new performance appraisal system was unfair and discriminatory.[3]

William C. Ford, Jr., exits his electric-powered Ford Ranger. Ford recently replaced Nasser as Ford Motor Co. CEO amid sighs of relief within the company.

On October 30, 2001, 44-year-old William C. Ford Jr., great grandson of founder Henry Ford and chairman of the board, replaced Nasser as CEO amid not only sighs of relief within Ford but even cheers.[4] While time will tell if Bill Ford can bring Ford back to an even keel, one wonders why things kept going from bad to worse at Ford under Nasser. Clearly, Nasser's intentions were good and well-meaning and many of Ford's problems during his reign of power were not of his doing such as the decline in the U.S. economy and the problems with Firestone tires.

The magnitude of Ford's problems when Nasser exited suggest how extraordinarily difficult it is to make major changes in an organization while keeping that organization focused on key initiatives and objectives and gaining the support of key stakeholders such as employees. To succeed at such a monumental undertaking, managers need to wisely use, exercise, and build their power. And at least some of Nasser's initiatives as CEO underscore the difficulties he had in this regard.

Some observers suggest that Nasser tried to do too many things too quickly, which caused Ford to drift from its major objective of efficiently producing high-quality vehicles. For example, in the early years of his tenure as CEO, Nasser acquired Volvo, Land Rover, repair shops, the Hertz car-rental agency, and even a driving company, consistent with his push to remake Ford as a major global company.[5]

While Nasser was initiating major internal changes such as the controversial performance appraisal system for middle managers, personnel changes, flattening of the hierarchy, eliminating seniority as a consideration for rewards, and institution of the Six Sigma quality improvement program, he failed to gain the support of key stakeholders for his initiatives and didn't even have a second in command to help spread the word and garner support.

While CEO, Nasser had 15 high level managers reporting directly to him and no second in command such as a head of operations. Nasser made major strategic decisions for Ford as well as handled day-to-day operations and one wonders if he spread himself too thin. Moreover, he didn't seem to have the allegiance of a loyal cadre of managers to enlist the support of Ford's employee base. Rather than gaining such support, Nasser eroded his support by the controversial performance appraisal system that alienated thousands of managers so much some have sought legal remedies (see the related "Focus on Diversity" in Chapter 4).

Six Sigma aside, according to J. D. Power & Associates which surveys consumers' perceptions of the product quality of major automobile manufacturers, Ford has some of the lowest quality ratings. For example, Ford's new Escape sports utility vehicle was just on the market for a few months when it had five recalls and the New Ford Explorer had two recalls in a month. In the first half of 2001, Ford lost more than $1.4 billion. News such as this made the replacement of Nasser as CEO seem more and more likely as the year progressed.[6] Let's hope that Bill Ford has the power and expertise to reinvent Ford once again and reverse its downward trajectory.

Overview

Successful leaders are able to effectively use their power to influence others and to bring about changes that allow them to achieve their goals. As illustrated in "A Manager's Challenge," this is a difficult undertaking which even accomplished managers such as Jacques Nasser, find challenging. In Chapter 13 we described how managers, as leaders, exert influence over other people to achieve group and organizational goals and how managers' sources of power enable them to exert such influence. In this chapter we describe why managers need to develop the skills necessary to manage organizational conflict, politics, and change if they are going to be effective and achieve their goals, skills Nasser seems to have lacked at Ford.

First, we describe conflict and the strategies that managers can use to resolve it effectively. We discuss one major conflict resolution technique, negotiation, in detail, outlining the steps managers can take to be good negotiators. Second, we describe organizational politics and the political strategies that managers can use to expand their power and use it effectively. Third, we examine the skills that managers must develop to analyze and change organizations to increase their efficiency and effectiveness. By the end of this chapter, you will appreciate why managers must develop the skills necessary to manage these important organizational processes if they are to be effective and achieve organizational goals.

Organizational Conflict

organizational conflict The discord that arises when the goals, interests, or values of different individuals or groups are incompatible and those individuals or groups block or thwart each other's attempts to achieve their objectives.

Organizational conflict is the discord that arises when the goals, interests, or values of different individuals or groups are incompatible and those individuals or groups block or thwart each other's attempts to achieve their objectives.[7] In "A Manager's Challenge," organizational conflict arose at Ford when Nasser implemented the new performance appraisal system that middle managers felt was unfair and discriminatory (see the related "Focus on Diversity" in Chapter 4). Conflict is an inevitable part of organizational life because the goals of different stakeholders such as managers and workers are often incompatible. Organizational conflict also can exist between departments and divisions that compete for resources or even between managers who may be competing for promotion to the next level in the organizational hierarchy.

It is important for managers to develop the skills necessary to manage conflict effectively. In addition, the level of conflict present in an organization has important implications for organizational performance. Figure 16.1 illustrates the relationship between organizational conflict and performance. At point A, there is little or no conflict and organizational performance suffers. Lack of conflict in an organization often signals that managers emphasize conformity at the expense of new ideas, are resistant to change, and strive for agreement rather than effective decision making. As the level of conflict increases from point A to point B, organizational effectiveness is likely to increase. When an organization has an optimum

Figure 16.1
The Effect of Conflict on Organizational Performance

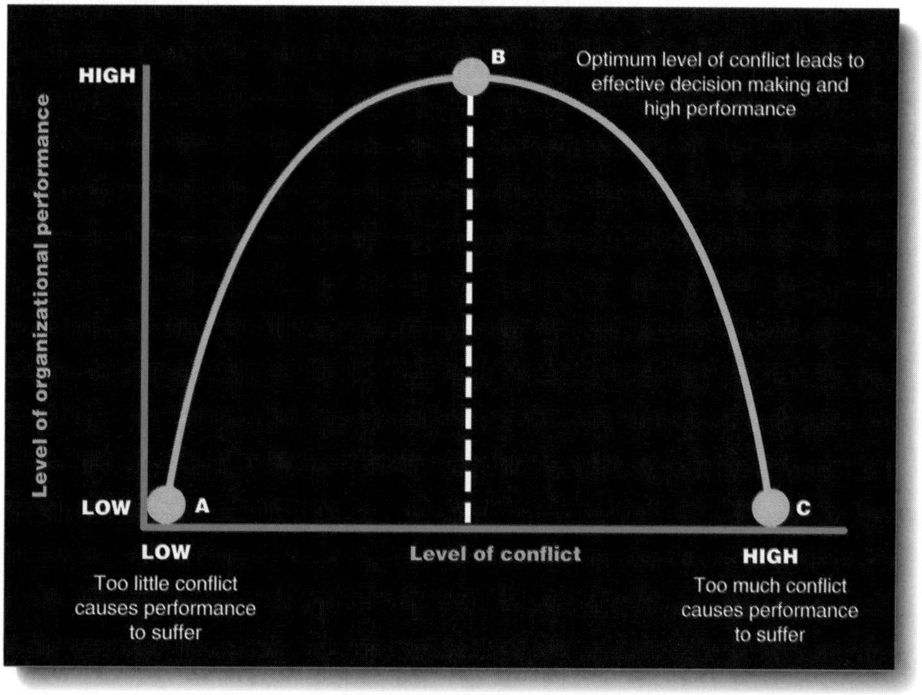

level of conflict (point B), managers are likely to be open to, and encourage, a variety of perspectives, look for ways to improve organizational functioning and effectiveness, and view debates and disagreements as a necessary ingredient for effective decision making. As the level of conflict increases from point B to point C, conflict escalates to the point where organizational performance suffers. When an organization has a dysfunctionally high level of conflict, managers are likely to waste organizational resources to achieve their own ends, to be more concerned about winning political battles than about doing what will lead to a competitive advantage for their organization, and to try to get even with their opponents rather than make good decisions.

Conflict is a force that needs to be managed rather than eliminated.[8] Managers should never try to eliminate all conflict but rather should try to keep conflict at a moderate and functional level to promote change efforts that benefit the organization. To manage conflict, managers must understand the types and sources of conflict and be familiar with certain strategies that can be effective in dealing with it.

Types of Conflict

There are several types of conflict in organizations: interpersonal, intragroup, intergroup, and interorganizational (see Figure 16.2).[9] Understanding how these types differ can help managers to deal with conflict.

INTERPERSONAL CONFLICT Interpersonal conflict is conflict between individual members of an organization, occurring because of differences in their goals or values. Two managers may experience interpersonal conflict when their values concerning protection of the environment differ. One manager may argue that the organization should do only what is required by law. The other manager may counter that the organization should invest in equipment to reduce emissions even though the organization's current level of emissions is below the legal limit.

INTRAGROUP CONFLICT Intragroup conflict is conflict that arises within a group, team, or department. When members of the marketing department in a clothing company disagree about how they should spend budgeted advertising dollars for a new line of men's designer jeans, they are experiencing intragroup conflict. Some of the members want to spend all the money on advertisements in magazines. Others want to devote half of the money to billboards and ads in city buses and subways.

Figure 16.2
Types of Conflict in Organizations

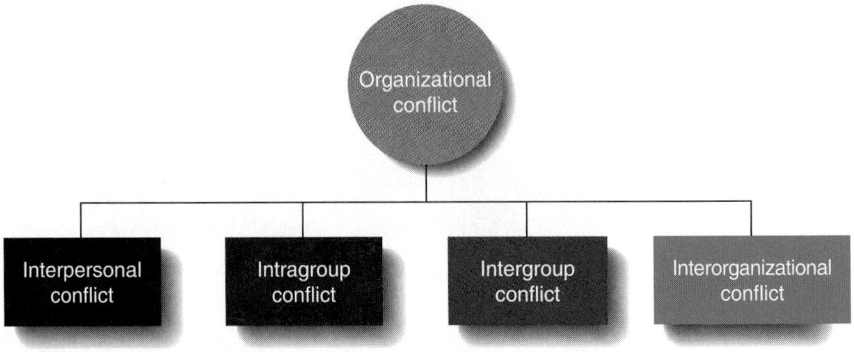

INTERGROUP CONFLICT Intergroup conflict is conflict between groups, teams, or departments. R&D departments, for example, sometimes experience intergroup conflict with production departments. Members of the R&D department may develop a new product that they think production can make inexpensively by using existing manufacturing capabilities. Members of the production department, however, may disagree and believe that the costs of making the product will be much higher. Managers of departments usually play a key role in managing intergroup conflicts such as these.

INTERORGANIZATIONAL CONFLICT Interorganizational conflict is conflict that arises across organizations. Sometimes interorganizational conflict arises when managers in one organization feel that another organization is not behaving ethically and is threatening the well-being of certain stakeholder groups.

Sources of Conflict

Conflict in organizations springs from a variety of sources. The ones that we examine here are incompatible goals and time horizons, overlapping authority, task interdependencies, incompatible evaluation or reward systems, scarce resources, and status inconsistencies (see Figure 16.3).[10]

INCOMPATIBLE GOALS AND TIME HORIZONS Recall from Chapter 8 that an important managerial activity is organizing people and tasks into departments and divisions to accomplish an organization's goals. Almost inevitably, this grouping results in the creation of departments and divisions that have incompatible goals and time horizons, and the result can be conflict. Production and production managers, for example, usually concentrate on efficiency and cost cutting; they have a relatively short time horizon and focus on producing quality goods or services in a timely and efficient manner. In contrast, marketing and marketing managers focus on sales and responsiveness to customers. Their time horizon is longer than that of production because they

Figure 16.3
Sources of Conflict in Organizations

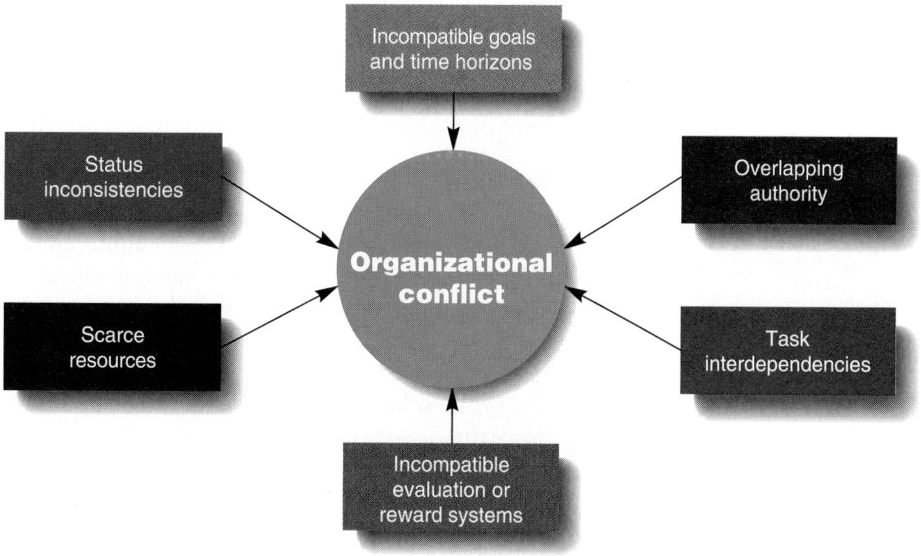

are trying to be responsive not only to customers' needs today but also to their changing needs in the future to build long-term customer loyalty. These fundamental differences between marketing and production are often breeding grounds for conflict.

Suppose production is behind schedule in its plan to produce a specialized product for a key customer. The marketing manager believes that the delay will reduce sales of the product and therefore insists that the product must be delivered on time even if saving the production schedule means increasing costs by paying production workers overtime. The production manager says that she will happily schedule overtime if marketing will pay for it. Both managers' positions are reasonable from the perspective of their own departments, and conflict is likely.

In "A Manager's Challenge," Nasser implemented the new performance appraisal system, which forced supervisors to rate and rank employees relative to each other rather than some objective standard to achieve the goal of improving performance. However, managers subject to the new system viewed it as discriminatory and incompatible with their own goals for a fair and equitable workplace.

OVERLAPPING AUTHORITY When two or more managers, departments, or functions claim authority for the same activities or tasks, conflict is likely.[11] This is precisely what happened when heirs of the Forman liquor distribution company based in Washington, D.C., inherited the company from their parents. One of the heirs, Barry Forman, wanted to control the company and was reluctant to share power with the other heirs. Several of the heirs felt that they had authority over certain tasks crucial to Forman's success (such as maintaining good relationships with the top managers of liquor companies). What emerged was a battle of wills and considerable conflict, which escalated to the point of being dysfunctional, requiring the family to hire a consulting firm to help resolve it.[12]

TASK INTERDEPENDENCIES Have you ever been assigned a group project for one of your classes in which one group member consistently failed to get things done on time? This probably created some conflict in your group because other group members were dependent on the late member's contributions to complete the project. Whenever individuals, groups, teams, or departments are interdependent, the potential for conflict exists.[13] With differing goals and time horizons, the managers of marketing and production, come into conflict precisely because these departments are interdependent. Marketing is dependent on production for the goods it markets and sells, and production is dependent on marketing for creating demand for the things it makes.

INCOMPATIBLE EVALUATION OR REWARD SYSTEMS The way in which interdependent groups, teams, or departments are evaluated and rewarded can be another source of conflict.[14] Production managers, for example, are evaluated and rewarded for their success in staying within the budget or lowering costs while maintaining quality. So they are reluctant to take any steps that will increase costs, such as paying workers high overtime rates to finish a late order for an important customer. Marketing managers, in contrast, are evaluated and rewarded for their success in generating sales and customer satisfaction. So they often think that overtime pay is a small price to pay for responsiveness to customers. Thus, conflict between production and marketing is rarely unexpected.

SCARCE RESOURCES Management is the process of acquiring, developing, protecting, and utilizing the resources that allow an organization to be efficient and effective (see Chapter 1). When resources are scarce, management is all the more difficult and conflict is likely.[15] When resources are scarce, for example, divisional managers may be in conflict over who has access to financial capital, and organizational members at all levels may be in conflict over who gets raises and promotions.

STATUS INCONSISTENCIES The fact that some individuals, groups, teams, or departments within an organization are more highly regarded than others in the organization can also create conflict. In some restaurants, for example, the chefs have relatively higher status than the people who wait on tables. Nevertheless, the chefs receive customers' orders from the wait staff and the wait staff can return to the chefs food that their customers or they think is not acceptable. This status inconsistency–high-status chefs taking orders from low-status wait staff–can be the source of considerable conflict between chefs and the wait staff. For this reason some restaurants require the wait staff to put orders on a spindle, thereby reducing the amount of direct order-giving from the wait staff to the chefs.[16]

Conflict Management Strategies

If an organization is to achieve its goals, managers must be able to resolve conflicts in a functional manner. *Functional conflict resolution* means that the conflict is settled by compromise or by collaboration between the parties in conflict. *Compromise* is possible when each party is concerned about its own goal accomplishment and the goal accomplishment of the other party and is willing to engage in a give-and-take exchange and to make concessions until a reasonable resolution of the conflict is reached. *Collaboration* is a way of handling conflict in which the parties to a conflict try to satisfy their goals without making any concessions and instead come up with a way to resolve their differences that leaves them both better off.[17]

When the parties to a conflict are willing to cooperate with each other and through compromise or collaboration devise a solution that each finds acceptable, an organization is more likely to achieve its goals. Conflict management strategies that managers can use to ensure that conflicts are resolved in a functional manner focus on individuals and on the organization as a whole. Below, we describe four strategies that focus on individuals: increasing awareness of the sources of conflict, increasing diversity awareness and skills, practicing job rotation or temporary assignments, and using permanent transfers or dismissals when necessary. We also describe two strategies that focus on the organization as a whole: changing an organization's structure or culture and directly altering the source of conflict.

STRATEGIES FOCUSED ON INDIVIDUALS

INCREASING AWARENESS OF THE SOURCES OF CONFLICT Sometimes conflict arises because of communication problems and interpersonal misunderstandings. For example, differences in linguistic styles (see Chapter 15) may lead some men in work teams to talk more, and take more credit for ideas, than women in those teams. These communication differences can result in conflict when the men incorrectly assume that the women are uninterested or less capable because they participate less and the women incorrectly assume that the men are being bossy and are not interested in their ideas because they seem to do all the talking. By increasing people's awareness of this source of conflict, managers can help to resolve conflict functionally. And once men and women realize that the source of their conflict is differences in linguistic styles, they can take steps to interact with each other more effectively. The men can give the women more of a chance to provide input, and the women can be more proactive in providing this input.

Sometimes personalities clash in an organization. In these situations, too, managers can help resolve conflicts functionally by increasing organizational members' awareness of the source of their difficulties. For example, some people who are not inclined to take risks may come in conflict with those who are prone to taking risks. The non-risk-takers might complain that those who welcome risk propose outlandish ideas without justification, while the risk-takers complain that their innovative ideas are always getting shot down. When both types of people are made aware that their conflicts are due to fundamental differences in their ways of approaching problems, they will likely be better able to cooperate in coming up with innovative ideas that entail only moderate levels of risk.

INCREASING DIVERSITY AWARENESS AND SKILLS Interpersonal conflicts also can arise because of diversity. Older workers may feel uncomfortable or resentful about reporting to a younger supervisor, a Hispanic may feel singled out in a group of white workers, or a female top manager may feel that members of her predominantly male top-management team band together whenever one of them disagrees with one of her proposals. Whether these feelings are justified, they are likely to cause recurring conflicts. Many of the techniques we described in Chapter 4 to increase diversity awareness and skills can help managers effectively manage diversity and resolve conflicts that have their origins in differences between organizational members.

Today one would hope that cases of overt discrimination would be on the decline (see Chapter 4). Disturbingly, recent statistics concerning racial discrimination and harassment suggest otherwise, as indicated in the following "Focus on Diversity."

Focus on Diversity

Alarming Accounts of Racial Harassment

Accounts of racial discrimination and harassment are surfacing in a variety of organizations ranging from Lockheed Martin, Boeing, and Texaco to Coca-Cola, Xerox, and Northwest Airlines. As society and organizations become more diverse and hopefully stereotypes are broken down, one would think that overt racial discrimination would be on the decline. However, according to the Equal Employment Opportunity Commission (EEOC), allegations of racial or national origin harassment in the workplace have doubled from 1990 to 2000, as compared to a 36 percent increase in minority employment.[18]

Especially disturbing is the threatening nature of some of the harassment that takes place. Some racial minorities are subject to not only derogatory comments but also threatening actions including depictions of hangman's nooses (harkening back to the tragic mob lynchings of African Americans decades ago). In a recent 18-month period, the EEOC received 25 hangman's noose–related complaints. An attorney and partner with Seyfarth, Shaw, Fairweather, and Geraldson which defends some organizations involved in discrimination lawsuits, Steve Poor says, "I've seen more of these cases in the last few years than in the previous 10, and it's bad stuff."[19]

Many times employees subject to discrimination are forced to go to the EEOC, because their complaints to supervisors and managers fall on deaf ears. It takes a lot of time and energy–never mind emotional stamina–to file such complaints, and experts suggest that the vast majority of complaints filed with the EEOC are based on documented problems. Moreover, employees who complain to the EEOC run the risk of retaliation on the job. The EEOC receives about 20,000 charges of retaliation per year by minorities who previously filed discrimination charges–twice the amount of retaliation charges filed 10 years ago. The harassment and retaliation that some employees experience is so severe that they require psychological help and find other aspects of their lives being disrupted by it.[20] Clearly, this is a deplorable state of affairs that managers cannot and should not tolerate (see Chapter 4 for more in-depth treatment of diversity and discrimination).

PRACTICING JOB ROTATION OR TEMPORARY ASSIGNMENTS Sometimes conflicts arise because individual organizational members simply do not have a good understanding of the work activities and demands that others in an organization face. A financial analyst, for example, may be required to submit monthly reports to a member of the accounting department. These reports have a low priority for the analyst, and she typically turns them in a couple of days late. On the due date, the accountant always calls up the financial analyst, and conflict ensues as the accountant describes in detail why she must have the reports on time and the financial analyst describes everything else she needs to do. In situations such as this, job rotation or temporary assignments, which expand organizational members' knowledge base and appreciation of other departments, can be a useful way of resolving the conflict. If the financial analyst spends some time working in the accounting department, she may appreciate better the need for timely reports. Similarly, a temporary assignment in the finance department may help the accountant realize the demands a financial analyst faces and the need to streamline unnecessary aspects of reporting.

USING PERMANENT TRANSFERS OR DISMISSALS WHEN NECESSARY Sometimes when other conflict resolution strategies do not work, managers may need to take more drastic steps, including permanent transfers or dismissals.

Suppose two first-line managers who work in the same department are always at each other's throats; frequent bitter conflicts arise between them even though they both seem to get along well with other employees. No matter what their supervisor does to increase their understanding of each other, these conflicts keep occurring. In this case, the supervisor may want to transfer one or both managers so that they do not have to interact as frequently.

When dysfunctionally high levels of conflict occur among top managers who cannot resolve their differences and understand each other, it may be necessary for one of them to leave the company. This is how Gerald Levin managed dysfunctionally high levels of conflict among top managers, when he was chairman of Time Warner (later Levin was CEO of AOL Time Warner). Robert Daly and Terry Semel, one of the most respected management teams in Hollywood and top managers in the Warner Brothers film company, had been in conflict with Michael Fuchs, a long-time veteran of Time Warner and head of the music division, for two years. As Semel described it, the company "was running like a dysfunctional family, and it needed one management team to run it."[21] Levin realized that Time Warner's future success rested on resolving this conflict, that it was unlikely that Fuchs would ever be able to work effectively with Daly and Semel, and that he risked losing Daly and Semel to another company if he did not resolve the conflict. Faced with that scenario, Levin asked Fuchs to resign.[22]

STRATEGIES FOCUSED ON THE WHOLE ORGANIZATION

CHANGING AN ORGANIZATION'S STRUCTURE OR CULTURE Conflict can signal the need for changes in an organization's structure or culture. Sometimes, managers can effectively resolve conflict by changing the organizational structure they use to group people and tasks.[23] As an organization grows, for example, the *functional structure* (composed of departments such as marketing, finance, and production) that was effective when the organization was small may cease to be effective, and a shift to a *product structure* might effectively resolve conflicts (see Chapter 8).

Managers also can effectively resolve conflicts by increasing levels of integration in an organization. Recall from Chapter 14 how Hallmark Cards increased integration by using cross-functional teams to produce new cards. The use of cross-functional teams speeded new card development and helped to resolve conflicts between different departments. When a writer and an artist have a conflict over the appropriateness of the artist's illustrations, they do not pass criticisms back and forth from one department to another, because now they are on the same team and can directly resolve the issue on the spot.

Sometimes managers may need to take steps to change an organization's culture to resolve conflict (see Chapter 9). Norms and values in an organizational culture might inadvertently promote dysfunctionally high levels of conflict that are difficult to resolve. For instance, norms that stress respect for formal authority may create conflict that is difficult to resolve when an organization creates self-managed work teams and managers' roles and the structure of authority in the organization change. Values stressing individual competition may make it difficult to resolve conflicts when organizational members need to put others' interests ahead of their own. In circumstances such as these, taking steps to change norms and values can be an effective conflict resolution strategy.

ALTERING THE SOURCE OF CONFLICT When conflict is due to overlapping authority, incompatible evaluation or reward systems, and status inconsistencies, managers can sometimes effectively resolve the conflict by directly altering the source of conflict–the overlapping authority, the evaluation or reward system, or the status inconsistency. For example, managers can clarify the chain of command and reassign tasks and responsibilities to resolve conflicts due to overlapping authority.

Tips for New Managers

Conflict

1. Try to handle conflicts by compromise or collaboration.
2. Analyze how the ways in which parties to a conflict differ from each other (such as linguistic styles, personality, age, or gender) may be contributing to misunderstandings and conflict.
3. Consider using job rotation or temporary assignments to help your subordinates understand the work activities and demands of other organizational members.
4. Analyze the extent to which conflict in your organization is due to a faulty organizational structure or a dysfunctional culture.

Negotiation Strategies for Integrative Bargaining

negotiation A method of conflict resolution in which the two parties in conflict consider various alternative ways to allocate resources to each other in order to come up with a solution acceptable to them both.

distributive negotiation Adversarial negotiation in which the parties in conflict compete to win the most resources while conceding as little as possible.

integrative bargaining Cooperative negotiation in which the parties in conflict work together to achieve a resolution that is good for them both.

A particularly important conflict resolution technique for managers and other organizational members to use in situations where the parties to a conflict have approximately equal levels of power is negotiation. During **negotiation,** the parties to a conflict try to come up with a solution acceptable to themselves by considering various alternative ways to allocate resources to each other.[24]

There are two major types of negotiation–distributive negotiation and integrative bargaining.[25] In **distributive negotiation,** the two parties perceive that they have a "fixed pie" of resources that they need to divide.[26] They take a competitive, adversarial stance. Each party realizes that he or she must concede something but is out to get the lion's share of resources.[27] The parties see no need to interact with each other in the future and do not care if their interpersonal relationship is damaged or destroyed by their competitive negotiations.[28]

In **integrative bargaining,** the parties perceive that they might be able to increase the resource pie by trying to come up with a creative solution to the conflict. They do not view the conflict competitively, as a win-or-lose situation; instead, they view it cooperatively, as a win-win situation in which both parties can gain. Integrative bargaining is characterized by trust, information sharing, and the desire of both parties to achieve a good resolution of the conflict.[29]

Consider how Adrian Hofbeck and Joseph Steinberg, partners in a successful German restaurant in the Midwest, resolved their recent conflict. Hofbeck and Steinberg founded the restaurant 15 years ago, share management responsibilities, and share equally in the restaurant's profits. Hofbeck recently decided that he wanted to retire and sell the restaurant, but retirement was the last thing Steinberg had in mind; he wanted to continue to own and manage the restaurant. Distributive negotiation was out of the question, for Hofbeck and Steinberg were close friends and valued their friendship; neither wanted to do something that would hurt the other or their continuing relationship. So they opted

Teamsters' President James P. Hoffa, right, shakes hands with Ian Hunter chief negotiator for the National Automobile Transporters labor division, after a tentative agreement was reached on a new labor contract in the spring of 1999. This agreement averted a potential Teamsters' strike against companies that haul new cars to auto dealers. Negotiation is an important conflict resolution technique for managers and other organizational members to use in situations in which the parties have approximately equal levels of power.

Table 16.1
Negotiation Strategies for Integrative Bargaining

- Emphasize superordinate goals.
- Focus on the problem, not the people.
- Focus on interests, not demands.
- Create new options for joint gain.
- Focus on what is fair.

for integrative bargaining, which they thought would help them resolve their conflict so that both could achieve their goals and maintain their friendship.

There are five strategies that managers in all kinds of organizations can rely on to facilitate integrative bargaining and avoid distributive negotiation: emphasizing superordinate goals; focusing on the problem, not the people; focusing on interests, not demands; creating new options for joint gain; and focusing on what is fair (see Table 16.1).[30] Hofbeck and Steinberg used each of these strategies to resolve their conflict.

EMPHASIZING SUPERORDINATE GOALS Superordinate goals are goals that both parties agree to regardless of the source of their conflict. Increasing organizational effectiveness, increasing responsiveness to customers, and gaining a competitive advantage are just a few of the many superordinate goals that members of an organization can emphasize during integrative bargaining. Superordinate goals help parties in conflict to keep in mind the big picture and the fact that they are working together for a larger purpose or goal despite their disagreements. Hofbeck and Steinberg emphasized three superordinate goals during their bargaining: ensuring that the restaurant continued to survive and prosper, allowing Hofbeck to retire, and allowing Steinberg to remain an owner and manager as long as he wished.

FOCUSING ON THE PROBLEM, NOT THE PEOPLE People who are in conflict may not be able to resist the temptation to focus on the other party's shortcomings and weaknesses, thereby personalizing the conflict. Instead of attacking the problem, the parties to the conflict attack each other. This approach is inconsistent with integrative bargaining and can easily lead both parties into a distributive negotiation mode. All parties to a conflict need to keep focused on the problem or on the source of the conflict and avoid the temptation to discredit each other.

Given their strong friendship, this was not much of an issue for Hofbeck and Steinberg, but they still had to be on their guard to avoid personalizing the conflict. Steinberg recalls that once when they were having a hard time coming up with a solution, he started thinking how lazy Hofbeck, a healthy 57-year-old, was to want to retire so young: "If only he wasn't so lazy, we would never be in the mess we're in right now." Steinberg never mentioned these thoughts to Hofbeck (who later admitted that sometimes he was annoyed with Steinberg for being such a workaholic), because he realized that they would hurt their chances for reaching an integrative solution.

FOCUSING ON INTERESTS, NOT DEMANDS Demands are *what* a person wants; interests are *why* the person wants them. When two people are in conflict, it is unlikely that the demands of both can be met. Their underlying interests, however, can be met and meeting them is what integrative bargaining is all about.

Hofbeck's demand was that they sell the restaurant and split the proceeds. Steinberg's demand was that they keep the restaurant and maintain the status quo. Obviously, both demands could not be met, but perhaps their interests could be. Hofbeck wanted to be able to retire, invest his share of the money from the restaurant, and live off the returns on the investment. Steinberg wanted to continue managing, owning, and deriving income from the restaurant.

CREATING NEW OPTIONS FOR JOINT GAIN Once two parties to a conflict focus on their interests, they are on the road toward achieving creative solutions to the conflict that will benefit them both. This win-win scenario means that rather than having a fixed set of alternatives from which to choose, the two parties can come up with new alternatives that might even expand the resource pie.

Hofbeck and Steinberg came up with three such alternatives. First, even though Steinberg did not have the capital, he could buy out Hofbeck's share of the restaurant. Hofbeck would provide the financing for the purchase, and in return Steinberg would pay him a reasonable return on his investment (the same kind of return he could have obtained had he taken his money out of the restaurant and invested it). Second, the partners could seek to sell Hofbeck's share in the restaurant to a third party under the stipulation that Steinberg would continue to manage the restaurant and receive income for his services. Third, the partners could continue to jointly own the restaurant. Steinberg would manage it and receive a proportionally greater share of its profits than Hofbeck, who would be an absentee owner not involved in day-to-day operations but would still receive a return on his investment in the restaurant.

FOCUSING ON WHAT IS FAIR Focusing on what is fair is consistent with the principle of distributive justice, which emphasizes the fair distribution of outcomes based on the meaningful contributions that people make to organizations (see Chapter 4). It is likely that two parties in conflict will disagree on certain points and prefer different alternatives that each party believes may better serve his or her own interests or maximize his or her own outcomes. Emphasizing fairness and distributive justice will help the two parties come to a mutual agreement about what is the best solution to the problem.

Steinberg and Hofbeck agreed that Hofbeck should be able to cut his ties with the restaurant if he chose to do so. They thus decided to pursue the second alternative described above and seek a suitable buyer for Hofbeck's share. They were successful in finding an investor who was willing to buy out Hofbeck's share and let Steinberg continue to manage the restaurant. And they remained good friends.

When managers pursue these five strategies and encourage other organizational members to do so, they are more likely to be able to effectively resolve their conflicts through integrative bargaining. In addition, throughout the negotiation process, managers and other organizational members need to be aware of, and on their guard against, the biases that can lead to faulty decision making (see Chapter 6).[31]

Tips for New Managers

Negotiation

1. Whenever feasible, use integrative bargaining rather than distributive negotiation.
2. To help ensure that conflicts are effectively resolved through integrative bargaining, emphasize superordinate goals, focus on the problem not the people, focus on interests not demands, create new options for joint gain, and focus on what is fair.

Organizational Politics

Managers must develop the skills necessary to manage organizational conflict in order for an organization to be effective. Suppose, however, that top managers are in conflict over the best strategy for an organization to pursue or the best structure to adopt to utilize organizational resources efficiently. In such situations, resolving conflict is often difficult, and the parties to the conflict resort to organizational politics and political strategies to try to resolve the conflict in their favor.

organizational politics Activities that managers engage in to increase their power and to use power effectively to achieve their goals and overcome resistance or opposition.

political strategies Tactics that managers use to increase their power and to use power effectively to influence and gain the support of other people while overcoming resistance or opposition.

Organizational politics are the activities that managers (and other members of an organization) engage in to increase their power and to use power effectively to achieve their goals and overcome resistance or opposition.[32] Managers often engage in organizational politics to resolve conflicts in their favor.

Political strategies are the specific tactics that managers (and other members of an organization) use to increase their power and to use power effectively to influence and gain the support of other people while overcoming resistance or opposition. Political strategies are especially important when managers are planning and implementing major changes in an organization: Managers not only need to gain support for their change initiatives and influence organizational members to behave in new ways but also to overcome often strong opposition from people who feel threatened by the change and prefer the status quo. By increasing their power, managers are better able to make needed changes. In addition to increasing their power, managers must make sure that they use their power in a way that actually enables them to influence others. In "A Manager's Challenge," it is apparent that Nasser experienced difficulties both in building power and in effectively exercising it; thus, he had trouble effectively implementing changes at Ford.

The Importance of Organizational Politics

The term *politics* has a negative connotation for many people. Some may think that managers who are political have risen to the top not because of their own merit and capabilities but because of who they know. Or people may think that political managers are self-interested and wield power to benefit themselves, not their organization. There is a grain of truth to this negative connotation. Some managers do appear to misuse their power for personal benefit at the expense of their organization's effectiveness.

Nevertheless, organizational politics are often a positive force. Managers striving to make needed changes often encounter resistance from individuals and groups that feel threatened and wish to preserve the status quo. Effective managers engage in politics to gain support for and implement needed changes. Similarly, managers often face resistance from other managers who disagree with their goals for a group or for the organization and with what they are trying to accomplish. Engaging in organizational politics can help managers overcome this resistance and achieve their goals.

Indeed, managers cannot afford to ignore organizational politics. Everyone engages in politics to a degree–other managers, coworkers, and subordinates, as well as people outside an organization such as suppliers. Those who try to ignore politics might as well bury their heads in the sand because in all likelihood they will be unable to gain support for their initiatives and goals.

Political Strategies for Increasing Power

Managers who use political strategies to increase their power are better able to influence others to work toward the achievement of group and organizational goals. By controlling uncertainty, making themselves irreplaceable, being in a central position, generating resources, and building alliances, managers can increase their power (see Figure 16.4).[33] We next look at each of these strategies.

Figure 16.4
Political Strategies for Increasing Power

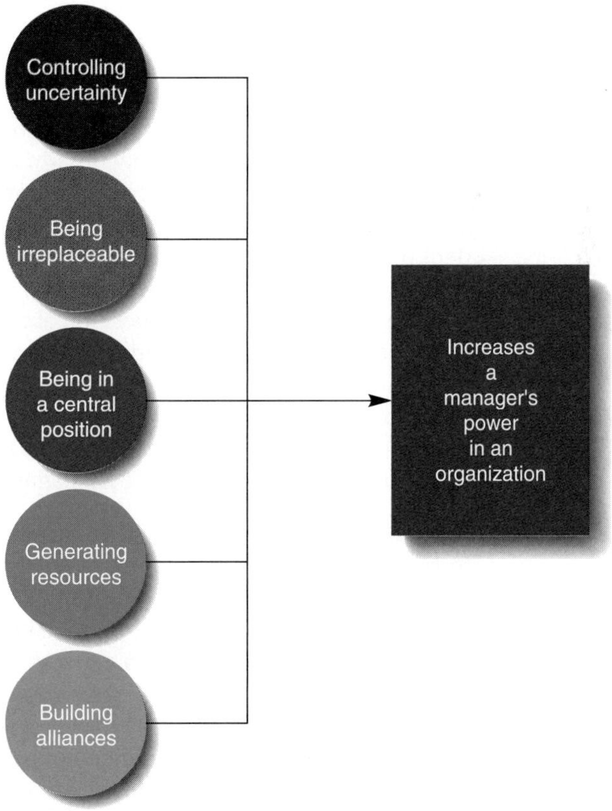

CONTROLLING UNCERTAINTY Uncertainty is a threat for individuals, groups, and whole organizations and can interfere with effective performance and goal attainment. For example, uncertainty about job security is threatening for many workers and may cause top performers (who have the best chance of finding another job) to quit and take a more secure position with another organization. When an R&D department faces uncertainty about customer preferences, its members may waste valuable resources to develop a product, such as smokeless cigarettes that customers do not want. When top managers face uncertainty about global demand, they may fail to export products to countries that want them and thus lose a source of competitive advantage.

Managers who are able to control and reduce uncertainty for other managers, teams, departments, and the organization as a whole are likely to see their power increase.[34] Managers of labor unions gain power when they can eliminate uncertainty over job security for workers. Marketing and sales managers gain power when they can eliminate uncertainty for other departments such as R&D by accurately forecasting customers' changing preferences. Top managers gain power when they are knowledgeable about global demand for an organization's products. Managers who are able to control uncertainty are likely to be in demand and sought after by other organizations.

MAKING ONESELF IRREPLACEABLE Managers gain power when they have valuable knowledge and expertise that allow them to perform activities that no one else can handle. This is the essence of being irreplaceable.[35] The more central these activities are to organizational effectiveness, the more power managers gain from being irreplaceable. Conversely, when managers are doing poorly, they often become replaceable, as was true with Nasser at Ford in "A Manager's Challenge."

BEING IN A CENTRAL POSITION Managers in central positions are responsible for activities that are directly connected to an organization's goals and sources of competitive advantage and often are located in central positions in important communication networks in an organization.[36] Managers in central positions have control over crucial organizational activities and initiatives and have access to important information. Other organizational members are dependent on them for their knowledge, expertise, advice, and support, and the success of the organization as a whole is seen as riding on these managers. These consequences of being in a central position are likely to increase managers' power.

Managers who are outstanding performers, have a wide knowledge base, and have made important and visible contributions to their organizations are likely to be offered central positions that will increase their power. And when those who are in central positions do not perform up to expectations, they become replaceable, as illustrated in "A Manager's Challenge."

GENERATING RESOURCES Organizations need three kinds of resources to be effective: (1) input resources such as raw materials, skilled workers, and financial capital; (2) technical resources such as machinery and computers; and (3) knowledge resources such as marketing or engineering expertise. To the extent that a manager is able to generate one or more of these kinds of resources for an organization, that manager's power is likely to increase.[37] In universities, for example, professors who win large grants to fund their research from associations such as the National Science Foundation and the Army Research Institute gain power because of the financial resources they are generating for their departments and universities as a whole.

Andrew C. Sigler, chairman of the board of paper producer Champion International Corporation, gained so much power from generating resources that he remained at the top of a Fortune 500 company for 20 years despite Champion's poor returns to shareholders. A sudden rise in paper prices turned Champion's fortunes around, but insiders attribute at least part of Sigler's staying power at the top to his close relationships with major investors such as billionaires Warren Buffett and Laurence Tisch; these ties enabled him to generate capital for Champion.[38]

BUILDING ALLIANCES When managers build alliances, they develop mutually beneficial relationships with people both inside and outside the organization. The two parties to an alliance support one another because doing so is in their best interests, and both parties benefit from the alliance. Alliances provide managers with power because they provide the managers with support for their initiatives. Partners to alliances provide support because they know that managers will reciprocate when their partners need support. Alliances can help managers achieve their goals and implement needed changes in organizations because they increase managers' levels of power. From "A Manager's Challenge," it is clear that Nasser probably could have done a better job of building alliances in Ford.

Many powerful top managers focus on building alliances not only inside their organizations but also with individuals, groups, and organizations in the task and general environments on which their organizations are dependent for resources. These individuals, groups, and organizations enter into alliances with managers because doing so is in their best interests and they know that they can count on the managers' support when they need it. As indicated in the following "Ethics in Action," when managers build alliances, they need to be on their guard to ensure that everything is aboveboard, ethical, and legal.

Ethics in Action

Unsavory Alliances in the Auction House World

Christie's and Sotheby's dominate the fine-art auction world with some 90 percent of the $4 billion market. Hence, it is not surprising that they have been fierce competitors. What is surprising is that when times were tough for both auction houses in the 1990s, they formed an illegal alliance to fix commissions. When their scheme became public, both auction houses were subject to a class-action lawsuit with fines in the hundreds of millions of dollars as well as federal investigations into price-fixing which is a violation of antitrust laws. David Boies, the attorney for former clients filing the class-action suit, hoped to pit each auction house against the other. This would maximize damages paid to his clients as well as his own fees since he negotiated a deal to obtain 25 percent of any damages paid on behalf of the suit in excess of $400 million.[39]

In the mid 1990s, Sotheby's and Christie's were hurting from a weak market that enabled their clients to negotiate lower and lower commissions, sometimes even lower than 2 percent. Essentially, clients would pit the two auction houses against each other, and whoever offered the lowest commission was given the business. Through a complicated chain of events, Sotheby's and Christie's formed an illegal alliance to not only fix prices on a sliding scale but also refuse to negotiate with customers. Thus, commissions would be higher for lower priced items (e.g., fine furniture in the tens of thousands of dollars) and lower for higher priced items (e.g., fine art in the millions) and both houses would refrain from negotiating downward to attract business. This scheme worked for both houses for a few years and they were back on their feet, at the expense of overcharging their clients.[40]

When their price-fixing scheme was exposed and they were facing the class-action lawsuit, Boies hoped to once again pit the two rivals against each other so whoever settled first would pay less in damages and cause the other to pay much more. Essentially, Boies told both houses that whichever settled first to the tune of $212 million would get the better deal and would help him go after the other house for significantly more in damages. He told each auction house that the other was the real scoundrel; hence, the proposed deal. The deal sounded good to both Christie's and Sotheby's and both decided to go for it. However, according to Boies' plan, they couldn't both have it as that would mean less money in damages for his clients. Once again, Sotheby's and Christie's allied forces and agreed to each pay $256 million in damages to avoid even costlier lawsuits.[41] As this tale of intrigue and deceit illustrates, organizations and their managers need to be aware of the temptation to form unsavory alliances when times are tough and to make sure that any alliances they enter into are legal and ethical.

A work of art is auctioned off at Sotheby's. In response to a weak market in the mid-1990s, Sotheby's agreed to an illegal price-fixing scheme with archrival Christie's.

Political Strategies for Exercising Power

Politically skilled managers not only have a good understanding of, and ability to use, those five strategies to increase their power; they also have a good appreciation of strategies for exercising their power. These strategies generally focus on how managers can use their power *unobtrusively*."[42] When managers exercise power unobtrusively, other members of an organization may not be aware that they are using their power to influence them. They may think that they support these managers for a variety of reasons: because they believe it is the rational or logical thing to do, because they believe that doing so is in their own best interests, or because they believe that the position or decision that these managers are advocating is legitimate or appropriate.

The unobtrusive use of power may sound devious, but managers typically use this strategy to bring about change and achieve organizational goals. Political strategies for exercising power to gain the support and concurrence of others include relying on objective information, bringing in an outside expert, controlling the agenda, and making everyone a winner (see Figure 16.5).[43]

RELYING ON OBJECTIVE INFORMATION Managers require the support of others to achieve their goals, implement changes, and overcome opposition. One way for a manager to gain this support and overcome opposition is to rely on objective information that supports the manager's initiatives. Reliance on objective information leads others to support the manager because of the facts; objective information causes others to believe that what the manager is proposing is the proper course of action. By relying on objective information, politically skilled managers unobtrusively exercise their power to influence others.

Figure 16.5
Political Strategies for Exercising Power

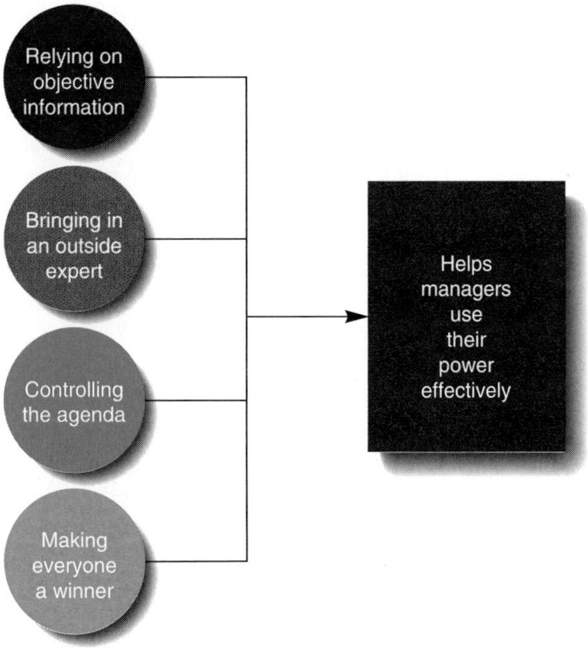

Take the case of Mary Callahan, vice president of Better Built Cabinets, a small cabinet company in the Southeast. Callahan is extremely influential in the company; practically every new initiative that she proposes to the president and owner of the company is implemented. Why is Callahan able to use her power in the company so effectively? Whenever she has an idea for a new initiative that she thinks the company might pursue, she and her subordinates begin by collecting objective information supporting the initiative. Recently, Callahan decided that Better Built should develop a line of high-priced European-style kitchen cabinets. Before presenting her proposal to Better Built's president, she compiled objective information showing that (1) there was strong unmet demand for these kinds of cabinets, (2) Better Built could manufacture them in its existing production facilities, and (3) the new line had the potential to increase Better Built's sales by 20 percent while not detracting from sales of the company's other cabinets. Presented with this information, the president agreed to Callahan's proposal. Moreover, the president and other members of Better Built whose cooperation was needed to implement the proposal supported it because they thought it would help Better Built gain a competitive advantage. Using objective information to support her position enabled Callahan to unobtrusively exercise her power and influence others to support her proposal.

BRINGING IN AN OUTSIDE EXPERT Bringing in an outside expert to support a proposal or decision can, at times, provide managers with some of the same benefits that the use of objective information does. It lends credibility to a manager's initiatives and causes others to believe that what the manager is proposing is the appropriate or rational thing to do. Suppose Callahan had hired a consultant to evaluate whether her idea was a good one. The consultant reports back to the president that the new European-style cabinets are likely to fulfill Callahan's promises and increase Better Built's sales and profits. Once again, this information provided by an objective expert can lend a sense of legitimacy to Callahan's proposal and allow her to unobtrusively exercise power to influence others.

Although you might think that consultants and other outside experts are neutral or objective, they sometimes are hired by managers who want them to support a certain position or decision in an organization. For instance, when managers are facing strong opposition from others who fear that a decision will harm their or their departments' interests, they may bring in an outside expert. They hope this expert will be perceived as a neutral observer to lend credibility and objectivity to their point of view. The support of such an outside expert may cause others to believe that a decision is indeed the right one. Of course, sometimes consultants and other outside experts actually are brought into organizations *to be* objective and provide managers with guidance on the appropriate course of action to take.

CONTROLLING THE AGENDA Managers also can exercise power unobtrusively by controlling the agenda–influencing what alternatives are considered or even whether a decision is made.[44] When managers influence the alternatives that are considered, they can make sure that each considered alternative is acceptable to them and that undesirable alternatives are not in the feasible set. In a hiring context, for example, managers can exert their power unobtrusively by ensuring that job candidates whom they do not find acceptable do not make their way onto the list of finalists for an open position. They do this by making sure that these candidates' drawbacks or deficiencies are communicated to everyone involved in making the hiring decision. When three finalists for an open position are discussed and evaluated in a hiring meeting, a manager may seem to exert little power or influence and just go along with what the rest of the group wants. However, the manager may have exerted power in the hiring process unobtrusively, by controlling which candidates made it to the final stage.

Sometimes managers can prevent a decision from being made. A manager in charge of a community relations committee, for example, may not favor a proposal for the organization to become more involved in local youth groups such as the Boy Scouts and the Girl Scouts. The manager can exert influence in this situation by not including the proposal on the agenda for the committee's next meeting. Alternatively, the manager could place the proposal at the end of the agenda for the meeting and feel confident that the committee will run out of time and not get to the last items on the agenda because that is what always happens. Either not including the proposal or putting it at the end of the agenda enables the manager to unobtrusively exercise power. Committee members do not perceive this manager as trying to influence them to turn down the proposal. Rather, the manager has made the proposal into a nonissue that is not even considered.

MAKING EVERYONE A WINNER Often, politically skilled managers are able to exercise their power unobtrusively because they make sure that everyone whose support they need benefits personally from providing that support. By making everyone a winner, a manager is able to influence other organizational members because these members see supporting the manager to be in their best interest. Making everyone a winner is something Nasser could have done more of as CEO of Ford.

Alternatively, the CEO of Nissan Motor Co., Carlos Ghosn, appears to be able to exercise his power by making others feel that it is in their best interest to go along with his initiatives, as indicated in the following "Managing Globally."

Managing Globally

Ghosn Shakes up Nissan

Carlos Ghosn has made some sweeping changes at Nissan Motor Corp., changes that signal a new era not only for Nissan but also for Japanese manufacturing. In 2001, Ghosn shut down one of Nissan's major factories in Murayama; in its heyday, the Murayama plant produced 453,000 vehicles annually and had 5,000 employees. In an effort to restore Nissan to profitability, Ghosn shut the plant and is embarking on a strategy to move Nissan's manufacturing outside Japan. For example, the all-export Maxima sedan will now be manufactured in Tennessee and plans are on the horizon to open a major minivan and SUV factory in Mississippi.[45]

Why the shift in production from Japan to the United States? Essentially, the Japanese market for cars is weak, the U.S. market is relatively stronger, currency problems are avoided, and it simply makes more sense to make cars in the markets in which they are sold.[46] Hence, this shift is not surprising from an economic perspective but it is surprising from a cultural perspective given Japan's emphasis on job security for employees.

Ghosn has been able to gain acceptance for his initiatives (which might eventually result in 21,000 job cuts worldwide by 2003) from the All Nissan Motor Workers' Union in Japan because he has been able to persuade them that the downsizing and cuts are necessary for Nissan to achieve a state of long-run and continued profitability. Thus, the union and its members believe that it is in their best interests to support Ghosn's initiatives. Moreover, Ghosn has offered positions to laid off Murayama workers in other Nissan plants and attesting to his good intentions, agreed to a better-than-anticipated pay hike after wages had been frozen for two years. According to research supported by the Confederation of Japan Automobile Workers' Unions (JAW), in the next five years, Japan may lose more than one-eighth of its 800,000 auto-related factory jobs after losing close to 100,000 such positions in the 1990s.[47] Managers overseeing these projected cutbacks are well advised to follow Ghosn's approach by which he has been, thus far, able to convince the union and its members that downsizing is in the long-run best interests of Nissan and its employees.[48]

Nissan Motor Co. President Carlos Ghosn, left, is applauded by employees as he arrives at a dealer in Fukuoka, southwestern Japan. Ghosn, who was sent in by French automaker Renault SA to fix the struggling Nissan, is now more than just an executive—he's a star.

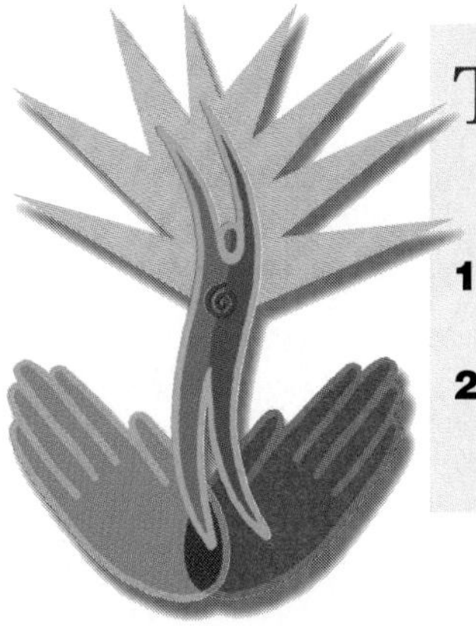

Tips for New Managers

Political Strategies

1. Determine the major source of uncertainty for your work group and organization and take steps to help control these sources of uncertainty.
2. Try to develop skills or expertise that are crucial to your organization and not possessed by other organizational members.

3. Determine which recourses are crucial for your organization and try to help generate these resources.
4. Build alliances with powerful organizational members to gain support for your ideas.
5. Whenever possible, use objective information to support positions that you advocate.

Managing Organizational Change

Both politics and conflict can signal to managers that the way an organization operates needs to change. For example, poor communication and a lack of cooperation between manufacturing and marketing may signal a need to increase the level of integration between these departments or even change the managers involved. However, organizational conflict and politics often arise because changes in the way an organization operates, particularly changes in strategy or structure, inevitably favor some individuals or groups over others (see Figure 16.6).

Because organizational conflict, politics, and change are intertwined as illustrated in "A Manager's Challenge," it is important for managers to develop the skills necessary to manage change effectively. Several experts have proposed a model that managers can follow to implement change successfully while effectively managing conflict and politics.[49] Figure 16.7 outlines the steps that managers must take to manage change effectively. In the rest of this section we examine each one.

Assessing the Need for Change

Organizational change can affect practically all aspects of organizational functioning, including an organization's structure, culture, strategies, control systems, groups and teams, and the human resource management system. It also affects critical organizational processes such as communication, motivation, and leadership. Organizational change can bring alterations in the ways managers

Figure 16.6
The Relationship Between Organizational Conflict, Politics, and Change

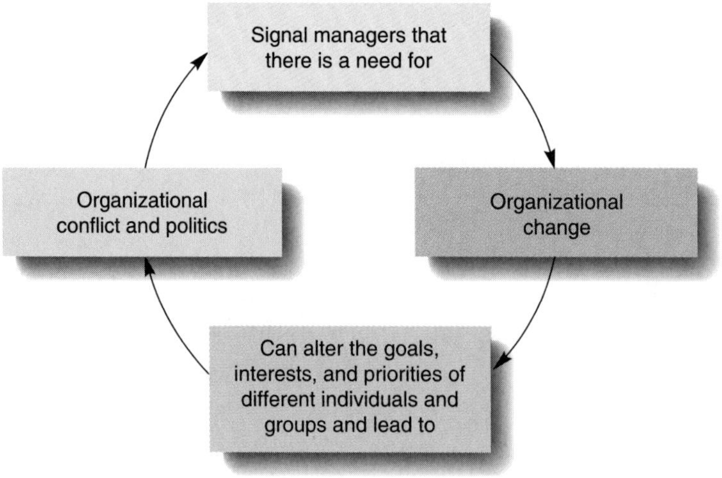

Figure 16.7
Four Steps in the Organizational Change Process

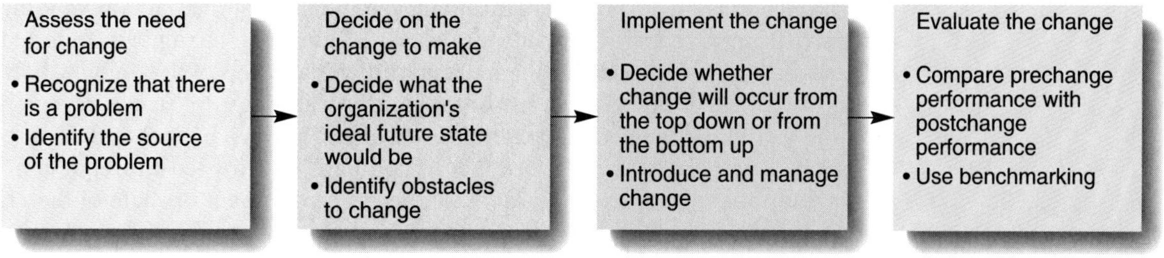
Assess the need for change
• Recognize that there is a problem
• Identify the source of the problem
Decide on the change to make
• Decide what the organization's ideal future state would be
• Identify obstacles to change
Implement the change
• Decide whether change will occur from the top down or from the bottom up
• Introduce and manage change
Evaluate the change
• Compare prechange performance with postchange performance
• Use benchmarking

carry out the critical tasks of planning, organizing, leading, and controlling, and the ways they perform their managerial roles.

Deciding how to change an organization is a complex matter, not least because change disrupts the status quo and poses a threat, prompting employees to resist attempts to alter work relationships and procedures. Organizational learning, the process through which managers try to increase organizational members' abilities to understand and appropriately respond to changing conditions (see Chapter 6), can be an important impetus for change and help all members of an organization, including managers, to effectively make decisions about needed changes.

Assessing the need for change includes two important activities: recognizing that there is a problem and identifying its source. Sometimes the need for change is obvious, such as when an organization's performance is suffering. Often, however, managers have trouble determining that something is going wrong because problems develop gradually; organizational performance may slip for a number of years before it becomes obvious. Thus, during the first step in the change process, managers need to recognize that there is a problem that requires change.

Often the problems that managers detect have produced a gap between desired performance and actual performance. To detect such a gap, managers need to look at performance measures, such as falling market share or profits, rising costs, or employees' failure to meet their established goals or stay within budgets, which indicate whether change is needed. These measures are provided by organizational control systems (discussed in Chapter 9).

To discover the source of the problem, managers need to look both inside and outside the organization. Outside the organization, they must examine how changes in environmental forces may be creating opportunities and threats that are affecting internal work relationships. Perhaps the emergence of low-cost foreign competitors has led to conflict among different departments that are trying to find new ways to gain a competitive advantage. Managers also need to look within the organization to see whether its structure and culture are causing problems between departments. Perhaps a company does not have the integrating mechanisms in place to allow different departments to respond to low-cost competition (see Chapter 8).

Deciding on the Change to Make

Once managers have identified the source of the problem, they must decide what they think the organization's ideal future state would be. In other words, they must decide where they would like their organization to be in the future–what kinds of goods and services it should be making, what its business-level strategy should be, how the organizational structure should be changed, and so on. During this step, managers also must engage in planning how they are going to attain the organization's ideal future state.

This step in the change process also includes identifying obstacles or sources of resistance to change. Managers must analyze the factors that may prevent the company from reaching its ideal future state. Obstacles to change are found at the corporate, divisional, departmental, and individual levels of the organization.

Corporate-level changes in an organization's strategy or structure, even seemingly trivial changes, may significantly affect how divisional and departmental managers behave. Suppose that to compete with low-cost foreign competitors, top managers decide to increase the resources spent on state-of-the-art machinery and reduce the resources spent on marketing or R&D. The power of manufacturing managers would increase, and the power of marketing and R&D managers would fall. This decision would alter the balance of power among departments and might lead to increased politics and conflict as departments start fighting to retain their status in the organization. An organization's present strategy and structure are powerful obstacles to change.

Organizational culture also can facilitate or obstruct change. Organizations with entrepreneurial, flexible cultures, such as high-tech companies, are much easier to change than are organizations with more rigid cultures such as those sometimes found in large bureaucratic organizations like the military or General Motors.

The same obstacles to change exist at the divisional and departmental levels as well. Division managers may differ in their attitudes toward the changes that top managers propose and will resist those changes if their interests and power seem threatened. Managers at all levels usually fight to protect their power and control over resources. Given that departments have different goals and time horizons, they may also react differently to the changes that other managers propose. When top managers are trying to reduce costs, for example, sales managers may resist attempts to cut back on sales expenditures if they believe that problems stem from manufacturing managers' inefficiencies.

At the individual level, too, people are often resistant to change because change brings uncertainty and uncertainty brings stress. For example, individuals may resist the introduction of a new technology because they are uncertain about their abilities to learn it and effectively use it.

These obstacles make organizational change a slow process. Managers must recognize these potential obstacles to change and take them into consideration. Some obstacles can be overcome by improving communication so all organizational members are aware of the need for change and of the nature of the changes being made. Empowering employees and inviting them to participate in the planning for change also can help overcome resistance and allay employees' fears. In addition, managers can sometimes overcome resistance by using the integrative bargaining strategies discussed earlier in this chapter. For example, emphasizing superordinate goals such as organizational effectiveness and gaining a competitive advantage can make organizational members who resist a change realize that the change is ultimately in everyone's best interests because it will increase organizational performance. The larger and more complex an organization is, the more complex is the change process.

Implementing the Change

top-down change Change that is implemented quickly throughout an organization by upper-level managers.

Generally, managers implement–that is, introduce and manage–change from the top down or from the bottom up.[50] **Top-down change** is implemented quickly: Top managers identify the need for change, decide what to do, and then move quickly to implement the changes throughout the organization. For example, top managers may decide to restructure and downsize the organization and then give divisional and departmental managers specific goals to achieve. With top-down change, the emphasis is on making the changes quickly and dealing with problems as they arise.

bottom-up change Change that is implemented gradually and involves managers and employees at all levels of an organization.

Bottom-up change is typically more gradual. Top managers consult with middle and first-line managers about the need for change. Then, over time, these low-level managers work with nonmanagerial employees to develop a detailed plan for change. A major advantage of bottom-up change is that it can co-opt resistance to change. Because the emphasis in bottom-up change is on participation and on keeping people informed about what is going on, uncertainty and resistance are minimized.

Evaluating the Change

The last step in the change process is to evaluate how successful the change effort has been in improving organizational performance.[51] Using measures such as changes in market share, profits, or the ability of managers to meet their goals, managers compare how well an organization is performing after the change with how well it was performing before. Managers also can use **benchmarking**, comparing their performance on specific dimensions with the performance of high-performing organizations to decide how successful the change effort has been. For example, when Xerox was doing poorly in the 1980s, it benchmarked the efficiency of its distribution operations against those of L. L. Bean, the efficiency of its central computer operations against those of John Deere, and its marketing abilities against those of Procter & Gamble. Those companies are renowned for their skills in those different areas, and by studying how they performed, Xerox was able to dramatically increase its own performance. Benchmarking is a key tool in total quality management, an important change program discussed at length in Chapter 18.

benchmarking Comparing performance on specific dimensions with the performance of high-performing organizations.

For some organizations, the need to be flexible and responsive to customers necessitates continuous change. One such organization, Igus Inc., is lead by Frank Blase and profiled in the following "Information Technology Byte."

Information Technology Byte

Change Is the Norm at Igus Inc.

Igus Inc. is a study in continuous change. Igus, headquartered in Cologne, Germany, manufactures polymer bearings, energy-chains, power-supply chains, and thousands of other products that are used in diverse applications ranging from factory assembly lines to the sets of Broadway shows. In Igus's flagship manufacturing facility everything is designed to be changed in a minute. Machinery and furniture are not welded down or fixed in place so they can be moved and reconfigured depending on the products Igus is developing and manufacturing. For example, during a recent five-year period, 50 major reconfigurations in the plant layout took place. Moreover, the plant is incredibly open–open to the outdoors via large windows and open internally through minimal glass walls.[52]

Igus operates 24 hours a day, seven days a week, manufactures over 25,000 products, and creates 2,500 new products or product variations each year.[53] Needless to say, responsiveness to customers' changing needs reigns at Igus and the flexible manufacturing facility and culture support it.

Lisa Forbush places products for shipment onto a conveyor belt at an L. L. Bean distribution center in Freeport, Maine. When Xerox was struggling in the 1980s, it benchmarked the efficiency of its distribution operations against those of L. L. Bean, a company known for its successful product distribution.

With their mobile phones at the ready, employees travel around the factory on motorized scooters; in the office areas where the only fixed glass walls are found, nonmotorized scooters do the trick. Consistent with the use of scooters is an emphasis on speed at Igus Inc. Blase is quick to praise teams that configure new products at breakneck speed and notes when problems occur in his weekly e-letter to employees. Everything about Igus Inc. exudes speed, flexibility, and change which may help to account for its rapid growth. Igus's current annual revenues of $100 million are ten times greater than they were in 1994 and this privately held company has over 800 employees.[54] While many managers might not need or want to embrace change as extensively as Blase does at Igus Inc., they can certainly learn a few lessons in flexibility, creativity, and responsiveness to customers from his change-oriented organization and factory.

Summary and Review

ORGANIZATIONAL CONFLICT Organizational conflict is the discord that arises when the goals, interests, or values of different individuals or groups are incompatible and those individuals or groups block or thwart each other's attempts to achieve their objectives. Four types of conflict arising in organizations are interpersonal conflict, intragroup conflict, intergroup conflict, and interorganizational conflict. Sources of conflict in organizations include incompatible goals and time horizons, overlapping authority, task interdependencies, incompatible evaluation or reward systems, scarce resources, and status inconsistencies. Conflict management strategies focused on individuals include increasing awareness of the sources of conflict, increasing diversity awareness and skills, practicing job rotation or temporary assignments, and using permanent transfers or dismissals when necessary. Strategies focused on the whole organization include changing an organization's structure or culture and altering the source of conflict.

NEGOTIATION STRATEGIES FOR INTEGRATION BARGAINING Negotiation is a conflict resolution technique used when parties to a conflict have approximately equal levels of power and try to come up with an acceptable way to allocate resources to each other. In distributive negotiation, the parties perceive that there is a fixed level of resources for them to allocate, and they compete to receive as much as possible at the expense of the other party, not caring about their relationship in the future. In integrative bargaining, both parties perceive that they may be able to increase the resource pie by coming up with a creative solution to the conflict, trusting each other, and cooperating with each other to achieve a win-win resolution. Five strategies that managers can use to facilitate integrative bargaining are to emphasize superordinate goals; focus on the problem, not the people; focus on interests, not demands; create new options for joint gain; and focus on what is fair.

ORGANIZATIONAL POLITICS Organizational politics are the activities that managers (and other members of an organization) engage in to increase their power and to use power effectively to achieve their goals and overcome resistance or opposition. Effective managers realize that politics can be a positive force that enables them to make needed changes in an organization. Five important political strategies for increasing power are controlling uncertainty, making oneself irreplaceable, being in a central position, generating resources, and building alliances. Political strategies for effectively exercising power focus on how to use power unobtrusively and include relying on objective information, bringing in an outside expert, controlling the agenda, and making everyone a winner.

MANAGING ORGANIZATIONAL CHANGE Managing organizational change is one of managers' most important and difficult tasks. Four steps in the organizational change process are assessing the need for change, deciding on the change to make, implementing the change, and evaluating how successful the change effort has been.

Management in Action

Topics for Discussion and Action

1. Discuss why too little conflict in an organization can be just as detrimental as too much conflict.
2. Interview a manager in a local organization to determine the kinds of conflicts that occur in that manager's organization and the strategies that are used to manage them.
3. Why is integrative bargaining a more effective way of resolving conflicts than distributive negotiation?
4. Why do organizational politics affect practically every organization? Why do effective managers need good political skills?
5. What steps can managers take to ensure that organizational politics are a positive force leading to a competitive advantage, not a negative force leading to personal advantage at the expense of organizational goal attainment?
6. Think of a member of an organization whom you know and who is particularly powerful. What political strategies does this person use to increase his or her power?
7. Why is it best to use power unobtrusively? How are people likely to react to power that is exercised obtrusively?
8. What are the main obstacles to change?
9. Interview a manager about a change effort that he or she was involved in. What issues were involved? What problems were encountered? What was the outcome of the change process?

Building Management Skills

Effective and Ineffective Conflict Resolution

Think about two recent conflicts that you had with other people, one conflict that you felt was effectively resolved (C1) and one that you felt was ineffectively resolved (C2). The other people involved could be coworkers, students, family members, friends, or members of an organization that you are a member of. Answer the following questions.

1. Briefly describe C1 and C2. What type of conflict was involved in each of these incidents?
2. What was the source of the conflict in C1 and in C2?
3. What conflict management strategies were used in C1 and in C2?
4. What could you have done differently to more effectively manage conflict in C2?
5. How was conflict resolved in C1 and in C2?

Small Group Breakout Exercise

Negotiating a Solution

Form groups of three or four people. One member of your group will play the role of Jane Rister, one member will play the role of Michael Schwartz, and one or two members will be observer(s) and spokesperson(s) for your group.

Jane Rister and Michael Schwartz are assistant managers in a large department store. They report directly to the store manager. Today they are meeting to discuss some important problems they need to solve but about which they disagree.

The first problem hinges around the fact that either Rister or Schwartz needs to be on duty whenever the store is open. For the last six months, Rister has taken most of the least desirable hours (nights and weekends). They are planning their schedules for the next six months. Rister thought Schwartz would take more of the undesirable times, but Schwartz has informed Rister that his wife has just gotten a nursing job that requires her to work weekends, so he needs to stay home weekends to take care of their infant daughter.

The second problem concerns a department manager who has had a hard time retaining salespeople in his department. The turnover rate in his department is twice that of the other departments in the store. Rister thinks the manager is ineffective and wants to fire him. Schwartz thinks the high turnover is just a fluke and the manager is effective.

The last problem concerns Rister's and Schwartz's vacation schedules. Both managers want to take off the week of July 4, but one of them needs to be in the store whenever it is open.

1. The group members playing Rister and Schwartz assume their roles and negotiate a solution to these three problems.
2. Observers take notes on how Rister and Schwartz negotiate solutions to their problems.
3. Observers determine the extent to which Rister and Schwartz use distributive negotiation or integrative bargaining to resolve their conflicts.
4. When called on by the instructor, observers communicate to the rest of the class how Rister and Schwartz resolved their conflicts, whether they used distributive negotiation or integrative bargaining, and their actual solutions.

Exploring the World Wide Web

Find the website of a company that is in the process of making major organizational changes. What are these changes? How are they being implemented? What kinds of obstacles to change do you think managers in this company may be encountering?

You're the Management Consultant

Mary Stevens is a middle manager in a large corporation who feels like she is caught between a rock and a hard place. Times are tough, her unit has experienced layoffs, the survivors are overworked and demoralized, and she feels she has no meaningful rewards such as the chance for a pay raise, bonus, or promotion to motivate them with. Her boss keeps increasing the demands on her and her unit as well as the unit's responsibilities. Moreover, Stevens believes she and her subordinates are being unfairly blamed for certain problems beyond their control. Stevens believes she has the expertise and skills to perform her job effectively and also that her subordinates are capable and effective in their jobs. Yet, she feels she is on shaky ground and powerless. As an expert in power, politics, and change, she has come to you for advice. What should she do?

BusinessWeek

Cases In the News

Is Kogan in a Corner?

Growing up in New York in the mid-1950s as the son of a bar-and-grill owner in Hell's Kitchen, Richard Jay Kogan knew when to back off from an uneven fight. Once, when he had a job selling peanuts in Yankee Stadium, a group of vendors pressed him to join their union. "He told them he didn't have to join any damn union, so they beat the hell out of him," says Gerald J. Mossinghoff, a longtime colleague. "Then he did join."

Kogan, 60, now chairman and chief executive of pharmaceutical company Schering-Plough Corp., seems to have lost some of his self-preservation skills. Over the past decade, he turned a niche-player company into one of the drug industry's top performers—nearly quintupling its market value between 1996 and 2000. But now the tightfisted and feisty Kogan is contending with manufacturing and regulatory problems big enough that he may be forced to sell Schering as distressed merchandise. This predicament would be difficult for any executive, but it must be particularly galling for Kogan. The traits that helped him fight his way to the top—a talent for making his numbers and an unusual amount of backroom savvy—may be responsible for his comedown.

Blockbuster

Kogan has been at war with one government agency no drug executive can afford to antagonize, the Food & Drug Administration. As he tried to wring a few more years of patent protection for the $3 billion-a-year blockbuster antihistamine Claritin, which accounts for a third of Schering's sales and about 40 percent of its profits, he has been anything but diplomatic. Kogan has come under attack in Washington for lavishly funded and ultimately unsuccessful congressional lobbying efforts to weaken the FDA's authority over patent issues. And he has publicly berated the agency for "extraordinarily lengthy" reviews of drug applications.

Meanwhile, just as Kogan has pressured his managers to cut costs aggressively, the FDA has repeatedly found fault with Schering's manufacturing practices. The FDA, fed up with the company's ineffective efforts to improve quality control and testing of drug ingredients, took drastic action in February. The agency told Schering it won't approve Clarinex, a follow-up drug to Claritin, until Kogan cleans up plants in New Jersey and Puerto Rico. And as if that weren't enough, the FDA wants Schering to sell Claritin over the counter, which would seriously hurt profits.

Belatedly, Kogan is trying to fix the company's manufacturing mess and placate regulators. "Right now, this is my No. 1 priority and the FDA is my No. 1 customer," Kogan told analysts on June 28. That was just six days after the company disclosed that it had failed new agency inspections. In a hurried effort begun this spring, Kogan is spending more than $60 million on manufacturing improvements and hiring 500 quality-control and production employees.

But that will take time, and the company's troubles have already taken a toll. Since February, the share price has fallen from $500 to about $36. Schering's first-quarter gains of $564 million were 10 percent below last year's, while sales shrank 3 percent, to $2.3 billion, as product shortages and higher research spending cut into results. That's quite a reversal for the CEO: From 1996, when Kogan took over, until the end of 2000, annual net income doubled, to $2.4 billion, while sales rose 73 percent to $9.8 billion. At best, net income might grow 1.6 percent to $2.5 billion this year, while Schering ekes out a 3 percent rise in sales, to $10.2 billion, estimates CIBC World markets analyst Mara Goldstein. "There's deep concern over the lack of care given to its underlying franchises," she says.

For Sale?

Indeed, much as Kogan says he'll tough it out, the company's problems may be more than he or other managers can handle. His heir apparent, Raul E. Cesan, resigned as president on June 27. Cesan, who was directly accountable for plant operations, may have taken the blame for the problems. Or he may have left because it looked likely that he wouldn't have a role in the company if it were sold. Merck & Co. could be interested since it is already working with Schering to develop a few new drugs. Kogan declined to be interviewed, though the company answered some questions in writing. He still insists Schering can remain independent.

As Kogan rose from executive vice-president to president to CEO over 14 years, he was the consummate drug executive: someone who understood the political and marketing challenges of the industry, as well as its scientific complexities. His decisions since 1993 to mount an all-out campaign for Claritin turned a modestly effective allergy reliever into one of the world's best-known and most lucrative medicines. And while he has contained manufacturing costs, he more than doubled R&D spending over the years, to $1.4 billion, which led to groundbreaking drugs for hepatitis C and cancer. It is those drugs that would attract bids for Schering. Plus, as a leader of the trade group Pharmaceutical Research & Manufacturers of America (PhRMA), Kogan helped defeat Clinton Administration efforts to impose drug price controls. For that, Mossinghoff, a former PhRMA president, says Kogan is "one of my heroes."

Over the years, Kogan has fared extremely well, too. He is one of the industry's best-paid chiefs, earning $21 million in cash and stock options in 2000. His salary, bonus, and stock options have netted him $86.8 million over the past three years. Only two drug execs pocketed more. They are the recently retired heads of Bristol-Myers Squibb Co. and Pfizer Inc.—bigger companies whose returns to shareholders substantially topped Schering's. Even as troubles have mounted, Kogan has been penalized only modestly: The board cut his 2000 bonus by $3000,000, to $1.87 million.

To his credit, and now detriment, Kogan has never managed by half-measures. In 1998, he cited "vigilant and rigorous control" over costs as a main goal. But his penny-pinching approach to manufacturing has cost Schering dearly. It faced a near-disaster in late 1999 and 2000 when it was forced to recall 59 million asthma inhalers after finding that some of the potentially life-saving devices didn't contain the active ingredient. Afterward, Schering conducted an audit of its Kenilworth (N.J.) plant. The scathing report by AAC Consulting Group of Rockville, Md., leaked to the consumer-advocacy group Public Citizen, found that managers felt "a continual push for increased production and decreased downtime sometimes at the expense of high-quality work." AAC also said that Schering supervisors "adopted a wait-and-see attitude, to determine if upper management will 'walk the talk' with respect to long-term commitment to product quality."

The FDA's lack of confidence will dog Kogan for a while. That means Schering has less time to switch patients to Clarinex before Claritin's patent expires at the end of 2002. Even if Kogan can deliver other new drugs, they may be too little, too late. The stubborn onetime peanut vendor may have to cry uncle again.

Source: J. Weber, "Is Kogan in a Corner?" *Business Week,* July 16, 2001, pp. 68–69.

Questions

1. To what extent and why might Kogan and Schering-Plough's actions be questionable on ethical grounds?
2. What should they do now? Why?

BusinessWeek Cases in the News

Staying the Course

You wouldn't know it to look at the place, but the cavernous gray shed near the central Javanese city of Yogyakarta is one of General Electric Co.'s most cost-effective lightbulb factories. Hang on. An ultracompetitive factory in the heart of Indonesia? Where reports of political turmoil and violence seem to presage the very disintegration of the nation?

It's true. Last year, GE Lighting Indonesia cranked out 90 million lightbulbs of all shapes and sizes. Sure, the factory can't match the speed of the company's automated plants in the United States and Europe. But thanks to an abundance of cheap labor, glass, and wire, it can make bulbs at a fraction of the cost. Best of all, the plant is miles from the ongoing unrest. "This is a relatively peaceful place," says General Manager Dhananjay Gupte. "We don't have bomb blasts, demonstrations, or riots."

When the Indonesian economy collapsed four years ago, a common belief was that multinational manufacturers would flee. In fact, management consultants estimate that fewer than 1 in 10 of the 3,000 foreign companies in Indonesia have left. Manufacturers of everything from Energizer batteries to Nike running shoes to L'Oréal cosmetics are determined to stay.

Risky Business

The math is simple: Indonesia boasts some of the lowest costs in the world, a big domestic market, and proximity to the rest of Asia. As a result, some companies are expanding. Coca-Cola Co. plans to open a new bottling plant next year, while Renault has announced a joint venture with Suzuki Motor

Corp. assembler Indomobil that will assemble and distribute Renault cars. Over the past three years, the government has approved $26.2 billion in new foreign investment.

Of course, operating in Indonesia is not risk-free. It requires patience, adaptability, and an ability to think like a local. U.S. or European execs are not necessarily equipped for the task. So companies such as Coca-Cola Co. and lensmaker Vision-Ease Lens Inc. are recruiting Indian managers to run their Indonesia operations. Indians are paid 60 percent less than Americans. And their experience in dealing with the vagaries of doing business in India prepares them better to do the same in Indonesia.

Multinationals, however, are being forced to accept a bottom-line truth. Because of the wealth-destroying impact of the 1997 financial crisis, foreign products are much more expensive for local consumers. To stay in the game, Procter & Gamble Co. and Unilever Group now make smaller shampoo and detergent sachets that the newly poor can afford. For its part, L'Oréal of France has give up on cracking the domestic market and switched to an export strategy. Now 70 percent of the cosmetics produced at L'Oréal's Jakarta plant go overseas to Malaysia, Singapore, Thailand, Hong Kong, Taiwan, and China.

Then there are those manufacturers that simply see opportunity in chaos. Minneapolis-based Vision-Ease broke ground on a plant near Jakarta amid nationwide riots. Months later the plant opened at a cost of just $2.5 million and is today exporting lenses to Europe and the United States.

Of course, not all companies are immune from Indonesia's political unrest. Nike Inc., for example, has a full-time labor-relations manager at its Jakarta headquarters. Her job is to prevent disruption of the company's operations. In mid-June, Indonesian workers went on strike to demand a minimum-wage hike. Mindful that local factories produce 31 percent of the footwear it sells worldwide, Nike dispatched its monitor to see if the production lines were in danger of being halted. It turned out to be a false alarm, but companies must be vigilant all the time.

Tamping down local unrest isn't so easy, however, for mining and oil companies. Exxon Mobil in Aceh, Freeport-McMoRan Copper & Gold in West Papau, and Caltex (a Chevron-Texaco joint venture) in Riau have all suffered production cuts as a result of protests from local communities, which are demanding a greater revenue split from the government in Jakarta.

While such problems may deter new investors, veterans take the long view. "If you're British Petroleum, you see 50 years of gas, not two years of political turmoil," says John Kurtz, country manager of management consultancy A.T. Kearney Inc. in Jakarta. "If you're Nestlé, you see 225 million people with long-term spending growth—not the sudden undertow of urban poverty." For all its turmoil, Indonesia represents not danger, but opportunity.

Source: M. Shari, "Staying the Course," *Business Week,* September 24, 2001, p. 112.

Questions

1. What are the pros and cons of manufacturing and doing business in Indonesia?
2. What obligation do multinationals have to citizens and employees in Indonesia?

Chapter 17

Managing Information Systems and Technologies

LEARNING OBJECTIVES

After studying this chapter, you should be able to:

- Differentiate between **data and information,** and list the **attributes of useful information.**
- Describe **three reasons why managers must have access to information** to perform their tasks and roles effectively.
- Describe the computer **hardware and software innovations** that have created the information technology revolution.
- Differentiate among **five kinds of management information systems.**
- Explain how advances in information systems can give an organization a **competitive advantage.**

A Manager's Challenge

How Herman Miller Designs the Office of the Future

How can managers create competitive advantage through information technology? At first glance, it might seem that advances in information technology would have a limited impact on the business of an office furniture maker (OFM) like Herman Miller, however, this assumption would be incorrect. Managers at Herman Miller have been finding countless ways to use IT and the Internet to give their company a competitive advantage over rival OFMs such as Steelcase and Hon.

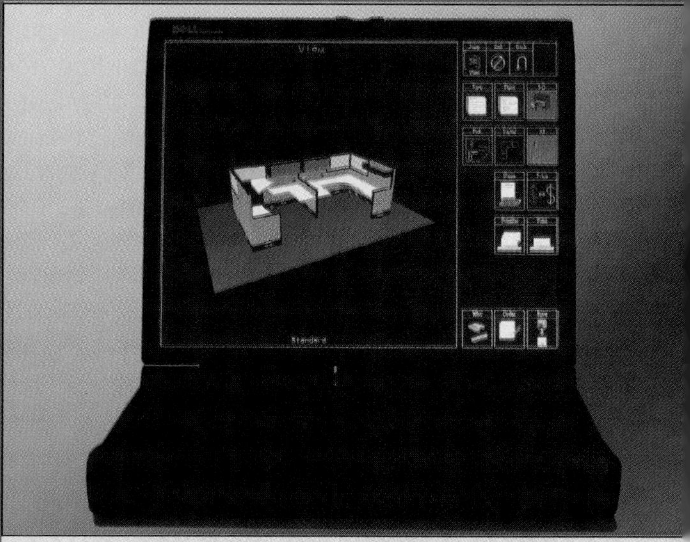
Hermann Miller's 2-Axis program allows customers to experiment with and customize the office furniture designs that Herman Miller's designers create. The result is a finished design that is best adapted to each customer's unique needs.

From the beginning, like the other OFMs, Miller's managers saw the potential of the Internet for selling their office furniture to potential business customers. These companies' websites were on-line advertisements for their products, services, capabilities, and other relevant marketing and historical information. However, very quickly, managers realized the true potential of email both inside a company on its intranet, and between companies over the Internet. In Herman Miller's case, the expanding use of the Internet followed a definite pattern.

First, Miller's managers developed information systems that linked all its dealers and salespeople to its manufacturing hub so that sales orders could be coordinated with the custom design department and with manufacturing so that customers could receive pricing and scheduling information promptly. Then with this customer delivery system in place, Miller developed information systems to link its manufacturing operations with its network of suppliers so that its input supply chain would be coordinated with its customer needs.

Miller's managers noticed that its competitors moved quickly to imitate its information systems and they began to search for new ways to take advantage of the opportunities provided by advanced IT. When they realized that IT could transform the very office furniture business, they began to define Herman Miller as a "digital" enterprise. Infused with e-business; the company's mission was not just to improve efficiency by reducing costs but also to change the way the customer experienced "Herman Miller" and increase value for the customer. Miller's managers accomplished this in several different ways.

One of their main Web initiatives was to establish an e-learning tool Uknowit.com which became Herman Miller's on-line university. Via the Web over 3,000 of Miller's employees and dealers are currently enrolled in Uknowit.com where they choose from 85 courses covering technology, products and services, product applications, consultative/selling skills, and industry competitive knowledge. The benefits to Miller, its dealers, and its customers from this IT initiative are improved speed to market and better ability to respond to competitors' tactics. That is, salespeople and dealers now have the information and tools they need to better compete for and keep customers. In the office furniture industry the average ramp up time for a new sales associate is typically 24 to 36 months due to the complexity of the products and sales cycle/process. Utilizing e-learning has reduced these times by 12 to 18 months.

Moreover, the office furniture business offers highly customized solutions to its customers. A main source of competitive advantage is the ability to give customers exactly what they want and at the right price. Traditionally, the contract furniture industry had a hard time meeting deadlines for customized furniture solutions and delivery to customers was often late. As a result of its new information systems, Herman Miller's salespeople are giving design and manufacturing more accurate and timely information that has reduced the incidence of sales and specification errors during the selling process.

Also, with these new systems time to market has been reduced and Miller is committed to being able to offer customers highly customized furniture in 10 business days or less. One important part of the information system is customer specific websites. On these websites, Miller's designers can offer clients the opportunity to comment on three-dimensional views of office workstations based on the clients' specifications. Working with its dealers and salespeople these workstations can be modified or adapted and then final specifications are sent electronically to the factories where they are produced. The primary advantage is speed to market and the fact that as clients become used to using Herman Miller's virtual tools, they become locked into its products and systems. Once all the relevant information has been captured, it is incorporated into relevant databases that provide ease of access and reuse by employees, dealers, suppliers, and customers.

Of course, all these IT initiatives have been costly to Herman Miller. Thousands of hours of management time have been spent developing these information systems and providing content, such as information on competitors in its on-line classes. Herman Miller's managers are looking long-term, they believe they have created a real source of competitive advantage for their company that will sustain it in the years ahead.

Overview

As the experience of Herman Miller suggests, there are enormous opportunities for managers to find new ways to use information systems and technologies to increase the flow of knowledge and speed communication and decision making in an organization. Thus, the adoption of new information technology can help give an organization a competitive advantage and lead to high performance.

In this chapter we begin by surveying information systems and information technology in general, looking at the relationship between information and the manager's job and the nature of the current information technology revolution. Then we discuss several types of information systems that managers can use to help themselves perform their jobs, and we examine the impact that rapidly evolving information systems and technologies may have on managers' jobs and on an organization's competitive advantage. By the end of this chapter, you will understand the profound ways in which new developments in information systems and technology are shaping managers' functions and roles.

Information and the Manager's Job

data Raw, unsummarized, and unanalyzed facts.

information Data that is organized in a meaningful fashion.

Managers cannot plan, organize, lead, and control effectively unless they have access to information. Information is the source of the knowledge and intelligence that they need to make the right decisions. Information, however, is not the same as data.[1] **Data** is raw, unsummarized, and unanalyzed facts such as volume of sales, level of costs, or number of customers. **Information** is data that is organized in a meaningful fashion, such as in a graph showing the change in sales volume or costs over time. By itself, data does not tell managers anything; information, in contrast, can communicate a great deal of useful knowledge to the person who receives it–such as a manager who sees sales falling or costs rising. The distinction between data and information is important because one of the uses of information technology is to help managers transform data into information in order to make better managerial decisions.

To further clarify the difference between data and information, consider the case of a manager in a supermarket who must decide how much shelf space to allocate to two breakfast cereal brands for children: Dentist's Delight and Sugar Supreme. Most supermarkets use checkout scanners to record individual sales and store the data on a computer. Accessing this computer, the manager might find that Dentist's Delight sells 50 boxes per day and Sugar Supreme sells 25 boxes per day. This raw data, however, is of little help in assisting the manager to decide about how to allocate shelf space. The manager also needs to know how much shelf space each cereal currently occupies and how much profit each cereal generates for the supermarket.

Suppose the manager discovers that Dentist's Delight occupies 10 feet of shelf space and Sugar Supreme occupies 4 feet and that Dentist's Delight generates 20 cents of profit a box while Sugar Supreme generates 40 cents of profit a box. By putting these three bits of data together (number of boxes sold, amount of shelf space, and profit per box), the manager gets some useful information on which to base a decision: Dentist's Delight generates $1 of profit per foot of shelf space per day [(50 boxes @ $.20)/10 feet], and Sugar Supreme generates $2.50 of profit per foot of shelf space per day [(25 boxes @ $.40)/4 feet]. Armed with this information, the manager might decide to allocate less shelf space to Dentist's Delight and more to Sugar Supreme.

Attributes of Useful Information

Four factors determine the usefulness of information to a manager: quality, timeliness, completeness, and relevance (see Figure 17.1).

Figure 17.1
Factors Affecting the Usefulness of Information

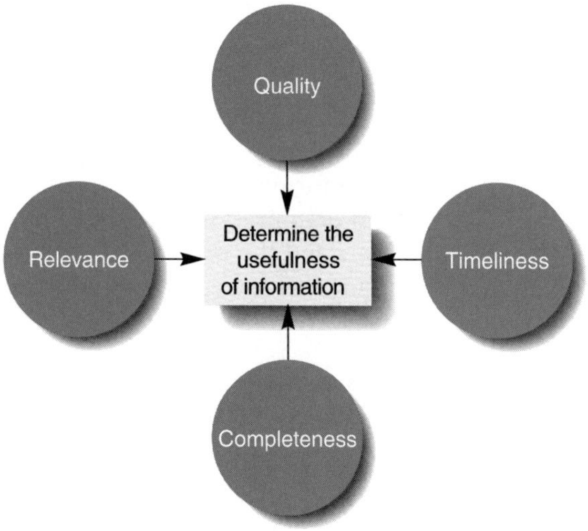

QUALITY Accuracy and reliability determine the quality of information.[2] The greater accuracy and reliability are, the higher is the quality of information. For an information system to work well, the information that it provides must be of high quality. If managers conclude that the quality of information provided by their information system is low, they are likely to lose confidence in the system and stop using it. Alternatively, if managers base decisions on low-quality information, poor and even disastrous decision making can result. For example, the partial meltdown of the nuclear reactor at Three Mile Island in Pennsylvania during the 1970s was the result of poor information caused by an information system malfunction. The information system indicated to engineers controlling the reactor that there was enough water in the reactor core to cool the nuclear pile, although this was in fact not the case. The consequences included the partial meltdown of the reactor and the release of radioactive gas into the atmosphere. At Herman Miller, if salespeople and dealers supply poor-quality information about customer needs, the result is expensive furniture redesign and high costs.

TIMELINESS Information that is timely is available when it is needed for managerial action, not after the decision has been made. In today's rapidly changing world, the need for timely information often means that information must be available on a real-time basis.[3] **Real-time information** is information that reflects current conditions. In an industry that experiences rapid changes, real-time information may need to be updated frequently.

real-time information Frequently updated information that reflects current conditions.

Airlines use real-time information on the number of flight bookings and competitors' prices to adjust their prices on an hour-to-hour basis to maximize their revenues. Thus, for example, the fare for flights from New York to Seattle might change from one hour to the next as fares are reduced to fill empty seats and raised when most seats have been sold. Airlines use real-time information on reservations to adjust fares at the last possible moment to fill planes and maximize revenues. U.S. airlines make more than 80,000 fare changes each day.[4] Obviously, the managers who make such pricing decisions need real-time information about the current state of demand in the marketplace. Herman Miller's designers need timely information about customers' changing needs and new furniture designs by competitors like Steelcase.

COMPLETENESS Information that is complete gives managers all the information they need to exercise control, achieve coordination, or make an effective decision. Recall from Chapter 7, however, that managers rarely have access to complete information. Instead, because of uncertainty, ambiguity, and bounded rationality, they have to make do with incomplete information.[5] One of the functions of information systems is to increase the completeness of the information that managers have at their disposal. Herman Miller's Uknowit.com information system provides its dealers with more knowledge on which to make competitive decisions.

RELEVANCE Information that is relevant is useful and suits a manager's particular needs and circumstances. Irrelevant information is useless and may actually hurt the performance of a busy manager who has to spend valuable time determining whether information is relevant. Given the massive amounts of information that managers are now exposed to and humans' limited information-processing capabilities, the people who design information systems need to make sure that managers receive only relevant information.

Today, software agents are increasingly being used by managers to scan and sort incoming email and prioritize it. A software agent is a software program that can be used to perform simple tasks such as scanning incoming information for relevance, taking some of the burden away from managers. Moreover, by recording and analyzing a manager's own efforts to prioritize incoming information, the software agent can mimic the manager's preferences and thus perform such tasks more effectively. For example, the software agent can automatically reprogram itself to place incoming email from the manager's boss at the top of the pile.[6]

Information Systems and Technology

information system A system for acquiring, organizing, storing, manipulating, and transmitting information.

management information system An information system that managers plan and design to provide themselves with the specific information they need.

information technology The means by which information is acquired, organized, stored, manipulated, and transmitted.

An **information system** is a system for acquiring, organizing, storing, manipulating, and transmitting information.[7] A **management information system (MIS)** is an information system that managers plan and design to provide themselves with the specific information they need to perform their roles effectively. Information systems have existed for as long as there have been organizations–a long time indeed. Before the computer age, most information systems were paper based: Clerks recorded important information on documents (often in duplicate or triplicate) in the form of words and numbers, sent a copy of the document to superiors, customers, or suppliers, as the case might be, and stored other copies in files for future reference.

Information technology is the means by which information is acquired, organized, stored, manipulated, and transmitted. Rapid advances in the power of information technology–specifically, through the use of computers–are having a fundamental impact on information systems, on managers, their organizations, and their suppliers and customers, as occurred in Herman Miller.[8] So important are these advances in information technology that organizations that have not adopted new information technology, or do so ineffectively, will become uncompetitive with those that do.[9] An interesting illustration of this can be found by comparing the on-line shopping information system of Amazon.com with that of walmart.com and bluelight.com, Kmart's on-line store.

Information Technology Byte

e-stores: amazon.com versus bluelight.com versus walmart.com

On-line stores live or die by their ability to provide customers with a satisfying shopping experience. Hundreds of now defunct dot-coms learned this lesson in the early 2000s when an inability to generate customer revenues caused their collapse. Among dot-com survivors, however, the different shopping experiences provide an interesting comparison. Amazon.com began as a virtual on-line enterprise, while bluelight.com and walmart.com, were outcomes of their bricks-and-mortar parents' desire to experiment with on-line retailing.

Amazon.com was the first of these on-line stores to be up and running; from the beginning its storefront was designed with the Internet in mind. Bluelight.com was next and walmart.com was last. Walmart.com had an inauspicious beginning when soon after it was up and running it was suddenly shut down for six months while its information systems were reworked to make them user-friendly. A close look at the three companies' websites in the summer of 2001 revealed major differences between the way their virtual information systems operate.(Take the opportunity to examine these websites now.)

Amazon.com's website possesses the IT most interactive with its customers. Its information systems remember customers' preferences, the items they have viewed, and past purchases; therefore, the systems can suggest related items that a customer might wish to consider purchasing based on life-style preferences. In addition, Amazon.com's customers can write reviews of its books and other products and in this way they can talk among themselves and develop a more satisfying shopping experience. By contrast, bluelight.com's information system has some limited ability to suggest items that a customer might consider purchasing but has no "customer history" to build the shopping experience. Finally, walmart.com's system simply brings into view items that a customer selects from the various product categories, it has no ability to provide a customized shopping experience. Another major difference among these on-line stores concerns the convenience of the checkout process.[10] Once again Amazon.com wins out with its "one-click" technology although in 2001 it seemed that the other stores were trying to imitate this.

This basic difference in information systems design is reflected in the degree to which customers make use of these on-line stores. Amazon.com is the most visited on-line store by far, however, bluelight.com is also much more popular than walmart.com. Thus, it seems that the ability of managers to create the IT that best meets the needs of their customers is a key determinant of the relative efficiency and effectiveness of these rival virtual businesses.

Amazon.com is widely regarded as having the best, most customer-responsive Internet storefront in the business.

Managers need information for three reasons: to make effective decisions; to control the activities of the organization; and to coordinate the activities of the organization. We examine these uses of information in detail below.

Information and Decisions

Much of management (planning, organizing, leading, and controlling) is about making decisions. For example, the marketing manager must decide what price to charge for a product, what distribution channels to use, and what promotional messages to emphasize. The manufacturing manager must decide how much of a product to make and how to make it. The purchasing manager must decide from whom to purchase inputs and what inventory of inputs to hold. The human relations manager must decide how much employees should be paid, how they should be trained, and what benefits they should be given. The engineering manager must make decisions about new product design. Top managers must decide how to allocate scarce financial resources among competing projects, how best to structure and control the organization, and what business-level strategy the organization should be pursuing. And, regardless of their functional orientation, all managers have to make decisions about matters such as what performance evaluation to give to a subordinate.

Decision making cannot be effective in an information vacuum. To make effective decisions, managers need information, both from inside the organization and from external stakeholders. When deciding how to price a product, for example, the marketing manager needs information about how consumers will react to different prices. She needs information about unit costs because she does not want to set the price below the costs of production. And she needs information about competitive strategy, since pricing strategy should be consistent with an organization's competitive strategy. Some of this information will come from outside the organization (for example, from consumer surveys) and some from inside the organization (information about unit production costs comes from manufacturing). As this example suggests, managers' ability to make effective decisions rests on their ability to acquire and process information. Recall that managers at Herman Miller designed their information systems both to collect this information and to educate their dealers so that they could make better decisions with regard to their customers.

Information and Control

As discussed in Chapter 9, controlling is the process whereby managers regulate how efficiently and effectively an organization and its members are performing the activities necessary to achieve organizational goals.[11] Managers achieve control over organizational activities by taking four steps (see Figure 9.2): (1) They establish measurable standards of performance or goals. (2) They measure actual performance. (3) They compare actual performance against established goals. (4) They evaluate the result and take corrective action if necessary.[12] Airborne Express, for example, has a delivery goal: to deliver 95 percent of the packages it picks up by noon the next day. Throughout the United States, Airborne has thousands of ground stations (branch offices that coordinate the pickup and delivery of packages in a particular area) that are responsible for the physical pickup and delivery of packages. Airborne managers monitor the delivery performance of these stations on a regular basis; if they find that the 95 percent goal is not being attained, they determine why and take corrective action if necessary.[13]

To achieve control over any organizational activity, managers must have information. To control a ground station, a manager at Airborne needs to know how many of that station's packages are being delivered by noon. To get this information, the manager needs to make sure that an information system is in place. Packages to be shipped by Airborne are scanned with a handheld scanner by the Airborne Express driver who first picks them up. The pickup information is sent by a wireless link to a central computer at Airborne's Seattle headquarters. The packages are scanned again by the truck driver when they are delivered. The delivery information is also transmitted to Airborne's central computer. By accessing the central computer, a manager can quickly find out not only what percentage of packages are delivered by noon of the day after they were picked up but also how this information breaks down on a station-by-station basis.[14]

Management information systems are used to control a variety of operations within organizations. In accounting, for example, information systems can be used to monitor expenditures and compare them against budgets.[15] To track expenditures against budgets, managers need information on current expenditures, broken down by relevant organizational units. Accounting information systems are designed to provide managers with such information. Another example of an information system used to monitor and control the daily activities of employees is the on-line MBO information system used by T.J. Rodgers at Cypress Semiconductor discussed in Chapter 10. Rodgers implemented a computer-based information system that allows him to review the goals of all his employees in about four hours.[16]

Information and Coordination

Coordinating department and divisional activities to achieve organizational goals is another basic task of management. As an extreme example of the size of the coordination task that managers face, consider the coordination effort involved in building Boeing's new commercial jet aircraft, the 777. The 777 is composed of 3 million individual parts and thousands of major components. Managers at Boeing have to coordinate the production and delivery of all of these parts so that they all arrive at Boeing's Everett, Washington, facility exactly when they are needed (for example, they want the wings to arrive before the engines). Boeing managers jokingly refer to this task as "coordinating 3 million parts in flying formation." To achieve this high level of coordination, managers need information about which supplier is producing what, when it is to be produced, and when it is to be delivered. Managers also need this information so that they are able to track the delivery performance of suppliers against expectations and receive advance warning of any likely problems. To meet these needs, managers at Boeing established a computer-based information system that links Boeing to all its suppliers and can track the flow of 3 million component parts through the production process–an immense task.

As noted in previous chapters, the coordination problems that managers face in managing their global supply chains to take advantage of national differences in the costs of production are increasing. To deal with global coordination problems, managers have been adopting sophisticated computer-based information systems that help them coordinate the flow of materials, semifinished goods, and finished products around the world. Consider, for example, how Bose Corporation which manufactures some of the world's best-known high-fidelity speakers manages its global supply chain.

Bose purchases almost all of the electronic and nonelectronic components for its speakers from independent suppliers. About 50 percent of its purchases are from foreign suppliers, the majority of which are in the Far East. The challenge for managers is to coordinate this globally dispersed supply chain to minimize Bose's inventory and transportation costs. Minimizing these costs requires that component parts arrive at Bose's assembly plant just in time to enter the production process and not before. Bose also has to remain responsive to customer demands. This requirement means that the company has to respond quickly to increases in demand for certain kinds of speakers, such as outdoor speakers in the summer. Failure to respond quickly can cause the loss of a big order to competitors. Since Bose does not want to hold extensive inventories at its Massachusetts plant, the need to remain responsive to customer demands requires that Bose's suppliers be able to respond rapidly to increased demand for component parts.

The responsibility for coordinating the supply chain to simultaneously minimize inventory and transportation costs and respond quickly to customer demands belongs to Bose's logistics managers. They have contracted with W. N. Procter, a Boston-based supply chain manager, to develop a sophisticated logistics information system. Procter offers Bose up-to-the-minute electronic data interchange (EDI) capabilities, which give Bose the real-time information it needs to track parts as they move through the global supply chain. The EDI system is known as ProcterLink. When a shipment leaves a supplier, it is logged into ProcterLink.[17] From that point on, Bose can track the supplies as they move across the globe toward Massachusetts. This system allows Bose to fine-tune its production scheduling so that supplies enter the production process exactly when they are needed.

How well this system can work was illustrated when one Japanese customer unexpectedly doubled its order for Bose speakers. Bose had to gear up its manufacturing in a hurry, but many of its components were stretched out across long distances. By using ProcterLink, Bose was able to locate the needed parts in its supply chain. It then broke them out of the normal delivery chain and moved them by air freight to get them to the assembly line in time for the accelerated schedule. As a result, Bose was able to meet the request of its customer.

The Information Technology Revolution

Computer-based information technology is an enabling technology. It has allowed managers to develop computer-based management information systems that provide timely, complete, relevant, and high-quality information. As we have discussed, IT allows companies like Herman Miller and Bose to improve their responsiveness to customers, minimize costs, and thus improve their competitive position. The link between information systems and competitive position is an important one that may determine the success or failure of organizations in an increasingly competitive global environment. To better understand the current revolution in information technology, in this section we examine several key aspects of computer-based information technology.

The Tumbling Price of Information

The information technology revolution began with the development of the first computers–the hardware of computer-based information technology–in the 1950s. The language of computers is a digital language of zeros and ones. Words, numbers, images, and sound can all be expressed in zeros and ones. Each letter in the alphabet has its own unique code of zeros and ones, as does each number, each color, and each sound. For example, the digital code for the number 20 is 10100. In the language of computers it takes a lot of zeros and ones to express even a simple sentence, to say nothing of complex color graphics or moving video images. Nevertheless, modern computers can read, process, and store millions of instructions per second (an instruction is a line of software code) and thus vast amounts of zeros and ones. It is this awesome power that forms the foundation of the current information technology revolution.

The brains of modern computers are microprocessors (Intel's Pentium chips and its newest chip the Itanium chip are microprocessors). Just in the last 10 years between 1991 and 2001, for example, the relative cost of computer processing has fallen so dramatically that Gordon Moore, a computer guru, noted that, "If the auto industry advanced as rapidly as the semiconductor industry, a Rolls Royce would get a half a million miles per gallon, and it would be cheaper to throw it away than to park it."[18] As the costs of acquiring, organizing, storing, and transmitting information have tumbled, computers have become almost as common as wireless phones and microwaves.[19] In addition, advances in microprocessor technology have led to dramatic reductions in the cost of communication between computers, which also have contributed to the falling price of information and information systems.

Wireless Communications

Another trend of considerable significance for information systems has been the rapid growth of wireless communication technologies, particularly digital communications. Wireless service was first offered in the United States in 1983. Initially, growth was slow, but since 1990 wireless service has spread rapidly. In 1984 there were 100,000 cellular subscribers in the United States[20]; in 1994 16 million, and by 2001 this figure had mushroomed to 110 million.[21] Some experts predict that worldwide subscribership will reach 1.2 billion people by 2005.[22]

Wireless communication is significant for the information technology revolution because it facilitates the linking together of computers, which greatly increases their power and adaptability. It is already possible to purchase a battery-operated laptop computer that has a wireless modem built in to facilitate communication with a "home" computer. An engineer or salesperson working in the field can send information to, and receive information from, the home office by using the wireless capabilities built into computers. Because a computer no longer has to be plugged into a hard-wired telephone line, accessing a large computer-based information system is much easier than it used to be.

Computer Networks

networking The exchange of information through a group or network of interlinked computers.

The tumbling price of computing power and information and the use of wireless communication channels has facilitated **networking,** the exchange of information through a group or network of interlinked computers. The most common arrangement now emerging is a three-tier network consisting of clients, servers, and a mainframe (see Figure 17.2). At the outer nodes of a typical three-tier network are the ***personal computers (PCs)*** that sit on the desks of individual users. These personal computers, referred to as *clients,* are linked to a local *server,* a high-powered midrange computer that "serves" the client personal computers. Servers often store power-hungry software programs that can be run more effectively on the server than on an individual's personal computer. Servers may also

Figure 17.2 A Typical Three-Tier Information System

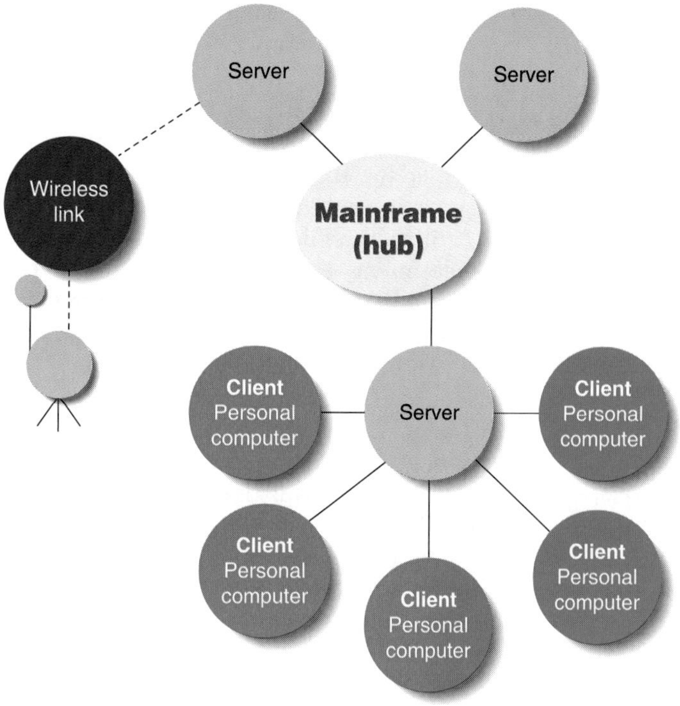

manage several printers that can be used by hundreds of clients, store data files, and handle email communications between clients. The client computers linked directly to a server constitute a *local area network (LAN)*. Within any organization there may be several LANs–for example, one in every division and function.

At the hub of a three-tier system are mainframe computers. *Mainframes* are large and powerful computers that can be used to store and process vast amounts of information. The mainframe can also be used to handle electronic communications between personal computers situated in different LANs. In addition, the mainframe may be connected to mainframes in other organizations and, through them, to LANs in other organizations. Increasingly, the Internet, a worldwide network of interlinked computers, is used as the conduit for connecting the computer systems of different organizations (see Chapter 15).

A manager with a personal computer hooked into a three-tier system can access data and software stored in the local server, in the mainframe, or through the Internet in computers based in another organization. A manager can therefore communicate electronically with other individuals hooked into the system, whether they are in the manager's LAN, in another LAN within the manager's organization, or in another organization altogether. Moreover, because of the growth of wireless communications, an individual with the proper equipment can hook into the system from any location–at home, on a boat, on the beach, in the air–anywhere a wireless communications link can be established.

operating system software Software that tells computer hardware how to run.

applications software Software designed for a specific task or use.

Software Developments

If computer hardware has been developing rapidly, so has computer software. **Operating system software** tells the computer hardware how to run. **Applications software,** such as programs for word processing, spreadsheets, graphics, and database management, is software developed for a specific task or use. The increase in the power of computer hardware has allowed software developers to write increasingly powerful programs that are, at the same time, increasingly user-friendly. By harnessing the rapidly growing power of microprocessors, applications software has vastly increased the ability of managers to acquire, organize, manipulate, and transmit information. In doing so, it also has increased the ability of managers to coordinate and control the activities of their organization and to make decisions, as discussed earlier.

artificial intelligence Behavior performed by a machine that, if performed by a human being, would be called intelligent.

Artificial intelligence is another interesting and potentially fruitful software development. **Artificial intelligence** has been defined as behavior by a machine that, if performed by a human being, would be called intelligent.[23] Artificial intelligence has already made it possible to write programs that can solve problems and perform simple tasks. For example, software programs variously called "software agents," "softbots," or "knowbots" can be used to perform simple managerial tasks such as sorting through reams of data or incoming e-mail messages to look for important data and messages. The interesting feature of these programs is that from "watching" a manager sort through such data they can "learn" what his or her preferences are. Having done this, they then can take over some of this work from the manager, freeing up more time to work on other tasks. Most of these programs are still in the development stage, but they may be commonplace within a decade.[24]

Another software development that is starting to have an impact on the manager's job is speech recognition software. Currently speech recognition software must be "trained" to recognize and understand each individual's voice, and it requires the speaker to pause after each word. The increasing power of microprocessors, however, has enabled the development of faster speech recognition programs that can handle more variables and much greater complexity. Now a manager driving down the road may be able to communicate with his computer through a wireless link and give that computer complex voice instructions.[25]

Types of Management Information Systems

Four types of computer-based management information systems can be particularly helpful in providing managers with the information they need to make decisions and to coordinate and control organizational resources: transaction-processing systems, operations information systems, decision support systems, and expert systems (see Figure 17.3). These systems are arranged along a continuum according to their increasing usefulness in providing managers with the information they need to make nonprogrammed decisions. (Recall from Chapter 7 that nonprogrammed decision making occurs in response to unusual, unpredictable opportunities and threats.) We examine each of these systems after focusing on the management information system that preceded them all: the organizational hierarchy.

The Organizational Hierarchy: The Traditional Information System

Traditionally, managers have used the organizational hierarchy as a system for gathering the information they need to achieve coordination and control and make decisions (see Chapter 9 for a detailed discussion of organizational structure and hierarchy). According to business historian Alfred Chandler, the use of

Figure 17.3
Four Computer-Based Management Information Systems

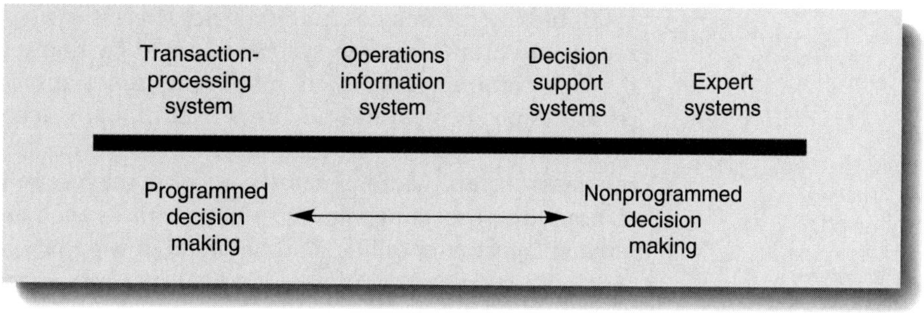

the hierarchy as an information network was perfected by railroad companies in the United States during the 1850s.[26] At that time, the railroads were the largest industrial organizations in the United States. By virtue of their size and geographical spread they faced unique problems of coordination and control. In the 1850s, railroad companies started to solve these problems by designing hierarchical management structures that provided senior managers with the information they needed to achieve coordination and control and to make decisions about the running of the railroads.

Daniel McCallum, superintendent of the Erie Railroad in the 1850s, realized that the lines of authority and responsibility defining the Erie's management hierarchy also represented channels of communication along which information traveled. McCallum established what was perhaps the first modern management information system. Regular daily and monthly reports were fed up the management chain so that top managers could make decisions about, for example, controlling costs and setting freight rates. Decisions were then relayed back down the hierarchy so they could be carried out. Imitating the railroads, most other organizations used their hierarchies as systems for collecting and channeling information. This practice began to change only when electronic information technologies became more reasonably priced in the 1960s.

Although hierarchy is a useful information system, several drawbacks are associated with it. First, in organizations with many layers of managers, it can take a long time for information to travel up the hierarchy and for decisions to travel back down. This slow pace can reduce the timeliness and usefulness of that information and prevent an organization from responding quickly to changing market conditions.[27] Second, information can be distorted as it moves from one layer of management to another, and information distortion reduces the quality of information.[28] Third, because managers have only a limited span of control, as an organization grows larger its hierarchy lengthens and this tall structure can make the hierarchy a very expensive information system. The popular idea that companies with tall management hierarchies are bureaucratic and unresponsive to the needs of their customers arises from the inability of tall hierarchies to effectively process data and provide managers with timely, complete, relevant, and high-quality information. Until modern computer-based information systems came along, however, the management hierarchy was the best information system available.

transaction-processing system A management information system designed to handle large volumes of routine, recurring transactions.

Transaction-Processing Systems

A **transaction-processing system** is a system designed to handle large volumes of routine, recurring transactions (see Figure 17.3). Transaction-processing systems began to appear in the early 1960s with the advent of commercially available mainframe computers. They were the first type of computer-based management information system adopted by many organizations, and today they are commonplace. Bank managers use a transaction-processing system to record deposits into, and payments out of, bank accounts. Supermarket managers use a transaction-processing system to record the sale of items and to track inventory levels. More generally, most managers in large organizations use a transaction-processing system to handle tasks such as payroll preparation and payment, customer billing, and payment of suppliers.

Operations Information Systems

operations information system A management information system that gathers, organizes, and summarizes comprehensive data in a form that managers can use in their nonroutine coordinating, controlling, and decision-making tasks.

Many types of management information systems followed hard on the heels of transaction-processing systems in the 1960s. An **operations information system** is a system that gathers comprehensive data, organizes it, and summarizes it in a form that is of value to managers. Whereas a transaction-processing system processes routine transactions, an operations information system provides managers with information that they can use in their nonroutine coordinating, controlling, and decision-making tasks. Most operations information systems are coupled with a transaction-processing system. An operations information system typically accesses data gathered by a transaction-processing system, processes that data into useful information, and organizes that information into a form accessible to managers. Managers often use an operations information system to get sales, inventory, accounting, and other performance-related information. For example, the information that T. J. Rodgers at Cypress Semiconductors gets on individual employee goals and performance is provided by an operations information system.

Airborne Express uses an operations information system to track the performance of its 500 or so ground stations. Each ground station is evaluated according to four criteria: delivery (the goal is to deliver 95 percent of all packages by noon the day after they were picked up), productivity (measured by the number

Airborne Express has one of the most sophisticated information control systems in the delivery business. At each step in the delivery process, it knows exactly how to best organize its delivery system to reduce time and money.

of packages shipped per employee hour), controllable cost, and station profitability. Each ground station also has specific delivery, efficiency, cost, and profitability targets that it must attain. Every month Airborne's operations information system is used to gather information on these four criteria and summarize it for top managers, who are then able to compare the performance of each station against its previously established targets. The system quickly alerts senior managers to underperforming ground stations, so they can intervene selectively to help solve any problems that may have given rise to the poor performance.[29]

Decision Support Systems

decision support system An interactive computer-based management information system that managers can use to make nonroutine decisions.

A **decision support system** is an interactive computer-based system that provides models that help managers make better nonprogrammed decisions.[30] Recall from Chapter 7 that *nonprogrammed decisions* are decisions that are relatively unusual or novel, such as decisions to invest in new productive capacity, develop a new product, launch a new promotional campaign, enter a new market, or expand internationally. Although an operations information system organizes important information for managers, a decision support system gives managers a model-building capability and so provides them with the ability to manipulate information in a variety of ways. Managers might use a decision support system to help them decide whether to cut prices for a product. The decision support system might contain models of how customers and competitors would respond to a price cut. Managers could run these models and use the results as an aid to decision making.

The stress on the word *aid* is important, for in the final analysis a decision support system is not meant to make decisions for managers. Rather, its function is to provide managers with valuable information that they can use to improve the quality of their decisions. A good example of a sophisticated decision support system, developed by Judy Lewent, chief financial officer of the U.S. pharmaceutical company Merck, is given in the next "Management Insight."

Management Insight

How Judy Lewent Became One of the Most Powerful Women in Corporate America

With annual sales of over $45 billion, Merck (www.merck.com) is one of the world's largest developers and marketers of advanced pharmaceuticals. In 2000, the company spent more than $3 billion on R&D to develop new drugs–an expensive and difficult process that is fraught with risks. Most new drug ideas fail to make it through the development process. It takes an average of $300 million and 10 years to bring a new drug to market, and 7 out of 10 new drugs fail to make a profit for the developing company.

Given the costs, risks, and uncertainties involved in the new drug development process, Judy Lewent, the former director of capital analysis at Merck, decided to develop a decision support system that could help managers make more effective R&D investment decisions. Her aim was to give Merck's top managers the information they needed to evaluate proposed R&D projects on a case-by-case basis. The system that Lewent and her staff developed is referred to in Merck as the "Research Planning Model."[31] At the heart of this decision support system is a sophisticated model. The input variables to the model include data on R&D spending, manufacturing costs, selling costs, and demand conditions. The relationships between the input variables are modeled by means of several equations that factor in the probability of a drug's making it through the development process and to market. The outputs of this modeling process are the revenues, cash flows, and profits that a project might generate.

The Merck model does not use a single value for an input variable, nor does it compute a single value for each output. Rather, a range is specified for each input variable (such as high, medium, and low R&D spending). The computer repeatedly samples at random from the range of values for each input variable and produces a probability distribution of values for each output. So, for example, instead of stating categorically that a proposed R&D project will yield a profit of $500 million, the decision support system produces a probability distribution. It might state that although $500 million is the most likely profit, there is a 25 percent chance that the profit will be less than $300 million and a 25 percent chance that it will be greater than $700 million.

Judy Lewent Chief Financial officer of Merck, consults with managers of Sweden's Astra Pharmaceuticals, as they work out the details of their global joint venture.

Merck now uses Lewent's decision support system to evaluate all proposed R&D investment decisions. In addition, Lewent has developed other decision support system models that Merck's managers can use to help them decide, for example, whether to enter into joint ventures with other companies or how best to hedge foreign exchange risk. As for Lewent, her reward was promotion to the position of chief financial officer of Merck. The 53-year-old Lewent is one of the most powerful women in corporate America.

Most decision support systems are geared toward aiding middle managers in the decision-making process. For example, a loan manager at a bank might use a decision support system to evaluate the credit risk involved in lending money to a particular client. Very rarely does a top manager use a decision support system. One reason for this may be that most electronic management information systems are not yet sophisticated enough to handle effectively the ambiguous types of problems facing top managers. To improve this situation, information systems professionals have been developing a variant of the decision support system: an executive support system.

executive support system A sophisticated version of a decision support system that is designed to meet the needs of top managers.

group decision support system An executive support system that links top managers so that they can function as a team.

An **executive support system** is a sophisticated version of a decision support system designed to meet the needs of top managers. Lewent's "Research Planning Model" is actually an executive support system. One of the defining characteristics of executive support systems is user-friendliness. Many of them include simple pull-down menus to take a manager through a decision analysis problem. Moreover, they may contain stunning graphics and other visual features to encourage top managers to use them.[32] Increasingly, executive support systems are being used to link top managers so that they can function as a team, and this type of executive support system is called a **group decision support system.**

Expert Systems and Artificial Intelligence

expert system A management information system that employs human knowledge captured in a computer to solve problems that ordinarily require human expertise.

Expert systems are the most advanced management information systems available. An **expert system** is a system that employs human knowledge captured in a computer to solve problems that ordinarily require human expertise.[33] Expert systems are a variant of artificial intelligence.[34] Mimicking human expertise (and intelligence) requires a computer that can at a minimum (1) recognize, formulate, and solve a problem, (2) explain the solution, and (3) learn from experience.

Recent developments in artificial intelligence that go by names such as "fuzzy logic" and "neural networks" have resulted in computer programs that, in a primitive way, try to mimic human thought processes. Although artificial intelligence is still at a fairly early stage of development, an increasing number of business applications are beginning to emerge in the form of expert systems. General Electric, for example, has developed an expert system to help troubleshooting problems in the diesel locomotive engines it manufactures. The expert system was originally based on knowledge collected from David Smith, GE's top locomotive troubleshooter, who retired in the 1980s after 40 years of service at GE. A novice engineer or technician can use the system to uncover a fault by spending only a few minutes at a computer terminal. The system also can explain to the user the logic of its advice, thereby serving as a teacher as well as a problem solver. The system is based on a flexible, humanlike thought process, and it can be updated to incorporate new knowledge as it becomes available. GE has installed the system in every railroad repair shop that it serves, thus eliminating delays and boosting maintenance productivity.[35]

The Impact and Limitations of Information Systems and Technology

The advances in management information systems and technology described in this chapter are having important effects on managers and organizations. By improving the ability of managers to coordinate and control the activities of the organization, and by helping managers make more effective decisions, modern computer-based information systems have become a central component of any organization's structure. And evidence that information systems can be a source of competitive advantage is growing; organizations that do not adopt leading-edge information systems are likely to be at a competitive disadvantage. In this section we examine how the rapid growth of computerized information systems is affecting organizational structure and competitive advantage. We also examine problems associated with implementing management information systems effectively, as well as their limitations.

Information Systems and Organizational Structure

Until the development of modern computer-based information systems, there was no viable alternative to the organizational hierarchy, despite the information problems associated with it. The rapid rise of computer-based information

Figure 17.4
How Computer-Based Information Systems Affect the Organizational Hierarchy

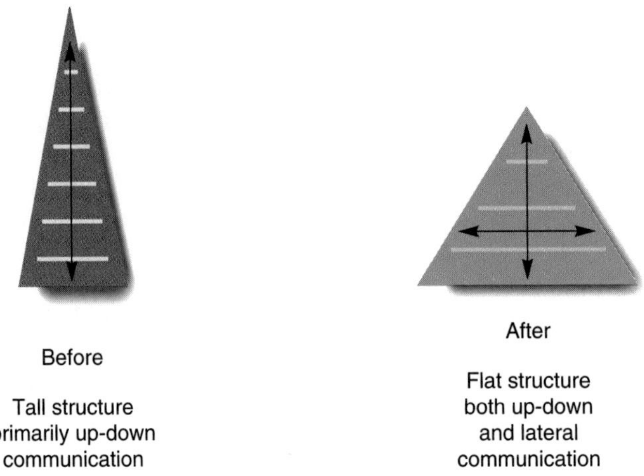

systems has been associated with a "delayering" (flattening) of the organizational hierarchy and a move toward greater decentralization and horizontal information flows within organizations (see Figure 17.4).[36]

FLATTENING ORGANIZATIONS By electronically providing managers with high-quality, timely, relevant, and relatively complete information, modern management information systems have reduced the need for tall management hierarchies. Consider again the computer-based operations information system that T. J. Rodgers uses at Cypress Semiconductor to review the performance of his 1,500 employees. Ten years ago, Rodgers might have needed 100 managers to conduct such performance reviews; now he can do them himself in four hours a week. Modern information systems have reduced the need for a hierarchy to function as a means to control the activities of the organization. In addition, they have reduced the need for a management hierarchy to coordinate organizational activities.

HORIZONTAL INFORMATION FLOWS Fired by the growth of three-tier mainframe-server-client computing architecture (see Figure 17.3), expansion of organizationwide computer networks has been rapid in recent years. Email systems, the development of software programs for sharing documents electronically, and the development of intranets (see Chapter 15) have accelerated this trend. An important consequence has been to increase horizontal information flows within organizations, something illustrated well by the experiences of Tel Co. and Soft Co.

Information Technology Byte

Information Flows at Tel Co. and Soft Co.

Despite being a high tech company, managers at Tel Co. were slow to adopt an internal electronic mail system (email) to facilitate communication throughout the company. Soft Co., by contrast, is a software company in which managers virtually "live on-line" and most communication between them takes place by means of email. Commenting on how the two companies differ, a manager who moved from Tel Co. to Soft Co. said:

At Tel Co. I would take two boxes of memos and company reports home with me each weekend to read. Then I had to go through all this stuff, most of which was irrelevant to my job, to find those pieces of paper that mattered to me. It was very time-consuming, very unproductive. At Soft Co. there is no paper to take home; most communication takes place via the company's email system. I use a software agent to scan all my incoming email and prioritize it (a software agent is a computer program that can perform certain tasks–such as sorting through and prioritizing incoming email). This saves a massive amount of time. The system alerts me instantly to email that is relevant to my job.[37]

This manager also noted that the use of an email system led to other communications differences between the two companies. At Tel Co. communication is primarily vertical; middle managers send information up the organizational hierarchy, and top managers send their responses back down. At Soft Co., however, communication between managers at different levels has become far less structured, and because of the email system there is much less emphasis on formal channels of communication. Email allows managers at any level to communicate easily with each other, so managers at Soft Co. communicate directly with whomever they need to contact to get the job done. Also, email has resulted in much more cross-functional, horizontal communication because it is so easy for managers in different functions to communicate.

The observations of this manager about communication flows at Tel Co. and Soft Co. were confirmed in a study undertaken by Alta Analytics, a management consulting company.[38] Figure 17.5 shows maps of the communication flows between managers based in different departments at Tel Co. and Soft Co. The boxes in these two maps are employees grouped by function. To make these maps, Alta asked employees to name every manager with whom they had communication in any form–phone, meeting, memo, email–in the past week. If two people agreed that they had three or more important contacts, the mapmakers drew a line between their boxes, indicating a significant link.

Figure 17.5
Communication Flows at Tel Co. and Soft Co.

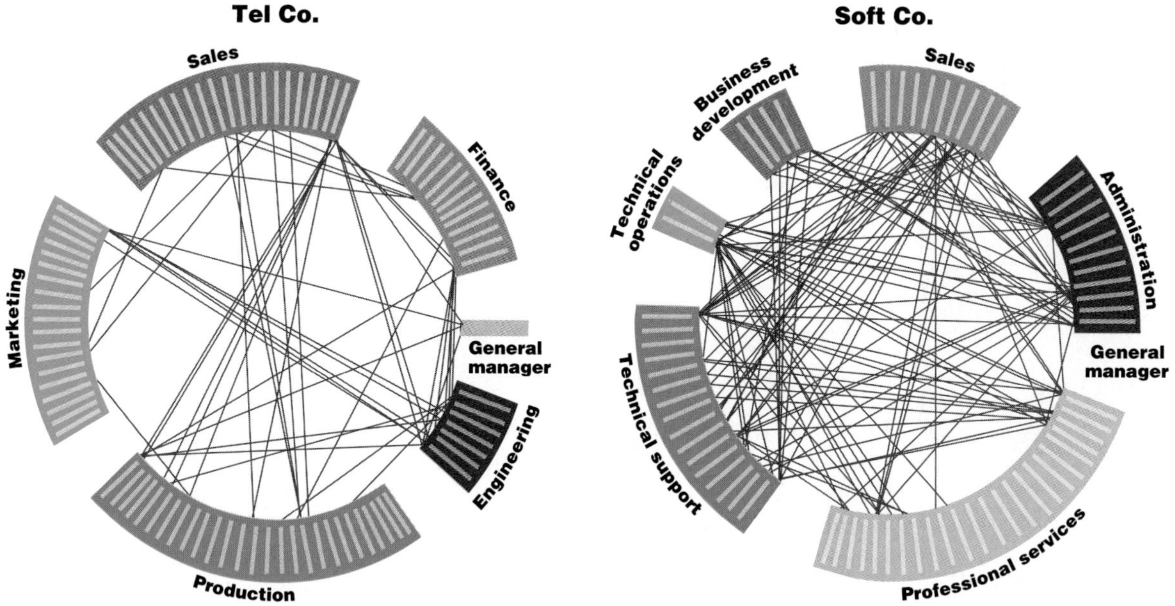

Source: T. A. Stewart, "Managing in a Wired Company," *Fortune,* July 11, 1994, 54. NETMAP® is a registered trademark for the NETMAP Software Systems, Alta Analytics, Inc., Westerville, OH.

The differences between the two companies are immediately apparent. At Tel Co., the general manager communicated only with four senior functional managers, all of whom had a direct reporting relationship to him; there were hardly any links between the marketing and production departments; and a handful of functional managers accounted for most of the interfunctional communication. At Soft Co., there was a much richer flow of communication between managers in the different functions, as indicated by the number of lines connecting the different boxes. Clearly, boundaries between functions mean little at Soft Co., as do differences in rank. Almost everybody talks to everybody else because of Soft Co.'s email system. At Tel Co. and Soft Co. the development of organizationwide computer networks has broken down the barriers that have traditionally separated functional departments and divisions and the result has been improved performance.

Information Systems and Competitive Advantage

State-of-the-art information technology can improve the competitiveness of an organization. Indeed, the search for competitive advantage is driving much of the rapid development and adoption of IT systems. By improving the decision-making capability of managers, for example, management information systems like executive support systems and decision support systems should help an organization enhance its competitive position. Similarly, by reducing the need for hierarchy, modern information systems can directly increase an organization's efficiency. One reason for an increase in efficiency is that the use of advanced information systems can reduce the number of employees required to perform organizational activities. At one time, for example, 13 layers of management separated Eastman Kodak's general manager of manufacturing and factory workers. With information systems, now the number of layers is four. Similarly, Intel found that by increasing the sophistication of its information systems it could cut the number of hierarchical layers in the organization from 10 to 5.[39]

William Davidow and Michael Malone, co-authors of The Virtual Corporation, coined the term virtual products to describe the way information systems can improve an organization's responsiveness to customers. They argue that information systems and technology are allowing companies to customize their product offerings without incurring any extra cost penalty, and indeed in ways that may reduce costs. For example, consider the way Merck Medco are using IT to revolutionize the distribution of drugs to patients.

Information Technology Byte

Merck Medco's Pharmacy of the Future

Merck, the pharmaceuticals company discussed earlier, is well known for its ability to discover new drugs and treatments to treat a wide variety of diseases. What is less known about Merck is that its drug distribution and supply subsidiary, Merck Medco, is redefining distribution in the pharmaceutical industry.[40] Medco's Internet pharmacy fills more prescriptions than all the other Internet pharmacies combined. It also delivers drugs via its free 800 number, mail order, and traditional means (manufacturer to warehouse to pharmacy). Although these advances have significantly reduced distribution

Gayle Wiggins, a systems control coordinator of Merck Medco, operates an automated packaging computer in the company's automated pharmacy center in Willingboro, NJ.

costs and have increased patient convenience, there are many significant new opportunities on the horizon to use IT in innovative ways.

Over the next two to five years, pharmacy benefit companies (PBC) like Merck Medco will equip physicians with the hardware and software needed to have each patient's medical record in an electronic file available through a laptop computer located in each patient treatment room in a physician's practice. The physician will have the patient's medical history including which drugs the patient has used and is currently using.[41] The physician will be able to enter the diagnosis and appropriate drug alternatives will automatically emerge. The file also contains information on the cost of the drug to the patient through the specific insurance plan. The physician will then be able to order the drug via an electronic prescription that will go to the patient's pharmacy or to the PBC and be delivered to the patient's house.

The benefits of using new IT in this way are significant. First, the risks of physicians prescribing the wrong drugs are far less likely so this service is safer, more effective, and less costly to patients and to the insurance companies. Second, this reduces the enormous amount of time physicians and their staffs have to spend dealing with HMOs and insurance companies. Third, PBMs like Medco–which Merck owns–generate revenues through these software and consulting services to health care providers, HMOs, and drug companies. Last, but not least, pharmacies will make far fewer mistakes filling prescriptions reducing the thousands of deaths each year that occur when mistakes are made. Thus, the result of IT and the Internet is higher-quality health-care solutions at lower costs and lower drug prices to consumers.

Limitations of Information Systems

For all of their usefulness, information systems have some limitations. A serious potential problem is that in all of the enthusiasm for management information systems, electronic communication by means of a computer network, and the like, a vital human element of communication might be lost. Some kinds of information cannot be aggregated and summarized on an MIS report. Henry Mintzberg noted that *thick information* is often required to coordinate and control an enterprise and to make informed decisions; Mintzberg means information rich in meaning and significance, far beyond that which can be quantified and aggregated.[42] According to Mintzberg, such information must be dug out, on site, by people closely involved in the events they wish to influence.

The importance of thick information is a strong argument in favor of using electronic communication to support face-to-face communication, not to replace it. For example, it would be wrong to make a judgment about an individual's performance merely by "reading the numbers" provided by a management information system. Instead, the numbers should be used to alert managers to individuals who may have a performance problem. The nature of this performance problem should then be explored in a face-to-face meeting, during which thick information can be gathered. As a top Boeing manager noted, "In our company, the use of email and videoconferencing has not reduced the need to visit people at other sites; it has increased it. Email has facilitated the establishment of communications channels between people who previously would not communicate, which is good, but direct visits are still required to cement any working relationships that evolve out of these electronic meetings."[43]

At Soft Co., discussed earlier, managers have been heard to complain that one drawback of their internal email system is that people spend a lot of time behind closed doors looking at computer screens and communicating electronically and very little time interacting directly with other managers.[44] When this is the case in an organization, management decisions may suffer because of a lack of thick information.

Another limitation of IT in organizations is that despite its many advantages there are still technological problems to be overcome.[45] One of these is the lack of consistent technological standards throughout the divisions or functions of an organization, and the use of different software systems that may impede communication and decision making. For example, different manufacturers of computer and communications equipment use different technical standards. For example, an IBM mainframe may be manufactured according to technical standards different from those of a Sun or Compaq server or an Apple personal computer. These different standards make it difficult to integrate various machines into a seamless computer network, and machines designed according to different standards may find it difficult to "talk" to one another.

An example of this problem is the emergence of the free operating system LINUX as an alternative to Microsoft's Windows platform. LINUX is a very stable platform and it is easy to write software for the LINUX platform. Indeed, Microsoft launched its Windows XP operating system in 2001, in part, as a response to the need to solve the problems of instability in it previous Windows system which was prone to crash often. Companies such as IBM and Sun Microsystems that wish to reduce Microsoft's dominance have been championing the LINUX systems and developing software for it. However, this software is not compatible with Windows and transferring files from one system to the other without, for example, losing the formatting of a word-processed document is difficult. This kind of connectivity problem can occur on a much larger scale within organizationwide computer networks. Currently the number of companies operating with LINUX is increasing because the software is relatively inexpensive compared with Microsoft's licensing charges. In the opening case of Chapter 19 we discuss how Maden Technologies is pioneering a new enterprise management systems software to overcome the communications problems associated with the use of different platforms in different parts of the organization.

Managers can take several steps to ease the implementation of information systems. First, they need to develop a list of the organization's principal goals and then decide on the major types of information they need to collect to measure how well they are achieving those goals. Second, after making this analysis, managers audit their current management information systems to determine the degree to which the information they are currently collecting is accurate, reliable, timely, and relevant. Third, managers need to investigate what other sources of information might be available to measure and improve efficiency, quality, innovation, and responsiveness to customers. For example, are organizational members using state-of-the-art information systems like email, computer-assisted design, and three-tier designs? It is useful to benchmark competitors to determine what kinds of systems they are using.

Fourth, when this analysis is complete, managers need to build support for the introduction of new information systems and convince employees that these systems will help raise job and organizational performance. Fifth, managers should create formal training programs, with appropriate backup support, to help train employees to use the new information systems and technology, making sure that these systems are as user-friendly as possible. Sixth, managers should emphasize that information systems are not a substitute for face-to-face communication and that employees at all levels should be involved in a continuing discussion about how best to exploit information technology to create a competitive advantage.

Tips for Future Managers

Managing **Information**

1. For effective decision making, design management information systems to ensure they provide high quality, timely, complete, and relevant information.
2. Train managers how to use advanced information systems to ensure that they make the best use of the information they receive to improve their planning and decision making.
3. Recognize that implementing an advanced MIS is a difficult process and that many technical and operational problems have to be overcome. Moreover, recognize that improving IT is a continuous process and IT evolves over time.
4. Make the improvement of information technology a priority at all levels in the organization and in all functions.

Summary and Review

INFORMATION AND THE MANAGER'S JOB Computer-based information systems are central to the operation of most organizations. By providing managers with high-quality, timely, relevant, and relatively complete information, properly implemented information systems can improve managers' ability to coordinate and control the operations of an organization and to make effective decisions. Moreover, information systems can help the organization to attain a competitive advantage through their beneficial impact on productivity, quality, innovation, and responsiveness to customers. Thus, modern information systems are an indispensable management tool.

THE INFORMATION TECHNOLOGY REVOLUTION Over the last 30 years there have been rapid advances in the power, and rapid declines in the cost, of information technology. Falling prices, wireless communication, computer networks, and software developments have all radically improved the power and efficacy of computer-based information systems.

TYPES OF MANAGEMENT INFORMATION SYSTEMS

Traditionally managers used the organizational hierarchy as the main system for gathering the information they needed to coordinate and control the organization and to make effective decisions. Today, managers use four main types of computer-based information systems. Listed in ascending order of sophistication, they are transaction-processing systems, operations information systems, decision support systems, and expert systems.

THE IMPACT AND LIMITATIONS OF INFORMATION SYSTEMS AND TECHNOLOGY Modern information systems and technology have changed organizational structure by making it flatter and by encouraging more cross-functional communication. In turn, this has helped organizations achieve a competitive advantage.

Management in Action

Topics for Discussion and Action

1. To be useful, information must be of high quality, timely, relevant, and as complete as possible. Describe the negative impact that a tall management hierarchy, when used as an information system, can have on these desirable attributes.
2. What is the relationship between information systems and competitive advantage?
3. Ask a manager to describe the main kinds of information systems that he or she uses on a routine basis at work.
4. Because of the growth of high-powered low-cost computing, wireless communications, and technologies such as videoconferencing, many managers soon may not need to come into the office to do their jobs. They will be able to work at home. What are the pros and cons of such an arrangement?
5. Many companies have reported that it is difficult to implement advanced management information and decision support systems. Why do you think this is so? How might the roadblocks to implementation be removed?
6. How can information systems help in the new product development process?
7. Why is face-to-face communication between managers still important in an organization?

Building Management Skills

Analyzing Information Systems

Pick an organization about which you have some direct knowledge. It may be an organization that you worked for in the past or are in contact with now (such as the college or school that you attend). For this organization, do the following.

1. Describe the information systems that managers use to coordinate and control organizational activities and to help make decisions. Are these information systems computer based or based on paper and hierarchy? Does the organization use a transaction-processing system, operations information system, decision support system, or expert system?
2. Do you think that the organization's existing information systems provide managers with high-quality, timely, relevant, and relatively complete information? Explain your answer.
3. What, if anything, might be done to improve the information systems in this organization?
4. How might advanced information systems be used to improve the competitive position of this organization? In particular, try to identify the impact the information systems might have on the organization's productivity, quality, innovation, and responsiveness to customers.

Small Group Breakout Exercise

Using New Information Systems

Form groups of three or four people, and appoint one member as the spokesperson who will communicate your findings to the whole class when called on by the instructor. Then discuss the following scenario.

You are a team of managing partners of a large firm of accountants. You are responsibile for auditing your firm's information systems to determine whether they are appropriate and up-to-date. To your surprise, you find that although your organization does have an email system in place and the accountants are connected into a powerful local area network (LAN), most of the accountants (including partners) are not using this technology. You also find that the organizational hierarchy is still the preferred information system of the managing partners.

Given this situation, you are concerned that your organization is not exploiting the opportunities offered by new information systems to obtain a competitive advantage. You have discussed this issue and are meeting to develop an action plan to get accountants to appreciate the need to learn, and to take advantage of, the potential of the new information technology.

1. What advantages can you tell the accountants they will obtain when they use the new information technology?
2. What problems do you think you may encounter in convincing the accountants to use the new information technology?
3. Discuss how you might make it easy for the accountants to learn to use the new technology.

Exploring the World Wide Web

Search for the website of a company that makes extensive use of information systems to deliver its goods or services to customers. What systems does it use, and how do they give the company a competitive advantage?

You're the Management Consultant

You are an IT consultant who has been called in by the managers of a small specialty furniture maker of custom-made tables, chairs, and cabinets. The goal of these managers is to use IT and the Internet to find new business opportunities and improve its competitive advantage. These managers want to find ways to reduce costs and attract customers and they are asking you for specific advice on the various ways in which IT might do this.

1. What are the various forces in a specialty furniture maker's task environment that have the most affect on its performance.
2. What kinds of IT can be used to help the company manage these forces?
3. In what ways can the Internet be used to help this organization improve its competitive position?

BusinessWeek Cases in the News

Rethinking the Internet

Everywhere we look, the once-limitless promise of the Internet appears to be fading. The dot-coms that were supposed to topple industry giants have mostly vanished. The last of the Net's bluest-chips are on the ropes. No. 1 e-tailer Amazon.com Inc. can't extract a profit from its $2.8 billion in sales, leading some to predict it will run out of money. And on March 7, one of the few profitable Web companies, portal Yahoo! Inc., said it would badly miss sales projections for the first quarter. Internet stocks are in free fall, many of them lucky to top a buck a share—sending billions of dollars of investment up in smoke.

And the collapse isn't stopping at the dot-coms, as the once-untouchable makers of the networking and computer gear that serve as the Internet's foundation are also on the run. On March 9, network equipment maker Cisco Systems Inc. jolted the market with its second warning of slower growth to come, announcing its first-ever widespread layoffs.That followed a warning of slowing sales in late February from Sun Microsystems Inc., whose servers run countless websites.

Now, the mounting woes of the Internet sector seem to be spreading to the rest of the economy. Just as the rollout of the Internet helped fuel the boom of the 1990s, the evaporation of Net euphoria is helping drag down consumer confidence and corporate capital spending, not to mention the stock market. Since the beginning of the year, the Standard & Poor's 500-stock index is down 12 percent, and the U.S. economy looks ready to slide into its first tech-triggered recession.

But look beyond the current economic and market plight, and a different picture emerges. As with any new technology, the early years of the Internet have been a learning process—and here's what we now know. First, the Internet was supposed to change everything. That's just plain wrong. The reality is, there was no way that a single technology could fulfill such an extravagant promise.

Instead, it turns out that the transformative power of the Internet is being felt unevenly. There are plenty of industries and situations where the Net has the potential to be revolutionary, as its most enthusiastic backers had predicted, and their number will only widen as new technologies such as broadband come into widespread use. But clearly in much of the economy, the Internet offers incremental payoffs without substantially altering core businesses. And even in industries where the Net can effect profound change, institutional barriers and business inertia mean the big gains may not come for years.

Strip away the highfalutin talk, and at bottom, the Internet is a tool that dramatically lowers the cost of communication. That means it can radically alter any industry or activity that depends heavily on the flow of information. In areas such as financial services, the process is well under way. In other information-intensive industries, such as entertainment, health care, government, and education, the potential lies in the future. But it's there. Says Gary E. Rieschel, executive managing director at Softbank Venture Capital, one of the biggest backers of Internet ventures: "The Internet is about communications, and people have never at any time in history stopped wanting to communicate."

That means the Internet can dramatically reduce the cost of both consumer and business transactions. It also can improve coordination, both within and across companies, while giving them direct contact with consumers. "The reality is that e-business is a tremendous tool for cost reduction, it's a tremendous tool to help you get closer to your customer, it's a tremendous tool for what used to be called Old Economy companies to apply to our current processes," says Brian P. Kelley, vice president of global consumer services at Ford Motor Co. and the architect of most of the auto maker's e-business initiatives.

Over the coming decade, the biggest gains will come from restructuring the way work is done within companies. The Net can become the communications backbone for everything from linking supply chains for speedy product turnarounds to storing employee expertise so that co-workers can tap into ready-made knowledge instead of starting from scratch. Says Massachusetts Institute of Technology economist Erik Brynjolfsson: "Most of [the Net's benefits] will come in changes to business practices and organization. What really matters is when companies and markets reorganize."

Given the crucial role of communication and information, the long-term impact on economic growth could be substantial. The Internet could add up to 0.4 percentage points to annual productivity growth over the next five years, according to new research from the Brookings Institution. "We're looking at an improvement in income per person of roughly $1,500 in 2010," says Robert E. Litan, director of economic studies at Brookings, who led the study, along with Alice M. Rivlin, former vice chairman of the Federal Reserve. And this estimate doesn't take into account the further gains that would come should broadband be affordably piped into every home, making interaction with the Internet far richer.

If applied right, ultimately, the Internet could boost the rate of innovation by increasing the speed at which ideas spread between companies, within economies, and across countries. With more information available, new ideas will get noticed and put into practice faster. "The Internet is the friend of companies making products that are truly unique and different," says Gary Hamel, chairman of the San Francisco office of consulting firm Strategos. "That means the premium for real innovation will go up."

True Grit

But the very strengths of the Internet are also its limitations. Just because communication is ubiquitous doesn't mean it's everything. The last five years have taught us that in industries such as retailing, manufacturing, and transportation, physical factors overpower the virtual. E-tailing turns out to be more about which company is best at moving boxes around rather than who has glitziest website or the biggest virtual store on earth. Linking supply chains over the Net cuts costs and improves response times, but ultimately manufacturers succeed or fail if they develop good products and figure out how to produce them at low cost and high quality. On-line airline reservation systems can improve customer convenience and boost the revenue yield per passenger, but they can't do anything about long delays caused by runaway congestion, too few loading gates, antiquated air traffic control systems, and mechanical difficulties on airplanes.

Even in areas where the Internet can play a central role, the big changes are not going to come overnight, as investors have found to their chagrin. Some of the information-intensive industries where the Internet could have its biggest effect are also the ones where institutional and regulatory barriers are the highest and vested interests are the strongest. In health care and education, for example, the possible benefits from widespread use of the Web are enormous, but it's going to happen in baby steps, over time. What's more, it's a difficult, painful, and slow process to restructure companies and markets. "We have cherry-picked some of the easy projects," says Andrew McAfee, a Harvard Business School professor who has studied how businesses use the Internet.

In the end, it turns out that the speed of Internet time has more to do with the capital markets than with the pace of technology adoption. The enormous amounts of venture capital available to startups drove companies to grow far faster in a few short years than the underlying infrastructure or consumer demand could support. In fact, the eventual benefits of the Web should be measured over a decade. "People had higher expectations for the next couple of years than are likely to be realized," says Jeffrey P. Bezos, CEO of Amazon.com. "And people have much lower expectations for the next couple of years than are likely to be realized over the next 10 years."

That may help explain the current confusion about the future of the Internet. On one hand, Internet usage continues to rise, and consumer e-commerce sales are up by 67 percent over a year earlier, according to the Census Bureau. "Our research doesn't show any downturn in consumer behavior," says Mary Modahl, vice president of marketing at Forrester Research.

Got Web?

That's why Internet optimists are refusing to retreat. Analyst Mary Meeker of Morgan Stanley Dean Witter is urging Net leaders such as Amazon, Yahoo, and AOL Time Warner to band together in a Got Milk?-style marketing campaign promoting the idea that the Web is alive and well. Another group, led by Michael Tchong, CEO of technology consultant Iconocast Inc., has launched a Back the Net campaign to urge people to buy something on-line or 10 shares in a Net company on April 3.

Such Webfests, however, aren't likely to change the minds of burned investors or restore the once-buoyant expectations for the Net. For instance, Merrill Lynch & Co. analyst Henry M. Blodget recently reduced his expectations for how much retail sales will go online to only 5 percent to 10 percent, down from 10 percent to 15 percent he envisioned just a few months ago. Even Bradford C. Koenig, head of the technology banking practice at Goldman, Sachs & Co., which underwrote many of the hottest Net initial public offerings, has lost confidence in pure Internet companies: "The notion of an Internet company is no longer viable."

But that's too pessimistic. In fact, part of the problem was that much of the investment flowed into areas where the Internet is incremental rather than revolutionary. Take retailing. The hyped consumer dotcoms were supposed to blow away their brick-and-mortar counterparts. But it turns out that the importance of information and communication in retailing—the Internet's forte—is much smaller than the role of logistics. How much smaller? According to Softbank's Rieschel, it takes between $15 million and $25 million to build a top-of-the-line website. Yet it costs at least $150 million to build a warehouse and distribution system for a consumer Web operation. "The Internet only solved 10 percent of the process, the front-end purchase process," says Rieschel. "What we really needed to do was fund the back end."

All across retailing, the Internet is no longer seen as the 800-pound gorilla. For example, a year ago, the prevailing wisdom was that old-fashioned auto dealers were going to be passe. But so far, that hasn't turned out to be true. "There hasn't been the massive shift to buying cars online that we thought there would be 18 months ago," admits Mark T. Hogan, president of e-GM, the auto maker's on-line consumer unit.

And there's growing evidence that shoppers on the Net are supersensitive to price, according to Austan Goolsbee, an economist at the University of Chicago. The implication is that any profits e-tailers might make could be short-lived as competition drives prices down on the Web. "Now, retail once again looks like a brutal, low-margin business," says Goolsbee.

The Internet was also supposed to transform markets by wiping out the middlemen. Real estate agents, for example, were expected to dwindle away as buyers located homes on the Web while paying lower commissions. But the reverse turned out to be true, since the number of real estate agents has grown rather than fallen. "Studies have shown that people who use the Internet use Realtors more than those who don't," says Stuart Wolff, CEO of Homestore.com Inc., the largest home and real estate related site.

Perhaps the biggest surprise is the comparatively limited impact that the Internet may have on manufacturing. To be sure, there is no doubt that e-business has become an essential part of any manufacturer's toolkit. The use of the Internet can reduce inventories, take costs out of the supply chain, and eliminate unnecessary transactions. Collaboration can also speed up product development, e-marketplaces can lower the cost of components and other supplies, and detailed info on customers can help customize products to snag bigger orders or even help determine which customers aren't cost-effective. At Procter & Gamble Co., a Web-based information-sharing network makes it easier to collect and evaluate new product ideas from the company's far-flung workforce of 110,000 people.

Nevertheless, at the end of the day, manufacturers are still in the business of making things, not simply moving bits and bytes around. Wheels have to be bolted onto the car, circuit boards have to be installed in the router—and that has to be done physically.

To understand how this limits the impact of the Internet in manufacturing, look at the example of Cisco, the communications equipment maker that is universally regarded as the poster company for using the Web. Some 68 percent of Cisco's orders are placed and fulfilled over the Web and 70 percent of its service calls are resolved online. Cisco is in the process of linking all of its contract manufacturers and key suppliers into an advanced Web supply-chain management system, dubbed eHub. This speeds up the rate at which information about demand is distributed to suppliers.

According to Cisco's own calculations, its payoff from its use of the Internet amounts to $1.4 billion per year, or 7 percent of sales. If the rest of manufacturing could even do half as well as Cisco in using the Internet, that would cut an impressive $150 billion from annual manufacturing costs. But these figures need to be put in perspective. A 7 percent reduction in costs is nothing to sneeze at, but it is not the radical reduction in costs that would signal a revolution.

Slow As Molasses

And while supply chains linked over the Net are more responsive than their predecessors, they have their limits, too. "The flexibility now being demanded by customers exceeds the physics of what the supply chain can actually deliver," says Kevin R. Burns, chief materials officer for contract manufacturer Solectron Corp. (SLR), whose big customers include Cisco and IBM (IBM). Now that companies have switched to Web-based models, he notes, they expect to be able to ramp up or halt production of a product within weeks. But it still takes at least three months to get a specially designed chip made in a Taiwanese foundry and around 40 weeks to order an LCD screen.

And while the unprecedented communications capabilities of the Web should enable corporations and markets to be organized in new ways, it's going to take longer than proponents expected. "At the marketplace level, I haven't seen radical changes brought on by the Internet," says McAfee. "It's going to be a much more gradual process."

While the obstacles don't disappear, it's easier to see the far-reaching potential of the Internet in those industries that are primarily about moving information rather than truckloads of goods. Take financial services. In many ways, financial products are ideally suited to the Internet, since they deal only with information. Indeed, a recent Goldman Sachs survey reported that 63 percent of financial companies had sold their products through an e-marketplace or a website, the highest of any industry.

The Internet is already well on its way to transforming financial services. On-line brokers such as E*Trade Group Inc. (EGRP) have completely changed how the retail brokerage business worked. And Internet services are now offered by nearly every U.S. bank and credit union. Bank of America (BAC) says it's signing up 130,000 on-line customers a month, giving it more than 3 million Internet customers. Citigroup (C) has 2.2 million, Wells Fargo & Co. (WFC) more than 2.5 million. FleetBoston Financial Corp. (FBF), the nation's seventh-largest bank, combined its on-line banking services with its on-line brokerage business, Quick & Reilly, and its on-line customer base jumped 50 percent, to more than 1 million customers, which is 35 percent of the total customer base.

But as in the case of entertainment, technological and institutional barriers are slowing down the eventual gains. Consider on-line bill-paying, widely anticipated to be the "sticky app" that drives traffic. The benefits of paying bills on the Net, for both consumers and businesses, could be enormous. But the technology has proven exceptionally complicated, and it has hit a wall trying to penetrate the banking industry. Among the problems: Banks and billers have been unable to agree on how bills should actually appear on-line. Still, Bank of America plans to launch a big ad campaign later this year to promote its bill-paying service.

And then there's health care. Despite the tangible nature of many medical services, health care has a very large information component that makes it a natural for Internet applications. Just shifting claims-processing to the Web could save $20 billion a year, according to the Brookings economists. At Merck Medco Managed Care, the nation's leading provider of prescription drug care, it costs a matter of cents to handle a prescription order on the Internet, as opposed to more than $1 through other methods, notes Stephen J. Gold, senior vice president.

Broadband's Promise

But there are enormous institutional barriers. For one, privacy considerations may slow down the full shift of health-care records to the Web. Moreover, health-insurance companies, doctors, and hospitals are unwilling to give up control of patient records and insurance payments to a third party. This reluctance helped frustrate WebMD (HLTH) and Healtheon, which expected to lead a restructuring of health care by moving many claims, payment, and related processing services to the Net. WebMD's efforts to provide real-time payment capabilities were shunned by insurers and HMOs, who prefer the current cumbersome process that lets them hold onto the money longer.

There's also the technology factor. In the long run, realizing the promise of the Net will depend on the widespread introduction of advanced technologies such as broadband to the home and high-speed wireless. With broadband connections over telephone or cable-television lines, consumers will be able to watch TV-quality video clips of the NCAA basketball tournament or download crystal-clear music files faster than ever before. What's more, they're more likely to use the Net because they'll always be connected and won't have to spend minutes dialing into the Net each time they want to visit a site.

The problem is that getting the new technologies in place may take longer than expected. Financially stressed telecom companies are slowing down the roll out of broadband. The failure of small telecom providers means that subscriber growth may slow down in second- or third-tier markets. And the prices for high-speed Internet access may rise. SBC Communications Inc. (SBC) recently raised the price of its residential high-speed Internet service by 25 percent, or $10 per month, which is likely to slow its adoption. "Until the foundation of Internet infrastructure gets built out, we're not going to see any consumer Net companies emerging," says Michael Parekh, managing director of Internet research at Goldman Sachs.

In the end, the Internet seems likely to revolutionize mainly communications-intensive industries and activities. If that seems too limited, remember that almost every breakthrough technology over the last 200 years affected some areas of the economy more than others. The automobile transformed personal transportation and patterns of housing while little affecting manufacturing. Electricity radically altered manufacturing practices and any industry that was power-intensive, while not having an enormous effect on health care. The Internet deserves to be put in such august company.

Source: M.J. Mandel, and R.D. Hof, "Rethinking the Internet," *Business Week,* March 26, 2001, pp. 117–22.

Questions

1. In what ways has IT and the Internet changed the way companies do business?

2. In what ways can the Internet help to reduce costs, increase quality, or increase responsiveness to customers?

3. Which kinds of businesses is the Internet likely to help most in the future? In what ways will it do this?

Chapter 18

Operations Management: Managing Quality, Efficiency, and Responsiveness to Customers

LEARNING OBJECTIVES

After studying this chapter, you should be able to:

- Explain the **role of operations management** in achieving superior quality, efficiency, and responsiveness to customers.
- Describe **what customers want,** and explain why it is so important for managers to be responsive to their needs.
- Explain why **achieving superior quality** is so important.
- Describe the **main features of total quality management.**
- Describe the challenges facing managers and organizations that seek to **implement total quality management.**
- Explain why **achieving superior efficiency** is so important.
- Differentiate among **facilities layout, flexible manufacturing, just-in-time inventory,** and **process reengineering.**

A Manager's Challenge

Bricks, Clicks, or Bricks and Clicks Supermarkets?

How can managers increase operating performance?

The potential uses of information technology and the Internet for improving responsiveness to customers became clear to companies in many industries in the late 1990s. One of these industries was the food delivery or supermarket industry. Entrepreneurs decided that developing an on-line ordering system that allowed customers to use the Internet to order their food on-line and creating a production system to deliver the food to their homes had enormous potential. For example, virtual grocer Webvan raised more than $1 billion to develop both the information system and physical infrastructure of warehouses and hot and cold delivery trucks that it needed to deliver food to customers. Other competitors like GroceryWorks.com and Homegrocer.com made similar kinds of investments. These on-line stores did attract customers, and by 2000 they had more than $1 billion in sales. Bricks-and-mortar (B&M) supermarkets like Kroger Company, Albertson's, and Safeway watched with some trepidation as their on-line rivals developed and managed their operations. Should they respond with their own on-line stores? What else should they do?

The on-line storefront and a delivery van of the now defunct on-line grocer Webvan.

One of the first responses by B&M supermarkets was to take steps to make their customers' shopping experience much more enjoyable. First, they improved their operations by building large, new, attractive stores that contained a wide variety of produce. Second, they increasingly incorporated IT into their operations to improve customer satisfaction with their stores. For example, Kroger experimented with a wide variety of self-serving technology kiosks. Kiosks are physical units within the store such as self-checkout units, check cashing units, bill payment units, and payment terminals that perform specific services for customers. These kiosks improved operations because they helped stores eliminate lengthy checkout lines and helped the company focus more on customer service. Together, these moves have helped B&M supermarkets improve responsiveness to customers, and increase the quality of their products and service. They have also helped reduce operating costs because customers perform their own services, including of course selecting their own products and delivering it to their homes.

By 2001, the question of which operating model was going to be the most successful was settled when many of the on-line grocers like Webvan announced that they were going out of business because of mounting losses. Why? First, the new egrocers did not possess the experience and ability to master the complex inventory management, sourcing, transportation, distribution, warehousing, and logistics necessary to operate successfully in this market unlike their well-established B&M rivals. Second, e-grocers had totally underestimated the problems and costs of operating the production and physical delivery service necessary to get products to customers. The average cost of home delivery for Webvan and other grocers was around $30, a cost they could not pass on to the customers they were trying to attract. In the future e-grocers hoped to attract only well-heeled customers who could afford to pay these high delivery costs—a very small market segment. The virtual grocery operating model was not working out.

After the collapse of Webvan, the other virtual grocers took a hard look at their operating systems. How could they provide high-quality, responsive customer service at a cost low enough to survive? Especially when the large supermarket chains had major cost advantages because of their huge purchasing power, market coverage, and ability to obtain economies of scale? Some e-grocers decided to form alliances with B&M supermarkets. For example, in several cities GroceryWorks.com now lets its customers order on its on-line store but then passes the orders onto the B&M supermarkets that process the order. GroceryWorks' trucks then deliver the orders; this avoids all the costs of sourcing and warehousing. Other Web grocers have just decided to focus on one market and develop an operating system to service the needs of customers inside just one city market. For example, grocerygateway.com just serves the needs of well-heeled customers in Toronto. •

Overview

Webvan and other virtual grocers used IT and the Internet to develop an operating and delivery system that may have been very responsive to customers but which was also very costly and inefficient compared to the operating systems of the B&M supermarket chains. Moreover, not only did they lack a viable operating system but they also lacked the skills to manage their operating systems efficiently. The B&M supermarkets, on the other hand, made innovations in their operating and information systems that allowed them to achieve superior quality, efficiency, and responsiveness to customers. These major sources of competitive advantage are still firmly in control of the $175-billion-a-year grocery market.

operations management The management of any aspect of the production system that transforms inputs into finished goods and services.

In this chapter we focus on the operations management techniques that managers can use to increase the quality of an organization's products, the efficiency of production, and the organization's responsiveness to customers. By the end of this chapter, you will understand the vital role operations management plays in building competitive advantage and creating a high-performing organization. In the next chapter we examine techniques that managers can use to enhance innovation and manage the product development process.

Operations Management and Competitive Advantage

production system The system that an organization uses to acquire inputs, convert the inputs into outputs, and dispose of the outputs.

operations manager A manager who is responsible for managing an organization's production system and for determining where operating improvements might be made.

Operations management is the management of any aspect of the production system that transforms inputs into finished goods and services. A **production system** is the system that an organization uses to acquire inputs, convert inputs into outputs, and dispose of the outputs (goods or services). **Operations managers** are managers who are responsible for managing an organization's production system. They do whatever it takes to transform inputs into outputs. Their job is to manage the three stages of production–acquisition of inputs, control of conversion processes, and disposal of goods and services–and to determine where operating improvements might be made in order to increase quality, efficiency, and responsiveness to customers and so give an organization a competitive advantage (see Figure 18.1).

Quality refers to goods and services that are reliable, dependable, or psychologically satisfying: They do the job they were designed for and do it well, or they possess some attribute that gives their users something they value.[1] *Efficiency* refers to the amount of inputs required to produce a given output. *Responsiveness to customers* refers to actions taken to meet the demands and needs of customers. Operations managers are responsible for ensuring that an organization has sufficient supplies of high-quality, low-cost inputs, and they are responsible for designing a production system that creates high-quality, low-cost products that customers are willing to buy.

Notice that achieving superior efficiency and quality is part of attaining superior responsiveness to customers. Customers want value for their money, and an

Figure 18.1
The Purpose of Operations Management

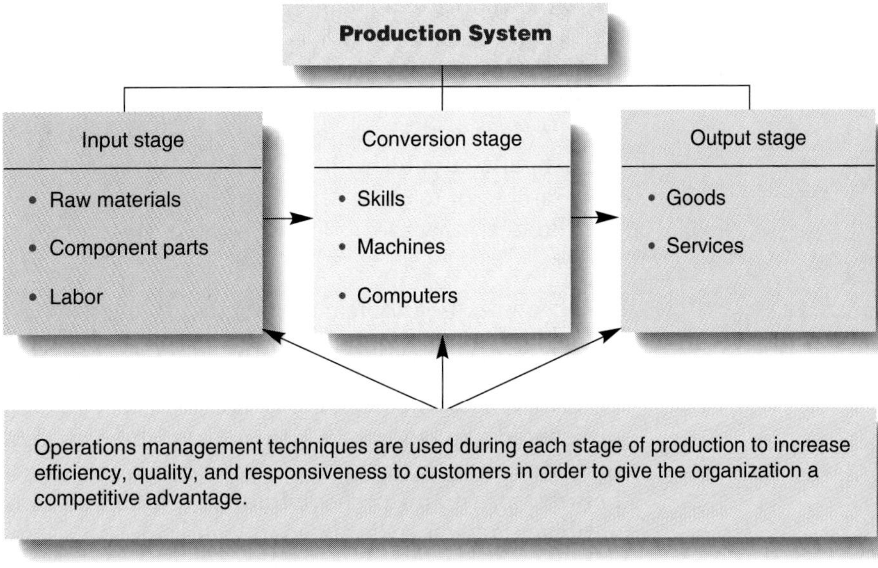
Production System
Input stage
• Raw materials
• Component parts
• Labor
Conversion stage
• Skills
• Machines
• Computers
Output stage
• Goods
• Services
Operations management techniques are used during each stage of production to increase efficiency, quality, and responsiveness to customers in order to give the organization a competitive advantage.

organization whose efficient production system creates high-quality, low-cost products is best able to deliver this value. For this reason, we begin by discussing how operations managers can design the production system to increase responsiveness to customers.

Improving Responsiveness to Customers

Organizations produce outputs–goods or services–that are consumed by customers. All organizations, profit seeking or not-for-profit, have customers. Without customers, most organizations would cease to exist. Because customers are vital to the survival of most organizations, managers must correctly identify customers and promote organizational strategies that respond to their needs. This is why management writers recommend that organizations define their business in terms of the customer needs they are satisfying, not the type of products they are producing.[2] The credo of pharmaceutical company Johnson & Johnson, for example, begins, "We believe our first responsibility is to the doctors, nurses and patients, to mothers and fathers and all others who use our products and services."[3] Through the credo Johnson & Johnson's managers emphasize their commitment to exemplary customer service. In contrast, in the early 2000s, Lucent Technologies decided that, given its expertise in transistor technology, it would focus on producing transistor-based Internet routers that could handle vast quantities of information. When it became clear that customers were choosing optical Internet routers because these routers could transfer information extremely quickly, Lucent lost a large part of its business.

What Do Customers Want?

Given that satisfying customer demands is central to the survival of an organization, an important question is, What do customers want? To specify exactly what they want is not possible because their wants vary from industry to industry. However, it is possible to identify some universal product attributes that most customers in most industries want. Generally, other things being equal, most customers prefer:

1. A lower price to a higher price
2. High-quality products to low-quality products
3. Quick service to slow service (They will always prefer good after-sales service and support to poor after-sales support.)
4. Products with many features to products with few features (They will prefer a personal computer with a CD-ROM drive, lots of memory, and a powerful microprocessor to one without these features.)
5. Products that are, as far as possible, customized or tailored to their unique needs

Of course, the problem is that other things are not equal. For example, providing high quality, quick service, and after-sales service and support, products with many features, and products that are customized raises costs and thus the price that must be charged to cover costs, as Webvan and other on-line grocers discovered.[4] So customers' demands for these attributes typically conflict with their demands for low prices. Accordingly, customers must make a trade-off between price and preferred attributes, and so must managers. This price/attribute trade-off is illustrated in Figure 18.2.

Figure 18.2
The Price/Attribute Relationship

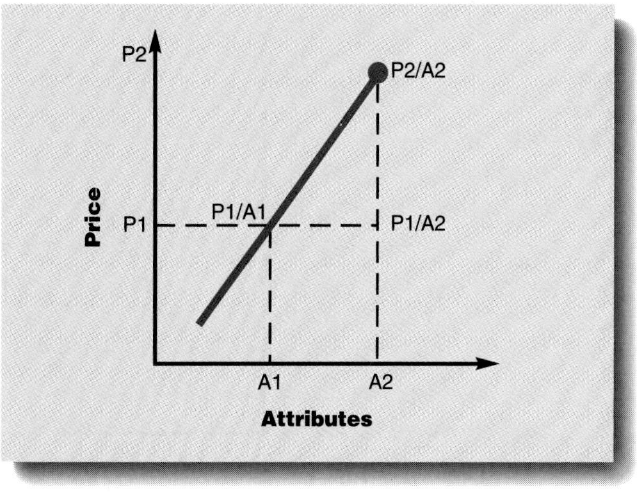

Desired attributes of a product–such as high quality, service, speed, after-sales support, features, and customization–are plotted on the horizontal axis; price is plotted on the vertical axis. The solid line shows the price/attribute relationship–that is, the combination of price and attributes an organization can offer and still make a profit. As the figure illustrates, the higher the price the customer is willing to pay for a product, the more desired attributes the customer is able to get. Or, in other words, the more desired attributes that an organization builds into its products, the higher is the price that the organization has to charge to cover its costs. At price P1 managers can offer a product with A1 attributes. If managers offer a product with A2 attributes at price P1, they will lose money because the price is too low to cover costs. A product with A2 attributes needs a price of P2 to be profitable for the organization. Thus, the nature of the organization's production system limits how responsive managers can be to customers.

Given the limits imposed on managers by their existing production system, what do the managers of a customer-responsive organization try to do? They try to push or shift the price/attribute curve to the right (toward the vertical dotted line in Figure 18.2) by developing new or improved production systems that are able to deliver either more desired product attributes for the same price or the same product attributes for a lower price.[5]

Figure 18.3 shows the price/attribute curves for the Kroger supermarket chain in 1991 before its customer-oriented IT kiosks were put in place and in 2001, when the IT and new store design was up and running. By accommodating customer demands for a greater variety of foods, increased quality, and quicker customer service, the new operating system allowed Kroger Company to offer more product attributes than previously at a similar or even lower price to customers. Kroger's shift from a traditional to a modern, IT-oriented store operation thus increased their responsiveness to customers and did so without imposing higher costs.

Designing Production Systems Responsive to Customers

Because satisfying customers is so important, managers try to design production systems that can produce the outputs that have the attributes customers desire. The attributes of an organization's outputs–their quality, cost, and features–are

Figure 18.3
Kroger's Price/Attribute Relationship in 1991 and 2001

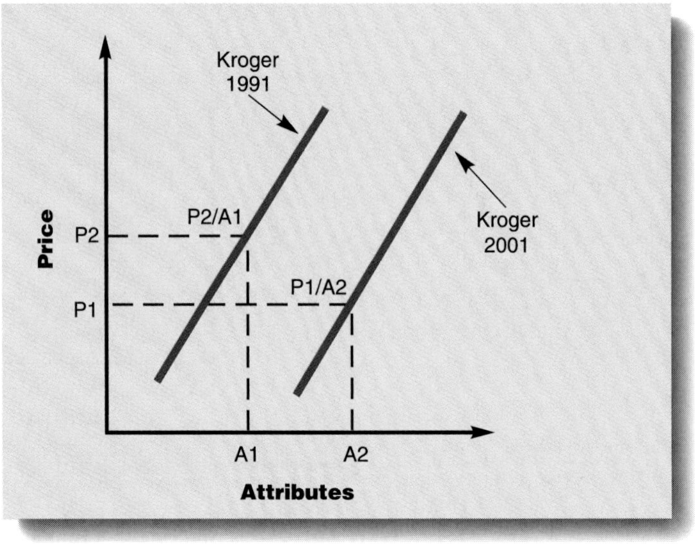

determined by the organization's production system.[6] As discussed earlier, for example, the need to respond to customer demands for competitively priced, quality food stuffs drove Kroger managers to choose a new store operations system. The imperative of satisfying customer needs shaped Kroger's "production" system. When managers focus on being responsive to their customers, and not just on producing or providing a product, they see new ways to reduce costs and increase quality–such as Kroger's introduction of kiosks.

Since the ability of an organization to satisfy the demands of its customers derives from its production system, managers need to devote considerable attention to constantly improving production systems. Managers' desire to attract customers by shifting the price/attribute line to the right explains their adoption of many new operations management techniques in recent years. These include total quality management, flexible manufacturing systems, just-in-time inventory, and, of course, new information systems and technologies discussed in detail later in this chapter.

As an example of the link between responsiveness to customers and an organization's production system, consider the success of Southwest Airlines. One of the most consistently successful airlines in the United States, Southwest Airlines has been expanding rapidly. One reason for Southwest's success is that its managers created a production system uniquely tailored to satisfy the demands of its customers: for low-priced, reliable (on-time), and convenient air travel. Southwest commands high customer loyalty precisely because its production system delivers products, such as flights from Houston to Dallas that have all the desired attributes: reliability, convenience, and low price.

Southwest's low-cost production system focuses not only on improving the maintenance of aircraft but also on the company's ticket reservation system, route structure, flight frequency, baggage-handling system, and in-flight services. Each of these elements of Southwest's production system is geared toward satisfying customer demands for low-priced, reliable, and convenient air travel. For example, Southwest offers a no-frills approach to in-flight customer service. No meals are served on board, and there are no first-class seats.

Southwest does not subscribe to the big reservation computers used by travel agents because the booking fees are too costly. Also, the airline flies only one aircraft, the fuel-efficient Boeing 737, which keeps training and maintenance costs down. All this translates into low prices for customers.

Southwest's reliability derives from the fact that it has the quickest aircraft turnaround time in the industry. A Southwest ground crew needs only 15 minutes to turn around an incoming aircraft and prepare it for departure. This speedy operation helps to keep flights on time. Southwest has such quick turnaround because it has a flexible workforce that has been cross-trained to perform multiple tasks. Thus, the person who checks tickets might also help with baggage loading if time is short.

Southwest's convenience comes from its scheduling multiple flights every day between its popular locations, such as Dallas and Houston, and its use of airports that are close to downtown (Hobby at Houston and Love Field at Dallas) instead of more distant major airports.[7]

Although managers must seek to improve their responsiveness to customers by improving their organizations' production systems, they should not offer a level of responsiveness to customers that is more than that production system can profitably sustain. The company that customizes every product to the unique demands of individual customers is likely to see its cost structure become so high that unit costs exceed unit revenues. This of course is what happened to Webvan and other on-line grocers. It also happened to Toyota in the 1990s when Toyota managers' drive to provide customers with many choices of car models and specifications increased costs faster than it generated additional revenues. At one point, literally thousands of variations of Toyota's basic models, such as the Camry and Corolla, were being produced by Toyota factories. Managers at Toyota concluded that the costs of extreme customization were exceeding the benefits and cut back on the number of models and specifications of its cars.[8]

Improving Quality

As noted earlier, high-quality products are reliable, dependable, and satisfying; they do the job they were designed for and meet customer requirements.[9] Quality is a concept that can be applied to the products of both manufacturing and service organizations–goods such as a Toyota car or a Kroger steak or services such as Southwest Airlines flight service or customer service in a Citibank branch. Why do managers seek to control and improve the quality of their organization's products?[10] There are two reasons (see Figure 18.4).

First, customers usually prefer a higher-quality product to a lower-quality product. So an organization able to provide, *for the same price,* a product of higher quality than a competitor's product is serving its customers better–it is being more responsive to its customers. Often, providing high-quality products creates a brand-name reputation for an organization's products. In turn, this enhanced reputation may allow the organization to charge more for its products than its competitors are able to charge and thus make even greater profits. In 2000, Lexus was number one on the J. D. Power list of the 10 most reliable car manufacturers. Toyota was number four and the top nonluxury car maker.[11] The high quality of Toyota/Lexus vehicles has enabled the company to charge higher prices for its cars than the prices charged by rival automakers.

Figure 18.4
The Impact of Increased Quality on Organizational Performance

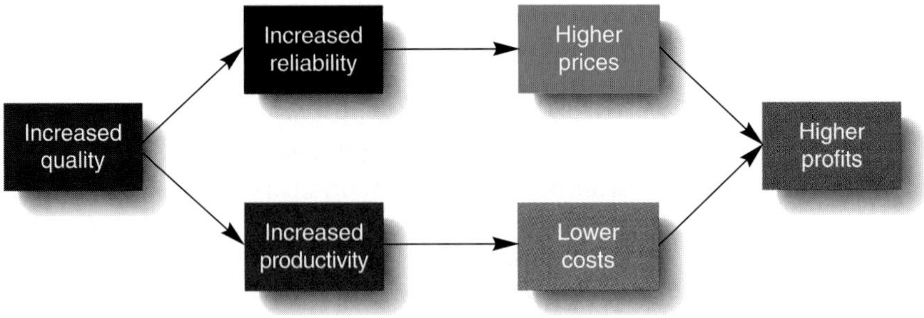

The second reason for trying to boost product quality is that higher product quality can increase efficiency and thereby lower operating costs and boost profits. Achieving high product quality lowers operating costs because of the effect of quality on employee productivity: Higher product quality means less employee time is wasted in making defective products that must be discarded or in providing substandard services, and less time has to be spent fixing mistakes. This translates into higher employee productivity, which means lower costs.

Total Quality Management

total quality management A management technique that focuses on improving the quality of an organization's products and services.

At the forefront of the drive to improve product quality is a technique known as total quality management.[12] **Total quality management (TQM)** focuses on improving the quality of an organization's products and services and stresses that all of an organization's functional activities should be directed toward this goal. Conceived as an organizationwide management program, TQM requires the cooperation of managers in every function of an organization if it is to succeed. The TQM concept was developed by a number of American consultants, including the late W. Edwards Deming, Joseph Juran, and A. V. Feigenbaum.[13]

What actions should managers take to implement a successful TQM program? The following 10 steps are necessary to make a TQM control system work.

1. *Build organizational commitment to quality.* TQM will do little to improve the performance of an organization unless all employees embrace it, and this often requires a change in an organization's culture.[14] At Citibank, discussed in detail in the "Management Insight," the process of changing culture began at the top. First, a group of top managers, including the CEO, received training in TQM from consultants from Motorola. Each member of the top-management group was then given the responsibility to train a group at the next level in the hierarchy, and so on down throughout the organization until all 100,000 employees had received basic TQM training.

2. *Focus on the customer.* TQM practitioners see a focus on the customer as the starting point.[15] According to TQM philosophy, the customer, not managers in quality control or engineering, defines what quality is. The challenge is fourfold: (1) to identify what customers want from the good or service that the company provides; (2) to identify what the company actually provides to customers; (3) to identify the gap that exists between what customers want and what they actually get (the quality gap); and (4) to formulate a plan for closing the quality gap. The efforts of Citibank managers to increase responsiveness to customers illustrates this aspect of TQM well.

Management Insight

Citibank Uses TQM to Increase Customer Loyalty

Citibank is one of the leading global financial institutions and has established a goal of becoming the premier institution in the 21st century. To achieve this lofty goal Citibank has started to use TQM to increase its responsiveness to customers recognizing that, ultimately, its customer base and customer loyalty determine the bank's future success.

As the first step in its TQM effort, Citibank identified the factors that dissatisfy its customers. When analyzing the complaints it found that most concerned the time it took to complete a customer's request, such as responding to an account problem or getting a loan. So Citibank's managers began to examine how they handled each kind of customer request. For each distinct request, they formed a cross-functional team that broke down a specific request into the steps between people and departments that were needed to complete the request. In analyzing them, teams found that oftentimes many steps in the process were unnecessary and could be replaced by using the right information systems. They also found that very often delays occurred because employees simply did not know how to handle a request. They were not being given the right kind of training and when they couldn't handle a request they simply put it aside until a supervisor could deal with it.

Pictured is a Citibank interactive center where customers can conduct their banking and through which they can talk to Citibank customer representatives who can help address any queries or solve any problems that might arise.

Citibank's second step to increase its responsiveness was to implement an organizationwide TQM program. Managers and supervisors were charged with reducing the complexity of the work process and finding the most effective way to process each particular request, such as a request for a loan. Managers were also charged with training employees to answer each specific request. The results were remarkable. For example, in the loan department the TQM program reduced the number of handoffs necessary to process a request by 75 percent: The department's average response time dropped from several hours to 30 minutes. By 2000, more than 92,000 employees worldwide had been trained in the new TQM processes and Citibank could easily measure TQM's effectiveness by the increased speed with which it was handling an increased volume of customer requests.

3. *Find ways to measure quality.* Another crucial element of any TQM program is the creation of a measuring system that managers can consistently use to evaluate quality. Devising appropriate measures is relatively easy in manufacturing companies where quality can be measured by criteria such as defects per million parts. It is more difficult in service companies where outputs are less tangible. However, with a little creativity, suitable quality measures can be devised as they were by managers at Citibank. Similarly, at L. L. Bean, the mail-order retailer, managers use the percentage of orders that are correctly filled as one of their quality measures. The common theme running through these examples is that managers must identify what quality means from a customer's perspective and devise some measure that captures this.

4. *Set goals and create incentives.* Once a measure has been devised, managers' next step is to set a challenging quality goal and to create incentives for reaching that goal. At Citibank, the CEO set an initial goal of reducing customer complaints by 50 percent. One way of creating incentives to attain a goal is to link rewards, such as bonus pay and promotional opportunities, to the goal.

5. *Solicit input from employees.* Employees can be a major source of information about the causes of poor quality. Therefore, it is important for managers to establish a framework for soliciting employee suggestions about improvements that can be made. Quality circles–groups of employees who meet regularly to discuss ways to increase quality–are often created to achieve this goal. Companies also create self-managed teams to further quality improvement efforts. Whatever the means chosen to solicit input from lower-level employees, managers must be open to receiving, and acting on, bad news and criticism from employees.

quality circles Groups of employees who meet regularly to discuss ways to increase quality.

6. *Identify defects and trace them to their source.* A major source of product defects is the production system. TQM preaches the need for managers to identify defects in the work process, trace those defects back to their source, find out why they occurred, and make corrections so that they do not occur again. To identify defects, Deming advocated the use of statistical procedures to spot variations in the quality of goods or services; however, IT makes the measurement of quality much easier.

7. *Introduce just-in-time inventory systems.* Inventory is the stock of raw materials, inputs, and component parts that an organization has on hand at a particular time. Just-in-time (JIT) inventory systems play a major role in the process of identifying and finding the source of defects in inputs. When an organization has a just-in-time inventory system, parts or supplies arrive at the organization when they are needed, not before. With a just-in-time inventory system component parts travel from suppliers to the assembly line in a small wheeled container known as a kanban. Assembly-line workers empty the kanbans and then the empty container is sent back to the supplier as the signal to produce another small batch of component parts, and so the process repeats itself. This system can be contrasted with a just-in-case view of inventory, which leads an organization to stockpile excess inputs in a warehouse just in case it needs them to meet sudden upturns in demand.

inventory The stock of raw materials, inputs, and component parts that an organization has on hand at a particular time.

just-in-time inventory system A system in which parts or supplies arrive at an organization when they are needed, not before.

Also, under a JIT inventory system, defective parts enter an organization's production system immediately; they are not warehoused for months before use. This means that defective inputs can be quickly spotted. Managers can then trace the problem to the supply source and fix it before more defective parts are produced.

8. *Work closely with suppliers.* A major cause of poor-quality finished goods is poor-quality component parts. To decrease product defects, managers must work closely with suppliers to improve the quality of the parts they supply. Managers at Xerox worked closely with suppliers to get them to adopt TQM programs, and the result was a huge reduction in the defect rate of component parts. Managers also need to work closely with suppliers to get them to adopt a JIT inventory system, also required for high quality.

To implement JIT systems with suppliers, and to get suppliers to set up their own TQM programs, two steps are necessary. First, managers must reduce the number of suppliers with which their organizations do business. Second, managers need to develop cooperative long-term relationships with remaining suppliers. Over the years, managers at Dell Computer have reduced the number of suppliers they need to a minimum which greatly streamlines their interactions with suppliers and leads to increased quality and lower-cost inputs.

9. *Design for ease of manufacture.* The more steps required to assemble a product, the more opportunities there are for making a mistake. It follows that designing products that have fewer parts and thus making their assembly easier should be linked to fewer defects. For example, Dell continually redesigns the way it assembles its computers to reduce the number of assembly steps required and to search for new ways to reduce the number of components that have to be linked together. The consequence of these redesign efforts has been a fall in assembly costs and marked improvement in product quality that led to it becoming the number one global PC maker.

10. *Break down barriers between functions.* Successful implementation of TQM requires substantial cooperation between the different functions of an organization. R&D managers have to cooperate with manufacturing managers to design products that are easy to manufacture; marketing managers have to cooperate with manufacturing and R&D managers so that customer problems identified by marketing can be acted on; human resource managers have to cooperate with all of the other functions of the company to devise suitable quality training programs, and so on.

In essence, to increase quality, managers need to develop strategic plans that state goals exactly and spell out how they will be achieved. Managers should embrace the philosophy that mistakes, defects, and poor-quality materials are not acceptable and should be eliminated. First-line managers should spend more time working with employees and providing them with the tools they need to do the job. Managers should create an environment in which employees will not be afraid to report problems or recommend improvements. Output goals and targets need to include not only numbers or quotas but also some notion of quality to promote the production of defect-free output. Managers also need to train employees in new skills to keep pace with changes in the workplace. Finally, achieving better quality requires managers to develop organizational values and norms centered on improving quality.

Improving Efficiency

The third goal of operations management is to increase the efficiency of an organization's production system. The fewer the inputs required to produce a given output, the higher will be the efficiency of the production system. Managers can measure efficiency at the organization level in two ways. The measure known as total factor productivity looks at how well an organization utilizes all of its resources–such as labor, capital, materials, or energy–to produce its outputs. It is expressed in the following equation:

$$\text{Total factor productivity} = \frac{\text{outputs}}{\text{all inputs}}$$

The problem with total factor productivity is that each input is typically measured in different units: Labor's contribution to producing an output is measured by hours worked; the contribution of materials is measured by the amount consumed (for example, tons of iron ore required to make a ton of steel); the contribution of energy is measured by the units of energy consumed (for example, kilowatt-hours), and so on. To compute total factor productivity, managers must convert all the inputs to a common unit, such as dollars, before they can work the equation.

Though sometimes a useful measure of efficiency overall, total factor productivity obscures the exact contribution of an individual input–such as labor–to the production of a given output. Consequently, most organizations focus on specific measures of efficiency, known as partial productivity, that measure the efficiency of an individual unit. For example, the efficiency of labor inputs is expressed as

$$\text{Labor productivity} = \frac{\text{outputs}}{\text{direct labor}}$$

Labor productivity is most commonly used to draw efficiency comparisons between different organizations. For example, one study found that in 1994 it took the average Japanese automobile components supplier half as many labor hours to produce a part, such as a car seat or exhaust system, as the average British company.[16] Thus, the study concluded, Japanese companies use labor more efficiently than British companies.

The management of efficiency is an extremely important issue in most organizations, because increased efficiency lowers production costs, thereby allowing the organization to make a greater profit or to attract more customers by lowering its price. For example, in 1990 the price of the average personal computer sold in the United States was $3,000, by 1995 the price was around $1,800, in 2001 it was $750. This decrease occurred despite the fact that the power and capabilities of the average personal computer increased dramatically during this time period (microprocessors became more powerful, memory increased, modems were built in, and multimedia capability was added).

Why was the decrease in price possible? As discussed above, manufacturers of personal computers such as Compaq and Dell focused on quality and used TQM to boost their efficiency by improving the quality of their components and making PCs easier to assemble. This allowed them to lower their costs and prices and still make a profit.[17] While TQM is an important step in the drive to raise efficiency, several other factors are also important as discussed below.

Facilities Layout, Flexible Manufacturing, and Efficiency

Another factor that influences efficiency is the way managers decide to lay out or design an organization's physical work facilities. This is important for two reasons. First, the way in which machines and workers are organized or grouped together into workstations affects the efficiency of the production system. Second, a major determinant of efficiency is the cost associated with setting up the equipment needed to make a particular product. **Facilities layout** is the operations management technique whose goal is to design the machine-worker interface to increase production system efficiency. **Flexible manufacturing** is the set of operations management techniques that attempt to reduce the setup costs associated with a production system.

facilities layout The operations management technique whose goal is to design the machine-worker interface to increase production system efficiency.

flexible manufacturing Operations management techniques that attempt to reduce the setup costs associated with a production system.

FACILITIES LAYOUT The way in which machines, robots, and people are grouped together affects how productive they can be. Figure 18.5 shows three basic ways of arranging workstations: product layout, process layout, and fixed-position layout.

Figure 18.5
Three Facilities Layouts

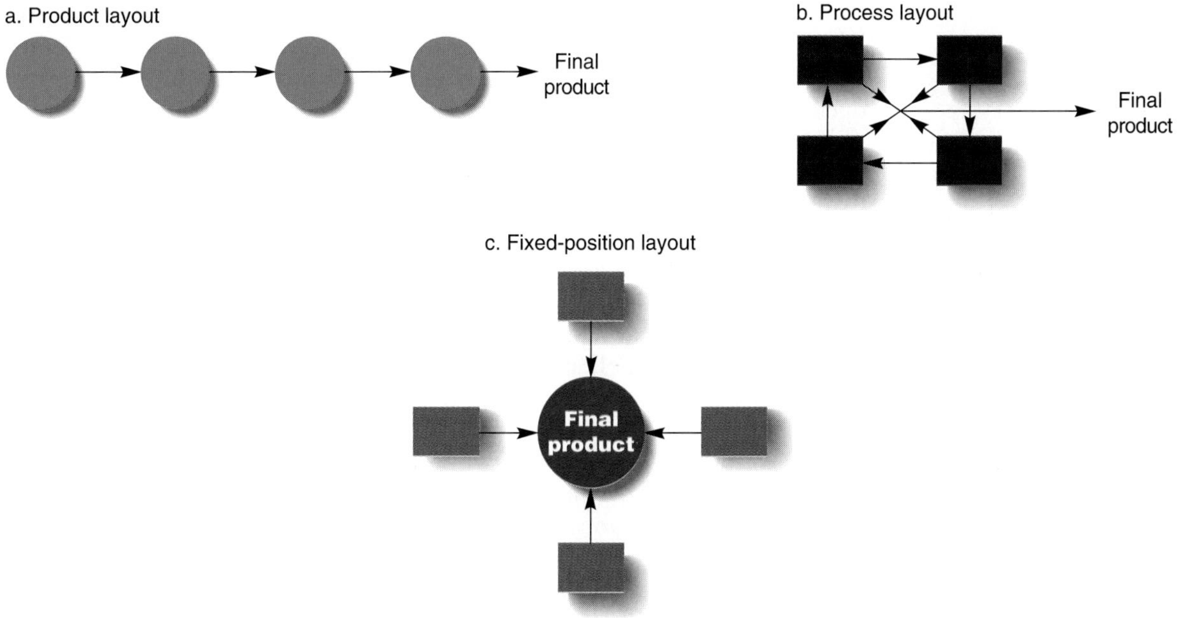

In a *product layout,* machines are organized so that each operation needed to manufacture a product is performed at workstations arranged in a fixed sequence. Typically, workers are stationary in this arrangement, and a moving conveyor belt takes the product being worked on to the next workstation so that it is progressively assembled. Mass production is the familiar name for this layout; car assembly lines are probably the best-known example. It used to be that product layout was efficient only when products were created in large quantities; however, the introduction of modular assembly lines controlled by computers is making it efficient to make products in small batches.

In a *process layout,* workstations are not organized in a fixed sequence. Rather, each workstation is relatively self-contained, and a product goes to whichever workstation is needed to perform the next operation to complete the product. Process layout is often suited to manufacturing settings that produce a variety of custom-made products, each tailored to the needs of a different kind of customer. For example, a custom furniture manufacturer might use a process layout so that different teams of workers can produce different styles of chairs or tables made from different kinds of woods and finishes. A process layout provides the flexibility needed to change the product. Such flexibility, however, often reduces efficiency because it is expensive.

In a *fixed-position layout,* the product stays in a fixed position. Its component parts are produced in remote workstations and brought to the production area for final assembly. Increasingly, self-managed teams are using fixed-position layouts. Different teams assemble each component part and then send these parts to the final assembly team, which makes the final product. A fixed-position layout is commonly used for products such as jet airlines, mainframe computers, and gas turbines–products that are complex and difficult to assemble or so large that moving them from one workstation to another would be difficult. The effects of moving from one facilities layout to another can be dramatic as the following "Managing Globally" suggests.

Managing Globally

How to Improve Facilities Layout

Paddy Hopkirk established his car accessories business in Bedfordshire, England, shortly after he had shot to motor car racing fame by winning the Monte Carlo Rally. Sales of Hopkirk's accessories, such as bicycle racks and axle stands, were always brisk, but Hopkirk was the first to admit that his production system left a lot to be desired so he invited consultants to help reorganize his production system.

After analyzing his factory's production system, the consultants realized that the source of the problem was the facilities layout Hopkirk had established. Over time, as sales grow, Hopkirk simply added new workstations to the production system as they were needed. The result was a process layout in which the product being assembled moved in the irregular sequences shown in the "Before Change" half of Figure 18.6. The consultants suggested that to save time and effort, the workstations should be reorganized into the sequential product layout shown in the "After Change" illustration.

Once this change was made, the results were dramatic. One morning the factory was an untidy sprawl of workstations surrounded by piles of crates holding semifinished components. Two days later, when the 170-person workforce came back to work, the machines had been brought together into tightly grouped workstations arranged in the fixed sequence shown in the illustration. The piles of components had disappeared, and the newly cleared floor space was neatly marked with color-coded lines mapping out the new flow of materials between workstations.

Figure 18.6
Changing a Facilities Layout

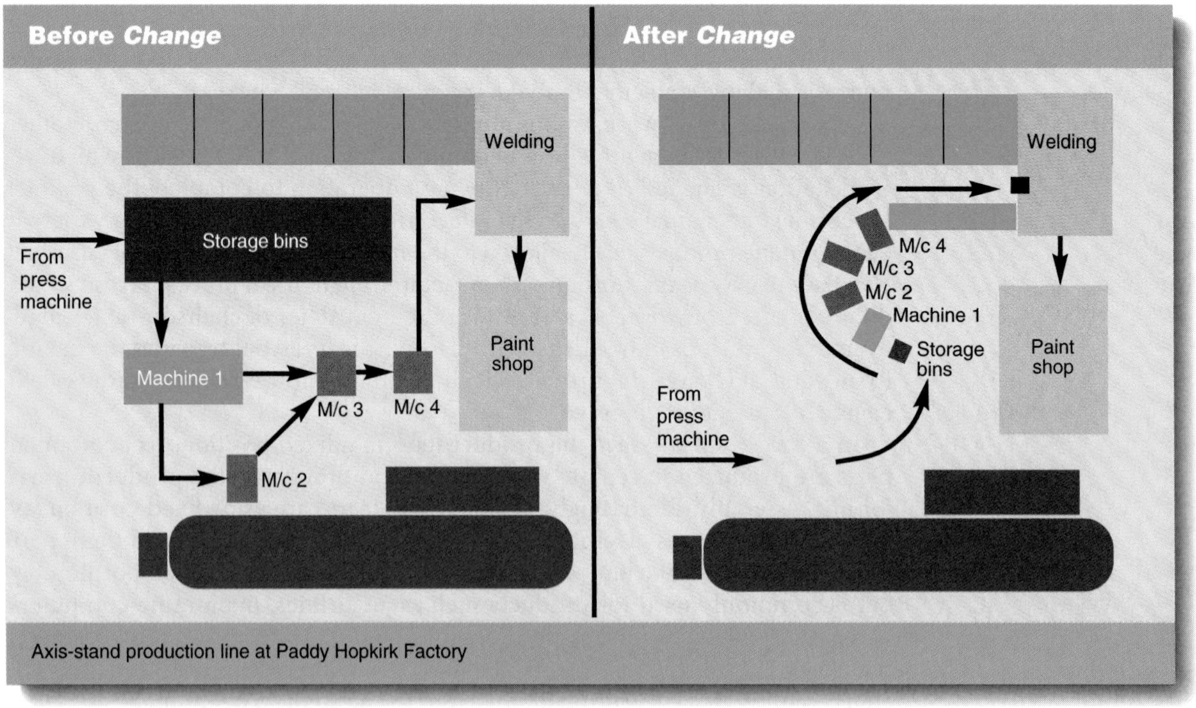

Axis-stand production line at Paddy Hopkirk Factory

Source: Reprinted from *Financial Times* of January 4, 1994 by permission of Financial Times Syndication, London.

In the first full day of production, efficiency increased by as much as 30 percent. The space needed for some operations had been cut in half, and work-in-progress had been cut considerably. Moreover, the improved layout allowed for some jobs to be combined, freeing operators for deployment elsewhere in the factory. An amazed Hopkirk exclaimed, "I was expecting a change but nothing as dramatic as this . . . it is fantastic."[18]

FLEXIBLE MANUFACTURING In a manufacturing company, a major source of costs is the costs associated with setting up the equipment needed to make a particular product. One of these costs is the cost of production that is forgone because nothing is produced while the equipment is being set up. For example, components manufacturers often need as much as half a day to set up automated production equipment when switching from production of one component part (such as a washer ring for the steering column of a car) to another (such as a washer ring for the steering column of a truck). During this half-day, a manufacturing plant is not producing anything but employees are paid for this "nonproductive" time.

It follows that if setup times for complex production equipment can be reduced, so can setup costs, and efficiency will rise. In other words, if setup times can be reduced, the time that plant and employees spend in actually producing something will increase. This simple insight has been the driving force behind the development of flexible manufacturing techniques.

Flexible manufacturing aims to reduce the time required to set up production equipment.[19] By redesigning the manufacturing process so that production equipment geared for manufacturing one product can be quickly replaced with equipment geared to make another product, setup times, and costs can be reduced dramatically. Another favorable outcome from flexible manufacturing is that a company is able to produce many more varieties of a product than before in the same amount of time. Thus flexible manufacturing increases a company's ability to be responsive to its customers.

Increasingly, organizations are experimenting with new designs for production systems that not only allow workers to be more productive but also make the work process more flexible, thus reducing setup costs. Some Japanese companies are experimenting with facilities layouts arranged as a spiral, as the letter Y, and as the number 6, to see how these various configurations affect setup costs and worker productivity. At a camcorder plant in Kohda, Japan, for example, Sony changed from a fixed-position layout in which 50 workers sequentially built a camcorder to a flexible spiral process design in which 4 workers perform all the operations necessary to produce the camcorder. This new layout allows the most efficient workers to work at the highest pace, and it reduces setup costs because workers can easily switch from one model to another, increasing efficiency by 10 percent.[20] An interesting example of a company that built a new factory to obtain the benefits from flexible manufacturing is profiled in the following "Managing Globally."

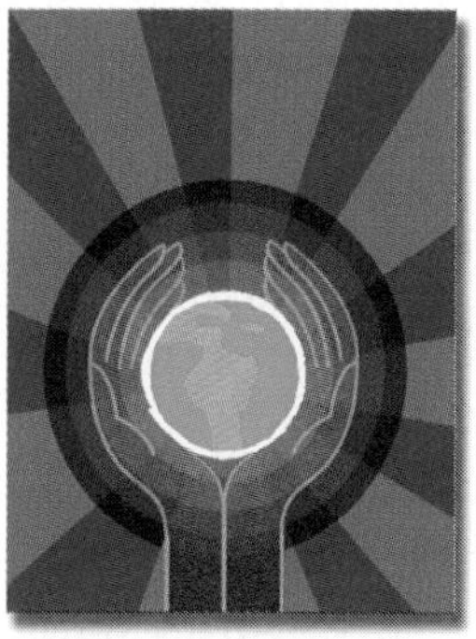

Managing Globally

Igus's Factory of the Future

Igus Inc., headquartered in Cologne, Germany, makes over 28,000 polymer bearings and energy supply cable products used in applications the world over. In the 1990s, the company's managers realized they needed to build a new factory that could handle the company's rapidly growing product line.

Assisted by Web-based on-line work instructions, an operator at Dell Computer determines the sequence in which Dell's customer-built computers are to be assembled by its computer-controlled flexible manufacturing system. This flexible system makes possible Dell's low-cost strategy.

Their product line was changing constantly as new products were innovated and old ones became obsolete. At Ingus new products are often introduced on a daily basis so this need for flexibility is the company's prime requirement. Moreover, because many of its products are highly customized, the specific and changing needs of its customers drive new product development.

Ingus's new factory was designed with the need for flexibility in mind. As big as three football fields, nothing in the factory is tied down or bolted to the floor. All the machines, computers, and equipment can be moved and repositioned to suit changing product requirements. Moreover, all its employees are trained to be flexible and can perform many of the production tasks necessary. For example, when one new product line proved popular with customers, its employees and production operations were relocated four times as it grew into larger spaces. Ingus can change its production system at a moment's notice and with minimal disruption, and since the company operates seven days a week, 24 hours a day these changes are occurring constantly.

To facilitate these changes, workers are equipped with power scooters to move around the plant quickly and reconfigure operations. This also allows them to move quickly to wherever in the factory their skills are most needed. Employees are also equipped with mobile phones so they are always on call.

Ingus's decision to create a flexible factory of the future has paid off. In the last five years its sales have increased from $10 to $100 million and its global staff has tripled.

Just-in-Time Inventory and Efficiency

Although JIT systems, such as Toyota's kanban system, were originally developed as part of the effort to improve product quality, they have major implications for efficiency. Major cost savings can result from increasing inventory turnover and reducing inventory holding costs, such as warehousing and stor-

crummy. Sure, there are no hot meals or fancy airport clubs. But Southwest's customer-service ethos is legendary. It's not unheard of for a gate agent to put a stranded passenger up for the night.

- **Keep employees happy.** They keep customers happy. Parties celebrating almost anything are epidemic. Employee photos cover the walls at Dallas headquarters, leaving no doubt who's most important here.

The pep-rally culture has its purpose: Southwest employees are more productive than most others in the industry, for similar pay, so maintaining morale is critical.

- **Keep it simple.** While Southwest has tweaked its formula over the years—adding more long-distance flights, for instance—it's still mainly a point-to-point, short-hop airline that uses one aircraft type to simplify training and maintenance.

For all his success, Kelleher faces one last challenge: managing the transition to his successors. Some management experts think it's a bad idea for a former CEO to remain as chairman of the board and the executive committee. A continued presence can undermine the new team or make things more difficult if change is needed. "There's a real question about who's in charge, and no company should have that doubt," warns Roger M. Kenny, managing partner of Boardroom Consultants. Which brings us to the last lesson. . .

- **Screw conventional wisdom.** That attitude has worked for Kelleher plenty of times before. He's counting on it one last time as he circles for retirement.

Source: W. Zellner, "Southwest: After Kelleher, More Blue Skies" *Business Week,* April 2, 2001, p. 45.

Questions

1. How did Herb Kelleher use operations management to reduce costs and build Southwest's competitive advantage?
2. How did Herb Kelleher use operations management to increase quality and responsiveness to customers and build Southwest's competitive advantage?

Chapter 19

The Management of Innovation, Product Development, and Entrepreneurship

Learning Objectives

After studying this chapter, you should be able to:

- Explain managers' role in facilitating **product development.**
- Identify the **factors that shorten the product life cycle,** and explain why reducing product development time increases the level of industry competition.
- Identify the **goals of product development,** and explain the relationships among them.
- Explain the **principles of product development,** and describe the way in which managers can encourage and promote innovation.
- Describe how managers can encourage and promote entrepreneurship to help create a **learning organization.**

A Manager's Challenge

Entrepreneurship and Innovation at Maden Technologies

How does an entrepreneur build an innovative business?

In 1962, fifteen-year old Omar Maden fled Cuba alone and penniless and was resettled with foster parents in Portland, Oregon. Five years later he was drafted into the U.S. Army during the Vietnam War and the former Afro-Cuban Maden found himself working on command and control communications technology for artillery and missiles. At the end of the war, Maden's superior officers encouraged him to remain in the Army because of his considerable technical skills. Maden became an Army information technology expert, and rose up the ranks to become a major. He was transferred to the Pentagon where he was responsible for implementing some key logistics communications technologies.[1]

After retiring from the Army in the mid-1980s, Maden decided he could use his IT-skills to become an independent consultant. Using a home equity loan and his personal savings he started Maden Technologies. Soon his previous employer, the Army, began to call on his services. Maden's big break came when he was hired to oversee deployment of the Army's logistics center for the Desert Storm campaign during the war with Iraq. He and his team of highly trained IT analysts fashioned a field communications system that offered Desert Storm's commanders instantaneous performance feedback which put them in total control of all mobile military resources. Maden's systems excelled and his success in managing this venture led to more contracts. Within 10 years Maden Technologies had become one of the Pentagon's largest research and development contractors.

Omar Maden has successfully guided his company through the transition from fulfilling government contracts to selling its high-tech expertise to the private sector.

Since 1995, Maden has organized his IT analysts into teams to develop the different communications products that the Army needed. For example, one team converted the military's internal email system into a battlefield tool that allows everyone to communicate with everyone else. Another team has developed a smart card that will have embedded in it a soldier's complete personal, medical, and military record. These cards are to be issued to 4 million Army personnel in 2002.

Realizing that his company's technological innovations and skills could be used more widely, Maden has been trying to reposition his company as a technology service provider to industry since the early 2000s. His employees have been pushing him to do this because they have received large stock options for their major contributions and are anxious to see their company succeed at a national level. Moreover, using his military experience, Maden has been careful to assign authority for each project to the members of the team responsible for developing each product to encourage innovation and entrepreneurial behavior. Team members are given wide authority to make decisions, and each team works closely with its customers—Army officers—so that they can be sure they are designing a product that matches the Army's current and future needs.[2] To further these ambitious goals Maden has moved to buy and take over many small companies that have technological skills complementary to his company. For example, he bought Reply Networks which facilitates delivery of bulk email. He also bought Enlighten for its cross-platform software for managing corporate networks. This means that one team of a company's managers can work across the Windows, Sun, or LINUX operating systems simultaneously—an enterprise management solution not previously possible. This software would revolutionize the way company networks are managed and is a potential blockbuster business.[3]

Clearly, entrepreneurship and innovation go hand-in-hand at Maden Technologies. Maden has taken advantage of the company's IT skills and used them to develop creative solutions for the Army's communications problems, and now for industry as a whole. Where Maden Technologies will be in 10 years time is an interesting question. Maden and his teams are confident they will soon be able to offer enterprise management solutions that are on a par with those offered by IBM, Computer Associates, and other software giants for a fraction of the cost. When this occurs Maden Technologies will join the ranks of the Fortune 100 and Maden will have achieved the American Dream.

Overview

Madden Technologies prospers because of the entrepreneurial genius of its founder and his ability to manage the product development process in ways that encourage his employees to be innovative. Managing innovation is an increasingly important aspect of a manager's job in an era of dramatic changes in advanced information technology. Promoting successful new product development is difficult and challenging and some product development efforts are much more successful than others. Madden Technology is performing at a high level while companies like Compaq and Lucent Technologies are struggling.

In Chapter 18 we examined the actions managers can take at the operational level to improve quality, efficiency, and responsiveness to customers. There we discussed one aspect of innovation–developing new and better ways to make goods and services by means of operations management techniques such as total quality management, just-in-time inventory systems, and process reengineering. In this chapter we examine the actions managers can take to improve the ability of their organizations to be innovative by developing new goods and services, another building block of competitive advantage. We discuss the relationship between technological change, product innovation, and competition.

We examine the goals of product development efforts. We explain several principles for structuring an organization's product development effort to attain these goals, and we examine the nature of entrepreneurship and discuss steps managers can take to promote entrepreneurship inside organizations. By the end of this chapter, you will understand why, in today's rapidly changing environment, managers' ability to effectively manage innovation, product development, and entrepreneurship is often the key to an organization's success and even survival.

Innovation, Technological Change, and Competition

As discussed in Chapter 5, *technology* is the skills, know-how, experience, body of scientific knowledge, tools, machines, computers, and equipment used in the design, production, and distribution of goods and services. Technology is involved in all organizational activities, and its rapid change makes technological change a significant factor in almost every organizational innovation.[4]

The two main types of technological change are quantum and incremental. **Quantum technological change** is a fundamental shift in technology that results in the innovation of new kinds of goods and services. Two examples are the development of the Internet, which has revolutionized the computer industry, and the development of genetic engineering (biotechnology), which is promising to revolutionize the treatment of illness with the development of genetically engineered medicines. McDonald's development of the principles behind the provision of fast food also qualifies as a quantum technological change.

quantum technological change A fundamental shift in technology that results in the innovation of new kinds of goods and services.

incremental technological change Change that refines existing technology and leads to gradual improvements or refinements in products over time.

quantum product innovations Products that result from quantum technological changes.

Incremental technological change is change that refines existing technology and leads to gradual improvements or refinements in products over time. Since 1971, for example, Intel has made a series of incremental improvements to its original 4004 microprocessor, leading to the introduction of its 8088, 8086, 286, 386, 486, its first Pentium chip in 1993, the Pentium 4 in 2000, and its Itanium chip in 2001.

Products that result from quantum technological changes are called **quantum product innovations** and are relatively rare. Managers in most organizations spend most of their time managing products that result from incremental technological changes, called incremental product innovations. For example, every time Dell Computer or Compaq Computer put a new, faster Intel chip into a PC they are making incremental product innovations. Similarly, every time engineers in an automobile company redesign a car model, and every time McDonald's managers try to improve the flavor and texture of burgers and fries, they are engaged in product development efforts designed to lead to incremental product innovations. Just because incremental change is less dramatic than quantum change does not imply that incremental product innovations are unimportant. In fact, as discussed below, it is often managers' ability to successfully manage incremental product development that results in success or failure in an industry.

The Effects of Technological Change

The consequences of quantum and incremental technological change are all around us. Microprocessors, personal computers, wireless phones, pagers, personal digital assistants, word-processing software, computer networks, digital cameras and camcorders, compact discs, VCRs and DVD players, genetically engineered medicines, fast food, on-line information services, superstores, and mass travel either did not exist a generation ago or were considered to be exotic and expensive products. Now these products are commonplace, and they are being improved all the time. Many of the organizations whose managers helped develop and exploit new technologies have reaped enormous gains. They include many of the most successful and rapidly growing organizations of our times, such as Dell Computer and Compaq Computer (personal computers), Microsoft (computer software), Intel (microprocessors), Nokia (microprocessors, wireless phones, and pagers), Sony (camcorders and compact discs), Matsushita (videocassette recorders), Amgen (biotechnology), McDonald's (fast food), Wal-Mart (superstores), and Carnival Cruises (cruise ships).

While some organizations have benefited from technological change, others have seen their markets threatened and their future in doubt. Traditional telephone companies the world over have seen their market dominance threatened by new companies offering Internet, broadband, and wireless telephone technology. For example, AT&T and other long distance companies have been suffering from increased competition because of advances in telecommunications. The decline of once-dominant consumer electronics companies such as RCA can be directly linked to their failure to innovate products such as VCRs and compact disc players.

Technological change offers both an opportunity and a threat.[5] On the one hand, it helps create new product opportunities that managers and their organizations can exploit. On the other hand, new and improved products can harm or even destroy demand for older, established products. Wal-Mart has put thousands of small stores out of business, and McDonald's has caused thousands of small diners to close, in part because both organizations have been so innovative in their production systems that they can give customers lower-priced products. Thousands of small specialized bookstores have closed in the United States in the last five years as a result of advances in IT that made on-line bookselling possible. Similarly, the development of the microprocessor by Intel has helped create a host of new product opportunities for entrepreneurs who have created thousands of companies that provide innovative computer software and hardware. At the same time, these microprocessors have destroyed demand for older products and ruined organizations whose managers who did not see the changes in time and act on them. Managers of typewriter companies, for example, might have noticed that the new technology would compete directly with their products and moved to acquire or merge with new computer companies. Most did not, however, and once-famous companies like Smith Corona are out of business. The nature of entrepreneurship is discussed in detail later in this chapter.

Product Life Cycles and Product Development

When technology is changing, organizational survival requires that managers quickly adopt and apply new technologies to innovate products. Managers who do not do so soon find that they have no market for their products–and destroy their organizations. The rate of technological change in an industry–and particularly the length of the product life cycle–determines how important it is for managers to innovate.

Figure 19.1
A Product Life Cycle

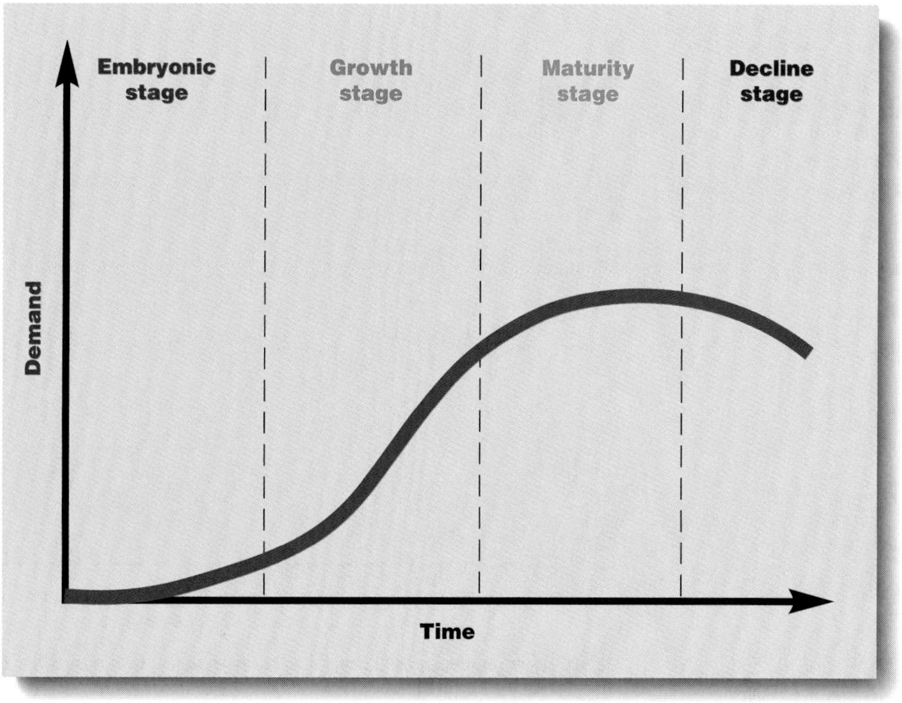

product life cycle
Changes in demand for a product that occur from its introduction through its growth and maturity to its decline.

The product life cycle reflects the changes in demand for a product that occur over time.[6] Demand for most successful products passes through four stages: the embryonic stage, growth, maturity, and decline (see Figure 19.1). In the *embryonic stage* a product has yet to gain widespread acceptance; customers are unsure what the product has to offer, and demand for it is minimal. If a product does become accepted by customers (and many do not), demand takes off, and the product enters its growth stage. In the *growth stage* many consumers are entering the market and buying the product for the first time; demand increases rapidly. This is the stage that personal digital assistants, such as Palm Pilots, are currently in.

The growth stage ends and the *mature stage* begins when market demand peaks because most customers have already bought the product (there are relatively few first-time buyers left). At this stage demand is typically replacement demand. In the car market, for example, most cars are bought by people who already have a car and are either trading up or replacing an old model. Products such as wireless telephones, personal computers for home use, and on-line information services are also currently in this stage. The *decline stage* follows the mature stage if and when demand for a product falls. Falling demand often occurs because a product has become technologically obsolescent and superseded by a more advanced product. For example, demand for every generation of VCR, CD, or DVD falls as they were superseded by newer, technically advanced models with more features.

THE RATE OF TECHNOLOGICAL CHANGE One of the main determinants of the length of a product's life cycle is the rate of technological change.[7] Figure 19.2 illustrates the relationship between the rate of technological change

Figure 19.2
The Relationship Between Technological Change and Length of the Product Life Cycle

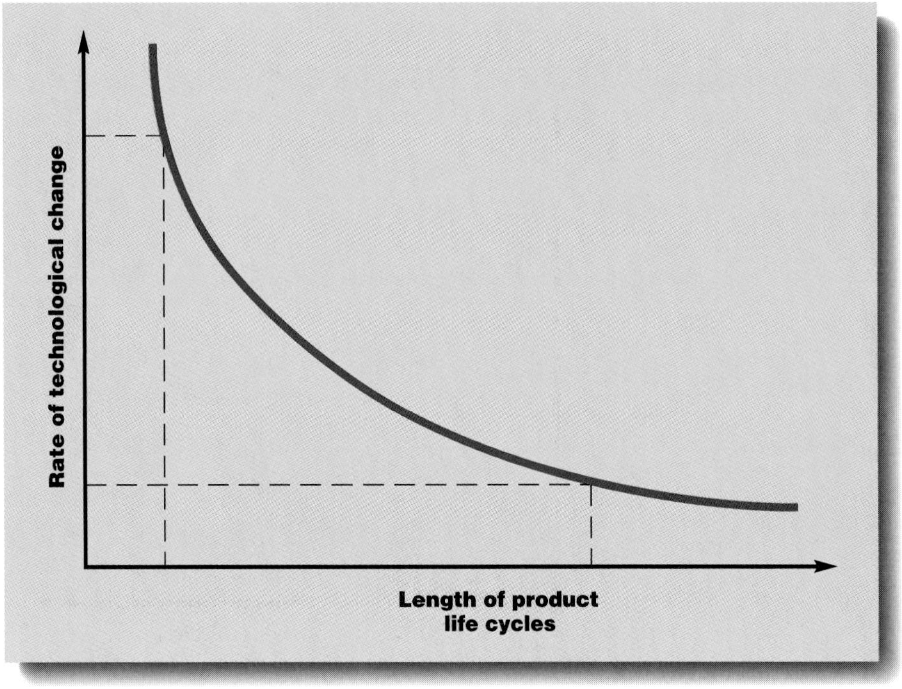

and the length of product life cycles. In some industries–such as personal computers, semiconductors, and disk drives–technological change is rapid and product life cycles are very short. For example, technological change is so rapid in the computer disk drive industry that a disk drive model becomes technologically obsolete about 12 months after introduction. The same is true in the personal computer industry, where product life cycles have shrunk from three years during the late 1980s to a few months today.

In other industries the product life cycle is somewhat longer. In the car industry, for example, the average product life cycle is about five years. The life cycle of a car is so short because fairly rapid technological change is producing a continual stream of incremental innovations in car design, such as the introduction of door airbags, advanced electronic microcontrollers, plastic body parts, and more fuel-efficient engines. In contrast, in many basic industries where the pace of technological change is slower, product life cycles tend to be much longer. In steel or electricity, for example, change in product technology is very limited, and products such as steel girders and electric cable can remain in the mature stage indefinitely.

THE ROLE OF FADS AND FASHIONS Fads and fashion are important determinants of the length of product life cycles.[8] A five-year-old car design is likely to be technologically outmoded and to look out-of-date and thus lose its attractiveness to customers. Similarly, in the restaurant business, the demand for certain kinds of food changes rapidly. The Cajun or Southwest cuisine popular one year may be history the next as Caribbean fare becomes the food of choice. Fashion considerations are even more important in the high-fashion end of the clothing industry, where last season's clothing line is usually out-of-date by the next season, and product life cycles may last no more than three months. Thus, fads and fashions are another reason why product life cycles may be short.

MANAGERIAL IMPLICATIONS Whether short product life cycles are caused by rapid technological change, changing fads and fashions, or some combination of the two, the message for managers is clear: The shorter the length of your product's life cycle, the more important it is to innovate products quickly and on a continuing basis. In industries where product life cycles are very short, managers must continually develop new products; otherwise, their organizations may go out of business. The personal computer company that cannot develop a new and improved product line every six months will soon find itself in trouble. The fashion house that fails to develop a new line of clothing for every season cannot succeed, nor can the small restaurant, club, or bar that is not alert to current fads and fashions. Car companies have a little more time, but even here it is vital that managers continually develop new and improved models every five years or so.

Increasingly, there is evidence that in a wide range of industries product life cycles are becoming more compressed as managers focus their organizations' resources on innovation to increase responsiveness to customers. To attract new customers, managers are trying to outdo each other by being the first to market with a product that incorporates a new technology or that plays to a new fashion trend.[9] In the automobile industry a typical five-year product life cycle is being reduced to three years as managers are increasingly competing with one another to attract new customers and encourage existing customers to upgrade and buy the newest product.[10] The way in which shrinking product life cycles for microprocessors have affected competition is considered in this "Management Insight."

Management Insight

Intel, AMD, and Shrinking Product Life Cycles

Intel's microprocessors are the brains of 85 percent of the personal computers sold worldwide. Intel's dominance in this business can be traced back to IBM's 1980 decision to use Intel's 8086 microprocessor in its first PC. Since then Intel has produced a series of ever-more-powerful microprocessors, including the 286, the 386, the 486, and the Pentium chips.

In 1965, Gordon Moore, one of Intel's founders, made a famous observation, now called "Moore's Law," in which he predicted that the number of transistors per integrated circuit would double every 18 months. Moore's law still holds true today thanks to the technology of companies like Intel as indicated in Figure 19.3 which shows how the power of Intel's chips has continued to increase.[11]

Intel has not had things all its own way, however. In the 1990s, several companies began making clones of Intel chips that can manipulate computer software in the same way as an Intel chip. Once a clone is introduced, chip prices fall, and so do Intel's profit margins. One of these companies, AMD, has been having increasing success.

In the past, the source of Intel's competitive advantage over companies like AMD was that these companies cannot start to design a clone of Intel's next microprocessor until they actually obtain it. So, for each new microprocessor, Intel normally had months or even years of lead time before AMD could develop a clone. The time it takes AMD to clone an Intel microprocessor has been shrinking, however. It took AMD five years to come up

Figure 19.3
Moore's Law: Intel's Evolving Microprocessors

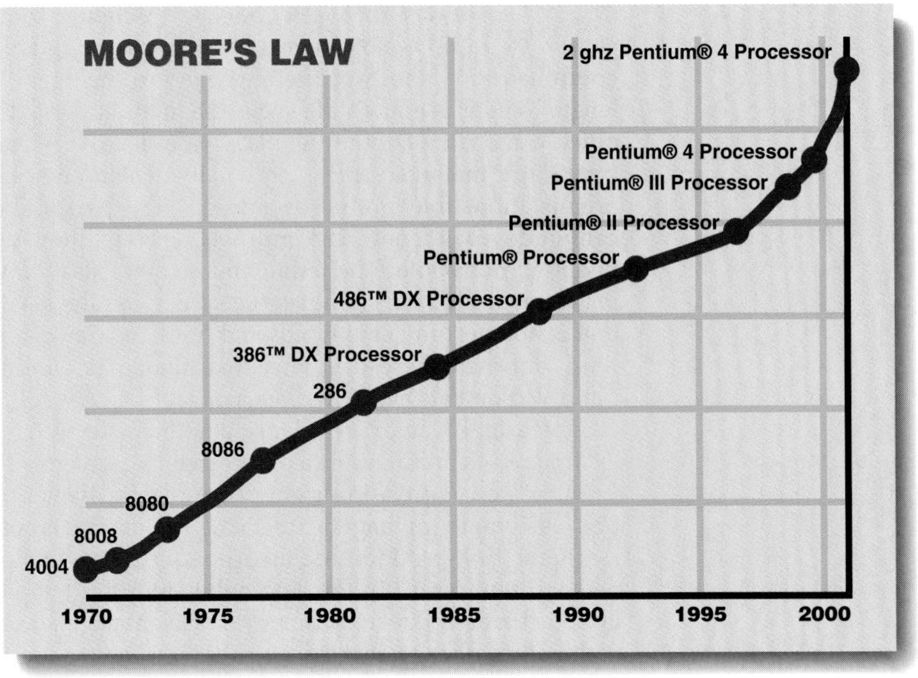

Source: http://intel.com/research/silicon/mooreslaw.htm. Reprinted by permission of Intel Corporation, Copyright Intel Corporation 2002.

with a compatible processor after Intel released its 386 chip in 1985. Matching Intel's next generation, the 486, took three years. Intel began volume production of the Pentium in early 1993. AMD introduced its clone, the P5, just two years later. To stay ahead of the competition, Intel responded by increasing the speed of its own product development process–effectively shrinking the length of its own product life cycles. Intel released its successor to the Pentium, the Pentium Pro, in 1995–twice as fast as it replaced the 486 with the Pentium–to keep the pressure on its rivals.

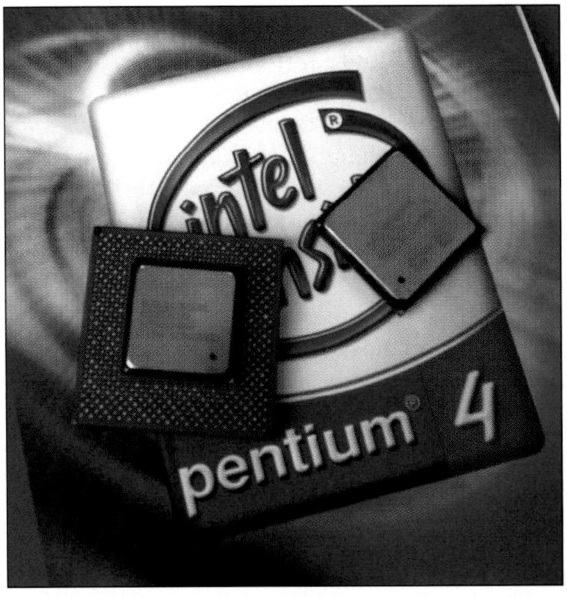

Intel's newest Pentium 2ghz chip. Will its next chip also come to market in 18 months?

The unthinkable happened in 2000 when AMD announced that it was introducing a new chip, the Athlon, that was faster than Intel's then fastest Pentium 4. AMD had the lead for several months. However, in August 2001 Intel announced that it had broken the key two gigahertz milestone, effectively doubling the speed of its computer processors in only 18 months, once again confirming Moore's Law.[12]

The increasingly rapid rate of both innovation and imitation has shrunk the time Intel has the market to itself and can reap its highest profit.[13] In the early 2000s, falling profits because of shrinking life cycles made it evident that Intel no longer had control of the market and Intel's share price began to fall. It remains, however, the dominant company in its industry although AMD claimed to have over 20 percent of the chip market in 2001.[14]

Tips for New Managers

Innovation

1. New product development is about trying to satisfy the future needs of customers with products that incorporate new, untried features.
2. Because the future is so unpredictable managers must try to increase their success rate by following the four principles of product development outlined in this chapter.
3. By encouraging employees to take risks and be innovative, managers develop a structure and culture that supports intrapreneurship.
4. Only those organizations that are successful at new product development survive and prosper.

Product Development

In this section we examine the steps that managers can take to promote innovation and encourage product development. Product development is the process or procedure that managers use to bring new or improved kinds of goods and services to the market. First, we discuss the goals of product development; second, we describe some principles for guiding and speeding the product development process; and third, we discuss some problems associated with managing product development successfully.

Goals of Product Development

When managers and organizations face the choice of innovating products or going out of business, what product development goals should they pursue? Most researchers and consultants recommend that managers aim to reduce development time, maximize a product's fit with customer needs, maximize product quality, and maximize manufacturability–the efficiency and ease of production (see Figure 19.4).[15]

REDUCING DEVELOPMENT TIME Product development time begins with the initial conception of a product and ends with its introduction into the market. Reducing product development time has become a key competitive priority of managers because this offers three important advantages.[16] First, the management team that reduces development time may be the first to market a product that incorporates new, state-of-the-art features.[17] Those managers will be able to charge a high price for the product and earn high profits. Moreover, the earlier managers are able to bring a new product to the market, relative to competitors, the longer is the period in which they will be able to charge high prices and obtain high profits.

This advantage is the reason why Intel's managers make such efforts to reduce the time required to develop a new microprocessor. This is also why disk drive manufacturers like Quantum Corporation put so much emphasis on shortening

Figure 19.4
Four Goals of New Product Development

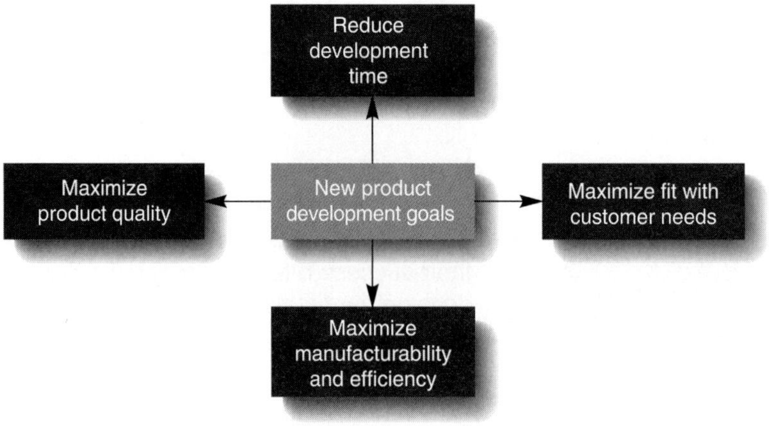

development time. Quantum's managers know that if they can get a new model disk drive to market before competitors such as Seagate Technologies, they can charge a higher price until competitors introduce their new models. In contrast, managers slow to introduce new products will have to charge lower prices to attract customers.

A second advantage of reducing product development time is that managers who can shorten times can upgrade their products relatively quickly and incorporate state-of-the-art technology as soon as it becomes available. Managers with more advanced products are better able to serve customer needs, build brand loyalty, and stay one step ahead of slower competitors.

A third advantage of reducing development time is that managers find it easier to experiment with new products and replace them with a superior product if they fail to meet customer needs. For example, Toyota's first minivan was a disaster. Recognizing this, Toyota's engineers were able to redesign the minivan within 18 months–instead of the three to five years typical at other car companies. The result was the Previa, one of the most successful minivans ever made.

MAXIMIZING THE FIT WITH CUSTOMER NEEDS Many new products fail when they reach the marketplace because they were not designed with customer needs in mind.[18] Surveys of companies have found that the most common reason why new products flop when they get to the marketplace is that managers did not understand or care about the needs of their customers.[19] It follows that maximizing the fit between a product's attributes and customers' needs is one of the main elements of successful product development.

Strange as it may seem, one reason why many managers fail to investigate whether a new technology can actually satisfy a customer need is that managers are dazzled by the technology itself. Take Steve Jobs, one of the two cofounders of Apple Computer. After Jobs left Apple in 1985, he started a company called NeXT to manufacture high-powered personal computers. Captivated by the most advanced technology, Jobs made sure that the NeXT machines incorporated innovative features such as optical disk drives and hi-fidelity sound. However, the NeXT system failed to gain market share because customers simply did not want many of these features. The optical disk drives turned customers off because they made it difficult to switch work from a personal computer using a regular disk drive to a NeXT machine. Moreover, the microprocessor for the NeXT machine could not run Microsoft's popular software. NeXT failed because Jobs was so dazzled by leading-edge technology that he lost sight of customer needs.[20]

In 2000, Jobs announced that Apple was opening Apple Stores nationwide to sell its products directly to customers.[21] In August 2001, Gateway Computer announced it was closing down its computer stores because they were losing money. Has Jobs tapped into a customer need for B&M computer stores? Or will Dell's virtual store continue to be the most effective way to capture customers?

MAXIMIZING PRODUCT QUALITY If managers introduce into the marketplace new products that have not been properly engineered and that suffer from substandard quality, their company's efforts to attract customers are doomed.[22] Poor quality is often the result of managers rushing a product to market in an attempt to reduce development time. Development time is important, but so is product quality. Meeting development time goals with a poor-quality product can be self-defeating.

MAXIMIZING MANUFACTURABILITY AND EFFICIENCY The production process used to manufacture a product can either shorten or lengthen development times and result in either low or high manufacturing costs–affecting efficiency.[23] Consider what happens when product engineers design a product but fail to keep manufacturing requirements in mind. After examining specifications for the product, the manufacturing managers tell the product engineers that the product cannot be manufactured efficiently and cost-effectively because of the way it is designed. The engineers then must redesign the product, thereby lengthening development times.

Poor design may raise manufacturing costs because, for example, the product has numerous components and is costly to assemble. Consultants recommend that ensuring that products can be made as efficiently as possible should be a key goal of managers' product development efforts.[24]

Principles of Product Development

How can managers increase their organizations' ability to innovate new goods and services and so increase competitive advantage? Here, we examine several ways in which managers can organize and control the product development process to reduce development time, maximize the product's fit with customer needs, maximize quality, and maximize both manufacturability and efficiency. Consider the steps that Thermos took to develop a barbecue grill as described in the "Management Insight."

Management Insight

Adventures in Barbecuing

Monte Peterson had no doubt about how to energize Thermos Company's sales of vacuum bottles and barbecue grills: Promote new product development and create new and improved models. Peterson assembled a cross-functional product development team of six middle managers from marketing, engineering, manufacturing, and finance. He told them to develop a new barbecue grill and to do it in 18 months. To ensure that managers were not spread too thin, he assigned these managers to this product development team only. Peterson also arranged for leadership of the team to rotate. Initially, to focus on what customers wanted, the marketing manager would take the lead; then, when technical developments became the main consideration, leadership would switch to engineering, and so on.

Team members christened the group the "Lifestyle team." To find out what people really wanted in a grill, the marketing manager and nine subordinates spent a month on the road visiting customers. While in the field the Lifestyle team set up focus groups, visited people's homes, and even videotaped barbecues. What team members found surprised them. The stereotype of Dad with apron and chef's hat slaving over a smoky barbecue grill was wrong. More women were barbecuing, and many cooks were tired of messy charcoal. Many homeowners were spending big money building decks, and they did not like rusty grills that spoiled the appearance of their decks. Moreover, environmental and safety issues were also increasing in importance. In California charcoal starter fluid is considered a pollutant and is banned; in New Jersey the use of charcoal and gas grills on the balconies of condos and apartments has been prohibited to avoid fires.

When the marketing group returned to Thermos headquarters and discussed their findings, they decided that Thermos had to produce a new kind of product. What they needed was a barbecue grill that looked like a handsome piece of furniture, required no pollutants such as charcoal starter fluid, and made the food taste good. The grill also had to be safe enough to be used by apartment and condo dwellers–which meant it had to be electric.

Within one year the basic attributes of the product were defined, and leadership of the team moved to engineering. The product engineers had been working on electric grill technology for about six months–ever since marketing had alerted them that an electric grill was a likely possibility. The critical task for engineering was to design a grill that gave food the cookout taste that conventional electric grills could not provide because they do not get hot enough. To raise the cooking temperature, Thermos drew on its vacuum technology to design a domed vacuum top that trapped heat inside the grill. They also built electric heat rods directly into the surface of the grill. These, along with the vacuum top, made the grill hot enough to sear meat and give it brown barbecue lines and a barbecue taste.[25]

The Thermos team with their new outdoor grill. The team concept proved so successful that Thermos now uses teams in all its divisions.

Manufacturing had been active from the early days of the development process, making sure that any proposed design could be produced economically. Because manufacturing was involved from the beginning, the team avoided some costly mistakes. At one critical team meeting the engineers said they wanted tapered legs on the grill. Manufacturing explained that tapered legs would have to be custom-made–and would raise manufacturing costs–and persuaded the team to go with straight legs.

When the product was introduced on schedule it was an immediate success. Indeed, it remains the best selling electric grill in the United States although it is now marketed as the Char-Broil Patio Bistro Grill.[26] In 1998, the Thermos Company sold its grill business to Char-Broil which has now taken up the challenge of developing innovative new grills for the 21st century.

The study of product development successes such as those of Thermos's Lifestyle team suggests four principles that managers can follow to increase the likelihood of success for their product development efforts.[27]

PRINCIPLE 1: ESTABLISH A STAGE-GATE DEVELOPMENT FUNNEL One of the most common mistakes that managers make in product development is trying to fund too many new projects at any one time.[28] The result is to spread limited financial, technical, and human resources too thinly over too many different projects. As a consequence, no single project is given the resources that are required to make it succeed.

stage-gate development funnel A planning model that forces managers to make choices among competing projects so that organizational resources are not spread thinly over too many projects.

Given this potential problem, managers need to develop a structured process for evaluating product development proposals and deciding which to support and which to reject. A common solution is to establish a **stage-gate development funnel,** a planning model that forces managers to make choices among competing projects so that organizational resources are not spread thinly over too many projects.[29] The funnel gives managers control over product development and allows them to intervene and take corrective action quickly and appropriately (see Figure 19.5).

At Stage 1, the development funnel has a wide mouth, so top managers initially can encourage employees to come up with as many new product ideas as possible. Managers can create incentives for employees to come up with ideas. Many organizations run "bright idea programs" that reward employees whose ideas eventually make it through the development process. Other organizations allow research scientists to devote a certain amount of work time to their own projects. Top managers at Hewlett-Packard and 3M, for example, have a 15 percent rule: They expect a research scientist to spend 15 percent of the workweek working on a project of his or her own choosing. Ideas may be submitted by individuals or by groups. Brainstorming (see Chapter 7) is a technique that managers frequently use to encourage new ideas.

New product ideas are written up as brief proposals. The proposals are submitted to a cross-functional team of managers, who evaluate the proposal at Gate 1. The cross-functional team considers the proposal's fit with the organization's strategy and its technical feasibility. Proposals that are consistent with the strategy of the organization and judged technically feasible pass through Gate 1 and into Stage 2. Other proposals are turned down (although the door is often left open for reconsidering a proposal at a later date).

Figure 19.5 A Stage-Gate Development Funnel

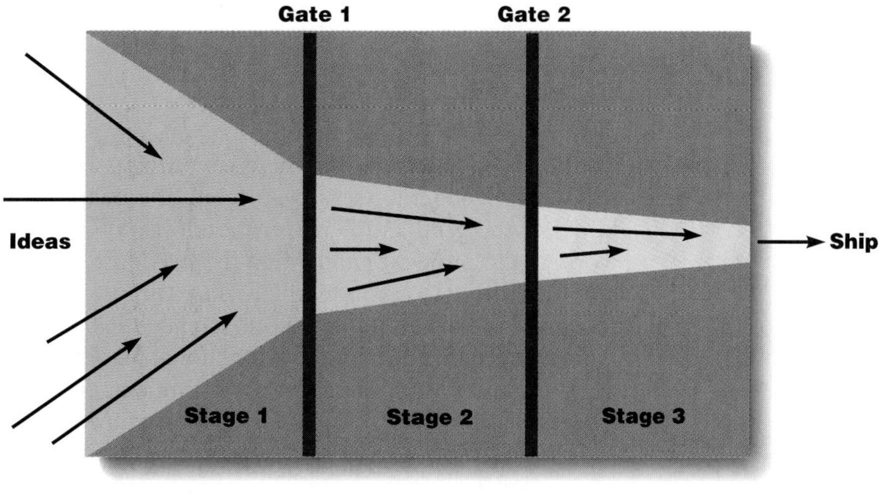

product development plan A plan that specifies all of the relevant information that managers need in order to decide whether to proceed with a full-blown product development effort.

The primary goal in Stage 2 is to draft a detailed product development plan. The **product development plan** specifies all of the relevant information that managers need to make a decision about whether to go ahead with a full-blown product development effort. The product development plan should include strategic and financial objectives, an analysis of the product's market potential, a list of desired product features, a list of technological requirements, a list of financial and human resource requirements, a detailed development budget, and a time line that contains specific milestones (for example, dates for prototype completion and final launch).

This plan is normally drafted by a cross-functional team of managers. Good planning requires a good strategic analysis (see Chapter 8), and team members must be prepared to spend considerable time out in the field with customers trying to understand their needs. Drafting a product development plan generally takes about three months. Once completed, the plan is reviewed by a senior management committee at Gate 2 (see Figure 19.5). These managers focus on the details of the plan to see whether the proposal is attractive (given its market potential) and viable (given the technological, financial, and human resources that would be needed to develop the product). Senior managers making this review keep in mind all other product development efforts currently being undertaken by the organization. One goal at this point is to ensure that limited organizational resources are used to their maximum effect.

contract book A written agreement that details product development factors such as responsibilities, resource commitments, budgets, time lines, and development milestones.

At Gate 2 projects are rejected, sent back for revision, or allowed to pass through into Stage 3, the development phase. Product development starts with the formation of a cross-functional team that is given primary responsibility for developing the product. In some companies, at the beginning of Stage 3 top managers and cross-functional team members sign a **contract book,** a written agreement that details factors such as responsibilities, resource commitments, budgets, time lines, and development milestones.[30] Signing the contract book is viewed as the symbolic launch of a product development effort. The contract book is also a document against which actual development progress can be measured. At Motorola, for example, team members and top management negotiate a contract and sign a contract book at the launch of a development effort, thereby signaling their commitment to the objectives contained in the contract.[31]

The Stage 3 development effort can last anywhere from six months to 10 years, depending on the industry and type of product. Some electronics products have development cycles of six months, but it takes from 3 to 5 years to develop a new car, about 5 years to develop a new jet aircraft, and as much as 10 years to develop a new medical drug.

core members The members of a team who bear primary responsibility for the success of a project and who stay with a project from inception to completion.

PRINCIPLE 2: ESTABLISH CROSS-FUNCTIONAL TEAMS A smooth-running cross-functional team seems to be a critical component of successful product development, as suggested by the experience of Thermos.[32] Marketing, engineering, and manufacturing personnel were **core members** of a successful product development team–the people who have primary responsibility for the product development effort. Other people besides core members work on the project as and when the need arises, but the core members (generally from three to six individuals) stay with the project from inception to completion of the development effort (see Figure 19.6).

The reason for using a cross-functional team is to ensure a high level of coordination and communication among managers in different functions, which increases group cohesiveness and performance, as we saw in Chapter 14. Input from both marketing and manufacturing members of Thermos's Lifestyle team

Figure 19.6
Members of a Cross-Functional Product Development Team

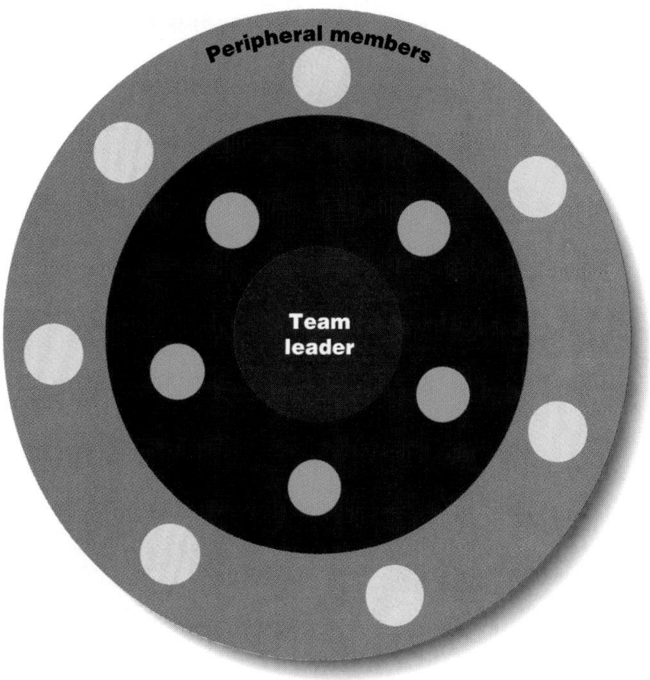

determined the characteristics of the barbecue that the engineers on the team ended up designing.

If a cross-functional team is to succeed, it must also have the right kind of leadership, and it must be managed in an effective manner.[33] To be successful, a product development team needs a team leader who can rise above a functional background and take a cross-functional view.[34] In addition to effective leadership, successful cross-functional product development teams have several other key characteristics.[35] Often, core members of successful teams are located close to each other in the same office space to foster a sense of shared mission and commitment to a development program. Successful teams develop a clear sense of their objectives and how they will be achieved, the purpose again being to create a sense of shared mission. A clear, explicit statement of objectives allows the team to measure its actual performance against its plan.

PRINCIPLE 3: USE CONCURRENT ENGINEERING Traditional product development is a sequential process consisting of five steps: opportunity identification, concept development, product design, process design, and commercial production (see Figure 19.7a). Opportunity development occurs at Stage 1 of the stage-gate funnel (see Figure 19.6), commercial production occurs at Stage 3, and the other three steps occur at Stage 2. The problem with sequential product development is that long product development times, poor product quality, and high manufacturing costs are likely if there is no direct communication among the manufacturing managers who develop the concept and the engineering or R&D managers who design the product. In many organizations engineers in R&D design a product and then "throw it over the wall" to manufacturing. The result can be a design that is too costly to manufacture. If solving this problem requires redesign, manufacturing sends the product back to the design engineers, thereby lengthening development time.

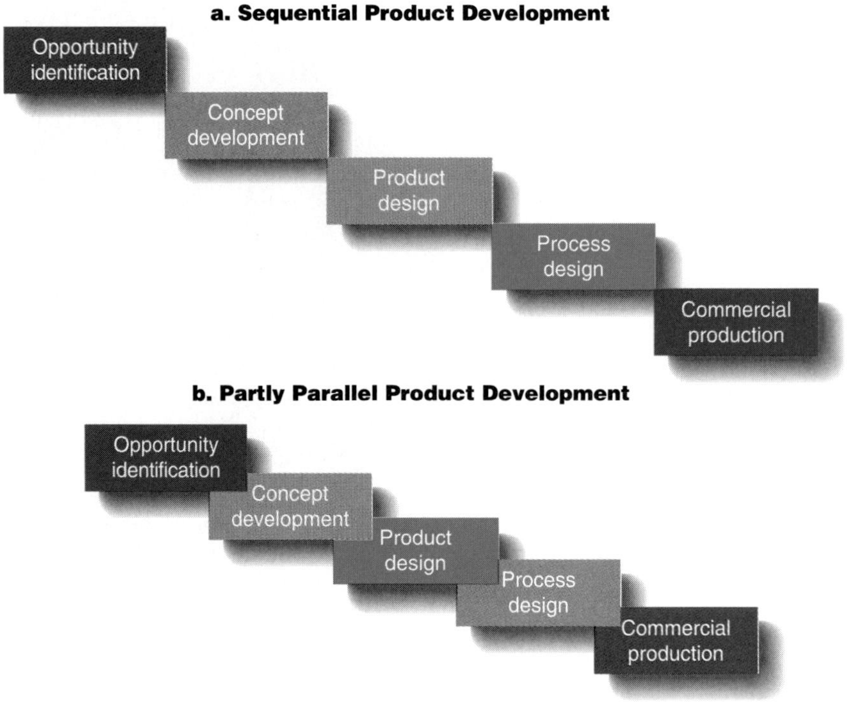

Figure 19.7
Sequential and Partly Parallel Development Processes

concurrent engineering The simultaneous design of the product and of the process for manufacturing the product.

Cross-functional teams can help solve this problem, and it is also helpful to alter the process so that it is partly parallel rather than sequential. In partly parallel product development, one step begins before the prior step is finished, and managers from one function are familiar with what is going on in other functions (see Figure 19.7b). The goal is to facilitate **concurrent engineering,** the simultaneous design of the product and of the process for manufacturing the product.[36] Recall that in the interests of reducing manufacturing costs, manufacturing members of the Lifestyle team at Thermos persuaded their colleagues in engineering to design an electric grill with straight legs. That is an example of concurrent engineering. The usual outcome of concurrent engineering is a product that is easy to manufacture. Concurrent engineering thus helps to reduce manufacturing costs and to increase product quality. The other benefit of a partly parallel process is that it reduces development time, for two reasons. The whole development process is compressed, and concurrent engineering reduces the probability that costly and time-consuming product redesigns will be needed.

PRINCIPLE 4: INVOLVE BOTH CUSTOMERS AND SUPPLIERS

Many new products fail when they reach the marketplace because they were designed with scant attention to customer needs. Successful product development requires inputs from more than just an organization's members; also needed are inputs from customers and suppliers.[37] At Thermos, team members spent a month on the road visiting customers to identify their needs. The revolutionary electric barbecue grill was a direct result of this process. In other cases, companies have found it worthwhile to include customer representatives as peripheral members of their product development team. Boeing's approach to designing its latest commercial jet aircraft, the 400-seat 777, provides an example of this, as shown in the "Management Insight."

Management Insight

Developing the Boeing 777

Boeing's most recent airliner, the wide-body 400-seat commercial jet aircraft, the Boeing 777, took only four years to develop from initial concept phase to take off. The relatively short development time for the 777 was a triumph for Boeing; the typical development time for jet aircraft is six years, which means Boeing saved billions of dollars. Moreover, on the day the 777 took off, Boeing already had 150 firm orders for the plane, and airlines had taken out options on another 150. This kind of advance ordering is a sure sign that Boeing had developed an aircraft that customers wanted.

To build a plane that was designed with customer needs in mind, Boeing invited eight U.S. and foreign airlines to help its engineers design the aircraft. The group included United, which launched the program with an order for 32 planes, American, Delta, British Airways, Japan Air Lines, All Nippon Airlines, Quantas, and Cathay Pacific. For almost a year, technical representatives from these airlines took up residence in Boeing's Everett facility and met with the engineering staff assigned to the 777 project. This was a dramatic shift for Boeing, which in the past had been very secretive about its design work.

Input from the eight carriers clearly determined the shape of the 777. They wanted a fuselage that was wider than rival McDonnell Douglas and Airbus models so that they could pack another 30 or so seats onto the aircraft. The result is an aircraft that is 5 inches wider than the McDonnell Douglas MD–11 and 25 inches wider than the Airbus A–330. They wanted a plane in which the galleys and lavatories could be relocated almost anywhere within the plane within hours. Boeing therefore designed a plane whose interior can be completely changed in three or four hours, configured with one, two, or three classes to fit whatever a carrier's market of the moment demands. And they wanted better overhead bins for carry-on baggage, so Boeing designed new overhead bins to meet their requirements.[38]

Besides customers, Boeing also brought 18 of its major suppliers into the 777 program and told them exactly what it wanted from them. Suppliers consulted with Boeing's project engineers. As a result, many potential production problems were solved ahead of time, thereby reducing the need for costly design changes late in the development process.

Including suppliers in the product development process is clearly another important factor in successful product development. When suppliers are responsible for major components of a product (such as the tail section of the 777), it is important to extend the principle of concurrent engineering to embrace them so that they too can manufacture quality components in a timely, cost-effective way.

Many of the information technologies discussed in Chapter 17 are becoming an increasingly important part of concurrent engineering. The way in which Boeing used computer-aided design (CAD) to design the 777, the first airliner to be designed entirely by computer, provides a graphic illustration of the advantages of CAD. Each of the thousands of components of the 777 was first engineered and tested in virtual space by means of three-dimensional CAD technology to make sure that everything fit together. If parts did not fit, they were redesigned on the computer until they did. Only then were real parts and subassemblies manufactured. By using CAD, Boeing dramatically reduced the need for expensive mockups and design changes and shortened development time.[39] The use of CAD technology in product development has exploded in recent years as design engineers employed by car makers, furniture makers, and architects have found that CAD allows them to cut down on design time and improve the accuracy of their engineering drawings.[40]

In sum, managers need to recognize that successful product development cuts across roles and functions and requires a high level of integration. They should recognize the importance of common values and norms in promoting the high levels of cooperation and cohesiveness necessary to build a culture for innovation. They also should be careful to reward successful innovators and make heroes of the employees and teams that develop successful new products. Finally, managers should fully utilize the four principles of product development to guide the process.

Problems with Product Development

Given today's rapid rate of technological change and its impact on the length of product life cycles, successful product development has become a major source of competitive advantage in many industries. To survive and compete successfully, managers must look for ways to reduce development time, achieve a close fit between new product attributes and customer demands, and maximize the quality and ease of production of new products. The four principles for effective product development described above indicate some of the actions that managers are taking to increase the effectiveness of product development efforts.

These principles, however, have not been universally adopted. The track record for product development is actually quite poor. Several studies have concluded that most product development projects either are terminated before completion or result in the production of new products that flop when they reach the marketplace.[41]

Although many managers know the theory underlying successful product development, making that theory work within an organization can be very difficult. Revolutionizing product development requires a break with traditional ways of thinking and managing. The establishment of cross-functional teams can help top managers redirect power and responsibility away from functional managers and toward the leaders and core members of product development teams. Not surprisingly, functional managers often resent such challenges to their authority and resist attempts to limit their power and influence within the organization. However, by assessing the need for change, deciding on the change to make, implementing the change, and evaluating the change (see Figure 16.7), top managers will be well positioned to overcome resistance and move the organization toward its desired future state.

Entrepreneurship

At the heart of innovation and product development are **entrepreneurs**, individuals who notice opportunities and take responsibility for mobilizing the resources necessary to produce new and improved goods and services. Entrepreneurs start new business ventures and do all of the planning, organizing, leading, and controlling necessary to meet organizational goals. Most commonly entrepreneurs assume all the risk and receive all the returns associated with the new business venture. These people are the

Houston Internet entrepreneur Dayna Steele Justiz samples a bite of meatloaf, one of NASA's culinary offerings she sells to the public through her Internet storefront, www.thespacestore.com. She sells overruns of ready-to-eat space food not required for astronauts aboard the space shuttle.

Bill Gates or Liz Claibornes of the world who make vast fortunes when their businesses succeed. Or they are among the millions of people who start new business ventures only to lose their money when they fail. Despite the fact that an estimated 80 percent of small businesses fail in the first three to five years, by some estimates 38 percent of men and 50 percent of women in today's workforce want to start their own companies.[42]

entrepreneur An individual who notices opportunities and takes responsibility for mobilizing the resources necessary to produce new and improved goods and services.

Some managers, scientists, or researchers employed by existing companies engage in entrepreneurial activity. They are involved in the innovation and product development process described in this chapter. To distinguish these individuals from entrepreneurs who found their own businesses, employees of existing organizations who notice opportunities for either quantum or incremental product improvements and are responsible for managing the product development process are known as **intrapreneurs.** In general, then, **entrepreneurship** is the mobilization of resources to take advantage of an opportunity to provide customers with new or improved goods and services.

intrapreneur A manager, scientist, or researcher who works inside an existing organization and notices opportunities for product improvements and is responsible for managing the product development process.

entrepreneurship The mobilization of resources to take advantage of an opportunity to provide customers with new or improved goods and services.

There is an interesting relationship between entrepreneurs and intrapreneurs. Many intrapreneurs become dissatisfied when their superiors decide neither to support nor to fund new product ideas and development efforts that the intrapreneurs think will succeed. What do intrapreneurs who feel that they are getting nowhere do? Very often they decide to leave their employers and start their own organizations to take advantage of their new product ideas. In other words, intrapreneurs become entrepreneurs and found companies that may compete with the companies they left.

Many of the world's most successful organizations have been started by frustrated intrapreneurs who became entrepreneurs. William Hewlett and David Packard left Fairchild Semiconductor, an early industry leader, when managers of that company would not support their ideas; their company soon outperformed Fairchild. Compaq Computer was founded by Rod Canion and some of his colleagues, who left Texas Instruments (TI) when managers there would not support Canion's idea that TI should develop its own personal computer. To prevent the departure of talented people, organizations need to take steps to promote internal entrepreneurship. In the remainder of this section we consider issues involved in promoting successful entrepreneurship in both new and existing organizations.

Entrepreneurship and New Ventures

The fact that a significant number of entrepreneurs were frustrated intrapreneurs provides a clue about the personal characteristics of people who are likely to start a new venture and bear all the uncertainty and risk associated with being an entrepreneur.

CHARACTERISTICS OF ENTREPRENEURS Entrepreneurs are likely to be high on the personality trait of *openness to experience,* meaning that they are predisposed to be original, to be open to a wide range of stimuli, to be daring, and to take risks. Entrepreneurs also are likely to have an *internal locus of control* and believe that they are responsible for what happens to themselves and that their own actions determine important outcomes such as the success or failure of a new business. People with an external locus of control, in contrast, would be very unlikely to leave a secure job in an organization and assume the risk associated with a new venture.

Entrepreneurs are likely to have a high level of self-esteem and feel competent and capable of handling most situations–including the stress and uncertainty surrounding a plunge into a risky new venture. Entrepreneurs are likely to have a high need for achievement and have a strong desire to perform challenging tasks and meet high personal standards of excellence.

ENTREPRENEURSHIP AND MANAGEMENT Given that entrepreneurs are predisposed to activities that are somewhat adventurous and risky, in what ways can people become involved in entrepreneurial ventures? One way is to start a business from scratch. Taking advantage of computer-based information systems, many people are starting solo ventures and going it alone. The total number of small office/home office workers is more than 40 million, and each year more than a million new solo entrepreneurs join the ranks of the more than 29 million self-employed.

When people who go it alone succeed, they frequently need to hire other people to help them run the business. Michael Dell, for example, began his computer business as a college student and within weeks had hired several people to help him to assemble computers from the component parts he bought from suppliers. From his solo venture grew Dell Computer, the largest personal computer company in the world today.

Entrepreneurs who found a new business often have difficulty managing the organization as it grows; entrepreneurship is not the same as management. Management encompasses all the decisions involved in planning, organizing, leading, and controlling resources. Entrepreneurship is noticing an opportunity to satisfy a customer need and then mobilizing resources to make a product that satisfies that need. When an entrepreneur has produced something that customers want, entrepreneurship gives way to management as the pressing need becomes to provide the product both efficiently and effectively.

Frequently, a founding entrepreneur lacks the skills, patience, and experience to engage in the difficult and challenging work of management. Some entrepreneurs find it very hard to delegate authority because they are afraid to risk their company by letting others manage it. As a result, they become overloaded, and the quality of their decision making declines. Other entrepreneurs lack the detailed knowledge necessary to establish state-of-the-art information systems and technology or to create the operations management procedures that are vital to increase the efficiency of their organizations' production systems. Thus, to succeed, it is necessary to do more than create a new product; an entrepreneur must hire managers who can create an operating system that will let a new venture survive and prosper.

DEVELOPING A PLAN FOR A NEW BUSINESS One crucial factor that can help promote the success of a new venture is a clear business plan. The purpose of a business plan is to guide the development of the new business, just as the stage-gate development funnel guides the product development effort. The steps in the development of a business plan are listed in Table 19.1.

Planning for a new business begins when an entrepreneur notices an opportunity to develop a new or improved good or service for the whole market or for a specific market niche. For example, an entrepreneur might notice an opportunity in the fast-food market to provide customers with healthy fast food such as rotisserie chicken served with fresh vegetables. This is what the founders of the Boston Market restaurant chain did.

The next step is to test the feasibility of the new product idea. The entrepreneur conducts as thorough a strategic planning exercise as possible, using the SWOT analysis technique discussed in Chapter 8. First, the entrepreneur analyzes opportunities and threats. For example, a potential threat might be that KFC will decide to imitate the idea and offer its customers rotisserie chicken (KFC actually did this after Boston Market identified the new market niche). The entrepreneur should conduct a thorough analysis of the external environment (see Chapter 5) to test the potential of a new product idea and must be willing to abandon an idea if it seems likely that the threats and risks may overwhelm the opportunities and returns. Entrepreneurship is always a very risky process, and many entrepreneurs become so committed to their new ideas that they ignore or discount the potential threats and forge ahead–only to lose their shirts.

Table 19.1
Developing a Business Plan

1. **Notice a product opportunity, and develop a basic business idea**
   - Goods/services
   - Customers/markets
2. **Conduct a strategic (SWOT) analysis**
   - Identify opportunities
   - Identify threats
   - Identify strengths
   - Identify weaknesses
3. **Decide whether the business opportunity is feasible**
4. **Prepare a detailed business plan**
   - Statement of mission, goals, and financial objectives
   - Statement of strategic objectives
   - List of necessary resources
   - Organizational time line of events

If the environmental analysis suggests that the product idea is feasible, the next step is to examine the strengths and weaknesses of the idea. At this stage the main strength is the resources possessed by the entrepreneur. Does the entrepreneur have access to an adequate source of funds? Does the entrepreneur have any experience in the fast-food industry such as having managed a restaurant? To identify weaknesses, the entrepreneur needs to assess how many and what kind of resources will be necessary to establish a viable new venture–such as a chain of chicken restaurants. Analysis might reveal that the new product idea will not generate an adequate return on investment. Or it might reveal that the entrepreneur needs to find partners to help provide the resources needed to open a chain on a sufficient scale to generate a high enough return on investment.

After conducting a thorough SWOT analysis, if the entrepreneur decides that the new product idea is feasible, the hard work begins of developing the actual business plan that will be used to attract investors or funds from banks. Included in the business plan should be the same basic elements as in the product development plan: (1) a statement of the organization's mission, goals, and financial objectives; (2) a statement of the organization's strategic objectives, including an analysis of the product's market potential, based on the SWOT analysis that has already been conducted; (3) a list of all the functional and organizational resources that will be required to successfully implement the new product idea, including a list of technological, financial, and human resource requirements; and (4) a time line that contains specific milestones for the entrepreneur and others to use to measure the progress of the venture, such as target dates for the final design and the opening of the first restaurant.

Many entrepreneurs do not have the luxury of having a team of cross-functional managers to help develop a detailed business plan. This is obviously true of solo ventures. One reason why franchising has become so popular in the United States is that an entrepreneur can purchase and draw on the business plan and experience of an already existing company, thereby reducing the risks associated with opening a new business. Entrepreneurs today can purchase the right to open a Subway Sandwich Shop. The founders of that chain, however, had to develop the business plan that made the franchise possible.

In sum, entrepreneurs have a number of significant challenges to confront and conquer if they are to be successful. It is not uncommon for an entrepreneur to fail repeatedly before finding a venture that proves successful. It also is not uncommon for an entrepreneur who establishes a successful new company to sell it in order to move on to new ventures that promise new risks and returns. An example of such an entrepreneur is Wayne Huizenga, who bought many small waste disposal companies to create the giant WMX waste disposal company, which he eventually sold. A few years later Huizenga took control of Blockbuster Video and, by opening and buying other video store chains, turned Blockbuster Video into the biggest video chain in the United States, only to sell it to Viacom.

Intrapreneurship and Organizational Learning

The intensity of competition today, particularly from agile, small companies, has made it increasingly important for large established organizations to promote and encourage intrapreneurship so as to raise the level of innovation and organizational learning. A learning organization (see Chapter 7) encourages all employees to identify opportunities and solve problems, thus enabling the organization to continuously experiment, improve, and increase its ability to provide customers with new and improved goods and services. The higher the level of intrapreneurship is, the higher will be the levels of learning and innovation. How can organizations promote organizational learning and intrapreneurship?

product champion A manager who takes "ownership" of a project and provides the leadership and vision that take a product from the idea stage to the final customer.

PRODUCT CHAMPIONS One way to promote intrapreneurship is to encourage individuals to assume the role of **product champion,** a manager who takes "ownership" of a project and provides the leadership and vision that take a product from the idea stage to the final customer. 3M, a company well known for its attempts to promote intrapreneurship, encourages all its managers to become product champions and identify new product ideas. Product champions become responsible for developing a business plan for the product. Armed with this business plan, they appear before 3M's product development committee, a team of senior 3M managers who probe the strengths and weaknesses of the plan to decide whether it should be funded. If the plan is accepted, the product champion assumes responsibility for product development. The "Management Insight" describes how Don Frey worked with Lee Iacocca to develop the Ford Mustang in the early 1960s and illustrates the importance of the product champion role.

Management Insight

How to Champion a Product at Ford

Don Frey, an engineer in Ford Motor Company's research laboratories was always assigned to projects that seemed new and interesting. However, he never got to talk to Ford's customers and never got involved in operational decision making about what to offer the customer and how much new developments would cost. As a result, for many years, he and other R&D engineers worked on products that never got to market because the work of the engineers was not linked to the needs of the customers. Frustrated by the lack of payoff from his work, Frey began to question the utility of a corporate research laboratory that was so far removed from operations and the market.

In 1957, he moved from the research laboratory to head Ford's passenger car design department so that he could be closer to market operations. In this new position, Frey was much closer to the customer and directed the energies of his department to producing innovations that customers wanted and were willing to pay for. Frey soon concluded that in the automobile business the best R&D was incremental; year by year innovations to better meet customer demands for safety, luxury, or utility should be the goal of product development. He also saw how important it was to use customer complaints as a guide for investing resources to get the most benefit.

Equipped with this new perspective on innovation, Frey was made a member of Ford's top planning committee in 1961. Quickly Frey and his staff saw the possibility of developing a new car for the emerging "sporty car segment" of the car market. Frey began to champion the development of a new car to meet this need. Ford, however, had just lost a fortune developing the ill-fated Edsel and was reluctant to invest in a brand new car. Frey could not get top management to support his idea.

Frey decided to go ahead, however. Because there was no corporate support for Frey's ideas, all of the early engineering and styling of what became the Mustang was carried out with bootleg funds–that is, funds earmarked for one project but used for something else. By 1962, Frey and his team had produced the first working prototype of the Mustang and believed they had a winner. Top management in general and Henry Ford II in particular were not impressed and offered no support, still fearing the new car might turn out to be another Edsel. Luckily for the Mustang team, Lee Iacocca became vice president and general manager of Ford in 1962, and he bought into the Mustang concept. Believing that the Mustang would be a huge success, Iacocca risked his reputation to convince top management to back the idea. In the fall of 1962, after much pressure, funds to produce the car were allocated.

With Frey as product champion, the Mustang raced from approval to market in only 18 months. When the Mustang was introduced in 1964, it was an instant success, and over 400,000 Mustangs were sold. Frey went on to champion other innovations in Ford vehicles, such as disc brakes and radial tires. Reflecting on his experiences as a product champion, he offered some "coaching tips" for future product champions: Innovation can start anywhere and from small beginnings, and product champions must be prepared to use all the skill they have to pull people and resources together and to resist top managers and financial experts who use numbers to kill new ideas.[43] As Frey's experiences suggest, innovation is a risky business, and product champions have to go out on a limb to take on the disbelievers.

Ford introduced the first Mustang in April 1964, its sporty look and peppy performance has always given it strong appeal to youthful car buyers.

SKUNKWORKS AND NEW VENTURE DIVISIONS The idea behind the product champion role is that employees who feel ownership for a project are inclined to act like outside entrepreneurs and go to great lengths to make the project succeed. This feeling of ownership can also be strengthened by using skunkworks and new venture divisions. A **skunkworks** is a group of intrapreneurs who are deliberately separated from the normal operation of an organization–for example, from the normal chain of command–to encourage them to devote all their attention to developing new products. The idea is that if these people are isolated they will become so intensely involved in a project that development time will be relatively brief and the quality of the final product will be enhanced. The term *skunkworks* was coined at the Lockheed Corporation, which formed a team of design engineers to develop special aircraft such as the U2 spy plane. The secrecy with which this unit functioned and speculation about its goals led others to refer to it as the skunkworks.

skunkworks A group of intrapreneurs who are deliberately separated from the normal operation of an organization to encourage them to devote all their attention to developing new products.

Large organizations can become tall, inflexible, and bureaucratic, and these conditions are not ideal for encouraging learning and experimentation. Recognizing this problem, many organizations create new venture divisions, separate from the parent organization and free from close scrutiny, to take charge of product development. A **new venture division** is an autonomous division that is given all the resources it needs to develop and market a new product. In essence, a new venture division functions in the same way that a new venture would; the division's managers become intrapreneurs in charge of product development. The hope is that this new setting will encourage a high level of organizational learning and entrepreneurship.

new venture division An autonomous division that is given all the resources it needs to develop and market a new product.

REWARDS FOR INNOVATION To encourage managers to bear the uncertainty and risk associated with the hard work of entrepreneurship, it is necessary to link performance to rewards. Increasingly, companies are rewarding intrapreneurs on the basis of the outcome of the product development process. Intrapreneurs are granted large bonuses if their projects succeed, or they are granted stock options that can make them millionaires if the product sells well. Both Microsoft and Cisco Systems, for example, have made hundreds of their employees multimillionaires as a result of the stock options they were granted as part of their reward package. In addition to money, successful intrapreneurs can expect to receive promotion to the ranks of top management. Most of 3M's top managers, for example, reached the executive suite because they had a track record of successful entrepreneurship. Organizations must reward intrapreneurs equitably if they wish to prevent them from leaving and becoming outside entrepreneurs who might form a new venture that competes directly against them. Nevertheless, they frequently do so.

Summary and Review

INNOVATION, TECHNOLOGICAL CHANGE, AND COMPETITION The high level of technological change in today's world creates new opportunities for managers to market new products but can destroy the market for older products. Rapid technological change and changing fads and fashions can shorten product life cycles. The shorter a product life cycle is, the greater is the importance of product development as a competitive weapon.

PRODUCT DEVELOPMENT Successful product development requires managers to pursue four goals: reducing development time and maximizing the product's fit with customer needs, its quality, and its manufacturability. To meet these goals, managers should follow four principles of product development: (1) establish a structured stage-gate development funnel for evaluating and controlling different product development efforts; (2) establish cross-functional teams composed of individuals from different functional departments, and give each team a leader who can rise above his or her functional background; (3) use concurrent engineering, the simultaneous design of the product and of the process for manufacturing the product, to reduce development time and increase manufacturability and product quality; (4) involve both customers and suppliers in the development process.

ENTREPRENEURSHIP Entrepreneurship is the mobilization of resources to take advantage of an opportunity to provide customers with new or improved goods and services. Entrepreneurs find new ventures of their own. Intrapreneurs work inside organizations and manage the product development process. Organizations need to encourage intrapreneurship because it leads to organizational learning and innovation.

Management in Action

Topics for Discussion and Action

1. Identify two industries where product life cycles are short and product development is an important competitive imperative. Identify two industries where product life cycles are long. What factors make the length of the product life cycle different in these industries?
2. When product life cycles are long, is product development not an important consideration for a company? Explain your answer.
3. The microprocessor that Intel developed can be classified as a quantum product innovation. Identify two other quantum product innovations, and explore their implications for product development.
4. What do you think are the greatest impediments to successful product development within an organization?
5. Why is it so important for managers to shorten the duration of product development? What steps can management take to reduce development time? What risks are associated with compressing development time?
6. Ask a manager to describe an example of incremental product improvement in which he or she was involved. What was it? What were the problems surrounding it? Did it succeed?
7. What are the four principles of successful product development? How do they affect one another?

Building Management Skills

Promoting Successful Product Development

Pick a well-known company that is operating in an industry characterized by technological change (such as Apple Computer in the personal computer industry, Amgen in biotechnology, America Online in information services, Microsoft in computer software). Then answer the following questions.

1. What is the source of technological change in the company's task and general environments?
2. What is the average length of the product life cycle in the company's industry?
3. Approximately how many new products has the company introduced over the last five years?
4. How successful have the company's product development efforts been?
5. What accounts for the company's product successes? What accounts for its failures?
6. From what you have been able to find out, do you think there is potential for improving the company's product development efforts? If so, how?

Small Group Breakout Exercise

Keeping Up with Your Customers

Form groups of three or four people, and appoint one member as the spokesperson who will communicate your findings to the whole class when called on by the instructor. Then discuss the following scenario.

You are the top managers in charge of a chain of stores selling high-quality, high-priced men's and women's clothing. Store sales are flat, and you are increasingly concerned that the clothing your stores offer to customers is failing to satisfy changing customer needs. You think that the purchasing managers are failing to spot changing fads and fashions in time, and you believe that store management is not doing enough to communicate to purchasing managers what customers are demanding. You want to revitalize your organization's product development process, which, in the case of your stores, means stocking the products that customers want.

1. Clearly state how and why each of the four goals of product development (development time, customer needs, quality, and manufacturability) is relevant to your organization.
2. Develop a program based on the four principles of product development that you intend to implement in your stores to achieve these goals. For example, how will you encourage input from employees and customers, and who will be responsible for managing the program?

Exploring the World Wide Web

Search for the website of a company that describes the company's approach to innovation or product development. What kind of activities does this company engage in, and how does it manage the product development process?

You're the Management Consultant

You have been called in to advise a team of entrepreneurs who have invented a new kind of soft drink flavored with South American herbs and spices. The drink has been tested in a small market and has received an enthusiastic response from tasters. The entrepreneurs wish to know how to best develop a business plan that will give them the most chance of establishing a competitive advantage.

1. Analyze the task environment of the soft drink industry to decide which forces are most likely to impact the new company.
2. Given this analysis what are the various means/strategies in which the company should produce, bottle, and distribute its new soft drink to customers to maximize its competitive advantage?
3. Which strategy do you think will be most effective for the company in the long run?

BusinessWeek Cases in the News

AOL vs. Microsoft

On July 26, [2001] in the heart of Microsoft Corp.'s Redmond (Wash.) campus, top executives at the software giant were deep into a presentation aimed at wowing Wall Street analysts. They started ticking off the technological triumphs in their upcoming Windows XP operating system and their new Xbox game player, when up popped a slide entitled "How to Beat AOL."

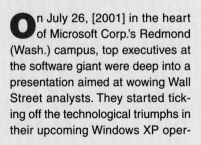

Microsoft has had many formidable adversaries through the years, including Netscape Communications, Lotus, Borland, and IBM, but it may have finally met its match. AOL Time Warner Inc. is the first company in years with the guts, money, and staying power to match the giant from Redmond. And it's gaining ground in a struggle that grows fiercer by the day. In recent weeks, skirmishes between the two have erupted over issues as diverse as control of the computer desktop, AOL's potential bid for AT&T's cable unit, and pricing of on-line services.

The latest: On July 26, the industry discovered that AOL had landed a coveted place on the desktop of the new Windows XP operating system that will ship with Compaq Computer Corp.'s machines, while MSN was relegated to a slot on the Windows start menu. "All we're trying to do is let consumers find AOL instead of being stuck with Microsoft," says AOL CEO Barry M. Schuler. Separately, AOL and Compaq are expected to announce an expanded strategic partnership in mid-August in which AOL will buy large amounts of Compaq technology while the PC maker advertises across AOL properties.

Not to be outdone, Microsoft is insisting that all PC makers that put AOL on the desktop put MSN there, too. "They're trying to not let people have the choice of using our software," said Chairman William H. Gates III at the company's July 26 analysts' meeting. Privately, the company is trying to match AOL's offers to PC makers, in hopes they'll promote MSN instead, a PC exec said.

While the two companies started in different corners of the tech business—Microsoft catering to PC users and AOL to the hordes of the on-line generation—they're increasingly on a collision course. Why? They're both facing slowing growth in their core businesses and see the same sources of long-term salvation: anywhere, anytime Web services—from stock quotes to on-line music to interactive TV—delivered lickety-split to the living room, office, or wireless device. And they're using their respective grips over PCs and on-line users to catapult into this new world. "Neither will cede dominance in any market," says John Corcoran, Internet analyst at CIBC World Markets. "They're saying: `I'm keeping my fingers in all your pies, and you're keeping a finger in all mine.'"

Tensions are only increasing as the scheduled Oct. 25 launch of XP draws closer. In June, AOL tried and failed to win a permanent slot on the new operating system after prolonged negotiations with Microsoft. That was a big strategic blow. But the government's antitrust case is giving AOL a once-in-a-lifetime chance to try to change the way Microsoft leverages its operating-system monopoly. According to industry sources, AOL supports a plan to force the software giant to license Windows to rivals who could then configure it their own way—an idea that was floated in the past but lacked wide support.

Both companies have big arsenals and little choice but to go mano-a-mano as they pursue the same markets. At its essence, this contest will be a duel between software vs. content. Microsoft is betting that its ubiquitous Windows operating system and its lock on the allegiances of software developers will win the race, while AOL is just as sure that its control over content and on-line subscribers' loyalties will triumph.

Both are taking whacks at each other's strongholds. Microsoft hopes its .Net technology, which lets PC software programs and websites communicate with one another, will lure PC users with a single, convenient sign-on to a raft of new services on the Net. With one click, consumers will be able to order their on-line broker to buy 100 shares of a company, transfer $1,000 from their bank to their brokerage, and update their personal stock-portfolio program. For this service, Microsoft will levy a small charge.

Meanwhile, AOL, fresh from its $103 billion acquisition of media giant Time Warner this year, is raring to tap Time Warner's enormous hoard of traditional print, film, television, and music content for distribution over the Net. AOL doesn't need to search for a market: It already has 30 million on-line subscribers primed to be guinea pigs for new services. When it launches potentially lucrative new offerings, such as on-line music or interactive TV, it will have a significant head start over Microsoft. What's more, AOL is trying to skirt Microsoft's iron grip over the PC by pushing TV, Sony Playstation, and other connected devices. Over the long term, predicts Mike Homer, a Netscape veteran and CEO of Kontiki, a Silicon Valley start-up, each is likely to maintain its sphere of influence. "AOL will win in the living room, and Microsoft will continue to march forward on the PC."

Pressure on Congress

Meanwhile, look for the dogfight to move into new battlegrounds. One of them is law and policymaking. AOL has been lobbying Congress on Microsoft's business plans and has talked to the Senate Judiciary Committee about the competitive issues surrounding Windows XP. In early March, AOL also briefed staff at the National Association of Attorneys General on the new operating system.

On another front, AOL believes that a good long-term remedy to the Microsoft antitrust case would be forcing the company to offer a version of the operating system to PC makers or other rivals, according to industry sources. AOL declined to discuss the idea. Such a proposal, which would be more politically acceptable than a breakup, was closely considered by trustbusters last year. Industry reaction to the idea, which would allow PC makers to load up their own bundle of applications rather than being forced to take those

Microsoft chooses, is mixed. "I love it," says Gateway Inc. (GTW) CEO Theodore W. Waitt. But it's not clear that other PC makers agree. One former Dell Computer Corp. (DELL) manager who has experience working with Microsoft said that while it might give PC makers more choice, it would also make configuring systems more complex—a big no-no in this time of cost-cutting. "It would make life more difficult for any PC [maker]," he says. Microsoft spokesperson Vivek Varma would not discuss the details of the idea and dismissed the proposal as having "no credibility and no weight."

Broadband is another arena where the combat is heating up. Both companies are working behind the scenes in the bidding for AT&T Broadband to keep the nation's leading cable operator out of the grasp of the other. Both AOL and Microsoft are betting that upgraded digital cable lines will be a winning conduit to deliver fast Internet services. AOL, especially, doesn't want to lose its dominance in Internet access when consumers migrate to broadband. And Microsoft wants to sell the software powering the set-top boxes that bring broadband services to the living room. If too many cable guys fall into AOL's camp, its market shrinks dramatically.

The battle was drawn after Comcast Corp. (CMCSA) made a bid for AT&T's cable assets in early July. Within two weeks, AOL execs met with AT&T in New York, according to industry sources. Under discussion: A new spin-off combining AT&T Broadband with AOL Time Warner's cable operations, with AT&T holding a 40% share. Comcast execs believe they can beat an AOL counteroffer with the help of Microsoft, which owns nearly 5% of Comcast.

No doubt about it, these two giants are going to collide more frequently as they rush into the broadband future. Consumers watching the brawl can only hope that this clash of the titans will mean better services for them.

Source: C. Yang, J. Greene, and A. Park, "AOL vs. Microsoft" *Business Week,* August 13, 2001, pp. 28–30.

Questions

1. What kinds of new products and services are both AOL and Microsoft trying to innovate to keep ahead in their fight for dominance over the Internet?
2. Which company do you think is going to have the most success in innovating new products and services? Why?

BusinessWeek Cases in the News

How a "Skunk Works" Kept Mustang Alive on a Tight Budget

Although the Ford Mustang is an American icon, it was almost killed because a projected $1 billion cost to overhaul the model seemed too much to Ford planners in 1989. However, a special 400-member group known inside Ford as "Team Mustang" worked for three years, instead of the usual four, and spent only $700 million to redesign the car, 25 percent to 30 percent less than any comparable new car program in Ford's recent history. The new model went on sale on December 9, 1993.

The Mustang team broke many of the rules that govern product development in the rigidly disciplined corporation. As the Mustang team fleshed out the plan in mid-1990, it agreed that the Mustang effort would need unprecedented freedom to make decisions without waiting for approval from headquarters or other departments. Team members wanted to think of themselves as independent stockholders of a "Mustang Car Co.," which happened to be financed by Ford.

The plan called for putting everyone involved under one roof—drafters sitting next to "bean counters," engineers one room away from stylists. That meant breaching the budgetary walls that divided departments and persuading department managers to cede some control over their subordinates. One of the boldest decisions was that Mr. Hothi, the program's manufacturing chief, would get veto power over changes to the body that threatened to derail his efforts to build the car with many of the factory tools used for the old one. All this cut sharply against the grain of Ford's corporate culture.

They set up Mustang Car Co. in a converted furniture warehouse in Allen Park, Michigan, a few miles south of Dearborn. They got approval to move engineers from various departments into their cramped offices, then grouped them into "chunk teams" with responsibility for every aspect of a particular piece, or "chunk" of the car.

They also did away with the arduous bidding process most Ford programs endure when selecting suppliers. With no time for that "rain dance" the Mustang team leaders agreed to pick the best available suppliers and simply ask them to join the Mustang process, from the start.

To save time and money, most of the convertible's designs were tested first on computer images, not on actual cars. Unfortunately, what happened on the screen didn't match what happened on the road. In July 1991, Mr. Zevalkink test-drove the first convertible prototype and discovered that it shimmied and shook. With Mr. Boddie's approval, he ordered a crash program to fix it. About a year later, in August 1992, Mr. Zevalkink took another test drive in another prototype convertible. To his dismay, it still shook.

Mr. Zevalkink felt queasy. Without a convertible, the Mustang line would lack its "image car" and miss out on sales. It had to be fixed. But that would mean ordering new reinforcement parts, new tooling. It might also require redesigning wiring and hoses under the hood. All that could make the car miss its September 1993 start-of-production target and overshoot the budget. The team went into a crisis drill. Mr. Boddie assembled a special team of about 50 people to attack the convertible's problems. Suppliers were called in, and round-the-clock work began.

For eight weeks, the team ran a blitz of re-engineering work, computer manipulations and tough budget sessions. Engineers slept on the floors at the Allen Park warehouse. Mr. Boddie was even emboldened to go further. After seeing a new Mercedes-Benz convertible parked in front of a restaurant, he instructed his engineers to get one and take it apart to find the secrets of its smooth ride. The result: Mustang engineers bolted a 25-pound steel cylinder to a spot behind the front fender. On the Mercedes, a similar "damper" muffled vibrations like a finger on a tuning fork. Mustang team leaders say the new convertibles and coupes are ready today.

Source: Joseph B. White and Oscar Suris, "How a 'Skunk Works' Kept Mustang Alive on a Tight Budget," *Wall Street Journal,* September 21, 1993, p. A1.

Questions

1. What factors account for the success of the Mustang new product development project at Ford?

2. Which of the principles of new product development outlined in this chapter did Ford use in the Mustang project?

Glossary

A

360-DEGREE APPRAISAL A performance appraisal by peers, subordinates, superiors, and sometimes clients who are in a position to evaluate a manager's performance.

ACHIEVEMENT ORIENTATION A worldview that values assertiveness, performance, success, and competition.

ADMINISTRATIVE MANAGEMENT The study of how to create an organizational structure that leads to high efficiency and effectiveness.

ADMINISTRATIVE MODEL An approach to decision making that explains why decision making is inherently uncertain and risky and why managers usually make satisfactory rather than optimum decisions.

AGREEABLENESS The tendency to get along well with other people.

ALDERFER'S ERG THEORY The theory that three universal needs–for existence, relatedness, and growth–constitute a hierarchy of needs and motivate behavior. Alderfer proposed that needs at more than one level can be motivational at the same time.

AMBIGUOUS INFORMATION Information that can be interpreted in multiple and often conflicting ways.

APPLICATIONS SOFTWARE Software designed for a specific task or use.

ARTIFICIAL INTELLIGENCE Behavior performed by a machine that, if performed by a human being, would be called intelligent.

ATTITUDE A collection of feelings and beliefs.

ATTRACTION-SELECTION-ATTRITION FRAMEWORK A model that explains how personality may influence organizational culture.

AUTHORITY The power to hold people accountable for their actions and to make decisions concerning the use of organizational resources.

B

BARRIERS TO ENTRY Factors that make it difficult and costly for an organization to enter a particular task environment or industry.

BEHAVIORAL MANAGEMENT The study of how managers should behave to motivate employees and encourage them to perform at high levels and be committed to the achievement of organizational goals.

BENCHMARKING Comparing performance on specific dimensions with the performance of high-performing organizations.

BIAS The systematic tendency to use information about others in ways that result in inaccurate perceptions.

BOTTOM-UP CHANGE Change that is implemented gradually and involves managers and employees at all levels of an organization.

BOUNDARY SPANNING Interacting with individuals and groups outside the organization to obtain valuable information from the task and general environments.

BOUNDARYLESS ORGANIZATION An organization whose members are linked by computers, faxes, computer-aided design systems, and videoteleconferencing and who rarely, if ever, see one another face-to-face.

BOUNDED RATIONALITY Cognitive limitations that constrain one's ability to interpret, process, and act on information.

BRAND LOYALTY Customers' preference for the products of organizations currently existing in the task environment.

BUREAUCRACY A formal system of organization and administration designed to ensure efficiency and effectiveness.

BUREAUCRATIC CONTROL Control of behavior by means of a comprehensive system of rules and standard operating procedures.

BUSINESS TO BUSINESS (B2B) NETWORK A group of organizations that join together and use IT to link themselves to potential global suppliers to increase efficiency and effectiveness.

BUSINESS-LEVEL PLAN Divisional managers' decisions pertaining to divisions' long-term goals, overall strategy, and structure.

BUSINESS-LEVEL STRATEGY A plan that indicates how a division intends to compete against its rivals in an industry.

C

CAFETERIA BENEFIT PLAN A plan from which employees can choose the benefits that they want.

CENTRALIZATION The concentration of authority at the top of the managerial hierarchy.

CHARISMATIC LEADER An enthusiastic, self-confident leader able to clearly communicate his or her vision of how good things could be.

CLAN CONTROL The control exerted on individuals and groups in an organization by shared values, norms, standards of behavior, and expectations.

CLASSICAL DECISION-MAKING MODEL A prescriptive approach to decision making based on the assumption that the decision maker can identify and evaluate all possible alternatives and their consequences and rationally choose the most appropriate course of action.

CLOSED SYSTEM A system that is self-contained and thus not affected by changes occurring in its external environment.

COERCIVE POWER The ability of a manager to punish others.

COLLECTIVE BARGAINING Negotiation between labor unions and managers to resolve conflicts and disputes about issues such as working hours, wages, benefits, working conditions, and job security.

COLLECTIVISM A worldview that values subordination of the individual to the goals of the group and adherence to the principle that people should be judged by their contribution to the group.

COMMAND ECONOMY An economic system in which the government owns all businesses and specifies which and how many goods and services are produced and the prices at which they are sold.

COMMAND GROUP A group composed of subordinates who report to the same supervisor; also called a department or unit.

COMMUNICATION The sharing of information between two or more individuals or groups to reach a common understanding.

COMMUNICATION NETWORKS The pathways along which information flows in groups and teams and throughout the organization.

COMPETITIVE ADVANTAGE The ability of one organization to outperform other organizations because it produces desired goods or services more efficiently and effectively than they do.

COMPETITORS Organizations that produce goods and services that are similar to a particular organization's goods and services.

CONCEPTUAL SKILLS The ability to analyze and diagnose a situation and to distinguish between cause and effect.

CONCURRENT CONTROL Control that gives managers immediate feedback on how efficiently inputs are being transformed into outputs so that managers can correct problems as they arise.

CONCURRENT ENGINEERING The simultaneous design of the product and of the process for manufacturing the product.

CONSCIENTIOUSNESS The tendency to be careful, scrupulous, and persevering.

CONSIDERATION Behavior indicating that a manager trusts, respects, and cares about subordinates.

CONTINGENCY THEORY The idea that the organizational structures and control systems managers choose depend on–are contingent on–characteristics of the external environment in which the organization operates.

CONTINUOUS-PROCESS TECHNOLOGY Technology that is almost totally mechanized and is based on the use of automated machines working in sequence and controlled through computers from a central monitoring station.

CONTRACT BOOK A written agreement that details product development factors such as responsibilities, resource commitments, budgets, time lines, and development milestones.

CONTROL SYSTEMS Formal target-setting, monitoring, evaluation, and feedback systems that provide managers with information about how well the organization's strategy and structure are working.

CONTROLLING Evaluating how well an organization is achieving its goals and taking action to maintain or improve performance; one of the four principal functions of management.

CORE MEMBERS The members of a team who bear primary responsibility for the success of a project and who stay with a project from inception to completion.

CORPORATE-LEVEL PLAN Top management's decisions pertaining to the organization's mission, overall strategy, and structure.

CORPORATE-LEVEL STRATEGY A plan that indicates in which industries and national markets an organization intends to compete.

CREATIVITY A decision maker's ability to discover original and novel ideas that lead to feasible alternative courses of action.

CROSS-FUNCTIONAL TEAM A group of managers from different departments brought together to perform organizational tasks.

CULTURE SHOCK The feelings of surprise and disorientation that people experience when they do not understand the values, folkways, and mores that guide behavior in a culture.

CUSTOMERS Individuals and groups that buy the goods and services that an organization produces.

D

DATA Raw, unsummarized, and unanalyzed facts.

DECISION MAKING The process by which managers respond to opportunities and threats by analyzing options and making determinations about specific organizational goals and courses of action.

DECISION SUPPORT SYSTEM An interactive computer-based management information system that managers can use to make nonroutine decisions.

DECODING Interpreting and trying to make sense of a message.

DELPHI TECHNIQUE A decision-making technique in which group members do not meet face to face but respond in writing to questions posed by the group leader.

DEMOGRAPHIC FORCES Outcomes of changes in, or changing attitudes toward, the characteristics of a population, such as age, gender, ethnic origin, race, sexual orientation, and social class.

DEPARTMENT A group of people who work together and possess similar skills or use the same knowledge, tools, or techniques to perform their jobs.

DEVELOPMENT Building the knowledge and skills of organizational members so that they will be prepared to take on new responsibilities and challenges.

DEVELOPMENTAL CONSIDERATION Behavior a leader engages in to support and encourage followers and help them develop and grow on the job.

DEVIL'S ADVOCACY Critical analysis of a preferred alternative, made in response to challenges raised by a group member who, playing the role of devil's advocate, defends unpopular or opposing alternatives for the sake of argument.

DIALECTICAL INQUIRY Critical analysis of two preferred alternatives in order to find an even better alternative for the organization to adopt.

DIFFERENTIATION STRATEGY Distinguishing an organization's products from the products of competitors in dimensions such as product design, quality, or after-sales service.

DISCIPLINE Obedience, energy, application, and other outward marks of respect for a superior's authority.

DISTRIBUTIVE JUSTICE A moral principle calling for the distribution of pay raises, promotions, and other organizational resources to be based on meaningful contributions that individuals have made and not on personal characteristics over which they have no control.

DISTRIBUTIVE NEGOTIATION Adversarial negotiation in which the parties in conflict compete to win the most resources while conceding as little as possible.

DISTRIBUTORS Organizations that help other organizations sell their goods or services to customers.

DIVERSIFICATION Expanding operations into a new business or industry and producing new goods or services.

DIVERSITY Differences among people in age, gender, race, ethnicity, religion, sexual orientation, socioeconomic background, and capabilities/disabilities.

DIVISION A business unit that has its own set of managers and functions or departments and competes in a distinct industry.

DIVISION OF LABOR Splitting the work to be performed into particular tasks and assigning tasks to individual workers.

DIVISIONAL MANAGERS Managers who control the various divisions of an organization.

DIVISIONAL STRUCTURE An organizational structure composed of separate business units within which are the functions that work together to produce a specific product for a specific customer.

E

ECONOMIC FORCES Interest rates, inflation, unemployment, economic growth, and other factors that affect the general health and well-being of a nation or the regional economy of an organization.

ECONOMIES OF SCALE Cost advantages associated with large operations.

EFFECTIVENESS A measure of the appropriateness of the goals an organization is pursuing and of the degree to which the organization achieves those goals.

EFFICIENCY A measure of how well or productively resources are used to achieve a goal.

EMOTIONAL INTELLIGENCE The ability to understand and manage one's own moods and emotions and the moods and emotions of other people.

EMOTIONS Intense, relatively short-lived feelings.

EMPLOYEE STOCK OPTION A financial instrument that entitles the bearer to buy shares of an organization's stock at a certain price during a certain period of time or under certain conditions.

EMPOWERMENT Expanding employees' tasks and responsibilities.

ENCODING Translating a message into understandable symbols or language.

ENTREPRENEUR An individual who notices opportunities and takes responsibility for mobilizing the resources necessary to produce new and improved goods and services.

ENTREPRENEURSHIP The mobilization of resources to take advantage of an opportunity to provide customers with new or improved goods and services.

ENTROPY The tendency of a system to lose its ability to control itself and thus to dissolve and disintegrate.

ENVIRONMENTAL CHANGE The degree to which forces in the task and general environments change and evolve over time.

EQUAL EMPLOYMENT OPPORTUNITY The equal right of all citizens to the opportunity to obtain employment regardless of their gender, age, race, country of origin, religion, or disabilities.

EQUITY The justice, impartiality, and fairness to which all organizational members are entitled.

EQUITY THEORY A theory of motivation that focuses on people's perceptions of the fairness of their work outcomes relative to their work inputs.

ESCALATING COMMITMENT A source of cognitive bias resulting from the tendency to commit additional resources to a project even if evidence shows that the project is failing.

ESPRIT DE CORPS Shared feelings of comradeship, enthusiasm, or devotion to a common cause among members of a group.

ETHICAL DECISION A decision that reasonable or typical stakeholders would find acceptable because it aids stakeholders, the organization, or society.

ETHICS Moral principles or beliefs about what is right or wrong.

ETHICS OMBUDSMAN An ethics officer who monitors an organization's practices and procedures to be sure they are ethical.

EXECUTIVE SUPPORT SYSTEM A sophisticated version of a decision support system that is designed to meet the needs of top managers.

EXPATRIATE MANAGERS Managers who go abroad to work for a global organization.

EXPECTANCY In expectancy theory, a perception about the extent to which effort results in a certain level of performance.

EXPECTANCY THEORY The theory that motivation will be high when workers believe that high levels of effort lead to high performance and high performance leads to the attainment of desired outcomes.

EXPERT POWER Power that is based in the special knowledge, skills, and expertise that a leader possesses.

EXPERT SYSTEM A management information system that employs human knowledge captured in a computer to solve problems that ordinarily require human expertise.

EXPORTING Making products at home and selling them abroad.

EXTERNAL LOCUS OF CONTROL The tendency to locate responsibility for one's fate within outside forces and to believe that one's own behavior has little impact on outcomes.

EXTINCTION Curtailing the performance of dysfunctional behaviors by eliminating whatever is reinforcing them.

EXTRAVERSION The tendency to experience positive emotions and moods and to feel good about oneself and the rest of the world.

EXTRINSICALLY MOTIVATED BEHAVIOR Behavior that is performed to acquire material or social rewards or to avoid punishment.

F

FACILITIES LAYOUT The operations management technique whose goal is to design the machine-worker interface to increase production system efficiency.

FEEDBACK CONTROL Control that gives managers information about customers' reactions to goods and services so that corrective action can be taken if necessary.

FEEDFORWARD CONTROL Control that allows managers to anticipate problems before they arise.

FILTERING Withholding part of a message out of the mistaken belief that the receiver does not need or will not want the information.

FIRST-LINE MANAGER A manager who is responsible for the daily supervision of nonmanagerial employees.

FLEXIBLE MANUFACTURING Operations management techniques that attempt to reduce the setup costs associated with a production system.

FOCUSED DIFFERENTIATION STRATEGY Serving only one segment of the overall market and trying to be the most differentiated organization serving that segment.

FOCUSED LOW-COST STRATEGY Serving only one segment of the overall market and being the lowest-cost organization serving that segment.

FOLKWAYS The routine social conventions of everyday life.

FORMAL APPRAISAL An appraisal conducted at a set time during the year and based on performance dimensions and measures that were specified in advance.

FORMAL GROUP A group that managers establish to achieve organizational goals.

FRANCHISING Selling to a foreign organization the rights to use a brand name and operating know-how in return for a lump-sum payment and a share of the profits.

FREE-MARKET ECONOMY An economic system in which private enterprise controls production and the interaction of supply and demand determines which and how many goods and services are produced and how much consumers pay for them.

FREE-TRADE DOCTRINE The idea that if each country specializes in the production of the goods and services that it can produce most efficiently, this will make the best use of global resources.

FRIENDSHIP GROUP An informal group composed of employees who enjoy each other's company and socialize with each other.

FUNCTION A unit or department in which people have the same skills or use the same resources to perform their jobs.

FUNCTIONAL MANAGERS Managers who supervise the various functions, such as manufacturing, accounting, and sales, within a division.

FUNCTIONAL STRUCTURE An organizational structure composed of all the departments that an organization requires to produce its goods or services.

FUNCTIONAL-LEVEL PLAN Functional managers' decisions pertaining to the goals that they propose to pursue to help the division attain its business-level goals.

FUNCTIONAL-LEVEL STRATEGY A plan that indicates how a function intends to achieve its goals.

G

GATEKEEPING Deciding what information to allow into the organization and what information to keep out.

GENDER SCHEMAS Preconceived beliefs or ideas about the nature of men and women, their traits, attitudes, behaviors, and preferences.

GENERAL ENVIRONMENT The wide-ranging economic, technological, sociocultural, demographic, political and legal, and global forces that affect an organization and its task environment.

GEOGRAPHIC STRUCTURE An organizational structure in which each region of a country or area of the world is served by a self-contained division.

GLASS CEILING A metaphor alluding to the invisible barriers that prevent minorities and women from being promoted to top corporate positions.

GLOBAL FORCES Outcomes of changes in international relationships, changes in nations' economic, political, and legal systems, and changes in technology, such as falling trade barriers, the growth of representative democracies, and reliable and instantaneous communication.

GLOBAL ORGANIZATION An organization that operates and competes in more than one country.

GLOBAL OUTSOURCING The purchase of inputs from foreign suppliers, or the production of inputs abroad, to lower production costs and improve product quality or design.

GLOBAL STRATEGY Selling the same standardized product and using the same basic marketing approach in each national market.

GOAL-SETTING THEORY A theory that focuses on identifying the types of goals that are most effective in producing high levels of motivation and performance and explaining why goals have these effects.

GRAPEVINE An informal communication network along which unofficial information flows.

GROUP Two or more people who interact with each other to accomplish certain goals or meet certain needs.

GROUP COHESIVENESS The degree to which members are attracted or loyal to a group.

GROUP DECISION SUPPORT SYSTEM An executive support system that links top managers so that they can function as a team.

GROUP NORMS Shared guidelines or rules for behavior that most group members follow.

GROUP ROLE A set of behaviors and tasks that a member of a group is expected to perform because of his or her position in the group.

GROUPTHINK A pattern of faulty and biased decision making that occurs in groups whose members strive for agreement among themselves at the expense of accurately assessing information relevant to a decision.

GROUPWARE Computer software that enables members of groups and teams to share information with each other.

H

HAWTHORNE EFFECT The finding that a manager's behavior or leadership approach can affect workers' level of performance.

HERZBERG'S MOTIVATOR-HYGIENE THEORY A need theory that distinguishes between motivator needs (related to the nature of the work itself) and hygiene needs (related to the physical and psychological context in which the work is performed) and proposes that motivator needs must be met for motivation and job satisfaction to be high.

HEURISTICS Rules of thumb that simplify decision making.

HIERARCHY OF AUTHORITY An organization's chain of command, specifying the relative authority of each manager.

HOSTILE WORK ENVIRONMENT SEXUAL HARASSMENT Telling lewd jokes, displaying pornography, making sexually oriented remarks about someone's personal appearance, and other sex-related actions that make the work environment unpleasant.

HUMAN RELATIONS MOVEMENT Advocates of the idea that supervisors receive behavioral training to manage subordinates in ways that elicit their cooperation and increase their productivity.

HUMAN RESOURCE MANAGEMENT Activities that managers engage in to attract and retain employees and to ensure that they perform at a high level and contribute to the accomplishment of organizational goals.

HUMAN RESOURCE PLANNING Activities that managers engage in to forecast their current and future needs for human resources.

HUMAN SKILLS The ability to understand, alter, lead, and control the behavior of other individuals and groups.

HYBRID STRUCTURE The structure of a large organization that has many divisions and simultaneously uses many different organizational structures.

I

ILLUSION OF CONTROL A source of cognitive bias resulting from the tendency to overestimate one's own ability to control activities and events.

IMPORTING Selling at home products that are made abroad.

INCREMENTAL PRODUCT INNOVATIONS Products that result from incremental technological changes.

INCREMENTAL TECHNOLOGICAL CHANGE Change that refines existing technology and leads to gradual improvements or refinements in products over time.

INDIVIDUAL ETHICS Personal standards that govern how individuals are to interact with other people.

INDIVIDUALISM A worldview that values individual freedom and self-expression and adherence to the principle that people should be judged by their individual achievements rather than by their social background.

INDUSTRY LIFE CYCLE The changes that take place in an industry as it goes through the stages of birth, growth, shakeout, maturity, and decline.

INEQUITY Lack of fairness.

INFORMAL APPRAISAL An unscheduled appraisal of ongoing progress and areas for improvement.

INFORMAL GROUP A group that managers or nonmanagerial employees form to help achieve their own goals or meet their own needs.

INFORMAL ORGANIZATION The system of behavioral rules and norms that emerge in a group.

INFORMATION Data that is organized in a meaningful fashion.

INFORMATION DISTORTION Changes in the meaning of a message as the message passes through a series of senders and receivers.

INFORMATION OVERLOAD The potential for important information to be ignored or overlooked while tangential information receives attention.

INFORMATION RICHNESS The amount of information that a communication medium can carry and the extent to which the medium enables the sender and receiver to reach a common understanding.

INFORMATION SYSTEM A system for acquiring, organizing, storing, manipulating, and transmitting information.

INFORMATION TECHNOLOGY The means by which information is acquired, organized, stored, manipulated, and transmitted.

INITIATING STRUCTURE Behavior that managers engage in to ensure that work gets done, subordinates perform their jobs acceptably, and the organization is efficient and effective.

INITIATIVE The ability to act on one's own, without direction from a superior.

INPUT Anything a person contributes to his or her job or organization.

INSTRUMENTAL VALUE A mode of conduct that an individual seeks to follow.

INSTRUMENTALITY In expectancy theory, a perception about the extent to which performance results in the attainment of outcomes.

INTEGRATING MECHANISMS Organizing tools that managers can use to increase communication and coordination among functions and divisions.

INTEGRATIVE BARGAINING Cooperative negotiation in which the parties in conflict work together to achieve a resolution that is good for them both.

INTELLECTUAL STIMULATION Behavior a leader engages in to make followers aware of problems and view these problems in new ways, consistent with the leader's vision.

INTEREST GROUP An informal group composed of employees seeking to achieve a common goal related to their membership in an organization.

INTERNAL LOCUS OF CONTROL The tendency to locate responsibility for one's fate within oneself.

INTERNET A global system of computer networks.

INTRANET A companywide system of computer networks.

INTRAPRENEUR A manager, scientist, or researcher who works inside an existing organization and notices opportunities for product improvements and is responsible for managing the product development process.

INTRINSICALLY MOTIVATED BEHAVIOR Behavior that is performed for its own sake.

INTUITION Ability to make sound decisions based on one's past experience and immediate feelings about the information at hand.

INVENTORY The stock of raw materials, inputs, and component parts that an organization has on hand at a particular time.

J

JARGON Specialized language that members of an occupation, group, or organization develop to facilitate communication among themselves.

JOB ANALYSIS Identifying the tasks, duties, and responsibilities that make up a job and the knowledge, skills, and abilities needed to perform the job.

JOB DESIGN The process by which managers decide how to divide tasks into specific jobs.

JOB ENLARGEMENT Increasing the number of different tasks in a given job by changing the division of labor.

JOB ENRICHMENT Increasing the degree of responsibility a worker has over his or her job.

JOB SATISFACTION The collection of feelings and beliefs that managers have about their current jobs.

JOB SIMPLIFICATION The process of reducing the number of tasks that each worker performs.

JOB SPECIALIZATION The process by which a division of labor occurs as different workers specialize in different tasks over time.

JOINT VENTURE A strategic alliance among two or more companies that agree to jointly establish and share the ownership of a new business.

JUDGMENT Ability to develop a sound opinion based on one's evaluation of the importance of the information at hand.

JUST-IN-TIME INVENTORY SYSTEM A system in which parts or supplies arrive at an organization when they are needed, not before.

K

KNOWLEDGE MANAGEMENT The sharing and integrating of expertise within and between functions and divisions through realtime, interconnected IT.

KNOWLEDGE MANAGEMENT SYSTEM A company-specific virtual information system that allows workers to share their knowledge and expertise and find others to help solve ongoing problems.

L

LABOR RELATIONS The activities that managers engage in to ensure that they have effective working relationships with the labor unions that represent their employees' interests.

LATERAL MOVE A job change that entails no major changes in responsibility or authority levels.

LEADER An individual who is able to exert influence over other people to help achieve group or organizational goals.

LEADER-MEMBER RELATIONS The extent to which followers like, trust, and are loyal to their leader; a determinant of how favorable a situation is for leading.

LEADERSHIP The process by which an individual exerts influence over other people and inspires, motivates, and directs their activities to help achieve group or organizational goals.

LEADERSHIP SUBSTITUTE Characteristics of subordinates or characteristics of a situation or context that act in place of the influence of a leader and make leadership unnecessary.

LEADING Articulating a clear vision and energizing and enabling organizational members so that they understand the part they play in achieving organizational goals; one of the four principal functions of management.

LEARNING A relatively permanent change in knowledge or behavior that results from practice or experience.

LEARNING ORGANIZATION An organization in which managers try to maximize the ability of individuals and groups to think and behave creatively and thus maximize the potential for organizational learning to take place.

LEARNING THEORIES Theories that focus on increasing employee motivation and performance by linking the outcomes that employees receive to the performance of desired behaviors and the attainment of goals.

LEGITIMATE POWER The authority that a manager has by virtue of his or her position in an organization's hierarchy.

LICENSING Allowing a foreign organization to take charge of manufacturing and distributing a product in its country or world region in return for a negotiated fee.

LINE MANAGER Someone in the direct line or chain of command who has formal authority over people and resources lower down.

LINE OF AUTHORITY The chain of command extending from the top to the bottom of an organization.

LINGUISTIC STYLE A person's characteristic way of speaking.

LONG-TERM ORIENTATION A worldview that values thrift and persistence in achieving goals.

LOW-COST STRATEGY Driving the organization's costs down below the costs of its rivals.

M

MANAGEMENT The planning, organizing, leading, and controlling of human and other resources to achieve organizational goals effectively and efficiently.

MANAGEMENT BY OBJECTIVES A goal-setting process in which a manager and his or her subordinates negotiate specific goals and objectives for the subordinate to achieve and then periodically evaluate the extent to which the subordinate is achieving those goals.

MANAGEMENT BY WANDERING AROUND A face-to-face communication technique in which a manager walks around a work area and talks informally with employees about issues and concerns.

MANAGEMENT INFORMATION SYSTEM An information system that managers plan and design to provide themselves with the specific information they need.

MANAGEMENT SCIENCE THEORY An approach to management that uses rigorous quantitative techniques to help managers make maximum use of organizational resources.

MARKET STRUCTURE An organizational structure in which each kind of customer is served by a self-contained division; also called customer structure.

MASLOW'S HIERARCHY OF NEEDS An arrangement of five basic needs that, according to Maslow, motivate behavior. Maslow proposed that the lowest level of unmet needs is the prime motivator and that only one level of needs is motivational at a time.

MASS-PRODUCTION TECHNOLOGY Technology that is based on the use of automated machines that are programmed to perform the same operations over and over.

MATRIX STRUCTURE An organizational structure that simultaneously groups people and resources by function and by product.

MECHANISTIC STRUCTURE An organizational structure in which authority is centralized, tasks and rules are clearly specified, and employees are closely supervised.

MEDIUM The pathway through which an encoded message is transmitted to a receiver.

MENTORING A process by which an experienced member of an organization (the mentor) provides advice and guidance to a less experienced member (the protégé) and helps the less experienced member learn how to advance in the organization and in his or her career.

MERIT PAY PLAN A compensation plan that bases pay on performance.

MESSAGE The information that a sender wants to share.

MIDDLE MANAGER A manager who supervises first-line managers and is responsible for finding the best way to use resources to achieve organizational goals.

MISSION STATEMENT A broad declaration of an organization's purpose that identifies the organization's products and customers and distinguishes the organization from its competitors.

MIXED ECONOMY An economic system in which some sectors of the economy are left to private ownership and free-market mechanisms and others are owned by the government and subject to government planning.

MOOD A feeling or state of mind.

MORES Norms that are considered to be central to the functioning of society and to social life.

MOTIVATION Psychological forces that determine the direction of a person's behavior in an organization, a person's level of effort, and a person's level of persistence.

MULTIDOMESTIC STRATEGY Customizing products and marketing strategies to specific national conditions.

N

NATIONAL CULTURE The set of values that a society considers important and the norms of behavior that are approved or sanctioned in that society.

NEED A requirement or necessity for survival and well-being.

NEED FOR ACHIEVEMENT The extent to which an individual has a strong desire to perform challenging tasks well and to meet personal standards for excellence.

NEED FOR AFFILIATION The extent to which an individual is concerned about establishing and maintaining good interpersonal relations, being liked, and having other people around them get along with each other.

NEED FOR POWER The extent to which an individual desires to control or influence others.

NEED THEORIES Theories of motivation that focus on what needs people are trying to satisfy at work and what outcomes will satisfy those needs.

NEEDS ASSESSMENT An assessment of which employees need training or development and what type of skills or knowledge they need to acquire.

NEGATIVE AFFECTIVITY The tendency to experience negative emotions and moods, to feel distressed, and to be critical of oneself and others.

NEGATIVE REINFORCEMENT Eliminating or removing undesired outcomes when people perform organizationally functional behaviors.

NEGOTIATION A method of conflict resolution in which the two parties in conflict consider various alternative ways to allocate resources to each other in order to come up with a solution acceptable to them both.

NETWORK STRUCTURE A series of strategic alliances that an organization creates with suppliers, manufacturers, and distributors to produce and market a product.

NETWORKING The exchange of information through a group or network of interlinked computers.

NEW VENTURE DIVISION An autonomous division that is given all the resources it needs to develop and market a new product.

NOISE Anything that hampers any stage of the communication process.

NOMINAL GROUP TECHNIQUE A decision-making technique in which group members write down ideas and solutions, read their suggestions to the whole group, and discuss and then rank the alternatives.

NONPROGRAMMED DECISION MAKING Nonroutine decision making that occurs in response to unusual, unpredictable opportunities and threats.

NONVERBAL COMMUNICATION The encoding of messages by means of facial expressions, body language, and styles of dress.

NORMS Unwritten rules and codes of conduct that prescribe how people should act in particular situations.

NURTURING ORIENTATION A worldview that values the quality of life, warm personal friendships, and services and care for the weak.

O

OBJECTIVE APPRAISAL An appraisal that is based on facts and is likely to be numerical.

ON-THE-JOB TRAINING Training that takes place in the work setting as employees perform their job tasks.

OPEN SYSTEM A system that takes in resources from its external environment and converts them into goods and services that are then sent back to that environment for purchase by customers.

OPENNESS TO EXPERIENCE The tendency to be original, have broad interests, be open to a wide range of stimuli, be daring, and take risks.

OPERANT CONDITIONING THEORY The theory that people learn to perform behaviors that lead to desired consequences and learn not to perform behaviors that lead to undesired consequences.

OPERATING BUDGET A budget that states how managers intend to use organizational resources to achieve organizational goals.

OPERATING SYSTEM SOFTWARE Software that tells computer hardware how to run.

OPERATIONS INFORMATION SYSTEM A management information system that gathers, organizes, and summarizes comprehensive data in a form that managers can use in their nonroutine coordinating, controlling, and decision-making tasks.

OPERATIONS MANAGEMENT The management of any aspect of the production system that transforms inputs into finished goods and services.

OPERATIONS MANAGER A manager who is responsible for managing an organization's production system and for determining where operating improvements might be made.

OPTIMUM DECISION The most appropriate decision in light of what managers believe to be the most desirable future consequences for their organization.

ORDER The methodical arrangement of positions to provide the organization with the greatest benefit and to provide employees with career opportunities.

ORGANIC STRUCTURE An organizational structure in which authority is decentralized to middle and first-line managers and tasks and roles are left ambiguous to encourage employees to cooperate and respond quickly to the unexpected.

ORGANIZATIONAL ARCHITECTURE The organizational structure, control systems, culture, and human resource management systems that together determine how efficiently and effectively organizational resources are used.

ORGANIZATIONAL BEHAVIOR The study of the factors that have an impact on how individuals and groups respond to and act in organizations.

ORGANIZATIONAL BEHAVIOR MODIFICATION The systematic application of operant conditioning techniques to promote the performance of organizationally functional behaviors and discourage the performance of dysfunctional behaviors.

ORGANIZATIONAL CITIZENSHIP BEHAVIORS Behaviors that are not required of organizational members but that contribute to and are necessary for organizational efficiency, effectiveness, and gaining a competitive advantage.

ORGANIZATIONAL COMMITMENT The collection of feelings and beliefs that managers have about their organization as a whole.

ORGANIZATIONAL CONFLICT The discord that arises when the goals, interests, or values of different individuals or groups are incompatible and those individuals or groups block or thwart each other's attempts to achieve their objectives.

ORGANIZATIONAL CULTURE The set of values, norms, standards for behavior, and shared expectations that influence the ways in which individuals, groups, and teams interact with each other and cooperate to achieve organizational goals.

ORGANIZATIONAL DESIGN The process by which managers make specific organizing choices that result in a particular kind of organizational structure.

ORGANIZATIONAL ENVIRONMENT The set of forces and conditions that operate beyond an organization's boundaries but affect a manager's ability to acquire and utilize resources.

ORGANIZATIONAL LEARNING The process through which managers seek to improve employees' desire and ability to understand and manage the organization and its task environment.

ORGANIZATIONAL PERFORMANCE A measure of how efficiently and effectively a manager uses resources to satisfy customers and achieve organizational goals.

ORGANIZATIONAL POLITICS Activities that managers engage in to increase their power and to use power effectively to achieve their goals and overcome resistance or opposition.

ORGANIZATIONAL SOCIALIZATION The process by which newcomers learn an organization's values and norms and acquire the work behaviors necessary to perform jobs effectively.

ORGANIZATIONAL STAKEHOLDERS Shareholders, employees, customers, suppliers, and others who have an interest, claim, or stake in an organization and in what it does.

ORGANIZATIONAL STRUCTURE A formal system of task and reporting relationships that coordinates and motivates organizational members so that they work together to achieve organizational goals.

ORGANIZING Structuring working relationships in a way that allows organizational members to work together to achieve organizational goals; one of the four principal functions of management.

OUTCOME Anything a person gets from a job or organization.

OUTSOURCE To use outside suppliers and manufacturers to produce goods and services.

OVERPAYMENT INEQUITY The inequity that exists when a person perceives that his or her own outcome/input ratio is greater than the ratio of a referent.

OVERT DISCRIMINATION Knowingly and willingly denying diverse individuals access to opportunities and outcomes in an organization.

P

PATH-GOAL THEORY A contingency model of leadership proposing that leaders can motivate subordinates by identifying their desired outcomes, rewarding them for high performance and the attainment of work goals with these desired outcomes, and clarifying for them the paths leading to the attainment of work goals.

PAY LEVEL The relative position of an organization's pay incentives in comparison with those of other organizations in the same industry employing similar kinds or workers.

PAY STRUCTURE The arrangement of jobs into categories reflecting their relative importance to the organization and its goals, level of skill required, and other characteristics.

PERCEPTION The process through which people select, organize, and interpret what they see, hear, touch, smell, and taste, to give meaning and order to the world around them.

PERFORMANCE APPRAISAL The evaluation of employees' job performance and contributions to their organization.

PERFORMANCE FEEDBACK The process through which managers share performance appraisal information with subordinates, give subordinates an opportunity to reflect on their own performance, and develop, with subordinates, plans for the future.

PERSONALITY TRAITS Enduring tendencies to feel, think, and act in certain ways.

PLANNING Identifying and selecting appropriate goals and courses of action; one of the four principal functions of management.

POLITICAL AND LEGAL FORCES Outcomes of changes in laws and regulations, such as the deregulation of industries, the privatization of organizations, and increased emphasis on environmental protection.

POLITICAL STRATEGIES Tactics that managers use to increase their power and to use power effectively to influence and gain the support of other people while overcoming resistance or opposition.

POOLED TASK INTERDEPENDENCE The task interdependence that exists when group members make separate and independent contributions to group performance.

POSITION POWER The amount of legitimate, reward, and coercive power that a leader has by virtue of his or her position in an organization; a determinant of how favorable a situation is for leading.

POSITIVE REINFORCEMENT Giving people outcomes they desire when they perform organizationally functional behaviors.

POTENTIAL COMPETITORS Organizations that presently are not in a task environment but could enter if they so chose.

POWER DISTANCE The degree to which societies accept the idea that inequalities in the power and well-being of their citizens are due to differences in individuals' physical and intellectual capabilities and heritage.

PRIOR HYPOTHESIS BIAS A cognitive bias resulting from the tendency to base decisions on strong prior beliefs even if evidence shows that those beliefs are wrong.

PROCEDURAL JUSTICE A moral principle calling for the use of fair procedures to determine how to distribute outcomes to organizational members.

PROCESS REENGINEERING The fundamental rethinking and radical redesign of business processes to achieve dramatic improvement in critical measures of performance such as cost, quality, service, and speed.

PRODUCT CHAMPION A manager who takes "ownership" of a project and provides the leadership and vision that take a product from the idea stage to the final customer.

PRODUCT DEVELOPMENT PLAN A plan that specifies all of the relevant information that managers need in order to decide whether to proceed with a full-blown product development effort.

PRODUCT LIFE CYCLE Changes in demand for a product that occur from its introduction through its growth and maturity to its decline.

PRODUCT STRUCTURE An organizational structure in which each product line or business is handled by a self-contained division.

PRODUCT TEAM STRUCTURE An organizational structure in which employees are permanently assigned to a cross-functional team and report only to the product team manager or to one of his or her direct subordinates.

PRODUCTION BLOCKING A loss of productivity in brainstorming sessions due to the unstructured nature of brainstorming.

PRODUCTION SYSTEM The system that an organization uses to acquire inputs, convert the inputs into outputs, and dispose of the outputs.

PROFESSIONAL ETHICS Standards that govern how members of a profession are to make decisions when the way they should behave is not clear-cut.

PROGRAMMED DECISION MAKING Routine, virtually automatic decision making that follows established rules or guidelines.

PUNISHMENT Administering an undesired or negative consequence when dysfunctional behavior occurs.

Q

QUALITY CIRCLES Groups of employees who meet regularly to discuss ways to increase quality.

QUANTUM PRODUCT INNOVATIONS Products that result from quantum technological changes.

QUANTUM TECHNOLOGICAL CHANGE A fundamental shift in technology that results in the innovation of new kinds of goods and services.

QUID PRO QUO SEXUAL HARASSMENT Asking for or forcing an employee to perform sexual favors in exchange for some reward or to avoid negative consequences.

R

REALISTIC JOB PREVIEW An honest assessment of the advantages and disadvantages of a job and organization.

REAL-TIME INFORMATION Frequently updated information that reflects current conditions.

RECEIVER The person or group for which a message is intended.

RECIPROCAL TASK INTERDEPENDENCE The task interdependence that exists when the work performed by each group member is fully dependent on the work performed by other group members.

RECRUITMENT Activities that managers engage in to develop a pool of qualified candidates for open positions.

REFERENT POWER Power that comes from subordinates' and co-workers' respect, admiration, and loyalty.

RELATED DIVERSIFICATION Entering a new business or industry to create a competitive advantage in one or more of an organization's existing divisions or businesses.

RELATIONSHIP-ORIENTED LEADERS Leaders whose primary concern is to develop good relationships with their subordinates and to be liked by them.

RELIABILITY The degree to which a tool or test measures the same thing each time it is used.

REPRESENTATIVE DEMOCRACY A political system in which representatives elected by citizens and legally accountable to the electorate form a government whose function is to make decisions on behalf of the electorate.

REPRESENTATIVENESS BIAS A cognitive bias resulting from the tendency to generalize inappropriately from a small sample or from a single vivid event or episode.

REPUTATION The esteem or high repute that individuals or organizations gain when they behave ethically.

RESEARCH AND DEVELOPMENT TEAM A team whose members have the expertise and experience needed to develop new products.

RESTRUCTURING Downsizing an organization by eliminating the jobs of large numbers of top, middle, and first-line managers and nonmanagerial employees.

REWARD POWER The ability of a manager to give or withhold tangible and intangible rewards.

RISK The degree of probability that the possible outcomes of a particular course of action will occur.

ROLE The specific tasks that a person is expected to perform because of the position he or she holds in an organization.

ROLE MAKING Taking the initiative to modify an assigned role by assuming additional responsibilities.

RULES Formal written instructions that specify actions to be taken under different circumstances to achieve specific goals.

RUMORS Unofficial pieces of information of interest to organizational members but with no identifiable source.

S

SATISFICING Searching for and choosing an acceptable, or satisfactory, response to problems and opportunities, rather than trying to make the best decision.

SCENARIO PLANNING The generation of multiple forecasts of future conditions followed by an analysis of how to respond effectively to each of those conditions; also called contingency planning.

SCHEMA An abstract knowledge structure that is stored in memory and makes possible the interpretation and organization of information about a person, event, or situation.

SCIENTIFIC MANAGEMENT The systematic study of relationships between people and tasks for the purpose of redesigning the work process to increase efficiency.

SELECTION The process that managers use to determine the relative qualifications of job applicants and their potential for performing well in a particular job.

SELF-EFFICACY A person's belief about his or her ability to perform a behavior successfully.

SELF-ESTEEM The degree to which individuals feel good about themselves and their capabilities.

SELF-MANAGED WORK TEAM A group of employees who supervise their own activities and monitor the quality of the goods and services they provide.

SELF-REINFORCER Any desired or attractive outcome or reward that a person gives to himself or herself for good performance.

SENDER The person or group wishing to share information.

SEQUENTIAL TASK INTERDEPENDENCE The task interdependence that exists when group members must perform specific tasks in a predetermined order.

SHORT-TERM ORIENTATION A worldview that values personal stability or happiness and living for the present.

SKUNKWORKS A group of intrapreneurs who are deliberately separated from the normal operation of an organization to encourage them to devote all their attention to developing new products.

SMALL-BATCH TECHNOLOGY Technology that is used to produce small quantities of customized, one-of-a-kind products and is based on the skills of people who work together in small groups.

SOCIAL LEARNING THEORY A theory that takes into account how learning and motivation are influenced by people's thoughts and beliefs and their observations of other people's behavior.

SOCIAL LOAFING The tendency of individuals to put forth less effort when they work in groups than when they work alone.

SOCIAL RESPONSIBILITY A manager's duty or obligation to make decisions that promote the welfare and well-being of stakeholders and society as a whole.

SOCIAL STRUCTURE The arrangement of relationships between individuals and groups in a society.

SOCIETAL ETHICS Standards that govern how members of a society are to deal with each other on issues such as fairness, justice, poverty, and the rights of the individual.

SOCIOCULTURAL FORCES Pressures emanating from the social structure of a country or society or from the national culture.

SPAN OF CONTROL The number of subordinates who report directly to a manager.

STAFF MANAGER A manager responsible for managing one of McDonald's specialist functions, like finance or marketing.

STAGE-GATE DEVELOPMENT FUNNEL A planning model that forces managers to make choices among competing projects so that organizational resources are not spread thinly over too many projects.

STANDARD OPERATING PROCEDURES Specific sets of written instructions about how to perform a certain aspect of a task.

STEREOTYPE Simplistic and often inaccurate beliefs about the typical characteristics of particular groups of people.

STRATEGIC ALLIANCE An agreement in which managers pool or share their organization's resources and know-how with a foreign company, and the two organizations share the rewards and risks of starting a new venture.

STRATEGIC HUMAN RESOURCE MANAGEMENT The process by which managers design the components of a human resource management system to be consistent with each other, with other elements of organizational architecture, and with the organization's strategy and goals.

STRATEGY A cluster of decisions about what goals to pursue, what actions to take, and how to use resources to achieve goals.

STRATEGY FORMULATION Analysis of an organization's current situation followed by the development of strategies to accomplish its mission and achieve its goals.

SUBJECTIVE APPRAISAL An appraisal that is based on perceptions of traits, behaviors, or results.

SUPPLIERS Individuals and organizations that provide an organization with the input resources that it needs to produce goods and services.

SWOT ANALYSIS A planning exercise in which managers identify organizational strengths (S), weaknesses (W), environmental opportunities (O), and threats (T).

SYNERGY Performance gains that result when individuals and departments coordinate their actions.

SYSTEMATIC ERRORS Errors that people make over and over and that result in poor decision making.

T

TARIFF A tax that a government imposes on imported or, occasionally, exported goods.

TASK ENVIRONMENT The set of forces and conditions that originate with suppliers, distributors, customers, and competitors and affect an organization's ability to obtain inputs and dispose of its outputs because they influence managers on a daily basis.

TASK FORCE A committee of managers or nonmanagerial employees from various departments or divisions who meet to solve a specific, mutual problem; also called an ad hoc committee.

TASK INTERDEPENDENCE The degree to which the work performed by one member of a group influences the work performed by other members.

TASK STRUCTURE The extent to which the work to be performed is clear-cut so that a leader's subordinates know what needs to be accomplished and how to go about doing it; a determinant of how favorable a situation is for leading.

TASK-ORIENTED LEADERS Leaders whose primary concern is to ensure that subordinates perform at a high level.

TEAM A group whose members work intensely with each other to achieve a specific, common goal or objective.

TECHNICAL SKILLS Job-specific knowledge and techniques that are required to perform an organizational role.

TECHNOLOGICAL FORCES Outcomes of changes in the technology that managers use to design, produce, or distribute goods and services.

TECHNOLOGY The combination of skills and equipment that managers use in the design, production, and distribution of goods and services.

TERMINAL VALUE A lifelong goal or objective that an individual seeks to achieve.

THEORY X Negative assumptions about workers that lead to the conclusion that a manager's task is to supervise them closely and control their behavior.

THEORY Y Positive assumptions about workers that lead to the conclusion that a manager's task is to create a work setting that encourages commitment to organizational goals and provides opportunities for workers to be imaginative and to exercise initiative and self-direction.

TIME HORIZON The intended duration of a plan.

TOP MANAGER A manager who establishes organizational goals, decides how departments should interact, and monitors the performance of middle managers.

TOP-DOWN CHANGE Change that is implemented quickly throughout an organization by upper-level managers.

TOP-MANAGEMENT TEAM A group composed of the CEO, COO president, and the heads of the most important departments.

TOTAL QUALITY MANAGEMENT A management technique that focuses on improving the quality of an organization's products and services.

TOTALITARIAN REGIME A political system in which a single party, individual, or group holds all political power and neither recognizes nor permits opposition.

TRAINING Teaching organizational members how to perform their current jobs and helping them acquire the knowledge and skills they need to be effective performers.

TRANSACTIONAL LEADERSHIP Leadership that motivates subordinates by rewarding high performance and reprimanding them for low performance.

TRANSACTION-PROCESSING SYSTEM A management information system designed to handle large volumes of routine, recurring transactions.

TRANSFORMATIONAL LEADERSHIP Leadership that makes subordinates aware of the importance of their jobs and performance to the organization and aware of their own needs for personal growth and that motivates subordinates to work for the good of the organization.

U

UNCERTAINTY Unpredictability.

UNCERTAINTY AVOIDANCE The degree to which societies are willing to tolerate uncertainty and risk.

UNDERPAYMENT INEQUITY The inequity that exists when a person perceives that his or her own outcome/input ratio is less than the ratio of a referent.

UNETHICAL DECISION A decision that a manager would prefer to disguise or hide from other people because it enables a company or a particular individual to gain at the expense of society or other stakeholders.

UNITY OF COMMAND A reporting relationship in which an employee receives orders from, and reports to, only one superior.

UNITY OF DIRECTION The singleness of purpose that makes possible the creation of one plan of action to guide managers and workers as they use organizational resources.

UNRELATED DIVERSIFICATION Entering a new industry or buying a company in a new industry that is not related in any way to an organization's current businesses or industries.

V

VALENCE In expectancy theory, how desirable each of the outcomes available from a job or organization is to a person.

VALIDITY The degree to which a tool or test measures what it purports to measure.

VALUES Ideas about what a society believes to be good, right, desirable, or beautiful.

VALUE SYSTEM The terminal and instrumental values that are guiding principles in an individual's life.

VERBAL COMMUNICATION The encoding of messages into words, either written or spoken.

VERTICAL INTEGRATION A strategy that allows an organization to create value by producing its own inputs or distributing and selling its own outputs.

VICARIOUS LEARNING Learning that occurs when the learner becomes motivated to perform a behavior by watching another person perform it; also called observational learning.

VIRTUAL TEAM A team whose members rarely or never meet face to face and interact by using various forms of information technology such as email, computer networks, telephone, fax, and video conferences.

W

WHOLLY OWNED FOREIGN SUBSIDIARY Production operations established in a foreign country independent of any local direct involvement.

Credits

Notes

Chapter 1

1. www.aol-timewarner.com, 2001.

2. C. Yang; R.Grover; and A. T. Palmer, "Show Time for AOL-Time Warner," *Business Week,* January 15, 2001, 57–64.

3. Ibid.

4. S. Prasso, "AOL-Time Warner's Power Towers," *Business Week,* June 11, 2001, 43.

5. G. R. Jones, *Organizational Theory* (Reading, MA: Addison-Wesley, 1995).

6. J. P. Campbell, "On the Nature of Organizational Effectiveness," in P. S. Goodman, J. M. Pennings, and others, *New Perspectives on Organizational Effectiveness* (San Francisco: Jossey Bass, 1977).

7. www.yahoo.marketguide.com. AOL-Time Warner, June 14, 2001.

8. H. Fayol, *General and Industrial Management* (New York: IEEE Press, 1984). Fayol actually identified five different managerial functions but most scholars today believe these four capture the essence of Fayol's ideas.

9. P. F. Drucker, *Management Tasks, Responsibilities, and Practices* (New York: Harper and Row, 1974).

10. D. McGraw, "The Kid Bytes Back," *U. S. News & World Report,* December 12, 1994, 70–71.

11. www.dell.com, press release, 2001.

12. J. A. Byrne, "A Potent Ingredient in Pepsi's Formula," *Business Week,* April 10, 2001, 180.

13. J. A. Byrne, "PepsiCo's New Formula," *Business Week,* April 10, 2000, 172–80.

14. www.pepsico.com, 2001.

15. N. Byrnes, "The Power of Two at PepsiCo," *Business Week,* January 29, 2001, 102–104.

16. www.pepsico.com, press release, May 2001.

17 G. McWilliams, "Lean Machine, How Dell Fine-Tunes Its PC Pricing to Gain Edge in a Slow Market," *The Wall Street Journal,* June 8, 2001, A.1.

18. J. Kotter, *The General Managers* (New York: Free Press, 1992).

19. C. P. Hales, "What Do Managers Do? A Critical Review of the Evidence," *Journal of Management Studies* (January 1986): 88–115; A. I. Kraul; P. R. Pedigo; D. D. McKenna; and M. D. Dunnette, "The Role of the Manager: What's Really Important in Different Management Jobs," *Academy of Management Executive,* November 1989, 286–93.

20. A. K. Gupta, "Contingency Perspectives on Strategic Leadership," in D. C. Hambrick, ed., *The Executive Effect: Concepts and Methods for Studying Top Managers* (Greenwich, CT: JAI Press, 1988), 147–78.

21. D. G. Ancona, "Top Management Teams: Preparing for the Revolution," in J. S. Carroll, ed., *Applied Social Psychology and Organizational Settings* (Hillsdale, NJ: Erlbaum, 1990); D. C. Hambrick and P. A Mason, "Upper Echelons: The Organization as a Reflection of Its Top Managers," *Academy of Management Journal* 9 (1984): 193–206.

22. T. A. Mahony; T. H. Jerdee; and S. J. Carroll, "The Jobs of Management," *Industrial Relations* 4 (1965): 97–110; L. Gomez-Mejia, J. McCann, and R. C. Page, "The Structure of Managerial Behaviors and Rewards," *Industrial Relations* 24 (1985): 147–54.

23. R. Stewart, "Middle Managers: Their Jobs and Behaviors," in J. W. Lorsch, ed., *Handbook of Organizational Behavior* (Englewood Cliffs, NJ: Prentice-Hall, 1987), 385–91.

24. K. Labich, "Making over Middle Managers," *Fortune,* May 8, 1989, 58–64.

25. B. Wysocki, "Some Companies Cut Costs Too Far, Suffer from Corporate Anorexia," *The Wall Street Journal,* July 5, 1995, A1.

26. W. Cascio, "Downsizing: What Do We Know? What Have We Learned?" *Academy of Management Executive,* February 1993, 95–104.

27. S. R. Parker; T. D. Wall; and P. R. Jackson, "That's Not My Job: Developing Flexible Work Orientations," *Academy of Management Journal* 40 (1997): 899–929

28. B. Dumaine, "The New Non-Manager," *Fortune,* February 22, 1993, 80–84.

29. A. Williams, "Arthur Andersen–IT Initiatives Support Shifts in Business Strategy," *Information Week,* September 11, 2000, 14–18.

30. T. Davenport and L. Prusak, *Information Ecology* (New York: Oxford University Press, 1997).

31. www.arthurandersen.com, 2000.

32. Williams, "Arthur Andersen," 172.

33. www.arthurandersen.com, 2000.

34. H. Mintzberg, "The Manager's Job: Folklore and Fact," *Harvard Business Review,* July–August 1975, 56–62.

35. H. Mintzberg, *The Nature of Managerial Work* (New York: Harper and Row, 1973).

36. Ibid.

37. N. Kelleher, "Short-Term Rentals Is All Booked Up," *Boston Herald,* January 17, 1995, 26.

38. R. H. Guest, "Of Time and the Foreman," *Personnel* 32 (1955): 478–86.

39. L. Hill, *Becoming a Manager: Mastery of a New Identity* (Boston: Harvard Business School Press, 1992).

40. Ibid.

41. R. L. Katz, "Skills of an Effective Administrator," *Harvard Business Review,* September–October 1974, 90–102.

42. Ibid.

43. A. Shama, "Management Under Fire: The Transformation of Management in the Soviet Union and Eastern Europe," *Academy of Management Executive* (1993), 22–35.

44. K. Seiders and L. L. Berry, "Service Fairness: What It Is and Why It Matters," *Academy of Management Executive* 12 (1998): 8–20.

45. C. Anderson, "Values-Based Management," *Academy of Management Executive* 11 (1997): 25–46.

46. W. H. Shaw and V. Barry, *Moral Issues in Business,* 6th ed. (Belmont, CA: Wadsworth, 1995); T. Donaldson, *Corporations and Morality* (Englewood Cliffs, NJ: Prentice-Hall, 1982).

47. A. B. Henderson, "Two Former Honda Officials Convicted of Accepting Bribes from Auto Dealers," *The Wall Street Journal,* June 22, 1995, A3.

48. "Hoffman-La Roche and BASF Agree to Pay Record Criminal Fines for Participating in International Vitamin Cartel," U.S. Department of Justice News Release, May 21, 1999.

49. J. R. Wilke and S. Warren, "Vitamin Firms Settle U.S. Charges, Agree to Pay $725 Million in Fines," *The Wall Street Journal,* 1999, May 21, A.3.

50. S. Jackson and others, *Diversity in the Workplace: Human Resource Initiatives* (New York: Guilford Press, 1992).

51. G. Robinson and C. S. Daus, "Building a Case for Diversity," *Academy of Management Executive,* 3 (1997), 21–31.

52. D. Jamieson and J. O'Mara, *Managing Workforce 2000: Gaining a Diversity Advantage* (San Francisco: Jossey-Bass, 1991).

53. www.uboc.com, 2001.

54. G. Colvin, "The 50 Best Companies for Asians, Blacks, and Hispanics," *Fortune,* July 19, 1999, 53–57.

55. "Union Bank of California Honored by U.S. Labor Department for Employment Practices," Press Release, September 11, 2000.

56. T. H. Cox and S. Blake, "Managing Cultural Diversity: Implications for Organizational Competitiveness," *Academy of Management Executive,* August 1991, 49–52.

57. D. R. Tobin, *The Knowledge Enabled Organization* (New York: AMACOM, 1998).

Chapter 2

1. H. Ford, "Progressive Manufacture," *Encyclopedia Britannica,* 13th ed. (New York: Encyclopedia Co., 1926).

2. R. Edwards, *Contested Terrain: The Transformation of the Workplace in the Twentieth Century* (New York: Basic Books, 1979).

3. A. Smith, *The Wealth of Nations* (London: Penguin, 1982).

4. Ibid., 110.

5. J. G. March and H. A. Simon, *Organizations* (New York: Wiley, 1958).

6. L. W. Fry, "The Maligned F. W. Taylor: A Reply to His Many Critics," *Academy of Management Review* 1 (1976): 124–29.

7. F. W. Taylor, *Shop Management* (New York: Harper, 1903); F. W. Taylor, *The Principles of Scientific Management* (New York: Harper, 1911).

8. J. A. Litterer, *The Emergence of Systematic Management as Shown by the Literature from 1870–1900* (New York: Garland, 1986).

9. H. R. Pollard, *Developments in Management Thought* (New York: Crane, 1974).

10. D. Wren, *The Evolution of Management Thought* (New York: Wiley, 1994), 134.

11. Edwards, *Contested Terrain.*

12. J. M. Staudenmaier, Jr., "Henry Ford's Big Flaw," *Invention and Technology* 10 (1994): 34–44.

13. H. Beynon, *Working for Ford* (London: Penguin, 1975).

14. Taylor, *Scientific Management.*

15. F. B. Gilbreth, *Primer of Scientific Management* (New York: Van Nostrand Reinhold, 1912).

16. F. B. Gilbreth, Jr., and E. G. Gilbreth, *Cheaper by the Dozen* (New York: Crowell, 1948).

17. D. Roy, "Efficiency and the Fix: Informal Intergroup Relations in a Piece Work Setting," *American Journal of Sociology* 60 (1954): 255–66.

18. M. Weber, *From Max Weber: Essays in Sociology,* ed. H. H. Gerth and C. W. Mills (New York: Oxford University Press, 1946); M. Weber, *Economy and Society,* ed. G. Roth and C. Wittich (Berkeley: University of California Press, 1978).

19. C. Perrow, *Complex Organizations,* 2nd ed. (Glenview IL: Scott, Foresman, 1979).

20. Weber, *From Max Weber,* 331.

21. See Perrow, *Complex Organizations,* Ch. 1, for a detailed discussion of these issues.

22. H. Fayol, *General and Industrial Management* (New York: IEEE Press, 1984).

23. Ibid., 79.

24. T. J. Peters and R. H. Waterman, Jr., *In Search of Excellence: Lessons from America's Best-Run Companies* (New York: Harper and Row, 1982).

25. R. E. Eccles and N. Nohira, *Beyond the Hype: Rediscovering the Essence of Management* (Boston: Harvard Business School Press, 1992).

26. L. D. Parker, "Control in Organizational Life: The Contribution of Mary Parker Follett," *Academy of Management Review* 9 (1984): 736–45.

27. P. Graham, *M. P. Follett–Prophet of Management: A Celebration of Writings from the 1920s* (Boston: Harvard Business School Press, 1995).

28. M. P. Follett, *Creative Experience* (London, Longmans, 1924).

29. E. Mayo, *The Human Problems of Industrial Civilization* (New York: Macmillan, 1933); F. J. Roethlisberger and W. J. Dickson, *Management and the Worker* (Cambridge: Harvard University Press, 1947).

30. D. W. Organ, "Review of Management and the Worker, by F. J. Roethlisberger and W. J. Dickson," *Academy of Management Review* 13 (1986): 460–64.

31. D. Roy, "Banana Time: Job Satisfaction and Informal Interaction," *Human Organization* 18 (1960): 158–61.

32. For an analysis of the problems in determining cause from effect in the Hawthorne studies and in social settings in general, see A. Carey, "The Hawthorne Studies: A Radical Criticism," *American Sociological Review* 33 (1967): 403–16.

33. D. McGregor, *The Human Side of Enterprise* (New York: McGraw-Hill, 1960).

34. Ibid., 48.

35. Peters and Waterman, *In Search of Excellence.*

36. J. Pitta, "It Had to Be Done and We Did It," *Forbes,* April 26, 1993, 148–52.

37. www.hp.com, press release, June 2001.

38. T. Dewett, and G. R. Jones, "The Role of Information Technology in the Organization: A Review, Model, and Assessment," *Journal of Management,* 2001 (forthcoming).

39. W. E. Deming, *Out of the Crisis* (Cambridge: MIT Press, 1986).

40. J. D. Thompson, *Organizations in Action* (New York: McGraw-Hill, 1967).

41. D. Katz and R. L. Kahn, *The Social Psychology of Organizations* (New York: Wiley, 1966); Thompson, *Organizations in Action.*

42. T. Burns and G. M. Stalker, *The Management of Innovation* (London: Tavistock, 1961); P. R. Lawrence and J. R. Lorsch, *Organization and Environment* (Boston: Graduate School of Business Administration, Harvard University, 1967).

43. Burns and Stalker, *The Management of Innovation.*

44. www.sony.com, 2001.

45. P. Abrahams, "Sony Celebrates the Results of Fine-tuning," *Financial Times,* April 4, 2001, p.5.

46. www.sony.com, 2001.

47. C. W. L. Hill and G. R. Jones, *Strategic Management: An Integrated Approach,* 3rd ed. (Boston: Houghton Mifflin, 1995).

Chapter 3

1. D. Whitford, "A Human Place to Work," *Fortune,* January 8, 2001, pp. 108–19.

2. Ibid.

3. Ibid.; www.medronic.com.

4. www.medronic.com, September 23, 2001.

5. Whitford, "A Human Place to Work," p. 118.

6. Whitford, "A Human Place to Work," p. 119.

7. C. Hymowitz and G. Stern, "At Procter & Gamble, Brands Face Pressure and So Do Executives," *The Wall Street Journal,* May 10, 1993, A1, A8; Z. Schiller, "Ed Artzt's Elbow Grease Has P&G Shining," *Business Week,* October 10, 1994, 84–86.

8. S. Carpenter, "Different Dispositions, Different Brains," *Monitor on Psychology,* February 2001, pp. 66–68.

9. J. M. Digman, "Personality Structure: Emergence of the Five-Factor Model," *Annual Review of Psychology* 41 (1990): 417–40; R. R. McCrae and P. T. Costa, "Validation of the Five-Factor Model of Personality Across Instruments and Observers," *Journal of Personality and Social Psychology* 52 (1987): 81–90; R. R. McCrae and P. T. Costa, "Discriminant Validity of NEO-PIR Facet Scales," *Educational and Psychological Measurement* 52 (1992): 229–37.

10. Digman, "Personality Structure"; McCrae and Costa, "Valuation of the Five-Factor Model"; and McCrae and Costa, "Discriminant Validity."

11. M. R. Barrick and M. K. Mount, "The Big Five Personality Dimensions and Job Performance: A Meta-Analysis," *Personnel Psychology* 44 (1991): 1–26.

12. Digman, "Personality Structure"; McCrae and Costa, "Validation of the Five-Factor Model"; McCrae and Costa, "Discriminant Validity."

13. J. B. Rotter, "Generalized Expectancies for Internal versus External Control of Reinforcement," *Psychological Monographs* 80 (1966): 1–28; P. Spector, "Behaviors in Organizations as a Function of Employees' Locus of Control," *Psychological Bulletin* 91 (1982): 482–97.

14. J. Brockner, *Self-Esteem at Work* (Lexington, MA: Lexington Books, 1988).

15. D. C. McClelland, *Human Motivation* (Glenview, IL: Scott, Foresman, 1985); D. C. McClelland, "How Motives, Skills, and Values Determine What People Do," *American Psychologist* 40 (1985): 812–25; D. C. McClelland, "Managing Motivation to Expand Human Freedom," *American Psychologist* 33 (1978): 201–10.

16. D. G. Winter, *The Power Motive* (New York: Free Press, 1973).

17. M. J. Stahl, "Achievement, Power, and Managerial Motivation: Selecting Managerial Talent with the Job Choice Exercise," *Personnel Psychology* 36 (1983): 775–89; D. C. McClelland and D. H. Burnham, "Power Is the Great Motivator," *Harvard Business Review* 54 (1976): 100–10.

18. R. J. House, W. D. Spangler, and J. Woycke, "Personality and Charisma in the U.S. Presidency: A Psychological Theory of Leader Effectiveness," *Administrative Science Quarterly* 36 (1991): 364–96.

19. G. H. Hines, "Achievement, Motivation, Occupations and Labor Turnover in New Zealand," *Journal of Applied Psychology* 58 (1973): 313–17; P. S. Hundal, "A Study of Entrepreneurial Motivation: Comparison of Fast- and Slow-Progressing Small Scale Industrial Entrepreneurs in Punjab, India," *Journal of Applied Psychology* 55 (1971): 317–23.

20. M. Rokeach, *The Nature of Human Values* (New York: Free Press, 1973).

21. Ibid.

22. Ibid.

23. L. Kraar, "The Overseas Chinese: Lessons from the World's Most Dynamic Capitalists," *Fortune,* October 31, 1994, 91–114.

24. M. Kripalani, "Commentary: India: Luring Investors Will Take Real Change," *Business Week,* June 4, 2001, *Business Week* Archives.

25. P. Edgardio, "A New High-Tech Dynasty?" *Business Week,* August 15, 1994, 90–91; "Formosa Plastics Corp.: Company Says Pretax Profit Doubled in the First Quarter," *The Wall Street Journal,* April 28, 1995, A1; Kraar, "The Overseas Chinese."

26. A. P. Brief, *Attitudes In and Around Organizations* (Thousand Oaks, CA: Sage, 1998).

27. D. W. Organ, *Organizational Citizenship Behavior: The Good Soldier Syndrome* (Lexington, MA: Lexington Books, 1988).

28. J. M. George and A. P. Brief, "Feeling Good–Doing Good: A Conceptual Analysis of the Mood at Work–Organizational Spontaneity Relationship," *Psychological Bulletin* 112 (1992): 310–29.

29. W. H. Mobley, "Intermediate Linkages in the Relationship Between Job Satisfaction and Employee Turnover," *Journal of Applied Psychology* 62 (1977): 237–40.

30. "Managers View Workplace Changes More Positively Than Employees," *The Wall Street Journal,* December 13, 1994, A1.

31. J. E. Mathieu and D. M. Zajac, "A Review and Meta-Analysis of the Antecedents, Correlates, and Consequences of Organizational Commitment," *Psychological Bulletin* 108 (1990): 171–94.

32. E. Slate. "Tips for Negotiations in Germany and France." *HR Focus* (July, 1994): 18.

33. D. Watson and A. Tellegen, "Toward a Consensual Structure of Mood," *Psychological Bulletin* 98 (1985): 219–35.

34. Ibid.

35. J. M. George, "The Role of Personality in Organizational Life: Issues and Evidence," *Journal of Management* 18 (1992): 185–213.

36. J. P. Forgas, "Affect in Social Judgments and Decisions: A Multi-Process Model," in M. Zanna, ed., *Advances in Experimental and Social Psychology,* vol. 25 (San Diego, CA: Academic Press, 1992) pp. 227–75; J. P. Forgas and J. M. George, "Affective Influences on Judgments and Behavior in Organizations: An Information Processing Perspective," *Organizational Behavior and Human Decision Processes* 86 (2001) pp. 3–34; J. M. George, "Leadership and Emotions: The Role of Emotional Intelligence," *Human Relations* 53(2000) 1027–1055; W. N. Morris, *Mood: The Frame of Mind* (New York: Springer-Verlag, 1989).

37. George, "Leadership and Emotions."

38. J. M. George and K. Bettenhausen, "Understanding Prosocial Behavior, Sales Performance, and Turnover: A Group Level Analysis in a Service Context," *Journal of Applied Psychology* 75 (1990): 698–709.

39. George and Brief, "Feeling Good–Doing Good"; J. M. George and J. Zhou; Understanding When Bad Moods Foster Creativity and Good Ones Don't: The Role of Context and Clarity of Feelings. Paper presented at the Academy of Management Annual Meeting, 2001; A. M. Isen and R. A. Baron, "Positive Affect as a Factor in Organizational Behavior," in B. M. Staw and L. L. Cummings, eds., *Research in Organizational Behavior,* vol. 13 (Greenwich, CT: JAI Press, 1991), 1–53.

40. J. D. Greene, R. B. Sommerville, L. E. Nystrom, J. M. Darley, and J. D. Cohen, "An FMRI Investigation of Emotional Engagement in Moral Judgment," *Science,* September 14, 2001, pp. 2105–2108; L. Neergaard, "Brain Scans Show Emotions Key to Resolving Ethical Dilemmas," *Houston Chronicle,* September 14, 2001, p. 13A.

41. L. Berton, "It's Audit Time! Send in the Clowns," *The Wall Street Journal,* January 18, 1995, B1, B6.

42. R. C. Sinclair, "Mood, Categorization Breadth, and Performance Appraisal: The Effects of Order of Information Acquisition and Affective State on Halo, Accuracy, Informational Retrieval, and Evaluations," *Organizational Behavior and Human Decision Processes* 42 (1988): 22–46.

43. D. Goleman, *Emotional Intelligence* (New York: Bantam Books, 1994); J. D. Mayer and P. Salovey, "The Intelligence of Emotional Intelligence," *Intelligence,* 1993, 17, pp. 433–42; J. D. Mayer and P. Salovey, "What Is Emotional Intelligence?," in P. Salovey and D. Sluyter, eds., *Emotional Development and Emotional Intelligence: Implications for Education* (New York: Basic Books, 1997); P. Salovey and J. D. Mayer, "Emotional Intelligence," *Imagination, Cognition, and Personality* 9 (1989–1990) pp. 185–211.

44. S. Epstein, *Constructive Thinking* (Westport, CT: Praeger, 1998).

45. J. M. George, "Emotions and Leadership: The Role of Emotional Intelligence," *Human Relations* 53 (2000) pp. 1027–1055; S. Begley, "The Boss Feels Your Pain," *Newsweek,* October 12, 1998, 74; D. Goleman, *Working With Emotional Intelligence* (New York: Bantam Books, 1998).

46. Harvey Golub and Kenneth I. Chenault, "American Express," *Business Week,* January 8, 2001, *Business Week* Archives; T. Schwartz, "How Do You Feel?" *Fast Company,* August 10, 2001, pp. 35–45; www.americanexpress.com.

47. Schwartz, "How Do You Feel?"

48. Schwartz, "How Do You Feel?"

49. Ibid.

50. J. A. Pearce, "The Company Mission as a Strategic Tool," *Sloan Management Review* (Spring 1982): 15–24.

51. C. I. Barnard, *The Functions of the Executive* (Cambridge, MA: Harvard University Press, 1948).

52. R. E. Freeman, *Strategic Management: A Stakeholder Approach* (Marshfield, MA: Pitman, 1984).

53. "The Jobs Challenge," *The Economist,* July 14, 2001, p. 56.

54. T. L. Beauchamp and N. E. Bowie, eds., *Ethical Theory and Business* (Englewood Cliffs, NJ: Prentice-Hall, 1979); A. MacIntyre, *After Virtue* (South Bend, IN: University of Notre Dame Press, 1981).

55. R. E. Goodin, "How to Determine Who Should Get What," *Ethics* (July 1975): 310–21.

56. Associated Press, "Firestone Agrees to Latest Recall of 3.5 Million Tires," *Houston Chronicle,* October 5, 2001, p. 2A.

57. J. Greenwald, "Inside the Ford/Firestone Fight," *Time,* May 29, 2001; Time.com, August 10, 2001; "More Recalls Ahead?" *Consumer Reports,* November, 2001, p. 8.

58. Greenwald, "Inside the Ford/Firestone Fight"; Time.com.

59. Ibid.

60. T. M. Jones, "Ethical Decision Making by Individuals in Organizations: An Issue Contingent Model," *Academy of Management Journal* 16 (1991): 366–95; G. F. Cavanaugh, D. J. Moberg, and M. Velasquez, " The Ethics of Organizational Politics," *Academy of Management Review* 6 (1981): 363–74.

61. L. K. Trevino, "Ethical Decision Making in Organizations: A Person–Situation Interactionist Model," *Academy of Management Review* 11 (1986): 601–17; W. H. Shaw and V. Barry, *Moral Issues in Business,* 6th ed. (Belmont, CA: Wadsworth, 1995).

62. B. Victor and J. B. Cullen, "The Organizational Bases of Ethical Work Climates," *Administrative Science Quarterly* 33 (1988): 101–25.

63. H. Demsetz, "Towards a Theory of Property Rights," *American Economic Review* 57 (1967): 347–59.

64. D. Collins, "Organizational Harm, Legal Consequences and Stakeholder Retaliation," *Journal of Business Ethics* 8 (1988): 1–13.

65. S. W. Gellerman, "Why Good Managers Make Bad Decisions," in K. R. Andrews, ed., *Ethics in Practice: Managing the Moral Corporation* (Boston: Harvard Business School Press, 1989).

66. L. K. Trevino, "Ethical Decision Making in Organizations," *Academy of Management Review* 11 (1986): 601–17.

67. M. S. Baucus and J. P. Near, "Can Illegal Corporate Behavior Be Predicted? An Event History Analysis," *Academy of Management Journal* 34 (1991): 9–36.

68. J. Flynn and C. Del Valle, "Did Sears Take Its Customers for a Ride?" *Business Week,* August 3, 1992, 24–25.

69. R. C. Soloman, *Ethics and Excellence* (New York: Oxford University Press, 1992).

70. J. Dobson, "Corporate Reputation: A Free Market Solution to Unethical Behavior," *Business and Society* 28 (1989): 1–5.

71. R. Johnson, "Ralston to Buy Beechnut, Gambling It Can Overcome Apple Juice Scandal," *The Wall Street Journal,* September 18, 1989, B11.

72. A. S. Waterman, "On the Uses of Psychological Theory and Research in the Process of Ethical Inquiry," *Psychological Bulletin* 103, no. 3 (1988): 283–98.

73. M. S. Frankel, "Professional Codes: Why, How, and with What Impact?" *Ethics* 8 (1989): 109–15.

74. J. Van Maanen and S. R. Barley, "Occupational Communities: Culture and Control in Organizations," in B. Staw and L. Cummings, eds., *Research in Organizational Behavior,* vol. 6 (Greenwich, CT: JAI Press, 1984), 287–365.

75. Jones, "Ethical Decision Making by Individuals in Organizations."

76. B. Schneider, "The People Make the Place," *Personnel Psychology* 40 (1987) 437–453.

77. B. Schneider, H. B. Goldstein, and D. B. Smith, "The ASA Framework: An Update," *Personnel Psychology,* 48 (1995) 747–73; J. Schaubroeck, D. C. Ganster, and J. R. Jones, "Organizational and Occupational Influences in the Attraction-Selection-Attrition Process," *Journal of Applied Psychology* 83 (1998) 869–91.

78. J. M. George, "Emotions and Leadership: The Role of Emotional Intelligence," *Human Relations* 53 (2000) 1027–55.

79. J. M. George, "Affect Regulation in Groups," in R. Lord, R. Klimoski, and R. Kanfer, eds., *Emotions and Work.* Organizational Frontiers Series: Jossey-Bass, forthcoming; E. Hatfield, J. Cacioppo, and R. L. Rapson, "Primitive Emotional Contagion," in M. S. Clark, ed., *Review of Personality and Social Psychology, vol. 14, Emotion and Social Behavior,* pp. 151–77. (Newbury Park, CA: Sage, 1992); E. Hatfield, J. T. Cacioppo, and R. L. Rapson. *Emotional Contagion.* (Paris: Cambridge University Press 1994).

80. W. Zellner, "Commentary: Earth to Herb Kelleher: Pick a Co-Pilot," *Business Week,* August 16, 1999, *Business Week* Archives.

81. Southwest Airlines Fact Sheet, June 19, 2001, www.swabiz.com.

82. M. Conlin, "Where Layoffs Are a Last Resort," *Business Week,* October 8, 2001, *Business Week* Archives.

83. "2000 Fun Facts," June 19, 2001, www.swabiz.com.

84. Conlin, "Where Layoffs Are a Last Resort" ; "Southwest Airlines Fact Sheet."

85. G. R. Jones, *Organizational Theory: Text and Cases* (Reading, MA: Addison-Wesley, 1997).

86. P. E. Murphy, "Creating Ethical Corporate Structure," *Sloan Management Review* (Winter 1989): 81–87.

87. E. Gatewood and A. B. Carroll, "The Anatomy of Corporate Social Response," *Business Horizons,* September–October 1981: 9–16.

88. M. Friedman, "A Friedman Doctrine: The Social Responsibility of Business Is to Increase Its Profits," *New York Times Magazine,* September 13, 1970: 33.

89. C. Stavraka, "Strong Corporate Reputation at J&J Boosts Diversity Recruiting Efforts," DiversityInc.com, February 16, 2001.

90. "Our Credo," www.jj.com, October 9, 2001.

91. Ibid.

92. L. L. Nash, *Good Intentions Aside* (Boston: Harvard Business School Press, 1993).

93. Nash, *Good Intentions Aside;* L. L. Nash, "Johnson & Johnson's Credo" in *Corporate Ethics: A Prime Business Asset* (New York: The Business Roundtable, February 1988).

94. Nash, *Good Intentions Aside.*

95. Stavraka, "Strong Corporate Reputation."

96. Nash, *Good Intentions Aside.*

Chapter 4

1. D. McCracken, "Winning the Talent War for Women," *Harvard Business Review,* November–December 2000, pp. 159–67.

2. McCracken, "Winning the Talent War for Women."

3. Ibid.

4. Ibid.

5. www.us.deloitte.com/US/believe/Diversity/div3.htm.

6. "Prejudice: Still on the Menu," *Business Week,* April 3, 1995, 42.

7. "She's a Woman, Offer Her Less," *Business Week,* May 7, 2001, p. 34.

8. "Glass Ceiling Is a Heavy Barrier for Minorities, Blocking Them from Top Jobs," *Wall Street Journal,* March 14, 1995, A1.

9. C. Gibson, "Nation's Median Age Highest Ever, But 65-and-Over Population's Growth Lags, Census 2000 Shows," U.S. Census Bureau News, May 30, 2001, www.census.gov.

10. U.S. Equal Employment Opportunity Commission, "Federal Laws Prohibiting Job Discrimination Questions and Answers," June 20, 2001, www.eeoc.gov.

11. N. Shirouzu and J. B. White, "Ford Assesses Job Ratings Amid Bias Suit," *Wall Street Journal,* July 9, 2001, A3, A14.

12. Ibid.

13. J. Muller, K. Kerwin, D. Welch, P. L. Moore, and Diane Brady, "Ford: Why It's Worse Than You Think," *Business Week,* June 25, 2001, *Business Week* Archives.

14. N. Shirouzu, "Nine Ford Workers File Bias Suit Saying Ratings Curb Older Staff," *Wall Street Journal,* February 15, 2001, p. B14.

15. Muller, Kerwin, Welch, Moore, and Brady, "Ford: Why It's Worse Than You Think."

16. Ibid.

17. "Sex by Industry by Class of Worker for the Employed Civilian Population 16 Years and Over," American FactFinder, October 15, 2001, http://factfinder.census.gov/.

18. "Profile of Selected Economic Characteristics: 2000," American FactFinder, October 15, 2001, http://factfinder.census.gov.

19. "2000 Catalyst Census of Women Corporate Officers and Top Earners of the Fortune 500," October 21, 2001, www.catalystwomen.org.

20. T. Gutner, "Wanted: More Diverse Directors," *Business Week,* April 30, 2001, p. 134.

21. Gutner, "Wanted: More Diverse Directors."

22. R. Sharpe, "As Leaders, Women Rule," *Business Week,* November 20, 2000, pp. 75–84.

23. Sharpe, "As Leaders, Women Rule."

24. B. Guzman, "The Hispanic Population," U.S. Census Bureau, May 2001; U.S. Census Bureau, "Profiles of General Demographic Characteristics," May 2001; U.S. Census Bureau, "Revisions to the Standards for the Classification of Federal Data on Race and Ethnicity," November 2, 2000, pp. 1–19. www.census.gov.

25. "Civilian Labor Force 16 and Older by Sex, Age, Race, and Hispanic Origin, 1978, 1988, 1998, and Projected 2008," Bureau of Labor Statistics, October 16, 2001, http://stats.bls.gov/emp/.

26. "Profile of General Demographic Characteristics: 2000," U.S. Census Bureau, Census 2000. www.census.gov.

27. L. Chavez, "Just Another Ethnic Group," *Wall Street Journal,* May 14, 2001, p. A22.

28. J. Flint, "NBC to Hire More Minorities on TV shows," *Wall Street Journal,* January 6, 2000, p. B13.

29. J. Poniewozik, "What's Wrong with This Picture?" *Time,* June 1, 2001, Time.com.

30. J. Poniewozik, "What's Wrong with This Picture?"

31. National Association of Realtors, PR Newswire, "Real Estate Industry Adapting to Increasing Cultural Diversity," May 16, 2001.

32. "Toyota Apologizes to African Americans over Controversial Ad," Kyodo News Service, Japan, May 23, 2001.

33. "Nissan Not Alone in Discrimination, Attorney Says," *Houston Chronicle,* July 6, 2001, C9.

34. Ibid.

35. "Toyota Apologizes to African Americans."

36. Ibid.

37. J. H. Coplan, "Putting a Little Faith in Diversity," *Business Week,* December 21, 2000, *Business Week* Online.

38. Ibid.

39. Ibid.

40. J. N. Cleveland, J. Barnes-Farrell, and J. M. Ratz, "Accommodation in the Workplace," *Human Resource Management Review,* 7(1997): 77–108; A. Colella, "Coworker Distributive Fairness Judgments of the Workplace Accommodations of Employees with Disabilities," *Academy of Management Review,* 26(2001) pp. 100–116.

41. Colella, "Coworker Distributive Fairness Judgments"; D. Stamps, "Just How Scary Is the ADA," *Training* 32(1995) 93–101; M. S. West and R. L. Cardy, "Accommodating Claims of Disability: The Potential Impact of Abuses," *Human Resource Management Review* 7(1997) 233–46.

42. G. Koretz, "How to Enable the Disabled," *Business Week,* November 6, 2000, *Business Week* Archives.

43. Colella, "Coworker Distributive Fairness Judgments."

44. P. Hewitt, "UH Highlights Abilities, Issues of the Disabled," *Houston Chronicle,* October 22, 2001, p. 24A.

45. Hewitt, "UH Highlights Abilities."

46. J. M. George, "AIDS/AIDS-Related Complex," in L. H. Peters, C. R. Greer, and S. A. Youngblood (eds), *The Blackwell Encyclopedic Dictionary of Human Resource Management* (Oxford, UK: Blackwell Publishers, 1997), pp. 6–7.

47. George, "AIDS Awareness Training."

48. S. Armour, "Firms Juggle Stigma, Needs of More Workers with HIV," *USA Today,* September 7, 2000, p. B1.

49. Armour, "Firms Juggle Stigma."

50. Armour, "Firms Juggle Stigma"; S. Vaughn, "Career Challenge; Companies' Work Not Over in HIV and AIDS Education," *Los Angeles Times,* July 8, 2001.

51. J. Carey, "Africa: The High Price of Denial," *Business Week,* February 19, 2001, *Business Week* Archives.

52. E. Licking, "AIDS: Taking Stock of the Devastation," *Business Week,* July 17, 2000, *Business Week* Archives; "Table: A Global View of HIV Infection," *Business Week, Business Week* Archives, July 17, 2000.

53. R. Maldonado, "Wall St. Bank Sued for AIDS Discrimination," *Crain's New York Business News,* May 7, 2001, p. 35.

54. Maldonado, "Wall St. Bank Sued."

55. R. Brownstein, "Honoring Work Is Key to Ending Poverty," *Detroit News,* October 2, 2001, p. 9; G. Koretz, "How Welfare to Work Worked," *Business Week,* September 24, 2001, *Business Week* Archives.

56. "As Ex-Welfare Recipients Lose Jobs, Offer Safety Net," *The Atlanta Constitution,* October 10, 2001, p. A18.

57. "Profile of Selected Economic Characteristics: 2000," American FactFinder, http://factfinder.census.gov/.

58. "Poverty–How the Census Bureau Measures Poverty," September 25, 2001, Census 2000, U.S. Census Bureau.

59. "Poverty 2000," U. S. Census Bureau, October 26, 2001, www.census.gov/.

60. I. Lelchuk, "Families Fear Hard Times Getting Worse/$30,000 in the Bay Area Won't Buy Necessities, Survey Says," *San Francisco Chronicle,* September 26, 2001, p. A13; S. R. Wheeler, "Activists: Welfare-to-Work Changes Needed," *Denver Post,* October 10, 2001, p. B6.

61. B. Carton, "Bedtime Stories: In 24-Hour Workplace, Day Care Is Moving to the Night Shift," *Wall Street Journal,* July 6, 2001, pp. A1, A4.

62. Carton, "Bedtime Stories."

63. Ibid.

64. Ibid.

65. M. Warner, "Building a Business," August 30, 2001, www.pbs.org/newshour/bb/business/july-dec01/plastics_8-30.html.

66. P. A. Toensmeier, "Visionary Makes a Commodity Pay Off with Lots of Hard Work," *Modern Plastics,* May 1999, p. 110.

67. Warner, "Building a Business."

68. Toensmeier, "Visionary Makes a Commodity Pay Off."

69. Warner, "Building a Business."

70. J. B. Arndorfer, "Industrial Investment: A Region Retools," *Crain's Chicago Business News,* September 3, 2001, p. 15.

71. Warner, "Building a Business."

72. G. Koretz, "Gays and the 'Marriage Tax'", *Business Week,* October 23, 2000, *Business Week* Archives.

73. "Company Benefits for Partners of Gays Increase," *Houston Chronicle,* September 26, 2000, p. 9A.

74. Ibid.

75. V. Valian, *Why So Slow? The Advancement of Women* (Cambridge, MA: MIT Press, 2000).

76. S. T. Fiske and S. E. Taylor, *Social Cognition,* 2nd ed. (New York: McGraw-Hill, 1991); Valian, *Why So Slow?*

77. Valian, Why So Slow?

78. S. Rynes and B. Rosen, "A Field Survey of Factors Affecting the Adoption and Perceived Success of Diversity Training," *Personnel Psychology,* 48(1995) 247–270; Valian, *Why So Slow?*

79. V. Brown and F. L. Geis, "Turning Lead into Gold: Leadership by Men and Women and the Alchemy of Social Consensus," *Journal of Personality and Social Psychology* 46(1984) 811–824; Valian, *Why So Slow?*

80. Valian, *Why So Slow?*

81. J. Cole and B. Singer, "A Theory of Limited Differences: Explaining the Productivity Puzzle in Science," in H. Zuckerman, J. R. Cole, and J. T. Bruer

(eds.), *The Outer Circle: Women in the Scientific Community* (New York, W. W. Norton, 1991) 277–310; M. F. Fox, "Sex, Salary, and Achievement: Reward-dualism in Academia," *Sociology of Education,* 54(1981) 71–84; J. S. Long, "The Origins of Sex Differences in Science," *Social Forces* 68(1990) 1297–1315; R. F. Martell, D. M. Lane, and C. Emrich, "Male-Female Differences: A Computer Simulation," *American Psychologist* 51(1996) 157–158; Valian, *Why So Slow?*

82. Cole and Singer, "A Theory of Limited Differences"; M. F. Fox, "Sex, Salary, and Achievement"; Long, "The Origins of Sex Differences in Science"; Martell, Lane, and Emrich, "Male-Female Differences: A Computer Simulation"; Valian, *Why So Slow?*

83. R. Folger and M. A. Konovsky, "Effects of Procedural and Distributive Justice on Reactions to Pay Raise Decisions," *Academy of Management Journal* 32 (1989): 115–30; J. Greenberg, "Organizational Justice: Yesterday, Today, and Tomorrow," *Journal of Management* 16 (1990): 399–402.

84. Catalyst, "The Glass Ceiling in 2000: Where Are Women Now?" October 21, 2001, www.catalystwomen.org.

85. Bureau of Labor Statistics, 1999; Catalyst, 1999 Census of Women Corporate Officers and Top Earners; 1999 Census of Women Board Directors of the Fortune 1000; Catalyst, "The Glass Ceiling in 2000."

86. 1999 Census of Women Corporate Officers and Top Earners; 1999 Census of Women Board Directors of the Fortune 1000.

87. Catalyst, "Women of Color in Corporate Management: Opportunities and Barriers, 1999," www.catalystwomen.org, October 21, 2001.

88. U.S. Department of Labor, Bureau of Labor Statistics, "Highlights of Women's Earnings in 1998," www.catalystwomen.org, October 21, 2001.

89. A. M. Jaffe, "At Texaco, the Diversity Skeleton Still Stalks the Halls," *New York Times,* December 11, 1994, sec. 3, p. 5.

90. Greenberg, "Organizational Justice."

91. W. M. Carley, "Salesman's Treatment Raises Bias Questions at Schering-Plough," *Wall Street Journal,* May 31, 1995, A1, A8.

92. G. Robinson and K. Dechant, "Building a Case for Business Diversity," *Academy of Management Executive* (1997):3, 32–47.

93. A. Patterson, "Target 'Micromarkets' Its Way to Success; No 2 Stores Are Alike," *Wall Street Journal,* May 31, 1995, A1, A9.

94. "The Business Case for Diversity: Experts Tell What Counts, What Works," DiversityInc.com, October 23, 2001.

95. B. Hetzer, "Find a Niche–and Start Scratching," *Business Week,* September 14, 1998, *Business Week* Archives.

96. K. Aaron, "Woman Laments Lack of Diversity on Boards of Major Companies," *The Times Union,* May 16, 2001, www.timesunion.com.

97. "The Business Case for Diversity."

98. B. Frankel, "Measuring Diversity Is One Sure Way of Convincing CEOs of Its Value," DiversityInc.com, October 5, 2001.

99. A. Stevens, "Lawyers and Clients," *Wall Street Journal,* June 19, 1995, B7.

100. B. McMenamin, "Diversity Hucksters," *Forbes,* May 22, 1995, 174–76.

101. J. Kahn, "Diversity Trumps the Downturn," *Fortune,* July 9, 2001, pp. 114–16.

102. H. R. Schiffmann, *Sensation and Perception: An Integrated Approach* (New York: Wiley, 1990).

103. A. E. Serwer, "McDonald's Conquers the World," *Fortune,* October 17, 1994, 103–16.

104. S. T. Fiske and S. E. Taylor, *Social Cognition* (Reading, MA: Addison-Wesley, 1984).

105. J. S. Bruner, "Going Beyond the Information Given," in H. Gruber, G. Terrell, and M. Wertheimer (eds.), *Contemporary Approaches to Cognition* (Cambridge: Harvard University Press, 1957); Fiske and Taylor, *Social Cognition.*

106. Fiske and Taylor, *Social Cognition.*

107. Valian, *Why So Slow?*

108. D. Bakan, *The Duality of Human Existence* (Chicago: Rand McNally, 1966); J. T. Spence and R. L. Helmreich, *Masculinity and Femininity: Their Psychological Dimensions, Correlates, and Antecedents* (Austin: University of Texas Press, 1978); J. T. Spence and L. L. Sawin, "Images of Masculinity and Femininity: A Reconceptualization, in V. E. O'Leary, R. K. Unger, & B. B. Wallston eds., *Women, Gender, and Social Psychology* (Hillsdale, NJ: Erlbaum, 1985), pp. 35–66; Valian, *Why So Slow?*

109. V. Valian, *Why So Slow?*

110. Serwer, "McDonald's Conquers the World."

111. M. Loden and J. B. Rosener, *Workforce America! Managing Employee Diversity as a Vital Resource* (Burr Ridge, IL: Irwin, 1991).

112. E. D. Pulakos and K. N. Wexley, "The Relationship Among Perceptual Similarity, Sex, and Performance Ratings in Manager-Subordinate Dyads," *Academy of Management Journal* 26 (1983): 129–39.

113. Fiske and Taylor, *Social Cognition.*

114. "Suit Alleges Gender Bias at Wal-Mart," *Houston Chronicle,* June 20, 2001, p. 10C.

115. "Suit Alleges Gender Bias at Wal-Mart."

116. M. Conlin and W. Zellner, "Is Wal-Mart Hostile to Women?" *Business Week,* July 16, 2001, *Business Week* Archives.

117. J. Floyd, "Wal-Mart Accused of Bias," June 19, 2001, abcNews.com.

118. Floyd, "Wal-Mart Accused of Bias."

119. Ibid.

120. A. G. Greenwald and M. Banaji, "Implicit Social Cognition: Attitudes, Self-Esteem, and Stereotypes," *Psychological Review* 102 (1995): 4–27.

121. A. P. Carnevale and S. C. Stone, "Diversity: Beyond the Golden Rule," *Training & Development,* October 1994, 22–39.

122. B. A. Battaglia, "Skills for Managing Multicultural Teams," *Cultural Diversity at Work* 4 (1992); Carnevale and Stone, "Diversity: Beyond the Golden Rule."

123. V. Valian, *Why So Slow?*

124. A. P. Brief, R. T. Buttram, R. M. Reizenstein, S. D. Pugh, J. D. Callahan, R. L. McCline, and J. B. Vaslow, "Beyond Good Intentions: The Next Steps Toward Racial Equality in the American Workplace," *Academy of Management Executive,* November 1997, pp. 59–72.

125. Brief, Buttram, Reizenstein, Pugh, Callahan, McCline, and Vaslow, "Beyond Good Intentions."

126. Ibid.

127 Ibid.

128. B. Mandell and S. Kohler-Gray, "Management Development That Values Diversity," *Personnel* (March 1990): 41–47.

129. B. Filipczak, "25 Years of Diversity at UPS," *Training,* August 1992, 42–46.

130. D. A. Thomas, "Race Matters: The Truth about Mentoring Minorities," *Harvard Business Review,* April 2001, pp. 99–107.

131. Thomas, "Race Matters."

132. S. N. Mehta, "Why Mentoring Works," *Fortune,* July 9, 2000.

133. S. N. Mehta, "Why Mentoring Works"; Thomas, "Race Matters."

134. "Chevron Settles Claims of 4 Women at Unit as Part of Sex Bias Suit," *Wall Street Journal,* January 22, 1995, B12.

135. D. K. Berman, "TWA Settles Harassment Claims at JFK Airport for $2.6 Million," *Wall Street Journal,* June 25, 2001, B6.

136. T. Segal, "Getting Serious About Sexual Harassment," *Business Week,* November 9, 1992, 78–82.

137. Carton, "Muscled Out? At Jenny Craig, Men are Ones Who Claim Sex Descrimintation," *Wall Street Journal,* November 29, 1994, A1, A7.

138. R. L. Paetzold and A. M. O'Leary-Kelly, "Organizational Communication and the Legal Dimensions of Hostile Work Environment Sexual Harassment," in G. L. Kreps, ed., *Sexual Harassment: Communication Implications* (Cresskill, NJ: Hampton Press, 1993).

139. M. Galen, J. Weber, and A. Z. Cuneo, "Sexual Harassment: Out of the Shadows," *Fortune,* October 28, 1991, 30–31.

140. A. M. O'Leary-Kelly, R. L. Paetzold, and R. W. Griffin, "Sexual Harassment as Aggressive Action: A Framework for Understanding Sexual Harassment" (paper presented at the annual meeting of the Academy of Management, Vancouver, August 1995).

141. S. J. Bresler and R. Thacker, "Four-Point Plan Helps Solve Harassment Problems," *HR Magazine,* May 1993, 117–24.

142. "Du Pont's Solution," *Training,* March 1992, 29.

143. J. S. Lublin, "Sexual Harassment Moves Atop Agenda in Many Executive Education Programs," *Wall Street Journal,* December 2, 1991, B1, B4.

144. "Navy Is Teaching Sailors What Proper Conduct Is," *Bryan/College Station Eagle,* April 19, 1993, A2.

145. S. B. Garland, "Finally, a Corporate Tip Sheet on Sexual Harassment," *Business Week,* July 13, 1998, 39.

Chapter 5

1. www.ebay.com, 2001; www.amazon.com, 2001.

2. L. J. Bourgeois, "Strategy and Environment: A Conceptual Integration," *Academy of Management Review* 5 (1985): 25–39.

3. M. E. Porter, *Competitive Strategy* (New York: Free Press, 1980).

4. "Coca-Cola Versus Pepsi-Cola and the Soft Drink Industry," *Harvard Business School Case* #9-391-179.

5. www.mcdonalds.com, press release, 2000.

6. www. mcdonalds.com, 2001.

7. M. E. Porter, *Competitive Advantage* (New York: Free Press, 1985).

8. "The Tech Slump Doesn't Scare Michael Dell," *Business Week,* April 16, 2001, p. 48.

9. "Dell CEO Would Like 40 Percent PC Market Share," www.daily news.yahoo.com, June 20, 2001.

10. For views on barriers to entry from an economics perspective, see Porter, *Competitive Strategy.* For the sociological perspective, see J. Pfeffer and G. R. Salancik, *The External Control of Organization: A Resource Dependence Perspective* (New York: Harper and Row, 1978).

11. Porter, *Competitive Strategy;* J. E. Bain, *Barriers to New Competition* (Cambridge: Harvard University Press, 1956); R. J. Gilbert, "Mobility Barriers and the Value of Incombency," in R. Schmalensee and R. D. Willig, eds., *Handbook of Industrial Organization,* vol. 1 (Amsterdam: North Holland, 1989).

12. www.amazon.com, press release, May 2001.

13. C. W. L. Hill, "The Computer Industry: The New Industry of Industries," in Hill and Jones, *Strategic Management.*

14. J. Muller and D. Brady, "A Kmart Special: Better Service," *Business Week,* September 4, 2000, pp. 80–84.

15. J. Muller and A. T. Palmer, "Kmart's Bright Idea," *Business Week,* April 9, 2001, pp. 48–52.

16. www.sony.com, press release, 2001; www.nokia.com, 2001.

17. G. G. Gordon, "Industry Determinants of Organizational Culture," *Academy of Management Review* 16 (1991): pp. 396–415. P. Tolbert, "Institutional Sources of Organizational Culture in Major Law Firms," in L. Zucker, ed. *Institutional Patterns and Organizations: Culture and Environment* (Cambridge, MA: Ballinger, 1988, pp. 101–113).

18. R. Lucas, "Political-Cultural Analysis of Organizations, *Academy of Management Review* 12 (1987): pp. 144–56.

19. J. Schumpeter, *Capitalism, Socialism and Democracy* (London: Macmillan, 1950), 68. Also see R. R. Winter and S. G. Winter, *An Evolutionary Theory of Economic Change* (Cambridge: Harvard University Press, 1982).

20. "The Coming Clash of Logic," *The Economist,* July 3, 1993, 21–23.

21. S. Sherman, "The New Computer Revolution," *Fortune,* June 14, 1993, 56–84.

22. www.cakebread.com, 2000.

23. N. Goodman, *An Introduction to Sociology* (New York: HarperCollins, 1991); C. Nakane, *Japanese Society* (Berkeley: University of California Press, 1970).

24. The Economist, *The Economist Book of Vital World Statistics* (New York: Random House, 1990).

25. For a detailed discussion of the importance of the structure of law as a factor explaining economic change and growth, see D. C. North, *Institutions, Institutional Change and Economic Performance* (Cambridge: Cambridge University Press, 1990).

26. R. B. Reich, *The Work of Nations* (New York: Knopf, 1991).

27. Jagdish Bhagwati, *Protectionism* (Cambridge: MIT Press, 1988).

28. R. B. Duncan, "Characteristics of Organization Environment and Perceived Environment," *Administrative Science Quarterly* 17 (1972): 313–27.

29. S. Brown and K. Eisenhardt, "Competing on the Edge," Boston, MA: Harvard Business School Press, 1998.

30. www.walmart.com, 2001.

31. W. Zellner, "Will Walmart.com Get It Right This Time?," *Business Week,* November 6, 2000, pp. 104–108.

32. J. S. Adams, "The Structure and Dynamics of Behavior in Boundary Spanning Roles," in M. D. Dunnette, ed., *The Handbook of Industrial and Organizational Psychology* (Chicago: Rand McNally, 1976).

33. For a discussion of sources of organizational inertia, see M. T. Hannah and J. Freeman, "Structural Inertia and Organizational Change," *American Sociological Review* 49 (1984): 149–64.

34. Not everyone agrees with this assessment. Some argue that organizations and individual managers have little impact on the environment. See Hannah and Freeman, "Structural Inertia and Organizational Change."

35. R. X. Cringeley, *Accidental Empires* (New York: Harper Business, 1993).

Chapter 6

1. www.amazon.com, 2001.

2. www.ebay.com, 2001.

3. A. Z. Cuneo, "Wieden Seeks a New "It" with Amazon.com" *Advertising Age,* June 4, 2001, p. 4.

4. C. Silva, "Globalization Slows in e-Retail," *Computerworld,* Inc., Jan. 29, 2001, pp. 1, 14.

5. J. Bhagwati, *Protectionism* (Cambridge, MA: MIT Press, 1988).

6. For a summary of these theories see P. Krugman and M. Obstfeld, *International Economics: Theory and Policy* (New York: HarperCollins, 1991). Also see C. W. L. Hill, *International Business* (New York: McGraw-Hill, 1997), Ch. 4.

7. www.wto.org.com, 2001.

8. C. A. Bartlett and S. Ghoshal, *Managing Across Borders* (Boston: Harvard Business School Press, 1989).

9. C. Arnst and G. Edmondson, "The Global Free-for-All," *Business Week,* September 26, 1994, 118–26.

10. W. Konrads, "Why Leslie Wexner Shops Overseas," *Business Week,* February 3, 1992, p. 30.

11. R. Dore, *Taking Japan Seriously: A Confusion Perspective on Leading Economic Issues* (Stanford, CA: Stanford University Press, 1987).

12. "Boeing's Worldwide Supplier Network," *Seattle Post-Intelligence,* April 9, 1994, 13.

13. I. Metthee, "Playing a Large Part," *Seattle Post-Intelligence,* April 9, 1994, 13.

14. R. B. Reich, *The Work of Nations* (New York: Knopf, 1991).

15. "Business: Link in the Global Chain," *The Economist,* June 2, 2001, pp. 62–63.

16. T. Levitt, "The Globalization of Markets," *Harvard Business Review,* May–June 1983: 92–102.

17. T. Deveny et al., "McWorld?" *Business Week,* October 13, 1986, 78–86.

18. R. Wesson, *Modern Government–Democracy and Authoritarianism,* 2d ed. (Englewood Cliffs, NJ: Prentice-Hall, 1992).

19. Nobel prize-winning economist Douglas North makes this argument. See D. C. North, *Institutions, Institutional Change, and Economic Performance* (Cambridge: Cambridge University Press, 1990).

20. For an accessible discussion of the reasons for this, see M. Friedman and R. Friedman, *Free to Choose* (London: Penguin Books, 1990).

21. P. M. Sweezy and H. Magdoff, *The Dynamics of U.S. Capitalism* (New York: Monthly Review Press, 1972).

22. The ideology is that of individualism, which dates back to Adam Smith, John Stuart Mill, and the like. See H. W. Spiegel, *The Growth of Economic Thought* (Durham, NC: Duke University Press, 1991).

23. www.wto.org, 2001.

24. www.wto.org, 2001.

25. M. Magnier, "Chiquita Bets Czechoslovakia Can Produce Banana Bonanza," *Journal of Commerce,* August 29, 1991, 1, 3.

26. www.ford.com, 2001.

27. www.gm.com, 2001; www.daimlerchrysler.com, 2001; www.renault.com, 2001.

28. J. Green, "Riding Together," *Business Week,* February 26, 2001, pp. 46–49.

29. L. Cohn, "GM Tries to Show Who's Boss," *Business Week,* March 12, 2001, pp. 54–56.

30. C. Tierney, A. Bowden, and I. M. Kunii, "Who Says It's Iffy Now," *Business Week,* October 23, 2001, p. 64.

31. E. B. Tylor, *Primitive Culture* (London: Murray, 1971).

32. For details on the forces that shape culture, see Hill, *International Business,* Ch. 2.

33. G. Hofstede, B. Neuijen, D. D. Ohayv, and G. Sanders, "Measuring Organizational Cultures: A Qualitative and Quantitative Study Across Twenty Cases," *Administrative Science Quarterly* 35 (1990): 286–316.

34. R. Bellah, *Habits of the Heart: Individualism and Commitment in American Life* (Berkeley: University of California Press, 1985).

35. R. Bellah, *The Tokugawa Religion* (New York: Free Press, 1957).

36. C. Nakane, *Japanese Society* (Berkeley: University of California Press, 1970).

37. For example, see Dore, *Taking Japan Seriously.*

38. G. Hofstede, "The Cultural Relativity of Organizational Practices and Theories," *Journal of International Business Studies* (Fall 1983): 75–89.

39. Hofstede, Neuijen, Ohayv, and Sanders, "Measuring Organizational Cultures."

40. J. Perlez, "GE Finds Tough Going in Hungary," *New York Times,* July 25, 1994, C1, C3.

41. www.ge.com, 2001.

42. J. P. Fernandez and M. Barr, *The Diversity Advantage* (New York: Lexington Books, 1994).

43. R. E. Caves, *Multinational Enterprise and Economic Analysis* (Cambridge: Cambridge University Press, 1982).

44. B. Kogut, "Joint Ventures: Theoretical and Empirical Perspectives," *Strategic Management Journal* 9 (1988): 319–33.

45. "Venture with Nestlé SA Is Slated for Expansion," *Wall Street Journal,* April 15, 2001, B2.

46. B. Bahree, "BP Amoco, Italy's ENI Plan $2.5 Billion Gas Plant," *Wall Street Journal,* March 6, 2001, A16.

47. N. Hood and S. Young, *The Economics of the Multinational Enterprise* (London: Longman, 1979).

48. www.wal-mart.com, 2000.

49. A. Chen and M. Hicks, "Going Global? Avoid Culture Clashes," *PC Week,* April 3, 2000, p. 65.

50. M. Troy, "Global Group Ready for New Growth Phase," *DSN Retailing Today,* June 5, 2000, p. 11.

51. Bhagwati, *Protectionism.*

52. www.yahoo.com, July 18, 2001.

53. "Free Trade or Foul," *The Economist,* June 4, 1994, 70. Also see Krugman and Obstfeld, *International Economics.*

54. A. Roddick, "Not Free Trade but Fair Trade," *Across the Board* (June 1994): 58; A. Jack and N. Buckley, "Halo Slips on the Raspberry Bubbles," *Financial Times,* August 27–28, 1994, 12.

55. M. Jordan, "From the Amazon to Your Armrest," *Wall Street Journal,* May 1, 2001, B1.

Chapter 7

1. J. Schlosser, "Jack? Jack Who?" *Fortune,* September 17, 2001, Fortune.com.

2. D. Shook, "Why Nike Is Dragging Its Feet," *Business Week,* March 19, 2001, *Business Week* Online.

3. D. Robson, "Just Do . . . Something: Nike's Insularity and Foot-Dragging Have It Running in Place," *Business Week,* July 2, 2001, pp. 70–71; Schlosser, "Jack? Jack Who?"; Shook, "Why Nike Is Dragging Its Feet"; "Still Waiting for Nike to Do It: Nike's Labor Practices in the Three Years Since CEO Phil Knight's Speech to the National Press Club," *Sweatshop Watch,* November 12, 2001, sweatshopwatch.org; "New Report Attacks Nike Work Practices," May 17, 2001, www.abc.net.

4. D. Robson, "Just Do . . . Something"; Schlosser, "Jack? Jack Who?"; Shook, "Why Nike Is Dragging Its Feet"; "Still Waiting for Nike to Do It"; "New Report Attacks Nike Work Practices."

5. Robson, "Just Do . . . Something."

6. Robson, "Just Do . . . Something."

7. Robson, "Just Do . . . Something."

8. Ibid.

9. Ibid.

10. G. P. Huber, *Managerial Decision Making* (Glenview, IL: Scott, Foresman, 1993).

11. H. A. Simon, *The New Science of Management* (Englewood Cliffs, NJ: Prentice-Hall, 1977).

12. One should be careful not to generalize too much here, however; for as Peter Senge has shown, programmed decisions rely on the implicit assumption that the environment is in a steady state. If environmental conditions change, then sticking to a routine decision rule can produce disastrous results. See P. Senge, *The Fifth Discipline: The Art and Practice of the Learning Organization* (New York: Doubleday, 1990).

13. H. A. Simon, *Administrative Behavior* (New York: Macmillan, 1947), 79.

14. H. A. Simon, *Models of Man* (New York: Wiley, 1957).

15. K. J. Arrow, *Aspects of the Theory of Risk Bearing* (Helsinki: Yrjo Johnssonis Saatio, 1965).

16. Ibid.

17. L. Braham, "Company Stock Could Sink Your Ship," *Business Week,* July 30, 2001, *Business Week* Archives; S. N. Mehta, "Lessons from the Lucent Debacle," *Fortune,* February 5, 2001, pp. 143–48; S. Rosenbush and A. Borrus, "Lucent's Dark Days," *Business Week,* May 7, 2001, *Business Week* Archives.

18. Mehta, "Lessons from the Lucent Debacle."

19. Mehta, "Lessons from the Lucent Debacle."

20. R. L. Daft and R. H. Lengel, "Organizational Information Requirements, Media Richness and Structural Design," *Management Science* 32 (1986): 554–71.

21. Robson, "Just Do . . . Something."

22. R. Cyert and J. March, *Behavioral Theory of the Firm* (Englewood Cliffs, NJ: Prentice-Hall, 1963).

23. J. G. March and H. A. Simon, *Organizations* (New York: Wiley, 1958).

24. H. A. Simon, "Making Management Decisions: The Role of Intuition and Emotion," *Academy of Management Executive* 1 (1987): 57–64.

25. M. H. Bazerman, *Judgment in Managerial Decision Making* (New York: Wiley, 1986). Also see Simon, *Administrative Behavior.*

26. R. Crockett, "Motorola: Can Chris Galvin Save His Family's Legacy?" *Business Week,* July 16, 2001, pp. 73–78.

27. Crockett, "Motorola: Can Chris Galvin Save His Family's Legacy?"

28. Crockett, "Motorola: Can Chris Galvin Save His Family's Legacy?"

29. Crockett, "Motorola: Can Chris Galvin Save His Family's Legacy?"; R. O. Crockett, "Motorola's Galvin Shakes Things Up–Again," *Business Week,* May 28, 2001, *Business Week* Archives; R. O. Crockett, "How an Ace Mechanic Could Fix Motorola," *Business Week,* October 22, 2001, *Business Week* Archives.

30. N. J. Langowitz and S. C. Wheelright, "Sun Microsystems, Inc. (A)," Harvard Business School Case #686–133.

31. R. D. Hof, "How to Kick the Mainframe Habit," *Business Week,* June 26, 1995, 102–04.

32. Bazerman, *Judgment in Managerial Decision Making*; Huber, *Managerial Decision Making*; J. E. Russo and P. J. Schoemaker, *Decision Traps* (New York: Simon & Schuster, 1989).

33. M. D. Cohen, J. G. March, and J. P. Olsen, "A Garbage Can Model of Organizational Choice," *Administrative Science Quarterly* 17 (1972): 1–25.

34. Ibid.

35. Bazerman, *Judgment in Managerial Decision Making.*

36. Senge, *The Fifth Discipline.*

37. E. de Bono, *Lateral Thinking* (London: Penguin 1968); Senge, *The Fifth Discipline.*

38. Russo and Schoemaker, *Decision Traps.*

39. Bazerman, *Judgment in Managerial Decision Making.*

40. N. Varchaver, "A Hot Stock's Dirty Secret," *Fortune,* July 9, 2001, pp. 106–110.

41. K. Holland, "The Fight Over 'Rambus Inside,'" *Business Week,* April 28, 1997, *Business Week* Archives; Varchaver, "A Hot Stock's Dirty Secret."

42. Varchaver, "A Hot Stock's Dirty Secret."

43. P. Burrows, "Does Crime Pay?" *Business Week,* September 3, 2001, pp. 62–68.

44. P. Burrows, "Does Crime Pay?"

45. Russo and Schoemaker, *Decision Traps.*

46. D. Kahneman and A. Tversky, "Judgment Under Uncertainty: Heuristics and Biases," *Science* 185 (1974): 1124–31.

47. C. R. Schwenk, "Cognitive Simplification Processes in Strategic Decision Making," *Strategic Management Journal* 5 (1984): 111–28.

48. Robson, "Just Do . . . Something."

49. An interesting example of the illusion of control is Richard Roll's hubris hypothesis of takeovers. See R. Roll, "The Hubris Hypothesis of Corporate Takeovers," *Journal of Business* 59 (1986): 197–216.

50. B. M. Staw, "The Escalation of Commitment to a Course of Action," *Academy of Management Review* 6 (1981): 577–87.

51. M. J. Tang, "An Economic Perspective on Escalating Commitment," *Strategic Management Journal* 9 (1988): 79–92.

52. Mehta, "Lessons from the Lucent Debacle."

53. Russo and Schoemaker, *Decision Traps.*

54. Ibid.

55. I. L. Janis, *Groupthink: Psychological Studies of Policy Decisions and Disasters,* 2d ed. (Boston: Houghton-Mifflin, 1982).

56. C. R. Schwenk, *The Essence of Strategic Decision Making* (Lexington, MA: Lexington Books, 1988).

57. See R. O. Mason, "A Dialectic Approach to Strategic Planning," *Management Science* 13 (1969): 403–14; R. A. Cosier and J. C. Aplin, "A Critical View of Dialectic Inquiry in Strategic Planning," *Strategic Management Journal* 1 (1980): 343–56; I. I. Mitroff and R. O. Mason, "Structuring III–Structured Policy Issues: Further Explorations in a Methodology for Messy Problems," *Strategic Management Journal* 1 (1980): 331–42.

58. Mason, "A Dialectic Approach to Strategic Planning."

59. D. M. Schweiger and P. A. Finger, "The Comparative Effectiveness of Dialectic Inquiry and Devil's Advocacy," *Strategic Management Journal* 5 (1984): 335–50.

60. Mary C. Gentile, *Differences That Work: Organizational Excellence Through Diversity* (Boston: Harvard Business School Press, 1994); F. Rice, "How to Make Diversity Pay," *Fortune,* August 8, 1994, 78–86.

61. B. Hedberg, "How Organizations Learn and Unlearn," in W. H. Starbuck and P. C. Nystrom, eds., *Handbook of Organizational Design,* vol. 1 (New York: Oxford University Press, 1981), 1–27.

62. Senge, *The Fifth Discipline.*

63. Ibid.

64. P. M. Senge, "The Leader's New Work: Building Learning Organizations," *Sloan Management Review* (Fall 1990): 7–23.

65. W. Zellner, K. A. Schmidt, M. Ihlwan, and H. Dawley, "How Well Does Wal-Mart Travel," *Business Week,* September 3, 2001, pp. 82–84.

66. Zellner, Schmidt, Ihlwan, and Dawley, "How Well Does Wal-Mart Travel."

67. Ibid.

68. Ibid.

69. R. W. Woodman, J. E. Sawyer, and R. W. Griffin, "Towards a Theory of Organizational Creativity," *Academy of Management Review* 18 (1993): 293–321.

70. T. J. Bouchard, Jr., J. Barsaloux, and G. Drauden, "Brainstorming Procedure, Group Size, and Sex as Determinants of Problem Solving Effectiveness of Individuals and Groups," *Journal of Applied Psychology* 59 (1974): 135–38.

71. M. Diehl and W. Stroebe, "Productivity Loss in Brainstorming Groups: Towards the Solution of a Riddle," *Journal of Personality and Social Psychology* 53 (1987): 497–509.

72. D. H. Gustafson, R. K. Shulka, A. Delbecq, and W. G. Walster, "A Comparative Study of Differences in Subjective Likelihood Estimates Made by Individuals, Interacting Groups, Delphi Groups, and Nominal Groups," *Organizational Behavior and Human Performance* 9 (1973): 280–91.

73. N. Dalkey, *The Delphi Method: An Experimental Study of Group Decision Making* (Santa Monica, CA: Rand Corp., 1989).

Chapter 8

1. www.federalexpress.com, 2001.

2. www.ups.com, 2001.

3. C. Haddad and J. Ewing, "Ground Wars," *Business Week,* May 21, 2001, pp. 64–68.

4. A. Chandler, *Strategy and Structure: Chapters in the History of the American Enterprise* (Cambridge, MA: MIT Press, 1962).

5. Ibid.

6. F. J. Aguilar, "General Electric: Reg Jones and Jack Welch," in *General Managers in Action* (Oxford: Oxford University Press, 1992).

7. www.ge.com, 2001.

8. Aguilar, *General Managers in Action.*

9. Aguilar, "General Electric."

10. C. W. Hofer and D. Schendel, *Strategy Formulation: Analytical Concepts* (St. Paul, MN: West, 1978).

11. H. Fayol, *General and Industrial Management* (1884; New York: IEEE Press, 1984).

12. Fayol, *General and Industrial Management,* 18.

13. A. P. De Geus, "Planning as Learning," *Harvard Business Review,* March–April 1988: 70–74.

14. P. Wack, "Scenarios: Shooting the Rapids," *Harvard Business Review* November–December, 1985: 139–50.

15. P. J. H. Schoemaker, "Multiple Scenario Development: Its Conceptual and Behavioral Foundation," *Strategic Management Journal* 14 (1993): 193–213.

16. R. Phelps, C. Chan, S. C. Kapsalis, "Does Scenario Planning Affect Firm Performance?" *Journal of Business Research,* March 2001, pp. 223–32.

17. J. A. Pearce, "The Company Mission as a Strategic Tool," *Sloan Management Review,* Spring 1992: 15–24.

18. D. F. Abell, *Defining the Business: The Starting Point of Strategic Planning* (Englewood Cliffs, NJ: Prentice-Hall, 1980).

19. C. Palmeri, "Mattel: Up the Hill Minus Jill," *Business Week,* April 9, 2001, pp. 53–54.

20. www.mattel.com, 2001.

21. G. Hamel and C. K. Prahalad, "Strategic Intent," *Harvard Business Review,* May-June 1989: 63–73.

22. J. Shinal, "Why Cisco's Comeback Plan Is a Long Shot," *Business Week,* May 21, 2001, p. 42.

23. E. A. Locke, G. P. Latham, M. Erez, "The Determinants of Goal Commitment," *Academy of Management Review* 13 (1988): 23–39.

24. Ibid.

25. M. Hammer and J. Champy, *Reengineering the Corporation* (New York: Harper Business, 1993).

26. K. R. Andrews, *The Concept of Corporate Strategy* (Homewood, IL: Irwin, 1971).

27. www.hitachi.com, 2001.

28. E. Penrose, *The Theory of the Growth of the Firm* (Oxford: Oxford University Press, 1959).

29. M. E. Porter, "From Competitive Advantage to Corporate Strategy," *Harvard Business Review* 65 (1987): 43–59.

30. D. J. Teece, "Economies of Scope and the Scope of the Enterprise," *Journal of Economic Behavior and Organization* 3 (1980): 223–47.

31. M. E. Porter, *Competitive Advantage: Creating and Sustaining Superior Performance* (New York: Free Press, 1985).

32. For a review of the evidence, see C. W. L. Hill and G. R. Jones, *Strategic Management: An Integrated Approach,* 3d ed. (Boston: Houghton Mifflin, 2000), Ch. 10.

33. C. R. Christensen et al., *Business Policy Text and Cases* (Homewood, IL: Irwin, 1987), 778.

34. C. W. L. Hill, "Conglomerate Performance over the Economic Cycle," *Journal of Industrial Economics* 32 (1983): 197–213.

35. V. Ramanujam and P. Varadarajan, "Research on Corporate Diversification: A Synthesis," *Strategic Management Journal* 10 (1989): 523–51. Also see A. Shleifer and R. W. Vishny, "Takeovers in the 1960s and 1980s: Evidence and Implications," in R. P. Rumelt, D. E. Schendel, and D. J. Teece, *Fundamental Issues in Strategy* (Boston: Harvard Business School Press, 1994).

36. J. R. Williams, B. L. Paez, and L. Sanders, "Conglomerates Revisited," *Strategic Management Journal* 9 (1988): 403–14.

37. C. A. Bartlett and S. Ghoshal, *Managing Across Borders* (Boston: Harvard Business School Press, 1989).

38. C. K. Prahalad and Y. L. Doz, *The Multinational Mission* (New York: Free Press, 1987).

39. www.gillette.com, 2001.

40. "Gillette Co.'s New $40 Million Razor Blade Factory in St Petersburg Russia," *Boston Globe,* June 7, 2000, p. C6.

41. www.gillette.com, 2000.

42. M. K. Perry, "Vertical Integration: Determinants and Effects," in R. Schmalensee and R. D. Willig, *Handbook of Industrial Organization,* vol. 1 (New York: Elsevier Science Publishing, 1989).

43. T. Muris, D. Scheffman, and P. Spiller, "Strategy and Transaction Costs: The Organization of Distribution in the Carbonated Soft Drink Industry," *Journal of Economics and Management Strategy* 1 (1992): 77–97.

44. "Matsushita Electric Industrial (MEI) in 1987," *Harvard Business School Case* #388-144.

45. P. Ghemawat, *Commitment: The Dynamic of Strategy* (New York: Free Press, 1991).

46. www.ibm.com, 2001.

47. M. E. Porter, *Competitive Strategy* (New York: Free Press, 1980).

48. C. W. L. Hill, "Differentiation Versus Low Cost or Differentiation and Low Cost: A Contingency Framework," *Academy of Management Review* 13 (1988): 401–12.

49. For details, see J. P. Womack, D. T. Jones, and D. Roos, *The Machine That Changed the World* (New York: Rawson Associates, 1990).

50. Porter, *Competitive Strategy.*

51. www.zara.com, 2001

52. C. Vitzthum, "Just-in-Time-Fashion," *Wall Street Journal,* May 18th, 2001, p. B.1, B.4.

53. www.zara.com, 2001.

54. Hill and Jones, *Strategic Management.*

55. Womack, Jones, and Roos, *The Machine That Changed the World.*

56. See D. Garvin, "What Does Product Quality Really Mean?" *Sloan Management Review* 26 (Fall 1984): 25–44; P. B. Crosby, *Quality Is Free* (New York: Mentor Books, 1980); A. Gabor, *The Man Who Discovered Quality* (New York: Times Books, 1990).

57. www.citicorp, 2001.

Chapter 9

1. www.lucent.com, 2001.

2. C. Arnst, R. O. Crockett, A. Reinhardt, and J. Shinai, "Lucent: Clean Break, Clean Slate," *Business Week,* November 6, 2000, pp. 172–180.

3. www.lucent.com, 2001.

4. G. R. Jones, *Organizational Theory: Text and Cases* (Reading, MA: Addison-Wesley, 1995).

5. J. Child, *Organization: A Guide for Managers and Administrators* (New York: Harper and Row, 1977).

6. P. R. Lawrence and J. W. Lorsch, *Organization and Environment* (Boston: Graduate School of Business Administration, Harvard University, 1967).

7. R. Duncan, "What Is the Right Organizational Design?" *Organizational Dynamics* (Winter 1979): 59–80.

8. T. Burns and G. R. Stalker, *The Management of Innovation* (London: Tavistock, 1966).

9. D. Miller, "Strategy Making and Structure: Analysis and Implications for Performance," *Academy of Management Journal* 30 (1987): 7–32.

10. A. D. Chandler, *Strategy and Structure* (Cambridge, MA: MIT Press, 1962).

11. J. Stopford and L. Wells, *Managing the Multinational Enterprise* (London: Longman, 1972).

12. C. Perrow, *Organizational Analysis: A Sociological View* (Belmont, CA: Wadsworth, 1970).

13. J. Woodward, *Management and Technology* (London: Her Majesty's Stationery Office, 1958).

14. J. Woodward, ibid.

15. F. W. Taylor, *The Principles of Scientific Management* (New York: Harper, 1911).

16. R. W. Griffin, *Task Design: An Integrative Approach* (Glenview, IL: Scott, Foresman, 1982).

17. Ibid.

18. J. R. Hackman and G. R. Oldham, *Work Redesign* (Reading, MA: Addison-Wesley, 1980).

19. J. R. Galbraith and R. K. Kazanjian, *Strategy Implementation: Structure, System, and Process,* 2d ed. (St. Paul, MN: West, 1986).

20. Lawrence and Lorsch, *Organization and Environment.*

21. www.pier1.com, 2001.

22. Jones, *Organizational Theory.*

23. Lawrence and Lorsch, *Organization and Environment.*

24. R. H. Hall, *Organizations: Structure and Process* (Englewood Cliffs, NJ: Prentice-Hall, 1972); R. Miles, *Macro Organizational Behavior* (Santa Monica, CA: Goodyear, 1980).

25. Chandler, *Strategy and Structure.*

26. G. R. Jones and C. W. L. Hill, "Transaction Cost Analysis of Strategy-Structure Choice," *Strategic Management Journal* 9 (1988): 159–72.

27. www.viacom.com, 2001.

28. www.viacom.com, 2001.

29. J. S. Lublin, "Division Problem–Place vs. Product: It's Tough to Choose a Management Model," *Wall Street Journal,* June 27, 2001, pp. A1, A4.

30. S. M. Davis and P. R. Lawrence, *Matrix* (Reading, MA: Addison-Wesley, 1977); J. R. Galbraith, "Matrix Organization Designs: How to Combine Functional and Project Forms," *Business Horizons* 14 (1971): 29–40.

31. L. R. Burns, "Matrix Management in Hospitals: Testing Theories of Matrix Structure and Development," *Administrative Science Quarterly* 34 (1989): 349–68.

32. C. W. L. Hill, *International Business* (New York: McGraw-Hill, 1997).

33. Jones, *Organizational Theory.*

34. A. Farnham, "America's Most Admired Company," *Fortune,* February 7, 1994, 50–54.

35. D. K. Denton, "Process Mapping Trims Cycle Times," *HRM Magazine,* February 1995, 56–59.

36. www.target.com, 2001.

37. P. Blau, "A Formal Theory of Differentiation in Organizations," *American Sociological Review* 35 (1970): 684–95.

38. www.mcdonalds.com, 2001.

39. www.mcdonalds.com, 2001.

40. Child, *Organization.*

41. S. McCartney, "Airline Industry's Top-Ranked Woman Keeps Southwest's Small-Fry Spirit Alive," *The Wall Street Journal,* November 30, 1995, B1.

42. P. M. Blau and R. A. Schoenherr, *The Structure of Organizations* (New York: Basic Books, 1971).

43. Jones, *Organizational Theory.*

44. C. Tierney and K. Schmidt, "Schrempp, the Survivor?" *Business Week,* March 5, 2001, p. 54.

45. www.yahoo.com, 2001.

46. Lawrence and Lorsch, *Organization and Environment,* 50–55.

47. J. R. Galbraith, *Designing Complex Organizations* (Reading, MA: Addison-Wesley, 1977), Ch. 1; Galbraith and Kazanjian, *Strategy Implementation,* Ch. 7.

48. Lawrence and Lorsch, *Organization and Environment,* 55.

49. B. Kogut, "Joint Ventures: Theoretical and Empirical Perspectives," *Strategic Management Journal* 9 (1988): 319–32.

50. G. S. Capowski, "Designing a Corporate Identity," *Management Review* (June 1993): 37–38.

51. J. Marcia, "Just Doing It," *Distribution* (January 1995): 36–40.

52. "Nike Battles Backlash from Overseas Sweatshops," *Marketing News,* November 9, 1998, p. 14.

53. J. Laabs, "Mike Gives Indonesian Workers a Raise," *Workforce,* December 1998, pp. 15–16.

54. W. Echikson, "It's Europe's Turn to Sweat about Sweatshops," *Business Week,* July 19, 1999, p. 96.

55. © 2001, Gareth R. Jones.

Chapter 10

1. W. G. Ouchi, "Markets, Bureaucracies, and Clans," *Administrative Science Quarterly* 25 (1980): 129–41.

2. P. Lorange, M. Morton, and S. Ghoshal, *Strategic Control* (St. Paul, MN: West, 1986).

3. H. Koontz and R. W. Bradspies, "Managing Through Feedforward Control," *Business Horizons* (June 1972): 25–36.

4. E. E. Lawler III and J. G. Rhode, *Information and Control in Organizations* (Pacific Palisades, CA: Goodyear, 1976).

5. C. W. L. Hill and G. R. Jones, *Strategic Management: An Integrated Approach,* 4th ed. (Boston: Houghton Mifflin, 1997).

6. W. M. Bulkeley and J. S. Lublin, "Xerox Appoints Insider Mulcahy to Execute Turnaround as CEO," *Wall Street Journal,* July, 27, 2001, p. A2.

7. E. Flamholtz, "Organizational Control Systems as a Management Tool," *California Management Review* (Winter 1979): 50–58.

8. W. G. Ouchi, "The Transmission of Control Through Organizational Hierarchy," *Academy of Management Journal* 21 (1978): 173–92.

9. W. G. Ouchi, "The Relationship Between Organizational Structure and Organizational Control," *Administrative Science Quarterly* 22 (1977): 95–113.

10. Ouchi, "Markets, Bureaucracies, and Clans."

11. W. H. Newman, *Constructive Control* (Englewood Cliffs, NJ: Prentice-Hall, 1975).

12. J. D. Thompson, *Organizations in Action* (New York: McGraw-Hill, 1967).

13. R. N. Anthony, *The Management Control Function* (Boston: Harvard Business School Press, 1988).

14. Ouchi, "Markets, Bureaucracies, and Clans."

15. Hill and Jones, *Strategic Management.*

16. R. Simons, "Strategic Orientation and Top Management Attention to Control Systems," *Strategic Management Journal* 12 (1991): 49–62.

17. G. Schreyogg and H. Steinmann, "Strategic Control: A New Perspective," *Academy of Management Review* 12 (1987): 91–103.

18. B. Woolridge and S. W. Floyd, "The Strategy Process, Middle Management Involvement, and Organizational Performance," *Strategic Management Journal* 11 (1990): 231–41.

19. J. A. Alexander, "Adaptive Changes in Corporate Control Practices," *Academy of Management Journal* 34 (1991): 162–93.

20. Hill and Jones, *Strategic Management.*

21. G. H. B. Ross, "Revolution in Management Control," *Management Accounting* 72 (1992): 23–27.

22. P. F. Drucker, *The Practice of Management* (New York: Harper and Row, 1954).

23. S. J. Carroll and H. L. Tosi, *Management by Objectives: Applications and Research* (New York: Macmillan, 1973).

24. R. Rodgers and J. E. Hunter, "Impact of Management by Objectives on Organizational Productivity," *Journal of Applied Psychology* 76 (1991): 322–26.

25. M. B. Gavin, S. G. Green, and G. T. Fairhurst, "Managerial Control Strategies for Poor Performance over Time and the Impact on Subordinate Reactions," *Organizational Behavior and Human Decision Processes* 63 (1995): 207–21.

26. www.cypress.com, 2001.

27. B. Dumaine, "The Bureaucracy Busters," *Fortune,* June 17, 1991, 46.

28. D. S. Pugh, D. J. Hickson, C. R. Hinings, and C. Turner, "Dimensions of Organizational Structure," *Administrative Science Quarterly* 13 (1968): 65–91.

29. B. Elgin, "Running the Tightest Ships on the Net," *Business Week,* January 29, 2001, pp. 125–26.

30. P. M. Blau, *The Dynamics of Bureaucracy* (Chicago: University of Chicago Press, 1955).

31. Ouchi, "Markets, Bureaucracies, and Clans"; M. Lebas and J. Weigenstein, "Management Control: The Roles of Rules, Markets, and Culture," *Journal of Management Studies* 23 (1986): 259–72.

32. M. Rokeach, *The Nature of Human Values* (New York: The Free Press, 1973).

33. D. C. Feldman, "The Development and Enforcement of Group Norms," *Academy of Management Review* 9 (1984): 47–53.

34. Jones, "Organizational Theory."

35. H. Schein, "The Role of the Founder in Creating Organizational Culture," *Organizational Dynamics* 12 (1983): 13–28.

36. J. M. George, "Personality, Affect, and Behavior in Groups," *Journal of Applied Psychology* 75 (1990): 107–16.

37. J. Van Maanen, "Police Socialization: A Longitudinal Examination of Job Attitudes in an Urban Police Department," *Administrative Science Quarterly* 20 (1975): 207–28.

38. P. L. Berger and T. Luckman, *The Social Construction of Reality* (Garden City, NY: Anchor Books, 1967).

39. H. M. Trice and J. M. Beyer, "Studying Organizational Culture Through Rites and Ceremonials," *Academy of Management Review* 9 (1984): 653–69.

40. H. M. Trice and J. M. Beyer, *The Cultures of Work Organizations* (Englewood Cliffs, NJ: Prentice Hall, 1993).

41. B. Ortega, "Wal-Mart's Meeting Is a Reason to Party," *The Wall Street Journal,* June 3, 1994, A1.

42. www.nokia.com, 2001.

43. P. de Bendern, "Quirky Culture Paves Nokia's Road to Fortune," www.yahoo.com, 2000.

44. Trice and Beyer, "Studying Organizational Culture."

45. S. Mcgee, "Garish Jackets Add to Clamor of Chicago Pits," *The Wall Street Journal,* July 31, 1995, C1.

46. S. Avery, "Many H-P Employees Accept Cuts," *Wall Street Journal,* June 24, 2001, p. A.3.

47. www.merck.com, 2001.

48. K. E. Weick, *The Social Psychology of Organization* (Reading, MA: Addison-Wesley, 1979).

49. J. W. Schulz, L. C. Hauck, R. M. Hauck, "Using the Power of Corporate Culture to Achieve Results: A Case Study of Sunflower Electric Power Corporation," *Management Quarterly,* 2, 2001, pp. 2–19.

50. J. P. Kotter and J. L. Heskett. *Corporate Culture and Performance* (New York: Free Press, 1992).

Chapter 11

1. http://www.trilogy.com; E. Ramstand, "How Trilogy Software Trains Its Raw Recruits to Be Risk Takers," *Wall Street Journal,* September 21, 1998; E. Thornton and H. Timmons, "Suing the Street Over Bum Advice," *Business Week,* March 5, 2001, *Business Week* Archives.

2. N. M. Tichy, "No Ordinary Boot Camp," *Harvard Business Review,* April, 2001, pp. 63–70.

3. Ramstand, "How Trilogy Software Trains Its Raw Recruits"; Tichy, "No Ordinary Boot Camp."

4. Ramstand, "How Trilogy Software Trains Its Raw Recruits"; Tichy, "No Ordinary Boot Camp."

5. Ramstand, "How Trilogy Software Trains Its Raw Recruits."

6. Tichy, "No Ordinary Boot Camp."

7. Ramstand, "How Trilogy Software Trains Its Raw Recruits."

8. J. E. Butler, G. R. Ferris, and N. K. Napier, *Strategy and Human Resource Management* (Cincinnati: Southwestern Publishing Co., 1991); P. M. Wright, and G. C. McMahan, "Theoretical Perspectives for Strategic Human Resource Management," *Journal of Management* 18 (1992): 295–320.

9. L. Clifford, "Why You Can Safely Ignore Six Sigma," *Fortune,* January 22, 2001, 140.

10. J. B. Quinn, P. Anderson, and S. Finkelstein, "Managing Professional Intellect: Making the Most of the Best," *Harvard Business Review,* March–April 1996, 71–80.

11. Ibid.

12. C. D. Fisher, L. F. Schoenfeldt, and J. B. Shaw, *Human Resource Management* (Boston: Houghton Mifflin, 1990).

13. P. M. Wright and G. C. McMahan, "Theoretical Perspectives for Strategic Human Resource Management," *Journal of Management* 18 (1992): 295–320.

14. L. Baird and I. Meshoulam, "Managing Two Fits for Strategic Human Resource Management," *Academy of Management Review,* 14, 116–28; J. Milliman, M. Von Glinow, and M. Nathan, "Organizational Life Cycles and Strategic International Human Resource Management in Multinational Companies: Implications for Congruence Theory," *Academy of Management Review,* 16, 318–39; R. S. Schuler and S. E. Jackson, "Linking Competitive Strategies with Human Resource Management Practices," *Academy of Management Executive,* 1 (1987): 207–219; P. M. Wright and S. A. Snell, "Toward an Integrative View of Strategic Human Resource Management," *Human Resource Management Review,* 1 (1991): 203–225.

15. Equal Employment Opportunity Commission, "Uniform Guidelines on Employee Selection Procedures," *Federal Register* 43 (1978): 38290–315.

16. R. Stogdill II, R. Mitchell, K. Thurston, and C. Del Valle, "Why AIDS Policy Must Be a Special Policy," *Business Week,* February 1, 1993, 53–54.

17 J. M. George, "AIDS/AIDS-Related Complex," in L. Peters, B. Greer, and S. Youngblood, eds., *The Blackwell Encyclopedic Dictionary of Human Resource Management.* Oxford, UK: Blackwell Publishers, 1997.

18. Ibid.

19. J. M. George, "AIDS Awareness Training," in L. Peters, B. Greer, and S. Youngblood, eds., *The Blackwell Encyclopedic Dictionary of Human Resource Management.* Oxford, UK: Blackwell Publishers, 1997; Stogdill, Mitchell, Thurston, and Del Valle, "Why AIDS Policy Must Be a Special Policy."

20. A. E. Cha, "Laid-Off Dot-Com Workers Get Chance to Reflect, Re-Energize," *Houston Chronicle,* May 13, 2001, p. 3D.

21. Ibid.

22. "Cheat Sheet: How to Fire or Be Fired," www.ecompany.com, April 2001.

23. M. Conlin, "Labor Laws Apply to Dot-Coms? Really?" *Business Week,* February 26, 2001, 96, 98.

24. "Advance Notice," www.ecompany.com, April, 2001; and Conlin, "Labor Laws Apply to Dot-Coms?"

25. M. Warner, "Pity the Poor Dot-Commer (a Little Bit)," *Fortune,* January 22, 2001, 40.

26. S. L. Rynes, "Recruitment, Job Choice, and Post-Hire Consequences: A Call for New Research Directions," in M. D. Dunnette and L. M. Hough, eds., *Handbook of Industrial and Organizational Psychology,* vol. 2 (Palo Alto, CA: Consulting Psychologists Press, 1991), 399–444.

27. R. L. Sullivan, "Lawyers a la Carte," *Forbes,* September 11, 1995, 44.

28. I. Sager and P. Burrows, "How IBM Uses the Net," April 3, 2000, *Business Week* Archives.

29. M. Roman, "At Microsoft, a Consolation Prize," December 25, 2000, *Business Week* Archives.

30. M. Gimein, "The Bugs in the Microsoft Culture: Is Redmond a Great Place to Work for Temps and Minorities," *Fortune,* January 8, 2001, 128.

31. M. Gimein, "Smart Is Not Enough," *Fortune,* January 8, 2001, 124–36.

32. Gimein, "The Bugs in the Microsoft Culture."

33. R. J. Harvey, "Job Analysis," in M. D. Dunnette and L. M. Hough eds., *Handbook of Industrial and Organizational Psychology,* vol. 2 (Palo Alto, CA: Consulting Psychologists Press, 1991), 71–163.

34. E. L. Levine, *Everything You Always Wanted to Know About Job Analysis: A Job Analysis Primer* (Tampa, FL: Mariner Publishing, 1983).

35. R. L. Mathis, and J. H. Jackson, *Human Resource Management,* 7th ed. (Minneapolis: West, 1994).

36. E. J. McCormick, P. R. Jeannerette, and R. C. Mecham, *Position Analysis Questionnaire* (West Lafayette, IN: Occupational Research Center, Dept. of Psychological Sciences, Purdue University, 1969).

37. C. D. Fisher, L. F. Schoenfeldt, and J. B. Shaw, *Human Resource Management* (Boston: Houghton Mifflin, 1990); Mathis and Jackson, *Human Resource Management;* R. A. Noe, J. R. Hollenbeck, B. Gerhart, and P. M. Wright, *Human Resource Management: Gaining a Competitive Advantage* (Burr Ridge, IL: Irwin, 1994).

38. Fisher, Schoenfeldt, and Shaw, *Human Resource Management;* E. J. McCormick, *Job Analysis: Methods and Applications* (New York: American Management Association, 1979); E. J. McCormick and P. R. Jeannerette, "The Position Analysis Questionnaire" in S. Gael ed., *The Job Analysis Handbook for Business, Industry, and Government* (New York: Wiley, 1988); Noe, Hollenbeck, Gerhart, and Wright, *Human Resource Management.*

39. Rynes, "Recruitment, Job Choice, and Post-Hire Consequences."

40. R. Sharpe, "The Life of the Party?: Can Jeff Taylor Keep the Good Times Rolling at Monster.com?," *Business Week,* June 4, 2001, *Business Week* Archives.

41. Ibid.

42. H. Green, R. Sharpe, and A. Weintraub, "How to Reach John Q. Public," *Business Week,* March 26, 2001, *Business Week* Archives; A. Salkever, "A Better Way to Float Your Resume," *Business Week,* October 9, 2000, *Business Week* Archives; R. Sharpe, "The Life of the Party?"

43. http://www.monster.com, June, 2001.

44. http://www.jobline.org/, June 2001; Jobline press releases, June 20, 2001, May 8, 2001, http://www.jobline.org.

45. S. L. Premack and J. P. Wanous, "A Meta-Analysis of Realistic Job Preview Experiments," *Journal of Applied Psychology* 70, 706–719; J. P. Wanous, "Realistic Job Previews: Can a Procedure to Reduce Turnover also Influence the Relationship Between Abilities and Performance?" *Personnel Psychology* 31, 249–58; J. P. Wanous, *Organizational Entry: Recruitment, Selection, and Socialization of Newcomers* (Reading, MA: Addison-Wesley, 1980).

46. R. M. Guion, "Personnel Assessment, Selection, and Placement." in M. D. Dunnette and L. M. Hough, *Handbook of Industrial and Organizational Psychology,* vol. 2, (Palo Alto, CA: Consulting Psychologists Press, 1991), 327–97.

47. Noe, Hollenbeck, Gerhart, and Wright, *Human Resource Management;* J. A. Wheeler and J. A. Gier, "Reliability and Validity of the Situational Interview for a Sales Position," *Journal of Applied Psychology* 2 (1987): 484–87.

48. Noe, Hollenbeck, Gerhart, and Wright, *Human Resource Management.*

49. J. Flint, "Can You Tell Applesauce from Pickles?" *Forbes,* October 9, 1995, 106–108.

50. Ibid.

51. "Wanted: Middle Managers, Audition Required," *Wall Street Journal,* December 28, 1995, A1.

52. R. B. Lieber, "The Fight to Legislate Incompetence out of the Cockpit," *Fortune,* February 5, 1996, 30.

53. J. Novack, "What if the Guy Shoots Somebody?" *Forbes,* December 4, 1995, 37.

54. Ibid.

55. Lieber, "The Fight to Legislate Incompetence."

56. A. S. Wellner, "Background Checks," *Business Week,* August 14, 2000, *Business Week* Archives; www.frauddefense.com, June 2001.

57. Ibid.

58. I. L. Goldstein, "Training in Work Organizations." in M. D. Dunnette and L. M. Hough, eds., *Handbook of Industrial and Organizational Psychology* vol. 2 (Palo Alto, CA: Consulting Psychologists Press, 1991), 507–619.

59. S. Overman, "Ethan Allen's Secret Weapon," *HRMagazine,* May, 1994, 61.

60. N. Banerjee, "For Mary Kay Sales Reps in Russia, Hottest Shade Is the Color of Money," *Wall Street Journal,* August 30, 1995, A8.

61. T. A. Stewart, "Mystified by Training? Here Are Some Clues," *Fortune,* April 2, 2001, 184.

62. J. Ewing, "Siemens: Building a 'B-School' in Its Own Backyard," *Business Week,* November 15, 1999, *Business Week* Archives.

63. J. Ewing and F. Keenan, "Sharing the Wealth: How Siemens Is Using Knowledge Management to Pool the Expertise of All Its Workers," *Business Week,* March 19, 2001, *Business Week Archives.*

64. J. A. Byrne, "Virtual B-Schools," *Business Week,* October 23, 1995, 64–68.

65. Fisher, Schoenfeldt, and Shaw, *Human Resource Management.*

66. Fisher, Schoenfeldt, and Shaw, *Human Resource Management;* G. P. Latham and K. N. Wexley, *Increasing Productivity Through Performance Appraisal.* (Reading, MA: Addison-Wesley, 1982).

67. T. A. DeCotiis, "An Analysis of the External Validity and Applied Relevance of Three Rating Formats," *Organizational Behavior and Human Performance* 19 (1977): 247–66; Fisher, Schoenfeldt, and Shaw, *Human Resource Management.*

68. J. Muller, K. Kerwin, D. Welch, P. L. Moore, D. Brady, "Ford: It's Worse Than You Think," *Business Week,* June 25, 2001, *Business Week* Archives.

69. Ibid.

70. L. M. Sixel, "Enron Rating Setup Irks Many Workers," *Houston Chronicle,* February 26, 2001, 1C.

71. J. S. Lublin, "It's Shape-Up Time for Performance Reviews." *Wall Street Journal,* October 3, 1994, B1, B2.

72. J. S. Lublin, "Turning the Tables: Underlings Evaluate Bosses," *Wall Street Journal,* October 4, 1994, B1, B14; S. Shellenbarger, "Reviews from Peers Instruct–and Sting," *Wall Street Journal,* October 4, 1994, B1, B4.

73. Lublin, "Turning the Tables."

74. Shellenbarger, "Reviews from Peers Instruct–and Sting."

75. C. Borman and D. W. Bracken, "360 Degree Appraisals," in C. L. Cooper and C. Argyris, eds., *The Concise Blackwell Encyclopedia of Management.* (Oxford, UK: Blackwell Publishers, 1998), 17; D. W. Bracken, "Straight Talk About Multi-Rater Feedback," *Training and Development* 48 (1994): pp. 44–51; M. R. Edwards, W. C. Borman, and J. R. Sproul, "Solving the Double-Bind in Performance Appraisal: A Saga of Solves, Sloths, and Eagles," *Business Horizons,* 85 (1985): 59–68.

76. M. A. Peiperl, "Getting 360° Feedback Right," *Harvard Business Review,* January 2001, 142–47.

77. A. Harrington, "Workers of the World, Rate Your Boss!" *Fortune,* September 18, 2000, 340, 342; http://www.ImproveNow.com, June, 2001.

78. Ibid.

79. Lublin, "It's Shape-Up Time for Performance Reviews."

80. J. Flynn and F. Nayeri, "Continental Divide Over Executive Pay," *Business Week,* July 3, 1995, 40–41.

81. J. A. Byrne, "How High Can CEO Pay Go?" *Business Week,* April 22, 1996, 100–106.

82. S. Premack and J. E. Hunter, "Individual Unionization Decisions," *Psychological Bulletin* 103 (1988): 223–34.

83. M. B. Regan, "Shattering the AFL-CIO's Glass Ceiling," *Business Week,* November 13, 1995, 46.

84. http://www.aflcio.org/, June, 2001.

85. G. P. Zachary, "Some Unions Step Up Organizing Campaigns and Get New Members," *Wall Street Journal,* September 1, 1995, A1, A2.

86. M. B. Regan, "Shattering the AFL-CIO's Glass Ceiling," *Business Week,* November 13, 1995, 46; www.aflcio.org, June 2001; R. S. Dunham, "Big Labor: So Out It's 'Off the Radar Screen,'" *Business Week,* March 26, 2001, *Business Week* Archives.

87. "The Honorable Elaine L. Chao United States Secretary of Labor," http://www.dol.gov/dol/_sec/public/aboutosec/chao.htm, June 25, 2001.

88. R. Blumenstein, "Ohio Strike That Is Crippling GM Plants Is Tied to Plan to Outsource Brake Work," *Wall Street Journal,* March 12, 1996, A3–A4.

89. J. Hannah, "GM Workers Agree to End Strike," *Bryan-College Station Eagle,* March 23, 1996, A12.

Chapter 12

1. "Learn About Us," www.containerstore.com, June 26, 2001.

2. Ibid.

3. J. Schlosser and J. Sung, "The 100 Best Companies to Work For," *Fortune,* January 8, 2001, 148–68.

4. D. Roth, "My Job at the Container Store," *Fortune,* January 10, 2000, www.fortune.com, June 26, 2001.

5. Schlosser and Sung, "The 100 Best Companies."

6. T. A. Stewart, "Just Think: No Permission Needed," *Fortune,* January 8, 2001, Fortune.com, June 26, 2001.

7. "The Container Store Tops *Fortune's* 100 Best List for Second Year in a Row," December 18, 2000, www.containerstore.com.

8. Roth, "My Job at the Container Store."

9. T. A. Stewart, "Just Think: No Permission Needed."

10. Roth, "My Job at the Container Store."

11. R. Kanfer, "Motivation Theory and Industrial and Organizational Psychology," in M. D. Dunnette and L. M. Hough, eds., *Handbook of Industrial and Organizational Psychology,* 2d ed., vol. 1 (Palo Alto, CA: Consulting Psychologists Press, 1990), 75–170.

12. Stewart, "Just Think: No Permission Needed."

13. Roth, "My Job at the Container Store."

14. J. P. Campbell and R. D. Pritchard, "Motivation Theory in Industrial and Organizational Psychology," in M. D. Dunnette, ed., *Handbook of Industrial and Organizational Psychology* (Chicago: Rand McNally, 1976) 63–130; T. R. Mitchell, "Expectancy-Value Models in Organizational Psychology," in N. T. Feather, ed., *Expectations and Actions: Expectancy-Value Models in Psychology* (Hillsdale, NJ: Erlbaum, 1982), 293–312; V. H. Vroom, *Work and Motivation* (New York: Wiley, 1964).

15. Stewart, "Just Think: No Permission Needed."

16. D. Milbank, "Long Viewed as Kaput, Many European Firms Seem to Be Reviving," *Wall Street Journal,* February 14, 1995, A1, A8.

17. J. Kaufman, "How Cambodians Came to Control California Doughnuts," *Wall Street Journal,* February 22, 1995, A1, A8.

18. A. H. Maslow, *Motivation and Personality* (New York: Harper and Row, 1954); Campbell and Pritchard, "Motivation Theory in Industrial and Organizational Psychology."

19. Kanfer, "Motivation Theory and Industrial and Organizational Psychology."

20. S. Ronen, "An Underlying Structure of Motivational Need Taxonomies: A Cross-Cultural Confirmation," in H. C. Triandis, M. D. Dunnette, and L. M. Hough, eds., *Handbook of Industrial and Organizational Psychology,* vol. 4 (Palo Alto, CA: Consulting Psychologists Press, 1994), 241–69.

21. N. J. Adler, *International Dimensions of Organizational Behavior,* 2d ed. (Boston: P.W.S.-Kent, 1991); G. Hofstede, "Motivation, Leadership and Organization: Do American Theories Apply Abroad?" *Organizational Dynamics* (Summer 1980): 42–63.

22. C. P. Alderfer, "An Empirical Test of a New Theory of Human Needs," *Organizational Behavior and Human Performance* 4 (1969): 142–75; C. P. Alderfer, *Existence, Relatedness, and Growth: Human Needs in Organizational Settings* (New York: Free Press, 1972); Campbell and Pritchard, "Motivation Theory in Industrial and Organizational Psychology."

23. Kanfer, "Motivation Theory and Industrial and Organizational Psychology."

24. F. Herzberg, *Work and the Nature of Man* (Cleveland: World, 1966).

25. N. King, "Clarification and Evaluation of the Two-Factor Theory of Job Satisfaction," *Psychological Bulletin* 74 (1970): 18–31; E. A. Locke, "The Nature and Causes of Job Satisfaction," in M. D. Dunnette, ed., *Handbook of Industrial and Organizational Psychology* (Chicago: Rand McNally, 1976), 1297–1349.

26. D. C. McClelland, *Human Motivation* (Glenview, IL: Scott, Foresman, 1985); D. C. McClelland, "How Motives, Skills, and Values Determine What People Do," *American Psychologist* 40 (1985): 812–25; D. C. McClelland, "Managing Motivation to Expand Human Freedom," *American Psychologist* 33 (1978): 201–10.

27. D. G. Winter, *The Power Motive* (New York: Free Press, 1973).

28. M. J. Stahl, "Achievement, Power, and Managerial Motivation: Selecting Managerial Talent with the Job Choice Exercise," *Personnel Psychology* 36 (1983): 775–89; D. C. McClelland and D. H. Burnham, "Power Is the Great Motivator," *Harvard Business Review* 54 (1976): 100–110.

29. R. J. House, W. D. Spangler, and J. Woycke, "Personality and Charisma in the U.S. Presidency: A Psychological Theory of Leader Effectiveness," *Administrative Science Quarterly* 36 (1991): 364–96.

30. G. H. Hines, "Achievement, Motivation, Occupations and Labor Turnover in New Zealand," *Journal of Applied Psychology* 58 (1973): 313–17; P. S. Hundal, "A Study of Entrepreneurial Motivation: Comparison of Fast- and Slow-Progressing Small Scale Industrial Entrepreneurs in Punjab, India," *Journal of Applied Psychology* 55 (1971): 317–23.

31. R. A. Clay, "Green Is Good for You," *Monitor on Psychology,* April 2001, pp. 40–42.

32. Schlosser and Sung, "The 100 Best Companies to Work For."

33. E. P. Dalesio, "Quiet Giant Ready to Raise Its Profits," *Houston Chronicle,* May 6, 2001, 4D.

34. J. Pfeffer, "SAS Institute: A Different Approach to Incentives and People Management Practices in the Software Industry," January, 1998, Harvard Business School Case HR-6; "Saluting the Global Awards Recipients of Arthur Andersen's Best Practices Awards 2000," September 6, 2000, www.fortune.com; N. Stein, "Winning the War to Keep Top Talent," www.fortune.com, September 6, 2000.

35. J. Pfeffer, "SAS Institute"; "Saluting the Global Awards Recipients"; N. Stein, "Winning the War to Keep Top Talent."

36. J. Pfeffer, "SAS Institute"; "Saluting the Global Awards Recipients"; N. Stein, "Winning the War to Keep Top Talent."

37. Dalesio, "Quiet Giant Ready."

38. J. Pfeffer, "SAS Institute"; "Saluting the Global Awards Recipients"; N. Stein, "Winning the War to Keep Top Talent."

39. J. S. Adams, "Toward an Understanding of Inequity," *Journal of Abnormal and Social Psychology* 67 (1963): 422–36.

40. Ibid.; J. Greenberg, "Approaching Equity and Avoiding Inequity in Groups and Organizations," in J. Greenberg and R. L. Cohen, eds., *Equity and Justice in Social Behavior* (New York: Academic Press, 1982), 389–435; J. Greenberg, "Equity and Workplace Status: A Field Experiment," *Journal of Applied Psychology* 73 (1988) 606–13; R. T. Mowday, "Equity Theory Predictions of Behavior in Organizations," in R. M. Steers and L. W. Porter, eds., *Motivation and Work Behavior* (New York: McGraw-Hill, 1987), 89–110.

41. A. Goldwasser, "Inhuman Resources," *ecompany.com,* March 2001, 154–55.

42. R. Greenberger, "More Web Workers Claim Unfair Labor Practices," *Wall Street Journal,* October 17, 2000, B1, B4.

43. M. Conlin, "Revenge of the Managers," *Business Week,* March 12, 2001, 60–61.

44. Ibid.

45. Ibid.

46. E. A. Locke and G. P. Latham, *A Theory of Goal Setting and Task Performance* (Englewood Cliffs, NJ: Prentice-Hall, 1990).

47. Ibid.; J. J. Donovan and D. J. Radosevich, "The Moderating Role of Goal Commitment on the Goal Difficulty-Performance Relationship: A Meta-Analytic Review and Critical Analysis," *Journal of Applied Psychology* 83 (1998): 308–315; M. E. Tubbs, "Goal Setting: A Meta-Analytic Examination of the Empirical Evidence," *Journal of Applied Psychology* 71 (1986): 474–83.

48. E. A. Locke, K. N. Shaw, L. M. Saari, and G. P. Latham, "Goal Setting and Task Performance: 1969–1980," *Psychological Bulletin,* 90 (1981): 125–52.

49. P. C. Earley, T. Connolly, and G. Ekegren, "Goals, Strategy Development, and Task Performance: Some Limits on the Efficacy of Goal Setting," *Journal of Applied Psychology* 74 (1989): 24–33; R. Kanfer and P. L. Ackerman, "Motivation and Cognitive Abilities: An Integrative/Aptitude-Treatment Interaction Approach to Skill Acquisition," *Journal of Applied Psychology* 74 (1989): 657–90.

50. W. C. Hamner, "Reinforcement Theory and Contingency Management in Organizational Settings," in H. Tosi and W. C. Hamner, eds., *Organizational Behavior and Management: A Contingency Approach* (Chicago: St. Clair Press, 1974).

51. B. F. Skinner, *Contingencies of Reinforcement* (New York: Appleton-Century-Crofts, 1969).

52. H. W. Weiss, "Learning Theory and Industrial and Organizational Psychology" in M. D. Dunnette and L. M. Hough, eds., *Handbook of Industrial and Organizational Psychology,* 2d ed., vol. 1 (Palo Alto, CA: Consulting Psychologists Press, 1990), 171–221.

53. Hamner, "Reinforcement Theory and Contingency Management."

54. "Who We Are," www.jcrew.com, June 28, 2001.

55. E. Kelly, "A Shift in Style," *Fortune,* November 13, 2000, 340–350.

56. Ibid.

57. "Store Listings," www.jcrew.com, June 28, 2001.

58. Kelly, "A Shift in Style."

59. "Why J. Crew," www.jcrew.com, June 28, 2001.

60. "A Dynamic, Friendly Workplace," www.jcrew.com, June 28, 2001.

61. F. Luthans and R. Kreitner, *Organizational Behavior Modification and Beyond* (Glenview, IL: Scott, Foresman, 1985); A. D. Stajkovic and F. Luthans, "A Meta-Analysis of the Effects of Organizational Behavior Modification on Task Performance, 1975–95," *Academy of Management Journal,* 40 (1997): 1122–49.

62. A. Bandura, *Principles of Behavior Modification* (New York: Holt, Rinehart and Winston, 1969); A. Bandura, *Social Learning Theory* (Englewood Cliffs, NJ: Prentice-Hall, 1977); T. R. V. Davis and F. Luthans, "A Social Learning Approach to Organizational Behavior," *Academy of Management Review* 5 (1980): 281–90.

63. A. P. Goldstein and M. Sorcher, *Changing Supervisor Behaviors* (New York: Pergamon Press, 1974); Luthans and Kreitner, *Organizational Behavior Modification and Beyond.*

64. A. Bandura, *Social Learning Theory*; Davis and Luthans, "A Social Learning Approach to Organizational Behavior"; F. Luthans and R. Kreitner, *Organizational Behavior Modification and Beyond.*

65. A. Bandura, "Self-Reinforcement: Theoretical and Methodological Considerations," *Behaviorism* 4 (1976): 135–55.

66. P. Engardio, "A Hothouse of High-Tech Talent," *Business Week/ 21st Century Capitalism* (1994): 126.

67. A. Bandura, "Self-Efficacy Mechanism in Human Agency," *American Psychologist* 37 (1982): 122–27; M. E. Gist and T. R. Mitchell, "Self-Efficacy: A Theoretical Analysis of Its Determinants and Malleability," *Academy of Management Review* 17 (1992): 183–211.

68. E. E. Lawler III, *Pay and Organization Development* (Reading, MA: Addison-Wesley, 1981).

69. "The Risky New Bonuses," *Newsweek,* January 16, 1995, 42.

70. Lawler, *Pay and Organization Development.*

71. Ibid.

72. J. F. Lincoln, *Incentive Management* (Cleveland: Lincoln Electric Company, 1951); R. Zager, "Managing Guaranteed Employment," *Harvard Business Review* 56 (1978): 103–15.

73. Lawler, *Pay and Organization Development.*

74. M. Gendron, "Gradient Named 'Small Business of Year,'" *Boston Herald,* May 11, 1994, 35.

75. W. Zeller, R. D. Hof, R. Brandt, S. Baker, and D. Greising. "Go-Go Goliaths," *Business Week,* February 13, 1995, 64–70.

76. "Stock option," *Encarta World English Dictionary,* www.dictionary.msn.com, June 28, 2001; Personal interview with Professor Bala Dharan, Jones Graduate School of Business, Rice University, June 28, 2001.

77. Personal interview with Professor Bala Dharan.

78. Ibid.

79. A. J. Michels, "Dallas Semiconductor," *Fortune,* May 16, 1994, 81.

80. M. Betts, "Big Things Come in Small Buttons," *Computerworld,* August 3, 1992, 30.

81. M. Boslet, "Metal Buttons Toted by Crop Pickers Act as Mini Databases," *Wall Street Journal,* June 1, 1994, B3.

82. C. D. Fisher, L. F. Schoenfeldt, and J. B. Shaw, *Human Resource Management* (Boston: Houghton Mifflin, 1990); B. E. Graham-Moore and T. L. Ross, *Productivity Gainsharing* (Englewood Cliffs, NJ: Prentice-Hall, 1983); A. J. Geare, "Productivity from Scanlon Type Plans," *Academy of Management Review* 1 (1976): 99–108.

83. J. Labate, "Deal Those Workers In," *Fortune,* April 19, 1993, 26.

84. K. Belson, "Japan's Net Generation," *Business Week,* March 19, 2001, *Business Week* Archives, June 27, 2001.

85. Belson, "Japan's Net Generation."

86. K. Belson, "Taking a Hint from the Upstarts," *Business Week,* March 19, 2001, *Business Week* Archives, June 27, 2001; "Going for the Gold," *Business Week,* March 19, 2001, *Business Week* Archives, June 27, 2001; "What the Government Can Do to Promote a Flexible Workforce," *Business Week,* March 19, 2001, *Business Week* Archives, June 27, 2001.

Chapter 13

1. S. B. Shepard, "A Talk with Meg Whitman," *Business Week,* March 19, 2001, pp. 98–99.

2. "*Business Week* eBiz–The eBiz 25: Meg Whitman," *Business Week,* May 14, 2001, *Business Week* Archives; J. Creswell, "eBay Remains Standing, But for How Long," *Fortune,* April 2, 2001, Fortune.com, July 8, 2001; R. D. Hoff, "Let's Get Crazier," *Business Week,* June 4, 2001, *Business Week* Archives; E. Nee, "10 Tech Trends to Bet On," *Fortune,* March 19, 2001, Fortune.com, July 8, 2001; S. B. Shepard, "A Talk with Meg Whitman," *Business Week,* March 19, 2001, pp. 98–99; J. Tanz, "Hot and Hotter: Meg Whitman," *Fortune,* May 14, 2001, Fortune.com, July 8, 2001.

3. E. Nee, "10 Tech Trends to Bet On," *Fortune,* March 19, 2001, Fortune.com, July 8, 2001.

4. "*Business Week* eBiz"; Creswell, "eBay Remains Standing"; Hoff, "Let's Get Crazier"; Nee, "10 Tech Trends to Bet On"; Shepard, "A Talk with Meg Whitman"; Tanz, "Hot and Hotter: Meg Whitman."

5. "eBay Stores Open for Business," June 11, 2001, press release, www.eBay.com, July 8, 2001.

6. "Community Values," www.eBay.com, July 8, 2001.

7. "The Top 25 Managers–Managers to Watch: Margaret C. Whitman, eBay," *Business Week,* January 8, 2000, *Business Week* Archives.

8. Shepard, "A Talk With Meg Whitman."

9. www.ebay.com, July 8, 2001.

10. "Careers," www.ebay.com, July 8, 2001.

11. G. Yukl, *Leadership in Organizations,* 2nd ed. (New York: Academic Press, 1989); R. M. Stogdill, *Handbook of Leadership: A Survey of the Literature* (New York: Free Press, 1974).

12. S. Koudsi, "Remedies for an Economic Hangover," *Fortune,* June 25, 2001, pp. 130–138.

13. Koudsi, "Remedies for an Economic Hangover"; www.starbucks.com, July 24, 2002.

14. www.bestbuy.com, July 24, 2002.

15. www.ibm.com, July 24, 2001.

16. Koudsi, "Remedies for an Economic Hangover."

17. R. Calori and B. Dufour, "Management European Style," *Academy of Management Executive* 9, no. 3 (1995): 61–70.

18. Ibid.

19. H. Mintzberg, *Power in and Around Organizations* (Englewood Cliffs, NJ: Prentice-Hall, 1983); J. Pfeffer, *Power in Organizations* (Marshfield, MA: Pitman, 1981).

20. R. P. French, Jr., and B. Raven, "The Bases of Social Power," in D. Cartwright and A. F. Zander, eds., *Group Dynamics* (Evanston, IL: Row, Peterson, 1960), 607–23.

21. R. L. Rose, "After Turning Around Giddings and Lewis, Fife Is Turned Out Himself," *The Wall Street Journal,* June 22, 1993, A1.

22. J. Fierman, "Winning Ideas from Maverick Managers," *Fortune,* February 6, 1995, 66–80.

23. Ibid., 70.

24. J. A. Lopez, "A Better Way? Setting Your Own Pay–and Other Unusual Compensation Plans," *The Wall Street Journal,* April 13, 1994, R6; "Maverick: The Success Story Behind the World's Most Unusual Workplace," *HRMagazine,* April 1994: 88–89; J. Pottinger, "Brazilian Maverick Reveals His Radical Recipe for Success," *Personnel Management,* September 1994: 71.

25. Fierman, "Winning Ideas from Maverick Managers."

26. G. Morgan and A. Zohar, "Ricardo Semler's Transformation at Semco (6/7)," www.yorku.ca/faculty/academic/gmorgan/semler.html, July, 24, 2001.

27. A. Grove, "How Intel Makes Spending Pay Off," *Fortune,* February 22, 1993, 56–61.

28. M. Loeb, "Jack Welch Lets Fly," 146.

29. L. Bird, "Lazarus's IBM Coup Was All About Relationships," *The Wall Street Journal,* May 26, 1994, B1, B7.

30. T. M. Burton, "Visionary's Reward: Combine 'Simple Ideas' and Some Failures; Result: Sweet Revenge," *The Wall Street Journal,* February 3, 1995, A1, A5.

31. L. Nakarmi, "A Flying Leap Toward the 21st Century? Pressure from Competitors and Seoul May Transform the Chaebol," *Business Week,* March 20, 1995, 78–80.

32. B. M. Bass, *Bass and Stogdill's Handbook of Leadership: Theory, Research, and Managerial Applications,* 3rd ed. (New York: Free Press, 1990); R. J. House and M. L. Baetz, "Leadership: Some Empirical Generalizations and New Research Directions," in B. M. Staw and L. L. Cummings, eds., *Research in Organizational Behavior,* vol. 1 (Greenwich, CT: JAI Press, 1979), 341–423; S. A. Kirpatrick and E. A. Locke, "Leadership: Do Traits Matter?" *Academy of Management Executive* (1991): 5, no. 2 48–60; Yukl, *Leadership in Organizations;* G. Yukl and D. D. Van Fleet, "Theory and Research on Leadership in Organizations," in M. D. Dunnette and L. M. Hough, eds., *Handbook of Industrial and Organizational Psychology,* 2nd ed., vol. 3 (Palo Alto, CA: Consulting Psychologists Press, 1992), 147–97.

33. E. A. Fleishman, "Performance Assessment Based on an Empirically Derived Task Taxonomy," *Human Factors* 9 (1967): 349–66; E. A. Fleishman, "The Description of Supervisory Behavior," *Personnel Psychology* 37 (1953): 1–6; A. W. Halpin and B. J. Winer, "A Factorial Study of the Leader Behavior Descriptions," in R. M. Stogdill and A. I. Coons, eds., *Leader Behavior: Its Description and Measurement* (Columbus: Bureau of Business Research, Ohio State University, 1957); D. Tscheulin, "Leader Behavior Measurement in German Industry," *Journal of Applied Psychology* 56 (1971): 28–31.

34. A. Taylor III, "Why GM Leads the Pack in Europe," *Fortune,* May 17, 1993, 83–86.

35. E. A. Fleishman and E. F. Harris, "Patterns of Leadership Behavior Related to Employee Grievances and Turnover," *Personnel Psychology* 15 (1962): 43–56.

36. M. Arndt, "Nardelli: Taking on a Fixer-Upper," *Business Week,* December 18, 2000, *Business Week* Archives.

37. P. Sellers, "Exit the Builder, Enter the Repairman," *Fortune,* March 19, 2001, pp. 87–88.

38. Sellers, "Exit the Builder, Enter the Repairman."

39. "Confronting Anti-Globalism," *Business Week,* August 6, 2001, *Business Week* Archives.

40. R. Likert, *New Patterns of Management* (New York: McGraw-Hill, 1961); N. C. Morse and E. Reimer, "The Experimental Change of a Major Organizational Variable," *Journal of Abnormal and Social Psychology* 52 (1956): 120–29.

41. R. R. Blake and J. S. Mouton, *The New Managerial Grid* (Houston: Gulf, 1978).

42. P. Hersey and K. Blanchard, *Management of Organizational Behavior: Utilizing Human Resources* (Englewood Cliffs, NJ: Prentice-Hall, 1982).

43. F. E. Fiedler, *A Theory of Leadership Effectiveness* (New York: McGraw-Hill, 1967); F. E. Fiedler, "The Contingency Model and the Dynamics of the Leadership Process," in L. Berkowitz, ed., *Advances in Experimental Social Psychology* (New York: Academic Press, 1978).

44. J. Rebello, "Radical Ways of Its CEO Are a Boon to Bank," *The Wall Street Journal,* March 20, 1995, B1, B3.

45. Fierman, "Winning Ideas from Maverick Managers," 78.

46. Fierman, "Winning Ideas from Maverick Managers."

47. M. Schuman, "Free to Be," *Forbes,* May 8, 1995, 78–80.

48. House and Baetz, "Leadership"; L. H. Peters, D. D. Hartke, and J. T. Pohlmann, "Fiedler's Contingency Theory of Leadership: An Application of the Meta-Analysis Procedures of Schmidt and Hunter," *Psychological Bulletin* 97 (1985): 274–85; C. A. Schriesheim, B. J. Tepper, and L. A. Tetrault, "Least Preferred Co-Worker Score, Situational Control, and Leadership Effectiveness: A Meta-Analysis of Contingency Model Performance Predictions," *Journal of Applied Psychology* 79 (1994): 561–73.

49. M. G. Evans, "The Effects of Supervisory Behavior on the Path-Goal Relationship," *Organizational Behavior and Human Performance* 5 (1970): 277–98; R. J. House, "A Path-Goal Theory of Leader Effectiveness," *Administrative Science Quarterly* 16 (1971): 321–38; J. C. Wofford and L. Z. Liska, "Path-Goal Theories of Leadership: A Meta-Analysis," *Journal of Management* 19 (1993): 857–76.

50. J. Rosenfeld, "Lead Softly, But Carry a Big Baton," *Fast Company,* July 2001, pp. 46–48.

51. Ibid.

52. C. Bangle, "The Ultimate Creativity Machine: How BMW Turns Art into Profit," *Harvard Business Review,* January 2001, pp. 47–55.

53. Bangle, "The Ultimate Creativity Machine," p. 48; *http:www.bmw.com,* September 11, 2001.

54. S. Kerr and J. M. Jermier, "Substitutes for Leadership: Their Meaning and Measurement," *Organizational Behavior and Human Performance* 22 (1978): 375–403; P. M. Podsakoff, B. P. Niehoff, S. B. MacKenzie, and M. L. Williams, "Do Substitutes for Leadership Really Substitute for Leadership? An Empirical Examination of Kerr and Jermier's Situational Leadership Model," *Organizational Behavior and Human Decision Processes* 54 (1993): 1–44.

55. Kerr and Jermier, "Substitutes for Leadership"; Podsakoff, Niehoff, MacKenzie, and Williams, "Do Substitutes for Leadership Really Substitute for Leadership?"

56. K. Miller, "Siemens Shapes Up," *Business Week,* May 1, 1995, 52–53.

57. B. M. Bass, *Leadership and Performance Beyond Expectations* (New York: Free Press, 1985); Bass, *Bass and Stogdill's Handbook of Leadership;* Yukl and Van Fleet, "Theory and Research on Leadership."

58. G. E. Schares, J. B. Levine, and P. Coy, "The New Generation at Siemens," *Business Week,* March 9, 1992, 46–48.

59. Miller, "Siemens Shapes Up."

60. Ibid.

61. J. A. Conger and R. N. Kanungo, "Behavioral Dimensions of Charismatic Leadership," in J. A. Conger, R. N. Kanungo, and Associates, *Charismatic Leadership* (San Francisco: Jossey-Bass, 1988).

62. A. L. Sprout, "Packard Bell," *Fortune,* June 12, 1995, 83.

63. Bass, *Leadership and Performance Beyond Expectations;* Bass, *Bass and Stogdill's Handbook of Leadership;* Yukl and Van Fleet, "Theory and Research on Leadership."

64. Ibid.

65. Miller, "Siemens Shapes Up."

66. S. Jones, "Colgate Cleans Up," *Fortune,* April 16, 2001, pp. 179–180.

67. P. Burrows, I. Sager, and S. Hamm, "The Era of Efficiency," *Business Week,* June 18, 2001, *Business Week* Archives; S. Jones, "Colgate Cleans Up," *Fortune,* April 16, 2001, pp. 179–180.

68. S. Jones, "Colgate Cleans Up," *Fortune,* April 16, 2001, pp. 179–180; M. Kripalani, "McCaw, Malone, Murdoch - Chandra?" *Business Week,* December 20, 1999, *Business Week* Archives.

69. Jones, "Colgate Cleans Up."

70. Bass, *Leadership and Performance Beyond Expectations.*

71. Bass, *Bass and Stogdill's Handbook of Leadership;* B. M. Bass and B. J. Avolio, "Transformational Leadership: A Response to Critiques," in M. M. Chemers and R. Ayman, eds., *Leadership Theory and Research: Perspectives and Directions.* San Diego: Academic Press, 1993, pp. 49–80; B. M. Bass, B. J. Avolio, and L. Goodheim, "Biography and the Assessment of Transformational Leadership at the World Class Level," *Journal of Management* 13 (1987): 7–20; J. J. Hater and B. M. Bass, "Supervisors Evaluations and Subordinates' Perceptions of Transformational and Transactional Leadership," *Journal of Applied Psychology* 73, 1988, 695–702; R. Pillai, "Crisis and Emergence of Charismatic Leadership in Groups: An Experimental Investigation," *Journal of Applied Psychology* 26, 1996, 543–62; J. Seltzer and B. M. Bass, "Transformational Leadership: Beyond Initiation and Consideration," *Journal of Management* 16 (1990) 693–703; D. A. Waldman, B. M. Bass, and W. O. Einstein, "Effort, Performance, Transformational Leadership in Industrial and Military Service," *Journal of Occupation Psychology* 60, 1987, 1–10.

72. R. Pillai, C. A. Schriesheim, and E. S. Williams, "Fairness Perceptions and Trust as Mediators of Transformational and Transactional Leadership: A Two-Sample Study," *Journal of Management* 25, 1999, 897–933.

73. G. Rifken, "Powering the Comeback at Coopers," *Forbes* ASAP, October 10, 1994, 118–20.

74. Ibid.

75. A. Crittenden, *The Price of Motherhood.* New York: Metropolitan Books, 2001.

76. A. H. Eagly and B. T. Johnson, "Gender and Leadership Style: A Meta-Analysis," *Psychological Bulletin* 108 (1990): 233–56.

77. Ibid.

78. The Economist, "Workers Resent Scoldings from Female Bosses," *Houston Chronicle,* August 19, 2000, p. 1C.

79. Ibid.

80. Ibid.

81. Ibid.

82. A. H. Eagly, S. J. Karau, and M. G. Makhijani, "Gender and the Effectiveness of Leaders: A Meta-Analysis," *Psychological Bulletin* 117 (1995): 125–45.

83. Ibid.

84. J. M. George and K. Bettenhausen, "Understanding Prosocial Behavior, Sales Performance, and Turnover: A Group-Level Analysis in a Service Context," *Journal of Applied Psychology* 75 (1990), 698–709.

85. J. M. George, "Emotions and Leadership: The Role of Emotional Intelligence," *Human Relations* 53 (2000), 1027–55.

86. George, "Emotions and Leadership."

Chapter 14

1. www.nucor.com, November 21, 2001.

2. M. Arndt, "Out of the Forge and into the Fire," *Business Week,* June 18, 2001, *Business Week* Archives.

3. S. Baker, "The Minimill That Acts Like a Biggie," *Business Week,* September 30, 1996, pp. 101–104; S. Baker, "Nucor," *Business Week,* February 13, 1995, p. 70; S. Overman, "No-Frills at Nucor," *HR Magazine,* July 1994, pp. 56–60.

4. www.nucor.com, November 21, 2001.

5. Baker, "The Minimill That Acts Like a Biggie"; Baker, "Nucor"; Overman, "No-Frills at Nucor"; www.nucor.com.

6. www.nucor.com, November 21, 2001.

7. M. Conlin, "Where Layoffs Are a Last Resort," *Business Week,* October 8, 2001, *Business Week* Archives.

8. W. R. Coradetti, "Teamwork Takes Time and a Lot of Energy," *HRMagazine* (June 1994): 74–77; D. Fenn, "Service Teams That Work," *Inc.* (August 1995): 99; "Team Selling Catches On, but Is Sales Really a Team Sport?" *The Wall Street Journal,* March 29, 1994, A1.

9. T. M. Mills, *The Sociology of Small Groups* (Englewood Cliffs, NJ: Prentice-Hall, 1967); M. E. Shaw, *Group Dynamics* (New York: McGraw-Hill, 1981).

10. R. S. Buday, "Reengineering One Firm's Product Development and Another's Service Delivery," *Planning Review* (March–April 1993): 14–19; J. M. Burcke, "Hallmark's Quest for Quality Is a Job Never Done," *Business Insurance,* April 26, 1993, 122; M. Hammer and J. Champy, *Reengineering the Corporation* (New York: Harper Business, 1993); T. A. Stewart, "The Search for the Organization of Tomorrow," *Fortune,* May 18, 1992, 92–98.

11. M. Sawhney, "Don't Homogenize, Synchronize," *Harvard Business Review,* July–August 2001, pp. 101–108.

12. Sawhney, "Don't Homogenize, Synchronize".

13. Sawhney, "Don't Homogenize, Synchronize"; www.3M.com, November 27, 2001; A. Johnson, "3M: Organized to Innovate," *Management Review,* July, 1986, pp. 35–36.

14. S. Dallas, "Rock Bottom Restaurants: Brewing Up Solid Profits," *Business Week,* May 22, 1995, 74.

15. L. Armstrong and L. Holyoke, "NASA's Tiny Camera Has a Wide-Angle Future," *Business Week,* March 6, 1995, 54–55.

16. J. A. Pearce II and E. C. Ravlin, "The Design and Activation of Self-Regulating Work Groups," *Human Relations* 11 (1987): 751–82.

17. R. Henkoff, "When to Take on the Giants," *Fortune,* May 30, 1994, 111, 114.

18. B. Dumaine, "Who Needs a Boss?" *Fortune,* May 7, 1990, 52–60; Pearce and Ravlin, "The Design and Activation of Self-Regulating Work Groups."

19. Dumaine, "Who Needs a Boss?"; A. R. Montebello and V. R. Buzzotta, "Work Teams That Work," *Training and Development* March 1993, 59–64.

20. T. D. Wall, N. J. Kemp, P. R. Jackson, and C. W. Clegg, "Outcomes of Autonomous Work Groups: A Long-Term Field Experiment," *Academy of Management Journal* 29 (1986): 280–304.

21. A. Markels, "A Power Producer Is Intent on Giving Power to Its People," *The Wall Street Journal,* July 3, 1995, A1, A12.

22. J. S. Lublin, "My Colleague, My Boss," *The Wall Street Journal,* April 12, 1995, R4, R12.

23. W. R. Pape, "Group Insurance," *Inc.* (Inc. Technology Supplement), June 17, 1997, 29–31; A. M. Townsend, S. M. DeMarie, and A. R. Hendrickson, "Are You Ready for Virtual Teams?" *HRMagazine,* September 1996, 122–26; A. M. Townsend, S. M. DeMarie, and A. M. Hendrickson, "Virtual Teams: Technology and the Workplace of the Future," *Academy of Management Executive* 12 (1998), 17–29.

24. Townsend, DeMarie, and Hendrickson, "Virtual Teams: Technology and the Workplace of the Future."

25. Pape, "Group Insurance"; Townsend, DeMarie, and Hendrickson, "Are You Ready for Virtual Teams?"

26. D. L. Duarte and N. T. Snyder, *Mastering Virtual Teams* (San Francisco: Jossey-Bass, 1999); K. A. Karl, "Book Reviews: Mastering Virtual Teams," *Academy of Management Executive,* August 1999, pp. 118–19.

27. B. Geber, "Virtual Teams," *Training* 32 (August 1995): pp. 36–40; T. Finholt and L. S. Sproull, "Electronic Groups at Work," *Organization Science* 1 (1990): pp. 41–64.

28. Geber, "Virtual Teams."

29. E. J. Hill, B. C. Miller, S. P. Weiner, and J. Colihan, "Influences of the Virtual Office on Aspects of Work and Work/Life Balance," *Personnel Psychology* 31 (1998): 667–83; S. G. Strauss, "Technology, Group Process, and Group Outcomes: Testing the Connections in Computer-Mediated and Face-to-Face Groups," *Human-Computer Interaction* 12 (1997): 227–66; M. E. Warkentin, L. Sayeed, and R. Hightower, "Virtual Teams versus Face-to-Face Teams: An Exploratory Study of a Web-based Conference System," *Decision Sciences* 28 (Fall 1997): 975–96.

30. Sawhney, "Don't Homogenize, Synchronize."

31. Sawhney, "Don't Homogenize, Synchronize"; www.thomson.com, November 27, 2001, P. E. Strom and H. Timmons, "Telecom Meltdowns," *Business Week,* April 23, 2001, *Business Week* Archives.

32. A. Deutschman, "The Managing Wisdom of High-Tech Superstars," *Fortune,* October 17, 1994, pp. 197–206.

33. J. D. Thompson, *Organizations in Action* (New York: McGraw-Hill, 1967).

34. Ibid.

35. Lublin, "My Colleague, My Boss."

36. R. G. LeFauve and A. C. Hax, "Managerial and Technological Innovations at Saturn Corporation," *MIT Management* Spring 1992, 8–19.

37. B. W. Tuckman, "Developmental Sequences in Small Groups," *Psychological Bulletin* 63 (1965): 384–99; B. W. Tuckman and M. C. Jensen, "Stages of Small Group Development," *Group and Organizational Studies* 2 (1977): 419–27.

38. C. J. G. Gersick, "Time and Transition in Work Teams: Toward a New Model of Group Development," *Academy of Management Journal* 31 (1988): 9–41; C. J. G. Gersick, "Marking Time: Predictable Transitions in Task Groups," *Academy of Management Journal* 32 (1989): 274–309.

39. J. R. Hackman, "Group Influences on Individuals in Organizations," in M. D. Dunnette and L. M. Hough, eds., *Handbook of Industrial and Organizational Psychology,* 2nd ed. vol. 3 (Palo Alto, CA: Consulting Psychologists Press, 1992), 199–267.

40. Ibid.

41. Ibid.

42. Lublin, "My Colleague, My Boss."

43. T. Kelley and J. Littman, *The Art of Innovation* (New York: Doubleday, 2001).

44. Kelley and Littman, *The Art of Innovation.*

45. Kelley and Littman, *The Art of Innovation*; www.ideo.com; "1999 Idea Winners," *Business Week,* June 7, 1999, *Business Week* Archives.

46. L. Festinger, "Informal Social Communication," *Psychological Review* 57 (1950): 271–82; Shaw, *Group Dynamics.*

47. Hackman, "Group Influences on Individuals in Organizations"; Shaw, *Group Dynamics.*

48. D. Cartwright, "The Nature of Group Cohesiveness," in D. Cartwright and A. Zander, eds., *Group Dynamics,* 3rd ed. (New York: Harper and Row, 1968); L. Festinger, S. Schacter, and K. Black, *Social Pressures in Informal Groups* (New York: Harper and Row, 1950); Shaw, *Group Dynamics.*

49. "Of High Priests and Pragmatists," *The Economist,* June 16, 2001, p. 13; www.unc.edu, November 21, 2001; C. M. Maclaggan, "New Cleaning Method Born in Chapel Hill Lab," *Chapel Hill News,* February 14, 2001, CHN.

50. "Of High Priests and Pragmatists," *The Economist;* www.unc.edu, November 21, 2001; Maclaggan, "New Cleaning Method Born in Chapel Hill Lab."

51. "Of High Priests and Pragmatists," *The Economist;* www.unc.edu, November 21, 2001; Maclaggan, "New Cleaning Method Born in Chapel Hill Lab."

52. T. F. O'Boyle, "A Manufacturer Grows Efficient by Soliciting Ideas from Employees," *The Wall Street Journal,* June 5, 1992, A1, A5.

53. Lublin, "My Colleague, My Boss."

54. Kelley and Littman, "The Art of Innovation."

55. Kelley and Littman, "The Art of Innovation."

56. P. C. Earley, "Social Loafing and Collectivism: A Comparison of the United States and the People's Republic of China," *Administrative Science Quarterly* 34 (1989): 565–81; J. M. George, "Extrinsic and Intrinsic Origins of Perceived Social Loafing in Organizations," *Academy of Management Journal* 35 (1992): 191–202; S. G. Harkins, B. Latane, and K. Williams, "Social Loafing: Allocating Effort or Taking It Easy," *Journal of Experimental Social Psychology* 16 (1980): 457–65; B. Latane, K. D. Williams, and S. Harkins, "Many Hands Make Light the Work: The Causes and Consequences of Social Loafing," *Journal of Personality and Social Psychology* 37 (1979): 822–32; J. A. Shepperd, "Productivity Loss in Performance Groups; A Motivation Analysis," *Psychological Bulletin* 113 (1993): 67–81.

57. George, "Extrinsic and Intrinsic Origins"; G. R. Jones, "Task Visibility, Free Riding, and Shirking: Explaining the Effect of Structure and Technology on Employee Behavior," *Academy of Management Review* 9 (1984): 684–95; K. Williams, S. Harkins, and B. Latane, "Identifiability as a Deterrent to Social

Loafing: Two Cheering Experiments," *Journal of Personality and Social Psychology* 40 (1981): 303–11.

58. S. Harkins and J. Jackson, "The Role of Evaluation in Eliminating Social Loafing," *Personality and Social Psychology Bulletin* 11 (1985): 457–65; N. L. Kerr and S. E. Bruun, "Ringelman Revisited: Alternative Explanations for the Social Loafing Effect," *Personality and Social Psychology Bulletin* 7 (1981): 224–31; Williams, Harkins, and Latane, "Identifiability as a Deterrent to Social Loafing."

59. M. A. Brickner, S. G. Harkins, and T. M. Ostrom, "Effects of Personal Involvement: Thought-Provoking Implications for Social Loafing," *Journal of Personality and Social Psychology* 51 (1986): 763–69; S. G. Harkins and R. E. Petty, "The Effects of Task Difficulty and Task Uniqueness on Social Loafing," *Journal of Personality and Social Psychology* 43 (1982): 1214–29.

60. B. Latane, "Responsibility and Effort in Organizations," in P. S. Goodman, ed., *Designing Effective Work Groups* (San Franciso: Jossey-Bass, 1986); Latane, Williams, and Harkins, "Many Hands Make Light the Work"; I. D. Steiner, *Group Process and Productivity* (New York: Academic Press, 1972).

Chapter 15

1. C. Dahle, "These, Days, Life in Internet Economy," *Fast Company,* July 2001, pp. 146–51.

2. Dahle, "These, Days, Life in Internet Economy."

3. R. D. Hof, "It's the People, Stupid," *Business Week* Online, October 23, 2000, EB138.

4. Hof, "It's the People, Stupid."

5. F. Keenan, "Friendly Spies on the Net," *Business Week* Online, July 9, 2001, pp. EB26–EB28.

6. Keenan, "Friendly Spies on the Net."

7. C. A. O'Reilly and L. R. Pondy, "Organizational Communication," in S. Kerr, ed., *Organizational Behavior* (Columbus, OH: Grid, 1979).

8. "The Cemex Way," *The Economist,* June 16, 2001, pp. 75–76.

9. Ibid.

10. Ibid.; www.cemex.com; "Keeping the Concrete–and the Cash–Flowing," *Business Week* Online, June 18, 2000, *Business Week* Archives.

11. E. M. Rogers and R. Agarwala-Rogers, *Communication in Organizations* (New York: Free Press, 1976).

12. W. Nabers, "The New Corporate Uniforms," *Fortune,* November 13, 1995, 132–56.

13. R. B. Schmitt, "Judges Try Curbing Lawyers' Body-Language Antics," *Wall Street Journal,* September 11, 1997, B1, B7.

14. D. A. Adams, P. A. Todd, and R. R. Nelson, "A Comparative Evaluation of the Impact of Electronic and Voice Mail on Organizational Communication," *Information & Management* 24 (1993): 9–21.

15. R. Winslow, "Hospitals' Weak Systems Hurt Patients, Study Says," *The Wall Street Journal,* July 5, 1995, B1, B6.

16. B. Newman, "Global Chatter," *The Wall Street Journal,* March 22, 1995, A1, A15.

17. "Miscommunications Plague Pilots and Air-Traffic Controllers," *The Wall Street Journal,* August 22, 1995, A1.

18. R. L. Daft, R. H. Lengel, and L. K. Trevino, "Message Equivocality, Media Selection, and Manager Performance: Implications for Information Systems," *MIS Quarterly* 11 (1987): 355–66; R. L. Daft and R. H. Lengel, "Information Richness: A New Approach to Managerial Behavior and Organization Design," in B. M. Staw and L. L. Cummings, eds., *Research in Organizational Behavior* (Greenwich, CT: JAI Press, 1984).

19. R. L. Daft, *Organization Theory and Design* (St. Paul, MN: West, 1992).

20. "Lights, Camera, Meeting: Teleconferencing Becomes a Time-Saving Tool," *The Wall Street Journal,* February 21, 1995, A1.

21. Daft, *Organization Theory and Design.*

22. T. J. Peters and R. H. Waterman, Jr., *In Search of Excellence* (New York: Harper and Row, 1982); T. Peters and N. Austin, *A Passion for Excellence: The Leadership Difference* (New York: Random House, 1985).

23. "Lights, Camera, Meeting."

24. B. Ziegler, "Virtual Power Lunches Will Make Passing the Salt an Impossibility," *The Wall Street Journal,* June 28, 1995, B1.

25. "E-Mail Etiquette Starts to Take Shape for Business Messaging," *The Wall Street Journal,* October 12, 1995, A1.

26. E. Baig, "Taking Care of Business–Without Leaving the House," *Business Week,* April 17, 1995, 106–07.

27. "Life Is Good for Telecommuters, but Some Problems Persist," *The Wall Street Journal,* August 3, 1995, A1.

28. "E-Mail Abuse: Workers Discover High-Tech Ways to Cause Trouble in the Office," *The Wall Street Journal,* November 22, 1994, A1; "E-Mail Alert: Companies Lag in Devising Policies on How It Should Be Used," *The Wall Street Journal,* December 29, 1994, A1.

29. A. T. Palmer, "Workers, Surf at Your Own Risk," *Business Week,* 2001, p. 14.

30. L. Armstrong, "Someone to Watch Over You," *Business Week,* July 10, 2000, *Business Week* Online.

31. Armstrong, "Someone to Watch Over You."

32. Palmer, "Workers, Surf at Your Own Risk."

33. Palmer, "Workers, Surf at Your Own Risk."

34. M. Conlin, "Workers, Surf at Your Own Risk." *Business Week,* July 10, 2000, 105–106.

35. "Employee-Newsletter Names Include the Good, the Bad, and the Boring," *The Wall Street Journal,* July 18, 1995, A1.

36. A. Overholt, "Intel's Got [Too Much] Mail," *Fast Company,* March 2001, 56–58.

37. Overholt, "Intel's Got [Too Much] Mail."

38. Overholt, "Intel's Got [Too Much] Mail."

39. O. W. Baskin and C. E. Aronoff, *Interpersonal Communication in Organizations* (Santa Monica, CA: Goodyear, 1989).

40. T. Gutner, "Move Over, Bohemian Grove," *Business Week,* February 19, 2001, p. 102.

41. Gutner, "Move Over, Bohemian Grove."

42. Gutner, "Move Over, Bohemian Grove."

43. T. Gutner, "Weaving an Old-Girls Network," *Business Week,* July 9, 2001, p. 115.

44. Gutner, "Weaving An Old-Girls Network."

45. "We've All Got Mail," *Newsweek,* May 15, 2001, 73K; "Diversity Deficit," *Business Week* Online, May 14, 2001.

46. P. M. Eng, "Big Business on the Net? Not Yet," *Business Week*, June 26, 1995, 100–01.

47. Ibid.; GCCGroup, "Internet Functions," http://www.gccgroup.com/netfacts.htm.

48. J. Sandberg, "Internet's Popularity in North America Appears to Be Soaring," *The Wall Street Journal*, October 30, 1995, B2.

49. Magnet Media Solutions, Inc., "Internet Facts."

50. Cyberv@lley, "Internet Demographics," http://www.cybersols.com/facts.html.

51. J. W. Verity and R. Hof, "Bullet-Proofing the Net," *Business Week*, November 13, 1995, 98–99.

52. Ibid.

53. M. J. Cronin, "Ford's Intranet Success," *Fortune*, March 30, 1998, 158; M. J. Cronin, "Intranets Reach the Factory Floor," *Fortune*, June 10, 1997; A. L. Sprout, "The Internet Inside Your Company," *Fortune*, November 27, 1995, 161–68; J. B. White, "Chrysler's Intranet: Promise vs. Reality," *Wall Street Journal*, May 13, 1997, B1, B6.

54. Ibid.

55. G. Rifkin, "A Skeptic's Guide to Groupware," *Forbes ASAP*, 1995: 76–91.

56. Ibid.

57. Ibid.

58. "Groupware Requires a Group Effort," *Business Week*, June 26, 1995, 154.

59. "On the Road," *Newsweek*, June 6, 1994, 8.

60. A. Wakizaka, "Faxes, E-Mail, Help the Deaf Get Office Jobs," *Wall Street Journal*, October 3, 1995, B1, B5.

61. D. Tannen, "The Power of Talk," *Harvard Business Review* (September–October 1995): 138–48; D. Tannen, *Talking from 9 to 5* (New York: Avon Books, 1995).

62. Ibid.

63. Ibid.

64. Ibid.

65. Tannen, "The Power of Talk."

66. Ibid.; Tannen, *Talking from 9 to 5*.

67. Ibid.

68. J. Cohen, "He Writes, She Writes," *Houston Chronicle*, July 7, 2001, C1–C2.

69. Cohen, "He Writes, She Writes."

70. Cohen, "He Writes, She Writes."

71. Tannen, "The Power of Talk," 148.

Chapter 16

1. J. Muller, K. Kerwin, D. Welch, P. L. Moore, and D. Brady, "Ford: Why It's Worse than You Think," *Business Week*, June 25, 2001, pp. 80–89.

2. Muller, et al., "Ford: Why It's Worse than You Think."

3. Muller, et al., "Ford: Why It's Worse than You Think"; K. Kerwin and J. Muller, "Bill Ford Takes the Wheel," *Business Week*, November 1, 2001, *Business Week* Online; J. Muller, D. Welch, and J. Green, "Ford's Gamble: Will It Backfire?" *Business Week*, June 4, 2001, *Business Week* Archives; A. Taylor II, "First Crunch Time for Jac," *Fortune*, June 25, 2001, pp. 34–36; "Nasser's Nightmare," *The Economist*, June 16, 2001, p. 65.

4. Kerwin and Muller, "Bill Ford Takes the Wheel."

5. Muller, et al., "Ford: Why It's Worse than You Think"; Kerwin and Muller, "Bill Ford Takes the Wheel"; Muller, Welch, and Green, "Ford's Gamble: Will It Backfire?"; Taylor, "First Crunch Time for Jac"; "Nasser's Nightmare," *The Economist*.

6. Muller, et al., "Ford: Why It's Worse than You Think"; Kerwin and Muller, "Bill Ford Takes the Wheel"; Muller, Welch, and Green, "Ford's Gamble: Will It Backfire?"; Taylor, "First Crunch Time for Jac"; "Nasser's Nightmare," *The Economist*.

7. J. A. Litterer, "Conflict in Organizations: A Reexamination," *Academy of Management Journal* 9 (1966): 178–86; S. M. Schmidt and T. A. Kochan, "Conflict: Towards Conceptual Clarity," *Administrative Science Quarterly* 13 (1972): 359–70; R. H. Miles, *Macro Organizational Behavior* (Santa Monica, CA: Goodyear, 1980).

8. S. P. Robbins, *Managing Organizational Conflict: A Nontraditional Approach* (Englewood Cliffs, NJ: Prentice-Hall, 1974); L. Coser, *The Functions of Social Conflict* (New York: Free Press, 1956).

9. L. L. Putnam and M. S. Poole, "Conflict and Negotiation," in F. M. Jablin, L. L. Putnam, K. H. Roberts, and L. W. Porter, eds., *Handbook of Organizational Communication: An Interdisciplinary Perspective* (Newbury Park, CA: Sage, 1987), 549–99.

10. L. R. Pondy, "Organizational Conflict: Concepts and Models," *Administrative Science Quarterly* 2 (1967): 296–320; R. E. Walton and J. M. Dutton, "The Management of Interdepartmental Conflict: A Model and Review," *Administrative Science Quarterly* 14 (1969): 62–73.

11. G. R. Jones and J. E. Butler, "Managing Internal Corporate Entrepreneurship: An Agency Theory Perspective," *Journal of Management* 18 (1992): 733–49.

12. T. Petzinger, Jr., "All Happy Businesses Are Alike, but Heirs Bring Unique Conflicts," *The Wall Street Journal*, November 17, 1995, B1.

13. J. A. Wall, Jr., "Conflict and Its Management," *Journal of Management* 21 (1995): 515–58.

14. Walton and Dutton, "The Management of Interdepartmental Conflict."

15. Pondy, "Organizational Conflict."

16. W. F. White, *Human Relations in the Restaurant Industry* (New York: McGraw-Hill, 1948).

17. K. W. Thomas, "Conflict and Negotiation Processes in Organizations," in M. D. Dunnette and L. M. Hough, eds., *Handbook of Industrial and Organizational Psychology*, 2d ed., vol. 3 (Palo Alto, CA: Consulting Psychologists Press, 1992), 651–717.

18. A. Bernstein and M. Arndt, "Racism in the Workplace," *Business Week* Online, July 30, 2001.

19. Bernstein and Arndt, "Racism in the Workplace."

20. Bernstein and Arndt, "Racism in the Workplace"; J. Muller, "Ford: The High Cost of Harassment," *Business Week* Online, November 15, 1999; "Sexual Harassment," *Business Week* Online, October 13, 1997.

21. E. Shapiro, J. A. Trachtenberg, and L. Landro, "Time Warner Settles Feud by Pushing Out Music Division's Fuchs," *The Wall Street Journal*, November 17, 1995, A1, A6.

22. Ibid.

23. P. R. Lawrence, L. B. Barnes, and J. W. Lorsch, *Organizational Behavior and Administration* (Homewood, IL: Irwin, 1976).

24. R. J. Lewicki and J. R. Litterer, *Negotiation* (Homewood, IL: Irwin, 1985); G. B. Northcraft and M. A. Neale, *Organizational Behavior* (Fort Worth, TX: Dryden, 1994); J. Z. Rubin and B. R.

Brown, *The Social Psychology of Bargaining and Negotiation* (New York: Academic Press, 1975).

25. L. Thompson and R. Hastie, "Social Perception in Negotiation," *Organizational Behavior and Human Decision Processes* 47 (1990): 98–123.

26. Thomas, "Conflict and Negotiation Processes in Organizations."

27. R. J. Lewicki, S. E. Weiss, and D. Lewin, "Models of Conflict, Negotiation and Third Party Intervention: A Review and Synthesis," *Journal of Organizational Behavior* 13 (1992): 209–52.

28. Northcraft and Neale, *Organizational Behavior.*

29. Lewicki, Weiss, and Lewin, "Models of Conflict, Negotiation and Third Party Intervention"; Northcraft and Neale, *Organizational Behavior;* D. G. Pruitt, "Integrative Agreements: Nature and Consequences," in M. H. Bazerman and R. J. Lewicki, eds., *Negotiating in Organizations* (Beverly Hills, CA: Sage, 1983).

30. R. Fischer and W. Ury, *Getting to Yes* (Boston: Houghton Mifflin, 1981); Northcraft and Neale, *Organizational Behavior.*

31. P. J. Carnevale and D. G. Pruitt, "Negotiation and Mediation," *Annual Review of Psychology* 43 (1992): 531–82.

32. A. M. Pettigrew, *The Politics of Organizational Decision Making* (London: Tavistock, 1973); Miles, *Macro Organizational Behavior.*

33. D. J. Hickson, C. R. Hinings, C. A. Lee, R. E. Schneck, and D. J. Pennings, "A Strategic Contingencies Theory of Intraorganizational Power," *Administrative Science Quarterly* 16 (1971): 216–27; C. R. Hinings, D. J. Hickson, J. M. Pennings, and R. E. Schneck, "Structural Conditions of Interorganizational Power," *Administrative Science Quarterly* 19 (1974): 22–44; J. Pfeffer, *Power in Organizations* (Boston: Pitman, 1981), 35.

34. Pfeffer, *Power in Organizations.*

35. Ibid.

36. M. Crozier, "Sources of Power of Lower Level Participants in Complex Organizations," *Administrative Science Quarterly* 7 (1962): 349–64; A. M. Pettigrew, "Information Control as a Power Resource," *Sociology* 6 (1972): 187–204.

37. Pfeffer, *Power in Organizations;* G. R. Salancik and J. Pfeffer, "The Bases and Uses of Power in Organizational Decision Making," *Administrative Science Quarterly* 19 (1974): 453–73; J. Pfeffer and G. R. Salancik, *The External Control of Organizations: A Resource Dependence View* (New York: Harper and Row, 1978).

38. J. S. Lublin, "Despite Poor Returns, Champion's Chairman Hangs On for 21 Years," *The Wall Street Journal,* October 31, 1995, A1, A5.

39. S. Tully, "A House Divided," *Fortune,* December 18, 2000, pp. 264–274; D. Brady and A. Davies, "Alfred Taubman: A Good Deal at Sotheby's, *Business Week,* October 9, 2000, *Business Week* Archives; "Worst Firing, Worst Hiring," *Business Week,* January 8, 2001.

40. Tully, "A House Divided." F

41. Tully, "A House Divided."

42. Pfeffer, *Power in Organizations.*

43. Ibid.

44. Ibid.

45. C. Dawson, "Nissan: Saying Sayonara," *Business Week,* September 24, 2001, *Business Week* Online.

46. Dawson, "Nissan: Saying Sayonara."

47. Dawson, "Nissan: Saying Sayonara."

48. Dawson, "Nissan: Saying Sayonara"; C. Dawson, "Machete Time: In a Cost-Cutting War with Nissan, Toyota Leans on Suppliers," *Business Week,* April 9, 2001, 42–43; C. Tierney, A. Bawden, I. M. Kunii, "Renault Nissan: Dynamic Duo," *Business Week,* October 23, 2000.

49. L. Brown, "Research Action: Organizational Feedback, Understanding and Change," *Journal of Applied Behavioral Research* 8 (1972): 697–711; P. A. Clark, *Action Research and Organizational Change* (New York: Harper and Row, 1972); N. Margulies and A. P. Raia, eds., *Conceptual Foundations of Organizational Development* (New York: McGraw-Hill, 1978).

50. W. L. French and C. H. Bell, *Organizational Development* (Englewood Cliffs, NJ: Prentice-Hall, 1990).

51. W. L. French, "A Checklist for Organizing and Implementing an OD Effort," in W. L. French, C. H. Bell, and R. A. Zawacki, eds., *Organizational Development and Transformation* (Homewood, IL: Irwin, 1994), 484–95.

52. C. Salter, "This is One Fast Factory," *Fast Company,* August, 2001, 32–33.

53. Salter, "This Is One Fast Factory."

54. C. Salter, "This Is One Fast Factory"; "Rock Around the Clock," *Design News,* June 19, 2000; R. T. Schneider, "Open-Top Carriers Simplify Hose and Cable Installation," *Hydraulics & Pneumatics,* March 2001, p. 14.

Chapter 17

1. N. B. Macintosh, *The Social Software of Accounting Information Systems* (New York: Wiley, 1995).

2. C. A. O'Reilly, "Variations in Decision Makers' Use of Information: The Impact of Quality and Accessibility," *Academy of Management Journal* 25 (1982): 756–71.

3. G. Stalk and T. H. Hout, *Competing Against Time* (New York: Free Press, 1990).

4. L. Uchitelle, "Airlines off Course," *San Francisco Chronicle,* September 15, 1991, 7.

5. R. Cyert and J. March, *Behavioral Theory of the Firm* (Englewood Cliffs, NJ: Prentice-Hall, 1963).

6. R. Brandt, "Agents and Artificial Life," *Business Week: The Information Revolution,* special issue (1994): 64–68.

7. E. Turban, *Decision Support and Expert Systems* (New York: Macmillan, 1988).

8. R. I. Benjamin and J. Blunt, "Critical IT Issues: The Next Ten Years," *Sloan Management Review* (Summer 1992): 7–19; W. H. Davidow and M. S. Malone, *The Virtual Corporation* (New York: Harper Business, 1992).

9. Davidow and Malone, ibid. M. E. Porter, *Competitive Advantage* (New York: Free Press, 1984).

10. T. J. Mullaney, "This Race Isn't Even Close," *Business Week,* 2000, December 18, pp. 208–209.

11. S. M. Dornbusch and W. R. Scott, *Evaluation and the Exercise of Authority* (San Francisco: Jossey-Bass, 1975).

12. J. Child, *Organization: A Guide to Problems and Practice* (London: Harper and Row, 1984).

13. C. W. L. Hill, "Airborne Express," in C. W. L. Hill and G. R. Jones, *Strategic Management: An Integrated Approach,* 2d ed. (Boston: Houghton Mifflin, 1992).

14. http://airborneexpress.com, 2001.

15. Macintosh, *The Social Software of Accounting Information Systems.*

16. B. Dumaine, "The Bureaucracy Busters," *Fortune,* June 17, 1991, 46.

17. P. Bradley, "Global Souring Takes Split-Second Timing," *Purchasing,* July 20, 1989, 52–58.

18. www.intel.com, 2001.

19. J. J. Donovan, *Business Re-engineering with Information Technology* (Englewood Cliffs, NJ: Prentice-Hall, 1994); C. W. L. Hill, "The Computer Industry: The New Industry of Industries," in C. W. L. Hill and G. R. Jones, *Strategic Management: An Integrated Approach,* 3d ed. (Boston: Houghton Mifflin, 1995).

20. M. B. Gordon, "The Wireless Services Industry: True Competition Emerges," *The Red Herring* (September/October 1994): 60–62.

21. www.nwfusion.com, 2001.

22. Ibid.

23. E. Rich, *Artificial Intelligence* (New York: McGraw-Hill, 1983).

24. Brandt, "Agents and Artificial Life."

25. www.ibm.com, 2001.

26. A. D. Chandler, *The Visible Hand* (Cambridge, MA: Harvard University Press, 1977).

27. C. W. L. Hill and J. F. Pickering, "Divisionalization, Decentralization, and Performance of Large United Kingdom Companies," *Journal of Management Studies* 23 (1986): 26–50.

28. O. E. Williamson, *Markets and Hierarchies: Analysis and Antitrust Implications* (New York: Free Press, 1975).

29. Hill, "Airborne Express."

30. Turban, *Decision Support and Expert Systems.*

31. N. A. Nichols, "Scientific Management at Merck: An Interview with CFO Judy Lewent," *Harvard Business Review* (January–February 1994): 88–91.

32. Turban, *Decision Support and Expert Systems.*

33. Ibid., 346.

34. Rich, *Artificial Intelligence.*

35. P. P. Bonisson and H. E. Johnson, "Expert Systems for Diesel Electric Locomotive Repair," *Human Systems Management* 4 (1985): 1–25.

36. Davidow and Malone, *The Virtual Corporation.*

37. The companies are real, but their names are fictitious. Information was obtained from a personal interview with a senior manager who had experience with both companies' information systems.

38. T. A. Stewart, "Managing in a Wired Company," *Fortune,* July 11, 1994, 54.

39. Ibid., 168.

40. www.merck.com, 2001

41. www.merckmedco.com, 2001

42. H. Mintzberg, *Mintzberg on Management: Inside Our Strange World of Organizations* (New York: Free Press, 1989).

43. From an interview conducted by C. W. L. Hill with a senior Boeing manager.

44. Stewart, "Managing in a Wired Company," 54.

45. See J. R. Meredith, "The Implementation of Computer Based Systems," *Journal of Operational Management* (October 1981); Turban, *Decision Support and Expert Systems;* R. J. Thierauf, *Effective Management and Evaluation of Information Technology* (London: Quorum Books, 1994).

Chapter 18

1. The view of quality as including reliability goes back to the work of W. Edwards Deming and Joseph Juran. See A. Gabor, *The Man Who Discovered Quality* (New York: Times Books, 1990).

2. D. F. Abell, *Defining the Business: The Starting Point of Strategic Planning* (Englewood Cliffs, NJ: Prentice-Hall, 1980).

3. For details, see "Johnson & Johnson (A)," *Harvard Business School Case* #384-053.

4. M. E. Porter, *Competitive Advantage* (New York: Free Press, 1985).

5. According to Richard D'Aveni, the process of pushing price/attribute curves to the right is a characteristic of the competitive process. See R. D'Aveni, *Hypercompetition* (New York: Free Press, 1994).

6. This is a central insight of the modern manufacturing literature. See R. H. Hayes and S. C. Wheelwright, "Link Manufacturing Process and Product Life Cycles," *Harvard Business Review,* (January–February 1979): 127–36; R. H. Hayes and S. C. Wheelwright, "Competing Through Manufacturing," *Harvard Business Review* (January–February 1985): 99–109.

7. B. O'Brian, "Flying on the Cheap," *Wall Street Journal,* October 26, 1992, A1; B. O'Reilly, "Where Service Flies Right," *Fortune,* August 24, 1992, 116–17; A. Salpukas, "Hurt in Expansion, Airlines Cut Back and May Sell Hubs," *Wall Street Journal,* April 1, 1993, A1, C8.

8. K. Done, "Toyota Warns of Continuing Decline," *Financial Times,* November 23, 1993, 23.

9. The view of quality as reliability goes back to the work of Deming and Juran; see Gabor, *The Man Who Discovered Quality.*

10. See D. Garvin, "What Does Product Quality Really Mean?" *Sloan Management Review* 26 (Fall 1984): 25–44; P. B. Crosby, *Quality Is Free* (New York: Mentor, 1980); Gabor, *The Man Who Discovered Quality.*

11. www.jdpa.com, 2001

12. See J. W. Dean and D. E. Bowen, "Management Theory and Total Quality: Improving Research and Practice Through Theory Development," *Academy of Management Review* 19 (1994): 392–418.

13. For general background information see J. C. Anderson, M. Rungtusanatham, and R. G. Schroeder, "A Theory of Quality Management Underlying the Deming Management Method," *Academy of Management Review* 19 (1994): 472–509; "How to Build Quality," *The Economist,* September 23, 1989, 91–92; Gabor, *The Man Who Discovered Quality;* Crosby, *Quality Is Free.*

14. Bowles, "Is American Management Really Committed to Quality?"

15. Gabor, *The Man Who Discovered Quality.*

16. J. Griffiths, "Europe's Manufacturing Quality and Productivity Still Lag Far Behind Japan's," *Financial Times,* November 4, 1994, 11.

17. S. McCartney, "Compaq Borrows Wal-Mart's Idea to Boost Production," *Wall Street Journal,* June 17, 1994, B4.

18. Gourlay, "Back to Basics on the Factory Floor."

19. P. Nemetz and L. Fry, "Flexible Manufacturing Organizations: Implications for Strategy Formulation," *Academy of Management Review* 13 (1988): 627–38; N. Greenwood, *Implementing Flexible Manufacturing Systems* (New York: Halstead Press, 1986).

20. M. Williams, "Back to the Past," *Wall Street Journal,* October 24, 1994, A1.

21. G. Stalk and T. M. Hout, *Competing Against Time* (New York: Free Press, 1990).

22. For an interesting discussion of some other drawbacks of JIT and other "Japanese" manufacturing techniques see S. M. Young, "A Framework for Successful Adoption and Performance of Japanese Manufacturing Practices in the United States," *Academy of Management Review* 17 (1992): 677–701.

23. T. Stundza, "Massachusetts Switch Maker Switches to Kanban," *Purchasing,* November 16, 2000, p. 103.

24. Dumaine, "The Trouble with Teams."

25. See C. W. L. Hill, "Transaction Cost Economizing as a Source of National Competitive Advantage: The Case of Japan," *Organization Science* (1994): M. Aoki, *Information, Incentives, and Bargaining in the Japanese Economy* (Cambridge: Cambridge University Press, 1989).

26. J. Hoerr, "The Payoff from Teamwork," *Business Week,* July 10, 1989, 56–62.

27. M. Hammer and J. Champy, *Re-engineering the Corporation* (New York: Harper Business, 1993), 35.

28. Ibid., 46.

29. Ibid.

30. For example, see Houlder, "Two Steps Forward, One Step Back"; Naj, "Shifting Gears"; D. Greising, "Quality: How to Make It Pay," *Business Week,* August 8, 1994, 54–59.

31. L. Helm and M. Edid, "Life on the Line: Two Auto Workers Who Are Worlds Apart," *Business Week,* September 30, 1994, 76–78.

32. Dumaine, "The Trouble with Teams."

Chapter 19

1. N.Irwin, "Defying the Slump," *Washington Post,* May 7, 2001, p. 3.

2. G. R. Simpson, "Maden Technologies Gets Ready to Make Its Presence Felt," *Wall Street Journal,* Feb. 15, 2001, p. A.2.

3. www.madentech.com, 2001.

4. See R. D'Aveni, *Hyper-Competition* (New York: Free Press, 1994); P. Anderson and M. L. Tushman, "Technological Discontinuities and Dominant Design: A Cyclical Model of Technological Change," *Administrative Science Quarterly* 35 (1990): 604–33.

5. J. A. Schumpeter, *Capitalism, Socialism and Democracy* (New York: Harper, 1942).

6. V. P. Buell, *Marketing Management* (New York: McGraw-Hill, 1985).

7. See M. M. J. Berry and J. H. Taggart, "Managing Technology and Innovation: A Review," *R & D Management* 24 (1994): 341–53; Clark and Wheelwright, *Managing New Product and Process Development.*

8. E. Abrahamson, "Managerial Fads and Fashions: The Diffusion and Rejection of Innovations," *Academy of Management Review* 16 (1991): 586–612.

9. See Berry and Taggart, "Managing Technology and Innovation"; M. Gort and J. Klepper, "Time Paths in the Diffusion of Product Innovations," *Economic Journal,* September 1982: 630–53. Looking at the history of 46 products, Gort and Klepper found that the length of time before other companies entered the markets created by a few inventive companies declined from an average of 14.4 years for products introduced before 1930 to 4.9 years for those introduced after 1949—implying that product life cycles were being compressed. Also see A. Griffin, "Metrics for Measuring Product Development Cycle Time," *Journal of Production and Innovation Management* 10 (1993): 112–25.

10. Clark and Wheelwright, *Managing New Product and Process Development.* Also see G. Stalk and T. M. Hout, *Competing Against Time* (New York: Free Press, 1990).

11. www.intel.com, 2001

12. "Intel Chip Hits 2 Gigahertz Milestone," yahoo.com, 2001.

13. C. W. L. Hill, "The New Industry of Industries?" in C. W. L. Hill and G. R. Jones, *Strategic Management: An Integrated Approach* 2nd ed. (Boston Houghton Mifflin, 1992), 135–54.

14. www.amd.com, 2001.

15. See Clark and Wheelwright, *Managing New Product and Process Development;* R. E. Gomory, "From the Ladder of Science to the Product Development Cycle," *Harvard Business Review* (November–December 1989): 99–105; Stalk and Hout, *Competing Against Time.*

16. See M. R. Millson, D. P. Raj, and D. Wilemon, "A Survey of Major Approaches for Accelerating New Product Development," *Journal of Product Innovation Management* 9 (1992): 53–69, Stalk and Hout, *Competing Against Time.*

17. In the language of strategic management, the company may be able to capture a first-mover advantage. See C. W. L. Hill, M. Heeley, and J. Sakson, "Strategies for Profiting from Technological Product Innovation," *Advances in Global High Technology Management* 3 (1993): 79–95.

18. See E. Mansfield, "How Economists See R&D," *Harvard Business Review,* November–December 1981: 98-106; B. Avishai and W. Taylor, "Customers Drive a Technology Driven Company," *Harvard Business Review,* November–December 1989: 107–14.

19. B. Dumaine, "Payoff from the New Management," *Fortune,* December 13, 1993, 103–10.

20. C. Power et al., "Flops: Too Many New Products Fall," *Business Week,* August 16, 1993, 76–82.

21. www.apple.com, Press Release, 2000.

22. K. B. Clark and T. Fujimoto, "The Power of Product Integrity," *Harvard Business Review,* November–December 1990: 107–19.

23. Ibid.

24. K. B. Clark and T. Fujimoto, "Lead Time in Automobile Product Development: Explaining the Japanese Advantage," *Journal of Engineering and Technology Management* 6 (1989): 25–58.

25. B. Dumaine, "Payoff from the New Management."

26. www.charbroil.com, 2001.

27. C. W. L. Hill, "The Efficacy of the New Product Development Process," working paper, University of Washington 1994.

28. Clark and Wheelwright, *Managing New Product and Process Development.*

29. Ibid.

30. G. K. Gill, "Motorola Inc.: Bandit Pager Project," *Harvard Business School* Case #690-043.

31. Ibid.

32. A. Griffin and J. R. Hauser, "Patterns of Communication Among Marketing, Engineering, and Manufacturing," *Management Science* 38 (1992): 360–73; R. K. Moenaert, W. E. Sounder, A. D. Meyer, and D. Deschoolmeester, "R&D-Marketing Integration Mechanisms, Communication Flows, and Innovation Success," *Journal of Production and Innovation Management* 11 (1994): 31–45.

33. See G. Barczak and D. Wileman, "Leadership Differences in New Product Development Teams," *Journal of Product Innovation Management* 6 (1989): 259–67; E. F. McDonough and G. Barczak, "Speeding Up New Product Development: The Effects of Leadership Style and Source of Technology," *Journal of Product Innovation Management* 8 (1991): 203–11; Clark and Fujimoto, "The Power of Product Integrity."

34. Clark and Wheelwright, *Managing New Product and Process Development.*

35. Clark and Fujimoto, "The Power of Product Integrity."

36. J. R. Heartly, *Concurrent Engineering* (Cambridge, MA: Productivity Press, 1992).

37. See B. Avishai and W. Taylor, "Customers Drive a Technology Driven Company."; W. E. Sounder, "Managing Relations Between R&D and Marketing in New Product Development Projects," *Journal of Product Innovation Management* 5 (1988): 6–19; B. J. Zinger and M. M. Madique, "A Model of New Product Development: An Empirical Test," *Management Science* 36 (1990): 867–83.

38. C. W. L. Hill, "The Boeing Corporation: Commercial Aircraft Operations," in C. W. L. Hill and G. R. Jones, *Strategic Management: An Integrated Approach,* 3d ed. (Boston: Houghton Mifflin, 1995).

39. Information from remarks made by Boeing Vice President Dean Cruze in a presentation to an MBA class at the University of Washington.

40. "The Mind's Eye," *The Economist,* survey of manufacturing technology; March 5, 1994, 11.

41. Mansfield, "How Economists See R&D."

42. T. Lonier, "Some Insights and Statistics on Working Solo," www.workingsolo.com.

43. D. Frey, "Learning the Ropes: My Life as a Product Champion." *Harvard Business Review,* September–October 1991, pp. 46–56.

Photo Credits

Chapter 1

Page 3, © Charlie Samuels

Page 9, AP Photo/Harry Cabluck

Page 10, AP Photo/John Keating/PEPSICO

Page 16, © Mark Richards/PhotoEdit

Page 20, © Mark Peterson/SABA

Page 26, © Charles Gupton/Stone

Page 28, © Darren McCollester/Getty Images

Page 29, © Bill Aron/PhotoEdit

Chapter 2

Page 39 (top), © Austrian Archives/CORBIS

Page 39 (bottom), © Chad Ehlers/International Stock

Page 43, © Bettmann/CORBIS

Page 45, © Bettmann/CORBIS

Page 47, 20th Century Fox (Courtesy Kobal)

Page 55, Courtesy Regina A. Greenwood and Henley Management College

Page 64, © AFP/CORBIS

Chapter 3

Page 73, © Reuters NewMedia Inc./CORBIS

Page 82, AP Photo/Mike Fiala

Page 90, AP Photo/Paul Sancya

Page 101, © Frank Ordonez/Syracuse Newspapers/The Image Works

Page 105, © Roger Ressmeyer/CORBIS

Chapter 4

Page 113, AP Photo/Lloyd Francis, Jr.

Page 115, © Mark Richards/PhotoEdit

Page 124, Courtesy of MacNeil/Lehrer Productions

Page 134, © Ed Quinn/SABA

Page 139 (left), Courtesy of United Parcel Service

Page 139 (right), Courtesy of United Parcel Service

Page 143, © Michael Schwarz/Liaison Agency

Chapter 5

Page 151 (bottom), © Michael Newman/PhotoEdit

Page 156, © Bruce Burkhardt/CORBIS

Page 159, AP Photo/Richard Drew

Page 164, © Charles O'Rear/CORBIS

Page 172 (bottom), AP Photo/April L. Brown

Chapter 6

Page 183, AP Photo/Koji Sasahara

Page 189, © John Chiasson/Liaison Agency

Page 194, © Fritz Hoffmann/The Image Works

Page 208, AP Photo/Tsugufumi Matsumoto

Page 210, © Rob Crandall/The Image Works

Chapter 7

Page 217, Digital Imagery © copyright 2001 PhotoDisc, Inc. Photographer: SW Productions

Page 219, © Macduff Everton/CORBIS

Page 224, © Reuters NewMedia Inc./CORBIS

Page 227, © Ted Goff

Page 230, © Paul S. Howell/Liaison Agency

Page 239, © AFP/CORBIS

Chapter 8

Page 249 (top), © Michael Newman/ PhotoEdit

Page 249 (bottom), © Rachel Epstein/ PhotoEdit

Page 260, AP Photo/Tiger Electronics/ Ray Stubblebine

Page 264, AP Photo/Gary Tramontina

Page 270, © Pablo Bartholomew/Liaison Agency

Page 275, AP Photo/Denis Doyle

Chapter 9

Page 287, Digital Imagery © copyright 2001 PhotoDisc, Inc. Photographer: Steve Cole

Page 292, © Alain Benainous/Liaison Agency

Page 294, © Bernard Boutrit/Woodfin Camp & Associates, Inc.

Page 304, AP Photo/Koji Sasahara

Page 307, Courtesy Hallmark Cards, Inc.

Page 319, AP Photo/Tina Fineberg

Chapter 10

Page 329, © AFP/CORBIS

Page 333, © Index Stock Imagery/ Tomas del Amo

Page 343, DILBERT reprinted by permission of United Features Syndicate, Inc.

Page 345, © James A. Sugar/CORBIS

Page 351, Courtesy Texas A&M University

Page 353, © Mark Richards/PhotoEdit

Chapter 11

Page 363, Photo by Kirk Tuck for Trilogy

Page 367, AP Photo/Jeff Carlick

Page 369, © Bob Daemmrich/CORBIS SYGMA

Page 378, AP Photo/Town Talk, Stephen Reed

Page 383, Courtesy Siemens AG

Page 393, © Richard Howard/Black Star

Chapter 12

Page 403, Courtesy The Container Store

Page 415, AP Photo/Karen Tam

Page 419, © Bill Varie/CORBIS

Page 422, Courtesy of The Lincoln Electric Company, Cleveland, Ohio

Page 431, AP Photo/Kasahara

Chapter 13

Page 441, AP Photo/Paul Sakuma

Page 444, © Robin Weiner/WirePix/ The Image Works

Page 451, AP Photo/NYSE, Mel Nudelman

Page 457, © Tony Freeman/PhotoEdit

Page 462, © Jeff Greenberg/PhotoEdit

Chapter 14

Page 475, AP Photo/Karen Tam

Page 486, Digital Imagery © copyright 2001 PhotoDisc, Inc. Photographer: Jules Frazier

Page 495, © Mark Richards/PhotoEdit

Page 498, © Michael Newman/ PhotoEdit

Chapter 15

Page 511, Courtesy of Intel Corporation

Page 514, © Reuters NewMedia Inc./ CORBIS

Page 519, © Corbis Stock Market /Jon Feingersh

Page 527, AP Photo/Autodesk, Court Mast

Page 538 (left), © Ellen Senisi/The Image Works

Page 538 (right), © Tony Freeman/ PhotoEdit

Chapter 16

Page 547, AP Photo/Paul Warner

Page 557, AP Photo/Khue Bui

Page 564, © AFP/CORBIS

Page 567, AP Photo/Katsumi Kasahara

Page 572, AP Photo/Joel Page

Chapter 17

Page 581, Herman Miller, Inc.

Page 594, Courtesy Airborne Express

Page 596, AP Photo/Richard Drew

Page 601, AP Photo/Brian Branch-Price

Chapter 18

Page 613 (top), AP Photo/Erik S. Lesser

Page 613 (bottom), © Michael Macor/ SF Chronicle/Corbis SABA

Page 621, © Mark Richards/PhotoEdit

Page 628, Courtesy of Dell Computer Corp.

Page 629, Courtesy Toyota Motor Manufacturing, Kentucky, Inc.

Page 630, © Joe McNally

Chapter 19

Page 641, Courtesy of Maden Technologies

Page 648, AP Photo/Peter Lennihan

Page 652, © James Schnepf/Liaison Agency

Page 659, AP Photo/Pat Sullivan

Page 664, AP Photo

Index

Names

D

E

F

J

K

L

M

N

O

P

Q

R

Subjects

D

J

K

L

N

O

T

U

Companies

C

D

E

F

G

H